Upfront

Colour pages giving you information about this guide and how to get the best out of it.

- 2 Welcome to the guide
- 4 Sure signs of where to stay
- 6 A look at some of the best
- 7 Tourist Information Centres
- 8 How to use the guide
- 10 England at a glance

contents

town within England's 11 tourist regions.

- 18 London
- 38 Cumbria
- 62 Northumbria
- 84 North West
- 100 Yorkshire & Humberside
- 134 Heart of England
- 192 Middle England
- 212 East Anglia
- 248 West Country
- 314 South of England
- 352 South East England

FRONT COVER:
THE OLD RECTORY, THORNTON WATLASS, N. YORKSHIRE

Plus...

- 384 Farm holiday groups
- 386 Group & youth section

where to stay '94

Information pages

Lots of useful information to help you choose the right place to stay.

- 400 The national accommodation rating scheme
- 402 The national wheelchair accessible scheme
- 403 General advice and information
- 406 About the guide entries
- 409 What's on in England 1994
- 415 Reader enquiry coupons
- 431 Index to advertisers

Town index and colour maps

Use these to find places with accommodation and the relevant page numbers.

- 425 Town index
- 433 Colour maps
- 448 Finding a place to stay

Key to symbols

The fold-out back cover gives a convenient key to all the symbols used in this guide.

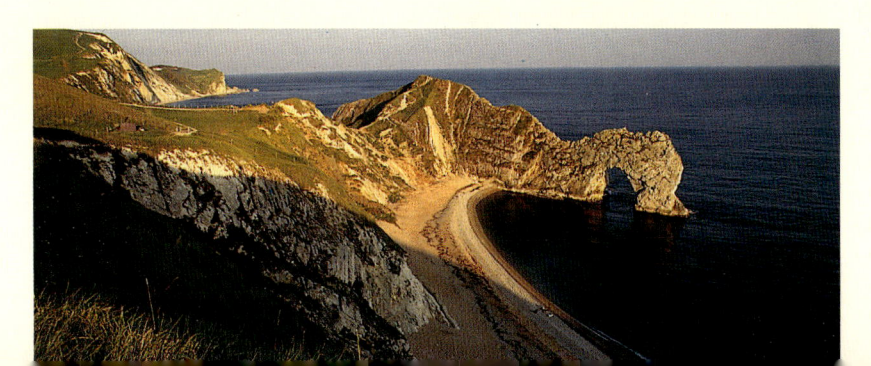

1

WHERE TO STAY 1994

This 'Where to Stay' guide is designed to give you all the information you need to help you find accommodation in England in the right place, at the right price and with the facilities and services that are right for you.

welcome to the guide

Whatever your reason for staying away from home – holiday, shopping trip, on business or visiting friends or relatives – you're sure to find in this guide accommodation that suits you best.

And to help in your selection, most of the accommodation entries in this guide show the national ratings awarded by the English Tourist Board (see pages 4–5).

A unique and helpful feature of this 'Where to Stay' guide is that all the essential information you need is presented in a straightforward and easy-to-read style, along with a brief description of the establishment.

Symbols are used only to give you all the very detailed – but perhaps necessary – information about additional services and facilities. But there's no need to flick back and forth between pages to find out what all the symbols mean – just fold out the back cover and you can check them as you go.

At the back of the guide you will find full-colour maps which not only pinpoint all those cities, towns and villages with accommodation listings, but are also useful as route maps. They show major towns, motorways, main 'A' roads, airports, BR InterCity stations, main ferry routes, and much, much more.

To complete the 'Where to Stay' package you'll find the Information Pages (starting on page 399) full of useful advice on such things as booking, cancellation, complaints, etc.

Also at the back is a comprehensive town index to make it easy for you to check out what accommodation is available in a particular place.

And there's more! Each of the 11 regional sections starts with lots of ideas on where to go and what to see in the region. Throughout the guide you'll also find thumbnail town descriptions to give you a quick picture of each place.

'Where to Stay' is a series of four guides, all available from your local bookshop:

Hotels & Guesthouses in England **£8.99**

Bed & Breakfast, Farmhouses, Inns & Hostels in England **£7.99**

Self-Catering Holiday Homes in England **£5.99**

Camping & Caravan Parks in Britain **£3.99**

3

WHERE TO STAY 1994

When you see a Crown or Lodge rating at an establishment or in its advertising you can be sure that the accommodation has been inspected and found to meet Tourist Board standards for facilities and services.

sure signs of *where to stay*

Since their introduction in 1987, the Tourist Board accommodation ratings have become recognised as the leading indicator of the standards you can expect to find at your selected establishment.

Over 30,000 places to stay throughout Britain now offer the reassurance of a national rating.

Crown ratings:

Listed You can be sure that the accommodation will be clean and comfortable, but the range of facilities and services may be limited.

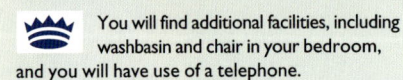

You will find additional facilities, including washbasin and chair in your bedroom, and you will have use of a telephone.

There will be a colour TV in your bedroom or in a lounge and you can enjoy morning tea/coffee in your bedroom. At least some of the bedrooms will have a private bath (or shower) and WC.

At least half of the bedrooms will have private bath (or shower) en-suite. You will also be able to order a hot evening meal.

Your bedroom will have a colour TV, radio and telephone, there will be lounge service until midnight and evening meals can be ordered up to 2030 hours. 90% of the bedrooms will have private bath and/or shower and WC en-suite.

Every bedroom will have private bath, fixed shower and WC en-suite. The restaurant will be open for breakfast, lunch and dinner (or you can take meals in your room from breakfast until midnight) and you will benefit from an all-night lounge service. A night porter will also be on duty.

More information on the national rating scheme is given on pages 400–401

4

All accommodation included in this 'Where to Stay' guide has been inspected – or is awaiting inspection – under the national rating scheme.

To help you find accommodation that offers the quality standard you seek, as well as the facilities and services you need, Crown and Lodge ratings contain two parts. The number of symbols indicates the range of facilities and services provided: the more symbols, the wider the range. Quality standards are shown by the terms **APPROVED, COMMENDED, HIGHLY COMMENDED** and **DE LUXE**.

Those places that have applied for a quality grade are subject to a more rigorous Tourist Board inspection, taking into account such important aspects as warmth of welcome, atmosphere and efficiency of service as well as the quality of furnishings, fitments and equipment.

If no quality grade appears alongside the symbols it means the proprietor has yet to invite us to do a quality assessment. However, you can still be sure of a high standard of cleanliness and service appropriate to the type of establishment.

Wheelchair Access Categories: These new symbols are sure signs of places to stay for wheelchair users and others who may have difficulty in walking. See page 402 for further information and a list of establishments in this guide which have received a wheelchair access category symbol following inspection by the Tourist Board.

Lodge ratings:

New 'Lodge' ratings acknowledge the purpose-built bedroom accommodation that is now appearing along major roads and motorways. The range of facilities is indicated by Moon symbols.

In a One Moon 'Lodge', your bedroom will have at least a washbasin and radio or colour TV. Tea/coffee may be from a vending machine in a public area.

Your bedroom in a Two Moon 'Lodge' will have colour TV, tea/coffee-making facilities and en-suite bath or shower with WC.

In a Three Moon 'Lodge', you will find colour TV and radio, tea/coffee-making facilities and comfortable seating in your bedroom and there will be a bath, shower and WC en-suite. The reception area will be manned throughout the night.

Quality standards:

The quality grades **APPROVED, COMMENDED, HIGHLY COMMENDED** and **DE LUXE** can apply to any of the Crown and Lodge ratings. A Listed or One Crown B&B can have a HIGHLY COMMENDED or even DE LUXE grade if what it provides is to a very high quality standard. A Four or Five Crown hotel might have an APPROVED grade if what it provides is to a relatively modest quality standard.

WHERE TO STAY 1994

MIDDLE ORD MANOR HOUSE, BERWICK-UPON-TWEED, NORTHUMBERLAND

a look at some of the best

Establishments included in this 'Where to Stay' guide which have achieved the highest quality grade of DE LUXE for the exceptionally high quality standard of the facilities and services they provide are featured on these pages.

Please use the Town Index on page 425 to find page numbers for their full entry listings.

TAVERN HOUSE, TETBURY, GLOUCESTERSHIRE

The Beeches, Carlisle, Cumbria
Broadview, Crewkerne, Somerset
The Grange, East Barkwith, Lincolnshire
Halfway House, Crayke, N. Yorkshire
Holmfield, Kendal, Cumbria
Hope House, Tynemouth, Tyne & Wear
Middle Ord Manor House, Berwick-upon-Tweed, Northumberland
The Old Rectory, Thornton Watlass, N. Yorkshire
Parkside House, Hastings, E. Sussex
Pickett Howe, Buttermere, Cumbria
Shawswell Country House, Rendcomb, Gloucestershire
Tavern House, Tetbury, Gloucestershire

**When it comes to your next England break, the first stage of your journey could be closer than you think. You've probably got a Tourist Information Centre nearby. But you might not have realised that it's there to serve the local community – as well as visitors.
So make us your first stop. We'll be happy to help you, wherever you're heading.**

use your *i*'s

Many Information Centres can provide you with maps and guides, helping you plan well in advance. And sometimes it's even possible for us to book your accommodation, too.

A visit to your nearest Information Centre can pay off in other ways as well. We can point you in the right direction when it comes to finding out about all the special events which are happening in the local region.

In fact, we can give you details of places to visit within easy reach... and perhaps tempt you to plan a day trip or weekend away.

Across the country, there are more than 550 Tourist Information Centres so you're never far away. You'll find the address of your nearest Tourist Information Centre in your local Phone Book.

WHERE TO STAY 1994

This 'Where to Stay' guide will make it easy for you to find accommodation to suit your mood and your pocket. The content has been structured to enable you to find a place to stay even if you have only a general idea of the area you are planning to visit. Just follow the notes below and you'll soon find accommodation that's right for you.

how to use the guide

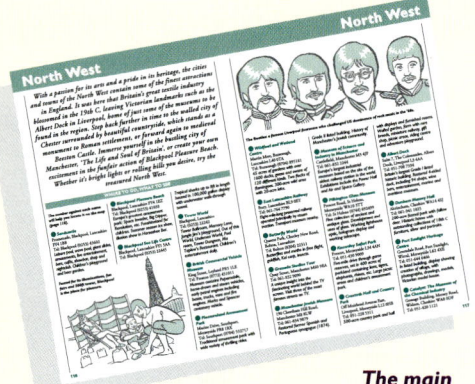

If the place you plan to visit is included in the town index – turn to the page number given to find accommodation available there. Also check that location on the colour maps to find other places nearby which also have accommodation listings.

If the place you want is not in the town index – or you have only a general idea of the area in which you wish to stay – use the colour maps to find places in the area which have accommodation listings.

The main body of this guide is divided into 11 sections corresponding to England's tourist regions. Each regional section has an introduction with ideas on where to go and what to see.

The region's cities, towns and villages with their accommodation are then listed alphabetically. Accompanying each place name is a map reference which refers to the colour maps at the back of the guide. This enables you to find the exact location.

There is a complete town index at the back which lists all the places with accommodation featured in the guide.

Accommodation information has been provided by the proprietors of the establishments. Some information is represented by symbols and you will find a key to these inside the back cover flap.

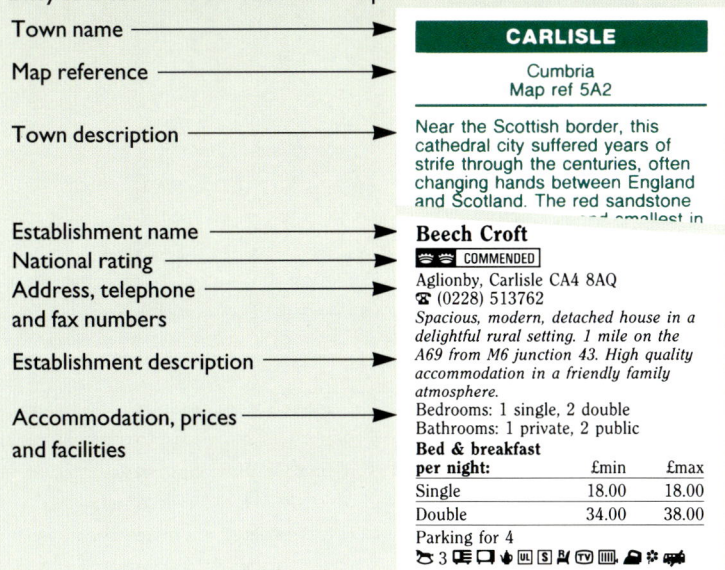

Town name	**CARLISLE**
Map reference	Cumbria Map ref 5A2
Town description	Near the Scottish border, this cathedral city suffered years of strife through the centuries, often changing hands between England and Scotland. The red sandstone
Establishment name National rating Address, telephone and fax numbers	**Beech Croft** COMMENDED Aglionby, Carlisle CA4 8AQ ☎ (0228) 513762
Establishment description	Spacious, modern, detached house in a delightful rural setting. 1 mile on the A69 from M6 junction 43. High quality accommodation in a friendly family atmosphere.
Accommodation, prices and facilities	Bedrooms: 1 single, 2 double Bathrooms: 1 private, 2 public **Bed & breakfast** **per night:** £min £max Single 18.00 18.00 Double 34.00 38.00 Parking for 4

Changes may have occurred since the guide went to press or may occur during 1994 – so please check any aspects which are important to you before booking. We also advise you to read the information pages towards the back of the guide, particularly the section on cancellations.

Enquiry coupons are included at the back of the guide. One type will help you when contacting establishments about accommodation; the other can be used to request information from advertisers.

WHERE TO STAY 1994

England
at a glance

England is divided into 11 tourist regions, each of which has its own section in this guide. The regions are shown on the map and also listed opposite together with an index which identifies the region in which each county is located.

- Northumbria
- Cumbria
- Yorkshire & Humberside
- North West
- Middle England
- East Anglia
- Heart of England
- London
- South East England
- South of England
- West Country

Colour maps showing all the places with accommodation listed in this guide and an index to the place names can be found at the back of the guide.

18 London
   Greater London

38 Cumbria
   The County of Cumbria, including
   English Lakeland

62 Northumbria
   Cleveland, County Durham,
   Northumberland, Tyne & Wear

84 North West
   Cheshire, Greater Manchester, Lancashire,
   Merseyside

100 Yorkshire & Humberside
   North, South and West Yorkshire,
   Humberside

134 Heart of England
   Gloucestershire, Hereford & Worcester,
   Shropshire, Staffordshire, Warwickshire,
   West Midlands

192 Middle England
   Derbyshire, Leicestershire, Lincolnshire,
   Northamptonshire, Nottinghamshire

212 East Anglia
   Bedfordshire, Cambridgeshire, Essex,
   Hertfordshire, Norfolk, Suffolk

248 West Country
   Avon, Cornwall, Devon, Somerset,
   Western Dorset, Wiltshire, Isles of Scilly

314 South of England
   Berkshire, Buckinghamshire, Eastern Dorset,
   Hampshire, Isle of Wight, Oxfordshire

352 South East England
   East and West Sussex, Kent, Surrey

County Index

Avon: West Country
Bedfordshire: East Anglia
Berkshire: South of England
Buckinghamshire: South of England
Cambridgeshire: East Anglia
Cheshire: North West
Cleveland: Northumbria
Cornwall: West Country
County Durham: Northumbria
Cumbria: Cumbria
Derbyshire: Middle England
Devon: West Country
Dorset (Eastern): South of England
Dorset (Western): West Country
East Sussex: South East England
Essex: East Anglia
Gloucestershire: Heart of England
Greater London: London
Greater Manchester: North West
Hampshire: South of England
Hereford & Worcester: Heart of England
Hertfordshire: East Anglia
Humberside: Yorkshire & Humberside
Isle of Wight: South of England
Isles of Scilly: West Country
Kent: South East England
Lancashire: North West
Leicestershire: Middle England
Lincolnshire: Middle England
Merseyside: North West
Norfolk: East Anglia
North Yorkshire: Yorkshire & Humberside
Northamptonshire: Middle England
Northumberland: Northumbria
Nottinghamshire: Middle England
Oxfordshire: South of England
Shropshire: Heart of England
Somerset: West Country
South Yorkshire: Yorkshire & Humberside
Staffordshire: Heart of England
Suffolk: East Anglia
Surrey: South East England
Tyne & Wear: Northumbria
Warwickshire: Heart of England
West Midlands: Heart of England
West Sussex: South East England
West Yorkshire: Yorkshire & Humberside
Wiltshire: West Country

THE ENGLAND FOR EXCELLENCE AWARDS 1992 WINNERS

The England for Excellence Awards were created by the English Tourist Board to recognise and reward the highest standards of excellence and quality in all major sectors of tourism in England. The coveted Leo statuette, presented each year to winners, has become firmly established as the ultimate accolade in the English tourism industry.

Over the past five years, the Leo has been won by all types and sizes of business with one common attribute – excellence in the facilities and services they offer.

Thames Tower
Black's Road
London W6 9EL

English Tourist Board

Resort of the Year sponsored by Marks & Spencer
BOURNEMOUTH

Bed and Breakfast Award sponsored by Le Shuttle
THE OLD RECTORY, Ripon

Attraction of the Year sponsored by Blackpool Pleasure Beach Limited
NATIONAL FISHING HERITAGE CENTRE

Hotel of the Year sponsored by Horwath Consulting
THE LANESBOROUGH

TIC of the Year sponsored by Holiday Property Bond Limited
FONTWELL TIC

Self-Catering Holiday of the Year sponsored by Hoseasons Holidays Limited
ANGLERS' PARADISE HOLIDAYS

Tourism and the Environment Award sponsored by Center Parcs Limited
LOSEHILL HALL, PEAK NATIONAL PARK CENTRE

Travel Journalist of the Year sponsored by Forte Plc
PAUL GOGARTY

Hotel Company of the Year sponsored by RCI Europe Limited
HILTON UNITED KINGDOM

Tourism for all Award sponsored by RAC Enterprises Limited
MUSEUM OF SCIENCE AND INDUSTRY IN MANCHESTER

Tourism and the Arts Award sponsored by First Leisure Corporation Plc
GREATER MANCHESTER VISITOR AND CONVENTION BUREAU/MANCHESTER INTERNATIONAL FESTIVAL OF EXPRESSIONISM

Caravan Holiday Park Award sponsored by the National Caravan Council
FOXHUNTER PARK

Tourism Training Award sponsored by The Tussauds Group Limited
LUCKETTS TRAVEL

English Travel Company of the Year sponsored by BTTF
BUTLIN'S LIMITED

Outstanding Contribution to English Tourism Award sponsored by Hilton UK
SIR ANDREW LLOYD WEBBER

VISIT BATH
for a
Memorable Riverside Experience
at the
OLD MILL HOTEL & RESTAURANT

Tollbridge Road, Bath, Avon BA1 7DE
☎ (0225) 858476 Fax: (0225) 852600

What could be more luxurious than enjoying your holiday on the banks of the River Avon, beside the historic Tollbridge and overlooking the Weir, with panoramic views which make the setting truly romantic!

Turn with the Wheel — in the new revolving restaurant with the unique rotating floor turned gently by the huge waterwheel, offering the diners varied breathtaking views, yet only $1\frac{1}{2}$ miles from Bath city centre with easy access by public transport.

Luxurious Accommodation — all ensuite rooms, most with river views.

Honeymooners' Paradise — with 4-poster beds and honeymoon packs.

Single from £35   Doubles from £48   Special short break offers

---

Special Budget Accommodation available at the Old Mill Lodge. Newly furbished rooms offer colour TV, radio, tea/coffee facilities, etc. Some rooms are ensuite and offer river views.

◆ Restaurant & Bar ◆ Fishing ◆ Car Park ◆

Singles from £18   Doubles from £24   Special short break offer

A LONG ESTABLISHED FAMILY RUN HOTEL OFFERING ALL THE COMFORTS OF HOME

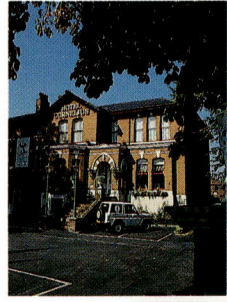

Hotel Cornelius
Your Comfort is Our Comfort

ROOMS FROM £25

- 36 EN SUITE WITH SATELLITE TV & D.D. TELEPHONE, TEA & COFFEE FACILITIES
- 24 HR. ROOM SERVICE
- LUXURIOUS BRIDAL SUITE
- 3 FAMILY ROOMS
- WEDDING RECEPTION ROOM FOR 100 GUESTS
- AUTHENTIC ITALIAN RESTAURANT OPEN TO THE PUBLIC
- ENGLISH/CONTINENTAL BREAKFAST
- FULL COLOUR BROCHURE

- 3 CONFERENCE ROOMS
- FROM 5 TO 100 PEOPLE
- FULL IN-HOUSE CONFERENCE FACILITIES INCLUDING AUDIO VISUAL & SOUND EQUIPMENT
- IDEAL FOR EXHIBITIONS, TRADE SHOWS, PRODUCT LAUNCHES & BUSINESS MEETINGS
- FREE SECURE PARKING FOR 50 CARS
- 10 MINUTES FROM MANCHESTER AIRPORT & MANCHESTER CITY CENTRE 5 MINS

175 MANCHESTER ROAD, CHORLTON CUM HARDY, MANCHESTER M16 0ED.
Tel:061 862 9565 Fax:061 862 9028

ALL MAJOR CREDIT CARDS WELCOME

FIVE MINUTES FROM MANCHESTER UNITED & CITY FOOTBALL CLUBS.

THE MANOR BORN
THREE STAR HOTEL - FIVE STAR VIEWS

FOR COLOUR BROCHURE & DETAILS OF BREAKS: CRAIG MANOR HOTEL LAKE ROAD WINDERMERE LA23 3AR TEL: 05394 88877

A former 17th Century Coaching Inn, the King's Head sits at the foot of Helvellyn midway between Grasmere and Keswick.
With oak beams and inglenooks, real fires in winter, beer gardens in summer, real ales, fine wines, traditional English fayre and genuine hospitality, this is a true Lakeland Inn.
We have 19 bedrooms (including family and single rooms) all with bathrooms, colour t.v., tea and coffee facilities and telephones.
Residents lounge, restaurant, traditional bar, games room and bar food dining area.
We offer very reasonable rates for both Bed and Breakfast and Dinner Bed and Breakfast.
Contact us now for a colour brochure and a quote for your short break or holiday.

APPROVED

THE KING'S HEAD HOTEL

ST' JOHN'S IN THE VALE

Contact:-
Derek Sweeney,
King's Head Hotel,
Thirlspot,
Nr. Keswick,
Cumbria CA12 4TN
Tel: (07687) 72393.
Fax: (07687) 72309.

National Accessible Scheme

If you are a wheelchair user or someone who has difficulty walking, look for the national 'Accessible' symbol when choosing where to stay.

All the places that display the symbol have been checked by a Tourist Board inspector against criteria that reflect the practical needs of wheelchair users.

There are three categories of accessibility, indicated by symbols:

Category 1: Accessible to all wheelchair users including those travelling independently

Category 2: Accessible to a wheelchair user with assistance

Category 3: Accessible to a wheelchair user able to walk short distances and up at least three steps

A leaflet giving more information on the scheme is available free from any Tourist Information Centre, whose staff will also be pleased to help with finding suitable accommodation in the area. Additional help and guidance can be obtained from the Holiday Care Service, 2 Old Bank Chambers, Station Road, Horley, Surrey RH6 9HW.
Tel: (0293) 774535. Fax: (0293) 784647.
Minicom: (0293) 776943 (24-hour answering).

Use your *i*'s

There are more than 550 Tourist Information Centres throughout England offering friendly help with accommodation and holiday ideas as well as suggestions of places to visit and things to do.

In your home town there may be a centre which can help you before you set out. You'll find the address of your nearest Tourist Information Centre in your local Phone Book.

"Where to Stay" customer survey

Win one of four holiday weekends* with Lyric Hotels!

Lyric Hotels

win

* Two night's accommodation for one person, to include evening meal and full English breakfast, at one of the following hotels:

Gainsborough House Hotel, Kidderminster COMMENDED
Hatherley Manor, Gloucester COMMENDED
Madeley Court Hotel, Ironbridge HIGHLY COMMENDED
Wyck Hill House Hotel, Stow-on-the-Wold DE LUXE

Please
Affix
Stamp

English Tourist Board

Sally Marshall
Managing Editor "Where to Stay"
English Tourist Board
Thames Tower
Black's Road
Hammersmith
London W6 9EL

Key to symbols

Information about many of the services and facilities at accommodation listed in this guide is given in the form of symbols. The key to these symbols is inside the back cover flap. You may find it helpful to keep the flap open when referring to the accommodation listings.

Bookings

When enquiring about accommodation you may find it helpful to use the booking enquiry coupons which can be found towards the end of the guide.
These should be cut out and mailed direct to the establishments in which you are interested.
Do remember to include your name and address.

Where to Stay in England

Published by: English Tourist Board, Thames Tower, Black's Road, Hammersmith, London W6 9EL.
Internal Reference Number: ETB/214/94 AS/1367/36M/93

Managing Editor: Sally Marshall
Compilation & Production: Guide Associates, Croydon
Design: Celsius, Winchester
Colour Photography: Nigel Corrie (front cover); Celsius, Glyn Williams and Syndication International
Illustrations: Susie Louis
Cartoons: David Austin
Cartography: Colin Earl Cartography, Alton
Typesetting: Computaprint, London, and Celsius
Printing & Binding: Bemrose Security Printing, Derby
Advertisement Sales: Madison Bell Ltd, 3 St. Peter's Street, Islington Green, London N1 8JD. Telephone: 071-359 7737.

© English Tourist Board (except where stated)

IMPORTANT:
The information contained in this guide has been published in good faith on the basis of information submitted to the English Tourist Board by the proprietors of the premises listed, who have paid for their entries to appear. The English Tourist Board cannot guarantee the accuracy of the information in this guide and accepts no responsibility for any error or misrepresentation. All liability for loss, disappointment, negligence or other damage caused by reliance on the information contained in this guide, or in the event of bankruptcy, or liquidation, or cessation of trade of any company, individual or firm mentioned, is hereby excluded. Please check carefully all prices and other details before confirming a reservation.

The English Tourist Board
The Board is a statutory body created by the Development of Tourism Act 1969 to develop and market England's tourism. Its main objectives are to provide a welcome for people visiting England; to encourage people living in England to take their holidays there; and to encourage the provision and improvement of tourist amenities and facilities in England. The Board has a statutory duty to advise the Government on tourism matters relating to England and, with Government approval and support, administers the national classification & grading schemes for tourist accommodation in England.

London

Come to London and you'll have a ball – and that's a promise! There is nothing predictable about this vibrant city, and that is its charm. Shopaholics should head for Oxford Street, Covent Garden and Knightsbridge. Those with a thirst for knowledge should drop into one of London's many attractions such as the Tower of London or take a look inside Buckingham Palace, newly opened to the public. For those who like the sights, the Thames alone is breathtaking: to the west is Henry VIII's Hampton Court with its maddening maze, to the east the awesome engineering achievement of the Thames Barrier. Art, science, entertainment and education, a day in London is unforgettable. And the evening is yet to come!

WHERE TO GO, WHAT TO SEE

Florence Nightingale (1820–1910) was known as the 'lady with the lamp' because of her practice of touring the wards at night in the hospital she ran in the Crimea. She became a national heroine and founded the Nightingale School and Home for Nurses in London – the forerunner of today's nurse training system. Her statue is to be found in Pall Mall.

Bank of England Museum
Bartholomew Lane, London
EC2 8AH
Tel: 071-601 5545
History of Bank of England. Interactive video illustrating place of the Bank in today's world economy. Bars of gold, banknote gallery.

Banqueting House
Whitehall, London SW1A 2ER
Tel: 071-930 4179
The last remaining part of the Palace of Whitehall, built between 1619–1622. Famous for Rubens ceiling paintings and Inigo Jones architecture.

British Museum
Great Russell Street, London
WC1B 3DG
Tel: 071-636 1555
One of the great museums of the world, showing the works of man from all over the world from prehistoric to comparatively modern times. British Library Exhibition Galleries.

Cabinet War Rooms
Clive Steps, King Charles Street, London SW1A 2AQ
Tel: 071-930 6961
Suite of 21 historic rooms,

London

including Cabinet Room, transatlantic telephone room, map room and Prime Minister's room. Were in operational use 1939–1945.

Chessington World of Adventures
Leatherhead Rd, Chessington, Surrey KT9 2NE
Tel: Epsom (0372) 729560
A world of adventure, fun, exciting theme areas, rides, circus and the famous zoo. Rides include 'Vampire' and 'Professor Burp's Bubble Works'.

Chislehurst Caves
Old Hill, Chislehurst, Kent BR7 5NB
Tel: 081-467 3264
Over 20 miles of caves, parts dating from 6,000 BC. Druids' altar, Roman well, haunted pool, World War II exhibits.

Design Museum
Butler's Wharf, Shad Thames, London SE1 2YD
Tel: 071-403 6933
Study collection showing the development of design in mass production. Review of new products, graphics gallery and changing programme of exhibitions.

Dickens House
48 Doughty Street, London WC1N 2LF
Tel: 071-405 2127
Home of Charles Dickens from 1837–1839. Letters, pictures, first editions, furniture, memorabilia, in restored rooms.

Dulwich Picture Gallery
College Road, London SE21 7AD
Tel: 081-693 5254
13 rooms and over 300 pictures on view. Includes works by Poussin and Claude, Rubens, Rembrandt, Van Dyck, Teniers, Gainsborough, Murillo and Canaletto.

One of the best ways to see London is by double-decker bus. Several operators run services (including open-top buses), with Victoria station being a key boarding point.

The Fan Museum
12 Crooms Hill, London SE10 8ER
Tel: 081-305 1441
The only venue in the world devoted entirely to the art and craft of the fan. Changing exhibitions, gift shop.

Geffrye Museum
Kingsland Road, London E2 8EA
Tel: 071-739 9893
English domestic interiors from 1600 to 1900s, set in delightful 18th C almshouses with pleasant gardens.

Guildhall
Gresham Street, London EC2P 2EJ
Tel: 071-606 3030
Centre of civic government for the square mile of the City of London where the Corporation of London has its offices.

Guinness World of Records
The Trocadero, Coventry Street, Piccadilly Circus, London W1V 7FD
Tel: 071-439 7331
Exhibition using models, videos, computers and electronic displays to bring to life the Guinness Book of Records.

Hampton Court Palace
Hampton Court, Surrey KT8 9AU
Tel: 081-781 9500
Oldest Tudor palace in England. Tudor kitchens, tennis courts, maze, state apartments and King's apartments.

Kenwood House (Iveagh Bequest)
Hampstead Lane, London NW3 7JR
Tel: 081-348 1286
Collection of English and foreign art. Shoe buckle collection and Hull Grundy collection of jewellery. Neo-classical villa by Robert Adam.

London Dungeon
28–34 Tooley Street, London SE1 2SZ
Tel: 071-403 0606
World's first medieval horror museum. Now featuring two major shows: 'The Jack the Ripper Experience' and 'The Theatre of the Guillotine'.

London

The Albert Bridge is one of the many bridges – ancient and modern – which span the Thames.

London Planetarium
Marylebone Road, London
NW1 5LR
Tel: 071-486 1121
Featuring the Space Trail and Star Show. No admission to children under 5.

London Toy and Model Museum
21–23 Craven Hill, London
W2 3EN
Tel: 071-262 9450
One of the most extensive collections of commercially made toys and models in Europe dating from 1850 onward. Including trains, cars, 'planes and nursery toys.

London Zoo
Regent's Park, London NW1 4RY
Tel: 071-722 3333
Over 8,000 animals including giant panda, venomous snakes, penguins and piranhas. Daily events, Lifewatch Conservation Centre and Moonlight World.

Museum of Mankind
6 Burlington Gardens, London
W1X 2EX
Tel: 071-323 8043
Ethnography department of the British Museum houses collections from Africa, Australia and the Pacific islands, North and South America.

Museum of the Moving Image
South Bank, London SE1 8XT
Tel: 071-928 3535
Celebration of cinema and television. 44 exhibition areas, offering plenty of hands-on participation, and a cast of actors to tell visitors more.

National Gallery
Trafalgar Square, London
WC2N 5DN
Tel: 071-839 3321
Western painting 13th to 19th C. Includes work by Van Gogh, Rembrandt, Cezanne, Turner, Gainsborough, Leonardo da Vinci, Renoir and Botticelli.

National Maritime Museum
Romney Road, Greenwich, London
SE10 9NF
Tel: 081-858 4422
Britain's maritime heritage illustrated through actual and model ships, paintings, uniforms, navigation and astronomy instruments, archives and photographs. Queen's House.

London

The Natural History Museum
Cromwell Road, London
SW7 5BD
Tel: 071-938 9123
Home of the wonders of the natural world, one of the most popular museums in the world, and one of London's finest landmarks.

Old Royal Observatory
Flamsteed House, Greenwich Park, Greenwich, London SE10 9NF
Tel: 081-858 4422
Museum of astronomy and time. Greenwich Meridian, working telescopes and planetarium, timeball, Wren's Octagon Room. Fully restored in 1993.

Operating Theatre Museum and Herb Garret
9A St Thomas' Street, London
SE1 9RT
Tel: 071-955 4791
Restored 1822 women's operating theatre is the only 19th C operating theatre in England. Exhibits tell the story of surgery, herbal medicine etc.

Osterley Park House
Jersey Road, Isleworth, Middlesex
TW7 4RB
Tel: 081-560 3918
The superb interiors contain one of the most complete examples of Robert Adam's work, including plasterwork, carpets and furniture.

Rock Circus
London Pavilion, Piccadilly Circus, London W1V 9LA
Tel: 071-734 7203
An amazing combination of stereo sound through personal headsets, audio animatronics and Madame Tussaud's figures of over 50 rock stars.

Royal Air Force Museum
Grahame Park Way, Hendon, London NW9 5LL
Tel: 081-205 2266
Three halls displaying almost 70 full-size aircraft. 'Battle of Britain Experience', flight simulator, jet trainer, free film shows. Shop and restaurant.

Royal Mews
Buckingham Palace, London
SW1A 1AA
Tel: 071-930 4832
Her Majesty The Queen's carriage horses, carriages and harness used on State occasions, including Coronation coach, built 1761.

Science Museum
Exhibition Road, South Kensington, London SW7 2DD
Tel: 071-938 8000
National Museum of Science and Industry. Full-size replica of Apollo II Lunar Lander, launch pad, Wellcome Museum of the History of Medicine, flight lab, food for thought, optics.

Sherlock Holmes Museum
221B Baker Street, London
NW1 6XE
Tel: 071-935 8866
Grade II listed lodging house. First floor Holmes' apartment. Second floor Mrs Hudson's and Dr Watson's rooms. Souvenir shop.

Spencer House
27 St James's Place, London
SW1A 1NR
Tel: 071-409 0526
Private palace built 1756–1766 for the first Earl Spencer, an ancestor of HRH the Princess of Wales. Nine state rooms with antique and neo-classical furniture.

Spitting Image Rubberworks
Cubitts Yard, James Street, Covent Garden, London WC2E 8PA
Tel: 071-240 0838
London's wackiest animated puppet exhibition stars over 30 of their most infamous puppets.

Thames Barrier Visitors' Centre
Unity Way, London SE18 5NJ
Tel: 081-854 1473
Exhibition with 10-minute video and working scale model. 18-minute multi-media show. Riverside walkways, Barrier Buffet and teaching rooms for schools.

The Theatre Museum
1E Tavistock Street, Covent Garden, London WC2E 7PA
Tel: 071-836 7891
Five galleries include permanent display of history of performance in the United Kingdom. Collection includes theatre, ballet, dance, rock and pop music, musical stage.

Tower Hill Pageant
1 Tower Hill Terrace, London
EC3N 4EE
Tel: 071-709 0081
Automatic vehicles transport visitors past tableaux depicting the history of the City and its port. Display of archaeological finds. Shop and restaurant.

Tower of London
Tower Hill, London EC3 4AB
Tel: 071-709 0765
Building spans 900 years of British history. The nation's Crown Jewels, regalia and coronation robes on display. Beefeaters and the ravens.

Victoria and Albert Museum
South Kensington, London
SW7 2RL
Tel: 071-938 8500
Magnificent Victorian building. Fine and decorative arts from 15th–20th C, jewellery, silver, textiles, fashions, ceramics.

Wimbledon Lawn Tennis Museum
Wimbledon, London SW19 5AE
Tel: 081-946 6131
Exhibits include Victorian parlour, racket maker's workshop, costumes, trophies, equipment. Films of matches, shop.

FIND OUT MORE
A free information pack about holidays and attractions in the London region is available on written request from:
London Tourist Board and Convention Bureau
26 Grosvenor Gardens, London SW1W 0DU.

London

TOURIST INFORMATION

Tourist and leisure information can be obtained from Tourist Information Centres throughout England. Details of centres and other information services in Greater London are given below. The symbol ⛱ means that an accommodation booking service is provided.

TOURIST INFORMATION CENTRES

POINTS OF ARRIVAL

Victoria Station, Forecourt, SW1 ⛱
Easter–October, daily 0800–1900. November–Easter, reduced opening hours.

Liverpool Street Underground Station, EC2 ⛱
Monday 0815–1900. Tuesday–Saturday 0815–1800. Sunday 0830–1645.

Heathrow Terminals 1, 2, 3 Underground Station Concourse (Heathrow Airport) ⛱
Daily 0830–1800.

The above information centres provide a London and Britain tourist information service, offer a hotel accommodation booking service, stock free and saleable publications on Britain and London and sell theatre tickets, tourist tickets for bus and underground and tickets for sightseeing tours.

INNER LONDON

British Travel Centre ⛱
12 Regent Street, Piccadilly Circus, SW1Y 4PQ
Monday–Friday 0900–1830. Saturday–Sunday 1000–1600 (0900–1700 Saturdays May–September).

Bloomsbury Tourist Information Centre ⛱
35–36 Woburn Place, WC1H 0JR
Tel: 071-580 4599
Daily 0945–1900.

Greenwich Tourist Information Centre ⛱
46 Greenwich Church Street, SE10 9BL
Tel: 081-858 6376
April–September, daily 1000–1700. October–March, reduced opening hours.

Islington Tourist Information Centre ⛱
44 Duncan Street, E1 8BL
Tel: 071-278 8787
Monday–Saturday 1000–1700. Reduced winter opening hours.

Lewisham Tourist Information Centre
Lewisham Library, 366 Lewisham High Street, SE13 6LG
Tel: 081-690 8325
Saturday, Monday 0930–1700. Tuesday, Thursday 0930–2000. Friday 0930–1300.

Selfridges ⛱
Oxford Street, W1. Basement Services Arcade – Duke Street entrance.
Open during normal store hours.

Tower Hamlets Tourist Information Centre
107a Commercial Street, E1 6BG
Tel: 081-375 2549
Monday–Friday 0930–1630.

OUTER LONDON

Bexley Tourist Information Centre ⛱
Central Library, Townley Road, Bexleyheath DA6 7HJ
Tel: 081-303 9052
Monday, Tuesday, Thursday 0930–2000. Friday 0930–1730. Saturday 0930–1700.

Also at Hall Place Visitor Centre ⛱
Bourne Road, Bexley
Tel: (0322) 558676
June–September, daily 1130–1630.

Croydon Tourist Information Centre
Katharine Street, Croydon CR9 1ET

Tel: 081-253 1009
Monday 0930–1900. Tuesday–Friday 0930–1800. Saturday 0900–1700.

Harrow Tourist Information Centre
Civic Centre, Station Road, Harrow HA1 2UJ
Tel: 081-424 1103
Monday–Friday 0900–1700.

Hillingdon Tourist Information Centre
Central Library, 14 High Street, Uxbridge UB8 1HD
Tel: Uxbridge (0895) 250706
Monday–Thursday 0930–2000. Friday 0930–1730. Saturday 0930–1600.

Hounslow Tourist Information Centre
24 The Treaty Centre, Hounslow High Street, Hounslow TW3 1ES
Tel: 081-572 8279
Monday, Wednesday 0930–1730. Tuesday, Thursday–Saturday 0930–2000.

Redbridge Tourist Information Centre
Town Hall, High Road, Ilford, Essex IG1 1DD
Tel: 081-478 3020
Monday–Friday 0830–1700.

Richmond Tourist Information Centre ⛱
Old Town Hall, Whittaker Avenue, Richmond upon Thames TW9 1TP
Tel: 081-940 9125
Monday–Friday 1000–1800. Saturday 1000–1700. May–October, also Sunday 1015–1615.

Twickenham Tourist Information Centre
The Atrium, Civic Centre, York Street, Twickenham, Middlesex TW1 3BZ
Tel: 081-891 7272
Monday–Friday 0900–1715.

London

VISITORCALL

LTB's 'phone guide to London operates 24 hours a day. To access a full range of information call 0839 123456. To access specific lines dial 0839 123 followed by:

    What's on this week – 400
    What's on next 3 months – 401
    Sunday in London – 407
    Rock and pop concerts – 422
    Popular attractions – 480
    Where to take children – 424
    Museums – 429
    Palaces (including Buckingham Palace) – 481
    Current exhibitions – 403
    Changing the Guard – 411
    Theatre – 423
    Historic sights – 427
    Pubs and restaurants – 485

Calls cost 36p per minute cheap rate, 48p per minute at all other times.
To order a Visitorcall card please call 071-971 0026. Information for callers using push-button telephones: 071-971 0027.

HOTEL ACCOMMODATION SERVICE

The London Tourist Board and Convention Bureau helps visitors to find and book accommodation at a wide range of prices in hotels and guesthouses, including budget accommodation, throughout the Greater London area. Reservations are made with hotels which are members of LTB denoted in this guide with the symbol ⋈ by their name.

Reservations can be made by credit card holders via the telephone accommodation reservations service on 071-824 8844 by simply giving the reservations clerk your card details (Access or Visa) and room requirements. LTB takes an administrative booking fee. The service operates Monday–Friday 0930–1730.

Reservations on arrival are handled at the Tourist Information Centres operated by LTB at Victoria Station forecourt, Heathrow Terminals 1, 2, 3 Underground Station Concourse, Liverpool Street Station and Selfridges. Go to any of them on the day when you need accommodation. A communication charge and a refundable deposit are payable when making a reservation.

WHICH PART OF LONDON?

The majority of tourist accommodation is situated in the central parts of London and is therefore very convenient for most of the city's attractions and night life.

However, there are many hotels in outer London which provide other advantages, such as easier parking. In the 'Places to Stay' pages which follow, you will find accommodation listed under INNER LONDON (covering the E1 to W14 London Postal Area) and OUTER LONDON (covering the remainder of Greater London). Colour maps 6 and 7 at the back of the guide show place names and London Postal Area codes and will help you to locate accommodation in your chosen area of London.

Use your *i*'s

There are more than 550 Tourist Information Centres throughout England offering friendly help with accommodation and holiday ideas as well as suggestions of places to visit and things to do.
In your home town there may be a centre which can help you before you set out. You'll find the address of your nearest Tourist Information Centre in your local Phone Book.

London index

If you are looking for accommodation in a particular establishment in London and you know its name, this index will give you the page number of the full entry in the guide.

A	page no
Aaron House SW5	29
Abbey Court Hotel W2	32
The Abbotts Hotel NW2	26
Abcone Hotel SW7	30
Albro House Hotel W2	32
Alexander Hotel SW1	28
Alexander House Hotel SW1	28
The Alice House West Drayton	37
Amsterdam Hotel SW5	29
Apple Tree Cottage West Drayton	37
Arena Hotel Wembley	37
Avonmore Hotel W14	35

B	page no
Barry House Hotel W2	32
Be My Guest SE26	27
Bedknobs SE22	27
Bentinck House Hotel W1	31
Beverley House Hotel W2	32
Blair House Hotel SW3	29

C	page no
Compton Guest House SW19	31
Mrs B Connolly N13	25
Corfton Guest House W5	35
Creffield Lodge W5	35
Crescent Lodge Hotel Harrow	36
Croydon Hotel Croydon	36

D	page no
Diana Hotel SE21	27

E	page no
Eaton Guesthouse W5	35
Elizabeth Hotel SW1	28
Elm Hotel Wembley	37
Europa House Hotel W2	32

F	page no
Five Kings Guest House N7	25
Five Sumner Place Hotel SW7	30

G	page no
George Hotel WC1	35
Georgian House Hotel SW1	28
Glynne Court Hotel W1	31
Grange Lodge W5	35
Grangewood Lodge Hotel E7	25

H	page no
Hamilton House Hotel SW1	28
Hyde Park Rooms Hotel W2	32

I	page no
Iverna Croydon	36

J	page no
J and T Guest House NW10	26

K	page no
Kandara Guest House N1	25
Kensbridge Hotel SW7	30
Kensington Garden Hotel W2	32
Kingsland House SE12	27

L	page no
The Langorf Hotel NW3	26
Lincoln House Hotel W1	31

M	page no
Meadow Croft Lodge SE9	26
Merlyn Court Hotel SW5	29
Mitre House Hotel W2	32
More House SW7	30

N	page no
Nayland Hotel W2	32
Hotel Number Sixteen SW7	30

P	page no
Pane Residence N22	26
Park Lodge Hotel W2	34
Parkland Walk Guest House N19	26
Parkwood Hotel W2	34
The Plough Inn SW14	31

R	page no
Regency Hotel W1	31
Rhodes House Hotel W2	34
Rilux House NW4	26
Rose Court Hotel W2	34

Royal Cambridge Hotel W2	34
Ruddimans Hotel W2	34

S	page no
St. Athan's Hotel WC1	35
Sass House Hotel W2	34
Simone House Hotel SW1	28
Sleeping Beauty Motel E10	25
Springfield Hotel W2	34
Stanley House Hotel SW1	28
Mrs J Stock Purley	37
Hotel Strand Continental WC2	36
Swiss House Hotel SW5	30

T	page no
Thanet Hotel WC1	36

V	page no
Vicarage Private Hotel W8	35

W	page no
Mrs Freda Ward SE6	26
Westbury Guest House E7	25
Westpoint Hotel W2	34
The White House W5	35
Wigmore Court Hotel W1	31
Windermere Hotel SW1	29
Windsor House SW5	30
Wyndham Hotel W1	31

Y	page no
York House Hotel SW5	30

Advertisers

When requesting further information from advertisers in this guide, you may find it helpful to use the advertisement enquiry coupons which can be found towards the end of the guide. These should be cut out and mailed direct to the companies in which you are interested. Do remember to include your name and address.

LONDON

Places to stay

Accommodation entries in this section are listed under **Inner London** (covering the E1 to W14 London Postal Area) and **Outer London** (covering the remainder of Greater London). See colour maps 6 and 7 at the back of the guide. If you want to look up a particular establishment, use the index to establishments (preceding page) to find the page number.

The symbols at the end of each accommodation entry give information about services and facilities. A 'key' to these symbols is inside the back cover flap, which can be kept open for easy reference.

INNER LONDON

Colour maps 6 & 7 at the back of the guide show place names and London Postal Area codes and will help you to locate accommodation in your chosen area of London.

LONDON E7

Grangewood Lodge Hotel
Listed
104 Clova Road, Forest Gate, London E7 9AF
☎ 081-534 0637 & 503 0941
Comfortable budget accommodation in a quiet road, pleasant garden. Easy access to central London, Docklands and M11. 12 minutes to Liverpool Street station.
Bedrooms: 9 single, 2 double, 6 twin, 3 triple
Bathrooms: 3 public, 1 private shower

Bed & breakfast
per night:	£min	£max
Single	15.00	18.00
Double	25.00	32.00

Parking for 3
Cards accepted: Access, Visa

Westbury Guest House
8 Westbury Road, Forest Gate, London E7 8BU
☎ 081-472 9848 & 518 2005
Victorian family house with all modern amenities and close to travel facilities. Ten minutes from London City Airport.
Bedrooms: 1 single, 2 twin
Bathrooms: 1 public

Bed & breakfast
per night:	£min	£max
Single	15.00	20.00
Double	30.00	40.00

Parking for 2

LONDON E10

Sleeping Beauty Motel
APPROVED
543 Lea Bridge Road, Leyton, London E10 7EB
☎ 081-556 8080
Fax 081-556 8080

All rooms en-suite with bath and showers, satellite TV. Lift, bar, car park. Warm and friendly atmosphere. Prices are per room.
Bedrooms: 26 double, 15 triple, 2 family rooms
Bathrooms: 43 private

Bed & breakfast
per night:	£min	£max
Single	30.00	35.00
Double	30.00	35.00

Parking for 34
Cards accepted: Access, Visa, Diners, Amex, Switch

LONDON N1

Kandara Guest House
Listed
68 Ockendon Road, London N1 3NW
☎ 071-226 5721 & 226 3379
Small family-run guesthouse near the Angel, Islington. Free street parking and good public transport to West End and City.
Bedrooms: 4 single, 2 double, 1 twin, 1 triple
Bathrooms: 2 public

LONDON N7

Five Kings Guest House
59 Anson Road, Tufnell Park, London N7 0AR
☎ 071-607 3996 & 607 6466
Privately-run guesthouse in a quiet residential area. 15 minutes to central London. Unrestricted parking in road.
Bedrooms: 6 single, 3 double, 3 twin, 2 triple, 2 family rooms
Bathrooms: 9 private, 3 public, 2 private showers

Bed & breakfast
per night:	£min	£max
Single	15.00	17.00
Double	26.00	30.00

Cards accepted: Access, Visa

LONDON N13

Mrs B Connolly
Listed
71 Berkshire Gardens, Palmers Green, London N13 6AA
☎ 081-888 5573
2-storey house with a garden, 5 minutes' bus ride from Wood Green Piccadilly line underground station. Car parking available.
Bedrooms: 1 single, 1 double
Bathrooms: 1 public

Continued ▶

We advise you to confirm your booking in writing.

25

LONDON

LONDON N13
Continued

Bed & breakfast
per night:	£min	£max
Single	9.00	10.00
Double	20.00	22.00

Lunch available
Parking for 1

LONDON N19
Parkland Walk Guest House
Listed COMMENDED

12 Hornsey Rise Gardens, London N19 3PR
☎ 071-263 3228
Fax 071-831 9489
Telex 262433

Friendly Victorian family house in residential area Highgate/Crouch End. Near many restaurants and convenient for central London. Non-smokers only. British Tourist Authority award winner - Best Small Hotel in London competition.
Bedrooms: 2 single, 1 twin, 1 double
Bathrooms: 2 public

Bed & breakfast
per night:	£min	£max
Single	22.00	28.00
Double	40.00	45.00

LONDON N22
Pane Residence
154 Boundary Road, Wood Green, London N22 6AE
☎ 081-889 3735

In a pleasant location 6 minutes' walk from Turnpike Lane underground station and near Alexandra Palace. Kitchen facilities available.
Bedrooms: 1 single, 1 double, 1 twin
Bathrooms: 1 public

Bed & breakfast
per night:	£min	£max
Single	16.00	17.00
Double	24.00	24.00

Parking for 2

LONDON NW2
The Abbotts Hotel
Listed

283-285 Willesden Lane, Willesden Green, London NW2 5JA
☎ 081-459 5387
Fax 081-208 3818

Please mention this guide when making a booking.

Homely and comfortable, a recently refurbished all en-suite hotel. Complimented for its friendly staff. Within easy reach of motorways, central London and Wembley complex.
Bedrooms: 6 single, 4 double, 4 twin, 4 triple, 4 family rooms
Bathrooms: 22 private

Bed & breakfast
per night:	£min	£max
Single	28.00	30.00
Double	36.00	38.00

Half board
per person:	£min	£max
Daily	35.00	38.00
Weekly	245.00	266.00

Evening meal 1800 (last orders 2030)
Parking for 15
Cards accepted: Access, Visa, Diners, Amex

Ad Display advertisement appears on page 29

LONDON NW3
The Langorf Hotel
COMMENDED

20 Frognal, Hampstead, London NW3 6AG
☎ 071-794 4483
Fax 071-435 9055

Three minutes' walk from Finchley Road underground, this elegant Edwardian residence in Hampstead boasts attractive bedrooms with full facilities. BTA Spencer Award runners-up.
Bedrooms: 1 single, 18 double, 8 twin, 4 triple
Bathrooms: 30 private

Bed & breakfast
per night:	£min	£max
Single	45.00	61.00
Double	50.00	90.00

Lunch available
Evening meal 1800 (last orders 2300)
Parking for 5
Cards accepted: Access, Visa, Diners, Amex

LONDON NW4
Rilux House

1 Lodge Road, London NW4 4DD
☎ 081-203 0933
Fax 081-203 6446

High standard, all private facilities, kitchenette and garden. Quiet. Close to underground, buses, M1, 20 minutes West End. Convenient for Wembley, easy route to Heathrow, direct trains to Gatwick and Luton airports. Languages spoken.
Bedrooms: 1 double
Bathrooms: 1 private

Bed & breakfast
per night:	£min	£max
Single	24.00	28.00
Double	39.00	48.00

Parking for 1

LONDON NW10
J and T Guest House
Listed

98 Park Ave North, Willesden Green, London NW10 1JY
☎ 081-452 4085
Fax 081-450 2503

Small guesthouse in north west London close to underground. Easy access to Wembley Stadium complex. 5 minutes from M1.
Bedrooms: 1 double, 3 twin, 1 triple
Bathrooms: 4 private, 1 public

Bed & breakfast
per night:	£min	£max
Single	25.00	27.00
Double	38.00	44.00

Parking for 2
Cards accepted: Access, Visa

LONDON SE6
Mrs Freda Ward
Listed

41 Minard Road, Catford, London SE6 1NP
☎ 081-697 2596

English home in quiet residential area off A205 South Circular road. 10 minutes' walk to 'Hither Green station for 20-minute journey to central London.
Bedrooms: 1 single, 2 twin
Bathrooms: 1 public

Bed & breakfast
per night:	£min	£max
Single	17.00	
Double	34.00	

Half board
per person:	£min	£max
Daily	22.50	

Evening meal 1700 (last orders 2000)

LONDON SE9
Meadow Croft Lodge
APPROVED

96-98 Southwood Road, New Eltham, London SE9 3QS
☎ 081-859 1488
Fax 081-850 8054

Between A2 and A20, near New Eltham station with easy access to London. Warm and friendly atmosphere. TV in

LONDON

rooms. British Tourist Authority London B&B award 1990.
Bedrooms: 4 single, 3 double, 9 twin, 1 family room
Bathrooms: 1 private, 4 public, 9 private showers

Bed & breakfast
per night:	£min	£max
Single	21.00	27.00
Double	37.00	42.00

Parking for 9
Cards accepted: Access, Visa

LONDON SE12
Kingsland House
Listed

45 Southbrook Road, Lee, London SE12 8LJ
☎ 081-318 4788
Detached house in conservation area, close to Blackheath and Greenwich and with easy access to City and West End. Homely atmosphere. Cooked breakfast when required.
Bedrooms: 2 single, 2 twin
Bathrooms: 1 public

Bed & breakfast
per night:	£min	£max
Single	18.00	20.00
Double	30.00	36.00

LONDON SE21
Diana Hotel

88 Thurlow Park Road, London SE21 8HY
☎ 081-670 3250
Small, friendly, family-run hotel in a pleasant suburb of Dulwich, 10 minutes from central London.
Bedrooms: 2 single, 4 double, 3 twin, 3 triple
Bathrooms: 2 private, 2 public, 2 private showers

Bed & breakfast
per night:	£min	£max
Single	28.00	38.00
Double	40.00	50.00

Evening meal 1800 (last orders 1930)
Parking for 3

LONDON SE22
Bedknobs
Listed COMMENDED

58 Glengarry Road, East Dulwich, London SE22 8QD
☎ 081-299 2004
Victorian family-run house, carefully restored, providing modern-day comforts and a friendly service. BTA London B & B award 1992.
Bedrooms: 1 single, 1 double, 1 twin, 1 triple

Bathrooms: 2 public

Bed & breakfast
per night:	£min	£max
Single	19.50	25.00
Double	35.00	42.00

LONDON SE26
Be My Guest

79 Venner Road, Sydenham, London SE26 5HU
☎ 081-659 5413
Fax 081-776 8151
Spacious Victorian residence, 15 minutes to central London from nearby stations. Free travel in London with reservations of 3 days or more. Car and driver service by arrangement.
Bedrooms: 1 twin, 2 family rooms
Bathrooms: 3 private

Bed & breakfast
per night:	£min	£max
Single	40.00	48.00
Double	48.00	57.00

Continued ▶

Please check prices and other details at the time of booking.

CORONA HOTEL

87-89 Belgrave Road, Victoria, London SW1V 2BQ
Tel : 071-828 9279   Fax : 071-931 8576

The Corona may be small in stature, but it is big on hospitality and prides itself on a homely personal service with the emphasis on immaculate cleanliness.

Our rooms have colour TV, radio, direct dial telephone, tea & coffee facilities, central heating and most have en suite bathrooms.

Major tourist attractions, West End theatres and the fashionable stores of Londonare all within easy reach.

ELIZABETH HOTEL

Friendly, private Hotel ideally located for all parts of the Capital
37 Eccleston Square, VICTORIA,
London SW1V 1PB.
Telephone: 071-828 6812

★ 1986 Winner of the ★
British Tourist Authority's
London Bed and Breakfast Award

CENTRAL LONDON SW1

Situated in stately garden square (c. 1835), close to Belgravia and a few doors from one of the residences of the late Sir Winston Churchill. Within two minutes' walk of Victoria Station/Coach Station/Air Terminals. Parking nearby.
Comfortable single, twin, double and family rooms.
Attractive lounge and pleasant Breakfast Room. Lift.
Good ENGLISH BREAKFAST, or Continental breakfast at any time for EARLY DEPARTURES.
MODERATE PRICES include accommodation, breakfast and Tax
FREE COLOUR BROCHURE AVAILABLE

English Tourist Board

LONDON

LONDON SE26
Continued

Half board per person:	£min	£max
Daily	34.00	63.00
Weekly	238.00	441.00

Lunch available
Evening meal 1900 (last orders 2000)
Parking for 2
Cards accepted: Access, Visa

LONDON SW1

Alexander Hotel
Listed

13 Belgrave Road, Victoria, London
SW1V 1RB
☎ 071-834 9718
Family-run hotel 3 minutes' walk from Victoria rail, coach and air terminal stations. Close to major attractions including Buckingham Palace.
Bedrooms: 1 single, 7 double, 2 twin, 2 triple, 1 family room
Bathrooms: 13 private

Bed & breakfast per night:	£min	£max
Single	25.00	40.00
Double	35.00	50.00

Cards accepted: Access, Visa

Alexander House Hotel
Listed APPROVED

32 Hugh Street, London SW1 1RT
☎ 071-834 5320
Guesthouse with TV in bedrooms. Full English breakfast.
Bedrooms: 2 single, 3 double, 2 twin, 2 triple
Bathrooms: 2 public

Bed & breakfast per night:	£min	£max
Single	20.00	25.00
Double	28.00	35.00

Elizabeth Hotel
37 Eccleston Square, London
SW1V 1PB
☎ 071-828 6812

Friendly, quiet hotel overlooking magnificent gardens of stately residential square (circa 1835), close to Belgravia and within 5 minutes' walk of Victoria.
Bedrooms: 12 single, 12 double, 6 twin, 4 triple, 9 family rooms
Bathrooms: 27 private, 6 public, 13 private showers

Bed & breakfast per night:	£min	£max
Single	36.00	57.00
Double	58.00	82.00

[Ad] Display advertisement appears on page 27

Georgian House Hotel
35 St. George's Drive, London
SW1V 4DG
☎ 071-834 1438
Fax 071-976 6085
Run by the direct descendants of the master builder who built the hotel in 1851. All facilities and extensive breakfast.
Bedrooms: 8 single, 14 double, 5 twin, 4 triple, 3 family rooms
Bathrooms: 23 private, 3 public, 8 private showers

Bed & breakfast per night:	£min	£max
Single	15.00	29.00
Double	28.00	44.00

Cards accepted: Access, Visa

Hamilton House Hotel
60 Warwick Way, London SW1V 1SA
☎ 071-821 7113
Fax 071-630 0806
Telex 262433 Ref B 1502
Hotel close to Victoria station and the West End. Warm and friendly atmosphere. Modern decor. Satellite TV. Comfortable family restaurant.
Bedrooms: 20 double, 21 twin, 2 triple
Bathrooms: 25 private, 6 public

Bed & breakfast per night:	£min	£max
Single	35.00	54.00
Double	45.00	65.00

Evening meal 1800 (last orders 2200)
Cards accepted: Access, Visa

Simone House Hotel
Listed

49 Belgrave Road, London SW1V 2BB
☎ 071-828 2474
Near Victoria station and within easy walking distance of numerous sightseeing attractions.
Bedrooms: 2 single, 5 double, 8 twin, 3 triple
Bathrooms: 8 private, 2 public

Bed & breakfast per night:	£min	£max
Single	18.00	24.00
Double	28.00	46.00

Stanley House Hotel
19-21 Belgrave Road, London
SW1V 1RB
☎ 071-834 5042 & 834 7292
Fax 071-834 8439
Telex 24699 KISMET G
Modern-style family hotel with spacious rooms, all with intercom and radio. Telex available.
Bedrooms: 5 double, 12 twin, 1 triple, 13 family rooms
Bathrooms: 18 private, 4 public

Sidney Hotel

Tel: 071-834 2738
Fax: 071-630 0973

74/76 BELGRAVE ROAD, VICTORIA, LONDON SW1V 2BP
WELCOME TO THE SIDNEY HOTEL

Noted for its friendly atmosphere and cleanliness, the Sidney Hotel is a few minutes walk from Victoria rail, tube and coach station.

Totally refurbished rooms, most with en suite bathrooms and colour TV, radio, direct dial telephone, tea/coffee facilities, hairdryers and irons.

We love old London and if we can help you enjoy it we will. Please book as far ahead as possible.

Home away from Home

LONDON

Bed & breakfast
per night:	£min	£max
Single	20.00	30.00
Double	30.00	40.00

Lunch available
Cards accepted: Access, Visa, Diners, Amex

Windermere Hotel ⋀
COMMENDED
142-144 Warwick Way, Victoria, London SW1V 4JE
☎ 071-834 5163 & 834 5480
Fax 071-630 8831
Telex 94017182 WIREG
Winner of the 1992 BTA Trophy, Small Hotel Award. Winner of the 1991 Certificate of Distinction. A friendly, charming hotel with well-appointed rooms and a licensed restaurant.
Bedrooms: 3 single, 11 double, 5 twin, 1 triple, 3 family rooms
Bathrooms: 19 private, 2 public

Bed & breakfast
per night:	£min	£max
Single	34.00	55.00
Double	48.00	73.00

Lunch available
Evening meal 1800 (last orders 2100)
Cards accepted: Access, Visa, Amex

LONDON SW3

Blair House Hotel ⋀
APPROVED
34 Draycott Place, London SW3 2SA
☎ 071-581 2323 & 581 2324
Fax 071-827 7752
A homely hotel in a quiet, elegant street close to Harrods and museums.
Bedrooms: 5 single, 4 double, 5 twin, 1 triple, 2 family rooms
Bathrooms: 10 private, 5 public

Bed & breakfast
per night:	£min	£max
Single	40.00	63.00
Double	60.00	73.00

Cards accepted: Access, Visa, Diners, Amex

LONDON SW5

Aaron House
17 Courtfield Gardens, London SW5 0PD
☎ 071-370 3991
Fax 071-373 2303
Victorian house overlooking a quiet garden square, providing rooms with original character but with modern facilities. Near public transport.
Bedrooms: 6 single, 6 double, 3 twin, 4 triple, 1 family room
Bathrooms: 12 private, 4 public

Bed & breakfast
per night:	£min	£max
Single	24.00	30.00
Double	34.00	42.00

Cards accepted: Access, Visa, Amex

Amsterdam Hotel ⋀
7 Trebovir Road, London SW5 9LS
☎ 071-370 5084
Fax 071-244 7608
Comfortable, attractively furnished rooms all with private bathroom, colour TV and direct dial telephone.
Bedrooms: 4 single, 8 double, 4 twin, 2 triple, 2 family rooms
Bathrooms: 20 private, 1 public

Bed & breakfast
per night:	£min	£max
Single	39.00	47.00
Double	51.00	60.00

Evening meal 1800 (last orders 2030)
Cards accepted: Access, Visa, Diners, Amex

Merlyn Court Hotel ⋀
2 Barkston Gardens, London SW5 0EN
☎ 071-370 1640
Fax 071-244 8024

Continued ▶

LONDON HOTEL

BEST RATES

SINGLES FROM £24 - £34
DOUBLES FROM £15 pp to £22 pp
FAMILIES 3/4/5 FROM £14 pp
GROUP RATES FROM £13 pp

**WINDSOR HOUSE HOTEL,
12 PENYWERN ROAD,
LONDON SW5 9ST**

Tel: 071 373 9087 Fax: 071 385 2417

5 Mins to Piccadilly

Call, fax or write now!
WELCOME TO LONDON

THE ABBOTT'S HOTEL

- Spacious Bedrooms all with En-Suite Facilities
- Furnished & Decorated to Highest Standard with all Modern Facilities
- Realistic Rates
- Family Rooms Available
- Private Car Park
- All Major Cards Accepted

**WEMBLEY STADIUM COMPLEX
LESS THAN 3 MILES AWAY**
2 Minutes from Local Tube
10 Minutes to Central London
M1 Motorway-7 Minutes Drive

**081-459 5387
Fax 081-208 3818**
24 Hours
283/285 Willesden Lane,
Willesden Green, London NW2 5JA

LONDON

LONDON SW5
Continued

Well-established, family-run, good value hotel in quiet Edwardian square, close to Earl's Court and Olympia. Direct underground link to Heathrow, the West End and rail stations. Car park nearby.
Bedrooms: 4 single, 4 double, 4 twin, 2 triple, 3 family rooms
Bathrooms: 8 private, 6 public, 2 private showers

Bed & breakfast
per night:	£min	£max
Single	25.00	35.00
Double	35.00	55.00

Cards accepted: Access, Visa

Swiss House Hotel
171 Old Brompton Road, London SW5 0AN
☎ 071-373 2769 & 373 9383
Fax 071-373 4983
Very clean, comfortable and conveniently situated hotel near London museums, shopping/exhibition centres. Gloucester Road underground station is within easy walking distance. Recent winner of BTA award for best value B&B in London.
Bedrooms: 2 single, 6 double, 2 twin, 6 triple
Bathrooms: 11 private, 1 public

Bed & breakfast
per night:	£min	£max
Single	34.00	48.00
Double	50.00	60.00

Cards accepted: Access, Visa, Diners, Amex

Windsor House
Listed
12 Penywern Road, London SW5 9ST
☎ 071-373 9087
Fax 081-385 2417

Budget-priced bed and breakfast establishment in Earl's Court. Easily reached from airports and motorway. The West End is minutes away by underground.
Bedrooms: 2 single, 5 double, 3 twin, 1 triple, 4 family rooms

Bathrooms: 1 private, 5 public, 11 private showers

Bed & breakfast
per night:	£min	£max
Single	24.00	34.00
Double	30.00	44.00

Parking for 10
Cards accepted: Access, Visa, Diners, Amex

Display advertisement appears on page 29

York House Hotel
28 Philbeach Gardens, London SW5 9EA
☎ 071-373 7519 & 373 7579
Fax 071-370 4641
Bed and breakfast hotel, conveniently located close to the Earl's Court and Olympia Exhibition Centres and the West End.
Bedrooms: 20 single, 9 double, 3 twin, 6 triple
Bathrooms: 1 private, 9 public

Bed & breakfast
per night:	£min	£max
Single	25.00	26.00
Double	40.00	57.00

Cards accepted: Access, Visa, Amex

LONDON SW7

Abcone Hotel
10 Ashburn Gardens, London SW7 4DG
☎ 071-370 3383
Fax 071-373 3082
Close to Gloucester Road underground and convenient for High Street Kensington, Knightsbridge, Olympia, Earl's Court, museums and Hyde Park.
Bedrooms: 16 single, 16 double, 3 twin
Bathrooms: 26 private, 3 public

Bed & breakfast
per night:	£min	£max
Single	35.00	65.00
Double	48.00	85.00

Evening meal 1900 (last orders 2130)
Cards accepted: Access, Visa, Diners, Amex

Five Sumner Place Hotel
HIGHLY COMMENDED
5 Sumner Place, South Kensington, London SW7 3EE
☎ 071-584 7586
Fax 071-823 9962
Winner of the Best Small Hotel in London Award. Situated in South Kensington, the most fashionable area. This family owned and run hotel offers first-class service and personal attention.
Bedrooms: 3 single, 6 double, 4 twin
Bathrooms: 13 private

Bed & breakfast
per night:	£min	£max
Single	72.00	84.00
Double	88.00	99.00

Cards accepted: Access, Visa, Amex

Kensbridge Hotel
Listed
31 Elvaston Place, London SW7 5NN
☎ 071-589 6265 & 589 2923
Fax 071-373 6183
Comfortable bed and breakfast hotel with refrigerator, colour TV and tea/coffee facilities in all rooms. Some self-catering suites available.
Bedrooms: 5 single, 4 double, 14 twin, 3 triple, 3 family rooms
Bathrooms: 18 private, 9 public, 7 private showers

Bed & breakfast
per night:	£min	£max
Single	20.00	28.00
Double	25.00	45.00

More House
53 Cromwell Road, South Kensington, London SW7 2EH
☎ 071-584 2040 & 584 2039
Large Victorian building in Kensington, close to museums and within walking distance of Hyde Park. Available July and August, only.
Bedrooms: 28 single, 20 twin
Bathrooms: 12 public

Bed & breakfast
per night:	£min	£max
Single		21.00
Double		36.00

Open July-August

Hotel Number Sixteen
16 Sumner Place, London SW7 3EG
☎ 071-589 5232
Fax 071-584 8615
Telex 266638

With atmosphere of a comfortable town house in very attractive street. Secluded award-winning gardens. Winner of the Spencer Trophy.
Bedrooms: 9 single, 27 double, 3 triple
Bathrooms: 37 private, 1 private shower

Bed & breakfast
per night:	£min	£max
Single	60.00	95.00
Double	110.00	135.00

LONDON

Cards accepted: Access, Visa, Diners, Amex

LONDON SW14

The Plough Inn
APPROVED

42 Christchurch Road, East Sheen, London SW14 7AF
☎ 081-876 7833 & 876 4533
A delightful old pub, established 1733. Next to Richmond Park. En-suite accommodation, traditional ales, home-cooked food.
Bedrooms: 7 double
Bathrooms: 7 private

Bed & breakfast
per night:	£min	£max
Single	47.00	50.00
Double	60.00	65.00

Half board
per person:	£min	£max
Daily	53.00	60.00

Lunch available
Evening meal 1930 (last orders 2130)
Parking for 6
Cards accepted: Access, Visa

LONDON SW19

Compton Guest House
Listed

65 Compton Road, Wimbledon, London SW19 7QA
☎ 081-947 4488 & 879 3245
Family-run guesthouse of a high standard, in a pleasant, sought-after, peaceful area. 5 minutes from Wimbledon station (British Rail and District Line), offering quick and easy access to the West End and central London, M1, M2, M3, M4, and M25. Quality rooms, good service.
Bedrooms: 2 single, 1 double, 2 twin, 1 triple, 2 family rooms
Bathrooms: 2 public

Bed & breakfast
per night:	£min	£max
Single	25.00	35.00
Double	35.00	55.00

Parking for 2

LONDON W1

Bentinck House Hotel ⚜

20 Bentinck Street, London W1M 5RL
☎ 071-935 9141
Fax 071-224 5903
Telex 8954111

We advise you to confirm your booking in writing.

Family-run bed and breakfast hotel in the heart of London's fashionable West End, close to Bond Street underground and Oxford Street.
Bedrooms: 6 single, 3 double, 4 twin, 3 triple, 1 family room
Bathrooms: 17 private, 4 public

Bed & breakfast
per night:	£min	£max
Single	39.00	52.00
Double	59.00	69.00

Half board
per person:	£min	£max
Daily	35.00	62.00
Weekly	240.00	360.00

Evening meal 1800 (last orders 2200)
Cards accepted: Access, Visa, Diners, Amex

Glynne Court Hotel
Listed

41 Great Cumberland Place, Marble Arch, London W1H 7GH
☎ 071-262 4344
Fax 071-724 2071
Friendly hotel, convenient for shops and theatres. 3 minutes' walk from Marble Arch, Hyde Park and Oxford Street.
Bedrooms: 2 single, 4 double, 3 twin, 2 triple, 1 family room
Bathrooms: 6 public

Bed & breakfast
per night:	£min	£max
Single		30.00
Double		40.00

Cards accepted: Access, Visa, Diners, Amex

Lincoln House Hotel ⚜
COMMENDED

33 Gloucester Place, London W1H 3PD
☎ 071-486 7630
Fax 071-486 0166
Newly refurbished Georgian hotel in heart of West End close to Oxford Street shops, theatres, etc. Ideal location for holiday or business trips. Well-appointed accommodation at economy rates.
Bedrooms: 4 single, 9 double, 5 twin, 4 triple
Bathrooms: 17 private, 1 public

Bed & breakfast
per night:	£min	£max
Single	35.00	49.00
Double	49.00	65.00

Cards accepted: Access, Visa, Diners, Amex, Switch

Regency Hotel ⚜

19 Nottingham Place, London W1M 3FF
☎ 071-486 5347
Fax 071-224 6057

Budget priced high quality hotel, tastefully furnished, with en-suite accommodation and facilities, in the heart of London's West End.
Bedrooms: 9 single, 7 double, 2 twin, 2 triple
Bathrooms: 18 private, 1 public

Bed & breakfast
per night:	£min	£max
Single	40.00	60.00
Double	60.00	75.00

Half board
per person:	£min	£max
Daily	50.00	70.00
Weekly	320.00	420.00

Lunch available
Evening meal 1800 (last orders 2030)
Cards accepted: Access, Visa, Diners, Amex, Switch

Wigmore Court Hotel ⚜
APPROVED

23 Gloucester Place, London W1H 3PB
☎ 071-935 0928
Fax 071-487 4254
Small, clean, fully refurbished family hotel. Large en-suite rooms - ideal for families. 3 minutes' walk to Oxford Street.
Bedrooms: 5 single, 6 double, 4 twin, 3 triple, 2 family rooms
Bathrooms: 18 private, 1 public

Bed & breakfast
per night:	£min	£max
Single	30.00	45.00
Double	45.00	60.00

Cards accepted: Access, Visa, Diners

Wyndham Hotel
Listed

30 Wyndham Street, London W1H 1DD
☎ 071-723 7204 & 723 9400
Small family-run bed and breakfast close to Baker Street and Marylebone stations. Well within walking distance of Oxford Street.
Bedrooms: 6 single, 2 double, 3 twin
Bathrooms: 1 public, 10 private showers

Continued ▶

LONDON

LONDON W1
Continued

Bed & breakfast per night:	£min	£max
Single	28.00	30.00
Double	38.00	40.00

LONDON W2

Abbey Court Hotel ⋒
Listed

174 Sussex Gardens, London W2 1TP
☎ 071-402 0704
Fax 071-262 2055
Central London hotel, reasonable prices. Within walking distance of Lancaster Gate, Paddington station and Hyde Park.
Bedrooms: 4 single, 7 double, 3 twin, 10 triple, 2 family rooms
Bathrooms: 10 private, 6 public, 6 private showers

Bed & breakfast per night:	£min	£max
Single	18.00	
Double	26.00	

Parking for 10
Cards accepted: Access, Visa, Amex

[Ad] Display advertisement appears on page 33, inside back cover

Albro House Hotel ⋒

155 Sussex Gardens, London W2 2RY
☎ 071-724 2931
Fax 071-724 2931
Ideally located in pleasant area near public transport. Nice rooms, mostly en-suite. English breakfast. Languages spoken. Friendly and safe. Some parking available.
Bedrooms: 2 single, 4 double, 6 twin, 3 triple, 1 family room
Bathrooms: 9 private, 3 public, 1 private shower

Bed & breakfast per night:	£min	£max
Single	18.00	38.00
Double	32.00	48.00

Parking for 1
Cards accepted: Access, Visa, Diners

Barry House Hotel ⋒
APPROVED

12 Sussex Place, London W2 2TP
☎ 071-723 7340 & 723 0994
Fax 071-723 9775
Family-run bed and breakfast hotel, 4 minutes' walking distance from Paddington station. Hyde Park, Marble Arch and Oxford Street close by. Direct-dial telephones.
Bedrooms: 3 single, 2 double, 11 twin, 2 family rooms
Bathrooms: 14 private, 2 public

Bed & breakfast per night:	£min	£max
Single	28.00	36.00
Double	50.00	56.00

Cards accepted: Access, Visa, Diners, Amex

Beverley House Hotel ⋒

142 Sussex Gardens, London W2 1UB
☎ 071-723 3380
Fax 071-402 3292
Recently refurbished bed and breakfast hotel, serving traditional English breakfast and offering high standards at low prices. Close to Paddington station, Hyde Park and museums.
Bedrooms: 6 single, 5 double, 6 twin, 6 triple
Bathrooms: 23 private

Bed & breakfast per night:	£min	£max
Single	35.00	45.00
Double	40.00	57.00

Evening meal 1800 (last orders 2200)
Parking for 2
Cards accepted: Access, Visa, Diners, Amex

Europa House Hotel ⋒
Listed APPROVED

151 Sussex Gardens, London W2 2RY
☎ 071-723 7343 & 402 1923
Fax 071-224 9331
Close to Hyde Park, and convenient for the Heathrow Airbus link. All rooms with en-suite facilities, tea and coffee making facilities, colour TV. English breakfast included.
Bedrooms: 2 single, 2 double, 7 twin, 5 triple, 2 family rooms
Bathrooms: 18 private, 1 public

Bed & breakfast per night:	£min	£max
Single	32.00	35.00
Double	45.00	50.00

Parking for 1
Cards accepted: Access, Visa

Hyde Park Rooms Hotel ⋒

137 Sussex Gardens, Hyde Park, London W2 2RX
☎ 071-723 0225 & 723 0965
Small centrally located private hotel with personal service. Within walking distance of Hyde Park and Kensington Gardens. Car parking available.
Bedrooms: 5 single, 6 double, 4 twin, 2 triple, 3 family rooms
Bathrooms: 5 private, 2 public

Bed & breakfast per night:	£min	£max
Single	20.00	30.00
Double	30.00	45.00

Parking for 3

Cards accepted: Access, Visa, Diners, Amex, Switch

Kensington Garden Hotel
HIGHLY COMMENDED

9 Kensington Gardens Square, London W2 4BH
☎ 071-221 7790
Fax 071-792 8612
Beautifully refurbished Victorian building, centrally situated close to Bayswater and Queensway underground station. Easy access to airports and British Rail stations.
Bedrooms: 8 single, 4 double, 3 twin, 2 triple
Bathrooms: 13 private, 4 private showers

Bed & breakfast per night:	£min	£max
Single	30.00	40.00
Double	55.00	65.00

Lunch available
Evening meal 1900 (last orders 2300)
Cards accepted: Access, Visa, Diners, Amex

Mitre House Hotel ⋒
COMMENDED

178-184 Sussex Gardens, Hyde Park, London W2 1TU
☎ 071-723 8040 & 402 5695
Fax 071-402 0990
Telex 914113 MITRE G
Family-run hotel, recently refurbished to a high standard, well located for shops and sights. Free car park. Junior and family suites available.
Bedrooms: 9 single, 18 double, 26 twin, 17 triple
Bathrooms: 70 private, 3 public

Bed & breakfast per night:	£min	£max
Single	45.00	55.00
Double	54.99	65.00

Parking for 20
Cards accepted: Access, Visa, Diners, Amex

Nayland Hotel ⋒

132-134 Sussex Gardens, London W2 1UB
☎ 071-723 4615
Fax 071-402 3292
Centrally located, close to many amenities and within walking distance of Hyde Park and Oxford Street. Quality you can afford.
Bedrooms: 11 single, 8 double, 17 twin, 5 triple
Bathrooms: 41 private

Bed & breakfast per night:	£min	£max
Single	40.00	50.00
Double	46.00	62.00

Evening meal 1800 (last orders 2100)

LONDON

ACCOMMODATION

Central London — WESTPOINT HOTEL — **Budget Prices**

WESTPOINT HOTEL

170 Sussex Gardens, Hyde Park, London W2 1PT.
Tel: 071-402 0281 (Reservations) Fax: 071-224 9114.

Most rooms with private shower & toilet, radio/intercom
& colour TV. Children welcome. TV lounge.

This hotel has long been a popular choice amongst tourists because of its central location, being near to Hyde Park and only 2 minutes from Paddington and Lancaster Gate tube stations. The West End's tourist attractions, including theatres, museums and Oxford Street stores, are within easy reach. Individuals, families and groups are all welcome.

• PRIVATE CAR PARK • DIRECT A2 BUS FROM HEATHROW •

RATES: Low Season
Singles from £18 per person.
Doubles from £13 per person.
Family rooms from £11 per person.

High Season
Singles from £24 per person.
Doubles from £15 per person.
Family rooms from £13 per person.

ABBEY COURT HOTEL

174 Sussex Gardens, Hyde Park, London W2 1TP.
Tel: 071-402 0704 Fax: 071-262 2055.

Open all year. Radio Intercom in every room. Children welcome.
Most rooms with private shower, toilet and colour TV.

• CAR PARKING AVAILABLE • A2 BUS FROM HEATHROW •

Central London hotel in a pleasant avenue near Hyde Park and within 2 minutes' walking distance of Paddington main line and tube station and Lancaster Gate tube station. The tourist attractions of the West End including theatres, museums and Oxford Street are within easy reach. Individuals, families, school parties and groups are all welcome and group tours can be arranged.

TERMS per person:
High Season: Single from £26.00, double from £18.00 p.p., family £13.00 p.p.
Low season: Single from £20.00, double from £14.50 p.p., family from £12.00 p.p.

Special Prices
SASS HOUSE HOTEL

11 Craven Terrace, Hyde Park, London W2 3QD.
Tel: 071-262 2325 Fax: 071-262 0889

★ Centrally located – within easy reach of London's most famous tourist attractions.
★ Nearest underground Paddington and Lancaster Gate. ★ Served by a network of bus routes.
★ Colour television lounge. ★ Centrally heated. ★ Radio and intercom in all rooms.
★ Special group and party booking rates. ★ Parking facilities available.
★ A2 bus from Heathrow.

RATES per person: single from £16.00. Double room from £12.00 p.p.
and family room or party booking rate from £12.00 p.p. inc.. bed & breakfast.

LONDON

LONDON W2
Continued

Parking for 5
Cards accepted: Access, Visa, Diners, Amex

Park Lodge Hotel
APPROVED

73 Queensborough Terrace,
Bayswater, London W2 3SU
☎ 071-229 6424
Fax 071-221 4772
Centrally located hotel, close to Hyde Park and convenient for Oxford Street, theatres and restaurants.
Bedrooms: 11 single, 10 double,
6 twin, 1 triple, 1 family room
Bathrooms: 29 private
Bed & breakfast

per night:	£min	£max
Single	30.00	38.00
Double	40.00	48.00

Cards accepted: Access, Visa, Diners, Amex

Parkwood Hotel
APPROVED

4 Stanhope Place, London W2 2HB
☎ 071-402 2241
Fax 071-402 1574
Smart townhouse convenient for Hyde Park and Oxford Street. Comfortable bedrooms and friendly atmosphere.
Bedrooms: 5 single, 2 double, 7 twin,
4 triple
Bathrooms: 12 private, 2 public
Bed & breakfast

per night:	£min	£max
Single	30.00	45.00
Double	45.00	55.00

Cards accepted: Access, Visa

Rhodes House Hotel
APPROVED

195 Sussex Gardens, London W2 2RJ
☎ 071-262 5617 & 262 0537
Fax 071-723 4054
Rooms with private facilities, TV and telephone. Friendly atmosphere. Families especially welcome. Near transport for sightseeing and shopping.
Bedrooms: 3 single, 3 double, 3 twin,
9 family
Bathrooms: 15 private, 2 public
Bed & breakfast

per night:	£min	£max
Single	35.25	47.00
Double	41.25	56.00

Cards accepted: Access, Visa

Rose Court Hotel

1-3 Talbot Square, London W2 1TR
☎ 071-723 5128
Fax 071-723 1855
Telex 262643
Privately-run Victorian town house in a quiet garden square. Close to Paddington and the West End.
Bedrooms: 3 single, 15 double,
12 twin, 7 triple, 3 family rooms
Bathrooms: 39 private, 2 public
Bed & breakfast

per night:	£min	£max
Single	36.00	46.00
Double	46.00	65.00

Half board

per person:	£min	£max
Daily	42.00	52.00
Weekly	270.00	310.00

Lunch available
Evening meal 1800 (last orders 2230)
Cards accepted: Access, Visa, Diners, Amex

Royal Cambridge Hotel

124 Sussex Gardens, London W2 1UB
☎ 071-873 0000
Fax 071-873 0830

Charming townhouse hotel, centrally located 10 minutes' walk from Oxford Street and Hyde Park. Thoughtfully refurbished and offering high standard amenities.
Bedrooms: 6 single, 10 double,
13 twin
Bathrooms: 29 private
Bed & breakfast

per night:	£min	£max
Single	35.00	55.00
Double	55.00	95.00

Half board

per person:	£min	£max
Daily	42.50	62.50
Weekly	262.50	420.00

Parking for 3
Cards accepted: Access, Visa, Diners, Amex, Switch

Ruddimans Hotel
Listed APPROVED

160-162 Sussex Gardens, London
W2 1UD
☎ 071-723 1026 & 723 6715
Fax 071-262 2983
Comfortable hotel close to West End and London's attractions, offering generous English breakfast and good service at reasonable prices. Car park.

Bedrooms: 10 single, 12 double,
12 twin, 6 triple
Bathrooms: 26 private, 4 public
Bed & breakfast

per night:	£min	£max
Single	24.00	30.00
Double	34.00	42.00

Parking for 6

Sass House Hotel
Listed

10 & 11 Craven Terrace, London
W2 3QD
☎ 071-262 2325
Fax 071-262 0889
Budget accommodation, convenient for central London, Hyde Park and the West End. Paddington and Lancaster Gate underground stations nearby. Easy access to tourist attractions.
Bedrooms: 4 single, 4 double, 4 twin,
6 triple
Bathrooms: 3 public
Bed & breakfast

per night:	£min	£max
Single	16.00	
Double	24.00	

Cards accepted: Access, Visa, Amex

Display advertisement appears on page 33, inside back cover

Springfield Hotel
Listed APPROVED

154 Sussex Gardens, London W2 1UD
☎ 071-723 9898
Fax 071-723 0874
Small hotel close to Hyde Park and Marble Arch.
Bedrooms: 3 single, 2 double, 8 twin,
3 family rooms
Bathrooms: 13 private, 3 public
Bed & breakfast

per night:	£min	£max
Single	25.00	30.00
Double	35.00	40.00

Parking for 2
Cards accepted: Access, Visa, Diners, Switch

Westpoint Hotel
Listed

170-172 Sussex Gardens, London
W2 1TP
☎ 071-402 0281
Fax 071-224 9114
Inexpensive accommodation in central London. Close to Paddington and Lancaster Gate underground stations. Easy access to tourist attractions and Hyde Park.
Bedrooms: 2 single, 17 double, 6 twin,
9 triple, 6 family rooms
Bathrooms: 23 private, 5 public,
1 private shower

LONDON

Bed & breakfast
per night:	£min	£max
Single	18.00	
Double	25.00	

Parking for 15
Cards accepted: Access, Visa, Diners, Amex

🛏 Display advertisement appears on page 33, inside back cover

LONDON W5

Corfton Guest House

42 Corfton Road, Ealing, London W5 2HT
☎ 081-998 1120
Close to Ealing Broadway station, in a quiet residential area of considerable character.
Bedrooms: 2 single, 4 double, 1 twin, 2 triple
Bathrooms: 4 private, 2 public

Bed & breakfast
per night:	£min	£max
Single	14.00	25.00
Double	22.00	30.00

Parking for 6

Creffield Lodge
Listed

2-4 Creffield Road, Ealing, London W5 3HN
☎ 081-993 2284
Fax 081-992 7082
Telex 935114

Victorian-style property on ground and two upper floors, located in quiet residential road, adjacent to 150-bedroom Carnarvon Hotel.
Bedrooms: 10 single, 4 double, 4 twin, 1 triple
Bathrooms: 5 private, 5 public

Bed & breakfast
per night:	£min	£max
Single	27.50	47.50
Double	42.50	62.50

Lunch available
Evening meal 1830 (last orders 2130)
Parking for 20
Cards accepted: Access, Visa, Diners, Amex

Eaton Guesthouse

60 Eaton Rise, London W5 2HA
☎ 081-998 2157
In a quiet residential area, 5 minutes' walk from Ealing Broadway British Rail and underground stations.

Bedrooms: 3 single, 2 double, 3 twin, 1 triple
Bathrooms: 3 private, 2 public

Bed & breakfast
per night:	£min	£max
Single	15.00	19.00
Double	25.00	32.00

Parking for 6

Grange Lodge

48-50 Grange Road, Ealing, London W5 5BX
☎ 081-567 1049
Fax 081-579 5350
Quiet, comfortable hotel within a few hundred yards of the underground station. Midway between central London and Heathrow.
Bedrooms: 7 single, 1 double, 4 twin, 2 triple
Bathrooms: 9 private, 2 public

Bed & breakfast
per night:	£min	£max
Single	22.00	35.00
Double	33.00	47.00

Parking for 10
Cards accepted: Access, Visa

The White House
HIGHLY COMMENDED

14 North Common Road, London W5 2QB
☎ 081-567 2224
Imposing Victorian detached family home overlooking Ealing Common, tastefully furnished with antiques. Conveniently near Heathrow and central London. Close to underground.
Bedrooms: 2 double
Bathrooms: 2 private

Bed & breakfast
per night:	£min	£max
Single	37.50	47.50
Double	47.50	62.50

Parking for 1

LONDON W8

Vicarage Private Hotel

10 Vicarage Gate, Kensington, London W8 4AG
☎ 071-229 4030
Delightful, family-run Victorian townhouse hotel, situated in a quiet garden square, offering a generous freshly-cooked English breakfast and a "home from home" atmosphere. Ideally located for all tourist attractions and transport facilities.
Bedrooms: 9 single, 2 double, 5 twin, 3 triple
Bathrooms: 5 public

Bed & breakfast
per night:	£min	£max
Single	30.00	32.00
Double	54.00	56.00

LONDON W14

Avonmore Hotel
COMMENDED

66 Avonmore Road, Kensington, London W14 8RS
☎ 071-603 3121 & 603 4296
Fax 071-603 4035
Privately owned, with a friendly atmosphere. 3 minutes' walk from West Kensington underground station, Olympia Exhibition Centre and Earl's Court.
Bedrooms: 1 single, 2 double, 3 twin, 3 triple
Bathrooms: 7 private, 1 public

Bed & breakfast
per night:	£min	£max
Single	45.00	56.00
Double	57.00	67.00

Cards accepted: Access, Visa

LONDON WC1

George Hotel

58-60 Cartwright Gardens, London WC1H 9EL
☎ 071-387 8777
Fax 071-383 5044
Central London hotel in a quiet square. Comfortable, bright rooms with TV. Gardens and tennis courts available for guests' use.
Bedrooms: 16 single, 1 double, 5 twin, 10 triple, 8 family rooms
Bathrooms: 3 private, 14 public, 4 private showers

Bed & breakfast
per night:	£min	£max
Single	29.50	39.50
Double	41.50	49.50

Cards accepted: Access, Visa, Switch

St. Athan's Hotel
Listed

20 Tavistock Place, Russell Square, London WC1H 9RE
☎ 071-837 9140 & 837 9627
Fax 071-833 8752
Small family-run hotel offering bed and breakfast.
Bedrooms: 16 single, 15 double, 15 twin, 5 family rooms
Bathrooms: 6 private, 12 public

Bed & breakfast
per night:	£min	£max
Single	28.00	40.00
Double	38.00	50.00

Cards accepted: Access, Visa, Diners, Amex

LONDON WC1
Continued

Thanet Hotel
Listed **COMMENDED**
8 Bedford Place, London WC1B 5JA
☎ 071-636 2869 & 580 3377
Fax 071-323 6676
Comfortable, family-run hotel, with colour TV, tea and coffee and direct-dial telephones. Mostly en-suite rooms. Next to British Museum, close to London's famous Theatreland. Full English breakfast.
Bedrooms: 2 single, 4 double, 3 twin, 3 triple, 1 family room
Bathrooms: 8 private, 2 public

Bed & breakfast
per night:	£min	£max
Single	40.00	50.00
Double	50.00	60.00

Cards accepted: Access, Visa

LONDON WC2

Hotel Strand Continental
Listed
143 The Strand, London WC2R 1JA
☎ 071-836 4880
Small hotel with friendly atmosphere, near theatres and famous London landmarks.
Bedrooms: 10 single, 8 double, 2 twin, 2 triple
Bathrooms: 6 public

Bed & breakfast
per night:	£min	£max
Single	24.00	27.00
Double	30.00	33.00

Colour maps at the back of this guide pinpoint all places which have accommodation listings in the guide.

OUTER LONDON
Colour maps 6 & 7 at the back of the guide show place names and London Postal Area codes and will help you to locate accommodation in your chosen area of London.

CROYDON

Croydon Hotel
112 Lower Addiscombe Road, Croydon CR0 6AD
☎ 081-656 7233
Fax 081-656 7233
Close to central Croydon - route A222 and 10 minutes' walk from East Croydon Station. Opposite shops and restaurants.
Bedrooms: 1 single, 4 double, 3 twin
Bathrooms: 6 private, 1 public

Bed & breakfast
per night:	£min	£max
Single	25.00	34.00
Double	42.00	42.00

Parking for 4
Cards accepted: Access, Visa

Ad Display advertisement appears on this page

Iverna
Listed
1 Annandale Road, Addiscombe, Croydon CR0 7HP
☎ 081-654 8639
Large house in a quiet road, close to East Croydon station. London Victoria 15 minutes away. No smoking in public areas.
Bedrooms: 2 single, 1 twin
Bathrooms: 1 public

Bed & breakfast
per night:	£min	£max
Single	18.00	20.00
Double	34.00	38.00

Parking for 1

HARROW

Crescent Lodge Hotel
COMMENDED
58-60 Welldon Crescent, Harrow, Middlesex HA1 1QR
☎ 081-863 5491 & 863 5163
Fax 081-427 5965
All rooms have colour TV with video and satellite, direct-dial telephone, refrigerator, hospitality tray. Residential restaurant and bar, garden. Wembley 10 minutes, West End 20 minutes, Heathrow 35 minutes. Special rates for corporate users.
Bedrooms: 9 single, 3 double, 7 twin, 1 triple, 1 family room
Bathrooms: 12 private, 4 public

Bed & breakfast
per night:	£min	£max
Single	32.00	43.00
Double	45.00	55.00

Half board
per person:	£min	£max
Daily	47.00	58.00
Weekly	315.00	385.00

Lunch available
Evening meal 1900 (last orders 2030)
Parking for 7
Cards accepted: Access, Visa, Diners, Amex

HEATHROW AIRPORT
See under West Drayton

PURLEY

Mrs J Stock
Listed
"Stocks", 51 Selcroft Road, Purley, Surrey CR8 1AJ
☎ 081-660 3054
Fax 081-660 3054
Central London 20 minutes by train. Convenient for M25, M23 and Gatwick Airport.
Bedrooms: 2 single, 1 double
Bathrooms: 1 public

CROYDON HOTEL

En-suite rooms with tea/coffee facilities and colour T.V. Parking on route A222.
8 minutes walk to East Croydon Station frequent direct trains to Victoria and Gatwick Airport.
Opp. restaurants and shops.

112 Lower Addiscombe Road, Croydon, CR0 6AD Tel and Fax: 081 656 7233

LONDON

Bed & breakfast
per night: £min £max
Single 20.00 25.00
Double 36.00 46.00

Evening meal 1800 (last orders 2100)
Parking for 3
Open January-November

WEMBLEY

Arena Hotel

6 Forty Lane, Wembley, Middlesex
HA9 9EB
☎ 081-908 0670 & 908 2850
Fax 081-908 2007
Spacious accommodation with TV and satellite link in every room. New refurbishment, only 1800 yards from Wembley Stadium complex. Easy access by all transport routes.
Bedrooms: 2 single, 1 double, 4 twin, 3 triple
Bathrooms: 8 private, 2 public

Bed & breakfast
per night: £min £max
Single 25.00 35.00
Double 35.00 49.00

Parking for 10
Cards accepted: Access, Visa

Elm Hotel
APPROVED

1-7 Elm Road, Wembley, Middlesex
HA9 7JA
☎ 081-902 1764
Fax 081-903 8365
Ten minutes' walk (1200 yards) from Wembley Stadium and Conference Centre. 150 yards from Wembley Central underground and mainline station.
Bedrooms: 7 single, 9 double, 9 twin, 5 triple
Bathrooms: 21 private, 4 public

Bed & breakfast
per night: £min £max
Single 35.00 45.00
Double 45.00 55.00

Parking for 6
Cards accepted: Access, Visa

WEST DRAYTON

The Alice House
Listed APPROVED

9 Hollycroft Close, Sipson, West Drayton, Middlesex UB7 OJJ
☎ 081-897 9032
Small, clean and comfortable guesthouse. Convenient for the airport, but with no noise from flight path. Car service to airport available. Evening meal by arrangement. Close M4, M25. London 40 minutes. Parking.

Bedrooms: 1 single, 1 double, 1 twin
Bathrooms: 1 public

Bed & breakfast
per night: £min £max
Single 28.00 32.00
Double 38.00 42.00

Evening meal 1800 (last orders 2000)
Parking for 6

Apple Tree Cottage

1a Frays Avenue, West Drayton, Middlesex UB7 7AF
☎ (0895) 448872
Charming and comfortable accommodation in cottage-style house. 10 minutes to Heathrow, 30 minutes to central London, close to M4, M40, M25.
Bedrooms: 1 single, 2 double
Bathrooms: 1 public, 1 private shower

Bed & breakfast
per night: £min £max
Single 20.00 28.00
Double 34.00 38.00

Evening meal 1900 (last orders 2130)
Parking for 2

Use your i's

There are more than 550 Tourist Information Centres throughout England offering friendly help with accommodation and holiday ideas as well as suggestions of places to visit and things to do.

In your home town there may be a centre which can help you before you set out. You'll find the address of your nearest Tourist Information Centre in your local Phone Book.

Cumbria

Home of the Great Lakes, this beautiful region has some of the most spectacular views in England, and so much more! Discover the secrets of Morecambe Bay, where many a stagecoach lost its race against the incoming tide, or visit Hadrian's Wall, built by the Romans as a defence against savage raids from the North. And there is Carlisle, the great border city, with a flavour all of its own. For total peace, seek out the stark beauty and solitude of the Pennine Way or the pretty villages and wooded hillsides cradled within the rich countryside of the Eden Valley. And throughout there is a chorus of inns, museums and attractions to suit all tastes.

WHERE TO GO, WHAT TO SEE

The number against each name will help you locate it on the map (page 41).

❶ Naworth Castle
Brampton, Cumbria
Tel: Brampton (069 77) 41156
Historic border fortress, built in 1335 and renovated in 1602. Great hall, Gobelin tapestries, Pre-Raphaelite library, 14th C dungeons.

❷ Carlisle Castle
Carlisle, Cumbria CA3 8UR
Tel: Carlisle (0228) 31777
Border stronghold – keep built 1092 on site of Roman fort. 12th C keep with vaulted passages, chambers, staircases, towers and dungeon. 14th C main gate with portcullis.

❷ Tullie House
Castle Street, Carlisle, Cumbria CA3 8TP
Tel: Carlisle (0228) 34781
Major tourist complex housing museum, art gallery, theatre, shops, restaurant, bars.

❸ South Tynedale Railway
Railway Station, Alston, Cumbria CA9 3JB
Tel: Alston (0434) 381696
2ft gauge railway following part of the route of the former Alston to Haltwhistle branch line through South Tynedale.

Valued by professional climbers for its high sugar content, Kendal Mint Cake will sustain you on strenuous fell walks.

❹ Flying Buzzard and Vic 96 – The Hold
Elizabeth Dock, South Quay, Maryport, Cumbria CA15 8AB
Tel: Maryport (0900) 815954
Restored 1951 Clyde tug. Guided tours of entire ship. Children's activity gallery in hold of restored 1945 steam lighter. Engine steamed on occasion.

❺ Hutton-in-the-Forest
Skelton, Cumbria CA11 9TH
Tel: Skelton (076 84) 84449
14th C Pele Tower with later additions. Tapestries, furniture, paintings, china, armour. Formal gardens, dovecote, lake and woods with specimen trees.

Cumbria

The steam launch 'Dolly', built around 1850, can be seen at Windermere Steamboat Museum.

⑥ Armathwaite Hall Farm Park
Coalbeck Farm, Bassenthwaite, Cumbria CA12 4RE
Tel: Keswick (076 87) 76236
Farm park with collection of rare and interesting farm animals and poultry.

⑦ Mirehouse
Underskiddaw, Cumbria CA12 4QE
Tel: Keswick (076 87) 72287
Manuscripts and portraits with many literary connections, Victorian schoolroom/nursery, antiques quiz, woodland and lakeside walk, 4 adventure playgrounds.

⑧ Dalemain
Dacre, Cumbria CA11 OHB
Tel: Pooley Bridge (076 84) 86290
Historic house, Georgian furniture, Westmorland and Cumberland Yeomanry Museum. Agricultural bygones, adventure playground, licensed restaurant, gardens.

⑨ Lowther Leisure Park
Hackthorpe, Cumbria CA10 2HG
Tel: Hackthorpe (0931) 712523
Over 40 attractions including Stevensons Crown Circus, Lowther adventure fort, Tarzan trail, assault course and train rides.

⑩ Whinlatter Visitor Centre
Braithwaite, Cumbria CA12 5TW
Tel: Braithwaite (076 87) 82469
Interpretative forestry exhibition with audio-visual presentations. Working model of forest operations, lecture theatre, walks, trails, orienteering.

⑪ Cumberland Pencil Museum
Southey Works, Keswick, Cumbria CA12 5NG
Tel: Keswick (076 87) 73626
Pencil story from discovery of graphite to present. Video presentation of operations inside pencil factory and mines exhibition.

⑪ Lingholm Gardens
Lingholm, Keswick, Cumbria CA12 5UA
Tel: Keswick (076 87) 72003
Formal and woodland gardens, azaleas, rhododendrons. Views of Borrowdale and Skiddaw. Plant centre.

⑫ Ponsonby Farm Park
Ponsonby, Cumbria CA20 1BX
Tel: Beckermet (0946) 841426
Working mixed farm, rare breeds of farm animals, old and modern farm buildings. Tearoom, shop, picnic and play area.

⑬ Dove Cottage and Wordsworth Museum
Grasmere, Cumbria LA22 9SH
Tel: Grasmere (053 94) 35544
Wordsworth's home 1799–1808. Poet's possessions, museum with manuscripts, farmhouse reconstruction, paintings and drawings. Special exhibitions throughout the year.

⑭ Muncaster Mill
Ravenglass, Cumbria CA18 1ST
Tel: Ravenglass (0229) 717323
Working water-powered corn mill. Early Victorian machinery in daily use producing a range of stone-ground flours and oatmeals.

⑭ Muncaster Castle, Gardens and Owl Centre
Ravenglass, Cumbria CA18 1RQ
Tel: Ravenglass (0229) 717614
14th C pele tower with 15th and 19th C additions. Gardens with exceptional collection of rhododendrons and azaleas. Extensive collection of owls.

⑮ Brantwood
Coniston, Cumbria LA21 8AD
Tel: Coniston (053 94) 41396
Beautiful home of John Ruskin. Superb lake and mountain views. Works by Ruskin and

39

Cumbria

Writer Beatrix Potter's love of nature took her from London to the Lake District, where her home is now a museum.

contemporaries, memorabilia. Craft and picture galleries.

⑯ Brockhole Lake District National Park Visitor Centre
Windermere, Cumbria LA23 1LJ
Tel: Windermere (053 94) 46601
Exhibitions include the National Park Story, slide shows and films. Shop, gardens, grounds, adventure playground, trails, events. Restaurant, tearoom.

⑯ Windermere Steamboat Museum
Rayrigg Road, Bowness-on-Windermere, Cumbria LA23 1BN
Tel: Windermere (053 94) 45565
Steamboats and other vintage craft, many afloat. Steam launch trips. Model boat pond, museum, shop and restaurant.

⑯ The World of Beatrix Potter Exhibition
The Old Laundry, Crag Brow, Bowness-on-Windermere, Cumbria LA23 3BT
Tel: Windermere (053 94) 88444
Exhibition interpreting the life and works of Beatrix Potter, comprising 9-screen video wall and film.

⑰ Grizedale Forest Park Visitor Centre
Grizedale, Hawkshead, Cumbria LA22 0QJ
Tel: Satterthwaite (0229) 860373
Displays show Grizedale from wildwood to woodland managed by the Forestry Commission for timber, wildlife and people. Trails, walks, hides, orienteering, books, maps.

⑱ Abbot Hall Art Gallery
Abbot Hall, Kirkland, Kendal, Cumbria LA9 5AL
Tel: Kendal (0539) 722464
18th C mansion house. Paintings by Romney, Ruskin and Turner. Furniture by Gillows. Variety of exhibitions.

⑲ Graythwaite Hall Gardens
Newby Bridge, Cumbria LA12 8BA
Tel: Newby Bridge (053 95) 31248
Rhododendrons, azaleas and flowering shrubs. Laid out by T. Mawson 1888–1890.

⑳ Gleaston Watermill
Gleaston, Ulverston, Cumbria LA12 0QH
Tel: Bardsea (0229) 869244
Water cornmill in working order. Impressive Grade II listed wooden machinery and watermill. Farm tools display. Craft workshop including videos.

⑳ The Country Store
Lindal Business Park, Lindal-in-Furness, Ulverston, Cumbria LA12 0LL
Tel: Dalton (0229) 65099
One of Britain's major candle manufacturers offering visitors the opportunity to learn about all aspects of candlemaking and to buy the products at reduced rates.

⑳ Laurel and Hardy Museum
4C Upper Brook Street, Ulverston, Cumbria LA12 7BQ
Tel: Ulverston (0229) 52292
Memorabilia of Laurel and Hardy including films, books, posters and film stills.

㉑ Lakeland Wildlife Oasis
Hale, Cumbria LA7 7BW
Tel: (053 95) 63027
A wildlife exhibition where both living animals and inanimate 'hands on' displays are used to illustrate evolution in the animal kingdom. Gift shop.

㉒ Lakeland Motor Museum
Cark in Cartmel, Cumbria LA11 7PL
Tel: Grange-over-Sands (053 95) 58509
Over 100 historic cars, motorcycles, bicycles and engines. 1920s replica garage. Many collections of transport-related items. Esso historic exhibition.

Cumbria

FIND OUT MORE

Further information about holidays and attractions in the Cumbria region is available from:
Cumbria Tourist Board
Ashleigh, Holly Road,
Windermere, Cumbria LA23 2AQ
Tel: (053 94) 44444

Use the map below to locate places in the 'Where to Go, What to See' section.

These publications are available from the Cumbria Tourist Board (post free):
Cumbria The Lake District Touring Map (including tourist information and touring caravan and camping parks) £2.95
Places to Visit and Things to Do in Cumbria The Lake District (over 200 ideas for a great day out) 95p
Short Walks - Good for Families (route descriptions, maps and information for 14 walks in the lesser-known areas of Cumbria) 95p
Wordsworth's Lake District (folded map showing major Wordsworthian sites plus biographical details) 45p. Japanese language version £1
Explore Cumbria by Car (route descriptions, maps and information for 10 circular motor tours) 95p

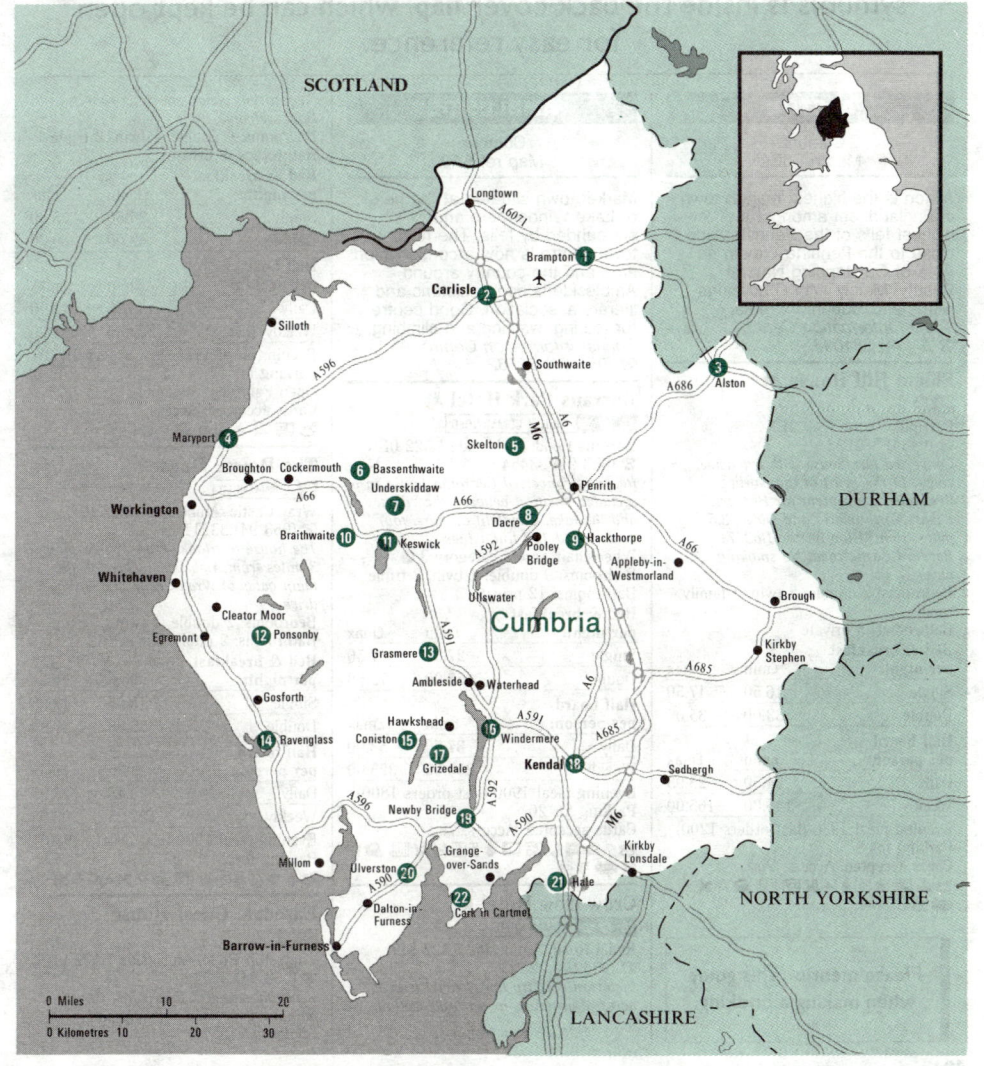

CUMBRIA

Places to stay

Accommodation entries in this regional section are listed in alphabetical order of place name, and then in alphabetical order of establishment.

The map references refer to the colour maps at the back of the guide. The first figure is the map number; the letter and figure which follow indicate the grid reference on the map.

The symbols at the end of each accommodation entry give information about services and facilities. A 'key' to these symbols is inside the back cover flap, which can be kept open for easy reference.

ALSTON

Cumbria
Map ref 5B2

Alston is the highest market town in England, set amongst the highest fells of the Pennines and close to the Pennine Way in an Area of Outstanding Natural Beauty. Mainly 17th C buildings with steep, cobbled streets.
Tourist Information Centre
☎ *(0434) 381696*

Shield Hill House **M**
※※
Garrigill, Alston CA9 3EX
☎ (0434) 381238
Converted farmhouse with extensive views. In the heart of the North Pennines. Convenient for Borders, Lakes, Northumbria and Dales. 3.5 miles from Alston on the B6277 Barnard Castle road. No smoking please.
Bedrooms: 2 double, 2 twin, 1 family room
Bathrooms: 5 private

Bed & breakfast
per night: £min £max
Single 16.50 17.50
Double 33.00 35.00

Half board
per person: £min £max
Daily 24.50 25.95
Weekly 145.00 165.00

Evening meal 1930 (last orders 1200)
Parking for 8
Cards accepted: Access, Visa
🛇💷🎨🔽🛁♿🍽📺💻🅿♨
🐕 SP

Please mention this guide when making a booking.

AMBLESIDE

Cumbria
Map ref 5A3

Market town situated at the head of Lake Windermere and surrounded by fells. The historic town centre is now a conservation area and the country around Ambleside is rich in historic and literary association. Good centre for touring, walking and climbing.
Tourist Information Centre
☎ *(053 94) 32582*

Borrans Park Hotel **M**
※※※ HIGHLY COMMENDED
Borrans Road, Ambleside LA22 0EN
☎ (053 94) 33454
Recently converted Georgian house in a secluded position between the village and the lake. Candlelit dinners, four-posters and 120 fine wines.
Wheelchair access category 3 ♿
Bedrooms: 9 double, 1 twin, 2 triple
Bathrooms: 12 private

Bed & breakfast
per night: £min £max
Single 27.50 47.50
Double 55.00 75.00

Half board
per person: £min £max
Daily 37.50 53.00
Weekly 260.00 325.00

Evening meal 1900 (last orders 1800)
Parking for 20
Cards accepted: Access, Visa
🛇♿💷🎨🛁🔽⑤📺♨🐕
🍽⭐ SP

Crow How Hotel **M**
※※ COMMENDED
Rydal Road, Ambleside LA22 9PN
☎ (053 94) 32193
Victorian country house hotel with 2 acres of grounds, in a rural location.

Magnificent views, spacious rooms. Dogs welcome.
Bedrooms: 6 double, 1 twin, 2 triple
Bathrooms: 9 private

Bed & breakfast
per night: £min £max
Single 24.50 25.50
Double 49.00 60.00

Half board
per person: £min £max
Daily 36.50 42.00
Weekly 229.50 264.00

Evening meal 1930 (last orders 1930)
Parking for 12
Open February-November
Cards accepted: Access, Visa
🛇💷🎨🛁♿⑤♨🐕⭐ SP

The Dower House
※ COMMENDED
Wray Castle, Ambleside LA22 0JA
☎ (053 94) 33211
The house overlooks Lake Windermere, 3 miles from Ambleside. Through the main gates of Wray Castle and up the drive.
Bedrooms: 2 double, 1 twin
Bathrooms: 2 public

Bed & breakfast
per night: £min £max
Single 18.95 18.95
Double 35.00 37.90

Half board
per person: £min £max
Daily 27.45 28.95
Weekly 192.25 202.65

Evening meal 1900 (last orders 1930)
Parking for 14
🛇5♨⑪⑤🎨📺♨🐕⭐ SP

Easedale Guest House
※※
Compston Road, Ambleside LA22 9DJ
☎ (053 94) 32112
Centrally situated, fine views, car parking, good food, friendly and comfortable.

42

CUMBRIA

Bedrooms: 1 single, 4 double, 1 twin
Bathrooms: 2 private, 2 public

Bed & breakfast
per night:	£min	£max
Single	13.00	16.00
Double	26.00	40.00

Half board
per person:	£min	£max
Daily	23.00	30.00
Weekly	161.00	205.00

Evening meal 1900 (last orders 1930)
Parking for 8

Foxghyll ♏
HIGHLY COMMENDED
Under Loughrigg, Rydal, Ambleside LA22 9LL
☎ (053 94) 33292

Large country house in secluded gardens with direct access to fells. All rooms en-suite, one with spa bath. Ample parking.
Bedrooms: 2 double, 1 twin
Bathrooms: 3 private

Bed & breakfast
per night:	£min	£max
Double	40.00	50.00

Parking for 7

The Gables Hotel ♏
Compston Road, Ambleside LA22 9DJ
☎ (053 94) 33272

In a quiet residential area overlooking the park, tennis courts, bowling green and Loughrigg Fell. Convenient for the shops, walking and water sports.
Bedrooms: 3 single, 5 double, 1 twin, 4 triple
Bathrooms: 13 private

Bed & breakfast
per night:	£min	£max
Single	18.75	23.50

Half board
per person:	£min	£max
Daily	29.75	34.50
Weekly	208.25	

Evening meal 1900 (last orders 1700)
Parking for 7
Open January-November

Glenside ♏
COMMENDED
Old Lake Road, Ambleside LA22 0DP
☎ (053 94) 32635

17th C farm cottage, comfortable bedrooms with original oak beams. TV lounge. Between town and lake, ideal centre for walking. Private parking.
Bedrooms: 2 double, 1 twin
Bathrooms: 1 public

Bed & breakfast
per night:	£min	£max
Single	13.00	15.00
Double	26.00	30.00

Parking for 3

High Wray Farm
Listed
High Wray, Ambleside LA22 0JE
☎ (053 94) 32280

173-acre livestock farm. Charming 17th C farmhouse once owned by Beatrix Potter. In quiet location, ideal centre for touring or walking. Panoramic views and lake shore walks close by.
Bedrooms: 2 double, 1 twin
Bathrooms: 1 private, 1 public

Bed & breakfast
per night:	£min	£max
Single	13.00	15.00
Double	26.00	30.00

Parking for 7

Lattendales ♏
Compston Road, Ambleside LA22 9DJ
☎ (053 94) 32368

Traditional Lakeland home in the heart of Ambleside. A central base for walking or touring, offering comfortable accommodation and local produce.
Bedrooms: 2 single, 2 double, 2 twin
Bathrooms: 4 private, 1 public

Bed & breakfast
per night:	£min	£max
Single	13.00	15.00
Double	30.00	39.00

Half board
per person:	£min	£max
Daily	25.00	30.00
Weekly	169.00	199.00

Evening meal 1830 (last orders 1700)

Laurel Villa ♏
HIGHLY COMMENDED
Lake Road, Ambleside LA22 0DB
☎ (053 94) 33240

Detached Victorian house, personally run by resident proprietors. En-suite bedrooms overlooking the fells. Within easy reach of the lake. Private car park.
Bedrooms: 8 double, 1 twin
Bathrooms: 9 private

Bed & breakfast
per night:	£min	£max
Single	50.00	50.00
Double	60.00	60.00

Half board
per person:	£min	£max
Daily	50.00	50.00

Evening meal 1900 (last orders 1700)

Parking for 10
Cards accepted: Access, Visa

The Old Vicarage ♏
APPROVED
Vicarage Road, Ambleside LA22 9DH
☎ (053 94) 33364
Fax (053 94) 34734

Quietly situated in own grounds in heart of village. Car park, quality en-suite accommodation, friendly service. Family-run. Pets welcome.
Bedrooms: 7 double, 1 twin, 1 triple, 1 family room
Bathrooms: 10 private

Bed & breakfast
per night:	£min	£max
Single	20.00	24.50
Double	40.00	49.00

Parking for 12

Raaesbeck
Fairview Road, Ambleside LA22 9EE
☎ (053 94) 33844
18th C building in the older, quiet and elevated part of the village, with a garden and views of Loughrigg Fell, yet only 3 minutes' walk from village.
Bedrooms: 2 double, 1 twin
Bathrooms: 2 public

Bed & breakfast
per night:	£min	£max
Double	25.00	27.00

Parking for 3
Cards accepted: Amex

Riverside Lodge Country House ♏
COMMENDED
Nr. Rothay Bridge, Ambleside LA22 0EH
☎ (053 94) 34208
Georgian country house of character with 2 acres of grounds through which the River Rothay flows. 500 yards from the centre of Ambleside.
Bedrooms: 4 double
Bathrooms: 4 private

Bed & breakfast
per night:	£min	£max
Double	44.00	58.00

Parking for 20
Cards accepted: Access, Visa

CUMBRIA

AMBLESIDE
Continued

Rowanfield Country Guesthouse
HIGHLY COMMENDED

Kirkstone Road, Ambleside LA22 9ET
☎ (053 94) 33686

Idyllic setting, panoramic lake and mountain views. Laura Ashley style decor. Scrumptious food created by proprietor/chef. Special break prices.
Bedrooms: 5 double, 1 twin, 1 triple
Bathrooms: 7 private

Bed & breakfast
per night:	£min	£max
Double	46.00	54.00

Half board
per person:	£min	£max
Daily	37.00	41.00
Weekly	222.00	237.00

Evening meal 1900 (last orders 1930)
Parking for 8
Open March-December
Cards accepted: Access, Visa

Smallwood House Hotel
APPROVED

Compston Road, Ambleside LA22 9DJ
☎ (053 94) 32330
Family-run hotel in central position, offering warm and friendly service, good home cooking and value-for-money quality and standards.
Bedrooms: 2 single, 6 double, 2 twin, 3 triple, 1 family room
Bathrooms: 14 private, 2 public

Bed & breakfast
per night:	£min	£max
Single	16.00	19.50
Double	32.00	39.00

Half board
per person:	£min	£max
Daily	26.00	29.50
Weekly	180.00	200.00

Lunch available
Evening meal 1900 (last orders 2000)
Parking for 11

Wanslea Guest House

Lake Road, Ambleside LA22 0DB
☎ (053 94) 33884
Fax (053 94) 31701
Spacious, comfortable, family-run Victorian house offering good food, wines and fine views. Easy walk to lake

and village. Honeymoons a speciality. Brochure available.
Bedrooms: 1 single, 3 double, 3 triple, 1 family room
Bathrooms: 4 private, 3 public

Bed & breakfast
per night:	£min	£max
Single	16.00	25.00
Double	32.00	55.00

Half board
per person:	£min	£max
Daily	26.00	39.50
Weekly	175.00	220.00

Lunch available
Evening meal 1845 (last orders 1500)

Windlehurst Guesthouse

Millans Park, Ambleside LA22 9AG
☎ (053 94) 33137
Elegant Victorian house on a peaceful road in Ambleside, with commanding views of Loughrigg Fell. Within easy walking distance of amenities. No-smoking establishment.
Bedrooms: 1 single, 2 double, 2 triple, 1 family room
Bathrooms: 2 private, 2 public

Bed & breakfast
per night:	£min	£max
Single	13.00	22.00
Double	26.00	44.00

Parking for 6
Open January-October and Christmas

APPLEBY-IN-WESTMORLAND
Cumbria
Map ref 5B3

Former county town of Westmorland, at the foot of the Pennines in the Eden Valley. The castle was rebuilt in the 17th C, except for its Norman keep, ditches and ramparts. It now houses a Rare Breeds Survival Trust Centre. Good centre for exploring the Eden Valley.
Tourist Information Centre
☎ (076 83) 51177

Asby Grange Farm
Listed

Great Asby, Appleby-in-Westmorland CA16 6HF
☎ (076 83) 52881
300-acre mixed farm. 18th C farmhouse in beautiful and peaceful countryside, 5 miles south of Appleby. Ideal for touring Lakes and Yorkshire Dales. Convenient for M6.
Bedrooms: 1 double, 1 triple
Bathrooms: 1 public

Bed & breakfast
per night:	£min	£max
Double	24.00	28.00

Parking for 4
Open April-October

Bongate House
APPROVED

Appleby-in-Westmorland CA16 6UE
☎ (076 83) 51245
Family-run Georgian guesthouse on the outskirts of a small market town. Large garden. Relaxed friendly atmosphere, good home cooking.
Bedrooms: 1 single, 4 double, 2 twin, 1 triple
Bathrooms: 5 private, 1 public

Bed & breakfast
per night:	£min	£max
Single	16.50	16.50
Double	33.00	37.00

Half board
per person:	£min	£max
Daily	23.50	26.00
Weekly	150.00	170.00

Evening meal 1900 (last orders 1800)
Parking for 10

Dufton Hall Farm

Dufton, Appleby-in-Westmorland CA16 6DD
☎ (076 83) 51573
60-acre mixed farm. Part of ancient hall, and working hill farm in village centre, 3.5 miles north-east of Appleby-in-Westmorland.
Bedrooms: 2 double, 1 twin
Bathrooms: 3 private

Bed & breakfast
per night:	£min	£max
Single	15.00	18.00
Double	27.00	30.00

Evening meal 1800 (last orders 1900)
Parking for 3
Open April-October

Howgill House

Appleby-in-Westmorland CA16 6UW
☎ (076 83) 51574
Private family-run house standing in a large garden. On the B6542, half a mile from the town centre.
Bedrooms: 1 single, 1 twin, 2 triple
Bathrooms: 2 public

Bed & breakfast
per night:	£min	£max
Single	14.00	
Double	27.00	

Parking for 6
Open May-September

CUMBRIA

Meadow Ing Farm
Listed COMMENDED

Crackenthorpe, Appleby-in-Westmorland CA16 6AE
☎ (076 83) 52543
105-acre dairy farm. Attractive sandstone farmhouse in Eden. Beautiful views, antique-furnished rooms, friendly atmosphere, wholesome food. Private fishing available on the River Eden.
Bedrooms: 1 twin, 1 double
Bathrooms: 2 public

Bed & breakfast
per night:	£min	£max
Single	15.50	
Double	29.00	

Half board
per person:	£min	£max
Daily	23.00	
Weekly	154.00	

Evening meal 1830 (last orders 1930)

BORROWDALE
Cumbria
Map ref 5A3

Stretching south of Derwentwater to Seathwaite in the heart of the Lake District, the valley is walled by high fellsides. It can justly claim to be the most scenically impressive valley in the Lake District. Excellent centre for walking and climbing.

Mary Mount

Borrowdale, Keswick CA12 5UU
☎ (076 87) 77223
Set in 4.5 acres of gardens and woodlands on the shores of Derwentwater, 2.5 miles from Keswick. Views across lake to Catbells and Maiden Moor. Families welcome.
Bedrooms: 1 single, 5 double, 5 twin, 3 triple
Bathrooms: 14 private

Bed & breakfast
per night:	£min	£max
Single	16.00	25.00
Double	32.00	50.00

Lunch available
Evening meal 1830 (last orders 2045)
Parking for 40
Open February-December
Cards accepted: Access, Visa

Yew Craggs Guest House
Listed

Rosthwaite, Keswick CA12 5XB
☎ (076 87) 77260
Beside Rosthwaite Bridge in the centre of the Borrowdale Valley. Good for walking, superb views in all directions.
Bedrooms: 3 double, 2 triple
Bathrooms: 1 public

Bed & breakfast
per night:	£min	£max
Double	26.00	38.00

Parking for 6
Open February-November

BRAITHWAITE
Cumbria
Map ref 5A3

Braithwaite nestles at the foot of the Whinlatter Pass and has a magnificent backdrop of the mountains forming the Coledale Horseshoe.

Coledale Inn

Braithwaite, Keswick CA12 5TN
☎ (076 87) 78272
Victorian country house hotel and Georgian inn, in a peaceful hillside position away from traffic, with superb mountain views.
Bedrooms: 1 single, 5 double, 2 twin, 3 triple, 1 family room
Bathrooms: 12 private

Bed & breakfast
per night:	£min	£max
Single	16.00	25.00
Double	32.00	50.00

Lunch available
Evening meal 1830 (last orders 2100)
Parking for 15
Cards accepted: Access, Visa

Thelmlea

Braithwaite, Keswick CA12 5TD
☎ (076 87) 78305
Country house in 1.75 acre grounds. Friendly relaxed atmosphere, log fire, home cooking. Superb views. Ideal base for walkers or touring. Within easy reach of all lakes, coast and Carlisle (30-40 minute drive).
Bedrooms: 2 double, 2 triple
Bathrooms: 3 private, 2 public

Bed & breakfast
per night:	£min	£max
Single	14.50	19.50
Double	29.00	39.00

Half board
per person:	£min	£max
Daily	24.50	29.50
Weekly	150.00	187.00

Evening meal from 1830
Parking for 9

Symbols are explained on the flap inside the back cover.

BRAMPTON
Cumbria
Map ref 5B2

Pleasant market town whose character has changed very little over the past 150 years. The Moot Hall, in the market square, is a fine octagonal building which stands next to the stocks. A good centre for exploring Hadrian's Wall.

Birtle Dene

Tree Road, Brampton CA8 1UA
☎ (069 77) 41013

House with family atmosphere, in ideal touring area close to Hadrian's Wall and borders. Lounge and dining room, colour TV, tea and coffee facilities. Reductions for children. No smoking.
Bedrooms: 1 double, 1 twin
Bathrooms: 1 private, 1 public

Bed & breakfast
per night:	£min	£max
Single	14.00	16.00
Double	28.00	32.00

Parking for 2

Halidon

4 Tree Terrace, Tree Road, Brampton CA8 1TY
☎ (069 77) 2106
Delightfully restored Edwardian terraced house five minutes from town centre. Close to Roman Wall amd Talkin Tarn. Home cooking and a warm welcome.
Bedrooms: 1 twin, 1 triple
Bathrooms: 1 public

Bed & breakfast
per night:	£min	£max
Single	13.50	15.00
Double	27.00	30.00

Hare & Hounds Inn

Talkin Village, Brampton CA8 1LE
☎ (069 77) 3456
Typical country inn with a cosy atmosphere and real ale, only 500 yards from the golf-course and Talkin Tarn with boating, fishing, swimming, windsurfing and birdwatching.
Bedrooms: 1 single, 2 double, 1 twin
Bathrooms: 2 private, 1 public

Continued ▶

CUMBRIA

BRAMPTON
Continued

Bed & breakfast
per night:	£min	£max
Single	20.00	25.00
Double	30.00	35.00

Half board
per person:	£min	£max
Daily	20.00	32.00
Weekly	130.00	180.00

Lunch available
Evening meal 1900 (last orders 2130)
Parking for 18

High Rigg Farm
APPROVED
Walton, Brampton CA8 2AZ
☎ (069 77) 2117
202-acre mixed farm. 18th C listed farmhouse on roadside, 1 mile from Walton and Roman Wall, 4 miles from Brampton. Family-run with pedigree cattle and sheep, farm trail.
Bedrooms: 1 triple
Bathrooms: 1 public

Bed & breakfast
per night:	£min	£max
Single	14.50	15.50
Double	27.00	29.00

Half board
per person:	£min	£max
Daily	21.50	22.50

Evening meal 1800 (last orders 1400)
Parking for 4

Howard House Farm
COMMENDED
Gilsland, Carlisle CA6 7AN
☎ Gilsland (069 77) 47285
250-acre livestock farm. Peaceful farm in comfortable and friendly surroundings, 7 miles north-east of Brampton and centre of Roman Wall.
Bedrooms: 1 double, 1 twin, 1 triple
Bathrooms: 1 private, 2 public

Bed & breakfast
per night:	£min	£max
Single		20.00
Double	30.00	36.00

Half board
per person:	£min	£max
Daily	25.00	
Weekly	105.00	

Evening meal 1800 (last orders 1800)
Parking for 4

Low Rigg Farm
Listed COMMENDED
Walton, Brampton CA8 2DX
☎ (069 77) 3233
60-acre dairy farm. Comfortable and friendly farmhouse accommodation, 3

miles from Brampton and 9 miles from Carlisle in beautiful Hadrian's Wall country.
Bedrooms: 1 twin, 1 family room
Bathrooms: 1 public

Bed & breakfast
per night:	£min	£max
Single	13.00	15.00
Double	26.00	30.00

Half board
per person:	£min	£max
Daily	22.00	24.00
Weekly	140.00	155.00

Evening meal 1900 (last orders 1300)
Parking for 3

BROUGHTON-IN-FURNESS
Cumbria
Map ref 5A3

Old market village whose historic charter to hold fairs is still proclaimed every year on the first day of August in the market square. Good centre for touring the pretty Duddon Valley.

Cobblers Cottage
APPROVED
Griffin Street, Broughton-in-Furness LA20 6HH
☎ (0229) 716413

Quaint 17th C cottage offering delicious food in a cosy and relaxed atmosphere. Ideally situated for exploring South Lakes and beautiful Duddon Valley.
Bedrooms: 2 double, 1 twin
Bathrooms: 1 private, 1 public

Bed & breakfast
per night:	£min	£max
Single	16.00	18.50
Double	32.00	37.00

Half board
per person:	£min	£max
Daily	25.00	31.00
Weekly	168.00	210.00

Evening meal 1900 (last orders 1700)

National Crown ratings were correct at the time of going to press but are subject to change. Please check at the time of booking.

BUTTERMERE
Cumbria
Map ref 5A3

Small village surrounded by high mountains, between Buttermere Lake and Crummock Water. An ideal centre for walking and climbing the nearby peaks and for touring.

Pickett Howe
DE LUXE
Brackenthwaite, Buttermere Valley, Cockermouth CA13 9UY
☎ Lorton (0900) 85444
Award-winning 17th C farmhouse, luxuriously appointed. Peacefully situated between Crummock Water and Loweswater lakes. Three miles from Buttermere. Renowned for creative cooking and relaxing atmosphere.
Bedrooms: 3 double, 1 twin
Bathrooms: 4 private

Half board
per person:	£min	£max
Daily	52.00	52.00
Weekly	336.00	336.00

Parking for 6
Open April-November
Cards accepted: Access, Visa

CALDBECK
Cumbria
Map ref 5A2

Quaint limestone village lying on the northern fringe of the Lake District National Park. John Peel, the famous huntsman who is immortalised in song, is buried in the churchyard. The fells surrounding Caldbeck were once heavily mined, being rich in lead, copper and barytes.

Friar Hall
Caldbeck, Wigton CA7 8DS
☎ (0697) 478633
140-acre mixed farm. In the lovely village of Caldbeck overlooking the river. Ideal for touring the Lakes and Scottish Borders. On Cumbria Way route.
Bedrooms: 2 double, 1 triple
Bathrooms: 2 public

Bed & breakfast
per night:	£min	£max
Single	16.00	17.00
Double	31.00	33.00

Parking for 3
Open March-October

CUMBRIA

Parkend Restaurant and Country Hotel
COMMENDED
Parkend, Caldbeck, Wigton CA7 8HH
☎ (069 74) 78494
17th C farmhouse restaurant with en-suite rooms, situated 1.5 miles west of Caldbeck. Birthplace of the legendary John Peel.
Bedrooms: 3 double
Bathrooms: 3 private

Bed & breakfast

per night:	£min	£max
Single	32.00	32.00
Double	48.00	48.00

Lunch available
Evening meal 1900 (last orders 2200)
Parking for 16
Cards accepted: Access, Visa, Amex

CARLISLE
Cumbria
Map ref 5A2

Near the Scottish border, this cathedral city suffered years of strife through the centuries, often changing hands between England and Scotland. The red sandstone cathedral is the second smallest in England. The castle, founded in 1092, now houses a museum.
Tourist Information Centre
☎ (0228) 512444

Beech Croft
COMMENDED
Aglionby, Carlisle CA4 8AQ
☎ (0228) 513762
Spacious, modern, detached house in a delightful rural setting. 1 mile on the A69 from M6 junction 43. High quality accommodation in a friendly family atmosphere.
Bedrooms: 1 single, 2 double
Bathrooms: 1 private, 2 public

Bed & breakfast

per night:	£min	£max
Single	18.00	18.00
Double	34.00	38.00

Parking for 4

The Beeches
Listed DE LUXE
Wood Street, Carlisle CA1 2SF
☎ (0228) 511962
Situated in Carlisle's unique award-winning street and quiet conservation area, an 18th C Grade II listed period residence. Laura Ashley furnishings, every attention to detail and comfort. Finalist in bed and breakfast category of England for Excellence 1991. 1 mile from M6 exit 43 and city centre. Private parking.
Bedrooms: 1 double, 2 twin
Bathrooms: 1 public

Bed & breakfast

per night:	£min	£max
Double	30.00	35.00

Parking for 6

Corner House
COMMENDED
87 Petteril Street, Carlisle CA1 2AW
☎ (0228) 41942
Entirely non-smoking environment. Beautifully furnished town house. Guests collected from rail and bus stations. Four-poster en-suite room with colour TV and all facilities.
Bedrooms: 2 double, 2 twin, 2 triple
Bathrooms: 4 private, 1 public

Bed & breakfast

per night:	£min	£max
Single	18.00	23.00
Double	32.00	40.00

Half board

per person:	£min	£max
Daily	22.00	27.50
Weekly	135.00	145.00

Evening meal 1800 (last orders 2030)
Parking for 3

Craighead
APPROVED
6 Hartington Place, Carlisle CA1 1HL
☎ (0228) 27443
Attractive Victorian town house with spacious rooms and original features. Minutes' walk to city centre, bus and rail stations. Friendly and comfortable. Fresh farm food.
Bedrooms: 2 double, 1 twin
Bathrooms: 2 public

Bed & breakfast

per night:	£min	£max
Single	15.00	17.00
Double	28.00	32.00

Croft End
Listed
Hurst, Ivegill, Carlisle CA4 0NL
☎ (076 84) 84362
Rural bungalow situated midway junction 41 and 42 of M6, 4 miles west of Southwaite service area.
Bedrooms: 1 single, 1 double
Bathrooms: 1 public

Bed & breakfast

per night:	£min	£max
Single	14.00	16.00
Double	26.00	28.00

Parking for 4

The Gill Farm
Blackford, Carlisle CA6 4EL
☎ Kirklinton (0228) 75521
124-acre arable & livestock farm. Ideal halfway stopping place or a good base for touring Cumbria's beauty spots. In peaceful countryside, 3 miles from the M6 junction 44. From Carlisle go north to Blackford, fork right at sign for Cliff and Kirklinton, after 100 yards turn right, half a mile turn left, Gill Farm on left up this road.
Bedrooms: 1 double, 1 twin, 1 triple
Bathrooms: 2 public

Bed & breakfast

per night:	£min	£max
Single	16.00	18.00
Double	29.00	33.00

Evening meal 1800 (last orders 1600)
Parking for 6
Open January-November

Howard House
HIGHLY COMMENDED
27 Howard Place, Carlisle CA1 1HR
☎ (0228) 29159
Lawrence and Sandra invite you to their spacious Victorian home in quiet location. City centre, bus/rail stations, riverside walks. Four-poster en-suite rooms. Home cooking. Family historians welcome. Come, let us spoil you.
Bedrooms: 1 single, 1 double, 1 twin, 2 family rooms
Bathrooms: 2 private, 1 public

Bed & breakfast

per night:	£min	£max
Single	14.00	16.00
Double	28.00	34.00

Half board

per person:	£min	£max
Daily	21.00	24.00
Weekly	140.00	161.00

Evening meal 1800 (last orders 1000)

Howard Lodge Guesthouse
90 Warwick Road, Carlisle CA1 1JW
☎ (0228) 29842
Victorian townhouse on main road 400 metres from city centre. Tastefully decorated and offering modern facilities. En-suite available.
Bedrooms: 1 double, 1 twin, 1 triple
Bathrooms: 1 private, 2 public

Bed & breakfast

per night:	£min	£max
Single	15.00	17.00
Double	26.00	34.00

Evening meal 1800 (last orders 1400)
Parking for 2

New Pallyards
COMMENDED
Hethersgill, Carlisle CA6 6HZ
☎ Nicholforest (0228) 577 308
Fax (0228) 577 308
65-acre mixed farm. Warmth and hospitality await you in this 18th C modernised farmhouse. Country setting, easily accessible from M6, A7, M74, all rooms en-suite. National award winner.

Continued ▶

47

CUMBRIA

CARLISLE
Continued

Bedrooms: 1 single, 2 double, 1 twin, 1 triple
Bathrooms: 3 private, 1 public, 1 private shower

Bed & breakfast
per night:	£min	£max
Single	16.50	18.50
Double	33.00	37.00

Half board
per person:	£min	£max
Daily	26.50	28.50
Weekly	125.00	160.00

Evening meal 1900 (last orders 1930)
Parking for 7
Cards accepted: Visa, Amex

Park House Hotel
Park House Road, Kingstown, Carlisle CA6 4BY
☎ (0228) 26028
Homely pub with good bar meals, a quarter of a mile from M6 junction 44.
Bedrooms: 4 single, 1 twin
Bathrooms: 2 public

Bed & breakfast
per night:	£min	£max
Single	18.50	18.50
Double	35.00	35.00

Lunch available
Evening meal 1800 (last orders 2045)
Parking for 40
Cards accepted: Access, Visa

Streethead Farm
Listed
Ivegill, Carlisle CA4 ONG
☎ Southwaite (069 74) 73287
211-acre mixed & dairy farm. Distant hills, log fires, home cooking on working farm between Penrith and Carlisle (8 miles). 10 minutes from junctions 41 and 42 of M6. Ideal for Lakes or Scotland. Brochure available.
Bedrooms: 1 double, 1 triple
Bathrooms: 1 public

Bed & breakfast
per night:	£min	£max
Single	16.00	16.00
Double	30.00	32.00

Half board
per person:	£min	£max
Daily		24.00
Weekly		147.00

Evening meal 1830 (last orders 1000)
Parking for 2
Open March-October

We advise you to confirm your booking in writing.

CARTMEL
Cumbria
Map ref 5A3

Picturesque conserved village based on a 12th C priory with a well-preserved church and gatehouse. Just half a mile outside the Lake District National Park, this is a peaceful base for walking and touring, with historic houses and beautiful scenery.

Eeabank House
123 Station Road, Cark in Cartmel, Grange-over-Sands LA11 7NY
☎ Flookburgh (053 95) 58818
Family-run guesthouse close to Holker Hall and gardens. Easy access to Lakes, good country walks. Ideal for touring.
Bedrooms: 1 double, 1 twin, 1 triple
Bathrooms: 1 private, 1 public

Bed & breakfast
per night:	£min	£max
Single	15.50	18.00
Double	31.00	36.00

Half board
per person:	£min	£max
Daily	22.00	30.00
Weekly	147.00	164.00

Lunch available
Evening meal 1830 (last orders 2100)
Parking for 3
Cards accepted: Access, Visa

CARTMEL FELL
Cumbria
Map ref 5A3

Small village set in tranquil countryside in an upland area of great beauty. Noted for its 16th C church with 3-tiered pulpit.

Lightwood Farmhouse
COMMENDED
Cartmel Fell, Bowland Bridge, Grange-over-Sands LA11 6NP
☎ Newby Bridge (053 95) 31454
17th C farmhouse with original oak beams. Extensive views, large garden with streams. Home cooking. Just off the A592 near Bowland Bridge.
Bedrooms: 5 double, 3 twin, 1 triple
Bathrooms: 9 private, 1 public

Bed & breakfast
per night:	£min	£max
Double	35.00	45.00

Evening meal from 1900
Parking for 9
Cards accepted: Access, Visa

CASTLE CARROCK
Cumbria
Map ref 5B2

Small village nestling at the north-western tip of the Pennines, in an Area of Outstanding Natural Beauty.

The Weary Sportsman
Castle Carrock, Carlisle CA4 9LU
☎ Carlisle (0228) 70230
17th C country inn, in pleasant surroundings 8 miles east of Carlisle. A peaceful retreat in which to relax and enjoy good homely meals.
Bedrooms: 1 single, 2 double, 1 twin
Bathrooms: 1 public

Bed & breakfast
per night:	£min	£max
Single	13.50	15.00
Double	27.00	29.00

Half board
per person:	£min	£max
Daily	17.50	
Weekly	112.00	

Lunch available
Evening meal 1800 (last orders 2100)
Parking for 8

CONISTON
Cumbria
Map ref 5A3

Born from the mining industry, this village lies at the north end of Coniston Water. The scenery to the rear of the village is dominated by Coniston Old Man. Its most famous resident was John Ruskin, whose home, Brantwood, is open to the public. Good centre for walking.

Arrowfield
HIGHLY COMMENDED
Little Arrow, Coniston LA21 8AU
☎ (053 94) 41741
Elegant 19th C Lakeland house in beautiful rural setting. Adjacent to Coniston/Torver road (A593). 2 miles from Coniston village.
Bedrooms: 1 single, 2 double, 2 twin
Bathrooms: 2 private, 1 public

Bed & breakfast
per night:	£min	£max
Single	17.00	19.00
Double	32.00	42.00

Half board
per person:	£min	£max
Daily	29.00	34.00
Weekly	192.00	224.00

Evening meal from 1900
Parking for 6
Open March-November

CUMBRIA

Yewdale Hotel
COMMENDED

Yewdale Road, Coniston LA21 8LU
☎ (053 94) 41280
Built of local materials in 1896 as a bank, now a modern hotel skilfully refurbished throughout. Reduced rate breaks available.
Bedrooms: 5 double, 2 twin, 3 triple
Bathrooms: 10 private, 2 public

Bed & breakfast
per night:	£min	£max
Double	43.90	63.00

Half board
per person:	£min	£max
Daily	32.90	42.45
Weekly	138.40	192.00

Lunch available
Evening meal (last orders 2100)
Parking for 6
Cards accepted: Access, Visa

DALSTON
Cumbria
Map ref 5A2

Village in undulating countryside on the banks of the River Caldew. The churchyard is burial place to two Bishops of Carlisle.

Smithy Cottage
Listed COMMENDED

Bridge End, Dalston, Carlisle CA5 7BJ
☎ Carlisle (0228) 711659

Conversion of original 300-year-old blacksmith's smithy.
Bedrooms: 1 double, 1 twin
Bathrooms: 1 public

Bed & breakfast
per night:	£min	£max
Single	16.50	17.50
Double	33.00	35.00

Parking for 3
Open January-November

Individual proprietors have supplied all details of accommodation. Although we do check for accuracy, we advise you to confirm the information at the time of booking.

EGREMONT
Cumbria
Map ref 5A3

Old market town with a wide tree-lined street. One of its attractions is the 12th C Norman castle built of red sandstone.
Tourist Information Centre
☎ (0946) 820693

Old Vicarage Guest House
Listed COMMENDED

Thornhill, Egremont CA22 2NX
☎ Beckermet (0946) 841577
Imposing 19th C vicarage of character in attractive grounds. Within easy reach of sea and mountains.
Bedrooms: 3 triple
Bathrooms: 2 public

Bed & breakfast
per night:	£min	£max
Single	13.00	14.00
Double	26.00	28.00

Parking for 6

GRASMERE
Cumbria
Map ref 5A3

Described by William Wordsworth as "the loveliest spot that man hath ever found", this village, famous for its gingerbread, is in a beautiful setting overlooked by Helm Crag. Wordsworth lived at Dove Cottage. The cottage and museum are open to the public.

Beck Allans
Listed HIGHLY COMMENDED

College Street, Grasmere, Ambleside LA22 9SZ
☎ (053 94) 35563
A new but traditional Lakeland house, hidden in the delightful well timbered grounds of Beck Allans Holiday Apartments. Centre of village, adjacent River Rothay, super views. Accommodation includes two-bedroom family suite.
Bedrooms: 3 double, 1 twin
Bathrooms: 4 private

Bed & breakfast
per night:	£min	£max
Single	30.75	35.25
Double	41.00	47.00

Parking for 15
Cards accepted: Access, Visa

Craigside House
COMMENDED

Grasmere, Ambleside LA22 9SG
☎ (053 94) 35292
Delightfully furnished Victorian house on the edge of the village near Dove Cottage. In a large, peaceful garden overlooking the lake and hills.
Bedrooms: 2 double, 1 twin
Bathrooms: 3 private

Bed & breakfast
per night:	£min	£max
Single	24.50	50.00
Double	49.00	57.00

Parking for 6

Eller Close Vegetarian Guest House
Listed

Grasmere, Ambleside LA22 9RW
☎ (053 94) 35786
Charming Victorian guesthouse with spectacular views from every room. Secluded gardens with mountain stream providing peace and tranquillity. Delicious vegetarian breakfasts. Non-smoking, warm, relaxed atmosphere.
Bedrooms: 1 double, 1 twin, 1 family room
Bathrooms: 2 private, 2 public

Bed & breakfast
per night:	£min	£max
Single	15.50	26.50
Double	27.00	39.00

Half board
per person:	£min	£max
Daily	23.00	29.00
Weekly	143.50	182.00

Lunch available
Evening meal 1830 (last orders 2000)
Parking for 5

Rothay Lodge Guest House

White Bridge, Grasmere, Ambleside LA22 9RH
☎ (053 94) 35341
Traditional Lakeland country house in peaceful surroundings by river. 5 minutes' walk from the village centre. Lovely views.
Bedrooms: 3 double, 2 twin
Bathrooms: 3 private, 1 public

Bed & breakfast
per night:	£min	£max
Single	17.00	22.00
Double	34.00	43.00

Parking for 6
Open February-October

Travellers Rest
Listed

Grasmere, Ambleside LA22 9RR
☎ (053 94) 35604
Charming 17th C inn nestling in the heart of Lakeland and with superb views. Cumbrian hospitality includes good food, lovely ales, open fires and comfortable accommodation.
Bedrooms: 1 single, 4 double, 2 twin
Bathrooms: 2 public

Continued ▶

49

CUMBRIA

GRASMERE
Continued

Bed & breakfast per night:	£min	£max
Single	18.50	22.50
Double	35.00	43.00
Half board per person:	£min	£max
Daily	22.50	31.50
Weekly	147.50	210.50

Lunch available
Evening meal 1900 (last orders 2130)
Parking for 45

GRAYRIGG
Cumbria
Map ref 5B3

Punchbowl House
COMMENDED

Grayrigg, Kendal LA8 9BU
☎ (0539) 824345
Renovated spacious Victorian farmhouse with log fires, in peaceful surroundings between Lakes and Dales. Non-smoking.
Bedrooms: 2 double, 1 twin
Bathrooms: 1 private, 1 public

Bed & breakfast per night:	£min	£max
Single	15.00	25.00
Double	30.00	36.00

Parking for 6

HAVERTHWAITE
Cumbria
Map ref 5A2

Set in the Levens Valley south-west of Newby Bridge, on the north bank of River Leven. Headquarters of the Lakeside and Haverthwaite Railway Company.

The Coach House

Hollow Oak, Haverthwaite, Ulverston LA12 8AD
☎ Ulverston (053 95) 31622
Friendly and comfortable coach house with original beams. Garden. Convenient for Holker Hall, Coniston and Windermere. Non-smokers only please.
Bedrooms: 2 double, 1 twin
Bathrooms: 2 public

Bed & breakfast per night:	£min	£max
Single	13.00	15.00
Double	26.00	30.00

Parking for 3
Open March-October

HAWKSHEAD
Cumbria
Map ref 5A3

Lying near Esthwaite Water, this village has great charm and character. Its small squares are linked by flagged or cobbled alleys and the main square is dominated by the market house or Shambles where the butchers had their stalls in days gone by.

The Drunken Duck Inn
COMMENDED

Barngates, Ambleside LA22 0NG
☎ Ambleside (053 94) 36347
An old fashioned inn amidst magnificent scenery, oak-beamed bars, cosy log fires and charming bedrooms. Good food and beers.
Bedrooms: 9 double, 1 twin
Bathrooms: 10 private

Bed & breakfast per night:	£min	£max
Single	35.00	45.00
Double	50.00	74.00

Lunch available
Evening meal 1830 (last orders 2100)
Parking for 30
Cards accepted: Access, Visa

Foxgloves
Listed

Hawkshead, Ambleside LA22 0NR
☎ (053 94) 36352
Comfortable accommodation quietly situated on the edge of village. Home cooking. Superb views from every room. Visitors' lounge with colour TV. Non-smokers only, please.
Bedrooms: 3 double
Bathrooms: 1 private, 1 public

Bed & breakfast per night:	£min	£max
Double	30.00	40.00
Half board per person:	£min	£max
Daily	25.50	28.00
Weekly	157.00	172.00

Evening meal from 1800
Parking for 3

There are separate sections in this guide listing groups specialising in farm holidays and accommodation which is especially suitable for young people and organised groups.

KENDAL
Cumbria
Map ref 5B3

The "Auld Grey Town" lies in the valley of the River Kent with a backcloth of limestone fells. Situated just outside the Lake District National Park, it is a good centre for touring the Lakes and surrounding country. Ruined castle was the birthplace of Catherine Parr.
Tourist Information Centre
☎ (0539) 725758

Fairways Guest House
COMMENDED

102 Windermere Road, Kendal LA9 5EZ
☎ (0539) 725564
On the main Kendal-Windermere road. Victorian guesthouse with en-suite facilities. TV, tea and coffee in all rooms. Four-poster bedrooms. Private parking.
Bedrooms: 1 single, 3 double
Bathrooms: 4 private, 1 public

Bed & breakfast per night:	£min	£max
Single	15.00	16.00
Double	30.00	34.00

Parking for 4

Gateside Farm
Listed COMMENDED

Windermere Road, Kendal LA9 5SE
☎ (0539) 722036
300-acre dairy & livestock farm. Traditional Lakeland farm easily accessible from the motorway and on the main tourist route through Lakeland. One night and short stays are welcomed.
Bedrooms: 3 double, 1 twin, 1 triple
Bathrooms: 2 private, 2 public

Bed & breakfast per night:	£min	£max
Single	17.00	20.00
Double	28.00	30.00
Half board per person:	£min	£max
Daily	21.00	23.00

Evening meal (last orders 1700)
Parking for 7

The Glen
COMMENDED

Oxenholme, Kendal LA9 7RF
☎ (0539) 726386
Large, modernised house in its own grounds. All rooms have TV, tea-making and private facilities.
Bedrooms: 2 double, 1 twin
Bathrooms: 3 private

CUMBRIA

Bed & breakfast per night:	£min	£max
Single	18.00	20.00
Double	32.00	36.00

Parking for 8
Open February-November

Higher House Farm ⚊
COMMENDED

Oxenholme Lane, Natland, Kendal LA9 7QH
☎ Sedgwick (053 95) 61177

17th C beamed farmhouse in tranquil village south of Kendal, overlooking Lakeland fells. Near M6 and Oxenholme station. Delicious cuisine. Four-poster bed.
Bedrooms: 2 double, 1 family room
Bathrooms: 3 private

Bed & breakfast per night:	£min	£max
Single	15.00	24.50
Double	35.00	39.00

Half board per person:	£min	£max
Daily	27.50	36.50

Evening meal 1900 (last orders 2130)
Parking for 9

Holmfield ⚊
Listed DE LUXE

41 Kendal Green, Kendal LA9 5PP
☎ (0539) 720790

Elegant Edwardian house on edge of town. Large gardens, panoramic views, swimming pool, croquet. Pretty bedrooms. Renowned hospitality. Non-smoking establishment. Tariff for single occupancy by arrangement.
Bedrooms: 2 double, 1 twin
Bathrooms: 2 public

Bed & breakfast per night:	£min	£max
Double	30.00	36.00

Parking for 7

Lyndhurst ⚊

8 South Road, Kendal LA9 5QH
☎ (0539) 727281

Terraced house providing comfortable accommodation, in a quiet area with river view. 10 minutes' walk from the town.
Bedrooms: 2 single, 2 double, 1 twin, 1 triple
Bathrooms: 2 public

Bed & breakfast per night:	£min	£max
Single	13.75	16.50
Double	27.50	33.00

Parking for 4

7 Thorny Hills
COMMENDED

Kendal LA9 7AL
☎ (0539) 720207

Beautiful, unspoilt Georgian town house. Peaceful, pretty location close to town centre. Good home cooking. Self-catering available. Non-smokers only please.
Bedrooms: 2 double, 1 twin
Bathrooms: 1 private, 1 public

Bed & breakfast per night:	£min	£max
Single	14.00	18.00
Double	28.00	34.00

Half board per person:	£min	£max
Daily	22.00	26.00

Evening meal from 1800
Parking for 3
Open January-November

Winlea
COMMENDED

88 Windermere Road, Kendal LA9 5EZ
☎ (0539) 723177

Friendly Victorian guesthouse in good location. Well furnished en-suite rooms with colour TV and tea/coffee facilities. Lovely views, private parking. Non-smoking.
Bedrooms: 2 double
Bathrooms: 2 private

Bed & breakfast per night:	£min	£max
Double	30.00	32.00

Parking for 4

Individual proprietors have supplied all details of accommodation. Although we do check for accuracy, we advise you to confirm the information at the time of booking.

KESWICK

Cumbria
Map ref 5A3

Beautifully positioned town beside Derwentwater and below the mountains of Skiddaw and Blencathra. Excellent base for walking, climbing, watersports and touring. Motor-launches operate on Derwentwater and motor boats, rowing boats and canoes can be hired.
Tourist Information Centre
☎ *(076 87) 72645*

Acorn House Hotel ⚊
HIGHLY COMMENDED

Ambleside Road, Keswick CA12 4DL
☎ (076 87) 72553

Detached Georgian house with newly refurbished rooms, set in own garden. Quiet location close to town centre and 10 minutes from Derwentwater.
Bedrooms: 6 double, 1 twin, 3 triple
Bathrooms: 10 private

Bed & breakfast per night:	£min	£max
Single	25.00	
Double	42.00	55.00

Parking for 10
Open February-November
Cards accepted: Access, Visa

Bank Tavern
Listed

47 Main Street, Keswick CA12 5DS
☎ (076 87) 72663

A country pub in the town centre.
Bedrooms: 2 double, 2 twin, 1 triple
Bathrooms: 1 public

Bed & breakfast per night:	£min	£max
Single	14.00	14.00
Double	28.00	28.00

Lunch available
Evening meal 1800 (last orders 2100)
Parking for 5

Beckstones Farm ⚊
COMMENDED

Thornthwaite, Keswick CA12 5SQ
☎ Braithwaite (076 87) 78510

4-acre smallholding. Converted Georgian farmhouse in a typical Lakeland setting, with extensive views of the mountains and Thornthwaite Forest. 3 miles west of Keswick.
Bedrooms: 4 double, 1 twin
Bathrooms: 3 private, 1 public

Bed & breakfast per night:	£min	£max
Single	17.00	19.00
Double	34.00	38.00

Continued ▶

51

CUMBRIA

KESWICK
Continued

Half board
per person:	£min	£max
Daily	28.00	30.00
Weekly	185.00	199.00

Evening meal 1830 (last orders 1000)
Parking for 8
Open February-November

Berkeley Guest House ♠
The Heads, Keswick CA12 5ER
☎ (076 87) 74222
On a quiet road overlooking Borrowdale Valley, with splendid views from each comfortable room. Close to the town centre and lake.
Bedrooms: 3 double, 1 twin, 1 triple
Bathrooms: 2 private, 1 public

Bed & breakfast
per night:	£min	£max
Double	29.00	39.00

Open February-December

Birkrigg Farm
Listed
Newlands, Keswick CA12 5TS
☎ Braithwaite (076 87) 78278
250-acre mixed farm. Pleasantly and peacefully located in the Newlands Valley. 5 miles from Keswick on the Braithwaite to Buttermere road.
Bedrooms: 1 single, 2 double, 1 twin, 1 triple, 1 family room
Bathrooms: 2 public

Bed & breakfast
per night:	£min	£max
Single	13.00	14.00
Double	26.00	28.00

Evening meal from 1900
Parking for 6
Open March-November

Hazeldene Hotel ♠
APPROVED
The Heads, Keswick CA12 5ER
☎ (076 87) 72106
Fax (076 87) 75435
Beautiful and central with open views over Derwentwater to Borrowdale and the Newlands Valley. Close to the town centre and shops.
Bedrooms: 5 single, 9 double, 4 twin, 4 triple
Bathrooms: 18 private, 3 public

Bed & breakfast
per night:	£min	£max
Single	21.00	27.00
Double	42.00	54.00

Half board
per person:	£min	£max
Daily	35.00	41.00
Weekly	238.00	277.00

Evening meal 1830 (last orders 1600)
Parking for 18
Open February-November

Heatherlea
Listed COMMENDED
26 Blencathra Street, Keswick CA12 4HP
☎ (076 87) 72430
Charming, friendly guesthouse, close to town centre, offering a warm welcome. Good home cooking, residential licence, own key. Lovely views.
Bedrooms: 2 double, 1 triple, 1 family room
Bathrooms: 4 private

Bed & breakfast
per night:	£min	£max
Double	30.00	34.00

Half board
per person:	£min	£max
Daily	23.00	26.00

Evening meal 1830 (last orders 1830)

Lynwood House ♠
COMMENDED
35 Helvellyn Street, Keswick CA12 4EP
☎ (076 87) 72398
Non-smoking, licensed guesthouse, five minutes from town centre. Comfortable lounge, colour TV in each room, own key. Home cooking a speciality.
Bedrooms: 1 single, 3 double, 1 triple
Bathrooms: 1 public

Bed & breakfast
per night:	£min	£max
Single	15.00	16.00
Double	30.00	32.00

Half board
per person:	£min	£max
Daily	24.00	25.00
Weekly	160.00	167.00

Evening meal 1830 (last orders 1900)

Pitcairn House ♠
7 Blencathra Street, Keswick CA12 4HW
☎ (076 87) 72453
Well established, family-run bed and breakfast accommodation in the town. Access to rooms all day. Colour TV in all rooms. Good value.
Bedrooms: 4 double, 2 twin, 1 triple
Bathrooms: 2 public

Bed & breakfast
per night:	£min	£max
Single	13.50	14.50
Double	23.00	28.00

Parking for 2
Open January-November and Christmas

Ravensworth Hotel ♠
HIGHLY COMMENDED
Station Street, Keswick CA12 5HH
☎ (076 87) 72476
Small family-run licensed hotel, decorated to a high standard of comfort, situated close to Keswick's amenities. An ideal Lake District base.
Bedrooms: 7 double, 1 twin
Bathrooms: 8 private

Bed & breakfast
per night:	£min	£max
Single	21.00	31.00
Double	30.00	44.00

Evening meal 1900 (last orders 1900)
Parking for 5
Open March-November
Cards accepted: Access, Visa

Richmond House ♠
37-39 Eskin Street, Keswick CA12 4DG
☎ (076 87) 73965
Family-run guesthouse, home-from-home, easy walking distance to town centre and lake. Vegetarians catered for. Non-smokers only please.
Bedrooms: 3 single, 5 double, 2 twin
Bathrooms: 6 private, 2 private showers

Bed & breakfast
per night:	£min	£max
Single	13.50	18.00
Double	27.00	36.00

Half board
per person:	£min	£max
Daily	22.00	27.00
Weekly	155.00	170.00

Evening meal 1900 (last orders 1700)
Cards accepted: Access, Visa

Rickerby Grange ♠
COMMENDED
Portinscale, Keswick CA12 5RH
☎ (076 87) 72344

Detached country hotel in its own gardens, in a quiet village on the outskirts of Keswick. Provides imaginative cooking, a cosy bar and quiet lounge. Ground floor bedrooms available.
Bedrooms: 1 single, 8 double, 1 twin, 3 triple
Bathrooms: 11 private, 1 public, 1 private shower

CUMBRIA

Bed & breakfast
per night:	£min	£max
Single	20.00	28.50
Double	40.00	47.00

Half board
per person:	£min	£max
Daily	30.00	33.50
Weekly	198.00	219.50

Evening meal 1900 (last orders 1800)
Parking for 14
⌂5♨⛏♿☐⬇♨⚿🛏♨🛋🍽♻
🚗SP

Rowling End ♠
Listed COMMENDED
31 Helvellyn Street, Keswick
CA12 4EP
☎ (076 87) 74108
Small, comfortable, family-run guesthouse. All rooms centrally-heated, with TV, tea and coffee facilities. Some en-suite available. Five minutes from town centre. Good home-cooked evening meals.
Bedrooms: 2 double, 1 triple, 1 family room
Bathrooms: 2 private, 1 public

Bed & breakfast
per night:	£min	£max
Single	15.00	18.00
Double	30.00	36.00

Half board
per person:	£min	£max
Daily	25.00	28.00
Weekly	165.00	185.00

Open March-December
⌂☐⬇♿♨⚿🛏♨🍽♻🚗SP

Scawdel
Listed
Grange-in-Borrowdale, Keswick
CA12 5UQ
☎ (076 87) 77171
Detached house with private parking in Grange village, 4 miles from Keswick. Excellent mountain views from most windows. Rooms have comfortable seating and orthopaedic beds.
Bedrooms: 2 double, 1 twin
Bathrooms: 1 public

Bed & breakfast
per night:	£min	£max
Single	15.00	25.00
Double	29.00	31.00

Parking for 4
⌂6☐⬇♿S⚿🍽♻

Strathmore Guest House ♠
COMMENDED
8 St Johns Terrace, Keswick
CA12 4DP
☎ (076 87) 72584
Warm, stone-built guesthouse in lovely part of Keswick, opposite St John's church, close to town centre and lake. Fine breakfasts, beautiful outlook.
Bedrooms: 1 single, 4 double, 1 twin, 1 triple, 1 family room
Bathrooms: 3 public

Bed & breakfast
per night:	£min	£max
Single	15.00	17.50
Double	30.00	35.00

Half board
per person:	£min	£max
Daily	25.00	27.50
Weekly	155.00	175.00

Evening meal 1830 (last orders 1900)
Parking for 6
Open February-December
⌂♨⬇♿☐S⚿🛏♨🍽♻🚗🐕
SP T

Watendlath Guest House ♠
Listed COMMENDED
15 Acorn Street, Keswick CA12 4EA
☎ (076 87) 74165
Within easy walking distance of the lake, hills and town centre. We offer a warm and friendly welcome and traditional English breakfast.
Bedrooms: 3 double, 1 twin
Bathrooms: 2 private, 1 public

Bed & breakfast
per night:	£min	£max
Double	25.00	32.00

Open January-October
⌂⬇☐⬇♿☐S🍽♻🚗🐕♻SP

Whitehouse Guest House
COMMENDED
15 Ambleside Road, Keswick
CA12 4DL
☎ (076 87) 73176
Fully refurbished small, friendly guesthouse 5 minutes' walk from the town centre. Colour TV, electric blankets, tea/coffee. Most rooms with en-suite facilities.
Bedrooms: 4 double
Bathrooms: 3 private, 1 public, 1 private shower

Bed & breakfast
per night:	£min	£max
Double	26.00	33.00

Parking for 3
Open March-October
⌂☐⬇♿☐S♨🛏♨🍽♻🚗

KIRKBY STEPHEN
Cumbria
Map ref 5B3

Old market town close to the River Eden, with many fine Georgian buildings and an attractive market square. St Stephen's Church is known as the "Cathedral of the Dales". Good base for exploring the Eden Valley and the Dales.
Tourist Information Centre
☎ (076 83) 71199

Augill House Farm
HIGHLY COMMENDED
Brough, Kirkby Stephen CA17 4DX
☎ Brough (076 83) 41305

40-acre mixed farm. Georgian farmhouse. Warm and comfortable. Good access from A66. Breakfasts and 5-course dinners served in conservatory overlooking garden.
Bedrooms: 2 double, 1 twin
Bathrooms: 3 private

Bed & breakfast
per night:	£min	£max
Double	36.00	40.00

Half board
per person:	£min	£max
Daily	26.50	28.50
Weekly	170.00	170.00

Evening meal from 1900
Parking for 6
⌂12☐⬇♿☐♨♿🛏♨🍽♻🚗✴
🚗SP

LAMPLUGH
Cumbria
Map ref 5A3

Near the A5086 between Cockermouth and Cleator Moor, Lamplugh is a scattered village famous for its "Lamplugh Pudding". Ideal touring base for the western Lake District.

Briscoe Close
Listed COMMENDED
Scalesmoor, Lamplugh, Workington
CA14 4TZ
☎ (0946) 861633
Bungalow close to family-run farm. Near Loweswater and Ennerdale, half a mile from A5086. Home cooking using produce grown on farm.
Bedrooms: 2 double
Bathrooms: 1 public

Bed & breakfast
per night:	£min	£max
Single	15.00	
Double	30.00	

Half board
per person:	£min	£max
Daily	21.00	
Weekly	145.00	

Evening meal from 1900
Parking for 2
⌂♨☐S🛏♨🍽♻🚗✴🐕

The enquiry coupons at the back will help you when contacting proprietors.

CUMBRIA

LANGDALE
Cumbria
Map ref 5A3

The two Langdale valleys (Great Langdale and Little Langdale) lie in the heart of beautiful mountain scenery. The craggy Langdale Pikes are almost 2500 ft high. An ideal walking and climbing area.

Britannia Inn
COMMENDED
Elterwater, Ambleside LA22 9HP
☎ (053 94) 37210
Fax (053 94) 37211

A 400-year-old traditional Lake District inn on a village green in the beautiful Langdale Valley. A warm welcome to all. TV available in bedrooms.
Bedrooms: 7 double, 2 twin
Bathrooms: 6 private, 2 public

Bed & breakfast per night:	£min	£max
Single	25.00	31.00
Double	50.00	62.00

Half board per person:	£min	£max
Daily	41.50	46.50
Weekly	273.00	322.00

Lunch available
Evening meal 1930 (last orders 1930)
Parking for 10
Cards accepted: Access, Visa, Switch

LONGTOWN
Cumbria
Map ref 5A2

The last town in England situated in the Parish of Arthuret, with its claim to connections with the legendary King Arthur. Once important for the Scottish drovers and now enjoyed by those touring the Border country. Hadrian's Wall is close by.
Tourist Information Centre
☎ (0228) 791876

Craigburn
COMMENDED
Penton, Longtown, Carlisle CA6 5QP
☎ Nicholforest (0228) 577214
250-acre mixed farm. Near the Scottish border. We provide comfort and farmhouse cooking for weekend breaks, longer stays or a stopover to or from Scotland.
Bedrooms: 3 double, 1 twin, 2 triple
Bathrooms: 6 private

Bed & breakfast per night:	£min	£max
Single	23.00	24.00
Double	36.00	38.00

Half board per person:	£min	£max
Daily	28.00	29.00
Weekly	156.80	157.80

Evening meal 1800 (last orders 1400)
Parking for 20

LORTON
Cumbria
Map ref 5A3

High and Low Lorton are set in a beautiful vale north of Crummock Water and at the foot of the Whinlatter Pass. Church of St Cuthbert is well worth a visit.

New House Farm
HIGHLY COMMENDED
Lorton, Cockermouth CA13 9UU
☎ (0900) 85404
15-acre mixed farm. Beautifully restored 17th C Lakeland house, converted into a very special country guesthouse. Superb views of the Lorton Vale and hills from every room. Fine traditional cooking.
Bedrooms: 3 double
Bathrooms: 3 private

Bed & breakfast per night:	£min	£max
Single	30.00	35.00
Double	50.00	60.00

Half board per person:	£min	£max
Daily	45.00	55.00

Lunch available
Evening meal 1930 (last orders 1930)
Parking for 20
Open February-November and Christmas

LOWESWATER
Cumbria
Map ref 5A3

This scattered village lies between Loweswater, one of the smaller lakes of the Lake District, and Crummock Water. Several mountains lie beyond the village, giving lovely views.

Brook Farm
COMMENDED
Thackthwaite, Loweswater, Cockermouth CA13 0RP
☎ Lorton (0900) 85506
300-acre hill farm. In quiet surroundings and a good walking area. 5 miles from Cockermouth. Carrying sheep and suckler cows.
Bedrooms: 1 double, 1 twin

Bathrooms: 1 public

Bed & breakfast per night:	£min	£max
Single	15.00	16.50
Double	30.00	33.00

Half board per person:	£min	£max
Daily	21.00	22.50
Weekly	147.00	157.50

Evening meal from 1900
Parking for 3
Open May-October

Kirkstile Inn
COMMENDED
Loweswater, Cockermouth CA13 0RU
☎ Lorton (090 085) 219
A 16th C inn near an oak-fringed beck running between Loweswater and Crummock Water lakes, surrounded by fells.
Bedrooms: 5 double, 2 twin, 3 triple
Bathrooms: 8 private, 2 public

Bed & breakfast per night:	£min	£max
Single	32.50	45.00
Double	45.00	55.00

Lunch available
Evening meal 1830 (last orders 2100)
Parking for 40
Cards accepted: Access, Visa

MARYPORT
Cumbria
Map ref 5A2

On the Solway Firth, this town was once an iron and coal port. The Romans built a fort here, one of their chain of defensive points along the coast. It now has a marina and museums. Good views across the firth to the Scottish hills.
Tourist Information Centre
☎ (0900) 813738

East Farm
Listed
Crosscanonby, Maryport CA15 6SJ
☎ (0900) 812153
236-acre mixed & dairy farm. Beautiful views of Scotland. Between Maryport and Allonby. Beach, golf-course, pony trekking, windsurfing nearby. TV lounge, tea making facilities.
Bedrooms: 1 double, 1 family room
Bathrooms: 1 public

Bed & breakfast per night:	£min	£max
Single	13.00	14.00
Double	26.00	28.00

Parking for 2

CUMBRIA

MAULDS MEABURN
Cumbria
Map ref 5B3

Meaburn Hill Farm
Listed HIGHLY COMMENDED

Meaburn Hill, Maulds Meaburn, Penrith CA10 3HN
☎ Ravensworth (0931) 715205
200-acre livestock farm. Lovely 16th C farmhouse overlooking village green and river, in hidden valley 6 miles west of Appleby. Enjoy real country breakfasts, afternoon teas, log fires and antique-furnished rooms. A warm welcome awaits.
Bedrooms: 2 double, 1 twin
Bathrooms: 3 private

Bed & breakfast
per night:	£min	£max
Single	18.00	21.00
Double	36.00	42.00

Parking for 3
Open April-November

MUNGRISDALE
Cumbria
Map ref 5A2

Set in an unspoilt valley the simple, white church in this hamlet has a 3-decker pulpit and box pews.

Near Howe Farm Hotel ⋒
COMMENDED

Mungrisdale, Penrith CA11 0SH
☎ Penrith (076 87) 79678
Farmhouse in quiet surroundings 1 mile from Mungrisdale, half a mile from the A66 and within easy reach of all the lakes.
Bedrooms: 3 double, 1 twin, 3 triple
Bathrooms: 5 private, 1 public

Bed & breakfast
per night:	£min	£max
Single	19.00	19.00
Double	34.00	38.00

Half board
per person:	£min	£max
Daily	27.00	29.00
Weekly	189.00	203.00

Evening meal 1900 (last orders 1700)
Parking for 12
Open April-November

National Crown ratings were correct at the time of going to press but are subject to change. Please check at the time of booking.

ORTON
Cumbria
Map ref 5B3

Small, attractive village with the background of Orton Scar, it has some old buildings and a spacious green. George Whitehead, the itinerant Quaker preacher, was born here in 1636.

The Vicarage ⋒
Listed

Orton, Penrith CA10 3RQ
☎ (053 96) 24873
Fax (053 96) 24873
Warm, comfortable accommodation in a working vicarage overlooking rooftops and fells. Ideal for walkers visiting the Lakes and Yorkshire Dales.
Bedrooms: 1 double, 2 twin
Bathrooms: 1 public

Bed & breakfast
per night:	£min	£max
Single		15.00
Double		30.00

Half board
per person:	£min	£max
Daily		23.00
Weekly		140.00

Evening meal 1900 (last orders 2100)
Parking for 2

PATTERDALE
Cumbria
Map ref 5A3

Amongst the fells at the southern end of the Ullswater Valley, this village is dominated by Helvellyn and St Sunday Crag. Ideal centre for touring and outdoor activities.

Fellside ⋒
Listed APPROVED

Hartsop, Patterdale, Penrith CA11 0NZ
☎ Glenridding (076 84) 82532
A 17th C Cumbrian farmhouse at the foot of Kirkstone Pass, perfect for fellwalkers; artists welcome. Magnificent scenery. Piano in the lounge.
Bedrooms: 1 single, 1 double, 1 twin
Bathrooms: 2 public

Bed & breakfast
per night:	£min	£max
Single	14.00	16.00
Double	28.00	32.00

Parking for 3

The town index towards the back of this guide gives page numbers of all places with accommodation.

PENRITH
Cumbria
Map ref 5B2

This ancient and historic market town is the northern gateway to the Lake District. Penrith Castle was built as a defence against the Scots. Its ruins, open to the public, stand in the public park. High above the town is the famous Penrith Beacon.
Tourist Information Centre
☎ *(0768) 67466*

Glendale ⋒
Listed APPROVED

4 Portland Place, Penrith CA11 7QN
☎ (0768) 62579
Victorian town house overlooking pleasant gardens. Spacious family rooms. Children and pets welcome.
Bedrooms: 1 single, 1 double, 3 triple
Bathrooms: 1 public

Bed & breakfast
per night:	£min	£max
Single		17.00
Double		30.00

Greenfields ⋒
Listed HIGHLY COMMENDED

Ellonby, Penrith CA11 9SJ
☎ Skelton (076 84) 84671
Alison and Ken invite you into their comfortable home amidst mountains and meadows. Six miles from junction 41 M6. Explore Eden Valley and Northern Lakes.
Bedrooms: 1 single, 2 double
Bathrooms: 2 public

Bed & breakfast
per night:	£min	£max
Single	13.50	13.50
Double	27.00	27.00

Half board
per person:	£min	£max
Daily	21.00	21.00
Weekly	133.00	133.00

Lunch available
Evening meal 1830 (last orders 2000)
Parking for 3
Open April-November

Holmewood Guesthouse
Listed

5 Portland Place, Penrith CA11 7QN
☎ (0768) 63072
Large Victorian terraced house run by proprietress and providing good facilities. Ideal for Lake District and stopover to or from Scotland.
Bedrooms: 1 double, 3 triple, 1 family room
Bathrooms: 1 private, 2 public

Continued ▶

CUMBRIA

PENRITH
Continued

Bed & breakfast
per night:	£min	£max
Single	15.00	18.50
Double	28.00	45.00

Parking for 1

Hornby Hall Country House
Listed HIGHLY COMMENDED

Hornby Hall Farm, Brougham, Penrith CA10 2AR
☎ Culgaith (0768) 891114
850-acre mixed farm. Farmhouse with interesting old hall. Fishing on Eamont available. Within easy reach of Lakes, Pennines and Yorkshire Dales. Home-cooked local produce.
Bedrooms: 2 single, 2 double, 3 twin
Bathrooms: 2 private, 3 public

Bed & breakfast
per night:	£min	£max
Single	15.00	28.00
Double	44.00	56.00

Half board
per person:	£min	£max
Daily	28.00	43.00
Weekly	196.00	300.00

Evening meal 1900 (last orders 2100)
Parking for 10
Cards accepted: Access, Visa, Amex

Newton Rigg College

Penrith CA11 0AH
☎ (0768) 63791
Fax (0768) 67249
College with single and twin room accommodation set on 2000-acre campus in a beautiful setting. TV, lounge bar. Discount for groups.
Bedrooms: 8 single, 2 twin
Bathrooms: 4 public

Bed & breakfast
per night:	£min	£max
Single	12.50	14.50
Double	24.00	28.00

Half board
per person:	£min	£max
Daily	18.00	20.00
Weekly	107.00	119.00

Lunch available
Evening meal 1800 (last orders 1900)
Parking for 300

The Old Vicarage
COMMENDED

Eden Hall, Penrith CA11 8SX
☎ Langwathby (0768) 881329
Grade II listed, elegant, Georgian house extended in the Victorian period. In three quarter acre garden, in a peaceful village with easy access to the Pennines and Lakes.
Bedrooms: 1 twin, 1 triple

Bathrooms: 2 private
Bed & breakfast
per night:	£min	£max
Single	18.00	18.00
Double	32.00	32.00

Parking for 3
Open January-November

Sockbridge Mill Trout Farm
Listed COMMENDED

Penrith CA10 2JT
☎ (0768) 65338
8-acre fish farm. Picturesque working trout farm on the River Eamont, off the B5320 between Pooley Bridge and Penrith.
Bedrooms: 2 double, 2 twin
Bathrooms: 2 public, 1 private shower

Bed & breakfast
per night:	£min	£max
Single	12.00	16.00
Double	22.00	30.00

Half board
per person:	£min	£max
Daily	22.00	26.00
Weekly	130.00	155.00

Parking for 6
Open April-October

PENRUDDOCK
Cumbria
Map ref 5A2

Low Garth Guest House
APPROVED

Penruddock, Penrith CA11 0QU
☎ Greystoke (076 84) 83492
Tastefully converted 18th C barn in peaceful surroundings with magnificent views. Easy access to A66.
Bedrooms: 1 twin, 1 triple
Bathrooms: 2 private, 1 public

Bed & breakfast
per night:	£min	£max
Single	15.00	17.00
Double	30.00	34.00

Half board
per person:	£min	£max
Daily	25.00	28.00
Weekly	175.00	196.00

Evening meal 1800 (last orders 2000)
Parking for 8

National Crown ratings were correct at the time of going to press but are subject to change. Please check at the time of booking.

SEDBERGH
Cumbria
Map ref 5B3

This busy market town set below the Howgill Fells is an excellent centre for walkers and touring the Dales. The noted boys' school was founded in 1525.

Dalesman Country Inn
COMMENDED

Main Street, Sedbergh LA10 5BN
☎ (053 96) 21183
On entering Sedbergh from the M6 the Dalesman is the first inn on the left. 17th C but recently refurbished by local craftsmen. 10% discount on weekly bookings. Winter breaks available.
Bedrooms: 1 double, 2 twin, 3 triple
Bathrooms: 4 private, 1 public

Bed & breakfast
per night:	£min	£max
Single	33.50	37.50
Double	45.00	50.00

Lunch available
Evening meal 1800 (last orders 2130)
Parking for 10
Cards accepted: Access, Visa

SILLOTH
Cumbria
Map ref 5A2

Small port and coastal resort on the Solway Firth with wide cobbled roads and an attractive green leading to the promenade and seashore known for its magnificent sunsets.
Tourist Information Centre
☎ (069 73) 31944

Nook Farm
Listed APPROVED

Beckfoot, Silloth, Carlisle CA5 4LG
☎ Allonby (0900) 881279
90-acre dairy farm. Within easy reach of all tourist areas, and with views of Lakeland. On Cumbrian coast cycle way.
Bedrooms: 1 double, 1 triple
Bathrooms: 1 public

Bed & breakfast
per night:	£min	£max
Single	13.00	15.00
Double	25.00	30.00

Parking for 3
Open April-October

Establishments should be open throughout the year unless otherwise stated in the entry.

CUMBRIA

STAVELEY
Cumbria
Map ref 5A3

Large village built in slate, set between Kendal and Windermere at the entrance to the lovely Kentmere Valley.

Stockbridge Farm ♠
Listed

Kendal Road, Staveley, Kendal
LA8 9LP
☎ (0539) 821581
20-acre mixed farm. Comfortable, well-appointed 17th C farmhouse on edge of bypassed village midway between Kendal and Windermere on A591. Central heating. English breakfast. Friendly personal attention.
Bedrooms: 1 single, 4 double, 1 triple
Bathrooms: 1 public

Bed & breakfast
per night:	£min	£max
Single	13.50	14.00
Double	27.00	28.00

Parking for 6
Open March-October

THRELKELD
Cumbria
Map ref 5A3

This village is a centre for climbing the Saddleback range of mountains, which tower high above it.

Scales Farm Country Guesthouse
HIGHLY COMMENDED

Scales, Threlkeld, Keswick CA12 4SY
☎ (076 87) 79660
Tastefully modernised 17th C farmhouse, conveniently situated for touring the Lakes. All bedrooms en-suite with colour TV and tea/coffee-making facilities. Friendly personal service provided by proprietors.
Bedrooms: 4 double, 1 twin
Bathrooms: 5 private

Bed & breakfast
per night:	£min	£max
Double	40.00	46.00

Parking for 6

The national Crown scheme is explained in full in the information pages towards the back of this guide.

TROUTBECK
Cumbria
Map ref 5A3

On the Penrith to Keswick road, Troutbeck was the site of a series of Roman camps. The village now hosts a busy weekly sheep market.

Netherdene Guest House ♠
COMMENDED

Troutbeck, Penrith CA11 0SJ
☎ Greystoke (076 84) 83475
Traditional country house in its own quiet grounds, with extensive mountain views, offering comfortable well-appointed rooms with personal attention. Ideal base for touring Lakeland.
Bedrooms: 2 double, 1 twin, 1 triple
Bathrooms: 2 private, 2 public

Bed & breakfast
per night:	£min	£max
Single	18.00	20.00
Double	29.00	37.00

Half board
per person:	£min	£max
Daily	22.00	27.00
Weekly	145.00	170.00

Evening meal 1830 (last orders 1600)
Parking for 6
Open February-November and Christmas

Troutbeck Inn ♠

Troutbeck, Penrith CA11 0SJ
☎ Greystoke (076 84) 83635
Small, family-run country inn halfway between Keswick and Penrith. Approximately 10 minutes from the M6, Ullswater and Keswick, and ideal for all Lakeland activities. Bar meals available.
Bedrooms: 3 double, 1 triple
Bathrooms: 3 private, 1 public

Bed & breakfast
per night:	£min	£max
Single	20.00	25.00
Double	30.00	37.00

Evening meal 1830 (last orders 2100)
Parking for 50

There are separate sections in this guide listing groups specialising in farm holidays and accommodation which is especially suitable for young people and organised groups.

ULLSWATER
Cumbria
Map ref 5A3

This beautiful lake, which is over 7 miles long, runs from Glenridding to Pooley Bridge. Lofty peaks ranging around the lake make an impressive background. A steamer service operates along the lake between Pooley Bridge, Howtown and Glenridding in the summer.

Bridge End Farm ♠
COMMENDED

Hutton, Hutton John, Penrith
CA11 0LZ
☎ Greystoke (076 84) 83273
14-acre mixed farm. Warmest hospitality in 17th C farmhouse, situated in own grounds with gardens to river. Lakeland fell views. 5 miles west of M6, half a mile A66, 3 miles Ullswater.
Bedrooms: 2 double, 1 twin, 1 triple
Bathrooms: 3 private, 1 public

Bed & breakfast
per night:	£min	£max
Double	28.00	35.00

Half board
per person:	£min	£max
Daily	20.50	25.00
Weekly	135.00	155.00

Evening meal 1830 (last orders 1700)
Parking for 6
Open April-October

Cragside Cottage ♠

Thackthwaite, Ullswater, Penrith
CA11 0ND
☎ Pooley Bridge (076 84) 86385
Mountainside location, 3 miles north of Ullswater. All rooms have toilet, shower and washbasin, tea making facilities, TV. Reserved parking space. Breakfast served in room. Brochure available.
Bedrooms: 4 double, 1 triple
Bathrooms: 5 private

Bed & breakfast
per night:	£min	£max
Single	21.00	21.00
Double	30.00	30.00

Parking for 5
Open March-October
Cards accepted: Access, Visa

Swiss Chalet Inn ♠
APPROVED

Pooley Bridge, Penrith CA10 2NN
☎ Pooley Bridge (076 84) 86215
Fax (076 84) 86215
Set in charming village near shores of beautiful Ullswater, 5 miles from M6. All rooms en-suite.
Swiss/Continental/English cuisine.
Bedrooms: 1 single, 5 double, 2 twin, 1 family room
Bathrooms: 9 private

Continued ▶

57

CUMBRIA

ULLSWATER
Continued

Bed & breakfast
per night:	£min	£max
Single	27.00	32.00
Double	44.00	52.00

Lunch available
Evening meal 1800 (last orders 2145)
Parking for 40
Open February-December
Cards accepted: Access, Visa

Ullswater House
COMMENDED

Pooley Bridge, Penrith CA10 2NN
☎ Pooley Bridge (076 84) 86259
Centrally situated in Pooley Bridge. The well appointed rooms are quiet, each having a fridge containing alcoholic and soft drinks.
Bedrooms: 2 double, 1 twin
Bathrooms: 3 private

Bed & breakfast
per night:	£min	£max
Single	18.00	28.00
Double	36.00	36.00

Half board
per person:	£min	£max
Daily	28.00	28.00
Weekly	180.00	180.00

Evening meal 1900 (last orders 1900)
Parking for 4

Waterside House
COMMENDED

Watermillock, Penrith CA11 0JH
☎ Pooley Bridge (076 84) 86038
A listed statesman's house, set in 10 acres of gardens and meadows on Ullswater's glorious shores. Peaceful and comfortable, an idyllic retreat from pressures. On A592 to Patterdale, 2 miles south of Pooley Bridge.
Wheelchair access category 3
Bedrooms: 5 double, 1 twin, 1 triple
Bathrooms: 4 private, 3 public

Bed & breakfast
per night:	£min	£max
Single	20.00	35.00
Double	40.00	70.00

Parking for 10

Whitbarrow Farm

Berrier, Penrith CA11 0XB
☎ Greystoke (076 84) 83266
220-acre dairy farm. Built in the late 1800s in typical farmhouse style. Only 8 miles from the M6, 10 miles from Keswick and 5 miles from Ullswater. Access to nearby leisure centre.
Bedrooms: 1 double, 1 family room
Bathrooms: 1 public

Bed & breakfast
per night:	£min	£max
Single	15.00	17.00
Double	30.00	34.00

Parking for 3
Open February-November

UNDERBARROW
Cumbria
Map ref 5A3

At the foot of limestone escarpment Scout Scar, Underbarrow is close to the National Trust's Brigsteer Woods, west of Kendal. A quiet, spread-out village, overlooking the Lyth Valley.

Tranthwaite Hall
Listed

Underbarrow, Kendal LA8 8HG
☎ Crosthwaite (053 95) 68285
On a working dairy/sheep farm, this magnificent 11th C farmhouse has oak doors and beams and a rare black iron fire range. Peaceful setting in beautiful grounds.
Bedrooms: 1 double, 1 triple
Bathrooms: 1 public

Bed & breakfast
per night:	£min	£max
Single	15.00	17.00
Double	30.00	34.00

Parking for 3

WASDALE
Cumbria
Map ref 5A3

A very dramatic valley with England's deepest lake, Wastwater; highest mountain, Scafell Pike; smallest church. The eastern shore of Wastwater is dominated by the 1,500 ft screes dropping steeply into the lake. A good centre for walking and climbing.

Low Wood Hall Hotel
COMMENDED

Nether Wasdale, Wasdale CA20 1ET
☎ (094 67) 26289
Fax (094 67) 26289

Gracious Victorian country house with fine views across Wasdale. Close to Scafell, Wastwater and sea. Bar, billiard room. Extensive dinner menu.
Bedrooms: 1 single, 6 double, 7 twin
Bathrooms: 14 private

Bed & breakfast
per night:	£min	£max
Single	35.00	
Double		57.00

Half board
per person:	£min	£max
Daily	37.50	
Weekly	231.00	

Evening meal 1830 (last orders 2045)
Parking for 24
Cards accepted: Access, Visa

WINDERMERE
Cumbria
Map ref 5A3

Once a tiny hamlet before the introduction of the railway in 1847, now adjoins Bowness which is on the lakeside. Centre for sailing and boating. A good way to see the lake is a trip on a passenger steamer. Steamboat Museum has a fine collection of old boats.
Tourist Information Centre
☎ *(053 94) 46499*

Aaron Slack
COMMENDED

48 Ellerthwaite Road, Windermere LA23 2BS
☎ (053 94) 44649
Small, friendly guesthouse for non-smokers in a quiet part of Windermere, close to all amenities and concentrating on personal service.
Bedrooms: 2 double, 1 twin
Bathrooms: 3 private

Bed & breakfast
per night:	£min	£max
Single	12.00	21.00
Double	24.00	36.00

Cards accepted: Access, Visa, Amex

Almaria House
APPROVED

17 Broad Street, Windermere LA23 2AB
☎ (053 94) 43026
Maria and Alan offer you a warm welcome close to all amenities, public car parking, great breakfast. Ideal holiday base.
Bedrooms: 4 double, 1 triple
Bathrooms: 3 private, 1 public

Bed & breakfast
per night:	£min	£max
Single	15.00	25.00
Double	22.00	36.00

Half board
per person:	£min	£max
Daily	18.00	26.00

Open January-November
Cards accepted: Access, Visa

CUMBRIA

Bankfield House
Listed
Ings, Kendal LA8 9PY
☎ Staveley (0539) 821135
Local turn-of-the-century, detached house in own grounds, 2 miles from Windermere. Meals, licensed bar and large family room. Open fire in winter.
Bedrooms: 2 double, 1 family room
Bathrooms: 1 public

Bed & breakfast
per night:	£min	£max
Single	17.00	30.00
Double	25.00	75.00

Half board
per person:	£min	£max
Daily	25.00	40.00
Weekly	150.00	280.00

Lunch available
Evening meal 1830 (last orders 2130)
Parking for 8
Open January, March-October, December
Cards accepted: Access, Visa

The Beaumont Hotel
HIGHLY COMMENDED
Holly Road, Windermere LA23 2AF
☎ (053 94) 47075

Elegant Victorian house hotel with high standard accommodation, beautiful lounge, car parking. All rooms (2 four-posters) have colour TV, hairdryers, tea-making facilities. Warm, personal service.
Bedrooms: 1 single, 7 double, 1 twin, 1 family room
Bathrooms: 10 private

Bed & breakfast
per night:	£min	£max
Single	25.00	35.00
Double	46.00	56.00

Half board
per person:	£min	£max
Daily	35.00	45.00
Weekly	230.00	295.00

Parking for 10
Open February-November

Beckmead House
COMMENDED
5 Park Avenue, Windermere LA23 2AR
☎ (053 94) 42757
Delightful stone-built Victorian house with reputation for high standards, comfort and friendliness. Our a la carte breakfasts are famous. Convenient for lake, shops, restaurants and golf-course.
Bedrooms: 1 single, 2 double, 1 twin, 1 family room
Bathrooms: 2 private, 1 public, 2 private showers

Bed & breakfast
per night:	£min	£max
Single	14.50	18.00
Double	30.00	38.00

Boston House
4 The Terrace, Windermere LA23 1AJ
☎ (053 94) 43654
Fax (053 94) 43654

Charmingly peaceful Victorian listed building within 5 minutes' walk of trains and town centre. Delicious food, panoramic views, relaxed comfortable atmosphere, private parking.
Bedrooms: 2 double, 2 twin, 1 triple, 1 family room
Bathrooms: 5 private, 2 public

Bed & breakfast
per night:	£min	£max
Double	30.00	44.00

Half board
per person:	£min	£max
Daily	24.00	31.00
Weekly	150.00	205.00

Evening meal 1900 (last orders 1930)
Parking for 6
Cards accepted: Access, Visa

The Burn How Garden House Hotel & Motel
HIGHLY COMMENDED
Back Belsfield Road, Windermere LA23 3HH
☎ (053 94) 46226
Fax (053 94) 47000
Unique combination of Victorian houses and private chalets in secluded gardens in the heart of a picturesque village. Full facilities. Four-poster beds available.
Wheelchair access category 3
Bedrooms: 2 single, 8 double, 8 twin, 8 triple
Bathrooms: 26 private

Bed & breakfast
per night:	£min	£max
Single	46.00	52.00
Double	58.00	78.00

Half board
per person:	£min	£max
Daily	38.00	55.00
Weekly	220.00	340.00

Lunch available
Evening meal 1900 (last orders 2100)
Parking for 30
Cards accepted: Access, Visa, Amex, Switch

Cambridge House
Listed COMMENDED
9 Oak Street, Windermere LA23 1EN
☎ (053 94) 43826
Village centre location convenient for all amenities. Modern, comfortable rooms with en-suite facilities. Full English, Continental or vegetarian breakfast.
Bedrooms: 5 double, 1 triple
Bathrooms: 6 private

Bed & breakfast
per night:	£min	£max
Single	14.00	18.00
Double	28.00	36.00

Fairfield Country House Hotel
COMMENDED
Brantfell Road, Bowness-on-Windermere, Windermere LA23 3AE
☎ (053 94) 46565
Fax (053 94) 46565
Small, friendly 200-year-old country house with half an acre of peaceful secluded gardens. 2 minutes' walk from Lake Windermere and village.
Bedrooms: 1 single, 4 double, 1 twin, 2 triple, 1 family room
Bathrooms: 9 private, 1 public

Bed & breakfast
per night:	£min	£max
Single	22.00	28.00
Double	44.00	56.00

Half board
per person:	£min	£max
Daily	37.00	43.00
Weekly	259.00	273.00

Evening meal 1930 (last orders 1930)
Parking for 14
Cards accepted: Access, Visa

Glenville
COMMENDED
Lake Road, Windermere LA23 2EQ
☎ (053 94) 43371

Standing in its own grounds, midway between Windermere and Bowness and perfectly positioned for access to all amenities. The lake is an easy 10 minute walk. Car park.

Continued ▶

CUMBRIA

WINDERMERE
Continued

Bedrooms: 1 single, 6 double, 1 twin, 1 triple
Bathrooms: 8 private, 1 public

Bed & breakfast
per night:	£min	£max
Single	18.00	24.00
Double	36.00	48.00

Evening meal 1830 (last orders 1400)
Parking for 12
Open January-November

Holly Lodge
COMMENDED
6 College Road, Windermere
LA23 1BX
☎ (053 94) 43873
Traditional Lakeland stone guesthouse, built in 1854. In a quiet area off the main road, close to the village centre, buses, railway station and all amenities.
Bedrooms: 1 single, 5 double, 2 twin, 3 triple
Bathrooms: 4 private, 2 public

Bed & breakfast
per night:	£min	£max
Single	16.00	20.00
Double	32.00	40.00

Half board
per person:	£min	£max
Daily	25.50	29.50

Evening meal from 1900
Parking for 7

Lakes Hotel
COMMENDED
1 High Street, Windermere LA23 1AF
☎ (053 94) 42751 & 88123
Fax (053 94) 46026
Attractive and small Victorian bed and breakfast hotel, just 1 minute's walk from rail/bus stations and local shops. Spacious rooms, all with private facilities. Warm hospitality, excellent breakfasts. Local mini-coach tours our speciality. Los Angeles Times recommended.
Bedrooms: 1 single, 4 double, 2 twin, 1 triple, 1 family room
Bathrooms: 9 private

Bed & breakfast
per night:	£min	£max
Single	22.00	25.00
Double	40.00	44.00

Half board
per person:	£min	£max
Daily	31.00	33.00
Weekly	210.00	224.00

Evening meal 1900 (last orders 2100)
Parking for 10
Cards accepted: Access, Visa, Amex, Switch

Laurel Cottage
COMMENDED
St. Martin's Square, Bowness-on-Windermere, Windermere LA23 3EF
☎ (053 94) 45594
Charming early 17th C cottage with front garden, situated in centre of Bowness. Superb selection of restaurants within one minute's stroll.
Bedrooms: 2 single, 10 double, 1 twin, 2 triple
Bathrooms: 10 private, 2 public

Bed & breakfast
per night:	£min	£max
Single	20.00	22.00
Double	34.00	50.00

Parking for 8

New Hall Bank
Listed
Fallbarrow Road, Bowness-on-Windermere, Windermere LA23 3AJ
☎ (053 94) 43558
In a quiet area within 2 minutes' walking distance of town centre and the lake. Ample parking space. Lake views.
Bedrooms: 2 single, 7 double, 3 triple, 2 family rooms
Bathrooms: 2 public, 1 private shower

Bed & breakfast
per night:	£min	£max
Single	14.00	20.00
Double	28.00	40.00

Parking for 16

Oldfield House
COMMENDED
Oldfield Road, Windermere LA23 2BY
☎ (053 94) 88445

Friendly, informal atmosphere within a traditionally-built Lakeland residence. Quiet central location, free use of swimming and leisure club.
Bedrooms: 2 single, 3 double, 1 triple, 1 family room
Bathrooms: 6 private, 1 public

Bed & breakfast
per night:	£min	£max
Single	19.00	26.00
Double	34.00	48.00

Parking for 7
Cards accepted: Access, Visa, Switch

Park Beck Guest House
Listed APPROVED
3 Park Road, Windermere LA23 2AW
☎ (053 94) 44025

Ideally situated Lakeland-stone
guesthouse, close to all facilities. En-suite rooms with colour TV and tea/coffee making facilities.
Bedrooms: 2 double, 1 twin, 1 triple
Bathrooms: 4 private

Bed & breakfast
per night:	£min	£max
Single	16.00	20.00
Double	28.00	40.00

Lunch available
Parking for 2
Open February-December

The Poplars
COMMENDED
Lake Road, Windermere LA23 2EQ
☎ (053 94) 42325 & 446690
Small family-run guesthouse on the main lake road, offering en-suite accommodation coupled with fine cuisine and homely atmosphere.
Bedrooms: 1 single, 3 double, 2 twin, 1 triple
Bathrooms: 6 private, 1 public

Bed & breakfast
per night:	£min	£max
Single	16.00	22.00
Double	32.00	44.00

Half board
per person:	£min	£max
Daily	26.00	32.00
Weekly	148.00	210.00

Evening meal 1830 (last orders 1900)
Parking for 7

Royal Hotel
APPROVED
Queens Square, Bowness-on-Windermere, Windermere LA23 3DB
☎ (053 94) 43045 & 45267
Fax (053 94) 44990
One of Lakeland's oldest hotels, offering modern amenities. Only 100 yards from the lake with most rooms having lake and mountain views. Free leisure facilities. Prices are for room only.
Bedrooms: 6 single, 11 double, 7 twin, 5 triple
Bathrooms: 29 private

Bed & breakfast
per night:	£min	£max
Single	22.50	22.50
Double	39.00	49.00

Lunch available
Evening meal 1900 (last orders 2130)
Parking for 21
Cards accepted: Access, Visa, Diners, Amex, Switch

St. John's Lodge
COMMENDED
Lake Road, Windermere LA23 2EQ
☎ (053 94) 43078
Small private hotel midway between Windermere and the lake, managed by

CUMBRIA

the chef/proprietor and convenient for all amenities and services. Facilities of local sports and leisure club available to guests.
Bedrooms: 1 single, 9 double, 2 twin, 2 triple
Bathrooms: 14 private

Bed & breakfast
per night:	£min	£max
Single	17.50	23.00
Double	33.00	46.00

Half board
per person:	£min	£max
Daily	26.50	33.00
Weekly	178.00	199.00

Evening meal 1900 (last orders 1800)
Parking for 11
Open February-November
Cards accepted: Access, Visa

South View

Cross Street, Windermere LA23 1AE
☎ (053 94) 42951

Unique in Windermere village - tourist accommodation with own heated indoor swimming pool open all year. Not a hotel or a guesthouse - just a country home taking a few B & B guests. Quiet yet central. Self-catering cottage also available.
Bedrooms: 4 double, 1 twin
Bathrooms: 5 private, 2 public

Bed & breakfast
per night:	£min	£max
Single	21.00	25.00
Double	42.00	50.00

Evening meal 1830 (last orders 1300)
Parking for 6
Cards accepted: Access, Visa, Amex

Westbourne Hotel
COMMENDED

Biskey Howe Road, Bowness-on-Windermere, Windermere LA23 2JR
☎ (053 94) 43625

In a peaceful area of Bowness within a short walk of the lake and shops. Highly recommended by our regular guests for comfort, decor and food.
Bedrooms: 1 single, 4 double, 1 twin, 1 triple
Bathrooms: 7 private

Bed & breakfast
per night:	£min	£max
Single	21.00	25.00
Double	38.00	50.00

Half board
per person:	£min	£max
Daily	29.00	35.00

Evening meal 1830 (last orders 1900)
Parking for 10
Cards accepted: Access, Visa

Westwood
COMMENDED

4 Ellerthwaite Road, Windermere LA23 2AH
☎ (053 94) 43514

Traditional Lakeland stone semi-detached house in a pleasant, central position overlooking a small park.
Bedrooms: 4 double, 1 twin
Bathrooms: 5 private

Bed & breakfast
per night:	£min	£max
Double	27.00	36.00

Parking for 4

White Lodge Hotel
COMMENDED

Lake Road, Windermere LA23 2JS
☎ (053 94) 43624

Family-owned hotel with home cooking, only a short walk from Bowness Bay. All bedrooms have private bathrooms, colour TV and tea making facilities. Some with lake views and four-posters.
Bedrooms: 2 single, 7 double, 2 twin, 1 triple
Bathrooms: 12 private

Bed & breakfast
per night:	£min	£max
Single	23.00	29.00
Double	46.00	55.00

Half board
per person:	£min	£max
Daily	32.00	39.00
Weekly	225.00	250.00

Lunch available
Evening meal 1900 (last orders 2000)
Parking for 20
Open March-November
Cards accepted: Access, Visa

Winbrook House
COMMENDED

30 Ellerthwaite Road, Windermere LA23 2AH
☎ (053 94) 44932

This immaculately kept guesthouse, in a quiet part of Windermere, offers en-suite facilities, tea/coffee making, private car park, good food, warm personal welcome.
Bedrooms: 1 single, 4 double, 1 twin
Bathrooms: 3 private, 3 private showers

Bed & breakfast
per night:	£min	£max
Single	15.00	20.00
Double	30.00	40.00

Parking for 7

WORKINGTON

Cumbria
Map ref 5A2

A deep-water port on the west Cumbrian coast. There are the ruins of the 14th C Workington Hall, where Mary Queen of Scots stayed in 1568.
Tourist Information Centre
☎ *(0900) 602923*

Morven Guest House

Siddick Road, Siddick, Workington CA14 1LE
☎ (0900) 602118

Detached house north-west of Workington. Ideal base for touring the Lake District and west Cumbria. Large car park.
Bedrooms: 2 single, 1 double, 2 twin, 1 triple
Bathrooms: 4 private, 1 public, 1 private shower

Bed & breakfast
per night:	£min	£max
Single	19.00	30.00
Double	32.00	42.00

Lunch available
Evening meal 1800 (last orders 1600)
Parking for 20

61

Northumbria

Whatever your holiday dream, Northumbria can provide it. Embracing the four contrasting counties of Tyne and Wear, Northumberland, Cleveland and Durham, it was once the kingdom of Eric Bloodaxe. Its rich heritage is evident everywhere from Pemburgh Castle in the north to medieval Raby Castle in the south and, of course, the mighty Hadrian's Wall which stretches 80 miles dividing the north and south. Follow in the footsteps of the nation's great men and women – Captain Cook in Cleveland; the Prince Bishops who ruled like kings from Durham; Catherine Cookson in South Tyneside; and St Aidan who established Christianity in the region. With attractions and shopping facilities that rival the best in Europe, Northumbria promises a memorable stay.

WHERE TO GO, WHAT TO SEE

The number against each name will help you locate it on the map (page 64).

1 Lindisfarne Castle
Holy Island, Berwick-upon-Tweed, Northumberland
Tel: Berwick-upon-Tweed (0289) 89244
Tudor fort converted into a private home in 1990 for Edward Hudson by the architect Edwin Lutyens.

2 Bamburgh Castle
Bamburgh, Northumberland NE69 7NF
Tel: Bamburgh (066 84) 208
Coastal castle completely restored in 1900. Collections of china, porcelain, furniture, paintings, arms and armour.

3 Farne Islands
Seahouses, Northumberland
Bird reserve holding around 55,000 pairs of breeding birds, of 21 species. Home to a large colony of grey seals.

4 Alnwick Castle
Alnwick, Northumberland NE66 1NQ
Tel: Alnwick (0665) 510777
Home of the Duke of Northumberland. *Magnificent border fortress dating back to the 11th C. Main restoration done by Salvin in the 19th C.*

5 Cragside House and Country Park
Cragside, Rothbury, Morpeth, Northumberland NE65 7PX
Tel: Rothbury (0669) 20333
House built 1864–95 for the first Lord Armstrong, Tyneside

In 1838, during a violent storm, Grace Darling and her father rescued nine men from a stricken steamship. There is a museum to her memory in Bamburgh.

Northumbria

industrialist. First house to be lit by electricity generated by water power.

6 Morpeth Chantry Bagpipe Museum
The Chantry, Bridge Street, Morpeth, Northumberland NE61 1PJ
Tel: Morpeth (0670) 519466
Craft centre, Tourist Information Centre and museum. Extensive collection of bagpipes, including Northumberland, Scottish, Irish and Border half-longs.

7 Chesters Roman Fort
Chollerford, Northumberland NE46 4EP
Tel: Humshaugh (0434) 681379
Fort built for 500 cavalrymen. Remains include 5 gateways, barrack blocks, commandant's house and headquarters. Finest military bathhouse in Britain.

8 The Fishing Experience
Neville House, Fishquay, North Shields, Tyne & Wear NE30 1HE
Tel: 091-296 5449
An exciting family visitor attraction telling the fascinating history of the North Sea and fishing industry.

9 Housesteads Roman Fort
Haydon Bridge, Hexham, Northumberland NE47 6NN
Tel: Hexham (0434) 344363
Best preserved and most impressive of the Roman forts. Vercovicium was 5-acre fort for 100 infantry, surrounded by extensive civil settlement.

10 Souter Point Lighthouse
Coast Road, Whitburn, South Shields, Tyne & Wear SR6 7NH
Tel: 091-529 3061
The lighthouse and associated buildings were constructed in 1871 and contained the most advanced lighthouse technology of the day.

11 MetroCentre
Gateshead, Tyne & Wear NE11 9XX
Tel: 091-493 2046

Newcastle's high suspension bridge (back) and swing bridge allow ships to pass up and down the Tyne.

Over 300 shops with spacious malls, garden court, Mediterranean village, antique court, Roman forum, over 50 eating outlets, cinema, superbowl and Metroland indoor theme park.

12 Gibside Chapel and Grounds
Gibside, Burnopfield, Newcastle upon Tyne, Tyne & Wear NE16 6BG
Tel: Consett (0207) 542255
Mausoleum of 5 members of the Bowes family, built to a design by James Paine between 1760 and 1812. Restored in 1965. Avenue of Turkey Oak trees.

13 The Wildfowl and Wetlands Trust
District 15, Washington, Tyne & Wear NE38 8LE
Tel: 091-416 5454
Collection of 1,250 wildfowl of 108 varieties. Viewing gallery, picnic areas, hides and winter wild bird feeding station. Flamingos. Bird food available.

14 Beamish – The North of England Open Air Museum
Beamish, Co Durham DH9 0RG
Tel: Stanley (0207) 231811
Open air museum of northern life around the turn of the century. Buildings re-erected to form a town with shops and houses. Colliery village, station and working farm.

15 Durham Castle
Palace Green, Durham City, Co Durham DH1 3RW
Tel: 091-374 3863
Castle with fine Bailey founded in 1072, Norman chapel dating from 1080, kitchens and great hall dating from 1499 and 1284 respectively.

15 Durham Cathedral
Durham City, Co Durham DH1 3EQ
Tel: 091-386 2367
Widely considered to be the finest example of Norman church architecture in England. Tombs of St Cuthbert and the Venerable Bede.

Northumbria

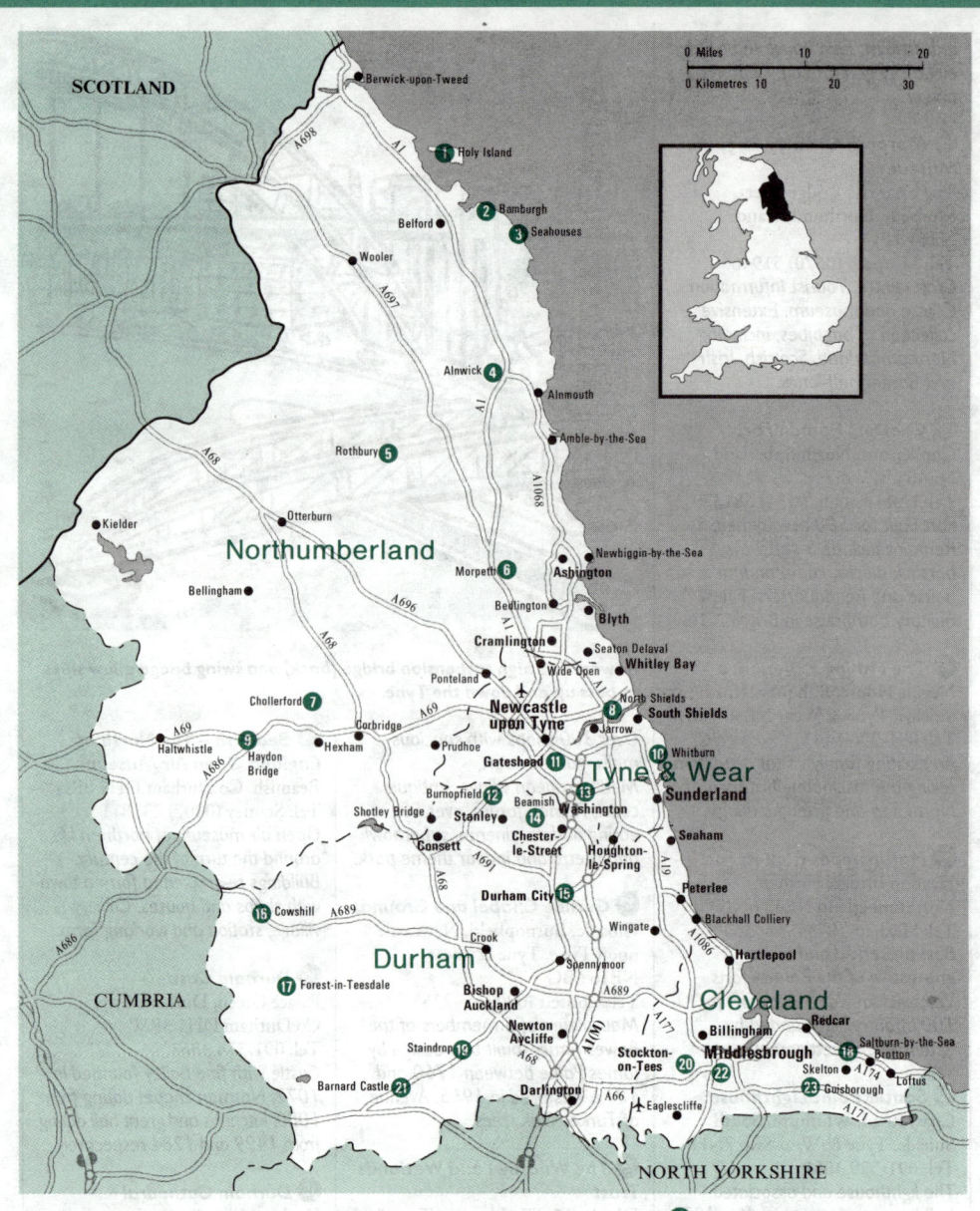

Use the map above to locate places in the 'Where to Go, What to See' section.

16 Killhope Leadmining Centre
Cowshill, St John's Chapel, Upper Weardale, Co Durham DL13 1AR
Tel: Weardale (0388) 537505

Most complete lead mining site in Great Britain. Includes crushing mill with 34ft water wheel, reconstruction of Victorian machinery, railway system and miners' accommodation.

17 High Force Waterfall
Forest-in-Teesdale, Co Durham
Tel: (0833) 40209
Most majestic of the waterfalls on the River Tees. The falls are only a short walk from a bus stop, car park and picnic area.

64

Northumbria

⑱ Saltburn Smugglers
Saltburn-by-the-Sea, Cleveland
TS12 1HF
Tel: Guisborough (0287) 625252
Discover the world of smuggling, experience the authentic sights, sounds and smells of Saltburn's smuggling heritage. Listen to tales of John Andrew, 'King of the Smugglers'.

⑲ Raby Castle
Staindrop, Darlington, Co Durham
DL2 3AH
Tel: Staindrop (0833) 660202
Medieval castle in 200-acre park. 600-year-old kitchen and carriage collection. Walled gardens and deer park.

⑳ Green Dragon Museum
Theatre Yard, Stockton-on-Tees, Cleveland TS18 1AT
Tel: Stockton (0642) 674308
Local history museum recording development of Stockton. Dawn of the 'railway age' is displayed in an exciting audio-visual show.

⑳ Preston Hall Museum
Yarm Road, Stockton-on-Tees, Cleveland TS18 3RH
Tel: Stockton (0642) 781184
Social history museum with period street and rooms, working craftsmen, arms, armour, costume and toys. Set in 116 acres of beautiful parkland. Aviary, pitch and putt.

㉑ The Bowes Museum
Barnard Castle, Co Durham
DL12 8NP
Tel: Teesdale (0833) 690690
French-style château housing art collections of national importance.

㉒ Captain Cook Birthplace Museum
Stewart Park, Marton, Middlesbrough, Cleveland
TS7 6AS
Tel: Middlesbrough (0642) 311211
Early life and voyages of Captain Cook and the countries he visited. Exhibitions changing monthly. One person free for every group of ten.

The delights of Newcastle Brown Ale can be sampled in pubs all around the country — but somehow it seems to taste even better when quaffed in its native city.

㉒ Ormesby Hall
Ormesby, Middlesbrough, Cleveland TS7 9AS
Tel: Middlesbrough (0642) 324188
Mid-18th C house with fine decorative plasterwork, Jacobean doorway, stable block. Attributed to Carr of York.

㉓ Gisborough Priory
Guisborough, Cleveland
TS14 6HL
Tel: Guisborough (0287) 38301
Remains of 12th C Augustinian priory founded by Robert de Brus, in the grounds of Gisborough Hall. Remains of 12th C gatehouse, 14th C church.

FIND OUT MORE

Further information about holidays and attractions in the Northumbria region is available from:
Northumbria Tourist Board
Aykley Heads, Durham DH1 5UX
Tel: 091-384 6905

These publications are available free from the Northumbria Tourist Board:
*Northumbria Holiday Guide 1994
Bed & Breakfast map - Northumbria and Cumbria
Where to Go map/gazetteer
Caravan and Camping Guide - Northumbria, Yorkshire & Humberside, Cumbria and North West
Educational brochure*

Also available is (price includes postage and packing):
Northumbria touring map and guide £5

NORTHUMBRIA

Places to stay

Accommodation entries in this regional section are listed in alphabetical order of place name, and then in alphabetical order of establishment.

The map references refer to the colour maps at the back of the guide. The first figure is the map number; the letter and figure which follow indicate the grid reference on the map.

The symbols at the end of each accommodation entry give information about services and facilities. A 'key' to these symbols is inside the back cover flap, which can be kept open for easy reference.

ALNMOUTH
Northumberland
Map ref 5C1

Quiet village with pleasant old buildings, at the mouth of the River Aln where extensive dunes and sands stretch along Alnmouth Bay. 18th C granaries, some converted to dwellings, still stand.

The Grange
HIGHLY COMMENDED
Northumberland Street, Alnmouth, Alnwick NE66 2RJ
☎ Alnwick (0665) 830401
Located in the heart of this unspoilt village. 200-year-old former granary in secluded gardens, with views over the River Aln.
Bedrooms: 1 single, 3 double, 1 twin
Bathrooms: 2 private, 1 public
Bed & breakfast
per night: £min £max
Single 18.00 19.00
Double 36.00 44.00
Parking for 8

High Buston Hall
HIGHLY COMMENDED
High Buston, Alnmouth, Alnwick NE66 3QH
☎ Alnwick (0665) 830341
Elegant listed Georgian country house in tranquil village setting, with commanding sea views. Traditional good food and warm hospitality.
Bedrooms: 2 double, 1 twin
Bathrooms: 3 private
Bed & breakfast
per night: £min £max
Single 30.00 40.00
Double 40.00 55.00

Half board
per person: £min £max
Daily 35.00 42.50
Evening meal from 1930
Parking for 9
Open March-December

ALNWICK
Northumberland
Map ref 5C1

Ancient and historic market town, entered through the Hotspur Tower, an original gate in the town walls. The medieval castle, the second biggest in England and still the seat of the Dukes of Northumberland, was restored from ruin in the 18th C.
Tourist Information Centre
☎ *(0665) 510665*

Cenac
COMMENDED
50 Swansfield Park Road, Alnwick NE66 1AR
☎ (0665) 603304
Quietly situated, comfortable house, offering well-appointed accommodation, only 10 minutes' stroll from the centre of Alnwick.
Bedrooms: 1 double, 1 twin
Bathrooms: 1 private, 1 private shower
Bed & breakfast
per night: £min £max
Single 17.00 17.00
Double 34.00 34.00
Half board
per person: £min £max
Daily 25.00 25.00
Weekly 165.00 165.00
Evening meal 1900 (last orders 1600)
Parking for 2
Open March-November

Clifton House
COMMENDED
Clifton Terrace, Alnwick NE66 1XF
☎ (0665) 510412
Regency town house in quiet location 3 minutes from Alnwick centre and close to golf-course. Off-street parking.
Bedrooms: 1 triple
Bathrooms: 1 private
Bed & breakfast
per night: £min £max
Single 15.00
Double 30.00
Parking for 2

New Moor House
Edlingham, Alnwick NE66 2BT
☎ Whittingham (066 574) 638
Old stone-built house with lots of character, oak beams, comfortable bedrooms and good food. Centrally situated for exploring Northumberland.
Bedrooms: 1 single, 1 double, 2 twin
Bathrooms: 1 private, 2 public
Bed & breakfast
per night: £min £max
Single 15.50 17.00
Double 31.00 34.00
Half board
per person: £min £max
Daily 24.50 27.00
Weekly 154.00 168.00
Evening meal 1900 (last orders 1900)
Parking for 8
Open March-November

Half board prices shown are per person but in some cases may be based on double/twin occupancy.

NORTHUMBRIA

AMBLE-BY-THE-SEA

Northumberland
Map ref 5C1

Small fishing town at the mouth of the River Coquet, with fine, quiet, sandy beaches to north and south. The harbour and estuary are popular for sailing and bird-watching. Coquet Island lies 1 mile offshore.

Togston Hall Farmhouse ♠

North Togston, Nr. Amble, Morpeth NE65 0HR
☎ Alnwick (0665) 712699
10-acre mixed farm. Tranquil farmhouse, with atmosphere and personal service. En-suite rooms, log fire, free-range eggs.
Bedrooms: 2 double, 1 twin
Bathrooms: 3 private, 1 public

Bed & breakfast per night:	£min	£max
Single	17.00	19.00
Double	34.00	40.00

Half board per person:	£min	£max
Daily	25.00	28.00
Weekly	193.00	200.00

Evening meal 1900 (last orders 2000)
Parking for 10
Open February-November

BALDERSDALE

Durham
Map ref 5B3

A quiet tributary of the River Tees lies in this valley in the attractive West Durham Moors. The River Balder has been dammed to create 3 attractive reservoirs.

West Schoon Bank

Baldersdale, Barnard Castle, County Durham DL12 9UP
☎ Teesdale (0833) 50201
156-acre hill farm. Newly renovated farmhouse overlooking Hury Reservoir. 3 miles from west end of Cotherstone, a peaceful location. Near Pennine Way. Walking and fishing available on reservoir.
Bedrooms: 1 double, 1 twin
Bathrooms: 1 public

Bed & breakfast per night:	£min	£max
Double	26.00	28.00

Half board per person:	£min	£max
Daily	20.00	21.00

Evening meal from 1800
Parking for 3
Open March-November

BAMBURGH

Northumberland
Map ref 5C1

Village with a spectacular red sandstone castle standing 150 ft above the sea. On the village green the magnificent Norman church stands opposite a museum containing mementoes of the heroine Grace Darling.

Burton Hall ♠
Listed COMMENDED

East Burton, Bamburgh NE69 7AR
☎ (0668) 214213
Fax (0668) 214213
Substantial countryside farmhouse with spacious rooms. 1.5 miles from Bamburgh, 3.5 miles from Seahouses. Head to Glororum crossroads, Burton signposted there.
Bedrooms: 6 double, 2 twin
Bathrooms: 4 private, 2 public

Bed & breakfast per night:	£min	£max
Single	18.00	25.00
Double	36.00	50.00

Parking for 10

1 Friars Court

Bamburgh NE69 7AE
☎ (066 84) 494 & 579
Detached house offering one double bedroom en-suite with colour TV and tea making facilities. Views of Bamburgh Castle and Lindisfarne.
Bedrooms: 1 double
Bathrooms: 1 private, 1 public

Bed & breakfast per night:	£min	£max
Single	20.00	22.00
Double	36.00	38.00

Parking for 4
Open March-October

Mizen Head Hotel ♠
APPROVED

Lucker Road, Bamburgh NE69 7BS
☎ (0668) 214254

Privately-owned, family-run hotel in its own grounds, with accent on good food and service. Convenient for beaches, castle and golf.
Bedrooms: 3 single, 5 double, 4 twin, 4 family rooms
Bathrooms: 7 private, 3 public

Bed & breakfast per night:	£min	£max
Single	19.00	30.00
Double	31.00	65.00

Half board per person:	£min	£max
Daily	29.00	43.00
Weekly	172.00	270.00

Lunch available
Evening meal 1830 (last orders 2000)
Parking for 30
Cards accepted: Access, Visa

BARNARD CASTLE

Durham
Map ref 5B3

High over the Tees, a thriving market town with a busy market square. Bernard Baliol's 12th C castle (now ruins) stands nearby. The Bowes Museum, housed in a grand 19th C French chateau, holds fine paintings and furniture. Nearby are some magnificent buildings.
Tourist Information Centre
☎ *(0833) 690909*

George & Dragon Inn
Listed

Boldron, Barnard Castle, County Durham DL12 9RF
☎ Teesdale (0833) 38215
Attractive inn in beautiful Teesdale, offering comfortable accommodation and friendly hospitality.
Bedrooms: 1 double, 1 twin
Bathrooms: 1 public

Bed & breakfast per night:	£min	£max
Single	14.00	15.00
Double	28.00	30.00

Half board per person:	£min	£max
Daily	19.00	20.00
Weekly	138.00	143.00

Lunch available
Evening meal 1900 (last orders 1730)
Parking for 20

Old Well Inn
COMMENDED

21 The Bank, Barnard Castle, County Durham DL12 8PH
☎ Teesdale (0833) 690130
Historic inn serving home cooking and real ales. Beer garden.
Bedrooms: 1 double, 2 twin
Bathrooms: 3 private, 1 public

Bed & breakfast per night:	£min	£max
Single	22.00	25.00
Double	38.00	45.00

Continued ▶

NORTHUMBRIA

BARNARD CASTLE
Continued

Half board

per person:	£min	£max
Daily	32.00	35.00

Lunch available
Evening meal 1900 (last orders 2150)
Cards accepted: Access, Visa

West Roods Tourism

West Roods Farm, Boldron, Barnard Castle, County Durham DL12 9SW
☎ Teesdale (0833) 690216
58-acre mixed & dairy farm. In Teesdale area, south of Barnard Castle, 2.5 miles east of Bowes on A66. Activities from water divining to table tennis. Home cooking using milk and eggs from our own farm.
Bedrooms: 1 single, 1 double, 1 twin
Bathrooms: 2 private, 2 public

Bed & breakfast

per night:	£min	£max
Single	16.00	20.00
Double	32.00	36.00

Half board

per person:	£min	£max
Daily	23.00	27.00
Weekly	149.00	

Evening meal 1700 (last orders 1800)
Parking for 6
Open March-October
Cards accepted: Visa, Diners, Amex

BEADNELL
Northumberland
Map ref 5C1

Charming fishing village on Beadnell Bay. Seashore lime kilns (National Trust), dating from the 18th C, recall busier days as a coal and lime port and a pub is built on to a medieval pele tower which survives from days of the border wars.

Beach Court
HIGHLY COMMENDED

Harbour Road, Beadnell, Chathill NE67 5BJ
☎ Alnwick (0665) 720225 & Mobile (0831) 889653
Fax (0665) 720225
Magnificent turreted beachside home with Cheviot Hills as a backdrop. Recapture a bygone era of personal service complemented by 20th C facilities. Secure courtyard parking.
Bedrooms: 2 double, 1 twin, 1 family room
Bathrooms: 4 private

Bed & breakfast

per night:	£min	£max
Double	40.00	55.00

Half board

per person:	£min	£max
Daily	27.95	40.00

Parking for 6

Low Dover
HIGHLY COMMENDED

Harbour Road, Beadnell, Chathill NE67 5BH
☎ Alnwick (0665) 720291 & Cellnet (0860) 730866
Quiet, comfortable accommodation in large residence in superb location overlooking Beadnell Bay. 20 yards to beach and 18th C harbour, 3 miles to Farne Islands. No dogs and no smoking. Free brochure.
Bedrooms: 1 double, 1 triple
Bathrooms: 2 private

Bed & breakfast

per night:	£min	£max
Double	40.00	50.00

Parking for 4

Shepherds Cottage
Listed COMMENDED

Beadnell, Chathill NE67 5AD
☎ Alnwick (0665) 720497
Character cottage near Beadnell, with spacious garden, tea and coffee facilities, comfortable sitting room. Ample off-road parking.
Bedrooms: 2 double, 1 twin
Bathrooms: 1 private, 1 public

Bed & breakfast

per night:	£min	£max
Single	15.00	17.50
Double	30.00	35.00

Parking for 6

BEAMISH
Durham
Map ref 5C2

Village made famous by the award-winning Beamish, North of England Open Air Museum, which covers every aspect of the life, buildings and artefacts of the North East of 1913. Also in the area are Causey Arch and Tanfield Railway.
Tourist Information Centre
☎ 091-370 2533

Mount Escob
Listed COMMENDED

Beamish Woods, Stanley, County Durham DH9 0SA
☎ 091-370 0289
4-acre smallholding. Country house on picturesque site of former water-powered papermill. Surrounded by wooded hills, 12 acres of grassland where horses are kept. Very close to A1 (M), Durham, MetroCentre, half a mile from Beamish Museum.

Bedrooms: 2 double, 1 twin
Bathrooms: 1 public

Bed & breakfast

per night:	£min	£max
Single	15.00	16.00
Double	30.00	30.00

Parking for 7

BELFORD
Northumberland
Map ref 5B1

Small market town on the old coaching road, close to the coast, the Scottish border and the north-east flank of the Cheviots. Built mostly in stone and very peaceful now that the A1 has by-passed the town, Belford makes an ideal centre for excursions to the moors and coast.

Blue Bell Farm House
Listed

West Street, Belford NE70 7QE
☎ (0668) 213890
Large house in own grounds. 150 yards down West Street to campsite. Private views from all sides.
Bedrooms: 2 double, 1 twin
Bathrooms: 1 private, 2 public

Bed & breakfast

per night:	£min	£max
Single	10.00	12.00
Double	24.00	30.00

Parking for 4

Woodview

Warenford, Belford NE70 7HY
☎ (0668) 213702
Victorian house in small village (just off A1) with spacious, well-equipped bedrooms. Within a few miles of beaches and local tourist attractions.
Bedrooms: 1 double, 1 twin
Bathrooms: 2 private

Bed & breakfast

per night:	£min	£max
Single	15.00	17.00
Double	30.00	34.00

Parking for 2
Open April-October

Individual proprietors have supplied all details of accommodation. Although we do check for accuracy, we advise you to confirm the information at the time of booking.

NORTHUMBRIA

BELLINGHAM

Northumberland
Map ref 5B2

Set in the beautiful valley of the North Tyne close to the Kielder Forest, Kielder Water and lonely moorland below the Cheviots. The church has an ancient stone wagon roof fortified in the 18th C with buttresses.
Tourist Information Centre
☎ (0434) 220616

Lyndale Guest House ⋒
COMMENDED

Off Main Square, Bellingham, Hexham NE48 2AW
☎ Hexham (0434) 220361
Attractive, comfortable bungalow with pleasant walled garden and sun lounge with panoramic views. Quality ground floor en-suites with tea making facilities and hairdryers. Good food, good walking and quiet roads. Close to Hadrian's Wall and Kielder Water.
Bedrooms: 1 single, 2 double, 1 twin, 1 triple
Bathrooms: 4 private, 1 public

Bed & breakfast
per night:	£min	£max
Single	16.00	20.00
Double	30.00	40.00

Half board
per person:	£min	£max
Daily	26.00	32.00
Weekly	160.00	209.00

Evening meal 1800 (last orders 1400)
Parking for 6

Mantle Hill ⋒
COMMENDED

Hesleyside, Bellingham, Hexham NE48 2LB
☎ (0434) 220428
Fax (0434) 220113
Family home, built as dower house to historic Hesleyside Hall. 200 yards from North Tyne River with lovely views over unspoilt countryside. Licensed.
Bedrooms: 1 double, 1 twin
Bathrooms: 2 private

Bed & breakfast
per night:	£min	£max
Single	18.00	23.50
Double	36.00	47.00

Half board
per person:	£min	£max
Daily	30.00	35.50

Evening meal 1900 (last orders 2100)
Parking for 8
Cards accepted: Visa

Riverdale Hall Hotel ⋒
COMMENDED

Bellingham, Hexham NE48 2JT
☎ Hexham (0434) 220254
Fax (0434) 220457
Spacious country hall in large grounds. Indoor swimming pool, sauna, fishing, cricket field and golf opposite. Award-winning restaurant in hospitable family-run hotel.
Bedrooms: 3 single, 4 double, 9 twin, 4 triple
Bathrooms: 20 private, 2 public

Bed & breakfast
per night:	£min	£max
Single	35.00	42.00
Double	59.00	72.00

Half board
per person:	£min	£max
Daily	46.00	59.00
Weekly	265.00	319.00

Lunch available
Evening meal 1900 (last orders 2130)
Parking for 60
Cards accepted: Access, Visa, Diners, Amex, Switch

BERWICK-UPON-TWEED

Northumberland
Map ref 5B1

Guarding the mouth of the Tweed, England's northernmost town with the best 16th C city walls in Europe. The handsome Guildhall and barracks date from the 18th C. Three bridges cross to Tweedmouth, the oldest built in 1634.
Tourist Information Centre
☎ (0289) 330733

22 Castle Terrace

Berwick-upon-Tweed TD15 1NP
☎ (0289) 306120
Attractive sandstone house in a secluded residential area of the town, retaining many original 19th C features.
Bedrooms: 1 double, 1 twin
Bathrooms: 1 public

Bed & breakfast
per night:	£min	£max
Double	28.00	30.00

Parking for 4

Drousha
COMMENDED

29 North Road, Berwick-upon-Tweed TD15 1PW
☎ (0289) 306659
Victorian house with many original features. Sea views, yet close to the centre of town and station.
Bedrooms: 1 single, 1 double, 1 triple
Bathrooms: 2 public

Bed & breakfast
per night:	£min	£max
Single	15.00	25.00
Double	25.00	32.00

Half board
per person:	£min	£max
Daily	20.00	31.50
Weekly	140.00	220.50

Evening meal 1830 (last orders 1900)
Parking for 3

Ladythorne House
Listed

Cheswick, Berwick-upon-Tweed TD15 2RW
☎ (0289) 387382
Grade II listed building, dated 1721, set in farmland. Only 15 minutes' walk from the beaches.
Bedrooms: 1 single, 1 double, 2 twin, 2 triple
Bathrooms: 3 public

Bed & breakfast
per night:	£min	£max
Single	12.50	15.00
Double	25.00	30.00

Parking for 8

Middle Ord Manor House ⋒
DE LUXE

Middle Ord Farm, Berwick-upon-Tweed TD15 2XQ
☎ (0289) 306323
320-acre mixed farm. Quality accommodation within Georgian farmhouse. Central for touring the Borders, coast and Holy Island. En-suites and four-poster bed available.
Bedrooms: 2 double, 1 twin
Bathrooms: 3 private, 1 public

Bed & breakfast
per night:	£min	£max
Single	16.50	22.00
Double	33.00	44.00

Parking for 6
Open April-October

The Old Vicarage Guest House ⋒
HIGHLY COMMENDED

24 Church Road, Tweedmouth, Berwick-upon-Tweed TD15 2AN
☎ (0289) 306909

Spacious, detached 19th C vicarage, recently refurbished to a high standard. 10 minutes' walk from town centre and beautiful beaches.

Continued ▶

69

NORTHUMBRIA

BERWICK-UPON-TWEED
Continued

Bedrooms: 1 single, 4 double, 1 twin, 1 triple
Bathrooms: 4 private, 1 public

Bed & breakfast
per night:	£min	£max
Single	13.00	16.00
Double	26.00	44.00

Parking for 4

8 Ravensdowne
COMMENDED

Berwick-upon-Tweed TD15 1HX
☎ (0289) 307883
Small, homely guesthouse, Grade II listed, within easy reach of river, golf, tennis and beaches. Residents' lounge. Access to historic town walls.
Bedrooms: 2 single, 1 double, 2 twin
Bathrooms: 2 private, 2 public

Bed & breakfast
per night:	£min	£max
Single		16.00
Double	32.00	40.00

Wallace Guest House
Listed COMMENDED

1 Wallace Green, Berwick-upon-Tweed TD15 1EB
☎ (0289) 306519
End terraced house facing Berwick Barracks. 2 minutes to sea, ramparts, golf-course and River Tweed.
Bedrooms: 1 double, 1 twin, 2 triple, 1 family room
Bathrooms: 2 private, 2 public, 1 private shower

Bed & breakfast
per night:	£min	£max
Single	16.50	17.50
Double	27.00	38.00

Half board
per person:	£min	£max
Daily	20.50	26.00
Weekly	134.05	168.70

Evening meal 1830 (last orders 1930)

BISHOP AUCKLAND
Durham
Map ref 5C2

Busy market town on the bank of the River Wear. The Palace, a castellated Norman manor house altered in the 18th C, stands in beautiful gardens. Open to the public and entered from the market square by a handsome 18th C gatehouse, the park is a peaceful retreat of trees and streams.

Five Gables
Listed

Binchester, Bishop Auckland, County Durham DL14 8AT
☎ Weardale (0388) 608204
300 yards from A688 between Bishop Auckland and Spennymoor. Victorian house with views over countryside and Weardale. Within easy reach of popular tourist attractions in the North of England.
Bedrooms: 1 double, 1 triple
Bathrooms: 1 public

Bed & breakfast
per night:	£min	£max
Single		15.00
Double		25.00

Open April-October

BOWES
Durham
Map ref 5B3

Old stone village high up on a Roman road crossing the Pennines. Settled since Roman times, the town has a sturdy Norman castle keep and an ancient church with a Norman font and Roman inscribed stone.

Ancient Unicorn Inn

Bowes, Barnard Castle, County Durham DL12 9HN
☎ Teesdale (0833) 28321 & 28386
16th C inn on the A66 with comfortable bedrooms, extensive bar menu. Ideal base for exploring the Lakes, Northumbria, Yorkshire Dales and Yorkshire Wolds.
Bedrooms: 2 twin, 1 triple
Bathrooms: 3 private

Bed & breakfast
per night:	£min	£max
Single	19.00	19.00
Double	30.00	35.00

Lunch available
Evening meal 1930 (last orders 2130)
Parking for 20

CASTLESIDE
Durham
Map ref 5B2

Village on the edge of the North Pennines on the A68, one of the main routes from England to Scotland.

Castlenook Guest House

18-20 Front Street, Castleside, Consett, County Durham DH8 9AR
☎ Consett (0207) 506634
On the A68 within easy reach of Durham City, Hadrian's Wall, Beamish Museum and MetroCentre. Excellent village amenities.
Bedrooms: 1 double, 2 twin
Bathrooms: 3 private

Bed & breakfast
per night:	£min	£max
Single	14.00	18.00
Double	28.00	30.00

Half board
per person:	£min	£max
Daily	19.00	22.00
Weekly	130.00	144.00

Evening meal 1700 (last orders 1850)
Parking for 5

Willerby Grange Farm
COMMENDED

Allensford, Castleside, Consett, County Durham DH8 9BA
☎ Consett (0207) 508752
Situated in beautiful Derwent Valley, self-contained apartments available also for bed and breakfast. Tree nursery, pony trekking/livery on site. Easy travelling distance to Beamish, Gateshead, Hadrian's Wall. Moorland and woodland walks. Approximately 1 kilometre off A68 at Allensford.
Bedrooms: 4 double
Bathrooms: 4 private

Bed & breakfast
per night:	£min	£max
Single	25.00	30.00
Double	40.00	50.00

Parking for 100
Cards accepted: Access, Visa, Diners, Amex

> There are separate sections in this guide listing groups specialising in farm holidays and accommodation which is especially suitable for young people and organised groups.

> Individual proprietors have supplied all details of accommodation. Although we do check for accuracy, we advise you to confirm the information at the time of booking.

70

NORTHUMBRIA

CHESTER-LE-STREET
Durham
Map ref 5C2

Originally a Roman military site, town with modern commerce and light industry on the River Wear. The ancient church replaced a wooden sanctuary which sheltered the remains of St Cuthbert for 113 years. The Anker's house beside the church is now a museum.

Low Urpeth Farm House
Listed HIGHLY COMMENDED
Ouston, Chester-Le-Street, County Durham DH2 1BD
☎ 091-410 2901
Fax 091-410 0081
500-acre arable & livestock farm. Leave A1(M) at Chester-le-Street. Take A693, signpost Beamish. At second roundabout turn right to Ouston. Pass garage, down hill, over roundabout and turn left into farm at "Trees Please" sign.
Bedrooms: 1 double, 2 twin
Bathrooms: 2 private, 1 public
Bed & breakfast
per night:	£min	£max
Single	17.00	
Double	30.00	

Parking for 6

Waldridge Fell House
COMMENDED
Waldridge Lane, Waldridge, Chester-Le-Street, County Durham DH2 3RY
☎ 091-389 1908
Former village chapel, stone-built in 1868. Panoramic views and country walks. Children half price. Winter weekend breaks.
Bedrooms: 4 triple
Bathrooms: 1 private, 1 public, 1 private shower
Bed & breakfast
per night:	£min	£max
Single	21.00	27.00
Double	32.00	40.00

Parking for 8

Waldridge Hall Farm
Listed HIGHLY COMMENDED
Old Waldridge, Chester-Le-Street, County Durham DH2 3SL
☎ 091-388 4210
40-acre arable farm. Listed 18th C farmhouse in pretty countryside, between Durham City and the Beamish Museum. A warm welcome with homely accommodation. Vegetarians catered for. No smoking in bedrooms.
Bedrooms: 1 double, 1 twin, 1 triple
Bathrooms: 1 public
Bed & breakfast
per night:	£min	£max
Single	22.00	25.00
Double	30.00	35.00

Parking for 8
Open March-October

CONSETT
Durham
Map ref 5B2

Former steel town on the edge of rolling moors. Modern development includes the shopping centre and a handsome Roman Catholic church, designed by a local architect. To the west, the Derwent Reservoir provides water sports and pleasant walks.

Bee Cottage Farm
HIGHLY COMMENDED
Castleside, Consett, County Durham DH8 9HW
☎ (0207) 508224

46-acre livestock farm. 1.5 miles west of the A68, between Castleside and Tow Law. Unspoilt views. Ideally located for Beamish Museum and Durham. No smoking in main farmhouse.
Bedrooms: 1 single, 3 double, 2 twin, 1 triple, 2 family rooms
Bathrooms: 3 private, 5 public
Bed & breakfast
per night:	£min	£max
Single	22.00	30.00
Double	35.00	54.00

Half board
per person:	£min	£max
Daily	18.50	41.00

Lunch available
Evening meal 2015 (last orders 2130)
Parking for 20

CORBRIDGE
Northumberland
Map ref 5B2

Small town on the River Tyne. Close by are extensive remains of the Roman military town Corstopitum, with a museum housing important discoveries from excavations. The town itself is attractive with shady trees, a 17th C bridge and interesting old buildings, notably a 14th C vicarage.

Fellcroft
HIGHLY COMMENDED
Station Road, Corbridge NE45 5AY
☎ Hexham (0434) 632384

Well-appointed stone-built Edwardian house with full private facilities and colour TV in all bedrooms. Quiet road in country setting, half a mile south of market square. Excellent choice of eating places nearby. Non-smokers only please.
Bedrooms: 2 twin
Bathrooms: 2 private
Bed & breakfast
per night:	£min	£max
Single	18.00	20.00
Double	28.00	32.00

Half board
per person:	£min	£max
Daily	20.00	26.00

Evening meal 1900 (last orders 1945)
Parking for 2

The Hayes Guest House
Newcastle Road, Corbridge NE45 5LP
☎ Hexham (0434) 632010
Large house set amidst 7.5 acres of woodland and gardens with delightful views. Self-catering flat, caravan and cottages also available.
Bedrooms: 2 single, 1 double, 2 twin, 1 triple
Bathrooms: 2 public, 2 private showers
Bed & breakfast
per night:	£min	£max
Single	16.50	16.50
Double	33.00	33.00

Evening meal 1900 (last orders 1600)
Parking for 14
Open January-November
Cards accepted: Amex

COTHERSTONE
Durham
Map ref 5B3

Glendale
Cotherstone, Barnard Castle, County Durham DL12 9UH
☎ Teesdale (0833) 650384
Dormer bungalow with beautiful gardens and large pond, in quiet, rural surroundings. Take Briscoe road from Cotherstone for 200 yards.
Bedrooms: 3 double
Bathrooms: 3 private, 1 public
Bed & breakfast
per night:	£min	£max
Double	28.00	30.00

Parking for 4
Open February-November

Please mention this guide when making a booking.

NORTHUMBRIA

CROOK
Durham
Map ref 5C2

Pleasant market town sometimes referred to as "the gateway to Weardale". The town's shopping centre surrounds a large, open green, attractively laid out with lawns and flowerbeds around the Devil's Stone, a relic from the Ice Age.

Greenhead Country House Hotel
COMMENDED

Fir Tree, Crook, County Durham DL15 8BL
☎ Bishop Auckland (0388) 763143
Superbly located in countryside, 10 miles from Durham. Comfortable well appointed hotel. Overlooks secluded fields and wooded area. Lounge with sandstone arches, log fire and oak beams. Brochure on request.
Bedrooms: 1 single, 4 double, 1 twin
Bathrooms: 6 private

Bed & breakfast
per night:	£min	£max
Single	30.00	35.00
Double	40.00	45.00

Half board
per person:	£min	£max
Daily	37.00	47.00

Evening meal 1800 (last orders 1700)
Parking for 15
Cards accepted: Access, Visa

DURHAM
Durham
Map ref 5C2

Ancient city with its Norman castle and cathedral set on a bluff high over the Wear. A market and university town and regional centre, spreading beyond the market-place on both banks of the river. July Miners' Gala is a celebrated Durham tradition.
Tourist Information Centre
☎ 091-384 3720

Acorn House
Listed APPROVED

5 Mowbray Street, Durham, County Durham DH1 4BH
☎ 091-386 3108
Built in 1840 and retaining original character. Town centre, bus and rail station 5 minutes away. Park and wooded walks with cathedral views nearby.
Bedrooms: 1 double, 1 triple
Bathrooms: 1 private, 1 public

Bed & breakfast
per night:	£min	£max
Single	16.00	28.00
Double	30.00	45.00

Half board
per person:	£min	£max
Daily	28.00	40.00
Weekly	185.00	260.00

Evening meal 1930 (last orders 1400)
Parking for 1

Bay Horse Inn
COMMENDED

Brandon Village, Durham, County Durham DH7 8ST
☎ 091-378 0498
3 miles from Durham city centre. Stone-built chalets all with shower, toilet, TV, tea and coffee facilities and telephone. Ample car parking.
Bedrooms: 3 double, 6 twin, 1 family room
Bathrooms: 10 private

Bed & breakfast
per night:	£min	£max
Single	28.00	28.00
Double	37.00	37.00

Lunch available
Evening meal 1900 (last orders 2200)
Parking for 25
Cards accepted: Access, Visa

Bees Cottage Guest House

Bridge Street, Durham, County Durham DH1 4RT
☎ 091-384 5775
Durham's oldest cottage. In city centre, close to rail and bus stations. All rooms en-suite with colour TV and hospitality tray. Private parking.
Bedrooms: 1 double, 2 twin, 1 triple
Bathrooms: 4 private

Bed & breakfast
per night:	£min	£max
Single	27.00	27.00
Double	40.00	40.00

Parking for 4

Castledene
Listed COMMENDED

37 Nevilledale Terrace, Durham, County Durham DH1 4QG
☎ Wearside 091-384 8586
Edwardian end-of-terrace house half a mile east of the market place. Within walking distance of the riverside, cathedral and castle.
Bedrooms: 1 single, 2 twin
Bathrooms: 1 public

Bed & breakfast
per night:	£min	£max
Single		16.00
Double		32.00

Parking for 5

Crakemarsh
Listed HIGHLY COMMENDED

Mill Lane, Plawsworth Gate, Chester-Le-Street, County Durham DH2 3LG
☎ 091-371 2464
Comfortable residence with country views. 10 minutes from Beamish Museum, 2.5 miles Durham, 30 yards to A167. Durham to Chester-le-Street, Leamside/Finchale Priory turning at Plawsworth Gate, first house on left. Evening meals on request. Strictly no smoking.
Bedrooms: 1 double, 1 triple
Bathrooms: 1 public

Bed & breakfast
per night:	£min	£max
Single	22.00	25.00
Double	34.00	38.00

Evening meal 1800 (last orders 1900)
Parking for 4

Lothlorien
COMMENDED

Front Street, Witton Gilbert, Durham DH7 6SY
☎ 091-371 0067
Country cottage only 5 minutes by car from Durham City centre and on a direct route to Hadrian's Wall. A good centre for touring.
Bedrooms: 1 single, 1 double, 1 twin
Bathrooms: 1 public

Bed & breakfast
per night:	£min	£max
Single	16.00	17.00
Double	32.00	34.00

Parking for 3

Trevelyan College

Elvet Hill Road, Durham DH1 3LN
☎ 091-374 3765 & 374 3768
Fax 091-374 3789
Set in parkland within easy walking distance of Durham City. Comfortable Cloister Bar, TV lounges, ample parking.
Bedrooms: 253 single, 8 double, 27 twin
Bathrooms: 58 private, 47 public

Bed & breakfast
per night:	£min	£max
Single	17.00	26.90
Double	31.30	49.50

Half board
per person:	£min	£max
Daily	25.80	35.70

Lunch available
Evening meal 1830 (last orders 1930)
Parking for 100
Open March-April, June-September, December

NORTHUMBRIA

EBCHESTER
Durham
Map ref 5B2

Old village standing on the 4-acre Roman fort Vindomara near to the place where the Roman road Dere Street crossed the River Derwent.

The Raven Hotel
HIGHLY COMMENDED
Broomhill, Ebchester, Consett, County Durham DH8 6RY
☎ (0207) 560367 & 560082
Fax (0207) 560262
Stone-built, traditionally decorated hotel with fine views over Derwent Valley. Conservatory Restaurant serving quality food. Lounge bar with excellent range of beers and bar meals. Twenty minutes from both Durham and Gateshead MetroCentre.
Bedrooms: 11 double, 14 twin, 3 triple
Bathrooms: 28 private

Bed & breakfast
per night:	£min	£max
Single	41.00	55.00
Double	57.00	72.00

Half board
per person:	£min	£max
Daily	51.00	65.00
Weekly	279.00	385.00

Lunch available
Evening meal 1900 (last orders 2200)
Parking for 100
Cards accepted: Access, Visa, Diners, Amex

EDMUNDBYERS
Durham
Map ref 5B2

Small village in hilly country beneath Muggleswick Common. A winding, man-made lake on the River Derwent just north complements smaller reservoirs southward across the common, traditionally offering fishing and picnic areas.

Redwell Hall Farm
APPROVED
Shotley Bridge, Consett, County Durham DH8 9TS
☎ Consett (0207) 55216
Traditional stone-built farm situated in picturesque valley and close to beautiful Derwent Reservoir. Accommodation is in farmhouse annexe. Ideal for visiting Durham, Hexham, Tynedale and the North Pennines. Conversational German.
Bedrooms: 1 double, 1 twin, 1 family room
Bathrooms: 2 public

Bed & breakfast
per night:	£min	£max
Single		18.50
Double	31.00	33.00

Lunch available
Evening meal 1800 (last orders 1900)
Parking for 50

EGGLESTON
Durham
Map ref 5B3

Small village between Barnard Castle and Middleton-in-Teesdale on the edge of the moors. Once a smelting centre for the North Pennines lead industry but no trace of it remains today.

Moorcock Inn
APPROVED
Hill Top, Gordon Bank, Eggleston, Barnard Castle, County Durham DL12 0AU
☎ Teesdale (0833) 50395
Country inn of character, with modern amenities and spectacular views from all rooms, popular with both tourists and locals.
Bedrooms: 1 single, 3 double, 1 twin, 1 triple
Bathrooms: 2 private, 3 public

Bed & breakfast
per night:	£min	£max
Single	22.00	25.00
Double	32.00	35.00

Half board
per person:	£min	£max
Daily	27.00	30.00
Weekly	167.00	175.00

Lunch available
Evening meal 1900 (last orders 2200)
Parking for 50

EMBLETON
Northumberland
Map ref 5C1

Coastal village spread along the edge of Embleton Bay. The old church was extensively restored in the 19th C. The vicarage incorporates a medieval pele tower.

Doxford Farm
COMMENDED
Chathill NE67 5DY
☎ Charlton Mires (066 579) 235

400-acre mixed farm. Listed Georgian farmhouse set in wooded grounds 4 miles from Embleton. Coast and moorland are within easy reach. Lake and woodland nature trail. Home cooking and home-made bread.
Bedrooms: 1 double, 1 twin, 1 triple, 1 family room
Bathrooms: 1 private, 1 public

Bed & breakfast
per night:	£min	£max
Single	15.00	22.00
Double	30.00	36.00

Half board
per person:	£min	£max
Daily	23.00	30.00
Weekly	150.00	200.00

Evening meal 1830 (last orders 1600)
Parking for 8
Cards accepted: Visa

FALSTONE
Northumberland
Map ref 5B2

Remote village on the edge of Kielder Forest where it spreads beneath the heathery slopes of the south-west Cheviots along the valley of the North Tyne. Just 1 mile west lies Kielder Water, a vast man-made lake which adds boating and fishing to forest recreations.

Blackcock Inn
COMMENDED
Falstone, Hexham NE48 1AA
☎ Hexham (0434) 240200
Fax (0434) 240036

Traditional old country village inn close to Kielder Water, offering cask ale, good food and comfortable accommodation. Non-smokers 10% discount.
Bedrooms: 2 single, 2 double
Bathrooms: 3 private, 1 public

Continued ▶

We advise you to confirm your booking in writing.

73

NORTHUMBRIA

FALSTONE
Continued

Bed & breakfast
per night:	£min	£max
Single	20.00	25.00
Double		45.00

Lunch available
Evening meal 1900 (last orders 2100)
Parking for 12

The Pheasant Inn (by Kielder Water) ⚜
COMMENDED

Stannersburn, Falstone, Hexham
NE48 1DD
☎ Hexham (0434) 240382
Historic inn with beamed ceilings and open fires. Home cooking. Fishing, riding and all water sports nearby. Close to Kielder Water, Hadrian's Wall and the Scottish border.
Bedrooms: 2 double, 5 twin, 1 family room
Bathrooms: 8 private

Bed & breakfast
per night:	£min	£max
Single	30.00	35.00
Double	50.00	55.00

Half board
per person:	£min	£max
Daily	35.00	45.00
Weekly	245.00	291.00

Lunch available
Evening meal 1900 (last orders 2100)
Parking for 30

FOREST-IN-TEESDALE
Durham
Map ref 5B2

An area in Upper Teesdale of widely-dispersed farmsteads set in wild but beautiful scenery with High Force Waterfall and Cauldron Snout. Once the hunting park of the Earls of Darlington.

Langdon Beck Hotel
Listed

Forest-in-Teesdale, Barnard Castle, County Durham DL12 0XP
☎ Teesdale (0833) 22267
A pleasant inn in the magnificent area of Upper Teesdale where a friendly welcome and home cooking are assured. Ideal for walkers and nature lovers.
Bedrooms: 3 single, 1 double, 1 twin, 1 triple
Bathrooms: 2 private, 2 public

Bed & breakfast
per night:	£min	£max
Single	18.00	21.00
Double	36.00	42.00

Half board
per person:	£min	£max
Daily	25.00	28.00
Weekly	170.00	190.00

Lunch available
Evening meal 1830 (last orders 1830)
Parking for 15
Open January-November

GREENHEAD
Northumberland
Map ref 5B2

Small hamlet, overlooked by the ruins of Thirlwall Castle, at the junction of the A69 and the B6318 which runs alongside Hadrian's Wall. Some of the finest sections of the wall and the Carvoran Roman Military Museum are nearby.

Holmhead Farm Licensed Guest House ⚜
COMMENDED

Hadrian's Wall, Greenhead, Carlisle, Cumbria CA6 7HY
☎ Gilsland (069 77) 47402
Fax (069 77) 47402
Modernised farmhouse on the most spectacular part of Hadrian's Wall and on the Pennine Way. Friendly service and home cooking (BTA award-winning breakfast). Hadrian's Wall information service for guests.
Bedrooms: 1 double, 2 twin, 1 triple
Bathrooms: 4 private

Bed & breakfast
per night:	£min	£max
Single	21.00	31.50
Double	42.00	43.00

Half board
per person:	£min	£max
Daily	37.00	38.00
Weekly	126.00	130.00

Evening meal 1930 (last orders 1600)
Parking for 6
Cards accepted: Access, Visa

There are separate sections in this guide listing groups specialising in farm holidays and accommodation which is especially suitable for young people and organised groups.

HALTWHISTLE
Northumberland
Map ref 5B2

Small market town with interesting 12th C church, old inns and blacksmith's smithy. North of the town are several important sites and interpretation centres of Hadrian's Wall. Ideal centre for archaeology, outdoor activity or touring holidays.
Tourist Information Centre
☎ *(0434) 322002*

Broomshaw Hill Farm ⚜
HIGHLY COMMENDED

Willia Road, Haltwhistle NE49 9NP
☎ Hexham (0434) 320866
5-acre livestock farm. Attractive modernised 18th C stone-built farmhouse. On conjunction of bridleway and footpath, both leading to Hadrian's Wall 1 mile away.
Bedrooms: 2 twin, 1 triple
Bathrooms: 1 public

Bed & breakfast
per night:	£min	£max
Single	14.00	15.00
Double	28.00	30.00

Half board
per person:	£min	£max
Daily	22.00	24.00
Weekly	150.00	160.00

Evening meal 1830 (last orders 0900)
Parking for 8
Open February-October

Hall Meadows ⚜
COMMENDED

Main Street, Haltwhistle NE49 0AZ
☎ (0434) 321021
Built in 1888, a large family house with pleasant garden in the centre of Haltwhistle. Ideally placed for Hadrian's Wall.
Bedrooms: 1 single, 1 double, 1 twin
Bathrooms: 1 public

Bed & breakfast
per night:	£min	£max
Single	15.00	15.00
Double	28.00	30.00

Parking for 3

Oaky Knowe Farm ⚜
Listed COMMENDED

Haltwhistle NE49 0NB
☎ Hexham (0434) 320648
300-acre livestock farm. Overlooking the Tyne Valley, within walking distance of Haltwhistle and the Roman Wall. This comfortable farmhouse offers friendly family holidays.
Bedrooms: 1 twin, 2 triple
Bathrooms: 1 public

NORTHUMBRIA

Bed & breakfast per night:	£min	£max
Single	15.00	16.00
Double	26.00	28.00

Half board per person:	£min	£max
Daily	19.00	22.00
Weekly	130.00	150.00

Evening meal 1700 (last orders 1530)
Parking for 8

HAMSTERLEY FOREST

Durham

See under Barnard Castle, Bishop Auckland, Crook, Tow Law

HAYDON BRIDGE

Northumberland
Map ref 5B2

Small town on the banks of the South Tyne with an ancient church, built of stone from sites along the Roman Wall just north. Ideally situated for exploring Hadrian's Wall and the Border country.

Geeswood House M
HIGHLY COMMENDED

Whittis Road, Haydon Bridge, Hexham NE47 6AQ
☎ Hexham (0434) 684220

Comfortable old house with a pleasant, informal atmosphere, lovely views and garden, personal service and true hospitality. Home-made bread, fresh produce, delicious breakfasts and dinners.
Bedrooms: 1 double, 2 twin
Bathrooms: 2 public

Bed & breakfast per night:	£min	£max
Double	32.00	32.00

Half board per person:	£min	£max
Daily	24.50	25.00
Weekly	155.00	155.00

Evening meal 1830 (last orders 1600)
Parking for 3

Sewing Shields Farm
Listed COMMENDED

Hadrian's Wall, Haydon Bridge, Hexham NE47 6NW
☎ Hexham (0434) 684418
2000-acre hill farm. 17th C listed farmhouse, situated on top of Hadrian's Wall, 1 mile east of Housesteads, 5 miles north of Haydon Bridge. Breathtaking views.
Bedrooms: 1 double, 1 twin, 1 family room
Bathrooms: 2 public

Bed & breakfast per night:	£min	£max
Single	13.00	14.00
Double	26.00	28.00

Half board per person:	£min	£max
Daily	21.00	21.00
Weekly	140.00	140.00

Evening meal from 1800
Parking for 6

HEIGHINGTON

Durham
Map ref 5C3

Eldon House M
HIGHLY COMMENDED

East Green, Heighington, Darlington, County Durham DL5 6PP
☎ Aycliffe (0325) 312270
17th C manor house with large garden overlooking the village green. Large, comfortable, well-appointed rooms. Ample parking. Tennis court.
Bedrooms: 3 twin
Bathrooms: 3 private

Bed & breakfast per night:	£min	£max
Single	25.00	30.00
Double	35.00	40.00

Parking for 6

HESLEDEN

Durham
Map ref 5C2

Small village south of the New Town of Peterlee near the County Durham coast.

Golden Calf Hotel

Front Street, Hesleden, Hartlepool, Cleveland TS27 4PH
☎ Wellfield (0429) 836493
Family-run hotel with friendly service. Only 1 mile from A19 on Castle Eden road. 15 minutes to Teesside, 35 minutes to Newcastle, 12 miles to A1.
Bedrooms: 2 double, 2 triple
Bathrooms: 1 public

Bed & breakfast per night:	£min	£max
Single	12.50	
Double	25.00	

Half board per person:	£min	£max
Daily	15.00	19.00

Lunch available
Evening meal 1900 (last orders 2200)
Parking for 20

HEXHAM

Northumberland
Map ref 5B2

Old coaching and market town near Hadrian's Wall. Since pre-Norman times a weekly market has been held in the centre with its market-place and abbey park, and the richly-furnished 12th C abbey church has a superb Anglo-Saxon crypt.
Tourist Information Centre
☎ *(0434) 605225*

Anick Grange
COMMENDED

Hexham NE46 4LP
☎ (0434) 603807
363-acre mixed farm. 17th C farmhouse 1 mile from Hexham. Superb open views. Home cooking and warm welcome.
Bedrooms: 1 single, 1 twin, 1 triple
Bathrooms: 1 private, 1 public

Bed & breakfast per night:	£min	£max
Single	15.00	17.00
Double	30.00	34.00

Parking for 4
Open April-September

Rye Hill Farm M
COMMENDED

Slaley, Hexham NE47 0AH
☎ (0434) 673259

30-acre livestock farm. Warm and comfortable barn conversion, 5 miles south of Hexham, where you can enjoy the peace of rural life. Noted for the food and the friendly atmosphere.
Bedrooms: 2 double, 2 twin, 2 triple
Bathrooms: 6 private, 1 public

Bed & breakfast per night:	£min	£max
Single	20.00	
Double	36.00	

Half board per person:	£min	£max
Daily	30.00	
Weekly	176.40	

Evening meal 1930 (last orders 1700)
Parking for 6

NORTHUMBRIA

HEXHAM
Continued

Stotsfold Hall
Steel, Hexham NE47 0HP
☎ (0434) 673270
Beautiful house surrounded by 15 acres of gardens and woodland with streams and flowers. 6 miles south of Hexham.
Bedrooms: 2 single, 1 double, 1 twin
Bathrooms: 3 public

Bed & breakfast per night:	£min	£max
Single	16.50	16.50
Double	33.00	33.00

Parking for 6

Topsy Turvy
Listed COMMENDED
9 Leazes Lane, Hexham NE46 3BA
☎ (0434) 603152
A cosy home, where you can rest for a while, put your feet up and be thoroughly spoilt.
Bedrooms: 2 double
Bathrooms: 1 private, 1 public

Bed & breakfast per night:	£min	£max
Single	15.00	15.00
Double	30.00	30.00

Half board per person:	£min	£max
Daily	20.00	

Parking for 3

HOLY ISLAND
Northumberland
Map ref 5B1

Still an idyllic retreat, tiny island and fishing village and cradle of northern Christianity. It is approached from the mainland at low water by a causeway. The clifftop castle (National Trust) was restored by Sir Edwin Lutyens.

Britannia
Holy Island, Berwick-upon-Tweed TD15 2RX
☎ Berwick-upon-Tweed (0289) 89218
Comfortable, friendly bed and breakfast in centre of Holy Island. Hot and cold water, tea-making facilities in all rooms. TV lounge. En-suite available.
Bedrooms: 1 double, 1 twin, 1 triple
Bathrooms: 1 private, 1 public

Bed & breakfast per night:	£min	£max
Double	30.00	31.00

Parking for 4
Open March-November

Crown & Anchor Hotel
Fenkle Street, Holy Island, Berwick-upon-Tweed TD15 2RX
☎ Berwick-upon-Tweed (0289) 89215
Old-fashioned inn with public bar, no-smoking lounge bar and dining room. Bedrooms en-suite and centrally heated. Beautiful views and quietly situated.
Bedrooms: 2 double, 1 twin
Bathrooms: 3 private, 1 public

Bed & breakfast per night:	£min	£max
Single	20.00	25.00
Double	32.00	40.00

Lunch available
Parking for 5

North View
COMMENDED
Marygate, Holy Island, Berwick-upon-Tweed TD15 2SD
☎ Berwick-upon-Tweed (0289) 89222
400-year-old listed building on historic and beautiful island. Ideally situated for visiting many of Northumberland's tourist attractions.
Bedrooms: 2 double, 1 twin
Bathrooms: 3 private

Bed & breakfast per night:	£min	£max
Single	20.00	25.00
Double		40.00

Half board per person:	£min	£max
Daily	28.00	35.00

Lunch available
Evening meal 1900 (last orders 2130)
Parking for 6

KIELDER FOREST
Northumberland

See under Bellingham, Falstone, Wark

LONGHORSLEY
Northumberland
Map ref 5C1

Village set between the hills and the sea, close to Longdike Beck. A battlemented tower here is thought to date from the 16th C. 3 miles north-westward at Brinkburn on the River Coquet a beautiful Augustinian Priory, restored in the 19th C, stands in idyllic surroundings.

Thistleyhaugh Farm
HIGHLY COMMENDED
Longhorsley, Morpeth NE65 8RG
☎ (0665) 570629
480-acre mixed farm. On the River Coquet, 2.5 miles off the A697 Wooler road.
Bedrooms: 1 single, 2 double, 1 twin

Bathrooms: 2 private, 1 public

Bed & breakfast per night:	£min	£max
Single	16.00	16.00
Double	20.00	20.00

Half board per person:	£min	£max
Daily	17.00	17.00
Weekly	112.00	112.00

Evening meal 1900 (last orders 2100)

LOWICK
Northumberland
Map ref 5B1

Inland from Holy Island and near the A1, Lowick has a long, wide main street with a few shops and inns and is in agricultural land between the foothills of the Cheviots and the coast.

The Old Manse
HIGHLY COMMENDED
5 Cheviot View, Lowick, Berwick-upon-Tweed TD15 2TY
☎ Berwick-upon-Tweed (0289) 88264
Grade II listed Georgian church manse on the outskirts of Lowick village, 3.5 miles off the A1. In the heart of rural Northumberland.
Bedrooms: 1 double, 2 twin
Bathrooms: 2 private, 1 public

Bed & breakfast per night:	£min	£max
Double	34.00	36.00

Half board per person:	£min	£max
Daily	27.00	28.00
Weekly	189.00	196.00

Evening meal 1830 (last orders 1500)
Parking for 3
Open March-October

MIDDLESBROUGH
Cleveland
Map ref 5C3

Boom-town of the mid 19th C, today's Teesside industrial and conference town has a modern shopping complex and predominantly modern buildings. An engineering miracle of the early 20th C is the Transporter Bridge which replaced an old ferry.
Tourist Information Centre
☎ (0642) 243425

Leven Close Farm
APPROVED
High Leven, Yarm TS15 9JP
☎ Stockton-on-Tees (0642) 750114
250-acre mixed farm. 18th C farmhouse. Easy access to stately homes, coast and market towns.
Bedrooms: 2 double, 1 triple

NORTHUMBRIA

Bathrooms: 1 public

Bed & breakfast
per night:	£min	£max
Single	15.00	
Double	30.00	

Half board
per person:	£min	£max
Daily	20.00	
Weekly	140.00	

Evening meal from 1800
Parking for 14
ॐ 🏛 ☎ ⌂ ♦ ⅲ ⚨ 🏴 🅣 🎷 ⚛ ✝ 🎭 ▶ ✓ ✱ 🏵

MIDDLETON-IN-TEESDALE
Durham
Map ref 5B3

Small stone town of hillside terraces overlooking the river, developed by the London Lead Company in the 18th C. 5 miles up-river is the spectacular 70-ft waterfall, High Force.
Tourist Information Centre
☎ (0833) 40400

Brunswick House ▲
⚜⚜⚜ COMMENDED

55 Market Place, Middleton-in-Teesdale, Barnard Castle, County Durham DL12 0QH
☎ Teesdale (0833) 40393
18th C listed stone-built guesthouse retaining much character and many original features. Comfort, friendly service and home cooking are assured.
Bedrooms: 2 double, 1 twin, 1 family room
Bathrooms: 4 private

Bed & breakfast
per night:	£min	£max
Single		27.50
Double		38.00

Half board
per person:	£min	£max
Daily		31.50
Weekly		190.00

Lunch available
Evening meal 1930 (last orders 1900)
Parking for 5
ॐ 🏛 ⌂ ♦ ⚛ 🏴 🅢 ⚙ ⅲ ▶ ✱ ✝ 🎭 🏵 SP ⚑

Wythes Hill Farm
⚜

Lunedale, Middleton-in-Teesdale, Barnard Castle, County Durham DL12 0NX
☎ Teesdale (0833) 40249
550-acre mixed farm. Farmhouse with panoramic views, on the Pennine Way in lovely walking area. Farmhouse cooking. Peace and quiet, friendliness and comfort guaranteed.
Bedrooms: 1 double, 1 twin, 1 triple
Bathrooms: 2 public

Bed & breakfast
per night:	£min	£max
Single	14.00	15.00
Double	28.00	30.00

Half board
per person:	£min	£max
Daily	21.00	22.00
Weekly		140.00

Evening meal 1800 (last orders 1830)
Parking for 3
Open April-October
ॐ ♦ ⚛ ⅲ 🅢 ⚨ 🏴 ⅲ ▶ ✱ 🎭 OAP

MORPETH
Northumberland
Map ref 5C2

Market town on the River Wansbeck. There are charming gardens and parks, among them Carlisle Park which lies close to the ancient remains of Morpeth Castle. The chantry building houses the Northumbrian Craft Centre and the bagpipe museum.
Tourist Information Centre
☎ (0670) 511323

The Shieling
Listed

2 Manor Farm, Ulgham, Morpeth NE61 3AT
☎ (0670) 790317
Old stone-built farm building converted into a bungalow. In a quiet village 5 miles from Morpeth, on the B1337.
Bedrooms: 3 twin
Bathrooms: 2 public

Bed & breakfast
per night:	£min	£max
Single	15.00	17.00
Double	25.00	28.00

Evening meal 1800 (last orders 2000)
Parking for 3
ॐ ⚛ ♦ ⅲ ♦ ⚑ ⅲ 🅢 🏴 ⅲ ▶ U ✱ ✝ 🏵

NEWCASTLE UPON TYNE
Tyne and Wear
Map ref 5C2

Commercial and cultural centre of the North East, with a large indoor shopping centre, Quayside market, museums and theatres which offer an annual 6 week season by the Royal Shakespeare Company. Norman castle keep, medieval alleys, old Guildhall.
Tourist Information Centre
☎ 091-261 0691 or 230 0030

Bywell
⚜⚜

Sanderson House, 59 Sanderson Road, Jesmond, Newcastle upon Tyne NE2 2DR
☎ 091-281 7615
Large Victorian house with spacious bedrooms, located in quiet residential area close to city centre and all amenities. No smoking.
Bedrooms: 1 double, 1 twin
Bathrooms: 1 private, 1 public

Bed & breakfast
per night:	£min	£max
Single		18.00
Double	30.00	38.00

Parking for 1
ॐ ⌂ ♦ ⅲ 🅢 ⚙ ⅲ ▶ ✱ 🎭

Grosvenor Hotel ▲
⚜⚜⚜ APPROVED

Grosvenor Road, Jesmond, Newcastle upon Tyne NE2 2RR
☎ 091-281 0543
Fax 091-281 9217
Friendly hotel in quiet residential suburb, offering a wide range of facilities. Close to city centre.
Bedrooms: 18 single, 9 double, 14 twin
Bathrooms: 33 private, 5 public

Bed & breakfast
per night:	£min	£max
Single	25.00	40.00
Double	40.00	60.00

Half board
per person:	£min	£max
Daily	29.50	49.50
Weekly	177.00	297.00

Lunch available
Evening meal 1830 (last orders 2100)
Parking for 30
Cards accepted: Access, Visa, Diners, Amex
ॐ ⚛ ☎ ⌂ ♦ ⅲ 🅢 ⚨ ⅲ ⅲ ● ⅲ ▶ T5-100 OAP ⚑ SP T

NORHAM
Northumberland
Map ref 5B1

Border village on the salmon-rich Tweed, dominated by its dramatic castle ruin. Near Castle Street is the church, like the castle destroyed after the Battle of Flodden, but rebuilt. Norham Station Railway Museum is just outside the town.

Dromore House ▲
Listed

12 Pedwell Way, Norham, Berwick-upon-Tweed TD15 2LD
☎ Berwick-upon-Tweed (0289) 382313
Guesthouse in a small village on the River Tweed, between the Cheviot and Lammermuir Hills. Quiet beaches are within easy reach.
Bedrooms: 1 double, 1 twin, 1 triple
Bathrooms: 1 private, 1 public, 1 private shower

Bed & breakfast
per night:	£min	£max
Single	13.00	16.00
Double	26.00	32.00

Continued ▶

77

NORHAM

Continued

Half board per person:	£min	£max
Daily	20.00	23.00
Weekly	140.00	161.00

Evening meal 1700 (last orders 1900)
Parking for 3

REDCAR

Cleveland
Map ref 5C3

Lively holiday resort near Teesside with broad sandy beaches, a fine racecourse, a large indoor funfair at Coatham and other seaside amusements. Britain's oldest existing lifeboat can be seen at the Zetland Museum.

Sunnyside House

22 Station Road, Redcar TS10 1AQ
☎ (0642) 477531
Well situated property close to town centre and beach.
Bedrooms: 1 single, 4 triple
Bathrooms: 2 public

Bed & breakfast per night:	£min	£max
Single	15.00	15.00
Double	25.00	26.00

Evening meal 1700 (last orders 1900)

Willow House

8 Newcomen Terrace, Redcar TS10 1AT
☎ (0642) 485330
Large, terraced property overlooking the sea and close to the town centre. Warm, friendly atmosphere and home cooking.
Bedrooms: 1 single, 2 triple, 3 family rooms
Bathrooms: 3 public

Bed & breakfast per night:	£min	£max
Single	15.00	15.00
Double	25.00	26.00

Evening meal 1700 (last orders 1900)

Individual proprietors have supplied all details of accommodation. Although we do check for accuracy, we advise you to confirm the information at the time of booking.

ROTHBURY

Northumberland
Map ref 5B1

Old market town on the River Coquet near the Simonside Hills. It makes an ideal centre for walking and fishing or for exploring this beautiful area from the coast to the Cheviots. Cragside House and Gardens (National Trust) are open to the public.

Bickerton Cottage Farm
Listed COMMENDED

Rothbury NE65 7LW
☎ (0669) 40264
500-acre livestock farm. Situated in the glorious open scenery of the Northumberland National Park, the perfect holiday base for exploring Northumberland and the Scottish Borders. A warm welcome awaits you.
Bedrooms: 1 double, 1 twin
Bathrooms: 1 public

Bed & breakfast per night:	£min	£max
Double	25.00	30.00

Parking for 2
Open March-October

Lorbottle West Steads
Listed

Thropton, Morpeth NE65 7JT
☎ Alnwick (0665) 574672
310-acre mixed farm. Stone farmhouse with panoramic views of the Coquet Valley and Cheviot Hills. B6341 to Thropton, turn for Whittingham, turn at Lorbottle, first right.
Bedrooms: 1 single, 1 double, 1 twin
Bathrooms: 1 public

Bed & breakfast per night:	£min	£max
Single	13.00	14.00
Double	27.00	30.00

Parking for 8
Open May-October

Silverton Lodge
COMMENDED

Silverton Lane, Rothbury, Morpeth NE65 7RJ
☎ (0669) 20144

Charming family home converted from a stone-built Victorian school. Set on the edge of Rothbury. Laura Ashley style. No smoking please.
Bedrooms: 1 double, 1 twin
Bathrooms: 2 private

Bed & breakfast per night:	£min	£max
Double	31.00	34.00

Half board per person:	£min	£max
Daily	24.00	25.50
Weekly	152.00	162.00

Evening meal 1900 (last orders 1930)
Parking for 4

Thropton Demesne
HIGHLY COMMENDED

Thropton, Morpeth NE65 7LT
☎ (0669) 20196
24-acre mixed farm. Traditional farmhouse peacefully situated in the picturesque Coquet Valley. Spectacular views. Ideally placed for fishing, golf and walking.
Bedrooms: 1 double, 1 twin, 1 triple
Bathrooms: 3 private

Bed & breakfast per night:	£min	£max
Single	20.50	25.00
Double	35.00	37.00

Parking for 6

ROWLANDS GILL

Tyne and Wear
Map ref 5C2

Adjacent to the Derwent Walk Country Park on the side of the River Derwent, opposite the National Trust Gibside Chapel.

Chopwell Wood House

Chopwell Woods, Rowlands Gill NE39 1LT
☎ (0207) 542765
Large, attractive house in 600 acres of woodland in the Derwent Valley, within easy reach of Newcastle, Durham and Hexham. Near MetroCentre and Beamish Museum.
Bedrooms: 1 double, 1 twin, 1 triple
Bathrooms: 1 public

Bed & breakfast per night:	£min	£max
Single	15.00	20.00
Double	25.00	30.00

Parking for 6

National Crown ratings were correct at the time of going to press but are subject to change. Please check at the time of booking.

NORTHUMBRIA

RYTON
Tyne and Wear
Map ref 5C2

On a wooded site above the Tyne, Ryton has a 12th C church with a Jacobean screen and good 19th C oak carving. Small pit working, notable for the spectacular 1826 Stargate Explosion, ceased in 1967. Easy access to the A1, Hadrian's Wall and rural Northumbria.

Barmoor Old Manse
Listed

The Old Manse, Barmoor, Ryton NE40 3BD
☎ 091-413 2438
Large stone Victorian house, built as Manse for Congregational Church in 1862. Delightful garden. Near MetroCentre, Roman Wall and Beamish Museum.
Bedrooms: 1 double, 2 twin
Bathrooms: 1 public
Bed & breakfast
per night: £min   £max
Single   15.00   18.00
Double   30.00   35.00
Parking for 2

SALTBURN-BY-THE-SEA
Cleveland
Map ref 5C3

Set on fine cliffs just north of the Cleveland Hills, a gracious Victorian resort with later developments and wide, firm sands. A handsome Jacobean mansion at Marske can be reached along the sands.
Tourist Information Centre
☎ (0287) 622422

Boulby Barns Farm
Listed

Easington, Loftus, Saltburn-by-the-Sea TS13 4UT
☎ Guisborough (0287) 641306
7-acre mixed farm. Traditional stone farmhouse with accommodation on a working smallholding in the national park. Situated half a mile from A174, close to Boulby Cliffs and the Cleveland Way, with views of moors and sea.
Bedrooms: 2 double, 2 twin
Bathrooms: 2 public
Bed & breakfast
per night: £min   £max
Single   15.00   15.50
Parking for 8
Open April-November

SEAHOUSES
Northumberland
Map ref 5C1

Small modern resort developed around a 19th C herring port. Just offshore, and reached by boat from here, are the rocky Farne Islands (National Trust) where there is an important bird reserve. The bird observatory occupies a medieval pele tower.

'Leeholme'
Listed

93 Main Street, Seahouses NE68 7TS
☎ (0665) 720230
A warm welcome awaits you at this small homely bed and breakfast. 5 minutes' walk to Seahouses harbour and shops. Hearty breakfast assured.
Bedrooms: 1 double, 1 twin
Bathrooms: 1 public
Bed & breakfast
per night: £min   £max
Single   13.00
Double   26.00   26.00
Parking for 2
Open March-October

Rowena
Listed

99 Main Street, Seahouses NE68 7TS
☎ (0665) 721309
Comfortable bed and breakfast accommodation, 5 minutes' walk from the harbour where boats leave to visit the Farne Islands.
Bedrooms: 1 single, 1 double, 1 twin, 1 triple
Bathrooms: 1 private, 1 public
Bed & breakfast
per night: £min   £max
Single   14.00
Double   29.00   34.00
Parking for 3

Slate Hall Riding Centre

174 Main Street, Seahouses NE68 7UA
☎ (0665) 720320
65-acre mixed farm. Comfortable farmhouse, en-suite rooms, tastefully decorated, home cooking. Ideally situated for touring coast and castles. Approved riding centre behind house.
Bedrooms: 2 triple
Bathrooms: 2 private
Bed & breakfast
per night: £min   £max
Double   30.00   40.00
Parking for 3

SLALEY
Northumberland
Map ref 5B2

Small hamlet, now a major golfing venue, south of Corbridge near the Derwent Reservoir.

Rose and Crown Inn
COMMENDED

Main Street, Slaley, Hexham NE47 0AA
☎ Hexham (0434) 673263
Warm, friendly, family-run business with good wholesome home cooking and a la carte restaurant. All bedrooms en-suite.
Bedrooms: 1 single, 2 twin
Bathrooms: 3 private
Bed & breakfast
per night: £min   £max
Single   17.50   22.50
Double   35.00   45.00
Half board
per person: £min   £max
Daily   25.00   30.00
Weekly   155.00 190.00
Lunch available
Evening meal 1830 (last orders 2200)
Parking for 32
Cards accepted: Access, Visa

SPENNYMOOR
Durham
Map ref 5C2

Booming coal and iron town from the 18th C until early in the present century when traditional industry gave way to lighter manufacturing and trading estates were built. On the moors south of the town there are fine views of the Wear Valley.

Idsley House
COMMENDED

4 Green Lane, Spennymoor, County Durham DL16 6HD
☎ Bishop Auckland (0388) 814237

Long-established Victorian guesthouse on A167/A688 run by local family. Ideal for Durham City. Suitable for business or pleasure. Ample parking on premises.
Bedrooms: 1 single, 1 double, 2 twin, 1 triple
Bathrooms: 2 private, 1 public

Continued ▶

NORTHUMBRIA

SPENNYMOOR
Continued

Bed & breakfast
per night:	£min	£max
Single	18.00	25.00
Double	33.00	33.00

Parking for 8

STAINDROP
Durham
Map ref 5B3

Gazebo House
HIGHLY COMMENDED

4 North Green, Staindrop, Darlington, County Durham DL2 3JN
☎ Teesdale (0833) 660222

18th C house with listed gazebo (illustrated) in garden. Adjacent Raby Park and Castle. Ideal base for Lake District and Yorkshire Dales.
Bedrooms: 1 double, 1 twin
Bathrooms: 2 private

Bed & breakfast
per night:	£min	£max
Single	15.00	15.00
Double	35.00	35.00

Half board
per person:	£min	£max
Daily	22.00	22.00
Weekly	140.00	140.00

Evening meal 1900 (last orders 2200)

STANLEY
Durham
Map ref 5C2

Small town on the site of a Roman cattle camp. At the Beamish North of England Open Air Museum numerous set-pieces and displays recreate industrial and social conditions prevalent during the area's past.

Bushblades Farm
Listed

Harperley, Stanley, County Durham DH9 9UA
☎ (0207) 232722
60-acre livestock farm. Comfortable Georgian farmhouse, in rural setting. Within easy reach of Durham City, Beamish Museum, A1M, MetroCentre and Roman Wall.
Bedrooms: 2 double, 1 twin
Bathrooms: 1 private, 1 public

Bed & breakfast
per night:	£min	£max
Single	20.00	25.00
Double	30.00	38.00

Parking for 6

STEEL
Northumberland
Map ref 5B2

Gairshield Farm
Listed HIGHLY COMMENDED

Whitley Chapel, Steel, Hexham NE47 0HS
☎ Hexham (0434) 673562
117-acre hill farm. Comfortable 17th C farmhouse set in superb open countryside with excellent views. Friendly family welcome. 8 miles south of Hexham.
Bedrooms: 1 triple
Bathrooms: 1 public

Bed & breakfast
per night:	£min	£max
Single	13.50	13.50
Double	17.00	17.00

Parking for 4
Open April-October

STOCKSFIELD
Northumberland
Map ref 5B2

Pretty rural village in Tyne Valley in area of good agricultural land. Bywell Hall, the home of Lord Allendale, is nearby as well as Cherryburn, the birthplace of Thomas Bewick, where a museum dedicated to the life and works of this famous local engraver can be found.

Old Ridley Hall
Listed

Stocksfield NE43 7RU
☎ (0661) 842816
Country house with rambling garden. Plenty of car parking. Pets welcome.
Bedrooms: 1 single, 3 twin
Bathrooms: 1 private, 2 public

Bed & breakfast
per night:	£min	£max
Single	15.00	20.00
Double	30.00	40.00

Half board
per person:	£min	£max
Daily	25.00	
Weekly	150.00	

Evening meal 1700 (last orders 2000)
Parking for 11

SUNDERLAND
Tyne and Wear
Map ref 5C2

Ancient coal and shipbuilding port on Wearside, with important glassworks since the 17th C. Today's industrial complex dates from the 19th C. Modern building includes the Civic Centre.
Tourist Information Centre
☎ 091-565 0960 or 091-565 0990

Bed & Breakfast Stop
Listed COMMENDED

183 Newcastle Road, Fulwell, Sunderland, Tyne & Wear SR5 1NR
☎ 091-548 2291
Tudor-style semi-detached house on the A1018 Newcastle to Sunderland road. 5 minutes to the railway station and 10 minutes to the seafront and city centre.
Bedrooms: 1 single, 1 twin, 1 triple
Bathrooms: 1 public

Bed & breakfast
per night:	£min	£max
Single	13.00	15.00
Double	26.00	28.00

Half board
per person:	£min	£max
Daily	19.00	21.00
Weekly	122.50	126.00

Evening meal 1800 (last orders 1200)
Parking for 3

TOW LAW
Durham
Map ref 5B2

Butsfield Abbey Farm
APPROVED

Satley, Tow Law, Bishop Auckland, County Durham DL13 4JD
☎ Bishop Auckland (0388) 730509
176-acre mixed farm. Farmhouse cottage in a quiet rural setting. 1 mile from A68 and 4 miles from Castleside.
Bedrooms: 1 double
Bathrooms: 1 private, 1 public

Bed & breakfast
per night:	£min	£max
Single	12.00	13.00
Double	24.00	26.00

Parking for 4

Individual proprietors have supplied all details of accommodation. Although we do check for accuracy, we advise you to confirm the information at the time of booking.

80

NORTHUMBRIA

TYNEMOUTH
Tyne and Wear
Map ref 5C2

At the mouth of the Tyne, old Tyneside resort adjoining North Shields with its fish quay and market. The pier is overlooked by the gaunt ruins of a Benedictine priory and a castle. Splendid sands, amusement centre and park.

Hope House
DE LUXE

47 Percy Gardens, Tynemouth, North Shields NE30 4HH
☎ 091-257 1989

Double-fronted Victorian house with superb coastal views from most rooms. Tastefully furnished, with large bedrooms. Fine cuisine and quality wines.
Bedrooms: 2 double, 1 twin
Bathrooms: 3 private, 1 public

Bed & breakfast
per night:	£min	£max
Single	18.75	23.50
Double	38.50	47.50

Half board
per person:	£min	£max
Daily	32.95	37.00
Weekly	220.00	250.00

Lunch available
Evening meal 1800 (last orders 2100)
Parking for 5
Cards accepted: Access, Visa, Diners, Amex

WARK
Northumberland
Map ref 5B2

Set in the beautiful Tyne Valley amid the Northumbrian fells, old village just above the meeting of Wark Burn with the Tyne. Grey stone houses surround the green with its shady chestnut trees and an iron bridge spans the stream. The mound of a Norman castle occupies the river bank.

Low Stead
HIGHLY COMMENDED

Wark, Hexham NE48 3DP
☎ Hexham (0434) 230352

16th C stone farmhouse in unspoilt country midway between Hadrian's Wall and Kielder. Good cooking, peaceful non-smoking haven for country lovers.
Bedrooms: 1 double, 1 twin
Bathrooms: 2 private

Bed & breakfast
per night:	£min	£max
Single	22.50	22.50
Double	45.00	45.00

Half board
per person:	£min	£max
Daily	35.00	35.00
Weekly	230.00	230.00

Evening meal 1900 (last orders 2000)
Parking for 6

WARKWORTH
Northumberland
Map ref 5C1

A pretty village overlooked by its medieval castle. A 14th C fortified bridge across the wooded Coquet gives a superb view of 18th C terraces climbing to the castle. Upstream is a curious 14th C Hermitage and in the market square is the Norman church of St Lawrence.

Beck 'N' Call
HIGHLY COMMENDED

Birling West Cottage, Warkworth, Morpeth NE65 0XS
☎ Alnwick (0665) 711653

Country cottage set in half an acre of terraced gardens with stream. First cottage on the right entering Warkworth from Alnwick.
Bedrooms: 2 double, 1 triple
Bathrooms: 1 private, 1 public

Bed & breakfast
per night:	£min	£max
Single	16.00	
Double	32.00	

Parking for 4

Bide A While
Listed

4 Beal Croft, Warkworth, Morpeth NE65 0XL
☎ Alnwick (0665) 711753

Bungalow on small executive housing estate of 8 dwellings.
Bedrooms: 1 double, 1 triple
Bathrooms: 1 private, 1 public

Bed & breakfast
per night:	£min	£max
Double	28.00	32.00

Parking for 3

North Cottage
HIGHLY COMMENDED

Birling, Warkworth, Morpeth NE65 0XS
☎ Alnwick (0665) 711263

Attractive cottage, with ground floor, en-suite non-smoking rooms. Extensive gardens, with patio where visitors are welcome to relax.
Bedrooms: 1 single, 2 double, 1 twin
Bathrooms: 3 private, 1 public

Bed & breakfast
per night:	£min	£max
Single	15.00	17.00
Double	30.00	34.00

Parking for 8

WESTGATE-IN-WEARDALE
Durham
Map ref 5B2

Small Weardale village with an old water-mill and a 19th C church. It is set at the entrance to the Bishops of Durham's former hunting ground, Old Park. Beautiful moorland, river and valley scenery to be explored.

Westgate House
HIGHLY COMMENDED

Westgate-in-Weardale, Bishop Auckland, County Durham DL13 1LW
☎ Bishop Auckland (0388) 517564

Experience northern hospitality in the heart of the magnificent North Pennines in a riverside country house with large secluded garden. All rooms have private facilities.
Bedrooms: 1 double, 2 twin
Bathrooms: 3 private

Bed & breakfast
per night:	£min	£max
Single	20.00	20.00
Double	40.00	40.00

Half board
per person:	£min	£max
Daily	30.00	30.00
Weekly	189.00	

Evening meal from 1900
Parking for 4
Open April-October

National Crown ratings were correct at the time of going to press but are subject to change. Please check at the time of booking.

WHITLEY BAY
Tyne and Wear
Map ref 5C2

Seaside resort with a large golfcourse, amusement parks and ice-rink. It is edged with wide sands which stretch northward toward a more rugged coastline. St Mary's Island, which can be reached at low tide, has a redundant lighthouse.
Tourist Information Centre
☎ 091-252 4494

Windsor Hotel ♨
HIGHLY COMMENDED
South Parade, Whitley Bay NE26 2RF
☎ 091-251 8888 & 297 0272

Private hotel close to the seafront and town centre. An excellent base in the north east for business or pleasure.

Bedrooms: 5 single, 16 double, 43 twin
Bathrooms: 64 private
Bed & breakfast

per night:	£min	£max
Single	30.00	55.00
Double	45.00	60.00

Half board

per person:	£min	£max
Daily	30.00	60.00

Lunch available
Evening meal 1800 (last orders 2130)
Parking for 26
Cards accepted: Access, Visa, Diners, Amex

There are separate sections in this guide listing groups specialising in farm holidays and accommodation which is especially suitable for young people and organised groups.

WYLAM
Northumberland
Map ref 5B2

Well-kept village on the River Tyne, famous as the birthplace of the railway pioneer, George Stephenson. The cottage in which he was born is open to the public, and the Wylam Railway Museum also commemorates William Hedley and Timothy Hackworth.

Wormald House ♨
HIGHLY COMMENDED
Main Street, Wylam NE41 8DN
☎ (0661) 852529 & 852552

Pleasant country home located near centre of Wylam, George Stephenson's birthplace. House stands on site of Timothy Hackworth's birthplace (Stephenson's contemporary).
Bedrooms: 2 double, 1 twin
Bathrooms: 3 private
Bed & breakfast

per night:	£min	£max
Single		17.00
Double		34.00

Parking for 4

National Accessible Scheme

If you are a wheelchair user or someone who has difficulty walking, look for the national 'Accessible' symbol when choosing where to stay.

All the places that display the symbol have been checked by a Tourist Board inspector against criteria that reflect the practical needs of wheelchair users.

There are three categories of accessibility, indicated by symbols:

Category 1: Accessible to all wheelchair users including those travelling independently

Category 2: Accessible to a wheelchair user with assistance

Category 3: Accessible to a wheelchair user able to walk short distances and up at least three steps

A leaflet giving more information on the scheme is available free from any Tourist Information Centre, whose staff will also be pleased to help with finding suitable accommodation in the area.
Additional help and guidance can be obtained from the Holiday Care Service,
2 Old Bank Chambers, Station Road, Horley, Surrey RH6 9HW.
Tel: (0293) 774535. Fax: (0293) 784647.
Minicom: (0293) 776943 (24-hour answering).

SURE SIGNS
OF WHERE TO STAY

Throughout Britain, the tourist boards now inspect over 30,000 places to stay, every year, to help you find the ones that suit you best.

Looking for a hotel, guesthouse, inn, B&B or farmhouse? Look for the **CROWN**. The classifications: 'Listed', and then **ONE to FIVE CROWN**, tell you the range of facilities and services you can expect. The more Crowns, the wider the range.

Looking for somewhere convenient to stop overnight on a motorway or major road route? Look for the 'Lodge' **MOON**. The classifications: **ONE to THREE MOON** tell you the range of facilities you can expect. The more Moons, the wider the range.

Looking for a self-catering holiday home? Look for the **KEY**. The classifications: **ONE to FIVE KEY**, tell you the range of facilities and equipment you can expect. The more Keys, the wider the range.

THE GRADES: **APPROVED, COMMENDED, HIGHLY COMMENDED and DE LUXE,** whether alongside the **CROWNS**, **KEYS** or **MOONS** show the quality standard of what is provided. If no grade is shown, you can still expect a high standard of cleanliness.

Looking for a holiday caravan, chalet or camping park? Look for the **Q** symbol. The more ✓s in the Q (from one to five), the higher the quality standard of what is provided.

English Tourist Board

We've checked them out before you check in!

More detailed information on the **CROWNS**, the **KEYS** and the **Q** is given in free *SURE SIGN* leaflets, available at any Tourist Information Centre.

North West

With a passion for its arts and a pride in its heritage, the cities and towns of the North West contain some of the finest attractions in England. It was here that Britain's great textile industry blossomed in the 19th C, leaving Victorian landmarks such as the Albert Dock in Liverpool, home of just some of the museums to be found in the region. Step back further in time to the walled city of Chester surrounded by beautiful countryside, which stands as a monument to Roman settlement, or forward again to medieval Beeston Castle. Immerse yourself in the bustling city of Manchester, 'The Life and Soul of Britain', or create your own excitement in the funfair action of Blackpool Pleasure Beach. Whether it's bright lights or rolling hills you desire, try the treasured North West.

WHERE TO GO, WHAT TO SEE

The number against each name will help you locate it on the map (page 86).

❶ Sandcastle
Promenade, Blackpool, Lancashire FY4 1BB
Tel: Blackpool (0253) 43602
Leisure pool, wave pool, giant slides, amusements, live entertainment, bars, cafés, showbar, shop and nightclub. Children's playground and beer garden.

Famed for its illuminations, fun fairs and 500ft tower, Blackpool is the place for pleasure.

❶ Blackpool Pleasure Beach
Blackpool, Lancashire FY4 1EZ
Tel: Blackpool (0253) 41033
Europe's greatest amusement park: Space Invader, Big Dipper, Revolution, etc. Funshineland for children. Summer season ice show, illusion show in Horseshoe Bar.

❶ Blackpool Sea Life Centre
Blackpool, Lancashire FY1 5AA
Tel: Blackpool (0253) 22445

Tropical sharks up to 8ft in length housed in 100,000 gallon display with underwater walk-through tunnel.

❶ Tower World
Blackpool, Lancashire
Tel: (0253) 22242
Tower Ballroom, Memory Lane, Jungle Jim's playground, Out of this World, Undersea World, Pool room, Tower Dungeon, Ma Taplow's Restaurant. Children's entertainment daily.

❷ British Commercial Vehicle Museum
King Street, Leyland PR5 1LE
Tel: Preston (0772) 451011
Museum contains Popemobile, horse-drawn and steam vehicles, early petrol engines including buses, trucks, vans and fire engines. Marks and Spencer centenary vehicle.

❸ Pleasureland Amusement Park
Marine Drive, Southport, Merseyside PR8 1RX
Tel: Southport (0704) 532717
Traditional amusement park with wide variety of thrilling rides.

84

North West

The Beatles: a famous Liverpool foursome who challenged US dominance of rock music in the '60s.

④ Wildfowl and Wetland Centre
Martin Mere, Burscough, Lancashire L40 0TA
Tel: Burscough (0704) 895181
45 acres of gardens with over 1600 ducks, geese and swans of 120 different kinds. Two flocks of flamingoes. 300-acre wild area with 20-acre lake.

⑤ East Lancashire Railway
Bury, Lancashire BL9 0EY
Tel: 061-764 7790
Eight-mile-long preserved railway operated principally by steam traction. Transport museum nearby.

⑥ Butterfly World
Queens Park, Chorley New Road, Bolton, Lancashire
Tel: Bolton (0204) 22311
Butterflies and moths in free flight, goldfish, Koi carp, insects.

⑦ Granada Studios Tour
Quay Street, Manchester M60 9EA
Tel: 061-832 9090
A unique insight into the fascinating world behind the TV screen. Visit three of the most famous streets on TV.

⑦ Manchester Jewish Museum
190 Cheetham Hill Road, Manchester M8 8LW
Tel: 061-834 9879
Restored former Spanish and Portuguese synagogue (1874).
Grade II listed building. History of Manchester's Jewish community.

⑦ Museum of Science and Industry in Manchester
Castlefield, Manchester M3 4JP
Tel: 061-832 2244
Europe's largest industrial museum based on the site of the oldest railway station in the world. Exhibitions include the Power Hall and Air and Space Gallery.

⑧ Pilkington Glass Museum
Prescot Road, St Helens, Merseyside WA10 3TT
Tel: St Helens (0744) 692499
Fine collection of ancient and antique glass. Development and uses of glass. Working lighthouse optic, hologram display and working telescope.

⑨ Knowsley Safari Park
Prescot, Merseyside L34 4AN
Tel: 051-430 9009
Five-mile drive through game reserves, set in 400 acres of parkland containing lions, tigers, elephants, rhinos, etc. Large picnic areas and children's amusement park.

⑩ Croxteth Hall and Country Park
Off Muirhead Avenue East, Liverpool, Merseyside L12 0HB
Tel: 051-228 5311
500-acre country park and hall with displays and furnished rooms. Walled garden, farm with rare breeds, miniature railway, gift shop, picnic areas, riding centre and adventure playground.

⑩ Albert Dock
Suite 7, The Colonnades, Albert Dock, Liverpool L3 4AA
Tel: 051-708 7334
Britain's largest Grade I listed historic building. Restored 4-sided dock, including 94 shops, wine bars, entertainment, marina and maritime museum.

⑪ Dunham Massey Hall
Altrincham, Cheshire WA14 4SJ
Tel: 061-941 1025
200-acre formal park with fallow deer. Historic house with outstanding collections of 18th C furniture, silver and portraits.

⑫ Port Sunlight Heritage Centre
Greendale Road, Port Sunlight, Wirral, Merseyside L62 4XE
Tel: 051-644 6466
In listed building, display showing creation of village, with photographs, drawings, models, Victorian model house.

⑬ Catalyst: The Museum of the Chemical Industry
Gossage Building, Mersey Road, Widnes, Cheshire WA8 0DF
Tel: 051-420 1121

North West

Use the map above to locate places in the 'Where to Go, What to See' section.

Dramatic riverside observation gallery with interactive microcomputers, video and other displays telling the story of the chemical industry in Widnes and Runcorn.

14 Gullivers World
Shackleton Close, Warrington
WA5 5YZ
Tel: Warrington (0925) 444888
Theme park with rides for the young and old.

15 Lyme Park
Disley, Stockport, Cheshire
SK12 2NX
Tel: Disley (0663) 762023
Nature trails and herds of red and fallow deer in 1377 acres of

North West

moorland, woodland and park. State rooms, period furniture, tapestry, Grinling Gibbons carvings in hall, clock collection.

16 Norton Priory Museum and Gardens
Tudor Road, Runcorn, Cheshire WA7 1SX
Tel: Runcorn (0928) 569895
Excavated Augustinian priory, remains of church, cloister and chapter house. Later site of Tudor mansion and Georgian house. Walled garden and woodland.

17 Hillside Ornamental Fowl
Damson Lane, Mobberley, Cheshire WA16 7HY
Tel: Mobberley (0565) 873282
A private collection of ornamental waterfowl, flamingoes, penguins, pheasants, bantams, pigeons and other rare species.

18 Quarry Bank Mill
Styal, Cheshire SK9 4LA
Tel: Wilmslow (0625) 527468
Georgian waterpowered cotton spinning mill, with 4 floors of displays and demonstrations. 275 acres of parkland to explore.

19 Boat Museum
Ellesmere Port, Cheshire L65 4EF
Tel: 051-355 5017
Over 50 historic craft, largest floating collection in the world with restored buildings, traditional cottages, workshops, steam engines, boat trips, etc.

20 Gawsworth Hall
Gawsworth, Macclesfield, Cheshire SK11 9RN
Tel: North Rode (0260) 223456
Fully furnished Tudor house and gardens. Open-air theatre June–July.

20 Silk Museum
Roe Street, Macclesfield, Cheshire SK11 6UT
Tel: Macclesfield (0625) 613210
Information centre, town history exhibition, silk museum, Sunday school, history exhibition, guided

trails, tearoom, shop, auditorium seats 450.

20 Capesthorne Hall
Siddington, Macclesfield, Cheshire SK11 9JY
Tel: Chelford (0625) 861221
Sculpture, paintings, furniture, Greek vases, family muniments. Georgian chapel, tea rooms, gardens, lakes, nature walks and caravan park.

21 Jodrell Bank Science Centre
Lower Withington, Cheshire SK11 9DL
Tel: Lower Withington (0477) 71339
Exhibition and interactive exhibits on astronomy. Planetarium and the Lovell telescope.

22 Chester Zoo
Upton-by-Chester, Chester, Cheshire CH2 1LH
Tel: Chester (0244) 380280
Penguin pool with underwater views, tropical house, spectacular displays of spring and summer bedding plants. Chimpanzee house and outdoor enclosure. New monorail.

FIND OUT MORE
Further information about holidays and attractions in the North West region is available from:
North West Tourist Board
Swan House, Swan Meadow Road, Wigan Pier, Wigan WN3 5BB
Tel: (0942) 821222

These publications are available free from the North West Tourist Board:
North West Welcome Guide
Discover England's North West (attractions map)
Overseas brochure
Group Visits
Bed & Breakfast map
Caravan and Camping Parks guide
Regional pub guide

The Lovell telescope at Jodrell Bank Science Centre is a fully steerable radio telescope used to 'look' deep into space.

87

NORTH WEST

Places to stay

Accommodation entries in this regional section are listed in alphabetical order of place name, and then in alphabetical order of establishment.

The map references refer to the colour maps at the back of the guide. The first figure is the map number; the letter and figure which follow indicate the grid reference on the map.

The symbols at the end of each accommodation entry give information about services and facilities. A 'key' to these symbols is inside the back cover flap, which can be kept open for easy reference.

ALDERLEY EDGE
Cheshire
Map ref 4B2

Residential town taking its name from the hill which rises to a height of 600 ft from the Cheshire Plain. The Edge is a well-known beauty spot with superb views. Many historic buildings including Chorley Old Hall (the oldest surviving manor house in Cheshire).

Dean Green Farm
HIGHLY COMMENDED

Nusery Lane, Nether Alderley, Macclesfield SK10 4TX
☎ Chelford (0625) 861401
131-acre beef farm. Situated between A34 and A535 at Nether Alderley. Grade II oak-beamed farmhouse surrounded by pastureland looking towards Alderley Edge, convenient for Knutsford, Wilmslow and Macclesfield.
Bedrooms: 1 double
Bathrooms: 1 private

Bed & breakfast
per night:	£min	£max
Single	29.37	
Double	58.75	

Half board
per person:	£min	£max
Daily	44.06	

Evening meal 1800 (last orders 2100)
Parking for 10

The enquiry coupons at the back will help you when contacting proprietors.

ALTRINCHAM
Greater Manchester
Map ref 4A2

Altrincham preserves the best of the old at its fascinating Old Market Place, with the best of the new on pedestrianised George Street. International fashion and high style interior design rub shoulders with unique boutiques and local speciality shops.
Tourist Information Centre
☎ 061-941 7337

Ashley Mill
Listed HIGHLY COMMENDED

Ashley Mill Lane, Ashley, Altrincham, Cheshire WA14 3PU
☎ 061-928 5751
17th C mill house in delightful Cheshire countryside. A haven of peace and tranquillity yet only 10 minutes from Manchester Airport.
Bedrooms: 1 single, 2 double, 1 twin
Bathrooms: 1 public

Bed & breakfast
per night:	£min	£max
Single	18.00	20.00
Double	36.00	40.00

Parking for 32

There are separate sections in this guide listing groups specialising in farm holidays and accommodation which is especially suitable for young people and organised groups.

BACUP
Lancashire
Map ref 4B1

Textile-manufacturing town in the Irwell Valley, surrounded by stretches of moorland and close to the South Yorkshire border. The Natural History Society Museum has collections of natural history, geology and old household items.

Pasture Bottom Farm
APPROVED

Bacup OL13 9UZ
☎ (0706) 873790
100-acre beef farm. Farmhouse bed and breakfast ideally situated for walking Rossendale and Lancashire Moor. Local attractions include a textile museum, Ski Rossendale and hang-gliding at Whitworth.
Bedrooms: 2 twin
Bathrooms: 1 public

Bed & breakfast
per night:	£min	£max
Single	13.50	13.50
Double	27.00	27.00

Half board
per person:	£min	£max
Daily	20.00	20.00
Weekly	140.00	140.00

Evening meal 1900 (last orders 1900)
Parking for 3

National Crown ratings were correct at the time of going to press but are subject to change. Please check at the time of booking.

88

NORTH WEST

BLACKBURN
Lancashire
Map ref 4A1

North east Lancashire market town. Waves Water Fun Centre; Lewis Textile Museum; Blackburn Museum; 19th C cathedral; Victorian landscaped Corporation Park.
Tourist Information Centre
☎ (0254) 53177

Mitton Hall Lodgings ♠
✦✦✦ APPROVED

Mitton Road, Mitton, Blackburn BB6 9PQ
☎ Stonyhurst (0254) 826455
Fax (0254) 826386

16th C listed hall in Ribble Valley. Restaurant, pizzeria, tavern, lodgings. Two miles Whalley Abbey, 3 miles Clitheroe Castle, close Trough of Bowland. Eleven miles junction 31 of M6, 7 miles M65.
Bedrooms: 2 single, 6 double, 4 twin, 2 triple
Bathrooms: 14 private
Bed & breakfast

per night:	£min	£max
Single	33.75	36.00
Double	36.50	41.00

Lunch available
Evening meal 1830 (last orders 2330)
Parking for 150
Cards accepted: Access, Visa, Amex

Rose Cottage ♠
✦✦✦

Longsight Road, Clayton Le Dale, Blackburn BB1 9EX
☎ Mellor (0254) 813223
Fax (0254) 813831
100-year-old cottage, on A59, at the gateway to the Ribble Valley, 5 miles from M6 junction 31.
Bedrooms: 1 double, 2 twin
Bathrooms: 2 private, 1 public
Bed & breakfast

per night:	£min	£max
Single	17.00	20.00
Double	28.00	32.00

Parking for 3

Please mention this guide when making a booking.

BLACKPOOL
Lancashire
Map ref 4A1

Largest fun resort in the North with Blackpool Pleasure Beach, piers, tram rides, sandy beaches and the famous Tower. Among its annual events are the Milk Race, the Veteran Car Run and the spectacular autumn illuminations.
Tourist Information Centre
☎ (0253) 21623 or 25212 or (high season) 403223

Ashcroft Hotel ♠
✦✦ COMMENDED

42 King Edward Avenue, Blackpool FY2 9TA
☎ (0253) 351538
Small friendly hotel off Queens Promenade, 2 minutes from sea and Gynn Gardens. Offering personal service. Cleanliness assured.
Bedrooms: 4 single, 2 double, 1 twin, 3 triple
Bathrooms: 2 public
Bed & breakfast

per night:	£min	£max
Single	15.00	18.00
Double	30.00	36.00

Half board

per person:	£min	£max
Daily	19.00	22.00
Weekly	123.00	151.00

Evening meal from 1700
Parking for 3
Cards accepted: Access, Visa

Sunray ♠
✦✦✦ COMMENDED

42 Knowle Avenue, Blackpool FY2 9TQ
☎ (0253) 351937
Modern semi in quiet residential part of north Blackpool. Friendly personal service and care. 1.75 miles north of tower along promenade. Turn right at Uncle Tom's Cabin. Sunray is about 300 yards on left.
Bedrooms: 3 single, 2 double, 2 twin, 2 triple
Bathrooms: 9 private, 1 public
Bed & breakfast

per night:	£min	£max
Single	23.00	29.00
Double	46.00	58.00

Half board

per person:	£min	£max
Daily	33.00	39.00
Weekly	198.00	234.00

Evening meal 1750 (last orders 1500)
Parking for 6
Open January-November
Cards accepted: Access, Visa

BOLTON
Greater Manchester
Map ref 4A1

Former cotton town with Civil War connections, now has one of the finest shopping centres in the region. Attractions include Hall i' th' Wood, Smithill's Hall, Central Museum, Art Gallery and the award-winning Octagon Theatre.
Tourist Information Centre
☎ (0204) 364333

Commercial Royal Hotel
✦✦✦ COMMENDED

13-15 Bolton Road, Moses Gate, Farnworth, Bolton BL4 7JN
☎ (0204) 73661
Fax (0204) 74147
New, quality hotel offering a high standard of service and facilities rarely found in small hotels. Two minutes from motorway network, 15 minutes from Manchester, 5 minutes from Bolton Tourist Information Centre.
Bedrooms: 6 single, 3 double, 1 twin
Bathrooms: 6 private, 2 public
Bed & breakfast

per night:	£min	£max
Single	22.00	37.00
Double	34.00	39.00

Half board

per person:	£min	£max
Daily	30.00	44.00
Weekly	200.00	290.00

Evening meal 1830 (last orders 2200)
Parking for 15
Cards accepted: Access, Visa, Diners, Amex

BOLTON-LE-SANDS
Lancashire
Map ref 5A3

Village on the main A6 trunk road with the picturesque Lancaster Canal passing through it. An ideal touring base.

Thwaite End Farm
✦✦

A6 Road, Bolton-le-Sands, Carnforth LA5 9TN
☎ Carnforth (0524) 732551
20-acre livestock farm. 17th C farmhouse in an ideal area for breaking your journey to and from Scotland. Well placed for touring the Lake District and Lancashire. Self-catering cottage also available.
Bedrooms: 2 double, 1 twin
Bathrooms: 2 private, 2 public

Continued ▶

NORTH WEST

BOLTON-LE-SANDS
Continued

Bed & breakfast
per night:	£min	£max
Single	17.50	18.50
Double	34.00	38.00

Parking for 4

BROXTON
Cheshire
Map ref 4A2

Egerton Arms Hotel
HIGHLY COMMENDED

Whitchurch Road, Broxton, Chester CH3 9JW
☎ Chester (0829) 782241
Fax (0829) 782352
Recently renovated rural public house/restaurant set in pleasant countryside on the main Chester to Whitchurch road (A41). Prices are per room.
Bedrooms: 2 single, 2 double, 1 twin, 2 triple
Bathrooms: 7 private

Bed & breakfast
per night:	£min	£max
Single	35.00	35.00
Double	40.00	40.00

Half board
per person:	£min	£max
Daily	60.00	75.00
Weekly	420.00	525.00

Lunch available
Evening meal 1800 (last orders 2200)
Parking for 100
Cards accepted: Access, Visa

BURNLEY
Lancashire
Map ref 4B1

"A town amidst the Pennines", alongside the Leeds-Liverpool canal. Townley Hall has fine period rooms and the entrance hall houses an art gallery and museum. The Kay-Shuttleworth collection of lace and embroidery can be seen at Gawthorpe Hall (National Trust).
Tourist Information Centre
☎ (0282) 455485

Ormerod Hotel
COMMENDED

121-123 Ormerod Road, Burnley BB11 3QW
☎ (0282) 423155
Small bed and breakfast hotel in quiet, pleasant surroundings facing local parks. Recently refurbished, all en-suite facilities. 5 minutes from town centre.
Bedrooms: 4 single, 2 double, 2 twin, 2 triple
Bathrooms: 10 private

Bed & breakfast
per night:	£min	£max
Single	19.00	23.00
Double	35.00	37.00

Parking for 7

BURY
Greater Manchester
Map ref 4B1

Famous for its huge open market and East Lancashire Steam Railway. Birthplace of Sir Robert Peel, founder of the police force and Prime Minister.
Tourist Information Centre
☎ 061-705 5111

Loe Farm Country House
COMMENDED

Redisher Lane, Hawkshaw, Bury, Lancashire BL8 4HX
☎ Tottington (0204) 883668
19-acre horses farm. Only 5 miles from M62, M61 and M66. All bedrooms have private facilities, radio, TV and tea/coffee making facilities.
Bedrooms: 4 double, 2 twin
Bathrooms: 6 private

Bed & breakfast
per night:	£min	£max
Single	25.00	
Double	38.00	

Half board
per person:	£min	£max
Daily	35.50	

Evening meal from 1800
Parking for 18
Cards accepted: Access, Visa

CHEADLE
Greater Manchester
Map ref 4B2

Curzon House
Listed

3 Curzon Road, Heald Green, Cheadle, Cheshire SK8 3LN
☎ 061-436 2804 & 430 5010
Detached house, fully modernised and tastefully decorated, in quarter acre of private beautiful gardens. Sun lounge. 5 minutes from Manchester Airport.
Bedrooms: 1 single, 1 double, 1 twin
Bathrooms: 2 public

Bed & breakfast
per night:	£min	£max
Single	15.00	20.00
Double	25.00	30.00

Parking for 3

CHESTER
Cheshire
Map ref 4A2

Roman and medieval walled city rich in architectural and archaeological treasures. Fine timber-framed and plaster buildings. Shopping in the Rows (galleried arcades reached by steps from the street). 14th C cathedral, castle and zoo.
Tourist Information Centre
☎ (0244) 317962 or 351609 or 318916

Cheyney Lodge Hotel
APPROVED

77-79 Cheyney Road, Chester CH1 4BS
☎ (0244) 381925
Small, friendly hotel of unusual design, featuring indoor garden and fish pond. 10 minutes' walk from city centre and on main bus route. Personally supervised with emphasis on good food.
Bedrooms: 5 double, 2 twin, 1 triple
Bathrooms: 7 private, 1 public

Bed & breakfast
per night:	£min	£max
Single		24.00
Double	38.00	42.00

Half board
per person:	£min	£max
Daily	26.50	29.50

Lunch available
Evening meal 1800 (last orders 2100)
Parking for 12
Cards accepted: Access, Visa

Eaton House

36 Eaton Road, Handbridge, Chester CH4 7EN
☎ (0244) 671346
140-year-old Victorian house with all modern facilities, in pleasant conservation area, near river and town centre.
Bedrooms: 2 double, 1 triple
Bathrooms: 2 private, 1 public

Bed & breakfast
per night:	£min	£max
Double	25.00	30.00

Parking for 5

Golborne Manor

Platts Lane, Hatton Heath, Chester CH3 9AN
☎ Tattenhall (0829) 70310
19th C manor house renovated to a high standard, set in 3.5 acres. Lovely rural setting with fine views. 5 miles south of Chester, off A41 Whitchurch road, turning right just after DP Motors. Ample parking.
Bedrooms: 1 twin, 1 family room
Bathrooms: 2 private, 1 public

NORTH WEST

Bed & breakfast
per night:	£min	£max
Single	20.00	25.00
Double	35.00	38.00

Parking for 6

Moorings
HIGHLY COMMENDED

14 Sandy Lane, Chester CH3 5UL
☎ (0244) 324485
Award-winning B & B in elegant riverside Victorian house with terraced gardens to River Dee. Idyllic rural aspect yet within easy walking distance of city centre.
Bedrooms: 1 double, 1 twin
Bathrooms: 1 private, 1 public
Bed & breakfast
per night:	£min	£max
Single	18.00	18.00
Double	28.00	36.00

Open February-December

Tickeridge House

Whitchurch Road, Milton Green, Chester CH3 9DS
☎ Tattenhall (0829) 70443
Chester 5 miles on A41. Set in 3 acres of gardens. All rooms on ground floor with comfortable beds and prettily decorated. A warm welcome awaits.
Bedrooms: 1 single, 1 double, 1 triple
Bathrooms: 1 private, 2 public
Bed & breakfast
per night:	£min	£max
Single	15.00	20.00
Double	30.00	38.00

Parking for 6
Cards accepted: Visa

CHORLEY
Lancashire
Map ref 4A1

Located in the heart of Lancashire, Chorley has a busy market town atmosphere. Jacobean Astley Hall, set in extensive parkland, has fine furniture and long gallery with shovel-board table.

Astley House Hotel
COMMENDED

3 Southport Road, Chorley PR7 1LB
☎ (0257) 272315
An elegant Victorian house with 20th C comforts. Just a few minutes' walk from Chorley town centre and park.
Bedrooms: 4 single, 2 twin
Bathrooms: 3 private, 1 public
Bed & breakfast
per night:	£min	£max
Single	19.00	24.00
Double	38.00	38.00

Evening meal from 1800
Parking for 6
Cards accepted: Access, Visa, Amex

The Original Farmers Arms
Listed COMMENDED

Towngate, Eccleston, Chorley PR7 5QS
☎ Eccleston (0257) 451594
Village pub and restaurant with a warm and friendly atmosphere offering an extensive menu of home-made dishes at reasonable prices, served all day and every day 12 noon to 10pm.
Bedrooms: 2 double, 2 twin
Bathrooms: 1 private, 1 public
Bed & breakfast
per night:	£min	£max
Single		20.00	25.00
Double		30.00	35.00

Lunch available
Evening meal 1200 (last orders 2200)
Parking for 36
Cards accepted: Access, Visa

CLITHEROE
Lancashire
Map ref 4A1

Intriguing town with the castle as its chief attraction. Excellent base for touring the Ribble Valley, Trough of Bowland and Pennine moorland. Country market on Tuesdays and Saturdays.
Tourist Information Centre
☎ (0200) 25566

Lower Standen Farm

Whalley Road, Clitheroe BB7 1PP
☎ (0200) 24176
140-acre mixed farm. 17th C farmhouse. Excellent for walking holidays.
Bedrooms: 2 double, 1 twin
Bathrooms: 1 public, 2 private showers
Bed & breakfast
per night:	£min	£max
Single	14.00	14.00
Double	28.00	28.00

Parking for 3

COLNE
Lancashire
Map ref 4B1

Old market town with mixed industries bordering the moorland Bronte country. Nearby are the ruins of Wycoller House, featured in Charlotte Bronte's "Jane Eyre" as Ferndean Manor.

148 Keighley Road
Listed HIGHLY COMMENDED

Colne BB8 0PJ
☎ (0282) 862002

Edwardian town house with many original features. Comfortable accommodation with easy access to Pendle, Bronte country and the Yorkshire Dales. Non-smokers only please.
Bedrooms: 1 single, 2 double
Bathrooms: 1 public
Bed & breakfast
per night:	£min	£max
Single	15.00	15.00
Double	30.00	30.00

Parking for 1

Middle Beardshaw Head Farm
Listed APPROVED

Burnley Road, Trawden, Colne BB8 8PP
☎ (0282) 865257
15-acre dairy farm. 17th-18th C Lancashire longhouse with oak beams, panelling, log fires. Panoramic views with pools, woods and stream. Half mile from Trawden. Self-catering cottage and caravan and camping site nearby.
Bedrooms: 2 single, 1 family room
Bathrooms: 1 public, 1 private shower
Bed & breakfast
per night:	£min	£max
Single	15.00	17.50
Double	30.00	35.00

Half board
per person:	£min	£max
Daily	23.00	25.50
Weekly	150.00	300.00

Lunch available
Evening meal 1900 (last orders 2030)
Parking for 10

Turnpike House
COMMENDED

6 Keighley Road, Colne BB8 OJL
☎ (0282) 869596
Large Victorian house, garden. Ideal for exploring Bronte country, Pendle, Forest of Bowland, Yorkshire Dales. Close to coach and rail stations. A warm welcome awaits you.
Bedrooms: 1 single, 1 double, 1 triple
Bathrooms: 1 public
Bed & breakfast
per night:	£min	£max
Single	13.00	14.00
Double	26.00	28.00

Evening meal 1800 (last orders 1930)
Parking for 1

National Crown ratings were correct at the time of going to press but are subject to change. Please check at the time of booking.

NORTH WEST

CONGLETON
Cheshire
Map ref 4B2

Important cattle market and silk town on the River Dane, now concerned with general textiles. Nearby are Little Moreton Hall, a Tudor house surrounded by a moat, the Bridestones, a chambered tomb, and Mow Cop, topped by a folly.
Tourist Information Centre
☎ *(0260) 271095*

Sandhole Farm
HIGHLY COMMENDED

Hulme Walfield, Congleton CW12 2JH
☎ Marton Heath (0260) 224419
Fax (0260) 224766
200-acre arable and mixed farm. Charming en-suite accommodation in tastefully converted stables adjacent to attractive traditional farmhouse. Two miles north of Congleton on A34.
Bedrooms: 3 single, 2 double, 7 twin, 1 triple
Bathrooms: 8 private, 2 public

Bed & breakfast
per night:	£min	£max
Single	25.00	28.00
Double	37.00	40.00

Parking for 40
Cards accepted: Access, Visa

Yew Tree Farm
Listed COMMENDED

North Rode, Congleton CW12 2PF
☎ North Rode (0260) 223569
77-acre mixed farm. Peaceful village setting. 20 minutes from M6. Guests are invited to look around the farm and get to know the animals.
Bedrooms: 1 double, 2 twin
Bathrooms: 1 private, 1 public

Bed & breakfast
per night:	£min	£max
Single	15.00	20.00
Double	28.00	35.00

Half board
per person:	£min	£max
Daily	23.00	26.00

Evening meal 1800 (last orders 1900)
Parking for 3

Individual proprietors have supplied all details of accommodation. Although we do check for accuracy, we advise you to confirm the information at the time of booking.

DUTTON
Lancashire
Map ref 4A1

Entirely surrounded by agricultural land, Dutton lies on the south-eastern side of Longridge Fell.

Smithy Farm
Listed

Huntingdonhall Lane, Dutton, Longridge, Preston PR3 2ZT
☎ Ribchester (0254) 878250
Set in the beautiful Ribble Valley, 20 minutes from the M6. Homely atmosphere, children half price.
Bedrooms: 2 double, 1 twin
Bathrooms: 1 public

Bed & breakfast
per night:	£min	£max
Single	12.00	12.00
Double	24.00	24.00

Evening meal 1900 (last orders 2130)
Parking for 4

GARSTANG
Lancashire
Map ref 4A1

Picturesque country market town. Regarded as the gateway to the fells, it stands on the Lancaster Canal and is popular as a cruising centre. Close by are the remains of Greenhalgh Castle (no public access) and the Bleasdale Circle. Discovery Centre.
Tourist Information Centre
☎ *(0995) 602125*

Guy's Thatched Hamlet Canal-Side
COMMENDED

St. Michael's Road, Bilsborrow, Garstang, Preston PR3 0RS
☎ Brock (0995) 640849 & 640010
Fax (0995) 640141

Friendly, family-run thatched canalside tavern, restaurant, pizzeria, lodgings, craft shops and cricket pitch. Off junction 32 of M6 then 3 miles north on A6 to Garstang. Preston 6 miles.
Bedrooms: 28 double, 4 triple
Bathrooms: 32 private

Bed & breakfast
per night:	£min	£max
Single	33.75	50.00
Double	36.50	55.00

Half board
per person:	£min	£max
Daily	33.00	48.50

Lunch available
Evening meal 1800 (last orders 2330)
Parking for 300
Cards accepted: Access, Visa, Amex, Switch

GREAT ECCLESTON
Lancashire
Map ref 4A1

Cartford Hotel

Cartford Lane, Little Eccleston, Preston PR3 0YP
☎ (0995) 70166
A country riverside pub and coaching inn, with 1.5 miles of fishing rights. Within easy reach of Blackpool and the Lake District.
Bedrooms: 1 single, 4 double, 1 twin
Bathrooms: 5 private, 1 public

Bed & breakfast
per night:	£min	£max
Single	24.50	28.50
Double	39.50	42.50

Lunch available
Evening meal 1900 (last orders 2130)
Parking for 100
Cards accepted: Access, Visa

HOLMES CHAPEL
Cheshire
Map ref 4A2

Large village with some interesting 18th C buildings and St Luke's Church encased in brick hiding the 15th C original.

Tiree
Listed

5 Middlewich Road, Cranage, Holmes Chapel, Crewe CW4 8HG
☎ (0477) 533716
Modern house set in open country 3 miles from the M6 (junction 18) and close to the A50, 2 miles north of Holmes Chapel.
Bedrooms: 1 single, 1 double, 1 twin
Bathrooms: 1 public

Bed & breakfast
per night:	£min	£max
Single	15.00	15.00
Double	28.00	28.00

Parking for 4

Map references apply to the colour maps at the back of this guide.

NORTH WEST

HOYLAKE
Merseyside
Map ref 4A2

Overlooking the North Wales coastline across the River Dee, this residential resort has good beaches, a 4-mile promenade and, nearby, the Royal Liverpool Golf Club. Variety of bird life on Hilbre Islands accessible on foot at low tide.

Green Lodge Hotel
COMMENDED
2 Stanley Road, Hoylake, Wirral L47 1HW
☎ 051-632 2321
Fax 051-632 6871
Recently renovated public house and restaurant with bedrooms offering high standard facilities. Close to Hoylake village and adjacent to Royal Liverpool Golf Club. Popular for golf holidays. Prices are per room.
Bedrooms: 3 double, 2 triple
Bathrooms: 5 private

Bed & breakfast
per night:	£min	£max
Double	34.50	34.50

Lunch available
Evening meal 1730 (last orders 2130)
Parking for 40
Cards accepted: Access, Visa

HYDE
Greater Manchester
Map ref 4B2

Needhams Farm
COMMENDED
Uplands Road, Werneth Low, Gee Cross, Hyde, Cheshire SK14 3AQ
☎ 061-368 4610
Fax 061-367 9106
30-acre beef farm. 500-year-old farmhouse with exposed beams in all rooms and an open fire in bar/dining room. Excellent views. Well placed for Manchester city and the airport.
Bedrooms: 1 single, 3 double, 1 twin, 1 triple
Bathrooms: 4 private, 1 public

Bed & breakfast
per night:	£min	£max
Single	18.00	20.00
Double	32.00	34.00

Half board
per person:	£min	£max
Daily	25.00	27.00

Lunch available
Evening meal 1900 (last orders 2130)
Parking for 12
Cards accepted: Access, Visa

INGLEWHITE
Lancashire
Map ref 4A1

Latus Hall Farm
Listed APPROVED
Inglewhite, Preston PR5 2LN
☎ Brock (0995) 40368

100-acre dairy farm. 300-year-old farmhouse, 7 miles north of Preston, 2.5 miles from A6 at Bilsborrow. Oak beams, log fires, and a warm welcome.
Bedrooms: 1 single, 1 double, 1 twin
Bathrooms: 1 public

Bed & breakfast
per night:	£min	£max
Single	13.50	
Double	27.00	

Parking for 6

KNUTSFORD
Cheshire
Map ref 4A2

Derives its name from Canute, King of the Danes, said to have forded the local stream. Ancient and colourful May Day celebrations. Nearby is the Georgian mansion of Tatton Park.
Tourist Information Centre
☎ *(0565) 632611 or 632210*

Laburnum Cottage Guest House
HIGHLY COMMENDED
Knutsford Road, Mobberley, Knutsford WA16 7PU
☎ Mobberley (0565) 872464
Fax (0565) 872464
Small country house set amidst Cheshire countryside on B5085 close to Tatton Park, 6 miles from Manchester Airport, 4 miles from Wilmslow, 4 miles from M6 exit 19 and 2 miles from M56. Pretty garden and log fires, taxi service to airport. Non-smokers only please.
Bedrooms: 2 single, 1 double, 2 twin
Bathrooms: 3 private, 1 public

Bed & breakfast
per night:	£min	£max
Single	25.00	38.00
Double	40.00	46.00

Evening meal from 1830
Parking for 8

LANCASTER
Lancashire
Map ref 4A1

Interesting old county town on the River Lune with history dating back to Roman times. Norman castle, St Mary's Church, Customs House, City and Maritime Museums, Ashton Memorial and Butterfly House are among places of note. Good centre for touring the Lake District.
Tourist Information Centre
☎ *(0524) 32878*

Lancaster Town House
COMMENDED
11 Newton Terrace, Caton Road, Lancaster LA1 3PB
☎ (0524) 65527
Ideal for touring the area, close to M6 motorway. All rooms en-suite with colour TV. Full breakfast menu.
Bedrooms: 2 single, 3 double, 1 twin
Bathrooms: 6 private

Bed & breakfast
per night:	£min	£max
Single		22.00
Double		34.50

Middle Holly Cottage
COMMENDED
Middle Holly, Forton, Preston PR3 1AH
☎ Forton (0524) 792399
Former coaching inn, set in rural surroundings. Adjacent A6 Lancaster road, 7 miles south of city, 3 miles south of M6 junction 33. Convenient for all North Lancashire areas and only 30 minutes' drive to Lakes.
Bedrooms: 1 single, 2 double, 1 twin, 1 triple
Bathrooms: 5 private

Bed & breakfast
per night:	£min	£max
Single	22.50	29.50
Double	34.50	39.50

Parking for 11
Cards accepted: Access, Visa

The Old Mill House
Waggon Road, Lower Dolphinholme, Lancaster LA2 9AX
☎ Forton (0524) 791855
17th C mill house with extensive landscaped gardens on River Wyre. Private woodland and ponds, adjacent to Forest of Bowland. 5 minutes from junction 33 of M6.
Bedrooms: 2 double, 1 twin
Bathrooms: 1 private, 1 public

Continued ▶

NORTH WEST

LANCASTER
Continued

Bed & breakfast
per night:	£min	£max
Single	16.50	25.00
Double	33.00	46.00

Half board
per person:	£min	£max
Daily	27.00	47.50
Weekly	175.00	225.00

Evening meal 1900 (last orders 1200)
Parking for 5

LIVERPOOL
Merseyside
Map ref 4A2

Exciting city, famous for the Beatles, football, the Grand National, theatres and nightlife. Liverpool has a magnificent waterfront, 2 cathedrals, 3 historic houses, museum, galleries and a host of attractions.
Tourist Information Centre
☎ 051-709 3631

Anna's

65 Dudlow Lane, Calderstones, Liverpool L18 2EY
☎ 051-722 3708
Fax 051-722 8699
Large family house with friendly atmosphere, in select residential area close to all amenities. Direct transport routes to city centre. 1 mile from end of M62 motorway.
Bedrooms: 1 double, 3 twin
Bathrooms: 1 public

Bed & breakfast
per night:	£min	£max
Single	17.50	18.50
Double	30.00	32.00

Parking for 6

Blenheim Guest House
Listed COMMENDED

37 Aigburth Drive, Liverpool L17 4JE
☎ 051-727 7380
Large Victorian villa overlooking Sefton Park, offering first class bed and breakfast accommodation at a very reasonable price.
Bedrooms: 3 single, 2 double, 4 twin, 5 triple
Bathrooms: 4 public

Bed & breakfast
per night:	£min	£max
Single	17.50	23.00
Double	29.00	35.00

Half board
per person:	£min	£max
Daily	21.00	24.00
Weekly	147.00	168.00

Parking for 10

Somersby Guest House
COMMENDED

57 Green Lane, off Menlove Avenue, Liverpool L18 2EP
☎ 051-722 7549
Attractive house with secure parking, delightfully situated in exclusive area with easy access to city centre, airport and M62.
Bedrooms: 2 double, 1 twin
Bathrooms: 2 public

Bed & breakfast
per night:	£min	£max
Single	17.50	20.00
Double	35.00	35.00

Parking for 6

MACCLESFIELD
Cheshire
Map ref 4B2

Former silk-manufacturing town with cobbled streets and picturesque cottages overlooking Bollin Valley. West Park Museum and Art Gallery and Gawsworth Hall are places of interest.
Tourist Information Centre
☎ (0625) 504114

Sandpit Farm

Messuage Lane, Marton, Macclesfield SK11 9HS
☎ Marton Heath (0260) 224254
110-acre arable farm. Comfortable, oak-beamed house. Hot and cold water in single. Twin and double rooms en-suite. Convenient for stately homes and National Trust properties. Easy access to the Peak District, Chester and Manchester Airport. 4 miles north of Congleton and 1 mile west of the A34.
Bedrooms: 1 single, 1 double, 1 twin
Bathrooms: 2 private, 1 public

Bed & breakfast
per night:	£min	£max
Single	13.00	17.00
Double	34.00	40.00

Parking for 4

MALPAS
Cheshire
Map ref 4A2

Millhey Farm

Barton, Malpas SY14 7HY
☎ Broxton (0829) 782431
140-acre mixed farm. Typical, lovely Cheshire black and white part-timbered farmhouse in conservation area, 9 miles from Chester, close to Welsh Border country. On A534, just off A41.
Bedrooms: 1 single, 1 triple, 1 family room
Bathrooms: 1 private, 1 public

Bed & breakfast
per night:	£min	£max
Single		14.00
Double	27.00	28.00

Parking for 2

The Old Stables
Listed

Threapwood, Malpas SY14 7AN
☎ Threapwood (0948) 770249
Walled garden and patio. Rooms with abundant beams. Off B5069 Malpas/Wrexham road from Malpas (3 miles) over Clywd border. Take second left turn into courtyard.
Bedrooms: 1 double, 1 twin
Bathrooms: 1 public

Bed & breakfast
per night:	£min	£max
Single		16.00
Double		32.00

Parking for 6

Tilston Lodge
HIGHLY COMMENDED

Tilston, Malpas SY14 7DR
☎ Broxton (0829) 250223
12-acre livestock & poultry farm. Comfortable Victorian farmhouse in conservation village. Rare breed farm animals. Spacious, beautifully decorated rooms, friendly service. Ideal for Chester and North Wales.
Bedrooms: 1 single, 1 twin, 1 triple
Bathrooms: 2 private, 2 public, 1 private shower

Bed & breakfast
per night:	£min	£max
Single	17.50	26.00
Double	40.00	44.00

Evening meal from 1830
Parking for 10

There are separate sections in this guide listing groups specialising in farm holidays and accommodation which is especially suitable for young people and organised groups.

NORTH WEST

MANCHESTER

Greater Manchester
Map ref 4B1

Manchester, City of Drama 1994, is full of variety and vitality. It offers the liveliest nightlife in Britain: exclusive restaurants jostle with pavement cafes; shops range from boutiques to antiques. The city is rich in historic interest.
Tourist Information Centre
☎ 061-234 3157/8

Baron Hotel ♠

116 Palatine Road, West Didsbury, Manchester M20 9ZA
☎ 061-445 3877 & 434 3688
Fax (0203) 520680
Comfortable, friendly, family-run hotel, all rooms with en-suite facilities. Ten minutes from Manchester Airport and city centre. Half a mile from the motorway network.
Bedrooms: 10 single, 5 twin, 1 double
Bathrooms: 16 private

Bed & breakfast
per night: £min £max
Single 25.00 30.00
Double 35.00 45.00
Half board
per person: £min £max
Daily 32.00 38.00
Evening meal 1900 (last orders 2030)
Parking for 25
Cards accepted: Access, Visa

Ebor Hotel ♠

402 Wilbraham Road, Chorlton-cum-Hardy, Manchester M21 1UH
☎ 061-881 1911 & 881 4855
Hotel offering comfortable accommodation and friendly service, within easy reach of airport, Manchester city centre and motorway network.
Bedrooms: 6 single, 3 double, 3 twin, 3 triple, 1 family room
Bathrooms: 7 private, 3 public

Bed & breakfast
per night: £min £max
Single 21.00 26.00
Double 31.00 36.00
Half board
per person: £min £max
Daily 27.00 32.00
Weekly 189.00 238.00
Evening meal 1830 (last orders 1700)
Parking for 20
Cards accepted: Access, Visa, Amex

Parkside Guest House ♠

58 Cromwell Road, Off Edge Lane, Stretford, Manchester M32 8QJ
☎ 061-865 2860
Clean, friendly guesthouse in a quiet, pleasant area near Old Trafford football/cricket grounds. 15 minutes from airport and city by Metro. M63 exit 7. Children over 7 welcome. Family rooms available.
Bedrooms: 1 double, 1 twin, 1 triple, 1 family room
Bathrooms: 4 private, 1 public
Bed & breakfast
per night: £min £max
Single 16.50 18.50
Double 30.00 32.00
Parking for 3

MANCHESTER AIRPORT

See under Alderley Edge, Altrincham, Hyde, Knutsford, Manchester, Salford, Stockport, Wilmslow

---

Individual proprietors have supplied all details of accommodation. Although we do check for accuracy, we advise you to confirm the information at the time of booking.

NANTWICH

Cheshire
Map ref 4A2

Old market town on the River Weaver made prosperous in Roman times by salt springs. Fire destroyed the town in 1583 and many buildings were rebuilt in Elizabethan style. Churche's Mansion (open to the public) survived the fire.
Tourist Information Centre
☎ (0270) 610983 or 610880

Henhull Hall

Welshmans Lane, Nantwich CW5 6AD
☎ (0270) 624158
240-acre mixed farm. Spacious and beautifully appointed farmhouse on the edge of the historic town of Nantwich and bordering the Shropshire Union Canal.
Bedrooms: 1 double, 1 twin
Bathrooms: 2 private, 1 public
Bed & breakfast
per night: £min £max
Single 18.00 20.00
Double 36.00 40.00
Parking for 4
Open January-November

Laburnum House Farm

Hearns Lane, Larden Green, Faddiley, Nantwich CW5 8JL
☎ Faddiley (0270) 74378

19-acre livestock farm. Lovely three-roomed suite with private balcony. Peace, privacy and a warm welcome guaranteed. Central for Chester and the
Continued ▶

Hotel Cornelius

YOUR COMFORT IS OUR COMFORT

* 36 EN-SUITES SATELLITE TV & D.D. TELEPHONE, TEA/COFFEE FACILITIES
* 24 HR. ROOM SERVICE
* LUXURIOUS BRIDAL SUITE
* 3 FAMILY ROOMS
* WEDDING RECEPTION ROOM FOR 100 GUESTS
* AUTHENTIC ITALIAN RESTAURANT OPEN TO THE PUBLIC
* ENGLISH/CONTINENTAL BREAKFAST
* FULL COLOUR BROCHURE
* MAJOR CREDIT CARDS ACCEPTED

* 3 CONFERENCE ROOMS
* FROM 5 TO 100 PEOPLE
* FULL IN-HOUSE CONFERENCE FACILITIES INCLUDING AUDIO VISUAL & SOUND EQUIPMENT
* IDEAL FOR EXHIBITIONS, TRADE SHOWS, PRODUCT LAUNCHES & BUSINESS MEETINGS
* FREE SECURE PARKING FOR 50 CARS
* 10 MINUTES FROM MANCHESTER AIRPORT & MANCHESTER CITY CENTRE

175 MANCHESTER ROAD, CHORLTON CUM HARDY, MANCHESTER, M16 OED.
TELEPHONE: 061 862 9565 FAX: 061 862 9028
5 Minutes from both Man UTD & CITY Football Clubs

NORTH WEST

NANTWICH
Continued

Potteries. Extra beds by arrangement. Discounts available.
Bedrooms: 1 double
Bathrooms: 1 private

Bed & breakfast
per night:	£min	£max
Single	27.00	33.00
Double	36.00	44.00

Parking for 4

Lea Farm

Wrinehill Road, Wybunbury, Nantwich CW5 7NS
☎ Crewe (0270) 841429
160-acre dairy farm. Charming farmhouse in beautiful gardens where peacocks roam. Comfortable lounge, pool/snooker, fishing pool. Ideal surroundings.
Bedrooms: 2 double, 1 triple
Bathrooms: 1 private, 1 public

Bed & breakfast
per night:	£min	£max
Single	13.00	16.00
Double	26.00	28.00

Half board
per person:	£min	£max
Daily	20.00	23.00
Weekly	130.00	160.00

Evening meal 1800 (last orders 1900)
Parking for 22

Oakland House
HIGHLY COMMENDED

252 Newcastle Road, Blakelow, Shavington, Nantwich CW5 7ET
☎ Crewe (0270) 67134
Friendly welcome, home comforts, rural views. Superior accommodation at reasonable rates. On A500 (A52) 5 miles from M6 junction 16. Within easy reach of historic Nantwich and Chester, Stapeley Water Gardens and Bridgemere Garden World.
Bedrooms: 3 double, 2 twin
Bathrooms: 5 private

Bed & breakfast
per night:	£min	£max
Single	18.00	
Double	30.00	

Parking for 10

Poole Bank Farm
COMMENDED

Poole, Nantwich CW5 6AL
☎ (0270) 625169
260-acre dairy farm. 17th C timbered farmhouse in delightful Cheshire countryside, close to the historic town of Nantwich.
Bedrooms: 2 double, 1 twin

Bathrooms: 1 private, 1 public

Bed & breakfast
per night:	£min	£max
Single	15.00	17.00
Double	25.00	30.00

Parking for 10

NORTHWICH
Cheshire
Map ref 4A2

An important salt-producing town since Roman times, Northwich has been replanned with a modern shopping centre and a number of black and white buildings. Unique Anderton boat-lift on northern outskirts of town.

Barratwich
Listed

Cuddington Lane, Cuddington, Northwich CW8 2SZ
☎ Sandiway (0606) 882412
Attractive cottage set in lovely countryside, yet only 1 mile from A49 and A556. Close to Delamere Forest, 12 miles from Chester. Comfortable rooms.
Bedrooms: 1 single, 2 twin
Bathrooms: 1 public

Bed & breakfast
per night:	£min	£max
Single	17.00	17.00
Double	30.00	30.00

Half board
per person:	£min	£max
Daily	22.50	22.50
Weekly	150.00	150.00

Evening meal 1900 (last orders 1400)
Parking for 4

Springfield Guest House
COMMENDED

Chester Road, Delamere, Oakmere, Northwich CW8 2HB
☎ Sandiway (0606) 882538
Family guesthouse erected in 1863. On A556 close to Delamere Forest, midway between Chester and M6 motorway junction 19. Manchester Airport 25 minutes' drive.
Bedrooms: 4 single, 1 double, 1 twin, 1 family room
Bathrooms: 2 private, 1 public

Bed & breakfast
per night:	£min	£max
Single	17.50	17.50
Double	30.00	30.00

Evening meal 1800 (last orders 2000)
Parking for 12

Check the introduction to this region for Where to Go, What to See.

OLDHAM
Greater Manchester
Map ref 4B1

The magnificent mill buildings which made Oldham one of the world's leading cotton-spinning towns still dominate the landscape. On the edge of the Peak District, it is now a centre of cultural entertainment and sport.
Tourist Information Centre
☎ 061-627 1024

Boothstead Farm
Listed

Rochdale Road, Denshaw, Oldham OL3 5UE
☎ Saddleworth (0457) 878622 & 874369
200-acre livestock farm. 18th C farmhouse on fringe of Saddleworth (A640) between junctions 21 and 22 of M62 motorway.
Bedrooms: 1 double, 1 twin
Bathrooms: 1 private

Bed & breakfast
per night:	£min	£max
Single	17.00	
Double	32.00	

Parking for 4

PRESTON
Lancashire
Map ref 4A1

Scene of decisive Royalist defeat by Cromwell in the Civil War and later of riots in the Industrial Revolution. Local history exhibited in Harris Museum.
Tourist Information Centre
☎ (0772) 253731

Brook House Guest House
COMMENDED

544 Blackpool Road, Ashton, Preston PR2 1HY
☎ (0772) 728684
Detached property 10 minutes from town centre and on bus route. TV lounge, car park, tea/coffee facilities, some en-suite rooms. Non-smoking establishment.
Bedrooms: 2 single, 1 double, 1 twin
Bathrooms: 2 private, 1 public

Bed & breakfast
per night:	£min	£max
Single	18.00	30.00
Double	41.00	45.00

Half board
per person:	£min	£max
Daily	27.50	39.00
Weekly	192.50	273.00

Evening meal 1800 (last orders 1800)
Parking for 4
Cards accepted: Access, Visa

NORTH WEST

Olde Duncombe House
HIGHLY COMMENDED

Garstang Road, Bilsborrow, Preston
PR3 0RE
☎ Brock (0995) 640336
In the beautiful Ribble Valley next to the Lancaster Canal, convenient for canal boat enthusiasts. 4 miles north of M6 junction 32.
Bedrooms: 1 single, 5 double, 2 twin, 2 triple
Bathrooms: 10 private

Bed & breakfast
per night:	£min	£max
Single	29.50	39.50
Double	39.50	49.50

Lunch available
Evening meal 1800 (last orders 2030)
Parking for 12
Cards accepted: Access, Visa

RIBBLE VALLEY
See under Clitheroe, Dutton

ROCHDALE
Greater Manchester
Map ref 4B1

Pennine mill town made prosperous by wool and later cotton-spinning, famous for the Co-operative Movement started in 1844 by a group of Rochdale working men. Birthplace of John Bright (Corn Law opponent) and more recently Gracie Fields. Roman and Bronze Age items in museum.
Tourist Information Centre
☎ (0706) 356192

Leaches Farm Bed and Breakfast
Listed

Leaches Farm, Ashworth Valley, Rochdale, Lancashire OL11 5UN
☎ (0706) 41116/7 & 228520
140-acre livestock farm. 18th C Pennine hill farmhouse with panoramic views and moorland walks. 10 minutes from the M62/M66.
Bedrooms: 1 single, 1 double, 1 twin
Bathrooms: 1 public

Bed & breakfast
per night:	£min	£max
Single	18.00	
Double	34.00	

Parking for 6

The town index towards the back of this guide gives page numbers of all places with accommodation.

ST MICHAEL'S ON WYRE
Lancashire
Map ref 4A1

Village near Blackpool with interesting 13th C church of St Michael containing medieval stained glass window depicting sheep shearing, and clock tower bell made in 1548.

Compton House
COMMENDED

Garstang Road, St Michael's on Wyre, Preston PR3 0TE
☎ (0995) 8378
Well-furnished country house in own grounds in a picturesque village, near M6 and 40 minutes from Lake District. Fishing in the Wyre. Antique restoration/reproduction of furniture undertaken on the premises.
Bedrooms: 1 single, 1 double, 2 twin
Bathrooms: 4 private

Bed & breakfast
per night:	£min	£max
Single	15.00	17.50
Double	30.00	35.00

Parking for 6

SALFORD
Greater Manchester
Map ref 4B1

Industrial city close to Manchester with Roman Catholic cathedral and university. Lowry often painted Salford's industrial architecture and much of his work is in the local art gallery.

White Lodge Private Hotel

87-89 Great Cheetham Street West, Broughton, Salford, Lancashire M7 9JA
☎ 061-792 3047
Small, family-run hotel, close to city centre amenities and sporting facilities.
Bedrooms: 3 single, 3 double, 3 twin
Bathrooms: 2 public

Bed & breakfast
per night:	£min	£max
Single	19.00	
Double	33.00	

Parking for 6

National Crown ratings were correct at the time of going to press but are subject to change. Please check at the time of booking.

SANDBACH
Cheshire
Map ref 4A2

Small Cheshire town, originally important for salt production. Contains narrow, winding streets, timbered houses and a cobbled market-place. Town square has 2 Anglo-Saxon crosses to commemorate the conversion to Christianity of the king of Mercia's son.
Tourist Information Centre
☎ (0270) 760460

Canal Centre and Village Store
Listed COMMENDED

Hassall Green, Sandbach CW11 0YB
☎ Crewe (0270) 762366

The house and shop, built circa 1777 at the side of Lock 57 on the Trent and Mersey Canal, have served canal users for over 200 years. Off A533 near Sandbach and junction 17 on M6 - signposted. Gift shop, tearooms, store and licensed restaurant (Tues-Sat from 7pm).
Bedrooms: 2 single, 1 double, 1 twin
Bathrooms: 1 public

Bed & breakfast
per night:	£min	£max
Single	14.50	16.00
Double	29.00	32.00

Evening meal 1900 (last orders 2130)
Parking for 5
Cards accepted: Access, Visa

Moss Cottage Farm
Listed COMMENDED

Hassall Road, Winterley, Sandbach CW11 0RU
☎ Crewe (0270) 583018
Beamed farmhouse in quiet location just off A534, with lovely walks, fishing and golf. All rooms have tea-making facilities.
Bedrooms: 1 single, 1 double, 1 twin
Bathrooms: 2 public

Bed & breakfast
per night:	£min	£max
Single	13.50	15.00
Double	27.00	30.00

Continued ▶

We advise you to confirm your booking in writing.

NORTH WEST

SANDBACH
Continued

**Half board
per person:** £min £max
Daily 22.00 22.00
Weekly 143.50 143.50
Evening meal 1700 (last orders 2000)
Parking for 10

SINGLETON
Lancashire
Map ref 4A1

Ancient parish dating from 1175, mentioned in Domesday Book. Chapel and day school dating back to 1865. Mainly rural area to the north of St Anne's.

Old Castle Farm
Listed APPROVED

Garstang Road, Singleton, Blackpool
FY6 8ND
☎ Poulton-le-Fylde (0253) 883839
Take junction 3 off M55, follow Fleetwood sign to first traffic lights. Turn right, travel 200 yards on A586 to bungalow on the right.
Bedrooms: 1 double, 1 twin, 1 triple
Bathrooms: 1 public
**Bed & breakfast
per night:** £min £max
Single 15.00
Double 30.00
Parking for 20
Open April-October

SOUTHPORT
Merseyside
Map ref 4A1

Delightful resort noted for its gardens, long sandy beach and many golf-courses, particularly Royal Birkdale. Attractions include Atkinson Art Gallery, Southport Railway Centre, funfair and the annual Southport Flower Show. Excellent shopping.
Tourist Information Centre
☎ (0704) 533333

Sandy Brook Farm

52 Wyke Cop Road, Scarisbrick, Southport PR8 5LR
☎ Scarisbrick (0704) 880337

27-acre arable farm. Small comfortable farmhouse in rural area of Scarisbrick, offering a friendly welcome. 3.5 miles from seaside town of Southport.
Bedrooms: 1 double, 3 twin, 1 triple, 1 family room
Bathrooms: 6 private
**Bed & breakfast
per night:** £min £max
Single 18.00
Double 29.00
Parking for 9

STOCKPORT
Greater Manchester
Map ref 4B2

Once an important cotton-spinning and manufacturing centre, Stockport has an impressive railway viaduct, a shopping precinct built over the River Mersey and a new leisure complex. Lyme Hall and Vernon Park Museum nearby.
Tourist Information Centre
☎ 061-474 3320/1

Waterfall Farm Cottage
COMMENDED

7 Motcombe Grove, Gatley, Cheadle, Cheshire SK8 3TL
☎ 061-436 4732
Large bungalow in secluded, gladed setting 5 minutes from Manchester Airport, close to motorways and well placed for north-west travel. Weekly terms and evening meals on request.
Bedrooms: 1 double, 1 twin
Bathrooms: 2 private, 1 public
**Bed & breakfast
per night:** £min £max
Single 25.00 30.00
Double 35.00 40.00
Evening meal 1900 (last orders 2100)
Parking for 5
Cards accepted: Amex

National Crown ratings were correct at the time of going to press but are subject to change. Please check at the time of booking.

WEETON
Lancashire
Map ref 4A1

Agricultural area to the north-west of Kirkham. Church dated 1843. Large army camp in parish.

Swarbrick Hall Farm

Singleton Road, Weeton, Preston
PR4 3JJ
☎ Blackpool (0253) 836465
200-acre mixed farm. Georgian farmhouse built in 1802, nestling in beautiful rural countryside of Lancashire.
Bedrooms: 1 family room
Bathrooms: 1 private
**Bed & breakfast
per night:** £min £max
Single 15.00 18.00
Double 30.00 36.00
Parking for 5

WILMSLOW
Cheshire
Map ref 4B2

Residential suburb of Manchester, on the River Bollin and bordered on 3 sides by open country.

Oversley Gardens
Listed COMMENDED

Altrincham Road, Styal, Wilmslow
SK9 4LJ
☎ (0625) 520258
Self-contained en-suite rooms set in rural Cheshire. Private secure car parking and own entrance to rooms. 5 minutes from Manchester Airport.
Bedrooms: 1 double, 2 twin
Bathrooms: 3 private
**Bed & breakfast
per night:** £min £max
Single 25.00
Double 35.00
Parking for 14
Cards accepted: Access, Visa

WIRRAL
Merseyside

See under Hoylake

THE ENGLAND FOR EXCELLENCE AWARDS 1992 WINNERS

The England for Excellence Awards were created by the English Tourist Board to recognise and reward the highest standards of excellence and quality in all major sectors of tourism in England. The coveted Leo statuette, presented each year to winners, has become firmly established as the ultimate accolade in the English tourism industry.

Over the past five years, the Leo has been won by all types and sizes of business with one common attribute – excellence in the facilities and services they offer.

Resort of the Year sponsored by Marks & Spencer
BOURNEMOUTH

Bed and Breakfast Award sponsored by Le Shuttle
THE OLD RECTORY, Ripon

Attraction of the Year sponsored by Blackpool Pleasure Beach Limited
NATIONAL FISHING HERITAGE CENTRE

Hotel of the Year sponsored by Horwath Consulting
THE LANESBOROUGH

TIC of the Year sponsored by Holiday Property Bond Limited
FONTWELL TIC

Self-Catering Holiday of the Year sponsored by Hoseasons Holidays Limited
ANGLERS' PARADISE HOLIDAYS

Tourism and the Environment Award sponsored by Center Parcs Limited
LOSEHILL HALL, PEAK NATIONAL PARK CENTRE

Travel Journalist of the Year sponsored by Forte Plc
PAUL GOGARTY

Hotel Company of the Year sponsored by RCI Europe Limited
HILTON UNITED KINGDOM

Tourism for all Award sponsored by RAC Enterprises Limited
MUSEUM OF SCIENCE AND INDUSTRY IN MANCHESTER

Tourism and the Arts Award sponsored by First Leisure Corporation Plc
GREATER MANCHESTER VISITOR AND CONVENTION BUREAU/MANCHESTER INTERNATIONAL FESTIVAL OF EXPRESSIONISM

Caravan Holiday Park Award sponsored by the National Caravan Council
FOXHUNTER PARK

Tourism Training Award sponsored by The Tussauds Group Limited
LUCKETTS TRAVEL

English Travel Company of the Year sponsored by BTTF
BUTLIN'S LIMITED

Outstanding Contribution to English Tourism Award sponsored by Hilton UK
SIR ANDREW LLOYD WEBBER

Thames Tower
Black's Road
London W6 9EL

English Tourist Board

Yorkshire & Humberside

A unique blend of history, beautiful countryside and coastline, lively cities and a host of attractions – whatever you want from your holiday, you'll find it in Yorkshire and Humberside. There are hundreds of square miles of National Park to explore in the Yorkshire Dales and the North York Moors, with their stunning landscapes, including wind-torn peaks and sleepy valleys, pretty villages and bustling market towns. Cliffs, coves and sandy beaches mingle with quiet fishing villages like Robin Hood's Bay and tiny Staithes, and each of the main resorts of Scarborough, Whitby, Filey, Cleethorpes and Bridlington has an atmosphere of its own. The powerful 19th C industrial heritage of south and west Yorkshire contrasts with the historic houses and abbeys, and for those who wish to learn more there are over 100 museums from award-winning centres to small folk museums.

WHERE TO GO, WHAT TO SEE

The number against each name will help you locate it on the map (page 103).

① Scarborough Millennium
55 Sandside, Scarborough, North Yorkshire YO11 1BR
Tel: Scarborough (0723) 501000
An exciting new attraction on Scarborough's harbourside. The sights, sounds and smells of 1000 years of Scarborough's history.

① Sea Life Centre
Scarborough, North Yorkshire YO12 6RP
Tel: Scarborough (0723) 376125
An opportunity to meet creatures that live in and around the oceans of the British Isles.

② North Yorkshire Moors Railway
Pickering Station, Pickering, North Yorkshire YO18 7AJ
Tel: Pickering (0751) 72508
18-mile railway through the national park. Steam and diesel trains.

③ Fountains Abbey and Studley Royal Park
Ripon, North Yorkshire HG4 3DZ
Tel: Sawley (0765) 608888
Largest monastic ruin in Britain, founded by Cistercian monks in 1132. Landscaped garden laid out 1720–40 with lake, formal watergarden and temples, deer park.

Amy Johnson (1903–41) is famed for her solo flight to Australia in 1930. Her statue stands in Prospect Street, Hull.

③ Newby Hall and Gardens
Ripon, North Yorkshire HG4 5AE
Tel: Harrogate (0423) 322583
Late 17th C house with additions, interior by Robert Adam, classical

Yorkshire & Humberside

Steam and diesel trains of the North Yorkshire Moors Railway at Pickering will take you through the national park.

sculpture, Gobelins tapestries, 25-acre gardens, miniature railway, picnic area, children's gardens.

④ Castle Howard
Malton, North Yorkshire YO6 7BZ
Tel: Coneysthorpe (065 384) 333
Set in 1,000 acres of parkland with nature walks, scenic lake and stunning rose gardens. Important furniture and works of art.

④ Eden Camp Modern History Theme Museum
Malton, North Yorkshire YO17 0SD
Tel: Malton (0653) 697777
Modern history theme museum depicting civilian way of life in Britain during World War II. Based in a genuine ex-PoW camp with original buildings.

⑤ Yorkshire Dales Falconry and Conservation Centre
Crows Nest, Giggleswick, North Yorkshire LA2 8AS
Tel: Settle (0729) 825164
Falconry centre with many species of birds of prey from around the world including vultures, eagles, hawks, falcons and owls. Free-flying displays, lecture room and aviaries.

⑥ Bridlington Leisure World
The Promenade, Bridlington, Humberside YO15 2QQ
Tel: Bridlington (0262) 606715
Wave pool, adult and junior pools. Multi-purpose hall with indoor bowling area, entertainment centre, club, disco.

⑥ Sewerby Hall, Park and Zoo
Sewerby, Bridlington, North Humberside YO15 1EA
Tel: Bridlington (0262) 673769
Zoo, aviary, old English walled garden, bowls, putting, golf, children's corner, museum, art gallery, Amy Johnson collection, novel train from park to North Beach.

⑦ Beningbrough Hall
Shipton-by-Beningbrough, York, North Yorkshire YO6 1DD
Tel: York (0904) 470666
Handsome Baroque house built in 1716 with nearly 100 pictures from the National Portrait Gallery. Victorian laundry, potting shed, garden, adventure playground, National Trust shop.

⑧ Jorvik Viking Centre
Coppergate, York, North Yorkshire YO1 1NT
Tel: York (0904) 643211
Visitors travel in electric cars down a time tunnel to a re-creation of Viking York. Excavated remains of Viking houses and display of objects found.

⑧ National Railway Museum
Leeman Road, York, North Yorkshire YO2 4XJ
Tel: York (0904) 621261
Collection of locomotives and carriages with displays depicting the technical, social and economic development of Britain's railway heritage.

⑧ The Arc
St Saviourgate, York, North Yorkshire YO1 2NN
Tel: York (0904) 654324
Visitors can 'touch the past', handling ancient finds of pottery and bone, stitching Roman sandals or picking a Viking padlock. Audio-visual display and exploration of dig by computer.

⑧ York Minster
Deangate, York, North Yorkshire YO1 2JA
Tel: York (0904) 624426
The largest Gothic cathedral in England. Museum of Saxon and Norman remains, chapter house and crypt. Unrivalled views from Norman tower.

⑨ Harewood House
Harewood, Leeds, West Yorkshire LS17 9LQ
Tel: Harewood (0532) 886225
18th C Carr/Adam house, Capability Brown landscape. Fine Sevres and Chinese porcelain, English and Italian paintings, Chippendale furniture. Exotic bird garden.

⑩ Temple Newsam House
Leeds, West Yorkshire LS15 0AE
Tel: Leeds (0532) 647321
Tudor and Jacobean house, birthplace of Lord Darnley. Paintings, furniture by Chippendale and others. Gold and silver c1600. Ceramics, especially Leeds pottery.

101

Yorkshire & Humberside

⑩ Leeds City Art Gallery and Henry Moore Centre
The Headrow, Leeds, West Yorkshire LS1 3AA
Tel: Leeds (0532) 478248
19th and 20th C paintings, sculptures, prints and drawings. Permanent collection of 20th C sculpture in Henry Moore Centre.

⑪ Museum of Army Transport
Beverley, Humberside HU17 ONG
Tel: Hull (0482) 860445
Army road, rail, sea and air exhibits excitingly displayed in two exhibition halls, plus the huge, last remaining Blackburn Beverley aircraft. Gulf exhibition.

⑫ Burton Constable Hall and Country Park
Burton Constable, Humberside HU11 4LN
Tel: Hornsea (0964) 562400
16th C house with outstanding additions in 18th C by Adam, Lightoller and others. Chippendale furniture, Chinese room and unique scientific collection.

⑬ National Museum of Photography, Film and Television
Prince's View, Bradford, West Yorkshire BD1 1NQ
Tel: Bradford (0274) 727488
The largest cinema screen (Imax) in Britain. Kodak Museum. Fly on a magic carpet, operate TV camera, become a newsreader for a day.

⑭ Hull and East Riding Museum
High Street, Hull, Humberside
Tel: Hull (0482) 593902
Humberside archaeology. Iron Age Hasholme boat and chariot burials, magnificent display of Romano-British mosaics.

⑮ Eureka!
Discovery Road, Halifax, West Yorkshire HX1 2NE
Tel: Halifax (0422) 330069
Eureka! is a new concept in children's museums, designed specifically for children aged 5 to 12 and accompanying adults. Visitors can touch, taste and smell.

⑯ Yorkshire Mining Museum
Caphouse Colliery, New Road, Overton, Wakefield, West Yorkshire WF4 4RH
Tel: Wakefield (0924) 848806
Exciting award-winning museum of the Yorkshire coalfield, including guided underground tour of authentic old workings.

⑰ Elsham Hall Country and Wildlife Park
Elsham, South Humberside DN20 0QZ
Tel: Barnetby (0652) 688698
Trout and carp lakes, wild butterfly garden walkway, animal farm, pets corner, adventure playground, new falconry centre, craft centre, art gallery and clock tower shop.

⑱ National Fishing Heritage Centre
Alexandra Dock, Grimsby, Humberside DN31 1UF
Tel: Grimsby (0472) 344867
Spectacular 1950s steam trawler experience. See, hear, smell and touch a series of re-created environments. Museum displays, aquarium, shop.

⑲ Pleasure Island Fun Park
Kings Road, Cleethorpes, South Humberside
Tel: Cleethorpes (0472) 211511
The East Coast's great new fun park. Rides include the Boomerang, Dream Boat, Wave Swinger, Mini Mine Train. Shows, restaurants and gift shops.

⑳ Cannon Hall Country Park
Cawthorne, South Yorkshire S75 4AT
Tel: Barnsley (0226) 774500
18th C landscaped parkland with lakes stocked with ornamental and indigenous waterfowl. Nearby Cannon Hall Museum and open farm.

㉑ Cusworth Hall Museum of South Yorkshire Life
Cusworth Lane, Doncaster, South Yorkshire DN5 7TU
Tel: Doncaster (0302) 782342

Grimsby is the place to go to learn about Britain's fishing traditions.

Yorkshire & Humberside

Georgian mansion in landscaped park containing Museum of South Yorkshire Life. Special educational facilities.

㉒ Thrybergh Country Park
Doncaster Road, Thrybergh, Rotherham, South Yorkshire
S65 4NU
Tel: Rotherham (0709) 850353
63-acre country park, including 35-acre lake. Fly fishing, sailing, windsurfing, canoeing, picnic area.

Use the map below to locate places in the 'Where to Go, What to See' section.

FIND OUT MORE

Further information about holidays and attractions in the Yorkshire & Humberside region is available from:
Yorkshire & Humberside Tourist Board
312 Tadcaster Road, York
YO2 2HF
Tel: (0904) 707961 or (0904) 707070 (24-hour brochure line).
Fax: (0904) 701414

These publications are available free from the Yorkshire & Humberside Tourist Board:
Main holiday guide (information on the region, including hotels, self-catering and caravan and camping parks)
Short Breaks and Winter Warmers
Bed & Breakfast touring map
Major events list
What's On (3 issues per year)
Attractions map
Overseas brochure (French, Dutch, German, Italian, Spanish)
Farm Holidays
Industrial Heritage map
'Freedom' Caravan and Camping guide

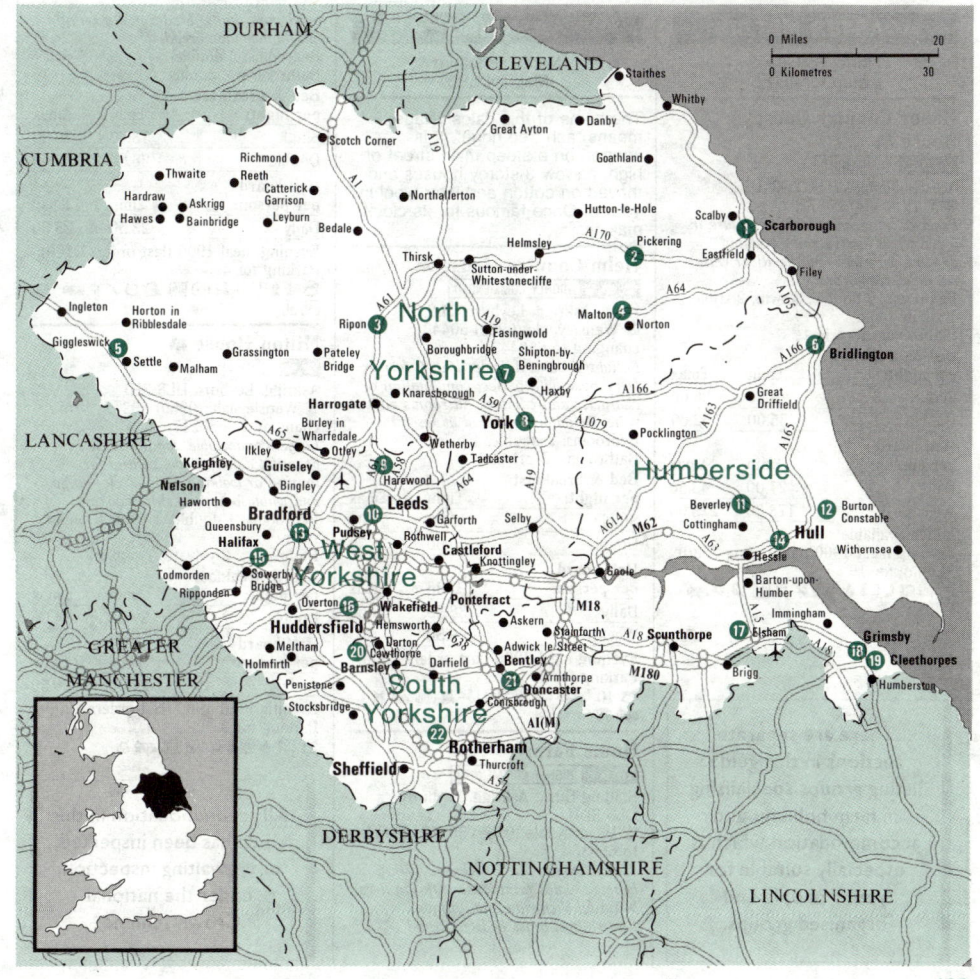

YORKSHIRE & HUMBERSIDE

Places to stay

Accommodation entries in this regional section are listed in alphabetical order of place name, and then in alphabetical order of establishment.

The map references refer to the colour maps at the back of the guide. The first figure is the map number; the letter and figure which follow indicate the grid reference on the map.

The symbols at the end of each accommodation entry give information about services and facilities. A 'key' to these symbols is inside the back cover flap, which can be kept open for easy reference.

ACASTER MALBIS
North Yorkshire
Map ref 4C1

Manor Country Guest House
COMMENDED
Acaster Malbis, York YO2 1UL
☎ York (0904) 706723
Peaceful, modernised 18th C house in 5.5 acres of landscaped woodland gardens with lake. By the River Ouse, 4.5 miles from York.
Bedrooms: 4 double, 3 twin, 2 triple, 1 family room
Bathrooms: 10 private

Bed & breakfast per night:	£min	£max
Single	19.50	36.00
Double	35.00	52.00

Half board per person:	£min	£max
Daily	27.00	43.50
Weekly	178.00	228.00

Lunch available
Evening meal 1900 (last orders 2030)
Parking for 19

There are separate sections in this guide listing groups specialising in farm holidays and accommodation which is especially suitable for young people and organised groups.

ASKRIGG
North Yorkshire
Map ref 5B3

The name of this dales village means "ash tree ridge". It is centred on a steep main street of high, narrow 3-storey houses and thrived on cotton and later wool in 18th C. Once famous for its clock making.

Helm Country House
HIGHLY COMMENDED
Helm, Askrigg, Leyburn DL8 3JF
☎ Wensleydale (0969) 50443
changing to 650443
Delightful dales hillside, 17th C former farmhouse with perfect combination of character and comfort. All rooms en-suite. Delicious food and wines.
Bedrooms: 2 double, 1 twin
Bathrooms: 3 private

Bed & breakfast per night:	£min	£max
Single	45.00	51.00
Double	50.00	56.00

Half board per person:	£min	£max
Daily	38.50	41.50
Weekly	269.50	

Evening meal 1900 (last orders 1900)
Parking for 5

Home Farm
Listed HIGHLY COMMENDED
Stalling Busk, Askrigg, Leyburn DL8 3DH
☎ Wensleydale (0969) 50360 changing to 650360
65-acre mixed farm. Licensed 17th C beamed, dales farmhouse with log fires, beautiful Victorian and antique furnishings, brass bedsteads and

patchwork quilts. Traditional cooking and home-made bread.
Bedrooms: 3 double
Bathrooms: 2 public

Bed & breakfast per night:	£min	£max
Single	18.00	20.00
Double	28.00	32.00

Half board per person:	£min	£max
Daily	23.50	25.50

Evening meal 1900 (last orders 2100)
Parking for 4

Milton House
Askrigg, Leyburn DL8 3HJ
☎ Wensleydale (0969) 50217
changing to 650217
Large, comfortable, family house in a beautiful dales village, central for touring or walking. Colour TV lounge and wholesome Yorkshire cooking.
Bedrooms: 1 double, 1 twin, 1 family room
Bathrooms: 2 private, 1 public

Bed & breakfast per night:	£min	£max
Double	29.00	34.00

Half board per person:	£min	£max
Daily	24.00	26.50

Evening meal 1900 (last orders 1900)
Parking for 3

All accommodation in this guide has been inspected, or is awaiting inspection, under the national Crown scheme.

104

YORKSHIRE & HUMBERSIDE

AYSGARTH
North Yorkshire
Map ref 5B3

Famous for its beautiful Falls - a series of 3 cascades extending for half a mile on the River Ure in Wensleydale. There is a coach and carriage museum with a crafts centre at Old Yore Mill and a National Park Centre.

George & Dragon Inn
COMMENDED
Aysgarth, Leyburn DL8 3AD
☎ (0969) 663358

Family-owned and run listed 17th C inn, with old beams and antiques. Lovely atmosphere and good food in a beautiful setting.
Bedrooms: 4 double, 1 twin
Bathrooms: 5 private

Bed & breakfast
per night:	£min	£max
Double	40.00	50.00

Lunch available
Evening meal 1800 (last orders 2100)
Parking for 40
Cards accepted: Access, Visa

Marlbeck
Listed
Aysgarth, Leyburn DL8 3AH
☎ Wensleydale (0969) 663610
Attractive B & B, a short walk from Aysgarth Falls. Pleasant service, gardens and views. Good food and amenities in the charming village.
Bedrooms: 1 twin, 1 triple
Bathrooms: 1 public

Bed & breakfast
per night:	£min	£max
Single	15.00	18.00
Double	28.00	30.00

Open April-October

Individual proprietors have supplied all details of accommodation. Although we do check for accuracy, we advise you to confirm the information at the time of booking.

BAINBRIDGE
North Yorkshire
Map ref 5B3

This Wensleydale grey-stone village, with fine views of the River Bain, reputedly England's shortest river, was once a Roman settlement, some of it still visible. Boating and water-skiing on nearby Semerwater. Ancient foresters' custom of hornblowing still continues.

Countersett Hall
HIGHLY COMMENDED
Countersett, Bainbridge, Leyburn DL8 3DD
☎ Wensleydale (0969) 650373
Peaceful and welcoming 17th C yeoman's farmhouse close to Semerwater, the largest natural lake in Yorkshire. Ideal centre for exploring the Dales. Wonderful scenery. Walk out of our door straight on to the hills. Delicious traditional or vegetarian meals.
Bedrooms: 2 single, 3 double
Bathrooms: 2 private, 2 public

Bed & breakfast
per night:	£min	£max
Single	17.00	19.00
Double	34.00	38.00

Half board
per person:	£min	£max
Daily	30.50	32.50

Evening meal 1930 (last orders 1700)
Parking for 6
Open March-October

High Force Farm
Listed APPROVED
Bainbridge, Leyburn DL8 3DL
☎ Wensleydale (0969) 50379
chnaging to 650379
470-acre hill farm. Working farm used in the James Herriot TV series, close to Semerwater Lake. Friendly, relaxed atmosphere in non-smoking establishment.
Bedrooms: 1 double, 1 family room
Bathrooms: 2 public

Bed & breakfast
per night:	£min	£max
Double	27.00	30.00

Parking for 3

BALK
North Yorkshire
Map ref 5C3

Barley Garth
Balk, Thirsk YO7 2AJ
☎ Thirsk (0845) 597524
Georgian house in a hamlet between Thirsk and the North York Moors National Park.
Bedrooms: 1 double, 1 twin, 1 triple

Bathrooms: 1 private, 1 public, 1 private shower

Bed & breakfast
per night:	£min	£max
Single	16.00	19.00
Double	24.00	37.00

Half board
per person:	£min	£max
Daily	18.50	27.00
Weekly	129.50	189.00

Parking for 3

BARNETBY
Humberside
Map ref 4C1

Holcombe House
COMMENDED
34 Victoria Road, Barnetby, South Humberside DN38 6JR
☎ (0652) 680655 & Mobile (0850) 764002
Pleasant, homely accommodation in centre of Barnetby village. 5 minutes from M180 and railway station, 3 miles from Humberside Airport, 15-30 minutes from Grimsby, Scunthorpe and Hull.
Bedrooms: 2 single, 1 double, 1 twin
Bathrooms: 2 private, 1 public, 1 private shower

Bed & breakfast
per night:	£min	£max
Single	17.50	23.00
Double	27.50	35.00

Evening meal 1900 (last orders 2000)
Parking for 4
Cards accepted: Access, Visa

BEDALE
North Yorkshire
Map ref 5C3

Ancient church of St Gregory and Georgian Bedale Hall occupy commanding positions over this market town situated in good hunting country. The Hall, which contains interesting architectural features including great ballroom and flying-type staircase, now houses a library and museum.

Elmfield House
Arrathorne, Bedale DL8 1NE
☎ (0677) 50558
Country house in its own grounds with open views of the countryside. Special emphasis on standards and home cooking. Solarium.
Bedrooms: 4 double, 3 twin, 2 triple
Bathrooms: 9 private

Continued ▶

105

YORKSHIRE & HUMBERSIDE

BEDALE
Continued

Bed & breakfast
per night:	£min	£max
Single	25.00	27.00
Double	38.00	44.00

Half board
per person:	£min	£max
Daily	30.00	36.00
Weekly	203.00	217.00

Evening meal from 1900
Parking for 10
Cards accepted: Access, Visa

BEVERLEY
Humberside
Map ref 4C1

Beverley's most famous landmark is its beautiful medieval Minster with Percy family tomb. Many attractive squares and streets, notably Wednesday and Saturday Market, North Bar Gateway and the Museum of Army Transport, Flemingate. Famous racecourse.
Tourist Information Centre
☎ (0482) 867430

Eastgate Guest House ⋀
COMMENDED

7 Eastgate, Beverley, North Humberside HU17 0DR
☎ Hull (0482) 868464
Fax (0482) 871899
Family-run Victorian guesthouse, established and run by the same proprietor for 26 years. Close to the town centre, Beverley Minster, Museum of Army Transport and railway station.
Bedrooms: 5 single, 5 double, 4 twin, 4 triple
Bathrooms: 7 private, 3 public

Bed & breakfast
per night:	£min	£max
Single	16.00	30.00
Double	26.00	42.00

Northumbria Bed and Breakfast
Listed

13 The Croft, Molescroft, Beverley, North Humberside HU17 7HT
☎ Hull (0482) 872254
Detached house with large gardens in quiet residential area, about 1 mile from town centre and Beverley Minster. Double rooms can be let as singles. Garden for guests' use. Village pub food nearby.
Bedrooms: 2 double
Bathrooms: 1 private, 1 public

Bed & breakfast
per night:	£min	£max
Single	16.00	18.00
Double	26.00	28.00

Parking for 2

Rudstone Walk Farm, Country House and Conference Centre ⋀
HIGHLY COMMENDED

South Cave, Beverley, North Humberside HU15 2AH
☎ North Cave (0430) 422230
303-acre arable farm. En-suite rooms overlooking lawned courtyard with meals served in the historic farmhouse. Excellent location for Beverley, York, moors and coast.
Wheelchair access category 3
Bedrooms: 7 double, 7 twin
Bathrooms: 14 private, 1 public

Bed & breakfast
per night:	£min	£max
Single	35.00	38.50
Double	44.00	65.00

Half board
per person:	£min	£max
Daily	31.50	57.00
Weekly	220.50	399.00

Evening meal 1900 (last orders 1600)
Parking for 30
Cards accepted: Access, Visa, Amex

BINGLEY
West Yorkshire
Map ref 4B1

Bingley Five-Rise is an impressive group of locks on the Leeds and Liverpool Canal. Town claims to have first bred the Airedale terrier originally used for otter hunting. Among fine Georgian houses is Myrtle Grove where John Wesley stayed. East Riddlesden Hall is nearby.

Ashley End
Listed

22 Ashley Road, Off Ashfield Crescent, Bingley BD16 1DZ
☎ Bradford (0274) 569679
Private house just off the main Bradford/Leeds road into Bingley. 5 minutes' walk to Bingley and 10 minutes' walk to the station. Twin room and single room have a wash basin.
Bedrooms: 1 single, 2 twin
Bathrooms: 1 public

Bed & breakfast
per night:	£min	£max
Single	14.00	15.00
Double	28.00	30.00

BISHOP THORNTON
North Yorkshire
Map ref 5C3

Small village in Nidderdale, near Brimham Rocks.

Hatton House Farm
HIGHLY COMMENDED

Bishop Thornton, Harrogate HG3 3JA
☎ Harrogate (0423) 770315
150-acre dairy & livestock farm. Farmhouse accommodation with special emphasis on well-presented, home-cooked food. Open all year round. No smoking indoors, please.
Bedrooms: 2 double, 1 twin
Bathrooms: 1 public

Bed & breakfast
per night:	£min	£max
Single	18.00	19.00
Double	36.00	38.00

Evening meal 1830 (last orders 1800)
Parking for 10

Raventofts Head House ⋀

Watergate Road, Bishop Thornton, Harrogate HG3 3JZ
☎ Ripon (0765) 620279
17-acre beef farm. Fully-modernised, stone-built farmhouse providing comfortable and inviting accommodation with a warm welcome. Picturesque countryside near places of historic interest. Evening meal by request only. Tea/coffee available at any time free of charge. Babies welcome.
Bedrooms: 1 single, 1 double, 1 twin
Bathrooms: 1 private, 1 public

Bed & breakfast
per night:	£min	£max
Single	15.00	18.00
Double	26.00	30.00

Half board
per person:	£min	£max
Daily	20.00	24.00
Weekly	120.00	150.00

Evening meal 1900 (last orders 2000)
Parking for 8

There are separate sections in this guide listing groups specialising in farm holidays and accommodation which is especially suitable for young people and organised groups.

YORKSHIRE & HUMBERSIDE

BOROUGHBRIDGE
North Yorkshire
Map ref 5C3

On the River Ure, Boroughbridge was once an important coaching centre with 22 inns and in the 18th C a port for Knaresborough's linens. It has fine old houses, many trees and a cobbled square with market cross. Nearby stand 3 megaliths known as the Devil's Arrows.

Treble Sykes Farm

Helperby, York YO6 2SB
☎ (0423) 360667
400-acre arable farm. Peaceful location with panoramic view over the Vale of York. Centrally situated for visits to historic York and the North York Moors and Dales. 4 miles from the A1.
Bedrooms: 1 single, 1 triple
Bathrooms: 2 public
Bed & breakfast

per night:	£min	£max
Single	14.00	15.00
Double	26.00	28.00

Parking for 10
Open March-October

BRADFORD
West Yorkshire
Map ref 4B1

City founded on wool, with fine Victorian and modern buildings. Attractions include the cathedral, city hall, Cartwright Hall, Lister Park, Moorside Mills Industrial Museum and National Museum of Photography, Film and Television.
Tourist Information Centre
☎ *(0274) 753678*

Brow Top Farm
COMMENDED

Baldwin Lane, Clayton, Bradford BD14 6PS
☎ (0274) 882178
300-acre mixed farm. Newly renovated farmhouse.
Bedrooms: 1 double, 1 twin, 1 triple
Bathrooms: 3 private
Bed & breakfast

per night:	£min	£max
Single	20.00	20.00
Double	30.00	30.00

Parking for 4

Carlton House Guest House
Listed

Thornton Road, Thornton, Bradford BD13 3QE
☎ (0274) 833397
Detached, Victorian house in open countryside between the Bronte villages of Thornton and Haworth.
Bedrooms: 1 single, 1 double, 1 twin, 1 triple
Bathrooms: 4 private
Bed & breakfast

per night:	£min	£max
Single	17.00	17.00
Double	29.00	29.00

Parking for 6

Carnoustie

8 Park Grove, Frizinghall, Bradford BD9 4JY
☎ (0274) 490561
Detached Victorian house 1.75 miles from Bradford city centre, close to Lister Park. En-suite rooms.
Bedrooms: 1 double, 1 twin
Bathrooms: 2 private
Bed & breakfast

per night:	£min	£max
Single	18.00	20.00
Double	29.00	31.00

Parking for 2

Ivy Guest House
Listed

3 Melbourne Place, Bradford BD5 0HZ
☎ (0274) 727060
Large, detached, listed house built of Yorkshire stone. Car park and gardens. Close to city centre, National Museum of Photography, Film and Television and Alhambra Theatre.
Bedrooms: 3 single, 2 double, 4 twin, 1 triple
Bathrooms: 3 public
Bed & breakfast

per night:	£min	£max
Single	20.00	20.00
Double	30.00	30.00

Half board

per person:	£min	£max
Daily	20.00	25.00
Weekly	140.00	175.00

Lunch available
Evening meal 1800 (last orders 2000)
Parking for 12
Cards accepted: Access, Visa, Amex

Park Grove Hotel
COMMENDED

Park Grove, Frizinghall, Bradford BD9 4JY
☎ (0274) 543444
Fax (0274) 495619
Victorian establishment in a secluded preserved area of Bradford, 1.5 miles from the city centre. Gateway to the dales.
Bedrooms: 5 single, 3 double, 1 twin, 2 triple
Bathrooms: 11 private
Bed & breakfast

per night:	£min	£max
Single	37.00	44.00
Double	48.00	55.00

Half board

per person:	£min	£max
Daily	46.00	50.00
Weekly	250.00	290.00

Evening meal 1900 (last orders 2100)
Parking for 8
Cards accepted: Access, Visa

BRIDLINGTON
Humberside
Map ref 5D3

Lively seaside resort with long sandy beaches, Leisureworld and busy harbour with fishing trips in cobles. Priory church of St Mary whose Bayle Gate is now a museum. Mementoes of flying pioneer, Amy Johnson, in Sewerby Hall. Harbour Museum and Aquarium.
Tourist Information Centre
☎ *(0262) 673474*

Central Guest House
Listed

1 Springfield Avenue, Bridlington, North Humberside YO15 3AA
☎ (0262) 400266
19th C Victorian guesthouse offering comfortable accommodation and fine cuisine. A good touring base for coast and country.
Bedrooms: 2 double, 1 family room
Bathrooms: 1 private, 1 public
Bed & breakfast

per night:	£min	£max
Single	10.00	20.00
Double	20.00	40.00

Half board

per person:	£min	£max
Daily	16.00	26.00
Weekly	96.00	150.00

Evening meal from 1630

BRIGG
Humberside
Map ref 4C1

Small town at an ancient crossing of the River Ancholme, granted a weekly Thursday market and annual horsefair by Henry III in 1235.
Tourist Information Centre
☎ *(0652) 657053*

Arties Mill
APPROVED

Wressle Road, Castlethorpe, Brigg, South Humberside DN20 9LF
☎ (0652) 652094 & 657107

Continued ▶

107

YORKSHIRE & HUMBERSIDE

BRIGG
Continued

Situated close to A18 between Brigg and Scunthorpe. Restaurant and bar meals available. Private functions, weddings. Motel and lodge adjacent to the mill.
Bedrooms: 1 single, 8 double, 16 twin, 1 triple
Bathrooms: 22 private, 1 public

Bed & breakfast
per night:	£min	£max
Single	32.50	45.00
Double	47.50	57.50

Half board
per person:	£min	£max
Daily	42.50	50.00

Lunch available
Evening meal 1830 (last orders 2200)
Parking for 100
Cards accepted: Access, Visa, Diners, Amex

CASTLETON
North Yorkshire
Map ref 5C3

Eskdale village, site of castle built by deBrus circa 1089. Castleton Moors are rich in prehistoric remains.

Moorlands Hotel

Castleton, Whitby YO21 2DB
☎ (0287) 660206
Family-run hotel/freehouse offering home cooking and a well stocked bar. In the national park with magnificent views of the Esk Valley and the North York Moors. Ideal for walking and touring.
Bedrooms: 3 single, 2 double, 3 twin, 1 triple
Bathrooms: 6 private, 2 public

Bed & breakfast
per night:	£min	£max
Single	20.00	20.00
Double	40.00	50.00

Half board
per person:	£min	£max
Daily	30.00	35.00
Weekly	189.00	210.00

Lunch available
Evening meal 1700 (last orders 2200)

Parking for 15
Cards accepted: Access, Visa

CLOUGHTON
North Yorkshire
Map ref 5D3

Village close to the east coast and North York Moors.

Gowland Farm
Listed

Gowland Lane, Cloughton, Scarborough YO13 0DU
☎ Scarborough (0723) 870924
In a quiet, peaceful location with superb views. 2 miles north of Cloughton on the A171 take a sharp left turn on to an unmarked road and house is half a mile down on the left.
Bedrooms: 1 single, 1 double, 1 twin
Bathrooms: 1 public

Bed & breakfast
per night:	£min	£max
Single	13.50	13.50
Double	27.00	27.00

Half board
per person:	£min	£max
Daily	20.00	20.00
Weekly	130.00	130.00

Evening meal 1900 (last orders 2000)
Parking for 8
Open April-October and Christmas

COXWOLD
North Yorkshire
Map ref 5C3

This well-known beauty spot in Hambleton and Howardian Hills is famous as home of Laurence Sterne, the 18th C country parson and author of "Tristram Shandy" books who, in 1760, lived at Shandy Hall, now open to the public.

Sunley Woods Farm
Listed

Husthwaite, York YO6 3TQ
☎ (0347) 868418
180-acre mixed farm. Comfortable farmhouse 18 miles north of York with glorious views overlooking the White Horse at Kilburn. Convenient for York and coast.
Bedrooms: 1 single, 1 double, 1 twin
Bathrooms: 1 public

Bed & breakfast
per night:	£min	£max
Single	12.00	12.50
Double	24.00	25.00

Parking for 10
Open April-October

Wakendale House
COMMENDED

Oldstead Grange, Coxwold, York YO6 4BJ
☎ (0347) 868351
160-acre mixed farm. Comfortable accommodation with a friendly family in an attractive farmhouse set in lovely countryside. No smoking in the house.
Bedrooms: 1 double, 1 twin, 1 triple
Bathrooms: 1 public

Bed & breakfast
per night:	£min	£max
Double		30.00

Parking for 5
Open February-November

Willows
Listed

12 Husthwaite Road, Coxwold, York YO6 4AE
☎ (0347) 868335
Attractive village 20 miles north of York and 6 miles from Thirsk. Lounge for sole use of guests. Continental breakfast available when required.
Bedrooms: 1 double
Bathrooms: 1 public

Bed & breakfast
per night:	£min	£max
Single	10.00	20.00
Double	20.00	30.00

Parking for 1

CRAKEHALL
North Yorkshire
Map ref 5C3

One of the prettiest of the lower dales villages, with its 5-acre green dominated by Crakehall Hall and enclosed by stone-built cottages dating back to the 1750s.

Waterside
COMMENDED

Glenaire, Crakehall, Bedale DL8 1HS
☎ Bedale (0677) 422908

Spacious, modern house with 1 acre of mature gardens and a trout stream. Central for the Yorkshire Dales and Moors, the gateway to Herriot country. All rooms have private facilities.
Bedrooms: 2 double, 2 twin
Bathrooms: 4 private

Bed & breakfast
per night:	£min	£max
Single	17.00	20.00
Double	34.00	40.00

YORKSHIRE & HUMBERSIDE

Half board per person:	£min	£max
Daily	29.00	32.00
Weekly	46.00	52.00

Evening meal from 1900
Parking for 5

CRAYKE

North Yorkshire
Map ref 5C3

Pretty hillside village once belonging to the Bishopric of Durham, hence the name of the village inn, the "Durham Ox".

Halfway House
DE LUXE

Easingwold Road, Crayke, York Y06 4TJ
☎ Easingwold (0347) 22614
Fax (0347) 22942
Elegant Victorian house set in secluded gardens with 7-acre paddock, halfway between the market town of Easingwold and pretty village of Crayke. Joint winner of 1992 Best Bed and Breakfast award.
Bedrooms: 2 double, 1 twin
Bathrooms: 1 private, 2 public

Bed & breakfast per night:	£min	£max
Single	25.00	35.00
Double	50.00	60.00

Half board per person:	£min	£max
Daily	41.50	51.50
Weekly	261.45	324.45

Evening meal from 2000
Parking for 13
Cards accepted: Access, Visa

CROPTON

North Yorkshire
Map ref 5C3

Moorland village at the top of a high ridge with stone houses, some of cruck construction, a Victorian church and the remains of a 12th C moated castle. Cropton Forest nearby.

High Farm
COMMENDED

Cropton, Pickering YO18 8HL
☎ Lastingham (075 15) 461
Lovely Victorian house with large gardens. Easy access to the moors, coast and York. Open fires and a warm welcome..
Bedrooms: 3 double
Bathrooms: 3 private

Bed & breakfast per night:	£min	£max
Single	16.00	20.00
Double	32.00	32.00

Parking for 10
Open March-October

DONCASTER

South Yorkshire
Map ref 4C1

Ancient Roman town famous for its heavy industries, butterscotch and racecourse (St Leger), also centre of agricultural area. Attractions include 18th C Mansion House, Cusworth Hall Museum, Doncaster Museum, St George's Church, The Dome and Doncaster Leisure Park.
Tourist Information Centre
☎ (0302) 734309

Canda Lodge
COMMENDED

Hampole Balk Lane, 5 Lane Ends, Skellow, Doncaster DN6 8LF
☎ (0302) 724028
Fax (0302) 738561
Charming guesthouse with TV, telephone, trouser press and tea/coffee facilities in all rooms (6 ground floor). Close to A1 and ideal for those travelling north/south. Non-smokers only please.
Bedrooms: 1 single, 5 double, 2 twin
Bathrooms: 4 private, 2 public, 1 private shower

Bed & breakfast per night:	£min	£max
Single	20.00	30.00
Double	30.00	38.00

Parking for 6
Cards accepted: Access, Visa

EASINGWOLD

North Yorkshire
Map ref 5C3

Market town of charm and character with a cobbled square and many fine Georgian buildings.

The Old Vicarage
COMMENDED

Market Place, Easingwold, York YO6 3AL
☎ (0347) 821015
Delightful 18th C country house with extensive lawned gardens and croquet lawn. In centre of market town, 12 miles north of York, and ideal as a touring centre for North Yorkshire.
Bedrooms: 1 single, 2 double, 2 twin
Bathrooms: 5 private

Bed & breakfast per night:	£min	£max
Single	20.00	22.00
Double	38.00	40.00

Parking for 5
Open March-October

Station Hotel
APPROVED

Knott Lane, Raskelf Road, Easingwold, York YO6 3NT
☎ (0347) 822635
Fax (0347) 823491
Historic Victorian remains of Britain's shortest standard gauge railway. Award winning food. Real ales and foreign beers. Ideal touring base for York, dales and moors. Discounts for longer stays.
Bedrooms: 3 double, 3 twin, 1 family room
Bathrooms: 7 private

Bed & breakfast per night:	£min	£max
Single	27.00	27.00
Double	40.00	40.00

Lunch available
Evening meal 1800 (last orders 2130)
Parking for 11
Cards accepted: Access, Visa

EBBERSTON

North Yorkshire
Map ref 5D3

Picturesque village with a Norman church and hall, overlooking the Vale of Pickering.

The Foxholm

Ebberston, Scarborough YO13 9NJ
☎ Scarborough (0723) 859550
Small, family-run, fully licensed country hotel in rural setting within easy reach of the moors, dales, sea and York.
Bedrooms: 2 single, 2 double, 2 twin, 1 triple
Bathrooms: 6 private, 3 public

Bed & breakfast per night:	£min	£max
Single	25.00	28.00
Double	46.00	52.00

Half board per person:	£min	£max
Daily	30.00	40.00

Lunch available
Evening meal 1830 (last orders 2030)
Parking for 14

Studley House
Listed

67 Main Street, Ebberston, Scarborough YO13 9NR
☎ Scarborough (0723) 859285

Continued ▶

109

YORKSHIRE & HUMBERSIDE

EBBERSTON
Continued

43-acre beef farm. Very clean, comfortable farmhouse in picturesque village. Full breakfast, central heating, tea makers. Own keys. Central for moors, forests, sea and York.
Bedrooms: 1 single, 2 triple
Bathrooms: 1 public
Bed & breakfast

per night:	£min	£max
Single	13.00	15.00
Double	26.00	30.00

Parking for 4

ELLERBY
North Yorkshire
Map ref 5C3

Ellerby Hotel
COMMENDED
Ellerby, Saltburn-by-the-Sea, Cleveland TS13 5LP
☎ Whitby (0947) 840342
Fax (0947) 841221
Residential country inn within the North York Moors National Park, 9 miles north of Whitby, 1 mile inland from Runswick Bay.
Bedrooms: 7 double, 2 triple
Bathrooms: 9 private
Bed & breakfast

per night:	£min	£max
Single	30.00	34.00
Double	46.00	52.00

Lunch available
Evening meal 1900 (last orders 2200)
Parking for 60
Cards accepted: Access, Visa, Switch

FLAMBOROUGH
Humberside
Map ref 5D3

Village with strong seafaring tradition, high on chalk headland dominated by cliffs of Flamborough Head, a fortress for over 2000 years. St Oswald's Church is in the oldest part of Flamborough.

The Grange
Listed
Flamborough, Bridlington, North Humberside YO15 1AS
☎ Bridlington (0262) 850207
Fax (0262) 851359
475-acre arable & livestock farm. Family-run Georgian farmhouse offering a warm welcome. Half a mile from the village, close to RSPB reserve at Bempton.
Bedrooms: 1 double, 1 twin, 1 triple
Bathrooms: 2 public

Bed & breakfast

per night:	£min	£max
Single	12.50	14.00
Double	25.00	28.00

Parking for 6

FLAXTON
North Yorkshire
Map ref 5C3

Attractive village with broad greens, just west of the A64 York to Malton highway.

Grange Farm
The Grange, Oak Busk Lane, Flaxton, York YO6 7RL
☎ York (0904) 468219
130-acre arable & livestock farm. South-facing, modernised farmhouse in its own grounds. 8 miles from York, off the A64 York to Scarborough road, through Flaxton village and right down Oak Busk Lane.
Bedrooms: 2 double, 1 family room
Bathrooms: 1 private, 1 public
Bed & breakfast

per night:	£min	£max
Single	13.00	
Double	26.00	30.00

Parking for 10

GARFORTH
West Yorkshire
Map ref 4B1

Myrtle House
Listed
31 Wakefield Road, Garforth, Leeds LS25 1AN
☎ Leeds (0532) 866445
Spacious Victorian terraced house between M62 and A1. All rooms have tea and coffee making facilities and TV.
Bedrooms: 1 single, 1 double, 3 twin, 1 triple
Bathrooms: 3 public
Bed & breakfast

per night:	£min	£max
Single	14.00	16.00
Double	28.00	32.00

There are separate sections in this guide listing groups specialising in farm holidays and accommodation which is especially suitable for young people and organised groups.

GIGGLESWICK
North Yorkshire
Map ref 5B3

Picturesque Pennine village of period stone cottages with ancient market cross, stocks and tithe barn. Parish church is dedicated to St Alkeda, an Anglo-Saxon saint. During restoration work the tomb of a 15th C knight with his horse was discovered.

Black Horse Hotel
Church Street, Giggleswick, Settle BD24 OBJ
☎ Settle (0729) 822506
Secluded, friendly hotel, within easy reach of the Yorkshire Dales and the Lake District. Bar meals/dining room.
Bedrooms: 2 double, 1 twin
Bathrooms: 3 private
Bed & breakfast

per night:	£min	£max
Single		25.00
Double		44.00

Half board

per person:	£min	£max
Daily		33.50

Lunch available
Evening meal 1900 (last orders 2100)
Parking for 20
Cards accepted: Access, Diners

GILLAMOOR
North Yorkshire
Map ref 5C3

Village much admired by photographers for its views of Farndale, including "Surprise View" from the churchyard.

Royal Oak Inn
COMMENDED
Gillamoor, York YO6 6HX
☎ Kirkbymoorside (0751) 31414
Old country inn on the edge of the North York Moors. Tastefully renovated, with plenty of character and charm. Open log fires.
Bedrooms: 5 double, 1 twin
Bathrooms: 6 private
Bed & breakfast

per night:	£min	£max
Single	30.00	
Double	44.00	46.00

Lunch available
Evening meal 1900 (last orders 2100)
Parking for 9

Please mention this guide when making a booking.

YORKSHIRE & HUMBERSIDE

GOATHLAND
North Yorkshire
Map ref 5D3

Spacious village has several large greens grazed by sheep and is an ideal centre for walking North York Moors. Nearby are several waterfalls, among them Mallyan Spout. Plough Monday celebrations held in January. Location for filming of TVs "Heartbeat" series.

Mallyan Spout Hotel ♠
COMMENDED
Goathland, Whitby YO22 5AN
☎ Whitby (0947) 86206 & 86486

Comfortable hotel with old-fashioned comforts, welcoming log fires and good dining facilities. An ideal centre for walking the North York Moors.
Bedrooms: 3 single, 13 double, 7 twin
Bathrooms: 23 private
Bed & breakfast

per night:	£min	£max
Single	40.00	55.00
Double	65.00	120.00

Half board

per person:	£min	£max
Daily	57.50	67.50

Lunch available
Evening meal 1900 (last orders 2100)
Parking for 100
Cards accepted: Access, Visa

GRAFTON
North Yorkshire
Map ref 5C3

Primrose Cottage
Listed
Lime Bar Lane, Grafton, York YO5 9QJ
☎ Harrogate (0423) 322835 & 322711
Fax (0423) 323985
In a quiet picturesque village, 1 mile east of A1, approximately 10 minutes north of Wetherby.
Bedrooms: 1 double, 2 twin
Bathrooms: 2 public
Bed & breakfast

per night:	£min	£max
Single	8.50	14.00
Double	17.00	28.00

Parking for 11
Open March-September and Christmas

GRASSINGTON
North Yorkshire
Map ref 5B3

Tourists visit this former lead-mining village to see its "smiddy", antique and craft shops and Upper Wharfedale Museum of Country Trades. Popular with fishermen and walkers. Numerous prehistoric sites. Grassington Feast in October. National Park Centre.

Clarendon Hotel ♠
COMMENDED
Hebden, Grassington, Skipton BD23 5DE
☎ Skipton (0756) 752446
Yorkshire Dales inn serving good food and ales. Personal supervision at all times by true Yorkshire people. Steaks and fish dishes are specialities.
Bedrooms: 2 double, 1 twin
Bathrooms: 3 private
Bed & breakfast

per night:	£min	£max
Double	40.00	50.00

Lunch available
Evening meal 1900 (last orders 2100)
Parking for 30

Foresters Arms Hotel
Listed
20 Main Street, Grassington, Skipton BD23 5AA
☎ (0756) 752349
Public house in Grassington, serving lunch and evening meals.
Bedrooms: 1 single, 3 double, 2 triple
Bathrooms: 1 private, 2 public
Bed & breakfast

per night:	£min	£max
Single	18.00	25.00
Double	36.00	50.00

Lunch available
Evening meal 1800 (last orders 2030)
Parking for 2

Franor House
3 Wharfeside Avenue, Threshfield, Skipton BD23 5BS
☎ (0756) 752115
Large semi-detached house in quiet surroundings. Take B6265 from Skipton, turning right for Grassington. Wharfeside Avenue is half a mile - first turning on left.
Bedrooms: 1 single, 1 twin, 1 triple
Bathrooms: 3 private
Bed & breakfast

per night:	£min	£max
Single	16.00	18.00
Double	30.00	34.00

Parking for 4

Grange Cottage ♠
HIGHLY COMMENDED
Linton, Skipton BD23 5HH
☎ (0756) 752527
Stone-built cottage with open fires and warm hospitality. In a quiet backwater of a picture postcard village, perfect for hiking and car touring in the dales.
Bedrooms: 1 double, 1 twin
Bathrooms: 1 public, 1 private shower
Bed & breakfast

per night:	£min	£max
Double	36.00	40.00

Parking for 4
Open March-October

GREEN HAMMERTON
North Yorkshire
Map ref 4C1

Bay Horse Inn & Motel ♠
COMMENDED
York Road, Green Hammerton, York YO5 8BN
☎ Boroughbridge (0423) 330338 & 331113
Fax (0423) 331279
Village inn 10 miles from York and Harrogate on the A59 and 3 miles off the A1. Restaurant and bar meals. Weekly rates on request.
Bedrooms: 2 single, 3 double, 4 twin, 1 triple
Bathrooms: 10 private
Bed & breakfast

per night:	£min	£max
Single	30.00	30.00
Double	45.00	45.00

Lunch available
Evening meal 1900 (last orders 2130)
Parking for 40
Cards accepted: Access, Visa, Diners

GUNNERSIDE
North Yorkshire
Map ref 5B3

Taking its name from the Viking chieftain "Gunner", the village has a humpbacked bridge known as 'Ivelet Bridge' spanning the river which is said to be haunted by a headless dog.

Oxnop Hall
COMMENDED
Low Oxnop, Gunnerside, Richmond DL11 6JJ
☎ Richmond (0748) 86253
600-acre hill farm. Traditional farmhouse in the heart of Swaledale, featuring oak beams and mullion windows. All rooms have private facilities.
Bedrooms: 1 single, 3 double, 1 triple
Bathrooms: 5 private, 1 public

Continued ▶

111

YORKSHIRE & HUMBERSIDE

GUNNERSIDE
Continued

Bed & breakfast
per night:	£min	£max
Single	20.00	21.00
Double	40.00	42.00

Half board
per person:	£min	£max
Daily	31.00	33.00
Weekly	217.00	231.00

Evening meal 1630 (last orders 1630)
Parking for 5

HALIFAX
West Yorkshire
Map ref 4B1

Founded on the cloth trade, and famous for its building society, textiles, carpets and toffee. Most notable landmark is Piece Hall where wool merchants traded, now restored to house shops, museums and art gallery. Home also to Eureka! The Museum for Children.
Tourist Information Centre
☎ *(0422) 368725*

The Elms

Keighley Road, Illingworth, Halifax HX2 8HT
☎ (0422) 244430
Victorian residence with gardens and original ornate ceilings, within 3 miles of Halifax.
Bedrooms: 2 single, 1 double, 1 triple
Bathrooms: 2 private, 1 public

Bed & breakfast
per night:	£min	£max
Single	18.00	20.00
Double	36.00	40.00

Half board
per person:	£min	£max
Daily	26.00	28.00
Weekly	170.00	190.00

Evening meal 1800 (last orders 2000)
Parking for 14

HAMPSTHWAITE
North Yorkshire
Map ref 4B1

Graystone View Farm
Listed

Grayston Plain, Hampsthwaite, Harrogate HG3 2LY
☎ Harrogate (0423) 770324
100-acre mixed farm. 18th C farmhouse peacefully located quarter of a mile off the A59 west of Harrogate.
Bedrooms: 1 double, 1 twin
Bathrooms: 1 public

Bed & breakfast
per night:	£min	£max
Single	14.50	15.00
Double	29.00	30.00

Parking for 2
Open April-November

HARMBY
North Yorkshire
Map ref 5B3

Village probably derives its name from the Saxon "Hernebrie" meaning heronry. There is a manor house and chapel.

Robin Garth
COMMENDED

Harmby, Leyburn DL8 5PD
☎ Wensleydale (0969) 23041
Large detached double-fronted house situated on the edge of Harmby village overlooking Lower Wensleydale, Middleham, Pen Hill and the River Ure.
Bedrooms: 1 double, 2 twin
Bathrooms: 2 public

Bed & breakfast
per night:	£min	£max
Single	15.00	15.00
Double	30.00	30.00

Half board
per person:	£min	£max
Daily	25.00	25.00
Weekly	150.00	150.00

Evening meal 1830 (last orders 1830)
Parking for 6
Open March-October

HARROGATE
North Yorkshire
Map ref 4B1

A major conference, exhibition and shopping centre, renowned for its spa heritage and award winning floral displays, spacious parks and gardens. Famous for antiques, toffee, fine shopping and excellent tea shops, also its Royal Pump Rooms and Baths.
Tourist Information Centre
☎ *(0423) 525666*

Acacia Lodge
COMMENDED

21 Ripon Road, Harrogate HG1 2JL
☎ (0423) 560752
Warm, beautifully appointed and furnished Victorian house in select area of town centre. En-suite rooms, pretty gardens and ample private parking. Warm hospitality and award-winning breakfasts.
Bedrooms: 1 single, 1 double, 2 twin, 1 triple
Bathrooms: 5 private

Bed & breakfast
per night:	£min	£max
Single	34.00	
Double	48.00	

Parking for 6

Alamah
COMMENDED

88 Kings Road, Harrogate HG1 5JX
☎ (0423) 502187
Spacious, comfortable rooms, personal attention, friendly atmosphere and full English breakfast. 300 metres from town centre. Garages/parking.
Bedrooms: 2 single, 2 double, 2 twin, 1 family room
Bathrooms: 5 private, 2 private showers

Bed & breakfast
per night:	£min	£max
Single	20.00	22.00
Double	42.00	45.00

Half board
per person:	£min	£max
Daily	32.00	

Evening meal 1830 (last orders 1630)
Parking for 8

Alexa House Hotel and Stable Cottages

26 Ripon Road, Harrogate HG1 2JJ
☎ (0423) 501988
Fax (0423) 504086
Small hotel, built for Baron de Ferrier in 1830. Maintains the old and gracious traditions of personal service and true Yorkshire hospitality.
Bedrooms: 3 single, 4 double, 5 twin
Bathrooms: 12 private

Bed & breakfast
per night:	£min	£max
Single	28.00	35.00
Double	48.00	52.00

Half board
per person:	£min	£max
Daily	34.00	36.00
Weekly	210.00	230.00

Evening meal 1830 (last orders 1900)
Parking for 10
Cards accepted: Access, Visa

Knabbs Ash
HIGHLY COMMENDED

Skipton Road, Felliscliffe, Harrogate HG3 2LT
☎ (0423) 771040

112

YORKSHIRE & HUMBERSIDE

Set back off the A59 Harrogate to Skipton road, 6 miles west of Harrogate, in its own grounds. In a panoramic, tranquil setting. Ideal area for walking and exploring the Yorkshire dales.
Bedrooms: 2 double, 1 twin
Bathrooms: 3 private

Bed & breakfast

per night:	£min	£max
Single	25.00	25.00
Double	40.00	40.00

Parking for 6

17 Peckfield Close
Listed APPROVED

Hampsthwaite, Harrogate HG3 2ES
☎ (0423) 770765
In picturesque village 4 miles from Harrogate off A59. Large, attractive garden. At start of Nidderdale Walk.
Bedrooms: 1 single, 2 twin
Bathrooms: 1 public

Bed & breakfast

per night:	£min	£max
Single	14.00	16.00
Double	28.00	32.00

Half board

per person:	£min	£max
Daily	20.00	22.00

Parking for 2

HARTOFT END
North Yorkshire
Map ref 5C3

In the heart of the North York Moors.

High Farm ₳
Listed

Hartoft End, Pickering YO18 8RP
☎ Lastingham (0751) 417648
16-acre beef farm. Overlooking a wooded valley in an ideal walking and touring area, 3 miles from Rosedale Abbey and 17 miles from the coast.
Bedrooms: 1 single, 1 double
Bathrooms: 1 public

Bed & breakfast

per night:	£min	£max
Single	12.00	12.00
Double	24.00	24.00

Parking for 2
Open April-November

National Crown ratings were correct at the time of going to press but are subject to change. Please check at the time of booking.

HAWES
North Yorkshire
Map ref 5B3

The capital of Upper Wensleydale on the famous Pennine Way, renowned for great cheeses. Popular with walkers. Dales National Park Information Centre and Folk Museum. Nearby is spectacular Hardraw Force waterfall.

Ebor Guest House ₳
Listed

Burtersett Road, Hawes DL8 3NT
☎ Wensleydale (0969) 667337
Small, family-run guesthouse, double-glazed and centrally-heated throughout. Walkers are particularly welcome. Centrally located for touring the dales.
Bedrooms: 1 single, 2 double, 1 twin
Bathrooms: 1 private, 1 public

Bed & breakfast

per night:	£min	£max
Single	14.00	16.00
Double	28.00	32.00

Parking for 5

Springbank House ₳
COMMENDED

Springbank, Towntoft, Hawes DL8 3NW
☎ Wensleydale (0969) 667376
Delightful Victorian house near the centre of Hawes with superb views over the surrounding fells.
Bedrooms: 1 twin, 1 triple
Bathrooms: 2 private

Bed & breakfast

per night:	£min	£max
Double	32.00	32.00

Parking for 3
Open February-October

White Hart Inn ₳
APPROVED

Main Street, Hawes DL8 3QL
☎ Wensleydale (0969) 667259
Small country inn with a friendly welcome, offering home-cooked meals using local produce. An ideal centre for exploring the Yorkshire Dales.
Bedrooms: 1 single, 4 double, 2 twin
Bathrooms: 2 public

Bed & breakfast

per night:	£min	£max
Single	17.50	33.00
Double	34.00	

Lunch available
Evening meal 1900 (last orders 2100)
Parking for 7
Cards accepted: Access, Visa

HAWORTH
West Yorkshire
Map ref 4B1

This Pennine town is famous as home of the Brontë family. The parsonage is now a Brontë Museum where furniture and possessions of the family are displayed. Moors and Brontë waterfalls nearby and steam trains on the Keighley and Worth Valley Railway pass through.
Tourist Information Centre
☎ (0535) 642329

Ebor House
APPROVED

Lees Lane, Haworth, Keighley BD22 8RA
☎ Keighley (0535) 645869
Yorkshire stone-built house of character, conveniently placed for the main tourist attractions of Haworth, including the Worth Valley Railway and Brontë Parsonage and Museum.
Bedrooms: 3 twin
Bathrooms: 1 public

Bed & breakfast

per night:	£min	£max
Single	14.00	14.00
Double	26.00	26.00

Parking for 2

Hole Farm
Listed COMMENDED

Dimples Lane, Haworth, Keighley BD22 8QS
☎ Keighley (0535) 644755
8-acre smallholding. 17th C farmhouse, 5 minutes' walk from Brontë Parsonage and 2 minutes' walk from the moors. Farm has peacocks, geese, cattle and horses. At the top of Haworth take first left after the Sun pub, first left again, then third drive on left.
Bedrooms: 2 double
Bathrooms: 2 private

Bed & breakfast

per night:	£min	£max
Double	32.00	32.00

Parking for 4

The Lee
Listed

Lee Lane, Oxenhope, Keighley BD22 9RB
☎ (0535) 646311
Detached 17th C house with 6 acres of land, 1.5 miles from the centre of Haworth. Close to the moors and waterfalls.
Bedrooms: 1 double, 1 triple
Bathrooms: 1 private, 1 public

Bed & breakfast

per night:	£min	£max
Double	27.00	29.00

Parking for 4

113

YORKSHIRE & HUMBERSIDE

HAWORTH
Continued

Old White Lion Hotel
COMMENDED
Haworth, Keighley BD22 8DU
☎ Keighley (0535) 642313
Fax (0535) 646222
Family-run, centuries old coaching inn. Candlelit restaurant using local fresh produce cooked to order and featured in food guides. Old world bars serving extensive range of bar snacks and real ales.
Bedrooms: 3 single, 6 double, 2 twin, 4 triple
Bathrooms: 15 private

Bed & breakfast
per night:	£min	£max
Single		32.00
Double		45.00

Lunch available
Evening meal 1900 (last orders 2200)
Parking for 10
Cards accepted: Access, Visa, Diners, Amex

HELLIFIELD
North Yorkshire
Map ref 4B1

Black Horse Hotel
COMMENDED
Main Road, Hellifield, Skipton
BD23 4HT
☎ (0729) 850223
Country pub on the A65 Skipton-Settle route. Restaurant, en-suite bedrooms, public bar, bar meals and function facilities.
Bedrooms: 1 single, 3 double, 2 twin, 1 triple
Bathrooms: 7 private

Bed & breakfast
per night:	£min	£max
Single	20.00	25.00
Double	40.00	60.00

Lunch available
Evening meal 1800 (last orders 2130)
Parking for 50
Cards accepted: Access, Visa, Amex

Wenningber Farm
HIGHLY COMMENDED
Airton Road, Hellifield, Skipton
BD23 4JR
☎ (0729) 850856
80-acre mixed farm. In a picturesque location between Hellifield and Otterburn, just 5 miles from Malham in the Yorkshire Dales National Park.
Bedrooms: 1 double, 1 twin
Bathrooms: 1 public

Bed & breakfast
per night:	£min	£max
Single	15.00	17.00
Double	29.00	30.00

Parking for 10
Open March-October

HELMSLEY
North Yorkshire
Map ref 5C3

Pretty town on the River Rye at the entrance to Ryedale and the North York Moors, with large square and remains of 12th C castle, several inns and All Saints' Church.

Sproxton Hall
HIGHLY COMMENDED
Sproxton, Helmsley, York YO6 5EQ
☎ (0439) 70225
300-acre mixed farm. 17th C Grade II listed stone farmhouse, beamed, beautifully decorated and comfortably furnished. In a peaceful setting with panoramic views, 1.5 miles from Helmsley. Excellent base for the North York Moors, York, the coast and dales. Non-smokers only please.
Bedrooms: 1 double, 1 twin
Bathrooms: 2 public

Bed & breakfast
per night:	£min	£max
Double	35.00	43.00

Parking for 10

Wether-Cote Farm
Listed
Bilsdale West, Helmsley, York
YO6 5NF
☎ Bilsdale (0439) 798260
300-acre mixed farm. Seven miles north of Helmsley in picturesque Bilsdale. Ideally placed for walking or touring. Short drive to Herriot and Heartbeat country. Cosy rooms with tea/coffee-making facilities. TV lounge, separate dining room, bathroom and shower room. Good home cooking and a real Yorkshire welcome.
Bedrooms: 1 double, 1 twin, 1 triple
Bathrooms: 2 public

Bed & breakfast
per night:	£min	£max
Single	14.00	15.00
Double	28.00	30.00

Half board
per person:	£min	£max
Daily	24.00	25.00
Weekly	163.00	168.00

Lunch available
Evening meal from 1830
Open March-October

HOLMFIRTH
West Yorkshire
Map ref 4B1

This village has become famous as the location for the filming of the TV series "Last of the Summer Wine". It has a postcard museum and is on the edge of the Peak District National Park.
Tourist Information Centre
☎ *(0484) 687603*

Spring Head House
Listed
15 Holmfirth Road, Shepley, Huddersfield HD8 8BB
☎ Huddersfield (0484) 606300
Fax (0484) 608030
Large Georgian house with a garden, close to Holmfirth and "Summer Wine" country and with easy access to the M1 and M62.
Bedrooms: 1 single, 1 twin
Bathrooms: 1 private, 1 public

Bed & breakfast
per night:	£min	£max
Single		17.00
Double		33.00

Parking for 3

29 Woodhead Road
COMMENDED
Holmfirth, Huddersfield HD7 1JU
☎ (0484) 683962
200-year-old family home, 5 minutes' walk from Holmfirth. Tea and coffee available at any time. Good walking area and pleasant countryside.
Bedrooms: 1 twin
Bathrooms: 1 private

Bed & breakfast
per night:	£min	£max
Single	13.50	14.00
Double	27.00	28.00

Parking for 2

HORTON-IN-RIBBLESDALE
North Yorkshire
Map ref 5B3

On the River Ribble and an ideal centre for pot-holing. The Pennine Way runs eastward over Pen-y-ghent, one of the famous "Three Peaks".
Tourist Information Centre
☎ *(0729) 860333*

Crown Hotel
Horton-in-Ribblesdale, Settle
BD24 0HF
☎ Settle (0729) 860209

YORKSHIRE & HUMBERSIDE

Small family-run country inn offering a warm welcome and friendly hospitality, in the heart of the dales.
Bedrooms: 2 single, 3 double, 4 triple
Bathrooms: 2 private, 2 public, 5 private showers
Bed & breakfast
per night:	£min	£max
Single	18.50	25.50
Double	37.00	51.00

Lunch available
Evening meal 1830 (last orders 2100)
Parking for 15
Cards accepted: Diners

HUBBERHOLME
North Yorkshire
Map ref 5B3

Ancient Upper Wharfedale village with a charming and interesting church noted for its rood loft dated 1558, a rare survival in England.

The George Inn
Listed
Kirk Gill, Hubberholme, Skipton BD23 5JE
☎ Kettlewell (0756) 760223
An ancient inn in the heart of the Yorkshire Dales. In "Good Pub Guide".
Bedrooms: 2 double, 1 twin
Bathrooms: 1 public
Bed & breakfast
per night:	£min	£max
Single	25.00	25.00
Double	36.00	36.00

Lunch available
Evening meal 1930 (last orders 2045)
Parking for 20

HUDDERSFIELD
West Yorkshire
Map ref 4B1

Founded on wool and cloth, has a famous choral society. Town centre redeveloped, but several good Victorian buildings remain, including railway station, St Peter's Church, Tolson Memorial Museum, art gallery and nearby Colne Valley Museum.
Tourist Information Centre
☎ (0484) 430808

Hollies Guest House
286 Halifax Old Road, Grimscar, Huddersfield HD2 2SP
☎ (0484) 427097

In woodland on the valley side with wildlife. A beautiful area, renowned for its industrial/historic heritage and music. All rooms with washbasins and colour TV. "Kirklees Way" long distance footpath.
Bedrooms: 1 single, 2 double
Bathrooms: 1 private, 1 public
Bed & breakfast
per night:	£min	£max
Single	14.00	16.00
Double	28.00	32.00

Lunch available
Parking for 4

HUNTON
North Yorkshire
Map ref 5C3

The Countryman's Inn
Hunton, Bedale DL8 1PY
☎ Bedale (0677) 50554
Recently modernised village inn and restaurant, retaining its old world charm, with log fires and beamed ceilings. Four-poster room. Just off the A684 between Bedale and Leyburn, convenient for the Yorkshire Dales.
Bedrooms: 5 double, 1 twin
Bathrooms: 6 private
Bed & breakfast
per night:	£min	£max
Single	25.00	30.00
Double	38.00	42.00

Parking for 20
Cards accepted: Access, Visa

HUSTHWAITE
North Yorkshire
Map ref 5C3

Attractive village beneath Hambleton Hills, of weathered brickwork houses and a green dominated by medieval church of St Nicholas with some Norman features.

Flower of May
Listed
Husthwaite, York YO6 3SG
☎ Coxwold (0347) 868317
153-acre mixed farm. Family-run farm with beautiful views of the Vale of York. Convenient for North York Moors, York and coast.
Bedrooms: 1 single, 1 double, 1 twin
Bathrooms: 1 public
Bed & breakfast
per night:	£min	£max
Single	11.00	11.00
Double	22.00	22.00

Parking for 5
Open February-November

ILKLEY
West Yorkshire
Map ref 4B1

This moorland town is famous for its ballad. The 16th C manor house, now a museum, displays local prehistoric and Roman relics. Popular walk leads up Heber's Ghyll to Ilkley Moor, with the mysterious Swastika Stone and White Wells, 18th C plunge baths.
Tourist Information Centre
☎ (0943) 602319

Briarwood
COMMENDED
Queens Drive, Ilkley LS29 9QW
☎ (0943) 600870
Victorian ladies' residence with spacious rooms and excellent views. Visitors are entertained as house guests. 5 minutes' walk from Ilkley Moor and Ilkley College.
Bedrooms: 2 twin
Bathrooms: 2 private, 1 public
Bed & breakfast
per night:	£min	£max
Single	15.00	17.00
Double	30.00	30.00

Parking for 5

Summerhill Guest House
24 Crossbeck Road, Ilkley LS29 9TN
☎ (0943) 607067
On the edge of Ilkley Moor with lovely views and within easy walking distance of the town.
Bedrooms: 1 single, 1 double, 5 twin
Bathrooms: 2 private, 1 public
Bed & breakfast
per night:	£min	£max
Single	12.00	16.00
Double	24.00	32.00

Half board
per person:	£min	£max
Daily	20.00	34.00

Evening meal 1830 (last orders 1830)
Parking for 5

There are separate sections in this guide listing groups specialising in farm holidays and accommodation which is especially suitable for young people and organised groups.

115

YORKSHIRE & HUMBERSIDE

INGLEBY GREENHOW
North Yorkshire
Map ref 5C3

Perched on the edge of Cleveland Hills, the village boasts the Norman church of St Andrew's with well-preserved carving and effigies of a priest and a knight. Ingleby Moor rises 1300 ft above village.

Manor House Farm
COMMENDED

Ingleby Greenhow, Middlesbrough, Cleveland TS9 6RB
☎ Great Ayton (0642) 722384
164-acre mixed farm. In a picture book setting surrounded by hills and forests, in the North York Moors National Park. Ideal for nature lovers, walking, touring, riding and relaxing. Fine food and wines.
Bedrooms: 1 double, 2 twin
Bathrooms: 2 private, 1 public

Half board
per person:	£min	£max
Daily	34.50	37.00
Weekly	224.00	

Evening meal 1900 (last orders 1600)
Parking for 66
Open January-November
Cards accepted: Amex

INGLETON
North Yorkshire
Map ref 5B3

Thriving tourist centre for fell-walkers, climbers and pot-holers. Popular walks up beautiful Twiss Valley to Ingleborough Summit, Whernside, White Scar Caves and waterfalls.

Bridge End Guest House

Mill Lane, Ingleton, Carnforth, Lancashire LA6 3EP
☎ (052 42) 41413
Georgian house pleasantly situated adjacent to the entrance to the Waterfalls walk. It features a cantilevered patio over the River Doe and retains an elegant staircase. All rooms en-suite. Vegetarians welcome.
Bedrooms: 1 single, 1 double, 1 triple
Bathrooms: 3 private, 1 public

Bed & breakfast
per night:	£min	£max
Single	18.00	19.50
Double	32.00	34.00

Half board
per person:	£min	£max
Daily	24.50	28.00
Weekly	162.00	185.00

Lunch available
Evening meal 1830 (last orders 2030)
Parking for 10

Ingleborough View
COMMENDED

Main Street, Ingleton, Carnforth, Lancashire LA6 3HH
☎ (052 42) 41523
Small, friendly guesthouse offering very comfortable accommodation. Panoramic views of river and mountain. Ideally situated for local walks, touring dales/Lake District.
Bedrooms: 2 double, 1 twin, 1 triple
Bathrooms: 1 private, 2 public

Bed & breakfast
per night:	£min	£max
Single	17.00	20.00
Double	26.00	32.00

Parking for 4

KETTLEWELL
North Yorkshire
Map ref 5B3

Set in the spectacular scenery of the Yorkshire Dales National Park in Wharfedale, this former market town is a convenient stopping place for climbers and walkers. Dramatic rock formation of Kilnsey Crag is 3 miles south.

Fold Farm
HIGHLY COMMENDED

Kettlewell, Skipton BD23 5RJ
☎ Skipton (0756) 760886
350-acre hill farm. 15th C stone-built farmhouse in the village. Close to all amenities. Private car parking.
Bedrooms: 2 double, 1 twin
Bathrooms: 3 private

Bed & breakfast
per night:	£min	£max
Single	25.00	25.00
Double	36.00	40.00

Parking for 6
Open April-October

KIRKBY
North Yorkshire
Map ref 5C3

Dromonby Hall Farm
COMMENDED

Busby Lane, Kirkby, Stokesley, Middlesbrough, Cleveland TS9 7AP
☎ Middlesbrough (0642) 712312
170-acre mixed farm. Modern farmhouse with superb views of hills and a short drive from coast. Beautiful walking and riding country (riding available on farm), ideal for touring by

car. One mile below Cringle Moor on the Coast to Coast and Cleveland Way.
Bedrooms: 1 double, 2 twin
Bathrooms: 1 private, 1 public

Bed & breakfast
per night:	£min	£max
Single	15.00	17.50
Double	30.00	35.00

Half board
per person:	£min	£max
Daily	25.00	
Weekly	150.00	

Parking for 6

KIRKBYMOORSIDE
North Yorkshire
Map ref 5C3

Attractive market town with remains of Norman castle. Good centre for exploring moors. Nearby are wild daffodils of Farndale.

Low Northolme Farm
HIGHLY COMMENDED

Salton, York YO6 6RP
☎ (0751) 32321
220-acre mixed farm. 18th C farmhouse set in peaceful area of Ryedale, 6 miles from Helmsley, just two miles south of A170.
Bedrooms: 1 single, 1 twin, 1 triple
Bathrooms: 3 private

Bed & breakfast
per night:	£min	£max
Double	32.00	35.00

Half board
per person:	£min	£max
Daily	24.50	26.00

Evening meal 1830 (last orders 1930)
Parking for 6
Open March-October

KNARESBOROUGH
North Yorkshire
Map ref 4B1

Picturesque market town on the River Nidd, famous for its 11th C castle ruins, overlooking town and river gorge. Attractions include oldest chemist's shop in country, prophetess Mother Shipton's cave, Dropping Well and Court House Museum. Boating on river.

Ebor Mount

18 York Place, Knaresborough HG5 0AA
☎ Harrogate (0423) 863315
Charming 18th C townhouse with private car park, providing bed and breakfast accommodation in recently refurbished rooms. Ideal touring centre.
Bedrooms: 1 single, 4 double, 1 twin, 2 triple

YORKSHIRE & HUMBERSIDE

Bathrooms: 8 private, 1 public

Bed & breakfast
per night:	£min	£max
Single	17.50	30.00
Double	35.00	40.00

Parking for 10
Cards accepted: Access, Visa

Yorkshire Lass ₳
APPROVED
High Bridge, Harrogate Road, Knaresborough HG5 8DA
☎ Harrogate (0423) 862962
Detached inn on main Harrogate/York road, with attractive bedrooms overlooking River Nidd. Real ales, wines, large selection of whiskies. Specialising in traditional Yorkshire dishes.
Bedrooms: 1 single, 2 double, 2 twin, 1 triple
Bathrooms: 6 private

Bed & breakfast
per night:	£min	£max
Single	30.00	40.00
Double	45.00	52.00

Half board
per person:	£min	£max
Daily	32.00	37.00
Weekly	224.00	224.00

Lunch available
Evening meal 1700 (last orders 2200)
Parking for 34
Cards accepted: Access, Visa, Amex

LEEDS
West Yorkshire
Map ref 4B1

Large city with excellent modern shopping centre and much splendid Victorian architecture. Museums and galleries including Temple Newsam House (the Hampton Court of the North). Home of Opera North and a new playhouse.
Tourist Information Centre
☎ (0532) 478101

Broomhurst Hotel ₳
COMMENDED
12 Chapel Lane, Headingley, Leeds LS6 3BW
☎ (0532) 786836
Fax (0532) 786836
Small, comfortable, owner-run hotel in a quiet, pleasantly wooded conservation area, 1.5 miles from the city centre. Convenient for Yorkshire County Cricket Ground and university.
Bedrooms: 4 double, 4 twin, 2 triple
Bathrooms: 8 private, 2 public

Bed & breakfast
per night:	£min	£max
Single	23.50	33.50
Double	37.00	45.00

Half board
per person:	£min	£max
Daily	34.00	44.00

Evening meal 1800 (last orders 0900)
Parking for 5
Cards accepted: Access, Visa

Eagle Tavern ₳
Listed
North Street, Leeds LS7 1AF
☎ (0532) 457146
Traditional pub in a commercial district of Leeds, offering friendly service at reasonable prices. Close to the city centre. Colour TV in all rooms. Voted CAMRA pub of the year 1989, 1990 and 1992.
Bedrooms: 1 single, 6 twin, 2 triple
Bathrooms: 2 public

Bed & breakfast
per night:	£min	£max
Single	20.00	22.00
Double	40.00	44.00

Evening meal 1730 (last orders 1900)
Parking for 12

Harewood Arms Hotel ₳
HIGHLY COMMENDED
Harrogate Road, Harewood, Leeds LS17 9LH
☎ (0532) 886566
Fax (0532) 886064
Stone-built hotel and restaurant of character with a rural aspect, 8 miles from Harrogate and Leeds. Opposite Harewood House and close to all amenities, including golf and racing.
Bedrooms: 2 single, 10 double, 10 twin, 2 triple
Bathrooms: 24 private

Bed & breakfast
per night:	£min	£max
Single	47.00	67.00
Double	62.00	80.00

Half board
per person:	£min	£max
Daily	62.50	82.50

Lunch available
Evening meal 1900 (last orders 2200)
Parking for 60
Cards accepted: Access, Visa, Diners, Amex, Switch

St Michael's Tower Hotel ₳
5 St Michael's Villas, Cardigan Road, Headingley, Leeds LS6 3AF
☎ (0532) 755557
Fax (0532) 755557
Comfortable, owner-run licensed hotel, 1.5 miles from city centre and close to Headingley cricket ground and university. Easy access to Yorkshire countryside.
Bedrooms: 7 single, 7 double, 7 twin, 1 triple, 1 family room
Bathrooms: 12 private, 4 public

Bed & breakfast
per night:	£min	£max
Single	19.50	26.00
Double	32.00	36.00

Half board
per person:	£min	£max
Daily	29.00	45.00

Evening meal 1830 (last orders 2000)
Parking for 26
Cards accepted: Access, Visa

The White House ₳
Listed APPROVED
157 Middleton Park Road, Leeds LS10 4LZ
☎ (0532) 711231
Spacious, detached house. Excellent local transport from near the door. Convenient for M1, M62 and West Riding towns and ideal stopover for North/South travel. Non-smokers only please.
Bedrooms: 1 double, 2 twin
Bathrooms: 1 public

Bed & breakfast
per night:	£min	£max
Single	16.00	16.00
Double	28.00	28.00

Parking for 2

LEEDS/BRADFORD AIRPORT
See under Bingley, Bradford, Leeds, Otley

LONG MARSTON
North Yorkshire
Map ref 4C1

Close to the site of the Battle of Marston Moor, a decisive Civil War battle of 1644. A monument commemorates the event.

Gill House Farm ₳
HIGHLY COMMENDED
Tockwith Road, Long Marston, York YO5 8PJ
☎ Rufforth (0904) 738379
500-acre mixed farm. Peaceful period farmhouse set in glorious countryside overlooking the Vale of York. Warm welcome. Good bus route and lots of local eating places.
Bedrooms: 2 double, 1 triple, 1 family room
Bathrooms: 4 private

Bed & breakfast
per night:	£min	£max
Double	40.00	

Parking for 5

117

YORKSHIRE & HUMBERSIDE

LOW ROW
North Yorkshire
Map ref 5B3

Swaledale village full of character with grey-stone houses. There is a village custom where children attending chapel who are able to recite psalms are given a Bible.

Crackpot Cottage
Listed COMMENDED

Crackpot, Low Row, Richmond
DL11 6NW
☎ Richmond (0748) 86486
Comfortably modernised dales farmhouse, dated 1721, in an elevated position three-quarters of a mile from Low Row village. Home cooking a speciality, vegetarians catered for.
Bedrooms: 1 double, 1 twin
Bathrooms: 1 private, 1 public

Bed & breakfast
per night:	£min	£max
Single	15.00	16.00
Double	30.00	32.00

Half board
per person:	£min	£max
Daily	20.50	27.00

Evening meal 1900 (last orders 1950)
Parking for 2

LUND
Humberside
Map ref 4C1

Clematis House, Farmhouse Bed & Breakfast

1 Eastgate, Lund, Driffield, North Humberside YO25 9TQ
☎ Driffield (0377) 217204
389-acre arable & livestock farm. Family-run working farm in pretty rural village. Farmhouse with character, spacious yet cosy, with en-suite rooms and tea/coffee making facilities. Secluded walled garden, TV lounge.
Bedrooms: 1 double, 1 twin
Bathrooms: 2 private

Bed & breakfast
per night:	£min	£max
Single	18.50	18.50
Double	34.00	34.00

Half board
per person:	£min	£max
Daily	26.00	26.00
Weekly	164.00	164.00

Evening meal 1800 (last orders 2000)
Parking for 4

MALHAM
North Yorkshire
Map ref 5B3

Hamlet of stone cottages amid magnificent rugged limestone scenery in the Yorkshire Dales National Park. Malham Cove is a curving, sheer white cliff 240 ft high. Malham Tarn, one of Yorkshire's few natural lakes, belongs to the National Trust. National Park Centre.

Beck Hall Guest House

Malham, Skipton BD23 4DJ
☎ Airton (0729) 830332
Family-run guesthouse set in a spacious riverside garden. Homely atmosphere, four-poster beds, log fires and home cooking.
Bedrooms: 11 double, 3 twin
Bathrooms: 11 private, 1 public

Bed & breakfast
per night:	£min	£max
Single	16.00	24.00
Double	30.00	38.00

Half board
per person:	£min	£max
Daily	21.50	25.50

Lunch available
Evening meal 1900 (last orders 2000)
Parking for 30

Miresfield Farm

Malham, Skipton BD23 4DA
☎ Airton (0729) 830414
In a beautiful garden bordering the village green and a tumbling stream. Ideal base for touring the national park.
Bedrooms: 6 double, 3 twin, 4 triple
Bathrooms: 11 private, 2 public

Bed & breakfast
per night:	£min	£max
Single	25.00	30.00
Double	40.00	44.00

Half board
per person:	£min	£max
Daily	28.00	30.00
Weekly	196.00	210.00

Evening meal 1830 (last orders 1200)
Parking for 16

Individual proprietors have supplied all details of accommodation. Although we do check for accuracy, we advise you to confirm the information at the time of booking.

MALTON
North Yorkshire
Map ref 5D3

Thriving farming town on the River Derwent with large livestock market. Famous for racehorse training. The local museum has Roman remains and many World War II relics from the "Eden" prisoner of war camp on site in the town. Castle Howard within easy reach.

Leonard House
COMMENDED

45 Old Maltongate, Malton YO17 0EH
☎ (0653) 697242
Comfortable Georgian house in market town, central for touring Ryedale, the moors and coast. Easy access by car, train or bus. Non-smokers only please.
Bedrooms: 1 double, 1 twin
Bathrooms: 1 public

Bed & breakfast
per night:	£min	£max
Single	14.00	14.00
Double	28.00	28.00

Parking for 3

MARKET WEIGHTON
Humberside
Map ref 4C1

Small town on the western side of the Yorkshire Wolds. A tablet in the parish church records the death of William Bradley in 1820 at which time he was 7 ft 9 in tall and weighed 27 stone!

Arras Farmhouse
Listed

Arras Farm, Market Weighton, York YO4 3RN
☎ (0430) 872404

460-acre arable farm. Large farmhouse and grounds, peaceful and comfortable, on A1079 between Market Weighton and Beverley. 3 miles from Market Weighton at crossroads.
Bedrooms: 2 double, 1 twin
Bathrooms: 2 private, 1 public

Bed & breakfast
per night:	£min	£max
Single	16.00	18.00
Double	28.00	32.00

Parking for 5

YORKSHIRE & HUMBERSIDE

MASHAM
North Yorkshire
Map ref 5C3

Famous market town on the River Ure, with a large market square. St Mary's Church has Norman tower and 13th C spire. Theakston's "Old Peculier" ale is brewed here.

Lamb Hill Farm
COMMENDED

Masham, Ripon HG4 4DJ
☎ Ripon (0765) 689274
390-acre mixed farm. Spacious and comfortable old farmhouse with views of the dales. Ideally situated for exploring Herriot country, yet only 45 minutes from York. 2 miles from Masham. A1 5 miles. Durham 1 hour.
Bedrooms: 1 double, 1 twin, 1 triple
Bathrooms: 3 private

Bed & breakfast per night:	£min	£max
Double	30.00	32.00

Half board per person:	£min	£max
Daily	25.00	25.00
Weekly	170.00	170.00

Evening meal from 1900
Parking for 5

Leighton Hall Farm
Listed APPROVED

Healey, Ripon HG4 4LS
☎ Ripon (0765) 689360
540-acre mixed farm. Farmhouse is a former monastery with beautiful panoramic views. Between the dales and 5 minutes from a fishing reservoir. Also near a pony trekking centre.
Bedrooms: 1 double, 2 twin
Bathrooms: 1 private, 1 public

Bed & breakfast per night:	£min	£max
Single	13.00	15.00
Double	26.00	30.00

Evening meal from 1830
Parking for 3
Open May-October

Pasture House
COMMENDED

Healey, Ripon HG4 4LJ
☎ Ripon (0765) 689149
100-year-old detached house in 3.5 acres at the foot of Colsterdale, a beautiful, small and quiet dale leading to grouse moors. Fishing and golf available by arrangement.
Bedrooms: 1 double, 1 twin, 1 triple
Bathrooms: 2 public

Bed & breakfast per night:	£min	£max
Single	12.00	12.00
Double	24.00	24.00

Half board per person:	£min	£max
Daily	20.00	20.00
Weekly	135.00	135.00

Lunch available
Evening meal from 1900
Parking for 6

MIDDLEHAM
North Yorkshire
Map ref 5C3

Town famous for racehorse training, with cobbled squares and houses of local stone. Norman castle, once principal residence of Warwick the Kingmaker and later Richard III. Ruins of Jervaulx Abbey nearby.

Black Swan Hotel
APPROVED

Market Place, Middleham, Leyburn DL8 4NP
☎ Wensleydale (0969) 22221
Unspoilt 17th C inn, with open fires and beamed ceilings, allied to 20th C comforts. Emphasis on food.
Bedrooms: 1 single, 4 double, 1 twin, 1 triple
Bathrooms: 7 private

Bed & breakfast per night:	£min	£max
Single	25.00	26.00
Double	40.00	56.00

Half board per person:	£min	£max
Daily	29.00	37.00

Lunch available
Evening meal 1900 (last orders 2100)
Parking for 3
Cards accepted: Access, Visa

Waterford House
HIGHLY COMMENDED

19 Kirkgate, Middleham, Leyburn DL8 4PG
☎ Wensleydale (0969) 22090
Fax (0969) 24020
Fine food and wine and a warm, friendly and comfortable stay in beautiful surroundings are assured. Lunch and full English afternoon tea available.
Bedrooms: 3 double, 1 triple, 1 family room
Bathrooms: 4 private

Bed & breakfast per night:	£min	£max
Single	35.00	45.00
Double	55.00	75.00

Half board per person:	£min	£max
Daily	43.00	61.00
Weekly	274.00	390.00

Lunch available
Evening meal 1900 (last orders 2200)

Parking for 8
Cards accepted: Access, Visa, Diners

MYTHOLMROYD
West Yorkshire
Map ref 4B1

Situated in the Calder Valley, the meaning of the name originates from "a clearance of woodland where streams join".

Riga Rose

Scout Close, Mytholmroyd, Hebden Bridge HX7 5JU
☎ Halifax (0422) 885415
Homely bed and breakfast accommodation designed with the visitor in mind.
Bedrooms: 1 double
Bathrooms: 1 private

Bed & breakfast per night:	£min	£max
Double		34.00

Parking for 2
Open March-December

MYTON-ON-SWALE
North Yorkshire
Map ref 5C3

Small village on the mighty River Swale.

Plump House Farm

Myton-on-Swale, York YO6 2RA
☎ Boroughbridge (0423) 360650
160-acre mixed farm. A warm welcome with comfortable en-suite accommodation on a working family farm. Easy access to York and Harrogate and an ideal centre for the coast, dales and moors. Reductions for children.
Bedrooms: 1 double, 1 family room
Bathrooms: 2 private

Bed & breakfast per night:	£min	£max
Single	12.00	

Half board per person:	£min	£max
Daily	18.00	

Evening meal 1800 (last orders 2000)
Parking for 4

Colour maps at the back of this guide pinpoint all places which have accommodation listings in the guide.

119

YORKSHIRE & HUMBERSIDE

NORTHALLERTON
North Yorkshire
Map ref 5C3

Formerly a staging post on coaching route to the North and later a railway town. Today a lively market town and administrative capital of North Yorkshire. Parish church of All Saints dates from 1200.
Tourist Information Centre
☎ (0609) 776864

Lovesome Hill Farm
COMMENDED
Lovesome Hill, Northallerton DL6 2PB
☎ (0609) 772311
165-acre mixed farm. 19th C farmhouse. Tastefully converted granary adjoins with spacious, quality en-suite rooms. "You'll love it". North of Northallerton, twixt dales and moors.
Bedrooms: 2 double, 1 triple
Bathrooms: 3 private, 1 public

Bed & breakfast
per night:	£min	£max
Single	20.00	30.00
Double	32.00	40.00

Half board
per person:	£min	£max
Daily	24.50	28.50

Evening meal from 1900
Parking for 10
Open February-November

NUNNINGTON
North Yorkshire
Map ref 5C3

On the River Rye, this picturesque village has a splendid Hall which houses some magnificent 17th C tapestries.

Sunley Court
COMMENDED
Nunnington, York YO6 5XQ
☎ Helmsley (0439) 748233
200-acre arable and mixed farm. On the A64 York to Malton road, turn left through Castle Howard and take Slingsby road to crossroads, then follow sign for Kirkbymoorside for 5 miles, farm is on left. 3 bedrooms have TV, twin and double room are en-suite.
Bedrooms: 2 single, 1 double, 1 twin
Bathrooms: 2 private, 1 public

Bed & breakfast
per night:	£min	£max
Single	15.00	
Double	30.00	

Half board
per person:	£min	£max
Daily	25.00	
Weekly	175.00	

Lunch available
Evening meal 1800 (last orders 2100)

Parking for 9
Open April-October

OAKWORTH
West Yorkshire
Map ref 4B1

This village lies on the route of the Worth Valley Railway which was the location of the film "The Railway Children", and is only 1 mile north of Haworth.

Broad Acre Farm
Listed COMMENDED
Broadhead Lane, Oakworth, Keighley BD22 DQN
☎ Haworth (0535) 643365
8-acre mixed farm. Large barn built 1992. Four miles from Keighley, 2 miles from Oakworth village and two and a half miles from Haworth. Large dining room, large sitting room. Good views.
Bedrooms: 1 twin, 1 family
Bathrooms: 1 private, 1 public

Bed & breakfast
per night:	£min	£max
Single	14.00	15.00
Double	28.00	30.00

Lunch available
Parking for 17
Open April-October

OSMOTHERLEY
North Yorkshire
Map ref 5C3

The famous "Lyke Wake Walk", across the Cleveland Hills to Ravenscar 40 miles away, starts here in this ancient village. Attached to the village cross is a large stone table used as a "pulpit" by John Wesley.

Quintana House
Listed COMMENDED
Back Lane, Osmotherley, Northallerton DL6 3BJ
☎ (0609) 883258
Detached, stone cottage near National Park village centre, within 90 metres of the Cleveland Way, affording panoramic views of Black Hambleton. Non-smokers only please.
Bedrooms: 1 double, 1 twin
Bathrooms: 1 public

Bed & breakfast
per night:	£min	£max
Double	28.00	30.00

Half board
per person:	£min	£max
Daily	20.00	33.00
Weekly	135.00	231.00

Evening meal 1830 (last orders 2000)
Parking for 5

OTLEY
West Yorkshire
Map ref 4B1

Market and manufacturing town in Lower Wharfedale, the birthplace of Thomas Chippendale. Has a Maypole, several old inns, rebuilt medieval bridge and a local history museum. All Saints Church dates from Norman times.
Tourist Information Centre
☎ (0532) 477707

Paddock Hill
APPROVED
Norwood, Otley LS21 2QU
☎ (0943) 465977
Converted farmhouse on the B6451 with open fires and lovely views. Within easy reach of Herriot, Bronte and Emmerdale country, the dales, Skipton, Harrogate and Leeds. Reservoir fishing nearby.
Bedrooms: 1 double, 2 twin
Bathrooms: 1 public, 1 private shower

Bed & breakfast
per night:	£min	£max
Single	13.50	16.00
Double	27.00	32.00

Parking for 3

PATELEY BRIDGE
North Yorkshire
Map ref 5C3

Small market town at centre of Upper Nidderdale. Flax and linen industries once flourished in this remote and beautiful setting.

North Pasture Farm
Brimham Rocks, Summer Bridge, Harrogate HG3 4DW
☎ Harrogate (0423) 711470
135-acre dairy farm. Parts of the house date back to 1400 and 1657. John Wesley preached in what is now the lounge.
Bedrooms: 2 double, 1 twin
Bathrooms: 3 private

Bed & breakfast
per night:	£min	£max
Single	20.00	
Double	40.00	

Half board
per person:	£min	£max
Daily	30.00	

Evening meal from 1830
Parking for 6
Open April-October

YORKSHIRE & HUMBERSIDE

PICKERING
North Yorkshire
Map ref 5D3

Market town and tourist centre on edge of North York Moors. Parish church has complete set of 15th C wall paintings depicting lives of saints. Part of 12th C castle still stands. Beck Isle Museum. The North York Moors Railway begins here.
Tourist Information Centre
☎ *(0751) 473791*

Grindale House ₳
COMMENDED
123 Eastgate, Pickering YO18 7DW
☎ (0751) 76636
Beautiful 18th C stone/pantile townhouse. Lovely rooms with antique furniture, private facilities, TVs. Car park. Friendly informal atmosphere. Non-smokers only please.
Bedrooms: 2 double, 1 twin
Bathrooms: 3 private
Bed & breakfast

per night:	£min	£max
Single	18.00	23.00
Double	32.00	44.00

Parking for 8

Heathcote Guest House ₳
100 Eastgate, Pickering YO18 7DW
☎ (0751) 76991
Early Victorian house 5 minutes from town centre. Ideal for walking and touring. All bedrooms have private facilities. Optional dinners. Relaxed, friendly atmosphere. Secluded parking. Non-smoking throughout.
Bedrooms: 1 single, 3 double, 1 twin
Bathrooms: 5 private, 1 public
Bed & breakfast

per night:	£min	£max
Single	18.00	19.50
Double	36.00	39.00

Half board

per person:	£min	£max
Daily	27.00	28.50
Weekly	177.00	177.00

Evening meal 1830 (last orders 1100)
Parking for 7
Open January, March-December
Cards accepted: Access, Visa

Marton Hill ₳
Listed
Marton, Sinnington, York YO6 6RG
☎ Kirkbymoorside (0751) 31478
55-acre livestock farm. 300-year-old country house with spectacular views. 3 miles from Kirkbymoorside on the Malton road, with good easy access.
Bedrooms: 1 double, 1 twin
Bathrooms: 1 public

Bed & breakfast

per night:	£min	£max
Double	20.00	24.00

Parking for 2
Open April-October

The Old Vicarage ₳
COMMENDED
Yedingham, Malton YO17 8SL
☎ West Heslerton (0944) 728426
Delightful, Georgian former vicarage set in large gardens with panoramic views of moors and wolds. Pretty village, with local inn, approximately 7 miles from Pickering, on River Derwent in the heart of Ryedale. Dinner by arrangement.
Bedrooms: 2 double, 1 twin
Bathrooms: 1 private, 1 public
Bed & breakfast

per night:	£min	£max
Single	13.00	17.00
Double	26.00	34.00

Half board

per person:	£min	£max
Daily	21.00	25.00

Parking for 4

Rains Farm
Allerston, Pickering YO18 7PQ
☎ Scarborough (0723) 859333
120-acre arable farm. Renovated farmhouse, peaceful, picturesque location in the Vale of Pickering. Ideal touring base for moors and coast. Good food, warm welcome.
Bedrooms: 2 double, 2 twin, 1 triple
Bathrooms: 5 private
Bed & breakfast

per night:	£min	£max
Single	20.00	
Double	30.00	35.00

Half board

per person:	£min	£max
Daily	24.00	

Evening meal 1800 (last orders 1400)
Parking for 6
Open April-October

RAVENSCAR
North Yorkshire
Map ref 5D3

Splendidly-positioned small coastal resort with magnificent views over Robin Hood's Bay. Its Old Peak is the end of the famous Lyke Wake Walk or "corpse way".

Foxcliffe Tea Rooms ₳
APPROVED
Station Square, Ravenscar, Scarborough YO13 OLU
☎ Scarborough (0723) 871028

Traditional country tea room set amongst beautiful countryside in the National Park. Sea views from every room. Non-smoking household.
Bedrooms: 1 single, 1 double, 2 twin
Bathrooms: 1 private, 1 public
Bed & breakfast

per night:	£min	£max
Single	15.00	15.00
Double	30.00	34.00

Half board

per person:	£min	£max
Daily	23.00	25.00
Weekly	161.00	175.00

Lunch available
Evening meal 1830 (last orders 1600)
Open March-September

Smugglers Rock Country Guest House ₳
Ravenscar, Scarborough YO13 0ER
☎ Scarborough (0723) 870044
Georgian country house, reputedly a former smugglers' haunt, with panoramic views over the surrounding national park and sea. Half a mile from the village. Ideal centre for touring, walking and pony trekking.
Bedrooms: 1 single, 3 double, 1 twin, 2 triple, 2 family rooms
Bathrooms: 9 private
Bed & breakfast

per night:	£min	£max
Single	18.50	19.00
Double	37.00	38.00

Half board

per person:	£min	£max
Daily		26.50
Weekly		169.00

Evening meal 1830 (last orders 1600)
Parking for 12
Open March-November

REDMIRE
North Yorkshire
Map ref 5B3

Peaceful and little-known dales village at east end of Wensleydale. Pale stone cottages scattered around a large green with ancient oak tree and pinfold where stray animals were penned.

Elm House ₳
HIGHLY COMMENDED
Elm House Estate, Redmire, Leyburn DL8 4EW
☎ Wensleydale (0969) 22313
Stone-built, 17th C manor house, fully modernised to provide every comfort. In a peaceful garden setting, overlooking beautiful Wensleydale. Personal service by resident owners.
Bedrooms: 1 double, 1 twin, 1 triple
Continued ▶

121

YORKSHIRE & HUMBERSIDE

REDMIRE
Continued

Bathrooms: 3 private
Bed & breakfast
per night:	£min	£max
Single	20.00	22.00
Double	39.00	42.00

Parking for 10

REETH
North Yorkshire
Map ref 5B3

Once a market town and lead-mining centre, Reeth today serves holiday-makers in Swaledale with its folk museum and 18th C shops and inns lining the green at High Row.

Springfield House
Listed

Quaker Close, Reeth, Richmond DL11 6UY
☎ Richmond (0748) 84634
Close to Swaledale, wonderful walks and superb views. Excellent base for touring the dales. Comfortable rooms with TV. Warm welcome assured.
Bedrooms: 1 single, 1 double, 1 twin
Bathrooms: 1 public
Bed & breakfast
per night:	£min	£max
Single	13.50	14.00
Double	27.00	28.00

Parking for 3
Open March-December

RICHMOND
North Yorkshire
Map ref 5C3

Market town on edge of Swaledale with 11th C castle, Georgian and Victorian buildings surrounding cobbled market-place. Green Howards' Museum is in the former Holy Trinity Church. Attractions include the Georgian Theatre, Richmondshire Museum and Easby Abbey.
Tourist Information Centre
☎ (0748) 850252

Holmedale
COMMENDED

Dalton, Richmond DL11 7HX
☎ Teesdale (0833) 21236
Georgian house in a quiet village, midway between Richmond and Barnard Castle. Ideal for the Yorkshire and Durham dales.
Bedrooms: 1 double, 1 triple
Bathrooms: 1 public

Bed & breakfast
per night:	£min	£max
Single	15.00	
Double	25.00	

Half board
per person:	£min	£max
Daily	20.00	
Weekly	125.00	

Evening meal 1800 (last orders 1200)
Parking for 2

Mount Pleasant Farm
COMMENDED

Whashton, Richmond DL11 7JP
☎ (0748) 822784

280-acre mixed farm. En-suite rooms in a converted stable, 1 suitable for disabled. Ideal for a family holiday and a pleasant place to stay. Noted for good food and warm welcome. Lots to see and do on the farm. Please ring for brochure and menus.
Wheelchair access category 3
Bedrooms: 4 double, 1 twin, 1 family room
Bathrooms: 6 private
Bed & breakfast
per night:	£min	£max
Single	15.00	17.00
Double	30.00	32.00

Half board
per person:	£min	£max
Daily	24.00	25.00
Weekly	163.00	170.00

Evening meal 1830 (last orders 1200)
Parking for 6

The Restaurant On The Green
Listed COMMENDED

5-7 Bridge Street, Richmond DL10 4RW
☎ (0748) 826229

Imposing William and Mary property with Georgian sundials. At corner of the Green at foot of castle bluff, near River Swale and countryside, yet 250 yards from Market Place. Good food, fine wines. No smoking.
Bedrooms: 1 double, 1 twin
Bathrooms: 2 private

Bed & breakfast
per night:	£min	£max
Single	24.00	28.00
Double	33.00	35.00

Evening meal 1900 (last orders 2130)
Cards accepted: Access, Visa

RIPON
North Yorkshire
Map ref 5C3

Small, ancient city with impressive cathedral containing Saxon crypt which houses church treasures from all over Yorkshire. "Setting the Watch" tradition kept nightly by horn-blower in Market Square. Fountains Abbey nearby.

Bishopton Grove House
APPROVED

Bishopton, Ripon HG4 2QL
☎ (0765) 600888
Restored Georgian house in a lovely rural corner of Ripon, near the River Laver and Fountains Abbey.
Bedrooms: 2 double, 1 twin
Bathrooms: 1 private, 2 public
Bed & breakfast
per night:	£min	£max
Single	16.50	18.00
Double	30.00	35.00

Half board
per person:	£min	£max
Daily	25.00	25.00

Evening meal 1800 (last orders 1930)
Parking for 5

The Coopers

36 College Road, Ripon HG4 2HA
☎ (0765) 603708
Spacious, comfortable Victorian house in quiet area. En-suite facilities available. Special rates for children. Cyclists welcome, storage for bicycles. Take-away meals acceptable in rooms.
Bedrooms: 1 single, 1 twin, 1 family room
Bathrooms: 1 private, 1 public
Bed & breakfast
per night:	£min	£max
Single	15.00	16.00
Double	26.00	34.00

Parking for 3

Lowgate Cottage
Listed COMMENDED

Lowgate Lane, Sawley, Ripon HG4 3EL
☎ Sawley (0765) 620302
Restored dwelling, peacefully located in one third of an acre of beautiful gardens. 10 minutes' walking distance from Fountains Abbey and Studley Park.
Bedrooms: 1 double, 1 twin
Bathrooms: 1 public

YORKSHIRE & HUMBERSIDE

Bed & breakfast
per night:	£min	£max
Single		25.00
Double		29.00

Half board
per person:	£min	£max
Daily	21.00	26.00
Weekly	140.00	

Parking for 4

Moor End Farm

Knaresborough Road, Littlethorpe, Ripon HG4 3LU
☎ (0765) 677419
41-acre livestock farm. 2.5 miles south of Ripon, between Bishop Monkton and Ripon on the Knaresborough road. Ideal centre for the dales and Herriot country. Home cooking and a warm Yorkshire welcome. Non-smokers only please.
Bedrooms: 2 double, 1 twin
Bathrooms: 1 private, 1 public

Bed & breakfast
per night:	£min	£max
Double	28.00	30.00

Half board
per person:	£min	£max
Daily	22.50	23.50
Weekly	150.00	157.00

Evening meal 1830 (last orders 1600)
Parking for 7
Open January-November

RUFFORTH

North Yorkshire
Map ref 4C1

Village west of York. There is a small airfield, and it is also the home of the York Gliding Centre.

Rosedale Guest House
COMMENDED

Wetherby Road, Rufforth, York YO2 3QB
☎ York (0904) 738297
Small, family-run guesthouse with a homely atmosphere and all facilities, in a delightful, unspoilt village 4 miles west of York on the B1224. Private parking available.
Bedrooms: 1 single, 2 double, 1 twin, 1 triple
Bathrooms: 1 private, 2 public, 2 private showers

Bed & breakfast
per night:	£min	£max
Single	13.00	15.00
Double	28.00	34.00

Parking for 5

Wellgarth House

Wetherby Road, Rufforth, York YO2 3QB
☎ York (0904) 738592/5
Individual and attractive country guesthouse in the delightful village of Rufforth. Ideal touring base for York and the Yorkshire Dales.
Bedrooms: 1 single, 3 double, 2 twin, 1 triple
Bathrooms: 4 private, 1 public

Bed & breakfast
per night:	£min	£max
Single	17.00	19.00
Double	28.00	40.00

Evening meal (last orders 1830)
Parking for 10
Cards accepted: Access, Visa

SCARBOROUGH

North Yorkshire
Map ref 5D3

Large, popular east coast seaside resort, formerly a spa town. Beautiful gardens and splendid sandy beaches in North and South Bays. Castle ruins date from 1100, fine Georgian and Victorian houses in old town. Angling, theatres, cricket festivals and seasonal entertainment.
Tourist Information Centre
☎ (0723) 373333

Howdale Hotel
COMMENDED

121 Queens Parade, Scarborough YO12 7HU
☎ (0723) 372696
Beautifully situated overlooking North Bay. Family-run hotel believing in high standards of comfort, cleanliness, and catering. Low season mini-breaks.
Bedrooms: 1 single, 10 double, 1 twin, 1 family room
Bathrooms: 11 private, 1 public

Bed & breakfast
per night:	£min	£max
Single	15.00	20.00
Double	30.00	40.00

Evening meal 1730 (last orders 1800)
Parking for 9
Open March-October
Cards accepted: Access, Visa

National Crown ratings were correct at the time of going to press but are subject to change. Please check at the time of booking.

SELBY

North Yorkshire
Map ref 4C1

Small market town on the River Ouse, believed to have been birthplace of Henry I, with a magnificent abbey containing much fine Norman and Early English architecture.
Tourist Information Centre
☎ (0757) 703263

Barff Lodge
HIGHLY COMMENDED

Mill Lane, Brayton, Selby YO8 9LB
☎ (0757) 213030
New bungalow built around central courtyard in open countryside. Off A19, adjacent to Selby Golf Club, and 20 minutes from York.
Bedrooms: 1 double, 1 twin
Bathrooms: 2 private

Bed & breakfast
per night:	£min	£max
Single	25.00	25.00
Double	36.00	36.00

Parking for 4
Cards accepted: Access, Visa

Hazeldene Guest House

34 Brook Street, Doncaster Road, Selby YO8 0AR
☎ (0757) 704809
Victorian town house, on the A19 and close to town centre. 12 miles from York, 7 miles from A1 and 6 miles from M52. Non-smokers only please.
Bedrooms: 2 single, 2 double, 3 triple
Bathrooms: 2 public

Bed & breakfast
per night:	£min	£max
Single	16.00	17.00
Double	30.00	33.00

Parking for 6

Villa Nurseries
Listed

33 York Road, Riccall, York YO4 6QG
☎ (0757) 248257
Family-run house in a quiet village 9 miles south of York, offering comfortable, friendly accommodation. Kitchen and laundry facilities.
Bedrooms: 1 single, 2 double, 2 twin, 1 triple, 1 family room
Bathrooms: 3 private, 1 public

Bed & breakfast
per night:	£min	£max
Single	14.00	18.00
Double	24.00	32.00

Parking for 10

YORKSHIRE & HUMBERSIDE

SETTLE
North Yorkshire
Map ref 5B3

Town of narrow streets and Georgian houses in an area of great limestone hills and crags. Panoramic view from Castleberg Crag which stands 300 ft above town.
Tourist Information Centre
☎ (0729) 825192

Maypole Inn
COMMENDED

Maypole Green, Main Street, Long Preston, Skipton BD23 4PH
☎ Long Preston (0729) 840219
17th C inn, with open fires, on the village green. Easy access to many attractive walks in the surrounding dales. 4 miles from Settle.
Bedrooms: 1 single, 2 double, 1 twin, 1 triple, 1 family room
Bathrooms: 6 private
Bed & breakfast

per night:	£min	£max
Single	26.00	26.00
Double	39.00	39.00

Lunch available
Evening meal 1830 (last orders 2100)
Parking for 25
Cards accepted: Access, Visa, Diners, Amex

The Riddings
HIGHLY COMMENDED

Long Preston, Skipton BD23 4QN
☎ Long Preston (0729) 840 231
Grade II listed country house with extensive formal and walled gardens, private woodland and landscaped waterfalls. Superb views over the Ribble Valley.
Bedrooms: 3 double, 1 twin
Bathrooms: 2 private, 1 public
Bed & breakfast

per night:	£min	£max
Single	26.00	35.00
Double	39.00	55.00

Half board

per person:	£min	£max
Daily	31.00	39.00
Weekly	195.00	245.00

Evening meal 1830 (last orders 1000)
Parking for 14

Scar Close Farm
COMMENDED

Feizor, Austwick, Lancaster LA2 8DF
☎ (0729) 823496
185-acre dairy & livestock farm. High standard en-suite farmhouse accommodation and food in a picturesque hamlet near Settle. A tourist centre for the dales, Lakes and seaside.
Bedrooms: 1 double, 1 twin, 1 triple

Bathrooms: 3 private
Bed & breakfast

per night:	£min	£max
Double	32.00	34.00

Half board

per person:	£min	£max
Daily	25.00	26.50

Evening meal 1800 (last orders 1830)
Parking for 5

SHEFFIELD
South Yorkshire
Map ref 4B2

Local iron ore and coal gave Sheffield its prosperous steel and cutlery industries. The modern city centre has many interesting buildings - cathedral, Cutlers' Hall, Crucible Theatre, Graves and Mappin Art Galleries - and Meadowhall shopping centre nearby.
Tourist Information Centre
☎ (0742) 734671 or 795901

28 Durlstone Crescent
Listed

Sheffield S12 2TS
☎ (0742) 651753
Three bedroomed semi-detached house with gardens to front and rear.
Bedrooms: 1 double
Bathrooms: 1 public
Bed & breakfast

per night:	£min	£max
Single	10.00	10.00
Double	20.00	20.00

Parking for 1
Open April-October

SHIPTONTHORPE
Humberside
Map ref 4C1

Robeanne House Farm
Listed

Driffield Lane, Shiptonthorpe, York YO4 3LB
☎ Howden (0430) 873312
Fax (0430) 873312
3-acre livestock farm. Comfortable, modern farmhouse on the main A163, in unspoilt countryside ideal for walking and touring. Convenient for York, east coast and Yorkshire Wolds, on route to Scotland. Quality and comfort with a wholesome breakfast will ensure a memorable stay.
Bedrooms: 2 double, 1 twin
Bathrooms: 1 private, 1 public

We advise you to confirm your booking in writing.

Bed & breakfast

per night:	£min	£max
Single	15.50	16.50
Double	31.00	33.00

Parking for 10
Cards accepted: Access, Visa

SINNINGTON
North Yorkshire
Map ref 5C3

Delightful village with broad greens and dried river beds. A tall maypole and the spired school overlook a curious packhorse bridge.

Fox & Hounds Hotel
COMMENDED

Main Street, Sinnington, York YO6 6SQ
☎ Pickering (0751) 431577
Old coaching inn, newly refurbished, with open fires and period furniture. In a rural setting. Fishing, riding and riverside walks close by. Private parking.
Bedrooms: 1 single, 5 double, 1 twin, 1 triple
Bathrooms: 8 private
Bed & breakfast

per night:	£min	£max
Single	25.00	30.00
Double	50.00	55.00

Half board

per person:	£min	£max
Daily	35.00	40.00
Weekly	227.50	262.50

Lunch available
Evening meal 1830 (last orders 2130)
Parking for 30
Cards accepted: Access, Visa

SPENNITHORNE
North Yorkshire
Map ref 5C3

Quiet, rural village with small fragments remaining of a castle and an interesting church.

Hayloft Suite
HIGHLY COMMENDED

Foal Barn, Spennithorne, Leyburn DL8 5PR
☎ Wensleydale (0969) 22580
200-year-old converted barn set around picturesque courtyard. Old world serviced cottage for 1 party of up to 4.
Bedrooms: 1 double, 1 twin
Bathrooms: 2 private
Bed & breakfast

per night:	£min	£max
Single	22.00	22.00
Double	44.00	44.00

Parking for 4

YORKSHIRE & HUMBERSIDE

STAINTONDALE
North Yorkshire
Map ref 5D3

Plane Tree Cottage Farm
Listed

Down Dale Road, Staintondale,
Scarborough YO13 0EY
☎ Scarborough (0723) 870796
60-acre mixed farm. Small, stone-built farm cottage of character with open views of lovely countryside and the sea. Eight miles north of Scarborough.
Bedrooms: 1 twin, 1 family room
Bathrooms: 1 public

Bed & breakfast
per night:	£min	£max
Single	14.00	14.00
Double	28.00	28.00

Half board
per person:	£min	£max
Daily	22.00	22.00
Weekly	140.00	140.00

Evening meal 1830 (last orders 1830)
Parking for 2
Open May-October

STOKESLEY
North Yorkshire
Map ref 5C3

Handsome market town midway between the North York Moors and the Cleveland border. Famous for its annual show in September.

Harker Hill Farm
Listed APPROVED

Harker Hill, Seamer, Stokesley,
Middlesbrough, Cleveland TS9 5NF
☎ (0642) 710431
55-acre mixed farm. Harker Hill has a warm, family atmosphere and is central for the North York Moors, east coastal resorts and Yorkshire Dales.
Bedrooms: 2 single, 2 double
Bathrooms: 1 public

Bed & breakfast
per night:	£min	£max
Single	15.00	16.00
Double	30.00	30.00

Half board
per person:	£min	£max
Daily	21.00	23.00
Weekly	140.00	140.00

Evening meal 1900 (last orders 2000)
Parking for 12

Establishments should be open throughout the year unless otherwise stated in the entry.

TADCASTER
North Yorkshire
Map ref 4C1

Known for its breweries which have been established here since 18th C. Wharfe Bridge has 7 arches. Above it stands the "virgin viaduct" built for the railway which never arrived.

Shann House Hotel

47 Kirkgate, Tadcaster LS24 9AQ
☎ (0937) 833931
Protected historic building, tastefully restored in the traditional manner. In peaceful seclusion, in the centre of the town and only minutes away from the A1.
Bedrooms: 2 single, 5 twin, 1 triple
Bathrooms: 8 private

Bed & breakfast
per night:	£min	£max
Single	20.50	
Double	36.00	41.00

Cards accepted: Access, Visa

TERRINGTON
North Yorkshire
Map ref 5C3

In the Howardian Hills, the name of this picturesque village is said to refer in Old English to the practice of sorcery. There is a church and an old rectory now known as Terrington Hall.

Gate Farm
Listed

Ganthorpe, Terrington, York YO6 4QD
☎ Coneysthorpe (065 384) 269
150-acre dairy farm. Stone-built farmhouse offering traditional Yorkshire hospitality in a quiet village near Castle Howard. Convenient for the moors, wolds, the east coast and York.
Bedrooms: 1 double, 1 twin, 1 family room
Bathrooms: 1 public, 1 private shower

Bed & breakfast
per night:	£min	£max
Single	12.50	15.00
Double	25.00	30.00

Half board
per person:	£min	£max
Daily	20.50	22.50

Evening meal 1830 (last orders 1600)
Parking for 3
Open March-October

Please mention this guide when making a booking.

THIRSK
North Yorkshire
Map ref 5C3

Thriving market town with cobbled square surrounded by old shops and inns and also with a local museum. St Mary's Church is probably the best example of Perpendicular work in Yorkshire.

Angel Inn

Long Street, Topcliffe, Thirsk
YO7 3RW
☎ (0845) 577237
Fax (0845) 578000
Attractive village inn with a warm, traditional atmosphere, renowned for good food and traditional ales. Ideal centre for touring York and Herriot country.
Bedrooms: 2 single, 7 double, 4 twin, 2 triple
Bathrooms: 15 private, 1 public

Bed & breakfast
per night:	£min	£max
Single	35.00	40.00
Double	50.00	60.00

Lunch available
Evening meal 1830 (last orders 2130)
Parking for 150
Cards accepted: Access, Visa

Doxford House

Front Street, Sowerby, Thirsk YO7 1JP
☎ (0845) 523238
Handsome, Georgian house with attractive gardens and paddock with animals, overlooking the greens of Sowerby. Comfortable rooms - all en-suite.
Wheelchair access category 3
Bedrooms: 1 double, 1 twin, 2 triple
Bathrooms: 4 private

Bed & breakfast
per night:	£min	£max
Single	15.00	20.00
Double	30.00	30.00

Half board
per person:	£min	£max
Daily	22.00	28.00

Evening meal 1830
Parking for 4

Firtree Farmhouse
Listed

Thormanby, Easingwold, York
YO6 3NN
☎ (0845) 501201 & 501220
650-acre arable farm. 18th C farmhouse set in beautiful countryside. 16 miles north of York, 5 miles south of Thirsk. Traditionally decorated rooms. Home cooked evening meals available. Dales and moors nearby.
Bedrooms: 1 double, 1 twin, 1 triple

Continued ▶

125

YORKSHIRE & HUMBERSIDE

THIRSK
Continued

Bathrooms: 2 private, 1 public

Bed & breakfast per night:	£min	£max
Single	15.00	17.00
Double	27.00	32.00

Half board per person:	£min	£max
Daily	20.00	24.00
Weekly	125.00	150.00

Evening meal 1900 (last orders 2100)
Parking for 5

Garth House
Listed
Dalton, Thirsk YO7 3HY
☎ (0845) 577310

50-acre livestock farm. Farmhouse set in a country village. Central for York, Harrogate and many historic, interesting places. Friendly welcome awaiting guests.
Bedrooms: 1 double, 1 twin, 1 triple
Bathrooms: 2 public

Bed & breakfast per night:	£min	£max
Single	12.00	14.00
Double	24.00	28.00

Parking for 6
Open March-November

High House Farm
Sutton Bank, Thirsk YO7 2HA
☎ (0845) 597557
113-acre mixed farm. Family-run, set in open countryside and offering some of the most magnificent views in North Yorkshire. Just half a mile from Sutton Bank Information Centre.
Bedrooms: 1 double, 1 triple
Bathrooms: 1 public

Bed & breakfast per night:	£min	£max
Double	28.00	30.00

Parking for 2
Open April-October

Otterington Shorthorn Inn
South Otterington, Northallerton DL7 9HP
☎ Northallerton (0609) 773816
Early 19th C inn with an open fire and oak beams, serving traditional ales and offering a warm welcome. Bar meals,

pool table and private entrance. In village north of Thirsk.
Bedrooms: 1 single, 3 double, 1 twin
Bathrooms: 1 public

Bed & breakfast per night:	£min	£max
Single	15.00	20.00
Double	30.00	36.00

Half board per person:	£min	£max
Daily	20.00	25.00
Weekly	140.00	175.00

Lunch available
Evening meal 1900 (last orders 2130)
Parking for 12

Plump Bank
COMMENDED
Felixkirk Road, Thirsk YO7 2EW
☎ (0845) 522406
From Thirsk take the A170 Scarborough road. After 1 mile turn left for Felixkirk and Boltby and house is on the left after 100 yards.
Bedrooms: 2 double, 1 twin
Bathrooms: 3 private

Bed & breakfast per night:	£min	£max
Double		32.00

Parking for 9
Open March-October

Thornborough House Farm
COMMENDED
South Kilvington, Thirsk YO7 2NP
☎ (0845) 522103
206-acre mixed farm. 200-year-old farmhouse in an ideal position for walking and touring in the North York Moors and Yorkshire Dales.
Bedrooms: 1 double, 1 twin, 1 family room
Bathrooms: 2 private, 1 public

Bed & breakfast per night:	£min	£max
Single	12.50	16.00
Double	25.00	32.00

Half board per person:	£min	£max
Daily	20.00	
Weekly	130.00	

Evening meal from 1830
Parking for 6

THORALBY
North Yorkshire
Map ref 5B3

Small village south of Aysgarth in Wensleydale.

High Green House
HIGHLY COMMENDED
Thoralby, Leyburn DL8 3SU
☎ Wensleydale (0969) 663420

Listed Georgian house with fine views, period furniture, beams, log fires. Walled garden to rear. Good traditional food. Excellent centre for touring and walking.
Wheelchair access category 3
Bedrooms: 2 double, 1 twin
Bathrooms: 3 private

Bed & breakfast per night:	£min	£max
Double	39.00	50.00

Half board per person:	£min	£max
Daily	32.50	38.00
Weekly	221.00	238.00

Evening meal from 1900
Parking for 4
Open April-October
Cards accepted: Access, Visa

THORNTON DALE
North Yorkshire
Map ref 5D3

Picturesque village with Thorntondale Beck, traversed by tiny stone footbridges at the edge of pretty cottage gardens.

Banavie
Roxby Road, Thornton Dale, Pickering YO18 7SX
☎ Pickering (0751) 74616
Stone-built, semi-detached house with splendid views overlooking this famous village. In a quiet residential area close to children's playing field.
Bedrooms: 3 double, 1 triple
Bathrooms: 1 public

Bed & breakfast per night:	£min	£max
Double	24.00	27.00

Parking for 4

THORNTON WATLASS
North Yorkshire
Map ref 5C3

The Buck Inn
COMMENDED
Thornton Watlass, Ripon HG4 4AH
☎ Bedale (0677) 422461
Friendly village inn overlooking the delightful cricket green in a small village, 3 miles from Bedale on the Masham road, and close to the A1. In James Herriot country. Walking holidays with experienced leader.
Bedrooms: 1 single, 2 double, 1 twin, 1 triple
Bathrooms: 5 private

Bed & breakfast per night:	£min	£max
Single	27.00	
Double	45.00	

126

YORKSHIRE & HUMBERSIDE

Lunch available
Evening meal 1830 (last orders 2130)
Parking for 40
Cards accepted: Access, Visa, Amex

The Old Rectory ⋀
Listed DE LUXE

Thornton Watlass, Ripon HG4 4AH
☎ Bedale (0677) 423456
Welcoming Georgian rectory in the centre of a peaceful Wensleydale village, an ideal base for exploring the Yorkshire Dales. 1992 winner ETB's Best B & B in England and 1992 winner Yorkshire & Humberside Best B & B White Rose Award.
Bedrooms: 2 double, 1 twin
Bathrooms: 3 private
Bed & breakfast
per night: £min   £max
Single   37.50   40.00
Double   60.00   65.00
Parking for 10

THURLSTONE
South Yorkshire
Map ref 4B1

On the River Don and close to the Peak District National Park. Has some 19th C weavers' cottages with long upper windows.

Weavers Cottages

3-5 Tenter Hill, Thurlstone, Sheffield S30 6RG
☎ Barnsley (0226) 763350
18th C weavers' cottages in conservation area and listed Grade II. Original workrooms converted into private suites with authentic furnishings.
Bedrooms: 1 single, 1 double, 1 twin
Bathrooms: 2 private, 1 public
Bed & breakfast
per night: £min   £max
Single   18.00   22.00
Double   36.00   44.00
Parking for 2

There are separate sections in this guide listing groups specialising in farm holidays and accommodation which is especially suitable for young people and organised groups.

WARTER
Humberside
Map ref 4C1

Picturesque Wolds village adjacent to the Wolds Way on the B1246 east coast road. Famous for its thatched cottages on the green and the priory, one of the "Lost great houses of East Yorkshire", destroyed in 1970.

Rickman House Bed & Breakfast ⋀
Listed COMMENDED

Huggate Road, Warter, York YO4 2SY
☎ Pocklington (0759) 304303
Secluded 17th C wolds farmhouse in large garden, surrounded by parkland overlooking Warter village. Period furniture, log fires. Convenient for York, Beverley, Hull and east coast.
Bedrooms: 2 double, 1 twin
Bathrooms: 1 private, 1 public
Bed & breakfast
per night: £min   £max
Single   16.00   17.00
Double   30.00   35.00
Half board
per person: £min   £max
Daily   27.00   37.00
Parking for 4
Cards accepted: Access, Visa

WEST WITTON
North Yorkshire
Map ref 5B3

Popular Wensleydale village, where the burning of "Owd Barle", effigy of an 18th C pig rustler, is held in August.

Old Vicarage Guest House ⋀

Main Street, West Witton, Leyburn DL8 4LX
☎ Wensleydale (0969) 22108
Substantially-built, tastefully-appointed, Grade II listed house of character converted to a guesthouse. Outstanding views of Wensleydale from the bedrooms.
Bedrooms: 2 double, 1 twin
Bathrooms: 3 private
Bed & breakfast
per night: £min   £max
Single   16.00   21.00
Double   28.00   34.00
Parking for 8
Open March-October

We advise you to confirm your booking in writing.

WETHERBY
West Yorkshire
Map ref 4B1

Prosperous market town on the River Wharfe, noted for horse-racing.
Tourist Information Centre
☎ *(0937) 582706*

Prospect House ⋀
Listed

8 Caxton Street, Wetherby LS22 6RU
☎ (0937) 582428
Established over 32 years. Near York, Harrogate, the dales, Herriot country. Midway London/Edinburgh. Restaurants nearby. Pets welcome.
Bedrooms: 1 single, 2 double, 2 twin, 1 triple
Bathrooms: 1 public
Bed & breakfast
per night: £min   £max
Single   15.50   16.00
Double   31.00   32.00
Parking for 6

14 Woodhill View ⋀
Listed APPROVED

Wetherby LS22 6PP
☎ (0937) 581200
Semi-detached house in a quiet residential area near the town centre.
Bedrooms: 1 double, 1 twin
Bathrooms: 1 public
Bed & breakfast
per night: £min   £max
Single   15.00   17.50
Double   25.00   27.00
Parking for 1
Cards accepted: Access, Visa

WHITBY
North Yorkshire
Map ref 5D3

Quaint holiday town with narrow streets and steep alleys at the mouth of the River Esk. Captain James Cook, the famous navigator, lived in Grape Lane. 199 steps lead to St Mary's Church and St Hilda's Abbey overlooking harbour. Dracula connections. Sandy beach.
Tourist Information Centre
☎ *(0947) 602674*

Cote Bank Farm

Egton, Whitby YO21 1UQ
☎ (0947) 85314

Continued ▶

127

YORKSHIRE & HUMBERSIDE

WHITBY
Continued

300-acre mixed farm. In national park, 18th C house with mullioned windows, spacious rooms, period furniture, log fires, home cooking. Many local places of interest, including Goathland (location for TV programme Heartbeat).
Bedrooms: 1 double, 1 family room
Bathrooms: 1 public

Bed & breakfast
per night:	£min	£max
Single	16.00	18.00
Double	32.00	64.00

Half board
per person:	£min	£max
Daily	25.00	30.00
Weekly	175.00	210.00

Evening meal from 1745
Parking for 3
Cards accepted: Amex

Falcon Guest House
29 Falcon Terrace, Whitby YO21 1EH
☎ (0947) 603507
Quiet area, 7 minutes' walk from harbour and town centre. Good street parking. Full breakfast, catering for all diets. Lounge available.
Bedrooms: 2 triple
Bathrooms: 2 private, 1 public

Bed & breakfast
per night:	£min	£max
Single	13.00	13.00
Double	26.00	26.00

Ryedale House M
154-158 Coach Road, Sleights, Whitby YO22 5EQ
☎ (0947) 810534
Welcoming Yorkshire house (non-smoking) 3.5 miles from Whitby, with large garden, magnificent views and relaxing atmosphere. Delicious traditional and vegetarian menus, picnics, light meals. Minimum stay 2 nights. Sorry, no pets.
Bedrooms: 2 double, 1 twin
Bathrooms: 2 public

Bed & breakfast
per night:	£min	£max
Double	28.00	30.00

Parking for 3
Open March-November

Weardale Guest House M
COMMENDED
12 Normanby Terrace, Whitby YO21 3ES
☎ (0947) 820389
Small, friendly guesthouse close to the town, shops and seafront. Freshly cooked breakfast from varied menu.
Bedrooms: 3 double, 1 twin, 1 triple, 1 family room
Bathrooms: 3 private, 1 public

Bed & breakfast
per night:	£min	£max
Single	14.50	17.00
Double	27.00	32.00

Evening meal 1800 (last orders 1930)

White House Hotel M
COMMENDED
Upgang Lane, West Cliff, Whitby YO21 3JJ
☎ (0947) 600469
Family-run hotel in a unique position with panoramic views, overlooking Sandsend Bay, adjoining a golf-course. Emphasis on food.
Bedrooms: 3 single, 4 double, 2 twin, 2 triple
Bathrooms: 9 private, 1 public

Bed & breakfast
per night:	£min	£max
Single	24.00	28.00
Double	48.00	56.00

Half board
per person:	£min	£max
Daily	34.00	38.00
Weekly	240.00	260.00

Lunch available
Evening meal 1830 (last orders 2130)
Parking for 50
Cards accepted: Access, Visa

YORK
North Yorkshire
Map ref 4C1

Ancient walled city nearly 2000 years old containing many well-preserved medieval buildings. Its Minster has over 100 stained glass windows. Attractions include Castle Museum, National Railway Museum, Jorvik Viking Centre and York Dungeon.
Tourist Information Centre
☎ (0904) 620557 or 621756 or 643700

Ardsley House M
Listed APPROVED
92 Main Street, Askham Bryan, York YO2 3QS
☎ (0904) 707521
Large detached house within rural village, 3 miles from York. Peaceful gardens. Easy access to racecourse, golf and Herriot country.
Bedrooms: 1 single, 1 double, 1 twin

Bathrooms: 1 public

Bed & breakfast
per night:	£min	£max
Single	15.00	15.00
Double	30.00	30.00

Parking for 7

Arnot House M
17 Grosvenor Terrace, Bootham, York YO3 7AG
☎ (0904) 641966
Beautifully preserved Victorian town house with original cornices, fireplaces and staircase. Large rooms, tastefully decorated and well appointed. 5 minutes' walk from York Minster. Brochure available.
Bedrooms: 1 single, 2 double, 2 twin, 1 triple
Bathrooms: 2 public

Bed & breakfast
per night:	£min	£max
Single	14.00	16.00
Double	28.00	32.00

Half board
per person:	£min	£max
Daily	23.75	25.75
Weekly	166.25	180.25

Evening meal from 1830
Parking for 2
Open February-November

Avimore House Hotel M
78 Stockton Lane, York YO3 0BS
☎ (0904) 425556
Edwardian house, now a family-run hotel in a pleasant residential area on the east side of the city.
Bedrooms: 2 single, 1 double, 2 twin, 1 triple
Bathrooms: 6 private

Bed & breakfast
per night:	£min	£max
Single	18.00	23.00
Double	32.00	42.00

Evening meal 1800 (last orders 1200)
Parking for 6

Beech House M
6-7 Longfield Terrace, Bootham, York YO3 7DJ
☎ (0904) 634581
Small, family-run guesthouse with a warm welcome and a relaxing atmosphere only 5 minutes' walk from York Minster.
Bedrooms: 1 single, 6 double, 1 twin
Bathrooms: 8 private

Please mention this guide when making a booking.

YORKSHIRE & HUMBERSIDE

Bed & breakfast

per night:	£min	£max
Single	18.00	25.00
Double	36.00	46.00

Evening meal from 1800
Parking for 5

Blue Bridge Hotel ♠

Fishergate, York YO1 4AP
☎ (0904) 621193
Fax (0904) 671571
Friendly, private hotel, reputation for food, relaxed atmosphere and a warm welcome. Short riverside walk to city. Private car park.
Bedrooms: 2 single, 6 double, 3 twin, 5 triple
Bathrooms: 14 private, 1 public

Bed & breakfast

per night:	£min	£max
Single	40.00	48.00
Double	50.00	58.00

Half board

per person:	£min	£max
Daily	39.50	73.00

Evening meal 1830 (last orders 2130)
Parking for 20
Cards accepted: Access, Visa

Bowen House ♠

4 Gladstone Street, Huntington Road, York YO3 7RF
☎ (0904) 636881

Close to York Minster, this late Victorian town house combines high quality facilities with old-style charm. Private car park. Traditional vegetarian breakfasts. Non-smoking throughout.
Bedrooms: 1 single, 2 double, 1 twin, 1 family room
Bathrooms: 3 private, 1 public

Bed & breakfast

per night:	£min	£max
Single	18.00	22.00
Double	32.00	44.00

Parking for 4
Cards accepted: Access, Visa

City Guest House ♠

68 Monkgate, York YO3 7PF
☎ (0904) 622483
Cosy guesthouse 3 minutes from York Minster. En-suite rooms and car parking. Non-smokers only please.

Bedrooms: 3 single, 2 double, 2 twin, 1 family room
Bathrooms: 6 private, 2 private showers

Bed & breakfast

per night:	£min	£max
Single	14.00	22.00
Double	30.00	44.00

Parking for 5
Cards accepted: Access, Visa

Clifton Guest House ♠

127 Clifton, York YO3 6BL
☎ (0904) 634031
Splendid Victorian family-run guesthouse with bedrooms on the ground and first floors. Within walking distance of city centre.
Bedrooms: 1 single, 3 double, 2 twin, 1 triple
Bathrooms: 4 private, 2 public

Bed & breakfast

per night:	£min	£max
Single	12.50	20.00
Double	25.00	38.00

Evening meal 1800 (last orders 0900)
Parking for 14

Cornerways Guest House

16 Murton Way, Osbaldwick, York YO1 3UN
☎ (0904) 413366 & 621888
Detached house in a village location, yet only five minutes from the city and close to York's outer ring road, convenient for the coast.
Bedrooms: 1 single, 1 double, 1 twin
Bathrooms: 3 private

Bed & breakfast

per night:	£min	£max
Single	12.00	16.00
Double	32.00	36.00

Parking for 4

Cumbria House ♠
Listed COMMENDED

2 Vyner Street, Haxby Road, York YO3 7HS
☎ (0904) 636817
Family-run guesthouse, 10 minutes' walk from York Minster. En-suites available. Easily located from ring road. Private car park. Brochure.
Bedrooms: 1 single, 2 double, 2 triple
Bathrooms: 3 private, 1 public

Bed & breakfast

per night:	£min	£max
Single	15.00	20.00
Double	30.00	40.00

Parking for 5

Curzon Lodge and Stable Cottages ♠
COMMENDED

23 Tadcaster Road, Dringhouses, York YO2 2QG
☎ (0904) 703157

Delightful 17th C listed house and former stables in pretty conservation area overlooking York racecourse, once a home of the Terry "chocolate" family. All en-suite, some four-posters. Many antiques. Large enclosed car park.
Bedrooms: 1 single, 4 double, 3 twin, 2 triple
Bathrooms: 10 private

Bed & breakfast

per night:	£min	£max
Single	30.00	38.00
Double	44.00	56.00

Parking for 16
Cards accepted: Access, Visa

Dairy Guest House
Listed COMMENDED

3 Scarcroft Road, York YO2 1ND
☎ (0904) 639367
Decorated in the style of Habitat, Sanderson and Laura Ashley. The breakfast choice ranges from traditional British to wholefood/vegetarian.
Bedrooms: 2 double, 2 twin, 2 family rooms
Bathrooms: 2 private, 1 public

Bed & breakfast

per night:	£min	£max
Single	24.00	
Double	30.00	38.00

Hotel Fairmount ♠

230 Tadcaster Road, Mount Vale, York YO2 2ES
☎ (0904) 638298
Fax (0904) 639724
Large, tastefully furnished, Victorian villa with open views over racecourse, 10 minutes from city centre. Ground floor rooms available for people with special needs.
Bedrooms: 2 single, 6 double, 2 twin, 2 triple
Bathrooms: 12 private

Bed & breakfast

per night:	£min	£max
Single	20.00	30.00
Double	52.00	56.00

Continued ▶

129

YORKSHIRE & HUMBERSIDE

YORK
Continued

Foss Bank Guest House
16 Huntington Road, York YO3 7RB
☎ (0904) 635548
Small Victorian family-run guesthouse, comfortable and friendly, on the north-east side of the city. 5 minutes' walk from the city wall.
Bedrooms: 2 single, 2 double, 1 twin
Bathrooms: 1 public, 1 private shower
Bed & breakfast

per night:	£min	£max
Single	13.00	17.50
Double	26.00	35.00

Parking for 4
Open February-December

Hedley House
APPROVED
3-4 Bootham Terrace, York YO3 7DH
☎ (0904) 637404
Family-run hotel close to the city centre. 1 ground floor bedroom. All rooms en-suite. Home cooking, special diets catered for.
Bedrooms: 2 single, 5 double, 5 twin, 2 triple, 1 family room
Bathrooms: 15 private
Bed & breakfast

per night:	£min	£max
Single	20.00	32.00
Double	36.00	50.00

Lunch available
Evening meal 1830 (last orders 1900)
Parking for 12
Cards accepted: Access, Visa, Amex

Heworth Guest House
Listed
126 East Parade, Heworth, York YO3 7YG
☎ (0904) 426184
Small, friendly guesthouse, 15 minutes' walk from city centre. En-suite available. Vegetarians, vegans and coeliacs catered for. Easy parking.
Bedrooms: 2 single, 2 double, 1 twin, 1 triple
Bathrooms: 1 private, 3 public
Bed & breakfast

per night:	£min	£max
Single	14.00	19.00
Double	28.00	38.00

Parking for 1

Hillcrest Guest House
110 Bishopthorpe Road, York YO2 1JX
☎ (0904) 653160
Two elegantly converted Victorian town houses, close to the city centre, racecourse and station. It is our pleasure to offer individual attention, home cooking, comfort and good value.
Bedrooms: 3 single, 5 double, 1 twin, 2 triple, 2 family rooms
Bathrooms: 3 private, 3 public
Bed & breakfast

per night:	£min	£max
Single	13.00	18.00
Double	26.00	36.00

Half board

per person:	£min	£max
Daily	20.00	25.50
Weekly	140.00	170.00

Evening meal 1800 (last orders 1500)
Parking for 8
Cards accepted: Access, Visa

Hobbits Hotel
COMMENDED
9 St Peter's Grove, York YO3 6AQ
☎ (0904) 624538 & 642926
Find a friendly and comfortable welcome in this lovely old house, in a quiet cul-de-sac 10 minutes' walk from centre.
Bedrooms: 1 single, 2 double, 1 twin, 1 triple
Bathrooms: 5 private
Bed & breakfast

per night:	£min	£max
Single	26.00	28.00
Double	52.00	56.00

Parking for 5
Cards accepted: Access, Visa

Holly Lodge
APPROVED
206 Fulford Road, York YO1 4DD
☎ (0904) 646005
Listed Georgian building on the A19, convenient for both the north and south and within walking distance of the city centre. Quiet rooms and private car park.
Bedrooms: 3 double, 1 twin, 1 family room
Bathrooms: 5 private
Bed & breakfast

per night:	£min	£max
Single	25.00	25.00
Double	30.00	45.00

Parking for 5
Open January-November
Cards accepted: Access, Visa

Horseshoe House
COMMENDED
York Road, Dunnington, York YO1 5QJ
☎ (0904) 489369
Well-appointed accommodation in a country setting, half a mile from the A1079 and 4 miles from York city centre. Easy access to the racecourse and golf-course. Restaurants close by.
Bedrooms: 2 double, 1 twin
Bathrooms: 2 private, 1 public, 1 private shower
Bed & breakfast

per night:	£min	£max
Single	15.00	22.00
Double	25.00	32.00

Parking for 4

Jacobean Lodge Hotel
COMMENDED
Plainville Lane, Wigginton, York YO3 8RG
☎ (0904) 762749
Fax (0904) 762749
Converted 17th C farmhouse, 4 miles north of York. Set in picturesque gardens with ample parking. Open log fire, warm, friendly atmosphere and traditional cuisine.
Bedrooms: 2 single, 3 double, 1 twin, 1 triple, 1 family room
Bathrooms: 4 private, 1 public
Bed & breakfast

per night:	£min	£max
Single	25.00	30.00
Double	34.00	52.00

Lunch available
Evening meal 1900 (last orders 2200)
Parking for 70
Cards accepted: Access, Visa

The Limes
APPROVED
135 Fulford Road, York YO1 4HE
☎ (0904) 624548
Small, family-run hotel, 10 minutes from the city centre. Licensed bar, colour TV, all rooms en-suite. Family rooms available. Private car park. Close to university and golf-course. Three-day breaks available.
Bedrooms: 7 double, 1 twin, 2 triple
Bathrooms: 10 private, 1 public
Bed & breakfast

per night:	£min	£max
Single	20.00	50.00
Double	30.00	50.00

Half board

per person:	£min	£max
Daily	25.00	30.00

Evening meal 1900 (last orders 1830)
Parking for 14
Cards accepted: Access, Visa

YORKSHIRE & HUMBERSIDE

The Lodge
Earswick Grange, Old Earswick, York
YO3 9SW
☎ (0904) 761387
Modern family house in its own grounds. Large comfortable rooms ideal for families. No smoking establishment. Easy access to York.
Bedrooms: 1 double, 1 family room
Bathrooms: 2 public

Bed & breakfast

per night:	£min	£max
Single	13.00	
Double	26.00	28.00

Parking for 3

Mont-Clare Guest House
32 Claremont Terrace, Gillygate, York
YO3 7EJ
☎ (0904) 627054 & 651011
Fax (0904) 627054
Take advantage of city centre accommodation in quiet location close to all historic attractions. Priorities are cleanliness, good food, pleasant surroundings and friendliness. Reduced rates for weekly stay.
Bedrooms: 6 double, 1 twin
Bathrooms: 6 private, 1 private shower

Bed & breakfast

per night:	£min	£max
Double	28.00	45.00

Parking for 6

Mulberry Guest House
COMMENDED
124 East Parade, Heworth, York
YO3 7YG
☎ (0904) 423468
Beautifully appointed Victorian town house, a short walk from city centre. Lovingly furnished throughout. Warm welcome assured. No smoking. Easy parking.
Bedrooms: 1 single, 1 double, 1 twin
Bathrooms: 1 private, 2 private showers

Bed & breakfast

per night:	£min	£max
Single	14.00	17.00
Double	28.00	40.00

Parking for 2

Orillia House
89 The Village, Stockton-on-the-Forest,
York YO3 9UP
☎ (0904) 400600
A warm welcome awaits you in this 300-year-old house of charm and character, opposite church. Three miles north east of York.
Bedrooms: 2 double, 1 twin, 2 triple
Bathrooms: 5 private

Bed & breakfast

per night:	£min	£max
Double	28.00	40.00

Parking for 10
Cards accepted: Access, Visa

Pauleda House Hotel
123 Clifton, York YO3 6BL
☎ (0904) 634745 & 621327
Fax (0904) 621327
Family-run hotel with well-decorated, spacious rooms. Less than 1 mile from the city centre on the A19 north. Managed by the owners.
Bedrooms: 4 double, 3 twin, 3 triple
Bathrooms: 10 private, 1 public

Bed & breakfast

per night:	£min	£max
Single	16.00	25.00
Double	32.00	50.00

Half board

per person:	£min	£max
Daily	24.00	35.00

Evening meal 1830 (last orders 2100)
Parking for 16
Cards accepted: Access, Visa, Diners, Switch

Primrose Lodge
Listed
Hull Road, Dunnington, York
YO1 5LR
☎ (0904) 489140
Spacious, modern rooms to which guests have their own private entrance. Colour TV, tea and coffee making facilities in every room. 5 minutes from York on the A1079.
Bedrooms: 2 double, 1 twin
Bathrooms: 3 private

Bed & breakfast

per night:	£min	£max
Double	30.00	34.00

Parking for 6

Priory Hotel
COMMENDED
126-128 Fulford Road, York YO1 4BE
☎ (0904) 625280
Family hotel in a residential area with an adjacent riverside walk to the city centre.
Bedrooms: 1 single, 9 double, 6 twin, 4 triple
Bathrooms: 20 private

Bed & breakfast

per night:	£min	£max
Single	30.00	40.00
Double	45.00	55.00

Evening meal 1830 (last orders 2130)
Parking for 24
Cards accepted: Access, Visa, Diners, Amex, Switch

23 St Marys
HIGHLY COMMENDED
Bootham, York YO3 7DD
☎ (0904) 622738
Situated near the city in a quiet location. Individually styled bedrooms with embroidered linen re-creating elegance and comfort of a bygone era.
Bedrooms: 2 single, 6 double, 1 triple
Bathrooms: 9 private

Bed & breakfast

per night:	£min	£max
Single	30.00	34.00
Double	46.00	54.00

Parking for 3

Ship Inn
Listed COMMENDED
Acaster Malbis, York YO2 1UH
☎ (0904) 705609 & 703888
Fax (0532) 439693
17th C coaching inn on the River Ouse, 3.5 miles from York city centre. Restaurant, bar meals, conservatory. Weddings catered for.
Bedrooms: 5 double, 2 twin, 1 family room
Bathrooms: 8 private

Bed & breakfast

per night:	£min	£max
Single	37.50	37.50
Double	39.50	65.00

Half board

per person:	£min	£max
Daily	40.00	49.50

Lunch available
Evening meal 1900 (last orders 2130)
Parking for 60
Cards accepted: Access, Visa

Stanley Guest House
COMMENDED
Stanley Street, Haxby Road, York
YO3 7NW
☎ (0904) 637111
Friendly, comfortable guesthouse close to the many attractions of York. 10 minutes' walk to York Minster and city.
Bedrooms: 2 single, 3 double, 1 twin, 1 triple
Bathrooms: 5 private, 1 public, 2 private showers

Bed & breakfast

per night:	£min	£max
Single	17.50	20.00
Double	35.00	35.00

Parking for 5
Cards accepted: Access, Visa

Tower Guest House
COMMENDED
2 Feversham Crescent, Wigginton
Road, York YO3 7HQ
☎ (0904) 655571 & 635924
Within strolling distance of York Minster and the city centre.

Continued ▶

131

YORKSHIRE & HUMBERSIDE

YORK
Continued

Bedrooms: 2 double, 1 twin, 2 triple
Bathrooms: 5 private

Bed & breakfast
per night:	£min	£max
Single	18.00	24.00
Double	34.00	40.00

Parking for 5
Cards accepted: Access, Visa

Victoria Villa
Listed

72 Heslington Road, York YO1 5AU
☎ (0904) 631647

Victorian town house, close to city centre. Offering clean and friendly accommodation and a full English breakfast.

Bedrooms: 1 single, 2 double, 1 twin, 2 triple
Bathrooms: 2 public

Bed & breakfast
per night:	£min	£max
Single	15.00	20.00
Double	26.00	35.00

Parking for 4

Winston House

4 Nunthorpe Drive, Bishopthorpe Road, York YO2 1DY
☎ (0904) 653171

Close to racecourse and 10 minutes' walk to city centre, railway station. Character en-suite room with all facilities. Private car park.

Bedrooms: 1 double
Bathrooms: 1 private

Bed & breakfast
per night:	£min	£max
Double	26.00	30.00

Parking for 6

Key to symbols

Information about many of the services and facilities at accommodation listed in this guide is given in the form of symbols. The key to these symbols is inside the back cover flap. You may find it helpful to keep the flap open when referring to the accommodation listings.

Check the maps

The colour maps at the back of this guide show all cities, towns and villages which have accommodation listings in the guide. They will enable you to check if there is suitable accommodation in the vicinity of the place you plan to visit.

132

SURE SIGNS
OF WHERE TO STAY

Throughout Britain, the tourist boards now inspect over 30,000 places to stay, every year, to help you find the ones that suit you best.

Looking for a hotel, guesthouse, inn, B&B or farmhouse? Look for the **CROWN**. The classifications: 'Listed', and then **ONE to FIVE CROWN**, tell you the range of facilities and services you can expect. The more Crowns, the wider the range.

Looking for somewhere convenient to stop overnight on a motorway or major road route? Look for the 'Lodge' **MOON**. The classifications: **ONE to THREE MOON** tell you the range of facilities you can expect. The more Moons, the wider the range.

Looking for a self-catering holiday home? Look for the **KEY**. The classifications: **ONE to FIVE KEY**, tell you the range of facilities and equipment you can expect. The more Keys, the wider the range.

THE GRADES: **APPROVED, COMMENDED, HIGHLY COMMENDED and DE LUXE,** whether alongside the **CROWNS**, **KEYS** or **MOONS** show the quality standard of what is provided. If no grade is shown, you can still expect a high standard of cleanliness.

Looking for a holiday caravan, chalet or camping park? Look for the Q symbol. The more ✓s in the Q (from one to five), the higher the quality standard of what is provided.

English Tourist Board
We've checked them out before you check in!

More detailed information on the **CROWNS**, the **KEYS** and the **Q** is given in free *SURE SIGN* leaflets, available at any Tourist Information Centre.

Heart of England

Enjoy the contrasts – the mellow charms of honey coloured Cotswold villages vie with the picturesque riverside hamlets of Worcestershire and its black and white cottages whilst the dramatic scenery of the Wye Valley does battle with the brooding magnificence of the Forest of Dean. Cycle alongside the apple orchards in Herefordshire's cider country or Worcestershire's Vale of Evesham, or take an invigorating stride into the Shropshire hills. There are the lively cities of Coventry and Birmingham with a generous range of entertainments, galleries and museums. In Stratford-upon-Avon you can enjoy Shakespeare's life and plays, whilst the origins of the industrial revolution can be seen at Ironbridge Gorge. Take tea in the stylish spa town of Cheltenham or marvel at the region's castles and cathedrals. Above all, take time to enjoy this great Heart of England.

WHERE TO GO, WHAT TO SEE

The number against each name will help you locate it on the map (page 136).

Naked at noon: Lady Godiva is reputed to have ridden naked through the streets of Coventry in a bid to get local taxes reduced.

① Chatterley Whitfield Mining Museum
Tunstall, Stoke-on-Trent, Staffordshire ST6 8UN
Tel: Stoke on Trent (0782) 813337
Underground guided tour, British Coal Collection, energy hall, winding engine, pit ponies, underground and surface locomotives.

② Alton Towers Theme Park
Alton, Staffordshire ST10 4DB
Tel: Oakamoor (0538) 702200
Over 125 rides and attractions including Haunted House, Runaway Mine Train, Congo Train, Congo River Rapids, Log Flume, New Beast, Corkscrew and Thunderlooper.

③ Bass Museum, Visitor Centre and Shire Horse Stables
Horninglow Street, Burton upon Trent, Staffordshire DE14 1JZ
Tel: Burton upon Trent (0283) 42031
First major museum of brewing industry. Story of different methods of transporting beer since the early 1800s.

④ Ironbridge Gorge Museum
Ironbridge, Shropshire TF8 7AW
Tel: Ironbridge (0952) 433522
World's first cast iron bridge, Museum of the River and visitor centre, tar tunnel, Jackfield Tile Museum, Coalport China Museum, Rosehill House and Blists Hill Museum.

134

Heart of England

⑤ Tamworth Castle and Museum Service
Tamworth, Staffordshire B79 7LR
Tel: Tamworth (0827) 63563
Norman motte and bailey castle, shell keep and Norman tower. Late medieval great hall, Tudor stairs, Jacobean state apartments. Local history museum.

⑥ Black Country Museum
Dudley, West Midlands DY1 4SQ
Tel: 021-557 9643
26-acre open-air museum with shops, chapel, chainmaker's house, canal. Underground mining display and electrical tramway.

⑥ Dudley Zoo and Castle
Dudley, West Midlands DY1 4QB
Tel: Dudley (0384) 252401
Set in 40-acre wooded grounds of Dudley Castle. Visitors can enjoy a varied day combining zoology, history and geology.

⑥ Broadfield House Glass Museum
Barnett Lane, Kingswinford, Dudley, West Midlands DY6 9QA
Tel: Kingswinford (0384) 273011
Collection of 19th and 20th C Stourbridge glass, housed in Georgian mansion.

⑦ Sandwell Park Farm Visitors Centre
Salters Lane, West Bromwich, West Midlands B71 4BG
Tel: 021-553 0220

Restored 19th C working farm with livestock breeds of the period, traditional farming methods, displays and exhibitions. Tearooms and Victorian kitchen and garden.

⑧ Arbury Hall
Nuneaton, Warwickshire CV10 7PT
Tel: Nuneaton (0203) 382804
Elizabethan building gothicised by Sir Roger Newdigate during second half of 18th C. Magnificent Georgian plasterwork ceilings, landscaped gardens.

⑨ Cadbury World
Linden Road, Bournville, Birmingham, West Midlands B30 2LD
Tel: 021-433 4334
Story of chocolate from Aztec times to present day includes chocolate-making demonstration and a guided visit to the packaging plant of the factory.

⑨ Birmingham Museum of Science and Industry
Birmingham, West Midlands B3 1RZ
Tel: 021-235 1661
Steam engines, aircraft, veteran cars and motorcycles. Steam locomotives and other items of industrial or scientific interest.

⑨ Patrick Collection
180 Lifford Lane, Birmingham, West Midlands B30 3NT
Tel: 021-459 9111
Features include 3 exhibition halls, housing cars from 1904–1990 in period settings. Terraced gardens, wildlife lake, children's play area, shop.

⑨ Birmingham Botanical Gardens and Glasshouses
Westbourne Road, Edgbaston, Birmingham, West Midlands B15 3TR
Tel: 021-454 1860
15 acres of ornamental gardens and glasshouses. Tropical plants of botanical interest. Aviaries with exotic birds and children's play area.

⑩ National Motorcycle Museum
Bickenhill, West Midlands B92 0EJ
Tel: Coleshill (0675) 443311
Museum with a collection of 650 British machines from 1898–1980.

⑪ Jewellery Quarter Discovery Centre
77–79 Vyse Street, Hockley, West Midlands B18 6HA
Tel: 021-554 3598
The story of jewellery making in Birmingham with a visit around a 'time capsule' jewellery works.

⑫ Severn Valley Railway
The Railway Station, Bewdley, Worcestershire DY12 1BG
Tel: Bewdley (0299) 403816
Preserved standard gauge steam railway running 16 miles between Kidderminster, Bewley and Bridgnorth. Collection of locomotives and passenger coaches.

⑬ Ryton Gardens, National Centre for Organic Gardening
Ryton-on-Dunsmore, Coventry CV8 3LG
Tel: Coventry (0203) 303517
Exhibition gardens where no pesticides or artificial fertilizers are used. Wildlife and bee garden, shrub borders, native tree walk.

Traditional canal boat on the Grand Union Canal in Birmingham.

Heart of England

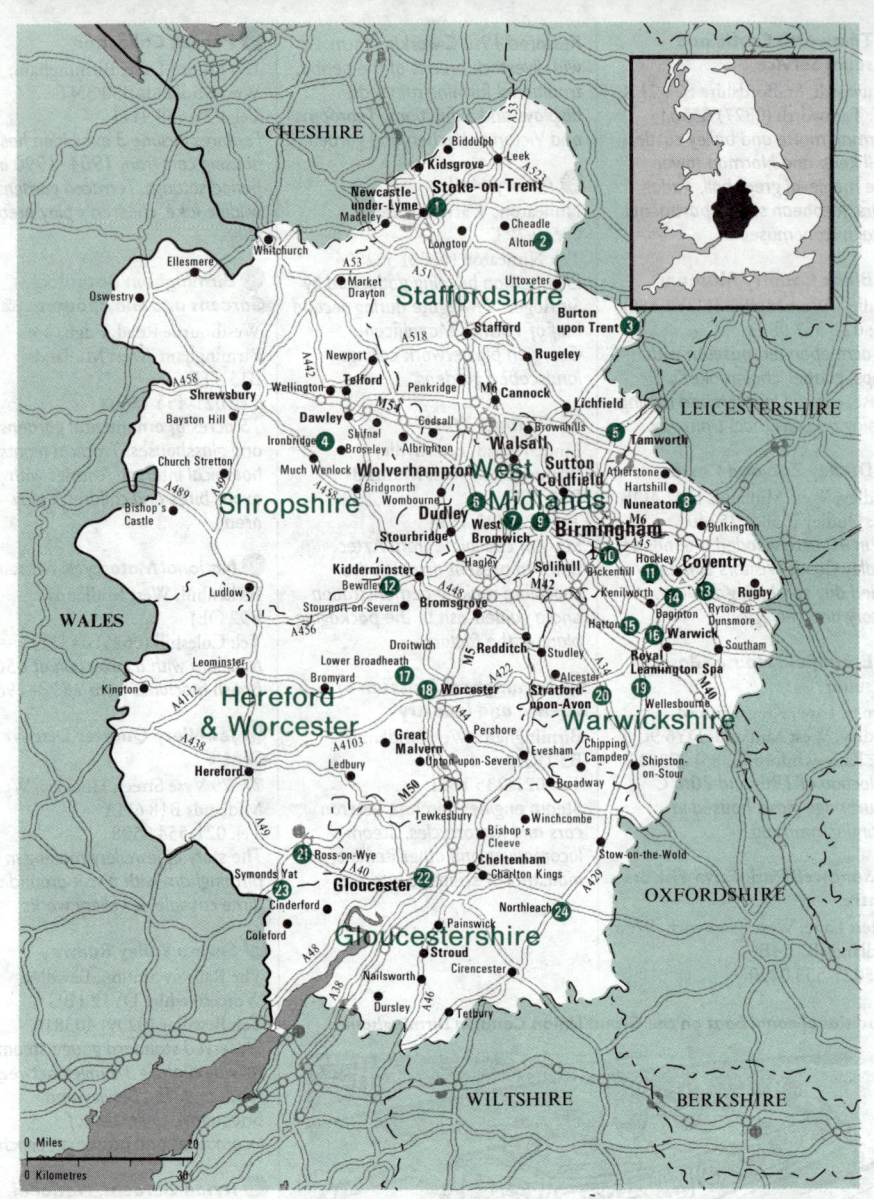

Use the map above to locate places in the 'Where to Go, What to See' section.

⑭ Midland Air Museum
Baginton, West Midlands CV8 3AZ
Tel: Coventry (0203) 301033
Collection of over 20 historic aeroplanes. Recently completed Sir Frank Whittle Jet Heritage Centre includes early jet aircraft and aero engines.

⑮ Hatton Country World
Hatton, Warwickshire CV35 0XA
Tel: Claverdon (0926) 842636
A 100-acre haven of rural attractions including over 40 breeds of rare farm animals. Craft centre.

⑯ Ashorne Hall
Ashorne Hill, Nr Warwick, Warwickshire CV33 9QN
Tel: Barford (0926) 651444

Heart of England

Britain's only 'nickelodeon' with unique presentation of automatic musical instruments. Vintage cinema showing silent films with organ accompaniment.

16 Warwick Castle
Warwick, Warwickshire CV34 4QU
Tel: Warwick (0926) 495421
Set in 60 acres of grounds and gardens. State rooms, armoury, dungeon, torture chamber, clock tower. 'A Royal Weekend Party 1898' by Madame Tussauds. Medieval banquets.

17 Elgar's Birthplace Museum
Crown East Lane, Lower Broadheath, Worcestershire WR2 6RH
Tel: Cotheridge (0905) 333294
Cottage in which Edward Elgar was born, now housing a museum of photographs, musical scores, letters and records associated with the composer.

18 The Commandery
Sidbury, Worcester, Worcestershire WR1 2HU
Tel: Worcester (0905) 355071
15th C timber-framed building with great hall and panelled rooms. Civil War audio-visual show and exhibition. Displays on Worcester's working past.

19 Wellesbourne Watermill
Mill Farm, Kineton Road, Wellesbourne, Warwickshire CV35 9HG
Tel: Leamington Spa (0926) 470279
Dramatic wooden waterwheel powering impressive machinery. Stoneground flour, conservation work, millpond, farm animals, local crafts and exhibition.

20 Shakespeare's Birthplace
Stratford-upon-Avon, Warwickshire CV37 6QW
Tel: Stratford-upon-Avon (0789) 204016
Half-timbered building furnished in period style, containing many fascinating books, manuscripts and objects. BBC TV Shakespeare costume exhibition.

The world's first cast iron bridge, erected in 1779, is now part of the Ironbridge Gorge Museum near Telford.

21 The Lost Street Museum
27 Brookend Street, Ross-on-Wye, Herefordshire HR9 7EE
Tel: Ross-on-Wye (0989) 62752
Complete Edwardian street of shops including tobacconist, glassware, grocer, chemist, clothes store, pub and many others.

22 Robert Opie Collection
Gloucester Docks, Gloucester GL1 2EH
Tel: Gloucester (0452) 302309
Steeped in nostalgia, the Robert Opie Collection of packaging and advertising brings over 100 years of shopping basket history vividly to life.

23 Jubilee Maze and Museum of Mazes
Symonds Yat, Herefordshire HR9 6DA
Tel: Symonds Yat (0600) 890360
A traditional hedge maze with carved stone temple centrepiece, created to celebrate Queen Elizabeth's Jubilee in 1977. World's only 'hands-on interactive' Museum of Mazes.

24 Keith Harding's World of Mechanical Music
Northleach, Gloucestershire GL54 3EU
Tel: Cotswold (0451) 60181
17th C wool merchant's house, antique clocks, musical boxes, automata and mechanical musical instruments presented as an entertainment. A unique experience of sound.

FIND OUT MORE

Further information about holidays and attractions in the Heart of England region is available from:
Heart of England Tourist Board
Lark Hill Road, Worcester WR5 2EF
Tel: (0905) 763436 or (0905) 763439 (24 hours)

These publications are available free from the Heart of England Tourist Board:
Bed & Breakfast touring map
Shakespeare's Country, Cotswolds and Heart of England
A Guide to Great Escapes in:
  The Cotswolds
  Peak and Potteries
  The Marches (where England and Wales meet)
  Shakespeare's Country
Events list
Fact sheets

Also available are:
Places to Visit in the Heart of England (over 700 attractions - with discounts, vouchers and places to visit in winter) £2.99
Heart of England map £1.95
Cotswolds map £2.95
Cotswold/Wyedean map £2.60
Shropshire/Staffordshire map £2.40
Please add 60p postage for up to 3 items, plus 25p for each additional 3 items.

137

HEART OF ENGLAND

Places to stay

Accommodation entries in this regional section are listed in alphabetical order of place name, and then in alphabetical order of establishment.

The map references refer to the colour maps at the back of the guide. The first figure is the map number; the letter and figure which follow indicate the grid reference on the map.

The symbols at the end of each accommodation entry give information about services and facilities. A 'key' to these symbols is inside the back cover flap, which can be kept open for easy reference.

ALCESTER
Warwickshire
Map ref 2B1

Town has Roman origins and many old buildings around the High Street. It is close to Ragley Hall, the 18th C Palladian mansion with its magnificent baroque Great Hall.

Icknield House

54 Birmingham Road, Alcester
B49 5EG
☎ (0789) 763287 & 763681
Comfortable, well-furnished Victorian house of character, on the Birmingham road, a few hundred yards off A435. Close to Warwick and the Cotswolds. 10 minutes from Stratford-upon-Avon. Excellent touring centre.
Bedrooms: 2 single, 2 double, 1 twin, 1 triple
Bathrooms: 3 private, 1 public, 1 private shower
Bed & breakfast
per night:	£min	£max
Single	17.00	23.00
Double	33.00	36.00

Half board
per person:	£min	£max
Daily	24.00	25.00
Weekly	160.00	170.00

Lunch available
Evening meal 1830 (last orders 1930)
Parking for 8

Orchard Lawns
HIGHLY COMMENDED
Wixford, Alcester B49 6DA
☎ Stratford-on-Avon (0789) 772668
Bed and breakfast accommodation in a small village on B4085, 7 miles from
Stratford-upon-Avon. TV lounge. Garden. Ideal touring centre.
Bedrooms: 1 single, 1 double, 1 twin
Bathrooms: 1 private, 1 public
Bed & breakfast
per night:	£min	£max
Single	15.50	18.50
Double	31.00	37.00

Parking for 6
Cards accepted: Access, Visa

Sambourne Hall Farm
COMMENDED
Wike Lane, Sambourne, Redditch, Worcestershire B96 6NZ
☎ Studley (0527) 852151
315-acre arable & livestock farm. Mid-17th C farmhouse in a peaceful village, close to local pub. Just off the A435 between Alcester and Studley and 9 miles from Stratford.
Bedrooms: 1 double, 1 triple
Bathrooms: 1 private
Bed & breakfast
per night:	£min	£max
Single	18.00	25.00
Double	35.00	35.00

Parking for 6

There are separate sections in this guide listing groups specialising in farm holidays and accommodation which is especially suitable for young people and organised groups.

ALTON
Staffordshire
Map ref 4B2

Alton Castle, an impressive 19th C building, dominates the village which is set in spectacular scenery. Nearby is Alton Towers, a romantic 19th C ruin with innumerable tourist attractions within one of England's largest theme parks in its 800 acres of magnificent gardens.

The Admiral Jervis Hotel

Mill Road, Oakamoor, Stoke-on-Trent ST10 3AG
☎ Oakamoor (0538) 702187
Country hotel of character, once an old coaching inn. Peaceful riverside location, quiet and comfortable. Chef/proprietor. Children welcome. 1.5 miles Alton Towers, 9 miles the Potteries.
Bedrooms: 2 double, 1 twin, 2 triple, 2 family rooms
Bathrooms: 7 private
Bed & breakfast
per night:	£min	£max
Double		39.00

Evening meal 1900 (last orders 2030)
Parking for 10
Open March-October
Cards accepted: Access, Visa

Bank House
APPROVED
Smithy Bank, Alton, Stoke-on-Trent ST10 4AA
☎ Oakamoor (0538) 702524
Central in Alton village, 1 mile from Alton Towers and close to Dovedale and Manifold Valley. 3 good inns serving meals within 200 metres. Family-run.
Bedrooms: 1 double, 3 triple
Bathrooms: 2 private, 1 public

HEART OF ENGLAND

Bed & breakfast per night:	£min	£max
Single	15.00	15.00
Double	30.00	30.00

Parking for 6

Bee Cottage ⋀
Listed

Saltersford Lane, Alton, Stoke-on-Trent ST10 4AU
☎ Oakamoor (0538) 702802
Traditional stone-built cottage, extended over a period of 200 years. In countryside, 1 mile from Alton Towers. Adjoining paddock and orchard extending to 2 acres.
Bedrooms: 3 double
Bathrooms: 1 public

Bed & breakfast per night:	£min	£max
Single	12.50	15.00
Double	25.00	30.00

Parking for 5
Open March-November

Bradley Elms Farm ⋀

Threapwood, Cheadle, Stoke-on-Trent ST10 4RA
☎ Cheadle (0538) 753135 & 750202
Well-appointed farm accommodation providing a comfortable and relaxing atmosphere for that well-earned break. On the edge of the Staffordshire Moorlands. 3 miles from Alton Towers, close to the Potteries and the Peak District National Park.
Bedrooms: 2 double, 1 twin, 1 triple, 1 family room
Bathrooms: 5 private, 1 public

Bed & breakfast per night:	£min	£max
Double	33.00	36.00

Half board per person:	£min	£max
Daily	27.00	31.50

Lunch available
Evening meal 1900 (last orders 2100)
Parking for 10

Bulls Head Inn ⋀
APPROVED

High Street, Alton, Stoke-on-Trent ST10 4AQ
☎ Oakamoor (0538) 702307
Fax (0538) 702065
In the village of Alton close to Alton Towers, an 18th C inn with real ale and home cooking.
Bedrooms: 3 double, 1 twin, 2 family rooms
Bathrooms: 6 private, 1 public

Bed & breakfast per night:	£min	£max
Single	25.00	35.00
Double	30.00	50.00

Lunch available
Evening meal 1900 (last orders 2200)
Parking for 10
Cards accepted: Access, Visa

Talbot Inn ⋀
Listed

Red Road, Alton, Stoke-on-Trent ST10 4BX
☎ Oakamoor (0538) 702767
Charming country inn, delightful setting within view of Alton Towers, offering varied, interesting home-cooked food, real ale and comfortable accommodation.
Bedrooms: 1 twin, 1 family room
Bathrooms: 1 public

Bed & breakfast per night:	£min	£max
Single	25.00	
Double	35.00	45.00

Lunch available
Evening meal 1830 (last orders 2100)
Parking for 20

Wild Duck Inn
Listed

New Road, Alton, Stoke-on-Trent ST10 4AF
☎ Oakamoor (0538) 702218
Large country inn, near Alton Towers Leisure Park. Comfortable bedrooms, restaurant, bar and family lounge.
Bedrooms: 7 triple
Bathrooms: 2 public

Bed & breakfast per night:	£min	£max
Double	34.00	40.00

Evening meal 1900 (last orders 2030)
Parking for 50
Open March-November
Cards accepted: Access, Visa

ALVECHURCH

Hereford and Worcester
Map ref 4B3

Close to industrial Redditch, Alvechurch has grown rapidly from village to town in recent years, but retains much of its old world charm. A centre for canal boat hire.

Alcott Farm
HIGHLY COMMENDED

Weatheroak, Alvechurch, Birmingham, Worcestershire B48 7EH
☎ Wythall (0564) 824051 & Mobile Phone (0374) 163253
77-acre horses farm. Owners Jane and John Poole offer a warm welcome at this attractive farmhouse. Stabling available. Birmingham Airport, National Exhibition Centre, Solihull, Stratford and Warwick all within 25 minutes. 5 minutes from M42 junction 3.
Bedrooms: 2 twin
Bathrooms: 2 private

Bed & breakfast per night:	£min	£max
Single	20.00	25.00
Double	40.00	40.00

Evening meal 1830 (last orders 2030)
Parking for 20

Ad Display advertisement appears on this page

Please check prices and other details at the time of booking.

IF YOU HAVE BUSINESS OR PLEASURE AT THE NEC BIRMINGHAM RELAX AT THE

ALCOTT FARM

Our large farmhouse is set in spectacular greenbelt and has luxurious en-suite bedrooms with all facilities, local pubs and restaurants nearby.
5 mins from junction 3 M42, 20 mins from Solihull, Birmingham NEC and Stratford upon Avon.

Contact Jane Poole
Tel: 0564 824051
Mobile: 0374 163253

HIGHLY COMMENDED

HEART OF ENGLAND

AMPNEY CRUCIS

Gloucestershire
Map ref 2B1

This is one of the 4 Ampney villages and is situated in pleasant countryside. Its church has Saxon features. The very attractive gardens at nearby Barnsley House are open Monday to Friday and offer plants for sale.

Waterton Garden Cottage

HIGHLY COMMENDED

Ampney Crucis, Cirencester GL7 5RX
☎ (0285) 851303
Sympathetically converted part of Victorian stable block, retaining many original features. Walled garden, heated pool, croquet lawn. Tranquil situation, not too far from Cirencester.
Bedrooms: 1 single, 2 double
Bathrooms: 3 private

Bed & breakfast

per night:	£min	£max
Single	25.00	35.00
Double	45.00	45.00

Half board

per person:	£min	£max
Daily	43.00	45.00

Lunch available
Parking for 6

AVON DASSETT

Warwickshire
Map ref 2C1

Village on the slopes of the Dasset Hills, with good views. The church, with its impressive tower and spire, dates from 1868 but incorporates a 14th C window with 15th C glass.

Crandon House

HIGHLY COMMENDED

Avon Dassett, Leamington Spa
CV33 0AA
☎ Fenny Compton (0295) 770652

20-acre mixed farm. Farmhouse offering a high standard of accommodation with superb views over unspoilt countryside. Quiet and peaceful. Easy access to Warwick, Stratford and Cotswolds. 4 miles from junctions 11 and 12 of M40.
Bedrooms: 1 double, 2 twin
Bathrooms: 3 private

Bed & breakfast

per night:	£min	£max
Single	20.00	25.00
Double	34.00	39.00

Half board

per person:	£min	£max
Daily	29.00	36.00
Weekly	180.00	240.00

Evening meal from 1900
Parking for 22
Cards accepted: Access, Visa

BALSALL COMMON

West Midlands
Map ref 4B3

Close to Kenilworth and within easy reach of Coventry.

Blythe Paddocks

Barston Lane, Balsall Common,
Coventry CV7 7BT
☎ Berkswell (0676) 533050
Family home standing in 5 acres. Ten minutes from Birmingham Airport and the National Exhibition Centre. NAC Stoneleigh 8 miles. Countryside location.
Bedrooms: 2 single, 1 double, 1 twin
Bathrooms: 1 public

Bed & breakfast

per night:	£min	£max
Single	15.00	20.00
Double	30.00	40.00

Parking for 10

BARLASTON

Staffordshire
Map ref 4B2

Wedgwood Memorial College

Station Road, Barlaston, Stoke-on-Trent ST12 9DG
☎ (0782) 372105 & 373427
Fax (0782) 372393
Pleasant, well-appointed adult residential college with relaxed, homely ambience, in a quiet village, yet close to National Trust downs and the Potteries. Convenient for the Peak District and Alton Towers. Good quality, home-cooked food with an imaginative repertoire of vegetarian dishes. Limited facilities for the disabled.
Bedrooms: 9 single, 7 twin, 3 triple, 2 family rooms
Bathrooms: 7 public

Bed & breakfast

per night:	£min	£max
Single	12.50	12.50
Double	25.00	25.00

Half board

per person:	£min	£max
Daily	18.50	18.50
Weekly	129.50	129.50

Lunch available
Evening meal 1830 (last orders 1830)
Parking for 40

BERKELEY

Gloucestershire
Map ref 2B1

Town dominated by the castle where Edward II was murdered. Dating from Norman times, it is still the home of the Berkeley family and is open to the public April to September. Slimbridge Wildfowl Trust is nearby.

Pickwick Farm

Listed

Berkeley GL13 9EU
☎ Dursley (0453) 810241
120-acre dairy farm. A warm welcome at this easily located family farm, formerly a coaching inn used by Charles Dickens. Close to Berkeley Castle and Slimbridge Wildfowl Trust. Non-smoking establishment.
Bedrooms: 1 double, 2 twin
Bathrooms: 1 public

Bed & breakfast

per night:	£min	£max
Single	16.00	17.50
Double	32.00	35.00

Parking for 3

BETLEY

Staffordshire
Map ref 4A2

Once a market town, now a village with many whitewashed and timber-framed houses. Much of the 17th C church was paid for by the Egerton family, whose monuments may be seen inside. Noteworthy is the unusual use of wood in the interior of the church.

Adderley Green Farm

Heighley Castle Lane, Betley, Crewe
CW3 9BA
☎ Crewe (0270) 820203
250-acre mixed & dairy farm. Elegant Georgian farmhouse in peaceful surroundings, furnished with antiques and four-poster beds. Ideal for Keele University and Alton Towers. 5 miles from M6 junction 16.
Bedrooms: 1 single, 2 double, 1 twin
Bathrooms: 2 private, 2 public

Bed & breakfast

per night:	£min	£max
Single	14.00	20.00
Double	24.00	34.00

Parking for 4

140

HEART OF ENGLAND

BIBURY
Gloucestershire
Map ref 2B1

Village on the River Coln with stone houses and the famous 17th C Arlington Row, former weavers' cottages. Arlington Mill is now a folk museum. Trout farm and Bansley House Gardens nearby are open to the public.

Cotteswold House
COMMENDED
Arlington, Bibury, Cirencester
GL7 5ND
☎ Cirencester (0285) 740609
Extensively refurbished Regency-style house in the Cotswold village of Bibury, offers purpose-built facilities in a friendly family atmosphere. All rooms en-suite with TV. Guest lounge/dining room. No smoking please.
Bedrooms: 2 double, 1 twin
Bathrooms: 3 private

Bed & breakfast
per night:	£min	£max
Single		22.00
Double		38.00

Parking for 4

Manor Farm
Ablington, Bibury, Cirencester
GL7 5NY
☎ (0285) 740266
700-acre arable and mixed farm. Cotswolds farmhouse in beautiful hamlet of Ablington. Good pubs/restaurants in Bibury (1 mile). Ideal base for touring Cotswolds. Undercover parking for bicycles.
Bedrooms: 1 double, 1 twin, 1 triple
Bathrooms: 1 private, 2 public

Bed & breakfast
per night:	£min	£max
Single	18.00	22.00
Double	30.00	36.00

Evening meal 1830 (last orders 1930)
Parking for 10

There are separate sections in this guide listing groups specialising in farm holidays and accommodation which is especially suitable for young people and organised groups.

BIRMINGHAM
West Midlands
Map ref 4B3

Britain's second city, with many attractions including the City Art Gallery, Barber Institute of Fine Arts, 17th C Aston Hall, science and railway museums, Jewellery Quarter, Cadbury World, 2 cathedrals and Botanical Gardens. Good base for exploring Shakespeare country.
Tourist Information Centre
☎ 021-643 2514

Heath Lodge Hotel
Coleshill Road, Marston Green,
Birmingham B37 7HT
☎ 021-779 2218
Fax 021-779 5673

Licensed family-run hotel, quietly situated yet just 1.5 miles from the National Exhibition Centre and Birmingham Airport. Courtesy car to airport.
Bedrooms: 8 single, 2 double, 6 twin
Bathrooms: 10 private, 1 public,
1 private shower

Bed & breakfast
per night:	£min	£max
Single	25.00	37.50
Double	35.00	48.00

Lunch available
Evening meal 1830 (last orders 2030)
Parking for 24
Cards accepted: Access, Visa, Amex

Prince Hotel
4 Stanmore Road, Edgbaston,
Birmingham B16 9TA
☎ 021-434 3123 & 429 2598
Ideally situated accommodation, with homely and friendly atmosphere. All rooms with satellite TV and tea-making facilities. Money-back guarantee.
Bedrooms: 4 single, 4 double, 1 twin
Bathrooms: 2 public, 3 private showers

Bed & breakfast
per night:	£min	£max
Single	20.00	25.00
Double	40.00	40.00

Parking for 6
Cards accepted: Access, Visa, Amex

BIRMINGHAM AIRPORT
West Midlands

See under Balsall Common, Coleshill, Coventry, Hampton in Arden, Meriden, Solihull

BLEDINGTON
Gloucestershire
Map ref 2B1

Village close to the Oxfordshire border, with a pleasant green and a beautiful church.

Kings Head Inn & Restaurant
COMMENDED
The Green, Bledington, Oxford
OX7 6HD
☎ Kingham (0608) 658365
Fax (0608) 658365
15th C inn located in the heart of the Cotswolds, facing the village green. Authentic lounge bars, full restaurant. Delightful en-suite rooms.
Bedrooms: 5 double, 1 twin
Bathrooms: 6 private

Bed & breakfast
per night:	£min	£max
Single	30.00	35.00
Double	52.00	55.00

Lunch available
Evening meal 1900 (last orders 2200)
Parking for 60
Cards accepted: Access, Visa

BLOCKLEY
Gloucestershire
Map ref 2B1

This village's prosperity was founded in silk mills and other factories but now it is a quiet, unspoilt place. An excellent centre for exploring pretty Cotswold villages, especially Chipping Campden and Broadway.

21 Station Road
COMMENDED
Blockley, Moreton-in-Marsh GL56 9ED
☎ (0386) 700402
Beautifully presented Cotswold-stone house on edge of delightful village. Ideal base for touring the Cotswolds and Shakespeare country. Tastefully decorated, comfortable, non-smoking accommodation with full en-suite facilities, colour TV, tea/coffee making facilities, radio/clock alarm and central heating. A warm welcome awaits you.
Bedrooms: 1 double, 2 twin
Bathrooms: 3 private

Continued ▶

141

HEART OF ENGLAND

BLOCKLEY
Continued

Bed & breakfast
per night:	£min	£max
Single	20.00	20.00
Double	35.00	35.00

Parking for 9

BODENHAM
Hereford and Worcester
Map ref 2A1

Attractive village with old timbered cottages and stone houses and an interesting church. Here the River Lugg makes a loop and flows under an ancient bridge at the end of the village.

Maund Court
HIGHLY COMMENDED

Bodenham, Hereford HR1 3JA
☎ (056 884) 282

150-acre mixed farm. Attractive 15th C farmhouse with a large garden, swimming pool and croquet. Riding, golf and pleasant walks nearby. Ideal centre for touring.

Bedrooms: 1 single, 2 double, 1 twin
Bathrooms: 4 private

Bed & breakfast
per night:	£min	£max
Single	16.00	17.00
Double	32.00	34.00

Evening meal 1800 (last orders 2000)
Parking for 8
Open March-November

BOURTON-ON-THE-WATER
Gloucestershire
Map ref 2B1

The River Windrush flows through this famous Cotswold village which has a green, and cottages and houses of Cotswold stone. Its many attractions include a model village, Birdland, a Motor Museum and the Cotswold Perfumery.

Berkeley Guesthouse
COMMENDED

Moore Road, Bourton-on-the-Water, Cheltenham GL54 2AZ
☎ Cotswolds (0451) 810388

Detached house with a homely, relaxed atmosphere, furnished to a high standard. Personal attention. Attractive gardens, sun lounge, car park. No smoking.

Bedrooms: 1 double, 1 twin, 1 triple
Bathrooms: 3 private

Bed & breakfast
per night:	£min	£max
Single	15.00	20.00
Double	30.00	35.00

Parking for 4

Coombe House
HIGHLY COMMENDED

Rissington Road, Bourton-on-the-Water, Cheltenham GL54 2DT
☎ Cotswold (0451) 821966

Bright, fresh, comfortable, family-run home. All en-suite facilities. Pretty garden, ample parking. Restaurants within walking distance. No smoking in house please.

Bedrooms: 3 double, 2 twin, 2 triple
Bathrooms: 7 private

Bed & breakfast
per night:	£min	£max
Single	35.00	42.00
Double	49.00	60.00

Parking for 10
Cards accepted: Access, Visa, Amex

Farncombe

Clapton, Bourton-on-the-Water, Cheltenham GL54 2LG
☎ Cotswold (0451) 820120

Quiet comfortable accommodation with superb views of the Windrush Valley. In the hamlet of Clapton, 2.5 miles from Bourton-on-the-Water. No-smoking house.

Bedrooms: 2 double, 1 twin
Bathrooms: 1 private, 1 public, 2 private showers

Bed & breakfast
per night:	£min	£max
Single	18.00	
Double	32.00	40.00

Parking for 3

Lamb Inn
COMMENDED

Great Rissington, Bourton-on-the-Water, Cheltenham GL54 2LP
☎ Cotswold (0451) 820388 & 820724

Country inn in rural setting, with home-cooked food, including steaks and local trout, served in attractive restaurant. Beer garden and real ale. Honeymoon suite also available.

Bedrooms: 10 double, 2 twin
Bathrooms: 10 private, 1 public

Bed & breakfast
per night:	£min	£max
Single	30.00	50.00
Double	38.00	72.00

Half board
per person:	£min	£max
Daily	40.00	65.00

Lunch available
Evening meal 1900 (last orders 2130)
Parking for 10
Cards accepted: Access, Visa

Lansdowne House
COMMENDED

Lansdowne, Bourton-on-the-Water, Cheltenham GL54 2AT
☎ Cotswold (0451) 820812

Large, period, stone family house, 2 minutes' level walk from the centre of this much visited and delightful Cotswold village.

Bedrooms: 2 double, 1 twin
Bathrooms: 3 private

Bed & breakfast
per night:	£min	£max
Single	18.00	28.00
Double	29.00	34.00

Parking for 4

The Lawns
Listed

Station Road, Bourton-on-the-Water, Cheltenham GL54 2ER
☎ Cotswold (0451) 821195

Newly built traditional Cotswold stone house, just 5 minutes' walk from the centre of this picturesque village. Relax in a comfortable lounge enjoying an open log fire. Families and children welcome. Discount winter breaks.

Bedrooms: 2 double, 1 twin, 2 triple
Bathrooms: 2 private, 1 public

Bed & breakfast
per night:	£min	£max
Single	20.00	25.00
Double	32.00	36.00

Parking for 9

Mousetrap Inn
APPROVED

Lansdowne, Bourton-on-the-Water, Cheltenham GL54 2AR
☎ Cotswold (0451) 820579

Small homely inn with beer garden. TV and tea/coffee makers in all rooms. Bar meals, and open fires in winter.

Bedrooms: 7 double, 2 twin

HEART OF ENGLAND

Bathrooms: 9 private
Bed & breakfast

per night:	£min	£max
Single	25.00	28.00
Double	40.00	45.00

Lunch available
Evening meal 1830 (last orders 2100)
Parking for 12

Old New Inn
COMMENDED
Bourton-on-the-Water, Cheltenham
GL54 2AF
☎ Cotswold (0451) 820467
Fax (0451) 810236

Built in 1712 and run by the same family for over 60 years. Traditional cooking and service. Log fires in winter. Large gardens. Ideal centre for touring.
Bedrooms: 5 single, 9 double, 5 twin, 1 triple
Bathrooms: 9 private, 3 public
Bed & breakfast

per night:	£min	£max
Single	27.00	34.00
Double	54.00	68.00

Half board

per person:	£min	£max
Daily	43.00	50.00

Lunch available
Evening meal 1930 (last orders 2030)
Parking for 32
Cards accepted: Access, Visa, Switch

The Ridge
Whiteshoots Hill, Bourton-on-the-Water, Cheltenham GL54 2LE
☎ Cotswold (0451) 820660
Large country house surrounded by beautiful grounds. Central for visiting many places of interest and close to all amenities. Ground floor en-suite bedroom available.
Bedrooms: 3 double, 1 twin, 1 triple
Bathrooms: 4 private, 1 public
Bed & breakfast

per night:	£min	£max
Single	20.00	25.00
Double	29.00	36.00

Parking for 12

Rooftrees Guesthouse
Rissington Road, Bourton-on-the-Water, Cheltenham GL54 2EB
☎ Cotswold (0451) 821943

Detached Cotswold-stone family house, all rooms individually decorated, 8 minutes' level walk from village centre. Home cooking with fresh local produce. 2 rooms are on ground floor and 2 have four-poster beds. No smoking.
Bedrooms: 3 double
Bathrooms: 3 private, 1 public
Bed & breakfast

per night:	£min	£max
Single	22.00	
Double	29.00	39.00

Half board

per person:	£min	£max
Daily	25.00	30.00

Evening meal 1830 (last orders 1200)
Parking for 8
Cards accepted: Access, Visa

Stepping Stone
Rectory Lane, Great Rissington, Cheltenham GL54 2LL
☎ Cotswold (0451) 821385
Large detached house in country village lane with private grounds and views across the Windrush Valley.
Bedrooms: 1 single, 2 double, 1 twin
Bathrooms: 2 private, 1 public
Bed & breakfast

per night:	£min	£max
Single	16.00	40.00
Double	32.00	42.00

Parking for 6

Strathspey
Listed APPROVED
Lansdown, Bourton-on-the-Water, Cheltenham GL54 2AR
☎ Cotswold (0451) 820694
Character, Cotswold-stone house 400 yards' walk from village centre. Quiet location with pretty riverside walk.
Bedrooms: 3 double
Bathrooms: 2 private, 1 public
Bed & breakfast

per night:	£min	£max
Double	32.00	36.00

Parking for 4

Upper Farm
Clapton on the Hill, Bourton-on-the-Water, Cheltenham GL54 2LG
☎ Cotswold (0451) 820453
130-acre mixed farm. 17th C Cotswold farmhouse in a quiet, unspoilt village 2.5 miles from Bourton-on-the-Water. Magnificent views. Fresh farm produce.
Bedrooms: 1 single, 2 double, 2 twin
Bathrooms: 2 private, 2 public
Bed & breakfast

per night:	£min	£max
Single	18.00	18.00
Double	28.00	38.00

Parking for 6
Open March-November

Willow Crest
COMMENDED
Rissington Road, Bourton-on-the-Water, Cheltenham GL54 2DZ
☎ Cotswold (0451) 822073
Chalet bungalow in a quiet position on the edge of the village.
Bedrooms: 2 double, 1 twin
Bathrooms: 1 private, 1 public
Bed & breakfast

per night:	£min	£max
Double	30.00	34.00

Parking for 6
Open March-October

Windrush Farm
COMMENDED
Bourton-on-the-Water, Cheltenham GL54 3BY
☎ Cotswold (0451) 820419

150-acre arable farm. Beautiful Cotswold-stone house on a family-run farm, in a peaceful setting 1.5 miles from Bourton-on-the-Water.
Bedrooms: 1 double, 1 twin
Bathrooms: 2 private
Bed & breakfast

per night:	£min	£max
Single	20.00	25.00
Double	35.00	38.00

Parking for 8
Open March-December

BREDENBURY
Hereford and Worcester
Map ref 2A1

Redhill Farm
Listed
Bredenbury, Bromyard, Herefordshire HR7 4SY
☎ Bromyard (0885) 483255 & 483535
Fax (0885) 483535
86-acre mixed farm. Farmhouse bed and breakfast in peaceful Herefordshire countryside. Children and pets welcome. Golf, tennis, fishing, leisure centre and riding nearby. On the A44 road. Ample parking.
Bedrooms: 1 double, 1 twin, 1 triple
Bathrooms: 1 public

Continued ▶

143

HEART OF ENGLAND

BREDENBURY
Continued

Bed & breakfast
per night:	£min	£max
Single	14.00	15.00
Double	26.00	28.00

Evening meal 1900 (last orders 2100)
Parking for 23

BREDON'S NORTON
Hereford and Worcester
Map ref 2B1

Hamlet at the foot of Bredon Hill with a substantial Victorian mansion in Tudor style.

Lampitt House
COMMENDED

Lampitt Lane, Bredon's Norton, Tewkesbury, Gloucestershire
GL20 7HB
☎ Bredon (0684) 72295

Large house set in 1.5 acre garden in picturesque Cotswold village at the foot of Bredon Hill. Extensive views. Tewkesbury 4 miles. Beautiful hill and riverside walks.
Bedrooms: 2 double, 1 twin
Bathrooms: 3 private

Bed & breakfast
per night:	£min	£max
Single	18.00	26.00
Double	32.00	36.00

Half board
per person:	£min	£max
Daily	28.00	36.00

Evening meal 1800 (last orders 2000)
Parking for 6

BRETFORTON
Hereford and Worcester
Map ref 2B1

The Pond House
COMMENDED

Lower Fields, Weston Road, Bretforton, Evesham, Worcestershire
WR11 5QA
☎ Evesham (0386) 831687

Superb country home in open farmland, with panoramic views of Cotswold Hills. Ideally placed for touring, 3 miles to Broadway and Chipping Campden, close to Stratford-upon-Avon.
Bedrooms: 2 double, 1 twin

144

Bathrooms: 1 public
Bed & breakfast
per night:	£min	£max
Single	20.00	21.50
Double	30.00	35.00

Parking for 10

BRIDGNORTH
Shropshire
Map ref 4A3

Interesting red sandstone town in 2 parts - High and Low - linked by a cliff railway. It has much of interest including a ruined Norman keep, half-timbered 16th C houses, Midland Motor Museum and Severn Valley Railway.
Tourist Information Centre
☎ (0746) 763358

The Albynes

Nordley, Bridgnorth WV16 4SX
☎ (0746) 762261

263-acre arable and mixed farm. Large country house, peacefully set in parkland with spectacular views of Shropshire countryside. On B4373 - Bridgnorth 3 miles, Ironbridge 4 miles.
Bedrooms: 2 twin
Bathrooms: 1 private, 2 public

Bed & breakfast
per night:	£min	£max
Single	17.00	20.00
Double	32.00	35.00

Parking for 8

Aldenham Weir
COMMENDED

Muckley Cross, Bridgnorth WV16 4RR
☎ Morville (074 631) 352

Superb country house, set in 11.5 acres, with working mill race, weir and trout stream for fishing. All rooms en-suite. Close to Ironbridge Gorge Museum. Quietly located off the A458, central between Much Wenlock and Bridgnorth.
Bedrooms: 3 double, 2 twin, 1 triple
Bathrooms: 6 private

Bed & breakfast
per night:	£min	£max
Single	24.00	24.00
Double	36.00	36.00

Parking for 5

Church House

Aston Eyre, Bridgnorth WV16 6XD
☎ Morville (074 631) 248

You are invited for a peaceful holiday in this oak-beamed cottage on a 6-acre smallholding. Overlooking Shropshire's rolling hils, it nestles behind a Norman church. Evening meals by arrangement.
Bedrooms: 1 double, 1 twin
Bathrooms: 2 private

Bed & breakfast
per night:	£min	£max
Double	28.00	32.00

Half board
per person:	£min	£max
Daily	26.00	26.00
Weekly		168.00

Evening meal 1800 (last orders 2000)
Parking for 4
Open February-November

Haven Pasture
COMMENDED

Underton, Bridgnorth WV16 6TY
☎ Middleton Scriven (074 635) 632
Fax (074 635) 632

Large country bungalow, set in 1 acre of gardens, with panoramic views. Outdoor heated swimming pool. Evening meals on request. Trout pools 400 yards.
Bedrooms: 1 double, 2 twin
Bathrooms: 3 private, 1 public

Bed & breakfast
per night:	£min	£max
Single	24.00	28.00
Double	32.00	38.00

Half board
per person:	£min	£max
Daily	23.50	26.50
Weekly	148.00	167.00

Evening meal 1830 (last orders 2100)
Parking for 8

Oldfield Cottage
Listed

2 Oldfield Cottage, Oldfield, Bridgnorth WV16 6AQ
☎ Middleton Scriven (074 635) 257

Traditional stone cottage in "Cadfael country". Exposed timbers and log fires. Large garden. Four miles from Bridgnorth.
Bedrooms: 1 double
Bathrooms: 1 public

Bed & breakfast
per night:	£min	£max
Double	35.00	35.00

Half board
per person:	£min	£max
Daily	25.00	27.50

Parking for 2
Open February-October

HEART OF ENGLAND

Park Grange

Morville, Bridgnorth WV16 4RN
☎ Morville (074 631) 285
Splendid beamed family house set in 12 acres, with goats, poultry, pony, wildlife and fishing pools. Children's play area. Panoramic views of Shropshire hills. Quiet location midway between Bridgnorth and Much Wenlock just off A458.
Bedrooms: 1 double
Bathrooms: 1 private

Bed & breakfast
per night:	£min	£max
Double	34.00	36.00

Parking for 10
Open March-October

BROADWAY
Hereford and Worcester
Map ref 2B1

Beautiful Cotswold village called the "Show village of England", with 16th C stone houses and cottages. Near the village is Broadway Tower with magnificent views over 12 counties and a country park with nature trails and adventure playground.

Broadway Court
Listed HIGHLY COMMENDED

89 High Street, Broadway, Worcestershire WR12 7AL
☎ (0386) 852237
Grade II listed barn conversion overlooking secluded, walled cottage garden with country views. Delightful and spacious en-suite bedrooms, beautiful panelled dining room. Two minutes' walk to village centre.
Bedrooms: 2 double
Bathrooms: 2 private

Bed & breakfast
per night:	£min	£max
Single	35.00	40.00
Double	45.00	50.00

Parking for 10

Cinnibar Cottage
Listed HIGHLY COMMENDED

45 Bury End, (Snowshill Rd.,), Broadway, Worcestershire WR12 7AF
☎ (0386) 858 623
150-year-old Cotswold-stone cottage. Quiet situation with open country views, half a mile from Broadway village green, along Snowshill road. Non-smoking establishment.
Bedrooms: 1 double, 1 twin
Bathrooms: 1 public

Bed & breakfast
per night:	£min	£max
Double	30.00	34.00

Parking for 1

Crown and Trumpet Inn
APPROVED

Church Street, Broadway, Worcestershire WR12 7AE
☎ (0386) 853202
Traditional English inn with log fires and oak beams, quietly located just off the village green. Home-cooked local and seasonal English food.
Bedrooms: 3 double, 1 twin
Bathrooms: 3 private, 1 public

Bed & breakfast
per night:	£min	£max
Double		37.00

Lunch available
Evening meal 1830 (last orders 2130)
Parking for 6

Eastbank

Station Drive, Broadway, Worcestershire WR12 7DF
☎ (0386) 852659
Quiet location, half a mile from village. All rooms fully en-suite (bath/shower), with colour TV and beverage facilities. Homely atmosphere. Free brochure.
Bedrooms: 2 double, 2 twin, 2 triple
Bathrooms: 6 private

Bed & breakfast
per night:	£min	£max
Single		15.00
Double	32.00	45.00

Half board
per person:	£min	£max
Daily	26.50	32.50

Evening meal 1900 (last orders 1000)
Parking for 6

Leasow House
HIGHLY COMMENDED

Laverton Meadow, Broadway, Worcestershire WR12 7NA
☎ Stanton (038 673) 526
Fax (038 673) 596

17th C Cotswold-stone farmhouse tranquilly set in open countryside close to Broadway village.
Bedrooms: 3 double, 2 twin, 2 triple
Bathrooms: 7 private

Bed & breakfast
per night:	£min	£max
Single	34.00	50.00
Double	48.00	60.00

Parking for 14
Cards accepted: Access, Visa, Amex

Manor Farm
COMMENDED

Wormington, Broadway, Worcestershire WR12 7NL
☎ Stanton (038 673) 302
280-acre arable & livestock farm. Attractive Tudor farmhouse in quiet village, 4 miles from Broadway. Access to farm with animals and river fishing.
Bedrooms: 2 double, 1 twin
Bathrooms: 1 private, 1 public, 1 private shower

Bed & breakfast
per night:	£min	£max
Single		17.00	25.00
Double	30.00	40.00

Parking for 6

Millhay Cottage
Listed

Bury End, Broadway, Worcestershire WR12 7JS
☎ (0386) 858241
House set in a superb garden off the Snowshill road and adjacent to Cotswold Way. The suite of two bedrooms, bathroom and WC is let as one family unit (1-4 persons).
Bedrooms: 1 double, 1 twin
Bathrooms: 2 private, 1 public

Bed & breakfast
per night:	£min	£max
Single	18.00	20.00
Double	33.00	36.00

Parking for 12

Mount Pleasant Farm
HIGHLY COMMENDED

Childswickham, Broadway, Worcestershire WR12 7HZ
☎ (0386) 853424
250-acre mixed farm. Large Victorian farmhouse with excellent views. Very quiet accommodation with all modern amenities. Approximately 3 miles from Broadway.
Bedrooms: 2 double, 1 twin
Bathrooms: 3 private

Bed & breakfast
per night:	£min	£max
Single		22.00
Double	35.00	40.00

Parking for 8

Olive Branch Guest House

78 High Street, Broadway, Worcestershire WR12 7AJ
☎ (0386) 853440
16th C house with modern amenities close to centre of village. Traditional English breakfast served. Reduced rates for 3 nights or more.
Bedrooms: 3 single, 2 double, 2 twin, 2 triple
Bathrooms: 5 private, 2 public

Continued ▶

145

HEART OF ENGLAND

BROADWAY
Continued

Bed & breakfast
per night:	£min	£max
Single	17.00	18.50
Double	35.00	44.00

Half board
per person:	£min	£max
Daily	24.50	26.50

Evening meal 1900 (last orders 2000)
Parking for 8
Cards accepted: Amex

Orchard Grove
HIGHLY COMMENDED

Station Road, Broadway,
Worcestershire WR12 7DE
☎ Evesham (0386) 853834
Attractive detached Cotswold house, just minutes from village centre, tastefully appointed for guests' every comfort. Warm welcome assured. Non-smokers only please.
Bedrooms: 1 double, 1 triple
Bathrooms: 2 private, 1 public

Bed & breakfast
per night:	£min	£max
Double	40.00	45.00

Parking for 3

Pine Tree Cottage
Listed COMMENDED

Laverton, Broadway, Worcestershire
WR12 7NA
☎ Stanton (038 673) 280
Fax (038 673) 280
Small family bed and breakfast, 2 miles from Broadway in peaceful village. Self-catering also available.
Bedrooms: 1 twin
Bathrooms: 1 private

Bed & breakfast
per night:	£min	£max
Single	18.00	18.00
Double	30.00	36.00

Parking for 3

Shenberrow Hill
Listed

Stanton, Broadway, Worcestershire
WR12 7NE
☎ (0386) 73468
9-acre horses farm. Attractive country house, quietly situated in beautiful unspoilt Cotswold village. Heated swimming pool. Friendly, helpful service. Inn nearby.
Bedrooms: 1 twin, 1 family room
Bathrooms: 1 private, 1 public

Bed & breakfast
per night:	£min	£max
Single	20.00	20.00
Double	39.00	39.00

Evening meal 1800 (last orders 2000)
Parking for 6

Southwold House
COMMENDED

Station Road, Broadway,
Worcestershire WR12 7DE
☎ (0386) 853681
Warm welcome, friendly service, good cooking at this large Edwardian house, only 4 minutes' walk from village centre. Reductions for 2 or more nights; bargain winter breaks.
Bedrooms: 1 single, 5 double, 2 twin
Bathrooms: 5 private, 2 public

Bed & breakfast
per night:	£min	£max
Single	18.00	
Double	36.00	47.00

Parking for 8
Cards accepted: Access, Visa, Amex

White Acres Guesthouse
COMMENDED

Station Road, Broadway,
Worcestershire WR12 7DE
☎ (0386) 852320
Spacious Victorian house providing a variety of en-suite bedrooms, 3 with four-poster beds. Ample off-the-road parking. Only 4 minutes' walk from the village centre. Brochure available.
Bedrooms: 5 double, 1 twin
Bathrooms: 6 private

Bed & breakfast
per night:	£min	£max
Double	38.00	42.00

Parking for 6
Open March-November

Windrush House
APPROVED

Station Road, Broadway,
Worcestershire WR12 7DE
☎ (0386) 853577
Edwardian guesthouse on the A44, half a mile from the village centre, offering personal service. Evening meals by arrangement. 10 per cent reduction in tariff after 2 nights. A no smoking establishment.
Bedrooms: 4 double, 1 twin
Bathrooms: 3 private, 1 public

Bed & breakfast
per night:	£min	£max
Single	18.00	20.00
Double	36.00	44.00

Parking for 5
Open March-October

We advise you to confirm your booking in writing.

BROMSGROVE
Hereford and Worcester
Map ref 4B3

This market town near the Lickey Hills has an interesting museum and craft centre and 14th C church with fine tombs and a Carillon tower. The Avoncroft Museum of Buildings is nearby where many old buildings have been re-assembled, having been saved from destruction.
Tourist Information Centre
☎ (0527) 31809

Astwood Court Farm
Listed

Astwood Lane, Stoke Prior,
Bromsgrove, Worcestershire B60 4BB
☎ Hanbury (0527) 821362
16th C farmhouse, within easy reach of Stratford-upon-Avon, Warwick and the Cotswolds. Exit 5 of the M5 to Stoke Works. After 1.5 miles, take first right after Bowling Green Inn.
Bedrooms: 1 double, 2 twin
Bathrooms: 1 private, 1 public

Bed & breakfast
per night:	£min	£max
Single	20.00	25.00
Double	30.00	35.00

Parking for 20

The Barn
COMMENDED

Woodman Lane, Clent, Stourbridge,
Worcestershire DY9 9PX
☎ Hagley (0562) 885879
Converted Georgian barn on smallholding. At foot of Clent Hills, access to hills from the property. Easy access to Birmingham and National Exhibition Centre.
Bedrooms: 1 double
Bathrooms: 1 private

Bed & breakfast
per night:	£min	£max
Single	20.00	25.00
Double	40.00	50.00

Parking for 11

Lower Bentley Farm

Lower Bentley Lane, Lower Bentley,
Bromsgrove, Worcestershire B60 4JB
☎ (0527) 821286
300-acre dairy & livestock farm. Victorian farmhouse 5 miles from Redditch, Bromsgrove, Droitwich, M5 and M42, in open countryside. Ideal base for business or pleasure.
Bedrooms: 1 double, 1 family room
Bathrooms: 2 private

HEART OF ENGLAND

Bed & breakfast per night:	£min	£max
Single	18.00	20.00
Double	30.00	32.00

Parking for 6

95 Old Station Road
Listed

Bromsgrove, Worcestershire B60 2AF
☎ (0527) 874463
Modern house in quiet pleasant location close to the A38, 3 miles from the M5 and 1.5 miles from the M42. Within easy reach of National Exhibition Centre, Worcester and Stratford. Car parking. TV lounge.
Bedrooms: 2 single, 1 twin
Bathrooms: 1 public

Bed & breakfast per night:	£min	£max
Single	15.00	15.00
Double	30.00	30.00

Half board per person:	£min	£max
Daily	20.00	20.00
Weekly	120.00	120.00

Evening meal 1800 (last orders 0900)
Parking for 2

BROMYARD
Hereford and Worcester
Map ref 2B1

Market town on the River Frome surrounded by orchards, with black and white houses and a Norman church. Nearby at Lower Brockhampton is a 14th C half-timbered moated manor house owned by the National Trust. Heritage Centre.

Littlebridge House
COMMENDED

Norton, Bromyard, Herefordshire HR7 4PN
☎ (0885) 482471
Set in open countryside 3 miles north of Bromyard on B4203. En-suite rooms available. All rooms tastefully decorated.
Bedrooms: 1 double, 1 twin, 1 family room
Bathrooms: 3 private, 1 public

Bed & breakfast per night:	£min	£max
Single	20.00	23.50
Double	30.00	37.00

Half board per person:	£min	£max
Daily	32.50	36.00

Evening meal 1830 (last orders 2000)
Parking for 3

Park House
28 Sherford Street, Bromyard, Herefordshire HR7 4DL
☎ (0885) 482294
Close to town centre, restaurant and shops, and a desirable location for touring. Ample parking.
Bedrooms: 1 single, 1 double, 1 twin, 2 triple
Bathrooms: 3 private, 1 public

Bed & breakfast per night:	£min	£max
Double	30.00	36.00

Parking for 6

BROSELEY
Shropshire
Map ref 4A3

Lord Hill Guest House
Listed

Duke Street, Broseley TF12 5LU
☎ Telford (0952) 884270
Former public house renovated to a high standard. Easy access to Ironbridge, Bridgnorth, Shrewsbury and Telford town centre.
Bedrooms: 1 single, 1 double, 5 twin
Bathrooms: 2 private, 2 public, 1 private shower

Bed & breakfast per night:	£min	£max
Single	15.00	18.00
Double	30.00	36.00

Half board per person:	£min	£max
Daily	20.00	23.00
Weekly	140.00	161.00

Parking for 9

BUCKNELL
Shropshire
Map ref 4A3

Village by the River Redlake with thatched black and white cottages, a Norman church and the remains of an Iron Age fort on a nearby hill. It is a designated Area of Outstanding Natural Beauty.

The Hall
COMMENDED

Bucknell SY7 0AA
☎ (054 74) 249
200-acre mixed farm. Georgian farmhouse in the picturesque village of Bucknell, with a peaceful and relaxed atmosphere.
Bedrooms: 2 double, 1 twin
Bathrooms: 1 private, 1 public

Bed & breakfast per night:	£min	£max
Single	15.00	16.00
Double	30.00	32.00

Half board per person:	£min	£max
Daily	23.00	24.00
Weekly	156.00	

Evening meal 1800 (last orders 1200)
Parking for 4
Open March-November

BURTON UPON TRENT
Staffordshire
Map ref 4B3

An important brewing town with the Bass Museum of Brewing, where the Bass shire horses are stabled. There are 3 bridges with views over the river and some interesting public buildings including the 18th C St Modwen's Church.
Tourist Information Centre
☎ (0283) 516609

Hayfield House
Listed

13 Ashby Road, Woodville, Swadlincote, Derbyshire DE11 7BZ
☎ (0283) 225620
Victorian villa on the A50 in South Derbyshire, close to the Leicestershire/Staffordshire/Derbyshire border.
Bedrooms: 1 triple, 1 family room
Bathrooms: 1 private, 1 public

Bed & breakfast per night:	£min	£max
Single	15.00	15.00
Double	28.00	28.00

Half board per person:	£min	£max
Daily	20.00	22.00
Weekly	130.00	140.00

Evening meal 1800 (last orders 1900)
Parking for 3

New Inn Farm
Listed

Needwood, Burton upon Trent DE13 9PB
☎ (0283) 75435
122-acre mixed & dairy farm. In the heart of Needwood Forest on the main B5234 Newborough to Burton upon Trent road. Central for Uttoxeter, Lichfield, Derby and A38 eastern access to Burton upon Trent.
Bedrooms: 1 single, 1 double, 1 triple
Bathrooms: 1 public

Bed & breakfast per night:	£min	£max
Single	15.00	
Double	30.00	

Parking for 6

HEART OF ENGLAND

CARDINGTON
Shropshire
Map ref 4A3

Grove Farm
Listed
Cardington, Church Stretton SY6 7JZ
☎ Longville (0694) 771251
7-acre mixed farm. Oak-beamed farmhouse built in 1667, in delightful village 5 miles from Church Stretton. Excellent walking country.
Bedrooms: 1 twin, 1 triple
Bathrooms: 1 public

Bed & breakfast
per night:	£min	£max
Single	11.00	12.00
Double	22.00	24.00

Parking for 10

CHELTENHAM
Gloucestershire
Map ref 2B1

Cheltenham was developed as a spa town in the 18th C and has some beautiful Regency architecture, in particular the Pittville Pump Room. It holds international music and literature festivals and is also famous for its race meetings and cricket.
Tourist Information Centre
☎ (0242) 522878

Cleyne Hage ⋀
APPROVED
Southam Lane, Southam, Cheltenham GL52 3NY
☎ (0242) 518569
Cotswold-stone house in secluded setting between B4632 and A435, on the Cotswold Way, 3 miles north of Cheltenham. Open view of hills and racecourse. Pets welcome. Parking. Non-smokers please.
Bedrooms: 2 single, 1 double, 1 twin
Bathrooms: 2 public

Bed & breakfast
per night:	£min	£max
Single	17.00	20.00
Double	26.00	30.00

Parking for 8
Cards accepted: Access, Visa

Elm Villa ⋀
49 London Road, Cheltenham GL52 6HE
☎ (0242) 231909
Beautiful, detached, listed Victorian house, with its own special original architecture. Three minutes town centre, theatre, swimming pool, parks.
Bedrooms: 1 double, 2 twin
Bathrooms: 1 public

Bed & breakfast
per night:	£min	£max
Single	20.00	25.00
Double	36.00	38.00

Parking for 4

Hamilton
Listed
46 All Saints Road, Cheltenham GL52 2HA
☎ (0242) 582845
Early Victorian town house, with spacious accommodation, near town centre. Ideal for visitors to Stratford-upon-Avon, the Cotswolds and Forest of Dean.
Bedrooms: 1 twin
Bathrooms: 1 public

Bed & breakfast
per night:	£min	£max
Double	28.00	45.00

Open January-November

Kielder ⋀
COMMENDED
222 London Road, Charlton Kings, Cheltenham GL52 6HW
☎ (0242) 237138
Comfortable family house on A40, near junction with A435. One and a quarter miles from town centre. Stair chairlift available. No smoking.
Bedrooms: 1 double, 1 twin, 1 triple
Bathrooms: 1 private, 1 public

Bed & breakfast
per night:	£min	£max
Single	16.00	17.00
Double	30.00	32.00

Half board
per person:	£min	£max
Daily	26.00	27.00
Weekly	175.00	180.00

Evening meal from 1830
Parking for 5

Lawn House
COMMENDED
11 London Road, Cheltenham GL52 6EX
☎ (0242) 578486
Elegant Grade II listed house. Good parking and close to town centre. Friendly atmosphere. Family-run. TVs, beverage trays, good food, comfortable rooms.
Bedrooms: 2 single, 3 double, 1 twin, 2 triple
Bathrooms: 2 private, 2 public

Bed & breakfast
per night:	£min	£max
Single	18.00	22.00
Double	36.00	44.00

Parking for 8
Cards accepted: Access, Visa

Lonsdale House ⋀
COMMENDED
Montpellier Drive, Cheltenham GL50 1TX
☎ (0242) 232379
Regency house situated 5 minutes' walk from the town hall, promenade, shopping centre, parks and theatre. Easy access to all main routes.
Bedrooms: 5 single, 2 double, 1 twin, 2 triple, 1 family room
Bathrooms: 3 private, 4 public

Bed & breakfast
per night:	£min	£max
Single	18.00	23.00
Double	36.00	44.00

Parking for 6
Cards accepted: Access, Visa

Old Rectory ⋀
COMMENDED
Woolstone, Cheltenham GL52 4RG
☎ Bishops Cleeve (024 267) 3766
Beautiful Victorian rectory in peaceful hamlet, 4 miles north of the Regency town of Cheltenham. Tranquil spot with lovely views.
Bedrooms: 1 double, 1 twin, 1 triple
Bathrooms: 3 private

Bed & breakfast
per night:	£min	£max
Single		23.00
Double		37.00

Parking for 6
Open March-November

The Original Yew Tree Farm
COMMENDED
Little Shurdinton, Cheltenham GL51 5TX
☎ (0242) 862022
Fax (0242) 862047
Grade II listed farmhouse, dating from about 1600, set in its own grounds with lovely views of the Cotswold Escarpment. Just off A46, 5 miles south of Cheltenham.
Bedrooms: 2 double
Bathrooms: 2 private

Bed & breakfast
per night:	£min	£max
Single		20.00
Double		40.00

Parking for 6

St. Michaels ⋀
COMMENDED
4 Montpellier Drive, Cheltenham GL50 1TX
☎ (0242) 513587
Elegant Edwardian guesthouse 5 minutes' stroll from town centre. Delightful rooms with central heating, refreshment tray, colour TV, clock/radio, hairdryer. Quiet location.
Bedrooms: 2 double, 1 twin, 1 triple

HEART OF ENGLAND

Bathrooms: 2 private, 1 public

Bed & breakfast

per night:	£min	£max
Single	18.00	25.00
Double	30.00	39.00

Parking for 3
Cards accepted: Access, Visa

The Wynyards
COMMENDED

Butts Lane, Woodmancote,
Cheltenham GL52 4QH
☎ Bishops Cleeve (024 267) 3876
Secluded old Cotswold stone house in elevated position with panoramic views. Set in open countryside on outskirts of small village. 4 miles from Cheltenham.
Bedrooms: 1 double, 2 twin
Bathrooms: 1 private, 2 public

Bed & breakfast

per night:	£min	£max
Single	12.50	18.00
Double	25.00	30.00

Parking for 6

CHIPPING CAMPDEN
Gloucestershire
Map ref 2B1

Outstanding Cotswold wool town with many old stone gabled houses, a splendid church, 17th C almshouses and Woolstaplers Hall Museum. Nearby are Kiftsgate Court Gardens and Hidcote Manor Gardens (National Trust).

Brymbo
Listed

Honeybourne Lane, Mickleton,
Chipping Campden GL55 6PU
☎ Mickleton (0386) 438876
Fax (0386) 438113
Comfortable, spacious farm building conversion with large garden in beautiful Cotswold countryside. 3 miles Chipping Campden, close to Stratford and Broadway. Free "4 wheel drive tour" offer.
Bedrooms: 2 double, 1 twin
Bathrooms: 2 private, 2 public

Bed & breakfast

per night:	£min	£max
Single	14.00	21.00
Double	28.00	36.00

Parking for 4

Haydon House
APPROVED

Church Street, Chipping Campden
GL55 6JG
☎ Evesham (0386) 840275

Comfortable historic house, converted from a dairy and bakehouse surrounding a secluded vine-hung courtyard. Centrally heated. No smoking.
Bedrooms: 1 single, 1 double, 1 twin
Bathrooms: 3 private

Bed & breakfast

per night:	£min	£max
Single	20.00	22.00
Double	40.00	42.00

Parking for 1

Lower High Street

Chipping Campden GL55 6DZ
☎ Evesham (0386) 840163
Cotswold-stone house in the Lower High Street, conveniently situated for tours and walks in the Cotswolds, shops and restaurants.
Bedrooms: 1 double, 1 twin
Bathrooms: 1 private, 1 public

Bed & breakfast

per night:	£min	£max
Double	30.00	35.00

Open April-October

Manor Farm
APPROVED

Weston Subedge, Chipping Campden
GL55 6QT
☎ Evesham (0386) 840390
Traditional 17th C farmhouse in the heart of the Cotswolds, completely refurbished and restored. All rooms en-suite. 1.5 miles from Chipping Campden.
Bedrooms: 2 double, 1 twin
Bathrooms: 3 private

Bed & breakfast

per night:	£min	£max
Single	18.00	20.00
Double	36.00	40.00

Parking for 8

Orchard Hill House
Listed HIGHLY COMMENDED

Broad Campden, Chipping Campden
GL55 6UU
☎ Evesham (0386) 841473

17th C Cotswold-stone restored farmhouse. Breakfast in our flagstoned dining room with inglenook fireplace around our 10 ft elm farmhouse table.
Bedrooms: 2 double, 1 triple
Bathrooms: 3 private

Bed & breakfast

per night:	£min	£max
Single	20.00	30.00
Double	40.00	50.00

Parking for 6

Sparlings
COMMENDED

Leysbourne, High Street, Chipping
Campden GL55 6HL
☎ Evesham (0386) 840505

Fully centrally heated, comfortable, attractive 18th C Cotswold house in Chipping Campden High Street. Walled garden. Easy parking. Children over 6 welcome.
Bedrooms: 1 double, 1 twin
Bathrooms: 2 private

Bed & breakfast

per night:	£min	£max
Single	25.00	25.00
Double	42.00	44.00

Weston Park Farm

Dovers Hill, Chipping Campden
GL55 6WW
☎ Evesham (0386) 840835
20-acre mixed farm. Self-contained wing of secluded, magnificently situated farmhouse, 1 mile from Chipping Campden, adjacent to National Trust land.
Bedrooms: 1 triple
Bathrooms: 1 private

Bed & breakfast

per night:	£min	£max
Single	20.00	20.00
Double	35.00	40.00

Parking for 10

Wyldlands
Listed COMMENDED

Broad Campden, Chipping Campden
GL55 6UR
☎ Evesham (0386) 840478
Non-smoking accommodation in quiet scenic village. Extensive views. Good food at traditional inn nearby.
Bedrooms: 2 double, 1 twin
Bathrooms: 1 private, 2 public

Continued ▶

HEART OF ENGLAND

CHIPPING CAMPDEN
Continued

Bed & breakfast
per night:	£min	£max
Single	18.00	20.00
Double	33.00	38.00

Parking for 4

CHURCH STRETTON
Shropshire
Map ref 4A3

Church Stretton lies under the eastern slope of the Longmynd surrounded by hills. It is ideal for walkers, with marvellous views, golf and gliding. Wenlock Edge is not far away.

Acton Scott Farm ᴀ
APPROVED

Acton Scott, Church Stretton SY6 6QN
☎ Marshbrook (0694) 781260
320-acre mixed farm. Conveniently situated 17th C farmhouse of character with comfortable, spacious rooms and log fires. Beautiful countryside.
Bedrooms: 1 double, 1 twin, 1 family room
Bathrooms: 1 private, 1 public
Bed & breakfast
per night:	£min	£max
Single	14.00	19.00
Double	26.00	36.00

Parking for 6
Open February-November

The Elms
Listed

Little Stretton, Church Stretton SY6 6RD
☎ (0694) 723084
Victorian country house in spacious grounds, decorated and furnished in Victorian style.
Bedrooms: 2 double, 1 twin
Bathrooms: 2 public
Bed & breakfast
per night:	£min	£max
Single	17.00	
Double	29.00	

Parking for 3

Gilberries Cottage ᴀ
COMMENDED

Wall-under-Heywood, Church Stretton SY6 7HZ
☎ Longville (0694) 771400
Country cottage adjoining family farm, in peaceful and beautiful countryside. Ideal for walking. Numerous places of interest nearby.
Bedrooms: 1 twin, 1 triple
Bathrooms: 1 public

Bed & breakfast
per night:	£min	£max
Double	32.00	34.00

Parking for 8
Open February-November

Rheingold

9 The Bridleways, Church Stretton SY6 7AN
☎ (0694) 723969
Comfortable family house set in peaceful location close to village centre. Lovely views across to the Longmynd.
Bedrooms: 1 double, 1 twin
Bathrooms: 1 private, 1 public
Bed & breakfast
per night:	£min	£max
Single	15.00	15.00
Double	30.00	30.00

Half board
per person:	£min	£max
Daily	22.50	22.50
Weekly	150.00	150.00

Parking for 2

Woolston Farm ᴀ

Church Stretton SY6 6QD
☎ Marshbrook (0694) 781201
312-acre mixed farm. Victorian farmhouse in the small hamlet of Woolston, off A49. Ideal position for touring Shropshire. Outstanding views and good farmhouse fare.
Bedrooms: 1 double, 1 triple
Bathrooms: 1 public
Bed & breakfast
per night:	£min	£max
Single	14.50	
Double	29.00	

Half board
per person:	£min	£max
Daily	22.50	
Weekly	154.00	

Evening meal 1850 (last orders 2000)
Parking for 2
Open January-November

There are separate sections in this guide listing groups specialising in farm holidays and accommodation which is especially suitable for young people and organised groups.

CIRENCESTER
Gloucestershire
Map ref 2B1

"Capital of the Cotswolds", Cirencester was Britain's second most important Roman town with many finds housed in the Corinium Museum. It has a very fine Perpendicular church and old houses around the market place.
Tourist Information Centre
☎ *(0285) 654180*

The Coach House ᴀ

Middle Duntisbourne, Cirencester GL7 7AR
☎ (0285) 653058
400-acre arable & livestock farm. Set in the beautiful Duntisbourne Valley. Pretty garden to sit in. Lounge with colour TV. Choice of breakfast.
Bedrooms: 1 double, 1 twin
Bathrooms: 2 private
Bed & breakfast
per night:	£min	£max
Single	15.00	20.00
Double	28.00	30.00

Parking for 8

1 Cove House ᴀ
COMMENDED

Park Place, Ashton Keynes, Cirencester SN6 6NS
☎ (0285) 861226
Part of 17th C manor house with southern aspect, beautiful walled garden. Elegant country house atmosphere, family service.
Bedrooms: 1 double, 1 twin
Bathrooms: 2 private
Bed & breakfast
per night:	£min	£max
Single	20.00	25.00
Double	40.00	48.00

Parking for 12

The Masons Arms ᴀ
High Street, Meysey Hampton, Cirencester GL7 5JT
☎ (0285) 850164

Seeking peace and tranquillity? Treat yourself to a break in this 17th C inn set beside the village green. A warm welcome awaits you.
Bedrooms: 1 single, 5 double, 1 twin, 2 triple
Bathrooms: 9 private

HEART OF ENGLAND

Bed & breakfast per night:	£min	£max
Single	24.50	29.50
Double	39.00	49.00

Lunch available
Evening meal 1900 (last orders 2130)
Parking for 8
Cards accepted: Access, Visa

The Old Rectory

Meysey Hampton, Cirencester GL7 5JX
☎ (0285) 851200

Delightful listed 17th C Cotswold house with 6 acres of grounds and superb views in quiet village cul-de-sac. M4 15 miles, M40 12 miles.
Bedrooms: 1 double, 1 twin
Bathrooms: 2 private

Bed & breakfast per night:	£min	£max
Single	25.00	27.00
Double	38.00	40.00

Parking for 10
Open February-November

Royal Agricultural College

Stroud Road, Cirencester GL7 6JS
☎ (0285) 652531 & 640644
Fax (0285) 640644
Set majestically on a 30-acre private Cotswold estate, bordering the Roman town of Cirencester.
Bedrooms: 50 single, 190 twin
Bathrooms: 48 private, 53 public

Bed & breakfast per night:	£min	£max
Single	23.50	36.00
Double	47.00	72.00

Half board per person:	£min	£max
Daily	32.20	60.00
Weekly	200.00	420.00

Lunch available
Evening meal 1800 (last orders 1900)
Parking for 700
Open January, March-April, July-September, December

Smerrill Barns

COMMENDED
Kemble, Cirencester GL7 6BW
☎ (0285) 770907

Accommodation in a listed barn, providing all modern facilities. Situated 3 miles from Cirencester on the A429.
Bedrooms: 1 single, 4 double, 1 twin, 1 triple
Bathrooms: 7 private, 1 public

Bed & breakfast per night:	£min	£max
Single	20.00	30.00
Double	40.00	60.00

Parking for 7
Cards accepted: Access, Visa

The Village Pub

Listed APPROVED
Barnsley, Cirencester GL7 5EF
☎ (0285) 740421
The Village Pub has 5 rooms, all with private facilities, and is situated in a pretty Cotswold village.
Bedrooms: 4 double, 1 twin
Bathrooms: 5 private

Bed & breakfast per night:	£min	£max
Single	29.00	30.00
Double	44.00	45.00

Lunch available
Evening meal 1900 (last orders 2130)
Parking for 40
Cards accepted: Access, Visa, Amex

Warwick Cottage Guest House

COMMENDED
75 Victoria Road, Cirencester GL7 1ES
☎ (0285) 656279
Attractive Victorian townhouse, 5 minutes from the town centre. Good base for touring the Cotswolds. Family rooms available as doubles or twins. Singles by arrangement.
Bedrooms: 2 double, 2 triple
Bathrooms: 4 private, 1 public

Bed & breakfast per night:	£min	£max
Double	30.00	34.00

Half board per person:	£min	£max
Daily	22.00	24.00
Weekly	135.00	155.00

Evening meal from 1830
Parking for 4

Wimborne House

COMMENDED
91 Victoria Road, Cirencester GL7 1ES
☎ (0285) 653890

Cotswold-stone house, built in 1886, with a warm and friendly atmosphere and spacious rooms. Four-poster room. Non-smokers only please.
Bedrooms: 4 double, 1 twin
Bathrooms: 5 private

Bed & breakfast per night:	£min	£max
Single	20.00	30.00
Double	28.00	45.00

Evening meal 1830 (last orders 1730)
Parking for 6

CLUN

Shropshire
Map ref 4A3

Small, ancient town on the Welsh border with flint and stone tools in its museum and Iron Age forts nearby. The impressive ruins of a Norman castle lie beside the River Clun and there are some interesting 17th C houses.

Hill House Farm

Listed
Church Bank, Clun, Craven Arms SY7 8LP
☎ Craven Arms (0588) 640325 & 640729
70-acre mixed farm. Set in beautiful, peaceful countryside overlooking Clun, with its Norman castle and medieval bridge. Ideal walking country, convenient for Offa's Dyke, Shropshire Way and the Longmynd.
Bedrooms: 1 single, 1 double, 1 triple
Bathrooms: 1 public

Bed & breakfast per night:	£min	£max
Single	13.00	14.00
Double	26.00	28.00

Lunch available
Evening meal 1800 (last orders 1900)
Parking for 4
Open February-November

Hurst Mill Farm

Clunton, Craven Arms SY7 0JA
☎ (0588) 640224
100-acre mixed farm. Attractive farmhouse and old mill in the lovely Clun Valley. River and woodland trails, 2 riding ponies, pets welcome. Winners of "Great Shropshire Breakfast" challenge.
Bedrooms: 1 double, 1 triple, 1 family room

Continued ▶

HEART OF ENGLAND

CLUN
Continued

Bathrooms: 2 public, 1 private shower

Bed & breakfast per night:	£min	£max
Single	14.00	16.00
Double	28.00	32.00

Half board per person:	£min	£max
Daily	22.00	23.00
Weekly	150.00	155.00

Evening meal 1800 (last orders 2000)
Parking for 8

New House Farm
COMMENDED

Clun, Craven Arms SY7 8NJ
☎ Bishops Castle (0588) 638314
325-acre mixed farm. Isolated 18th C stone farmhouse set high in the Clun hills, near Offa's Dyke. Scenic views, peaceful walking in unspoilt countryside.
Bedrooms: 1 double, 1 twin, 1 triple
Bathrooms: 1 private, 2 public

Bed & breakfast per night:	£min	£max
Single	16.00	17.50
Double	32.00	35.00

Half board per person:	£min	£max
Daily	24.50	26.50
Weekly	165.00	185.00

Evening meal 1900 (last orders 2100)
Parking for 5
Open February-November

CLUNGUNFORD
Shropshire
Map ref 4A3

Village near the River Clun and Stokesay Castle, a 13th C fortified manor house with an Elizabethan gatehouse.

Broadward Hall
Listed

Clungunford, Craven Arms SY7 0QA
☎ Bucknell (054 74) 357
176-acre mixed farm. Grade II listed, castellated building. 9 miles west of Ludlow in rural Clun Valley surroundings.
Bedrooms: 2 twin, 1 triple
Bathrooms: 2 public

Bed & breakfast per night:	£min	£max
Single	13.00	14.00
Double	26.00	28.00

Half board per person:	£min	£max
Daily	22.00	23.00
Weekly	154.00	154.00

Evening meal 1900 (last orders 0900)
Parking for 15
Open March-November

CODSALL
Staffordshire
Map ref 4B3

Expanding residential village a few miles from Wolverhampton.

Moors Farm and Country Restaurant

Chillington Lane, Codsall, Wolverhampton WV8 1QF
☎ (0902) 842330
Fax (0902) 842330
100-acre mixed farm. 200-year-old farmhouse, 1 mile from pretty village. All home produce used. Many local walks and places of interest.
Bedrooms: 2 double, 2 twin, 1 triple, 1 family room
Bathrooms: 2 private, 2 public

Bed & breakfast per night:	£min	£max
Single	24.00	29.00
Double	40.00	48.00

Half board per person:	£min	£max
Daily	29.00	38.00

Evening meal 1830 (last orders 1900)
Parking for 20

COLESHILL
Warwickshire
Map ref 4B3

Close to Birmingham's many attractions including the 17th C Aston Hall with its plasterwork and furnishings, the Railway Museum and Sarehole Mill, an 18th C water-powered mill restored to working order.

Maxstoke Hall Farm
COMMENDED

Maxstoke, Coleshill, Birmingham B46 2QT
☎ (0675) 463237
Fax (0675) 463237
230-acre arable farm. Elegant farmhouse, 1634, with en-suite rooms. 10 minutes from M42 and M6, 15 minutes from National Exhibition Centre and Birmingham Airport.
Bedrooms: 1 single, 1 twin
Bathrooms: 2 private

Bed & breakfast per night:	£min	£max
Single	23.00	23.00
Double	40.00	40.00

Half board per person:	£min	£max
Daily	33.00	33.00
Weekly	231.00	231.00

Evening meal 1830 (last orders 2000)
Parking for 30

COLWALL
Hereford and Worcester
Map ref 2B1

Village on the slopes of the Malvern Hills close to the famous Herefordshire Beacon, site of a large Iron Age camp. The area offers excellent walks with the Worcestershire Beacon to the north.

Hacketts
Listed APPROVED

Mathon Road, Colwall, Malvern, Worcestershire WR13 6EW
☎ (0684) 40261
3-acre arable farm. Well-built black and white house, completely remodernised and tastefully decorated. Situated on the roadside, with pleasant garden.
Bedrooms: 1 single, 1 double, 1 twin
Bathrooms: 2 public

Bed & breakfast per night:	£min	£max
Single	16.00	16.00
Double	32.00	32.00

Parking for 6
Open April-October

CORSE
Gloucestershire
Map ref 2B1

Kilmorie Guest House

Gloucester Road, Corse, Snigs End, Staunton, Coleford GL19 3RQ
☎ Gloucester (0452) 840224

7-acre livestock & fruit farm. Built by Chartists in 1848. Grade II listed smallholding in conservation area. Modernised, comfortable and friendly. Ideally situated for touring Cotswolds, Forest of Dean and Malvern Hills. Pony riding.
Bedrooms: 1 single, 3 double, 1 twin, 1 family room
Bathrooms: 2 private, 1 public

HEART OF ENGLAND

Bed & breakfast
per night:	£min	£max
Single	11.00	
Double	22.00	

Half board
per person:	£min	£max
Daily	17.50	
Weekly	122.50	

Lunch available
Evening meal from 1800
Parking for 8

COTSWOLDS

See under Ampney Crucis, Bibury, Bledington, Blockley, Bourton-on-the-Water, Bretforton, Broadway, Cheltenham, Chipping Campden, Cirencester, Cowley, Donnington, Fairford, Gloucester, Great Rissington, Guiting Power, Lechlade, Long Compton, Mickleton, Minchinhampton, Moreton-in-Marsh, Nailsworth, Naunton, Northleach, Nympsfield, Painswick, Rendcomb, Slimbridge, Stonehouse, Stow-on-the-Wold, Stroud, Teddington, Tetbury, Tewkesbury, Winchcombe

COVENTRY
West Midlands
Map ref 4B3

Modern city with a long history. It has many places of interest including the post-war and ruined medieval cathedrals, art gallery and museums, some 16th C almshouses, St Mary's Guildhall, Lunt Roman fort and the Belgrade Theatre.
Tourist Information Centre
☎ *(0203) 832303*

Acorn Lodge Private Guest House ⋔

Pond Farm, Upper Eastern Green Lane, Coventry CV5 7DP
☎ (0203) 465182
300-year-old beamed farmhouse of character in secluded position. Ideally situated for touring Stratford and Warwick and 20 miles from National Exhibition Centre and Birmingham Airport. Friendly, informal atmosphere. Paddocks and ponies.
Bedrooms: 2 single, 1 double, 1 twin
Bathrooms: 1 private, 2 public

Bed & breakfast
per night:	£min	£max
Single		15.00
Double	30.00	35.00

Parking for 6

Falcon Hotel ⋔
13-19 Manor Road, Coventry CV1 2LH
☎ (0203) 258615
Fax (0203) 520680
Situated close to Coventry railway station, ideal for the National Exhibition Centre and the travelling businessman. Shops, social and cultural activities readily at hand.
Bedrooms: 10 single, 11 double, 6 twin, 7 triple
Bathrooms: 34 private, 4 public

Bed & breakfast
per night:	£min	£max
Single	25.00	39.00
Double	39.00	55.00

Half board
per person:	£min	£max
Daily	32.00	45.00

Lunch available
Evening meal 1900 (last orders 2145)
Parking for 50
Cards accepted: Access, Visa, Diners, Amex

Mill Farmhouse ⋔

Mill Lane, Fillongley, Coventry CV7 8EE
☎ Fillongley (0676) 41898
Beautiful farmhouse set in rolling countryside, offering peace and tranquillity. Detached bed and breakfast apartments with en-suite bathrooms. Private car park and gardens. 15 minutes from Coventry, NEC, Birmingham Airport.
Bedrooms: 1 double, 1 twin
Bathrooms: 2 private

Bed & breakfast
per night:	£min	£max
Single	18.00	35.00
Double	40.00	45.00

Half board
per person:	£min	£max
Daily	28.00	45.00
Weekly	196.00	315.00

Lunch available
Evening meal 1800 (last orders 2000)
Parking for 8

Northanger House ⋔

35 Westminster Road, Coventry CV1 3GB
☎ (0203) 226780
Friendly home 5 minutes from the city centre. Close to railway and bus stations. Convenient for all amenities.
Bedrooms: 2 single, 2 double, 3 twin, 2 triple
Bathrooms: 3 public

Bed & breakfast
per night:	£min	£max
Single	17.00	17.00
Double	30.00	30.00

Parking for 1

Westwood Cottage

79 Westwood Heath Road, Westwood Heath, Coventry CV4 8GN
☎ (0203) 471084
One of 4 sandstone farm cottages, circa 1834, in rural surroundings. Recently converted but with character maintained and offering comfortable accommodation for a small number of guests.
Bedrooms: 2 single, 1 double, 1 twin
Bathrooms: 4 private, 4 public

Bed & breakfast
per night:	£min	£max
Single	18.00	18.00
Double	33.00	35.00

Parking for 5

Woodlands ⋔

Oak Lane, Allesley, Coventry CV5 9BX
☎ Meriden (0676) 22688
Comfortable, detached and privately situated in a beautiful country lane only 150 yards from the A45. Ten minutes from NEC and Birmingham Airport, ideal for Coventry, Stratford-upon-Avon and Warwick.
Bedrooms: 3 twin
Bathrooms: 1 public

Bed & breakfast
per night:	£min	£max
Single	16.00	18.00
Double	32.00	34.00

Parking for 6

COWLEY
Gloucestershire
Map ref 2B1

Butlers Hill Farm
APPROVED

Cockleford, Cowley, Cheltenham GL53 9NW
☎ Cheltenham (0242) 870455
130-acre livestock farm. A spacious, modern farmhouse in a quiet unspoilt river valley with attractive walks.
Bedrooms: 1 double, 1 twin
Bathrooms: 2 public

Bed & breakfast
per night:	£min	£max
Double	30.00	30.00

Continued ▶

153

HEART OF ENGLAND

COWLEY
Continued

Half board
per person:	£min	£max
Daily	22.00	22.00

Evening meal from 1900
Parking for 6
Open April-September

DEERHURST
Gloucestershire
Map ref 2B1

Deerhurst House
Deerhurst, Gloucester GL19 4BX
☎ Tewkesbury (0684) 292255
Classical Georgian country house set in 3 acres on edge of ancient riverside village of Deerhurst midway between Cheltenham, Tewkesbury and Gloucester.
Bedrooms: 1 twin, 1 family room
Bathrooms: 2 private

Bed & breakfast
per night:	£min	£max
Single	20.00	20.00
Double	39.00	40.00

Parking for 10

DIDDLEBURY
Shropshire
Map ref 4A3

Village close to the beautiful countryside of Wenlock Edge and the Longmynd.

Glebe Farm
HIGHLY COMMENDED
Diddlebury, Craven Arms SY7 9DH
☎ Munslow (058 476) 221
123-acre livestock farm. Listed 16th C farmhouse, an idyllic retreat, set in an old-fashioned garden by a stream amid the rolling hills of south Shropshire. Country-style cooking, joint runner up Best Breakfast 1991.
Bedrooms: 1 single, 3 double, 2 twin
Bathrooms: 4 private, 1 public

Bed & breakfast
per night:	£min	£max
Single	20.00	24.00
Double	37.00	48.00

Parking for 12
Open March-November

Please mention this guide when making a booking.

DONNINGTON
Gloucestershire
Map ref 2B1

Holmleigh
Listed
Donnington, Moreton-in-Marsh GL56 0XX
☎ Cotswold (0451) 830792
15-acre dairy farm. Farmhouse accommodation with friendly welcome. In a peaceful setting with own private lane from the village of Donnington, 1 mile from Stow-on-the-Wold.
Bedrooms: 2 twin
Bathrooms: 1 private, 1 public

Bed & breakfast
per night:	£min	£max
Single	12.00	12.00
Double	24.00	24.00

Parking for 3
Open April-October

DROITWICH
Hereford and Worcester
Map ref 2B1

Old town with natural brine springs, developed as a spa town at the beginning of the 19th C. It has some interesting churches, in particular the Church of the Sacred Heart with splendid mosaics. There are several fine parks and a Heritage Centre.
Tourist Information Centre
☎ (0905) 774312

Caulin Court
Listed
Ladywood, Droitwich, Worcestershire WR9 0AL
☎ (0905) 756382
20-acre horses farm. Lovely old country house set in 20 acres, 2 miles from Droitwich, 3 miles from Worcester. Easy access to motorways.
Bedrooms: 1 double
Bathrooms: 1 private

Bed & breakfast
per night:	£min	£max
Single	14.00	17.50
Double	32.00	35.00

Parking for 6

Church Farm
HIGHLY COMMENDED
Elmbridge, Droitwich, Worcestershire WR9 0DA
☎ Cutnall Green (0299) 851627
Beautiful listed Georgian farmhouse with panoramic views of Malvern Hills. Situated in peaceful village of Elmbridge yet only 2 miles from M5.
Bedrooms: 2 twin
Bathrooms: 2 private

Bed & breakfast
per night:	£min	£max
Single	25.00	25.00
Double	40.00	40.00

Parking for 7

Droitwich Bed and Breakfast
Listed
Merrivale, 216 Worcester Road, Droitwich, Worcestershire WR9 8AY
☎ Worcester (0905) 778213

Friendly domestic residence on main road on south side of Droitwich, 3 miles from M5 junction 5 or 6. Four-poster beds, TV, tea and coffee facilities.
Bedrooms: 2 double, 1 twin
Bathrooms: 1 private, 1 public

Bed & breakfast
per night:	£min	£max
Single	18.00	20.00
Double	30.00	35.00

Parking for 3

Richmond Guest House
Listed
3 Ombersley St. West, Droitwich, Worcestershire WR9 8HZ
☎ Worcester (0905) 775722
Victorian-built guesthouse in the town centre, 5 minutes from railway station and bus route. English breakfast. 30 minutes from National Exhibition Centre via M5/M42.
Bedrooms: 6 single, 2 double, 4 twin, 3 triple
Bathrooms: 3 public

Bed & breakfast
per night:	£min	£max
Single	15.00	16.00
Double	26.00	27.00

Parking for 12

Wessex House Farm
Trench Lane, Oddingley, Droitwich, Worcestershire WR9 7NB
☎ (0905) 772826
50-acre mixed farm. Modern farmhouse in pleasant surroundings 4 miles from the M5 motorway, 3 miles from Droitwich and within easy reach of Cotswolds. Farmhouse food. Also food available locally.
Bedrooms: 1 double, 1 triple
Bathrooms: 1 public

HEART OF ENGLAND

Bed & breakfast per night:	£min	£max
Single	13.00	15.00
Double	26.00	28.00

Parking for 3
Open March-November

ECCLESHALL

Staffordshire
Map ref 4B3

Small market town has long associations with the Bishops of Lichfield, 6 of whom are buried in the large 12th C parish church. The ruined castle was formerly the residence of these bishops.

Cobblers Cottage
Kerry Lane, Eccleshall, Stafford ST21 6EJ
☎ Stafford (0785) 850116
Country cottage with en-suite bedrooms, in a quiet lane on the edge of village, with several pubs and restaurants in walking distance.
Bedrooms: 1 double, 1 twin
Bathrooms: 2 private

Bed & breakfast per night:	£min	£max
Single	16.00	19.00
Double	28.00	34.00

Parking for 3

Glenwood
COMMENDED
Croxton, Eccleshall, Stafford ST21 6PF
☎ Wetwood (063 082) 238
16th C timber-framed cottage in an ideal position for visiting the many attractions of Staffordshire and Shropshire.
Bedrooms: 1 double, 2 twin, 1 triple
Bathrooms: 1 private, 1 public

Bed & breakfast per night:	£min	£max
Single	15.00	19.00
Double	28.00	36.00

Parking for 6
Cards accepted: Access, Visa

The Round House
COMMENDED
Butters Bank, Croxton, Eccleshall, Stafford ST21 6NN
☎ Wetwood (063 082) 631
A warm welcome awaits in this lovely country house, standing in 1.5 acres overlooking the surrounding countryside. Four miles from Eccleshall on the B5026, 15 minutes from M6 junction 14.
Bedrooms: 3 double
Bathrooms: 1 private, 2 private showers

Bed & breakfast per night:	£min	£max
Single		18.00
Double		30.00

Evening meal 1730 (last orders 2100)
Parking for 4

[Ad] Display advertisement appears on this page

ECKINGTON

Hereford and Worcester
Map ref 2B1

Large and expanding village in a fruit growing and market gardening area beside the Avon, which is crossed here by a 15th C bridge. Half-timbered houses are much in evidence.

The Anchor Inn & Restaurant
COMMENDED
Cotheridge Lane, Eckington, Pershore, Worcestershire WR10 3BA
☎ Evesham (0386) 750356
Fax (0386) 750356
Traditional village inn off the main road, comfortable lounge, separate restaurant. Chef prepared cuisine. Central for Worcester, Evesham, Cheltenham and Tewkesbury.
Bedrooms: 2 double, 3 twin
Bathrooms: 5 private

Bed & breakfast per night:	£min	£max
Single	25.00	25.00
Double	35.00	35.00

Half board per person:	£min	£max
Daily	32.50	40.00
Weekly	140.00	280.00

Lunch available
Evening meal 1900 (last orders 2130)
Parking for 30
Cards accepted: Access, Visa

ELLESMERE

Shropshire
Map ref 4A2

Small market town with old streets and houses and situated close to 9 lakes. The largest, the Mere, has many recreational facilities and some of the other meres have sailing and fishing.

Elson House Farm
COMMENDED
Elson, Ellesmere SY12 9EZ
☎ Dudleston Heath (069 175) 276
117-acre dairy farm. Spacious farmhouse set amongst Shropshire meres. Centrally heated. Guests' own lounge with television. Dining room, bathroom/shower. Tea/coffee provided on arrival.
Bedrooms: 1 single, 2 double, 1 twin
Bathrooms: 1 private, 1 public

Bed & breakfast per night:	£min	£max
Single	15.00	15.00
Double	30.00	32.00

Parking for 6

Half board prices shown are per person but in some cases may be based on double/twin occupancy.

The Round House

Butters Bank, Croxton, Eccleshall, Staffordshire, ST21 6NN

A warm friendly welcome awaits you at this picturesque country home.
Luxurious Accomodation all rooms en-suite tea/coffee and TV included.
Convenient for many local attractions.
From £20 Single person
£30 Double.
RAC acclaimed
Commended * plus
Please contact Caroline Hoggarth on 063 082 631

155

HEART OF ENGLAND

ELMLEY CASTLE
Hereford and Worcester
Map ref 2B1

The Cloisters
HIGHLY COMMENDED

Main Street, Elmley Castle, Pershore, Worcestershire WR10 3HS
☎ Pershore (0386) 710241
A stone and half-timbered Tudor house, part of which dates back to the 14th C. Located towards the end of the main street, on the left-hand corner of Ashton-under-Hill Lane. Elmley Castle, at the foot of Bredon Hill, is one of the most attractive villages in the Vale of Evesham.
Bedrooms: 1 double, 1 family room
Bathrooms: 2 private

Bed & breakfast

per night:	£min	£max
Single	18.50	19.50
Double	37.00	39.00

Parking for 3

ENGLISH BICKNOR
Gloucestershire
Map ref 2A1

Village with views of the River Wye and the Forest of Dean. The 13th-15th C sandstone church is built on the foundations of a Norman castle and boasts the original Norman nave.

Lower Tump Farm

Eastbach, English Bicknor, Coleford GL16 7EU
☎ Dean (0594) 860253
150-acre mixed farm. Attractive 16th C farmhouse. Spectacular views. Take turning signposted English Bicknor from A4136 Monmouth to Gloucester road, or take turning signposted Eastbach from B4234 Ross to Coleford road.
Bedrooms: 1 double, 1 triple
Bathrooms: 2 private

Bed & breakfast

per night:	£min	£max
Single		16.00
Double		25.00

Parking for 6

Individual proprietors have supplied all details of accommodation. Although we do check for accuracy, we advise you to confirm the information at the time of booking.

EVESHAM
Hereford and Worcester
Map ref 2B1

Evesham is a market town in the centre of a fruit-growing area. There are pleasant walks along the River Avon and many old houses and inns. A fine 16th C bell tower stands between 2 churches near the medieval Almonry Museum.
Tourist Information Centre
☎ *(0386) 446944*

Far Horizon
COMMENDED

Long Hyde Road, South Littleton, Evesham, Worcestershire WR11 5TH
☎ (0386) 831691
Elegant family home of character, with fine views over surrounding Cotswolds and Malvern Hills. Rural location 3 miles from Evesham.
Bedrooms: 1 single, 1 double, 1 twin
Bathrooms: 3 private

Bed & breakfast

per night:	£min	£max
Single	16.00	17.50
Double	32.00	35.00

Parking for 3
Open March-November

Hill Barn Orchard
Listed

Church Lench, Evesham, Worcestershire WR11 4UB
☎ (0386) 871035

50-acre arable farm. North of Evesham overlooking Church Lench and lakes in orchard setting. Close to Cotswolds and Stratford-upon-Avon. Fishing, good pub food locally.
Bedrooms: 1 double, 2 twin
Bathrooms: 1 private, 1 public

Bed & breakfast

per night:	£min	£max
Single	20.00	30.00
Double	30.00	40.00

Half board

per person:	£min	£max
Weekly	210.00	280.00

Parking for 12

Park View Hotel

Waterside, Evesham, Worcestershire WR11 6BS
☎ (0386) 442639

Family-run hotel offering comfortable accommodation in a friendly atmosphere. Riverside situation, close to town centre. Ideal base for touring the Cotswolds and Shakespeare country.
Bedrooms: 10 single, 4 double, 10 twin, 1 triple, 1 family room
Bathrooms: 7 public

Bed & breakfast

per night:	£min	£max
Single	19.50	22.00
Double	33.00	38.00

Half board

per person:	£min	£max
Daily	29.00	32.00

Lunch available
Evening meal 1800 (last orders 1900)
Parking for 50
Cards accepted: Access, Visa, Diners, Amex

EWEN
Gloucestershire
Map ref 2B1

Village in the South Cotswolds of attractive stone cottages and houses.

Wild Duck Inn
APPROVED

Drakes Island, Ewen, Cirencester GL7 6BY
☎ Cirencester (0285) 770310 & 770364
Fax (0285) 770310
15th C Cotswold stone inn, set in a rural position in the village. Two four-poster rooms in the oldest part of the building. All rooms with private facilities. Delightful garden.
Bedrooms: 5 double, 4 twin
Bathrooms: 9 private

Bed & breakfast

per night:	£min	£max
Single	48.00	48.00
Double	65.00	75.00

Half board

per person:	£min	£max
Weekly	280.00	385.00

Lunch available
Evening meal 1900 (last orders 2145)
Parking for 50
Cards accepted: Access, Visa

National Crown ratings were correct at the time of going to press but are subject to change. Please check at the time of booking.

HEART OF ENGLAND

FAIRFORD
Gloucestershire
Map ref 2B1

Small town with a 15th C wool church famous for its complete 15th C stained glass windows, interesting carvings and original wall paintings. It is an excellent touring centre and the Cotswolds Wildlife Park is nearby.

Waiten Hill Farm ⚜
Fairford GL7 4JG
☎ Cirencester (0285) 712652
350-acre mixed farm. Imposing 19th C farmhouse, overlooking River Coln, old mill and famous church. Short walk to shops and restaurants. Ideal for touring the Cotswolds and water parks.
Bedrooms: 1 double, 2 twin
Bathrooms: 1 private, 1 public, 1 private shower

Bed & breakfast
per night:	£min	£max
Single	15.00	20.00
Double	30.00	40.00

Parking for 6

FECKENHAM
Hereford and Worcester
Map ref 2B1

Large and lovely village containing a number of elegant Georgian houses and an interesting church with a Norman arcade and a chancel rebuilt by William Butterfield in 1853.

The Steps
COMMENDED
6 High Street, Feckenham, Redditch, Worcestershire B96 6HS
☎ Astwood Bank (052 789) 2678

Ducks paddle and cats doze while you relax by log fires amid antiques in an elegant Georgian home, situated near the site of King John's hunting lodge.
Bedrooms: 1 single, 1 double, 1 twin
Bathrooms: 1 private, 1 public

Bed & breakfast
per night:	£min	£max
Single	17.00	21.00
Double	28.00	32.00

Half board
per person:	£min	£max
Daily	24.00	28.00
Weekly	150.00	180.00

Evening meal 1930 (last orders 1700)
Parking for 3

FOREST OF DEAN
See under Corse, English Bicknor, Newent, Newland, Parkend

GLOUCESTER
Gloucestershire
Map ref 2B1

A Roman city and inland port, its cathedral is one of the most beautiful in Britain. Gloucester's many attractions include museums and the restored warehouses in the Victorian docks containing the National Waterways Museum, Robert Opie Collection and other attractions.
Tourist Information Centre
☎ (0452) 421188

Hill Farm ⚜
Wainlodes Lane, Bishops Norton, Gloucester GL2 9LN
☎ (0452) 730351
14th C thatched farmhouse in rural setting, close to River Severn, offering facilities for "get away from it all" breaks.
Bedrooms: 3 double, 1 twin
Bathrooms: 2 private, 1 public

Bed & breakfast
per night:	£min	£max
Single	15.00	21.50
Double	30.00	43.00

Half board
per person:	£min	£max
Daily	25.00	31.50
Weekly	175.00	220.50

Evening meal 1845 (last orders 2030)
Parking for 12

Longford Lodge ⚜
68 Tewkesbury Road, Longford, Gloucester GL2 9EH
☎ (0452) 526430
Friendly, family-run guesthouse on A38, 1.25 miles from Gloucester. Close to junction 11 of M5 and the Cotswolds.
Bedrooms: 2 single, 3 twin, 2 triple
Bathrooms: 1 private, 2 public

Bed & breakfast
per night:	£min	£max
Single	16.00	
Double	30.00	

Parking for 8

Merrivale ⚜
COMMENDED
Tewkesbury Road, Norton, Gloucester GL2 9LQ
☎ (0452) 730412
Large private house with a pleasant garden, 3 miles from Gloucester. TV and tea/coffee-making facilities in all bedrooms.
Bedrooms: 2 double, 3 twin, 1 triple
Bathrooms: 1 public, 2 private showers

Bed & breakfast
per night:	£min	£max
Single	14.50	17.00
Double	29.00	34.00

Parking for 8

Notley House and Coach House ⚜
COMMENDED
93 Hucclecote Road, Hucclecote, Gloucester GL3 3TR
☎ (0452) 611584
Affordable quality accommodation. Ideal for historic Gloucester and the Cotswolds. Tastefully furnished en-suite rooms, suite with four-poster bed.
Bedrooms: 1 single, 2 double, 2 twin, 2 triple
Bathrooms: 5 private, 2 private showers

Bed & breakfast
per night:	£min	£max
Single	23.00	25.00
Double	41.00	45.00

Half board
per person:	£min	£max
Daily	33.00	35.00
Weekly	208.00	220.00

Lunch available
Evening meal 1800 (last orders 2030)
Parking for 8
Cards accepted: Access, Visa

GREAT RISSINGTON
Gloucestershire
Map ref 2B1

The Malthouse
Great Rissington, Cheltenham GL54 2LH
☎ Cotswolds (0451) 820582
Cotswold-stone malthouse built in 1648, in sought after, quiet Cotswold village. Accommodation is a private suite with gallery bedroom. Non-smokers please.
Bedrooms: 1 double
Bathrooms: 1 private

Continued ▶

HEART OF ENGLAND

GREAT RISSINGTON
Continued

Bed & breakfast
per night:	£min	£max
Double	40.00	

Parking for 2

GUITING POWER
Gloucestershire
Map ref 2B1

Unspoilt village with stone cottages and a green. The Cotswold Farm Park, with a collection of rare breeds, an adventure playground and farm trail, is nearby.

Guiting Guesthouse ⋒
HIGHLY COMMENDED

Post Office Lane, Guiting Power, Cheltenham GL54 5TZ
☎ (0451) 850470

Cotswold-stone farmhouse with inglenooks and four-posters. In centre of delightful village, convenient for Stratford-upon-Avon, Cheltenham, Oxford, Stow, etc.
Bedrooms: 3 double
Bathrooms: 3 private

Bed & breakfast
per night:	£min	£max
Single	20.00	24.00
Double	40.00	43.00

Half board
per person:	£min	£max
Daily	34.00	38.00
Weekly	230.00	260.00

Evening meal 1845 (last orders 1845)
Parking for 6

HAMPTON IN ARDEN
West Midlands
Map ref 4B3

The Hollies ⋒
Listed

Kenilworth Road, Hampton in Arden, Solihull B92 0LW
☎ (0675) 442941 & 442681
On the A452, ideally located for many major attractions of the Midlands, including the National Agricultural Centre, Warwick Castle and Stratford-upon-Avon. Only 5 minutes to National Motorcycle Museum and the National Exhibition Centre.
Bedrooms: 1 single, 3 double, 4 twin
Bathrooms: 5 private, 1 public

Bed & breakfast
per night:	£min	£max
Single	17.00	20.00
Double	34.00	40.00

Parking for 10

HARMER HILL
Shropshire
Map ref 4A3

Yorton House ⋒

Godings Lane, Harmer Hill, Shrewsbury SY4 3HB
☎ Bomere Heath (0939) 290510
Very comfortable sandstone and brick house with exceptional views in open countryside. Only 6 miles due north of centre of Shrewsbury, 300 yards from B5476.
Bedrooms: 2 double, 1 twin
Bathrooms: 3 private

Bed & breakfast
per night:	£min	£max
Single	24.00	24.00
Double	40.00	40.00

Parking for 6

HENLEY-IN-ARDEN
Warwickshire
Map ref 2B1

Old market town which in Tudor times stood in the Forest of Arden. It has many ancient inns, a 15th C Guildhall and parish church. Coughton Court with its Gunpowder Plot connections is nearby.

Irelands Farm ⋒
HIGHLY COMMENDED

Irelands Lane, Henley-in-Arden, Solihull, West Midlands B95 5SA
☎ (0564) 792476
220-acre arable & livestock farm. Secluded farmhouse in peaceful countryside. Close to Stratford, Warwick, National Exhibition Centre and the Cotswolds. 1 mile off A3400 between Henley and M42.
Bedrooms: 2 double, 1 twin
Bathrooms: 3 private

Bed & breakfast
per night:	£min	£max
Single	17.00	20.00
Double	35.00	40.00

Parking for 6

HEREFORD
Hereford and Worcester
Map ref 2A1

Agricultural county town, its cathedral containing much Norman work and a large chained library. The city's varied attractions include the Bulmer Railway Centre and several museums including the Cider Museum and the Old House.
Tourist Information Centre
☎ (0432) 268430

The Ancient Camp Inn ⋒
COMMENDED

Ruckhall, Eaton Bishop, Hereford HR2 9QX
☎ Golden Valley (0981) 250449
This inn is on the site of an Iron Age fort dating from the 4th-5th C BC. Spectacular views of the River Wye. Restaurant and bar food a speciality.
Bedrooms: 4 double, 1 twin
Bathrooms: 5 private

Bed & breakfast
per night:	£min	£max
Single	35.00	45.00
Double	48.00	58.00

Lunch available
Evening meal 1900 (last orders 2130)
Parking for 45
Cards accepted: Access, Visa

Cwm Craig Farm
COMMENDED

Little Dewchurch, Hereford HR2 6PS
☎ Carey (0432) 840250
190-acre arable & livestock farm. Spacious Georgian farmhouse on edge of Wye Valley, surrounded by superb, unspoilt countryside. 5 miles south of Hereford. Easy access from M50.
Bedrooms: 1 double, 1 twin, 1 triple
Bathrooms: 2 public

Bed & breakfast
per night:	£min	£max
Single	14.00	16.00
Double	28.00	30.00

Parking for 6

Felton House
HIGHLY COMMENDED

Felton, Hereford HR1 3PH
☎ (0432) 820366
Tranquil stone-built rectory with four-poster and brass beds . 3-acre gardens with small church in tiny hamlet 8 miles from Hereford, Leominster and Bromyard in the heart of unspoilt countryside.
Bedrooms: 1 single, 2 double, 1 twin
Bathrooms: 2 public

158

HEART OF ENGLAND

Bed & breakfast per night:	£min	£max
Single		14.50
Double	26.00	32.00

Parking for 6
Open January-November

Grafton Villa Farm House
HIGHLY COMMENDED

Grafton, Hereford HR2 8ED
☎ (0432) 268689
180-acre mixed farm. Family farmhouse of great character and warmth. Set back from the main Hereford to Ross-on-Wye road, surrounded by peaceful countryside. Ideal for touring the Wye Valley.
Bedrooms: 1 double, 1 twin, 1 triple
Bathrooms: 3 private

Bed & breakfast per night:	£min	£max
Single	18.00	20.00
Double	30.00	36.00

Half board per person:	£min	£max
Daily	30.00	32.00

Evening meal 1900 (last orders 1600)
Parking for 10

Lakes Farm
Listed

Wyatt Road, Sutton St Nicholas, Hereford HR1 3NS
☎ (0432) 880278
40-acre mixed farm. Small farm in quiet location, north east of Hereford. Fishing, golfing, horse riding and walking available.
Bedrooms: 1 single, 1 double, 1 twin
Bathrooms: 1 public

Bed & breakfast per night:	£min	£max
Single	15.50	15.50
Double	30.00	30.00

Half board per person:	£min	£max
Daily	23.50	23.50
Weekly	159.00	159.00

Parking for 4
Open January-October

Lower Bartestree Farm

Bartestree, Hereford HR1 4DT
☎ (0432) 851005
Comfortable accommodation in a peaceful setting with splendid views. Home-made bread, preserves and crafts available. Off A438, 4 miles from city centre.
Bedrooms: 1 twin, 1 triple
Bathrooms: 1 public

Bed & breakfast per night:	£min	£max
Single		16.00
Double		28.00

Parking for 5

ILMINGTON
Warwickshire
Map ref 2B1

Howard Arms
APPROVED

Lower Green, Ilmington, Shipston-on-Stour CV36 4LN
☎ Shipston-on-Stour (0608) 682226
Fax (0608) 682226
Delightful 17th and 18th C Cotswold inn, 8 miles south of Stratford-upon-Avon. Large bedrooms, imaginative food served in half-timbered bar or restaurant.
Bedrooms: 1 double, 1 triple
Bathrooms: 2 private

Bed & breakfast per night:	£min	£max
Single	30.00	30.00
Double	50.00	50.00

Half board per person:	£min	£max
Daily	37.75	49.00
Weekly	226.50	299.00

Lunch available
Evening meal 1900 (last orders 2130)
Parking for 18
Cards accepted: Access, Visa, Amex

IRONBRIDGE
Shropshire
Map ref 4A3

Small town on the Severn where the Industrial Revolution began. It has the world's first iron bridge built in 1774. The Ironbridge Gorge Museum contains several industrial sites and museums spread over 2 miles and is exceptionally interesting.
Tourist Information Centre
☎ *(0952) 432166*

Paradise House
APPROVED

Coalbrookdale, Telford TF8 7NR
☎ Telford (095 243) 3379
Georgian family home with large airy rooms, overlooking the valley. Central for museums and adjacent to the Shropshire Way footpath.
Bedrooms: 1 double, 1 family room
Bathrooms: 1 private, 1 public

Bed & breakfast per night:	£min	£max
Single	18.00	24.00
Double	34.00	38.00

Parking for 2
Open February-November

46 Wigmore
Listed

Woodside, Telford TF7 5NB
☎ Telford (0952) 583748
Privately-owned house with garden and garage at rear. TV in all rooms.
Bedrooms: 1 single, 1 twin
Bathrooms: 1 public

Bed & breakfast per night:	£min	£max
Single	10.00	12.00
Double	20.00	24.00

Half board per person:	£min	£max
Daily	13.00	15.00
Weekly	80.00	120.00

Evening meal from 1700
Parking for 2

KENILWORTH
Warwickshire
Map ref 4B3

The main feature of the town is the ruined 12th C castle. It has many royal associations but was damaged by Cromwell. A good base for visiting Coventry, Leamington Spa and Warwick.
Tourist Information Centre
☎ *(0926) 52595*

Banner Hill Farmhouse

Rouncil Lane, Kenilworth CV8 1NN
☎ (0926) 52850
250-acre mixed farm. Farmhouse set in Warwickshire countryside with local walks - bicycles available. Also a 30-foot residential van with 2 bedrooms, bathroom and kitchen.
Bedrooms: 3 twin
Bathrooms: 1 private, 1 public

Bed & breakfast per night:	£min	£max
Single	12.50	20.00
Double	32.00	35.00

Half board per person:	£min	£max
Daily	20.00	27.00
Weekly	75.00	120.00

Lunch available
Parking for 8

We advise you to confirm your booking in writing.

Please mention this guide when making a booking.

HEART OF ENGLAND

KIDDERMINSTER
Hereford and Worcester
Map ref 4B3

The town is the centre for carpet manufacturing. It has a medieval church with good monuments and a statue of Sir Rowland Hill, a native of the town and founder of the penny post. West Midlands Safari Park is nearby. Severn Valley railway station.

Cedars Hotel
APPROVED
Mason Road, Kidderminster, Worcestershire DY11 6AL
☎ (0562) 515595
Fax (0562) 751103

Charming conversion of a Georgian building close to the River Severn, Severn Valley Railway and Worcestershire countryside. 15 minutes from the M5.
Bedrooms: 1 single, 7 double, 7 twin, 1 triple, 4 family rooms
Bathrooms: 20 private
Bed & breakfast
per night:	£min	£max
Single	27.00	47.00
Double	36.00	57.00

Half board
per person:	£min	£max
Daily	39.00	60.00

Evening meal 1900 (last orders 2030)
Parking for 21
Cards accepted: Access, Visa, Diners, Amex

Clay Farm
HIGHLY COMMENDED
Clows Top, Kidderminster, Worcestershire DY14 9NN
☎ Clows Top (0299) 832421
98-acre mixed farm. Modern farmhouse with outstanding views. Bedrooms en-suite with tea-making facilities. TV, lounge, central heating. Fly and coarse fishing pools. Brochures on request. On the B4202 Clows Top to Cleobury Mortimer road.
Bedrooms: 2 double, 1 twin
Bathrooms: 2 private, 1 public
Bed & breakfast
per night:	£min	£max
Single	15.00	18.00
Double	30.00	30.00

Parking for 10

KINETON
Warwickshire
Map ref 2C1

Attractive old village in rolling countryside. 1 mile from site of famous battle of Edgehill. Medieval church of St Peter.

Willowbrook House
Lighthorne Road, Kineton, Warwick CV35 0JL
☎ (0926) 640475
Fax (0926) 641747
4-acre smallholding. Very comfortable house surrounded by lovely countryside, 3 miles to M40 (junction 12) and B4100, half a mile from Kineton village. Handy for Stratford-upon-Avon, Warwick and Cotswolds. Tea trays, antiques and friendly service.
Bedrooms: 2 double, 1 twin
Bathrooms: 1 private, 2 public
Bed & breakfast
per night:	£min	£max
Double	30.00	37.00

Parking for 6

KINGSTONE
Hereford and Worcester
Map ref 2A1

Village near the Golden Valley, Abbey Dore Church and Kilpeck church.

Webton Court Farmhouse
Kingstone, Hereford HR2 9NF
☎ Golden Valley (0981) 250220
280-acre mixed farm. Large black and white Georgian farmhouse in a quiet and peaceful part of Herefordshire. Lunch provided upon request.
Bedrooms: 1 single, 2 double, 2 twin, 1 triple, 2 family rooms
Bathrooms: 2 private, 3 public
Bed & breakfast
per night:	£min	£max
Single	15.00	15.00
Double	24.00	28.00

Half board
per person:	£min	£max
Daily	21.50	21.50
Weekly	136.50	136.50

Lunch available
Evening meal 1900 (last orders 2000)
Parking for 10

The enquiry coupons at the back will help you when contacting proprietors.

LEAMINGTON SPA
Warwickshire
Map ref 4B3

18th C spa town with many fine Georgian and Regency houses. Tea can be taken in the 19th C Pump Room. The attractive Jephson Gardens are laid out alongside the river and there is a museum and art gallery.
Tourist Information Centre
☎ *(0926) 311470*

Agape
Listed
26 St. Mary's Road, Leamington Spa CV31 1JW
☎ (0926) 882896
A private house to refresh the visitor to Regency Royal Leamington Spa. Close to historic Warwick and Stratford-upon-Avon.
Bedrooms: 1 single, 1 double, 1 twin
Bathrooms: 1 public, 1 private shower
Bed & breakfast
per night:	£min	£max
Single	17.50	
Double	35.00	

Parking for 2

Glendower Guesthouse
APPROVED
8 Warwick Place, Leamington Spa CV32 5BJ
☎ (0926) 422784
Charming Victorian building with many original features in a central but quiet location, offering comfortable accommodation with evening meals. Ideal for National Agricultural Centre, M40, NEC, Warwick Castle and for touring the Cotswolds.
Bedrooms: 3 single, 2 double, 2 twin, 2 triple
Bathrooms: 2 private, 2 public
Bed & breakfast
per night:	£min	£max
Single	16.00	
Double	32.00	

Half board
per person:	£min	£max
Daily	24.00	

Evening meal 1900 (last orders 2100)
Parking for 4

Hill Farm
APPROVED
Lewis Road, Radford Semele, Leamington Spa CV31 1UX
☎ (0926) 337571
350-acre mixed farm. Farmhouse set in large attractive garden, 2 miles from Leamington town centre and close to Warwick Castle and Stratford-upon-Avon.
Bedrooms: 3 double, 2 twin
Bathrooms: 3 private, 1 public

160

HEART OF ENGLAND

Bed & breakfast per night:	£min	£max
Single	15.00	18.00
Double	26.00	32.00
Parking for 4		

Northton
COMMENDED
77 Telford Avenue, Lillington, Leamington Spa CV32 7HQ
☎ (0926) 425609
Detached family home with large garden in quiet residential area off A445, 2.5 miles from National Agricultural Centre. No smoking and no pets please.
Bedrooms: 1 single, 1 twin
Bathrooms: 2 private

Bed & breakfast per night:	£min	£max
Single	15.00	
Double	30.00	
Parking for 4		
Open February-October		

The Orchard
Listed
3 Sherbourne Terrace, Clarendon Street, Leamington Spa CV32 5SP
☎ (0926) 428198
Victorian double-fronted terrace with walled garden. 5 minutes' walk to town centre. Overseas visitors welcome.
Bedrooms: 1 single, 1 twin, 1 triple
Bathrooms: 2 public

Bed & breakfast per night:	£min	£max
Single	15.00	16.00
Double	26.00	28.00

Half board per person:	£min	£max
Daily	18.00	18.00
Weekly	100.00	110.00
Lunch available		
Evening meal from 1800		

Snowford Hall Farmhouse Bed & Breakfast
COMMENDED
Snowford Hall Farm, Hunningham, Leamington Spa CV33 9ES
☎ Marton (0926) 632297
250-acre arable and mixed farm. 18th C farmhouse off the Fosse Way, on the edge of Hunningham village. On elevated ground overlooking quiet surrounding countryside. Self-catering also available.
Bedrooms: 1 double, 2 twin
Bathrooms: 1 private, 1 public, 1 private shower

Bed & breakfast per night:	£min	£max
Double	32.00	38.00
Parking for 4		

The Willis
11 Eastnor Grove, Leamington Spa CV31 1LD
☎ (0926) 425820
Spacious Victorian family house with large garden, in quiet cul-de-sac near town centre. Supper and diets by arrangement. Summer meals in conservatory. Non-smokers only please.
Bedrooms: 1 single, 1 double, 1 twin
Bathrooms: 1 private, 2 public

Bed & breakfast per night:	£min	£max
Single	20.00	25.00
Double	35.00	45.00
Evening meal 1830 (last orders 0830)		
Parking for 2		

LECHLADE
Gloucestershire
Map ref 2B1

Attractive village on the River Thames and a popular spot for boating. It has a number of fine Georgian houses and a 15th C church. Nearby is Kelmscott Manor, with its William Morris furnishings, and 18th C Buscot House (National Trust).

Cambrai Lodge
Oak Street, Spring Gardens, Lechlade-on-Thames, Fairford GL7 3AY
☎ Faringdon (0367) 253173
Family-run guesthouse, newly modernised, close to River Thames. Ideal base for touring the Cotswolds. Garden and ample parking.
Bedrooms: 1 single, 2 double
Bathrooms: 2 private, 1 public

Bed & breakfast per night:	£min	£max
Single	15.00	23.00
Double	28.00	35.00
Parking for 13		

There are separate sections in this guide listing groups specialising in farm holidays and accommodation which is especially suitable for young people and organised groups.

LEDBURY
Hereford and Worcester
Map ref 2B1

Town with cobbled streets and many black and white timbered houses, including the 17th C market house and old inns. Nearby is Eastnor Castle with an interesting collection of tapestries and armour.
Tourist Information Centre
☎ *(0531) 636147*

Wall Hills Country Guest House
COMMENDED
Hereford Road, Ledbury, Herefordshire HR8 2PR
☎ (0531) 632833
Georgian country house, now a guesthouse with spacious rooms. Chef/proprietor provides delicious modern British cuisine. Quiet secluded location, glorious views, overlooking Ledbury and hills.
Bedrooms: 1 double, 1 twin, 1 triple
Bathrooms: 3 private

Bed & breakfast per night:	£min	£max
Single	29.00	35.00
Double	39.00	46.00
Evening meal 1930 (last orders 2030)		
Parking for 20		
Cards accepted: Access, Visa		

LEEK
Staffordshire
Map ref 4B2

Old silk and textile town, with some interesting buildings and a number of inns dating from the 17th C. Its art gallery has displays of embroidery. Brindley Mill, designed by James Brindley, has been restored as a museum.
Tourist Information Centre
☎ *(0538) 381000*

Abbey Inn
APPROVED
Abbey Green Road, Leek ST13 8SA
☎ (0538) 382865
17th C inn with accommodation in a separate annexe, set in beautiful countryside. 1 mile from the town and just off the main A523.
Bedrooms: 2 single, 5 double
Bathrooms: 7 private

Bed & breakfast per night:	£min	£max
Single	27.00	27.00
Double	42.00	42.00

Continued ▶

161

HEART OF ENGLAND

LEEK
Continued

Lunch available
Evening meal 1830 (last orders 2100)
Parking for 60
Cards accepted: Access, Visa, Diners, Amex

Bank End Farm Motel
COMMENDED

Old Leek Road, Longsdon, Stoke-on-Trent ST9 9QJ
☎ (0538) 383638

62-acre mixed farm. Pleasant motel in converted dairy and old stone barn, in a quiet lane close to Leek, Peak District National Park and Alton Towers.
Bedrooms: 1 single, 3 double, 3 twin, 1 triple, 2 family rooms
Bathrooms: 8 private, 1 public

Bed & breakfast
per night:	£min	£max
Single	25.00	30.00
Double	42.00	48.00

Half board
per person:	£min	£max
Daily	36.00	40.00

Evening meal from 1830
Parking for 10

Fairboroughs Farm

Rudyard, Leek ST13 8PR
☎ Rushton Spencer (0260) 226341

150-acre livestock farm. Comfortable, oak-beamed, 17C listed stone house, with log fires and splendid views. Potteries, Peak District, Cheshire and Alton Towers, Biddulph Grange Gardens within easy reach.
Bedrooms: 1 double, 1 family room
Bathrooms: 1 public

Bed & breakfast
per night:	£min	£max
Single	15.00	
Double	28.00	

Parking for 4
Open March-November

Three Horseshoes Inn
COMMENDED

Buxton Road, Blackshaw Moor, Leek ST13 8TW
☎ (0538) 300296
Fax (0538) 300320

Log fire, slate floor, oak and pine beams, good food and wines. Cottage-style rooms. Convenient for Peak District National Park and Alton Towers.
Bedrooms: 4 double, 2 twin
Bathrooms: 6 private

Bed & breakfast
per night:	£min	£max
Single	40.00	46.00
Double	46.00	54.00

Half board
per person:	£min	£max
Daily	38.00	46.00

Lunch available
Evening meal 1900 (last orders 2130)
Parking for 100
Cards accepted: Access, Visa, Switch

LEINTWARDINE
Hereford and Worcester
Map ref 4A3

Attractive border village where the Rivers Teme and Clun meet. It has some black and white cottages, old inns and an impressive church. It is near Hopton Castle and the beautiful scenery around Clun.

Lower House

Adforton, Leintwardine, Craven Arms, Shropshire SY7 0NF
☎ Wigmore (056 886) 223

House dates from early 17th C. Set in peaceful unspoilt countryside. Excellent walking in surrounding hills. Home cooking using local produce. A no smoking establishment.
Bedrooms: 2 double, 2 twin
Bathrooms: 4 private

Bed & breakfast
per night:	£min	£max
Single	19.00	21.00
Double	38.00	42.00

Half board
per person:	£min	£max
Daily	32.00	34.00
Weekly	215.00	215.00

Evening meal 1900 (last orders 1930)
Parking for 10
Open March-October

There are separate sections in this guide listing groups specialising in farm holidays and accommodation which is especially suitable for young people and organised groups.

LEOMINSTER
Hereford and Worcester
Map ref 2A1

The town owed its prosperity to wool and has many interesting buildings, notably the timber-framed Grange Court, a former town hall. The impressive Norman priory church has 3 naves and a ducking stool. Berrington Hall (National Trust) is nearby.
Tourist Information Centre
☎ *(0568) 616460*

Heath House
HIGHLY COMMENDED

Humber, Stoke Prior, Leominster, Herefordshire HR6 0NF
☎ Steens Bridge (056 882) 385 changing to (0568) 760385

Attractive stone farmhouse full of beams and history, set in peaceful countryside. Room to move and relax in comfort.
Bedrooms: 1 double, 1 twin, 1 triple
Bathrooms: 3 private

Bed & breakfast
per night:	£min	£max
Single	16.00	21.50
Double	40.00	40.00

Half board
per person:	£min	£max
Daily	26.00	36.50
Weekly	168.00	231.00

Evening meal 1900 (last orders 2100)
Parking for 6

Home Farm

Bircher, Leominster, Herefordshire HR6 0AX
☎ Yarpole (056 885) 525 changing to (0568) 780525

150-acre mixed farm. Traditional farmhouse accommodation with tea room on Welsh border, 4 miles north of Leominster and 7 miles south of Ludlow. On B4362. Paradise for walkers and country-lovers.
Bedrooms: 1 double, 1 twin, 1 triple
Bathrooms: 2 public, 1 private shower

Bed & breakfast
per night:	£min	£max
Single	16.00	20.00
Double	30.00	35.00

Parking for 6
Open February-November

Withenfield
HIGHLY COMMENDED

South Street, Leominster, Herefordshire HR6 8JN
☎ (0568) 612011

162

HEART OF ENGLAND

Elegantly furnished Georgian house with modern facilities and conservatory overlooking garden. Conveniently situated for touring countryside, castles, black and white villages.
Bedrooms: 2 double, 2 twin
Bathrooms: 4 private
Bed & breakfast

per night:	£min	£max
Single	36.00	39.00
Double	49.00	56.00

Evening meal from 1830
Parking for 5
Cards accepted: Access, Visa

LICHFIELD
Staffordshire
Map ref 4B3

Lichfield is Dr Samuel Johnson's birthplace and commemorates him with a museum and statue. The 13th C cathedral has 3 spires and the west front is full of statues. There is a regimental museum and Heritage Centre.
Tourist Information Centre
☎ (0543) 252109

Main View
APPROVED
18 Burton Road, Alrewas, Burton upon Trent DE13 7BB
☎ Burton-upon-Trent (0283) 790725
Detached house on the main A38 northbound. Country village convenient for Birmingham and the North. Pleasant views.
Bedrooms: 1 single, 1 double, 1 twin
Bathrooms: 1 public
Bed & breakfast

per night:	£min	£max
Single	15.00	17.00
Double	29.00	32.00

Evening meal 1700 (last orders 1800)
Parking for 6

Individual proprietors have supplied all details of accommodation. Although we do check for accuracy, we advise you to confirm the information at the time of booking.

LONG COMPTON
Warwickshire
Map ref 2B1

Village with a restored church displaying Norman doorways and a thatched room above the lych gate. Several interesting old houses exist in the area.

Ascott House Farm
Whichford, Long Compton, Shipston-on-Stour CV36 5PP
☎ (060 884) 655 changing to (0608) 684655

500-acre arable & livestock farm. Old stone farmhouse in beautiful countryside on edge of Cotswolds. 3 miles off A3400 between Stratford-upon-Avon and Oxford. 10 miles from M40 at Banbury. Swimming pool, games room and walks. Riding and golf within 3 miles.
Bedrooms: 2 double, 1 twin
Bathrooms: 2 private, 2 public
Bed & breakfast

per night:	£min	£max
Single	15.00	18.00
Double	28.00	34.00

Parking for 12

LONGNOR
Staffordshire
Map ref 4B2

Remote village in farming country between Buxton and Hartington and close to the River Dove.

Mount Pleasant Farm
COMMENDED
Elkstone, Longnor, Buxton, Derbyshire SK17 0LU
☎ Blackshaw (0538) 300380
A truly peaceful farmhouse with wonderful views over the Manifold Valley. Home cooking using local produce wherever possible.
Bedrooms: 1 twin, 1 triple
Bathrooms: 2 private, 1 public
Bed & breakfast

per night:	£min	£max
Single	17.00	19.00
Double	34.00	38.00

Half board

per person:	£min	£max
Daily		27.00
Weekly		175.00

Evening meal from 1830
Parking for 5
Open March-November

LUDLOW
Shropshire
Map ref 4A3

Outstandingly interesting border town with a magnificent castle high above the River Teme, 2 half-timbered old inns and an impressive 15th C church. The Reader's House, with its 3-storey Jacobean porch, should also be seen.
Tourist Information Centre
☎ (0584) 875053

Church Bank
Listed
Burrington, Ludlow SY8 2HT
☎ Wigmore (056 886) 426
Stone cottage guesthouse in tiny village. Walking in hills and forests, and historic places to visit. Four-course dinner.
Bedrooms: 1 double, 2 twin
Bathrooms: 2 public
Bed & breakfast

per night:	£min	£max
Single		13.50
Double		27.00

Half board

per person:	£min	£max
Daily		24.00
Weekly		154.00

Evening meal from 1900
Parking for 4
Open April-September

The Church Inn
Butter Cross, Ludlow SY8 1AW
☎ (0584) 872174
Georgian inn, centrally located on one of the most ancient sites in Ludlow. Good food and CAMRA listed for ales.
Bedrooms: 6 double, 2 twin, 1 triple
Bathrooms: 9 private
Bed & breakfast

per night:	£min	£max
Single	28.00	28.00
Double	40.00	40.00

Lunch available
Evening meal 1900 (last orders 2130)
Cards accepted: Access, Visa

Corndene
Coreley, Ludlow SY8 3AW
☎ (0584) 890324
Country house of character in the heart of rural Shropshire. Beautiful and secluded situation only 5 minutes off A4117 (Ludlow 7 miles). Spacious en-suite rooms, wholesome home cooking
Continued ▶

163

HEART OF ENGLAND

LUDLOW
Continued

and relaxing atmosphere. No smoking indoors please.
Bedrooms: 3 twin
Bathrooms: 3 private

Bed & breakfast

per night:	£min	£max
Single	20.50	21.50
Double	36.00	41.00

Half board

per person:	£min	£max
Daily	26.00	28.50
Weekly	160.00	175.00

Evening meal 1830 (last orders 2000)
Parking for 5

Fairview
HIGHLY COMMENDED

Green Lane, Onibury, Craven Arms SY7 9BL
☎ Bromfield (058 477) 505
5-acre smallholding. 300-year-old cottage 6 miles north of Ludlow. Panoramic views of Wenlock Edge, Long Mynd and Clee Hills.
Bedrooms: 2 double, 1 twin
Bathrooms: 1 private, 1 public

Bed & breakfast

per night:	£min	£max
Single	15.00	16.50
Double	30.00	33.00

Half board

per person:	£min	£max
Daily	25.00	26.50
Weekly	157.50	167.00

Evening meal 1930 (last orders 1930)
Parking for 8
Open April-October

Haynall Villa
COMMENDED

Haynall Lane, Little Hereford, Ludlow SY8 4BG
☎ Brimfield (0584) 711589
72-acre mixed & livestock farm. Early 19th C farmhouse set in the peaceful Teme Valley, 6 miles from historic Ludlow. Friendly atmosphere, comfortable rooms, lounge with log fires. Tasty home cooking. Holiday makers and business people welcome. Fishing available.
Bedrooms: 1 double, 1 twin, 1 family room
Bathrooms: 1 private, 2 public

Bed & breakfast

per night:	£min	£max
Single	16.00	
Double	30.00	

Half board

per person:	£min	£max
Daily		26.00
Weekly		175.00

Evening meal 1900 (last orders 1600)
Parking for 6

Longlands
Listed

Woodhouse Lane, Richards Castle, Ludlow SY8 4EU
☎ Richards Castle (058 474) 636
35-acre livestock farm. Farmhouse set in lovely rural landscape. Home-grown produce. Convenient for Ludlow, Mortimer Forest and Croft Castle. Interesting 14th C church and remains of 11th C castle in village.
Bedrooms: 1 double, 1 twin
Bathrooms: 2 private, 1 public

Bed & breakfast

per night:	£min	£max
Single	16.50	
Double	31.00	

Half board

per person:	£min	£max
Daily	24.00	
Weekly	154.00	

Evening meal 1830 (last orders 1930)
Parking for 2
Open April-December

28 Lower Broad Street
COMMENDED

Ludlow SY8 1PQ
☎ (0584) 876996

Listed town house of charm and character. Secluded walled garden. Emphasis on good food and wines, warm hospitality and quiet relaxed atmosphere.
Bedrooms: 1 double, 1 twin
Bathrooms: 2 private, 1 public

Bed & breakfast

per night:	£min	£max
Single	35.00	45.00
Double	45.00	50.00

Half board

per person:	£min	£max
Daily	35.00	40.00
Weekly	250.00	275.00

Evening meal 1930 (last orders 2030)

Middleton Court
Listed

Middleton, Ludlow SY8 2DZ
☎ (0584) 872842

245-acre mixed farm. Attractive country house offering comfort and good home cooking. Wonderful peace and tranquillity, lovely views of Clee Hills. Non-smoking household. Ludlow two miles.
Bedrooms: 1 single, 1 double, 1 triple
Bathrooms: 1 private, 1 public

Bed & breakfast

per night:	£min	£max
Single	18.00	23.00
Double	36.00	40.00

Half board

per person:	£min	£max
Daily	30.50	35.50
Weekly	220.50	

Evening meal 1900 (last orders 1600)
Parking for 10
Open March-October

Pengwern
Listed

5 St. Julians Avenue, Ludlow SY8 1ET
☎ (0584) 872587
Detached Edwardian house situated in quiet road within level walking distance of town centre.
Bedrooms: 1 single, 1 double
Bathrooms: 1 public

Bed & breakfast

per night:	£min	£max
Single		15.50
Double		30.00

Parking for 1

Seifton Court
COMMENDED

Culmington, Ludlow SY8 2DG
☎ Seifton (0584 473) 214
50-acre mixed farm. Period farmhouse, 5 miles from Ludlow on the B4365 road. Set in the beautiful Corve Dale valley. Near Longmynd, Ironbridge. Ideal for walking and visiting National Trust properties. Farmhouse fare using home-grown produce.
Bedrooms: 1 single, 2 double, 1 twin
Bathrooms: 2 private, 1 public

Bed & breakfast

per night:	£min	£max
Single	18.00	25.00
Double	34.00	40.00

Half board

per person:	£min	£max
Daily	29.00	36.00
Weekly	170.00	190.00

HEART OF ENGLAND

Lunch available
Evening meal 1800 (last orders 1900)
Parking for 7

The Wheatsheaf Inn
APPROVED

Lower Broad Street, Ludlow SY8 1PH
☎ (0584) 872980
Family-run mid 17th C beamed inn, 100 yards from the town centre, nestling under Ludlow's historic 13th C Broad Gate, the last remaining of 7 town gates.
Bedrooms: 4 double, 1 twin
Bathrooms: 5 private, 1 public

Bed & breakfast
per night:	£min	£max
Single	20.00	25.00
Double	35.00	40.00

Lunch available
Evening meal 1830 (last orders 2100)

MALVERN
Hereford and Worcester
Map ref 2B1

Spa town in Victorian times, its water is today bottled and sold worldwide. 6 resorts, set on the slopes of the Hills, form part of Malvern. Great Malvern Priory has splendid 15th C windows. It is an excellent walking centre.
Tourist Information Centre
☎ (0684) 892289

Cowleigh Park Farm
HIGHLY COMMENDED

Cowleigh Road, Malvern,
Worcestershire WR13 5HJ
☎ (0684) 566750

Beautifully restored, Grade II listed timbered farmhouse set in 2.5 acres of landscaped gardens. In a tranquil setting at the foot of the Malvern Hills. Ample secure parking.
Bedrooms: 1 double, 2 twin
Bathrooms: 3 private

Bed & breakfast
per night:	£min	£max
Double	36.00	40.00

Evening meal 1830 (last orders 1000)
Parking for 6

We advise you to confirm your booking in writing.

Grove House Farm
COMMENDED

Guarlford, Malvern, Worcestershire
WR14 3QZ
☎ (0684) 574256
Fax (0684) 574256
370-acre mixed farm. Large farmhouse at the foot of the Malvern Hills, in peaceful surroundings. Close to the Three Counties Showground.
Bedrooms: 1 double, 1 twin, 1 triple
Bathrooms: 2 public

Bed & breakfast
per night:	£min	£max
Single	20.00	
Double	35.00	40.00

Parking for 8
Open January-November

Mellbreak

177 Wells Road, Malvern Wells,
Malvern, Worcestershire WR14 4HE
☎ (0684) 561287
Comfortable Regency house with garden and views, near Three Counties Showground. English cooking of old-world style and substance. Extensive wine list.
Bedrooms: 1 single, 2 double, 1 twin
Bathrooms: 1 private, 1 public, 3 private showers

Bed & breakfast
per night:	£min	£max
Single	18.00	

Half board
per person:	£min	£max
Daily	28.00	

Evening meal from 1800
Parking for 4

The Red Lion Inn
Listed COMMENDED

Stiffords Bridge, Malvern,
Worcestershire WR13 5NN
☎ Ridgeway Cross (0886) 880318
Traditional country inn offering traditional ales and home-cooked bar fare, also a la carte restaurant. Attractive patio and gardens. Ideally situated on A4103, 3 miles from Malvern and 9 miles west of Worcester.
Bedrooms: 1 twin, 1 triple
Bathrooms: 1 public

Bed & breakfast
per night:	£min	£max
Single	23.00	25.00
Double	38.00	40.00

Lunch available
Evening meal 1900 (last orders 2130)
Parking for 60
Cards accepted: Access, Visa

Sidney House
COMMENDED

40 Worcester Road, Malvern,
Worcestershire WR14 4AA
☎ (0684) 574994 & 563065

Small, attractive Georgian hotel with personal and friendly service. Magnificent views over the Worcestershire countryside. Close to town centre and hills. Dinner by arrangement. Stay for 8 nights bed and breakfast - pay for 7. Winter weekend breaks - stay for 3 pay for 2. Prices below are from 1 March.
Bedrooms: 1 single, 4 double, 2 twin, 1 triple
Bathrooms: 5 private, 1 public

Bed & breakfast
per night:	£min	£max
Single	20.00	40.00
Double	40.00	60.00

Half board
per person:	£min	£max
Daily	35.00	55.00
Weekly	245.00	385.00

Lunch available
Evening meal 1900 (last orders 1500)
Parking for 10
Cards accepted: Access, Visa, Amex

The Wyche Inn
Listed

74 Wyche Road, Malvern,
Worcestershire WR14 4EQ
☎ (0684) 575396
The highest inn in Worcestershire, nestling on top of the Malvern Hills and with spectacular views across the Severn Valley.
Bedrooms: 2 double, 2 twin, 1 triple
Bathrooms: 5 private

Bed & breakfast
per night:	£min	£max
Single	22.00	24.00
Double	36.00	38.00

Lunch available
Evening meal 1900 (last orders 2200)
Parking for 12
Cards accepted: Access, Visa

MARKET DRAYTON
Shropshire
Map ref 4A2

Old market town with black and white buildings and 17th C houses. Hodnet Hall is in the vicinity with its beautiful landscaped gardens covering 60 acres.
Tourist Information Centre
☎ (0630) 652139

Old Colehurst Manor

Sutton upon Tern, Market Drayton
TF9 2JB
☎ (0630) 638833
Fax (0630) 638647

Continued ▶

Please mention this guide when making a booking.

HEART OF ENGLAND

MARKET DRAYTON
Continued

17th C manor with timber framed beams in all rooms, open fires in bedrooms and antique furniture.
Bedrooms: 7 double, 2 twin
Bathrooms: 5 private, 2 public
Bed & breakfast

per night:	£min	£max
Single	45.00	75.00
Double	60.00	105.00

Half board

per person:	£min	£max
Daily	60.00	150.00
Weekly	350.00	950.00

Lunch available
Evening meal 1900 (last orders 2200)
Parking for 12
Cards accepted: Access, Visa, Switch

MARTON
Warwickshire
Map ref 4B3

Bright little village on the road from Banbury to Coventry, with an ancient stone bridge across the River Leam.

Elms Farm
Listed

Oxford Road, Marton, Rugby
CV23 9RQ
☎ (0926) 632770
800-acre mixed farm. Come and stay in our beautiful listed farmhouse. Large gardens, lovely riverside walks. Close to NAC/NEC, Stratford and Warwick.
Bedrooms: 2 double, 1 twin
Bathrooms: 1 private, 1 public
Bed & breakfast

per night:	£min	£max
Single	15.00	20.00
Double	30.00	40.00

Parking for 6
Open January-November

MAXSTOKE
Warwickshire
Map ref 4B3

The Old Rectory
HIGHLY COMMENDED

Church Lane, Maxstoke, Coleshill, Birmingham B46 2QW
☎ Coleshill (0675) 462248
Fax (0675) 481615

Victorian rectory built from local sandstone, set in 5 acres of walled garden, originally the gardens of Maxstoke Priory.
Bedrooms: 1 double, 1 twin, 1 triple
Bathrooms: 3 private
Bed & breakfast

per night:	£min	£max
Single	25.00	29.00
Double	40.00	46.00

Parking for 10

MERIDEN
West Midlands
Map ref 4B3

Village halfway between Coventry and Birmingham. Said to be the centre of England, marked by a cross on the green.

Cooperage Farm Bed and Breakfast

Old Road, Meriden, Coventry CV7 7JP
☎ (0676) 23493
Fax (0676) 23876
6-acre mixed farm. 300-year-old red brick, Grade II listed farmhouse, set in beautiful countryside. Ideally situated for the National Exhibition Centre, airport and touring the centre of England.
Bedrooms: 1 double, 3 twin, 2 triple
Bathrooms: 4 private, 2 public
Bed & breakfast

per night:	£min	£max
Single	20.00	30.00
Double	36.00	46.00

Evening meal 1800 (last orders 1900)
Parking for 6

MICKLETON
Gloucestershire
Map ref 2B1

Mickleton lies in the Vale of Evesham and is close to Hidcote Manor Gardens (National Trust) and to the beautiful Cotswold town of Chipping Campden.

Bank House
APPROVED

Mickleton, Chipping Campden
GL55 6RX
☎ (0386) 438302
Period house with a tranquil old world garden. Excellent restaurant and inns within 2 minutes' walk. Hidcote Gardens 1 mile, Broadway 6 miles.
Bedrooms: 1 double, 2 twin
Bathrooms: 3 private
Bed & breakfast

per night:	£min	£max
Double	33.50	38.00

Parking for 4
Open April-October

MINCHINHAMPTON
Gloucestershire
Map ref 2B1

Stone-built town, with many 17th/18th C buildings, owing its existence to the wool and cloth trades. A 17th C pillared market house may be found in the town square, near which is the Norman and 14th C church.

Hunters Lodge
COMMENDED

Dr Brown's Road, Minchinhampton, Stroud GL6 9BT
☎ Brimscombe (0453) 883588
Cotswold stone house adjoining Minchinhampton common and golf-course. Ideal centre for Bath, Gloucester, Cheltenham and Cotswolds. Located 2 miles from A419 Stroud-Cirencester road 1.5 miles from A46 (first house on right going into Minchinhampton).
Bedrooms: 1 twin, 1 triple
Bathrooms: 2 private
Bed & breakfast

per night:	£min	£max
Single	20.00	25.00
Double	30.00	38.00

Parking for 8

MINSTERLEY
Shropshire
Map ref 4A3

Village with a curious little church of 1692 and a fine old black and white hall. The lofty ridge known as the Stiperstones is 4 miles to the south.

Cricklewood Cottage
HIGHLY COMMENDED

Plox Green, Minsterley, Shrewsbury SY5 0HT
☎ Shrewsbury (0743) 791229
Delightful 18th C cottage with countryside views, at foot of Stiperstones Hills. Exposed beams, inglenook fireplace, traditional furnishings. Lovely cottage garden. Wholesome food.
Bedrooms: 1 double, 2 twin
Bathrooms: 3 private

HEART OF ENGLAND

Bed & breakfast

per night:	£min	£max
Single	19.00	28.50
Double	38.00	38.00

Half board

per person:	£min	£max
Daily	29.00	38.50
Weekly	189.00	249.55

Evening meal 1900 (last orders 1000)
Parking for 4

Sycamore Cottage

5 Perkins Beach, Stiperstones, Minsterley, Shrewsbury SY5 0PQ
☎ Shrewsbury (0743) 790914

Comfortable stone cottage standing on 3.5 acres of land, 1100 feet up and with wonderful views all around. Direct access on to Stiperstones Hills.
Bedrooms: 1 twin
Bathrooms: 1 private

Bed & breakfast

per night:	£min	£max
Single	16.00	
Double	32.00	

Half board

per person:	£min	£max
Daily	25.00	

Evening meal 1930 (last orders 2200)
Parking for 3

MORETON-IN-MARSH

Gloucestershire
Map ref 2B1

Attractive town of Cotswold stone with 17th C houses, an ideal base for touring the Cotswolds. Some of the local attractions include Batsford Park Arboretum, the Jacobean Chastleton House and Sezincote Garden.

Blue Cedar House ⋒

Stow Road, Moreton-in-Marsh GL56 0DW
☎ (0608) 50299

Attractive detached residence set in half-acre garden in the Cotswolds, with pleasantly decorated, well-equipped accommodation and garden room. Close to village centre.
Bedrooms: 2 double, 1 twin, 1 triple
Bathrooms: 2 private, 2 public, 1 private shower

Bed & breakfast

per night:	£min	£max
Single	18.00	26.00
Double	31.00	39.00

Half board

per person:	£min	£max
Daily	23.00	27.00

Evening meal 1800 (last orders 1800)

Parking for 7
Open February-November

Dorn Priory
COMMENDED

Dorn, Moreton-in-Marsh GL56 9NS
☎ (0608) 650152

17th C Cotswold house in peaceful surroundings. Set in a small hamlet on edge of Cotswolds, within easy reach of Stratford and Oxford.
Bedrooms: 1 twin, 1 family room
Bathrooms: 1 public

Bed & breakfast

per night:	£min	£max
Double	28.00	30.00

Parking for 10

Honeybrook Cottage

Main Street, Adlestrop, Moreton-in-Marsh GL56 0YN
☎ (0608) 658884

Natural stone cottage in quiet village 4 miles from Stow-on-the-Wold, Moreton-in-Marsh and Chipping Norton. South-facing gardens with stream.
Bedrooms: 1 double, 1 twin
Bathrooms: 2 private, 1 public

Bed & breakfast

per night:	£min	£max
Single	22.00	24.00
Double	36.00	38.00

Parking for 3

Lines Farm ⋒

Chastleton Road, Little Compton, Moreton-in-Marsh GL56 0SL
☎ Barton on the Heath (060 874) 343

27-acre livestock farm. Detached Cotswold-stone house with good facilities and beautiful views. Easily accessible from A44 between Chipping Norton and Moreton-in-Marsh.
Bedrooms: 1 double, 1 triple
Bathrooms: 1 private, 1 public

Bed & breakfast

per night:	£min	£max
Single	20.00	20.00
Double	30.00	34.00

Parking for 10

Lower Farm Barn ⋒

Great Wolford, Shipston-on-Stour, Warwickshire CV36 5NQ
☎ Barton on the Heath (060 874) 435

900-acre arable farm. 18th C converted barn combines modern comforts with exposed beams and ancient stonework. Use of attractive drawing room. Quiet village between A34, A44 and A429.
Bedrooms: 1 double, 1 twin, 1 triple
Bathrooms: 2 private, 1 public

Bed & breakfast

per night:	£min	£max
Single	16.00	17.00
Double	28.00	31.00

Parking for 10

Manor Farm ⋒
Listed

Great Wolford, Shipston-on-Stour, Warwickshire CV36 5NQ
☎ Barton-on-the-Heath (060 874) 247

270-acre mixed farm. Comfortable listed farmhouse in a small village with traditional pub, close to Moreton-in-Marsh. Open fire, TV lounge, lovely views. Ideal for Cotswolds and Stratford.
Bedrooms: 1 double, 1 twin
Bathrooms: 1 public

Bed & breakfast

per night:	£min	£max
Single	16.00	18.00
Double	28.00	30.00

Parking for 12
Open March-November

New Farm ⋒
COMMENDED

Dorn, Moreton-in-Marsh GL56 9NS
☎ (0608) 650782

250-acre dairy farm. Old Cotswold farmhouse. All rooms spacious, en-suite and furnished with antiques. Colour TV, coffee and tea facilities. Dining room with large impressive fireplace. Full English breakfast served with hot crispy bread.
Bedrooms: 1 double, 1 twin, 1 multiple
Bathrooms: 3 private, 1 public

Bed & breakfast

per night:	£min	£max
Single	15.00	17.00
Double	30.00	32.00

Continued ▶

167

HEART OF ENGLAND

MORETON-IN-MARSH
Continued

Half board
per person:	£min	£max
Daily	40.00	42.00
Weekly	175.00	180.00

Parking for 10

Old Farm
COMMENDED

Dorn, Moreton-in-Marsh GL56 9NS
☎ (0608) 50394

250-acre mixed farm. Enjoy the delights of a 15th C farmhouse - a comfortable family home. Spacious bedrooms. Tennis and croquet. Children welcome.
Bedrooms: 1 double, 1 twin, 1 triple
Bathrooms: 1 private, 1 public

Bed & breakfast
per night:	£min	£max
Single	18.00	20.00
Double	28.00	32.00

Parking for 8
Open March-October

Red Lion Inn
APPROVED

Little Compton, Moreton-in-Marsh GL56 0RT
☎ Barton-on-the-Heath (060 874) 397
Fax (060 874) 521

16th C village inn with large garden, offering comfortable accommodation, bar meals, home-made dishes and quality rump steaks. 4 miles from Moreton-in-Marsh off A44.
Bedrooms: 2 double, 1 twin
Bathrooms: 1 public

Bed & breakfast
per night:	£min	£max
Single		24.00
Double		36.00

Lunch available
Evening meal 1900 (last orders 2045)
Parking for 20
Cards accepted: Access, Visa, Switch

Rest Harrow
APPROVED

Evenlode Road, Moreton-in-Marsh GL56 0NJ
☎ (0608) 50653

Large four-bedroomed house in rural location. Take Evenlode turning by Wellington public house on main Oxford-London road, then half a mile on left.
Bedrooms: 1 double, 1 triple
Bathrooms: 1 public

Bed & breakfast
per night:	£min	£max
Single	13.00	14.00
Double	26.00	26.00

Parking for 3

Twostones
COMMENDED

Evenlode, Moreton-in-Marsh GL56 0NY
☎ (0608) 51104

16th C priest cottage, on smallholding, in quiet village, 3 miles from Stow-on-the-Wold and 2.5 miles from Moreton-in-Marsh. Ideal for Stratford and Cotswolds.
Bedrooms: 1 double, 2 twin
Bathrooms: 3 private

Bed & breakfast
per night:	£min	£max
Single	17.00	18.00
Double	34.00	36.00

Parking for 6

MUCH WENLOCK
Shropshire
Map ref 4A3

Small town close to Wenlock Edge in beautiful scenery and full of interest. In particular there are the remains of an 11th C priory with fine carving and the black and white 16th C Guildhall.

The Longville Arms
Listed

Longville in the Dale, Much Wenlock TF13 6DR
☎ Longville (0694) 771206

18th C rural pub, home-cooked food, friendly atmosphere, good walking. National Trust buildings nearby. Garden. Children welcome. Self-catering accommodation available.
Bedrooms: 1 family room
Bathrooms: 1 public

Bed & breakfast
per night:	£min	£max
Single	20.00	20.00
Double	30.00	30.00

Half board
per person:	£min	£max
Daily	35.00	45.00

Lunch available
Evening meal 1900 (last orders 2100)
Parking for 24

The Old Barn

45 Sheinton Street, Much Wenlock TF13 6HR
☎ Telford (0952) 728191

18th C barn, converted to cottage-style accommodation, in the beautiful town of Much Wenlock.
Bedrooms: 2 double, 2 twin
Bathrooms: 4 private

Bed & breakfast
per night:	£min	£max
Single	25.00	28.00
Double	34.00	38.00

Parking for 4
Open January-November

Perkley House
HIGHLY COMMENDED

5 Bourton Westwood, Much Wenlock TF13 6QB
☎ (0952) 727252

Comfortable, traditional stone house quietly situated in 2 acres with spectacular views. One mile from Much Wenlock on B4378.
Bedrooms: 2 double
Bathrooms: 2 private

Bed & breakfast
per night:	£min	£max
Single	25.00	28.00
Double	40.00	42.00

Parking for 6
Open February-November

Walton House
Listed COMMENDED

35 Barrow Street, Much Wenlock TF13 6EP
☎ (0952) 727139

Two minutes' walk from town centre. 5 miles from Ironbridge Gorge, 13 miles from Shrewsbury, 8 miles from Bridgnorth and 10 miles from Telford town centre. Lawns and patio.
Bedrooms: 1 single, 2 twin
Bathrooms: 1 public

Bed & breakfast
per night:	£min	£max
Single		14.00
Double		26.00

Parking for 2
Open April-October
Cards accepted: Visa

NAILSWORTH
Gloucestershire
Map ref 2B1

Ancient wool town with several elegant Jacobean and Georgian houses, surrounded by wooded hillsides with fine views.

Apple Orchard House
COMMENDED

Orchard Close, Springhill, Nailsworth, Stroud GL6 0LX
☎ (0453) 832503
Fax (0453) 836213

Elegant and spacious Cotswold house in pretty 1 acre garden. Panoramic views from bedrooms and sitting room of picturesque Cotswold hills. Excellent touring centre. Close to restaurants, M5, M4.
Wheelchair access category 3
Bedrooms: 1 double, 2 twin

HEART OF ENGLAND

Bathrooms: 3 private

Bed & breakfast per night:	£min	£max
Single	15.00	24.00
Double	30.00	34.00
Half board per person:	£min	£max
Daily	25.00	27.00
Weekly	157.50	170.10

Evening meal 1900 (last orders 1700)
Parking for 3
Cards accepted: Access, Visa

Ad Display advertisement appears on this page

North Farm
COMMENDED
Nympsfield Road, Nailsworth, Stroud GL6 0ET
☎ Stroud (0453) 833598
Modernised former farmhouse, 3 large bedrooms, all with bathroom en-suite. Panoramic views of surrounding countryside. Convenient for touring. Brochure on request.
Bedrooms: 1 double, 2 twin
Bathrooms: 3 private

Bed & breakfast per night:	£min	£max
Single	18.00	20.00
Double	30.00	32.00
Half board per person:	£min	£max
Daily	27.50	32.00
Weekly	173.25	201.60

Evening meal 1800 (last orders 2000)
Parking for 4

National Crown ratings were correct at the time of going to press but are subject to change. Please check at the time of booking.

NAUNTON
Gloucestershire
Map ref 2B1

A high place on the Windrush, renowned for its wild flowers and with an attractive dovecote.

Eastern Hill Farm
Listed
Naunton, Cheltenham GL54 3AF
☎ Guiting Power (0451) 850716
77-acre arable and mixed farm. Traditional-style Cotswolds farmhouse, within walking distance of Bourton-on-the-Water and the Slaughters. Breathtaking views.
Bedrooms: 1 double, 1 twin, 1 triple
Bathrooms: 3 public

Bed & breakfast per night:	£min	£max
Single	17.00	18.00
Double	34.00	36.00

Evening meal from 1900
Parking for 6

NEWCASTLE-UNDER-LYME
Staffordshire
Map ref 4B2

Industrial town whose museum and art gallery give evidence of its past. The Guildhall was built in the 18th C and there is the modern university of Keele.
Tourist Information Centre
☎ (0782) 711964

Graythwaite Guest House
106 Lancaster Road, Newcastle-under-Lyme ST5 1DS
☎ (0782) 612875
Comfortable Victorian villa in conservation area. Town centre 5 minutes' walk. Ideal for Pottery factory visits. 10 minutes from M6, off the A34.
Bedrooms: 4 single, 1 double, 1 twin, 1 triple
Bathrooms: 3 private, 2 public

Bed & breakfast per night:	£min	£max
Single	16.00	25.00
Double	32.00	38.00

Parking for 10
Cards accepted: Access, Visa

NEWENT
Gloucestershire
Map ref 2B1

Small town with the largest collection of birds of prey in Europe at the Falconry Centre. Flying demonstrations daily. Glass workshop where visitors can watch glass being blown. There is a "seconds" shop. North of the village are Three Choirs Vineyards.
Tourist Information Centre
☎ (0531) 822145

George Hotel
Church Street, Newent GL18 1PU
☎ (0531) 820203
Family-run 17th C coaching house in Newent town centre, offering bed and breakfast and extensive bar and restaurant menus.
Bedrooms: 2 double, 6 twin, 2 triple
Bathrooms: 4 public

Bed & breakfast per night:	£min	£max
Single		20.00
Double		30.00

Lunch available
Evening meal 1900 (last orders 2230)
Parking for 12
Cards accepted: Access, Visa, Diners

5 Onslow Road
Listed
Newent GL18 1TL
☎ (0531) 821677
Modern 4 bedroom house, south side of Newent. Last right turn out of town off old Gloucester Road, third house on left.
Bedrooms: 1 double, 1 twin
Continued ▶

RAC Highly Acclaimed   AA Selected

APPLE ORCHARD HOUSE
NAILSWORTH–SOUTH COTSWOLDS
COMMENDED

Stay in beautifully situated touring centre, surrounded by National Trust hills and commons, and recognised as one of the best eating centres of the South Cotswolds. Enjoy easy quick access to:

Lovely gardens/historic houses and castles/interesting towns and villages/ancient monuments and cathedrals/nature conservation areas including Slimbridge wildfowl trust and Westonbirt Arboretum/panoramic views.
Price: from £16.00pp 10% reduction on 7 nights. (Book before Feb 28th to get 1993 prices). 3 Course Dinner £10pp by arrangement. Laundry Facilities. Colour TV All Bedrooms, Panoramic Views All Rooms.
Discovery of this interesting yet unspoilt part of England takes at least a week!
1 Ground floor room - suit disabled person.
Group bookings up to 24. Ideal for Walking Parties.
1/2 Hour North of Bath / 40 Mins Bourton-on-the-Water
Free Brochure from:
Apple Orchard House, Springhill, Nailsworth,
Gloucestershire GL6 0IX ☎ **(0453) 832503 Fax (0453) 836213**

169

HEART OF ENGLAND

NEWENT
Continued

Bathrooms: 1 private, 1 public

Bed & breakfast
per night:	£min	£max
Single	13.50	15.00
Double	27.00	30.00

Parking for 2

NEWLAND
Gloucestershire
Map ref 2A1

Probably the most attractive of the villages of the Forest of Dean. The church is often referred to as "the Cathedral of the Forest"; it contains a number of interesting monuments and the Forest Miner's Brass. Almshouses nearby were endowed by William Jones, founder of Monmouth School.

Scatterford Farm

Newland, Coleford GL16 8NG
☎ Dean (0594) 836562
Fax (0594) 836323

A beautiful 15th C farmhouse with spacious rooms set in the midst of glorious walking country. Half-a-mile from Newland village.

Bedrooms: 2 double, 1 twin
Bathrooms: 3 private

Bed & breakfast
per night:	£min	£max
Single	17.50	17.50
Double	35.00	35.00

Parking for 8

NEWPORT
Shropshire
Map ref 4A3

Small market town on the Shropshire Union Canal has a wide High Street and a church with some interesting monuments. Newport is close to Aqualate Mere which is the largest lake in Staffordshire.

Lane End Farm

Chetwynd, Newport TF10 8BN
☎ Sambrook (0952) 550337

Delightful period farmhouse set in lovely countryside. Located on A41 near Newport for ideal touring base and beautiful local walks.

Bedrooms: 2 double
Bathrooms: 2 private

Bed & breakfast
per night:	£min	£max
Single	15.00	25.00
Double	30.00	40.00

Half board
per person:	£min	£max
Daily	22.50	33.00
Weekly	157.50	175.00

Evening meal 1800 (last orders 2100)
Parking for 5

Sambrook Manor
Listed

Sambrook, Newport TF10 8AL
☎ Sambrook (0952) 550256

260-acre mixed farm. Old manor farmhouse built in 1702. Close to Stoke Potteries, Shrewsbury, Ironbridge, Wolverhampton and many places of historic interest.

Bedrooms: 1 single, 1 double, 1 triple
Bathrooms: 2 public

Bed & breakfast
per night:	£min	£max
Single	15.00	15.00
Double	30.00	30.00

Parking for 10

NORTHLEACH
Gloucestershire
Map ref 2B1

Village famous for its beautiful 15th C wool church with its lovely porch and interesting interior. There are also some fine houses including a 17th C wool merchant's house containing Keith Harding's World of Mechanical Music, and the Cotswold Countryside Collection is in the former prison.

Market House

The Square, Northleach, Cheltenham GL54 3EJ
☎ Cotswold (0451) 860557

400-year-old guesthouse with exposed beams and inglenook fireplace, in the heart of the Cotswolds.

Bedrooms: 2 double, 1 twin
Bathrooms: 1 private, 1 public

Bed & breakfast
per night:	£min	£max
Single	15.00	17.00
Double	30.00	40.00

Parking for 4

Northfield Bed & Breakfast
COMMENDED

Cirencester Road (A429), Northleach, Cheltenham GL54 3JL
☎ Cotswold (0451) 860427

Detached family house in the country with large gardens and home-grown produce. Excellent centre for visiting the Cotswolds and close to local services.

Bedrooms: 1 double, 1 twin, 1 triple
Bathrooms: 3 private

Bed & breakfast
per night:	£min	£max
Single	20.00	20.00
Double	30.00	36.00

Half board
per person:	£min	£max
Daily	40.00	

Evening meal 1900 (last orders 2000)
Parking for 10

NUNEATON
Warwickshire
Map ref 4B3

Busy town with an art gallery and museum which has a permanent exhibition of the work of George Eliot. The library also has an interesting collection of material. Arbury Hall, a fine example of Gothic architecture, is nearby.
Tourist Information Centre
☎ *(0203) 384027*

Triple 'A' Lodge Guest House
Listed

94-96 Coleshill Road, Chapel End, Nuneaton CV10 0PH
☎ Coventry (0203) 394515
Fax (0203) 394515

Family-run guesthouse on the outskirts of Nuneaton, in the pleasant village of Chapel End. Tea/coffee facilities and colour TV in all rooms. Evening meals available.

Bedrooms: 3 double, 3 twin
Bathrooms: 2 public

Bed & breakfast
per night:	£min	£max
Single	15.00	18.00
Double	24.00	30.00

Evening meal 1800 (last orders 2130)
Parking for 12
Cards accepted: Diners, Amex

National Crown ratings were correct at the time of going to press but are subject to change. Please check at the time of booking.

HEART OF ENGLAND

NYMPSFIELD
Gloucestershire
Map ref 2B1

Pretty village high up in the Cotswolds, with a simple mid-Victorian church and a prehistoric long barrow nearby.

Rose and Crown Inn
Listed COMMENDED
Nympsfield, Stonehouse GL10 3TU
☎ Dursley (0453) 860240
Fax (0453) 860900

300-year-old inn, in quiet Cotswold village, close to Cotswold Way and Nympsfield Gliding Club. Easy access to M4/M5.
Bedrooms: 3 double, 1 triple
Bathrooms: 1 private, 1 public

Bed & breakfast
per night:	£min	£max
Single	27.00	36.00
Double	36.00	48.00

Half board
per person:	£min	£max
Daily	25.00	50.00
Weekly	150.00	350.00

Lunch available
Evening meal 1830 (last orders 2130)
Parking for 30
Cards accepted: Access, Visa, Amex

OAKAMOOR
Staffordshire
Map ref 4B2

Small village below a steep hill amid the glorious beauty of the Churnet Valley. Its industrial links have now gone, as the site of the factory which made 20,000 miles of copper wire for the first Atlantic cable has been transformed into an attractive picnic site on the riverside.

Bank House
HIGHLY COMMENDED
Farley Road, Oakamoor, Stoke-on-Trent ST10 3BD
☎ Leek (0538) 702810

Symbols are explained on the flap inside the back cover.

Peaceful, elegantly furnished home with log fires and beautiful views. Good food, home-made breads. Close to Alton Towers and the Peak District National Park.
Bedrooms: 1 single, 2 twin
Bathrooms: 3 private

Bed & breakfast
per night:	£min	£max
Single	28.00	28.00
Double	46.00	64.00

Half board
per person:	£min	£max
Daily	41.00	50.00
Weekly	224.00	273.00

Lunch available
Evening meal 1900 (last orders 2130)
Parking for 10
Cards accepted: Access, Visa

Ribden Farm
Listed COMMENDED
Oakamoor, Stoke-on-Trent ST10 3BW
☎ (0538) 702830
98-acre livestock farm. Grade II listed 18th C farmhouse, open countryside, 1.5 miles from Alton Towers.
Bedrooms: 2 double, 1 twin
Bathrooms: 3 private

Bed & breakfast
per night:	£min	£max
Single	20.00	25.00
Double	30.00	32.00

Parking for 3

Tenement Farm
Three Lows, Ribden, Oakamoor, Stoke-on-Trent ST10 3BW
☎ (0538) 702333
100-acre livestock farm. Traditional farmhouse bed and breakfast in the heart of the Midlands. Alton Towers 2 miles. Close to Manifold Valley and Dovedale. No smoking preferred.
Bedrooms: 2 double, 1 triple, 2 family rooms
Bathrooms: 5 private

Bed & breakfast
per night:	£min	£max
Double	30.00	32.00

Evening meal 1830 (last orders 1930)
Parking for 10
Open April-November

OMBERSLEY
Hereford and Worcester
Map ref 2B1

A particularly fine village full of black and white houses including the 17th C Dower House and some old inns. The church contains the original box pews.

The Crown and Sandys Arms
APPROVED
Ombersley, Droitwich, Worcestershire WR9 0EW
☎ Worcester (0905) 620252
Fax (0905) 620767
Freehouse with comfortable bedrooms, draught beers and open fires. Home-cooked meals available lunch and evenings, 7 days a week.
Bedrooms: 1 single, 5 double, 1 twin
Bathrooms: 5 private, 1 public

Bed & breakfast
per night:	£min	£max
Single	20.00	35.00
Double	40.00	45.00

Lunch available
Evening meal 1800 (last orders 2200)
Parking for 100
Cards accepted: Access, Visa, Switch

Greenlands
Listed HIGHLY COMMENDED
Uphampton, Ombersley, Droitwich, Worcestershire WR9 0JP
☎ Worcester (0905) 620873

Dated 1580, in beautiful conservation area. Tastefully furnished bedrooms with every comfort. Sitting room with open fire. Breakfast served in delightful gardens or in beamed room overlooking them. Situated in lane adjacent "Reindeer Inn" on A449.
Bedrooms: 1 single, 1 double, 1 twin
Bathrooms: 1 private, 1 public

Bed & breakfast
per night:	£min	£max
Single	14.00	16.00
Double	28.00	36.00

Parking for 6

The town index towards the back of this guide gives page numbers of all places with accommodation.

171

HEART OF ENGLAND

ONNELEY
Staffordshire
Map ref 4A2

The Wheatsheaf Inn at Onneley
COMMENDED

Bar Hill Road, Onneley CW3 9QF
☎ Stoke-on-Trent (0782) 751581
Fax (0782) 751499

18th C country inn with bars, restaurant, conference and function facilities. On the A525, 3 miles from Bridgemere and Keele University, 7 miles from Newcastle-under-Lyme. Prices are per room.

Bedrooms: 4 double, 1 twin
Bathrooms: 5 private

Bed & breakfast
per night:	£min	£max
Single	45.00	45.00
Double	45.00	55.00

Half board
per person:	£min	£max
Daily	38.50	56.00

Lunch available
Evening meal 1800 (last orders 2200)
Parking for 150
Cards accepted: Access, Visa, Diners, Amex

OSWESTRY
Shropshire
Map ref 4A3

Town close to the Welsh border, the scene of many battles. To the north are the remains of a large Iron Age hill fort. An excellent centre for exploring Shropshire and Offa's Dyke.
Tourist Information Centre
☎ *(0691) 662488*

Pant-Hir

Croesaubach, Oswestry SY10 9BH
☎ Llansilin (069 170) 457

25-acre horses farm. Just outside Oswestry in beautiful rural surroundings lies this attractive smallholding. The bedrooms are en-suite with TV. Added attraction is the miniature horse stud.

Bedrooms: 1 double, 1 twin
Bathrooms: 2 private

Bed & breakfast
per night:	£min	£max
Double	32.00	32.00

Half board
per person:	£min	£max
Weekly		160.00

Evening meal 1900 (last orders 2000)
Parking for 10
Open January-November

Rhoswiel Lodge
Listed

Weston Rhyn, Oswestry SY10 7TG
☎ Chirk (0691) 777609

Victorian country house with modern annexe in pleasant surroundings beside Llangollen Canal, 4 miles north of Oswestry. 300 yards from the A5.

Bedrooms: 2 single, 2 double, 2 twin
Bathrooms: 3 public

Bed & breakfast
per night:	£min	£max
Single	12.00	15.00
Double	24.00	28.00

Parking for 6

PAINSWICK
Gloucestershire
Map ref 2B1

Picturesque wool town with inns and houses dating from the 14th C. Painswick House is a Palladian mansion with Chinese wallpaper. The churchyard is famous for its yew trees.

The Dream Factory
APPROVED

Friday Street, Painswick, Stroud GL6 6QJ
☎ (0452) 812379

Grade II listed building, in the centre of the village known as the Queen of the Cotswolds.

Bedrooms: 1 double
Bathrooms: 1 private

Bed & breakfast
per night:	£min	£max
Single	15.00	
Double	30.00	

Upper Doreys Mill

Edge, Painswick, Stroud GL6 6NF
☎ (0452) 812459

18th C cloth mill with log fires and old beams. By a stream and in a rural setting. Half a mile from Painswick, down Edge Lane.

Bedrooms: 2 double, 1 twin
Bathrooms: 3 private

Bed & breakfast
per night:	£min	£max
Single	20.00	
Double	36.00	

Parking for 6

Establishments should be open throughout the year unless otherwise stated in the entry.

PARKEND
Gloucestershire
Map ref 2A1

Village in the Forest of Dean, once an important industrial and railway centre, but now quiet and peaceful and a good base for exploring the forest.

The Fountain Inn

Fountain Way, Parkend, Lydney GL15 4JD
☎ Dean (0594) 562189
Fax (0594) 564438

Beautifully renovated village pub, at Parkend, 3.5 miles from Lydney on the A48 Chepstow to Gloucester road. Ideal for walking and cycling.
Wheelchair access category 3
Bedrooms: 2 single, 4 double, 2 twin
Bathrooms: 8 private

Bed & breakfast
per night:	£min	£max
Single	24.00	
Double	44.00	

Half board
per person:	£min	£max
Daily	25.00	27.00

Lunch available
Evening meal 1800 (last orders 2130)
Parking for 30
Cards accepted: Access, Visa, Diners, Amex

PUTLEY
Hereford and Worcester
Map ref 2B1

The Coach House
Listed

Putley, Ledbury, Herefordshire HR8 2QP
☎ Ledbury (0531) 670684

18th C coach house and stables with cobbled courtyard, originally part of the nearby Putley Court.

Bedrooms: 2 double
Bathrooms: 2 private

Half board
per person:	£min	£max
Daily	13.00	15.50

Parking for 6

RENDCOMB
Gloucestershire
Map ref 2B1

Shawswell Country House
DE LUXE

Rendcomb, Cirencester GL7 7HD
☎ Cirencester (0285) 831779

"Far from the madding crowd". 17th C country house offering quality accommodation, wealth of beams. Idyllic hillside setting. From A435, take

HEART OF ENGLAND

turning to Rendcomb and follow "no through road".
Bedrooms: 1 single, 3 double, 1 twin
Bathrooms: 5 private

Bed & breakfast
per night:	£min	£max
Single	25.00	35.00
Double	45.00	55.00

Half board
per person:	£min	£max
Daily	41.00	51.00

Evening meal 1900 (last orders 2000)
Parking for 8
Open February-November

ROCK
Hereford and Worcester
Map ref 4A3

The Old Forge
Listed

Gorst Hill, Rock, Kidderminster,
Worcestershire DY14 9YG
☎ (0299) 266745

Recently renovated country cottage, near the Wyre Forest. Ideal for country walks and visiting local places of interest. Short and midweek breaks.
Bedrooms: 1 double, 1 twin
Bathrooms: 1 public

Bed & breakfast
per night:	£min	£max
Single	13.25	
Double	25.00	

Parking for 5

ROSS-ON-WYE
Hereford and Worcester
Map ref 2A1

Attractive market town with a 17th C market hall, set above the River Wye. There are lovely views over the surrounding countryside from the Prospect and the town is close to Goodrich Castle and the Welsh border.
Tourist Information Centre
☎ (0989) 62768

The Arches Country House

Walford Road, Ross-on-Wye,
Herefordshire HR9 5TP
☎ (0989) 63348

Family-run hotel set in half an acre of lawns, half a mile from the town centre. All bedrooms are furnished to a high standard and have views of the lawned garden. Warm, friendly atmosphere and personal service.
Bedrooms: 1 single, 4 double, 2 twin, 1 triple
Bathrooms: 6 private, 2 public, 1 private shower

Bed & breakfast
per night:	£min	£max
Single	18.00	21.00
Double	32.00	42.00

Parking for 8

The Ashe

Bridstow, Ross-on-Wye, Herefordshire
HR9 6QA
☎ (0989) 63336

200-acre mixed farm. 15th C sandstone farmhouse with oak beams and panelling. Situated in beautiful countryside. Ideal for walking and touring Wye Valley, Forest of Dean and Wales. 2 miles north of Ross-on-Wye, turn right off the A49 to Backney and Foy.
Bedrooms: 1 double, 1 twin
Bathrooms: 2 private

Bed & breakfast
per night:	£min	£max
Single	14.50	15.50
Double	29.00	31.00

Parking for 8

Brook House

Lea, Ross-on-Wye, Herefordshire
HR9 7JZ
☎ (0989) 750710

Fine Queen Anne Grade II listed house offering a warm welcome, comfortable rooms and open fires. Home-cooked and produced fare. Home-made muffins a speciality.
Bedrooms: 2 double, 1 twin
Bathrooms: 1 private, 1 public, 2 private showers

Bed & breakfast
per night:	£min	£max
Single	17.75	
Double	31.50	35.50

Evening meal 1900 (last orders 1800)
Parking for 2

Brookfield House

Over Ross, Ross-on-Wye, Herefordshire
HR9 7AT
☎ (0989) 62188

Queen Anne/Georgian listed building close to the town centre. Private car park. Easy reach of M50 and A40.
Bedrooms: 2 single, 3 double, 3 twin
Bathrooms: 3 private, 3 public

Bed & breakfast
per night:	£min	£max
Single	17.00	18.00
Double	34.00	39.00

Parking for 11
Cards accepted: Access, Visa

Edde Cross House
HIGHLY COMMENDED

Edde Cross Street, Ross-on-Wye,
Herefordshire HR9 7BZ
☎ (0989) 65088

Delightful Georgian town house overlooking river, with the atmosphere and character of a comfortable private home. Close to town centre. Bedrooms with colour TV and beverage tray, some en-suite. No smoking house.
Bedrooms: 1 single, 3 double, 1 twin
Bathrooms: 2 private, 1 public

Bed & breakfast
per night:	£min	£max
Single	18.00	30.00
Double	35.00	45.00

Open February-November

The Grange

Pencoyd, St Owens Cross, Hereford
HR2 8JY
☎ Harewood End (098 987) 267

Sympathetically renovated farm barn constructed in 1818, with many exposed timbers and cruck beams. Set in walled garden next to 11th C church. Heated outdoor swimming pool, tennis court.
Bedrooms: 1 family room
Bathrooms: 1 private

Bed & breakfast
per night:	£min	£max
Single	17.00	19.50
Double	34.00	39.00

Parking for 10

Lavender Cottage
Listed

Bridstow, Ross-on-Wye, Herefordshire
HR9 6QB
☎ (0989) 62836

Part 17th C character property, 1 mile from Ross-on-Wye. Take Hereford road, turn right to Foy and then first turning on left.
Bedrooms: 1 double, 2 twin
Bathrooms: 1 public

Bed & breakfast
per night:	£min	£max
Single	18.00	20.00
Double	28.00	32.00

Continued ▶

We advise you to confirm your booking in writing.

173

HEART OF ENGLAND

ROSS-ON-WYE
Continued

Half board
per person:	£min	£max
Daily	23.50	24.50
Weekly	154.00	161.00

Evening meal from 1830
Parking for 3

Merrivale Place
APPROVED

The Avenue, Ross-on-Wye, Herefordshire HR9 5AW
☎ (0989) 64929
Fine Victorian house in quiet tree-lined avenue. Large comfortable rooms and lovely views. Home cooking. Near town and river.
Bedrooms: 1 double, 1 twin, 1 triple
Bathrooms: 2 public

Bed & breakfast
per night:	£min	£max
Double	32.00	34.00

Half board
per person:	£min	£max
Daily	25.00	26.00

Evening meal 1830 (last orders 1600)
Parking for 6
Open February-October

Norton House
COMMENDED

Whitchurch, Ross-on-Wye, Herefordshire HR9 6DJ
☎ (0600) 890046
300-year-old former farmhouse, tastefully improved, with wealth of original features. Renowned home cooking, friendly atmosphere, quality and comfort paramount.
Bedrooms: 3 double
Bathrooms: 3 private

Bed & breakfast
per night:	£min	£max
Single	30.00	30.00
Double	40.00	40.00

Half board
per person:	£min	£max
Daily	32.95	32.95

Evening meal from 1900
Parking for 7

Rosswyn Hotel
APPROVED

17 High Street, Ross-on-Wye, Herefordshire HR9 5BZ
☎ (0989) 62733
Conveniently situated 15th C freehouse, just off the market square in a thriving small town. Oak beams, antiques and four-poster beds contribute to the friendly atmosphere.
Bedrooms: 1 single, 5 double, 2 twin
Bathrooms: 7 private, 1 public

Bed & breakfast
per night:	£min	£max
Single	30.00	35.00
Double	40.00	60.00

Half board
per person:	£min	£max
Daily	38.00	45.00

Lunch available
Evening meal 1730 (last orders 1930)
Parking for 6
Cards accepted: Access, Visa, Diners, Amex

Rudhall Farm
HIGHLY COMMENDED

Ross-on-Wye, Herefordshire HR9 7TL
☎ Upton Bishop (098 985) 240

Savour the tranquillity of our elegant farmhouse offering style with comfort. Acclaimed for hospitality. Aga cooked breakfasts. In picturesque valley with lake and millstream. Ideal for exploring the Wye Valley.
Bedrooms: 1 single, 1 double, 1 twin
Bathrooms: 1 private, 1 public

Bed & breakfast
per night:	£min	£max
Single	18.50	20.00
Double	33.00	36.00

Parking for 10

The Skakes

Glewstone, Ross-on-Wye, Herefordshire HR9 6AZ
☎ (0989) 770456
Country guesthouse combining 18th C character with 20th C comforts. Perfect for Symonds Yat, Wye Valley, Forest of Dean. Home cooking.
Bedrooms: 2 single, 4 double, 2 twin
Bathrooms: 2 private, 3 public

Bed & breakfast
per night:	£min	£max
Single	20.00	
Double	30.00	

Half board
per person:	£min	£max
Daily	25.50	
Weekly	157.00	

Evening meal 1900 (last orders 1900)
Parking for 8
Cards accepted: Access, Visa

Thatch Close
COMMENDED

Llangrove, Ross-on-Wye, Herefordshire HR9 6EL
☎ Llangarron (0989) 770300
13-acre mixed farm. Secluded Georgian country farmhouse midway between Ross-on-Wye and Monmouth. Home-produced vegetables and meat. Ideal for country lovers of any age. Guests welcome to help with animals. Map sent on request. Ordnance Survey: 51535196.
Bedrooms: 1 double, 1 twin, 1 triple
Bathrooms: 3 private

Bed & breakfast
per night:	£min	£max
Double	28.00	36.00

Half board
per person:	£min	£max
Daily	24.00	28.00
Weekly	155.00	175.00

Lunch available
Evening meal 1830 (last orders 1800)
Parking for 7

RUGBY
Warwickshire
Map ref 4C3

Town famous for its public school which gave its name to Rugby Union football and which featured in "Tom Brown's Schooldays".
Tourist Information Centre
☎ (0788) 535348

Tibbits Farm

Nethercote, Flecknoe, Rugby CV23 8AS
☎ (0788) 890239
1200-acre mixed farm. 17th C farmhouse offering a high standard of accommodation in beautiful rural setting but close to motorway exits. Two golf-courses, fishing and places of historic interest nearby.
Bedrooms: 2 double
Bathrooms: 2 private

Bed & breakfast
per night:	£min	£max
Single	20.00	25.00
Double	40.00	50.00

Parking for 42

White Lion Inn
Listed APPROVED

Coventry Road, Pailton, Rugby CV23 0QD
☎ (0788) 832359
17th C coaching inn, recently refurbished but maintaining all old world features. Close to Rugby, Coventry and Stratford. Within 2 miles of motorways.
Bedrooms: 6 twin
Bathrooms: 6 private, 2 public

HEART OF ENGLAND

Bed & breakfast per night:	£min	£max
Single		17.50
Double		35.00

Lunch available
Evening meal 1830 (last orders 2200)
Parking for 60
Cards accepted: Access, Visa

RUYTON-XI-TOWNS
Shropshire
Map ref 4A3

Town got its name from the time when, at the beginning of the 14th C, it was one of 11 towns "joined" into 1 manor. It is situated above the River Perry and has the remains of a castle in the churchyard.

Brownhill House
COMMENDED
Ruyton-XI-Towns, Shrewsbury
SY4 1LR
☎ Baschurch (0939) 260226
Comfortable accommodation, relaxed atmosphere, good food and home-grown produce. Extensive breakfast menu. Unique garden bordering River Perry, as seen on TV. Fishing, canoeing, walks, local pubs. Golf and horseriding nearby.
Bedrooms: 1 single, 1 double, 1 twin
Bathrooms: 1 private, 1 public

Bed & breakfast per night:	£min	£max
Single	14.00	15.00
Double	28.00	32.00

Half board per person:	£min	£max
Daily	22.00	24.00

Lunch available
Evening meal from 1800
Parking for 5

SEVERN STOKE
Hereford and Worcester
Map ref 2B1

Village to the south of Worcester with a picturesque group of houses surrounding the church and magnificent views across the Severn to the Malvern Hills.

Madge Hill House
Severn Stoke, Worcester WR8 9JN
☎ (0905) 371362
Georgian house in peaceful country setting, between Tewkesbury and Worcester on A38. En-suite bedrooms with TV.
Bedrooms: 1 double, 1 twin
Bathrooms: 2 private

Bed & breakfast per night:	£min	£max
Single	17.00	17.00
Double	34.00	34.00

Parking for 2

SHELSLEY BEAUCHAMP
Hereford and Worcester
Map ref 2B1

Village on the banks of the River Teme, with hop fields and cherry orchards much in evidence. Nearby Shelsley Walsh is famous for its twice-yearly motor hill climb.

Church House Farm
Shelsley Beauchamp, Worcester
WR6 6RA
☎ (0886) 812393
200-acre mixed farm. 18th C family-run farm on River Teme, with sheep and cattle. Farmhouse food with home-grown vegetables and meats, when available.
Bedrooms: 2 twin
Bathrooms: 2 private

Bed & breakfast per night:	£min	£max
Single	18.00	
Double	30.00	

Half board per person:	£min	£max
Daily	24.50	

Evening meal 1900 (last orders 1100)
Parking for 10
Open April-October

SHIFNAL
Shropshire
Map ref 4A3

Small market town, once an important staging centre for coaches on the Holyhead road. Where industrialism has not prevailed, the predominating architectural impression is Georgian, though some timber-framed houses survived the Great Fire of 1591.

Beech House
COMMENDED
Wolverhampton Road, Shifnal
TF11 9HA
☎ Telford (0952) 460261
Quiet country house with large garden and tennis court. Just under 1 mile from Shifnal on A464. Comfortable rooms.
Bedrooms: 2 twin
Bathrooms: 1 public

Bed & breakfast per night:	£min	£max
Single		17.50
Double		35.00

Parking for 4

SHREWSBURY
Shropshire
Map ref 4A3

Beautiful historic town on the River Severn retaining many fine old timber-framed houses. Its attractions include Rowley's Museum with Roman finds, remains of a castle, Clive House Museum, St Chad's 18th C round church and rowing on the river.
Tourist Information Centre
☎ *(0743) 350761*

Abbey Lodge Guest House
Listed APPROVED
68 Abbey Foregate, Shrewsbury
SY2 6BE
☎ (0743) 235832
Friendly family-run business close to town centre. Evening meals available, parking at rear. Children welcome.
Bedrooms: 4 single, 2 double, 1 twin, 2 triple, 2 family rooms
Bathrooms: 2 private, 2 public, 4 private showers

Bed & breakfast per night:	£min	£max
Single	13.00	18.00
Double	26.00	36.00

Half board per person:	£min	£max
Daily	18.00	23.00
Weekly	126.00	161.00

Evening meal 1800 (last orders 0830)
Parking for 10
Cards accepted: Access, Visa

Ashton Lees
COMMENDED
Dorrington, Shrewsbury SY5 7JW
☎ Dorrington (0743) 718378
Comfortable family home set in large secluded garden, 6 miles south of Shrewsbury on A49. Convenient for exploring Shropshire.
Bedrooms: 2 double, 1 twin
Bathrooms: 1 private, 1 public

Bed & breakfast per night:	£min	£max
Single	16.00	19.00
Double	32.00	38.00

Parking for 6

Cardeston Park Farm
COMMENDED
Ford, Shrewsbury SY5 9NH
☎ (0743) 884265
150-acre mixed farm. Spacious farmhouse set in countryside on the

Continued ▶

175

HEART OF ENGLAND

SHREWSBURY
Continued

English/Welsh border. On A458 Shrewsbury to Welshpool road, 7 miles from Shrewsbury, 13 miles from Welshpool.
Bedrooms: 1 single, 1 double, 1 twin
Bathrooms: 2 private, 1 public

Bed & breakfast

per night:	£min	£max
Single	14.00	20.00
Double	28.00	30.00

Parking for 4

The Castle Vaults Inn
Listed

16 Castle Gates, Shrewsbury SY1 2AB
☎ (0743) 358807

Public house/inn with an open Mexican eating house, situated in the shadows of Shrewsbury Castle. Roof garden. Fully automatic fire alarm system throughout the building.
Bedrooms: 3 single, 2 double, 1 twin, 1 triple
Bathrooms: 4 private, 1 public

Bed & breakfast

per night:	£min	£max
Single	19.00	25.00
Double	38.00	40.00

Lunch available
Evening meal 1800 (last orders 2200)

Chatford House

Bayston Hill, Shrewsbury SY3 0AY
☎ (0743) 718301

5-acre mixed farm. Comfortable farmhouse built in 1776, 5.5 miles south of Shrewsbury off A49. Through Bayston Hill, take third right (Stapleton) then right to Chatford.
Bedrooms: 3 twin
Bathrooms: 1 public

Bed & breakfast

per night:	£min	£max
Double	26.00	

Parking for 4
Open April-October

Haughmond Cottage
Listed

Ebrey Wood, Astley, Shrewsbury SY4 4DD
☎ (0939) 250689

Separate accommodation in a beautifully converted barn in the countryside, 5 miles north of Shrewsbury off the A53 towards Haughton.
Bedrooms: 1 single, 1 double, 1 triple
Bathrooms: 2 public

Bed & breakfast

per night:	£min	£max
Single	15.00	17.50
Double	30.00	35.00

Parking for 8
Open February-December

Hillsboro
Listed

1 Port Hill Gardens, Shrewsbury SY3 8SH
☎ (0743) 231033

Charming Edwardian private house in quiet residential area, near park, river and Shrewsbury School. 5 minutes from town centre. Traditional breakfast a speciality. Parking.
Bedrooms: 1 double, 1 twin
Bathrooms: 1 public

Bed & breakfast

per night:	£min	£max
Single	14.50	14.50
Double	29.00	29.00

Parking for 2

Merevale House
Listed COMMENDED

66 Ellesmere Road, Shrewsbury SY1 2QP
☎ (0743) 243677

Comfortable, attractive, detached Victorian house, 10 minutes' walk from town and railway station. On bus route. Private parking. Many extra home comforts. Brochure. Weekly reductions. Two nights for one October–March.
Bedrooms: 1 single, 3 double
Bathrooms: 1 public

Bed & breakfast

per night:	£min	£max
Single	15.00	15.00
Double	30.00	30.00

Parking for 8

Roseville
HIGHLY COMMENDED

12 Berwick Road, Shrewsbury SY1 2LN
☎ (0743) 236470

Late Victorian detached town house, close to town centre. Comfortable, relaxed atmosphere and fine food. A no-smoking establishment.
Bedrooms: 1 single, 1 double, 1 twin
Bathrooms: 3 private

Bed & breakfast

per night:	£min	£max
Single	17.00	25.00
Double	36.00	40.00

Half board

per person:	£min	£max
Daily	23.50	29.00
Weekly	160.00	200.00

Evening meal 1800 (last orders 2000)
Parking for 3

Shorthill Lodge
COMMENDED

Shorthill, Lea Cross, Shrewsbury SY5 8JE
☎ (0743) 860864

Attractive, comfortable house in open country setting, inglenook log fire and centrally heated in winter. Five miles south of Shrewsbury, off A488. Nearby pub, restaurant and golf course. Brochure available.
Bedrooms: 1 double, 1 twin
Bathrooms: 2 private

Bed & breakfast

per night:	£min	£max
Single	16.00	20.00
Double	30.00	36.00

Parking for 3

The Stiperstones Guest House
COMMENDED

18 Coton Crescent, Coton Hill, Shrewsbury SY1 2NZ
☎ (0743) 246720
Fax (0743) 350303

100-year-old half-timbered property a short stroll from the River Severn and town centre. Located near beautiful countryside.
Bedrooms: 1 single, 1 double, 1 triple
Bathrooms: 2 public

Bed & breakfast

per night:	£min	£max
Single	17.00	18.00
Double	30.00	32.00

Half board

per person:	£min	£max
Daily	23.00	25.50
Weekly	145.00	160.00

Evening meal 1900 (last orders 1200)
Parking for 8

Sydney House Hotel
APPROVED

Coton Crescent, Coton Hill, Shrewsbury SY1 2LJ
☎ (0743) 354681

Edwardian town house with period features, 10 minutes' walk from town

176

HEART OF ENGLAND

centre and railway station. Most rooms en-suite. All with direct dial telephone, colour TV, hot drink facilities and hairdryer.
Bedrooms: 2 single, 2 double, 2 twin, 1 triple
Bathrooms: 4 private, 2 public

Bed & breakfast
per night:	£min	£max
Single	32.00	45.00
Double	42.00	65.00

Half board
per person:	£min	£max
Daily	30.00	50.00
Weekly	200.00	340.00

Lunch available
Evening meal 1930 (last orders 2100)
Parking for 7
Cards accepted: Access, Visa, Amex

SLIMBRIDGE
Gloucestershire
Map ref 2B1

The Wildfowl and Wetlands Trust Centre was founded by Sir Peter Scott and has the world's largest collection of wildfowl. Of special interest are the wild swans and the geese which wander around the grounds.

Tudor Arms Lodge
Shepherds Patch, Slimbridge, Gloucester GL2 7BP
☎ Dursley (0453) 890306
Newly-built lodge adjoining an 18th C freehouse, alongside Gloucester and Sharpness Canal. Renowned Slimbridge Wildfowl and Wetlands Trust centre only 800 yards away.
Bedrooms: 4 double, 5 twin, 2 triple, 1 family room
Bathrooms: 12 private

Bed & breakfast
per night:	£min	£max
Single	29.50	32.50
Double	39.50	42.50

Half board
per person:	£min	£max
Daily	28.00	40.00

Lunch available
Evening meal 1900 (last orders 2200)
Parking for 70
Cards accepted: Access, Visa

National Crown ratings were correct at the time of going to press but are subject to change. Please check at the time of booking.

SOLIHULL
West Midlands
Map ref 4B3

On the outskirts of Birmingham. Some Tudor houses and a 13th C church remain amongst the new public buildings and shopping centre. The 16th C Malvern Hall is now a school and the 15th C Chester House at Knowle is now a library.
Tourist Information Centre
☎ 021-704 6130

The Gate House
Listed
Barston Lane, Barston, Solihull B92 0JN
☎ Barston (0675) 443274
Early Victorian mansion house set in beautiful countryside. Close to the National Exhibition Centre, International Convention Centre, airport and motorway.
Bedrooms: 1 single, 1 double, 2 twin
Bathrooms: 3 private, 1 public

Bed & breakfast
per night:	£min	£max
Single	20.00	25.00
Double	36.00	40.00

Parking for 20

STAFFORD
Staffordshire
Map ref 4B3

The town has a long history and some half-timbered buildings still remain, notably the 16th C High House. There are several museums in the town and Shugborough Hall and the famous angler Izaak Walton's cottage, now a museum, are nearby.
Tourist Information Centre
☎ (0785) 40204

Oakleigh
Salters Lane, Enson, Stafford ST18 9TA
☎ Sandon (088 97) 432
A converted barn offering privacy and quietness in the countryside. Fresh food served in a large conservatory. 4 miles north of Stafford off A34.
Bedrooms: 1 double, 1 twin
Bathrooms: 2 private

Bed & breakfast
per night:	£min	£max
Single	24.00	
Double	36.00	

Parking for 4

Park Farm
Weston Road, Stafford ST18 0BD
☎ (0785) 40257

250-acre dairy farm. Three-hundred-year-old farmhouse situated on the A518 by the county showground with lovely views over surrounding countryside.
Bedrooms: 1 twin, 1 triple
Bathrooms: 2 private

Bed & breakfast
per night:	£min	£max
Single	17.50	17.50
Double	30.00	30.00

Parking for 4

STIPERSTONES
Shropshire
Map ref 4A3

Below the spectacular ridge of the same name, from which superb views over moorland, forest and hills may be enjoyed.

Tankerville Lodge
COMMENDED
Stiperstones, Minsterley, Shrewsbury SY5 0NB
☎ Shrewsbury (0743) 791401
Country house noted for warm hospitality, set in superb landscape which offers breathtaking views. Ideal touring base for Shropshire and Welsh borderland. Adjacent to Stiperstones Nature Reserve.
Bedrooms: 1 double, 3 twin
Bathrooms: 2 public

Bed & breakfast
per night:	£min	£max
Single	15.25	17.75
Double	30.50	30.50

Half board
per person:	£min	£max
Daily	23.25	25.75
Weekly	152.07	169.57

Evening meal 1900 (last orders 1600)
Parking for 5

STOKE LACY
Hereford and Worcester
Map ref 2A1

Small village by the River Leadon a few miles from Bromyard and Lower Brockhampton Manor House. The 14th C half-timbered manor house of Lower Brockhampton (National Trust) is nearby.

Nether Court
COMMENDED
Stoke Lacy, Bromyard, Herefordshire HR7 4HJ
☎ Hereford (0432) 820247

Continued ▶

HEART OF ENGLAND

STOKE LACY
Continued

300-acre mixed farm. Victorian farmhouse in peaceful village surroundings. Tennis court. Small lake for wildlife. Good restaurant within walking distance. Near Hereford, Ludlow, Malvern, Leominster and Worcester.
Bedrooms: 1 single, 1 double, 1 triple
Bathrooms: 2 private, 1 public

Bed & breakfast

per night:	£min	£max
Single	18.00	
Double	28.00	

Evening meal from 1800

STOKE-ON-TRENT

Staffordshire
Map ref 4B2

Famous for its pottery. Factories of several famous makers, including Josiah Wedgwood, can be visited. The City Museum has one of the finest pottery and porcelain collections in the world.
Tourist Information Centre
☎ (0782) 284600

The Hollies

Clay Lake, Endon, Stoke-on-Trent ST9 9DD
☎ (0782) 503252
Delightful Victorian house in a quiet country setting off B5051. Convenient for M6, the Potteries and Alton Towers. Non-smokers only, please.
Bedrooms: 2 double, 1 twin, 2 triple
Bathrooms: 3 private, 1 public

Bed & breakfast

per night:	£min	£max
Single	20.00	25.00
Double	30.00	36.00

Parking for 5

The Limes

Cheadle Road, Blythe Bridge, Stoke-on-Trent ST11 9PW
☎ Blythe Bridge (0782) 393278
Victorian residence of character in large, landscaped gardens, near Alton Towers, Wedgwood, the Potteries and Staffordshire Moorlands.
Bedrooms: 1 single, 1 double, 1 triple
Bathrooms: 1 public, 2 private showers

Bed & breakfast

per night:	£min	£max
Single	19.00	20.00
Double	34.00	36.00

Parking for 8

White Gables Hotel

Trentham Road, Blurton, Stoke-on-Trent ST3 3DT
☎ (0782) 324882
Fax (0782) 598302
Elegant, peaceful country house style hotel in own grounds. Beautifully maintained, with good facilities for discerning businessmen and families alike. Owner run. 1 mile from Wedgwood, 10 miles from Alton Towers.
Bedrooms: 1 single, 2 double, 3 twin, 1 triple, 2 family rooms
Bathrooms: 3 private, 2 public, 1 private shower

Bed & breakfast

per night:	£min	£max
Single	15.00	25.00
Double	30.00	50.00

Half board

per person:	£min	£max
Daily	20.00	30.00

Evening meal 1700 (last orders 1900)
Parking for 11
Cards accepted: Access, Visa, Diners, Amex

White House Hotel

94 Stone Road, Trent Vale, Stoke-on-Trent ST4 6SP
☎ (0782) 642460 & 657189
A warm, friendly, early Victorian house. 1 mile from M6 motorway, junction 15. Easy access to the world-famous Potteries and local tourist attractions.
Bedrooms: 5 single, 2 double, 2 twin, 1 triple
Bathrooms: 4 private, 2 public

Bed & breakfast

per night:	£min	£max
Single	23.00	35.00
Double	36.00	46.00

Evening meal 1900 (last orders 1730)
Parking for 11
Cards accepted: Access, Visa, Diners, Amex

STONE

Staffordshire
Map ref 4B2

Town on the River Trent with the remains of a 12th C Augustinian priory. It is surrounded by pleasant countryside. Trentham Gardens with 500 acres of parklands and recreational facilities is within easy reach.

Couldreys
COMMENDED

8 Airdale Road, Stone ST15 8DW
☎ (0785) 812500
Fax (0785) 811761
Large Edwardian house and garden, quietly situated on the outskirts of a small market town. Convenient for M6, Wedgwood and Potteries. Non-smokers only please.
Bedrooms: 1 twin
Bathrooms: 1 private

Bed & breakfast

per night:	£min	£max
Single		20.00
Double		30.00

Parking for 2

STONEHOUSE

Gloucestershire
Map ref 2B1

Village in the Stroud Valley with an Elizabethan Court, later restored and altered by Lutyens.

Merton Lodge

8 Ebley Road, Stonehouse GL10 2LQ
☎ (0453) 822018
Former gentleman's residence offering a warm welcome. No smoking in the house. Three miles from junction 13 of M5. Take A419 to Stroud, over 3 roundabouts, under footbridge - located opposite garden centre.
Bedrooms: 3 double
Bathrooms: 1 private, 2 public

Bed & breakfast

per night:	£min	£max
Single	13.00	13.00
Double	26.00	26.00

Parking for 6

National Crown ratings were correct at the time of going to press but are subject to change. Please check at the time of booking.

Individual proprietors have supplied all details of accommodation. Although we do check for accuracy, we advise you to confirm the information at the time of booking.

178

HEART OF ENGLAND

STOURBRIDGE
West Midlands
Map ref 4B3

Town on the River Stour, famous for its glassworks. Several of the factories can be visited and glassware purchased at the factory shops.

St. Elizabeth's Cottage
COMMENDED

Woodman Lane, Clent, Stourbridge DY9 9PX
☎ Hagley (0562) 883883
Beautiful country cottage with lovely gardens and interior professionally decorated throughout. 20 minutes from Birmingham and close to motorway links.
Bedrooms: 1 twin
Bathrooms: 1 public

Bed & breakfast
per night:	£min	£max
Single	19.00	20.00
Double	38.00	40.00

Parking for 2

STOURPORT-ON-SEVERN
Hereford and Worcester
Map ref 4B3

Town standing at the confluence of the Rivers Stour and Severn and on the Staffordshire and Worcestershire Canal which was built in the 18th C and is now a popular place for pleasure boats. Some fine Georgian houses remain.

Worrall's Farm
Listed

Netherton Lane, Dunley, Stourport-on-Severn, Worcestershire DY13 0UL
☎ Great Witley (0299) 896245
5-acre smallholding. Early 18th C mill house near the Severn Valley. A millstream setting amid rolling Worcestershire countryside.
Bedrooms: 1 triple
Bathrooms: 1 public

Bed & breakfast
per night:	£min	£max
Double	25.00	28.00

Parking for 2
Open April-October

The national Crown scheme is explained in full in the information pages towards the back of this guide.

STOW-ON-THE-WOLD
Gloucestershire
Map ref 2B1

Attractive Cotswold wool town with a large market-place and some fine houses, especially the old grammar school. There is an interesting church dating from Norman times. Stow-on-the-Wold is surrounded by lovely countryside and Cotswold villages.
Tourist Information Centre
☎ *(0451) 31082*

Bretton House
HIGHLY COMMENDED

Fosseway, Stow-on-the-Wold, Cheltenham GL54 1JU
☎ Cotswold (0451) 830388
Fine Victorian house in own grounds with glorious views of the Cotswolds. Tastefully refurbished, providing accommodation of a good standard and friendly atmosphere.
Bedrooms: 2 double, 1 twin
Bathrooms: 3 private

Bed & breakfast
per night:	£min	£max
Double		40.00

Half board
per person:	£min	£max
Daily		32.50

Evening meal 1900 (last orders 2100)
Parking for 10

Corsham Field Farmhouse
Listed

Bledington Road, Stow-on-the-Wold, Cheltenham GL54 1JH
☎ Cotswold (0451) 831750
100-acre mixed farm. Homely farmhouse with breathtaking views. Heating, TVs, washbasins, tea and coffee making facilities in all bedrooms. Good pub food 5 minutes' walk away.
Bedrooms: 1 double, 1 twin, 1 triple
Bathrooms: 1 private, 2 public

Bed & breakfast
per night:	£min	£max
Single	15.00	25.00
Double	24.00	35.00

Parking for 10

Journeys End
Listed APPROVED

Evenlode, Moreton-in-Marsh GL56 0NN
☎ Moreton-in-Marsh (0608) 650786
20-acre mixed farm. Peaceful, comfortable, modernised 18th C farmhouse in quiet village. Approximately 3 miles from Moreton-in-Marsh and Stow-on-the-Wold. One ground floor bedroom.
Bedrooms: 1 double, 1 triple
Bathrooms: 2 private

Bed & breakfast
per night:	£min	£max
Single	16.00	20.00
Double	32.00	38.00

Parking for 5

Old Farmhouse Hotel
APPROVED

Lower Swell, Stow-on-the-Wold, Cheltenham GL54 1LF
☎ Cotswold (0451) 830232
Fax (0451) 870962
Sympathetically converted 16th C Cotswold-stone farmhouse in a quiet hamlet, 1 mile west of Stow-on-the-Wold. Offers warm and unpretentious hospitality.
Bedrooms: 9 double, 4 twin, 1 family room
Bathrooms: 12 private, 1 public

Bed & breakfast
per night:	£min	£max
Single	22.00	48.00
Double	41.00	84.00

Half board
per person:	£min	£max
Daily	36.50	62.50
Weekly	250.00	425.00

Lunch available
Evening meal 1900 (last orders 2100)
Parking for 25
Cards accepted: Access, Visa

Royalist Hotel

Digbeth Street, Stow-on-the-Wold, Cheltenham GL54 1BN
☎ Cotswold (0451) 830670
The oldest inn in England (947 AD) with all the inherent charm and character of the past, yet every modern day facility as well.
Bedrooms: 7 double, 2 twin, 3 triple
Bathrooms: 12 private

Bed & breakfast
per night:	£min	£max
Single	35.00	50.00
Double	50.00	75.00

Lunch available
Parking for 10
Cards accepted: Access, Visa, Amex

South Hill Farmhouse

Fosseway, Stow-on-the-Wold, Cheltenham GL54 1JU
☎ Cotswold (0451) 831219
Fax (0451) 831219
Base your touring holiday in this Victorian farmhouse. Individually furnished and spacious rooms, a hearty breakfast, lounge with open fires.
Bedrooms: 2 double, 1 twin, 2 triple
Bathrooms: 4 private, 1 public

Continued ▶

HEART OF ENGLAND

STOW-ON-THE-WOLD
Continued

Bed & breakfast
per night:	£min	£max
Double	30.00	36.00

Parking for 6

South Hill Lodge
Fosseway, Stow-on-the-Wold,
Cheltenham GL54 1JU
☎ Cotswold (0451) 831083
Homely, family-run Victorian lodge house with superb views over the Cotswold Hills.
Bedrooms: 2 double, 1 twin
Bathrooms: 1 private, 1 public

Bed & breakfast
per night:	£min	£max
Double	30.00	36.00

Parking for 6
Open February-November

Map references apply to the colour maps at the back of this guide.

STRATFORD-UPON-AVON
Warwickshire
Map ref 2B1

Famous as Shakespeare's home town, Stratford's many attractions include his birthplace, New Place where he died, the Royal Shakespeare Theatre and Gallery, "The World of Shakespeare" audio-visual theatre and Hall's Croft (his daughter's house).
Tourist Information Centre
☎ (0789) 293127

Abberley
COMMENDED
12 Albany Road, Stratford-upon-Avon CV37 6PG
☎ (0789) 295934
Comfortable home set in a quiet residential area yet within easy walking distance of theatres and town centre. Non-smokers only please.
Bedrooms: 1 twin
Bathrooms: 1 private

Bed & breakfast
per night:	£min	£max
Double	40.00	44.00

Parking for 2

Allors
Listed
62 Evesham Road, Stratford-upon-Avon CV37 9BA
☎ (0789) 269982
Comfortable en-suite accommodation in detached house with private sitting facilities. Non-smoking. TV. Parking. Reductions two or more nights.
Bedrooms: 1 double, 1 twin
Bathrooms: 2 private

Bed & breakfast
per night:	£min	£max
Double	30.00	36.00

Parking for 3
Open March-October

Cherangani
COMMENDED
61 Maidenhead Road, Stratford-upon-Avon CV37 6XU
☎ (0789) 292655
Pleasant detached house in a quiet, residential area, offering warm, attractive accommodation. Within walking distance of the town and theatre.
Bedrooms: 1 twin
Bathrooms: 1 public

English Tourist Board COMMENDED

Oxstalls Farm Stud
For Farmhouse Bed & Breakfast

Warwick Road
Stratford on Avon
Warwickshire. CV37 4NR
[0789] 205277

The Barn
Built 1840 & a Listed Building

- Five minutes from The Royal Shakespeare Theatre.
- One mile from town centre Shakespeare properties
- Thoroughbred Stud Farm, overlooking beautiful Welcombe Hills
- Adjacent to 18 hole Golf Course
- All rooms are pleasantly furnished many with ensuite facilities and TV, Tea & Coffee making etc.
- Convenient for touring the Cotswolds
- Twenty minutes from the N.E.C. Birmingham.
- Additional en suite rooms in the Cow Shed & Stables Complex
- Easy access from Junction 15 M40.

* Also the Old Cowshed has now been renovated into delightful ensuite bedrooms

Prices
From £15.00 per person
to
£25.00 per person

Main House

Oxstalls Farm is situated on the A439. Stratford Road to Warwick. 1 mile from Stratford on Avon

HEART OF ENGLAND

Bed & breakfast

per night:	£min	£max
Single	15.00	17.00
Double	30.00	34.00

Parking for 3

Church Farm ⋒
COMMENDED

Dorsington, Stratford-upon-Avon
CV37 8AX
☎ (0789) 720471 & (0831) 504194
127-acre mixed farm. Situated in beautiful countryside, some rooms en-suite, TV, tea and coffee facilities. Close to Stratford-upon-Avon, Warwick, the Cotswolds and Evesham.
Bedrooms: 3 double, 2 twin, 2 family rooms
Bathrooms: 4 private, 2 public

Bed & breakfast

per night:	£min	£max
Double	27.00	32.00

Parking for 12

Clomendy Guest House ⋒

157 Evesham Road, Stratford-upon-Avon CV37 9BP
☎ (0789) 266957

Small, detached, mock-Tudor family-run guesthouse, convenient for town centre, Anne Hathaway's cottage and theatres. Stratford-in-Bloom commendation winner. Rail/coach guests met and returned.
Bedrooms: 1 single, 1 double, 1 twin
Bathrooms: 1 public, 1 private shower

Bed & breakfast

per night:	£min	£max
Single	14.00	16.00
Double	24.00	32.00

Parking for 4

Curtain Call
Listed

142 Alcester Road, Stratford-upon-Avon CV37 9DR
☎ (0789) 267734
One mile from centre of Stratford. All rooms have own TV, shower, WC, tea/coffee-making facilities and hairdryer. Non-smoking establishment.
Bedrooms: 2 single, 1 double, 1 twin, 1 triple
Bathrooms: 3 private, 1 public

Bed & breakfast

per night:	£min	£max
Single	15.00	16.50
Double	30.00	35.00

Half board

per person:	£min	£max
Daily	20.00	24.00
Weekly	147.00	160.00

Evening meal 1730 (last orders 2000)
Parking for 5

Field View ⋒
APPROVED

35 Banbury Road, Stratford-upon-Avon CV37 7HW
☎ (0789) 292694
10 minutes' walk from Stratford town centre, offering comfortable, family-type accommodation.
Bedrooms: 1 double
Bathrooms: 1 public

Bed & breakfast

per night:	£min	£max
Single	14.00	16.00
Double	28.00	32.00

Parking for 3

Gravelside Barn ⋒
HIGHLY COMMENDED

Binton, Stratford-upon-Avon
CV37 9TU
☎ (0789) 750502 & 297000
Fax (0789) 298056
A peaceful converted barn, set on a hill in farmland. Magnificent views, great breakfasts. Easy access to motorways and Stratford-upon-Avon.
Bedrooms: 2 double, 1 twin
Bathrooms: 3 private

Bed & breakfast

per night:	£min	£max
Single	35.00	40.00
Double	50.00	60.00

Parking for 6
Cards accepted: Access, Visa

Green Gables ⋒
COMMENDED

47 Banbury Road, Stratford-upon-Avon CV37 7HW
☎ (0789) 205557
Edwardian house in a residential area, within 10 minutes' walk of the town centre and theatre.
Bedrooms: 1 double
Bathrooms: 1 private, 1 public

Bed & breakfast

per night:	£min	£max
Double	31.00	37.00

Parking for 3

Highcroft ⋒
APPROVED

Banbury Road, Stratford-upon-Avon CV37 7NF
☎ (0789) 296293

Lovely country house in 2-acre garden, only 2 miles from Stratford-upon-Avon, on A422. Families welcome. Friendly, relaxed atmosphere.
Bedrooms: 1 double, 1 family room
Bathrooms: 2 private

Bed & breakfast

per night:	£min	£max
Single	17.50	20.00
Double	30.00	36.00

Parking for 3

Kawartha House ⋒
Listed

39 Grove Road, Stratford-upon-Avon CV37 6PB
☎ (0789) 204469
Fax (0789) 262076

Well-appointed townhouse with friendly atmosphere, overlooking old town park. Few minutes' walk from town centre and places of historic interest. En-suite facilities, parking.
Bedrooms: 1 single, 1 double, 2 twin, 2 triple, 1 family room
Bathrooms: 2 private, 1 public, 2 private showers

Bed & breakfast

per night:	£min	£max
Single	13.00	19.00
Double	28.00	41.00

Parking for 4

Moonlight Bed & Breakfast ⋒
Listed

144 Alcester Road, Stratford-upon-Avon CV37 9DR
☎ (0789) 298213
Small family guesthouse near town centre, offering comfortable accommodation at reasonable prices. All rooms en-suite and with tea/coffee making facilities.
Bedrooms: 1 double, 1 twin, 1 triple
Bathrooms: 3 private

Bed & breakfast

per night:	£min	£max
Single	13.00	15.00
Double	26.00	30.00

Parking for 3

181

HEART OF ENGLAND

STRATFORD-UPON-AVON
Continued

Moonraker House
COMMENDED
40 Alcester Road, Stratford-upon-Avon
CV37 9DB
☎ (0789) 299346 & 267115
Fax (0789) 295504

Family-run, near town centre. Beautifully co-ordinated decor throughout. Some rooms with four-poster beds and garden terrace available for non-smokers.
Bedrooms: 19 double, 3 twin, 2 triple
Bathrooms: 24 private

Bed & breakfast
per night:	£min	£max
Single	28.00	36.00
Double	39.00	62.00

Parking for 24
Cards accepted: Access, Visa

Moss Cottage
COMMENDED
61 Evesham Road, Stratford-upon-Avon CV37 9BA
☎ (0789) 294770

Attractive detached cottage. Spacious full en-suite accommodation. English breakfast (and free range eggs). Hospitality tray and TV in bedroom. Reduction for 2 or more nights.
Bedrooms: 2 double
Bathrooms: 2 private

Bed & breakfast
per night:	£min	£max
Single	28.00	30.00
Double	34.00	38.00

Parking for 3
Open March-November

Newlands
COMMENDED
7 Broad Walk, Stratford-upon-Avon
CV37 6HS
☎ (0789) 298449

Park your car at Sue Boston's home and take a short walk to the Royal Shakespeare Theatre, town centre and Shakespeare properties.
Bedrooms: 1 single, 1 double, 1 twin
Bathrooms: 2 private, 1 public

Please mention this guide when making a booking.

Bed & breakfast
per night:	£min	£max
Single	15.00	17.50
Double	30.00	40.00

Parking for 2

One Acre Guest House
One Acre, Barton Road, Welford-on-Avon, Stratford-upon-Avon CV37 8EZ
☎ (0789) 750477

Family house in Shakespearean village with countryside views and a warm friendly atmosphere. 4 miles from Stratford-upon-Avon, off B439.
Bedrooms: 1 double, 1 twin, 1 triple
Bathrooms: 3 private

Bed & breakfast
per night:	£min	£max
Single	18.00	22.00
Double	30.00	33.00

Half board
per person:	£min	£max
Daily	22.50	25.50

Evening meal 1800 (last orders 2100)
Parking for 6

Oxstalls Farm
COMMENDED
Warwick Road, Stratford-upon-Avon
CV37 0NS
☎ (0789) 205277

60-acre stud farm. Beautifully situated overlooking the Welcome Hills and golf course. 1 mile from Stratford-upon-Avon town centre and the Royal Shakespeare Theatre.
Bedrooms: 1 single, 7 double, 4 twin, 7 triple
Bathrooms: 11 private, 2 public, 3 private showers

Bed & breakfast
per night:	£min	£max
Single	15.00	25.00
Double	32.00	50.00

Parking for 20

Ad Display advertisement appears on page 180

Penshurst Guesthouse
APPROVED
34 Evesham Place, Stratford-upon-Avon CV37 6HT
☎ (0789) 205259 & 295322
Fax (0789) 295322

Centrally located family-run guesthouse offering a warm welcome and en-suite facilities in most rooms. Fluent French spoken.
Bedrooms: 2 single, 1 double, 1 twin, 2 triple, 2 family rooms
Bathrooms: 2 private, 2 public

Bed & breakfast
per night:	£min	£max
Single	15.00	22.00
Double	29.00	44.00

Half board
per person:	£min	£max
Daily	22.00	32.00
Weekly	150.00	200.00

Evening meal 1800 (last orders 1400)

The Poplars
Listed
Mansell Farm, Newbold-on-Stour, Stratford-upon-Avon CV37 8BZ
☎ (0789) 450540

172-acre dairy farm. Modern farmhouse, within walking distance of village with shop, church and 2 pubs which serve good food. Six miles south of Stratford-upon-Avon on A3400.
Bedrooms: 1 single, 1 double, 1 twin
Bathrooms: 1 private, 1 public

Bed & breakfast
per night:	£min	£max
Single	13.00	15.00
Double	30.00	35.00

Half board
per person:	£min	£max
Daily	20.50	22.50
Weekly	130.00	140.00

Evening meal 1830 (last orders 2000)
Parking for 3
Open March-October

Ravenhurst
2 Broad Walk, Stratford-upon-Avon
CV37 6HS
☎ (0789) 292515

Quietly situated, a few minutes' walk from the town centre and places of historic interest. Comfortable home, with substantial breakfast provided. Four-poster en-suite available.
Bedrooms: 5 double, 1 twin
Bathrooms: 4 private, 1 public

Bed & breakfast
per night:	£min	£max
Double	32.00	44.00

Parking for 4
Cards accepted: Access, Visa, Diners, Amex

Sequoia House
51-53 Shipston Road, Stratford-upon-Avon CV37 7LN
☎ (0789) 268852 & 294940
Fax (0789) 414559

HEART OF ENGLAND

Beautifully-appointed private hotel with large car park and delightful garden walk to the theatre, riverside gardens and Shakespeare properties. Fully air-conditioned dining room.
Bedrooms: 2 single, 10 double, 12 twin
Bathrooms: 20 private, 3 public, 1 private shower

Bed & breakfast

per night:	£min	£max
Single	29.00	49.00
Double	39.00	72.00

Lunch available
Evening meal 1800 (last orders 1930)
Parking for 33
Cards accepted: Access, Visa, Diners, Amex

Thirkleby
Listed
60 Evesham Road, Stratford-upon-Avon CV37 9BA
☎ (0789) 298640
Elegant town house, tastefully furnished, within walking distance of town and theatre. Parking. En-suite rooms overlooking delightful secluded gardens.
Bedrooms: 1 single, 1 double, 1 twin
Bathrooms: 1 public, 2 private showers

Bed & breakfast

per night:	£min	£max
Single	16.00	18.00
Double	30.00	36.00

Parking for 3

Whitchurch Farm
Wimpston, Stratford-upon-Avon CV37 8NS
☎ Alderminster (0789) 450275
260-acre mixed farm. Listed Georgian farmhouse set in park-like surroundings on the edge of the Cotswolds. Ideal for a touring holiday. Small village 4 miles south of Stratford-upon-Avon.
Bedrooms: 2 double, 1 twin
Bathrooms: 3 private, 2 public

Bed & breakfast

per night:	£min	£max
Single	14.00	18.00
Double	28.00	36.00

Half board

per person:	£min	£max
Daily	23.00	27.00

Evening meal from 1830
Parking for 3

Wood View
HIGHLY COMMENDED
Pathlow, Stratford-upon-Avon CV37 0RQ
☎ (0789) 295778
Beautifully situated comfortable home, with fine views over fields and woods. Ideal for touring Stratford-upon-Avon and the Cotswolds.

Bedrooms: 2 twin
Bathrooms: 2 private

Bed & breakfast

per night:	£min	£max
Single	20.00	28.00
Double	40.00	56.00

Parking for 6

STROUD
Gloucestershire
Map ref 2B1

This old town has been producing broadcloth for centuries and the local museum has an interesting display on the subject. It is surrounded by attractive hilly country.
Tourist Information Centre
☎ (0453) 765768

Cairngall Guest House
APPROVED
65 Bisley Old Road, Stroud GL5 1NF
☎ (0453) 764595
Unique, Bath-stone house in French style with porticoed west front, furnished to complement the architectural design.
Bedrooms: 1 double, 1 triple
Bathrooms: 1 public

Bed & breakfast

per night:	£min	£max
Single	12.00	16.00
Double	28.00	32.00

Parking for 3
Open February-December

Downfield Hotel
134 Cainscross Road, Stroud GL5 4HN
☎ (0453) 764496

Imposing Georgian house in quiet location. Home cooking. 1 mile from town centre, 5 miles from M5 motorway, junction 13, on main A419 road.
Bedrooms: 4 single, 9 double, 7 twin, 1 triple
Bathrooms: 11 private, 3 public

Bed & breakfast

per night:	£min	£max
Single	20.00	29.00
Double	29.00	35.00

Half board

per person:	£min	£max
Daily	25.00	50.00
Weekly	175.00	273.00

Evening meal 1830 (last orders 2000)
Parking for 23
Cards accepted: Access, Visa

The Frith
COMMENDED
Slad, Stroud GL6 7QD
☎ Painswick (0452) 814117
Family house set in one and a half acres, on B4070 Stroud to Birdlip road. Panoramic views of the Slad Valley, in an area of outstanding natural beauty near the Cotswold Way. Golf and riding nearby.
Bedrooms: 3 double
Bathrooms: 1 private, 1 public

Bed & breakfast

per night:	£min	£max
Single	22.00	25.00
Double	30.00	36.00

Parking for 6

Hawthorns
Lower Littleworth, Amberley, Stroud GL5 5AW
☎ Amberley (0453) 873535
Grade II listed Queen Anne house in National Trust setting. Glorious 20-mile views. Wild badgers (floodlit) feed at nightfall within touching distance. Exceptional walking country, riding, hot-air ballooning. Warm welcome.
Bedrooms: 2 double, 1 twin
Bathrooms: 3 private

Bed & breakfast

per night:	£min	£max
Single	20.00	30.00
Double	28.00	38.00

Parking for 3
Open March-October and Christmas

SYMONDS YAT WEST
Hereford and Worcester
Map ref 2A1

Jubilee Maze and Exhibition was created here in 1977 to commemorate Queen Elizabeth II's Jubilee, and there are other attractions beside the river. The area of Symonds Yat is a world-renowned beauty spot.

Riversdale Lodge Hotel
COMMENDED
Symonds Yat West, Ross-on-Wye, Herefordshire HR9 6BL
☎ (0600) 890445
High standard accommodation, set in 2 acres on the banks of the River Wye. Spectacular views of the rapids and gorge. Traditional food.
Bedrooms: 4 double, 1 family room
Bathrooms: 5 private, 1 public

Continued ▶

183

HEART OF ENGLAND

SYMONDS YAT WEST
Continued

Bed & breakfast per night:	£min	£max
Single	24.00	27.00
Double	46.00	54.00

Half board per person:	£min	£max
Daily	34.00	36.00
Weekly	238.00	252.00

Evening meal 1900 (last orders 1300)
Parking for 11

TEDDINGTON
Gloucestershire
Map ref 2B1

Village a few miles east of Tewkesbury and north of Cheltenham, with just a few farms and houses, but an interesting church.

Bengrove Farm
APPROVED
Bengrove, Teddington, Tewkesbury GL20 8JB
☎ Cheltenham (0242) 620332
10-acre mixed farm. Large, interesting 14th C farmhouse with attractive rooms, timbered and beamed. 2 twin rooms, lounge and guests' bathroom. Comfortably furnished.
Bedrooms: 2 twin
Bathrooms: 1 public

Bed & breakfast per night:	£min	£max
Single	16.00	16.00
Double	28.00	28.00

Parking for 10

TELFORD
Shropshire
Map ref 4A3

New Town named after Thomas Telford, the famous engineer who designed many of the country's canals, bridges and viaducts. It is close to Ironbridge with its monuments and museums to the Industrial Revolution, including restored 18th C buildings.
Tourist Information Centre
☎ *(0952) 291370*

Allscott Inn
APPROVED
Walcot, Wellington, Telford TF6 5EQ
☎ (0952) 248484
Homely country inn offering delicious food and comfortable accommodation. Beer garden. Easy access Shrewsbury, Ironbridge and Telford.
Bedrooms: 2 double, 2 twin
Bathrooms: 2 private, 1 public

Bed & breakfast per night:	£min	£max
Single	22.00	30.00
Double	35.00	40.00

Lunch available
Evening meal 1900 (last orders 2200)
Parking for 50
Cards accepted: Amex

The Lodge
Listed
Adeney, Newport TF10 8LY
☎ Newport (0952) 820255
Old farmhouse in quiet surroundings, conveniently situated for Telford, historic Ironbridge, Shrewsbury, the Potteries and Lilleshall National Sports Centre.
Bedrooms: 1 single, 2 twin
Bathrooms: 2 public

Bed & breakfast per night:	£min	£max
Single	12.00	15.00
Double	24.00	30.00

Parking for 4

Old Rectory
Stirchley Village, Telford TF3 1DY
☎ (0952) 596308
Large, comfortable guesthouse dating from 1734. Set in an acre of secluded gardens, on edge of town park. Convenient for town centre and Ironbridge museums. Three miles from M54 junction 4.
Bedrooms: 2 single, 2 twin, 1 family room
Bathrooms: 1 private, 2 public

Bed & breakfast per night:	£min	£max
Single	20.00	
Double	30.00	

Half board per person:	£min	£max
Daily		27.00
Weekly		189.00

Evening meal 1800 (last orders 2100)
Parking for 6

Old Vicarage
Church Street, St Georges, Telford TF2 9LZ
☎ (0952) 616437
Former Victorian vicarage with extensive landscaped gardens, close to M54 junction 4, convenient for Telford town centre and Ironbridge.
Bedrooms: 2 double, 1 twin
Bathrooms: 2 private, 1 public

We advise you to confirm your booking in writing.

Bed & breakfast per night:	£min	£max
Single	22.00	27.00
Double	34.00	37.00

Parking for 6

TETBURY
Gloucestershire
Map ref 2B2

Small market town with 18th C houses and an attractive 17th C Town Hall. It is a good touring centre with many places of interest nearby including Badminton House and Westonbirt Arboretum.

Tavern House
DE LUXE
Willesley, Tetbury GL8 8QU
☎ (0666) 880444

A Grade II listed Cotswold stone house (formerly a staging post) on the A433 Bath road, 1 mile from Westonbirt Arboretum and 4 miles from Tetbury.
Bedrooms: 3 double, 1 twin
Bathrooms: 4 private

Bed & breakfast per night:	£min	£max
Single	35.00	55.00
Double	49.00	57.00

Parking for 4
Cards accepted: Access, Visa

TEWKESBURY
Gloucestershire
Map ref 2B1

Tewkesbury's outstanding possession is its magnificent church, built as an abbey, with a great Norman tower and beautiful 14th C interior. The town stands at the confluence of the Severn and Avon and has many old houses, inns and several museums.
Tourist Information Centre
☎ *(0684) 295027*

Abbots Court Farm
APPROVED
Church End, Twyning, Tewkesbury GL20 6DA
☎ (0684) 292515
450-acre arable & dairy farm. Large, comfortable farmhouse in excellent touring area. Most rooms en-suite, 3 games rooms, grass tennis court. Fishing available.

HEART OF ENGLAND

Bedrooms: 1 single, 1 double, 2 twin,
1 triple, 2 family rooms
Bathrooms: 3 private, 1 public

Bed & breakfast
per night:	£min	£max
Single	16.50	18.50
Double	27.00	31.00

Half board
per person:	£min	£max
Daily	22.00	24.00
Weekly	139.00	154.00

Evening meal 1830 (last orders 1830)
Parking for 20
Cards accepted: Visa

Newton Farm
APPROVED

Ashchurch, Tewkesbury GL20 7BE
☎ (0684) 295903
10-acre smallholding. Easy to find accommodation, half a mile off the M5 at junction 9, then on the A438 heading towards Stow. All rooms en-suite with TV and tea-making facilities.
Bedrooms: 3 family rooms
Bathrooms: 3 private

Bed & breakfast
per night:	£min	£max
Single	14.00	14.00
Double	28.00	28.00

Half board
per person:	£min	£max
Daily	20.00	20.00
Weekly	120.00	120.00

Evening meal 1830 (last orders 1700)
Parking for 10

Personal Touch
Listed

37 Tirle Bank Way, Tewkesbury
GL20 8ES
☎ (0684) 297692
Semi-detached overlooking farmland. Leave M5 at junction 9, Tewkesbury. Second left past traffic lights, then left and immediately right, follow road round to right.
Bedrooms: 2 twin
Bathrooms: 1 public

Bed & breakfast
per night:	£min	£max
Single	15.00	
Double	30.00	

Half board
per person:	£min	£max
Daily	20.00	
Weekly	140.00	

Lunch available
Evening meal from 1830
Parking for 2
Open February-October

Town Street Farm
APPROVED

Tirley, Gloucester GL19 4HG
☎ Gloucester (0452) 780442
500-acre mixed farm. 18th C farmhouse set in beautiful surroundings and within half a mile of the River Severn.
Bedrooms: 1 double, 1 twin, 1 triple
Bathrooms: 3 private, 1 public

Bed & breakfast
per night:	£min	£max
Single	20.00	21.00
Double	30.00	32.00

Parking for 4

Willow Cottages
Listed

Shuthonger Common, Tewkesbury
GL20 6ED
☎ (0684) 298599
Secluded former farmhouse on Shuthonger Common offering a warm welcome. Excellent touring, walking and fishing. One mile north of Tewkesbury on A38.
Bedrooms: 2 twin, 1 triple
Bathrooms: 1 public

Bed & breakfast
per night:	£min	£max
Single	14.00	15.00
Double	28.00	30.00

Evening meal 1930 (last orders 1700)
Parking for 5

UPPER HULME
Staffordshire
Map ref 4B2

Picturesque hamlet in the Manifold Valley where a former narrow gauge railway line, which ran between Hulme End and Waterhouses, is now a macadamised walkers' path.

Keekorok Lodge Farm Guest House
Listed

Upper Hulme, Leek ST13 8UA
☎ Blackshaw (0538) 300218
15-acre mixed farm. Secluded farmhouse with panoramic views, rocks at rear. Very peaceful. Chatsworth, Alton Towers and the Potteries all close by. Ideal walking and climbing area.
Bedrooms: 1 double, 1 twin
Bathrooms: 1 public

Bed & breakfast
per night:	£min	£max
Single	20.00	22.00
Double	28.00	32.00

Half board
per person:	£min	£max
Weekly	203.00	

Evening meal from 1800
Parking for 10
Open April-October

UPTON-UPON-SEVERN
Hereford and Worcester
Map ref 2B1

Attractive country town on the banks of the Severn and a good river cruising centre. It has many pleasant old houses and inns, and the pepperpot landmark is now the Heritage Centre.
Tourist Information Centre
☎ (0684) 594200

Jessamine Cottage

1 Laburnum Walk, Upton-upon-Severn, Worcester WR8 0LW
☎ (0684) 593179
Modernised 19th C cottage, set in 1 acre of market garden, within walking distance of town centre. Fresh garden produce available. Reduced tariff for 3 or more nights.
Bedrooms: 1 single, 1 double, 1 twin
Bathrooms: 2 public

Bed & breakfast
per night:	£min	£max
Single	15.00	15.00
Double	30.00	30.00

Parking for 6

Pool House Riverside Country House Hotel

Hanley Road, Upton-upon-Severn, Worcester WR8 0PA
☎ (0684) 592151
Fine Queen Anne country house in large picturesque garden running down to the River Severn. Quiet, comfortable accommodation.
Bedrooms: 3 double, 4 twin, 2 triple
Bathrooms: 6 private, 1 public

Bed & breakfast
per night:	£min	£max
Single	22.00	35.00
Double	35.00	50.00

Parking for 20
Open February-November
Cards accepted: Access, Visa

Tiltridge Farm
COMMENDED

Upper Hook Road, Upton-upon-Severn, Worcester WR8 0SA
☎ (0684) 592906
Fax (0684) 594142

9-acre vineyard & grazing farm. Large fully renovated farmhouse close to

Continued ▶

185

HEART OF ENGLAND

UPTON-UPON-SEVERN
Continued

Upton and Malvern showground. Good food, warm welcome and wine from our own vineyard!
Bedrooms: 1 double, 1 triple
Bathrooms: 1 public

Bed & breakfast

per night:	£min	£max
Single	17.50	17.50
Double	32.00	32.00

Half board

per person:	£min	£max
Daily	24.50	30.00
Weekly	161.00	199.50

Evening meal 1800 (last orders 2000)
Parking for 12

UTTOXETER
Staffordshire
Map ref 4B2

Small market town famous for its racecourse. There are half-timbered buildings around the Market Square.

Stramshall Farm ₳
Listed COMMENDED

Stramshall, Uttoxeter ST14 5AG
☎ (0889) 562363
140-acre dairy & livestock farm. A large late-Victorian house of typical architecture. Set in attractive garden and in the centre of Stramshall village, 2 miles north of Uttoxeter.
Bedrooms: 2 triple
Bathrooms: 1 public

Bed & breakfast

per night:	£min	£max
Single	16.00	20.00
Double	28.00	32.00

Parking for 4
Open March-October

West Lodge ₳
Listed HIGHLY COMMENDED

Bramshall, Uttoxeter ST14 5BC
☎ (0889) 566000
Detached residence in 1 acre of attractive garden, on the B5027, 2 miles from Uttoxeter. Easy access to the Derbyshire Dales and Alton Towers.
Bedrooms: 1 double, 2 twin
Bathrooms: 2 public

Bed & breakfast

per night:	£min	£max
Single	18.50	21.00
Double	28.00	32.00

Parking for 8

VOWCHURCH
Hereford and Worcester
Map ref 2A1

Village in the Golden Valley by the River Dore and set in beautiful countryside. It has an interesting 14th C church and is close to Abbey Dore with its famous Cistercian church.

Upper Gilvach Farm
COMMENDED

St. Margarets, Vowchurch, Hereford HR2 0QY
☎ Michaelchurch (098 123) 618
90-acre dairy farm. Between Golden Valley and Black Mountains. Very quiet with much historic interest. Family-run.
Bedrooms: 2 double, 1 triple
Bathrooms: 3 private, 1 public

Bed & breakfast

per night:	£min	£max
Single	15.00	17.00
Double	30.00	34.00

Half board

per person:	£min	£max
Daily	20.00	25.00
Weekly	120.00	150.00

Parking for 20

WARWICK
Warwickshire
Map ref 2B1

Castle rising above the River Avon and 15th C Beauchamp Chapel attached to St Mary's Church, medieval Lord Leycester's Hospital almshouses and several museums. Nearby is Ashorne Hall Nickelodeon and the new National Heritage museum at Gaydon.
Tourist Information Centre
☎ (0926) 492212

The Croft ₳
COMMENDED

Haseley Knob, Warwick CV35 7NL
☎ Haseley Knob (0926) 484447
Fax (0926) 484447
With friendly family atmosphere in picturesque rural setting. On A4177 between Balsall Common and Warwick, convenient for the NEC, National Agricultural Centre, Stratford and Coventry. 15 minutes from Birmingham Airport.
Bedrooms: 1 single, 2 double, 1 twin, 1 triple
Bathrooms: 5 private, 2 public

Bed & breakfast

per night:	£min	£max
Single	18.50	25.00
Double	35.00	39.00

Half board

per person:	£min	£max
Daily	27.00	35.00

Evening meal 1800 (last orders 2000)
Parking for 10

30 Eastley Crescent ₳
HIGHLY COMMENDED

Warwick CV34 5RX
☎ (0926) 496480
Next to A46 and 5 minutes from the M40. Use of garden. Hairdryer, shoe cleaning, trouser press. Non-smoking establishment.
Bedrooms: 1 single, 1 double
Bathrooms: 1 private, 1 public

Bed & breakfast

per night:	£min	£max
Single	16.00	16.00
Double	32.00	32.00

Parking for 2

Forth House ₳
HIGHLY COMMENDED

44 High Street, Warwick CV34 4AX
☎ (0926) 401512
Ground floor and first floor guest suites with sitting room and bathroom at the back of the house. Overlooking peaceful garden, in town centre.
Bedrooms: 1 twin, 1 family room
Bathrooms: 2 private

Bed & breakfast

per night:	£min	£max
Single	25.00	35.00
Double	38.00	48.00

Parking for 2

Fulbrook Edge ₳
COMMENDED

Sherbourne Hill, Warwick CV35 8AG
☎ (0926) 624242
Old-fashioned hospitality in spectacular panoramic surroundings. All rooms at ground level. Croquet lawn. Midway Stratford/Warwick on the A46, a few minutes from the M40, junction 15. Wheelchair access category 3 ♿
Bedrooms: 1 double, 2 twin
Bathrooms: 1 public

Bed & breakfast

per night:	£min	£max
Single	27.00	29.00
Double	36.00	40.00

Parking for 12

The Gate House ₳
Listed COMMENDED

75 West Street, Warwick CV34 6AH
☎ (0926) 496965

Please mention this guide when making a booking.

HEART OF ENGLAND

Centre of Warwick (A429) 15th C timbered property, 100 yards from Warwick Castle. One and a quarter miles from M40 motorway.
Bedrooms: 1 double, 1 twin
Bathrooms: 2 private
Bed & breakfast

per night:	£min	£max
Single	25.00	35.00
Double	35.00	45.00

Parking for 4

Merrywood
Listed   HIGHLY COMMENDED
Hampton on the Hill, Warwick
CV35 8QR
☎ (0926) 492766
Family house in small village 2 miles from Warwick, with open views from 2 of the rooms.
Bedrooms: 1 single, 1 twin
Bathrooms: 2 public
Bed & breakfast

per night:	£min	£max
Single	15.00	17.50
Double	25.00	27.50

Parking for 3

Northleigh House ₳
HIGHLY COMMENDED
Five Ways Road, Hatton, Warwick
CV35 7HZ
☎ (0926) 484203
Comfortable, peaceful country house where the elegant rooms are individually designed and have en-suite bathroom, fridge, kettle and remote-control TV.
Bedrooms: 1 single, 4 double, 1 twin
Bathrooms: 6 private
Bed & breakfast

per night:	£min	£max
Single	29.00	38.00
Double	40.00	55.00

Parking for 8
Open February-November
Cards accepted: Access, Visa

Old Rectory ₳
COMMENDED
Vicarage Lane, Sherbourne, Warwick
CV35 8AB
☎ Barford (0926) 624562
Fax (0926) 624562

Georgian country house with beams and inglenook fireplaces, furnished with antiques. Well-appointed bedrooms, many with brass beds, all with en-suite facilities and colour TV. Hearty breakfast, tray supper. Situated half a mile from M40 junction 15.
Bedrooms: 4 single, 6 double, 2 twin, 1 triple, 1 family room
Bathrooms: 14 private
Bed & breakfast

per night:	£min	£max
Single	30.00	35.00
Double	39.00	49.00

Evening meal 1800 (last orders 2200)
Parking for 14
Cards accepted: Access, Visa

Redlands Farm House
Banbury Road, Lighthorne, Warwick
CV35 0AH
☎ Leamington Spa (0926) 651241
Built in local stone, mainly 17th C, tastefully restored with a wealth of timber beams. Centrally located for Warwick and Stratford-upon-Avon, 2 miles from M40 junction 12.
Bedrooms: 1 single, 1 double, 1 family room
Bathrooms: 1 private, 1 public
Bed & breakfast

per night:	£min	£max
Single	15.00	17.50
Double	30.00	36.00

Parking for 6
Open April-September

Shrewley House ₳
HIGHLY COMMENDED
Hockley Road, Shrewley, Warwick
CV35 7AT
☎ Claverdon (092 684) 2549
Fax (092 684) 2216
Listed 17th C farmhouse and home set amidst beautiful 1.5 acre gardens. King-sized four-poster bedrooms, all en-suite, with many thoughtful extras. Four miles from Warwick.
Bedrooms: 2 double, 1 family room
Bathrooms: 3 private
Bed & breakfast

per night:	£min	£max
Single	32.00	37.00
Double	45.00	55.00

Evening meal from 1930
Parking for 22
Cards accepted: Access, Visa

Tudor House Inn ₳
90-92 West Street, Warwick
CV34 6AW
☎ (0926) 495447
Fax (0926) 492948
Inn of character dating from 1472, with a wealth of beams. One of the few buildings to survive the great fire of Warwick in 1694. Opposite Warwick Castle and close to Warwick racecourse.
Bedrooms: 3 single, 5 double, 2 twin, 1 family room
Bathrooms: 6 private, 1 public, 2 private showers
Bed & breakfast

per night:	£min	£max
Single	24.00	
Double	54.00	

Half board

per person:	£min	£max
Daily	34.00	

Lunch available
Evening meal 1800 (last orders 2300)
Parking for 6
Cards accepted: Access, Visa, Diners, Amex, Switch

WATERHOUSES
Staffordshire
Map ref 4B2

Village in the valley of the River Hamps, once the terminus of the Leek and Manifold Light Railway, 8 miles of which is now a macadamised walkers' path.

Ye Olde Crown ₳
APPROVED
Leek Road, Waterhouses, Stoke-on-Trent ST10 3HL
☎ (0538) 308204
On the edge of the Peak District National Park and at the start of the beautiful Manifold Valley. It is built of natural stone and has a wealth of original oak beams.
Bedrooms: 2 single, 3 double, 1 twin, 1 family room
Bathrooms: 5 private, 1 public
Bed & breakfast

per night:	£min	£max
Single	14.00	21.50
Double	33.00	33.00

Half board

per person:	£min	£max
Daily	22.50	36.50
Weekly	157.00	255.00

Lunch available
Evening meal 1900 (last orders 2200)
Parking for 50

HEART OF ENGLAND

WEM
Shropshire
Map ref 4A3

Small town connected with Judge Jeffreys who lived in Lowe Hall. Well known for its ales.

Forncet
Listed COMMENDED

Soulton Road, Wem, Shrewsbury SY4 5HR
☎ (0939) 232996
Spacious, centrally heated Victorian house on the edge of this small market town, 200 yards from British Rail station.
Bedrooms: 1 single, 1 twin, 1 triple
Bathrooms: 2 public

Bed & breakfast per night:	£min	£max
Single	11.00	14.00
Double	22.00	28.00
Half board per person:	£min	£max
Daily	18.00	21.00

Evening meal 1830 (last orders 1930)
Parking for 4

Foxleigh House
COMMENDED

Foxleigh Drive, Wem, Shrewsbury SY4 5BP
☎ (0939) 233528

Pretty bedrooms, private bathrooms in elegant country house on Shropshire Way. Ideal for touring. Comfort and warm welcome.
Bedrooms: 2 twin
Bathrooms: 2 private

Bed & breakfast per night:	£min	£max
Single	20.00	20.00
Double	36.00	40.00
Half board per person:	£min	£max
Daily	25.00	27.00
Weekly	170.00	180.00

Evening meal 1830 (last orders 2000)
Parking for 7

Lowe Hall Farm

Wem, Shrewsbury SY4 5UE
☎ (0939) 232236
150-acre dairy farm. Historically famous Grade II listed farmhouse, once the country residence of Judge Jeffreys, 1648-1689. High standard of food, decor and accommodation is guaranteed.
Bedrooms: 1 double, 1 twin, 1 triple
Bathrooms: 1 private, 2 public

Bed & breakfast per night:	£min	£max
Single	17.00	17.00
Double	32.00	32.00

Evening meal 1830 (last orders 1930)
Parking for 8

WEOBLEY
Hereford and Worcester
Map ref 2A1

One of the most beautiful Herefordshire villages and full of attractive black and white timber-framed houses. It is dominated by the church which has a fine spire.

Ye Olde Salutation Inn
HIGHLY COMMENDED

Market Pitch, Weobley, Hereford HR4 8SJ
☎ (0544) 318443
Fax (0544) 318216
Traditional black and white country inn overlooking the main Broad Street. Quality home-cooked bar meals and a la carte menu. Inglenook fireplace. Homely atmosphere.
Bedrooms: 4 double, 1 twin
Bathrooms: 3 private, 1 public

Bed & breakfast per night:	£min	£max
Single	23.00	32.00
Double	35.00	54.00

Lunch available
Evening meal 1900 (last orders 2130)
Parking for 20
Cards accepted: Access, Visa

WHITTINGTON
Shropshire
Map ref 4A2

The Mount

35 Top Street, Whittington, Oswestry SY11 4DR
☎ Oswestry (0691) 657384

18th/19th C family house with beams and inglenook. Large comfortable rooms have lovely views. Extensive gardens. Chester, Shrewsbury, North and Mid-Wales within easy reach.
Bedrooms: 2 triple
Bathrooms: 2 private

Bed & breakfast per night:	£min	£max
Single	22.00	
Double	35.00	

Parking for 3

WINCHCOMBE
Gloucestershire
Map ref 2B1

Ancient town with a folk museum and railway museum. To the south lies Sudeley Castle with its fine collection of paintings and toys and an Elizabethan garden.
Tourist Information Centre
☎ *(0242) 602925*

Ireley Grounds Farm
HIGHLY COMMENDED

Broadway Road, Winchcombe, Cheltenham GL54 5NY
☎ Cheltenham (0242) 603582 & 603928
Fax (0242) 603443
Impressive farmhouse, offering comfortable accommodation, with four-poster beds in double rooms. Standing in 6 acres, with spectacular views, 1 mile from Winchcombe.
Bedrooms: 1 single, 1 double, 1 twin
Bathrooms: 3 private

Bed & breakfast per night:	£min	£max
Single	20.00	22.50
Double	45.00	50.00

Parking for 15

Isbourne House
COMMENDED

Castle Street, Winchcombe, Cheltenham GL54 5JA
☎ Cheltenham (0242) 602281
Listed part-Georgian part-Elizabethan house overlooking the grounds of Sudeley Castle, situated within attractive gardens bordered by the River Isbourne. 2 minutes from both open countryside and town centre. Spacious rooms with en-suite facilities.
Bedrooms: 1 single, 1 double, 1 triple
Bathrooms: 3 private

Bed & breakfast per night:	£min	£max
Single	25.00	36.00
Double	45.00	50.00

Parking for 2

Manor Farm
Listed

Greet, Winchcombe, Cheltenham GL54 5BJ
☎ Cheltenham (0242) 602423
400-acre mixed farm. Cotswolds manor in quiet hamlet. Good views of Cotswold Escarpment and steam railway. Near

HEART OF ENGLAND

racecourse. Picturesque well-equipped holiday cottages also available.
Bedrooms: 1 double, 1 twin
Bathrooms: 2 private

Bed & breakfast

per night:	£min	£max
Single	18.50	22.00
Double	37.00	44.00

Parking for 10
Open January-November

Mercia
COMMENDED

Hailes Street, Winchcombe,
Cheltenham GL54 5HU
☎ Cheltenham (0242) 602251
Black and white Cotswold-stone Tudor cottage with beamed walls and ceilings. Private parking at rear. Pleasant garden and views. 15 minutes from M5.
Bedrooms: 2 double, 1 twin
Bathrooms: 3 private

Bed & breakfast

per night:	£min	£max
Single	16.00	18.00
Double	32.00	36.00

Parking for 3

The Plaisterers Arms

Abbey Terrace, Winchcombe,
Cheltenham GL54 5LL
☎ Cheltenham (0242) 602358
Fax (0242) 602358
Old Cotswold stone inn with en-suite bed and breakfast accommodation, close to Sudeley Castle and town centre. Extensive menu, pub lunches, bar snacks and evening meals available every day. Large garden, patio and children's area.
Bedrooms: 3 double, 1 twin
Bathrooms: 4 private, 1 public

Bed & breakfast

per night:	£min	£max
Single	18.00	22.00
Double	30.00	35.00

Lunch available
Evening meal 1830 (last orders 2130)
Cards accepted: Access, Visa, Amex

Postlip Hall Farm
COMMENDED

Winchcombe, Cheltenham GL54 5AQ
☎ Cheltenham (0242) 603351
300-acre mixed farm. Family farm in superb scenic location a mile from Winchcombe on the side of Cleeve Hill. Perfect centre for touring the Cotswolds, Bath and Warwick. Tranquil, friendly atmosphere.
Bedrooms: 1 double, 1 triple
Bathrooms: 2 private

Bed & breakfast

per night:	£min	£max
Single	16.00	26.00
Double	32.00	35.00

Parking for 6

Slade Barn
Listed COMMENDED

Stow Road, Hawling, Cheltenham
☎ Guiting Power (0451) 850634
3-acre smallholding. Lovely position in beautiful countryside, yet only 10 minutes from town. Pretty bedrooms, log fire. Evening meals on request. We want you to enjoy your stay.
Bedrooms: 1 single, 1 twin
Bathrooms: 1 public

Bed & breakfast

per night:	£min	£max
Single	18.00	23.00
Double	36.00	46.00

Half board

per person:	£min	£max
Daily	28.00	33.00
Weekly	126.00	161.00

Lunch available
Evening meal 1600 (last orders 1800)
Parking for 10
Cards accepted: Switch

WOLVERHAMPTON

West Midlands
Map ref 4B3

Modern industrial town with a long history, a fine parish church and an excellent art gallery. There are several places of interest in the vicinity including Moseley Old Hall and Wightwick Manor with its William Morris influence.
Tourist Information Centre
☎ *(0902) 312051*

Pavilion Lodge
COMMENDED

Hilton Park Services, M6 Motorway,
Between exits 10a & 11,
Wolverhampton WV11 2DR
☎ Cheslyn Hay (0922) 412237
Fax (0922) 418762
Ideally situated for all major tourist attractions in the area, including Alton Towers and National Exhibition Centre. En-suite bedrooms and facilities for the disabled.
Bedrooms: 6 double, 36 twin, 22 triple
Bathrooms: 64 private

Bed & breakfast

per night:	£min	£max
Single	35.95	35.95
Double	43.95	43.95

Lunch available
Evening meal (last orders 2200)

Parking for 60
Cards accepted: Access, Visa, Diners, Amex, Switch

WOOTTON WAWEN

Warwickshire
Map ref 2B1

Attractive village which has an unspoilt church with an Anglo-Saxon tower, the only chained library in Warwickshire and some good brasses and monuments.

Wootton Park Farm
APPROVED

Alcester Road, Wootton Wawen,
Solihull, West Midlands B95 6HJ
☎ Henley-in-Arden (0564) 792673

340-acre arable & dairy farm. Delightful 16th C half-timbered farmhouse with a wealth of oak beams. 5 miles north of Stratford-upon-Avon in quiet countryside. Conveniently situated for the National Agricultural Centre and the National Exhibition Centre.
Bedrooms: 1 double, 1 twin, 1 triple
Bathrooms: 1 private, 1 public

Bed & breakfast

per night:	£min	£max
Single	22.00	25.00
Double	36.00	40.00

Parking for 6

WORCESTER

Hereford and Worcester
Map ref 2B1

Lovely riverside city dominated by its Norman and Early English cathedral, King John's burial place. Many old buildings including the 15th C Commandery and the 18th C Guildhall. There are several museums and the Royal Worcester porcelain factory.
Tourist Information Centre
☎ *(0905) 726311*

Burgage House
Listed

4 College Precincts, Worcester
WR1 2LG
☎ (0905) 25796
Comfortable accommodation in elegant Georgian mews house in quiet cobbled street next to cathedral. Close to River Severn and cricket ground.

Continued ▶

189

HEART OF ENGLAND

WORCESTER
Continued

Bedrooms: 1 single, 1 double, 1 twin, 1 triple
Bathrooms: 2 private, 2 public
Bed & breakfast
per night:	£min	£max
Single	20.00	24.00
Double	32.00	35.00

Ivy Cottage
COMMENDED
Sinton Green, Hallow, Worcester WR2 6NP
☎ (0905) 641123
Cottage-style house in small village, 4 miles north of Worcester, half a mile off A443 Worcester to Tenbury road.
Bedrooms: 1 double, 1 twin, 1 triple
Bathrooms: 2 private
Bed & breakfast
per night:	£min	£max
Single		16.00
Double	32.00	35.00

Parking for 4

Little Lightwood Farm
COMMENDED
Lightwood Lane, Cotheridge, Worcester WR6 5LT
☎ Cotheridge (0905) 333236
56-acre dairy farm. Farmhouse accommodation with en-suite rooms, tea-making facilities and heating in all bedrooms. Delightful views of the Malvern Hills. Just off the A44 from Worcester to Leominster, 3.5 miles from Worcester.
Bedrooms: 2 double, 1 twin
Bathrooms: 3 private
Bed & breakfast
per night:	£min	£max
Single	18.00	20.00
Double	32.00	36.00

Half board
per person:	£min	£max
Daily	25.00	29.00
Weekly	162.00	190.00

Evening meal from 1800
Parking for 6
Open February-November

Loch Ryan Hotel
119 Sidbury, Worcester WR5 2DH
☎ (0905) 351143
Fax (0905) 764407
Historic hotel, once home of Bishop Gore, close to cathedral, Royal Worcester Porcelain factory and Commandery. Attractive terraced garden. Imaginative food. Holders of Heartbeat and Worcester City clean food awards.
Bedrooms: 1 single, 3 double, 5 twin, 1 family room
Bathrooms: 10 private

Bed & breakfast
per night:	£min	£max
Single	35.00	45.00
Double	45.00	55.00

Evening meal 1800 (last orders 1900)
Cards accepted: Access, Visa, Diners, Amex

WYE VALLEY
See under Hereford, Ross-on-Wye, Symonds Yat West

YOXALL
Staffordshire
Map ref 4B3

The Moat
HIGHLY COMMENDED
Town Hill, Yoxall, Burton upon Trent DE13 8NN
☎ Burton upon Trent (0543) 472210
Country house sited in 2.5 acres of garden, dry moated, of historic interest. Grounds listed Grade II.
Bedrooms: 3 twin
Bathrooms: 3 private, 1 public
Bed & breakfast
per night:	£min	£max
Single	25.00	30.00
Double	45.00	50.00

Parking for 6

Key to symbols

Information about many of the services and facilities at accommodation listed in this guide is given in the form of symbols. The key to these symbols is inside the back cover flap. You may find it helpful to keep the flap open when referring to the accommodation listings.

THE ENGLAND FOR EXCELLENCE AWARDS 1992 WINNERS

The England for Excellence Awards were created by the English Tourist Board to recognise and reward the highest standards of excellence and quality in all major sectors of tourism in England. The coveted Leo statuette, presented each year to winners, has become firmly established as the ultimate accolade in the English tourism industry.

Over the past five years, the Leo has been won by all types and sizes of business with one common attribute – excellence in the facilities and services they offer.

Thames Tower
Black's Road
London W6 9EL

English Tourist Board

Resort of the Year sponsored by Marks & Spencer
BOURNEMOUTH

Bed and Breakfast Award sponsored by Le Shuttle
THE OLD RECTORY, Ripon

Attraction of the Year sponsored by Blackpool Pleasure Beach Limited
NATIONAL FISHING HERITAGE CENTRE

Hotel of the Year sponsored by Horwath Consulting
THE LANESBOROUGH

TIC of the Year sponsored by Holiday Property Bond Limited
FONTWELL TIC

Self-Catering Holiday of the Year sponsored by Hoseasons Holidays Limited
ANGLERS' PARADISE HOLIDAYS

Tourism and the Environment Award sponsored by Center Parcs Limited
LOSEHILL HALL, PEAK NATIONAL PARK CENTRE

Travel Journalist of the Year sponsored by Forte Plc
PAUL GOGARTY

Hotel Company of the Year sponsored by RCI Europe Limited
HILTON UNITED KINGDOM

Tourism for all Award sponsored by RAC Enterprises Limited
MUSEUM OF SCIENCE AND INDUSTRY IN MANCHESTER

Tourism and the Arts Award sponsored by First Leisure Corporation Plc
GREATER MANCHESTER VISITOR AND CONVENTION BUREAU/MANCHESTER INTERNATIONAL FESTIVAL OF EXPRESSIONISM

Caravan Holiday Park Award sponsored by the National Caravan Council
FOXHUNTER PARK

Tourism Training Award sponsored by The Tussauds Group Limited
LUCKETTS TRAVEL

English Travel Company of the Year sponsored by BTTF
BUTLIN'S LIMITED

Outstanding Contribution to English Tourism Award sponsored by Hilton UK
SIR ANDREW LLOYD WEBBER

Middle England

Conjuring up images of kings, queens and their courts, the wonderful variety of 'The Shires of Middle England' is yours to discover. Join the medieval adventure of Robin Hood in Sherwood Forest, visit the theme park at Ilkeston and test your mettle, or enjoy the thrill of the racing at Silverstone. Alternatively, walk and relax in the beautiful Peak District, visit nature reserves or muse in the museums and heritage centres scattered through the region. From the tranquil seaside resorts of Skegness and Mablethorpe to the bustling cities of Nottingham and Leicester with their up-to-the-minute shopping and entertainment, Middle England offers something for even the most bohemian of tastes, and above all a warm welcome for all.

WHERE TO GO, WHAT TO SEE

The number against each name will help you locate it on the map (page 194).

① Gainsborough Old Hall
Parnell Street, Gainsborough, Lincolnshire DN21 2NB
Tel: Gainsborough (0427) 612669
Late medieval timber-framed manor house built c1460, with fine medieval kitchen. Displays on the building and its restoration.

② Buxton Micrarium
Buxton, Derbyshire SK17 6BQ
Tel: Buxton (0298) 78662
Unique exhibition of the natural world under the microscope, using special push-button projection microscopes operated by visitors.

③ Lincoln Cathedral
Lincoln, Lincolnshire LN2 1PZ
Tel: Lincoln (0522) 544544
Triple-towered cathedral founded 1072, with Norman west front, 12th C work, Angel Choir of 1280. Wren library of 1674. Treasury. Regular services.

③ Museum of Lincolnshire Life
Burton Road, Lincoln, Lincolnshire LN1 3LY
Tel: Lincoln (0522) 528448
Agricultural, industrial and social history of Lincolnshire from 1800. Edwardian room setting. Display of craftwork in progress. First World War tank on display.

④ Chatsworth House, Farmyard and Adventure Playground
Bakewell, Derbyshire DE4 1PP
Tel: Baslow (0246) 582204

The crooked spire of All Saints' Church, Chesterfield – caused by the use of unseasoned timber.

Built 1687–1707. Collection of fine pictures, books, drawings, furniture. Garden laid out by Capability Brown with fountains, cascade. Farmyard and adventure playground.

⑤ Rufford Country Park and Craft Centre
Ollerton, Nottinghamshire NG22 9DF
Tel: Mansfield (0623) 824153
Parkland and 25-acre lake with ruins of Cistercian abbey. Woodland walks, formal gardens, sculpture garden. Craft centre with exhibitions of British craftsmanship.

⑥ White Post Modern Farm Centre
Farnsfield, Nr Newark, Nottinghamshire NG22 8HL
Tel: Mansfield (0623) 882977
Working farm with llama, ostriches, egg incubator, free-range hens, lakes, picnic areas, tea gardens.

⑦ The Heights of Abraham
Matlock Bath, Derbyshire DE4 3PD
Tel: Matlock (0629) 582365
Cable car ride across Derwent Valley gives access to Alpine

Middle England

Centre with refreshments, superb views, woodland, prospect tower and two show caves.

8 The National Tramway Museum
Crich, Matlock, Derbyshire DE4 5DP
Tel: Ambergate (0773) 852565
Collection of 50 tramcars from Britain and overseas built 1873–1953. Tram rides on one-mile route, period street scene, depots, power station, workshops.

Midland and LMS origin. Steam-hauled passenger service. Museum site. Country park.

11 American Adventure
Pit Lane, Ilkeston, Derbyshire DE7 5SX
Tel: Langley Mill (0773) 531521
American theme park with more than 100 rides including Great Niagara Rapids Ride, The Missile, Cherokee Falls, log flume and many other attractions. Shoot-out and shows daily.

The fenland around Spalding is the centre of Britain's bulb industry, with magnificent displays to be seen in the spring.

9 Millgate Museum of Social and Folk Life
Newark, Nottinghamshire NG24 4TS
Tel: Newark (0636) 79403
Museum portraying local social and folk life. Series of street scenes with period shops. Mezzanine gallery with regular programme of temporary exhibitions.

10 Midland Railway Centre
Butterley Station, Ripley, Derbyshire DE5 3TL
Tel: Ripley (0773) 747674
Over 25 locomotives and over 80 items of historic rolling stock of

12 Nottingham Industrial Museum
Woolaton Park, Nottingham NG8 2AE
Tel: Nottingham (0602) 284602
18th C stables presenting history of Nottingham's industries: printing, pharmacy, hosiery and lace. Victorian beam engine, horse gin, transport.

12 The Tales of Robin Hood
Nottingham, Nottinghamshire NG1 6GF
Tel: Nottingham (0602) 414414
Join the world's greatest medieval adventure and hide out in the Sheriff's eerie cave. Ride through

the magical Greenwood and play the Silver Arrow game.

13 Heckington Windmill
Hale Road, Heckington, Lincolnshire NG34 0JW
Tel: Sleaford (0529) 60765
Unique 8-sailed tower mill, built 1830 and restored to full order. Millings at weekends (wind permitting). Wholemeal flour on sale.

14 Belvoir Castle
Belvoir, Lincolnshire NG32 1PD
Tel: Grantham (0476) 870262
Seat of Dukes of Rutland since Henry VIII. Rebuilt in 1816. Museum of 17th/21st Lancers, picture gallery, magnificent state rooms.

15 Belton House, Park and Gardens
Grantham, Lincolnshire NG32 2LS
Tel: Grantham (0476) 66116
The crowning achievement of Restoration country house architecture, built in 1685–88 for Sir John Brownlow. Alterations by James Wyatt in 1777.

16 Sudbury Hall
Sudbury, Derbyshire DE6 5HT
Tel: Burton (0283) 585305
Grand 17th C house. Plasterwork ceilings, ceiling paintings, carved staircase and overmantel. Museum of childhood in former servants' wing.

17 Derby Industrial Museum
Full Street, Derby, Derbyshire DE1 3AR
Tel: Derby (0332) 255308
Displays on industries of Derbyshire, including Rolls-Royce aero engines. New railway engineering gallery. Museum is in former silk mill.

18 Springfields
Camelgate, Spalding, Lincolnshire PE12 6ET
Tel: Spalding (0775) 724843
25 acres of landscaped gardens with lake, maze, woodland walks

193

Middle England

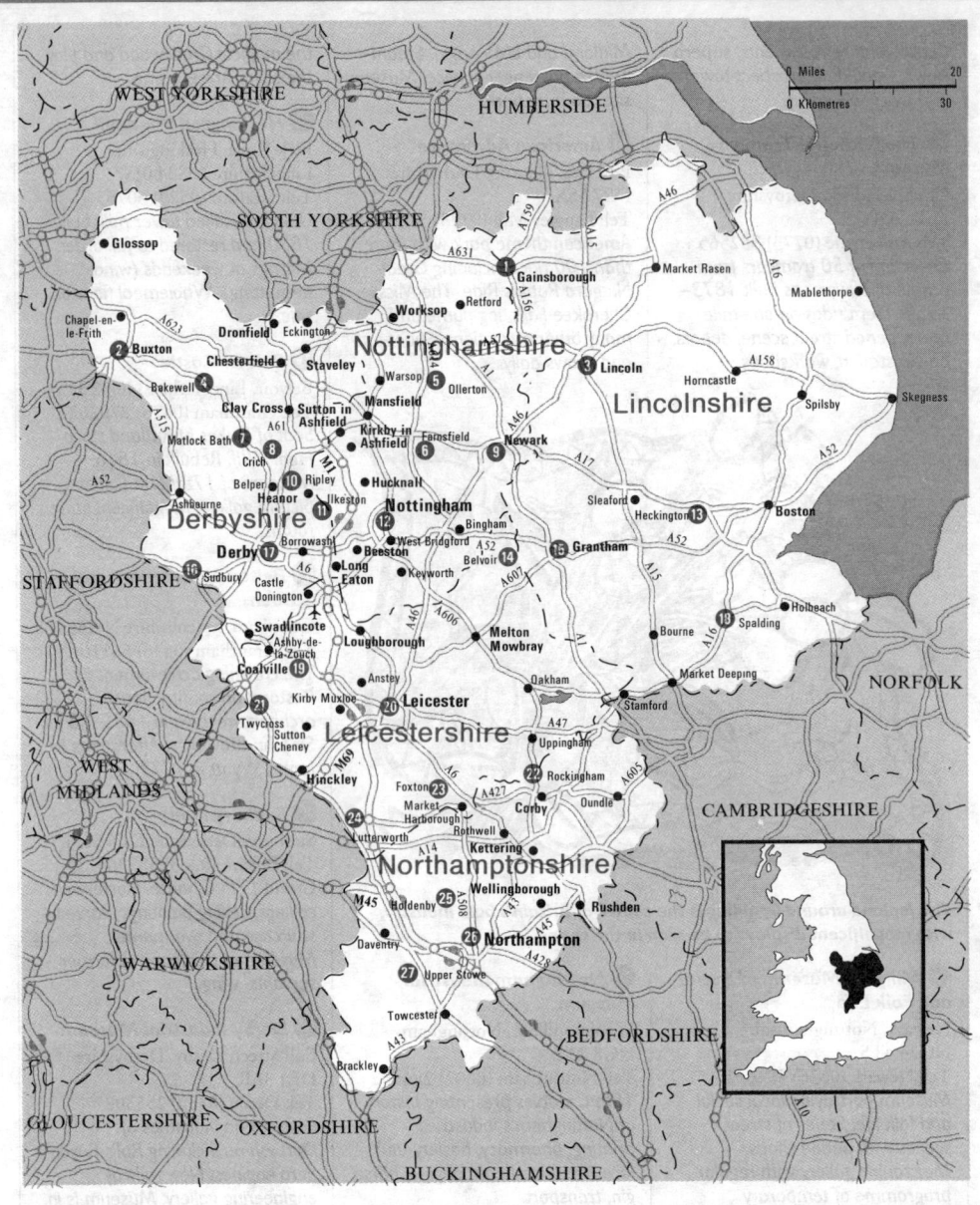

and glasshouse. Displays of over 1 million spring bulbs, 100,000 summer roses and bedding plants.

⑲ Snibston Discovery Park
Coalville, Leicestershire LE67 3LN
Tel: Coalville (0530) 510851
Former coal mine site with new museum building, nature trail.

⑳ Newarke Houses Museum
The Newarke, Leicester, Leicestershire LE2 7BY
Tel: Leicester (0533) 473222
Local history and crafts from 1485. Toys and games, clocks, mechanical instruments. 19th C street scene, early 20th C shop. Furniture by Gimson/Waals/Barnsley Brothers.

Use the map above to locate places in the 'Where to Go, What to See' section.

Middle England

㉑ Twycross Zoo
Twycross, Warwickshire CV9 3PX
Tel: Tamworth (0827) 880250
Gorillas, orang-utans, chimpanzees, modern gibbon complex, elephants, lions, cheetahs, giraffes, reptile house, pets' corner, rides.

㉒ Rockingham Castle
Rockingham, Leicestershire
LE16 8TH
Tel: Rockingham (0536) 770240
Elizabethan house within walls of Norman castle. Fine pictures. Extensive views and gardens with roses and ancient yew hedge.

㉓ Foxton Locks
Gumley Road, Foxton, Leicestershire
Tel: Leicester (0533) 656914
Landscaped picnic site with woodland footpath to Grand Union Canal towpath, long flight of locks and remains of barge lift.

㉔ Stanford Hall and Motorcycle Museum
Lutterworth, Leicestershire
LE17 6DH
Tel: Rugby (0788) 860250
William and Mary house on River Avon. Family costumes, furniture and pictures. Replica 1898 flying machine. Motorcycle museum. Rose garden. Nature trail. Craft centre on Sundays.

㉕ Holdenby House Gardens
Holdenby, Northampton
NN6 8DJ
Tel: Northampton (0604) 770074
Remains of Elizabethan gardens. Original entrance, arches and terraces. King Charles Walk. Museum. Craft shop. Rare breeds of farm animals. Falconry centre.

㉕ Central Museum and Art Gallery
Guildhall Road, Northampton, Northamptonshire NN1 1DP
Tel: Northampton (0604) 39415
Displays on Northampton's history from earliest times to present, using objects, sound and film.

Footwear through the ages, ceramics.

㉖ Church of the Holy Sepulchre
Sheep Street, Northampton
NN1 3NL
Tel: Northampton (0604) 754782
England's largest Norman round church built c1100 with tower c1300. Restored by Gilbert Scott. Crusader window, Northamptonshire Regiment memorial chapel.

㉗ Old Dairy Farm Centre
Upper Stowe, Northampton, Northamptonshire NN7 4SH
Tel: Weedon (0327) 40525
Wood turning, picture framing and various craft workshops.

There are many tales of Robin Hood and his merry men to be told in and around Nottingham and Sherwood Forest.

FIND OUT MORE

Further information about holidays and attractions in Middle England is available from:
East Midlands Tourist Board
Exchequergate, Lincoln LN2 1PZ
Tel: (0522) 531521

These publications are available free from the East Midlands Tourist Board:
Middle England '94 (general brochure including accommodation)
The Peak District 1994
Derbyshire - A Guide to Short Breaks
Events list (please send large stamped and addressed envelope)

Also available is (price includes postage and packing):
Shires of Middle England Leisure Map £3.50

MIDDLE ENGLAND

Places to stay

Accommodation entries in this regional section are listed in alphabetical order of place name, and then in alphabetical order of establishment.

The map references refer to the colour maps at the back of the guide. The first figure is the map number; the letter and figure which follow indicate the grid reference on the map.

The symbols at the end of each accommodation entry give information about services and facilities. A 'key' to these symbols is inside the back cover flap, which can be kept open for easy reference.

ABTHORPE
Northamptonshire
Map ref 2C1

Stone Cottage
Listed
Main Street, Abthorpe, Towcester
NN12 8QN
☎ Silverstone (0327) 857544
Grade II listed cottage in delightful secluded position on edge of conservation village. Convenient for Silverstone, Cotswolds and Oxford.
Bedrooms: 1 single, 2 twin
Bathrooms: 2 public

Bed & breakfast
per night:	£min	£max
Single	17.50	17.50
Double	30.00	30.00

Parking for 8

ADSTONE
Northamptonshire
Map ref 2C1

Stonedene
Listed
The Green, Adstone, Towcester
NN12 8DY
☎ Towcester (0327) 860434
A stone built family home in a quiet, rural area. Midway between Northampton and Banbury on the B4525.
Bedrooms: 1 double, 1 twin
Bathrooms: 1 public

Bed & breakfast
per night:	£min	£max
Single	12.00	15.00
Double	22.00	28.00

Half board
per person:	£min	£max
Daily	23.00	23.00
Weekly	149.50	149.50

Evening meal 1830 (last orders 2100)
Parking for 8

ALDWARK
Derbyshire
Map ref 4B2

Tithe Farm ⋀
COMMENDED
Aldwark, Grange Mill, Matlock
DE4 4HX
☎ Carsington (062 985) 263
Peacefully situated, within 10 miles of Matlock, Bakewell, Ashbourne, the dales and historic houses. Extensive breakfast menu with home-made bread and preserves.
Bedrooms: 1 twin, 1 triple
Bathrooms: 2 private

Bed & breakfast
per night:	£min	£max
Single	19.00	20.00
Double	32.00	34.00

Parking for 6
Open April-October

There are separate sections in this guide listing groups specialising in farm holidays and accommodation which is especially suitable for young people and organised groups.

ALFORD
Lincolnshire
Map ref 4D2

Busy market town with attractive Georgian houses and shops and a Folk Museum in the thatched manor house. A craft market is held on Fridays in the summer months and there is a restored and working 5-sailed tower mill.

Halton House
50 East Street, Alford LN13 9EH
☎ Louth (0507) 462058
Detached house in own gardens in the rural setting of a small market town on the edge of the Lincolnshire Wolds. A warm welcome awaits you. Non-smokers preferred.
Bedrooms: 1 double, 1 twin
Bathrooms: 2 public

Bed & breakfast
per night:	£min	£max
Single	14.00	15.00
Double	28.00	30.00

Parking for 3

ALKMONTON
Derbyshire
Map ref 4B2

Dairy House Farm ⋀
COMMENDED
Alkmonton, Longford, Ashbourne
DE6 3DG
☎ Ashbourne (0335) 330359
Fax (0335) 330359
82-acre livestock farm. Old red brick farmhouse with oak beams, inglenook fireplace and a comfortable atmosphere. Guests have their own lounge and dining room. Non-smokers only and no pets please.

196

MIDDLE ENGLAND

Bedrooms: 3 single, 2 double, 1 twin, 1 triple
Bathrooms: 5 private, 1 public

Bed & breakfast

per night:	£min	£max
Single	15.00	22.00
Double	30.00	36.00

Half board

per person:	£min	£max
Daily	25.00	32.00
Weekly	168.00	215.00

Lunch available
Evening meal 1830 (last orders 2030)
Parking for 8
⛱5 ♦ 🛈 § ⌿ ⌦ ⊺⊽ ⊞ ⧆ ♪ ✴ ✕ 🦮

ANCASTER
Lincolnshire
Map ref 3A1

Large village on the Roman Ermine Street, within easy drive of Belton House, Grantham and the cathedral city of Lincoln.

Woodlands
Listed

West Willoughby, Ancaster, Grantham NG32 3SH
☎ Loveden (0400) 30340 changing to 230340

12-acre mixed farm. Victorian stone farmhouse, in peaceful rural surroundings. A warm welcome, comfortable accommodation and traditional farmhouse breakfast. Within easy reach of (A1) Grantham, Lincoln and many places of historic interest.
Bedrooms: 1 twin, 1 triple
Bathrooms: 1 public

Bed & breakfast

per night:	£min	£max
Single	15.00	16.00
Double	28.00	30.00

Half board

per person:	£min	£max
Daily	21.00	23.00

Evening meal 1700 (last orders 2000)
Parking for 6
Open March-November
⛱ ⎕ ♦ ⊞ ⊺⊽ ⧆ ✴ 🦮

All accommodation in this guide has been inspected, or is awaiting inspection, under the national Crown scheme.

ASHBOURNE
Derbyshire
Map ref 4B2

Market town on the edge of the Peak District National Park and an excellent centre for walking. Its impressive church with 212-ft spire stands in an unspoilt old street. Ashbourne is well-known for gingerbread and its Shrovetide football match.
Tourist Information Centre
☎ (0335) 343666

Little Park Farm
COMMENDED

Mappleton, Ashbourne DE6 2BR
☎ Thorpe Cloud (033 529) 341
123-acre mixed farm. 300-year-old listed oak-beamed farmhouse, tastefully furnished. In the peaceful Dove Valley, 3 miles from Ashbourne. Superb views.
Bedrooms: 2 double, 1 twin
Bathrooms: 1 public

Bed & breakfast

per night:	£min	£max
Double	26.00	30.00

Half board

per person:	£min	£max
Daily	22.50	22.50

Evening meal from 1830
Parking for 3
Open March-October
⛱ 12 ⊞ ⌿ ⊺⊽ ⧆ ✕ 🦮 🏠

Mercaston Hall ♨

Mercaston, Brailsford, Derby DE6 3BL
☎ (0335) 60243
55-acre mixed farm. Listed buildings in attractive, quiet countryside. Hard tennis court. Kedleston Hall (National Trust) 1 mile, Carsington Reservoir 5 minutes away.
Bedrooms: 1 double, 1 twin
Bathrooms: 2 private, 1 public

Bed & breakfast

per night:	£min	£max
Double	29.00	33.00

Parking for 16
⛱8 ⎕ ⊟ ♦ ⌖ ⊞ § ⌿ ⌦ ⊺⊽ ⧆ ⧈ ♪ ♿ ⌣ ✴ 🦮 🏠

Shirley Hall Farm
HIGHLY COMMENDED

Shirley, Ashbourne DE6 3AS
☎ (0335) 60346
200-acre mixed farm. This peaceful timbered manor house, complete with part of its moat, is adjacent to superb woodland walks and makes an excellent centre for Sudbury and Kedleston Hall, Chatsworth and Alton Towers.
Bedrooms: 2 double, 1 twin
Bathrooms: 2 private, 1 public

Bed & breakfast

per night:	£min	£max
Single	16.00	19.00
Double	30.00	36.00

Parking for 5
⛱3 ⊟ ⎕ ♦ ⊞ 🛈 § ⊺⊽ ⧆ ♪ ✴ ✕ 🦮 🏠

ASHFORD IN THE WATER
Derbyshire
Map ref 4B2

Limestone village in attractive surroundings of the Peak District approached by 3 bridges over the River Wye. There is an annual well-dressing ceremony and the village was well-known in the 18th C for its black marble quarries.

Gritstone House ♨
HIGHLY COMMENDED

Greaves Lane, Ashford in the Water, Bakewell DE45 1QH
☎ Bakewell (0629) 813563
Charming 18th C Georgian house offering friendly service and accommodation designed with comfort and style in mind. Ideal centre for exploring the Peak District's scenery and country houses, and close to an extensive range of dining-out facilities.
Bedrooms: 2 double, 1 twin
Bathrooms: 1 private, 1 public

Bed & breakfast

per night:	£min	£max
Double		32.00

⊞ ⎕ ♦ ⌖ ⊞ § ⌿ ⌦ ⧆ ✕ 🦮 🏠

ASHOVER
Derbyshire
Map ref 4B2

Unspoilt village with a 13th C church.

Old School Farm

Uppertown, Ashover, Chesterfield S45 0JF
☎ Chesterfield (0246) 590813
25-acre mixed farm. A working farm welcoming children but not pets, suitable for visitors with their own transport. In a small hamlet bordering the Peak District, ideal for Chatsworth House, Chesterfield and Matlock Bath.
Bedrooms: 1 single, 1 double, 2 family rooms
Bathrooms: 2 private, 1 public

Bed & breakfast

per night:	£min	£max
Single	14.00	16.00
Double	28.00	32.00

Continued ▶

197

MIDDLE ENGLAND

ASHOVER
Continued

Half board
per person:	£min	£max
Daily	20.00	22.00
Weekly	140.00	154.00

Evening meal 1900 (last orders 0930)
Parking for 10
Open March-November

BAKEWELL
Derbyshire
Map ref 4B2

Pleasant market town, famous for its pudding. It is set in beautiful countryside on the River Wye and is an excellent centre for exploring the Derbyshire Dales, the Peak District National Park, Chatsworth and Haddon Hall.
Tourist Information Centre
☎ *(0629) 813227*

Castle Cliffe Private Hotel
COMMENDED
Monsal Head, Bakewell DE45 1NL
☎ Great Longstone (0629) 640258
A Victorian stone house overlooking beautiful Monsal Dale. Noted for its friendly atmosphere, good food and exceptional views.
Bedrooms: 3 double, 4 twin, 2 family rooms
Bathrooms: 2 private, 2 public, 6 private showers

Bed & breakfast
per night:	£min	£max
Double	40.00	44.00

Half board
per person:	£min	£max
Daily	30.00	42.00
Weekly	190.00	220.00

Evening meal 1900 (last orders 1700)
Parking for 15
Cards accepted: Access, Visa

BELPER
Derbyshire
Map ref 4B2

Chevin Green Farm
COMMENDED
Chevin Road, Belper, Derby DE56 2UN
☎ (0773) 822328
38-acre mixed farm. Extended and improved 300-year-old beamed farmhouse accommodation with all bedrooms en-suite, an ideal base for exploring Derbyshire.
Bedrooms: 2 single, 2 double, 1 twin, 1 triple
Bathrooms: 6 private

Bed & breakfast
per night:	£min	£max
Single	16.00	20.00
Double	26.00	36.00

Parking for 6

BLYTH
Nottinghamshire
Map ref 4C2

Village on the old Great North Road. A busy staging post in Georgian times with many examples of Georgian Gothic architecture. The remains of a Norman Benedictine priory survive as the parish church.

Priory Farm Guesthouse
Hodsock Priory Estate, Blyth, Worksop S81 0TY
☎ (0909) 591768 & 474299
1000-acre mixed farm. Farmhouse in peaceful surroundings on a private country estate. Easy access from the A1 (M).
Bedrooms: 2 single, 1 double, 1 twin
Bathrooms: 2 private, 1 public

Bed & breakfast
per night:	£min	£max
Single	14.50	16.00
Double	29.00	32.00

Half board
per person:	£min	£max
Daily	21.00	22.50
Weekly	118.50	130.00

Evening meal 1800 (last orders 2000)
Parking for 6

BOSTON
Lincolnshire
Map ref 3A1

Historic town famous for its church tower, the Boston Stump, 272 ft high. Still a busy port, the town is full of interest and has links with Boston Massachusetts through the Pilgrim Fathers. The cells where they were imprisoned can be seen in the medieval Guildhall.
Tourist Information Centre
☎ *(0205) 356656*

Bramley House
Listed COMMENDED
267 Sleaford Road, Boston PE21 7PQ
☎ (0205) 354538
Small guesthouse, charmingly decorated, with warm and friendly personal service. Ample parking.
Bedrooms: 2 single, 1 double, 1 twin
Bathrooms: 1 public

Bed & breakfast
per night:	£min	£max
Single	17.50	20.00
Double	30.00	40.00

Half board
per person:	£min	£max
Daily	23.50	26.00
Weekly	147.00	164.50

Evening meal 1700 (last orders 1900)
Parking for 10

BRACKLEY
Northamptonshire
Map ref 2C1

Historic market town of mellow stone, with many fine buildings lining the wide High Street and Market Place. Sulgrave Manor (George Washington's ancestral home) and Silverstone Circuit are nearby.
Tourist Information Centre
☎ *(0280) 700111*

Walltree House Farm
Steane, Brackley NN13 5NS
☎ Banbury (0295) 811235
200-acre arable farm. Individual ground floor rooms in the courtyard attached to Victorian farmhouse, mostly en-suite. Gardens and woods to relax in. Near historic sites, shopping and sports.
Bedrooms: 2 double, 3 twin, 3 triple
Bathrooms: 7 private, 1 public

Bed & breakfast
per night:	£min	£max
Single	27.00	30.00
Double	38.00	40.00

Half board
per person:	£min	£max
Daily	35.00	40.00
Weekly	220.50	252.00

Evening meal 1900 (last orders 1900)
Parking for 10
Cards accepted: Access, Visa

Welbeck House
Pebble Lane, Brackley NN13 5DA
☎ (0280) 702364
A large house in a quiet, attractive area of Brackley, close to the A43, M40 and many places of interest. We pride ourselves on our full-scale breakfasts and a warm welcome to all.
Bedrooms: 2 double, 1 twin
Bathrooms: 2 public

Bed & breakfast
per night:	£min	£max
Single	14.00	16.00
Double	25.00	30.00

Parking for 4

We advise you to confirm your booking in writing.

MIDDLE ENGLAND

BRANSTON
Lincolnshire
Map ref 4C2

Branston Hall Hotel ⋔
COMMENDED

Lincoln Road, Branston, Lincoln
LN4 1PD
☎ Lincoln (0522) 793305
Fax (0522) 790549
Country house hotel in lovely parkland, on the B1188, 4 miles south of Lincoln.
Bedrooms: 6 single, 8 double, 4 twin, 1 triple, 1 family room
Bathrooms: 20 private
Bed & breakfast

per night:	£min	£max
Single	57.50	70.00
Double	77.50	90.00

Half board

per person:	£min	£max
Daily	70.00	82.50
Weekly	315.00	420.00

Lunch available
Evening meal 1900 (last orders 2145)
Parking for 70
Cards accepted: Access, Visa, Diners, Amex, Switch

BROUGHTON ASTLEY
Leicestershire
Map ref 4C3

The Old Farm House
Listed

Old Mill Road, Broughton Astley, Leicester LE9 6PQ
☎ Sutton in the Elms (0455) 282254
Fax (0455) 284301
Recently converted Georgian farmhouse overlooking grass fields. Quietly situated behind the church, 1 minute from village centre. Near junctions 20/21 of M1, junction 1 of M69.
Bedrooms: 1 double, 3 twin
Bathrooms: 2 public
Bed & breakfast

per night:	£min	£max
Single	16.00	16.00
Double	32.00	32.00

Parking for 4

BURTON LATIMER
Northamptonshire
Map ref 3A2

The Wold
Listed COMMENDED

34 Church Street, Burton Latimer, Kettering NN15 5LU
☎ (0536) 722685
A detached house of generous proportions, in a semi-rural area in the old part of Burton Latimer. Non-smokers preferred.
Bedrooms: 1 single, 1 double, 1 twin

Bathrooms: 2 public, 1 private shower
Bed & breakfast

per night:	£min	£max
Single	16.00	17.50
Double	28.00	30.00

Half board

per person:	£min	£max
Daily	22.50	24.00

Evening meal from 1900
Parking for 3

BUXTON
Derbyshire
Map ref 4B2

The highest market town in England and one of the oldest spas, with an elegant Crescent, Micrarium, Poole's Cavern, Opera House and attractive Pavilion Gardens. An excellent centre for exploring the Peak District.
Tourist Information Centre
☎ *(0298) 25106*

Coningsby ⋔
HIGHLY COMMENDED

6 Macclesfield Road, Buxton
SK17 9AH
☎ (0298) 26735

Substantial Victorian detached house set in a pretty garden in a pleasant area. A friendly welcome, superior accommodation, good food and wine are assured but non-smoking guests only please.
Bedrooms: 3 double
Bathrooms: 3 private
Bed & breakfast

per night:	£min	£max
Double	38.00	40.00

Half board

per person:	£min	£max
Daily	31.50	32.50
Weekly	207.50	213.50

Evening meal 1900 (last orders 1600)
Parking for 6
Open January-November

Edge Lee Guesthouse ⋔
COMMENDED

Edge Lee, Bishops Lane, Burbage, Buxton SK17 6UW
☎ (0298) 22870
Peacefully situated in one acre, two-thirds of a mile from Buxton centre, overlooking golf-course. All rooms tastefully decorated and with full facilities. Warm friendly welcome to everyone.

Bedrooms: 2 double, 1 triple
Bathrooms: 3 private
Bed & breakfast

per night:	£min	£max
Single	25.00	30.00
Double	30.00	35.00

Parking for 6
Open April-October

Fairhaven ⋔
Listed APPROVED

1 Dale Terrace, Buxton SK17 6LU
☎ (0298) 24481
Centrally placed with ample roadside parking, offering English home cooking in a warm and friendly atmosphere.
Bedrooms: 1 single, 1 double, 1 twin, 3 triple
Bathrooms: 1 public
Bed & breakfast

per night:	£min	£max
Single	16.00	20.00
Double	28.00	40.00

Half board

per person:	£min	£max
Daily	20.00	26.00
Weekly	132.00	150.00

Evening meal 1800 (last orders 1600)
Cards accepted: Access, Visa

Hawthorn Farm Guesthouse
COMMENDED

Fairfield Road, Buxton SK17 7ED
☎ (0298) 23230
A 400-year-old former farmhouse which has been in the family for 10 generations. Full English breakfast.
Bedrooms: 3 single, 2 double, 2 twin, 4 triple
Bathrooms: 5 private, 2 public
Bed & breakfast

per night:	£min	£max
Single	18.50	19.50
Double	37.00	45.00

Parking for 15
Open April-October

Lynstone Guesthouse

3 Grange Road, Buxton SK17 6NH
☎ (0298) 77043
A spacious homely house. Home cooking, traditional and vegetarian. Ideal base for touring and walking. Children welcome, cleanliness assured. Off-street parking. No smoking and no pets please.
Bedrooms: 1 triple, 1 family room
Bathrooms: 1 private, 2 public
Bed & breakfast

per night:	£min	£max
Double		28.00

Continued ▶

199

MIDDLE ENGLAND

BUXTON
Continued

Half board
per person:	£min	£max
Daily	22.00	
Weekly	140.00	

Evening meal 1800 (last orders 1800)
Parking for 3
Open March-December

Oldfield House
COMMENDED
8 Macclesfield Road, Buxton
SK17 9AH
☎ (0298) 24371
Attractive detached Victorian guesthouse with gardens, close to the town centre and Pavilion Gardens. Spacious en-suite bedrooms. Non-smoking.
Bedrooms: 2 double, 1 triple
Bathrooms: 3 private, 1 public

Bed & breakfast
per night:	£min	£max
Single	20.00	20.00
Double	32.00	33.00

Half board
per person:	£min	£max
Daily	24.00	25.00
Weekly	165.00	165.00

Parking for 8

Pedlicote Farm
Listed
Peak Forest, Buxton SK17 8EG
☎ (0298) 22241
Old farmhouse conversion in the Peak District National Park, full of character, with a charming atmosphere and magnificent views.
Bedrooms: 1 double, 2 twin
Bathrooms: 2 public

Bed & breakfast
per night:	£min	£max
Single	18.00	18.00
Double	30.00	30.00

Half board
per person:	£min	£max
Daily	25.00	25.00
Weekly	165.00	165.00

Lunch available
Parking for 9

The Victorian Guesthouse
COMMENDED
5 Wye Grove, Off Macclesfield Road, Buxton SK17 9AJ
☎ (0298) 78159
Set in attractive and comfortable surroundings, furnished in a tasteful Victorian manner, with a beautiful conservatory to relax in. En-suite available. Telephone for brochure.
Bedrooms: 2 double, 1 twin
Bathrooms: 2 private, 1 public

Bed & breakfast
per night:	£min	£max
Single	18.00	24.00
Double	30.00	35.00

Half board
per person:	£min	£max
Daily	25.00	27.50
Weekly	165.00	200.00

Parking for 4

CASTLE BYTHAM
Lincolnshire
Map ref 3A1

Attractive village with castle earthworks dating from Saxon times and a parish church, churchyard and several houses of interest. It also has a duck pond and stream.

School Farm House
4 High Street, Castle Bytham, Grantham NG33 4RZ
☎ Stamford (0780) 410245
Fax (0780) 410245
A family home in one of Lincolnshire's attractive villages, 3 miles off A1. Stamford is 8 miles south and Grantham is 10 miles north. Non-smokers only.
Bedrooms: 1 single, 2 double
Bathrooms: 3 private, 1 public

Bed & breakfast
per night:	£min	£max
Single	20.00	25.00
Double	40.00	48.00

Parking for 4

CASTLE DONINGTON
Leicestershire
Map ref 4C3

A Norman castle once stood here. The world's largest collection of single-seater racing cars is displayed at Donington Park alongside the racing circuit, and an Aeropark Visitor Centre can be seen at nearby East Midlands International Airport.

High Barn Farm
Listed
Isley Walton, Castle Donington, Derby DE7 2RL
☎ Derby (0332) 810360
84-acre mixed farm. Accommodation in delightfully converted barn, cottage and farmhouse. Small and friendly, peacefully rural, warm welcome assured.
Bedrooms: 2 single, 1 double, 5 twin, 1 family room
Bathrooms: 3 private, 3 public

Bed & breakfast
per night:	£min	£max
Single	16.00	21.00
Double	32.00	40.00

Parking for 16

CASTLETON
Derbyshire
Map ref 4B2

Large village in a spectacular Peak District setting with ruined Peveril Castle and 4 great show caverns, where the Blue John stone and lead were mined. One cavern offers a mile-long underground boat journey.

Bargate Cottage
COMMENDED
Bargate, Pindale Road, Castleton, Sheffield S30 2WG
☎ Hope Valley (0433) 620201
Fax (0433) 627739
Unspoilt, renovated 17th C cottage adjacent to Peveril Castle in the centre of the village. An ideal base for relaxing, walking or touring. Many recreational facilities available locally. Non-smokers only please.
Bedrooms: 3 double, 1 twin
Bathrooms: 4 private

Bed & breakfast
per night:	£min	£max
Double	37.00	45.00

Half board
per person:	£min	£max
Daily	28.50	32.50

Evening meal from 1830
Parking for 6

COTGRAVE
Nottinghamshire
Map ref 4C2

Jerico Farm
COMMENDED
Fosse Way, Cotgrave, Nottingham NG12 3HG
☎ Kinoulton (0949) 81733

120-acre mixed farm. Attractive, warm, comfortable accommodation with views over the Nottinghamshire Wolds. Only 8 miles from Nottingham off the Fosse Way between Newark and Leicester. A warm welcome assured. Family-run.
Bedrooms: 1 double, 2 twin
Bathrooms: 1 private, 1 public

MIDDLE ENGLAND

Bed & breakfast
per night:	£min	£max
Single	16.00	20.00
Double	30.00	35.00

Parking for 4

CRANFORD ST ANDREW

Northamptonshire
Map ref 3A1

Dairy Farm
COMMENDED

Cranford St Andrew, Kettering
NN14 4AQ
☎ (053 678) 273
350-acre mixed farm. 17th C thatched house with inglenook fireplaces and a garden with an ancient circular dovecote and mature trees. Good food.
Bedrooms: 1 double, 2 twin
Bathrooms: 2 private, 1 public

Bed & breakfast
per night:	£min	£max
Single	18.00	25.00
Double	36.00	40.00

Half board
per person:	£min	£max
Daily	28.00	30.00
Weekly	160.00	200.00

Evening meal 1900 (last orders 1200)
Parking for 5

There are separate sections in this guide listing groups specialising in farm holidays and accommodation which is especially suitable for young people and organised groups.

DERBY

Derbyshire
Map ref 4B2

Modern industrial city but with ancient origins. There is a wide range of attractions including several museums (notably Royal Crown Derby), a theatre, a concert hall, and the cathedral with fine ironwork and Bess of Hardwick's tomb.
Tourist Information Centre
☎ (0332) 255802

Bonehill Farm
Listed

Etwall Road, Mickleover, Derby
DE3 5DN
☎ (0332) 513553
120-acre mixed farm. A traditional farmhouse in a rural setting, 3 miles from Derby. Alton Towers, the Peak District, historic houses and the Potteries are all within easy reach.
Bedrooms: 1 double, 1 twin, 1 triple
Bathrooms: 1 public

Bed & breakfast
per night:	£min	£max
Single	15.00	17.00
Double	30.00	32.00

Parking for 6

DESBOROUGH

Northamptonshire
Map ref 4C3

West Lodge Farm
HIGHLY COMMENDED

Pipewell Road, Desborough, Kettering
NN14 2SH
☎ Kettering (0536) 760552
570-acre arable farm. Spacious Georgian farmhouse set in extensive gardens. Breakfast overlooking 600 acres of countryside. Experience freedom from neighbours. Close to A1/M1 link.
Bedrooms: 1 double, 1 twin
Bathrooms: 1 private, 1 public, 1 private shower

Bed & breakfast
per night:	£min	£max
Single	18.00	22.00
Double	36.00	40.00

Parking for 5
Open January-July, September-December

DOVERIDGE

Derbyshire
Map ref 4B2

The Beeches Farmhouse
HIGHLY COMMENDED

The Beeches, Waldley, Doveridge, Derby DE6 5LR
☎ Rocester (0889) 590288
Fax (0889) 590288
160-acre dairy farm. 18th C farmhouse with licensed restaurant in beautiful Derbyshire, close to Alton Towers and Dovedale. Won top national award for farm-based catering.
Bedrooms: 2 double, 3 twin, 7 family rooms
Bathrooms: 8 private, 2 public

Bed & breakfast
per night:	£min	£max
Single	19.30	38.50
Double	30.00	48.00

Half board
per person:	£min	£max
Daily	24.75	48.50
Weekly	171.80	335.00

Evening meal 1830 (last orders 2030)
Parking for 15
Cards accepted: Access, Visa, Amex

[Ad] Display advertisement appears on this page

Half board prices shown are per person but in some cases may be based on double/twin occupancy.

The Beeches
Farmhouse Hotel and Award Winning Restaurant

Winners of the top national award for farm based catering. 18th Century farmhouse, licensed restaurant, fresh food and homemade desserts. Convenient for exploring the beautiful Derbyshire countryside or enjoying the thrills of AltonTowers.

Excellent en-suite family rooms. Children love feeding the many animals on our working dairy farm.

TELEPHONE OR FAX: 0889 590288

BARBARA TUNNICLIFFE
The Beeches,
Waldley, Doveridge, Derbyshire.

A WARM WELCOME AWAITS YOU

201

MIDDLE ENGLAND

EAST BARKWITH
Lincolnshire
Map ref 4D2

The Grange ⋔
DE LUXE
Torrington Lane, East Barkwith, Lincoln LN3 5RY
☎ Wragby (0673) 858249
315-acre mixed farm. A special stay in a welcoming, spacious Georgian farmhouse offering en-suite accommodation, traditional breakfasts and candlelit dinners. Extensive grounds with lawn tennis. Quiet location halfway between Lincoln and Louth.
Bedrooms: 2 double, 1 twin
Bathrooms: 3 private

Bed & breakfast
per night:	£min	£max
Single	25.00	
Double	40.00	

Half board
per person:	£min	£max
Daily	32.00	

Lunch available
Evening meal 1830 (last orders 1930)
Parking for 16

EDWINSTOWE
Nottinghamshire
Map ref 4C2

Village close to Sherwood Forest, famous for the legend of Robin Hood. The Visitor Centre and Country Park includes a Robin Hood exhibition, and there are guided walks and many special events.
Tourist Information Centre
☎ (0623) 824490

Duncan Wood Lodge ⋔
Listed COMMENDED
Carburton, Worksop S80 3BP
☎ Worksop (0909) 483614
Countryside lodge in the heart of Sherwood Forest. One acre of gardens and orchard in woodland setting. Home-grown produce.
Bedrooms: 1 single, 3 double, 3 twin, 1 family room
Bathrooms: 4 private, 2 public

Bed & breakfast
per night:	£min	£max
Single	17.00	28.00
Double	33.00	38.00

Half board
per person:	£min	£max
Daily	24.00	35.00
Weekly	150.00	215.00

Lunch available
Evening meal 1830 (last orders 2030)

Parking for 9
Cards accepted: Access, Visa

ELMESTHORPE
Leicestershire
Map ref 4C3

Water Meadows Farm
Listed COMMENDED
22 Billington Road East, Elmesthorpe, Leicester LE9 7SB
☎ Earl Shilton (0455) 843417
15-acre beef farm. Tudor-style, oak-beamed farmhouse with extensive gardens, including private woodland and stream. Own produce, home cooking. Located along a private road. Central for visiting many places of scenic and historic interest.
Bedrooms: 1 double, 1 twin, 1 family room
Bathrooms: 1 public

Bed & breakfast
per night:	£min	£max
Single	16.00	16.00
Double	26.00	26.00

Half board
per person:	£min	£max
Daily	20.00	23.00
Weekly	120.00	120.00

Evening meal from 1900
Parking for 10

EYAM
Derbyshire
Map ref 4B2

Attractive village famous for the courage it showed during the plague of 1665. The church has several memorials to this time and there is a well-dressing ceremony in August. The fine 17th C manor house of Eyam Hall is open in summer, and Chatsworth is nearby.

Miners Arms Inn & Restaurant
COMMENDED
Water Lane, Eyam, Sheffield S30 2RA
☎ Hope Valley (0433) 630853
Charming 17th C inn nestling in the famous plague village of Eyam. All rooms recently refurbished. Full a la carte restaurant.
Bedrooms: 1 single, 3 double, 2 twin
Bathrooms: 6 private

Bed & breakfast
per night:	£min	£max
Single	25.00	30.00
Double	40.00	45.00

Lunch available
Evening meal 1900 (last orders 2100)
Parking for 101

FOXTON
Leicestershire
Map ref 4C3

Attractive village established in the 8th C. The 13th C church contains part of a Saxon Cross and a "lepers window". The Grand Union Canal passes through the village. Within walking distance is historic Foxton Locks with its unique staircase flight of 10 locks, and Inclined Plane Museum.

The Old Manse
Swingbridge Street, Foxton, Market Harborough LE16 7RH
☎ East Langton (0858) 84 456
Period house in large gardens with warm and friendly atmosphere, on edge of conservation village, 3 miles north of Market Harborough.
Bedrooms: 1 double, 2 twin
Bathrooms: 1 public

Bed & breakfast
per night:	£min	£max
Single	20.00	22.00
Double	35.00	38.00

Parking for 6

FROGGATT
Derbyshire
Map ref 4B2

Chequers Inn ⋔
HIGHLY COMMENDED
Froggatt, Calver, Sheffield S30 1ZB
☎ Hope Valley (0433) 630231
In the heart of the Peak District National Park, 3 miles from Chatsworth, 6 miles from Bakewell. Traditional ales, log fire and always a warm welcome.
Bedrooms: 4 double, 2 twin
Bathrooms: 6 private

Bed & breakfast
per night:	£min	£max
Single	38.00	45.00
Double	48.00	58.00

Lunch available
Evening meal 1900 (last orders 2130)
Parking for 60
Cards accepted: Access, Visa

GLOOSTON
Leicestershire
Map ref 4C3

The Old Barn Inn ⋔
COMMENDED
Glooston, Market Harborough LE16 7ST
☎ East Langton (085 884) 215
A 16th C oak-beamed inn with log fires offering home-cooked food and a selection of traditional ales. In the village on a no-through-road.
Bedrooms: 2 double, 1 twin

MIDDLE ENGLAND

Bathrooms: 3 private
Bed & breakfast
per night: £min £max
Single 39.50
Double 49.50
Half board
per person: £min £max
Daily 54.00
Lunch available
Evening meal 1900 (last orders 2130)
Parking for 13
Cards accepted: Access, Visa

GRANTHAM
Lincolnshire
Map ref 3A1

On the old Great North Road (A1), Grantham's splendid parish church has a fine spire and chained library. Sir Isaac Newton was educated here and his statue stands in front of the museum which includes displays on Newton and other famous local people.
Tourist Information Centre
☎ (0476) 66444

Lanchester Guesthouse

84 Harrowby Road, Grantham
NG31 9DS
☎ (0476) 74169
Well established and run professionally to high standards but retaining its warm and friendly atmosphere. All rooms can be let as singles. Light suppers can be served until 9pm.
Bedrooms: 1 double, 2 twin
Bathrooms: 1 private, 1 public
Bed & breakfast
per night: £min £max
Single 15.00 25.00
Double 28.00 40.00
Half board
per person: £min £max
Daily 25.00 35.00
Evening meal 1800 (last orders 1200)
Parking for 3

HAINTON
Lincolnshire
Map ref 4D2

Old Vicarage

School Lane, Hainton, Lincoln
LN3 6LW
☎ Burgh on Bain (0507) 313660
Quiet country household in the Wolds, in 1 acre of secluded gardens. We offer home baking and produce, and are convenient for the Viking Way, the coast and Lincoln. Evening meals by arrangement. Non-smokers only please.
Bedrooms: 1 double, 2 twin

Bathrooms: 2 public
Bed & breakfast
per night: £min £max
Single 15.00
Double 30.00
Half board
per person: £min £max
Daily 22.50
Weekly 140.00
Evening meal from 1900
Parking for 6

HATHERSAGE
Derbyshire
Map ref 4B2

Hillside village in the Peak District, dominated by the church with many good brasses and monuments to the Eyre family which provide a link with Charlotte Bronte. Little John, friend of Robin Hood, is said to be buried here.

The Old Vicarage
Listed

Church Bank, Hathersage, Sheffield
S30 1AB
☎ Hope Valley (0433) 651099
In 1845 Charlotte Bronte stayed in this listed building which is beside Little John's grave overlooking the Hope Valley. Central for Chatsworth House, the caves, fishing and walking.
Bedrooms: 2 double, 1 twin
Bathrooms: 1 private, 2 public,
1 private shower
Bed & breakfast
per night: £min £max
Single 19.00 19.00
Double 32.00 40.00
Parking for 3

HINCKLEY
Leicestershire
Map ref 4B3

The town has an excellent leisure centre. Bosworth Battlefield, with its Visitor Centre and Battle Trail, is 5 miles away.
Tourist Information Centre
☎ (0455) 635106

Woodside Farm Guesthouse
COMMENDED

Ashby Road, Stapleton, Leicester
LE9 8JE
☎ Market Bosworth (0455) 291929
16-acre arable & horses farm. Close to the Battle of Bosworth site and Kirkby Mallory race track. 3 miles north of Hinckley on A447.
Bedrooms: 1 single, 3 double, 1 twin, 1 triple
Bathrooms: 3 private, 2 public, 1 private shower

Bed & breakfast
per night: £min £max
Single 19.50 25.00
Double 38.00 45.00
Lunch available
Evening meal 1830 (last orders 2130)
Parking for 17
Cards accepted: Access, Visa

HUSBANDS BOSWORTH
Leicestershire
Map ref 4C3

Armitage's B & B
APPROVED

31-33 High Street, Husbands Bosworth, Lutterworth LE17 6LJ
☎ Market Harborough (0858) 880066
Village centre home of character on A427, with wholesome cooking and warm welcome. Good choice of reasonably-priced evening meals at nearby inn.
Bedrooms: 3 twin
Bathrooms: 1 public
Bed & breakfast
per night: £min £max
Single 14.00 15.00
Double 28.00 30.00
Parking for 6

KIRBY MUXLOE
Leicestershire
Map ref 4C3

Faith Cottage
Listed

400 Ratby Lane, Kirby Muxloe, Leicester LE9 9AQ
☎ Leicester (0533) 387435
Old world cottage, convenient for Leicester and surrounding places of interest.
Bedrooms: 1 single, 1 twin
Bathrooms: 1 private, 1 public
Bed & breakfast
per night: £min £max
Single 17.50 17.50
Double 35.00 35.00
Parking for 3

There are separate sections in this guide listing groups specialising in farm holidays and accommodation which is especially suitable for young people and organised groups.

203

MIDDLE ENGLAND

LINCOLN
Lincolnshire
Map ref 4C2

Ancient city dominated by the magnificent 11th C cathedral with its triple towers. A Roman gateway is still used and there are medieval houses lining narrow, cobbled streets. Other attractions include the Norman castle, several museums and the Usher Gallery.
Tourist Information Centre
☎ *(0522) 529828*

Garden House M
COMMENDED

Burton-By-Lincoln, Lincoln LN1 2RD
☎ (0522) 526120
Fax (0522) 523787
Fully restored 300-year-old house with oak beams. A stair lift and wheelchair ramp are available. 1 mile north of Lincoln off the B1398.
Wheelchair access category 3
Bedrooms: 1 double, 2 twin
Bathrooms: 2 private, 1 public

Bed & breakfast
per night:	£min	£max
Single	17.00	21.00
Double	34.00	42.00

Parking for 3

New Farm

Burton, Lincoln LN1 2RD
☎ (0522) 527326
360-acre arable & dairy farm. Twin-bedded room with private bathroom. Use of lounge with colour TV. 2 miles north of Lincoln. Evening meal by prior arrangement. Coarse fishing in private lakes. Nature reserve close by.
Bedrooms: 1 twin
Bathrooms: 1 private

Bed & breakfast
per night:	£min	£max
Single	22.00	22.00
Double	30.00	30.00

Half board
per person:	£min	£max
Daily	23.00	30.00
Weekly	155.00	

Parking for 3
Open March-November

Newport Guesthouse M

26-28 Newport, Lincoln LN1 3DP
☎ (0522) 528590
Part of a Victorian terrace only 4 minutes' walk from cathedral and castle.
Bedrooms: 1 single, 1 double, 3 twin, 1 triple, 1 family room
Bathrooms: 2 public

Bed & breakfast
per night:	£min	£max
Single	17.00	17.00
Double	34.00	34.00

Parking for 6

LONG BUCKBY
Northamptonshire
Map ref 4C3

Murcott Mill
COMMENDED

Murcott, Long Buckby, Northampton NN6 7QR
☎ (0327) 842236
100-acre livestock farm. Imposing Georgian mill house overlooking open countryside. Recently renovated to a high standard, with open fires and en-suite bedrooms. Ideal stopover for M1 travellers.
Bedrooms: 1 double, 2 twin
Bathrooms: 3 private, 1 public

Bed & breakfast
per night:	£min	£max
Single	15.00	20.00
Double	30.00	35.00

Half board
per person:	£min	£max
Daily	21.50	26.50

Evening meal 1900 (last orders 2030)
Parking for 32

LOUTH
Lincolnshire
Map ref 4D2

Attractive old market town set on the eastern edge of the Lincolnshire Wolds. St James's Church has an impressive tower and spire and there are the remains of a Cistercian abbey. The museum contains an interesting collection of local material.
Tourist Information Centre
☎ *(0507) 609289*

Wickham House
HIGHLY COMMENDED

Church Lane, Conisholme, Louth LN11 7LX
☎ North Somercotes (0507) 358465
Attractive 18th C cottage, in country setting. En-suite bedrooms, separate tables, home cooking. Convenient for coast, bird reserves, Cadwell Park and Wolds. Non-smokers only please.
Bedrooms: 1 single, 1 double, 1 twin
Bathrooms: 3 private

Bed & breakfast
per night:	£min	£max
Double		35.00

Evening meal 1900 (last orders 1300)
Parking for 4
Open January-November

LUDFORD
Lincolnshire
Map ref 4D2

Walk Farm
Listed COMMENDED

Ludford, Lincoln LN3 6AP
☎ Burgh on Bain (0507) 313242
4-acre smallholding. Very peaceful and beautiful area on Lincolnshire Wolds. Outstanding views. Good food and homely atmosphere. Small pets welcome.
Bedrooms: 1 single, 1 double, 1 triple
Bathrooms: 1 public

Bed & breakfast
per night:	£min	£max
Single	13.00	13.00
Double	26.00	28.00

Half board
per person:	£min	£max
Daily	19.50	20.50
Weekly	115.50	122.50

Evening meal 1900 (last orders 2130)
Parking for 7

MARKET DEEPING
Lincolnshire
Map ref 3A1

Attractive Fenland market town.

Abbey House and Coach House
APPROVED

West End Road, Maxey, Peterborough PE6 9EJ
☎ (0778) 344642

Listed former rectory, dating in part from 1190 AD, close to historic Stamford. Ideal for touring the eastern shires with their abundance of abbeys, cathedrals, stately homes and attractive stone villages.
Bedrooms: 1 single, 3 double, 2 twin, 1 triple
Bathrooms: 5 private, 1 public

Bed & breakfast
per night:	£min	£max
Single	18.00	28.50
Double	32.00	44.00

Parking for 12

MIDDLE ENGLAND

MARKET HARBOROUGH
Leicestershire
Map ref 4C3

There have been markets here since the early 13th C, and the town was also an important coaching centre, with several ancient hostelries. The early 17th C grammar school was once the butter market.
Tourist Information Centre
☎ (0858) 462649 or 462699

The Fox Inn
COMMENDED

Church Street, Wilbarston, Market Harborough LE16 8QG
☎ Rockingham (0536) 771270
An old ironstone village inn offering home-cooked food, real ales and traditional pub games. Near Rockingham Forest and Castle.
Bedrooms: 1 double, 2 twin, 1 family room
Bathrooms: 3 private, 1 private shower
Bed & breakfast
per night:	£min	£max
Single	20.00	30.00
Double	30.00	40.00

Lunch available
Evening meal 1900 (last orders 2200)
Parking for 10
Cards accepted: Access, Visa

MARKET RASEN
Lincolnshire
Map ref 4D2

Market town on the edge of the Lincolnshire Wolds. The racecourse and the picnic site and forest walks at Willingham Woods are to the east of the town.

East Farm House
HIGHLY COMMENDED

Middle Rasen Road, Buslingthorpe, Market Rasen LN3 5AQ
☎ (0673) 842283
410-acre arable farm. In a pretty, rural location, 4 miles south-west of Market Rasen on the Middle Rasen to Lissington road. Guests' sitting room, colour TV, tea/coffee facilities. En-suite available.
Bedrooms: 1 double, 1 twin
Bathrooms: 1 private, 1 public, 1 private shower
Bed & breakfast
per night:	£min	£max
Single	18.00	20.00
Double	34.00	36.00

Half board
per person:	£min	£max
Daily		29.00
Weekly		203.00

Evening meal from 1800
Parking for 6

MATLOCK
Derbyshire
Map ref 4B2

The town lies beside the narrow valley of the River Derwent surrounded by steep wooded hills. Good centre for exploring Derbyshire's best scenery.

Farley Farm

Farley, Matlock DE4 5LR
☎ (0629) 582533
250-acre mixed farm. Built in 1610 of natural stone, set in open countryside close to Peak District and many places of interest.
Bedrooms: 1 double, 1 twin, 1 family room
Bathrooms: 2 public
Bed & breakfast
per night:	£min	£max
Single	16.00	16.00
Double	30.00	30.00

Half board
per person:	£min	£max
Daily	21.00	22.00
Weekly	147.00	147.00

Evening meal 1700 (last orders 1900)
Parking for 10

Thornleigh ᛙ

11 Lime Grove Walk, Matlock DE4 3FD
☎ (0629) 57626
Large Edwardian house with private parking, convenient for bus/rail stations and shops. Non-smokers only please.
Bedrooms: 1 single, 1 double, 1 triple
Bathrooms: 1 public
Bed & breakfast
per night:	£min	£max
Single	14.00	14.00
Double	28.00	28.00

Parking for 3
Open March-November

MEDBOURNE
Leicestershire
Map ref 4C3

Picturesque village with medieval bridge.

Homestead House
HIGHLY COMMENDED

5 Ashley Road, Medbourne, Market Harborough LE16 8DL
☎ (085 883) 724

In an elevated position overlooking the Welland Valley on the outskirts of Medbourne, a picturesque village dating back to Roman times.
Bedrooms: 3 twin
Bathrooms: 3 private
Bed & breakfast
per night:	£min	£max
Single	20.00	22.00
Double	35.00	40.00

Half board
per person:	£min	£max
Daily	25.50	28.00
Weekly	160.00	178.00

Evening meal 1800 (last orders 2000)
Parking for 6
Cards accepted: Access, Visa, Diners, Switch

MELTON MOWBRAY
Leicestershire
Map ref 4C3

Close to the attractive Vale of Belvoir and famous for its pork pies and Stilton cheese which are the subjects of special displays in the museum. It has a beautiful church with a tower 100 ft high.
Tourist Information Centre
☎ (0664) 69946

Manor House ᛙ
COMMENDED

Church Lane, Saxelby, Melton Mowbray LE14 3PA
☎ (0664) 812269
125-acre livestock farm. Home cooking and a warm welcome in this oak-beamed farmhouse. Parts date back several hundred years including a unique 400-year-old staircase.
Bedrooms: 2 double, 1 family room
Bathrooms: 1 private, 1 public
Bed & breakfast
per night:	£min	£max
Double		35.00

Half board
per person:	£min	£max
Daily		27.50
Weekly		170.00

Evening meal 1900 (last orders 1200)
Parking for 6
Open April-October

MIDDLETON
Northamptonshire
Map ref 4C3

Valley View

3 Camsdale Walk, Middleton, Market Harborough, Leicestershire LE16 8YR
☎ Rockingham (0536) 770874
An elevated, stone-built house with panoramic views of the Welland Valley.

Continued ▶

205

MIDDLE ENGLAND

MIDDLETON
Continued

Within easy distance of Market Harborough and Corby.
Bedrooms: 1 double, 1 twin
Bathrooms: 1 public
Bed & breakfast

per night:	£min	£max
Single	15.00	17.00
Double	30.00	34.00

Parking for 2

NEWARK
Nottinghamshire
Map ref 4C2

The town has many fine old houses and ancient inns near the large, cobbled market-place. Substantial ruins of the 12th C castle, where King John died, dominate the riverside walk and there are several interesting museums. Sherwood Forest is nearby.
Tourist Information Centre
☎ *(0636) 78962*

High Barn
Listed
Main Street, Upton, Newark NG23 5TE
☎ Southwell (0636) 813444
Converted barn in a conservation village near Newark. Friendly atmosphere in family home of watercolourist Jennie Searle. Studio open to view.
Bedrooms: 1 single, 1 double, 1 twin
Bathrooms: 1 public
Bed & breakfast

per night:	£min	£max
Single	14.00	
Double	26.00	

Parking for 3

Willow Tree Inn
Listed
Front Street, Barnby-in-the-Willows, Newark NG24 2SA
☎ Fenton Claypole (0636) 626613
Heavily beamed inn in a conservation village surrounded by historic places. Close to the Trent and Witham Fisheries, and Newark, off the A17 and A1.
Bedrooms: 1 single, 2 double, 2 triple
Bathrooms: 2 private, 1 public
Bed & breakfast

per night:	£min	£max
Single	20.00	28.00
Double	30.00	40.00

Lunch available
Evening meal 1900 (last orders 2230)
Parking for 50
Cards accepted: Access, Visa

NOTTINGHAM
Nottinghamshire
Map ref 4C2

Attractive modern city with a rich history. Outside its castle, now a museum, is Robin Hood's statue. Attractions include "The Tales of Robin Hood"; the Lace Hall; Wollaton Hall; museums and excellent facilities for shopping, sports and entertainment.
Tourist Information Centre
☎ *(0602) 470661 or 773558*

Adams Castle View Guesthouse
Listed
85 Castle Boulevard, Nottingham NG7 1FE
☎ (0602) 500022
Late-Victorian private dwelling, completely refurbished in 1989 to accommodate guests. Close to city centre and railway station.
Bedrooms: 3 single, 1 twin
Bathrooms: 1 public
Bed & breakfast

per night:	£min	£max
Single	15.00	16.00
Double	30.00	32.00

Grantham Hotel
APPROVED
24-26 Radcliffe Road, West Bridgford, Nottingham NG2 5FW
☎ (0602) 811373
Family-run hotel offering modern accommodation in a comfortable atmosphere. Convenient for the centre of Nottingham, Trent Bridge and the National Water Sports Centre.
Bedrooms: 13 single, 2 double, 5 twin, 1 triple, 1 family room
Bathrooms: 13 private, 3 public
Bed & breakfast

per night:	£min	£max
Single	19.50	26.00
Double	32.00	36.00

Half board

per person:	£min	£max
Daily	24.50	31.00
Weekly	138.00	156.00

Parking for 20
Cards accepted: Access, Visa

Nelson & Railway Inn
Listed APPROVED
Station Road, Kimberley, Nottingham NG16 2NR
☎ (0602) 382177
A family-run village inn 1 mile north of junction 26 of the M1. Listed in Good Beer Guide.
Bedrooms: 2 twin
Bathrooms: 1 public

Bed & breakfast

per night:	£min	£max
Single	19.50	
Double	35.00	

Lunch available
Evening meal 1700 (last orders 2200)
Parking for 50

OAKHAM
Leicestershire
Map ref 4C3

Pleasant former county town of Rutland. Fine 12th C Great Hall, part of its castle, with a historic collection of horseshoes. An octagonal Butter Cross stands in the market-place and Rutland County Museum, Rutland Farm Park and Rutland Water are of interest.
Tourist Information Centre
☎ *(0572) 724329*

Milburn Motel
Listed
South Street, Oakham LE15 6EA
☎ (0572) 723330
Modern residence with a bright, comfortable atmosphere, in a central part of Oakham.
Bedrooms: 1 single, 1 double, 4 twin, 1 triple
Bathrooms: 3 private, 1 public
Bed & breakfast

per night:	£min	£max
Single	15.00	25.00
Double	25.00	35.00

Parking for 7

Yew Tree Farm
Listed
Teigh, Oakham LE15 7RT
☎ Wymondham (057 284) 497
700-acre mixed farm. A listed, stone-built farmhouse, in small quiet village 5 miles north of Oakham. Near A1, Rutland Water and Melton Mowbray. Good walking, cycling and riding. Good pub food locally.
Bedrooms: 1 double, 2 twin
Bathrooms: 1 public
Bed & breakfast

per night:	£min	£max
Single	11.00	13.00
Double	22.00	26.00

Parking for 3
Open January-November

Colour maps at the back of this guide pinpoint all places which have accommodation listings in the guide.

MIDDLE ENGLAND

OUNDLE
Northamptonshire
Map ref 3A1

Historic town situated on the River Nene with narrow alleys and courtyards and many stone buildings, including a fine church and historic inns.
Tourist Information Centre
☎ (0832) 274333

Castle Farm Guesthouse ⋒
☺☺☺
Castle Farm, Fotheringhay, Peterborough PE8 5HZ
☎ Cotterstock (083 26) 200
850-acre mixed farm. An early 19th C stone farmhouse in beautiful surroundings, with lawns running down to the River Nene and adjoining the Fotheringhay Castle site. 2 rooms can be adapted to family rooms. Packed lunches by arrangement.
Bedrooms: 1 single, 1 double, 4 twin
Bathrooms: 5 private, 1 public
Bed & breakfast
per night: £min £max
Single 22.00 29.00
Double 33.00 46.00
Half board
per person: £min £max
Daily 31.00 38.00
Weekly 217.00 266.00
Evening meal from 1915
Parking for 12

PEAK DISTRICT
See under Aldwark, Ashbourne, Ashford in the Water, Bakewell, Buxton, Castleton, Eyam, Froggatt, Hathersage, Tideswell, Winster

ROWLAND
Derbyshire
Map ref 4B2

Rowland Cottage ⋒
Listed
Rowland, Bakewell DE45 1NR
☎ Great Longstone (0629) 640365
Nestling peacefully below Longstone Edge since 1667. A warm welcome, comfortable beds, delicious food and relaxation await you. Come and share our lovely home!
Bedrooms: 1 double, 1 triple
Bathrooms: 1 private, 1 public
Bed & breakfast
per night: £min £max
Single 17.50 20.00
Double 30.00 35.00
Half board
per person: £min £max
Daily 23.50 26.00
Weekly 157.00 175.00

Evening meal 1900 (last orders 2100)
Parking for 3

SHERWOOD FOREST
See under Edwinstowe, Newark, Southwell, Upton

SKEGNESS
Lincolnshire
Map ref 4D2

Famous seaside resort with 6 miles of sandy beaches and bracing air. Attractions include swimming pools, bowling greens, gardens, Natureland Marine Zoo, golf-courses and a wide range of entertainment at the Embassy Centre. Nearby is Gibraltar Point Nature Reserve.
Tourist Information Centre
☎ (0754) 764821

Victoria Inn ⋒
☺☺
Wainfleet Road, Skegness PE25 3RG
☎ (0754) 767333
Friendly, traditional inn with hotel annexe providing home-cooked food. Central for town and beach facilities.
Bedrooms: 1 single, 3 double, 1 twin, 2 triple
Bathrooms: 4 private, 1 public
Bed & breakfast
per night: £min £max
Single 14.00 15.00
Double 28.00 30.00
Half board
per person: £min £max
Daily 17.00 25.00
Weekly 102.00 150.00
Lunch available
Evening meal 1800 (last orders 2200)
Parking for 20
Cards accepted: Access, Visa

SOUTHWELL
Nottinghamshire
Map ref 4C2

Town dominated by the Norman minster which has some beautiful 13th C stone carvings in the Chapter House. Charles I spent his last night of freedom in one of the inns. The original Bramley apple tree can still be seen.

Barn Lodge
Listed COMMENDED
Duckers Cottage, Brinkley, Southwell NG25 0TP
☎ (0636) 813435
Smallholding with panoramic views, 1 mile from the centre of Southwell and close to the racecourse, railway station and River Trent.
Bedrooms: 1 double, 1 twin, 1 triple

Bathrooms: 3 private
Bed & breakfast
per night: £min £max
Single 20.00 20.00
Double 40.00 40.00
Parking for 3

Old Forge ⋒
☺☺ HIGHLY COMMENDED
2 Burgage Lane, Southwell NG25 0ER
☎ Newark (0636) 812809
Carefully restored old forge with an attractive garden, peacefully located in a small minster town. A few minutes' walk from shops and restaurants. Private parking facilities and 10% reduction on longer stays.
Bedrooms: 3 double, 2 twin
Bathrooms: 5 private, 1 public
Bed & breakfast
per night: £min £max
Single 26.00 32.00
Double 40.00 46.00
Parking for 5
Cards accepted: Access, Visa

STAMFORD
Lincolnshire
Map ref 3A1

Exceptionally beautiful and historic town with many houses of architectural interest, notable churches and other public buildings all in the local stone. Burghley House, built by William Cecil, is a magnificent Tudor mansion on the edge of the town.
Tourist Information Centre
☎ (0780) 55611

Birch House
Listed
4 Lonsdale Road, Stamford PE9 2RW
☎ (0780) 54876
Comfortable, family-run detached house on the outskirts of Stamford. All rooms have TV and tea/coffee making facilities. Non-smokers only, please.
Bedrooms: 2 single, 1 double, 1 twin
Bathrooms: 1 public
Bed & breakfast
per night: £min £max
Single 15.00
Double 30.00
Parking for 4

The Manor Cottage
Listed HIGHLY COMMENDED
Main Road, Collyweston, Stamford PE9 3PN
☎ (0780) 83209
Large stone-built Georgian house with panoramic views, in the picturesque village of Collyweston, just 3 miles from historic Stamford.

Continued ▶

MIDDLE ENGLAND

STAMFORD
Continued

Bedrooms: 2 single, 1 double, 1 twin
Bathrooms: 1 private, 1 public

Bed & breakfast per night:	£min	£max
Single	15.00	35.00
Double	25.00	60.00

Parking for 10
Cards accepted: Access, Visa

Martins
Listed

20 High Street, Saint Martin's, Stamford PE9 2LF
☎ (0780) 52106
Elegant, 17th C house near the town centre. Large rooms furnished with antiques. Walled garden and street parking.
Bedrooms: 3 twin
Bathrooms: 2 public

Bed & breakfast per night:	£min	£max
Single	22.50	
Double	45.00	

Half board per person:	£min	£max
Daily	35.00	
Weekly	213.00	

Evening meal 1930 (last orders 2030)

Midstone Farm House
Listed

Southorpe, Stamford PE9 3BX
☎ (0780) 740136
20-acre mixed farm. A Grade II listed farmhouse in beautiful countryside with lovely walks. Children welcome - animals to see on this working farm.
Bedrooms: 1 triple, 1 family room
Bathrooms: 2 public

Bed & breakfast per night:	£min	£max
Single	18.00	19.50
Double	32.00	35.00

Half board per person:	£min	£max
Daily	25.00	30.00
Weekly	147.00	160.00

Evening meal 1700 (last orders 1900)
Parking for 5

The Priory
HIGHLY COMMENDED

Church Road, Ketton, Stamford PE9 3RD
☎ (0780) 720215
Fax (0780) 721881

Large historic house with en-suite rooms overlooking splendid gardens. Room phone, colour TV. Large conservatory and feature dining room. Licensed.
Bedrooms: 2 double, 1 twin
Bathrooms: 2 private, 1 public

Bed & breakfast per night:	£min	£max
Single	24.00	30.00
Double	36.00	50.00

Half board per person:	£min	£max
Daily	30.50	42.50

Lunch available
Evening meal 1900 (last orders 2100)
Parking for 10
Cards accepted: Access, Visa

SUTTON-ON-TRENT
Nottinghamshire
Map ref 4C2

Leylands
Listed COMMENDED

Great North Road, Sutton-on-Trent, Newark NG23 6QN
☎ Newark (0636) 821710
Fax (0636) 822177
Spacious accommodation with "old world charm" in a rural setting, designed and built by proprietors. Convenient for Sherwood Forest, Lincoln and Newark, and just 5 minutes off the A1.
Bedrooms: 1 single, 1 double, 1 twin
Bathrooms: 1 private, 1 public

Bed & breakfast per night:	£min	£max
Single	15.00	15.00
Double	36.00	40.00

Half board per person:	£min	£max
Daily	23.00	28.00

Evening meal 1830 (last orders 2000)
Parking for 6

Individual proprietors have supplied all details of accommodation. Although we do check for accuracy, we advise you to confirm the information at the time of booking.

TIDESWELL
Derbyshire
Map ref 4B2

Small town with a large 14th C church known as the "Cathedral of the Peak". There is a well-dressing ceremony each June with Morris dancing, and many choral events throughout the year.

Poppies
Listed

Bank Square, Tideswell, Buxton SK17 8LA
☎ (0298) 871083
Poppies offers a warm welcome, comfortable accommodation and good vegetarian and traditional home cooking in a small restaurant, at the centre of this picturesque mid Peak District village.
Bedrooms: 1 double, 1 twin, 1 triple
Bathrooms: 1 private, 1 public

Bed & breakfast per night:	£min	£max
Single	13.00	17.50
Double	26.00	35.00

Half board per person:	£min	£max
Daily	21.50	36.00
Weekly	137.50	200.00

Lunch available
Evening meal 1900 (last orders 2130)
Open February-December
Cards accepted: Access, Visa

UPPINGHAM
Leicestershire
Map ref 4C3

Quiet market town dominated by its famous public school which was founded in 1584. It has many stone houses and is surrounded by attractive countryside.

Old Rectory

Belton in Rutland, Oakham LE15 9LE
☎ Belton (057 286) 279
Fax (057 286) 343
14-acre horses farm. A Victorian country house on the edge of charming village. Quiet, friendly atmosphere. Three miles from Uppingham and 10 minutes from Rutland Water. Accessible from the A47, following signs.
Bedrooms: 1 single, 2 double, 1 twin, 1 triple
Bathrooms: 5 private, 1 public

Bed & breakfast per night:	£min	£max
Single	15.00	28.00
Double	35.00	42.00

Half board per person:	£min	£max
Daily	27.50	40.50
Weekly	175.00	252.00

MIDDLE ENGLAND

Evening meal 1800 (last orders 1900)
Parking for 6
Cards accepted: Access, Visa

UPTON
Nottinghamshire
Map ref 4C2

Honey Cottage
HIGHLY COMMENDED

The Green, Upton, Newark NG23 5SU
☎ Southwell (0636) 813318
Attractive cottage in the heart of a conservation village, ideal for touring Robin Hood country. Bar and restaurant meals are available in the village pubs. Within easy reach of the A1.
Bedrooms: 2 twin
Bathrooms: 2 private

Bed & breakfast
per night:	£min	£max
Single		24.00
Double		36.00

Parking for 4

WEEDON
Northamptonshire
Map ref 2C1

Globe Hotel
COMMENDED

High Street, Weedon, Northampton NN7 4QD
☎ (0327) 40136
Fax (0327) 349058
19th C countryside inn. Old world atmosphere and freehouse hospitality with good English cooking, available all day. Meeting rooms. Close to M1, Stratford and many tourist spots. Send for information pack.
Bedrooms: 4 single, 6 double, 5 twin, 3 triple
Bathrooms: 18 private

Bed & breakfast
per night:	£min	£max
Single	28.50	42.00
Double	39.00	49.50

Half board
per person:	£min	£max
Daily		68.00

Lunch available
Evening meal (last orders 2200)
Parking for 40
Cards accepted: Access, Visa, Diners, Amex

Check the introduction to this region for Where to Go, What to See.

WESSINGTON
Derbyshire
Map ref 4B2

Crich Lane Farm

Moorwood Moor Lane, Wessington, Derby DE55 6DU
☎ Alfreton (0773) 835186
44-acre dairy farm. 17th C farmhouse just off the A615 Alfreton to Matlock road. Pets for children and a friendly welcome.
Bedrooms: 1 single, 1 double, 1 twin
Bathrooms: 2 public

Bed & breakfast
per night:	£min	£max
Single	14.00	15.00
Double	27.00	30.00

Parking for 10

WEST HADDON
Northamptonshire
Map ref 4C3

Pear Trees
31 Station Road, West Haddon, Northampton NN6 7AU
☎ (0788) 510389
Attractive 18th C Northamptonshire-stone detached house in village, with good pubs/restaurants within walking distance. Four miles junction 18 M1/M6. Rugby 10 miles, Daventry 7 miles, Northampton 13 miles, nearest main line station 2 miles.
Bedrooms: 1 double, 1 twin, 1 triple
Bathrooms: 2 private, 1 public

Bed & breakfast
per night:	£min	£max
Single	15.50	17.50
Double	30.00	35.00

Half board
per person:	£min	£max
Daily	20.00	23.00
Weekly	135.00	165.00

Evening meal 1900 (last orders 2030)

WESTON UNDERWOOD
Derbyshire
Map ref 4B2

Parkview Farm
HIGHLY COMMENDED

Weston Underwood, Ashbourne DE6 4PE
☎ Ashbourne (0335) 60352 changing to 360352
370-acre arable & dairy farm. Victorian farmhouse with country house atmosphere. Elegant four-poster bedrooms overlooking the garden and the National Trust's Kedleston Hall and Park.
Bedrooms: 2 double, 1 twin
Bathrooms: 2 public

Bed & breakfast
per night:	£min	£max
Single	20.00	25.00
Double	36.00	38.00

Parking for 10

WINSTER
Derbyshire
Map ref 4B2

Village with some interesting old gritstone houses and cottages, including the 17th C stone market hall now owned by the National Trust. It is a former lead mining centre.

The Dower House
HIGHLY COMMENDED

Main Street, Winster, Matlock DE4 2DH
☎ Matlock (0629) 650213
Fax (0629) 650894

Elizabethan country house offering peace and relaxation in a homely atmosphere. Home-made jams and marmalade. Close to Chatsworth and Haddon Hall. Resident Blue Badge Derbyshire tourist guide.
Bedrooms: 1 double, 2 twin
Bathrooms: 3 private, 1 public

Bed & breakfast
per night:	£min	£max
Single	30.00	35.00
Double	45.00	55.00

Parking for 6
Open March-October

WIRKSWORTH
Derbyshire
Map ref 4B2

Small town which was once the centre of the lead-mining industry in Derbyshire. It has many old buildings of interest, including the church of St Mary, narrow streets and alleys, a Heritage Centre and the National Stone Centre. There is a well-dressing ceremony in May.

Avondale Farm

Grangemill, Wirksworth, Derby DE4 4HT
☎ Winster (0629) 650820
Tastefully converted barn offering peaceful, private ground floor

Continued ▶

209

MIDDLE ENGLAND

WIRKSWORTH
Continued

accommodation. A delightful rural setting just off A5012, 4 miles north of Wirksworth.
Bedrooms: 1 twin
Bathrooms: 1 private
Bed & breakfast

per night:	£min	£max
Double	39.00	43.00

Parking for 1

YARDLEY GOBION
Northamptonshire
Map ref 2C1

Old Wharf Farm
Listed
Yardley Gobion, Towcester NN12 7UE
☎ Milton Keynes (0908) 542454

9-acre smallholding. This unique complex of old farm buildings, with its own working wharf and dry dock on to the Grand Union Canal, is now a family home, smallholding and canal boat maintenance base.
Bedrooms: 1 single, 1 double, 1 triple
Bathrooms: 2 public
Bed & breakfast

per night:	£min	£max
Single	17.00	20.00
Double	34.00	40.00

Parking for 5

> The enquiry coupons at the back will help you when contacting proprietors.

Check the maps

The colour maps at the back of this guide show all cities, towns and villages which have accommodation listings in the guide. They will enable you to check if there is suitable accommodation in the vicinity of the place you plan to visit.

Bookings

When enquiring about accommodation you may find it helpful to use the booking enquiry coupons which can be found towards the end of the guide.
These should be cut out and mailed direct to the establishments in which you are interested.
Do remember to include your name and address.

210

SURE SIGNS
OF WHERE TO STAY

Throughout Britain, the tourist boards now inspect over 30,000 places to stay, every year, to help you find the ones that suit you best.

Looking for a hotel, guesthouse, inn, B&B or farmhouse? Look for the **CROWN**. The classifications: 'Listed', and then **ONE to FIVE CROWN**, tell you the range of facilities and services you can expect. The more Crowns, the wider the range.

Looking for somewhere convenient to stop overnight on a motorway or major road route? Look for the 'Lodge' **MOON.** The classifications: **ONE to THREE MOON** tell you the range of facilities you can expect. The more Moons, the wider the range.

Looking for a self-catering holiday home? Look for the **KEY**. The classifications: **ONE to FIVE KEY,** tell you the range of facilities and equipment you can expect. The more Keys, the wider the range.

THE GRADES: **APPROVED, COMMENDED, HIGHLY COMMENDED and DE LUXE,** whether alongside the **CROWNS**, **KEYS** or **MOONS** show the quality standard of what is provided. If no grade is shown, you can still expect a high standard of cleanliness.

Looking for a holiday caravan, chalet or camping park? Look for the **Q** symbol. The more ✓s in the Q (from one to five), the higher the quality standard of what is provided.

English Tourist Board

We've checked them out before you check in!

More detailed information on the **CROWNS**, the **KEYS** and the **Q** is given in free *SURE SIGN* leaflets, available at any Tourist Information Centre.

East Anglia

The spiritual heartland of England's great artists Constable and Gainsborough and author John Bunyan, East Anglia is an unsurprisingly beautiful and romantic region. At one time it was England's most populous area, and this is reflected in the riotous colour and diversity of its cities and monuments. Visit the Roman remains in Colchester and St Albans, and the historic cities of Cambridge and Peterborough. There are magnificent cathedrals, churches and stately homes like Woburn Abbey, villages to explore, miles of coastline and the tranquillity of the Norfolk Broads. For the energetic, activities abound from watersports and cross-country walks, to amusement parks such as Yarmouth's Pleasure Beach – one of the top tourist attractions in the country.

WHERE TO GO, WHAT TO SEE

The number against each name will help you locate it on the map (page 215).

① Holkham Hall
Wells-next-the-Sea, Norfolk NR23 1AB
Tel: Fakenham (0328) 710227
Classic 18th C Palladian-style mansion, part of a great agricultural estate, and a living treasure house of artistic and architectural history.

Boadicea: Queen of the Iceni tribe in East Anglia.

② Kingdom of the Sea
Southern Promenade, Hunstanton, Norfolk PE36 5BH
Tel: Hunstanton (0485) 533576
See a world only divers see, from the ocean tunnel. View and touch a variety of rock pool creatures. Also a seal rehabilitation centre.

③ Norfolk Lavender Ltd
Caley Mill, Heacham, Norfolk PE31 7JE
Tel: Heacham (0485) 70384
Lavender is distilled from the flowers and the oil is made into a wide range of gifts. Slide show when distillery not working.

④ Blickling Hall
Blickling, Norfolk NR11 6NF
Tel: Aylsham (0263) 733084
Jacobean red brick mansion. Garden, orangery, parkland and lake. Fine tapestries and furniture.

⑤ Pensthorpe Waterfowl Park
Pensthorpe, Fakenham, Norfolk NR21 0LN
Tel: Fakenham (0328) 851465
Large waterfowl and wildfowl collection. Information centre, conservation shop, adventure play area, walks and nature trails. Licensed restaurant.

⑥ Old Gaol House
Undercroft of Town Hall, King's Lynn, Norfolk PE30 1HY
Tel: King's Lynn (0553) 763044
Treasures of King's Lynn including King John cup, Royal Charters, mayoral insignia. In undercroft of Guildhall of Holy Trinity.

⑦ Sainsbury Centre for Visual Arts
Norwich, Norfolk NR4 7TJ
Tel: Norwich (0603) 56060

East Anglia

The windmill at Cley next the Sea – now a guesthouse.

Robert and Lisa Sainsbury Collection is wide ranging and of international importance, with the recent addition of new Crescent Wing.

⑧ Sacrewell Farm and Country Centre
Sacrewell, Thornhaugh, Peterborough, Cambridgeshire PE8 6HJ
Tel: Stamford (0780) 782222
500-acre farm, with working watermill, gardens, shrubberies, nature and general interest trails. 18th C buildings, displays of farm, rural and domestic bygones.

⑨ Pleasurewood Hills American Theme Park
Lowestoft, Suffolk NR32 5DZ
Tel: Lowestoft (0493) 441611
Tempest chair lift, cine 180, railway pirate ship, fort, Aladdin's cave, parrot shows, rollercoaster, waveswinger, haunted castle, star ride Enterprise.

⑩ Otter Trust
Earsham, Suffolk NR35 2AF
Tel: Bungay (0986) 893470

A breeding and conservation headquarters with the largest collection of otters in the world. Also lakes with collection of waterfowl, deer, etc.

⑪ Bressingham Steam Museum and Gardens
Bressingham, Norfolk IP22 2AB
Tel: Bressingham (037 988) 386
Steam rides through 5 miles of woodland, garden and nursery. Rides on footplate of mainline locomotive. The Victorian Gallopers and over 50 steam engines. Alan Bloom's 'Dell' garden.

⑫ Ancient House Museum
White Hart Street, Thetford, Norfolk IP24 1AA
Tel: Thetford (0842) 752599
Museum of Thetford and Breckland life in a remarkable early Tudor house. Displays on local history, flint, archaeology and natural history.

⑬ Ely Cathedral
Chapter House, The College, Ely, Cambridgeshire CB7 4DN
Tel: Ely (0353) 667735

One of England's finest cathedrals. Octagon is the crowning glory. Fine outbuildings. Guided tours and tower tours available. Brass rubbing and stained glass museum.

⑬ Oliver Cromwell's House
29 St Mary's Street, Ely, Cambridgeshire CB7 4HF
Tel: Ely (0353) 662062
Family home of Oliver Cromwell. 17th C kitchen and parlour scenes, tourist information centre, souvenirs and craft shop. Video of fens drainage story.

⑭ Pakenham Watermill
Grimestone End, Pakenham, Suffolk
Tel: Lavenham (0787) 247179
Fine 18th C working watermill on Domesday site complete with oil engine and other subsidiary machinery. Recently restored by Suffolk Preservation Society.

⑮ Ickworth Rotunda
Ickworth, Bury St Edmunds, Suffolk IP29 5QE
Tel: Bury St Edmunds (0284) 735270
Possibly the most unusual house in England – a unique and impressive oval rotunda. Sumptuous collections of furniture, silver and art.

⑯ The National Horseracing Museum
99 High Street, Newmarket, Suffolk CB8 8JL
Tel: Newmarket (0638) 667333
5 permanent galleries telling the great story of the development of horseracing. British sporting art.

⑰ Cambridge and County Folk Museum
Cambridge, Cambridgeshire CB3 0AQ
Tel: Cambridge (0223) 355159
16th C former farmhouse, an inn from 17th C to 1934. Wide variety of objects relating to everyday life of the people of Cambridge.

213

East Anglia

⑱ The Priory
Lavenham, Suffolk CO10 9RW
Tel: Lavenham (0787) 247417
Timber-framed house which through the ages has been the home of Benedictine monks, medieval wool merchants and an Elizabethan rector. Herb garden.

⑲ Imperial War Museum
Duxford, Cambridgeshire
CB2 4QR
Tel: Duxford (0223) 835000
Over 120 aircraft plus tanks, vehicles and guns on display. Adventure playground, shops, restaurant, narrow gauge railway.

Punting on the River Cam.

⑳ Woburn Abbey
Woburn, Bedfordshire MK43 0TP
Tel: Woburn (0525) 290666
18th C Palladian mansion altered by Henry Holland, the Prince Regent's architect. Contains a collection of English silver, French and English furniture and an important art collection.

㉑ Leighton Buzzard Railway
Page's Park Station, Billington Road, Leighton Buzzard, Bedfordshire LU7 8TN
Tel: Leighton Buzzard (0525) 373888
Preserved 2ft gauge industrial railway built 1919, with nine steam locomotives from around the world. Diesel collection, return trips of 5½ miles.

㉒ Whipsnade Wild Animal Park
Zoological Society of London, Dunstable, Bedfordshire LU6 2LF
Tel: Whipsnade (0582) 872171
Over 2,000 animals of 200 species in 600 acres of parkland. Children's playground, railway, Tiger Falls, sea-lions and birds of prey.

㉓ The Mossman Collection
Stockwood Country Park, Farley Hill, Luton, Bedfordshire
LU1 4BH
Tel: Luton (0582) 38714
Britain's largest collection of horse-drawn carriages, displayed in a new purpose-built building.

㉔ Colne Valley Railway
Castle Hedingham, Essex C09 3DZ
Tel: Hedingham (0787) 61174
Complete reconstruction of Victorian/Edwardian rural branch line stations, signal boxes, vintage engines and carriage displays. Museum.

㉕ Knebworth House, Gardens and Park
Knebworth, Hertfordshire
SG3 6PY
Tel: Stevenage (0438) 812661
Tudor mansion house refashioned in the 19th C by Bulwer-Lytton. Houses a collection of manuscripts, portraits, Jacobean banquetting hall, adventure playground and gift shop.

㉖ The Working Silk Museum
New Mills, Braintree, Essex
CM7 6GB
Tel: Braintree (0376) 553393
Show of textiles and mill shop. Looms and ancient textile machines restored and working. Weaving demonstrations. Evening tours by appointment.

㉗ Paycockes
West Street, Coggeshall, Essex
CO6 1NS
Tel: Coggeshall (0376) 61305
Half-timbered merchant's house built c1500. Richly carved interior. Special display of local crafts.

㉘ Tymperleys Clock Museum
Trinity Street, Colchester, Essex
C01 1JN
Tel: Colchester (0206) 712931
Selection of Colchester-made clocks from the Mason Collection, displayed in 15th C house which Bernard Mason restored and presented to the town.

㉙ Hatfield House
Hatfield Park, Hatfield, Hertfordshire AL9 5NQ
Tel: Hatfield (0707) 262823
Jacobean house built in 1611 and Old Palace built in 1497. Contains famous paintings, fine furniture and possessions of Queen Elizabeth I. Park and gardens.

㉚ The Gardens of the Rose
The Royal National Rose Society, Chiswell Green, St Albans, Hertfordshire AL2 3NR
Tel: St Albans (0727) 50461
The Royal National Rose Society's garden, 20 acres of showground and trial ground for new varieties of rose. 30,000 roses of all types with 1,700 different varieties.

㉚ Museum of St Albans
Hatfield Road, St Albans, Hertfordshire AL1 3RR
Tel: St Albans (0727) 819340
Purpose-built as a museum in 1898, displays include craft tools and local and natural history telling the St Albans story from Roman times to the present day. Wildlife garden.

㉚ Verulamium Museum
St Michaels, St Albans, Hertfordshire AL3 4SW
Tel: St Albans (0727) 819339
The museum of everyday life in Roman Britain re-displayed for 1992. Recreated Roman rooms, 'hands-on' areas and excavation videos of coins to coffins and mosaics to mercury.

East Anglia

(31) Paradise Wildlife Park
White Stubbs Lane, Broxbourne, Hertfordshire EN10 7QA
Tel: Hoddesdon (0992) 468001
Over 16 acres of park and woodland with large, enclosed animal paddocks and path-linked picnic sites. Rides, nature trail, crazy golf, shop, restaurant and cafeteria.

Use the map below to locate places in the 'Where to Go, What to See' section.

FIND OUT MORE

Further information about holidays and attractions in the East Anglia region is available from:
East Anglia Tourist Board
Toppesfield Hall, Hadleigh, Suffolk
IP7 5DN
Tel: (0473) 822922

These publications are available free from the East Anglia Tourist Board:
Bed & Breakfast Touring Map for the East of England
East Anglia, the Real England
Places to Stay:
  Hotels, Guesthouses and Inns
  Self-Catering
  Camping and Caravanning

Also available are (prices include postage and packing):
East Anglia Guide £3.50
East Anglia Leisure Map £4
A Day out of London Map £3.50
Gardens to Visit in East Anglia £1

EAST ANGLIA

Places to stay

Accommodation entries in this regional section are listed in alphabetical order of place name, and then in alphabetical order of establishment.

The map references refer to the colour maps at the back of the guide. The first figure is the map number; the letter and figure which follow indicate the grid reference on the map.

The symbols at the end of each accommodation entry give information about services and facilities. A 'key' to these symbols is inside the back cover flap, which can be kept open for easy reference.

ABBERTON
Essex
Map ref 3B3

Manwood Cottage
Listed
Mersea Road, Abberton, Colchester
CO5 7NR
☎ Peldon (0206) 735395
Small establishment 4 miles from Colchester on B1025. Non-smokers given clean, comfortable accommodation and good breakfasts. Spacious parking. Frequent bus service to stations. Free tea/coffee as requested.
Bedrooms: 1 single, 1 twin
Bathrooms: 1 public
Bed & breakfast
per night: £min £max
Single 15.00 17.00
Double 30.00 34.00
Parking for 3

ACLE
Norfolk
Map ref 3C1

Market town has church with 11th C round tower and font dating from 1410.

East Norwich Inn
Old Road, Acle, Norwich NR13 3QN
☎ Great Yarmouth (0493) 751112
Family-run inn, with broad range of food and real ales. Rooms separate from public areas. Ten miles from Yarmouth and Norwich off A47.
Bedrooms: 4 double, 2 twin, 2 triple, 1 family room
Bathrooms: 9 private

Bed & breakfast
per night: £min £max
Single 24.50 26.00
Double 32.00 35.00
Lunch available
Evening meal 1900 (last orders 2200)
Parking for 35
Cards accepted: Access, Visa, Diners

ALDHAM
Essex
Map ref 3B2

Old House
Listed COMMENDED
Ford Street, Aldham, Colchester
CO6 3PH
☎ Colchester (0206) 240456
Bed and breakfast in 14th C family home with friendly atmosphere, oak beams, log fires, large garden and ample parking. Between Harwich and Cambridge, Felixstowe and London. On A604, 5 miles west of Colchester.
Bedrooms: 2 single, 2 double, 1 twin, 1 triple
Bathrooms: 3 private, 1 public
Bed & breakfast
per night: £min £max
Single 20.00 28.00
Double 30.00 45.00
Parking for 8

Individual proprietors have supplied all details of accommodation. Although we do check for accuracy, we advise you to confirm the information at the time of booking.

AMPTHILL
Bedfordshire
Map ref 2D1

Busy market town with houses of distinctive Georgian character. Market established in 13th C, where traders sell their wares around the town pump, a Portland-stone obelisk presented to the town in 1785 by Lord Ossory.
Tourist Information Centre
☎ (0525) 402051

Pond Farm
Listed
7 High Street, Pulloxhill, Bedford
MK45 5HA
☎ Flitwick (0525) 712316
70-acre arable & horses farm. Listed building, an ideal base for touring. Close to Woburn Abbey, Whipsnade Zoo, the Shuttleworth Collection of old aircraft and Luton Airport. Resident Great Dane.
Bedrooms: 1 double, 1 twin, 1 triple
Bathrooms: 1 public
Bed & breakfast
per night: £min £max
Single 16.00 20.00
Double 28.00
Parking for 6

There are separate sections in this guide listing groups specialising in farm holidays and accommodation which is especially suitable for young people and organised groups.

216

EAST ANGLIA

AYLSHAM
Norfolk
Map ref 3B1

Small town on the River Bure with an attractive market place and interesting church. Nearby is Blickling Hall (National Trust). Also the terminal of the Bure Valley narrow gauge steam railway which runs on 9 miles of the old Great Eastern trackbed, between Wroxham and Aylsham.

The Old Bank House
3 Norwich Road, Aylsham, Norwich NR11 6BN
☎ (0263) 733843
A warm welcome and elegant accommodation in our listed Georgian house with panelled rooms, Victorian bathrooms, half-tester bed and games room.
Bedrooms: 1 double, 1 twin, 1 triple
Bathrooms: 1 private, 2 public

Bed & breakfast
per night:	£min	£max
Single	16.00	20.00
Double	32.00	40.00

Parking for 3

The Old Pump House
Holman Road, Aylsham, Norwich NR11 6BY
☎ (0263) 733789
Spacious 1780s family home, opposite thatched pump near marketplace. Central for Broads, coast, steam railways, Norwich. Pine shuttered breakfast room overlooking garden. Non-smoking.
Bedrooms: 2 double, 2 twin, 1 triple
Bathrooms: 2 private, 2 public

Bed & breakfast
per night:	£min	£max
Single	16.00	20.00
Double	32.00	40.00

Parking for 7

BARDFIELD SALING
Essex
Map ref 3B2

Taborsfield
Listed
Woolpits Road, Bardfield Saling, Braintree CM7 5EA
☎ Great Dunmow (0371) 850391
Detached house with attractive garden situated on edge of small village.
Bedrooms: 1 single, 1 double, 1 triple
Bathrooms: 1 private, 1 public

Bed & breakfast
per night:	£min	£max
Single	13.00	14.00
Double	29.00	30.00

Parking for 10

BARROW
Suffolk
Map ref 3B2

30 Brittons Crescent
Listed
Barrow, Bury St Edmunds IP29 5AG
☎ Bury St Edmunds (0284) 810148
Bungalow between Bury St Edmunds and Newmarket, 2 miles off A45. Spacious bedrooms with TV and tea/coffee facilities. Garden, patio. Local bus service. Meals in village.
Bedrooms: 1 twin
Bathrooms: 1 private

Bed & breakfast
per night:	£min	£max
Single	12.50	12.50
Double	25.00	25.00

Parking for 2

Fentons
Listed
The Green, Barrow, Bury St Edmunds IP29 5DT
☎ Bury St Edmunds (0284) 810015

Attractive early 19th C former farmhouse with outbuildings. From A45 follow sign to Barrow. Fentons is beside the Green Veterinary Centre.
Bedrooms: 1 double, 1 twin
Bathrooms: 1 private, 1 public

Bed & breakfast
per night:	£min	£max
Single	16.00	19.00
Double	32.00	38.00

Half board
per person:	£min	£max
Daily	26.00	31.00

Evening meal 1900 (last orders 2000)
Parking for 8

National Crown ratings were correct at the time of going to press but are subject to change. Please check at the time of booking.

BECCLES
Suffolk
Map ref 3C1

Fire destroyed the town in the 16th C and it was rebuilt in Georgian red brick. The River Waveney, on which the town stands, is popular with boating enthusiasts and has an annual regatta. Home of Beccles and District Museum and the William Clowes Printing Museum.

Rose Cottage
Listed COMMENDED
21 Kells Way, Geldeston, Beccles NR34 0LU
☎ Kirby Cane (050 845) 451
Parts of the cottage date back to 1600, with inglenook fireplaces, beams and studwork. Quiet Waveney Valley position in south Norfolk.
Bedrooms: 2 single, 2 double
Bathrooms: 1 public

Bed & breakfast
per night:	£min	£max
Single	14.00	14.00
Double	25.00	25.00

Parking for 3

BEDFORD
Bedfordshire
Map ref 2D1

Busy county town with interesting buildings and churches near the River Ouse which has pleasant riverside walks. Many associations with John Bunyan including Bunyan Meeting House, museum and statue. The Bedford Museum and Cecil Higgins Art Gallery are of interest.
Tourist Information Centre
☎ (0234) 215226

Firs Farm
Stagsden, Bedford MK43 8TB
☎ (0234) 822344
504-acre arable farm. Family-run farm, set in quiet surroundings quarter-of-a-mile south of A422, midway between Bedford and Milton Keynes (M1 junction 14).
Bedrooms: 2 double, 1 twin
Bathrooms: 1 public, 1 private shower

Bed & breakfast
per night:	£min	£max
Single	15.00	17.50
Double	30.00	35.00

Parking for 4

Please mention this guide when making a booking.

217

EAST ANGLIA

BEDFORD
Continued

No 1 The Grange
COMMENDED
Sunderland Hill, Ravensden, Bedford MK44 2SH
☎ (0234) 771771
Elegant, spacious, family-run accommodation in rural surroundings. Two riding schools and Mosbray golf course nearby. Non-smokers only please.
Bedrooms: 1 single, 1 double, 1 twin
Bathrooms: 1 private, 2 public

Bed & breakfast
per night:	£min	£max
Single		20.00
Double		38.00

Half board
per person:	£min	£max
Daily		32.00
Weekly		220.00

Lunch available
Evening meal 1830 (last orders 1200)
Parking for 10

BEETLEY
Norfolk
Map ref 3B1

Peacock House
Listed HIGHLY COMMENDED
Peacock Lane, Old Beetley, Dereham NR20 4DG
☎ Dereham (0362) 860371
Beautiful period farmhouse in rural setting, 3.5 miles from Dereham. Ideal for Norwich, Sandringham and coast. Full English breakfast and a warm welcome.
Bedrooms: 1 single, 2 double
Bathrooms: 3 private, 1 public

Bed & breakfast
per night:	£min	£max
Single	15.00	18.00
Double	32.00	36.00

Parking for 4

BILLERICAY
Essex
Map ref 3B3

Oakwood House
126 Norsey Road, Billericay CM11 1BH
☎ (0277) 655865
Detached property with large garden backing on to woodland. Ideally situated for High Street and station. Non-smoking establishment.
Bedrooms: 1 single, 1 double, 1 triple
Bathrooms: 2 private, 1 public

Bed & breakfast
per night:	£min	£max
Single		18.00
Double		35.00

Bed & breakfast
per night:	£min	£max
Single	18.00	20.00
Double	35.00	36.00

Parking for 4

BLAKENEY
Norfolk
Map ref 3B1

Picturesque village on the north coast of Norfolk and a former port and fishing village. 15th C Guildhall. Marshy creeks extend towards Blakeney Point (National Trust) and are a paradise for naturalists, with trips to the reserve and to see the seals from Blakeney Quay.

Flintstones Guest House
Listed COMMENDED
Wiveton, Holt NR25 7TL
☎ Cley (0263) 740337
Attractive licensed guesthouse in picturesque rural surroundings near village green. 1 mile from Cley and Blakeney with good sailing and bird-watching. All rooms with private facilities. Non-smokers only please.
Bedrooms: 1 double, 1 twin, 3 triple
Bathrooms: 5 private

Bed & breakfast
per night:	£min	£max
Single	20.50	22.50
Double	30.00	34.00

Half board
per person:	£min	£max
Daily	24.50	26.50
Weekly	171.50	

Evening meal 1900 (last orders 1700)
Parking for 5

BLYTHBURGH
Suffolk
Map ref 3C2

Little Thorbyns
Listed COMMENDED
The Street, Blythburgh, Halesworth IP19 9LS
☎ (050 270) 664
Charming country cottage in village of outstanding natural beauty. Good comfortable accommodation. Close to Minsmere/Southwold and all East Anglia's attractions.
Bedrooms: 1 single, 1 double, 1 twin
Bathrooms: 2 public

Bed & breakfast
per night:	£min	£max
Single	16.00	16.00
Double	32.00	32.00

Half board
per person:	£min	£max
Daily	22.50	22.50
Weekly	150.00	150.00

Parking for 4

BORLEY
Essex
Map ref 3B2

Borley Place
Borley, Sudbury, Suffolk CO10 7AE
☎ Sudbury (0787) 371120
18th C farmhouse, set in rolling countryside on the Essex/Suffolk border. The picturesque village of Long Melford (England's longest village) is just down the road. The market town of Sudbury is close by.
Bedrooms: 1 single, 1 double
Bathrooms: 1 private, 1 public

Bed & breakfast
per night:	£min	£max
Single	13.50	15.00
Double	30.00	33.00

Parking for 6

BOXFORD
Suffolk
Map ref 3B2

Cox Hill House
Listed COMMENDED
Boxford, Sudbury CO10 5JG
☎ (0787) 210449

Delightful Suffolk country house overlooking the lovely old wool village of Boxford. On hilltop between Hadleigh, Kersey and Sudbury. Easy access to Lavenham, Dedham, Colchester, Cambridge and Harwich.
Bedrooms: 1 double, 2 twin
Bathrooms: 3 private

Bed & breakfast
per night:	£min	£max
Single	18.00	26.00
Double	34.00	46.00

Parking for 8

Please check prices and other details at the time of booking.

EAST ANGLIA

BRAINTREE
Essex
Map ref 3B2

The Heritage Centre in the Town Hall describes Braintree's former international importance in wool, silk and engineering. St Michael's parish church includes some Roman bricks and Braintree market was first chartered in 1199.
Tourist Information Centre
☎ (0376) 550066

Corkers
Shalford Green, Braintree CM7 5AZ
☎ Great Dunmow (0371) 850276
Two 16th C original farm cottages, tastefully converted. Lathe and plaster with oak beams. Half a mile from Shalford.
Bedrooms: 2 single, 1 double
Bathrooms: 1 public
Bed & breakfast

per night:	£min	£max
Single	15.00	
Double	30.00	

Parking for 3

Spicers Farm
COMMENDED
Rotten End, Wethersfield, Braintree CM7 4AL
☎ Great Dunmow (0371) 851021
70-acre mixed & arable farm. Farmhouse with large garden in area designated of special landscape value. Lovely views of quiet rural countryside yet convenient for Harwich, Stansted, Cambridge and Constable country. 6 miles north west of Braintree.
Bedrooms: 1 double, 2 twin
Bathrooms: 3 private, 1 public
Bed & breakfast

per night:	£min	£max
Single	15.00	18.00
Double	30.00	36.00

Parking for 10

BRUISYARD
Suffolk
Map ref 3C2

High House Farm
Listed
Badingham Road, Bruisyard, Saxmundham IP17 2EQ
☎ Badingham (072 875) 429
Comfortable accommodation in a quiet setting close to A12 and the market towns of Framlingham and Saxmundham, convenient for touring heritage coast and rural Suffolk.
Bedrooms: 1 single, 2 twin
Bathrooms: 1 public

Bed & breakfast

per night:	£min	£max
Single	12.50	12.50
Double	30.00	30.00

BULPHAN
Essex
Map ref 3B3

Bonny Downs Farm
Listed APPROVED
Doesgate Lane, Bulphan, Upminster RM14 3TB
☎ Basildon (0268) 542129
60-acre mixed farm. Large comfortable farmhouse offering home-cooked food. Conveniently placed for all road links: M25, A13 and A127 to London and south-east England.
Bedrooms: 2 twin, 1 triple
Bathrooms: 1 private, 1 public
Bed & breakfast

per night:	£min	£max
Single	20.00	20.00
Double	30.00	30.00

Half board

per person:	£min	£max
Daily	28.00	28.00
Weekly	160.00	160.00

Evening meal 1800 (last orders 2000)
Parking for 4

BUNGAY
Suffolk
Map ref 3C1

Market town and yachting centre on the River Waveney with the remains of a great 12th C castle. In the market-place stands the Butter Cross, rebuilt in 1689 after being largely destroyed by fire. Nearby at Earsham is the Otter Trust.

Dove Restaurant
Wortwell, Harleston, Norfolk IP20 0EN
☎ Homersfield (098 686) 315
A former railway hotel, now an established international restaurant offering accommodation. On the Norfolk/Suffolk border. Good centre for the Waveney Valley.
Bedrooms: 2 double, 1 twin
Bathrooms: 1 private, 1 public
Bed & breakfast

per night:	£min	£max
Single	16.00	
Double	30.00	

Half board

per person:	£min	£max
Daily	23.50	30.00

Lunch available
Evening meal 1900 (last orders 2130)
Parking for 16
Cards accepted: Access, Visa

Shoo-Devil Farmhouse
Ilketshall Saint Margaret, Bungay NR35 1QU
☎ Ilketshall (0986) 781303
16th C thatched farmhouse with attractive gardens, set in peaceful surroundings. Ideal for touring East Anglia. Comfortable, spacious bedrooms with en-suite facilities.
Bedrooms: 1 double, 1 twin
Bathrooms: 2 private
Bed & breakfast

per night:	£min	£max
Single	13.50	15.00
Double	27.00	30.00

Parking for 2
Open March-October

BURES
Suffolk
Map ref 3B2

Butlers Farm
HIGHLY COMMENDED
Colne Road, Bures CO8 5DN
☎ Sudbury (0787) 227243
100-acre mixed farm. Warm welcome guaranteed at this restored 17th C farmhouse in quiet undulating countryside, 1 mile outside Bures. Adjoins public footpaths.
Bedrooms: 1 double, 2 twin
Bathrooms: 2 private, 1 public
Bed & breakfast

per night:	£min	£max
Single	19.00	27.50
Double	38.00	55.00

Evening meal 1930 (last orders 2100)
Parking for 6

BURGH ST PETER
Norfolk
Map ref 3C1

Church with unusually narrow thatched nave and 16th C tower overlooking Oulton Broad.

Shrublands Farm
COMMENDED
Burgh St Peter, Beccles, Suffolk NR34 0BB
☎ Aldeby (050 277) 241
480-acre mixed farm. Family-run, offering a choice of home-cooked English breakfast. Beccles, Bungay, Lowestoft, Great Yarmouth and Norwich all within easy reach. Indoor pool and food at nearby River Centre.
Bedrooms: 2 double, 1 twin

Continued ▶

EAST ANGLIA

BURGH ST PETER
Continued

Bathrooms: 2 public

Bed & breakfast

per night:	£min	£max
Single	15.50	16.50
Double	31.00	33.00

Parking for 6

BURY ST EDMUNDS
Suffolk
Map ref 3B2

Ancient market and cathedral town which takes its name from the martyred Saxon King, St Edmund. Bury St Edmunds has many fine buildings including the Athenaeum and Moyses Hall, reputed to be the oldest Norman house in the county.
Tourist Information Centre
☎ *(0284) 764667*

Copper Beech
Listed

Grindle Gardens, Bury St Edmunds
IP33 2QG
☎ (0284) 767757
Modern family house set in two thirds of an acre close to town centre and trunk road network. Excellent parking facilities.
Bedrooms: 1 double, 1 twin
Bathrooms: 1 public

Bed & breakfast

per night:	£min	£max
Single	15.50	17.50
Double	30.00	35.00

Parking for 8

Elms Farm
COMMENDED

Depden, Bury St Edmunds IP29 4BS
☎ Chevington (0284) 850289
470-acre mixed farm. 17th C farmhouse in a quiet rural position at the highest point in Suffolk. 7 miles south-west of Bury St Edmunds.
Bedrooms: 1 double, 1 twin
Bathrooms: 1 public

Bed & breakfast

per night:	£min	£max
Single	16.00	18.00
Double	30.00	32.00

Parking for 10

The Leys

113 Fornham Road, Bury St Edmunds
IP32 6AT
☎ (0284) 760225
Lovely, spacious Victorian house in own grounds, close to the A45 and railway station. Pay-phone, home-made bread and preserves.

Bedrooms: 1 double, 1 twin, 1 triple
Bathrooms: 1 private, 1 public

Bed & breakfast

per night:	£min	£max
Single	20.00	30.00
Double	32.00	40.00

Parking for 6

Malthouse
Listed

20 Eastern Way, Bury St Edmunds
IP32 7AB
☎ (0284) 753185
Peacefully located away from main road but only 15 minutes' walk from town centre. Dining room overlooks the garden.
Bedrooms: 1 single, 2 twin
Bathrooms: 1 public

Bed & breakfast

per night:	£min	£max
Single	14.50	15.00
Double	29.00	30.00

Parking for 4

Manorhouse
HIGHLY COMMENDED

The Green, Beyton, Bury St Edmunds
IP30 9AF
☎ Beyton (0359) 70960 & (After May 94) 270960
Fax (0284) 752561

Listed 16th C former farmhouse with 20th C comforts, overlooking delightful village green. Good local hostelries. 4 miles east of Bury St Edmunds, off A45.
Bedrooms: 1 double, 1 twin
Bathrooms: 2 private

Bed & breakfast

per night:	£min	£max
Single	25.00	30.00
Double	36.00	38.00

Parking for 5

South Hill House
Listed COMMENDED

43 Southgate Street, Bury St Edmunds IP33 2AZ
☎ (0284) 755650
Fax (0284) 755650
Grade II* listed townhouse, reputed to be the school mentioned in Charles Dickens' Pickwick Papers. 10 minutes' walk from town centre, 2 minutes' drive from A45.
Bedrooms: 1 twin, 1 family room
Bathrooms: 2 private

Bed & breakfast

per night:	£min	£max
Single	20.00	25.00
Double	35.00	40.00

Parking for 4

39/40 Well Street
Listed

Bury St Edmunds IP33 1EQ
☎ (0284) 768986
Spacious 19th C town centre house. Car parking available and all amenities within easy walking distance. Warm welcome guaranteed.
Bedrooms: 2 single, 2 double, 1 twin
Bathrooms: 3 public

Bed & breakfast

per night:	£min	£max
Single	16.50	18.00
Double	32.00	34.00

CAMBRIDGE
Cambridgeshire
Map ref 2D1

A most important and beautiful city on the River Cam with 31 colleges forming one of the oldest universities in the world. Numerous museums, good shopping centre, restaurants, theatres, cinema and fine bookshops.
Tourist Information Centre
☎ *(0223) 322640*

Antwerp Guest House ₩

36 Brookfields, Mill Road, Cambridge
CB1 3NW
☎ (0223) 247690
On A1134 ring road between Addenbrookes Hospital and Cambridge Airport. Near the city's amenities, and bus and railway stations. Pleasant gardens.
Bedrooms: 4 double, 4 twin
Bathrooms: 2 private, 2 public

Bed & breakfast

per night:	£min	£max
Single	20.00	25.00
Double	30.00	35.00

Half board

per person:	£min	£max
Daily	22.00	24.50

Lunch available
Evening meal 1830 (last orders 1600)
Parking for 8

Bon Accord House ₩

20 St. Margarets Square, Cambridge
CB1 4AP
☎ (0223) 246568 & 411188
Quietly but conveniently situated, south of the fascinating historic centre of Cambridge. Non-smokers only please.

EAST ANGLIA

Bedrooms: 5 single, 2 double, 1 twin, 1 triple
Bathrooms: 1 private, 2 public
Bed & breakfast

per night:	£min	£max
Single	20.50	32.00
Double	34.00	48.00

Parking for 13
Cards accepted: Access, Visa

Carlton Lodge
Listed

245 Chesterton Road, Cambridge CB4 1AS
☎ (0223) 67792
Small family-run business within 1 mile of the city centre.
Bedrooms: 1 double, 1 twin, 1 triple
Bathrooms: 3 private, 1 public
Bed & breakfast

per night:	£min	£max
Double	34.00	36.00

Parking for 6

Cristinas

47 St. Andrews Road, Cambridge CB4 1DL
☎ (0223) 65855 & 327700
Small family-run business in quiet location, a short walk from city centre and colleges.
Bedrooms: 3 double, 2 twin, 1 triple
Bathrooms: 5 private, 2 public
Bed & breakfast

per night:	£min	£max
Single	23.00	25.00
Double	34.00	42.00

Parking for 8

Dykelands Guest House ♠

157 Mowbray Road, Cambridge CB1 4SP
☎ (0223) 244300
Detached guesthouse offering modern accommodation. On south side of city. Ideally located for city centre and for touring the secrets of the Cambridgeshire countryside. Children and vegetarians especially welcome.
Bedrooms: 1 single, 2 double, 2 twin, 3 triple
Bathrooms: 4 private, 1 public, 2 private showers
Bed & breakfast

per night:	£min	£max
Single	19.00	23.50
Double	33.00	38.00

Evening meal 1800 (last orders 1930)
Parking for 7
Cards accepted: Access, Visa

Foxhounds
Listed

71 Cambridge Road, Wimpole, Royston, Hertfordshire SG8 5QD
☎ (0223) 207344
Former pub, part 17th C, now a family home. On A603, 9 miles from Cambridge and within easy reach of Wimpole Hall (National Trust). Private residents' sitting room.
Bedrooms: 1 single, 2 twin
Bathrooms: 2 public
Bed & breakfast

per night:	£min	£max
Single	16.00	16.00
Double	30.00	32.00

Parking for 3

King's Tithe
HIGHLY COMMENDED

13a Comberton Road, Barton, Cambridge CB3 7BA
☎ (0223) 263610
Very quiet private house, 2 twin bedrooms with adjacent bathroom and separate toilet. Good bar food available at pubs in local villages; one pub is approximately 300 yards from house. On B1046 off A603.
Bedrooms: 2 twin
Bathrooms: 1 public
Bed & breakfast

per night:	£min	£max
Single	21.00	25.00
Double	32.00	38.00

Parking for 3
Open February-December

Leys Cottage ♠
Listed APPROVED

56 Wimpole Road, Barton, Cambridge CB3 7AB
☎ (0223) 262482
Fax (0223) 264166
Part 17th C house with modern extension in a quiet and secluded spot but within easy reach of Cambridge, M11 and A45. On A603 Cambridge-Sandy road.
Bedrooms: 1 single, 1 double, 1 twin
Bathrooms: 2 private, 1 public
Bed & breakfast

per night:	£min	£max
Single	20.00	25.00
Double	26.00	36.00

Evening meal 1900 (last orders 2030)
Parking for 4

Manor Farm
COMMENDED

Landbeach, Cambridge CB4 4ED
☎ (0223) 860165
620-acre mixed farm. Grade II listed, double-fronted, Georgian farmhouse, surrounded by enclosed garden, in centre of village next to church.
Bedrooms: 2 double, 1 twin

Bathrooms: 1 private, 1 public
Bed & breakfast

per night:	£min	£max
Single	20.00	25.00
Double	32.00	36.00

Parking for 4
Open January-November

31 Newton Road

Little Shelford, Cambridge CB2 5HL
☎ (0223) 842276
Countryside location 4 miles south of Cambridge. Spacious, well-appointed private suite in owner's house with own sitting room and kitchen.
Bedrooms: 1 twin
Bathrooms: 1 private
Bed & breakfast

per night:	£min	£max
Single	30.00	30.00
Double	40.00	42.00

Parking for 2

The Old Rectory
Listed

Green End, Landbeach, Cambridge CB4 4ED
☎ (0223) 861507
Fax (0223) 441276
Spacious, historic former rectory, 4 miles north of Cambridge. Period furnishings throughout. Mural on staircase. Grounds with paddock, rare breed animals. Aga home cooking.
Bedrooms: 1 double, 2 twin, 1 family room
Bathrooms: 4 private, 1 public
Bed & breakfast

per night:	£min	£max
Single	22.00	22.00
Double	34.00	36.00

Parking for 11

The Old Rectory
Listed COMMENDED

High Street, Swaffham Bulbeck, Cambridge CB5 0LX
☎ (0223) 811986 & 812009
Georgian former vicarage set in own grounds. Located 6 miles from Cambridge and 4 miles from Newmarket.
Bedrooms: 1 double, 1 twin, 1 triple
Bathrooms: 1 private, 1 public
Bed & breakfast

per night:	£min	£max
Single	16.00	21.00
Double	32.00	42.00

Parking for 10

221

EAST ANGLIA

CAMBRIDGE
Continued

Segovia Lodge
2 Barton Road, Newnham, Cambridge CB3 9JZ
☎ (0223) 354105 & 323011
Within walking distance of the city centre and colleges. Next to cricket and tennis fields. Warm welcome, personal service and both rooms with private facilities. Non-smokers only please.
Bedrooms: 1 double, 1 twin
Bathrooms: 2 private, 1 public

Bed & breakfast
per night:	£min	£max
Double	37.00	42.00

Parking for 4

CASTLE HEDINGHAM
Essex
Map ref 3B2

Little Chelmshoe House
HIGHLY COMMENDED
Gestingthorpe Road, Great Maplestead CO9 3AB
☎ Sudbury (0787) 62385 & 60532
Mobile (0836) 329560
Fax (0787) 62312
Secluded 17th C farmhouse, offering quality accommodation surrounded by lovely countryside. Croquet lawn, swimming pool, whirlpool bath. Free transport to local restaurants.
Bedrooms: 2 double
Bathrooms: 2 private

Bed & breakfast
per night:	£min	£max
Single	35.00	35.00
Double	55.00	55.00

Parking for 9
Cards accepted: Visa, Amex

CAWSTON
Norfolk
Map ref 3B1

Village with one of the finest churches in the country. St Agnes, built in the Perpendicular style, was much patronised by Michael de la Pole, Earl of Suffolk (1414), and has a magnificent hammer-beam roof and numerous carved angels.

Grey Gables Country House Hotel & Restaurant
Norwich Road, Cawston, Norwich NR10 4EY
☎ Norwich (0603) 871259
Former rectory in pleasant, rural setting, 10 miles from Norwich, coast

and Broads. Wine cellar, emphasis on food. Comfortably furnished with many antiques.
Bedrooms: 2 single, 5 double, 1 twin
Bathrooms: 6 private, 1 public

Bed & breakfast
per night:	£min	£max
Single	19.00	40.00
Double	48.00	58.00

Half board
per person:	£min	£max
Daily	33.00	45.00
Weekly	212.00	231.00

Lunch available
Evening meal 1900 (last orders 2100)
Parking for 15
Cards accepted: Access, Visa

CHATTERIS
Cambridgeshire
Map ref 3A2

Cross Keys Inn Hotel
APPROVED
16 Market Hill, Chatteris PE16 6BA
☎ March (0354) 693036 & 692644

Elizabethan coaching inn built around 1540, Grade II listed. A la carte menu and bar meals available. Friendly atmosphere, oak-beamed lounge with open log fires.
Bedrooms: 1 double, 5 twin, 1 triple
Bathrooms: 5 private, 1 public

Bed & breakfast
per night:	£min	£max
Single	21.00	32.50
Double	32.50	45.00

Lunch available
Evening meal 1900 (last orders 2200)
Parking for 10
Cards accepted: Access, Visa, Diners, Amex

CHEDISTON
Suffolk
Map ref 3C2

Saskiavill
Chediston, Halesworth IP19 OAR
☎ Halesworth (0986) 873067
Travelling west from Halesworth on the B1123, turn right after 2 miles at the signpost for Chediston Green. After crossing the hump-backed bridge over the stream, Saskiavill is the fourth property on the left.
Bedrooms: 1 double, 1 twin, 1 triple

Bathrooms: 3 private, 2 public

Bed & breakfast
per night:	£min	£max
Single	17.50	18.50
Double	33.00	37.00

Half board
per person:	£min	£max
Daily	19.50	21.50
Weekly	114.00	127.00

Evening meal from 1830
Parking for 8
Open January-October

CHELMSFORD
Essex
Map ref 3B3

The county town of Essex, originally a Roman settlement, Caesaromagus, thought to have been destroyed by Boudicca. Growth of the town's industry can be traced in the excellent museum in Oaklands Park. 15th C parish church has been Chelmsford Cathedral since 1914.
Tourist Information Centre
☎ *(0245) 283400*

Springfield
Listed APPROVED
8 Well Lane, Galleywood, Chelmsford CM2 8QY
☎ (0245) 257821
Family home at Galleywood, south of Chelmsford. Take B1007 out of the town or Galleywood turn-off from A12. Well Lane is near White Boar pub.
Bedrooms: 1 single, 2 twin
Bathrooms: 1 public

Bed & breakfast
per night:	£min	£max
Single	14.00	15.00
Double	28.00	30.00

Half board
per person:	£min	£max
Daily	21.00	22.00

Evening meal 1700 (last orders 2030)
Parking for 3

25 West Avenue
Listed
Maylandsea, Chelmsford CM3 6AE
☎ Maldon (0621) 740972
Fax (0621) 740945
Detached four-bedroomed private residence. From Maldon on B1018 or from South Woodham Ferrers on B1012 to Latchingdon, then on to Steeple Road to Maylandsea (about 2 miles).
Bedrooms: 1 double, 1 twin
Bathrooms: 1 public

EAST ANGLIA

Bed & breakfast per night:	£min	£max
Single	14.00	16.00
Double	28.00	32.00

Parking for 5

CHOSELEY
Norfolk
Map ref 3B1

Choseley Farmhouse
Listed

Choseley, Docking, King's Lynn
PE31 8PQ
☎ Thornham (048 526) 331
17th C Norfolk farmhouse with Tudor chimneys. Foundations are thought to date back to original abbey of 1250.
Bedrooms: 1 double, 2 twin
Bathrooms: 1 public

Bed & breakfast per night:	£min	£max
Double	30.00	30.00

Parking for 10
Open July-September

CLARE
Suffolk
Map ref 3B2

Attractive village with many of the houses displaying pargetting work and the site of a castle first mentioned in 1090. Clare Country Park occupies the site of the castle bailey and old railway station. Ancient House Museum in the 15th C priest's house contains local bygones.

Cobwebs
Listed

26 Nethergate Street, Clare, Sudbury
CO10 8NP
☎ Sudbury (0787) 277539
Beamed Grade II listed family house near town centre on A1092. Excellent base for touring. Set in delightful walled garden.
Bedrooms: 1 single, 2 twin
Bathrooms: 1 private, 1 public

Bed & breakfast per night:	£min	£max
Single	16.00	21.00
Double	32.00	36.00

CLOPHILL
Bedfordshire
Map ref 2D1

House Beautiful
Listed

14 The Slade, Clophill, Bedford
MK45 4BZ
☎ Silsoe (0525) 860517

Quiet, country cottage in lovely summer gardens - log fire in winter. M1 junction 12 10 minutes, Luton Airport 20 minutes.
Bedrooms: 1 single, 1 double, 1 twin
Bathrooms: 1 public

Bed & breakfast per night:	£min	£max
Single	15.00	20.00
Double	30.00	40.00

Evening meal 1800 (last orders 2000)
Parking for 4

CODDENHAM
Suffolk
Map ref 3B2

Spinney's End
Listed

Spring Lane, Coddenham, Ipswich
IP6 9TW
☎ (0449) 79451
100-acre mixed farm. Large spacious bungalow set in attractive landscaped gardens with farmland views, in a peaceful location. Full English breakfast is served and evening meals are available at public houses and inns within 1-2 mile radius.
Bedrooms: 2 double, 1 twin
Bathrooms: 1 public

Bed & breakfast per night:	£min	£max
Single	15.00	15.00
Double	27.00	27.00

Parking for 12

CODICOTE
Hertfordshire
Map ref 2D1

The Bell Inn & Motel M
High Street, Codicote SG4 8XD
☎ Stevenage (0438) 820278
Fax (0438) 821671

Recently refurbished traditional inn and restaurant with 25 en-suite motel rooms. Beautiful village setting, with gardens. Very close to A1(M), M25 and M1. Family-run and very welcoming.
Bedrooms: 8 double, 17 twin
Bathrooms: 25 private

Bed & breakfast per night:	£min	£max
Single	30.00	42.50
Double	35.00	47.50

Half board per person:	£min	£max
Daily	40.00	52.50
Weekly	300.00	380.00

Lunch available
Evening meal 1900 (last orders 2200)
Parking for 60
Cards accepted: Access, Visa, Diners, Amex, Switch

COLCHESTER
Essex
Map ref 3B2

Britain's oldest recorded town standing on the River Colne and famous for its oysters. Numerous historic buildings, ancient remains and museums. Plenty of parks and gardens, extensive shopping centre, theatre and zoo.
Tourist Information Centre ☎ (0206) 712920

2 The Chase
Listed HIGHLY COMMENDED

Straight Road, Lexden, Colchester
CO3 5BU
☎ (0206) 540587

60-year-old house of real character. Quiet yet convenient for town and other facilities. In large beautiful secluded gardens.
Bedrooms: 3 twin
Bathrooms: 2 private, 1 public

Bed & breakfast per night:	£min	£max
Single	21.00	24.00
Double	32.00	35.00

Parking for 6

The Maltings
Listed

Mersea Road, Abberton, Colchester
CO5 7NR
☎ Peldon (0206) 735780
Attractive period house with a wealth of beams and an open log fire, in walled garden with swimming pool.
Bedrooms: 1 single, 1 twin, 1 triple
Bathrooms: 2 public

Bed & breakfast per night:	£min	£max
Single	15.00	20.00
Double	30.00	35.00

Parking for 8

223

EAST ANGLIA

COLCHESTER
Continued

The Old Manse
Listed
15 Roman Road, Colchester CO1 1UR
☎ (0206) 45154
Victorian family house in a quiet square beside the castle park. 3 minutes' walk from town centre. Roman wall in the garden. Non-smokers only please.
Bedrooms: 1 double, 2 twin
Bathrooms: 1 private, 3 public

Bed & breakfast
per night:	£min	£max
Single	22.00	26.00
Double	34.00	38.00

Parking for 1

Rose & Crown
APPROVED
East Street, Colchester CO1 2TZ
☎ (0206) 867676 & 866677
Fax (0206) 866616

The oldest inn in the oldest recorded town in England. Early 15th C inn with charming en-suite bedrooms, log fire bar and noted restaurant. On Ipswich road 2 miles off A12 and half a mile from town centre.
Bedrooms: 2 single, 20 double, 9 twin, 2 triple
Bathrooms: 33 private

Bed & breakfast
per night:	£min	£max
Single	39.00	49.00
Double	49.00	59.00

Half board
per person:	£min	£max
Daily	39.50	39.50

Lunch available
Evening meal 1900 (last orders 2200)
Parking for 60
Cards accepted: Access, Visa, Diners, Amex

Scheregate Hotel
Listed APPROVED
36 Osborne Street, via St John's Street, Colchester CO2 7DB
☎ (0206) 573014
Interesting 15th C building, centrally situated, providing accommodation at moderate prices.
Bedrooms: 12 single, 9 twin, 1 triple, 1 family room
Bathrooms: 1 private, 5 public

Bed & breakfast
per night:	£min	£max
Single	15.00	18.00
Double	30.00	47.00

Parking for 30
Cards accepted: Access, Visa

COLTISHALL
Norfolk
Map ref 3C1

On the River Bure, with an RAF station nearby. The village is attractive with many pleasant 18th C brick houses and a thatched church.

Risings
Listed
Church Street, Coltishall, Norwich NR12 7DW
☎ Norwich (0603) 737549
Delightful 17th C Dutch gabled country home with enclosed garden, 200 yards from Coltishall Staithe, central for all Broadland touring. All diets catered for, vegetarian a speciality.
Bedrooms: 1 double, 2 twin
Bathrooms: 1 public

Bed & breakfast
per night:	£min	£max
Single	17.00	20.00
Double	30.00	34.00

Parking for 3
Cards accepted: Access, Visa

CROMER
Norfolk
Map ref 3C1

Once a small fishing village and now famous for its fishing boats that still work off the beach and offer freshly caught crabs. Excellent bathing on sandy beaches fringed by cliffs. The town boasts a fine pier, theatre, museum and a lifeboat station.
Tourist Information Centre
☎ *(0263) 512497*

Aylestone Lodge
20 Alfred Road, Cromer NR27 9AN
☎ (0263) 514394
Victorian terraced house. Spacious, comfortable rooms with continental quilts and razor points. Tea and coffee making facilities in all rooms.
Bedrooms: 2 double, 1 twin, 2 triple
Bathrooms: 2 public

Bed & breakfast
per night:	£min	£max
Single	14.00	16.00
Double	28.00	

The Grove Guest House
COMMENDED
95 Overstrand Road, Cromer NR27 0DJ
☎ (0263) 512412
Fax (0263) 513416
Georgian holiday home in 3 acres, with beautiful walks through fields and woods to the cliffs and beach.
Bedrooms: 2 single, 3 double, 3 twin, 2 family rooms
Bathrooms: 7 private, 2 public

Bed & breakfast
per night:	£min	£max
Single	16.50	20.50
Double	33.00	41.00

Half board
per person:	£min	£max
Daily	24.00	27.50
Weekly	144.00	179.00

Evening meal 1830 (last orders 1830)
Parking for 15
Open March-September

Shrublands Farm
HIGHLY COMMENDED
Northrepps, Cromer NR27 0AA
☎ Overstrand (0263) 78297
300-acre arable farm. Traditional Norfolk farmhouse in centre of Northrepps village, 1 mile off A149 and 2 miles from Cromer.
Bedrooms: 1 double, 2 twin
Bathrooms: 1 private, 2 public

Bed & breakfast
per night:	£min	£max
Single	20.00	23.00
Double	34.00	38.00

Half board
per person:	£min	£max
Daily	27.00	29.00

Evening meal 1900 (last orders 2000)
Parking for 4

DANBURY
Essex
Map ref 3B3

Southways
Listed
Copt Hill, Danbury, Chelmsford CM3 4NN
☎ Chelmsford (0245) 223428
Pleasant country house with large garden adjoining an area of National Trust common land.
Bedrooms: 2 twin
Bathrooms: 1 public

Bed & breakfast
per night:	£min	£max
Single	16.00	
Double	30.00	

Parking for 2

EAST ANGLIA

DARSHAM
Suffolk
Map ref 3C2

Priory Farm ⋒
Listed

Darsham, Saxmundham IP17 3QD
☎ Yoxford (072 877) 459
135-acre mixed farm. Comfortable 17th C farmhouse, ideally situated for exploring Suffolk and heritage coast. Cycle hire available from own hire fleet.
Bedrooms: 1 single, 1 double, 1 twin
Bathrooms: 1 public

Bed & breakfast
per night:	£min	£max
Single	15.00	25.00
Double	30.00	40.00

Parking for 10
Open March-October

DEBDEN GREEN
Essex
Map ref 2D1

Wigmores Farm
Listed COMMENDED

Debden Green, Saffron Walden CB11 3LX
☎ Thaxted (0371) 830050

16th C thatched farmhouse in open countryside, 1.5 miles from Thaxted just off the Thaxted to Debden road.
Bedrooms: 2 double, 1 twin
Bathrooms: 1 private, 2 public

Bed & breakfast
per night:	£min	£max
Single	18.00	
Double	34.00	

Half board
per person:	£min	£max
Daily	28.00	30.00
Weekly	200.00	210.00

Lunch available
Evening meal 1900 (last orders 2100)
Parking for 12

National Crown ratings were correct at the time of going to press but are subject to change. Please check at the time of booking.

DEDHAM
Essex
Map ref 3B2

A former wool town. Dedham Vale is an area of outstanding natural beauty and there is a countryside centre in the village. This is John Constable country and Sir Alfred Munnings lived at Castle House which is open to the public.

May's Barn Farm ⋒
❦❦❦ HIGHLY COMMENDED

May's Lane Off Long Rd. West, Dedham, Colchester CO7 6EW
☎ Colchester (0206) 323191
300-acre arable farm. Tranquil old farmhouse with outstanding views over Dedham Vale in Constable country. Quarter mile down unmade lane off Long Road West from B1029 between Dedham and Ardleigh.
Bedrooms: 1 double, 1 twin
Bathrooms: 2 private

Bed & breakfast
per night:	£min	£max
Single	20.00	20.00
Double	32.00	35.00

Parking for 7

DEREHAM
Norfolk
Map ref 3B1

East Dereham is famous for its associations with the poet William Cowper and also Bishop Bonner, chaplain to Cardinal Wolsey. His home is now a museum. Around the charming market-place are many notable buildings.

Chapel Farm
Dereham Road, Whinburgh, Dereham NR19 1AA
☎ (0362) 698433
Farmhouse with heated swimming pool, full-sized snooker table. Dinner can be taken at pub next door. Norwich and coast 30 minutes.
Bedrooms: 4 double, 1 twin
Bathrooms: 2 private, 1 public, 1 private shower

Bed & breakfast
per night:	£min	£max
Single	15.00	15.00
Double	30.00	30.00

Parking for 10

The town index towards the back of this guide gives page numbers of all places with accommodation.

DICKLEBURGH
Norfolk
Map ref 3B2

Lowbrook Farm
❦

Semere Green Lane, Dickleburgh, Diss IP21 4NT
☎ Diss (0379) 741265
Fax (0379) 741265
Exceptional barn conversion with gracious oak-beamed rooms overlooking fields, vineyard and watergarden. Convenient for Suffolk and Norfolk coasts, historic buildings and gardens.
Bedrooms: 2 twin
Bathrooms: 1 public

Bed & breakfast
per night:	£min	£max
Single	20.00	25.00
Double	35.00	45.00

Parking for 4
Open April-September

DISS
Norfolk
Map ref 3B2

Old market town built around 3 sides of the Mere, a placid water of 6 acres. Although modernised, some interesting Tudor, Georgian and Victorian buildings around the market-place remain. St Mary's church has a fine knapped flint chancel.
Tourist Information Centre
☎ *(0379) 650523*

Abbey Farm
❦❦

Great Green, Thrandeston, Diss IP21 4BN
☎ Mellis (0379) 783422
3-acre horses farm. Beautifully restored listed Elizabethan farmhouse set in 3 acres of peaceful wooded grounds where Shetland ponies roam. Open all year.
Bedrooms: 1 single, 1 double
Bathrooms: 1 private, 1 public

Bed & breakfast
per night:	£min	£max
Single	20.00	25.00
Double	40.00	50.00

Parking for 6

ELMDON
Essex
Map ref 2D1

Elmdon Bury
❦❦

Elmdon, Saffron Walden CB11 4NF
☎ Royston (0763) 838220

Continued ▶

225

EAST ANGLIA

ELMDON
Continued

350-acre arable farm. Recently restored red brick Essex farmhouse with outstanding thatched barns. Set in beautiful grounds behind church, in village centre.
Bedrooms: 1 double, 1 twin
Bathrooms: 2 private
Bed & breakfast

per night:	£min	£max
Single	18.50	25.00
Double	37.00	50.00

Evening meal 1930 (last orders 2030)
Parking for 10

ELMSWELL
Suffolk
Map ref 3B2

Kiln Farm Guest House
COMMENDED

Kiln Lane, Elmswell, Bury St Edmunds IP30 9QR
☎ (0359) 240442
Victorian farmhouse and converted barns set in 3 acres. In quiet lane half a mile from A1088 roundabout off A45. Self-catering accommodation available.
Bedrooms: 1 single, 1 double, 1 twin, 1 family room
Bathrooms: 4 private
Bed & breakfast

per night:	£min	£max
Single	18.00	24.00
Double	32.00	36.00

Evening meal 1830 (last orders 1900)
Parking for 7

ELSING
Norfolk
Map ref 3B1

Bartles Lodge
COMMENDED

Elsing, East Dereham NR20 3EA
☎ Dereham (0362) 637177
Rural setting in 5 acres, own private fishing lake. Perfect peace and tranquillity yet central for Broads, coast and city of Norwich.
Bedrooms: 3 double, 3 twin, 1 triple
Bathrooms: 7 private
Bed & breakfast

per night:	£min	£max
Single	22.00	28.00
Double	44.00	50.00

Half board

per person:	£min	£max
Daily	29.50	35.50
Weekly	165.00	220.00

Evening meal 1830 (last orders 2000)

Parking for 30
Cards accepted: Access, Visa

ELSTREE
Hertfordshire
Map ref 2D1

North Medburn Farm
Watling Street, Elstree, Borehamwood WD6 3AA
☎ 081-953 1522
100-acre arable farm. 150-year-old farmhouse on A5 between Elstree and Radlett. Five minutes from nearest station, 12 miles from centre of London.
Bedrooms: 1 single, 1 double, 3 twin
Bathrooms: 1 private, 1 public
Bed & breakfast

per night:	£min	£max
Single	17.50	
Double	35.00	

Parking for 4

ELY
Cambridgeshire
Map ref 3A2

Until the 17th C when the Fens were drained, Ely was an island. The cathedral, completed in 1189, dominates the surrounding area. One particular feature is the central octagonal tower with a fan-vaulted timber roof and wooden lantern.
Tourist Information Centre
☎ *(0353) 662062*

Forge Cottage
HIGHLY COMMENDED

Lower Road, Stuntney, Ely CB7 5TN
☎ (0353) 663275 & (Mobile) (0831) 833932
Fax (0353) 662260

Stunning views overlooking Ely Cathedral. This 17th C farmhouse has beams and inglenook fireplaces. Furnished with antiques and attractive chintz fabrics. Very comfortable.
Bedrooms: 1 double, 1 twin
Bathrooms: 2 private
Bed & breakfast

per night:	£min	£max
Single	30.00	30.00
Double	45.00	45.00

Parking for 4

38 Lynn Road
APPROVED

Ely CB6 1DA
☎ (0353) 664706
Family home built in 1927, offering bed and breakfast. Evening meal on request. Five minutes' walk from Cathedral, on A10.
Bedrooms: 2 twin, 1 triple
Bathrooms: 1 public
Bed & breakfast

per night:	£min	£max
Single	15.00	18.00
Double	25.00	30.00

Half board

per person:	£min	£max
Daily	17.00	22.50
Weekly	121.00	139.50

Evening meal 1800 (last orders 1900)
Parking for 3

Spinney Abbey

Stretham Road, Wicken, Ely CB7 5XQ
☎ (0353) 720971
200-acre mixed farm. Spacious Georgian farmhouse set in 1 acre of garden. All rooms with private facilities. Farm borders Wicken Fen Nature Reserve.
Bedrooms: 1 double, 1 twin, 1 triple
Bathrooms: 3 private
Bed & breakfast

per night:	£min	£max
Double	34.00	36.00

Parking for 4

EPPING
Essex
Map ref 2D1

Epping retains its identity as a small market town despite its nearness to London. Epping Forest covers 2000 acres and at Chingford Queen Elizabeth I's Hunting Lodge houses a display on the forest's history and wildlife.

Uplands
Listed APPROVED

181a Lindsey Street, Epping CM16 6RF
☎ Waltham Cross (0992) 573733
Private house with rural views. Close to M25, M11 for Stansted Airport and Central Line underground for London. Pay phone available.
Bedrooms: 2 single, 2 triple
Bathrooms: 2 public
Bed & breakfast

per night:	£min	£max
Single	16.00	
Double	32.00	

Parking for 6

EAST ANGLIA

EYE
Suffolk
Map ref 3B2

"Eye" means island and this town was once surrounded by marsh. The fine church of SS Peter and Paul has a tower over 100 ft high and a carving of the Archangel Gabriel can be seen on the 16th C Guildhall.

Laundry House
Listed
Langton Green, Eye IP23 7HL
☎ (0379) 870313

Country house with family atmosphere on outskirts of small town, 1 mile from A40 and 3 miles south of Scole. Easy reach of Bressingham Gardens, Minsmere, Aldeburgh. Interesting garden, free-range poultry, kitchen breakfasts.
Bedrooms: 1 double, 1 twin
Bathrooms: 1 public
Bed & breakfast
per night:	£min	£max
Single	15.00	15.00
Double	30.00	30.00

Parking for 2
Open April-December

EYKE
Suffolk
Map ref 3C2

The Old House ♏
COMMENDED
Eyke, Woodbridge IP12 2QW
☎ (0394) 460213
Lovely Grade II listed house, 1620. Comfortable and friendly, with beams, open fires, large, interesting garden and views over Deben Valley. Centre of village and edge of heritage coast. Good choice of food.
Bedrooms: 1 double, 2 triple
Bathrooms: 1 private, 2 public
Bed & breakfast
per night:	£min	£max
Single	15.00	22.00
Double	30.00	36.00

Half board
per person:	£min	£max
Daily	24.00	28.00

Evening meal 1800 (last orders 1000)
Parking for 9

FELIXSTOWE
Suffolk
Map ref 3C2

Seaside resort that developed at the end of the 19th C. Lying in a gently curving bay with a 2-mile-long beach and backed by a wide promenade of lawns and floral gardens. Ferry links to the continent.
Tourist Information Centre
☎ *(0394) 276770*

Dolphin Hotel ♏
41 Beach Station Road, Felixstowe IP11 8EY
☎ (0394) 282261
Private hotel, 5 minutes from beach and passenger terminal, 10 minutes from town centre.
Bedrooms: 3 single, 4 double, 1 twin
Bathrooms: 2 private, 2 public
Bed & breakfast
per night:	£min	£max
Single	18.00	26.00
Double	26.00	36.00

Lunch available
Evening meal 1900 (last orders 2130)
Parking for 24
Cards accepted: Access, Visa

Fludyer Arms Hotel ♏
APPROVED
Undercliff Rd. East, Felixstowe IP11 7LU
☎ (0394) 283279
Fax (0394) 670754

Closest hotel to the sea in Felixstowe. Two fully licensed bars and family room overlooking the sea. All rooms have superb sea views. Colour TV. Specialises in home-cooked food, with children's and vegetarian menus available.
Bedrooms: 3 single, 4 double, 1 twin
Bathrooms: 4 private, 1 public
Bed & breakfast
per night:	£min	£max
Single	24.00	32.00
Double	38.00	46.00

Lunch available
Evening meal 1900 (last orders 2100)
Parking for 14
Cards accepted: Access, Visa, Amex

We advise you to confirm your booking in writing.

FRAMLINGHAM
Suffolk
Map ref 3C2

Pleasant old market town with an interesting church, impressive castle and some attractive houses round Market Hill. The town's history can be traced at the Lanman Museum.

Boundary Farm
Listed COMMENDED
Saxmundham Road, Framlingham, Woodbridge IP13 9NU
☎ (0728) 723401

17th C listed farmhouse in 1.5 acres of garden amidst open countryside. Log fires, warm, friendly atmosphere. Pleasant stay is assured. 1.5 miles out of Framlingham on B1119 road. Ideal location for touring.
Bedrooms: 2 double, 1 twin
Bathrooms: 2 public
Bed & breakfast
per night:	£min	£max
Single	18.00	20.00
Double	32.00	36.00

Half board
per person:	£min	£max
Daily	24.50	29.50

Parking for 6

The Falcon Inn
Listed
Earl Soham, Framlingham, Woodbridge IP13 7SA
☎ Earl Soham (0728) 685263
15th C inn with exposed beams opposite bowls green and overlooking open fields. 3 miles from Framlingham. Ideal for touring East Anglia.
Bedrooms: 1 double, 2 twin
Bathrooms: 2 private, 1 public
Bed & breakfast
per night:	£min	£max
Single	19.00	25.00
Double	38.00	45.00

Lunch available
Evening meal 1800 (last orders 2130)
Parking for 24

Please mention this guide when making a booking.

EAST ANGLIA

FRAMLINGHAM
Continued

High House Farm ⚑
👑👑 **COMMENDED**

Cransford, Framlingham, Woodbridge IP13 9PD
☎ Rendham (072 878) 461 changing to (0728) 663461
240-acre arable farm. Beautifully restored 15th C farmhouse featuring exposed beams, inglenooks and attractive gardens. Large family room. Situated between Framlingham and Saxmundham.
Bedrooms: 1 double, 1 family room
Bathrooms: 2 private
Bed & breakfast

per night:	£min	£max
Double	32.00	36.00

Parking for 4

Shimmens Pightle ⚑
Listed **COMMENDED**

Dennington Road, Framlingham, Woodbridge IP13 9JT
☎ (0728) 724036
Brian and Phyllis Collett's home is set in an acre of landscaped garden overlooking fields, on outskirts of Framlingham. Ground floor rooms with washbasins. Locally-cured bacon and home-made marmalade.
Bedrooms: 1 double, 2 twin
Bathrooms: 1 public
Bed & breakfast

per night:	£min	£max
Double	33.00	35.00

Parking for 4

FRESSINGFIELD
Suffolk
Map ref 3C2

Chippenhall Hall ⚑
👑👑 **HIGHLY COMMENDED**

Fressingfield, Eye IP21 5TD
☎ (037 986) 8180 & 733
Fax (037 986) 272
Listed Tudor manor house, heavily beamed and with inglenook fireplaces, in 7 acres, one mile outside Fressingfield on B1116 to Framlingham.
Bedrooms: 3 double
Bathrooms: 3 private
Bed & breakfast

per night:	£min	£max
Single	38.00	48.00
Double	48.00	58.00

Half board

per person:	£min	£max
Daily	44.00	49.00
Weekly	308.00	343.00

Lunch available
Evening meal 1930 (last orders 1930)

Parking for 12
Cards accepted: Access, Visa

FRINTON-ON-SEA
Essex
Map ref 3C2

Sedate town that developed as a resort at the end of the 19th C and still retains an air of Victorian gentility. Fine sandy beaches, good fishing and golf.

Hodgenolls Farmhouse
👑 **COMMENDED**

Pork Lane, Great Holland, Frinton-on-Sea CO13 0ES
☎ Clacton (0255) 672054
Early 17th C timber-framed farmhouse in rural setting close to sandy beaches, Constable country, historic Colchester and Harwich. Non-smoking establishment.
Bedrooms: 2 double, 1 twin
Bathrooms: 1 public
Bed & breakfast

per night:	£min	£max
Single	17.00	17.00
Double	34.00	34.00

Parking for 5
Open April-October

GARBOLDISHAM
Norfolk
Map ref 3B2

Fox Inn
👑

The Street, Garboldisham, Diss IP22 2RZ
☎ (095 381) 8151
17th C coaching inn set on the edge of Thetford Forest Park.
Bedrooms: 2 twin
Bathrooms: 2 private
Bed & breakfast

per night:	£min	£max
Single	17.50	
Double	35.00	

Lunch available
Evening meal 1900 (last orders 2200)
Parking for 50

Ingleneuk Lodge ⚑
👑👑 **COMMENDED**

Hopton Road, Garboldisham, Diss IP22 2RQ
☎ (095 381) 541

Modern single-level home in 10 acres of wooded countryside. South-facing patio, riverside walk. Very friendly atmosphere. On B1111, 1 mile south of village.
Bedrooms: 3 single, 3 double, 2 twin, 2 triple
Bathrooms: 10 private, 1 public
Bed & breakfast

per night:	£min	£max
Single	22.00	31.50
Double	36.00	49.00

Half board

per person:	£min	£max
Daily	32.00	45.50
Weekly	210.00	294.00

Evening meal 1830 (last orders 1300)
Parking for 20
Cards accepted: Access, Visa, Amex

GISSING
Norfolk
Map ref 3B2

The Old Rectory ⚑
👑👑 **HIGHLY COMMENDED**

Gissing, Diss IP22 3XB
☎ Tivetshall (037 977) 575
Fax (037 977) 4427
Elegant Victorian house in 3 acres. Peaceful, comfortable, tastefully decorated and furnished. Four-course, candlelit dinner available, except Monday and Thursday. Tea/coffee-making facilities, colour TV, and an extensive range of toiletries available in all rooms. Indoor pool.
Bedrooms: 1 double, 2 twin
Bathrooms: 3 private
Bed & breakfast

per night:	£min	£max
Single	34.00	40.00
Double	46.00	54.00

Half board

per person:	£min	£max
Daily	42.50	46.50
Weekly	246.00	274.00

Evening meal 1945 (last orders 1945)
Parking for 6
Cards accepted: Access, Visa

> There are separate sections in this guide listing groups specialising in farm holidays and accommodation which is especially suitable for young people and organised groups.

EAST ANGLIA

GORLESTON-ON-SEA
Norfolk
Map ref 3C1

A well-frequented seaside resort separated from Great Yarmouth by the River Yare. The long, sandy beach is backed by cliffs and there is a pavilion and a swimming pool. Fishing and sailing are popular.

Balmoral Guest House

65 Avondale Road, Gorleston-on-Sea, Great Yarmouth NR31 6DJ
☎ Great Yarmouth (0493) 662538
Small, friendly guesthouse with personal service and a nice welcoming atmosphere. Good home cooking. One minute from beach and amenities.
Bedrooms: 1 single, 4 double, 1 triple, 1 family room
Bathrooms: 2 private, 2 public
Bed & breakfast

per night:	£min	£max
Single	15.00	20.00
Double	30.00	40.00

Half board

per person:	£min	£max
Daily	22.00	27.00
Weekly	140.00	175.00

Evening meal 1800 (last orders 1600)

GOSFIELD
Essex
Map ref 3B2

Gosfield Lake Resort
Listed

Church Road, Gosfield, Halstead CO9 1UE
☎ Halstead (0787) 475043
Situated by the lakeside with restaurant, water ski site, fishing, pitch 'n' putt and picnic area. 5 miles from Braintree via A131-A1017. 3 miles from Halstead via A604-A1017.
Bedrooms: 3 double, 3 twin
Bathrooms: 3 private, 2 public
Bed & breakfast

per night:	£min	£max
Single	13.50	18.50
Double	27.00	37.00

Lunch available
Evening meal 1900 (last orders 2100)
Parking for 100
Open January, March-December
Cards accepted: Access, Visa

Establishments should be open throughout the year unless otherwise stated in the entry.

GRAYS
Essex
Map ref 3B3

Stifford Clays Farmhouse
COMMENDED

Stifford Clays Road, North Stifford, Grays RM16 3NL
☎ (0375) 375918
200-year-old farmhouse with 3 acres of gardens and spacious, en-suite bedrooms. Close to Thurrock Lakeside, M25 Dartford crossing.
Bedrooms: 6 single, 4 double, 5 twin, 2 family rooms
Bathrooms: 17 private
Bed & breakfast

per night:	£min	£max
Single	17.00	22.00
Double	25.00	27.00

Parking for 18
Cards accepted: Access, Visa

GREAT BIRCHAM
Norfolk
Map ref 3B1

King's Head Hotel

Great Bircham, King's Lynn PE31 6RJ
☎ Syderstone (048 523) 265
Country inn with 3 bars, restaurant and beer garden, near Sandringham, King's Lynn and the coast. English and Italian cuisine, fresh Norfolk seafood and produce, traditional Sunday lunch.
Bedrooms: 2 double, 3 twin
Bathrooms: 5 private
Bed & breakfast

per night:	£min	£max
Double	48.00	50.00

Lunch available
Evening meal 1900 (last orders 2200)
Parking for 80
Cards accepted: Access, Visa

GREAT DUNMOW
Essex
Map ref 3B2

On the main Roman road from Bishop's Stortford to Braintree. Doctor's Pond near the square, was where the first lifeboat was tested in 1785. Home of the Dunmow Flitch trials held every 4 years on Whit Monday.

Homelye Farm
Listed

Homelye Chase, Braintree Road, Dunmow CM6 3AW
☎ Great Dunmow (0371) 872127
Bed and breakfast accommodation on quiet farm situated off the A120 one mile east of Dunmow. Convenient for Stansted Airport and M11 to London.
Bedrooms: 1 single, 1 double, 1 twin
Bathrooms: 3 private
Bed & breakfast

per night:	£min	£max
Single	18.50	20.00
Double	37.00	40.00

Parking for 6

Yarrow
APPROVED

27 Station Road, Felsted, Great Dunmow CM6 3HD
☎ (0371) 820878
Edwardian house. South-facing bedrooms with garden and countryside views. Ample parking. Quarter-of-a-mile to restaurants and pub in lovely village.
Bedrooms: 2 double, 1 twin
Bathrooms: 1 private, 2 public
Bed & breakfast

per night:	£min	£max
Single	14.00	16.00
Double	28.00	32.00

Parking for 8

GREAT YARMOUTH
Norfolk
Map ref 3C1

One of Britain's major seaside resorts with 5 miles of seafront and every possible amenity including an award winning leisure complex offering a huge variety of all-weather facilities. Busy harbour and fishing centre.
Tourist Information Centre
☎ *(0493) 846345 or (accommodation) 846344*

Furzedown Private Hotel
COMMENDED

19-20 North Drive, Great Yarmouth NR30 4EW
☎ (0493) 844138
Hotel overlooking the sea and 5 minutes' walk from town centre. Centrally heated throughout. Established over 30 years.
Bedrooms: 2 single, 9 double, 6 twin, 6 triple
Bathrooms: 19 private, 4 public, 4 private showers
Bed & breakfast

per night:	£min	£max
Single	22.50	23.50
Double	45.00	51.00

Half board

per person:	£min	£max
Daily	32.50	32.50
Weekly	180.00	195.00

Lunch available
Evening meal 1800 (last orders 1900)
Parking for 25
Cards accepted: Access, Visa

EAST ANGLIA

GREAT YARMOUTH
Continued

Spindrift Private Hotel
APPROVED

36 Wellesley Road, Great Yarmouth
NR30 1EU
☎ (0493) 858674

Attractively situated small private hotel, close to all amenities and with Beach Coach Station and car park at rear. Front bedrooms have sea views.
Bedrooms: 2 single, 2 double, 1 twin, 1 triple, 1 family room
Bathrooms: 5 private, 1 public

Bed & breakfast

per night:	£min	£max
Single	16.00	25.00
Double	25.00	40.00

Cards accepted: Access, Visa

HACHESTON
Suffolk
Map ref 3C2

Cherry Tree House
Listed

Hacheston, Woodbridge IP13 0DR
☎ Wickham Market (0728) 746371
Fax (0728) 746371

Large farmhouse built in 1641, with mature garden for guests' use. Ample parking. Imaginative English and continental cooking using fresh garden produce. Evening meal by arrangement.
Bedrooms: 1 single, 1 twin, 1 triple
Bathrooms: 2 public

Bed & breakfast

per night:	£min	£max
Single	18.00	20.00
Double	32.00	35.00

Half board

per person:	£min	£max
Daily	23.00	44.00
Weekly	150.00	180.00

Evening meal 1830 (last orders 2000)
Parking for 3

HADLEIGH
Suffolk
Map ref 3B2

Former wool town, lying on a tributary of the River Stour. The church of St Mary stands among a remarkable cluster of medieval buildings.
Tourist Information Centre
☎ (0473) 822922

Ash Street Farm
COMMENDED

Ash Street, Semer, Ipswich IP7 6QZ
☎ Bildeston (0449) 741493

Approached down a single track country lane, this fine 15th C farmhouse has lovely views and comfortable, spacious accommodation. Beautiful garden. Children and dogs welcome; most eccentricities catered for!
Bedrooms: 1 double, 1 triple
Bathrooms: 2 private

Bed & breakfast

per night:	£min	£max
Single	18.00	20.00
Double	30.00	34.00

Half board

per person:	£min	£max
Daily	25.00	27.00
Weekly	157.00	170.00

Evening meal 1830 (last orders 2030)
Parking for 8

French's Farm
Listed

Hadleigh, Ipswich IP7 5PQ
☎ Ipswich (0473) 824215

Large period country house set in magnificent grounds, offering well-appointed, peaceful accommodation and friendly service. Horse riding facilities available.
Bedrooms: 2 double, 1 twin
Bathrooms: 2 private, 1 public

Bed & breakfast

per night:	£min	£max
Single	20.00	25.00
Double	38.00	48.00

Evening meal 1800 (last orders 2000)
Parking for 15

Gables Hotel
COMMENDED

Angel Street, Hadleigh, Ipswich
IP7 5EY
☎ (0473) 827169

15th C timbered hall residence in historic market town, recently converted to private hotel offering all modern amenities.
Bedrooms: 1 single, 2 double, 1 twin
Bathrooms: 2 private, 2 public

Bed & breakfast

per night:	£min	£max
Single	22.00	42.00
Double	44.00	64.00

Half board

per person:	£min	£max
Daily	38.00	58.00
Weekly	244.00	496.00

Parking for 6

The Marquis of Cornwallis

Upper Layham, Hadleigh, Ipswich
IP7 5JZ
☎ (0473) 822051
Fax (0473) 822051

Large public house, situated in 2 acres of ground leading down to River Brett, between Constable country and Lavenham.
Bedrooms: 2 double, 1 twin
Bathrooms: 1 private, 1 public

Bed & breakfast

per night:	£min	£max
Single	25.00	28.00
Double	35.00	41.00

Lunch available
Evening meal 1900 (last orders 2130)
Parking for 22
Cards accepted: Access, Visa, Diners, Amex, Switch

Mount Pleasant Farm
APPROVED

Offton, Ipswich IP8 4RP
☎ Ipswich (0473) 658896
Fax (0473) 658896

8-acre mixed farm. Genuinely secluded, typical Suffolk farmhouse. 30 minutes from the sea and 5 minutes from water park. Many local beauty spots. Evening meals a speciality.
Bedrooms: 2 double, 1 twin
Bathrooms: 2 private, 1 public

Bed & breakfast

per night:	£min	£max
Single	15.00	
Double	25.00	

Half board

per person:	£min	£max
Daily	20.50	23.00

Lunch available
Evening meal 1900 (last orders 1000)
Parking for 10

Town House Fruit Farm
Listed

Hook Lane, Hadleigh, Ipswich
IP7 5PH
☎ (0473) 823260

85-acre fruit farm. Converted barn close to Constable country and East Anglian wool villages. Near Harwich and Felixstowe.
Bedrooms: 2 double, 1 twin
Bathrooms: 2 public

Bed & breakfast

per night:	£min	£max
Single	13.00	
Double	26.00	

Parking for 6

HADSTOCK
Essex
Map ref 2D1

Yardley's
COMMENDED

Orchard Pightle, Hadstock, Cambridge
CB1 6PQ
☎ Cambridge (0223) 891822

Comfortable modern house with conservatory and gardens, in quiet village location. Hadstock is off A604 Colchester/Cambridge road at Linton, 20 minutes from Cambridge. Non-smoking establishment.
Bedrooms: 1 single, 1 double, 1 twin
Bathrooms: 2 private, 2 public

EAST ANGLIA

Bed & breakfast per night:	£min	£max
Single	16.00	20.00
Double	32.00	36.00

Half board per person:	£min	£max
Daily	23.50	26.00
Weekly	154.00	175.00

Parking for 6

HARDWICK
Cambridgeshire
Map ref 2D1

Wallis Farm
Listed

98 Main Street, Hardwick, Cambridge CB3 7QU
☎ Madingley (0954) 210347

270-acre arable & livestock farm. Traditional family farmhouse in village of Hardwick, 5 miles from Cambridge and close to M11. Ground floor accommodation with patio doors opening on to large gardens.
Bedrooms: 1 double, 1 family room
Bathrooms: 2 private

Bed & breakfast per night:	£min	£max
Double	34.00	38.00

Parking for 6

HEMINGFORD GREY
Cambridgeshire
Map ref 3A2

38 High Street
COMMENDED

Hemingford Grey, Huntingdon PE18 9BJ
☎ Saint Ives (0480) 301203

Private detached house in centre of village, with large garden and quiet surroundings. All home cooking. 1 mile from the A604. Sorry, no smoking or pets.
Bedrooms: 2 single, 2 double
Bathrooms: 1 public

Bed & breakfast per night:	£min	£max
Single	18.00	18.00
Double	36.00	36.00

Half board per person:	£min	£max
Daily	28.00	28.00
Weekly	126.00	126.00

Evening meal 1930 (last orders 1600)
Parking for 4
Open January-November

HERTFORD
Hertfordshire
Map ref 2D1

Old county town with attractive cottages and houses and fine public buildings. The remains of the ancient castle, childhood home of Elizabeth I, now form the Council offices and the grounds are open to the public.
Tourist Information Centre
☎ (0992) 584322

Bengeo Hall
COMMENDED

St Leonards Road, Hertford SG14 3JN
☎ (0992) 582033
Fax (0604) 706835

Grade II mansion, c1660, in the Rib Valley close to town centre. Extensive gardens, doves and 500-year-old oak. 40 minutes fast train to central London. Peaceful, spacious and gracious. Will meet guests at Stansted Airport.
Bedrooms: 1 double, 2 twin
Bathrooms: 1 private, 2 public, 1 private shower

Bed & breakfast per night:	£min	£max
Single	20.00	35.00
Double	40.00	50.00

Evening meal 2000 (last orders 2000)
Parking for 6

HETHERSETT
Norfolk
Map ref 3B1

Magnolia House
Listed

Cromwell Close, Hethersett NR9 3HD
☎ Norwich (0603) 810749

Family-run B & B. All rooms centrally heated, colour TV, hot and cold water, tea/coffee making facilities, own key. Laundry available. Private car park.
Bedrooms: 2 single, 3 double, 1 twin
Bathrooms: 3 public

Bed & breakfast per night:	£min	£max
Single	15.00	18.00
Double	28.00	32.00

Parking for 7

Half board prices shown are per person but in some cases may be based on double/twin occupancy.

HEVINGHAM
Norfolk
Map ref 3B1

Marsham Arms Inn
COMMENDED

Holt Road, Hevingham, Norwich NR10 5NP
☎ (060 548) 268
Fax (060 548) 839

Old established freehouse and restaurant in heart of Norfolk countryside, 5 miles from Norwich airport on the B1149.
Bedrooms: 3 double, 5 twin
Bathrooms: 8 private

Bed & breakfast per night:	£min	£max
Single	32.00	40.00
Double	40.00	55.00

Half board per person:	£min	£max
Daily	40.00	55.00
Weekly	220.00	280.00

Lunch available
Evening meal 1800 (last orders 2200)
Parking for 100
Cards accepted: Access, Visa, Amex, Switch

HIGHAM
Suffolk
Map ref 3B2

The Bauble
HIGHLY COMMENDED

Higham, Colchester CO7 6LA
☎ (0206) 37254
Fax (0206) 37263

Modernised country house in mature gardens adjacent to the Rivers Brett and Stour. Ideal for touring Constable country and wool industry villages. Will accept children over 12 years old.
Bedrooms: 1 single, 2 twin
Bathrooms: 1 private, 2 public

Bed & breakfast per night:	£min	£max
Single	20.00	25.00
Double	35.00	40.00

Parking for 5

HINDOLVESTON
Norfolk
Map ref 3B1

The Windmill Guest House

56 The Street, Hindolveston, Dereham NR20 5DF
☎ Melton Constable (0263) 861095

Recently renovated 19th C farm cottage in rural village. Easy access to north

Continued ▶

231

EAST ANGLIA

HINDOLVESTON
Continued

Norfolk coast, nature reserves and many stately homes.
Bedrooms: 1 double, 1 twin
Bathrooms: 1 public
Bed & breakfast

per night:	£min	£max
Single	16.00	20.00
Double	32.00	32.00

Parking for 6

HINTLESHAM
Suffolk
Map ref 3B2

College Farm
HIGHLY COMMENDED

Hintlesham, Ipswich IP8 3NT
☎ (0473) 652253
Fax (0473) 652253

600-acre arable & livestock farm. Beamed 15th C farmhouse in rural setting 6 miles west of Ipswich, offers a warm welcome and comfortable accommodation. Close to Constable country and Lavenham.
Bedrooms: 1 single, 1 double, 1 triple
Bathrooms: 1 private, 1 public
Bed & breakfast

per night:	£min	£max
Single	15.00	20.00
Double	30.00	35.00

Parking for 10

The Old Barn
Listed COMMENDED

Chattisham Lane, Hintlesham, Ipswich IP8 3PU
☎ (0473) 87498 & 87731
Fax (0473) 87732

17th C Suffolk barn with wealth of exposed timbers, grounds of 3.5 acres. Comfortable family atmosphere. Idyllic country setting. Self-contained holiday cottage also available.
Bedrooms: 1 double
Bathrooms: 1 private
Bed & breakfast

per night:	£min	£max
Single		25.00
Double		35.00

Parking for 3

HITCHAM
Suffolk
Map ref 3B2

Mill House
Water Run, Hitcham, Ipswich IP7 7LN
☎ Bildeston (0449) 740315
On B1115 Stowmarket to Sudbury road. Late Regency house, in 4 acres of grounds, with garden and tennis court. Lavenham, Kersey, Long Melford and Hadleigh within 10 mile radius. Convenient for Constable country.
Bedrooms: 2 double, 1 twin
Bathrooms: 1 private, 1 public
Bed & breakfast

per night:	£min	£max
Single	12.50	13.00
Double	25.00	26.00

Half board

per person:	£min	£max
Daily	18.00	

Evening meal 1800 (last orders 2000)
Parking for 10

HOLT
Norfolk
Map ref 3B1

Much of the town centre was destroyed by fire in 1708 but has since been restored. The famous Gresham's School founded by Sir Thomas Gresham is sited here.

Hempstead Hall
Listed
Holt NR25 6TN
☎ (0263) 712224

1.5 miles off A148 near Holt. Elegant listed 19th C country house built from traditional Norfolk flint, conveniently situated near the north Norfolk coast and its many attractions.
Bedrooms: 1 double, 1 family room
Bathrooms: 2 private
Bed & breakfast

per night:	£min	£max
Single	16.00	21.00
Double	28.00	38.00

Parking for 6

HUNSTANTON
Norfolk
Map ref 3B1

Seaside resort which faces the Wash. The shingle and sand beach is backed by striped cliffs and many unusual fossils can be found here. The town is predominantly Victorian. The Oasis family leisure centre has indoor and outdoor pools.
Tourist Information Centre
☎ (0485) 532610

Caley Hall Motel and Restaurant
COMMENDED

Old Hunstanton, Hunstanton PE36 6HH
☎ (0485) 533486
The bar, restaurant and chalets have been converted from 17th C farm buildings.
Bedrooms: 5 single, 9 double, 11 twin, 4 triple
Bathrooms: 29 private
Bed & breakfast

per night:	£min	£max
Single	27.00	37.00
Double	54.00	60.00

Half board

per person:	£min	£max
Daily	40.75	50.75
Weekly	234.00	255.00

Lunch available
Evening meal 1900 (last orders 2100)
Parking for 70
Open March-December
Cards accepted: Access, Visa

Fieldsend House
COMMENDED

Homefields Road, Hunstanton PE36 5HL
☎ (0485) 532593
Country house style bed and breakfast. Tastefully furnished rooms with sea views, ample parking in grounds.
Bedrooms: 1 double, 1 twin, 1 family room
Bathrooms: 1 private, 1 public
Bed & breakfast

per night:	£min	£max
Single	16.00	20.00
Double	32.00	40.00

Parking for 6

Symbols are explained on the flap inside the back cover.

The enquiry coupons at the back will help you when contacting proprietors.

232

EAST ANGLIA

HUNTINGDON
Cambridgeshire
Map ref 3A2

Attractive, interesting town which abounds in associations with the Cromwell family. The town is connected to Godmanchester by a beautiful 14th C bridge over the great River Ouse.
Tourist Information Centre
☎ (0480) 425831

The Elms
APPROVED
Banks End, Wyton, Huntingdon
PE17 2AA
☎ (0480) 453523
Rambling Edwardian house in open countryside on outskirts of picturesque riverside village, 3 miles from Huntingdon. Friendly and welcoming. En-suite double converts to twin/family. No smoking please.
Bedrooms: 1 single, 1 double, 1 twin
Bathrooms: 2 private, 1 public
Bed & breakfast

per night:	£min	£max
Single	15.00	22.00
Double	30.00	35.00

Parking for 4

Prince of Wales
COMMENDED
Potton Road, Hilton, Huntingdon
PE18 9NG
☎ (0480) 830257

Traditional village inn with comfortable and well-equipped en-suite bedrooms. Convenient for St Ives, Huntingdon, St Neots and Cambridge. On B1040, midway between A604 (to become A14) and A45.
Bedrooms: 2 single, 1 double, 1 twin
Bathrooms: 4 private
Bed & breakfast

per night:	£min	£max
Single	20.00	30.00
Double	40.00	45.00

Lunch available
Evening meal 1900 (last orders 2115)
Parking for 9
Cards accepted: Access, Visa, Switch

Map references apply to the colour maps at the back of this guide.

ICKLETON
Cambridgeshire
Map ref 2D1

Shepherds Cottage
Grange Road, Ickleton, Saffron Walden, Essex CB10 1TA
☎ Saffron Walden (0799) 531171
Converted from two farm cottages, our house is surrounded by fields, half-a-mile outside Ickleton in the Elmdon direction.
Bedrooms: 1 twin
Bathrooms: 1 private
Bed & breakfast

per night:	£min	£max
Single	16.00	16.00
Double	32.00	32.00

Evening meal 1900 (last orders 2030)
Parking for 2

INGATESTONE
Essex
Map ref 3B3

Eibiswald
Listed HIGHLY COMMENDED
85 Mill Road, Stock, Ingatestone
CM4 9LR
☎ Stock (0277) 840631
Fax (0277) 840631
Anglo-Austrian hospitality. Comfortable, modern house in quiet, pleasant rural surroundings. Close to village centre. Railway 4 miles. Convenient for Chelmsford, Brentwood, Basildon. 5 minutes from A12 on B1007, signposted Billericay.
Bedrooms: 3 double
Bathrooms: 1 private, 1 public
Bed & breakfast

per night:	£min	£max
Single	24.00	30.00
Double	34.00	40.00

Parking for 7

We advise you to confirm your booking in writing.

There are separate sections in this guide listing groups specialising in farm holidays and accommodation which is especially suitable for young people and organised groups.

IPSWICH
Suffolk
Map ref 3B2

Interesting county town and major port on the River Orwell. Birthplace of Cardinal Wolsey. Christchurch Mansion, set in a fine park, contains a good collection of furniture and pictures, with works by Gainsborough, Constable and Munnings.
Tourist Information Centre
☎ (0473) 258070

School Barn
COMMENDED
Holbrook Road, Stutton, Ipswich
IP9 2RY
☎ Holbrook (0473) 327397
Fax (0473) 327397
Traditional Suffolk barn in attractive garden. In centre of Stutton village (south of Ipswich), opposite Post Office. On B1080, close to Alton Water on the Shotley Peninsula. Good holiday location.
Bedrooms: 2 double, 1 twin
Bathrooms: 1 private, 2 public
Bed & breakfast

per night:	£min	£max
Single	24.00	24.00
Double	38.00	46.00

Parking for 3

KERSEY
Suffolk
Map ref 3B2

A most picturesque village, which was famous for cloth-making, set in a valley with a water-splash. The church of St Mary is an impressive building at the top of the hill.

Red House Farm
Listed COMMENDED
Kersey, Ipswich IP7 6EY
☎ Boxford (0787) 210245
Listed farmhouse between Kersey and Boxford, central for Constable country. Rooms with wash basins, TV and tea-making facilities. Twin bedroom is en-suite.
Bedrooms: 1 double, 1 twin
Bathrooms: 1 private, 1 public
Bed & breakfast

per night:	£min	£max
Single	18.00	20.00
Double	32.00	34.00

Half board

per person:	£min	£max
Daily	26.00	28.00
Weekly	182.00	196.00

Evening meal 1900 (last orders 1000)
Parking for 5

EAST ANGLIA

KESSINGLAND
Suffolk
Map ref 3C1

Seaside village whose church tower has served as a landmark to sailors for generations. Nearby is the Suffolk Wildlife and Country Park.

The Old Rectory
HIGHLY COMMENDED

157 Church Road, Kessingland, Lowestoft NR33 7SQ
☎ Lowestoft (0502) 740020
Beautiful late Georgian house in 2 acres of garden, well back from road ensuring peace and quiet. A warm welcome awaits. Spacious, comfortable, delightfully furnished rooms, most with antiques.
Bedrooms: 2 double, 1 twin, 1 family room
Bathrooms: 3 private, 2 public
Bed & breakfast
per night:	£min	£max
Single	21.00	23.00
Double	38.00	42.00

Parking for 6
Open May-September

KING'S LYNN
Norfolk
Map ref 3B1

A busy town with many outstanding buildings. The Guildhall and Town Hall are both built of flint in a striking chequer design. Behind the Guildhall in the Old Gaol House the sounds and smells of prison life 2 centuries ago are recreated.
Tourist Information Centre
☎ (0553) 763044

Maranatha Guest House

115 Gaywood Road, Gaywood, King's Lynn PE30 2PU
☎ (0553) 774596
Large carrstone and brick residence with gardens front and rear. 10 minutes' walk from the town centre. Direct road to Sandringham and the coast.
Bedrooms: 2 single, 2 double, 2 twin
Bathrooms: 1 private, 2 public
Bed & breakfast
per night:	£min	£max
Single	15.00	
Double	24.00	26.00

Half board
per person:	£min	£max
Daily	16.00	19.00

Lunch available
Evening meal 1800 (last orders 1800)
Parking for 9

KNEESWORTH
Cambridgeshire
Map ref 2D1

The Grange
COMMENDED

Old North Road, Kneesworth SG8 5DS
☎ Royston (0763) 248674
18th C farmhouse set in pretty well-stocked gardens overlooking farmland. Breakfast served in Victorian conservatory, evening meal by arrangement. Large en-suite bedrooms. 20 minutes Cambridge, M11 and A1(M).
Bedrooms: 2 double, 1 twin
Bathrooms: 3 private
Bed & breakfast
per night:	£min	£max
Single	25.00	35.00
Double	36.00	50.00

Half board
per person:	£min	£max
Daily	32.50	50.00

Evening meal 1900 (last orders 2000)
Parking for 12

LAVENHAM
Suffolk
Map ref 3B2

A former prosperous wool town of timber-framed buildings with the cathedral-like church and its tall tower. The market-place is 13th C and the Guildhall now houses a museum.

The Great House Restaurant and Hotel

Market Place, Lavenham, Sudbury CO10 9QZ
☎ Sudbury (0787) 247431
Famous and historic 15th C house with covered outside courtyard, quietly and ideally located, full of warmth and oak furniture for a relaxing stay. French cuisine. Menu changing daily.
Bedrooms: 1 double, 1 twin, 1 triple, 1 family room
Bathrooms: 4 private
Bed & breakfast
per night:	£min	£max
Single	49.50	75.00
Double	66.00	80.00

Half board
per person:	£min	£max
Daily		49.75

Lunch available
Evening meal 1900 (last orders 2230)
Parking for 10
Open February-December
Cards accepted: Access, Visa

Hill House Farm

Preston St Mary, Lavenham, Sudbury CO10 9LT
☎ (0787) 247571
Beautiful listed Elizabethan farmhouse furnished with antiques, in peaceful rural setting close to Lavenham. Spacious accommodation with private access, lovely gardens and large pond with waterfowl.
Bedrooms: 1 twin
Bathrooms: 1 private
Bed & breakfast
per night:	£min	£max
Single		35.00
Double		60.00

Lunch available
Parking for 8
Open March-September
Cards accepted: Access

Meathe House
HIGHLY COMMENDED

Hill Green, Lavenham, Sudbury CO10 9LS
☎ (0787) 247809
Interesting, spacious house and friendly hospitality, beautifully situated in quiet countryside, 1 mile north of Lavenham. Ideal touring base. Non-smokers only please.
Bedrooms: 1 single, 1 double, 1 twin
Bathrooms: 1 public
Bed & breakfast
per night:	£min	£max
Single	18.00	20.00
Double	32.00	36.00

Parking for 5
Open April-October

Street Farm
Listed

Brent Eleigh, Sudbury CO10 9NU
☎ (0787) 247271
140-acre arable farm. Attractive 16th C farmhouse furnished to a high standard, set in large grounds 2 miles from historic Lavenham. En-suite bath or shower room. Tea and coffee making facilities.
Bedrooms: 2 double, 1 twin
Bathrooms: 2 private
Half board
per person:	£min	£max
Daily	18.00	20.00

Parking for 3
Open February-November

The town index towards the back of this guide gives page numbers of all places with accommodation.

EAST ANGLIA

LAWSHALL
Suffolk
Map ref 3B2

Brighthouse Farm
COMMENDED

Melford Road, Lawshall, Bury St Edmunds IP29 4PX
☎ Bury St Edmunds (0284) 830385
300-acre arable & livestock farm. A warm welcome awaits you at this 200-year-old farmhouse set in 3 acres of gardens. Close to many places of historic interest. Good pubs and restaurants nearby.
Bedrooms: 2 double, 1 twin
Bathrooms: 3 private, 1 public
Bed & breakfast

per night:	£min	£max
Single	16.00	25.00
Double	32.00	40.00

Parking for 10

LITTLE TEY
Essex
Map ref 3B2

Knaves Farm House
Listed

Great Tey Road, Little Tey, Colchester CO6 1JA
☎ Colchester (0206) 211039
Charming early Victorian farmhouse in 1 acre of well-kept garden with traditional Essex barns. 400 yards from A120 towards Great Tey.
Bedrooms: 1 double
Bathrooms: 1 private
Bed & breakfast

per night:	£min	£max
Single	18.50	24.00
Double	29.00	35.00

Evening meal 1800 (last orders 2000)
Parking for 1

LITTLE WALSINGHAM
Norfolk
Map ref 3B1

Little Walsingham is larger than its neighbour Great Walsingham and more important because of its long history as a religious shrine to which many pilgrimages were made. The village has many picturesque buildings of the 16th C and later.

St David's House
Friday Market, Little Walsingham, Walsingham NR22 6BY
☎ Fakenham (0328) 820633
16th C brick house in a delightful medieval village. From Fakenham (A148) take the B1105 - the village is fully signposted.
Bedrooms: 1 twin, 2 triple

Bathrooms: 2 public
Bed & breakfast

per night:	£min	£max
Single		15.00
Double		30.00

Half board

per person:	£min	£max
Daily		21.50

Lunch available
Evening meal from 1800

LITTLEPORT
Cambridgeshire
Map ref 3B2

Walnut Tree Bungalow

50 High Street, Littleport, Ely CB6 1HE
☎ Ely (0353) 861059
Spacious pleasant bungalow with large well-kept garden, on the A10 trunk road at Littleport between Cambridge and King's Lynn.
Bedrooms: 2 single, 2 double, 1 twin
Bathrooms: 5 private
Bed & breakfast

per night:	£min	£max
Single	15.00	18.00
Double	30.00	36.00

Half board

per person:	£min	£max
Daily	38.00	45.00
Weekly	266.00	315.00

Evening meal 1900 (last orders 1800)
Parking for 5
Open March-November

LODDON
Norfolk
Map ref 3C1

Small town on the River Chet. Round the square are some good buildings and the large church of Holy Trinity has many interesting contents. Close by is the 18th C Loddon House.

Mundham Grange

Mundham, Loddon, Norwich NR14 6EP
☎ Brooke (0508) 50067
Grade II listed modernised farmhouse. Peaceful rural situation for touring coast, Broads and historic city of Norwich. 2 miles from Loddon.
Bedrooms: 1 twin, 1 triple
Bathrooms: 1 private, 1 public
Bed & breakfast

per night:	£min	£max
Single	15.00	18.00
Double	30.00	36.00

Half board

per person:	£min	£max
Daily	22.50	25.50
Weekly	250.00	259.00

Evening meal 1800 (last orders 2000)
Parking for 10

LOWESTOFT
Suffolk
Map ref 3C1

Seaside town with wide sandy beaches. Important fishing port with picturesque fishing quarter. Home of the famous Lowestoft porcelain and birthplace of Benjamin Britten. East Point Pavilion's exhibition describes the Lowestoft story.
Tourist Information Centre
☎ (0502) 523000

Church Farm
Listed HIGHLY COMMENDED

Corton, Lowestoft NR32 5HX
☎ (0502) 730359
220-acre arable farm. Victorian farmhouse with a warm, welcoming atmosphere. Quietly situated on the Suffolk coast between Lowestoft and Great Yarmouth. Clean, comfortable, en-suite rooms, generous English breakfast. Non-smoking establishment.
Bedrooms: 2 double
Bathrooms: 2 private
Bed & breakfast

per night:	£min	£max
Single		25.00
Double		34.00

Parking for 4
Open March-October

Hall Farm
Listed

Jay Lane, Church Lane, Lound, Lowestoft NR32 5LJ
☎ (0502) 730415
101-acre arable farm. Traditional 16th C Suffolk farmhouse within 2 miles of the sea. Clean, comfortable accommodation with generous English breakfast. Farm down a quiet, private lane half-a-mile from A12.
Bedrooms: 1 single, 1 double, 1 twin, 1 triple
Bathrooms: 2 private, 1 public
Bed & breakfast

per night:	£min	£max
Single		15.00
Double	28.00	34.00

Parking for 6
Open March-October

EAST ANGLIA

MARGARET RODING
Essex
Map ref 2D1

Greys
Listed
Ongar Road, Margaret Roding, Dunmow CM6 1QR
☎ Good Easter (0245) 231509
340-acre arable and mixed farm. Formerly 2 cottages pleasantly situated on family farm just off A1060 with telephone kiosk. Beamed throughout, large garden. Tea/coffee available. Singles by arrangement.
Bedrooms: 2 double, 1 twin
Bathrooms: 1 public
Bed & breakfast
per night: £min £max
Single 16.00 18.00
Double 32.00 36.00
Parking for 6

MUCH HADHAM
Hertfordshire
Map ref 2D1

Daneswood
HIGHLY COMMENDED
Much Hadham SG10 6DT
☎ (027 984) 2519
A small, listed country house, built in the style of Edwin Lutyens, in 25 acres of gardens and bluebell woods. 15 minutes Stansted Airport.
Bedrooms: 1 twin
Bathrooms: 1 private
Bed & breakfast
per night: £min £max
Single 22.00
Double 35.00
Parking for 4

NEATISHEAD
Norfolk
Map ref 3C1

Regency Guest House
The Street, Neatishead, Norwich NR12 8AD
☎ Horning (0692) 630233
Ideal location for Broads boating/fishing activities. Accent on personal service. 10 miles from Norwich off A1151. 6 miles from coast. Tea-making facilities/TV in all rooms. Renowned for generous English breakfasts.
Bedrooms: 2 double, 1 twin
Bathrooms: 3 private, 2 public
Bed & breakfast
per night: £min £max
Single 19.00
Double 35.00

Parking for 8
Cards accepted: Diners

NEWMARKET
Suffolk
Map ref 3B2

Centre of the English horse-racing world and the headquarters of the Jockey Club and National Stud. Racecourse and horse sales. The National Horse Racing Museum traces the history and development of the Sport of Kings.
Tourist Information Centre
☎ (0638) 667200

Bechers
Listed
Hamilton Road, Newmarket CB8 7JQ
☎ (0638) 666546
Fax (0638) 561989

"Bechers" - home of the Champions. Guests can become involved in the hour by hour activities of this sporting family in their racing yard home.
Bedrooms: 1 single, 2 double, 1 twin
Bathrooms: 2 public
Bed & breakfast
per night: £min £max
Single 20.00 20.00
Double 40.00 40.00
Half board
per person: £min £max
Daily 34.00 36.00
Weekly 225.00 238.00
Evening meal 1800 (last orders 2100)
Parking for 10

Beechcroft Guest House
Listed
11 and 13 Park Lane, Newmarket CB8 8AX
☎ (0638) 669213
Small friendly guesthouse. Quiet but within walking distance of the town centre, station and buses.
Bedrooms: 1 single, 3 double, 3 twin, 2 triple, 2 family rooms
Bathrooms: 2 public
Bed & breakfast
per night: £min £max
Single 24.50
Double 43.00
Evening meal from 2000
Parking for 4
Cards accepted: Access, Visa, Switch

Westley House
Listed
Westley Waterless, Newmarket CB8 0RG
☎ (0638) 508112
Fax (0638) 508113
Spacious Georgian-style former rectory in quiet rural area 5 miles south of Newmarket and convenient for Cambridge. Large comfortable bedrooms and drawing room opening on to 5 acres of garden, trees and paddocks. Visitors are our guests. Advance bookings only please.
Bedrooms: 1 single, 2 twin
Bathrooms: 2 public
Bed & breakfast
per night: £min £max
Single 18.50 20.00
Double 37.00 40.00
Evening meal 1930 (last orders 2100)
Parking for 6

NORFOLK BROADS
See under Acle, Aylsham, Beccles, Bungay, Burgh St Peter, Cawston, Coltishall, Gorleston-on-Sea, Great Yarmouth, Hevingham, Loddon, Lowestoft, Neatishead, North Walsham, Norwich, Oulton Broad, Rackheath, Rollesby, Salhouse, Wroxham

NORTH WALSHAM
Norfolk
Map ref 3C1

Weekly market has been held here for 700 years. 1 mile south of town is a cross commemorating the Peasants' Revolt of 1381. Nelson attended the local Paston Grammar School, founded in 1606 and still flourishing.

Beechwood Hotel
COMMENDED
20 Cromer Road, North Walsham NR28 0HD
☎ (0692) 403231
In its own gardens with many roses, shrubs, large trees, extensive lawns and numerous rhododendrons.
Bedrooms: 1 single, 4 double, 3 twin, 1 triple, 2 family rooms
Bathrooms: 9 private, 2 public
Bed & breakfast
per night: £min £max
Single 22.00 26.00
Double 44.00 52.00
Half board
per person: £min £max
Daily 34.00 38.00
Weekly 169.00 209.00
Evening meal 1900 (last orders 1930)
Parking for 11

EAST ANGLIA

Geoffrey the Dyer House

Church Plain, Worstead, North Walsham NR28 9AL
☎ Smallburgh (0692) 536562
Carefully restored 17th C weaver's residence, full of character and comfort, close to beach, Broads and Norwich. In centre of conservation village.
Bedrooms: 2 double, 1 twin
Bathrooms: 3 private

Bed & breakfast per night:	£min	£max
Single	16.00	20.00
Double	32.00	40.00

Lunch available
Evening meal 1830 (last orders 2200)
Parking for 4

NORWICH
Norfolk
Map ref 3C1

Beautiful cathedral city and county town on the River Wensum with many fine museums and medieval churches. Norman castle, Guildhall and interesting medieval streets. Good shopping centre and market.
Tourist Information Centre
☎ (0603) 666071 or (accommodation) 761082

Arodet House

132 Earlham Road, Norwich NR2 3HF
☎ (0603) 503522
Convenient for university. Walking distance to city centre. Separate guest lounge. Tea/coffee facilities. Personal keys.
Bedrooms: 2 single, 2 double
Bathrooms: 1 private, 1 public

Bed & breakfast per night:	£min	£max
Single	16.00	17.00
Double	32.00	35.00

Blue Cedar Lodge
Listed

391 Earlham Road, Norwich NR2 3RQ
☎ (0603) 58131
Quiet modern house run by friendly family, set in wooded grounds. Convenient for city centre and University of East Anglia. Full fire certificate.
Bedrooms: 1 single, 2 double, 1 twin, 1 triple
Bathrooms: 2 private, 1 public

Bed & breakfast per night:	£min	£max
Single	16.00	18.00
Double	30.00	35.00

Parking for 8

Cavell House
Listed

Swardeston, Norwich NR14 8D2
☎ Mulbarton (0508) 78195
Birthplace of Nurse Edith Cavell. Georgian farmhouse on edge of Swardeston village. Off B1113 south of Norwich (5 miles from centre) in rural setting. Tennis coaching available.
Bedrooms: 1 single, 1 double, 1 twin
Bathrooms: 1 public

Bed & breakfast per night:	£min	£max
Single	10.00	18.00
Double	30.00	35.00

Parking for 10

Church Farm Guest House
COMMENDED

Church Street, Horsford, Norwich NR10 3DB
☎ (0603) 898020 & 898582
Quiet, modernised 17th C farmhouse. Separate entrance, lounge and dining room for guests. Approximately 4 miles north of Norwich.
Bedrooms: 1 double, 2 twin, 2 triple
Bathrooms: 5 private

Bed & breakfast per night:	£min	£max
Single	14.00	20.00
Double	32.00	36.00

Parking for 20

Gables Farm
HIGHLY COMMENDED

Hemblington Hall Road, Hemblington, Norwich NR13 4PT
☎ South Walsham (060 549) 239 & Mobile (0860) 786263
Fax (060 549) 548

Delightful, secluded listed 17th C thatched farmhouse in large garden surrounded by farmland. Within easy reach of Norwich, Norfolk Broads, the coast and many nature reserves.
Bedrooms: 1 twin, 1 family room
Bathrooms: 2 private

Bed & breakfast per night:	£min	£max
Single	21.00	21.00
Double	35.00	35.00

Parking for 6

Kingsley Lodge
COMMENDED

3 Kingsley Road, Norwich NR1 3RB
☎ (0603) 615819

Quiet house in the city centre close to bus station, offering spacious rooms, each with en-suite bathroom and WC. Non-smokers only please.
Bedrooms: 1 single, 2 double, 1 twin
Bathrooms: 4 private

Bed & breakfast per night:	£min	£max
Single	22.00	25.00
Double	36.00	36.00

Open February-December

The Limes
Listed

188 Unthank Road, Norwich NR2 2AH
☎ (0603) 54282
Large, comfortable rooms, close to the city centre and university. Run by a young, friendly family.
Bedrooms: 2 single, 1 double, 1 triple
Bathrooms: 2 public

Bed & breakfast per night:	£min	£max
Single	15.00	17.00
Double	30.00	32.00

Oakfield
HIGHLY COMMENDED

Yelverton Road, Framingham Earl, Norwich NR14 7SD
☎ Framingham Earl (0508) 492605
Superior accommodation in beautiful, quiet setting on edge of village 4 miles south-east of Norwich. Fine breakfasts. Local pubs serve good evening meals.
Bedrooms: 1 single, 1 double, 1 twin
Bathrooms: 1 private, 1 public

Bed & breakfast per night:	£min	£max
Single	16.00	20.00
Double	30.00	38.00

Parking for 6

Witton Hall Farm

Witton, Norwich NR13 5DN
☎ (0603) 714580
500-acre dairy farm. Elegant Georgian farmhouse in the heart of Norfolk. Peaceful, mature grounds. Swimming pool in walled garden.
Bedrooms: 1 double, 1 twin, 1 family room
Bathrooms: 3 private

Bed & breakfast per night:	£min	£max
Single	16.50	20.00
Double	30.00	33.00

Parking for 4

Please mention this guide when making a booking.

EAST ANGLIA

OAKINGTON
Cambridgeshire
Map ref 3A2

The Manor House
High Street, Oakington, Cambridge
CB4 5AG
☎ Cambridge (0223) 232450
Enjoy a quiet, relaxing stay at this 16th C manor house with antique furniture throughout, spacious country garden, heated covered swimming pool, drawing room and children's playroom.
Bedrooms: 3 double
Bathrooms: 2 public

Bed & breakfast
per night:	£min	£max
Single	20.00	20.00
Double	35.00	35.00

Half board
per person:	£min	£max
Daily	27.50	27.50

Evening meal 1830 (last orders 2000)
Parking for 8
Cards accepted: Access, Visa

ORFORD
Suffolk
Map ref 3C2

Once a thriving port, now a quiet village of brick and timber buildings, famous for its castle. Orford comes to life during the summer when boats tie up at the quay.

King's Head Inn
Listed
Front Street, Orford, Woodbridge
IP12 2LW
☎ (0394) 450271
Tiny inn with open fires, friendly atmosphere and personal service. Proprietor's own cooking with seafood specialities.
Bedrooms: 4 double, 1 twin, 1 triple
Bathrooms: 2 public

Bed & breakfast
per night:	£min	£max
Single	23.00	25.00
Double	38.00	42.00

Lunch available
Evening meal 1900 (last orders 2100)
Parking for 52
Cards accepted: Diners

National Crown ratings were correct at the time of going to press but are subject to change. Please check at the time of booking.

OULTON BROAD
Suffolk
Map ref 3C1

Oulton Broad is the most southerly of the Broads and is the centre of a very busy boating industry.

Ivy House Farm
HIGHLY COMMENDED
Ivy Lane, Oulton Broad, Lowestoft
NR33 8HY
☎ Lowestoft (0502) 501353
Farmhouse set in 30 acres beside Oulton Broad and nature reserve. Well-appointed en-suite rooms with views. Log fires.
Bedrooms: 1 double, 1 twin, 1 triple
Bathrooms: 3 private

Bed & breakfast
per night:	£min	£max
Single	30.00	34.00
Double	45.00	49.00

Parking for 8
Cards accepted: Access, Visa

PEASENHALL
Suffolk
Map ref 3C2

Bay House
COMMENDED
Rendham Road, Peasenhall, Saxmundham IP17 2NQ
☎ (072 879) 221
Comfortable country house on the outskirts of pretty village. Within easy reach of heritage coast and bird reserves.
Bedrooms: 1 twin
Bathrooms: 1 private, 2 public

Bed & breakfast
per night:	£min	£max
Single	17.00	17.00
Double	34.00	34.00

Parking for 1

PETERBOROUGH
Cambridgeshire
Map ref 3A1

Prosperous and rapidly expanding cathedral city on the edge of the Fens on the River Nene. Catherine of Aragon is buried in the cathedral. City Museum and Art Gallery. Ferry Meadows Country Park has numerous leisure facilities.
Tourist Information Centre
☎ (0733) 317336

Stoneacre
Elton Road, Wansford, Peterborough
PE8 6JT
☎ Stamford (0780) 783283

Rural and secluded with delightful views across the River Nene Valley. Half a mile from A1, 10 minutes from Peterborough and Stamford. Large grounds with mini golf-course.
Bedrooms: 3 double, 1 twin, 1 triple
Bathrooms: 3 private, 2 public

Bed & breakfast
per night:	£min	£max
Single	21.00	34.00
Double	27.00	48.00

Parking for 24

POTTON
Bedfordshire
Map ref 2D1

Westbury Bed and Breakfast
HIGHLY COMMENDED
Deepdale, Potton, Sandy SG19 2NH
☎ (0767) 260770

Country house set in garden and situated in the hamlet of Deepdale, 2 miles east of Sandy on B1042 Bedford-Cambridge road.
Bedrooms: 1 double, 2 twin
Bathrooms: 1 private, 1 public

Bed & breakfast
per night:	£min	£max
Single	16.00	20.00
Double	26.00	30.00

Parking for 3

PULHAM MARKET
Norfolk
Map ref 3B2

The Old Bakery
COMMENDED
Church Walk, Pulham Market, Diss
IP21 4SJ
☎ Diss (0379) 676492

1580 listed spiral-staircased oak-framed house in award-winning village. Fine traditional cooking by master chef. En-suite rooms with TV and beverage facilities. 15 miles south of Norwich, 1 mile off A140 on B1134.
Bedrooms: 1 twin, 1 family room
Bathrooms: 2 private

EAST ANGLIA

Bed & breakfast per night:	£min	£max
Single	28.00	32.00
Double	36.00	44.00

Half board per person:	£min	£max
Weekly	150.00	175.00

Evening meal 1800 (last orders 2000)
Parking for 3

QUIDENHAM
Norfolk
Map ref 3B1

Manor Farm
Listed

Quidenham, Norwich NR16 2NY
☎ (0953) 87540
950-acre arable farm. Large secluded farmhouse set in beautiful surroundings. Home cooking, fresh vegetables, own eggs.
Bedrooms: 2 single, 1 double, 1 twin
Bathrooms: 1 public

Bed & breakfast per night:	£min	£max
Single	15.00	16.00
Double	30.00	32.00

Half board per person:	£min	£max
Daily	25.00	

Evening meal 1900 (last orders 2000)
Parking for 10

RACKHEATH
Norfolk
Map ref 3C1

Barn Court
Listed APPROVED

6 Back Lane, Rackheath, Norwich NR13 6NN
☎ Norwich (0603) 782536
Fax (0603) 782536
Spacious accommodation in a traditional Norfolk barn conversion, built around a courtyard. Friendly atmosphere, good food. French spoken.
Bedrooms: 2 twin, 1 triple
Bathrooms: 2 public

Bed & breakfast per night:	£min	£max
Single	16.00	18.00
Double	30.00	36.00

Parking for 4
Open February-December

Check the introduction to this region for Where to Go, What to See.

RADWINTER
Essex
Map ref 3B2

The Plough Inn
Listed APPROVED

Sampford Road, Radwinter, Saffron Walden CB10 2TL
☎ Saffron Walden (0799) 599222
16th C inn with lovely garden views of countryside. Self-contained accommodation in garden. Lunch and evening meal available in the pub. 5 miles from Saffron Walden and 6 miles from Finchingfield.
Bedrooms: 1 double, 1 twin
Bathrooms: 2 private

Bed & breakfast per night:	£min	£max
Single	22.00	
Double	36.00	

Lunch available
Evening meal 1900 (last orders 2200)
Parking for 20

RAMSEY
Cambridgeshire
Map ref 3A2

The Leys M
Listed

25 Bury Road, Ramsey, Huntingdon PE17 1NE
☎ (0487) 813221 & 710053
Large family house with a friendly atmosphere. On B1040 on the southern outskirts of Ramsey, between Huntingdon and Peterborough.
Bedrooms: 1 single, 1 twin, 2 triple
Bathrooms: 2 public

Bed & breakfast per night:	£min	£max
Single	12.00	15.00
Double	24.00	30.00

Evening meal 1930 (last orders 1930)
Parking for 10

REEPHAM
Norfolk
Map ref 3B1

An important market town in the 18th C and an air of prosperity lingers on. Bordering the attractive market-place are Dial House, a large town house, and St Michael's Church. Nearby is the Norfolk Wildlife Park.

Malthouse Cottage
3-4 Malthouse Yard, Reepham, Norwich NR10 4EJ
☎ Norwich (0603) 871346
Delightful old malthouse and garden cottage set in secluded gardens within conservation area of small market town.

Bedrooms: 1 double, 1 twin, 1 family room
Bathrooms: 3 private

Bed & breakfast per night:	£min	£max
Single	20.00	20.00
Double	35.00	35.00

Open February-December
Parking for 2

ROLLESBY
Norfolk
Map ref 3C1

Rollesby Broad forms part of the Ormesby Broad complex and fine views can be seen from the road which runs through the middle.

The Old Court House M
COMMENDED

Court Road, Rollesby, Great Yarmouth NR29 5HG
☎ Great Yarmouth (0493) 369665

Small family-run hotel set in 4 acres in a peaceful, rural location near the Broads. Private bar and swimming pool, games area. Bicycles for hire. Tennis, fishing and riding nearby. Home cooking.
Bedrooms: 2 double, 1 twin, 1 triple, 3 family rooms
Bathrooms: 6 private, 2 public

Bed & breakfast per night:	£min	£max
Double	36.00	43.00

Half board per person:	£min	£max
Daily	28.00	31.50
Weekly	178.00	199.00

Evening meal 1830 (last orders 1830)
Parking for 20
Open February-November

RUSHALL
Norfolk
Map ref 3B2

The Half Moon Inn M
Rushall, Diss IP21 4QG
☎ Diss (0379) 740793

Continued ▶

We advise you to confirm your booking in writing.

239

EAST ANGLIA

RUSHALL
Continued

14th C coaching inn, offering a warm welcome and a fine range of reasonably priced meals. Family rooms available. Well situated for visiting the coast, Norfolk Broads, Norwich and Bury St Edmunds.
Bedrooms: 4 double, 3 triple
Bathrooms: 5 private, 1 public

Bed & breakfast

per night:	£min	£max
Single	25.00	30.00
Double	45.00	50.00

Lunch available
Evening meal 1800 (last orders 2200)
Parking for 40

SAFFRON WALDEN
Essex
Map ref 2D1

Takes its name from the saffron crocus once grown around the town. The church of St Mary has superb carvings, magnificent roofs and brasses. A town maze can be seen on the common. Two miles south-west is Audley End, a magnificent Jacobean mansion owned by English Heritage.
Tourist Information Centre
☎ *(0799) 510444*

Pond Mead

Widdington, Saffron Walden
CB11 3SB
☎ (0799) 40201
Large rambling old house with 1.5 acres of garden on the edge of the village of Widdington (population of 650), about 4 miles south of Saffron Walden.
Bedrooms: 1 single, 1 double, 1 triple
Bathrooms: 1 public

Bed & breakfast

per night:	£min	£max
Single	12.00	17.00
Double	24.00	30.00

Parking for 5

Rockells Farm

Duddenhoe End, Saffron Walden
CB11 4UY
☎ Royston (0763) 838253
420-acre arable farm. Georgian house in rolling countryside with plenty of opportunities for walking and

sightseeing. The 3-acre lake provides excellent fishing. Stansted Airport 20 minutes by car, Cambridge 30 minutes.
Bedrooms: 1 single, 1 twin, 1 triple
Bathrooms: 3 private, 1 public

Bed & breakfast

per night:	£min	£max
Single	16.00	18.00
Double	32.00	36.00

Half board

per person:	£min	£max
Daily	23.50	25.50

Evening meal from 1800
Parking for 4

Rowley Hill Lodge
Listed COMMENDED

Little Walden, Saffron Walden
CB10 1UZ
☎ (0799) 525975
Quiet farm lodge with large garden, 1 mile from centre of Saffron Walden. Stansted Airport and Cambridge 20 minutes.
Bedrooms: 1 single, 1 twin
Bathrooms: 1 private, 2 public

Bed & breakfast

per night:	£min	£max
Single	16.00	18.00
Double	32.00	32.00

Parking for 4

Yeoman Cottage

Hempstead, Saffron Walden
CB10 2PH
☎ Radwinter (0799) 599345
Comfortable timbered 14th C house with antique furniture and charming gardens, in village famous for William Harvey and Dick Turpin. Convenient for Cambridge, Thaxted and Stansted. Good local restaurants.
Bedrooms: 1 single, 1 twin
Bathrooms: 1 public

Bed & breakfast

per night:	£min	£max
Single	14.00	18.00
Double	28.00	28.00

Parking for 3

There are separate sections in this guide listing groups specialising in farm holidays and accommodation which is especially suitable for young people and organised groups.

ST ALBANS
Hertfordshire
Map ref 2D1

As Verulamium this was one of the largest towns in Roman Britain and its remains can be seen in the museum. The Norman cathedral was built from Roman materials to commemorate Alban, the first British Christian martyr.
Tourist Information Centre
☎ *(0727) 864511*

Amaryllis
Listed

25 Ridgmont Road, St Albans
AL1 3AG
☎ (0727) 862755

Friendly, informal family home close to city centre. Convenient for M1 and M25. Central London 20 minutes by train. Non-smokers only please.
Bedrooms: 1 single, 1 twin, 1 triple
Bathrooms: 1 public

Bed & breakfast

per night:	£min	£max
Single	13.00	20.00
Double	28.00	32.00

Parking for 1

Care Inns

29 Alma Road, St Albans AL1 3AT
☎ (0727) 867310
Comfortable family atmosphere. Ideally located close to station, town and cathedral. All rooms have en-suite bath/shower and toilet.
Bedrooms: 1 single, 1 double, 1 twin
Bathrooms: 3 private

Bed & breakfast

per night:	£min	£max
Single	20.00	25.00
Double	36.00	

Parking for 5

Newpark House Hotel

North Orbital Road (A414), St Albans
AL1 1EG
☎ Bowmansgreen (0727) 824839
Fax (0727) 826800
On A414 trunk road eastbound to A1 (M). Pebbledash, 3-storey house, small landscaped garden with patio and fish pond.
Bedrooms: 9 single, 5 twin
Bathrooms: 5 public

EAST ANGLIA

Bed & breakfast
per night:	£min	£max
Single	22.50	25.00
Double	40.00	45.00

Half board
per person:	£min	£max
Daily	30.50	33.50

Evening meal 1800 (last orders 2030)
Parking for 30
Cards accepted: Access, Visa

The Squirrels
Listed APPROVED

74 Sandridge Road, St Albans
AL1 4AR
☎ (0727) 840497
Edwardian terraced house, 10 minutes' walk from town centre.
Bedrooms: 1 twin
Bathrooms: 1 private

Bed & breakfast
per night:	£min	£max
Single		15.00
Double		25.00

SALHOUSE
Norfolk
Map ref 3C1

Village above the tree-fringed Salhouse Broad. The church of All Saints has a thatched roof and a 14th C arcade.

Brooks Bank
COMMENDED

Lower Street, Salhouse, Norwich
NR13 6RW
☎ Norwich (0603) 720420
18th C house situated in the centre of Broadland. Guests' own private accommodation. Illustrated brochure. Our pleasure is your comfort.
Bedrooms: 1 double, 1 twin, 1 triple
Bathrooms: 3 private

Bed & breakfast
per night:	£min	£max
Single	18.00	22.00
Double	30.00	35.00

Parking for 4

SANDY
Bedfordshire
Map ref 2D1

Small town on the River Ivel on the site of a Roman settlement. Sandy is mentioned in Domesday.

Highfield Farm
HIGHLY COMMENDED

Great North Road, Sandy SG19 2AQ
☎ (0767) 682332
300-acre arable farm. Attractive period farmhouse set back in its own grounds.

1 mile north of Sandy roundabout on A1 (southbound).
Bedrooms: 2 double, 3 twin, 1 triple
Bathrooms: 4 private, 1 public

Bed & breakfast
per night:	£min	£max
Single		19.00	25.00
Double		30.00	35.00

Parking for 8

The Pantiles
APPROVED

7 Swaden, Everton Road, Sandy
SG19 2DA
☎ (0767) 680668
Converted barn set in a wooded valley, in the grounds of a 16th C thatched cottage. Take the first left after the railway bridge. The house is 400 yards on the left-hand side.
Bedrooms: 2 double, 1 twin
Bathrooms: 3 private

Bed & breakfast
per night:	£min	£max
Single	20.00	25.00
Double	30.00	35.00

Parking for 6

SHERINGHAM
Norfolk
Map ref 3B1

Holiday resort with Victorian and Edwardian hotels and a sand and shingle beach where the fishing boats are hauled up. The North Norfolk Railway operates from Sheringham Station during the summer. Other attractions include museums, theatre and Splash Fun Pool.

Camberley
APPROVED

62 Cliff Road, Sheringham NR26 8BJ
☎ (0263) 823101
In its own grounds, overlooking sea, town and surrounding countryside. Slipway to beach directly opposite. Family-run.
Bedrooms: 3 double
Bathrooms: 3 private, 1 public

Bed & breakfast
per night:	£min	£max
Single	17.00	19.00
Double	34.00	38.00

Parking for 3

The national Crown scheme is explained in full in the information pages towards the back of this guide.

SOUTH MIMMS
Hertfordshire
Map ref 2D1

Best known today for its location at the junction of the M25 and the A1M.
Tourist Information Centre
☎ (0707) 643233

The Black Swan
Listed

62-64 Blanche Lane, South Mimms, Potters Bar EN6 3PD
☎ Potters Bar (0707) 644180
Comfortable accommodation in oak-beamed bedrooms or self-contained flats in quietly located listed building. Breakfast provided.
Bedrooms: 2 double
Bathrooms: 2 private, 1 public

Bed & breakfast
per night:	£min	£max
Single	25.00	25.00
Double	30.00	35.00

Parking for 7

SOUTHEND-ON-SEA
Essex
Map ref 3B3

On the Thames Estuary and the nearest seaside resort to London. Famous for its pier and unique pier trains. Other attractions include Peter Pan's Playground, indoor swimming pools, indoor rollerskating and ten pin bowling.
Tourist Information Centre
☎ (0702) 355122 or 355120

Aldridge Guest House
Listed APPROVED

17 Hartington Road, Southend-on-Sea
SS1 2HR
☎ (0702) 614555
Friendly accommodation with comfortable bedrooms, close to seafront, pier and shops. Choice of breakfast served in your room.
Bedrooms: 1 single, 1 double, 2 twin, 1 triple
Bathrooms: 1 private, 1 public, 1 private shower

Bed & breakfast
per night:	£min	£max
Single	12.00	14.00
Double	24.00	28.00

The Bay Guest House

187 Eastern Esplanade, Thorpe Bay, Southend-on-Sea SS1 3AA
☎ (0702) 588415
On seafront half-a-mile east of Sea Life Centre. Lounge overlooking estuary. Choice of breakfast cooked to order. Free public car park at rear.

Continued ▶

EAST ANGLIA

SOUTHEND-ON-SEA
Continued

Bedrooms: 2 single, 5 double, 1 twin, 1 triple
Bathrooms: 2 private, 2 public
Bed & breakfast

per night:	£min	£max
Single	15.00	20.00
Double	25.00	30.00

Roslin Hotel
COMMENDED

Thorpe Esplanade, Thorpe Bay,
Southend-on-Sea SS1 3BG
☎ (0702) 586375
Fax (0702) 586663

Hotel overlooking the Thames Estuary in residential Thorpe. Within easy reach of Southend and 45 minutes from London. Live entertainment Friday and Saturday.
Bedrooms: 20 single, 7 double, 9 twin, 4 triple
Bathrooms: 40 private
Bed & breakfast

per night:	£min	£max
Single	38.00	60.00
Double	60.00	70.00

Half board

per person:	£min	£max
Weekly	255.00	280.00

Lunch available
Evening meal 1830 (last orders 2200)
Parking for 34
Cards accepted: Access, Visa, Diners, Amex, Switch

SOUTHWOLD
Suffolk
Map ref 3C2

Pleasant and attractive seaside town with a triangular market square and spacious greens around which stand flint, brick and colour-washed cottages. The parish church of St Edmund is one of the greatest churches in Suffolk.

Albert House
Listed

16 Dunwich Road, Southwold
IP18 6LJ
☎ (0502) 722218

Victorian terrace with yesterday's charm and today's standard, peacefully situated just off the seafront in the heart of Southwold.

Bedrooms: 2 double, 1 twin
Bathrooms: 1 public
Bed & breakfast

per night:	£min	£max
Single	18.00	25.00
Double	32.00	38.00

Saxon House
APPROVED

86 Pier Avenue, Southwold IP18 6BL
☎ (0502) 723651

Comfortable detached guesthouse, 100 yards from beach. All rooms with sea views, clock radios, wash hand basins and tea/coffee making facilities. TV lounge, full English breakfast. Non-smoking establishment.
Bedrooms: 2 double, 1 twin, 1 family room
Bathrooms: 1 public
Bed & breakfast

per night:	£min	£max
Single	21.50	22.50
Double	40.00	44.00

STANWAY
Essex
Map ref 3B2

11 Harvest End
Listed

Stanway, Colchester CO3 5YX
☎ Colchester (0206) 43202
Family home in quiet residential area, convenient for A12. Easy access to coast, ferries and Constable country. Spacious bedrooms, parking.
Bedrooms: 1 single, 1 double, 1 twin
Bathrooms: 1 public
Bed & breakfast

per night:	£min	£max
Single	16.00	18.00
Double	32.00	36.00

Parking for 2

STEEPLE BUMPSTEAD
Essex
Map ref 3B2

An interesting building in the village is the Moot Hall, which in the 17th C served as a village school and was restored as part of the 1977 Jubilee celebrations.

Yew Tree House
Listed

15 Chapel Street, Steeple Bumpstead, Haverhill, Suffolk CB9 7DQ
☎ (0440) 730364
Charming Victorian house, with many period features, and comfortable accommodation, in the centre of Steeple Bumpstead.
Bedrooms: 1 double, 1 twin
Bathrooms: 1 private, 1 public

Bed & breakfast

per night:	£min	£max
Single	17.00	21.00
Double	28.00	35.00

Half board

per person:	£min	£max
Daily	22.00	26.00
Weekly	154.00	182.00

Evening meal 1800 (last orders 2000)
Parking for 3
Open March-December

STOKE HOLY CROSS
Norfolk
Map ref 3C1

Salamanca Farm

Stoke Holy Cross, Norwich NR14 8QJ
☎ Framingham (0508) 492322
175-acre mixed farm. Victorian house offering full English breakfast. Set in beautiful undulating country, 4 miles from Norwich.
Bedrooms: 3 double, 1 twin
Bathrooms: 4 private, 2 public
Bed & breakfast

per night:	£min	£max
Single	16.00	
Double	32.00	

Parking for 8

STRATFORD ST MARY
Suffolk
Map ref 3B2

Set in countryside known as Constable country.

Teazles
Listed APPROVED

Stratford St Mary, Colchester
CO7 6LU
☎ Colchester (0206) 323148
Attractive 16th C country house in heart of Constable country. Just off A12 on B1029 to Dedham, leaving church on right. Refurbished in 1971, now our family home to which we welcome guests.
Bedrooms: 1 single, 1 double, 1 twin
Bathrooms: 2 public
Bed & breakfast

per night:	£min	£max
Single	16.00	19.00
Double	32.00	37.00

Parking for 7

Establishments should be open throughout the year unless otherwise stated in the entry.

EAST ANGLIA

THAXTED
Essex
Map ref 3B2

Small town rich in outstanding buildings and dominated by its hilltop medieval church. The magnificent Guildhall was built by the Cutlers' Guild in the late 14th C. A windmill built in 1804 has been restored and houses a rural museum.

Folly House
COMMENDED

Watling Lane, Thaxted, Dunmow CM6 2QY
☎ (0371) 830618
Sunny, light, spacious house, with sweeping views over hills, in the historic and picturesque village of Thaxted. Attentive friendly service. Sky TV in all rooms. Transport to Stansted Airport.
Bedrooms: 1 double, 2 twin
Bathrooms: 1 private, 1 public

Bed & breakfast

per night:	£min	£max
Single	16.00	18.00
Double	36.00	40.00

Half board

per person:	£min	£max
Daily	25.00	28.00
Weekly	120.00	150.00

Evening meal 1800 (last orders 2030)
Parking for 4

Piggots Mill
HIGHLY COMMENDED

Watling Lane, Thaxted, Dunmow CM6 2QY
☎ (0371) 830379
850-acre arable farm. Traditional Essex barn, now a secluded farmhouse in the centre of Thaxted. Garden leads into meadow giving access to attractive walks. Children over 12 welcome.
Bedrooms: 1 double, 1 twin
Bathrooms: 2 private

Bed & breakfast

per night:	£min	£max
Single	27.00	29.00
Double	40.00	42.00

Parking for 10

Individual proprietors have supplied all details of accommodation. Although we do check for accuracy, we advise you to confirm the information at the time of booking.

THETFORD
Norfolk
Map ref 3B2

Small, medieval market town with numerous reminders of its long history: the ruins of the 12th C priory, Iron Age earthworks at Castle Hill and a Norman castle mound. Timber-framed Ancient House is now a museum.

East Farm

Barnham, Thetford IP24 2PB
☎ Elveden (084 289) 0231
Friendly, comfortable farmhouse with large rooms and country views. On outskirts of village. No smoking in bedrooms. En-suite and tea/coffee-making facilities.
Bedrooms: 1 double, 1 twin
Bathrooms: 2 private

Bed & breakfast

per night:	£min	£max
Single	21.00	22.00
Double	36.00	38.00

Parking for 4

THOMPSON
Norfolk
Map ref 3B1

College Farm
Listed

Thompson, Thetford IP24 1QG
☎ Caston (095 383) 318 changing to (0953) 483318
14th C farmhouse, formerly a college of priests. In quiet village away from main road. Meals provided at nearby inns.
Bedrooms: 1 single, 1 double, 2 twin
Bathrooms: 2 public

Bed & breakfast

per night:	£min	£max
Single	17.00	18.00
Double	34.00	36.00

Parking for 10

Rose Cottage
Listed COMMENDED

Butters Hall Lane, Thompson, Thetford IP24 1QQ
☎ Attleborough (0953) 488104
Spacious and comfortable flint walled period house peacefully situated 3 miles south of Watton on A1075.
Bedrooms: 1 single, 1 double
Bathrooms: 1 public

Bed & breakfast

per night:	£min	£max
Single	14.00	18.00
Double	32.00	32.00

Half board

per person:	£min	£max
Daily	21.00	26.00
Weekly	133.00	164.00

Evening meal 1800 (last orders 2100)
Parking for 4

THORNHAM
Norfolk
Map ref 3B1

The Chequers Inn
Thornham, Hunstanton PE36 6LY
☎ (048 526) 229
Picturesque Grade II listed freehouse with beams and low ceilings, open fires and real ales. On main A149 road.
Bedrooms: 1 single, 2 double
Bathrooms: 3 private

Bed & breakfast

per night:	£min	£max
Single	20.00	25.00
Double	40.00	50.00

Lunch available
Evening meal 1800 (last orders 2200)
Parking for 31
Cards accepted: Access, Visa

Ilex Cottage
Listed COMMENDED

High Street, Thornham, Hunstanton PE36 6LY
☎ (0485) 512310
Fully modernised traditional style property with large garden, situated in picturesque coastal village of Thornham, approximately 5 minutes by car from beaches and bird reserves.
Bedrooms: 1 double, 2 twin
Bathrooms: 2 private, 1 public

Bed & breakfast

per night:	£min	£max
Single	19.00	30.00
Double	30.00	38.00

Parking for 6

THROCKING
Hertfordshire
Map ref 2D1

Southfields Farm
Listed

Throcking, Buntingford SG9 9RD
☎ Royston (0763) 281224
Warm, comfortable farmhouse 1.5 miles off A10 midway between London and Cambridge. TV, tea and coffee facilities. Closed at Christmas. No smoking in bedrooms.
Bedrooms: 1 single, 1 twin
Bathrooms: 1 public

Bed & breakfast

per night:	£min	£max
Single		15.00
Double		30.00

Parking for 5

EAST ANGLIA

TIPTREE
Essex
Map ref 3B3

Linden
Listed

8 Clarkesmead, Maldon Road, Tiptree, Colchester CO5 OBX
☎ (0261) 819737
Fax (0261) 818033

Modern architect-designed house in quiet cul-de-sac, off Maldon Road on edge of Tiptree.

Bedrooms: 1 single, 1 double, 1 twin
Bathrooms: 2 public, 1 private shower

Bed & breakfast

per night:	£min	£max
Single	20.00	22.50
Double	38.00	38.00

Parking for 6
Cards accepted: Visa

TRING
Hertfordshire
Map ref 2C1

Pleasant town near lovely countryside and woods. Tring has a fine church with a large 14th C tower. Tring Park houses the Rothschild Zoological Collection, now part of the Natural History Museum. The Tring Reservoir's National Nature Reserve is nearby.

The Royal Hotel

Tring HP23 5QR
☎ (0442) 827616 & 828588
Fax (0442) 890383

On the famous Ridgeway Path, close to the pretty village of Aldbury.

Bedrooms: 8 double, 8 twin, 2 family rooms
Bathrooms: 18 private, 1 public

Bed & breakfast

per night:	£min	£max
Single	30.00	42.00
Double	40.00	50.00

Half board

per person:	£min	£max
Weekly	125.00	200.00

Lunch available
Evening meal 1930 (last orders 2100)
Parking for 50
Cards accepted: Access, Visa, Diners, Amex

All accommodation in this guide has been inspected, or is awaiting inspection, under the national Crown scheme.

UGLEY
Essex
Map ref 2D1

The Thatch
COMMENDED

Cambridge Road, Ugley, Bishop's Stortford, Hertfordshire CM22 6HZ
☎ Rickling (079 988) 440 changing to (0799) 543440

Partly thatched cottage in half-an-acre of garden backing on to farmland. Between Stansted and Newport, close to the airport and M11.

Bedrooms: 2 double, 1 twin, 1 triple
Bathrooms: 3 private, 1 public

Bed & breakfast

per night:	£min	£max
Single	18.00	20.00
Double	30.00	40.00

Parking for 7

WARE
Hertfordshire
Map ref 2D1

Interesting riverside town with picturesque summer-houses lining the tow-path of the River Lea. The town has many timber-framed and Georgian houses and the famous Great Bed of Ware is now in the Victoria and Albert Museum.

Ashridge
COMMENDED

3 Belle Vue Road, Ware SG12 7BD
☎ (0920) 463895

Comfortable, Edwardian residence in quiet cul-de-sac. 10 minutes' walk from Ware and station. Non-smokers only please.

Bedrooms: 2 single, 1 double, 1 twin
Bathrooms: 2 public

Bed & breakfast

per night:	£min	£max
Single	16.50	20.00
Double	33.00	40.00

Half board

per person:	£min	£max
Daily	22.50	26.00

Evening meal 1830 (last orders 1200)
Parking for 4

Individual proprietors have supplied all details of accommodation. Although we do check for accuracy, we advise you to confirm the information at the time of booking.

WATFORD
Hertfordshire
Map ref 2D1

Large town with many industries but with some old buildings, particularly around St Mary's Church which contains some fine monuments. The grounds of Cassiobury Park, once the home of the Earls of Essex, form a public park and golf-course.

The Millwards

30 Hazelwood Road, Croxley Green, Rickmansworth WD3 3EB
☎ (0923) 233751 & 226666

Quiet, homely canalside residence. Pleasant location. Convenient London (Metropolitan line), Moor Park, Wembley, Heathrow, Rickmansworth, M1 and M25, Watford and Croxley Business Centre.

Bedrooms: 1 single, 3 twin
Bathrooms: 2 public

Bed & breakfast

per night:	£min	£max
Single	15.00	20.00
Double	28.00	30.00

Parking for 2

WATTON
Norfolk
Map ref 3B1

Moat Farm
Listed

Ashill, Thetford IP25 7BX
☎ Holme Hale (0760) 440357

600-acre mixed farm. Old farmhouse on edge of Breckland, close to Peddars Way between Watton and Swaffham.

Bedrooms: 1 double, 2 twin
Bathrooms: 2 public

Bed & breakfast

per night:	£min	£max
Single	17.00	
Double	34.00	

Evening meal 1900 (last orders 2000)
Parking for 10

WELLS-NEXT-THE-SEA
Norfolk
Map ref 3B1

Seaside resort and small port on the north coast. The Buttlands is a large tree-lined green surrounded by Georgian houses and from here narrow streets lead to the quay.

Hideaway
APPROVED

Red Lion Yard, Wells-next-the-Sea NR23 1AX
☎ Fakenham (0328) 710524

244

EAST ANGLIA

Single-storey extension built on to house. Own entrance and garden for guests with 24-hour access. All en-suite.
Bedrooms: 1 double, 2 twin
Bathrooms: 3 private, 1 public
Bed & breakfast
per night:	£min	£max
Double	32.00	36.00

Half board
per person:	£min	£max
Daily	24.00	27.00
Weekly	158.50	172.50

Evening meal 1820 (last orders 1930)
Parking for 4

WEST BERGHOLT
Essex
Map ref 3B2

Farthings
Listed

Manor Lane, West Bergholt, Colchester CO6 3JJ
☎ Colchester (0206) 241749
Comfortable house with large garden in quiet country setting on edge of village. Good eating places locally. Ideal touring centre.
Bedrooms: 1 single, 1 twin
Bathrooms: 1 private, 2 public
Bed & breakfast
per night:	£min	£max
Single	16.00	20.00
Double	32.00	38.00

Parking for 4

WEST STOW
Suffolk
Map ref 3B2

Eastleigh
Listed

Icklingham Road, West Stow, Bury St Edmunds IP28 6EZ
☎ Bury St Edmunds (0284) 728264
Cottage in village. Country park with Saxon village. Forest walks. Trout fishing available.
Bedrooms: 1 double
Bathrooms: 1 public
Bed & breakfast
per night:	£min	£max
Single	12.00	
Double	24.00	

Parking for 2

WETHERDEN
Suffolk
Map ref 3B2

Brickwall Farmhouse
Wetherden, Stowmarket IP14 3JW
☎ Elmswell (0359) 242732
Fax (0359) 42711

16th C timber-framed farmhouse overlooking open fields and duck pond, set in 0.75 acre of gardens. Half-a-mile from A45, between Bury St Edmunds and Ipswich.
Bedrooms: 1 double, 1 twin
Bathrooms: 1 public
Bed & breakfast
per night:	£min	£max
Single	15.00	15.00
Double	30.00	30.00

Evening meal from 1800
Parking for 4

WEYBREAD
Suffolk
Map ref 3C2

Pear Tree Farm
Listed

The Street, Weybread, Diss, Norfolk IP21 5TH
☎ Fressingfield (037 986) 753
15th C farmhouse with most beams exposed. Surrounded by fields. Large garden and lawns. Good parking space.
Bedrooms: 1 single, 1 twin, 1 triple
Bathrooms: 1 public
Bed & breakfast
per night:	£min	£max
Single	12.00	14.00
Double	24.00	28.00

Half board
per person:	£min	£max
Daily	17.00	19.00
Weekly	119.00	122.00

Evening meal 1800 (last orders 2000)
Parking for 5
Open January-October

WISBECH
Cambridgeshire
Map ref 3A1

The town is the centre of the agricultural and flower-growing industries of Fenland. Peckover House (National Trust) is an important example of domestic architecture.
Tourist Information Centre
☎ (0945) 583260

Holly Gap
Listed

Mile Tree Lane, Wisbech PE13 4TR
☎ (0945) 63119
Rural bungalow surrounded by orchards, approximately 2 miles from the market town of Wisbech. Hens, goats, ponies and miniature horses. Guests' own horse welcome.
Bedrooms: 2 double
Bathrooms: 1 public
Bed & breakfast
per night:	£min	£max
Single	20.00	20.00
Double	25.00	30.00

Parking for 10

Stratton Farm
COMMENDED

West Drove North, Walton Highway, Wisbech PE14 7DP
☎ (0945) 880162
22-acre livestock farm. All ground floor en-suite accommodation in peaceful setting, with heated swimming pool and private fishing. Wheelchair facilities. Non-smokers only please.
Bedrooms: 2 double, 1 twin
Bathrooms: 3 private
Bed & breakfast
per night:	£min	£max
Single	21.00	22.00
Double	42.00	44.00

Parking for 10

WIX
Essex
Map ref 3B2

New Farm House
COMMENDED

Spinnell's Lane, Wix, Manningtree CO11 2UJ
☎ Clacton (0255) 870365
Fax (0255) 870837
50-acre arable farm. Modern comfortable farmhouse in large garden, 10 minutes' drive to Harwich and convenient for Constable country. From Wix village crossroads, take Bradfield Road, turn right at top of hill; first house on left.
Bedrooms: 3 single, 1 double, 3 twin, 5 family rooms
Bathrooms: 7 private, 2 public
Bed & breakfast
per night:	£min	£max
Single	18.50	22.00
Double	35.00	42.00

Half board
per person:	£min	£max
Daily	28.50	32.00
Weekly	186.50	208.60

Evening meal 1830 (last orders 1730)
Parking for 18
Cards accepted: Access, Visa

EAST ANGLIA

WIX
Continued

Spring Farm
Colchester Road, Wix, Manningtree
CO11 2RN
☎ (0255) 870246
Fax (0255) 870884

2-acre arable farm. Grade II listed Georgian fronted farmhouse, set in landscaped gardens with heated outdoor swimming pool and hard tennis court. Situated three-quarters of a mile from A120 at Wix - 6 miles from Harwich.
Bedrooms: 1 twin, 1 family room
Bathrooms: 2 private

Bed & breakfast per night:
	£min	£max
Single	18.00	
Double	34.00	36.00

Parking for 10

WOODBRIDGE
Suffolk
Map ref 3C2

Once a busy seaport, the town is now a sailing centre on the River Deben. There are many buildings of architectural merit including the Bell and Angel Inns. The 18th C Tide Mill is now restored and open to the public.

Fen House
Fen Walk, Woodbridge IP12
☎ (0394) 387343
Accommodation in private family home set in wooded location. Five minutes' walk from town centre. TV and welcome tray. Adjacent bathroom with shower unit.
Bedrooms: 2 single, 1 twin
Bathrooms: 1 private, 2 public

Bed & breakfast per night:
	£min	£max
Single	15.00	20.00
Double	30.00	40.00

Parking for 6

Moat Barn
HIGHLY COMMENDED
Bredfield, Woodbridge IP13 6DD
☎ Charsfield (047 337) 520
Renovated Suffolk barn with exposed beams and original features, standing in grounds of over 1 acre. In Bredfield village, with pub and church, just 3

miles from the market town of Woodbridge.
Bedrooms: 1 single, 1 double, 1 triple, 1 family room
Bathrooms: 1 private, 2 public

Bed & breakfast per night:
	£min	£max
Single	20.00	20.00
Double	30.00	40.00

Parking for 10

Otley House
HIGHLY COMMENDED
Helmingham Road, Otley, Ipswich
IP6 9NR
☎ Helmingham (0473) 890253
Fax (0473) 890059

17th C country house set in mature peaceful grounds with lakes and croquet lawn, 5 miles north-west of Woodbridge. Billiard room, drawing room, Regency dining room. Open fires. English and Scandinavian cooking. Smoking in billiard room only.
Bedrooms: 2 double, 2 twin
Bathrooms: 4 private

Bed & breakfast per night:
	£min	£max
Single	34.00	38.00
Double	44.00	50.00

Half board per person:
	£min	£max
Daily	37.00	40.00
Weekly	259.00	280.00

Evening meal 1930 (last orders 1600)
Parking for 8
Open April-October

WOODHAM FERRERS
Essex
Map ref 3B3

Woolfe's Cottage
Listed
The Street, Woodham Ferrers, Chelmsford CM3 5RG
☎ Chelmsford (0245) 320037
Large converted Victorian cottage in historic village, 12 miles from Chelmsford on the B1418. Many excellent walking trails for ramblers.
Bedrooms: 1 double, 1 twin
Bathrooms: 1 public

Bed & breakfast per night:
	£min	£max
Single	15.00	17.00
Double	28.00	30.00

Evening meal 1900 (last orders 2000)
Parking for 2

WOOLLEY
Cambridgeshire
Map ref 3A2

New Manor Farm
Listed
Woolley, Huntingdon PE18 0YJ
☎ Huntingdon (0480) 890092
80-acre livestock farm. Spacious, comfortable family farmhouse in quiet pastoral hamlet only 2 miles from A1. Large secluded garden.
Bedrooms: 2 double, 1 twin
Bathrooms: 1 public, 2 private showers

Bed & breakfast per night:
	£min	£max
Single	18.00	22.00
Double	28.00	32.00

Half board per person:
	£min	£max
Daily	32.00	36.00
Weekly	210.00	238.00

Evening meal 1900 (last orders 2100)
Parking for 6
Open April-October

WOOLPIT
Suffolk
Map ref 3B2

Village with a number of attractive timber-framed Tudor and Georgian houses. St Mary's Church is one of the most beautiful churches in Suffolk and has a fine porch. The brass eagle lectern is said to have been donated by Elizabeth I.

The Swan Inn
Listed COMMENDED
Woolpit, Bury St Edmunds IP30 9QN
☎ Elmswell (0359) 40482
16th C inn at centre of popular village. Well-appointed ground floor bedrooms in a quiet annexe, overlooking a walled garden.
Bedrooms: 1 single, 1 double, 1 twin, 1 triple
Bathrooms: 1 private, 1 public

Bed & breakfast per night:
	£min	£max
Single	17.00	21.00
Double	32.00	36.00

Parking for 12

Please mention this guide when making a booking.

EAST ANGLIA

WROXHAM
Norfolk
Map ref 3C1

Yachting centre on the River Bure which houses the headquarters of the Norfolk Broads Yacht Club. The church of St Mary has a famous doorway and the manor house nearby dates back to 1623.

Manor Barn House
COMMENDED

Back Lane, Rackheath, Wroxham, Norwich NR13 6NN
☎ Norwich (0603) 783543
Traditional Norfolk barn conversion with exposed beams, in quiet setting with pleasant gardens. Just off the A1151, 2 miles from Wroxham.
Bedrooms: 3 double, 2 twin
Bathrooms: 5 private

Bed & breakfast
per night:	£min	£max
Single	18.00	22.00
Double	32.00	35.00

Parking for 8

Staitheway House

Staitheway Road, Wroxham, Norwich NR12 8TH
☎ (0603) 782148
Fine Victorian house in quiet location but within easy walking distance of village, river and all amenities.
Bedrooms: 1 single, 1 twin, 1 triple
Bathrooms: 2 private, 1 public

Bed & breakfast
per night:	£min	£max
Single	17.50	20.00
Double	28.00	36.00

Evening meal 1900 (last orders 2050)
Parking for 3
Open January-November

Wroxham Park Lodge
COMMENDED

142 Norwich Road, Wroxham, Norwich NR12 8SA
☎ (0603) 782991
Comfortable Victorian house in lovely gardens, 1 mile from Wroxham Broads and town centre. Central for all Broads amenities. Open all year round.
Bedrooms: 2 double, 1 twin

Bathrooms: 3 private, 1 public

Bed & breakfast
per night:	£min	£max
Single	18.00	20.00
Double	36.00	40.00

Parking for 6

WYMONDHAM
Norfolk
Map ref 3B1

Busy market town with a charming octagonal market cross. In 1615 a great fire destroyed most of its buildings but the Green Dragon Inn, now one of the oldest in the country, survived.

Cobweb Cottage
Listed APPROVED

Queens Street, Spooner Row, Wymondham NR18 9JU
☎ (0953) 604070
Delightful old world cottage in quiet location 2.5 miles from Wymondham, 15 minutes from Norwich, central for touring Norfolk. Homely accommodation and cooking. No smoking in accommodation.
Bedrooms: 2 single, 2 double, 1 twin
Bathrooms: 3 public

Bed & breakfast
per night:	£min	£max
Single	15.00	17.00
Double	30.00	34.00

Half board
per person:	£min	£max
Daily	25.00	27.00
Weekly	175.00	175.00

Evening meal 1900 (last orders 2200)
Parking for 6
Cards accepted: Access, Visa

Rose Farm
Listed

School Lane, Suton, Wymondham NR18 9JN
☎ (0953) 603512
2-acre poultry farm. Homely farmhouse accommodation within easy reach of Norwich, Broads and Breckland. Bus and train services close by.
Bedrooms: 2 single, 1 double, 1 triple
Bathrooms: 2 public

Bed & breakfast
per night:	£min	£max
Single	17.00	19.00
Double	34.00	38.00

Half board
per person:	£min	£max
Daily	25.00	27.00
Weekly	170.00	180.00

Parking for 4

Turret House
Listed

27 Middleton Street, Wymondham NR18 0AB
☎ (0953) 603462
Large Victorian house in centre of Wymondham within walking distance of shops, restaurants and historic abbey. Convenient for Norwich.
Bedrooms: 1 double, 1 twin
Bathrooms: 1 public

Bed & breakfast
per night:	£min	£max
Single	13.50	13.50
Double	27.00	27.00

Parking for 2
Cards accepted: Visa

Willow Farm
Listed COMMENDED

Wattlefield, Wymondham NR18 9PA
☎ (0953) 604679

Comfortable farmhouse offering high standard of hospitality in relaxed atmosphere. Two miles south down B1135 from Wymondham fork right. Willow Farm three quarters of a mile on the left.
Bedrooms: 1 single, 1 double, 1 twin
Bathrooms: 2 public

Bed & breakfast
per night:	£min	£max
Single	14.00	15.00
Double	28.00	30.00

Parking for 3

West Country

From legendary King Arthur's court to the infamous 'Bloody Assize' of Judge Jeffreys, the West Country offers a powerful cocktail of magic to charm its visitors. A vast and rugged coastline offers some of the most breathtaking scenery in England: golden sands, implacable cliffs, sheltered coves which protect pretty fishing villages and the off-shore treasures of the Isles of Scilly and Lundy. Inland there are historic cities and towns, cathedrals and abbeys, castles and stately homes, zoos and wildlife parks and the great National Parks of Dartmoor and Exmoor. There are the Georgian attractions of Bath, the mediterranean atmosphere of Torbay and many museums in which to unearth the secrets of the West Country.

WHERE TO GO, WHAT TO SEE

With its rolling Atlantic breakers, the north coast of Cornwall is a paradise for surfers.

The number against each name will help you locate it on the map (pages 250 and 251).

❶ The Exploratory Hands-on Science Centre
Bristol Old Station, Clock Tower Yard, Temple Gate, Bristol, Avon BS1 6QU
Tel: Bristol (0272) 252008
Exhibition of lights, lenses, lasers, bubbles, bridges, illusions, gyroscopes and much more, all housed in Brunel's original engine shed and drawing office.

❶ SS Great Britain
Great Western Dock, Gas Ferry Road, Bristol, Avon BS1 6TY
Tel: Bristol (0272) 260680
Now being restored in her original dock, SS Great Britain was the first ocean-going, screw-propelled iron ship in history. Designed by Brunel and launched 1843.

❷ Bowood House and Gardens
Calne, Wiltshire SN11 0LZ
Tel: Calne (0249) 812102
18th C house by Robert Adam. Collections of paintings, watercolours, Victoriana, Indiana and porcelain. Landscaped park with lake, terraces, waterfall, grottos.

❸ Avebury Museum
Avebury, Nr Marlborough, Wiltshire SN8 1RF
Tel: Avebury (067 23) 250
Founded by Alexander Keiller in 1930s and containing one of the most important prehistoric archaeological collections in Britain. Remains from Avebury area.

❹ Fox Talbot Museum of Photography
Lacock, Wiltshire SN15 2LG
Tel: Lacock (0249) 730459
Displays of apparatus and photographs related to Fox Talbot. Gallery with seasonal exhibitions.

❺ Roman Baths Museum
Pump Room, Abbey Church Yard, Bath, Avon BA1 1LZ
Tel: Bath (0225) 461111
Roman baths and temple precinct, hot springs and Roman monuments. Jewellery, coins, curses and votive offerings from the sacred spring.

❻ The Tropical Bird Gardens
Rode, Somerset BA3 6QW
Tel: Frome (0373) 830326
Hundreds of exotic birds in lovely

West Country

natural surroundings. 17 acres of woodland, gardens and lakes with children's play areas, pets' corner, miniature steam railway, clematis collection.

⑦ Cheddar Showcaves
Cheddar Gorge, Somerset BS27 3QF
Tel: Cheddar (0934) 742343
Beautiful caves located in Cheddar Gorge. Gough's Cave with its cathedral-like caverns and Cox's Cave with its stalagmites and stalactites. Also 'The Crystal Quest' fantasy adventure.

⑧ Wookey Hole Caves and Mill
Wookey Hole, Wells, Somerset BA5 1BB
Tel: Wells (0749) 672243
The most spectacular caves in Britain and home to the Witch of Wookey. Working Victorian paper mill, 'Fairground by Night' exhibition, Edwardian Penny Pier Arcade, archaeological museum, mirror maze.

⑨ Glastonbury Abbey
The Abbey Gate House, Glastonbury, Somerset BA6 9EL
Tel: Glastonbury (0458) 832267
Ruins of 12th/13th C abbey. Modern display with model of the 1539 abbey. According to legend, founded by Joseph of Arimathea in 1st C and the burial place of King Arthur.

⑩ Clark's Village Factory Centre
High Street, Street, Somerset BA16
Tel: Street (0458) 43131
A variety of attractions including demonstrations of shoe manufacture, shoe museum, landscaped 'heritage' walkway, children's play area and factory shopping.

⑪ Stourhead House and Gardens
Stourton, Wiltshire
Tel: Bourton (0747) 840348
Landscaped garden laid out 1741–80, with lakes and temples,

rare trees and plants. House begun in 1721 contains fine paintings and Chippendale furniture.

⑫ Salisbury and South Wiltshire Museum
The King's House, 65 The Close, Salisbury, Wiltshire SP1 2EN
Tel: Salisbury (0722) 332151
Grade I listed building. Stonehenge collection, the Salisbury Giant and early man. History of Old Sarum, Salisbury, Romans to Saxons, ceramics, Wedgwood, picture and costume exhibitions.

⑬ The Big Sheep
Abbotsham Barton, Abbotsham, Devon EX39 5AP
Tel: Bideford (0237) 472366
Award-winning attraction combining sheep racing, 'One Man and His Dog' sheepdog trials, sheep milking, lamb and duck trials. Adventure playground and nature trail.

⑭ Haynes Motor Museum
Sparkford, Somerset BA22 7LH
Tel: North Cadbury (0963) 40804
Motor vehicles and memorabilia covering the years from the turn of the century to the present day. Video cinema, exhibition.

⑮ Fleet Air Arm Museum
Royal Naval Air Station, Yeovilton, Somerset BA22 8HT
Tel: Ilchester (0935) 840565
Over 50 historic aircraft, displays and equipment, including Concorde prototype. Falklands campaign, Kamikaze, RNAS 1914–1918, The Wrens and Harrier Jump Jet Story exhibitions.

⑯ Rosemoor Garden – Royal Horticultural Society
Rosemoor, Torrington, Devon EX38 8PH
Tel: Torrington (0805) 24067
Garden of rare horticultural interest. Trees, shrubs, roses,

Arthur: legendary English king, said to have been born at Tintagel and buried at Glastonbury.

249

West Country

alpines and arboretum. Nursery of rare plants.

17 Killerton House
Broadclyst, Nr Exeter, Devon
EX5 3LE
Tel: Exeter (0392) 881345
18th C house built for the Acland family, now houses collection of costumes shown in various room settings. 15 acres of hillside garden with rare trees and shrubs.

18 Parnham House
Beaminster, Dorset DT8 3NA
Tel: Beaminster (0308) 862204
Tudor manor house with additions and embellishments by John Nash in 1810. Home of John Makepeace and his famous furniture-making workshops. 14 acres of gardens.

19 'Tales of Lyme' – The Experience
Marine Parade, Lyme Regis, Dorset DT7 3JH
Tel: Lyme Regis (0297) 443039
Historical tableaux and audio-visual display depicting the history of Lyme from the salt-boiling monks of 774 AD to the present day.

20 The Dinosaur Museum
Icen Way, Dorchester, Dorset
DT1 1EW
Tel: Dorchester (0305) 269880
Only museum in Britain devoted

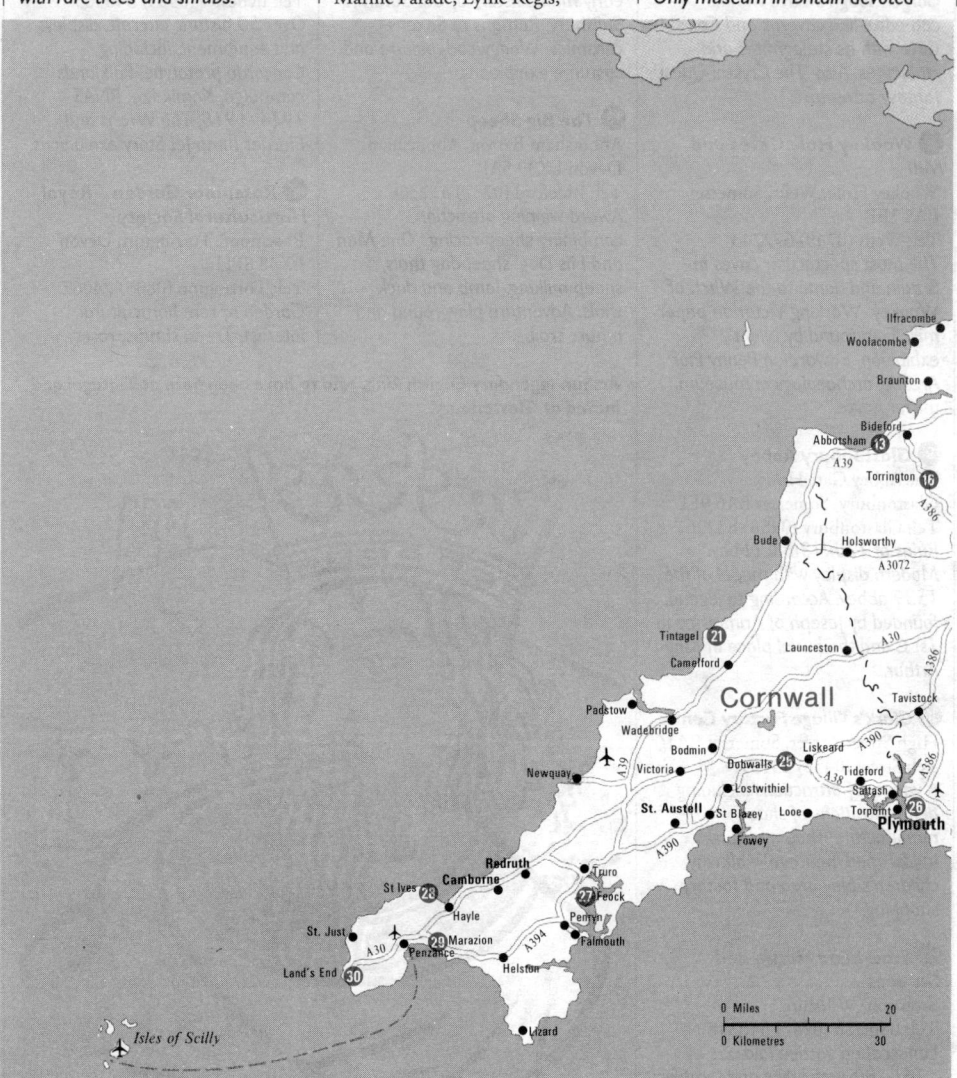

250

West Country

exclusively to dinosaurs. Fossils, full-size models, computerised, mechanical and electronic displays. Video gallery.

㉑ Tintagel Castle
Tintagel, Cornwall PL34 0AA
Tel: Camelford (0840) 770328
Medieval ruined castle on wild, windswept coast. Famous for associations with Arthurian legend.

Built largely in 13th C by Richard, Earl of Cornwall, and used as a prison in 14th C.

㉒ Weymouth Sea Life Park
Lodmoor Country Park,
Weymouth, Dorset DT4 7SX
Tel: Weymouth (0305) 761070
Spectacular marine life displays – shark observatory, fascinating

tropical jungle and trail, Captain Kidd's Adventureland, pets' paddock and splashpool.

㉓ Buckfast Abbey
Buckfastleigh, Devon TQ11 0EE
Tel: Buckfastleigh (0364) 42519
Large Benedictine monastery rebuilt on medieval foundations. Many art treasures in the abbey

Use the map below to locate places in the 'Where to Go, What to See' section.

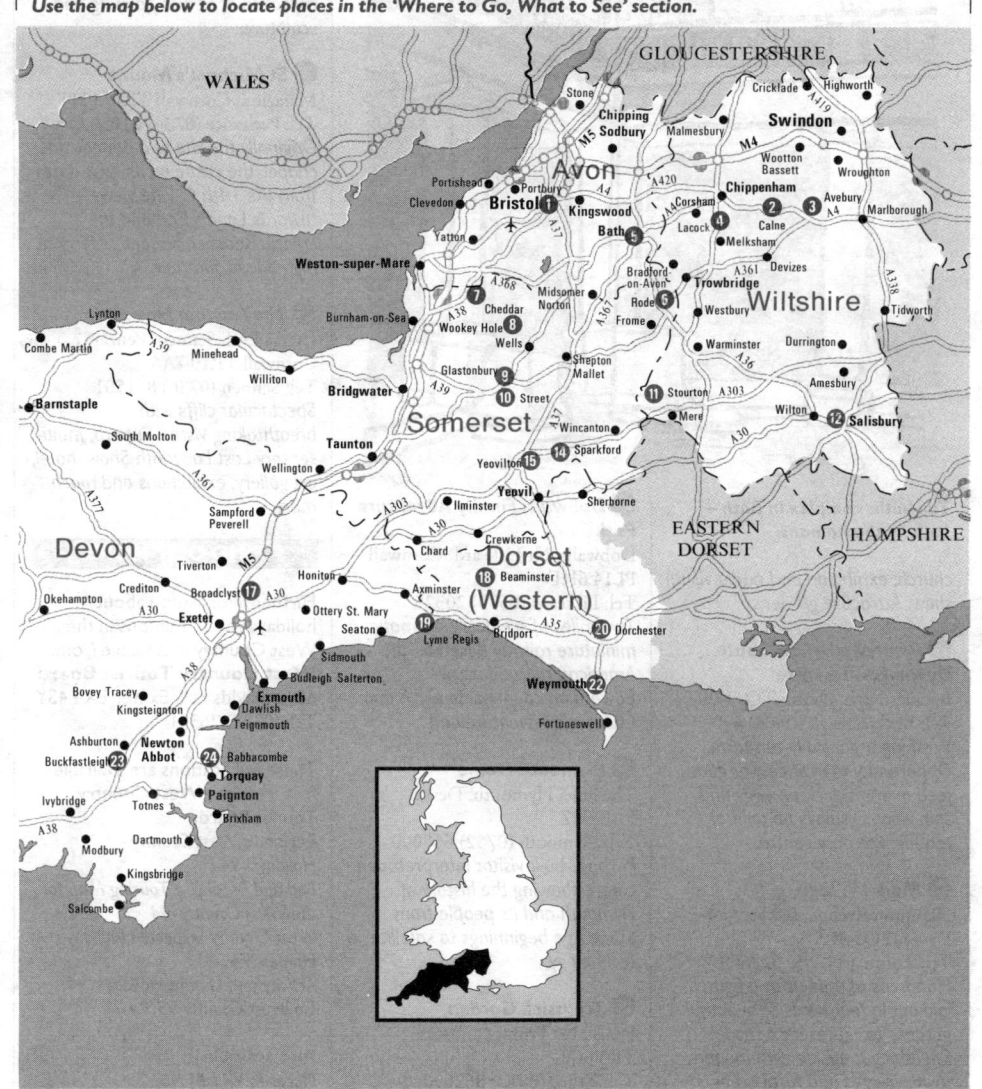

West Country

The baths complex in Bath – built by the Romans.

church, exhibition and audio-visual show. Attractive gardens.

㉔ Pennywell – The South Devon Farm Centre
Buckfastleigh, Devon TQ11 0LT
Tel: Buckfastleigh (0364) 42023
Working organically-run farm. Opportunity to milk cow or goat, feed animals, pick up eggs and spin wool. Displays on animal rearing. Falconry centre.

㉕ Model Village
Hampton Avenue, Babbacombe, Devon TQ1 3LA
Tel: Torquay (0803) 328669
Hundreds of models and figures laid out in four acres of beautiful gardens to represent a model English countryside with modern town, villages and rural areas.

㉕ Dobwalls Family Adventure Park
Dobwalls, Nr Liskeard, Cornwall PL14 6HD
Tel: Liskeard (0579) 20325
Two miles of scenically dramatic miniature railway based on the American railroad scene. Edwardian countryside exhibition. Children's Adventureland.

㉖ Plymouth Dome
The Hoe, Plymouth, Devon PL1 2NZ
Tel: Plymouth (0752) 668000
Purpose-built visitor interpretation centre showing the history of Plymouth and its people from Stone Age beginnings to satellite technology.

㉗ Trelissick Garden
Feock, Nr Truro, Cornwall TR3 6QL
Tel: Truro (0872) 862090
Large garden, lovely in all seasons. Superb views of estuary and Falmouth harbour. Woodland walks beside the River Fal.

㉘ Tate Gallery St Ives
Porthmeor Beach, St Ives, Cornwall
Tel: Penzance (0736) 796226
A major new gallery showing changing groups of work from the Tate Gallery's pre-eminent collection of St Ives painting and sculpture.

㉙ St Michael's Mount
Marazion, Cornwall TR17 0HT
Tel: Penzance (0736) 710507
Originally the site of a Benedictine chapel, the castle on its rock dates from the 14th C. Fine views towards Land's End and the Lizard. Reached by foot or ferry at high tide in summer.

㉚ The Custom House
Land's End, Sennen, Penzance, Cornwall TR19 7AA
Tel: Sennen (0736) 871501
Spectacular cliffs with breathtaking vistas. Superb, multi-sensory Last Labyrinth Show, hotel, art gallery, exhibitions and much more.

FIND OUT MORE

Further information about holidays and attractions in the West Country is available from:
West Country Tourist Board
60 St Davids Hill, Exeter EX4 4SY
Tel: (0392) 76351

These publications are available free from the West Country Tourist Board:
England's West Country - Holidays '94
Bed and Breakfast Touring Map for the West Country '94
West Country Inspected Holiday Homes '94
Activity and Leisure Holidays '94
Go West Country 93/94

Also available is:
Places to Visit £1.95

WEST COUNTRY

Places to stay

Accommodation entries in this regional section are listed in alphabetical order of place name, and then in alphabetical order of establishment.

The map references refer to the colour maps at the back of the guide. The first figure is the map number; the letter and figure which follow indicate the grid reference on the map.

The symbols at the end of each accommodation entry give information about services and facilities. A 'key' to these symbols is inside the back cover flap, which can be kept open for easy reference.

ABBOTSBURY
Dorset
Map ref 2A3

Beautiful village near Chesil Beach, with a long main street of mellow stone and thatched cottages and the ruins of a Benedictine monastery. High above the village on a hill is a prominent 15th C chapel. Abbotsbury's famous swannery and sub-tropical gardens lie just outside the village.

Swan Lodge
APPROVED
Rodden Row, Abbotsbury, Weymouth DT3 4JL
☎ (0305) 871249
Situated on the B3157 coastal road between Weymouth and Bridport. Swan Inn public house opposite, where food is served all day, is under the same ownership.
Bedrooms: 2 double, 2 twin, 1 triple
Bathrooms: 1 public
Bed & breakfast
per night: £min   £max
Single   30.00   38.00
Double   40.00   48.00
Lunch available
Evening meal 1800 (last orders 2200)
Parking for 10
Cards accepted: Access, Visa

Colour maps at the back of this guide pinpoint all places which have accommodation listings in the guide.

ALLERFORD
Somerset
Map ref 1D1

Village with picturesque stone and thatch cottages and a packhorse bridge, set in the beautiful Vale of Porlock.

Fern Cottage
COMMENDED
Allerford, Minehead TA24 8HN
☎ Porlock (0643) 862215

Large 16th C traditional Exmoor cottage in National Trust wooded vale. Dramatic scenery and wildlife. Fine classic cooking and comprehensive wine list.
Bedrooms: 3 double, 1 twin, 1 triple
Bathrooms: 1 public
Bed & breakfast
per night: £min   £max
Single   19.25   19.25
Double   38.50   38.50
Half board
per person: £min   £max
Daily   29.50   29.50
Weekly   185.85 185.85
Evening meal 1900 (last orders 1800)
Parking for 7
Cards accepted: Access, Visa, Switch

We advise you to confirm your booking in writing.

AMESBURY
Wiltshire
Map ref 2B2

Standing on the banks of the River Avon, this is the nearest town to Stonehenge on Salisbury Plain. The area is rich in prehistoric sites.
Tourist Information Centre
☎ *(0980) 623255*

Church Cottage
Listed HIGHLY COMMENDED
Church Street, Amesbury, Salisbury SP4 7EY
☎ (0980) 624650
Period 18th C property with beams and antiques, only 2 miles from Stonehenge. Attractive patio and gardens, lovely bedrooms, delicious English breakfast. Evening meal available.
Bedrooms: 3 double
Bathrooms: 3 private
Bed & breakfast
per night: £min   £max
Single   22.00   27.00
Double   30.00   33.00

Mandalay Guest House
HIGHLY COMMENDED
15 Stonehenge Road, Amesbury, Salisbury SP4 7BA
☎ Shrewton (0980) 623733
Beautiful bedrooms in house of great character. Fine breakfast served in classical breakfast room overlooking the garden temple. No-smoking policy.
Bedrooms: 1 twin, 1 triple, 1 family room
Bathrooms: 3 private, 1 public

Continued ▶

253

WEST COUNTRY

AMESBURY
Continued

Bed & breakfast
per night:	£min	£max
Single	22.00	23.00
Double	35.00	35.00

Parking for 5

Ratfyn Barrow House
Listed

Ratfyn Road, Amesbury, Salisbury
SP4 7DZ
☎ Shrewton (0980) 623422

Comfortable accommodation in pleasant surroundings off main road. Site of ancient barrow, a listed monument.
Bedrooms: 1 double, 2 twin
Bathrooms: 1 private, 1 public

Bed & breakfast
per night:	£min	£max
Single	18.00	
Double	24.00	38.00

Parking for 4
Open April-October

ASHBRITTLE
Somerset
Map ref 1D1

Higher Westcott Farm
APPROVED

Ashbrittle, Wellington TA21 0HZ
☎ Clayhanger (039 86) 258
230-acre mixed farm. Family-run, situated in lovely countryside on the Devon/Somerset border. Traditional farmhouse cooking with home-produced food. Coarse and fly fishing nearby. Ideal for touring Exmoor and Quantock Hills. Warm welcome assured.
Bedrooms: 2 triple
Bathrooms: 1 private, 1 public

Bed & breakfast
per night:	£min	£max
Single	15.00	16.00
Double	30.00	32.00

Half board
per person:	£min	£max
Daily	20.00	21.00
Weekly	125.00	130.00

Evening meal 1830 (last orders 1730)
Parking for 4
Open April-October

Lower Westcott Farm

Ashbrittle, Wellington TA21 0HZ
☎ Clayhanger (039 86) 296
220-acre mixed farm. On Devon/Somerset borders in peaceful, scenic countryside. Ideal for touring Exmoor, Quantocks, coast. Noted for comfort, homeliness and farmhouse cooking. All rooms have spectacular views across valley.
Bedrooms: 1 double, 1 twin, 1 triple
Bathrooms: 2 private, 1 public

Bed & breakfast
per night:	£min	£max
Single	14.00	16.00
Double	28.00	32.00

Half board
per person:	£min	£max
Daily	20.00	22.00
Weekly	140.00	150.00

Evening meal 1800 (last orders 1700)
Parking for 4

ASHBURTON
Devon
Map ref 1C2

Formerly a thriving wool centre and important as one of Dartmoor's four stannary towns. Today's busy market town has many period buildings. Ancient tradition is maintained in the annual ale-tasting and bread-weighing ceremony. Good centre for exploring Dartmoor or the south Devon coast.

New Cott Farm
COMMENDED

Poundsgate, Newton Abbot TQ13 7PD
☎ Poundsgate (036 43) 421
Fax (036 43) 338
130-acre mixed farm. Friendly welcome, pleasing accommodation, lots of lovely home-made food. Beautiful views. On Two Moors Way and an ideal area for walking or just enjoying Dartmoor.
Bedrooms: 1 double, 1 twin, 1 triple
Bathrooms: 3 private

Bed & breakfast
per night:	£min	£max
Double	32.00	34.00

Half board
per person:	£min	£max
Daily	25.00	26.00
Weekly	156.00	

Evening meal 1830 (last orders 1600)
Parking for 3

Wellpritton Farm
HIGHLY COMMENDED

Holne, Newton Abbot TQ13 7RX
☎ Poundsgate (036 43) 273
15-acre mixed farm. Plenty of mouthwatering farm-produced food in a

tastefully modernised farmhouse on the edge of Dartmoor. Special diets catered for by arrangement. A warm welcome and caring personal attention.
Bedrooms: 2 double, 2 twin
Bathrooms: 3 private, 1 public

Bed & breakfast
per night:	£min	£max
Single	16.00	17.00
Double	32.00	34.00

Half board
per person:	£min	£max
Daily	24.00	25.00
Weekly	147.00	147.00

Evening meal from 1900
Parking for 4

ASHTON KEYNES
Wiltshire
Map ref 2B2

Village beside the River Thames, with houses standing along the edge of the stream reached by bridges from the road on the opposite bank. Nearby stands the manor, Ashton House.

Corner Cottage
APPROVED

Fore Street, Ashton Keynes, Swindon
SN6 6NP
☎ Cirencester (0285) 861454
Homely 17th C Cotswold stone cottage in centre of best kept village within the Cotswold Water Park. Ideal for water sports and touring Cotswolds.
Bedrooms: 1 double, 1 family room
Bathrooms: 2 private

Bed & breakfast
per night:	£min	£max
Single	18.00	22.00
Double	35.00	37.00

Parking for 4

BANTHAM
Devon
Map ref 1C3

Village at the mouth of the River Avon, with a fine sandy beach.

Sloop Inn
COMMENDED

Bantham, Kingsbridge TQ7 3AJ
☎ Kingsbridge (0548) 560489 & 5560215
Part 16th C inn in old world fishing village. Some rooms overlook sea and river estuary. Menu majors on local seafood.
Bedrooms: 3 double, 2 triple
Bathrooms: 5 private

Bed & breakfast
per night:	£min	£max
Double	49.00	55.00

254

WEST COUNTRY

Lunch available
Evening meal 1900 (last orders 2200)
Parking for 35

BARNSTAPLE
Devon
Map ref 1C1

At the head of the Taw Estuary, once a ship-building and textile town, now an agricultural centre with attractive period buildings, a modern civic centre and leisure centre. Attractions include Queen Anne's Walk, a charming colonnaded arcade and Pannier Market.
Tourist Information Centre
☎ (0271) 388583

The Cedars Lodge Inn
COMMENDED
Bickington Road, Barnstaple
EX31 2HP
☎ (0271) 71784
Fax (0271) 25733
Country house with lodges in 3 acres. All en-suite, satellite TV. Pub and restaurant. Just off North Devon link road.
Bedrooms: 9 double, 8 twin, 6 family rooms
Bathrooms: 23 private

Bed & breakfast
per night:	£min	£max
Single	34.00	38.00
Double	48.50	52.00

Lunch available
Evening meal 1830 (last orders 2200)
Parking for 100
Cards accepted: Access, Visa, Amex

Home Park Farm Accommodation
COMMENDED
Lower Blakewell, Muddiford,
Barnstaple EX31 4ET
☎ (0271) 42955

70-acre livestock farm. An away-from-it-all paradise for country and garden lovers, off the beaten track. Ideal situation for touring. Take A39 Lynton road from Barnstaple, fork left B3230, second left and continue to end of road. SAE for brochure.
Bedrooms: 1 double, 1 triple, 1 family room
Bathrooms: 3 private

Bed & breakfast
per night:	£min	£max
Single	18.50	20.00
Double	35.00	40.00

Half board
per person:	£min	£max
Daily	24.50	30.00
Weekly	135.00	150.00

Lunch available
Evening meal 1800 (last orders 1800)
Parking for 4
Open April, June-October

Waytown Farm
COMMENDED
Shirwell, Barnstaple EX31 4JN
☎ Shirwell (0271) 850396
240-acre mixed farm. Pleasantly situated 17th C farmhouse 3 miles from Barnstaple. Exmoor and beaches within easy reach. Home cooking, relaxed atmosphere. Access at all times.
Bedrooms: 2 double, 1 twin
Bathrooms: 2 private, 1 public

Bed & breakfast
per night:	£min	£max
Single	20.00	21.00
Double	36.00	38.00

Half board
per person:	£min	£max
Daily	24.00	26.00
Weekly	145.00	150.00

Evening meal 1830 (last orders 1600)
Parking for 6
Open January-November

BATH
Avon
Map ref 2B2

Georgian spa city beside the River Avon. Important Roman site with impressive reconstructed baths, uncovered in 19th C. Bath Abbey built on site of monastery where first king of England was crowned (AD 973). Fine architecture in mellow local stone. Pump Room and museums.
Tourist Information Centre
☎ (0225) 462831

Aaron House Number Ninety Three
COMMENDED
93 Wells Road, Bath BA2 3AN
☎ (0225) 317977
Pleasant Victorian house, all rooms en-suite. Within very easy walking distance of city centre, British Rail and national coach stations.
Bedrooms: 1 double, 1 twin, 1 triple
Bathrooms: 3 private

Bed & breakfast
per night:	£min	£max
Single	19.00	35.00
Double	38.00	45.00

Half board
per person:	£min	£max
Daily	28.00	44.00
Weekly	196.00	308.00

Evening meal from 1830
Cards accepted: Access, Visa, Amex

Ashley Villa Hotel
26 Newbridge Road, Bath BA1 3JZ
☎ (0225) 421683 & 428887
Comfortably furnished licensed hotel with relaxing informal atmosphere, close to city centre. All rooms en-suite. Swimming pool.
Bedrooms: 2 single, 7 double, 2 twin, 3 triple
Bathrooms: 14 private

Bed & breakfast
per night:	£min	£max
Single	39.00	39.00
Double	45.00	59.00

Evening meal 1800 (last orders 2100)
Parking for 10
Cards accepted: Access, Visa

Astor House
14 Oldfield Road, Bath BA2 3ND
☎ (0225) 429134
Lovely Victorian house with comfortable, spacious rooms and large secluded garden. Peaceful, elegant atmosphere.
Bedrooms: 2 double, 1 twin
Bathrooms: 2 public

Bed & breakfast
per night:	£min	£max
Double	30.00	34.00

Parking for 4
Open April-October

Bailbrook Lodge
APPROVED
35/37 London Road West, Bath
BA1 7HZ
☎ (0225) 859090

Fine Georgian house with many original features - ceilings, staircase and fireplaces - all carefully restored. Splendid views overlooking the Avon Valley. Near M4 and on the outskirts of Bath.

Continued ▶

WEST COUNTRY

BATH
Continued

Bedrooms: 4 double, 2 twin
Bathrooms: 6 private
Bed & breakfast
per night:	£min	£max
Single	30.00	40.00
Double	45.00	60.00

Lunch available
Parking for 20
Cards accepted: Access, Visa, Diners, Amex

Cherry Tree Villa

7 Newbridge Hill, Bath BA1 3PW
☎ (0225) 331671
Modernised, tastefully decorated Victorian house with friendly atmosphere, within easy walking distance of city centre through pleasant park.
Bedrooms: 1 single, 1 double, 1 triple
Bathrooms: 1 public
Bed & breakfast
per night:	£min	£max
Single	15.00	18.00
Double	30.00	36.00

Parking for 4

Church Farm

Monkton Farleigh, Bradford-on-Avon, Wiltshire BA15 2QJ
☎ (0225) 858583 & Mobile (0374) 277665
52-acre mixed farm. Large converted barn with en-suite rooms and guest lounge on working farm with livery stables. 10 minutes to Bath.
Bedrooms: 3 double
Bathrooms: 1 private, 1 public
Bed & breakfast
per night:	£min	£max
Single	18.50	18.50
Double	30.00	35.00

Parking for 5

Cranleigh

159 Newbridge Hill, Bath BA1 3PX
☎ (0225) 310197

Lovely Victorian house with beautiful views, spacious en-suite bedrooms (four-poster available), generous breakfasts.

Quiet residential area. Private parking. Non-smoking.
Bedrooms: 2 double, 2 twin, 1 triple
Bathrooms: 5 private
Bed & breakfast
per night:	£min	£max
Single	32.00	35.00
Double	48.00	56.00

Parking for 5
Cards accepted: Access, Visa, Switch

Fern Cottage
COMMENDED

74 Monkton Farleigh, Bradford-on-Avon, Wiltshire BA15 2QJ
☎ (0225) 859412
Delightful stone-built 17th C cottage, set in fine gardens in peaceful conservation village between Bath and Bradford-on-Avon. Well-appointed rooms.
Bedrooms: 1 double, 1 twin, 1 triple
Bathrooms: 1 private, 1 public
Bed & breakfast
per night:	£min	£max
Single	20.00	25.00
Double	35.00	40.00

Parking for 5

The Old Mill Hotel & Restaurant

Tollbridge Road, Bath, Avon BA1 7DE
☎ (0225) 858476/31/32/33/19/42
Fax: (0225) 852600

wine & dine by the riverside

What could be more luxurious than a peaceful riverside experience on the banks of the River Avon beside the historic Toll Bridge overlooking the Weir & panoramic views.

New water-wheel Restaurant with a rotating base for "That Riviera Touch!" offering a varied menu.

Most rooms have river views, 18 bedrooms all en suite with colour T.V., Radio, telephone, tea/coffee making facilities, 4 poster beds available.
Riverside restaurant, bar and lounge, fishing and parking available. **Prices from: Single £35.00 Doubles £48.00 Short breaks from £65.00**
HONYMOONERS PARADISE to celebrate honeymoons, anniversaries etc. Rooms with 4-poster beds and river views, in a peaceful setting, yet only 2 minutes from Bath city. Complimented with special event welcoming pack. Interested?

WEST COUNTRY

Forres Guest House
172 Newbridge Road, Lower Weston, Bath BA1 3LE
☎ (0225) 427698
Edwardian family guesthouse with friendly, informative hosts, who are ex-teachers and love Bath. River Avon and Cotswold Way close by. Traditional and vegetarian breakfasts. Colour TV in all rooms.
Bedrooms: 2 double, 2 twin, 1 triple
Bathrooms: 5 private

Bed & breakfast
per night:	£min	£max
Single	20.00	22.00
Double	28.00	38.00

Parking for 5
Open April-October

Gainsborough Hotel
APPROVED
Weston Lane, Bath BA1 4AB
☎ (0225) 311380

Spacious and comfortable country house hotel in own lovely grounds near the city centre and botanical gardens. High ground, nice views, own large car park. 5-course breakfast, friendly staff, warm welcome.
Bedrooms: 2 single, 8 double, 4 twin, 1 triple, 1 family room
Bathrooms: 16 private

Bed & breakfast
per night:	£min	£max
Single	30.00	40.00
Double	48.00	60.00

Evening meal 1845 (last orders 1945)
Parking for 18
Cards accepted: Access, Visa, Diners, Amex

Green Lane House
Green Lane, Hinton Charterhouse, Bath BA3 6BL
☎ (0225) 723631
Fully renovated, attractive stone house built in 1725, and comfortably furnished. Quiet village in beautiful countryside, convenient for Bath, Somerset and Cotswolds.
Bedrooms: 2 double, 2 twin
Bathrooms: 2 private, 1 public

Please mention this guide when making a booking.

Bed & breakfast
per night:	£min	£max
Single	24.00	37.00
Double	37.00	49.00

Parking for 2
Cards accepted: Access, Visa, Amex

Hatt Farm
Listed COMMENDED
Old Jockey, Box, Corsham, Wiltshire SN14 9DJ
☎ (0225) 742989
800-acre arable & livestock farm. 18th C farmhouse in peaceful location, commanding magnificent views of Wiltshire countryside. Bath 5 miles. Many places of interest within easy distance. Double room can be used as a family room.
Bedrooms: 1 double, 1 twin
Bathrooms: 2 private, 1 public

Bed & breakfast
per night:	£min	£max
Single	20.00	
Double	30.00	35.00

Parking for 5
Open January-November

Haute Combe House
176 Newbridge Road, Bath BA1 3LE
☎ (0225) 420061
Fax (0225) 420461
Sunny south-facing period property with hotel facilities at affordable prices. Nearby park-and-ride for city attractions.
Bedrooms: 1 single, 3 double, 1 twin, 2 triple, 1 family room
Bathrooms: 8 private

Bed & breakfast
per night:	£min	£max
Single	22.00	34.00
Double	32.00	48.00

Half board
per person:	£min	£max
Daily	28.00	36.00

Evening meal 1900 (last orders 1800)
Parking for 8
Cards accepted: Access, Visa, Amex

The Hollies
COMMENDED
Hatfield Road, Wellsway, Bath BA2 2BD
☎ (0225) 313366

Grade II early Victorian family house, 1 mile from city centre, overlooking parish church and gardens. Pretty

---

guestrooms, comfortably furnished. Sunny secluded garden.
Bedrooms: 2 double, 1 twin
Bathrooms: 2 private, 1 private shower

Bed & breakfast
per night:	£min	£max
Single	18.00	24.00
Double	32.00	42.00

Parking for 6

Kennard Hotel
COMMENDED
11 Henrietta Street, Bath BA2 6LL
☎ (0225) 310472
Fax (0225) 442456

Converted Georgian house in quiet street. A few minutes' level walk to city centre, abbey, Roman Baths, Pump Room and Henrietta Park.
Bedrooms: 2 single, 7 double, 2 twin, 1 triple, 1 family room
Bathrooms: 10 private, 2 public

Bed & breakfast
per night:	£min	£max
Single	25.00	35.00
Double	35.00	55.00

Cards accepted: Access, Visa, Diners, Amex, Switch

Kinlet Villa Guest House
COMMENDED
99 Wellsway, Bath BA2 4RX
☎ (0225) 420268
Edwardian villa retaining original features and furnishings. Walking distance from city centre, good bus service, unrestricted parking. Non-smokers only, please.
Bedrooms: 1 double, 1 triple
Bathrooms: 1 public

Bed & breakfast
per night:	£min	£max
Double	30.00	32.00

Leighton House
HIGHLY COMMENDED
139 Wells Road, Bath BA2 3AL
☎ (0225) 314769

Continued ▶

257

WEST COUNTRY

BATH
Continued

Elegant and spacious Victorian guesthouse set in award-winning gardens with own car park. 10 minutes' walk from city centre.
Bedrooms: 3 double, 3 twin, 2 triple
Bathrooms: 8 private

Bed & breakfast

per night:	£min	£max
Single	42.00	48.00
Double	56.00	64.00

Parking for 8
Cards accepted: Access, Visa

The Manor House
APPROVED

Mill Lane, Monkton Combe, Bath
BA2 7HD
☎ (0225) 723128

Restful, rambling 16th C manor beside mill stream in wooded valley designated as an Area of Outstanding Natural Beauty, just 2 miles south of city. Inglenook fires, Victorian conservatory, spacious bedrooms. Fine breakfasts served until noon.
Bedrooms: 2 double, 2 family rooms
Bathrooms: 4 private, 1 public

Bed & breakfast

per night:	£min	£max
Single	20.00	25.00
Double	38.00	45.00

Parking for 6

Marlborough House

1 Marlborough Lane, Bath BA1 2NQ
☎ (0225) 318175 & 466127
Victorian house situated within 5 minutes' level walk of city centre and Royal Crescent. A non-smokers' house. Friendly atmosphere. Parking.
Bedrooms: 2 single, 1 double, 1 twin, 1 triple
Bathrooms: 3 private, 1 public, 1 private shower

Bed & breakfast

per night:	£min	£max
Single	20.00	25.00
Double	38.00	50.00

Parking for 3
Cards accepted: Access, Visa

Meadowland
HIGHLY COMMENDED

36 Bloomfield Park, Bath BA2 2BX
☎ (0225) 311079
Set in its own quiet secluded grounds, offering the highest standards in beautifully appointed en-suite accommodation. Private parking, lovely gardens. Non-smokers only please. A peaceful retreat for the discerning traveller.
Bedrooms: 2 double, 1 twin
Bathrooms: 3 private

Bed & breakfast

per night:	£min	£max
Single	40.00	45.00
Double	48.00	55.00

Parking for 6
Cards accepted: Access, Visa

Membland Guest House
Listed COMMENDED

7 Pulteney Terrace, Pulteney Road, Bath BA2 4HJ
☎ (0225) 336712
5 minutes' walk to Roman baths, abbey, train/coach stations, city shops, tranquil canalside. Private parking, comfortable rooms and generous breakfast.
Bedrooms: 1 twin, 1 triple
Bathrooms: 1 public, 1 private shower

Bed & breakfast

per night:	£min	£max
Single	22.00	33.00
Double	27.00	37.00

Parking for 2
Open February-December

Oakleigh House
COMMENDED

19 Upper Oldfield Park, Bath BA2 3JX
☎ (0225) 315698
Quietly situated Victorian home only 10 minutes from city centre. All rooms en-suite with colour TV, tea/coffee making facilities, etc. Private car park.
Bedrooms: 3 double, 1 twin
Bathrooms: 4 private

Bed & breakfast

per night:	£min	£max
Single	35.00	45.00
Double	45.00	60.00

Parking for 4
Cards accepted: Access, Visa

Old Mill Hotel & Waterwheel Restaurant

Tollbridge Road, Bath BA1 7DE
☎ (0225) 858476
Fax (0225) 852600
Riverside hotel with breathtaking views, 2 miles from centre of Bath. Unique water wheel restaurant with a rotating floor. Most rooms with river views.
Bedrooms: 10 double, 4 twin, 3 triple
Bathrooms: 17 private

Bed & breakfast

per night:	£min	£max
Single	35.00	45.00
Double	48.00	58.00

Lunch available
Evening meal 1900 (last orders 2100)
Parking for 35
Cards accepted: Access, Visa, Amex

Ad Display advertisement appears on page 13, 256, inside back cover

The Old Red House
COMMENDED

37 Newbridge Road, Bath BA1 3HE
☎ (0225) 330464

Welcome to this charming Victorian "gingerbread house" with stained-glass windows. The romantic bedrooms are colourful and warm, with canopied or king size beds. Breakfast in sunny conservatory. Special rates for 3 or more nights. Brochure. No smoking.
Bedrooms: 2 double, 1 twin
Bathrooms: 2 private, 1 public, 1 private shower

Bed & breakfast

per night:	£min	£max
Single	25.00	
Double	36.00	50.00

Parking for 3
Cards accepted: Access, Visa

The Old School House
HIGHLY COMMENDED

Church Street, Bathford, Bath
BA1 7RR
☎ (0225) 859593

Pretty Victorian schoolhouse of Bath stone in peaceful conservation area. Views and fine walks overlooking Avon Valley. 3 miles to Bath centre. All rooms have full private facilities. Dinners, licensed. Non-smoking.
Bedrooms: 3 double, 1 twin
Bathrooms: 4 private

Bed & breakfast

per night:	£min	£max
Single	45.00	45.00
Double	60.00	65.00

WEST COUNTRY

Half board per person:	£min	£max
Daily	48.50	63.50
Weekly	320.00	420.00

Evening meal 1900 (last orders 2000)
Parking for 6
Cards accepted: Access, Visa

Orchard House M

24 Box Road, Bathford, Bath
BA1 7QD
☎ (0225) 859072
Small family-run guesthouse which aims to please, close to city and open countryside. Ideal location for walking the Avon Canal and Cotswold Way. Non-smoking house.
Bedrooms: 3 twin, 1 triple
Bathrooms: 3 private, 1 public

Bed & breakfast per night:	£min	£max
Single	19.00	22.00
Double	30.00	34.00

Parking for 4

Poplar Farm M

Listed COMMENDED

Stanton Prior, Bath BA2 9HX
☎ Mendip (0761) 470382
350-acre mixed farm. Large 17th C farmhouse on working farm producing cereals and beef. Situated in beautiful countryside beneath Iron Age fort on Stantonbury Hill. Just 5 miles west of Bath.
Bedrooms: 1 double, 1 twin, 1 family room
Bathrooms: 3 private, 2 public

Bed & breakfast per night:	£min	£max
Single	15.00	20.00
Double	30.00	40.00

Parking for 8

The Priory Wing

54 Lyncombe Hill, Bath BA2 4PJ
☎ (0225) 336395
Peaceful Georgian listed building bordering meadowland yet only 10 minutes from city centre and railway/bus stations. Original fireplaces in both bedrooms, one adjoining flagstone, panelled, entrance hall. Non-smokers only please.
Bedrooms: 1 double, 1 twin
Bathrooms: 2 private

Bed & breakfast per night:	£min	£max
Single	17.50	17.50
Double	35.00	35.00

Parking for 2

Hotel Saint Clair

APPROVED

1 Crescent Gardens, Upper Bristol Road, Bath BA1 2NA
☎ (0225) 425543
Small family guesthouse 5 minutes' walk from city, 2 minutes from Royal Crescent. Large public car park 1 minute away. One night stays welcome.
Bedrooms: 3 single, 4 double, 2 twin, 1 triple
Bathrooms: 2 private, 2 public

Bed & breakfast per night:	£min	£max
Single	20.00	27.00
Double	34.00	40.00

Cards accepted: Access, Visa

Sampford

11 Oldfield Road, Bath BA2 3ND
☎ (0225) 310053
In a quiet residential area half a mile south of city centre off the A367 Exeter road.
Bedrooms: 1 double, 1 twin, 1 triple
Bathrooms: 1 public, 3 private showers

Bed & breakfast per night:	£min	£max
Double		30.00

Parking for 2

Seven Springs

Listed APPROVED

4 High Street, Woolley, Bath BA1 8AR
☎ (0225) 858001
In small country hamlet of Woolley, 3 miles from Bath city centre and 4 miles from M4. Lovely walks on public footpaths. Ideal for touring West Country.
Bedrooms: 2 family rooms
Bathrooms: 2 private

Bed & breakfast per night:	£min	£max
Single	16.00	17.50
Double	32.00	35.00

Parking for 8

Sheridan

95 Wellsway, Bearflat, Bath BA2 4RU
☎ (0225) 429562
Quiet, comfortable family guesthouse. A few minutes' drive from city centre and on main bus route to city and railway station. A non-smoking house.
Bedrooms: 1 single, 1 twin, 1 triple
Bathrooms: 2 public

Bed & breakfast per night:	£min	£max
Single	15.00	15.00
Double	30.00	34.00

Siena Hotel M

HIGHLY COMMENDED

25 Pulteney Road, Bath BA2 4EZ
☎ (0225) 425495
Fax (0225) 469029
Fine Victorian building overlooking Bath Abbey, a few minutes' level walk from centre. Refurbished to provide spacious well-appointed en-suite rooms.
Bedrooms: 2 single, 7 double, 3 triple, 1 family room
Bathrooms: 13 private

Bed & breakfast per night:	£min	£max
Single		32.50
Double		52.50

Lunch available
Evening meal 1900 (last orders 2000)
Parking for 13
Cards accepted: Access, Visa

Tivoli House

70 Greenway Lane, Bath BA2 4LL
☎ (0225) 335288
Georgian detached house with swimming pool in rural setting with wonderful views. Bath railway station 10 minutes' walk.
Bedrooms: 2 double, 1 twin
Bathrooms: 2 private, 1 public

Bed & breakfast per night:	£min	£max
Single	20.00	28.00
Double	35.00	48.00

Parking for 3

Toghill House Farm

Listed COMMENDED

Doynton, Bristol BS15 5RT
☎ (0225) 891261

50-acre mixed farm. Warm and cosy 17th C farmhouse, formerly a resting home for monks travelling from Malmesbury to Glastonbury. Views over historic Bath, Bristol and Welsh hills.
Bedrooms: 1 double, 1 triple, 1 family room
Bathrooms: 3 private, 1 public

Bed & breakfast per night:	£min	£max
Single	22.00	
Double	36.00	

Parking for 50

259

WEST COUNTRY

BATH
Continued

Wansdyke Cottage
Listed **APPROVED**
Marksbury Gate, Bath BA2 9HE
☎ Saltford (0225) 873674

Cottage-style accommodation including self-contained suite of bedroom, bathroom, kitchen and lounge. 5 miles west of Bath on A39.
Bedrooms: 1 single, 2 double, 1 twin
Bathrooms: 1 private, 2 public

Bed & breakfast
per night:	£min	£max
Single	15.00	20.00
Double	30.00	35.00

Half board
per person:	£min	£max
Daily	18.50	27.00
Weekly	129.50	189.00

Lunch available
Evening meal 1900 (last orders 1700)
Parking for 4

Wellsway Guest House
51 Wellsway, Bath BA2 4RS
☎ (0225) 423434
Comfortable, clean, warm, small guesthouse on bus route. Close to local shops, only a few minutes' walk from city centre.
Bedrooms: 1 single, 1 double, 1 twin, 1 triple
Bathrooms: 1 public

Bed & breakfast
per night:	£min	£max
Single	16.00	18.00
Double	24.00	33.00

Parking for 3

There are separate sections in this guide listing groups specialising in farm holidays and accommodation which is especially suitable for young people and organised groups.

BEAMINSTER
Dorset
Map ref 2A3

Old country town of mellow local stone set amid hills and rural vales. Mainly Georgian buildings; attractive almshouses date from 1603. The 17th C church with its ornate, pinnacled tower was restored inside by the Victorians. Parnham, a Tudor manor house, lies 1 mile south.

Jenny Wrens
COMMENDED
1 Hogshill Street, Beaminster DT8 3AE
☎ (0308) 862814
17th C tea shop with bed and breakfast accommodation. Full English breakfast.
Bedrooms: 2 double, 1 twin
Bathrooms: 2 private, 1 public

Bed & breakfast
per night:	£min	£max
Single	16.50	20.00
Double	33.00	40.00

Lunch available
Parking for 1

Kitwhistle Farm
Listed
Beaminster Down, Beaminster DT8 3SG
☎ (0308) 862458
141-acre dairy farm. Downland farm in quiet location 8 miles from sea. All facilities on ground floor, one family only. Personal attention.
Bedrooms: 1 double, 1 twin
Bathrooms: 1 public

Bed & breakfast
per night:	£min	£max
Single	15.00	26.00
Double	25.00	30.00

Parking for 2

The Old Vicarage
Listed
Clay Lane, Beaminster DT8 3BU
☎ (0308) 863200
Large, spacious mid-Victorian vicarage close to town centre, set in its own grounds of three-quarters of an acre. Hardy's Emminster Vicarage (as in "Tess of the D'Urbervilles").
Bedrooms: 2 double, 1 twin
Bathrooms: 2 private, 1 public

Bed & breakfast
per night:	£min	£max
Single	13.50	16.00
Double	27.00	32.00

Parking for 6
Open May-October

BECKINGTON
Somerset
Map ref 2B2

Woolpack Inn
Beckington, Bath BA3 6SP
☎ Frome (0373) 831244
Small 16th C coaching inn set in an historic Somerset village close to Bath, Salisbury and Wells.
Bedrooms: 3 single, 2 double, 4 twin, 1 triple
Bathrooms: 10 private

Bed & breakfast
per night:	£min	£max
Single	39.50	44.50
Double	49.50	54.50

Half board
per person:	£min	£max
Daily	57.00	67.00

Lunch available
Evening meal 1800 (last orders 2200)
Parking for 16
Cards accepted: Access, Visa, Amex, Switch

BERRYNARBOR
Devon
Map ref 1C1

Small village set in a wooded valley, close to Exmoor and to the wild North Devon coast.

Langleigh House
APPROVED
The Village, Berrynarbor, Ilfracombe EX34 9SG
☎ Combe Martin (0271) 883410
Friendly family-run guesthouse providing all home-cooked food, in the beautiful North Devon village of Berrynarbor.
Bedrooms: 1 single, 3 double, 1 triple, 1 family room
Bathrooms: 4 private, 1 public

Bed & breakfast
per night:	£min	£max
Single	15.00	16.00
Double	30.00	32.00

Half board
per person:	£min	£max
Daily	22.00	23.00
Weekly	145.00	151.00

Evening meal 1830 (last orders 1200)
Parking for 6

BICKINGTON
Devon
Map ref 1D2

Kellinch Farm
COMMENDED
Bickington, Newton Abbot TQ12 6PB
☎ Newton Abbot (0626) 821252

260

WEST COUNTRY

44-acre mixed farm. Attractive 17th C farmhouse, idyllically set in the heart of the Devonshire countryside. Central for the moors and sea.
Bedrooms: 1 double, 1 twin
Bathrooms: 2 private, 1 public
Bed & breakfast
per night:	£min	£max
Single	14.50	16.00
Double	29.00	32.00

Half board
per person:	£min	£max
Daily	23.00	24.50
Weekly	157.50	

Evening meal from 1900
Parking for 10

BIDEFORD
Devon
Map ref 1C1

The home port of Sir Richard Grenville, the town with its 17th C merchants' houses flourished as a shipbuilding and cloth town. The bridge of 24 arches was built about 1460. Charles Kingsley stayed here while writing Westward Ho!
Tourist Information Centre
☎ *(0237) 477676*

Sunset Hotel M

Landcross, Bideford EX39 5JA
☎ (0237) 472962
Small, elegant country hotel in peaceful, picturesque location, specialising in home cooking. Delightful en-suite bedrooms with beverages and colour TVs. Book with confidence. Non-smoking establishment.
Bedrooms: 1 single, 1 double, 1 twin, 1 triple
Bathrooms: 4 private
Bed & breakfast
per night:	£min	£max
Single	26.00	29.00
Double	47.00	50.00

Half board
per person:	£min	£max
Daily	33.50	35.00
Weekly	225.00	245.00

Evening meal 1900 (last orders 1900)
Parking for 6
Open February-November
Cards accepted: Access, Visa

Half board prices shown are per person but in some cases may be based on double/twin occupancy.

BISHOP SUTTON
Avon
Map ref 2A2

Village at edge of Chew Valley Lake.

Overbrook
COMMENDED

Stowey Bottom, Bishop Sutton, Bristol BS18 4TN
☎ (0275) 332648
Delightful house of character, in quiet lane by a stream in Chew Valley. Near Bath, Bristol, Wells and Cheddar Gorge.
Bedrooms: 1 double, 1 twin
Bathrooms: 2 private
Bed & breakfast
per night:	£min	£max
Single	17.50	18.50
Double	31.00	32.00

Evening meal 1900 (last orders 2000)
Parking for 8

BISHOP'S LYDEARD
Somerset
Map ref 1D1

Slimbridge Station Farm
COMMENDED

Bishop's Lydeard, Taunton TA4 3BX
☎ Bishops Lydeard (0823) 432223
120-acre dairy farm. Victorian house next to the privately-owned West Somerset Steam Railway which has a limited number of trains running in the summer.
Bedrooms: 1 single, 1 double, 1 twin
Bathrooms: 1 public
Bed & breakfast
per night:	£min	£max
Single	14.00	16.00
Double	28.00	32.00

Parking for 4

BLUNSDON
Wiltshire
Map ref 2B2

Portqvin Guest House
COMMENDED

Highworth Road, Blunsdon, Swindon SN2 4DH
☎ Swindon (0793) 721261
A quality guesthouse overlooking the Wiltshire/Berkshire Downs. Situated 5 miles from Swindon town centre off the A419 Cirencester road.
Bedrooms: 3 single, 2 double, 2 twin, 1 triple
Bathrooms: 8 private
Bed & breakfast
per night:	£min	£max
Single	24.00	28.00
Double	34.00	40.00

Parking for 10

BODMIN
Cornwall
Map ref 1B2

County town south-west of Bodmin Moor with a ruined priory and church, containing the casket said to have held relics of St Petroc, to whom the church is dedicated. Nearby are Lanhydrock House and Pencarrow House.
Tourist Information Centre
☎ *(0208) 76616*

Treffry Farm M
HIGHLY COMMENDED

Lanhydrock, Bodmin PL30 5AF
☎ (0208) 74405

200-acre dairy farm. Lovely Georgian farmhouse in beautiful countryside adjoining National Trust Lanhydrock. Central for coast, moors and walks.
Bedrooms: 1 double, 2 twin
Bathrooms: 2 private, 1 public, 1 private shower
Bed & breakfast
per night:	£min	£max
Single		18.50
Double		37.00

Half board
per person:	£min	£max
Daily		27.50
Weekly		180.00

Evening meal 1830 (last orders 1200)
Parking for 3
Open March-October

BOSCASTLE
Cornwall
Map ref 1B2

Small, unspoilt village in Valency Valley. Active as a port until onset of railway era, its natural harbour affords rare shelter on this wild coast. Attractions include spectacular blow-hole, Celtic field strips, part-Norman church. St Juliot Church nearby, was restored by Thomas Hardy.

The Old Coach House M

Tintagel Road, Boscastle PL35 0AS
☎ (0840) 250398
Relax and enjoy this beautiful 300-year-old former coach house. All rooms en-suite with colour TV, teamakers,

Continued ▶

261

WEST COUNTRY

BOSCASTLE
Continued

hairdryers, etc. Friendly and helpful owners.
Wheelchair access category 3
Bedrooms: 1 single, 3 double, 1 twin, 1 triple
Bathrooms: 6 private

Bed & breakfast
per night:	£min	£max
Single	15.00	22.00
Double	30.00	44.00

Lunch available
Parking for 9
Open March-October
Cards accepted: Access, Visa, Amex

Tolcarne Hotel
COMMENDED
Tintagel Road, Boscastle PL35 0AS
☎ (0840) 250654

Delightful house of character in own grounds with lovely views, near beautiful coastal paths along the dramatic Cornish coastline. Home cooking, including vegetarian. Warm welcome. Licensed.
Bedrooms: 1 single, 4 double, 3 twin, 1 family room
Bathrooms: 8 private, 1 public

Bed & breakfast
per night:	£min	£max
Single	18.00	21.00
Double	36.00	42.00

Half board
per person:	£min	£max
Daily	27.50	29.50
Weekly	175.00	189.00

Evening meal 1900 (last orders 1730)
Parking for 15
Open March-October
Cards accepted: Access, Visa

There are separate sections in this guide listing groups specialising in farm holidays and accommodation which is especially suitable for young people and organised groups.

BOVEY TRACEY
Devon
Map ref 1D2

Standing by the river just east of Dartmoor National Park, this old town has good moorland views. Its church, with a 14th C tower, holds one of Devon's finest medieval rood screens.

Lower Elsford Cottage
Listed HIGHLY COMMENDED
Bovey Tracey, Newton Abbot TQ13 9NY
☎ Lustleigh (064 77) 408
17th C stone cottage near the reservoirs at Hennock, overlooking village of Lustleigh with outstanding scenic views. Fishing available.
Bedrooms: 1 single, 1 double
Bathrooms: 1 private, 1 public

Bed & breakfast
per night:	£min	£max
Single	17.00	20.00
Double	34.00	36.00

Parking for 4

BRADFORD-ON-AVON
Wiltshire
Map ref 2B2

Huddled beside the river, the buildings of this former cloth-weaving town reflect continuing prosperity from the Middle Ages. There is a tiny Anglo-Saxon church, part of a monastery. The part-14th C bridge carries a medieval chapel, later used as a gaol.
Tourist Information Centre ☎ (0225) 865797

Barge Inn
17 Frome Road, Bradford-on-Avon BA15 2EA
☎ (0225) 863403
Grade II listed inn on the banks of Kennet and Avon Canal. Canalside gardens. Restaurant open every day.
Bedrooms: 1 double, 2 twin
Bathrooms: 1 private, 1 public

Bed & breakfast
per night:	£min	£max
Single	18.00	25.00
Double	36.00	55.00

Lunch available
Evening meal 1900 (last orders 2200)
Parking for 40

Brookfield House
HIGHLY COMMENDED
Vaggs Hill, Southwick, Trowbridge BA14 9NA
☎ Frome (0373) 830615
150-acre dairy farm. Barn converted in 1989, in completely rural location on boundary between Somerset and Wiltshire. South-facing aspects. Farm is 100 yards away.
Bedrooms: 2 double, 1 twin
Bathrooms: 2 private, 2 public

Bed & breakfast
per night:	£min	£max
Single	15.00	30.00
Double	34.00	38.00

Parking for 10

BRENDON
Devon
Map ref 1C1

Small village on the East Lyn River, in beautiful Lorna Doone country between Exmoor and the dramatic North Devon coast. Watersmeet (National Trust) is nearby.

Brendon House Hotel
Brendon, Lynton EX35 6PS
☎ (059 87) 206
Comfortable 18th C house set in beautiful gardens overlooking the East Lyn river, with an informal and friendly atmosphere. Home-produced food and interesting wine list. Dogs welcome.
Bedrooms: 2 double, 1 twin, 1 family room
Bathrooms: 4 private, 1 public

Bed & breakfast
per night:	£min	£max
Single	16.50	18.50
Double	33.00	37.00

Half board
per person:	£min	£max
Daily	27.50	30.00
Weekly	172.00	193.00

Evening meal 1930 (last orders 2000)
Parking for 5
Open March-November

BRIDESTOWE
Devon
Map ref 1C2

Small Dartmoor village with a much restored 15th C church, and Great Links Tor rising to the south-east.

White Hart Inn
Fore Street, Bridestowe, Okehampton EX20 4EL
☎ (083 786) 318
17th C inn, family-run for 30 years, primarily noted for good food. En-suite accommodation. Close to Dartmoor National Park, Lydford Gorge and fishing at Roadford Lake.
Bedrooms: 2 double
Bathrooms: 2 private

WEST COUNTRY

Bed & breakfast per night:	£min	£max
Single	25.00	
Double	40.00	

Lunch available
Evening meal 1900 (last orders 2130)
Parking for 20
Cards accepted: Access, Visa, Diners, Amex

BRIDGERULE
Devon
Map ref 1C2

Lodgeworthy Farm
COMMENDED
Bridgerule, Holsworthy EX22 7EH
☎ (028 881) 351

210-acre dairy farm. Old Devon longhouse in centre of village, offering a warm welcome and every comfort. Ideal touring centre, good local amenities.
Bedrooms: 1 single, 1 double, 1 family room
Bathrooms: 2 private, 1 public

Bed & breakfast per night:	£min	£max
Single	15.00	
Double	30.00	

Half board per person:	£min	£max
Daily	21.00	
Weekly	140.00	

Evening meal 1830 (last orders 1830)
Parking for 5

The Villa
Bridgerule, Holsworthy EX22 7ET
☎ (028 881) 452

Secluded stone-built farmhouse in an acre of gardens, overlooking dairy and beef farm. Centre of village, convenient for sea or touring. Warm welcome, home-grown produce.
Bedrooms: 2 double
Bathrooms: 2 private, 1 public

Bed & breakfast per night:	£min	£max
Single	15.00	
Double	30.00	

Half board per person:	£min	£max
Daily	21.00	
Weekly	140.00	

Evening meal 1830 (last orders 1830)
Parking for 3
Open March-October

We advise you to confirm your booking in writing.

BRIDGWATER
Somerset
Map ref 1D1

Former medieval port on the River Parrett, now small industrial town with mostly 19th C or modern architecture. Georgian Castle Street leads to West Quay and site of 13th C castle razed to the ground by Cromwell. Birthplace of Cromwellian admiral Robert Blake is now museum. Arts centre.

Cokerhurst Farm
COMMENDED
87 Wembdon Hill, Bridgwater TA6 7QA
☎ (0278) 422330 & Mobile (0850) 692065

105-acre arable farm. West of Bridgwater, off A39. Old farmhouse set in quiet countryside with peaceful garden overlooking the lake and farm.
Bedrooms: 1 double, 1 twin, 1 triple
Bathrooms: 1 private, 1 public

Bed & breakfast per night:	£min	£max
Single	17.00	20.00
Double	34.00	40.00

Parking for 143
Open April-September

Wembdon Farm
Hollow Lane, Wembdon, Bridgwater TA5 2BD
☎ (0278) 453097

380-acre arable & dairy farm. Enjoy bed and breakfast at this homely farmhouse. En-suite rooms with tea/coffee making facilities, lounge, dining room and lovely gardens. Convenient for Quantock, Mendip and Polden Hills, Somerset Levels and coast. Golf and fishing nearby. Non-smokers only please.
Bedrooms: 2 double
Bathrooms: 2 private

Bed & breakfast per night:	£min	£max
Double	33.00	39.00

Parking for 4
Open April-December

West Bower Manor
Listed COMMENDED
West Bower Lane, Durleigh, Bridgwater TA5 2AT
☎ (0278) 422895

Peaceful medieval manor house beside a lake. Home-made bread, free-range breakfasts.
Bedrooms: 2 double, 1 twin
Bathrooms: 3 private, 2 public

Bed & breakfast per night:	£min	£max
Single	17.50	30.00
Double	25.00	40.00

Parking for 6

BRIDPORT
Dorset
Map ref 2A3

Market town and chief producer of nets and ropes just inland of dramatic Dorset coast. Old, broad streets built for drying and twisting, long gardens for rope-walks. Grand arcaded Town Hall and Georgian buildings. Local history museum has Roman relics.
Tourist Information Centre
☎ *(0308) 24901*

Britmead House
COMMENDED
154 West Bay Road, Bridport DT6 4EG
☎ (0308) 422941

Elegant, spacious, tastefully decorated house. Lounge and dining room overlooking garden. West Bay Harbour/Coastal Path, 10 minutes' walk away. Renowned for hospitality, delicious meals and comfort.
Bedrooms: 4 double, 3 twin
Bathrooms: 6 private, 1 private shower

Bed & breakfast per night:	£min	£max
Single	23.00	32.00
Double	36.00	50.00

Half board per person:	£min	£max
Daily	29.50	36.50

Evening meal 1900 (last orders 1700)
Parking for 8
Cards accepted: Access, Visa, Diners, Amex

WEST COUNTRY

BRIDPORT
Continued

Lancombes House ⋒
Listed APPROVED
West Milton, Bridport DT6 3TN
☎ Powerstock (0308) 485375

35-acre mixed farm. 200-year-old barn converted to comfortable accommodation, 300 feet above sea level with exceptional views. On the Poorton road out of West Milton.
Bedrooms: 1 double, 1 triple
Bathrooms: 2 private, 3 public

Bed & breakfast
per night:	£min	£max
Single	15.00	20.00
Double	36.00	46.00

Half board
per person:	£min	£max
Daily	23.00	30.00
Weekly	160.00	210.00

Lunch available
Evening meal 1830 (last orders 2100)
Parking for 20
Cards accepted Diners, Amex

The Mill House
Listed COMMENDED
East Road, Bridport DT6 4AG
☎ (0308) 25147
Converted Georgian cornmill with lovely garden, own stream and meadows. Noted for our English breakfasts and high standards. Non-smokers only please.
Bedrooms: 1 single, 2 double
Bathrooms: 1 private, 1 public

Bed & breakfast
per night:	£min	£max
Single	12.60	14.00
Double	24.40	31.00

Parking for 4
Open March-December

There are separate sections in this guide listing groups specialising in farm holidays and accommodation which is especially suitable for young people and organised groups.

BRISTOL
Avon
Map ref 2A2

A university town and major port. City grew around medieval river docks (Cabot sailed for Newfoundland in 1497). Merchant Venturers founded here 1552. Fine old churches and cathedral; wide views of Avon Gorge from Brunel's Clifton Bridge.
Tourist Information Centre
☎ *(0272) 260767*

Albany Guest House
500 Bath Road, Brislington, Bristol BS4 3JY
☎ (0272) 778710
Comfortable, tastefully-furnished Victorian semi, on main A4 2 miles from city centre and 1 mile from station. Off-road parking.
Bedrooms: 1 single, 2 double, 1 twin
Bathrooms: 2 private, 1 public

Bed & breakfast
per night:	£min	£max
Single	18.00	21.00
Double	27.00	31.00

Parking for 3

The Bowl Inn and Restaurant ⋒
COMMENDED
16 Church Road, Lower Almondsbury, Bristol BS12 4DT
☎ Almondsbury (0454) 612757 & 613717
Fax (0454) 619910

12th C building, once a priory, nestling on the edge of the Severn Vale. 3 minutes from M4/M5 interchange.
Bedrooms: 2 double, 6 twin
Bathrooms: 8 private

Bed & breakfast
per night:	£min	£max
Single	38.50	49.50
Double	74.50	95.75

Half board
per person:	£min	£max
Daily	48.00	70.00

Lunch available
Evening meal 1830 (last orders 2200)
Parking for 40
Cards accepted: Access, Visa, Diners, Amex, Switch

Sunderland Guest House ⋒
Listed APPROVED
4 Sunderland Place, Clifton, Bristol BS8 1NA
☎ (0272) 737249
Small friendly guesthouse, well situated for Bristol centre or Clifton village. Within 5 minutes' walk of BBC, Bristol University, Victoria Rooms. Close to coach and train stations.
Bedrooms: 5 single, 2 double, 2 twin, 1 triple
Bathrooms: 2 public

Bed & breakfast
per night:	£min	£max
Single	27.00	30.00
Double	38.00	48.00

Parking for 3

BRIXHAM
Devon
Map ref 1D2

Famous for its trawling fleet in the 19th C, a steeply-built fishing port overlooking the harbour and fish market. A statue of William of Orange recalls his landing here before deposing James II. There is an aquarium and museum. Good cliff views and walks.
Tourist Information Centre
☎ *(0803) 852861*

Richmond House Private Hotel ⋒
COMMENDED
Higher Manor Road, Brixham TQ5 8HA
☎ (0803) 882391
Detached Victorian house with Laura Ashley interior, sun trap garden and adjacent car park. En-suite available. Convenient for shops and harbour, yet quiet location. First left after Golden Lion.
Bedrooms: 2 single, 1 double, 1 twin, 3 triple, 1 family room
Bathrooms: 2 private, 2 public

Bed & breakfast
per night:	£min	£max
Single	18.00	
Double	32.00	

Parking for 5
Cards accepted: Access, Visa

Individual proprietors have supplied all details of accommodation. Although we do check for accuracy, we advise you to confirm the information at the time of booking.

WEST COUNTRY

BROAD CHALKE
Wiltshire
Map ref 2B3

Delightful River Ebble Valley village with a 13th C church displaying a notable porch and central tower.

The Queens Head Inn
Broad Chalke, Salisbury SP5 5EN
☎ Salisbury (0722) 780344
15th C building with stone walls and old beams. Set in the beautiful Chalke Valley, 8 miles from Salisbury.
Bedrooms: 3 double, 1 twin
Bathrooms: 4 private

Bed & breakfast per night:	£min	£max
Single	30.00	30.00
Double	45.00	45.00

Lunch available
Evening meal 1900 (last orders 2115)
Parking for 40
Cards accepted: Access, Visa

BROAD HINTON
Wiltshire
Map ref 2B2

Weir Farm
Listed
Broad Hinton, Swindon SN4 9NE
☎ Swindon (0793) 731207
Fax (0793) 731207
800-acre mixed farm. Large farmhouse 6 miles from Swindon.
Bedrooms: 1 single, 1 double, 1 twin
Bathrooms: 1 public

Bed & breakfast per night:	£min	£max
Single	16.00	20.00
Double	28.00	34.00

Parking for 4

BROADHEMBURY
Devon
Map ref 1D2

Lane End Farm
Broadhembury, Honiton EX14 OLU
☎ Honiton (0404) 84263
220-acre arable & livestock farm. Walk through delightful unspoilt farmland, or relax on the flower-surrounded lawn. Home-grown fruit and vegetables, good home cooking. Easy reach of M5.
Bedrooms: 1 double, 1 twin, 1 triple
Bathrooms: 2 public

Bed & breakfast per night:	£min	£max
Single	13.00	15.00
Double	26.00	30.00

Half board per person:	£min	£max
Daily	21.50	23.50
Weekly	149.50	

Lunch available
Evening meal 1630 (last orders 0900)
Parking for 4
Open March-November

BUCKFASTLEIGH
Devon
Map ref 1C2

Small manufacturing and market town just south of Buckfast Abbey on the fringe of Dartmoor. Return trips can be taken by steam train on a reopened line along the beautiful Dart Valley.

Wellpark Farm
Listed COMMENDED
Wellpark Bungalow, Dean Prior, Buckfastleigh TQ11 OLY
☎ (0364) 43775
500-acre dairy farm. Enjoy a farmhouse holiday on this working farm overlooking Dartmoor. Delicious food, comfortable/relaxing atmosphere. Large enclosed garden with children's play area.
Bedrooms: 1 double, 1 family room
Bathrooms: 1 public

Bed & breakfast per night:	£min	£max
Single	10.00	15.00
Double	20.00	30.00

Half board per person:	£min	£max
Daily	17.50	22.50
Weekly	110.00	125.00

Evening meal 1800 (last orders 0800)
Parking for 3
Open March-October

BUDE
Cornwall
Map ref 1C2

Resort on dramatic Atlantic coast. High cliffs give spectacular sea and inland views. Golf-course, cricket pitch, folly, surfing, coarse-fishing and boating. Mother-town Stratton was base of Royalist Sir Bevil Grenville.
Tourist Information Centre
☎ *(0288) 354240*

Cliff Hotel
COMMENDED
Crooklets Beach, Bude EX23 8NG
☎ (0288) 353110
Fax (0288) 353110

Indoor pool and spa, solarium, putting, tennis court. 5 acres of land, near National Trust cliffs, 200 yards from the beach. Chef/proprietor.
Bedrooms: 2 single, 3 double, 1 twin, 9 triple
Bathrooms: 15 private

Bed & breakfast per night:	£min	£max
Single	21.00	30.00
Double	42.00	60.00

Half board per person:	£min	£max
Daily	26.00	36.00
Weekly	200.00	250.00

Lunch available
Evening meal 1830 (last orders 1930)
Parking for 15
Open April-October

Clovelly House
COMMENDED
4 Burn View, Bude EX23 8BY
☎ (0288) 352761
In a level location, opposite golf club and close to all amenities. All rooms with tea/coffee facilities, satellite TV, some en-suite.
Bedrooms: 2 single, 2 double, 1 twin, 1 triple
Bathrooms: 3 private, 1 public

Bed & breakfast per night:	£min	£max
Single	14.00	17.00
Double	28.00	36.00

Parking for 2

Lower Northcott Farm
APPROVED
Poughill, Bude EX23 9EL
☎ (0288) 352350
400-acre mixed farm. Georgian farmhouse in secluded grounds with children's safe play area. Visitors welcome to wander around and meet the animals.
Bedrooms: 1 single, 1 twin, 3 family rooms
Bathrooms: 3 private, 1 public, 1 private shower

Bed & breakfast per night:	£min	£max
Single	15.00	
Double	30.00	

Continued ▶

WEST COUNTRY

BUDE
Continued

Half board
per person:	£min	£max
Daily	21.00	
Weekly	140.00	

Evening meal 1830 (last orders 1830)
Parking for 4

BUDLEIGH SALTERTON
Devon
Map ref 1D2

Small resort with pebble beach on coast of red cliffs, setting for famous Victorian painting "The Boyhood of Raleigh". Sir Walter Raleigh was born at Hayes Barton. A salt-panning village in medieval times, today's resort has some Georgian houses.
Tourist Information Centre
☎ (0395) 445275

East Cliff
HIGHLY COMMENDED

14 Marine Parade, Budleigh Salterton EX9 6NS
☎ (0395) 445555
Large detached family house on seafront, situated on the south west coastal path and offering comfortable accommodation and a beautiful garden. Golf-course and bird watching locally.
Bedrooms: 2 twin
Bathrooms: 2 private

Bed & breakfast
per night:	£min	£max
Single	28.00	30.00
Double	42.00	50.00

Parking for 2

BURBAGE
Wiltshire
Map ref 2B2

Village close to Savernake Forest, famous as a habitat for deer. Close by are the remains of Wolf Hall mansion, where a great banquet in honour of Jane Seymour took place in 1536.

The Old Vicarage ♠
HIGHLY COMMENDED

Burbage, Marlborough SN8 3AG
☎ Marlborough (0672) 810495
Fax (0672) 810663
Victorian country house in 2-acre garden, offering peace, comfort and delicious food. Within easy reach of Avebury, Bath, Oxford and Salisbury.
Bedrooms: 1 single, 1 double, 1 twin
Bathrooms: 3 private

Bed & breakfast
per night:	£min	£max
Single		35.00
Double		60.00

Half board
per person:	£min	£max
Daily	55.00	60.00

Evening meal 2000 (last orders 1200)
Parking for 10
Cards accepted: Access, Visa, Amex

BURTON BRADSTOCK
Dorset
Map ref 2A3

Lying amid fields beside the River Bride, a village of old stone houses, a 14th C church and a village green. The beautiful coast road from Abbotsbury to Bridport passes by and Iron Age forts top the surrounding hills. The sheltered river valley makes a staging post for migrating birds.

Three Horseshoes
APPROVED

Mill Street, Burton Bradstock, Bridport DT6 4QZ
☎ (0308) 897259
Thatched inn with car park and garden on the B3157 Bridport to Weymouth road.
Bedrooms: 2 double, 1 twin
Bathrooms: 1 public

Bed & breakfast
per night:	£min	£max
Single	16.50	17.50
Double	30.00	33.00

Lunch available
Evening meal 1830 (last orders 2115)
Parking for 14

CALLINGTON
Cornwall
Map ref 1C2

A quiet market town standing on high ground above the River Lynher. The 15th C church of St Mary's has an alabaster monument to Lord Willoughby de Broke, Henry VII's marshal. A 15th C chapel, 1 mile east, houses Dupath Well, one of the Cornish Holy Wells.

Dozmary ♠
Listed COMMENDED

Tors View Close, Tavistock Road, Callington PL17 7DY
☎ Liskeard (0579) 83677
A deceptively spacious dormer bungalow providing comfortable accommodation with good facilities, just a few minutes from Callington town centre.
Bedrooms: 1 double, 2 twin
Bathrooms: 1 private, 1 public

Bed & breakfast
per night:	£min	£max
Single	15.00	16.00
Double	26.00	28.00

Parking for 4
Open January-November

East Cornwall Farmhouse
HIGHLY COMMENDED

Fullaford Road, Callington PL17 8AN
☎ Liskeard (0579) 50018
Beautifully situated former court house sympathetically restored in farmhouse style. Close to Cotehele House. Ideal for touring. 1 mile from A390.
Bedrooms: 1 single, 2 double, 1 twin
Bathrooms: 2 private, 1 public

Bed & breakfast
per night:	£min	£max
Single	15.00	15.00
Double	30.00	38.00

Half board
per person:	£min	£max
Daily	22.00	31.00
Weekly	154.00	217.00

Lunch available
Evening meal 1830 (last orders 2030)
Parking for 6
Open March-November

CALNE
Wiltshire
Map ref 2B2

Prosperity from wool in the 15th C endowed this ancient market town with a fine church in the Perpendicular style. To the east are chalk downlands and at Oldbury Castle, an Iron Age fort, a 17th C white horse is carved into the hillside.

Fenwicks
HIGHLY COMMENDED

Buccabank, Lower Goatacre, Lyneham, Calne SN11 9HY
☎ Hilmarton (0249) 760645
Secluded house with charming accommodation and grounds. Close to M4 junctions 16 and 17, Avebury, Marlborough, Castle Combe, Lacock. Within easy reach of Bath and Cotswolds. "Good food" pub 1 mile away.
Bedrooms: 1 twin, 1 triple
Bathrooms: 2 private

Bed & breakfast
per night:	£min	£max
Single	25.00	28.00
Double	32.50	37.50

Parking for 5
Cards accepted: Amex

WEST COUNTRY

CANNINGTON
Somerset
Map ref 1D1

Quantock Hills village with Brymore House, birthplace of John Pym, a leading statesman in the reign of Charles I, lying to the west. Three fine old 16th C houses are close by.

Blackmore Farm
HIGHLY COMMENDED

Cannington, Bridgwater TA5 2NE
☎ Combwich (0278) 653442
Fax (0278) 653442

650-acre mixed farm. Tastefully restored and historic 14th C manor house with four-poster and oak bedsteads. Pleasant rural surroundings. All rooms en-suite.
Bedrooms: 2 double, 1 triple
Bathrooms: 3 private

Bed & breakfast
per night:	£min	£max
Single	16.00	25.00
Double	32.00	42.00

Parking for 6

CASTLE CARY
Somerset
Map ref 2B2

One of south Somerset's most attractive market towns, with a picturesque winding high street of golden stone and thatch, markethouse and famous round 18th C lock-up.

George Hotel
COMMENDED

Market Place, Castle Cary BA7 7AH
☎ (0963) 50761

15th C thatched coaching inn with en-suite rooms, 2 bars and noted restaurant. Centrally located for many National Trust houses and gardens, Cheddar, Wells, Glastonbury and Bath.
Bedrooms: 4 single, 6 double, 5 twin
Bathrooms: 15 private

Bed & breakfast
per night:	£min	£max
Single	40.00	50.00
Double	50.00	65.00

Half board
per person:	£min	£max
Daily	45.00	62.00

Lunch available
Evening meal 1900 (last orders 2130)
Parking for 10
Cards accepted: Access, Visa

CHACEWATER
Cornwall
Map ref 1B3

Kings Head Inn
Listed APPROVED

Fore Street, Chacewater, Truro TR4 8LN
☎ Truro (0872) 560652
Comfortable country village inn, 6 miles from county town of Truro. Close to both north and south coast beaches and tourist attractions.
Bedrooms: 2 family rooms
Bathrooms: 1 public

Bed & breakfast
per night:	£min	£max
Single	12.00	12.00
Double	24.00	24.00

Half board
per person:	£min	£max
Daily	15.00	24.50
Weekly	92.50	160.00

Lunch available
Evening meal 1800 (last orders 2100)
Parking for 12

CHAGFORD
Devon
Map ref 1C2

Handsome stone houses, some from the Middle Ages, grace this former stannary town on northern Dartmoor. It is a popular centre for walking expeditions and for tours of the antiquities on the rugged moor. There is a splendid 15th C granite church, said to be haunted by the poet Godolphin.

St. Johns West

Murchington, Chagford, Newton Abbot TQ13 8HJ
☎ (0647) 432468
Splendid country house within Dartmoor National Park, 1.5 miles north-west of Chagford. Walkers welcome. Sorry - non-smoking throughout. Brochure with pleasure.
Bedrooms: 1 double, 1 twin, 1 family room
Bathrooms: 2 private, 1 public

Bed & breakfast
per night:	£min	£max
Single	14.00	18.00
Double	28.00	36.00

Evening meal 1800 (last orders 2000)
Parking for 6

Three Crowns Hotel
APPROVED

High Street, Chagford, Newton Abbot TQ13 8AJ
☎ (0647) 433444
Fax (0647) 433117
13th C hotel of character in picturesque village within Dartmoor National Park. Good cuisine. Function room. Four-poster beds. Log fires.
Bedrooms: 2 single, 13 double, 1 triple
Bathrooms: 13 private, 2 public

Bed & breakfast
per night:	£min	£max
Single	25.00	35.00
Double	50.00	60.00

Half board
per person:	£min	£max
Daily	42.50	47.50
Weekly	200.00	250.00

Lunch available
Evening meal 1900 (last orders 2130)
Parking for 21
Cards accepted: Access, Visa, Diners, Amex

CHARD
Somerset
Map ref 1D2

Market town in hilly countryside. The wide main street has some handsome buildings, among them the Guildhall, court house and almshouses. Modern light industry and dairy produce have replaced 19th C lace making which came at decline of cloth trade.
Tourist Information Centre
☎ (0460) 67463

Wambrook Farm
Listed

Wambrook, Chard TA20 3DF
☎ (0460) 62371
300-acre mixed farm. Attractive listed farmhouse 2 miles from Chard in beautiful rural village. Children welcome. From Chard take A30 towards Honiton, follow signs.
Bedrooms: 1 double, 1 twin, 1 triple
Bathrooms: 1 private, 1 public

Bed & breakfast
per night:	£min	£max
Single	15.50	18.50
Double	27.00	31.00

Parking for 8
Open April-November

267

WEST COUNTRY

CHEDDAR
Somerset
Map ref 1D1

Large village at foot of Mendips just south of the spectacular Cheddar Gorge. Close by are Roman and Saxon sites and famous show caves. Traditional Cheddar cheese is still made here.

Tor Farm
HIGHLY COMMENDED
Nyland, Cheddar BS27 3UD
☎ (0934) 743710
33-acre mixed farm. On A371 between Cheddar and Draycott (take the road signposted Nyland). Quiet and peaceful on Somerset Levels. Private fishing. Ideally situated for visiting Cheddar, Bath, Wookey Hole, Glastonbury, Wells and coast.
Bedrooms: 2 single, 4 double, 1 twin, 1 family room
Bathrooms: 6 private, 2 public

Bed & breakfast per night:	£min	£max
Single	17.50	
Double	30.00	43.00

Half board per person:	£min	£max
Daily	27.50	31.50
Weekly	164.50	205.50

Evening meal 1900 (last orders 1800)
Parking for 10
Cards accepted: Access, Visa

CHEW MAGNA
Avon
Map ref 2A2

Prosperous redstone village in the Mendip Hills with fine houses, cottages and inns of varying periods. High Street rises between railed, raised pavements from a part-Norman church with lofty 15th C tower.

Woodbarn Farm
Listed
Denny Lane, Chew Magna, Bristol BS18 8SZ
☎ (0275) 332599
125-acre mixed farm. Central for touring Bath, Bristol, Wells and Cheddar. 3 minutes from Chew Valley Lake. Friendly, flexible atmosphere. Large farmhouse breakfasts. Warm welcome.
Bedrooms: 1 double, 1 family room
Bathrooms: 1 private, 1 public

Please mention this guide when making a booking.

Bed & breakfast per night:	£min	£max
Single	17.00	20.00
Double	32.00	38.00

Parking for 6
Open March-December

CHEWTON MENDIP
Somerset
Map ref 2A2

Franklyns Farm
APPROVED
Chewton Mendip, Bath BA3 4NB
☎ (0761) 241372
350-acre arable & dairy farm. Comfortable and cosy modern farmhouse in heart of Mendips, in a peaceful setting with superb views. Situated on Emborough B3114 road.
Bedrooms: 1 double, 1 twin
Bathrooms: 2 public

Bed & breakfast per night:	£min	£max
Double	30.00	

Parking for 5

CHICKERELL
Dorset
Map ref 2B3

Stonebank
14 West Street, Chickerell, Weymouth DT3 4DY
☎ Weymouth (0305) 760120
Charming 17th C former farmhouse, close to coastal path and Chesil Beach. Ideal for exploring the Dorset coast and countryside.
Bedrooms: 2 double
Bathrooms: 2 private

Bed & breakfast per night:	£min	£max
Single	20.00	25.00
Double	30.00	35.00

Parking for 2
Open April-September

There are separate sections in this guide listing groups specialising in farm holidays and accommodation which is especially suitable for young people and organised groups.

CHIPPENHAM
Wiltshire
Map ref 2B2

Ancient market town with modern industry. Notable early buildings include the medieval Town Hall and the gabled 15th C Yelde Hall, now a local history museum. On the outskirts Hardenhuish has a charming hilltop church by the Georgian architect John Wood of Bath.
Tourist Information Centre
☎ (0249) 657733

Frogwell House
132 Hungerdown Lane, Chippenham SN14 0BD
☎ (0249) 650328

An imposing late 19th C house built of local stone, modernised to provide comfortable and appealing accommodation.
Bedrooms: 1 single, 1 double, 2 twin
Bathrooms: 2 private, 1 public

Bed & breakfast per night:	£min	£max
Single	20.00	22.00
Double	30.00	37.00

Evening meal 1800 (last orders 1900)
Parking for 6

75 Rowden Hill
Chippenham SN15 2AL
☎ (0249) 652981
Near National Trust village of Lacock and attractive Castle Combe. Corsham Court also nearby. Friendly welcome assured.
Bedrooms: 1 single, 1 double, 1 twin
Bathrooms: 1 public

Bed & breakfast per night:	£min	£max
Single	15.00	
Double	25.00	

Parking for 5
Open April-October

CHISELBOROUGH
Somerset
Map ref 2A3

Manor Farm
COMMENDED
Chiselborough, Stoke sub Hamdon TA14 6TQ
☎ (093 588) 1203

WEST COUNTRY

450-acre mixed farm. Mellow hamstone farmhouse offering comfortable facilities, colour TV, tea-making in all bedrooms. Ideal for touring or walking in the area.
Bedrooms: 2 double, 1 twin, 1 triple
Bathrooms: 2 public

Bed & breakfast
per night:	£min	£max
Single	17.00	19.00
Double	34.00	38.00

Parking for 4
Open April-October

CHITTOE HEATH

Wiltshire
Map ref 2B2

Wayside
COMMENDED

Chittoe Heath SN15 2EH
☎ Devizes (0380) 850458
Family-run establishment with informal atmosphere, in the heart of Wiltshire, with downs, historic houses and ancient sites. Bath, Salisbury and Marlborough all within 20 mile radius.
Bedrooms: 1 double, 1 triple
Bathrooms: 2 private

Bed & breakfast
per night:	£min	£max
Single	18.00	20.00
Double	35.00	38.00

Half board
per person:	£min	£max
Daily	28.00	30.00

Lunch available
Evening meal 1900 (last orders 2100)
Parking for 14

CHUDLEIGH

Devon
Map ref 1D2

Small market town close to main Exeter to Plymouth road. To the south is Chudleigh Rock, a dramatic limestone outcrop containing prehistoric caves.

Glen Cottage

Rock Road, Chudleigh, Newton Abbot TQ13 0JJ
☎ (0626) 852209
In 10 acres of secluded gardens with river and swimming pool, surrounded by woodlands. Rocks, caves and waterfalls.
Bedrooms: 3 double, 1 twin, 1 family room
Bathrooms: 1 private, 1 public

Bed & breakfast
per night:	£min	£max
Single	14.00	
Double	28.00	

Half board
per person:	£min	£max
Daily		20.00

Evening meal from 1900
Parking for 7

CLEVEDON

Avon
Map ref 1D1

Handsome Victorian resort on shingly shores of Severn Estuary. Pier, golf links with ruined folly, part-Norman clifftop church. Tennyson and Thackeray stayed at nearby Clevedon Court just to the east. Medieval with later additions, the manor overlooks terraces with rare plants.

Apple Trees
Listed APPROVED

161 Old Church Road, Clevedon BS21 7UB
☎ (0275) 872919
Lovely Victorian house. Excellent beds, beautiful lounge, home-made bread and marmalade. Quiet location, warm welcome, backing on to headland, lovely walks.
Bedrooms: 1 double, 1 triple
Bathrooms: 1 public

Bed & breakfast
per night:	£min	£max
Single	12.50	14.00
Double	26.00	26.00

Parking for 3
Open March-October

Harcot
Listed

18 Leagrove Road, Clevedon BS21 7QR
☎ Lulsgate (0275) 871509
Family-run guesthouse, 100 yards from seafront and 5 minutes from M5. Spacious rooms, sea views.
Bedrooms: 2 double, 1 twin
Bathrooms: 2 public

Bed & breakfast
per night:	£min	£max
Single	15.00	25.00
Double	25.00	27.00

Parking for 3

Individual proprietors have supplied all details of accommodation. Although we do check for accuracy, we advise you to confirm the information at the time of booking.

CLOVELLY

Devon
Map ref 1C1

Clinging to wooded cliffs, fishing village with steep cobbled street zigzagging, or cut in steps, to harbour. Carrying sleds stand beside whitewashed flower-decked cottages. Charles Kingsley's father was rector of the church set high up near the Hamlyn family's Clovelly Court.

Fuchsia Cottage
Listed APPROVED

Burscott, Clovelly, Bideford EX39 5RR
☎ (0237) 431398
Private house with comfortable ground and first floor en-suite accommodation. Surrounded by beautiful views of sea and country. Evening meal by arrangement.
Bedrooms: 1 single, 1 double, 1 triple
Bathrooms: 2 private, 1 public

Bed & breakfast
per night:	£min	£max
Single		14.00
Double		28.00

Half board
per person:	£min	£max
Daily		20.00
Weekly		140.00

Evening meal from 1830
Parking for 3

COLYTON

Devon
Map ref 1D2

Surrounded by fertile farmland, this small riverside town was an early Saxon settlement. Medieval prosperity from the wool trade built the grand church tower with its octagonal lantern and the church's fine west window.

Smallicombe Farm

Northleigh, Colyton EX13 6BU
☎ Wilmington (0404) 831310
17-acre mixed farm. Small farm with friendly cows, pigs, sheep and goats. In Area of Outstanding Natural Beauty. Glorious rural views from the farmhouse. All rooms en-suite. Reduced rates for children and weekly stays.
Bedrooms: 1 double, 1 twin, 1 family room
Bathrooms: 3 private

Bed & breakfast
per night:	£min	£max
Single	16.50	18.50
Double	33.00	37.00

Continued ▶

269

WEST COUNTRY

COLYTON
Continued

Half board per person:	£min	£max
Daily	24.50	26.50
Weekly	150.00	165.00

Evening meal (last orders 1600)
Open April-October

COMBE MARTIN
Devon
Map ref 1C1

On edge of the Exmoor National Park, this seaside village is set in a long narrow valley between towering cliffs. The main beach is a mixture of sand, rocks and pebbles and the lack of stong currents ensures safe bathing.

Channel Vista
COMMENDED
Woodlands, Combe Martin EX34 0AT
☎ (0271) 883514
Charming, Edwardian period house, with comfortable en-suite rooms. Close to picturesque cove. Superb coastal walks - discover beautiful Exmoor's wildlife and flowers. Dogs welcome.
Bedrooms: 1 single, 2 double, 2 triple, 2 family rooms
Bathrooms: 6 private, 1 public

Bed & breakfast per night:	£min	£max
Single	16.00	18.00
Double	32.00	36.00

Half board per person:	£min	£max
Daily	24.50	26.50
Weekly	136.50	156.50

Evening meal 1900 (last orders 2000)
Parking for 9
Open March-October and Christmas
Cards accepted: Access, Visa

CONSTANTINE
Cornwall
Map ref 1B3

Hilltop quarrying village overlooking wooded valley at the head of a creek on the Helford River. Shops, quarrymen's terraces, handsome church and chapel are all of granite. A granite-walled prehistoric cave, just north, can be explored.

Trengilly Wartha Inn
COMMENDED
Nancenoy, Constantine, Falmouth
TR11 5RP
☎ Falmouth (0326) 40332

Inn with restaurant, serving real ales and bar meals. From Falmouth follow signs to Constantine then signs to Gweek. Close to the Helford River and convenient for beaches. Gweek is also near.
Bedrooms: 4 double, 2 twin
Bathrooms: 5 private, 1 public

Bed & breakfast per night:	£min	£max
Single	32.00	40.00
Double	45.00	56.00

Half board per person:	£min	£max
Daily	30.00	60.00
Weekly	150.00	300.00

Lunch available
Evening meal 1830 (last orders 2130)
Parking for 80
Cards accepted: Access, Visa, Amex

COOMBE BISSETT
Wiltshire
Map ref 2B3

Two Bridges
COMMENDED
Homington Road, Coombe Bissett, Salisbury SP5 4LR
☎ (072 277) 531
Comfortable riverside bed and breakfast, set in idyllic village location near Salisbury. TV, private lounge area and use of garden. Non-smokers only please.
Bedrooms: 1 twin
Bathrooms: 1 private

Bed & breakfast per night:	£min	£max
Single	24.00	26.00
Double	36.00	38.00

Parking for 1

CORSHAM
Wiltshire
Map ref 2B2

Growing town with old centre showing Flemish influence, legacy of former prosperity from weaving. The church, restored last century, retains Norman features. The Elizabethan Corsham Court, with additions by Capability Brown, has fine furniture.

Boyds Farm
COMMENDED
Gastard, Corsham SN13 9PT
☎ (0249) 713146
211-acre arable farm. Attractive 16th C listed farmhouse in the peaceful village of Gastard. Bath, Lacock, Castle Combe and numerous attractions are close by.
Bedrooms: 2 double, 1 triple
Bathrooms: 1 private, 2 public

Bed & breakfast per night:	£min	£max
Single	16.00	18.00
Double	30.00	32.00

Parking for 6

Halfway Firs
Listed
5 Halfway Firs, Corsham SN13 0PJ
☎ Bath (0225) 810552
Situated 7 miles from Bath on A4, 5 miles from Chippenham and 1 mile from Corsham, overlooking open farmland.
Bedrooms: 1 single, 1 double, 1 triple
Bathrooms: 1 public

Bed & breakfast per night:	£min	£max
Single	15.00	16.00
Double	26.00	30.00

Parking for 4

Saltbox Farm
COMMENDED
Drewetts Mill, Box, Corsham
SN14 9PT
☎ Bath (0225) 742608

166-acre dairy farm. Country retreat in quiet conservation and walking location of the Box Valley. Six miles from Bath and ideal for exploring Wiltshire and Cotswolds.
Bedrooms: 1 double, 1 twin
Bathrooms: 1 public

Bed & breakfast per night:	£min	£max
Single	13.00	16.00
Double	26.00	32.00

Parking for 2
Open March-December

COVERACK
Cornwall
Map ref 1B3

Fishing village with thatched cottages on the Lizard Peninsula. Inland, Goonhilly Downs is an area of botanical importance. Three miles offshore are the notorious Manacles rocks, scene of numerous shipwrecks.

Bakery Cottage
Listed
Coverack, Helston TR12 6TD
☎ St. Keverne (0326) 280474

WEST COUNTRY

Old fisherman's cottage. Home cooking and friendly service in quiet fishing village. Safe bathing beach nearby.
Bedrooms: 1 double, 1 triple
Bathrooms: 1 public

Bed & breakfast
per night:	£min	£max
Single		13.50
Double		27.00

Half board
per person:	£min	£max
Daily		20.00

Evening meal 1830 (last orders 1830)
Parking for 2

CRACKINGTON HAVEN
Cornwall
Map ref 1C2

Tiny village on the North Cornwall coast, with a small sandy beach and surf bathing. The highest cliffs in Cornwall lie to the south.

Coombe Barton Inn

Crackington Haven, Bude EX23 0JG
☎ St. Gennys (0840) 230345
Warm and friendly inn beside the beach, serving good food, local ales and fine wines and offering comfortable accommodation.
Bedrooms: 1 single, 3 double, 1 twin, 1 family room
Bathrooms: 4 private, 2 public

Bed & breakfast
per night:	£min	£max
Single	15.00	22.50
Double	32.00	48.00

Lunch available
Evening meal 1800 (last orders 2200)
Parking for 40
Open March-October
Cards accepted: Access, Visa, Amex

Treworgie Barton
HIGHLY COMMENDED

Crackington Haven, Bude EX23 0NL
☎ St Gennys (0840) 230233
106-acre mixed farm. In secluded setting 2 miles from unspoilt cove. Good farmhouse cooking. Turn right at Wainhouse corner 10 miles south of Bude on A39, then follow farm signs.
Bedrooms: 3 double, 1 twin, 1 single room
Bathrooms: 5 private

Bed & breakfast
per night:	£min	£max
Single	16.00	22.00
Double	32.00	44.00

Half board
per person:	£min	£max
Daily	28.00	34.00
Weekly	186.00	228.00

Evening meal 1830 (last orders 1800)

Parking for 5
Open February-September, November

CREDITON
Devon
Map ref 1D2

Ancient town in fertile valley, once prosperous from wool, now active in cider-making. Said to be the birthplace of St Boniface. The 13th C Chapter House, the church governors' meeting place, holds a collection of armour from the Civil War.

Birchmans Farm
COMMENDED

Colebrooke, Crediton EX17 5AD
☎ Bow (0363) 82393
200-acre mixed farm. In the centre of Devon within easy reach of Exeter and Dartmoor. Home produce. All rooms en-suite with tea and coffee-making facilities.
Bedrooms: 2 double, 1 twin
Bathrooms: 3 private

Bed & breakfast
per night:	£min	£max
Single	15.00	16.00
Double	28.00	32.00

Half board
per person:	£min	£max
Daily	20.00	22.00
Weekly	135.00	150.00

Evening meal (last orders 1830)
Parking for 6

CREWKERNE
Somerset
Map ref 1D2

This charming little market town on the Dorset border nestles in undulating farmland and orchards in a conservation area. Built of local sandstone with Roman and Saxon origins. The magnificent St Bartholomew's Church dates from 15th C; St Bartholomew's Fair is held in September.

Broadview
DE LUXE

43 East Street, Crewkerne TA18 7AG
☎ (0460) 73424
Unusual colonial bungalow residence c1926. Set in an acre of secluded feature gardens with many unusual plants. Friendly, relaxing atmosphere and carefully furnished en-suite rooms. Quality, traditional home cooking.
Bedrooms: 1 double, 2 twin
Bathrooms: 3 private

Bed & breakfast
per night:	£min	£max
Single	25.00	35.00
Double		40.00

Half board
per person:	£min	£max
Daily		30.00
Weekly		210.00

Evening meal 1830 (last orders 1200)
Parking for 6

The George Hotel

Market Square, Crewkerne TA18 7LP
☎ (0460) 73650
Fax (0460) 72974

17th C Grade II listed coaching inn situated in the market square. Ideally located for touring. Fine food, real ales. Log fire. Warm welcome!
Bedrooms: 3 single, 8 double, 2 twin
Bathrooms: 7 private, 2 public, 3 private showers

Bed & breakfast
per night:	£min	£max
Single	22.00	30.00
Double	44.00	65.00

Lunch available
Evening meal 1900 (last orders 2100)
Cards accepted: Access, Visa, Amex

Home Farm
Listed

Roundham, Crewkerne TA18 8RH
☎ (0460) 73447
110-acre livestock farm. Situated on A30, 1 mile west of Crewkerne, 3 miles from Cricket St Thomas. TV and tea/coffee-making facilities in all rooms.
Bedrooms: 1 double, 1 twin, 1 triple
Bathrooms: 1 public, 1 private shower

Bed & breakfast
per night:	£min	£max
Single	15.00	19.00
Double	29.00	35.00

Parking for 5

National Crown ratings were correct at the time of going to press but are subject to change. Please check at the time of booking.

WEST COUNTRY

CROYDE
Devon
Map ref 1C1

Pretty village with thatched cottages near Croyde Bay. To the south stretch Saunton Sands and their dunelands Braunton Burrows with interesting flowers and plants, nature reserve and golf-course. Cliff walks and bird-watching at Baggy Point, west of the village.

Denham Country House
COMMENDED
North Buckland, Braunton EX33 1HY
☎ (0271) 890297

160-acre mixed farm. Sample home cooking in this delightful country house, a "little gem" off the beaten track. Enjoy peace and tranquillity amid beautiful unspoilt countryside, near miles of golden sands.
Bedrooms: 6 double, 1 twin, 1 triple, 2 family rooms
Bathrooms: 10 private, 1 public

Bed & breakfast

per night:	£min	£max
Double	40.00	48.00

Half board

per person:	£min	£max
Daily	32.00	36.00
Weekly	198.00	210.00

Evening meal 1900 (last orders 1900)
Parking for 8

DARTMOOR

See under Ashburton, Bickington, Bovey Tracey, Bridestowe, Buckfastleigh, Chagford, Dunsford, Holne, Lustleigh, Lydford, Moretonhampstead, Okehampton, Peter Tavy, Poundsgate, Tavistock, Two Bridges, Widecombe-in-the-Moor, Yelverton

---

There are separate sections in this guide listing groups specialising in farm holidays and accommodation which is especially suitable for young people and organised groups.

DARTMOUTH
Devon
Map ref 1D3

Ancient port at mouth of Dart. Has fine period buildings, notably town houses near Quay and Butterwalk of 1635. Harbour castle ruin. In 12th C Crusader fleets assembled here. Royal Naval College dominates from Hill. Carnival, June; Regatta, August.
Tourist Information Centre
☎ *(0803) 834224*

Boringdon House
HIGHLY COMMENDED
1 Church Road, Dartmouth TQ6 9HQ
☎ (0803) 832235
Welcoming Georgian house in large secluded garden overlooking Dartmouth town and harbour. Spacious attractive rooms. Courtyard parking. Short walk to town centre. No smoking please.
Bedrooms: 1 double, 2 twin
Bathrooms: 3 private

Bed & breakfast

per night:	£min	£max
Single	36.00	43.00
Double	42.00	49.00

Parking for 3
Open March-December

The Captains House
COMMENDED
18 Clarence Street, Dartmouth TQ6 9NW
☎ Torquay (0803) 832133
18th C listed house. Tasteful decor and personal service. Close to river and shops.
Bedrooms: 1 single, 3 double, 1 twin
Bathrooms: 5 private

Bed & breakfast

per night:	£min	£max
Single	25.00	30.00
Double	35.00	48.00

Cards accepted: Amex

Courtyard House
HIGHLY COMMENDED
10 Clarence Hill, Dartmouth TQ6 9NX
☎ (0803) 834916
Well-appointed bedrooms for comfortable overnight accommodation with full English breakfast. Located in quaint old street 2 minutes from town centre and river.
Bedrooms: 1 single, 2 double
Bathrooms: 3 private

Bed & breakfast

per night:	£min	£max
Single	20.00	25.00
Double	36.00	44.00

Lunch available
Parking for 2

Open March-October
Cards accepted: Access, Visa

Royal Castle Hotel
COMMENDED
11 The Quay, Dartmouth TQ6 9PS
☎ Torbay (0803) 833033
Fax (0803) 835445

Historic 17th C quayside coaching inn with resident proprietors, offering traditional-style food and service. Open fires, comfortable bedrooms.
Bedrooms: 4 single, 10 double, 7 twin, 4 triple
Bathrooms: 25 private

Bed & breakfast

per night:	£min	£max
Single	39.00	49.00
Double	70.00	90.00

Half board

per person:	£min	£max
Daily	54.00	64.00
Weekly	240.00	320.00

Lunch available
Evening meal 1845 (last orders 2145)
Parking for 4
Cards accepted: Access, Visa, Switch

DAWLISH
Devon
Map ref 1D2

Small resort, developed in Regency and Victorian periods beside Dawlish Water. Town centre has ornamental riverside gardens with black swans. One of British Rail's most scenic stretches was built by Brunel alongside jagged red cliffs between the sands and the town.
Tourist Information Centre
☎ *(0626) 863589.*

Smallacombe Farm
Dawlish EX7 0PS
☎ (0626) 862536
140-acre livestock farm. Secluded farm, 10 minutes from Dawlish and within easy reach of Dartmoor, Exeter and Torquay. En-suite available, children welcome. Ring for a brochure.
Bedrooms: 1 double, 1 twin, 1 triple
Bathrooms: 1 public

Bed & breakfast

per night:	£min	£max
Single	14.50	
Double	29.00	33.00

WEST COUNTRY

Half board per person:	£min	£max
Daily	22.50	
Weekly	147.00	

Evening meal 1830 (last orders 1830)
Parking for 10

DEVIZES
Wiltshire
Map ref 2B2

Old market town standing on the Kennet and Avon Canal. Rebuilt Norman castle, good 18th C buildings. St John's church has 12th C work and Norman tower. Museum of Wiltshire's archaeology and natural history reflects wealth of prehistoric sites in the county.
Tourist Information Centre
☎ *(0380) 729408*

Aspiro
46 The Green, Poulshot, Devizes SN10 1RT
☎ (0380) 828465
On green in exceptionally quiet village. Large secluded garden with much birdlife. Delightful old pub with restaurant nearby. German spoken.
Bedrooms: 1 double, 1 twin, 1 triple
Bathrooms: 1 public

Bed & breakfast per night:	£min	£max
Single	16.00	18.00
Double	28.00	32.00

Evening meal 1900 (last orders 2000)
Parking for 11

Pinecroft
Potterne Road (A360), Devizes SN10 5DA
☎ (0380) 721433
Fax (0380) 728368

Comfortable Georgian family house with spacious rooms, exquisite garden and private parking. Only 3 minutes' walk from town centre.
Bedrooms: 2 double, 1 twin, 1 family room
Bathrooms: 4 private

Bed & breakfast per night:	£min	£max
Single	18.00	22.00
Double	30.00	36.00

Half board per person:	£min	£max
Weekly	155.00	175.00

Parking for 6
Cards accepted: Access, Visa, Amex

Rathlin Guest House
COMMENDED
Wick Lane, Devizes SN10 5DP
☎ (0380) 721999
Elegant period charm, all rooms en-suite and individually furnished. Quiet location close to town centre. Tranquil gardens. Ample parking.
Bedrooms: 1 double, 2 twin
Bathrooms: 3 private

Bed & breakfast per night:	£min	£max
Single		25.00
Double		38.00

Half board per person:	£min	£max
Daily	27.00	33.00

Evening meal 1800 (last orders 1930)
Parking for 5

Roundway Hill Farm
Listed
Folly Road, Devizes SN10 2HU
☎ (0380) 722928
740-acre arable & livestock farm. Grade II listed farmhouse set in beautiful scenery at the bottom of Roundway Hill, 1 mile east of Devizes. Ample parking.
Bedrooms: 1 double, 1 family room
Bathrooms: 1 public

Bed & breakfast per night:	£min	£max
Single	16.00	16.00
Double	29.00	29.00

Half board per person:	£min	£max
Daily	23.00	25.00
Weekly	138.00	150.00

Evening meal 1900 (last orders 2115)
Parking for 12

DODDISCOMBSLEIGH
Devon
Map ref 1D2

Riverside village amid hilly countryside just east of Dartmoor. Former manor house stands beside granite church. Spared from the Roundheads by its remoteness, the church's chief interest lies in glowing 15th C windows said to contain Devon's finest collection of medieval glass.

Whitemoor Farm
Doddiscombsleigh, Exeter EX6 7PU
☎ Christow (0647) 52423

284-acre mixed farm. Homely 16th C thatched farmhouse, surrounded by garden and own farmland. Within easy reach of Dartmoor, the coast, Exeter, forest walks, birdwatching and Haldon Racecourse. Evening meal on request with good local inn nearby.
Bedrooms: 2 single, 1 double, 1 twin
Bathrooms: 1 public

Bed & breakfast per night:	£min	£max
Single	15.00	17.00
Double	30.00	34.00

Half board per person:	£min	£max
Daily	22.50	25.00
Weekly		168.00

Evening meal 1900 (last orders 2000)
Parking for 5
Cards accepted: Visa

DORCHESTER
Dorset
Map ref 2B3

Busy medieval county town destroyed by fires in 17th and 18th C. Cromwellian stronghold and scene of Judge Jeffrey's Bloody Assize after Monmouth Rebellion of 1685. Tolpuddle Martyrs were tried in Shire Hall. Museum has Roman and earlier exhibits and Hardy relics.
Tourist Information Centre
☎ *(0305) 267992*

Castleview
Listed
8 Edward Road, Dorchester DT1 2HJ
☎ (0305) 263507
Excellent base for touring beautiful Dorset, offering TVs, washbasins with softened water and tea/coffee-making facilities in all rooms.
Bedrooms: 2 single, 2 double
Bathrooms: 1 private, 1 public

Bed & breakfast per night:	£min	£max
Single	12.00	18.00
Double	26.00	36.00

Parking for 4

Churchview Guest House
Winterbourne Abbas, Dorchester DT2 9LS
☎ Martinstown (0305) 889296

Continued ▶

WEST COUNTRY

DORCHESTER
Continued

Beautiful 17th C guesthouse set in a small village 5 miles west of Dorchester. Noted for its warm welcome, comfort and delicious home cooking.
Bedrooms: 6 double, 4 twin
Bathrooms: 4 private, 2 public

Bed & breakfast
per night:	£min	£max
Single	16.00	18.00
Double	32.00	36.00

Half board
per person:	£min	£max
Daily	24.00	26.00
Weekly	165.00	180.00

Evening meal 1900 (last orders 1900)
Parking for 10
Cards accepted: Access, Visa

The Dower House
Bradford Peverell, Dorchester DT2 9SF
☎ (0305) 266125
Grade II listed village house set in 4.5 acres of partially walled garden. Warm welcome and home baking. Three miles north-west of Dorchester.
Bedrooms: 1 single, 1 double, 1 twin
Bathrooms: 3 private

Bed & breakfast
per night:	£min	£max
Single	16.00	17.50
Double	32.00	35.00

Parking for 3
Open March-October

Mountain Ash
APPROVED
Dorchester DT1 2PB
☎ (0305) 264811
Comfortable accommodation close to transport, Records Office and museums. Washbasins, TV, beverage facilities in bedrooms. Owner knowledgeable about Dorset.
Bedrooms: 1 single, 1 double, 1 twin
Bathrooms: 1 public

Bed & breakfast
per night:	£min	£max
Single	15.00	20.00
Double	30.00	40.00

Parking for 5

Riverhill House
COMMENDED
7 East Hill, Charminster, Dorchester DT2 9QL
☎ (0305) 265614
Well-appointed accommodation in lovely country house, rural setting 1.5 miles from Dorchester. Full English breakfast and optional home-cooked evening meals. Off-street parking. Every comfort and warm welcome assured. Ideal touring centre.
Bedrooms: 1 double, 2 twin
Bathrooms: 1 private, 2 public

Bed & breakfast
per night:	£min	£max
Single	14.00	14.00
Double	28.00	34.00

Half board
per person:	£min	£max
Daily	22.00	25.00
Weekly	140.00	165.00

Evening meal 1800 (last orders 2030)
Parking for 6

Yalbury Park
HIGHLY COMMENDED
Frome Whitfield Farm, Frome Whitfield, Dorchester DT2 7SE
☎ (0305) 250336
170-acre mixed farm. New stone farmhouse with large garden in parkland to River Frome. Warm welcome for all country lovers. 1 mile north of Dorchester.
Bedrooms: 1 twin, 1 triple
Bathrooms: 2 private

Bed & breakfast
per night:	£min	£max
Single	20.00	22.00
Double	40.00	44.00

Parking for 6
Open February-November

DULVERTON
Somerset
Map ref 1D1

Set among woods and hills of south-west Exmoor, a busy riverside town with a 13th C church. The Rivers Barle and Exe are rich in salmon and trout. The information centre at the Exmoor National Park Headquarters at Dulverton is open throughout the year.

Highercombe
COMMENDED
Dulverton TA22 9PT
☎ (0398) 23451
Relaxing, peacefully situated former hunting lodge, 14th C origins. Close to open moorland.
Bedrooms: 2 double, 1 twin
Bathrooms: 3 private

Bed & breakfast
per night:	£min	£max
Single	16.50	19.00
Double	33.00	38.00

Parking for 10

Lower Chilcott Farm
Dulverton TA22 9QQ
☎ (0398) 23439
Fax (0398) 24006
25-acre hill farm. Warm, welcoming Exmoor farmhouse with home produced food. Set amongst the beautiful Stream Coombe Valley. Tranquil, happy family atmosphere. Children, pets, horses and mothers-in-law welcome.
Bedrooms: 1 double, 1 triple
Bathrooms: 1 public

Bed & breakfast
per night:	£min	£max
Single	15.00	16.00
Double	30.00	32.00

Half board
per person:	£min	£max
Daily	23.00	24.00
Weekly	150.00	160.00

Evening meal 2000 (last orders 2000)
Parking for 6

Newhouse Farm
Oakford, Tiverton, Devon EX16 9JE
☎ Oakford (039 85) 347
42-acre livestock farm. Charming 16th C farmhouse featuring oak beams and inglenook fireplace. Pretty en-suite bedrooms. Home-baked bread, delicious country cooking, warm hospitality.
Bedrooms: 3 double
Bathrooms: 3 private

Bed & breakfast
per night:	£min	£max
Double	33.00	35.00

Half board
per person:	£min	£max
Daily	26.25	27.25
Weekly	165.00	170.00

Evening meal 1930 (last orders 1700)
Parking for 3

Springfield Farm
COMMENDED
Dulverton TA22 9QD
☎ (0398) 23722
270-acre livestock farm. Exmoor farm, peacefully situated 1.25 miles walk from Tarr Steps, with magnificent moorland and woodland views. Comfortable accommodation with friendly service and good food.
Bedrooms: 1 single, 1 double, 1 twin
Bathrooms: 1 private, 2 public

Bed & breakfast
per night:	£min	£max
Single	15.00	20.00
Double	30.00	36.00

WEST COUNTRY

Half board per person:	£min	£max
Daily	25.00	28.00
Weekly	175.00	195.00

Evening meal 1800 (last orders 2000)
Parking for 11
Open April-October

Town Mills
COMMENDED

High Street, Dulverton TA22 9HB
☎ (0398) 23124
Secluded 18th C millhouse in centre of Dulverton. Spacious bedrooms providing bedsitting facilities with breakfast served in rooms, some with log fires.
Bedrooms: 3 double, 1 twin
Bathrooms: 2 private, 1 public

Bed & breakfast per night:	£min	£max
Single	16.00	30.00
Double	29.00	38.00

Parking for 4

DUNSFORD
Devon
Map ref 1D2

Royal Oak Inn
Listed APPROVED

Dunsford, Exeter EX6 7DA
☎ Christow (0647) 52256
Beautiful en-suite rooms in Victorian country inn, in the heart of a charming thatched village in the Teign Valley. Always 6 real ales and unusual home-made meals served 7 days a week.
Bedrooms: 5 double, 2 twin, 1 triple
Bathrooms: 6 private, 1 public

Bed & breakfast per night:	£min	£max
Single	20.00	25.00
Double	35.00	40.00

Lunch available
Evening meal 1830 (last orders 2100)
Parking for 40
Cards accepted: Access, Visa

We advise you to confirm your booking in writing.

There are separate sections in this guide listing groups specialising in farm holidays and accommodation which is especially suitable for young people and organised groups.

DUNSTER
Somerset
Map ref 1D1

Ancient town with views of Exmoor. The hilltop castle has been continuously occupied since 1070. Medieval prosperity from cloth built 16th C octagonal Yarn Market and the church. A riverside mill, packhorse bridge and 18th C hilltop folly occupy other interesting corners in the town.

Yarn Market Hotel (Exmoor)

25 High Street, Dunster, Minehead TA24 6SF
☎ (0643) 821425
Fax (0643) 821199
Central and accessible hotel in quaint English village, an ideal location from which to explore the Exmoor National Park.
Bedrooms: 1 double, 1 twin, 1 triple, 1 family room
Bathrooms: 4 private

Bed & breakfast per night:	£min	£max
Single	22.50	27.50
Double	45.00	55.00

Half board per person:	£min	£max
Daily	30.00	38.00
Weekly	180.00	228.00

Evening meal 1800 (last orders 2000)
Parking for 6
Cards accepted: Access, Visa, Amex

EAST BUDLEIGH
Devon
Map ref 1D2

Thorn Mill Farm
COMMENDED

Frogmore Road, East Budleigh, Budleigh Salterton EX9 7BB
☎ Exmouth (0395) 444088

Country hosts, David and Jennie, welcome you to share their picturesque 16th C family home, with beamed lounge, inglenook fireplace, period features. Overlooking River Otter valley and footpaths to coastal paths.
Bedrooms: 1 single, 1 double, 1 twin
Bathrooms: 1 private, 1 public

Bed & breakfast per night:	£min	£max
Single	17.00	22.00
Double	34.00	50.00

Parking for 3

EGGESFORD
Devon
Map ref 1C2

Quiet village among rolling hills and on the west side of the River Taw. Close by is Eggesford Forest.

Fox and Hounds, Eggesford House Hotel

Eggesford, Chulmleigh EX18 7JZ
☎ Chulmleigh (0769) 80345
Country house hotel offering peace and tranquillity. Set in some 30 acres of woodland. Fishing for trout, salmon and sea trout on the River Taw. New 9-hole par 3 golf-course in hotel grounds.
Bedrooms: 3 single, 6 double, 10 twin, 1 triple
Bathrooms: 19 private, 1 public

Bed & breakfast per night:	£min	£max
Single	31.50	35.50
Double	63.00	63.00

Half board per person:	£min	£max
Daily	40.00	42.50
Weekly	200.00	250.00

Lunch available
Evening meal 1800 (last orders 2100)
Parking for 100
Cards accepted: Access, Visa

ERLESTOKE
Wiltshire
Map ref 2B2

Longwater
COMMENDED

Lower Road, Erlestoke, Devizes SN10 5UE
☎ Devizes (0380) 830095
Fax (0380) 830095

160-acre organic farm. Overlooking own parkland, lakes and water bird conservation area. Coarse fishing, adjacent to golf-course. Rare sheep and cattle on farm. Near National Trust properties.
Wheelchair access category 3
Bedrooms: 2 double, 2 twin, 1 triple

Continued ▶

275

WEST COUNTRY

ERLESTOKE
Continued

Bathrooms: 5 private

Bed & breakfast

per night:	£min	£max
Single	19.50	22.50
Double	39.00	39.00

Half board

per person:	£min	£max
Daily	30.00	33.00
Weekly	195.00	215.00

Evening meal 1900 (last orders 1000)
Parking for 8

EXETER
Devon
Map ref 1D2

University city rebuilt after the 1940s around its cathedral. Attractions include 13th C cathedral with fine west front; notable waterfront buildings; Maritime Museum; Guildhall; Royal Albert Memorial Museum; underground passages; Northcott Theatre.
Tourist Information Centre
☎ (0392) 265700

Clock Tower Hotel M

16 New North Road, Exeter EX4 4HF
☎ (0392) 424545
Fax (0392) 218445
Homely accommodation in the city centre. Coach and railway stations within 10 minutes' walk. All modern facilities. En-suite rooms.
Bedrooms: 3 single, 7 double, 2 twin, 2 triple
Bathrooms: 8 private, 3 public

Bed & breakfast

per night:	£min	£max
Single	15.00	19.00
Double	25.00	45.00

Half board

per person:	£min	£max
Daily	17.50	27.50
Weekly	110.00	170.00

Evening meal 1800 (last orders 1600)
Cards accepted: Access, Visa, Amex

Culm Vale Country House

Stoke Canon, Exeter EX5 4EG
☎ (0392) 841615
Comfortable accommodation in beautiful old country house 4 miles north east of Exeter. Friendly relaxed atmosphere, lovely gardens, ample free parking. Ideal touring centre.
Bedrooms: 2 double, 1 twin
Bathrooms: 1 public, 1 private shower

Bed & breakfast

per night:	£min	£max
Single	13.00	15.00
Double	26.00	30.00

Half board

per person:	£min	£max
Daily	19.00	21.00
Weekly	133.00	147.00

Evening meal from 1830
Parking for 6

Dolphin Inn

Thorverton, Exeter EX5 5NT
☎ (0392) 860205
16th C inn, in heart of beautiful, unspoilt village, one mile off the old Tiverton road, six miles north of Exeter. Originally an important coaching inn.
Bedrooms: 3 single, 1 double, 2 twin, 1 triple
Bathrooms: 4 private, 1 public

Bed & breakfast

per night:	£min	£max
Single	19.50	28.50
Double	37.00	48.00

Half board

per person:	£min	£max
Daily	26.50	40.00
Weekly	159.00	240.00

Lunch available
Evening meal 1800 (last orders 2200)
Parking for 30
Cards accepted: Access, Visa

The Grange

Stoke Hill, Exeter EX4 7JH
☎ (0392) 59723
Country house set in 3 acres of woodlands, 1.5 miles from the city centre. Ideal for holidays and off-season breaks.
Bedrooms: 2 double, 2 twin
Bathrooms: 2 private, 2 public

Bed & breakfast

per night:	£min	£max
Single	18.00	20.00
Double	28.00	30.00

Parking for 11

Hayne Barton
COMMENDED

Whitestone, Exeter EX4 2JN
☎ Longdown (039 281) 268
16-acre mixed farm. Listed farmhouse dating from 1086 (Domesday Book) set in gardens, woodland and fields overlooking Alphinbrook Valley. Exeter Cathedral, 4 miles.
Bedrooms: 2 double, 1 twin
Bathrooms: 3 private

Bed & breakfast

per night:	£min	£max
Single	24.00	30.00
Double	42.00	50.00

Half board

per person:	£min	£max
Daily	32.00	38.00
Weekly	210.00	250.00

Evening meal 1930 (last orders 2030)
Parking for 10

Marianne Pool Farm
Listed

Clyst St George, Exeter EX3 0NZ
☎ Topsham (0392) 874939

THE NEW INN

Winterbourne Monkton, Swindon, Wiltshire. Tel: 06723 240

A quiet and peaceful country pub with its own separate restaurant serving good wholesome food. Situated on the edge of Marlborough Downs and close to Avebury Village: situated in the World Heritage site. Good central touring position such as Bath, Oxford and Salisbury only one hour away.

WEST COUNTRY

200-acre mixed farm. Peacefully situated thatched Devon longhouse, overlooking countryside in quiet rural area near Exeter. Comfortably furnished, spacious rooms. 5 minutes from junction 30 of M5.
Bedrooms: 1 twin, 1 family room
Bathrooms: 1 public
Bed & breakfast

per night:	£min	£max
Single	15.00	16.00
Double	29.00	30.00

Parking for 2
Open April-October

Rydon Farm

Woodbury, Exeter EX5 1LB
☎ Woodbury (0395) 232341

280-acre dairy farm. 16th C Devon longhouse with exposed beams and inglenook fireplace. All rooms individually decorated. Large walled garden. Colour brochure available.
Bedrooms: 1 double, 1 twin, 1 triple
Bathrooms: 1 private, 1 public
Bed & breakfast

per night:	£min	£max
Single	17.00	23.00
Double	32.00	42.00

Parking for 5

EXFORD

Somerset
Map ref 1D1

Sheltered village on the River Exe close to Exmoor. Attractive old houses, shops and inns face the village green and the Methodist chapel has 2 windows by Burne-Jones. A footpath north-eastward leads to Dunkery Beacon, Exmoor's highest point.

Ashott Barton

Listed COMMENDED
Exford, Minehead TA24 7NP
☎ (064 383) 294

Recently renovated character farmhouse. Lots of old pine with Laura Ashley furnishings. Central to Exmoor and ideal for hunting, walking and touring the North Devon coast.
Bedrooms: 1 double, 1 twin
Bathrooms: 1 public
Bed & breakfast

per night:	£min	£max
Single	14.00	18.00
Double	32.00	32.00

Evening meal from 1800
Open April-October

EXMOOR

See under Allerford, Brendon, Combe Martin, Dulverton, Dunster, Exford, Kentisbury, Lynmouth, Lynton, Simonsbath, West Anstey, Winsford

EXMOUTH

Devon
Map ref 1D2

Developed as a seaside resort in George III's reign, set against the woods of the Exe Estuary and red cliffs of Orcombe Point. Extensive sands, small harbour, chapel and almshouses, a model railway and A la Ronde, a 16-sided house.
Tourist Information Centre
☎ *(0395) 263744*

The Mews

Knappe Cross, Brixington Lane, Exmouth EX8 5DL
☎ (0395) 272198
Large part of a delightfully secluded mews building in a country setting. Midway between Exmouth and Woodbury Common. Non-smokers only please.
Bedrooms: 1 single, 2 twin
Bathrooms: 1 public
Bed & breakfast

per night:	£min	£max
Single	13.50	15.00
Double	27.00	30.00

Parking for 10

The Swallows

COMMENDED
11 Carlton Hill, Exmouth EX8 2AJ
☎ (0395) 263937
Attractive Georgian house only 300 yards from seafront, pleasantly converted to modern standards and providing comfortable guest accommodation.
Bedrooms: 1 single, 2 double, 2 twin, 1 family room
Bathrooms: 5 private, 1 public
Bed & breakfast

per night:	£min	£max
Single	17.00	25.00
Double	32.00	40.00

Half board

per person:	£min	£max
Daily	26.00	34.00
Weekly	173.00	220.00

Evening meal from 1800
Parking for 3

FENNY BRIDGES

Devon
Map ref 1D2

Skinners Ash Farm

Listed APPROVED
Fenny Bridges, Honiton EX14 0BH
☎ Honiton (0404) 850231
127-acre mixed farm. Traditional farmhouse offering cream teas to order and with rare animals and birds. Situated on A30, 3 miles from Honiton and close to local beaches.
Bedrooms: 1 twin, 1 family room
Bathrooms: 1 public
Bed & breakfast

per night:	£min	£max
Single		15.00
Double		30.00

Half board

per person:	£min	£max
Daily		21.00
Weekly		143.00

Evening meal 1900 (last orders 2100)
Parking for 7
Open February-November

FIGHELDEAN

Wiltshire
Map ref 2B2

Vale House

Listed
Figheldean, Salisbury SP4 8JJ
☎ Stonehenge (0980) 70713
Secluded house in centre of picturesque village, 4 miles north of Amesbury on A345. Pub food nearby. Stonehenge 2 miles.
Bedrooms: 1 single, 2 twin
Bathrooms: 2 public
Bed & breakfast

per night:	£min	£max
Single	13.50	13.50
Double	27.00	27.00

Parking for 3

WEST COUNTRY

FONTHILL GIFFORD
Wiltshire
Map ref 2B3

Beckford Arms
HIGHLY COMMENDED
Fonthill Gifford, Tisbury, Salisbury
SP3 6PX
☎ Tisbury (0747) 870385
Fax (0747) 851496

Tastefully refurbished, stylish and comfortable 18th C inn, between Tisbury and Hindon in area of outstanding beauty. 2 miles A303. Convenient for Salisbury and Shaftesbury.
Bedrooms: 2 single, 4 double, 1 twin
Bathrooms: 5 private, 2 private showers

Bed & breakfast

per night:	£min	£max
Single	19.50	29.50
Double	39.00	54.50

Half board

per person:	£min	£max
Weekly	192.50	192.50

Lunch available
Evening meal 1900 (last orders 2200)
Parking for 42
Cards accepted: Access, Visa, Amex

FROME
Somerset
Map ref 2B2

Old market town with modern light industry, its medieval centre watered by the River Frome. Above Cheap Street with its flagstones and watercourse is the church showing work of varying periods. Interesting buildings include 18th C wool merchants' houses. Local history museum.

Fourwinds Guest House
COMMENDED
19 Bath Road, Frome BA11 2HJ
☎ (0373) 462618
Chalet bungalow with some bedrooms on ground floor. TV and tea-making facilities. Licensed, good food.
Bedrooms: 1 single, 2 double, 1 twin, 1 triple, 1 family room
Bathrooms: 4 private, 2 public

Bed & breakfast

per night:	£min	£max
Single	20.00	25.00
Double	35.00	40.00

Half board

per person:	£min	£max
Daily		30.00

Lunch available
Evening meal 1800 (last orders 1900)
Parking for 12

GLASTONBURY
Somerset
Map ref 2A2

Market town associated with Joseph of Arimathea and the birth of English Christianity. Built around its 7th C abbey said to be the site of King Arthur's burial. Glastonbury Tor with its ancient tower gives panoramic views over flat country and the Mendip Hills.
Tourist Information Centre
☎ (0458) 832954

Laverley House
West Pennard, Glastonbury BA6 8NE
☎ Pilton (0749) 890696
Grade II listed Georgian farmhouse in rural position with views towards Mendips. On the A361, 4 miles east of Glastonbury.
Bedrooms: 2 double, 1 family room
Bathrooms: 3 private, 1 public

Bed & breakfast

per night:	£min	£max
Single	25.00	25.00
Double	37.00	37.00

Half board

per person:	£min	£max
Daily	32.50	32.50
Weekly	204.50	

Evening meal 1900 (last orders 0900)
Parking for 6
Open March-October

Middlewick Farm
Wick, Glastonbury BA6 8JW
☎ (0458) 832351
20-acre beef farm. Tasteful barn conversion with ground floor accommodation, set in 20 acres of gardens and apple orchards with indoor heated swimming pool. From Glastonbury take the Wells road for 2 miles, take first right turn past Waggon and Horses public house, then first left. Follow lane for 1 mile. Farm is on right.
Bedrooms: 2 double, 1 twin
Bathrooms: 3 private

Bed & breakfast

per night:	£min	£max
Single	16.00	18.00
Double	30.00	32.00

Half board

per person:	£min	£max
Daily	25.00	27.00
Weekly	175.00	189.00

Evening meal 1900 (last orders 2030)
Parking for 20

Pippin
Listed
4 Ridgeway Gardens, Glastonbury
BA6 8ER
☎ (0458) 834262
Peaceful location with short walk to town centre or the Tor. Superb views over Chalice Hill. Every comfort.
Bedrooms: 1 single, 1 double, 1 twin
Bathrooms: 1 private, 1 public

Bed & breakfast

per night:	£min	£max
Single	12.50	14.00
Double	25.00	31.00

Parking for 2

Wick Hollow House
8 Wick Hollow, Glastonbury BA6 8JJ
☎ (0458) 833595
Peaceful, self-contained accommodation with private sitting room, on ground floor of lovely house overlooking Chalice Hill and the Tor. Special rates for stays of more than 3 nights. Children half price.
Bedrooms: 1 family room
Bathrooms: 1 private, 1 public

Bed & breakfast

per night:	£min	£max
Single	16.00	25.00
Double	32.00	37.00

Parking for 2

GRAMPOUND
Cornwall
Map ref 1B3

Perran House
Fore Street, Grampound, Truro
TR2 4RS
☎ St. Austell (0726) 882066
Delightful listed cottage in the pretty village of Grampound, between St Austell and Truro. Central for touring.
Bedrooms: 1 single, 3 double, 1 twin
Bathrooms: 3 private, 1 public

Bed & breakfast

per night:	£min	£max
Single	13.00	14.50
Double	26.00	33.00

Parking for 6
Cards accepted: Access, Visa

WEST COUNTRY

GREINTON
Somerset
Map ref 1D1

West Town Farm
APPROVED

Greinton, Bridgwater TA7 9BW
☎ Ashcott (0458) 210277

Original part of house is over 200 years old, with large inglenook fire and bread oven, flagstone floors and Georgian front. Listed building. Non-smoking establishment.
Bedrooms: 1 double, 1 twin
Bathrooms: 2 private
Bed & breakfast

per night:	£min	£max
Single	17.00	19.00
Double	34.00	38.00

Parking for 2
Open March-September
🛌 03 📞 ♦ ⛔ S ✗ ♨ ♿ ✱ ✈

HALSETOWN
Cornwall
Map ref 1B3

Carn Margh Guest House
HIGHLY COMMENDED

Polmanter Water, Halsetown, St Ives TR26 3AW
☎ Penzance (0736) 797380

Country guesthouse 1.5 miles from St Ives on the B3311 road from St Ives to Penzance at Halsetown.
Bedrooms: 4 double, 2 twin
Bathrooms: 3 private, 2 private showers
Bed & breakfast

per night:	£min	£max
Single	14.00	19.00
Double	28.00	38.00

Half board

per person:	£min	£max
Daily	25.00	30.00
Weekly	170.00	250.00

Evening meal 1930 (last orders 2000)
Parking for 25
Cards accepted: Access, Visa
🛌 ♨ 🍴 📞 ♦ ⛔ S ♨ U ✱ ✈ SP

HARTLAND
Devon
Map ref 1C1

Hamlet on high, wild country near Hartland Point. Just west, the parish church tower makes a magnificent landmark; the light, unrestored interior holds one of Devon's finest rood screens. There are spectacular cliffs around Hartland Point and the lighthouse.

Elmscott Farm

Hartland, Bideford EX39 6ES
☎ (0237) 441276

650-acre mixed farm. In a coastal setting, quietly situated near the Devon/Cornwall border. Signposted from the main A39, about 4 miles away.
Bedrooms: 2 double, 1 twin
Bathrooms: 1 private, 1 public
Bed & breakfast

per night:	£min	£max
Single	12.50	13.00
Double	25.00	26.00

Half board

per person:	£min	£max
Daily	20.00	21.50
Weekly	120.00	127.50

Evening meal 1800 (last orders 2000)
Parking for 8
Open April-October
🛌 ♦ ⛔ S ♨ ✱ U ✱ ✈ ✈

HELSTON
Cornwall
Map ref 1B3

Handsome town with steep, main street and narrow alleys. In medieval times it was a major port and stannary town. Most buildings date from Regency and Victorian periods. The famous May dance, the Furry, is thought to have pre-Christian origins. A museum occupies the old Butter Market.

Longstone Farm
APPROVED

Trenear, Helston TR13 0HG
☎ (0326) 572483

62-acre dairy farm. In peaceful countryside in west Cornwall. Ideal for touring and beaches. Flambards, horse riding and swimming pool nearby. B3297 to Redruth, left for Coverack Bridges. Right at bottom of hill, continue left for about 1.5 miles to Longstone Farm.
Bedrooms: 1 single, 3 double, 1 twin, 1 triple
Bathrooms: 2 private, 2 public
Bed & breakfast

per night:	£min	£max
Single	13.00	15.00
Double	26.00	30.00

Half board

per person:	£min	£max
Daily	20.00	22.50
Weekly	130.00	

Evening meal 1800 (last orders 0900)
Parking for 6
Open March-October
🛌 ♨ ⛔ S ♨ TV 🍴 ♦ ✱ ✈ OAP

Lyndale Guest House

4 Greenbank, Meneage Road, Helston TR13 8JA
☎ (0326) 561082

Delightful cottage-style accommodation near town and with ample parking. Ideally situated for touring Cornwall. Children welcome. Evening meal available. German spoken.
Bedrooms: 4 double, 1 twin, 1 triple
Bathrooms: 3 private, 1 public
Bed & breakfast

per night:	£min	£max
Single	16.50	19.50
Double	27.00	33.00

Evening meal 1800 (last orders 1900)
Parking for 8
🛌 ♨ ⛔ 📞 ♦ ♨ TV 🍴 ♦ ✈ 🐕

Riverside ♨
COMMENDED

Nantithet, Cury, Helston TR12 7RB
☎ Mullion (0326) 241027

Small guesthouse, friendly and relaxing, in rural situation midway between Helston and Mullion. Enjoy home cooking with fresh local produce. Ideal for touring and walking. Within 2 miles of beaches, Mullion Golf Club and Flambards Theme Park.
Bedrooms: 2 double, 1 twin, 1 family room
Bathrooms: 1 private, 2 public
Bed & breakfast

per night:	£min	£max
Single	13.50	18.50
Double	27.00	37.00

Half board

per person:	£min	£max
Daily	22.50	27.50
Weekly	155.00	175.00

Lunch available
Evening meal 1900 (last orders 2030)
Parking for 6
🛌 ♨ ⛔ 🍴 S ♨ TV 🍴 ♦ ✱ ✈ OAP SP

Please check prices and other details at the time of booking.

WEST COUNTRY

HENSTRIDGE
Somerset
Map ref 2B3

Village with a rebuilt church containing the Tudor Carent tomb.

Quiet Corner Farm
COMMENDED

Henstridge, Templecombe BA8 0RA
☎ Stalbridge (0963) 63045 changing to 363045
Fax (0963) 63045 changing to 363045
5-acre livestock & fruit farm. Stone farmhouse, part 18th C/Victorian, set within a complex of lovely old barns, some converted to holiday cottages. Marvellous views across Blackmoor Vale. In conservation village with post office, pubs, restaurant and shops all within walking distance. Miniature Shetland pony stud.
Bedrooms: 2 double, 1 twin
Bathrooms: 1 private, 1 public, 1 private shower

Bed & breakfast
per night:	£min	£max
Single	22.00	25.00
Double	34.00	38.00

Parking for 8

HERMITAGE
Dorset
Map ref 2B3

Almshouse Farm

Hermitage, Sherborne DT9 6HA
☎ Holnest (0963) 210296
140-acre dairy farm. Attractive stone-built farmhouse restored from a monastery, with a large inglenook fireplace. Overlooking the unspoilt countryside of Blackmoor Vale.
Bedrooms: 2 double, 1 twin
Bathrooms: 1 private, 2 public

Bed & breakfast
per night:	£min	£max
Single	15.00	17.00
Double	30.00	34.00

Parking for 4

HIGHWORTH
Wiltshire
Map ref 2B2

Roves Farm
COMMENDED

Sevenhampton, Highworth, Swindon SN6 7QG
☎ Swindon (0793) 763939
450-acre arable & livestock farm. Spacious, comfortable, quiet accommodation surrounded by beautiful countryside. Panoramic views, farm trail to woods, ponds and river. Signposted in Sevenhampton village.

Bedrooms: 1 twin, 1 triple
Bathrooms: 2 private

Bed & breakfast
per night:	£min	£max
Single	19.00	20.00
Double	31.00	32.00

Parking for 5

HOLNE
Devon
Map ref 1C2

Woodland village on south-east edge of Dartmoor. Its 15th C church has a painted medieval screen. Charles Kingsley was born at the vicarage. Holne Woods slope to the River Dart.

Dodbrooke Farm
Listed

Michelcombe, Holne, Newton Abbot TQ13 7SP
☎ Poundsgate (036 43) 461
23-acre livestock farm. Listed 17th C longhouse in idyllic setting at foot of Dartmoor, on farm with animals and large gardens. From Ashburton on A38 take road to Two Bridges, fork left for Holne then follow signs to Michelcombe.
Bedrooms: 2 single, 2 twin
Bathrooms: 1 public

Bed & breakfast
per night:	£min	£max
Single	13.00	14.00
Double	29.00	30.00

Half board
per person:	£min	£max
Daily	20.50	21.50

Evening meal from 1930
Parking for 3
Open January-November

HOLNEST
Dorset
Map ref 2B3

Bookham Stud and Ryewater Farm
Listed COMMENDED

Holnest, Sherborne DT9 5PL
☎ (0963) 210248
80-acre horses farm. Old stone farmhouse in peaceful situation, surrounded by beautiful garden. Take A352 from Sherborne, 5 miles on turn left at signpost to Boyshill, half-a-mile on turn left.
Bedrooms: 1 single, 2 twin
Bathrooms: 1 private, 1 public

Bed & breakfast
per night:	£min	£max
Single	14.00	20.00
Double	40.00	50.00

Parking for 22

HOLSWORTHY
Devon
Map ref 1C2

Busy rural town and centre of a large farming community. Market day attracts many visitors.

The Barton

Pancrasweek, Holsworthy EX22 7JT
☎ Bridgerule (028 881) 315
200-acre dairy farm. At the Devon/Cornwall border on the A3072, 3.5 miles from Holsworthy and 6 miles from the Cornish coast. Friendly atmosphere and home cooking with home-produced vegetables.
Bedrooms: 2 double, 1 twin
Bathrooms: 3 private

Bed & breakfast
per night:	£min	£max
Single	13.00	13.50
Double	26.00	27.00

Half board
per person:	£min	£max
Daily	20.00	20.50
Weekly	140.00	143.50

Evening meal 1800 (last orders 1600)
Parking for 5
Open May-September

ILFRACOMBE
Devon
Map ref 1C1

Resort of Victorian grandeur set on hillside between cliffs with sandy coves. At the mouth of the harbour stands an 18th C lighthouse, built over a medieval chapel. There are fine formal gardens, museum, Chambercombe Manor, interesting old house, nearby.
Tourist Information Centre
☎ (0271) 863001

Cairn House Hotel
APPROVED

43 St. Brannocks Road, Ilfracombe EX34 8EH
☎ (0271) 863911
Comfortable small licensed detached hotel with super views. Wide and varied menu and personal service. Ample parking.
Bedrooms: 2 single, 3 double, 3 triple, 2 family rooms
Bathrooms: 10 private

Bed & breakfast
per night:	£min	£max
Single	18.00	20.00
Double	36.00	40.00

Half board
per person:	£min	£max
Daily	28.00	30.00
Weekly	180.00	190.00

Evening meal 1800 (last orders 1900)

280

WEST COUNTRY

Parking for 10
Cards accepted: Access, Visa

Sunnymeade Country House Hotel ♠
APPROVED

Dean Cross, West Down, Ilfracombe
EX34 8NT
☎ (0271) 863668
Set in over half an acre amid beautiful rolling Devon countryside. Close to beaches and Exmoor. West Down is 4 miles south of Ilfracombe.
Bedrooms: 1 single, 6 double, 1 twin, 1 triple, 1 family room
Bathrooms: 8 private, 2 public

Bed & breakfast
per night:	£min	£max
Single	15.50	19.00
Double	31.00	38.00

Half board
per person:	£min	£max
Daily	23.50	
Weekly	147.00	175.00

Evening meal 1900 (last orders 1830)
Parking for 14
Open April-October
Cards accepted: Access, Visa, Diners, Amex

ISLES OF SCILLY

Picturesque group of granitic rocks and islands south-west of Land's End. Peaceful and unspoilt, they are noted for natural beauty, romantic maritime history, silver sands, early flowers and sub-tropical gardens on Tresco. Main island is St Mary's.
Tourist Information Centre
☎ (0720) 22536

Old School House
Listed

Bryher, Isles of Scilly TR23 0PR
☎ Scillonia (0720) 22671
Remote, age-old cottage within inches of water's edge on secluded cove. Informal, Scillonian family-run.
Bedrooms: 1 twin, 1 family room
Bathrooms: 1 public

Bed & breakfast
per night:	£min	£max
Single	18.00	19.00

Half board
per person:	£min	£max
Daily	25.00	26.00

Evening meal 1800 (last orders 1930)
Open April-September

Seaview Moorings
COMMENDED

The Strand, St Mary's, Isles of Scilly
TR21 0PT
☎ Scillonia (0720) 22327

Overlooking harbour, close to town, 15 yards from beach. Large choice breakfast menu. Friendly and comfortable home from home. Pets and children welcome.
Bedrooms: 3 double, 3 twin
Bathrooms: 2 public

Bed & breakfast
per night:	£min	£max
Single	19.97	21.15
Double	39.94	42.30

Open January-November

IVYBRIDGE
Devon
Map ref 1C2

Town set in delightful woodlands on the River Erme. Brunel designed the local railway viaduct. South Dartmoor Leisure Centre.
Tourist Information Centre
☎ (0752) 897035

Hillhead Farm
Listed

Ugborough, Ivybridge PL21 0HQ
☎ Plymouth (0752) 892674
77-acre mixed farm. Spacious family farmhouse, surrounded by fields. All home-cooked and largely home-grown food. From A38 turn off at Wrangton Cross, turn left, take third right over crossroads, after half a mile go straight over next crossroads, after three-quarters of a mile turn left, farm is 75 yards on left.
Bedrooms: 2 double, 2 twin
Bathrooms: 1 public

Bed & breakfast
per night:	£min	£max
Single	12.00	12.00
Double	24.00	24.00

Half board
per person:	£min	£max
Daily	18.00	18.00
Weekly	112.00	112.00

Evening meal 1900 (last orders 2100)
Parking for 5

National Crown ratings were correct at the time of going to press but are subject to change. Please check at the time of booking.

KENTISBEARE
Devon
Map ref 1D2

Pretty village at the foot of the Blackdown Hills. The church has a magnificent carved 15th C screen, and nearby is a medieval priest's house with a minstrels' gallery and oak screens.

Knowles House
Listed

Broad Road, Kentisbeare, Cullompton
EX15 2EU
☎ (088 46) 209
Country house with beautiful gardens and woodland on edge of the Blackdown Hills. 5 minutes M5, junction 28, left on A373, left to Shaldon, 1.5 miles on left.
Bedrooms: 1 double, 1 twin
Bathrooms: 2 private

Bed & breakfast
per night:	£min	£max
Single	15.00	15.00
Double	30.00	30.00

Parking for 4

Millhayes
Listed **HIGHLY COMMENDED**

Kentisbeare, Cullompton EX15 2AF
☎ (088 46) 412
Fax (088 46) 412
Situated in the picturesque village of Kentisbeare, only 3 miles from the M5 junction 28. It is approximately half way between Taunton and Exeter and within easy reach of both north and south coasts.
Bedrooms: 2 single, 1 double, 1 twin
Bathrooms: 2 private, 1 public

Bed & breakfast
per night:	£min	£max
Single	17.50	17.50
Double	39.00	39.00

Parking for 8

KENTISBURY
Devon
Map ref 1C1

Hollacombe Farm
Listed **COMMENDED**

Kentisbury, Barnstaple EX31 4NR
☎ Parracombe (059 83) 286

120-acre livestock farm. Comfortable farmhouse with spacious accommodation in beautiful scenery on

Continued ▶

281

WEST COUNTRY

KENTISBURY
Continued

the A399 close to Blackmoor Gate crossroads, in Exmoor National Park.
Bedrooms: 1 single, 1 double, 1 triple
Bathrooms: 1 private, 1 public

Bed & breakfast per night:	£min	£max
Single	15.00	20.00
Double	30.00	36.00

Evening meal 1900 (last orders 0930)
Parking for 8
Open April-October

KING'S NYMPTON
Devon
Map ref 1C1

Great Oakwell Farm
Listed

King's Nympton, Umberleigh
EX37 9TE
☎ South Molton (0769) 572810
200-acre dairy farm. Friendly, comfortable, relaxing farmhouse, with glorious views. Ideal for touring Exmoor and the Devon coast from Hartland Point to Minehead.
Bedrooms: 1 single, 2 double
Bathrooms: 2 public

Bed & breakfast per night:	£min	£max
Single	14.00	16.00
Double	28.00	32.00

Half board per person:	£min	£max
Daily	21.50	23.50
Weekly	150.50	164.50

Evening meal 1900 (last orders 1630)
Parking for 8

KINGSAND
Cornwall
Map ref 1C3

Friary Manor
APPROVED

Maker Heights, Mount Edgcumbe, Kingsand, Torpoint PL10 1JB
☎ Plymouth (0752) 822112
Fax (0752) 822112

Bordering the Mount Edgcumbe country park, set above a private wooded valley. Lovely country house, 1717, in its own 4-acre landscaped garden.

Bedrooms: 2 double, 1 twin, 1 triple, 2 family rooms
Bathrooms: 4 private, 1 public

Bed & breakfast per night:	£min	£max
Single	24.70	38.78
Double	42.30	49.40

Half board per person:	£min	£max
Daily	34.65	38.20
Weekly	199.75	270.25

Lunch available
Evening meal 1900 (last orders 2100)
Parking for 32
Cards accepted: Access, Visa, Switch

KINGSBRIDGE
Devon
Map ref 1C3

Formerly important as a port, now a market town overlooking head of beautiful, wooded estuary winding deep into rural countryside. Summer art exhibitions; Cookworthy Museum.
Tourist Information Centre
☎ (0548) 853195

The Ashburton Arms
Listed COMMENDED

West Charleton, Kingsbridge TQ7 2AH
☎ (0548) 531242
Friendly village freehouse serving real ale and home-cooked food. Comfortable accommodation. Sorry, no pets. No smoking on first floor.
Bedrooms: 2 single, 1 double, 1 twin
Bathrooms: 1 public

Bed & breakfast per night:	£min	£max
Single	18.00	20.00
Double	33.00	38.00

Lunch available
Evening meal 1900 (last orders 2130)
Parking for 15
Cards accepted: Access, Visa

Court Barton Farmhouse
COMMENDED

Aveton Gifford, Kingsbridge TQ7 4LE
☎ (0548) 550312

40-acre mixed farm. Beautiful 16th C manor farmhouse, below the church 100 yards from A379. Splendid hospitality guaranteed.
Bedrooms: 1 single, 3 double, 2 twin, 1 triple
Bathrooms: 6 private, 1 public, 1 private shower

Bed & breakfast per night:	£min	£max
Single	16.00	25.00
Double	32.00	48.00

Parking for 10

Crannacombe Farm

Hazelwood, Loddiswell, Kingsbridge TQ7 4DX
☎ (0548) 550256
80-acre mixed farm. Period farmhouse in the Avon Valley - an Area of Outstanding Natural Beauty. Private bathrooms and TV in bedrooms. Lovely river walks and views. Ten minutes from Kingsbridge.
Bedrooms: 1 double, 1 family room
Bathrooms: 2 private

Bed & breakfast per night:	£min	£max
Single	16.00	16.50
Double	31.00	32.00

Half board per person:	£min	£max
Daily	24.50	24.50
Weekly	171.50	171.50

Evening meal 1830 (last orders 1900)
Parking for 8
Open February-November

Globe Inn

Frogmore, Kingsbridge TQ7 2NR
☎ Frogmore (0548) 531351
Friendly village freehouse at the head of Frogmore Creek. Atmospheric restaurant and bars. Real ales, good food, open fires, beer garden and parking.
Bedrooms: 3 double, 2 twin, 1 triple
Bathrooms: 2 private, 2 public

Bed & breakfast per night:	£min	£max
Single	12.50	25.00
Double	25.00	40.00

Lunch available
Evening meal 1800 (last orders 2200)
Parking for 20
Cards accepted: Access, Visa, Switch

There are separate sections in this guide listing groups specialising in farm holidays and accommodation which is especially suitable for young people and organised groups.

WEST COUNTRY

LANGPORT
Somerset
Map ref 1D1

Small market town with Anglo-Saxon origins, sloping to River Parrett. Well-known for glove making and, formerly, for eels. Interesting old buildings include some fine local churches.

Gothic House

Muchelney, Langport TA10 ODW
☎ (0458) 250626
Gothic style Victorian former farmhouse. Spacious and comfortable. Large gardens. Situated on the Langport and Crewkerne road on the edge of the Somerset Levels.
Bedrooms: 3 double
Bathrooms: 2 private, 1 public

Bed & breakfast
per night:	£min	£max
Single	15.00	18.00
Double	26.00	34.00

Half board
per person:	£min	£max
Daily	22.00	26.00
Weekly	150.00	180.00

Evening meal 1800 (last orders 2030)
Parking for 10

LAUNCESTON
Cornwall
Map ref 1C2

Medieval "Gateway to Cornwall", county town until 1838, founded by the Normans under their hilltop castle near the original monastic settlement. This market town, overlooked by its castle ruin, has a square with Georgian houses and an elaborately-carved granite church.
Tourist Information Centre
☎ (0566) 772321

Eagle House Hotel

Castle Street, Launceston PL15 8BA
☎ (0566) 772036
Townhouse hotel within the wall of Launceston Castle, 2 minutes' walk from town centre and overlooking Cornish countryside. Golf and fishing nearby.
Bedrooms: 1 single, 8 double, 6 twin
Bathrooms: 15 private

Bed & breakfast
per night:	£min	£max
Single	22.50	
Double	44.00	

Half board
per person:	£min	£max
Daily	30.00	
Weekly	200.00	

Evening meal 1830 (last orders 2130)

Parking for 50
Cards accepted: Access, Visa

Wheatley Farm
HIGHLY COMMENDED

Maxworthy, Launceston PL15 8LY
☎ Canworthy Water (056 681) 232 changing to (0566) 781232
Fax (056 681) 232 changing to (0566) 781232
232-acre mixed farm. The warmest of welcomes awaits you at Wheatley Farm. Ten minutes' drive to spectacular north coast. En-suite rooms, one with romantic four-poster. Colour TV. Delicious cooking our speciality.
Bedrooms: 2 double, 2 family rooms
Bathrooms: 4 private

Bed & breakfast
per night	£min	£max
Double	36.00	40.00

Half board
per person:	£min	£max
Daily	28.00	32.00

Evening meal 1830 (last orders 1400)
Parking for 4
Open April-September

LEIGH
Wiltshire
Map ref 2B2

Grove Farmhouse

Ashton Road, Leigh, Swindon SN6 6RF
☎ Cirencester (0285) 860964
Fax (0285) 862441
Traditional 17th C farmhouse with stableyard, paddocks, ponds and gardens. Quiet rural location near water parks, riding and Cotswolds.
Bedrooms: 1 double, 1 twin, 1 triple
Bathrooms: 3 private

Bed & breakfast
per night:	£min	£max
Single	25.00	
Double	36.00	38.00

Parking for 4

Individual proprietors have supplied all details of accommodation. Although we do check for accuracy, we advise you to confirm the information at the time of booking.

LISKEARD
Cornwall
Map ref 1C2

Former stannary town with a livestock market and light industry, at the head of a valley running to the coast. Handsome Georgian and Victorian residences and a Victorian Guildhall reflect the prosperity of the mining boom. The large church has an early 20th C tower and a Norman font.

Tregondale Farm
HIGHLY COMMENDED

Menheniot, Liskeard PL14 3RG
☎ (0579) 342407
180-acre mixed farm. Characteristic farmhouse in beautiful countryside. En-suite facilities. Home-produced food our speciality. Log fires, tennis court. North east of Menheniot, between A38 and A390.
Bedrooms: 1 double, 1 twin, 1 triple
Bathrooms: 1 private, 2 public

Bed & breakfast
per night:	£min	£max
Single	15.00	18.00
Double	30.00	36.00

Half board
per person:	£min	£max
Daily	24.00	27.00
Weekly	168.00	180.00

Evening meal 1900 (last orders 1800)
Parking for 3

Tresulgan Farm
HIGHLY COMMENDED

Menheniot Station, Liskeard PL14 3PU
☎ Widegates (050 34) 268
145-acre dairy farm. Picturesque views from modernised 17th C farmhouse which has retained its character. Lots to do in this beautiful area and a warm and friendly welcome awaits you.
Bedrooms: 1 double, 1 triple, 1 family room
Bathrooms: 3 private

Bed & breakfast
per night:	£min	£max
Single	16.00	17.00
Double	32.00	34.00

Half board
per person:	£min	£max
Daily	23.00	24.00
Weekly	160.00	167.00

Evening meal 1830 (last orders 1930)
Parking for 4
Open March-November

Please mention this guide when making a booking.

WEST COUNTRY

LITTLE BEDWYN
Wiltshire
Map ref 2C2

Harrow Inn
COMMENDED

Little Bedwyn, Marlborough SN8 3JP
☎ Marlborough (0672) 870871
Fax (0672) 870140
Country inn on south-east side of quiet, unspoilt village close to Kennet and Avon Canal. Excellent restaurant, attractive garden.
Bedrooms: 1 single, 2 twin
Bathrooms: 3 private

Bed & breakfast per night:	£min	£max
Single	22.00	28.00
Double	37.00	45.00

Lunch available
Evening meal 1930 (last orders 2100)
Parking for 1
Cards accepted: Access, Visa

LOOE
Cornwall
Map ref 1C2

Small resort developed around former fishing and smuggling ports occupying the deep estuary of the East and West Looe Rivers. Narrow winding streets, with old inns; museum and art gallery are housed in interesting old buildings. Shark fishing centre, boat trips; busy harbour.

Bucklawren Farm
HIGHLY COMMENDED

St. Martin-by-Looe, Looe PL13 1NZ
☎ Widegates (050 34) 738

534-acre arable & dairy farm. Set in glorious countryside with beautiful sea views. Only 1.5 miles from beach. Family and en-suite accommodation with colour TV. Delicious farmhouse cooking.
Bedrooms: 1 double, 1 twin, 1 triple, 2 family rooms
Bathrooms: 4 private, 1 public

Bed & breakfast per night:	£min	£max
Single	15.00	23.00
Double	30.00	36.00

Half board per person:	£min	£max
Daily	24.00	26.50
Weekly	157.50	168.00

Evening meal 1800 (last orders 1800)

Parking for 10
Open March-November
Cards accepted: Access, Visa

Coombe Farm
HIGHLY COMMENDED

Widegates, Looe PL13 1QN
☎ Widegates (050 34) 223

10-acre smallholding. Country house in lovely grounds with superb views to sea. All rooms en-suite. Candlelit dining. Home cooking. Glorious walks and beaches nearby. Ideally situated for touring Cornwall and Devon.
Bedrooms: 1 single, 2 double, 2 twin, 2 triple, 3 family rooms
Bathrooms: 10 private

Bed & breakfast per night:	£min	£max
Single	16.50	22.50
Double	33.00	45.00

Half board per person:	£min	£max
Daily	27.00	33.00
Weekly	182.00	224.00

Evening meal 1900 (last orders 1900)
Parking for 12
Open March-October

Kantara Guest House
APPROVED

7 Trelawney Terrace, Looe PL13 2AG
☎ (0503) 262093
Family-run guesthouse, 5 minutes' walking distance to the beach and town. Friendly atmosphere - home from home.
Bedrooms: 1 single, 1 twin, 3 triple
Bathrooms: 2 public

Bed & breakfast per night:	£min	£max
Single	11.50	15.00
Double	23.00	30.00

Half board per person:	£min	£max
Daily	19.00	22.50
Weekly	128.50	152.50

Lunch available
Evening meal 1800 (last orders 1900)
Parking for 2
Cards accepted: Access, Visa, Amex

Pixies Holt
Shutta, Looe PL13 1JD
☎ (0503) 262726
Built in 1878 for a ship's captain, with views across the two rivers. Only 10 minutes' walk to the fishing port of Looe.
Bedrooms: 1 single, 4 double, 1 twin, 1 triple
Bathrooms: 4 private, 1 public

Bed & breakfast per night:	£min	£max
Single	14.40	20.00
Double	28.80	40.00

Parking for 8
Open February-November
Cards accepted: Access, Visa, Amex

Stonerock Cottage
COMMENDED

Portuan Road, Hannafore, Looe PL13 2DN
☎ (0503) 263651
Modernised, old world cottage facing south to the Channel. Ample free parking. 2 minutes from the beach, shops, tennis and other amenities.
Bedrooms: 1 single, 2 double, 1 twin
Bathrooms: 1 private, 2 public

Bed & breakfast per night:	£min	£max
Single	14.00	15.00
Double	28.00	30.00

Parking for 4
Open February-October

LUSTLEIGH
Devon
Map ref 1D2

Riverside village of pretty thatched cottages gathered around its 15th C church. The traditional Mayday festival has dancing round the maypole. Just west is Lustleigh Cleave, where Dartmoor is breached by the River Bovey which flows through a deep valley of boulders and trees.

Eastwrey Barton Hotel
HIGHLY COMMENDED

Lustleigh, Newton Abbot TQ13 9SN
☎ (064 77) 338
Well-appointed 17th C country house hotel. Peaceful, relaxing and renowned for good food and personal service.
Bedrooms: 3 double, 3 twin
Bathrooms: 6 private

Bed & breakfast per night:	£min	£max
Single	29.00	29.00
Double	58.00	58.00

Half board per person:	£min	£max
Daily	42.00	42.00
Weekly	264.00	264.00

Evening meal 1930 (last orders 1930)
Parking for 20
Open March-October
Cards accepted: Access, Visa

WEST COUNTRY

The Mill ♠
Listed
Lustleigh, Newton Abbot TQ13 9SS
☎ (064 77) 357
12-acre smallholding. Historic riverside millhouse on edge of beautiful Dartmoor village. Exposed beams, antique furniture, home-grown produce.
Bedrooms: 1 single, 1 double, 1 triple
Bathrooms: 2 public

Bed & breakfast
per night:	£min	£max
Single	17.50	17.50
Double	32.00	32.00

Half board
per person:	£min	£max
Daily	26.00	28.00
Weekly	180.00	190.00

Parking for 3

LYDFORD
Devon
Map ref 1C2

Former important tin mining town, a small village on edge of West Dartmoor. Remains of Norman castle where all falling foul of tinners' notorious "Lydford Law" were incarcerated. Bridge crosses River Lyd where it rushes through a mile-long gorge of boulders and trees.

Castle Inn and Hotel ♠
Listed COMMENDED
Lydford, Okehampton EX20 4BH
☎ (0822) 82242
Fax (0822) 82454
Unspoilt 16th C inn serving fine food and real ales in beamed bar/restaurant with slate floors and open fires.
Bedrooms: 1 single, 5 double, 2 twin
Bathrooms: 5 private, 1 public, 1 private shower

Bed & breakfast
per night:	£min	£max
Single	25.00	45.00
Double	37.50	52.50

Half board
per person:	£min	£max
Daily	33.25	45.50
Weekly	175.00	255.00

Lunch available
Evening meal 1830 (last orders 2130)
Parking for 50
Cards accepted: Access, Visa, Amex, Switch

The enquiry coupons at the back will help you when contacting proprietors.

LYME REGIS
Dorset
Map ref 1D2

Pretty, historic fishing town and resort set against the fossil-rich cliffs of Lyme Bay. In medieval times it was an important port and cloth centre. The Cobb, a massive stone breakwater, shelters the ancient harbour which is still lively with boats.
Tourist Information Centre
☎ (0297) 442138

Kersbrook Hotel ♠
HIGHLY COMMENDED
Pound Road, Lyme Regis DT7 3HX
☎ (0297) 442596 & 442576

Thatched, 18th C listed hotel and restaurant in its own picturesque gardens, set high above Lyme Bay. For those who prefer peace and tranquillity.
Bedrooms: 2 single, 7 double, 3 twin
Bathrooms: 12 private

Bed & breakfast
per night:	£min	£max
Double	60.00	70.00

Half board
per person:	£min	£max
Daily	45.50	50.50
Weekly	300.00	340.00

Lunch available
Evening meal 1930 (last orders 2100)
Parking for 16
Open February-November
Cards accepted: Access, Visa, Amex, Switch

Quambi
HIGHLY COMMENDED
Charmouth Road, Lyme Regis DT7 3DP
☎ (0297) 443117

Detached house in own gardens with pleasant views across Lyme Bay and Lyme Regis, only 5 minutes' walk from seafront.
Bedrooms: 1 single, 3 double, 1 twin, 1 triple
Bathrooms: 4 private, 1 public

Bed & breakfast
per night:	£min	£max
Single	20.00	22.00
Double	30.00	40.00

Parking for 7
Open March-October

Southernhaye
COMMENDED
Pound Road, Lyme Regis DT7 3HX
☎ (0297) 443077
Distinctive Edwardian house in quiet location with panoramic views over Lyme Bay, about ten minutes' walk from town and beach.
Bedrooms: 1 double, 1 twin
Bathrooms: 1 public

Bed & breakfast
per night:	£min	£max
Single	16.00	16.00
Double	28.00	32.00

Parking for 2

Springfield
COMMENDED
Woodmead Road, Lyme Regis DT7 3LJ
☎ (0297) 443409
Elegant Georgian house in walled garden, with well-proportioned, tastefully decorated rooms, many enjoying views over the sea.
Bedrooms: 1 single, 2 double, 2 twin, 1 triple, 1 family room
Bathrooms: 3 private, 2 public

Bed & breakfast
per night:	£min	£max
Single	15.00	18.00
Double	26.00	40.00

Parking for 9
Open February-November

White House
COMMENDED
47 Silver Street, Lyme Regis DT7 3HR
☎ (0297) 443420
Fine views of Dorset coastline from rear of this 18th C guesthouse. A short walk from beach, gardens and shops.
Bedrooms: 5 double, 2 twin
Bathrooms: 7 private

Bed & breakfast
per night:	£min	£max
Double	36.00	40.00

Parking for 6
Open April-October

National Crown ratings were correct at the time of going to press but are subject to change. Please check at the time of booking.

WEST COUNTRY

LYNMOUTH
Devon
Map ref 1C1

Resort set beneath bracken-covered cliffs and pinewood gorges where 2 rivers meet, and cascade between boulders to the town. Lynton, set on cliffs above, can be reached by water-operated cliff railway from the Victorian esplanade. Valley of the Rocks, to the west, gives dramatic walks.

Coombe Farm
COMMENDED
Countisbury, Lynton EX35 6NF
☎ Brendon (059 87) 236
365-acre hill farm. Located half a mile off the A39 and 3 miles from Lynmouth.
Bedrooms: 2 double, 1 twin, 1 triple, 1 family room
Bathrooms: 2 private, 2 public

Bed & breakfast per night:	£min	£max
Double	33.00	42.00
Half board per person:	£min	£max
Daily	28.50	32.00
Weekly	185.00	210.00

Evening meal 1900 (last orders 1700)
Parking for 6
Open March-November

LYNTON
Devon
Map ref 1C1

Hilltop resort on Exmoor coast linked to its seaside twin, Lynmouth, by a water-operated cliff railway which descends from the town hall. Spectacular surroundings of moorland cliffs with steep chasms of conifer and rocks through which rivers cascade.
Tourist Information Centre
☎ (0598) 52225

Sandrock Hotel
COMMENDED
Longmead, Lynton EX35 6DH
☎ (0598) 53307
Comfortable family-run hotel, quietly situated near local beauty spots, bowls green and tennis courts.
Bedrooms: 2 single, 4 double, 3 twin
Bathrooms: 7 private, 1 public

Bed & breakfast per night:	£min	£max
Single	19.50	22.50
Double	39.00	46.80
Half board per person:	£min	£max
Daily	30.00	35.00
Weekly	195.50	225.00

Evening meal 1900 (last orders 2000)

Parking for 9
Open February-November
Cards accepted: Access, Visa, Amex

MALMESBURY
Wiltshire
Map ref 2B2

Overlooking the River Avon, an old town dominated by its great church, once a Benedictine abbey. The surviving Norman nave and porch are noted for fine sculptures, 12th C arches and musicians' gallery.
Tourist Information Centre
☎ (0666) 823748

Bullocks Horn Farm
Listed COMMENDED
Charlton, Malmesbury SN16 9OZ
☎ (0666) 577458
12-acre livestock & horses farm. Well-appointed farmhouse in beautiful peaceful surroundings, with large well-tended gardens. 2 miles east of Malmesbury, close to Cotswolds and M4.
Bedrooms: 2 single, 1 double, 1 twin
Bathrooms: 2 public

Bed & breakfast per night:	£min	£max
Single	15.00	16.00
Double	30.00	32.00

Parking for 6

Flisteridge Cottage
Listed COMMENDED
Flisteridge Road, Upper Minety, Malmesbury SN16 9PS
☎ (0666) 860343
Quiet secluded country cottage in rural surroundings. Take A429 Cirencester/Malmesbury road, turn off at Crudwell, signpost Oaksey and Minety, on to C class road, through Eastcourt and Flisteridge woods. Cottage is down gravel drive signposted on right.
Bedrooms: 1 single, 1 double, 1 twin
Bathrooms: 1 private, 1 public

Bed & breakfast per night:	£min	£max
Single	13.50	15.00
Double	26.00	31.50

Parking for 8
Open March-November

Lovett Farm
Little Somerford, Malmesbury SN15 5BP
☎ (0666) 823268
65-acre livestock farm. Modern farmhouse ideally situated for visiting Bath and the Cotswolds. Close to M4, 3 miles east of Malmesbury.
Bedrooms: 1 double, 1 twin
Bathrooms: 1 private, 1 public

Bed & breakfast per night:	£min	£max
Single	15.00	17.00
Double	28.00	32.00

Parking for 5

Manor Farm
COMMENDED
Corston, Malmesbury SN16 0HF
☎ (0666) 822148

436-acre mixed farm. Relax and unwind in charming 17th C Cotswolds farmhouse. Excellent meals available in village pub. Ideally situated for visiting Cotswolds, Bath and Stonehenge.
Bedrooms: 2 double, 2 triple, 1 family room
Bathrooms: 1 private, 1 public, 1 private shower

Bed & breakfast per night:	£min	£max
Single	14.00	22.00
Double	28.00	40.00

Parking for 12
Cards accepted: Access, Visa, Diners, Amex

MARKET LAVINGTON
Wiltshire
Map ref 2B2

The Old Coach House
21 Church Street, Market Lavington, Devizes SN10 4DU
☎ Devizes (0380) 812879
Fax (0380) 812074
Comfortable 18th C home close to many places of interest. Residential English language tuition by qualified host-teachers also available.
Bedrooms: 1 double, 1 twin
Bathrooms: 2 private

Bed & breakfast per night:	£min	£max
Single	20.00	22.50
Double	35.00	38.00

Parking for 3

The town index towards the back of this guide gives page numbers of all places with accommodation.

WEST COUNTRY

MARLBOROUGH
Wiltshire
Map ref 2B2

Important market town, in a river valley cutting through chalk downlands. The broad main street, with colonnaded shops on one side, shows a medley of building styles, mainly from the Georgian period. Lanes wind away on either side and a church stands at each end.
Tourist Information Centre
☎ *(0672) 513989*

Laurel Cottage Guest House
HIGHLY COMMENDED

Southend, Ogbourne St George, Marlborough SN8 1SG
☎ Ogbourne St George (0672) 841288

16th C thatched cottage, in a delightful rural setting, a fully modernised family home. Low beamed ceilings and inglenook fireplace. Non-smokers only please.
Bedrooms: 2 double, 2 twin
Bathrooms: 2 private, 1 public

Bed & breakfast
per night:	£min	£max
Single	25.00	34.00
Double	32.00	47.00

Half board
per person:	£min	£max
Daily	26.00	33.50

Evening meal from 1900
Parking for 5
Open April-October

MARTINSTOWN
Dorset
Map ref 2B3

Old Post Office
Listed

Martinstown, Dorchester DT2 9LF
☎ (0305) 889254
Grade II listed Georgian cottage tastefully modernised throughout. Large garden with many small animals. Good rural base, children and pets welcome.
Bedrooms: 1 double, 2 twin
Bathrooms: 2 public

Bed & breakfast
per night:	£min	£max
Single	15.00	17.50
Double	30.00	35.00

Half board
per person:	£min	£max
Daily		25.00

Evening meal 2000 (last orders 1630)
Parking for 3

MARTOCK
Somerset
Map ref 2A3

Small town with many handsome buildings of Ham stone and a beautiful old church with tie-beam roof. Medieval treasurer's house, Georgian market house, 17th C manor.

Wychwood
COMMENDED

7 Bearley Road, Martock TA12 6PG
☎ (0935) 825601
Quality, comfortable accommodation in modern detached house. Quiet position just off A303. Close Montacute House (National Trust) and other historic houses and gardens. Near Glastonbury Abbey and Wells Cathedral. Brochure.
Bedrooms: 1 single, 1 double, 1 twin
Bathrooms: 2 private, 3 public, 1 private shower

Bed & breakfast
per night:	£min	£max
Single	16.00	18.00
Double	30.00	34.00

Half board
per person:	£min	£max
Daily	24.00	27.00
Weekly	161.00	182.00

Evening meal 1830 (last orders 2000)
Parking for 3

MELKSHAM
Wiltshire
Map ref 2B2

Small industrial town standing on the banks of the River Avon. Old weavers' cottages and Regency houses are grouped around the attractive church which has traces of Norman work. The 18th C Round House, once used for dyeing fleeces, is now a craft centre.
Tourist Information Centre
☎ *(0225) 707424*

Longhope Hotel

9 Beanacre Road, Melksham SN12 8AG
☎ (0225) 706737
Situated in its own grounds on the A350 Melksham - Chippenham road. Half a mile from Melksham town centre, 10 miles from M4 junction 17.
Bedrooms: 1 single, 3 double, 1 twin, 2 triple

Bathrooms: 7 private

Bed & breakfast
per night:	£min	£max
Single	22.00	24.00
Double	32.00	35.00

Half board
per person:	£min	£max
Daily	29.00	32.00
Weekly	160.00	180.00

Evening meal 1830 (last orders 1900)
Parking for 12

MERE
Wiltshire
Map ref 2B2

Small town with a grand Perpendicular church surrounded by Georgian houses, with old inns and a 15th C chantry house. On the chalk downs overlooking the town is an Iron Age fort.
Tourist Information Centre
☎ *(0747) 861211*

Talbot Hotel
APPROVED

The Square, Mere BA12 6DR
☎ (0747) 860427
Fax (0747) 861210
16th C coaching inn with interesting features. Ideal for visits to Stourhead, Longleat, Stonehenge, Salisbury, Bath, Sherborne and Cheddar areas. Two-night breaks available.
Bedrooms: 2 single, 2 double, 1 twin, 2 triple
Bathrooms: 7 private

Bed & breakfast
per night:	£min	£max
Single	20.00	32.50
Double	40.00	53.00

Lunch available
Evening meal 1830 (last orders 2130)
Parking for 20
Cards accepted: Access, Visa, Amex

MEVAGISSEY
Cornwall
Map ref 1B3

Small fishing town, a favourite with holidaymakers. Earlier prosperity came from pilchard fisheries, boat-building and smuggling. By the harbour are fish cellars, some converted, and a local history museum is housed in an old boat-building shed. Handsome Methodist chapel; shark fishing, sailing.

Auraville

The Drive, Trevarth, Mevagissey, St Austell PL26 6RX
☎ (0726) 843293

Continued ▶

287

WEST COUNTRY

MEVAGISSEY
Continued

Private residence in quiet and peaceful surroundings, a short walk from the harbour. Central for touring Cornwall.
Bedrooms: 1 single, 2 double, 1 twin
Bathrooms: 2 public
Bed & breakfast
per night:	£min	£max
Single	12.50	14.50
Double	25.00	29.00

Parking for 4

Kerry Anna Country House
COMMENDED
Treleaven Farm, Mevagissey, St Austell PL26 6RZ
☎ (0726) 843558
200-acre mixed farm. Country house overlooking village, surrounded by rambling farmland, wild flowers and wildlife. Outdoor swimming pool, games barn, putting green. Farm cooking.
Bedrooms: 3 double, 2 twin, 1 family room
Bathrooms: 6 private
Bed & breakfast
per night:	£min	£max
Double	16.00	25.00

Half board
per person:	£min	£max
Daily	26.00	35.00
Weekly	170.00	220.00

Evening meal 1830 (last orders 1200)
Parking for 6
Open April-October

Rising Sun Inn
Portmellon Cove, Mevagissey, St Austell PL26 6PL
☎ (0726) 843235
17th C inn right next to the beach at Portmellon Cove, and overlooking Chapel Point and surrounding countryside.
Bedrooms: 3 double, 1 twin, 1 triple
Bathrooms: 5 private
Bed & breakfast
per night:	£min	£max
Double	32.00	45.00

Lunch available
Evening meal 1830 (last orders 2130)
Parking for 60
Open March-October
Cards accepted: Access, Visa

Steep House
Portmellon Cove, Mevagissey, St Austell PL26 2PH
☎ (0726) 843732

Refreshingly clean and comfortable house with large garden and covered (summertime) heated pool. Superb views, private parking, barbecues, Christmas celebrations.
Bedrooms: 6 double, 1 twin
Bathrooms: 1 private, 2 public, 1 private shower
Bed & breakfast
per night:	£min	£max
Double	30.00	50.00

Half board
per person:	£min	£max
Daily	25.00	36.00

Lunch available
Evening meal 1900 (last orders 1700)
Parking for 12
Cards accepted: Access, Visa, Amex

MINEHEAD
Somerset
Map ref 1D1

Victorian resort with spreading sands developed around old fishing port on the coast below Exmoor. Former fishermen's cottages stand beside the 17th C harbour; cobbled streets climb the hill in steps to the church. Boat trips, steam railway. Hobby Horse festival 1 May.
Tourist Information Centre ☎ (0643) 702624

Kildare Lodge
COMMENDED
Townsend Road, Minehead TA24 5RQ
☎ (0643) 702009
Fax (0643) 706516
Edwin Lutyens designed Grade II listed building. Elegant a la carte restaurant. Licensed bar with bar meals. Comfortable en-suite accommodation.
Bedrooms: 2 single, 4 double, 2 twin, 2 triple
Bathrooms: 10 private
Bed & breakfast
per night:	£min	£max
Single	24.50	29.50
Double	42.50	62.50

Half board
per person:	£min	£max
Daily	31.50	35.00
Weekly	199.00	235.00

Lunch available
Evening meal 1830 (last orders 2130)
Parking for 38
Cards accepted: Access, Visa, Diners

MODBURY
Devon
Map ref 1C3

Attractive South Hams town set in rolling countryside, whose Perpendicular church has a rare Devon spire.

Weeke Farm
Listed
Modbury, Ivybridge PL21 0TT
☎ (0548) 830219
114-acre dairy farm. 19th C farmhouse, one mile from Modbury. One double, one family bedroom, bathroom with toilet for guests' use only. Lounge/diner with colour TV.
Bedrooms: 1 double, 1 triple
Bathrooms: 1 public
Bed & breakfast
per night:	£min	£max
Single	12.00	14.00
Double	24.00	28.00

Parking for 3
Open March-October

MORETONHAMPSTEAD
Devon
Map ref 1C2

Small market town with a row of 17th C almshouses standing on the Exeter road. Surrounding moorland is scattered with ancient farmhouses, prehistoric sites.

Cookshayes Country Guest House
COMMENDED
33 Court Street, Moretonhampstead, Newton Abbot TQ13 8LG
☎ (0647) 40374
Licensed guesthouse on edge of Dartmoor. Ornamental gardens with ample parking. Traditionally furnished. Accent on food and comfort.
Bedrooms: 1 single, 4 double, 2 twin, 1 triple
Bathrooms: 6 private, 2 public
Bed & breakfast
per night:	£min	£max
Single	20.00	20.00
Double	32.00	39.00

Half board
per person:	£min	£max
Daily	30.00	33.50
Weekly	203.00	227.50

Evening meal 1900 (last orders 1700)
Parking for 15
Open March-October
Cards accepted: Access, Visa, Amex

WEST COUNTRY

Great Doccombe Farm
COMMENDED

Doccombe, Moretonhampstead, Newton Abbot TQ13 8SS
☎ (0647) 40694

8-acre mixed farm. 300-year-old farmhouse in Dartmoor National Park. Comfortable rooms, farmhouse cooking. Ideal for walking the Teign Valley and Dartmoor.
Bedrooms: 2 double, 1 twin
Bathrooms: 2 private, 2 public

Bed & breakfast
per night:	£min	£max
Single	16.00	16.00
Double	30.00	34.00

Half board
per person:	£min	£max
Daily	24.00	26.00

Evening meal 1800 (last orders 1000)
Parking for 6
Open February-November

Great Sloncombe Farm
COMMENDED

Moretonhampstead, Newton Abbot TQ13 8QF
☎ (0647) 40595

170-acre dairy farm. 13th C Dartmoor farmhouse. Comfortable rooms, central heating, en-suite. Large wholesome farmhouse breakfasts and delicious dinners. Friendly Devonshire welcome.
Bedrooms: 2 double, 1 twin
Bathrooms: 3 private

Bed & breakfast
per night:	£min	£max
Single	16.00	19.00
Double	32.00	38.00

Half board
per person:	£min	£max
Daily	25.00	29.00

Evening meal 1830 (last orders 1000)
Parking for 3

White Hart Hotel
COMMENDED

The Square, Moretonhampstead, Newton Abbot TQ13 8NF
☎ (0647) 40406
Fax (0647) 40565

Historic inn in centre of Dartmoor town. Antiques, log fires, cosy bar. Fine restaurant and bar meals. Comfortable bedrooms with courtesy trays.
Bedrooms: 1 single, 9 double, 6 twin, 4 triple
Bathrooms: 20 private

Bed & breakfast
per night:	£min	£max
Single		43.00
Double		63.00

Half board
per person:	£min	£max
Daily	43.00	48.00
Weekly	301.00	336.00

Lunch available
Evening meal 1800 (last orders 2030)
Parking for 12
Cards accepted: Access, Visa, Diners, Amex, Switch

Wooston Farm
HIGHLY COMMENDED

Moretonhampstead, Newton Abbot TQ13 8QA
☎ (0647) 40367

280-acre mixed farm. Situated within Dartmoor National Park above the Teign Valley, with scenic views and walks. Two rooms are en-suite, one with 4-poster bed.
Bedrooms: 2 double, 1 twin
Bathrooms: 2 private, 1 public

Bed & breakfast
per night:	£min	£max
Single	15.00	18.00
Double	30.00	40.00

Half board
per person:	£min	£max
Daily	24.00	29.00
Weekly	168.00	203.00

Evening meal 1800 (last orders 1830)
Parking for 5

MORWENSTOW

Cornwall
Map ref 1C2

Scattered parish on the wild north Cornish coast. The church, beautifully situated in a deep combe by the sea, has a fine Norman doorway and 15th C bench-ends. Its unique vicarage was built by the 19th C poet-priest Robert Hawker. Nearby are Cornwall's highest cliffs.

Cornakey Farm

Morwenstow, Bude EX23 9SS
☎ (028 883) 260 changing to (0288) 331260

220-acre mixed farm. Convenient coastal walking area with extensive views of sea and cliffs from bedrooms. Home cooking, games room, children welcome. Good touring centre.
Bedrooms: 2 triple
Bathrooms: 1 private, 1 public

Bed & breakfast
per night:	£min	£max
Single	14.00	15.00
Double	28.00	30.00

Half board
per person:	£min	£max
Daily	18.00	20.00
Weekly	126.00	140.00

Evening meal 1830 (last orders 1730)
Parking for 2

MULLION

Cornwall
Map ref 1B3

Small holiday village with a golf-course, set back from the coast. The church has a serpentine tower of 1500, carved roof and beautiful medieval bench-ends. Beyond Mullion Cove, with its tiny harbour, wild untouched cliffs stretch south-eastward toward Lizard Point.

Tregaddra Farm
COMMENDED

Cury, Helston TR12 7BB
☎ (0326) 240235

220-acre arable & livestock farm. 18th C farmhouse with modern facilities and set in well kept gardens. Inglenook fireplace, sun lounge, balconies and a view of coast and countryside for a 15 mile radius. Home produce used.
Bedrooms: 1 single, 2 double, 2 triple
Bathrooms: 5 private

Bed & breakfast
per night:	£min	£max
Single	17.50	19.50
Double	35.00	39.00

Half board
per person:	£min	£max
Daily	23.50	26.00
Weekly	164.50	182.00

Evening meal from 1830
Parking for 8

MYLOR BRIDGE

Cornwall
Map ref 1B3

Penmere Guest House

10 Rosehill, Mylor Bridge, Falmouth TR11 5LZ
☎ Falmouth (0326) 374370

Continued ▶

WEST COUNTRY

MYLOR BRIDGE
Continued

Beautifully restored Victorian property enjoying splendid creek views, close to yachting centres. Lovely garden, perfect for a relaxing stay.
Bedrooms: 2 double, 2 twin, 2 triple
Bathrooms: 4 private, 1 public

Bed & breakfast
per night:	£min	£max
Single	20.00	27.50
Double	40.00	48.00

Parking for 6

NEWQUAY
Cornwall
Map ref 1B2

Popular resort spread over dramatic cliffs around its old fishing port. Many beaches with abundant sands, caves and rock pools; excellent surf. Pilots' gigs are still raced from the harbour and on the headland stands the stone Huer's House from the pilchard-fishing days.
Tourist Information Centre
☎ (0637) 871345

Degembris Farmhouse
👑 COMMENDED

St Newlyn East, Newquay TR8 5HY
☎ Mitchell (0872) 510555
Fax (0872) 510230
165-acre arable farm. 18th C listed Cornish farmhouse overlooking beautiful wooded valley. Our country trail will take you through natural woodland and fields visiting the pond and exploring the valley of the bluebells.
Bedrooms: 1 single, 1 double, 1 twin, 1 triple, 1 family room
Bathrooms: 2 public

Bed & breakfast
per night:	£min	£max
Single	15.00	
Double	30.00	

Half board
per person:	£min	£max
Daily	23.00	

Evening meal 1800 (last orders 1000)
Parking for 8
Open April-October

Manuels Farm
👑👑 HIGHLY COMMENDED

Quintrell Downs, Newquay TR8 4NY
☎ (0637) 873177
44-acre mixed farm. In a sheltered valley 2 miles inland from Newquay, offering the peace of the countryside with the charm of a traditional 17th C farmhouse.
Bedrooms: 1 double, 1 triple, 1 family room
Bathrooms: 1 private, 2 public

Bed & breakfast
per night:	£min	£max
Single	16.00	18.00
Double	32.00	36.00

Half board
per person:	£min	£max
Daily	25.50	30.00
Weekly	175.00	200.00

Evening meal 1830 (last orders 1630)
Parking for 6

Rose Cottage
👑

Shepherds Farm, St Newlyn East, Newquay TR8 5NW
☎ Zelah (0872) 540502
600-acre mixed farm. Decorated to a high standard, all rooms are en-suite with colour TV and tea-making facilities. Ideal for touring and beaches, one mile from A30. A warm welcome awaits.
Bedrooms: 2 double, 1 twin
Bathrooms: 3 private

Bed & breakfast
per night:	£min	£max
Single	15.00	17.00
Double	30.00	34.00

Half board
per person:	£min	£max
Daily	22.50	24.50
Weekly	150.00	160.00

Parking for 3

Tregurrian Hotel M
👑👑

Watergate Bay, Newquay TR8 4AB
☎ St. Mawgan (0637) 860280
On coast road between Newquay and Padstow, just 100 yards from golden sandy beach in an area reputed to have some of the finest beaches and coastline in Europe.
Bedrooms: 4 single, 11 double, 4 twin, 2 triple, 6 family rooms
Bathrooms: 22 private, 2 public

Bed & breakfast
per night:	£min	£max
Single	16.00	27.50

Half board
per person:	£min	£max
Daily	29.50	36.00
Weekly	120.00	225.00

Lunch available
Evening meal 1845 (last orders 1930)
Parking for 25
Open March-October
Cards accepted: Access, Visa

Symbols are explained on the flap inside the back cover.

NEWTON ABBOT
Devon
Map ref 1D2

Lively market town at the head of the Teign Estuary. A former railway town, well placed for moorland or seaside excursions. Interesting old houses nearby include Bradley Manor dating from the 15th C and Forde House, visited by Charles I and William of Orange.
Tourist Information Centre
☎ (0626) 67494

Bulleigh Park
👑👑

Ipplepen, Newton Abbot TQ12 5UA
☎ Kingskerswell (0803) 872254
40-acre mixed farm. Well situated family farm in delightful rural setting with extensive views. Home cooking. Take Totnes road out of Newton Abbot for 2.5 miles, turn left to Marldon road, 1 mile.
Bedrooms: 1 double, 1 triple
Bathrooms: 1 private, 1 public

Bed & breakfast
per night:	£min	£max
Single	13.50	17.50
Double	27.00	35.00

Evening meal 1830 (last orders 1930)
Parking for 8

NEWTON FERRERS
Devon
Map ref 1C3

Hillside village overlooking wooded estuary of the River Yealm, with attractive waterside cottages and yacht anchorage.

Maywood Cottage
👑👑 COMMENDED

Bridgend, Newton Ferrers, Plymouth PL81 ALO
☎ Plymouth (0752) 872372
Cottage on 3 levels, close to River Yealm estuary. Part old, all modernised. Take Bridgend - Noss Mayo road off B3186 (leading to Newton Ferrers). Maywood is at bottom of hill on right just before estuary.
Bedrooms: 3 twin
Bathrooms: 2 private, 1 public

Bed & breakfast
per night:	£min	£max
Single	15.00	25.00
Double	25.00	45.00

Half board
per person:	£min	£max
Daily	23.50	33.50
Weekly	150.00	200.00

Evening meal 1800 (last orders 2030)
Parking for 3

290

WEST COUNTRY

NORTH TAWTON
Devon
Map ref 1C2

Oaklands Farm
North Tawton EX20 2BQ
☎ Okehampton (0837) 82340
130-acre mixed farm. Centrally situated for north and south Devon coasts and Dartmoor. Very warm welcome. Easy access on level drive. Farmhouse cooking.
Bedrooms: 2 double, 1 triple
Bathrooms: 1 public

Bed & breakfast
per night:	£min	£max
Single	13.00	14.00
Double	26.00	28.00

Half board
per person:	£min	£max
Daily	20.00	21.00
Weekly	120.00	120.00

Parking for 4

OKEHAMPTON
Devon
Map ref 1C2

Busy market town near the high tors of northern Dartmoor. The Victorian church, with William Morris windows and a 15th C tower, stands on the site of a Saxon church. A Norman castle ruin overlooks the river to the west of the town. Museum of Dartmoor Life in a restored mill.

Higher Cadham Farm
COMMENDED
Jacobstowe, Okehampton EX20 3RB
☎ Exbourne (083 785) 647

139-acre mixed farm. 16th C farmhouse on a traditional Devon farm, 5 miles from Dartmoor and within easy reach of coast. On the Tarka trail.
Bedrooms: 1 single, 1 double, 1 twin, 1 family room
Bathrooms: 1 public

Bed & breakfast
per night:	£min	£max
Single	13.00	14.00
Double	26.00	28.00

Half board
per person:	£min	£max
Daily	20.00	21.00
Weekly	122.00	122.00

Evening meal 1900 (last orders 1700)

Parking for 6
Open March-November

Week Farm
COMMENDED
Bridestowe, Okehampton EX20 4HZ
☎ Bridestowe (083 786) 221

180-acre dairy & livestock farm. A warm welcome awaits you at this homely 17th C farmhouse three-quarters of a mile from the old A30 and 6 miles from Okehampton. Home cooking and every comfort. Come and spoil yourselves.
Bedrooms: 2 double, 2 triple, 1 family room
Bathrooms: 3 private, 1 public

Bed & breakfast
per night:	£min	£max
Single	18.00	20.00
Double	36.00	40.00

Half board
per person:	£min	£max
Daily	27.00	30.00
Weekly	190.00	210.00

Evening meal 1900 (last orders 1700)
Parking for 10
Cards accepted: Amex

OTTERTON
Devon
Map ref 1D2

Village on the banks of the River Otter, close to the sea. Beautiful thatched cottages of cob or pinkish stone and a church with a 15th C tower, overlooking the river. A craft centre is housed in an ancient mill nearby. Spectacular red sandstone cliffs rise to 500 ft toward Sidmouth.

Ropers Cottage
Ropers Lane, Otterton, Budleigh Salterton EX9 7JF
☎ Colaton Raleigh (0395) 68628
16th C modernised cottage with inglenook fireplace and beams.
Bedrooms: 1 double, 2 twin
Bathrooms: 1 private, 1 public

Bed & breakfast
per night:	£min	£max
Single	15.00	18.00
Double	30.00	36.00

Parking for 4
Open April-October

OTTERY ST MARY
Devon
Map ref 1D2

Former wool town with modern light industry set in countryside on the River Otter. The Cromwellian commander, Fairfax, made his headquarters here briefly during the Civil War. The interesting church, dating from the 14th C, is built to cathedral plan.

Fluxton Farm Hotel ₳
Ottery St Mary EX11 1RJ
☎ (0404) 812818
Spacious hotel in former farmhouse in beautiful country setting. Comfortable en-suite bedrooms, 2 sitting rooms, and large gardens. Locally grown home-cooked food served in candlelit dining room. Log fires in season.
Bedrooms: 3 single, 3 double, 4 twin, 2 triple
Bathrooms: 10 private, 1 public

Bed & breakfast
per night:	£min	£max
Single	23.00	25.00
Double	46.00	50.00

Half board
per person:	£min	£max
Daily	29.00	32.00
Weekly	195.00	210.00

Evening meal 1850 (last orders 1800)
Parking for 20

Home Farm
Escott, Ottery St Mary EX11 1LU
☎ Honiton (0404) 850241
300-acre mixed farm. Comfortable old farmhouse with oak beams, in parkland setting, off B3176. 1 mile from A30, 6 miles from coast.
Bedrooms: 1 double, 1 family room
Bathrooms: 2 public

Bed & breakfast
per night:	£min	£max
Double	30.00	36.00

Parking for 2
Open April-September

Pitt Farm
Listed
Ottery St Mary EX11 1NL
☎ (0404) 812439
190-acre mixed farm. Thatched 16th C farmhouse offering country fare. On B3176, half a mile off A30 and within easy reach of all east Devon coastal resorts.
Bedrooms: 1 double, 1 twin, 2 triple
Bathrooms: 3 public

Continued ▶

WEST COUNTRY

OTTERY ST MARY
Continued

Bed & breakfast per night:	£min	£max
Single	14.00	17.00
Double	28.00	34.00

Half board per person:	£min	£max
Daily	21.50	25.00

Evening meal 1900 (last orders 1700)
Parking for 6
Cards accepted: Amex

PADSTOW
Cornwall
Map ref 1B2

Old town encircling its harbour on the Camel Estuary. The 15th C church has notable bench-ends. There are fine houses on North Quay and Raleigh's Court House on South Quay. Tall cliffs and golden sands along the coast and ferry to Rock. Famous 'Obby 'Oss Festival on May Day.

Trevorrick Farm
Listed HIGHLY COMMENDED

St Issey, Wadebridge PL27 7QH
☎ Rumford (0841) 540574
11-acre mixed farm. Delightful, comfortable farmhouse where quality and service come first. Located 1 mile from Padstow, overlooking Little Petherick Creek and the Camel Estuary.
Bedrooms: 2 double, 1 twin
Bathrooms: 2 public

Bed & breakfast per night:	£min	£max
Single	16.00	18.50
Double	32.00	37.00

Parking for 20

PAIGNTON
Devon
Map ref 1D2

Lively seaside resort with a pretty harbour on Torbay. Bronze Age and Saxon sites are occupied by the 15th C church, which has a Norman door and font. The beautiful Chantry Chapel was built by local landowners, the Kirkhams.
Tourist Information Centre
☎ *(0803) 558383*

Dainton Hotel & Restaurant
APPROVED

95 Dartmouth Road, Goodrington, Paignton TQ4 6NA
☎ (0803) 550067 & 525901
Fax (0803) 666339

Delightful old world Tudor-style hotel overlooking Torbay. 150 yards from beach and shops. All rooms en-suite. Winners of Torquay in Bloom. A warm welcome awaits you from the Richards family.
Bedrooms: 2 single, 5 double, 1 twin, 3 triple
Bathrooms: 11 private

Bed & breakfast per night:	£min	£max
Single	25.00	28.00
Double	44.00	50.00

Half board per person:	£min	£max
Daily	30.00	32.00
Weekly	195.00	210.00

Lunch available
Evening meal 1800 (last orders 2130)
Parking for 20
Cards accepted: Access, Visa, Switch

New Barn Farm and Angling Centre

Totnes Road, Paignton TQ4 7PT
☎ (0803) 553602
64-acre mixed farm. On the A385, midway between Paignton and Totnes, amid beautiful countryside with panoramic views. Coarse fishing and fun trout fishing.
Bedrooms: 1 double, 1 twin, 1 triple
Bathrooms: 1 private, 1 public

Bed & breakfast per night:	£min	£max
Single	14.00	14.00
Double	28.00	28.00

Parking for 4
Open April-September

PARRACOMBE
Devon
Map ref 1C1

Pretty village spreading over the slopes of a river valley on the western edge of Exmoor.

Fox and Goose Inn
APPROVED

Parracombe, Barnstaple EX31 4PE
☎ (059 83) 239
19th C country coaching inn next to Heddon River, set in Exmoor National Park in the quiet village of Parracombe. Good home-cooked food.
Bedrooms: 4 double, 1 twin

Bathrooms: 1 public, 5 private showers

Bed & breakfast per night:	£min	£max
Single	15.00	16.50
Double	30.00	33.00

Half board per person:	£min	£max
Daily	25.00	26.50
Weekly	140.00	160.00

Evening meal 1900 (last orders 2100)
Parking for 20
Cards accepted: Access, Visa

PELYNT
Cornwall
Map ref 1C2

Trenake Farm
COMMENDED

Pelynt, Looe PL13 2LT
☎ Lanreath (0503) 220216
286-acre mixed farm. 14th C farmhouse, 5 miles from Looe and 3 miles from Talland Bay beach.
Bedrooms: 1 single, 1 double, 1 triple
Bathrooms: 1 public

Bed & breakfast per night:	£min	£max
Single	13.50	14.50
Double	27.00	29.00

Parking for 6
Open April-October

PENDEEN
Cornwall
Map ref 1A3

Small village on the beautiful coast road from Land's End to St Ives. A romantic landscape of craggy inland cliffs covered with bracken shelving to a rocky shore. There are numerous prehistoric sites, disused tin mines, a mine museum at Geevor and a lighthouse at Pendeen.

Trewellard Manor Farm
COMMENDED

Pendeen, Penzance TR19 7SU
☎ Penzance (0736) 788526
300-acre dairy farm. Friendly and comfortable atmosphere, home cooking and seasonal open fires.
Bedrooms: 2 double, 1 twin
Bathrooms: 1 private, 1 public, 1 private shower

Bed & breakfast per night:	£min	£max
Single	15.00	
Double	32.00	

Parking for 2

292

WEST COUNTRY

PENSFORD
Avon
Map ref 2A2

Green Acres
Listed

Stanton Wick, Pensford BS18 4BX
☎ Mendip (0761) 490397
A friendly welcome awaits you in peaceful setting, off A37/A368. Relax and enjoy panoramic views across Chew Valley to Dundry Hills.
Bedrooms: 1 single, 1 double, 1 twin
Bathrooms: 4 public
Bed & breakfast
per night:	£min	£max
Single	16.00	20.00
Double	30.00	34.00

Parking for 21

PENTEWAN
Cornwall
Map ref 1B3

Tiny 19th C port with a pretty square, hidden from the main road, overlooked by a Regency terrace with luxuriant flower gardens and a Methodist chapel. Separated by the River Winnick from a broad, sandy beach.

Polrudden Farm
Listed

Pentewan, St Austell PL26 6BJ
☎ St Austell (0726) 843213
75-acre mixed farm. Modern farmhouse with fantastic views and walks, 3 miles from St Austell and 2 miles from Mevagissey. Peace and tranquillity.
Bedrooms: 1 double, 2 twin
Bathrooms: 2 public
Bed & breakfast
per night:	£min	£max
Double	25.00	30.00

Half board
per person:	£min	£max
Daily	15.00	20.00

Parking for 13

There are separate sections in this guide listing groups specialising in farm holidays and accommodation which is especially suitable for young people and organised groups.

PENZANCE
Cornwall
Map ref 1A3

Resort and fishing port on Mount's Bay with mainly Victorian promenade and some fine Regency terraces. Former prosperity came from tin trade and pilchard fishing. Grand Georgian style church by harbour. Georgian Egyptian building at head of Chapel Street and Morrab Gardens.
Tourist Information Centre
☎ (0736) 62207

Halcyon Guest House

6 Chyandour Square, Penzance TR18 3LW
☎ (0736) 66302
Granite Tudor-style house overlooking Mount's Bay and St Michael's Mount in a private road between town and beach. Private parking.
Bedrooms: 1 double, 1 twin, 1 triple, 1 family room
Bathrooms: 4 private
Bed & breakfast
per night:	£min	£max
Single	20.00	22.00
Double	34.00	38.00

Half board
per person:	£min	£max
Daily	24.50	26.50
Weekly	147.00	154.00

Evening meal 1830 (last orders 1830)
Parking for 4
Open March-October

Lynwood Guest House

41 Morrab Road, Penzance TR18 4EX
☎ (0736) 65871
Lynwood offers a warm welcome and is situated between promenade and town centre, close to all amenities.
Bedrooms: 1 single, 1 double, 2 twin, 2 triple
Bathrooms: 3 public
Bed & breakfast
per night:	£min	£max
Single	11.00	14.00
Double	22.00	28.00

Cards accepted: Access, Visa, Amex

Menwidden Farm
Listed **APPROVED**

Ludgvan, Penzance TR20 8BN
☎ (0736) 740415
40-acre dairy farm. Centrally situated in west Cornwall. Warm family atmosphere and home cooking. Turn right at Crowlas crossroads on the A30 from Hayle, signpost Vellanoweth on right turn. Last farm on left.
Bedrooms: 4 double, 1 triple, 1 family room

Bathrooms: 2 public
Bed & breakfast
per night:	£min	£max
Single	13.00	
Double	26.00	

Half board
per person:	£min	£max
Daily	18.00	
Weekly	120.00	

Evening meal 1800 (last orders 1800)
Parking for 8
Open February-November
Cards accepted: Amex

Penalva
APPROVED

Alexandra Road, Penzance TR18 4LZ
☎ (0736) 69060
Well positioned imposing Victorian hotel, near all amenities, offering full central heating, good food and service. Non-smokers only please.
Bedrooms: 1 single, 3 double, 1 twin
Bathrooms: 5 private
Bed & breakfast
per night:	£min	£max
Single	10.00	16.00
Double	20.00	32.00

Half board
per person:	£min	£max
Daily	18.00	24.00
Weekly	120.00	160.00

Evening meal 1830 (last orders 1900)

Tregoddick House
Listed

Madron, Penzance TR20 8SS
☎ (0736) 62643
Detached period house with walled gardens. Interior has some original fittings, granite fireplaces, etc. Located in attractive village close to West Penwith moors.
Bedrooms: 2 twin
Bathrooms: 2 private
Bed & breakfast
per night:	£min	£max
Single	16.00	17.50
Double	32.00	35.00

Parking for 2
Open January-November

Woodstock Guest House

29 Morrab Road, Penzance TR18 4AZ
☎ (0736) 69049
Well-appointed, centrally situated guesthouse. Helpful, friendly service. Tea-making facilities, radio, TV and hairdryer all inclusive.
Bedrooms: 1 single, 1 double, 1 twin, 2 triple
Bathrooms: 1 private, 2 public

Continued ▶

WEST COUNTRY

PENZANCE
Continued

Bed & breakfast per night:	£min	£max
Single	10.00	14.00
Double	20.00	35.00

Cards accepted: Access, Visa, Diners, Amex

PERRANUTHNOE
Cornwall
Map ref 1B3

Small village on Mount's Bay, with lovely cliff walks.

Ednovean Farm
COMMENDED

Perranuthnoe, Penzance TR20 9LZ
☎ Penzance (0736) 711883
30-acre mixed farm. 17th C barn with charming country-style bedrooms, nestling above Mount's Bay, close to secluded coves. Fresh flowers, flagstones.
Bedrooms: 2 double, 1 twin
Bathrooms: 2 private, 1 public, 1 private shower

Bed & breakfast per night:	£min	£max
Single	18.00	
Double	35.00	50.00

Half board per person:	£min	£max
Daily	25.00	35.00
Weekly	175.00	245.00

Lunch available
Evening meal 1800 (last orders 1900)
Parking for 4

PETER TAVY
Devon
Map ref 1C2

Churchtown
Listed

Peter Tavy, Tavistock PL19 9NN
☎ Mary Tavy (0822) 810477
Peaceful Victorian house in own grounds on edge of village. Beautiful moorland views. 5 minutes' walk to excellent pub food.
Bedrooms: 1 single, 2 double
Bathrooms: 2 public

Bed & breakfast per night:	£min	£max
Single	12.00	14.00
Double	24.00	28.00

Parking for 6

PIDDLETRENTHIDE
Dorset
Map ref 2B3

The Poachers Inn
COMMENDED

Piddletrenthide, Dorchester DT2 7QX
☎ (0300) 348358
Country inn with riverside garden, in beautiful Piddle Valley. Swimming pool. All rooms en-suite, colour TV, tea-making facilities, telephone. Residents' lounge. Brochure available.
Bedrooms: 8 double, 1 twin, 2 family rooms
Bathrooms: 11 private

Bed & breakfast per night:	£min	£max
Single	28.00	32.00
Double	42.00	50.00

Half board per person:	£min	£max
Daily	31.00	35.00
Weekly	195.00	220.00

Lunch available
Evening meal 1700 (last orders 2130)
Parking for 30
Cards accepted: Access, Visa

PLYMOUTH
Devon
Map ref 1C2

Devon's largest city, major port and naval base. Old houses on the Barbican and ambitious architecture in modern centre, with aquarium, museum and art gallery, the Dome - a new heritage centre on the Hoe. Superb coastal views over Plymouth Sound from the Hoe.

Tourist Information Centre
☎ *(0752) 264849*

Athenaeum Lodge
Listed COMMENDED

4 Athenaeum Street, The Hoe, Plymouth PL1 2RH
☎ (0752) 665005
Elegant Georgian Grade II listed guesthouse, close to the Hoe, historic Barbican, town centre and ferry port. Satellite TV in all rooms. Run by resident owners.
Bedrooms: 1 single, 2 double, 5 triple
Bathrooms: 3 private, 2 public, 1 private shower

Bed & breakfast per night:	£min	£max
Single	15.00	16.00
Double	26.00	33.00

Parking for 5

Bowling Green Hotel
HIGHLY COMMENDED

9-10 Osborne Place, Lockyer Street, Plymouth PL1 2PU
☎ (0752) 667485

Rebuilt Victorian property with views of Dartmoor. Overlooking Sir Francis Drake's bowling green on beautiful Plymouth Hoe. Centrally situated for the Barbican, Theatre Royal and leisure/conference centre.
Bedrooms: 1 single, 6 double, 2 twin, 3 triple
Bathrooms: 8 private, 4 private showers

Bed & breakfast per night:	£min	£max
Single	26.00	32.00
Double	34.00	42.00

Parking for 4
Cards accepted: Access, Visa, Diners, Amex

Gabber Farm
COMMENDED

Down Thomas, Plymouth PL9 0AW
☎ (0752) 862269
120-acre mixed & dairy farm. On the south Devon coast, near Bovisand and Wembury. Directions are provided. Friendly welcome assured. Special rates for OAPs.
Bedrooms: 1 double, 2 twin, 1 triple, 1 family room
Bathrooms: 2 private, 1 public

Bed & breakfast per night:	£min	£max
Single	14.00	16.00
Double	28.00	32.00

Half board per person:	£min	£max
Daily	22.00	24.00
Weekly	140.00	160.00

Evening meal 1900 (last orders 1800)
Parking for 4
Open March-November

Phantele Guest House
COMMENDED

176 Devonport Road, Stoke, Plymouth PL1 5RD
☎ (0752) 561506
Small family-run guesthouse about 2 miles from city centre. Convenient base for touring. Close to continental and Torpoint ferries.
Bedrooms: 2 single, 1 double, 1 twin, 2 triple
Bathrooms: 2 private, 2 public

294

WEST COUNTRY

Bed & breakfast per night:	£min	£max
Single	13.50	14.50
Double	25.00	32.00

Half board per person:	£min	£max
Daily	18.50	25.50
Weekly	120.00	132.00

Evening meal 1830 (last orders 1700)

POLZEATH
Cornwall
Map ref 1B2

Small resort on Padstow Bay and the widening Camel Estuary, with excellent sands and bathing. Pentire Head (National Trust), a notable viewpoint, lies to the north.

Pheasants Rise
Trebetherick, Polzeath, Wadebridge PL27 6SA
☎ Trebetherick (0208) 863190
Bungalow with superb country views. All rooms have TV, tea-maker. 5 minutes from Polzeath/Daymer Bay beaches. Excellent walks, surfing, golf-course.
Bedrooms: 1 double, 2 twin
Bathrooms: 2 private, 1 public, 1 private shower

Bed & breakfast per night:	£min	£max
Double	30.00	34.00

Parking for 6
Open March-October

PORTHLEVEN
Cornwall
Map ref 1B3

Old fishing port with handsome Victorian buildings overlooking Mount's Bay. An extensive, shingly beach reaches south-east towards the Loe Bar, where the pebbles make a lake on the landward side.

Harbour Inn ♠
COMMENDED
Commercial Road, Porthleven, Helston TR13 9JD
☎ Helston (0326) 573876
150-year-old inn on harbour edge. Restaurant open 7 days per week. Most bedrooms en-suite, many with harbour views.
Bedrooms: 1 single, 6 double, 2 twin, 1 family room
Bathrooms: 8 private, 1 public, 2 private showers

Bed & breakfast per night:	£min	£max
Single	33.50	33.50
Double	60.00	60.00

Half board per person:	£min	£max
Daily	45.00	45.00
Weekly	285.00	285.00

Lunch available
Evening meal 1830 (last orders 2130)
Parking for 10
Cards accepted: Access, Visa, Diners, Amex

PORTISHEAD
Avon
Map ref 2A2

The Poacher
106 High Street, Portishead, Bristol BS20 9AJ
☎ (0275) 844002
The Poacher is over 300 years old and is still dispensing fine food, ale and hospitality to this day.
Bedrooms: 1 single, 2 double
Bathrooms: 1 public

Bed & breakfast per night:	£min	£max
Single	15.00	

Lunch available
Evening meal 1830 (last orders 2100)
Parking for 40

PORTLAND
Dorset
Map ref 2B3

Joined by a narrow isthmus to the coast, a stony promontory sloping from the lofty landward side to a lighthouse on Portland Bill at its southern tip. Villages are built of the white limestone for which the "isle" is famous.

Alessandria Hotel and Italian Restaurant
APPROVED
71 Wakeham Easton, Portland, Weymouth DT5 1HW
☎ (0305) 822270 & 820108
Well-equipped hotel with comfortable bedrooms and a la carte Italian restaurant. All fresh food cooked to order by Giovanni himself. Warm, intimate and friendly Italian atmosphere.
Bedrooms: 4 single, 6 double, 4 twin, 2 family rooms
Bathrooms: 12 private, 3 public, 4 private showers

Bed & breakfast per night:	£min	£max
Single	20.00	30.00
Double	40.00	60.00

Half board per person:	£min	£max
Daily	30.00	40.00
Weekly	175.00	225.00

Lunch available
Evening meal 1900 (last orders 2200)
Parking for 17
Cards accepted: Access, Visa, Diners, Amex, Switch

6-20

PORTREATH
Cornwall
Map ref 1B3

Formerly developed as a mining port, small resort with some handsome 19th C buildings. Cliffs, sands and good surf.

Cliff House
Listed
The Square, Portreath, Redruth TR16 4LB
☎ Redruth (0209) 842008
200-year-old whitewashed cottage near the harbour, 2 minutes from the beach. Situated on the North Atlantic coast.
Bedrooms: 2 single, 1 double, 1 twin
Bathrooms: 2 public

Bed & breakfast per night:	£min	£max
Single	15.00	15.00
Double	30.00	30.00

Parking for 6

The Portreath Arms
APPROVED
Portreath, Redruth TR16 4LA
☎ Redruth (0209) 842259
Typical Cornish public house, originally a Victorian coaching inn, with letting rooms. Situated in a small coastal village with beach and harbour.
Bedrooms: 1 double, 6 twin
Bathrooms: 5 private, 1 public

Bed & breakfast per night:	£min	£max
Single	15.00	20.00
Double	30.00	35.00

Half board per person:	£min	£max
Daily	20.00	30.00
Weekly	140.00	210.00

Lunch available
Evening meal 1830 (last orders 2200)
Parking for 50

There are separate sections in this guide listing groups specialising in farm holidays and accommodation which is especially suitable for young people and organised groups.

WEST COUNTRY

POUNDSGATE
Devon
Map ref 1C2

Dartmoor village near the Dart Valley. River Dart Country Park is 2 miles to the south-east.

Leusdon Lodge Country House Hotel ⋈
COMMENDED
Poundsgate, Newton Abbot TQ13 7PE
☎ (036 43) 304 & 573
Fax (036 43) 599

Family run country house on Dartmoor. Delightful garden, splendid views. Local riding and fishing, short breaks, walking weekends.
Bedrooms: 1 double, 5 twin, 1 triple
Bathrooms: 7 private

Bed & breakfast
per night:	£min	£max
Double	47.00	78.00

Half board
per person:	£min	£max
Daily	38.50	54.00

Lunch available
Evening meal 1930 (last orders 1945)
Parking for 12
Cards accepted: Access, Visa, Diners, Amex

POWERSTOCK
Dorset
Map ref 2A3

Hilly village of mellow stone houses, overlooked by its church. Partly rebuilt in the 19th C, the church retains a fine Norman chancel arch, gargoyles and 15th C carvings in the south porch.

Oakleigh House
HIGHLY COMMENDED
Townsend, Powerstock, Bridport DT6 3TE
☎ (0308) 485126
Large country house with outstanding views. In the heart of a beautiful Dorset village, full of charm and character, 5 miles north-east of the market town of Bridport and the coastline.
Bedrooms: 1 double, 1 twin
Bathrooms: 2 private

Bed & breakfast
per night:	£min	£max
Single		26.00
Double		38.00

Parking for 4
Open February-November

Powerstock Mill
COMMENDED
Powerstock, Bridport DT6 3SL
☎ (030 885) 213
50-acre dairy farm. Comfortable old farmhouse nestling in a valley, in an Area of Outstanding Natural Beauty. Only 4 miles away from beautiful coastline. High tea and babysitting provided on request.
Bedrooms: 1 double, 1 twin
Bathrooms: 1 public

Bed & breakfast
per night:	£min	£max
Single	18.00	20.00
Double	36.00	40.00

Half board
per person:	£min	£max
Daily	25.00	30.00
Weekly	199.00	210.00

Evening meal 1800 (last orders 2000)
Parking for 7

PRIDDY
Somerset
Map ref 2A2

Village in the Mendips, formerly a lead-mining centre, with old inns dating from the mining era. The area is rich in Bronze Age remains, among them the Priddy nine barrows. There is a sheep fair in the village every August.

Highcroft
COMMENDED
Wells Road, Priddy, Wells BA5 3AU
☎ Wells (0749) 673446
A natural stone country house with large lawns. From Wells take A39 to Bristol for 3 miles, turn left to Priddy and Highcroft is on right after about 2 miles.
Bedrooms: 1 single, 1 double, 1 twin, 1 triple
Bathrooms: 2 private, 1 public

Bed & breakfast
per night:	£min	£max
Single	15.00	15.00
Double	30.00	34.00

Parking for 5

Map references apply to the colour maps at the back of this guide.

REDLYNCH
Wiltshire
Map ref 2B3

Templeman's Old Farmhouse
COMMENDED
Redlynch, Salisbury SP5 2JS
☎ Downton (0725) 20331
Gracious country house in its own peaceful rural setting with panoramic views. Spacious accommodation, no en-suite but ample facilities.
Bedrooms: 1 single, 1 double, 1 twin
Bathrooms: 1 public

Bed & breakfast
per night:	£min	£max
Single	17.00	19.00
Double	34.00	38.00

Parking for 12
Open April-October

Yew Tree Cottage
Listed
Grove Lane, Redlynch, Salisbury SP5 2NR
☎ Downton (0725) 21730 changing to 511730
Delightful spacious country cottage and smallholding (rare sheep and ducks), in New Forest heritage village, near Salisbury. Ideal southern touring centre. Non-smoking.
Bedrooms: 1 single, 1 double, 1 twin
Bathrooms: 1 public

Bed & breakfast
per night:	£min	£max
Single	16.00	18.00
Double	32.00	36.00

Parking for 6

ROADWATER
Somerset
Map ref 1D1

Glasses Farm
Roadwater, Watchet TA23 0QH
☎ Washford (0984) 40552
220-acre arable & dairy farm. Thatched 16th C farmhouse near the Brendon Hills. Ideal for walking, riding, quiet holidays looking at local beauty spots. Closed at Christmas.
Bedrooms: 1 double, 2 twin
Bathrooms: 2 public

Bed & breakfast
per night:	£min	£max
Single	16.50	

Parking for 6
Open February-November

WEST COUNTRY

RODE
Somerset
Map ref 2B2

Irondale House
67 High Street, Rode BA3 6PB
☎ Frome (0373) 830730
Large and comfortable private house. Easy for sightseeing visits to Bath, Wells, Longleat. High standard of cooking. Fresh food used.
Bedrooms: 2 twin
Bathrooms: 2 private

Bed & breakfast
per night:	£min	£max
Single	24.00	30.00
Double	38.00	40.00

Half board
per person:	£min	£max
Daily	37.00	41.00
Weekly	259.00	

Parking for 1

ST AGNES
Cornwall
Map ref 1B3

Small town in a once-rich mining area on the north coast. Terraced cottages and granite houses slope to the church. Some old mine workings remain, but the attraction must be the magnificent coastal scenery and superb walks. St Agnes Beacon offers one of Cornwall's most extensive views.

Penkerris ♨
Penwinnick Road, St Agnes TR5 0PA
☎ (0872) 552262

Enchanting Edwardian residence with own grounds in unspoilt Cornish village. Beautiful rooms, log fires in winter, good home cooking. Dramatic cliff walks and beaches nearby.
Bedrooms: 1 single, 2 double, 2 twin, 2 triple
Bathrooms: 2 private, 3 public

Bed & breakfast
per night:	£min	£max
Single	12.50	20.00
Double	25.00	35.00

Half board
per person:	£min	£max
Daily	20.00	25.00
Weekly	125.00	155.00

Lunch available
Evening meal from 1830
Parking for 8
Cards accepted: Access, Visa

ST AUSTELL
Cornwall
Map ref 1B3

Cornwall's china-clay town, on a slope between the clay district's spoil-cones and the clay ports and bathing beaches on St Austell Bay. The traffic-free centre has a fine church of Pentewan stone and an Italianate Town and Market Hall, still a busy market-place.

Poltarrow Farm
HIGHLY COMMENDED
St Mewan, St Austell PL26 7DR
☎ (0726) 67111
45-acre mixed farm. Delightful farmhouse set in peaceful countryside, central for discovering Cornwall. Traditional farm cooking with comfortable surroundings. Half-a-mile St Austell - Truro A390, turn right at St Mewan school. Entrance on left.
Bedrooms: 2 double, 1 twin
Bathrooms: 3 private

Bed & breakfast
per night:	£min	£max
Single	18.00	20.00
Double	32.00	36.00

Half board
per person:	£min	£max
Daily	25.00	27.00
Weekly	175.00	189.00

Evening meal from 1830
Parking for 5
Cards accepted: Access, Visa

ST DOMINICK
Cornwall
Map ref 1C2

Burcombe Farm
APPROVED
St Dominick, Saltash PL12 6SH
☎ Liskeard (0579) 50217
170-acre arable and mixed farm. Farm dates back to 1722.
Bedrooms: 1 double, 2 twin
Bathrooms: 2 private, 1 public

Bed & breakfast
per night:	£min	£max
Single	18.50	21.00
Double	37.00	42.00

Parking for 5

We advise you to confirm your booking in writing.

ST IVES
Cornwall
Map ref 1B3

Old fishing port, artists' colony and holiday town with good surfing beach. Fishermen's cottages, granite fish cellars, a sandy harbour and magnificent headlands typify a charm that has survived since the 19th C pilchard boom. Tate Gallery opened in 1993.
Tourist Information Centre
☎ *(0736) 796297*

Seagulls Guest House
4 Godrevy Terrace, St Ives TR26 1JA
☎ Penzance (0736) 797273
Panoramic sea views overlooking island and beaches. Superior rooms with private facilities. Reputation for comfort and hospitality. Free private parking.
Bedrooms: 1 single, 3 double, 1 triple
Bathrooms: 3 private, 1 public, 1 private shower

Bed & breakfast
per night:	£min	£max
Single	10.00	19.50
Double	20.00	39.00

Parking for 10

ST KEW
Cornwall
Map ref 1B2

Old village sheltered by trees standing beside a stream. The church is noted for its medieval glass showing the Passion and the remains of a scene of the Tree of Jesse.

Tregellist Farm
COMMENDED
Tregellist, St Kew, Bodmin PL30 3HG
☎ Bodmin (0208) 880537
125-acre mixed farm. Farmhouse, built in 1989, offering old-fashioned hospitality. Set in tiny hamlet with lovely views and pleasant walks. Central for coast and moors. Children welcome. 1.5 miles from A39.
Bedrooms: 1 double, 1 twin, 1 triple
Bathrooms: 3 private, 1 public

Bed & breakfast
per night:	£min	£max
Single	16.00	18.00

Half board
per person:	£min	£max
Daily	24.00	26.00

Evening meal from 1800
Parking for 6
Open February-October

WEST COUNTRY

ST MAWGAN
Cornwall
Map ref 1B2

Pretty village on wooded slopes in the Vale of Lanherne. At its centre, an old stone bridge is overlooked by the church with its lofty buttressed tower. Among the ancient stone crosses in the churchyard is a 15th C lantern cross with carved figures.

The Falcon Inn
Listed COMMENDED
St Mawgan, Newquay TR8 4EP
☎ Newquay (0637) 860225
16th C wisteria-covered inn with beautiful gardens in the vale of Lanherne. Unspoilt peaceful situation.
Bedrooms: 2 double, 1 twin
Bathrooms: 2 private, 1 public

Bed & breakfast
per night:	£min	£max
Single	15.00	25.00
Double	34.00	42.00

Lunch available
Evening meal 1830 (last orders 2200)
Parking for 25
Cards accepted: Access, Visa

SALCOMBE
Devon
Map ref 1C3

Sheltered yachting resort of whitewashed houses and narrow streets in a balmy setting on the Salcombe Estuary. Palm, myrtle and other Mediterranean plants flourish. There are sandy bays and creeks for boating.

Torre View Hotel
COMMENDED
Devon Road, Salcombe TQ8 8HJ
☎ (0548) 842633
Large detached residence with every modern comfort, commanding extensive views of the estuary and surrounding countryside.
Bedrooms: 4 double, 2 twin, 2 triple
Bathrooms: 8 private

Bed & breakfast
per night:	£min	£max
Single	23.00	28.00
Double	44.00	52.00

Half board
per person:	£min	£max
Daily	32.50	36.50
Weekly	210.00	239.00

Evening meal 1900 (last orders 1800)
Parking for 5
Open February-October
Cards accepted: Access, Visa

SALISBURY
Wiltshire
Map ref 2B3

Beautiful city and ancient regional capital set amid water meadows. Buildings of all periods are dominated by the cathedral whose spire is the tallest in England. Built between 1220 and 1258, it is one of the purest examples of Early English architecture.
Tourist Information Centre
☎ *(0722) 334956*

Avon Lodge Guest House
28 Castle Road, Salisbury SP1 3RJ
☎ (0722) 331359
Victorian house offering a warm welcome and pleasant homely atmosphere. City centre a few minutes' walk. Ideal base for touring the south. A non-smoking establishment.
Bedrooms: 1 double, 1 twin, 1 triple
Bathrooms: 1 public

Bed & breakfast
per night:	£min	£max
Single	20.00	25.00
Double	32.00	36.00

Parking for 3

The Bell Inn
Warminster Road, South Newton, Salisbury SP2 0QD
☎ (0722) 743336
300-year-old roadside inn offering full en-suite facilities. Extensive range of bar meals. 6 miles north west of Salisbury.
Bedrooms: 1 single, 1 double, 1 twin
Bathrooms: 3 private

Bed & breakfast
per night:	£min	£max
Single	18.00	
Double	30.00	34.00

Lunch available
Evening meal 1900 (last orders 2100)
Parking for 60

Beulah
Listed
144 Britford Lane, Salisbury SP2 8AL
☎ (0722) 333517
Bungalow in quiet road 1.25 miles from city centre, overlooking meadows. Evening meal served on request. No-smoking establishment.
Bedrooms: 1 single, 1 family room
Bathrooms: 1 public

Bed & breakfast
per night:	£min	£max
Single	14.50	16.00
Double	29.00	32.00

Half board
per person:	£min	£max
Daily	21.00	22.50

Evening meal 1800 (last orders 1600)
Parking for 4

Byways House
31 Fowlers Road, Salisbury SP1 2QP
☎ (0722) 328364
Fax (0722) 322146
Attractive family-run Victorian house close to cathedral in quiet area of city centre. Car park. Bedrooms en-suite with colour TV. Traditional English and vegetarian breakfasts.
Bedrooms: 4 single, 8 double, 8 twin, 2 triple, 1 family room
Bathrooms: 19 private, 1 public

Bed & breakfast
per night:	£min	£max
Single	20.00	28.00
Double	35.00	44.00

Parking for 15
Cards accepted: Access, Visa

Castlewood
45 Castle Road, Salisbury SP1 3RH
☎ (0722) 421494 & 324809
Large Edwardian house, tastefully restored throughout. Pleasant 10 minutes' riverside walk to city centre and cathedral.
Bedrooms: 1 single, 1 double, 1 twin, 1 family room
Bathrooms: 2 private, 1 public

Bed & breakfast
per night:	£min	£max
Single	18.00	20.00
Double	28.00	35.00

Parking for 4

Cranston Guest House
5 Wain-a-Long Road, Salisbury SP1 1LJ
☎ (0722) 336776
Large detached town house covered in Virginia creeper. 10 minutes' walk from town centre and cathedral.
Bedrooms: 1 single, 2 double, 1 twin, 1 family room
Bathrooms: 4 private, 1 public

Bed & breakfast
per night:	£min	£max
Single	16.00	17.00
Double	32.00	34.00

Evening meal 1800 (last orders 1900)
Parking for 4

The Gallery
Listed COMMENDED
36 Wyndham Road, Salisbury SP1 3AB
☎ (0722) 324586
A warm welcome awaits you at The Gallery, situated within easy walking distance of cathedral, museum and shopping centre. A non-smoking establishment.
Bedrooms: 1 double, 2 twin
Bathrooms: 3 private

WEST COUNTRY

Bed & breakfast per night:	£min	£max
Double	28.00	34.00

Hayburn Wyke Guest House

72 Castle Road, Salisbury SP1 3RL
☎ (0722) 412627
Family-run spacious guesthouse adjacent to Victoria Park. Short walk from the cathedral and city centre and Old Sarum. Stonehenge 9 miles.
Bedrooms: 2 double, 2 twin, 2 triple
Bathrooms: 2 private, 1 public

Bed & breakfast per night:	£min	£max
Single	21.00	34.00
Double	32.00	38.00

Parking for 6

Kelebrae

101 Castle Road, Salisbury SP1 3RP
☎ (0722) 333628
A family home, opposite Victoria Park within walking distance of city centre. Convenient for Stonehenge. Parking.
Bedrooms: 2 double, 1 twin
Bathrooms: 1 private, 1 public

Bed & breakfast per night:	£min	£max
Double	30.00	32.00

Parking for 4

Leena's Guest House

50 Castle Road, Salisbury SP1 3RL
☎ (0722) 335419
Attractive Edwardian house with friendly atmosphere, close to riverside walks and park. Modern facilities include en-suite and ground-floor rooms.
Bedrooms: 1 single, 2 double, 2 twin, 1 family room
Bathrooms: 3 private, 1 public, 1 private shower

Bed & breakfast per night:	£min	£max
Single	17.00	19.00
Double	28.00	36.00

Parking for 7

Newton Cottage

South Newton, Salisbury SP2 0QW
☎ (0722) 743111
Typically English thatched cottage with inglenook, built in 1679. Offering hospitality and personal attention. Chalk stream fly fishing tuition by prior arrangement. Easy for Wilton House, Stourhead and Bath.
Bedrooms: 2 double, 1 twin
Bathrooms: 2 public

Bed & breakfast per night:	£min	£max
Single	14.00	15.00
Double	29.00	31.00

Parking for 4

The Old Bakery

35 Bedwin Street, Salisbury SP1 3UT
☎ (0722) 320100
15th C house of charm and character, conveniently situated in one of the oldest parts of the city centre.
Bedrooms: 1 single, 1 double, 1 twin
Bathrooms: 2 private, 1 public

Bed & breakfast per night:	£min	£max
Single	15.00	20.00
Double	30.00	40.00

Richburn Guest House

APPROVED

23 & 25 Estcourt Road, Salisbury SP1 3AP
☎ (0722) 325189
Large, tastefully renovated Victorian house with homely family atmosphere. All modern amenities and large car park. Close to city centre and parks.
Bedrooms: 1 single, 5 double, 2 twin, 1 triple, 1 family room
Bathrooms: 2 private, 2 public

Bed & breakfast per night:	£min	£max
Single	16.50	17.00
Double	27.00	36.00

Parking for 10

Swaynes Firs Farm

APPROVED

Grimsdyke, Coombe Bissett, Salisbury SP5 5RF
☎ Martin Cross (072 589) 240
15-acre mixed farm. Country farmhouse in pleasant position with good views. Ancient Roman ditch on farm. Peacocks, ducks, chickens and horses are reared on the farm.
Bedrooms: 2 twin, 1 family room
Bathrooms: 3 private

Bed & breakfast per night:	£min	£max
Single	15.00	18.00
Double	30.00	36.00

Parking for 9

SALISBURY PLAIN

See under Amesbury, Figheldean, Market Lavington, Salisbury, Shrewton, Winterbourne Stoke

Please mention this guide when making a booking.

SEATON

Devon
Map ref 1D2

Small resort lying near the mouth of the River Axe. A mile-long beach extends to the dramatic cliffs of Beer Head. Annual arts and drama festival.
Tourist Information Centre
☎ (0297) 21660

Beaumont

Castle Hill, Seaton EX12 2QW
☎ (0297) 20832
Attractive and spacious guesthouse in select seafront position, offering en-suite comfort, personal attention and traditional home cooking.
Bedrooms: 1 double, 2 triple, 2 family rooms
Bathrooms: 5 private

Bed & breakfast per night:	£min	£max
Single	16.00	18.00
Double	32.00	36.00

Half board per person:	£min	£max
Daily	25.00	27.00
Weekly	160.00	175.00

Evening meal 1900 (last orders 1900)
Parking for 6
Open January-October, December

SHALDON

Devon
Map ref 1D2

Pretty resort facing Teignmouth from the south bank of the Teign Estuary. Regency houses harmonise with others of later periods; there are old cottages and narrow lanes. On the Ness, a sandstone promontory nearby, a tunnel built in the 19th C leads to a beach revealed at low tide.

Fonthill

HIGHLY COMMENDED

Torquay Road, Shaldon, Teignmouth TQ14 0AX
☎ (0626) 872344
Fax (0626) 872344

Lovely Georgian family home in superb grounds overlooking River Teign. Very comfortable rooms in a peaceful setting. Restaurants nearby.
Bedrooms: 3 twin

Continued ▶

299

WEST COUNTRY

SHALDON
Continued

Bathrooms: 1 private, 1 public
Bed & breakfast

per night:	£min	£max
Single	25.00	28.00
Double	37.00	44.00

Parking for 5
Open February-December

SHEPTON MALLET
Somerset
Map ref 2A2

Important, stone-built market town beneath the south-west slopes of the Mendips. Thriving rural industries include glove and shoe making, dairying and cider making; the remains of a medieval "shambles" in the square date from the town's prosperity as a wool centre.

Hurlingpot Farm
COMMENDED

Chelynch, Doulting, Shepton Mallet BA4 4PY
☎ (0749) 880256
Lovely old farmhouse in an open country setting, 2 miles from Shepton Mallet. A361 Chelynch road turn left just past Poachers Pocket Pub. 16 miles from Bath and Bristol, 8 miles from Wells.
Bedrooms: 1 double, 1 twin, 1 triple
Bathrooms: 3 private
Bed & breakfast

per night:	£min	£max
Single	20.00	25.00
Double		35.00

Parking for 6

SHERBORNE
Dorset
Map ref 2B3

Historic town of Ham stone, a business and market centre for a wide area and a developing cultural centre with a range of activities. The home of Dorset Opera. In Anglo-Saxon times it was a cathedral city and until the Dissolution there was a monastery here.
Tourist Information Centre
☎ (0935) 815181

Quinns
HIGHLY COMMENDED

Marston Road, Sherborne DT9 4BL
☎ (0935) 815008
Delightful accommodation in modern house. All rooms en-suite, TV, tea/coffee making facilities. Spacious lounge. Dinners by arrangement. Car park.

Bedrooms: 1 single, 1 double, 1 twin
Bathrooms: 3 private
Bed & breakfast

per night:	£min	£max
Single	21.00	25.00
Double	42.00	50.00

Half board

per person:	£min	£max
Daily	34.50	38.50

Evening meal from 1900
Parking for 4

SHIRWELL
Devon
Map ref 1C1

The Spinney
COMMENDED

Shirwell, Barnstaple EX31 4JR
☎ (0271) 850282
Regency former rectory with spacious accommodation, set in over an acre of grounds with views of Exmoor. Meals made from local market-day produce.
Bedrooms: 1 single, 1 double, 1 twin, 2 triple
Bathrooms: 1 private, 2 public
Bed & breakfast

per night:	£min	£max
Single	16.00	20.00
Double	32.00	40.00

Half board

per person:	£min	£max
Daily	23.00	27.00
Weekly	132.00	160.00

Evening meal 1900 (last orders 1730)
Parking for 7

SHREWTON
Wiltshire
Map ref 2B2

Maddington House
Listed APPROVED

Shrewton, Salisbury SP3 4JD
☎ (0980) 620406
Beautiful listed 17th C family home, with attractive period hall and dining room. Stonehenge 2 miles and Salisbury 9 miles.
Bedrooms: 1 double, 1 twin, 1 family room
Bathrooms: 1 public, 3 private showers
Bed & breakfast

per night:	£min	£max
Single	17.00	19.50
Double	30.00	34.00

Parking for 7

We advise you to confirm your booking in writing.

SIDMOUTH
Devon
Map ref 1D2

Charming resort set amid lofty red cliffs where the River Sid meets the sea. The wealth of ornate Regency and Victorian villas recalls the time when this was one of the south coast's most exclusive resorts. Museum; August International Festival of Folk Arts.
Tourist Information Centre
☎ (0395) 516441

Broad Oak
HIGHLY COMMENDED

Sid Road, Sidmouth EX10 8QP
☎ (0395) 513713

Listed Victorian villa in delightful gardens overlooking "The Byes". A peaceful location, only a short stroll from the town centre and Esplanade.
Bedrooms: 1 single, 1 double, 1 twin
Bathrooms: 2 private, 1 public
Bed & breakfast

per night:	£min	£max
Single	18.00	18.00
Double	44.00	48.00

Parking for 4
Open February-November

Ferndale
COMMENDED

92 Winslade Road, Sidmouth EX10 9EZ
☎ (0395) 515495
Quiet, comfortable, well-modernised Victorian property offering spacious, well-equipped accommodation. Within easy reach of seafront and town centre.
Bedrooms: 1 double, 2 twin
Bathrooms: 1 private, 1 public
Bed & breakfast

per night:	£min	£max
Single	16.00	19.00
Double	30.00	36.00

Open March-November

Lower Pinn Farm

Pinn, Sidmouth EX10 0NN
☎ (0395) 513733
220-acre mixed farm. Situated in an Area of Outstanding Natural Beauty, 2 miles west of unspoilt coastal resort of Sidmouth. Comfortable, spacious rooms.
Bedrooms: 2 double, 1 twin
Bathrooms: 2 private, 1 public

WEST COUNTRY

Bed & breakfast per night:	£min	£max
Double	35.00	38.00

Parking for 3
Open April-November

Lynstead

Vicarage Road, Sidmouth EX10 8UQ
☎ (0395) 514635
Small, comfortable guesthouse on level near shops, sea and all amenities, bordering National Trust parkland. Non-smoking lounge and dining room.
Bedrooms: 1 single, 1 double, 1 twin, 1 triple, 1 family room
Bathrooms: 2 private, 2 public

Bed & breakfast per night:	£min	£max
Single	15.00	17.00
Double	30.00	34.00

Parking for 6

Pinn Barton Farm
COMMENDED

Peak Hill, Pinn Lane, Sidmouth EX10 0NN
☎ (0395) 514004
330-acre mixed farm. Two miles from seafront in an Area of Outstanding Natural Beauty. A friendly welcome in comfortable surroundings awaits guests. Closed at Christmas.
Bedrooms: 1 double, 1 twin, 1 triple
Bathrooms: 3 private

Bed & breakfast per night:	£min	£max
Single	25.00	
Double	36.00	38.00

Parking for 4

SIMONSBATH

Somerset
Map ref 1C1

Village beside the beautiful River Barle, deep in Exmoor. From the Middle Ages until the 19th C this was stag-hunting country.

Emmetts Grange Farm Guest House
COMMENDED

Simonsbath, Minehead TA24 7LD
☎ Exford (064 383) 282
1200-acre livestock farm. 16th century country house on a large moorland farm, in a lovely, quiet position 2.5 miles out of Simonsbath on the South Molton road.
Bedrooms: 1 single, 1 double, 2 twin
Bathrooms: 2 private, 1 public

Bed & breakfast per night:	£min	£max
Single	20.00	23.00
Double	40.00	46.00

Evening meal 2000 (last orders 1800)
Parking for 6
Open March-October

SLAPTON

Devon
Map ref 1D3

Start House
COMMENDED

Start, Slapton, Kingsbridge TQ7 2QD
☎ Kingsbridge (0548) 580254
Situated in quiet hamlet, 1 mile from Slapton. Comfortable house overlooking beautiful valley. Large garden. Ideal for wildlife and walking.
Bedrooms: 1 single, 2 double, 1 twin
Bathrooms: 2 private, 1 public

Bed & breakfast per night:	£min	£max
Single	15.00	17.00
Double	33.00	37.00

Half board per person:	£min	£max
Daily	27.00	29.00
Weekly	173.00	183.00

Evening meal 1830 (last orders 1000)
Parking for 4
Open January-November

SOUTH MOLTON

Devon
Map ref 1C1

Busy market town at the mouth of the Yeo Valley near southern Exmoor. Wool, mining and coaching brought prosperity between the Middle Ages and the 19th C and the fine square with Georgian buildings, a Guildhall and Assembly Rooms reflect this former affluence.

Huxtable Farm
COMMENDED

West Buckland, Barnstaple EX32 0SR
☎ Filleigh (0598) 760254
Fax (0598) 760254
80-acre livestock farm. Medieval longhouse and barn carefully restored and furnished with antiques. Four-course candlelit dinners with farm/local produce, including complimentary home-made wine and bread rolls. Games room and sauna. Log fire in winter.
Bedrooms: 1 single, 2 double, 1 twin, 2 triple
Bathrooms: 4 private, 1 public, 1 private shower

Bed & breakfast per night:	£min	£max
Single	22.00	25.00
Double	44.00	44.00

Half board per person:	£min	£max
Daily	34.00	34.00
Weekly	223.00	238.00

Evening meal 1930 (last orders 1730)
Parking for 8

Kerscott Farm
COMMENDED

Bishop's Nympton, South Molton EX36 4QG
☎ Bishop's Nympton (0769) 550262
40-acre mixed farm. 16th C heavily beamed farmhouse mentioned in Domesday Book. Idyllic, peaceful, rural location. Breathtaking views of Exmoor. Interesting interior and antiques. Good country cooking, bread, preserves. Varied breakfasts. Non-smokers only please.
Bedrooms: 2 double, 1 twin
Bathrooms: 1 private, 1 public

Bed & breakfast per night:	£min	£max
Double	26.00	29.00

Half board per person:	£min	£max
Daily	19.50	21.50
Weekly		133.00

Evening meal 1830 (last orders 1400)
Parking for 8
Open March-October

The White House
COMMENDED

Bottreaux Mill, South Molton EX36 3PT
☎ Anstey Mills (039 84) 331
Detached house on B3227, 7 miles east of South Molton, with panoramic views over Exmoor. Warm welcome and personal attention. Comfortable accommodation, log fires, garden produce used.
Bedrooms: 1 double, 1 twin
Bathrooms: 2 private

Bed & breakfast per night:	£min	£max
Single	15.00	18.00
Double	28.00	36.00

Half board per person:	£min	£max
Daily	20.00	24.00
Weekly	112.00	135.00

Evening meal from 1900
Parking for 3
Open April-October

STATHE

Somerset
Map ref 1D1

Black Smock Inn
Listed APPROVED

Langport Road, Stathe, Bridgwater TA7 0JN
☎ Burrowbridge (0823) 698352
Traditional moorland inn 3 miles west of Langport. High standard

Continued ▶

301

WEST COUNTRY

STATHE
Continued

accommodation. Panoramic views over Somerset Levels. Fishing, hiking, bird watching.
Bedrooms: 4 twin
Bathrooms: 2 private, 1 public

Bed & breakfast
per night:	£min	£max
Single	15.50	17.50
Double	31.00	35.00

Lunch available
Evening meal 1900 (last orders 2200)
Parking for 40

STAWELL
Somerset
Map ref 1D1

The Grange
Listed   HIGHLY COMMENDED
Stawell, Bridgwater TA7 9AF
☎ Chilton Polden (0278) 722452
Lovely old house on south side of Polden Hills, 10 minutes from exit 23 on M5.
Bedrooms: 3 double
Bathrooms: 1 private, 1 public

Bed & breakfast
per night:	£min	£max
Double	29.00	32.00

Parking for 3

STOKE ST GREGORY
Somerset
Map ref 1D1

Parsonage Farm
Listed
Stoke St Gregory, Taunton TA3 6ET
☎ Burrowbridge (0823) 698205
120-acre dairy farm. Large Georgian farmhouse and garden on ridge overlooking the Somerset Levels. Lovely views, good base for touring. Well-stocked coarse fishing half a mile away.
Bedrooms: 2 twin, 1 family room
Bathrooms: 1 public

Bed & breakfast
per night:	£min	£max
Single	15.00	17.50
Double	30.00	35.00

Parking for 8

National Crown ratings were correct at the time of going to press but are subject to change. Please check at the time of booking.

SWINDON
Wiltshire
Map ref 2B2

Wiltshire's industrial and commercial centre, an important railway town in the 19th C, situated just north of the Marlborough Downs. The railway village created in the mid-19th C has been preserved. Railway museum, art gallery, theatre and leisure centre.
Tourist Information Centre
☎ (0793) 530328

L'Hotel Du Nord ♏
100 County Road, Swindon SN1 2EP
☎ (0793) 491120
Small, privately-owned hotel, centrally situated, offering comfortable accommodation in a friendly atmosphere.
Bedrooms: 1 single, 1 double, 1 twin
Bathrooms: 2 private, 1 public

Bed & breakfast
per night:	£min	£max
Single	17.00	25.00
Double	32.00	38.00

Half board
per person:	£min	£max
Daily	25.50	33.50

Evening meal 1800 (last orders 2030)
Parking for 4
Cards accepted: Access, Visa

Internos
3 Turnpike Road, Blunsdon, Swindon SN2 4EA
☎ (0793) 721496
Detached red brick house off A419, 4 miles north of Swindon and 6 miles from M4 junction 15.
Bedrooms: 1 single, 1 twin, 1 triple
Bathrooms: 2 public

Bed & breakfast
per night:	£min	£max
Single	19.00	23.00
Double	32.00	32.00

Parking for 6

The Live and Let Live
COMMENDED
Upper Pavenhill, Purton, Swindon SN5 9DQ
☎ (0793) 770627
Converted stable, 5 miles west of Swindon, north of M4 (junction 16) and Wootton Bassett. At Londis shop turn into Pavenhill. Proceed for half a mile to right turning - Upper Pavenhill. House is 200 yards on left. Non-smokers preferred.
Bedrooms: 1 twin, 1 triple
Bathrooms: 1 public

Bed & breakfast
per night:	£min	£max
Single		18.00
Double		35.00

Parking for 3

Relian Guest House
151-153 County Road, Swindon SN1 2EB
☎ (0793) 521416
Quiet house adjacent to Swindon Town Football Club and near town centre. Close to bus and rail stations. Free car parking.
Bedrooms: 4 single, 2 double, 2 twin
Bathrooms: 3 private, 2 public, 3 private showers

Bed & breakfast
per night:	£min	£max
Single	20.00	25.00

Parking for 7

SYDLING ST NICHOLAS
Dorset
Map ref 2B3

Magiston Farm
Listed
Sydling St Nicholas DT2 9NR
☎ Maiden Newton (0300) 320295
400-acre arable farm. 350-year-old farmhouse, set beside the Sydling River in the heart of Dorset's peaceful countryside. 5 miles north of Dorchester.
Bedrooms: 2 single, 1 double, 2 twin
Bathrooms: 1 private, 1 public

Bed & breakfast
per night:	£min	£max
Single	14.50	15.50
Double	29.00	31.00

Half board
per person:	£min	£max
Daily	24.00	25.50
Weekly	168.00	178.00

Evening meal from 1900
Parking for 10

There are separate sections in this guide listing groups specialising in farm holidays and accommodation which is especially suitable for young people and organised groups.

WEST COUNTRY

TAUNTON
Somerset
Map ref 1D1

County town, well-known for its public schools, sheltered by gentle hill-ranges on the River Tone. Medieval prosperity from wool has continued in marketing and manufacturing and the town retains many fine period buildings.
Tourist Information Centre
☎ *(0823) 274785*

Higher Dipford Farm
COMMENDED

Dipford, Trull, Taunton TA3 7NU
☎ (0823) 275770

120-acre dairy farm. Old Somerset longhouse with inglenook fireplaces. Real farmhouse fare using own produce from the dairy. Fresh salmon a speciality. Friendly atmosphere.
Bedrooms: 1 double, 2 twin
Bathrooms: 3 private

Bed & breakfast
per night:	£min	£max
Single	27.00	30.00
Double	46.00	50.00

Half board
per person:	£min	£max
Daily	40.00	45.00
Weekly	238.00	269.00

Lunch available
Evening meal 1900 (last orders 2130)
Parking for 6
Open January, March-December
Cards accepted: Amex

Prockters Farm

West Monkton, Taunton TA2 8QN
☎ West Monkton (0823) 412269
300-acre mixed farm. 300-year-old farmhouse, 3 miles from M5. Inglenook fireplaces, brass beds, collection of farm antiques. Large garden. Tea and cake on arrival.
Bedrooms: 3 double, 2 twin
Bathrooms: 2 private, 3 public

Bed & breakfast
per night:	£min	£max
Single	20.00	25.00
Double	32.00	42.00

Parking for 6
Cards accepted: Amex

Strawbridges Farm Guest House
HIGHLY COMMENDED

Strawbridges Farm, Churchstanton, Taunton TA3 7DP
☎ Churchstanton (0823) 60591
Former farm set in peaceful Blackdown Hills, 6 miles Taunton and M5. Excellent facilities with good home cooking. Ideal for touring.
Bedrooms: 1 single, 2 double, 2 twin
Bathrooms: 2 private, 1 public

Bed & breakfast
per night:	£min	£max
Single	15.00	24.00
Double	32.00	40.00

Half board
per person:	£min	£max
Daily	26.50	31.50
Weekly	179.50	215.50

Evening meal 1900 (last orders 1900)
Parking for 10

TAVISTOCK
Devon
Map ref 1C2

Old market town beside the River Tavy on the western edge of Dartmoor. Developed around its 10th C abbey, of which some fragments remain, it became a stannary town in 1305 when tin-streaming thrived on the moors. Tavistock Goose Fair, October.

April Cottage
HIGHLY COMMENDED

Mount Tavy Road, Tavistock PL19 9JB
☎ (0822) 613280
Lovely Victorian riverside character cottage in beautiful setting. Dining room overlooks river. 150 metres from town centre. Modern comforts include en-suite. Homely and welcoming.
Bedrooms: 2 double, 1 twin
Bathrooms: 1 private, 1 public

Bed & breakfast
per night:	£min	£max
Single	14.50	16.00
Double	25.00	32.00

Parking for 4

Wringworthy Farm
Listed

Mary Tavy, Tavistock PL19 9LT
☎ Mary Tavy (0822) 810431
120-acre livestock farm. Elizabethan farmhouse with modern comforts, in quiet valley near the moors. Within easy reach of sea and well placed for touring.
Bedrooms: 1 double, 1 twin, 1 triple
Bathrooms: 2 public

Bed & breakfast
per night:	£min	£max
Single	15.00	16.00
Double	30.00	32.00

Parking for 3
Open February-November

TINTAGEL
Cornwall
Map ref 1B2

Coastal village near the legendary home of King Arthur. There is a lofty headland with the ruin of a Norman castle and traces of a Celtic monastery are still visible in the turf.

Castle Villa
COMMENDED

Molesworth Street, Tintagel PL34 0BZ
☎ Camelford (0840) 770373 & 770203
Over 150 years old, Castle Villa is within easy walking distance of the 11th C church, post office and King Arthur's castle.
Bedrooms: 1 single, 3 double, 1 twin
Bathrooms: 1 private, 2 public

Bed & breakfast
per night:	£min	£max
Single	13.50	15.50
Double	27.00	36.00

Half board
per person:	£min	£max
Daily	23.50	26.50
Weekly	148.05	166.95

Evening meal 1900 (last orders 1000)
Parking for 6
Cards accepted: Access, Visa

Polkerr Guest House ♏

HIGHLY COMMENDED

Tintagel PL34 0BY
☎ Camelford (0840) 770382
Period country house offering quality accommodation, central heating, TV and tea-making facilities in all rooms. Ideal for touring, bathing, golf and coastal walks.
Bedrooms: 1 single, 4 double, 2 triple
Bathrooms: 5 private, 1 public

Bed & breakfast
per night:	£min	£max
Single	12.50	17.00
Double	30.00	34.00

Half board
per person:	£min	£max
Daily	20.00	24.50
Weekly	140.00	168.00

Evening meal 1830 (last orders 1730)
Parking for 9

303

WEST COUNTRY

TINTAGEL
Continued

Tintagel Arms Hotel & Zorba's Tavern
COMMENDED
Fore Street, Tintagel PL34 ODB
☎ Camelford (0840) 770780
Main street position close to Old Post Office and King Arthur's Castle.
Bedrooms: 1 single, 5 double, 1 triple
Bathrooms: 7 private

Bed & breakfast
per night:	£min	£max
Single	16.50	25.00
Double	36.00	50.00

Lunch available
Evening meal 1800 (last orders 2200)
Parking for 10
Cards accepted: Access, Visa

TIVERTON
Devon
Map ref 1D2

Busy market and textile town, settled since the 9th C, at the meeting of 2 rivers. Town houses, Tudor almshouses and parts of the fine church were built by wealthy cloth merchants; a medieval castle is incorporated into a private house; Blundells School.
Tourist Information Centre
☎ (0884) 255827

Great Bradley Farm
HIGHLY COMMENDED
Withleigh, Tiverton EX16 8JL
☎ (0884) 256946

155-acre dairy farm. Enjoy peaceful, beautiful countryside, 20 minutes from M5. Lovely, historic farmhouse offering comfortable, attractive bedrooms and delicious food. Non-smokers only please.
Bedrooms: 1 double, 1 twin
Bathrooms: 2 private

Bed & breakfast
per night:	£min	£max
Double	30.00	35.00

Half board
per person:	£min	£max
Daily	25.00	27.00
Weekly	160.00	165.00

Parking for 2
Open March-November

Hornhill
HIGHLY COMMENDED
Exeter Hill, Tiverton EX16 4PL
☎ (0884) 253352

75-acre mixed farm. Country house with superb views. Home cooking using local produce. Comfortable bedrooms, one with Victorian four poster. Peaceful relaxed atmosphere. Ten minutes from M5.
Bedrooms: 2 double, 1 twin
Bathrooms: 3 private

Bed & breakfast
per night:	£min	£max
Single	16.00	17.00
Double	30.00	34.00

Half board
per person:	£min	£max
Daily	25.00	

Evening meal 1830 (last orders 1930)
Parking for 4

Lodge Hill Farm Guesthouse
APPROVED
Ashley, Tiverton EX16 5PA
☎ (0884) 252907
10-acre mixed farm. Ideally situated in a peaceful rural setting in the beautiful Exe Valley. Perfect base for exploring Devon. Easily accessible on A396, 1 mile south of Tiverton.
Bedrooms: 3 single, 2 double, 1 twin, 2 family rooms
Bathrooms: 6 private, 2 public

Bed & breakfast
per night:	£min	£max
Single	13.50	16.00
Double	27.00	32.00

Parking for 12
Cards accepted: Access, Visa

Lower Collipriest Farm
HIGHLY COMMENDED
Tiverton EX16 4PT
☎ (0884) 252321
221-acre dairy & livestock farm. Lovely thatched farmhouse in beautiful Exe Valley. Of particular interest to naturalists. Traditional and speciality cooking. Coasts and moors within easy reach. Brochure available.
Bedrooms: 2 single, 2 twin
Bathrooms: 4 private

Bed & breakfast
per night:	£min	£max
Single	17.00	18.00
Double	36.00	38.00

Half board
per person:	£min	£max
Daily	26.00	27.00
Weekly	182.00	186.00

Evening meal 1900 (last orders 1200)
Parking for 4
Open March-November

TORQUAY
Devon
Map ref 1D2

Devon's grandest resort, developed from a fishing village. Smart apartments and terraces rise from the seafront and Marine Drive along the headland gives views of beaches and colourful cliffs.
Tourist Information Centre
☎ (0803) 297428

Aries House
Listed
1 Morgan Avenue, Torquay TQ2 5RP
☎ (0803) 215655
Family-run guesthouse in the town centre, offering easy access to all amenities. Seafront 10 minutes' walk. Courtesy car from rail/coach stations.
Bedrooms: 2 single, 2 double, 5 triple
Bathrooms: 2 public

Bed & breakfast
per night:	£min	£max
Single	11.00	15.00

Parking for 2

Barn Hayes Country Hotel
HIGHLY COMMENDED
Brim Hill, Maidencombe, Torquay TQ1 4TR
☎ (0803) 327980

Warm, friendly and comfortable country house hotel in an Area of Outstanding Natural Beauty overlooking countryside and sea. Relaxation is guaranteed in these lovely surroundings by personal service, good food and fine wines.
Bedrooms: 2 single, 4 double, 2 twin, 2 triple, 2 family rooms
Bathrooms: 10 private, 1 public

Bed & breakfast
per night:	£min	£max
Single	22.00	24.00
Double	44.00	48.00

Half board
per person:	£min	£max
Daily	32.00	34.00
Weekly	216.00	231.00

WEST COUNTRY

Lunch available
Evening meal 1830 (last orders 1900)
Parking for 16
Open February-December
Cards accepted: Access, Visa

The Beehive
Listed

Steep Hill, Maidencombe, Torquay
TQ1 4TS
☎ (0803) 314647
In a peaceful valley 4 minutes' walk from the beach, close to Torquay harbour and within easy reach of Dartmoor. All rooms have magnificent sea views. Non-smokers only, please.
Bedrooms: 2 double, 1 twin
Bathrooms: 1 public

Bed & breakfast
per night:	£min	£max
Single	14.00	16.00
Double	28.00	32.00

Parking for 6

Claver Guest House
Listed

119 Abbey Road, Torquay TQ2 5NP
☎ (0803) 297118
A warm welcome awaits you. Close to beach, harbour and all entertainments. Home-cooked food, you'll never leave the table hungry!
Bedrooms: 1 single, 2 double, 1 twin, 2 triple, 2 family rooms
Bathrooms: 1 private, 2 public

Bed & breakfast
per night:	£min	£max
Single	12.00	
Double	24.00	

Half board
per person:	£min	£max
Daily	19.00	
Weekly	110.00	

Evening meal 1800 (last orders 1800)
Parking for 4
Open January-November

Craig Court Hotel
APPROVED

10 Ash Hill Road, Torquay TQ1 3HZ
☎ (0803) 294400
Small hotel situated a short distance from the town centre and the harbour. Quiet location with a lovely garden and choice of menus.
Bedrooms: 2 single, 4 double, 2 twin, 2 family rooms
Bathrooms: 5 private, 3 public

Bed & breakfast
per night:	£min	£max
Single	16.50	22.50
Double	33.00	43.00

Half board
per person:	£min	£max
Daily	22.00	28.00
Weekly	154.00	196.00

Evening meal 1800 (last orders 0900)
Parking for 10
Open April-October

Gainsboro Hotel
APPROVED

22 Rathmore Road, Torquay TQ2 6NY
☎ (0803) 292032
Family-run hotel providing friendly atmosphere. Close to station, seafront and amenities.
Bedrooms: 1 single, 3 double, 1 twin, 1 triple, 1 family room
Bathrooms: 2 private, 1 public

Bed & breakfast
per night:	£min	£max
Single	11.00	15.00
Double	22.00	30.00

Evening meal from 1800
Parking for 5
Open March-October
Cards accepted: Access, Visa

Maple Lodge
COMMENDED

36 Ash Hill Road, Torquay TQ1 3JD
☎ (0803) 297391

Detached guesthouse with beautiful views. Relaxed atmosphere, home cooking, en-suite and shower rooms. Centrally situated for town and beaches.
Bedrooms: 1 single, 2 double, 1 twin, 2 triple, 1 family room
Bathrooms: 4 private, 1 public, 2 private showers

Bed & breakfast
per night:	£min	£max
Single	12.50	17.50
Double	25.00	35.00

Half board
per person:	£min	£max
Daily	17.50	22.50
Weekly	122.00	149.00

Evening meal from 1800
Parking for 5
Open March-October

Newton House
COMMENDED

31 Newton Road, Torre, Torquay
TQ2 5DB
☎ (0803) 297520
Detached guesthouse, family-run for 10 years. Tastefully decorated, well-appointed rooms, separate tables. Cleanliness assured. Bus and walking distance to town centre amenities.
Bedrooms: 1 single, 4 double, 2 twin, 1 triple
Bathrooms: 6 private, 1 public

Bed & breakfast
per night:	£min	£max
Single	12.00	24.00
Double	24.00	40.00

Parking for 15

Two Palms Guest House

216 Newton Road, Torquay TQ2 7JN
☎ (0803) 613793
Small guesthouse at the Scotts Bridge end of Newton Road. Resident proprietor ensures a warm welcome and an enjoyable stay.
Bedrooms: 1 single, 2 double, 1 twin
Bathrooms: 1 private, 2 public

Bed & breakfast
per night:	£min	£max
Single	12.50	17.50
Double	24.50	31.50

Parking for 5
Open April-October

TORRINGTON
Devon
Map ref 1C1

Perched high above the River Torridge, with a charming market square, Georgian Town Hall and a museum. The famous Dartington Crystal Factory, Rosemoor Gardens and Plough Arts Centre are all located in the town.

Flavills Farm
Listed

Kingscott, St Giles in the Wood,
Torrington EX38 7JW
☎ (080 52) 3530 & 3250
125-acre mixed farm. 15th C farmhouse in conservation area of picturesque hamlet. Peaceful atmosphere.
Bedrooms: 1 single, 1 double, 1 triple
Bathrooms: 1 public

Bed & breakfast
per night:	£min	£max
Single	12.00	12.00
Double	24.00	24.00

Parking for 6
Open April-September

There are separate sections in this guide listing groups specialising in farm holidays and accommodation which is especially suitable for young people and organised groups.

WEST COUNTRY

TOTNES
Devon
Map ref 1D2

Old market town steeply built near the head of the Dart Estuary. Remains of medieval gateways, a noble church, 16th C Guildhall and medley of period houses recall former wealth from cloth and shipping, continued in rural and water industries.
Tourist Information Centre
☎ *(0803) 863168*

Dorsley Park
Listed

Higher Plymouth Road, Totnes
TQ9 6DN
☎ (0803) 863680
23-acre mixed farm. 160-year-old stone-built cottages offering comfortable accommodation, in a relaxed and friendly atmosphere. Tea and coffee making facilities.
Bedrooms: 1 single, 1 twin, 1 triple
Bathrooms: 2 public

Bed & breakfast

per night:	£min	£max
Single	13.00	14.00
Double	25.00	27.00

Parking for 5

Old Church House Inn ⋔
COMMENDED

Torbryan, Newton Abbot TQ12 5UR
☎ Ipplepen (0803) 812372

13th C coaching house of immense character and old world charm with inglenook fireplaces, stone walls and oak beamed ceilings. Situated in a beautiful valley between Dartmoor and Torquay.
Bedrooms: 5 double, 1 twin, 1 triple
Bathrooms: 7 private

Bed & breakfast

per night:	£min	£max
Single	27.50	35.00
Double	55.00	70.00

Half board

per person:	£min	£max
Daily	37.50	45.00
Weekly	260.00	315.00

Lunch available
Evening meal 1900 (last orders 2130)
Parking for 30
Cards accepted: Access, Visa

The Old Forge at Totnes ⋔
HIGHLY COMMENDED

Seymour Place, Totnes TQ9 5AY
☎ (0803) 862174
All modern comforts in a delightful 600-year-old stone building, with beautiful walled garden, cobbled driveway and fully operational smithy workshop. Weekly and off-season discount. Cottage suite suitable for family or disabled guests.
Bedrooms: 1 single, 3 double, 2 twin, 2 triple, 2 family rooms
Bathrooms: 7 private, 1 public

Bed & breakfast

per night:	£min	£max
Single	30.00	45.00
Double	40.00	60.00

Parking for 10
Cards accepted: Access, Visa

TROWBRIDGE
Wiltshire
Map ref 2B2

Wiltshire's administrative centre, a handsome market and manufacturing town with a wealth of merchants' houses and other Georgian buildings.
Tourist Information Centre
☎ *(0225) 777054*

Welam House
COMMENDED

Bratton Road, West Ashton,
Trowbridge BA14 6AZ
☎ (0225) 755908
Located in quiet village, garden with trees and lawn with a view of Westbury White Horse. Ideally situated for touring. Bowls and mini-golf for guests.
Bedrooms: 1 double, 1 twin, 1 triple
Bathrooms: 3 private

Bed & breakfast

per night:	£min	£max
Double	28.00	32.00

Parking for 6
Open March-November

There are separate sections in this guide listing groups specialising in farm holidays and accommodation which is especially suitable for young people and organised groups.

TRURO
Cornwall
Map ref 1B3

Cornwall's administrative centre and cathedral city, set at the head of Truro River on the Fal Estuary. A medieval stannary town, it handled mineral ore from west Cornwall; fine Georgian buildings recall its heyday as a society haunt in the second mining boom.
Tourist Information Centre
☎ *(0872) 74555*

Arrallas
COMMENDED

Ladock, Truro TR2 4NP
☎ Mitchell (0872) 510379
320-acre arable & dairy farm. Signed from opposite the Clock Garage, Summercourt. Farmhouse accommodation set in truly rural situation. Good food, warm welcome, attention to detail. Closed at Christmas. Listed building.
Bedrooms: 2 double, 1 twin
Bathrooms: 3 private

Bed & breakfast

per night:	£min	£max
Double	32.00	36.00

Half board

per person:	£min	£max
Daily	24.50	31.50
Weekly	166.50	198.50

Evening meal from 1900
Parking for 8
Open January-November

Marcorrie Hotel ⋔
APPROVED

20 Falmouth Road, Truro TR1 2HX
☎ (0872) 77374
Fax (0872) 41666
Family-run hotel close to the city centre. Ideal for business or holiday, central for visiting the country houses and gardens of Cornwall.
Bedrooms: 3 single, 3 double, 2 twin, 1 triple, 3 family rooms
Bathrooms: 10 private, 1 public, 1 private shower

Bed & breakfast

per night:	£min	£max
Single	19.75	29.50
Double	39.50	42.00

Half board

per person:	£min	£max
Daily	27.75	37.50
Weekly	180.00	

Evening meal 1900 (last orders 1700)
Parking for 16
Cards accepted: Access, Visa, Amex

WEST COUNTRY

Nanteague Farm Guest House
HIGHLY COMMENDED
Marazanvose, Truro TR4 9DH
☎ (0872) 540351
130-acre beef farm. Ideal base from which to explore Cornwall. Wonderful views. En-suite rooms, pool, lake, golf-course, floatarium.
Bedrooms: 1 double, 1 triple, 2 single rooms
Bathrooms: 4 private, 1 public

Bed & breakfast
per night:	£min	£max
Single	14.00	16.50
Double	28.00	33.00

Half board
per person:	£min	£max
Daily	22.50	24.50
Weekly	157.50	171.50

Evening meal from 1900
Parking for 8
Open April-October
Cards accepted: Access, Visa, Amex

Rock Cottage
HIGHLY COMMENDED
Blackwater, Truro TR4 8EU
☎ (0872) 560252

18th C beamed cottage, old world charm. Haven for non-smokers. Warm, friendly hospitality, personal service. Informal atmosphere. Varied a la carte menu.
Bedrooms: 2 double, 1 twin
Bathrooms: 3 private

Bed & breakfast
per night:	£min	£max
Double	30.00	35.00

Evening meal 1900 (last orders 1500)
Parking for 4

TWO BRIDGES
Devon
Map ref 1C2

Dartmoor hamlet on the banks of the West Dart River, at the heart of the moor.

Two Bridges Hotel
APPROVED
Two Bridges Dartmoor, Princetown PL20 6SQ
☎ Princetown (0822) 890581
Fax (0822) 890575

18th C inn fronting river, old world log fires, good food, wine and ales. Ideal for walking, riding, fishing and golf. In middle of Dartmoor. Addictive.
Bedrooms: 1 single, 13 double, 8 twin, 2 triple
Bathrooms: 20 private, 2 public

Bed & breakfast
per night:	£min	£max
Single	24.50	39.50
Double	42.50	85.00

Half board
per person:	£min	£max
Daily	24.25	52.00
Weekly	169.00	364.00

Lunch available
Evening meal 1800 (last orders 2100)
Parking for 120
Cards accepted: Access, Visa, Diners, Amex, Switch

WATCHET
Somerset
Map ref 1D1

Small port on Bridgwater Bay, sheltered by the Quantocks and the Brendon Hills. A thriving paper industry keeps the harbour busy; in the 19th C it handled iron from the Brendon Hills. Cleeve Abbey, a ruined Cistercian monastery, is 3 miles to the south-west.

Wood Advent Farm
COMMENDED
Roadwater, Watchet TA23 0RR
☎ Washford (0984) 40920
350-acre mixed farm. Situated in Exmoor National Park, ideal for touring the many beauty spots. Country cooking, using mostly home-produced food.
Bedrooms: 1 single, 2 double, 1 twin, 2 family rooms
Bathrooms: 6 private

Bed & breakfast
per night:	£min	£max
Single	16.50	25.50
Double	33.00	40.00

Half board
per person:	£min	£max
Daily	29.00	32.50
Weekly	165.00	220.00

Lunch available
Evening meal 1900 (last orders 2100)
Parking for 13

WELLINGTON
Somerset
Map ref 1D1

Pinksmoor Millhouse
COMMENDED
Pinksmoor Farm, Wellington TA21 0HD
☎ Greenham (0823) 672361
98-acre dairy & livestock farm. Personal service and home cooking. House adjoins old mill and stream with abundant wildlife and scenic walks. Conservation area. En-suite bedrooms with beverage-making facilities and TV.
Bedrooms: 1 double, 1 twin, 1 triple
Bathrooms: 2 private, 1 public

Bed & breakfast
per night:	£min	£max
Single	19.50	20.50
Double	34.00	36.00

Half board
per person:	£min	£max
Daily	28.50	31.50
Weekly	189.00	213.50

Evening meal 1900 (last orders 1600)
Parking for 5

WELLOW
Avon
Map ref 2B2

The Manor House
Listed
Wellow, Bath BA2 8QQ
☎ Combe Down (0225) 832027
17th C stone manor house in heart of farming village 7 miles south of Bath. Home-baked bread and organic food. Convenient for Longleat, Stourhead, Wells and Glastonbury.
Bedrooms: 1 single, 2 double
Bathrooms: 1 private, 1 public

Bed & breakfast
per night:	£min	£max
Single	16.00	18.00
Double	30.00	35.00

Parking for 3

Individual proprietors have supplied all details of accommodation. Although we do check for accuracy, we advise you to confirm the information at the time of booking.

WEST COUNTRY

WELLS
Somerset
Map ref 2A2

Small city set beneath the southern slopes of the Mendips. Built between 1180 and 1424, the magnificent cathedral is preserved in much of its original glory and with its ancient precincts forms one of our loveliest and most unified groups of medieval buildings.
Tourist Information Centre
☎ *(0749) 672552*

Beaconsfield Farm
COMMENDED
Easton, Wells BA5 1DU
☎ (0749) 870308
Period character farmhouse in 4 acres with magnificent views. Beautifully decorated rooms with en-suites available. Village pub/restaurant 100 yards.
Bedrooms: 2 double, 1 twin
Bathrooms: 2 private, 1 public
Bed & breakfast

per night:	£min	£max
Double	28.00	34.00

Parking for 10
Open March-October

Bekynton House
COMMENDED
7 St Thomas Street, Wells BA5 2UU
☎ (0749) 672222
A central setting close to the cathedral and Bishop's Palace makes this period home an ideal choice for a weekend or a special holiday. Wells is an excellent touring centre and walkers' paradise.
Bedrooms: 1 single, 3 double, 2 twin, 2 triple
Bathrooms: 6 private, 2 public
Bed & breakfast

per night:	£min	£max
Single	22.00	24.00
Double	38.00	46.00

Parking for 7
Cards accepted: Access, Visa

Burcott Mill
Burcott, Wells BA5 1NJ
☎ (0749) 673118
Restored working watermill with attached house and craft workshops. Friendly country atmosphere. Birds and animals. Home cooking. Opposite good country pub.
Bedrooms: 1 single, 1 double, 1 twin, 2 triple
Bathrooms: 3 private, 1 public
Bed & breakfast

per night:	£min	£max
Single	15.00	19.00
Double	30.00	38.00

Half board

per person:	£min	£max
Daily	25.00	29.00
Weekly	158.00	183.00

Parking for 10

The Coach House
HIGHLY COMMENDED
Stoberry Park, Wells BA5 3AA
☎ (0749) 676535
Old coach house in private parkland. Short walk from centre of Wells. Superb views over city and countryside.
Bedrooms: 1 double, 2 twin
Bathrooms: 3 private
Bed & breakfast

per night:	£min	£max
Double	36.00	40.00

Parking for 6

Home Farm
Stoppers Lane, Coxley, Wells BA5 1QS
☎ (0749) 672434
15-acre pig farm. 1.5 miles from Wells, in a quiet spot just off A39. Extensive views of Mendip Hills. Pleasant rooms.
Bedrooms: 1 single, 3 double, 2 twin, 1 triple
Bathrooms: 3 private, 2 public
Bed & breakfast

per night:	£min	£max
Single	15.50	16.00
Double	31.00	38.00

Parking for 12

Littlewell Farm Guest House
HIGHLY COMMENDED
Coxley, Wells BA5 1QP
☎ (0749) 677914
Converted 200-year-old farmhouse enjoying extensive rural views of beautiful countryside. All bedrooms have shower or bathroom en-suite. Located 1 mile south-west of Wells.
Bedrooms: 1 single, 2 double, 2 twin
Bathrooms: 5 private
Bed & breakfast

per night:	£min	£max
Single	19.50	22.00
Double	35.00	40.00

Half board

per person:	£min	£max
Daily	30.00	35.00

Evening meal 1900 (last orders 2000)
Parking for 11

Manor Farm
Old Bristol Road, Upper Milton, Wells BA5 3AH
☎ (0749) 673394
130-acre beef farm. Elizabethan manor house, Grade II listed, on the southern slopes of the Mendips, 1 mile north of Wells. Superb view.*
Bedrooms: 2 double, 1 twin
Bathrooms: 1 public
Bed & breakfast

per night:	£min	£max
Single	16.00	17.00
Double	27.00	30.00

Parking for 6

Tor Guest House
APPROVED
20 Tor Street, Wells BA5 2US
☎ (0749) 672322 & 672084
Historic, sympathetically restored 17th C building in delightful grounds overlooking the cathedral. Attractive, comfortable, warm bedrooms. 3 minutes' walk to town centre.
Bedrooms: 1 single, 2 double, 2 twin, 3 family rooms
Bathrooms: 8 private
Bed & breakfast

per night:	£min	£max
Single	20.00	30.00
Double	34.00	48.00

Evening meal 1830 (last orders 1000)
Parking for 10
Cards accepted: Access, Visa

WEST ANSTEY
Devon
Map ref 1D1

Partridge Arms Farm
COMMENDED
Yeo Mill, West Anstey, South Molton EX36 3NU
☎ Anstey Mills (039 84) 217
200-acre mixed farm. Old established family farm. Well placed for touring, walking, riding, fishing, Exmoor National Park, north Devon, west Somerset and coastal resorts.
Bedrooms: 3 double, 2 twin, 2 family rooms
Bathrooms: 4 private, 1 public
Bed & breakfast

per night:	£min	£max
Single	17.50	22.00
Double	35.00	44.00

Half board

per person:	£min	£max
Daily	25.00	30.00
Weekly	175.00	203.00

Evening meal 1845 (last orders 1600)
Parking for 10

Check the introduction to this region for Where to Go, What to See.

WEST COUNTRY

WEST BAGBOROUGH
Somerset
Map ref 1D1

Bashfords Farmhouse
HIGHLY COMMENDED
West Bagborough, Taunton TA4 3EF
☎ Bishops Lydeard (0823) 432015
Delightful old farmhouse, built of local stone, set in the centre of a quiet village in the Quantock Hills. One mile off the A358 Taunton-Minehead road.
Bedrooms: 2 double, 1 twin
Bathrooms: 1 private, 1 public

Bed & breakfast
per night:	£min	£max
Single	15.00	20.00
Double	30.00	35.00

Parking for 5

WEST GRAFTON
Wiltshire
Map ref 2B2

Mayfield
Listed HIGHLY COMMENDED
West Grafton, Marlborough SN8 3BY
☎ Marlborough (0672) 810339
Beautifully decorated 15th C thatched house with happy family atmosphere. Lovely grounds with heated swimming pool and tennis court. Set in peaceful hamlet off A338.
Bedrooms: 1 double, 2 twin
Bathrooms: 2 public

Bed & breakfast
per night:	£min	£max
Single	24.00	28.00
Double	38.00	42.00

Parking for 6

WESTON-SUPER-MARE
Avon
Map ref 1D1

Large, friendly resort developed in the 19th C. Traditional seaside attractions include theatres and a dance hall. The museum shows a Victorian seaside gallery and has Iron Age finds from a hill fort on Worlebury Hill in Weston Woods.
Tourist Information Centre
☎ (0934) 626838

Conifers
63 Milton Road, Weston-super-Mare
BS23 2SP
☎ (0934) 624404
Semi-detached corner guesthouse standing back in a large garden. Completely refurbished for bed and breakfast use. 20 years' experience.
Bedrooms: 1 single, 1 double, 1 twin
Bathrooms: 1 private, 1 public

Bed & breakfast
per night:	£min	£max
Single	15.00	18.00
Double	28.00	34.00

Parking for 4
Open January-November

Purn House Farm
APPROVED
Bleadon, Weston-super-Mare
BS24 0QE
☎ Bleadon (0934) 812324
700-acre mixed farm. Comfortable 17th C farmhouse only 3 miles from Weston-super-Mare. Hot and cold water, tea-making facilities in all rooms, en-suite available with TV. Peaceful yet not isolated, on bus route to town centre and station.
Bedrooms: 1 double, 1 twin, 1 triple, 3 family rooms
Bathrooms: 3 private, 1 public

Bed & breakfast
per night:	£min	£max
Single	16.00	20.00
Double	32.00	40.00

Half board
per person:	£min	£max
Daily	23.00	27.00
Weekly	135.00	155.00

Evening meal 1830 (last orders 1000)
Parking for 10
Open March-October

WEYMOUTH
Dorset
Map ref 2B3

Ancient port and one of the south's earliest resorts. Curving beside a long, sandy beach, the elegant Georgian esplanade is graced with a statue of George III and a cheerful Victorian Jubilee clock tower.
Tourist Information Centre
☎ (0305) 765221

Fairlight
Listed
50 Littlemoor Road, Preston, Weymouth DT3 6AA
☎ (0305) 832293
Homely atmosphere in family bungalow. Children and one-nighters welcome. Freshly cooked food. Half a mile Boleaze Cove, 3 miles Weymouth.
Bedrooms: 1 double, 1 family room
Bathrooms: 1 public

Bed & breakfast
per night:	£min	£max
Single	15.00	17.50
Double	27.00	35.00

Half board
per person:	£min	£max
Daily	20.50	24.50
Weekly	123.00	147.00

Evening meal from 1900
Parking for 2

Green Acre
Listed
83 Preston Road, Preston, Weymouth DT3 6PY
☎ Preston (0305) 832047
Close to Bowleaze Cove at the east end of Weymouth. Detached house with wood-clad gables.
Bedrooms: 1 single, 3 double, 1 twin, 2 triple
Bathrooms: 2 public

Bed & breakfast
per night:	£min	£max
Single	13.50	15.50
Double	27.00	31.00

Parking for 8

Pebbles Guest House
COMMENDED
18 Kirtelton Avenue, Weymouth DT4 7PT
☎ (0305) 784331
Guesthouse with a friendly, relaxing atmosphere. Well equipped and comfortable bedrooms. Home cooking. Walking distance to the seafront and town centre.
Bedrooms: 2 single, 3 double, 2 triple, 1 family room
Bathrooms: 1 private, 1 public

Bed & breakfast
per night:	£min	£max
Single	12.50	15.50
Double	25.00	31.00

Half board
per person:	£min	£max
Daily	15.00	18.50
Weekly	105.00	129.50

Evening meal 1730 (last orders 1830)
Parking for 7

WICK ST LAWRENCE
Avon
Map ref 1D1

Icelton Farm
Listed
Wick St Lawrence, Weston-super-Mare BS22 OYJ
☎ Weston-super-Mare (0934) 515704
188-acre dairy farm. Situated off junction 21 of M5. Accommodation comprises a double room and family room. Good breakfasts.
Bedrooms: 1 double, 1 triple
Bathrooms: 1 public, 1 private shower

Continued ▶

Please mention this guide when making a booking.

309

WEST COUNTRY

WICK ST LAWRENCE
Continued

Bed & breakfast
per night:	£min	£max
Single	15.00	18.00
Double	30.00	33.00

Parking for 2
Open March-October

WIDECOMBE-IN-THE-MOOR
Devon
Map ref 1C2

Old village in pastoral country under the high tors of East Dartmoor. The "Cathedral of the Moor" stands near a tiny square, once used for archery practice, which has a 16th C Church House among other old buildings.

Heather Bank
Listed

Widecombe Hill, Widecombe-in-the-Moor, Newton Abbot TQ13 7TE
☎ (036 42) 205

Extensive views from comfortable en-suite accommodation with own access, adjoining moorland house overlooking the Widecombe Valley. Private parking and access to open moorland. Ideal for touring Dartmoor, Devon and Cornwall.

Bedrooms: 3 double
Bathrooms: 3 private

Bed & breakfast
per night:	£min	£max
Double		30.00

Parking for 20

Higher Venton Farm
Listed

Widecombe-in-the-Moor, Newton Abbot TQ13 7TF
☎ (036 42) 235

40-acre beef farm. 17th C thatched farmhouse with a homely atmosphere and farmhouse cooking. Ideal for touring Dartmoor. 16 miles from the coast.

Bedrooms: 2 double, 1 twin
Bathrooms: 1 private, 1 public

Bed & breakfast
per night:	£min	£max
Single	16.00	17.00
Double	28.00	30.00

Evening meal 1800 (last orders 1900)
Parking for 5

Sheena Tower ⋀

Widecombe-in-the-Moor, Newton Abbot TQ13 7TE
☎ (036 42) 308

Comfortable moorland guesthouse overlooking Widecombe village, offering a relaxed holiday in picturesque surroundings. Well placed for discovering Dartmoor.

Bedrooms: 1 single, 2 double, 1 twin, 1 triple, 1 family room
Bathrooms: 2 private, 2 public

Bed & breakfast
per night:	£min	£max
Single	14.00	16.00
Double	28.00	32.00

Half board
per person:	£min	£max
Daily	21.50	23.50
Weekly	147.50	161.50

Evening meal 1900 (last orders 1200)
Parking for 10
Open February-October

WINCANTON
Somerset
Map ref 2B3

Thriving market town, rising from the rich pastures of Blackmoor Vale near the Dorset border, with many attractive 18th C stone buildings. Steeplechase racecourse.

Lower Church Farm

Rectory Lane, Charlton Musgrove, Wincanton BA9 8ES
☎ (0963) 32307

60-acre dairy farm. 18th C brick farmhouse with beams and inglenooks, in a quiet area surrounded by lovely countryside. Ideal for touring.

Bedrooms: 2 double, 1 twin
Bathrooms: 3 private

Bed & breakfast
per night:	£min	£max
Double	26.00	30.00

Parking for 4

WINSFORD
Somerset
Map ref 1D1

Small village on the River Exe in splendid walking country under Winsford Hill. On the other side of the hill is a Celtic standing stone, the Caratacus Stone, and nearby across the River Barle stretches an ancient packhorse bridge, Tarr Steps, built of great stone slabs.

Larcombe Foot
COMMENDED

Winsford, Minehead TA24 7HS
☎ (064 385) 306

Comfortable country house in tranquil, beautiful setting, overlooking River Exe. Lovely walks on doorstep. Ideal for touring Exmoor and north Devon coast.

Bedrooms: 1 single, 1 double, 1 twin
Bathrooms: 3 private

Bed & breakfast
per night:	£min	£max
Single	16.00	17.00
Double	32.00	34.00

Parking for 3
Open April-October

WINTERBOURNE STEEPLETON
Dorset
Map ref 2B3

Redmays
Listed

Winterbourne Steepleton, Dorchester DT2 9LZ
☎ Martinstown (0305) 889506

Delightful village bungalow set in half an acre of lovely garden, off the A35, 5 miles west of Dorchester. Central for many interesting places.

Bedrooms: 1 double, 1 twin
Bathrooms: 1 public

Bed & breakfast
per night:	£min	£max
Single	15.00	18.00
Double	25.00	30.00

Half board
per person:	£min	£max
Daily	24.00	28.00
Weekly	150.00	175.00

Evening meal from 1830
Parking for 4

WINTERBOURNE STOKE
Wiltshire
Map ref 2B2

Scotland Lodge ⋀
COMMENDED

Winterbourne Stoke, Salisbury SP3 4TF
☎ Shrewton (0980) 620943 & Mobile (0860) 272599
Fax (0980) 620943

Historic, comfortable country house with private bathrooms. Helpful service, delicious breakfasts. Ideal touring base. French and some German spoken. Self-contained unit also available for self-catering.

Bedrooms: 1 double, 2 twin
Bathrooms: 3 private

Bed & breakfast
per night:	£min	£max
Single	25.00	30.00
Double	35.00	45.00

Parking for 5

We advise you to confirm your booking in writing.

310

WEST COUNTRY

WOODBURY
Devon
Map ref 1D2

Attractive village, with Woodbury Common to the east, affording a panoramic coastal view from Berry Head to Portland Bill. Woodbury Castle Iron Age fort lies at a height of some 600 ft.

Higher Bagmores Farm

Woodbury, Exeter EX5 1LA
☎ (0395) 232261
200-acre mixed farm. A brick-built farmhouse set in its own garden overlooking the Exe estuary. 2 miles from M5, 5 miles from seaside.
Bedrooms: 1 single, 1 double, 1 twin
Bathrooms: 2 public

Bed & breakfast
per night:	£min	£max
Single	14.00	14.00
Double	28.00	28.00

Parking for 4
Open January-November

WOOKEY
Somerset
Map ref 2A2

Small village below the southern slopes of the Mendips, near the River Axe. A mile or so north-east, the river runs through spectacular limestone caverns at Wookey Hole.

Fenny Castle House
COMMENDED

Fenny Castle, Wookey, Wells BA5 1NN
☎ Wells (0749) 672265
Riverside setting overlooking motte and bailey castle. Country house in 60 acres on boundary of Levels. Restaurant, lounge bar, delightful accommodation.
Bedrooms: 1 single, 3 double, 2 twin
Bathrooms: 6 private

Bed & breakfast
per night:	£min	£max
Single	25.00	28.00
Double	50.00	55.00

Half board
per person:	£min	£max
Daily	38.00	40.00
Weekly	245.00	260.00

Lunch available
Evening meal 1800 (last orders 2100)
Parking for 60
Cards accepted: Access, Visa, Amex

Please mention this guide when making a booking.

WOOLACOMBE
Devon
Map ref 1C1

Between Morte Point and Baggy Point, Woolacombe and Mortehoe offer 3 miles of the finest sand and surf on this outstanding coastline. Much of the area is owned by the National Trust.

Holmesdale Hotel

Bayview Road, Woolacombe EX34 7DQ
☎ (0271) 870335
Fax (0271) 870088
South facing, overlooking beach. Intercom and baby listener. Continental and English cuisine available. Beautiful bar and dining room. Honeymoon suite four-poster. Sea view balcony.
Bedrooms: 2 single, 2 double, 2 twin, 1 triple, 9 family rooms
Bathrooms: 7 private, 9 private showers

Half board
per person:	£min	£max
Weekly	145.00	218.00

Evening meal 1900 (last orders 2100)
Parking for 20
Open March-December
Cards accepted: Access, Visa

YELVERTON
Devon
Map ref 1C2

Village on the edge of Dartmoor, where ponies wander over the flat common. Buckland Abbey is 2 miles south-west, while Burrator Reservoir is 2 miles to the east.

Eggworthy Farm
APPROVED

Sampford Spiney, Yelverton PL20 6LJ
☎ (0822) 852142
650-acre livestock farm. Farmhouse amidst the Walkham Valley. 2 miles from Walkhampton Village in Dartmoor National Park. Ideal centre for walking.
Bedrooms: 1 single, 2 double
Bathrooms: 1 public

Bed & breakfast
per night:	£min	£max
Single	14.00	
Double	28.00	

Parking for 4

Greenwell Farm
COMMENDED

Meavy, Yelverton PL20 6PY
☎ (0822) 853563
220-acre hill farm. Fresh country air, breathtaking views and scrumptious farmhouse cuisine. This busy family

---

farm welcomes you to share our countryside and wildlife.
Bedrooms: 1 double, 1 twin, 1 triple
Bathrooms: 3 private

Bed & breakfast
per night:	£min	£max
Double	38.00	44.00

Half board
per person:	£min	£max
Daily	29.00	33.00
Weekly	195.00	210.00

Evening meal 1900 (last orders 1200)
Parking for 8

Rosemont Hotel
COMMENDED

Greenbank Terrace, Yelverton PL20 6DR
☎ (0822) 852175
Small, friendly, family-run hotel in quiet village on edge of Dartmoor. An ideal spot for touring the West Country. Quality food.
Bedrooms: 2 single, 1 double, 2 twin, 2 triple, 1 family room
Bathrooms: 2 public

Bed & breakfast
per night:	£min	£max
Single	18.00	18.00
Double	36.00	36.00

Half board
per person:	£min	£max
Daily	32.50	32.50
Weekly	209.50	209.50

Lunch available
Evening meal 1830 (last orders 2300)
Parking for 9

YEOVIL
Somerset
Map ref 2A3

Lively market town set in dairying country beside the River Yeo, famous for glove making. Interesting parish church. Museum of South Somerset at Hendford Manor.
Tourist Information Centre
☎ (0935) 71279

Holywell House
HIGHLY COMMENDED

Holywell, East Coker, Yeovil BA22 9NQ
☎ West Coker (0935) 862612
Fax (0935) 863035

Continued ▶

311

WEST COUNTRY

YEOVIL
Continued

Beautifully renovated country home with fine amenities. Three acres of lovely grounds, tennis court, idyllic rural setting. Quiet location off A30 2 miles west of Yeovil. Suites available.
Bedrooms: 2 double, 1 family room
Bathrooms: 3 private

Bed & breakfast
per night:	£min	£max
Single	25.00	30.00
Double	45.00	55.00

Evening meal 1900 (last orders 2030)
Parking for 15

Southwoods
APPROVED

3 Southwoods, Yeovil BA20 2QQ
☎ (0935) 22178
Charming Edwardian house, close to town centre, ski-slope, leisure centre/swimming pool and wooded beauty spot. Relaxed, friendly atmosphere.
Bedrooms: 1 single, 1 double, 1 twin
Bathrooms: 1 public

Bed & breakfast
per night:	£min	£max
Single	14.00	18.00
Double	28.00	32.00

Parking for 3

YEOVILTON
Somerset
Map ref 2A3

Cary Fitzpaine
APPROVED

Yeovilton, Yeovil BA22 8JB
☎ Charlton Mackerell (045 822) 3250
600-acre mixed farm. Elegant Georgian manor farmhouse in idyllic setting. 2 acres of gardens. High standard of accommodation.
Bedrooms: 1 single, 1 double, 1 twin, 1 triple
Bathrooms: 1 private, 2 public

Bed & breakfast
per night:	£min	£max
Single	15.00	18.00
Double	30.00	35.00

Parking for 11
Open April-November

Courtry Farm
Listed APPROVED

Bridgehampton, Yeovil BA22 8HF
☎ Ilchester (0935) 840327
590-acre mixed farm. Farmhouse with ground floor rooms, en-suite, TV, tea-making facilities. Tennis court. Fleet Air Arm Museum half a mile.
Bedrooms: 1 twin, 1 triple
Bathrooms: 2 private

Bed & breakfast
per night:	£min	£max
Single	18.00	20.00
Double	30.00	

Parking for 20

ZEALS
Wiltshire
Map ref 2B2

Pretty village of thatched cottages set high over the Dorset border. Zeals House dates from the medieval period and has some 19th C work. The Palladian Stourhead House (National Trust), in its magnificent gardens, lies further north.

Cornerways Cottage

Longcross, Zeals, Warminster BA12 6LL
☎ Bourton (0747) 840477
18th C cottage with original beams. Ideal position for touring Stourhead, Stonehenge, Shaftesbury and other local attractions. Riding, fishing and walking locally. Close to A303, midway for London or Devon and Cornwall. Two miles from Stourhead House and Gardens, 4 miles from Longleat.
Bedrooms: 3 double
Bathrooms: 3 private

Bed & breakfast
per night:	£min	£max
Single	16.00	18.00
Double	30.00	32.00

Parking for 6

We advise you to confirm your booking in writing.

Country Code

♣ Enjoy the countryside and respect its life and work
♣ Guard against all risk of fire ♣ Fasten all gates
♣ Keep your dogs under close control ♣ Keep to public paths across farmland ♣ Use gates and stiles to cross fences, hedges and walls ♣ Leave livestock, crops and machinery alone ♣ Take your litter home
♣ Help to keep all water clean ♣ Protect wildlife, plants and trees ♣ Take special care on country roads ♣ Make no unnecessary noise

SURE SIGNS
OF WHERE TO STAY

Throughout Britain, the tourist boards now inspect over 30,000 places to stay, every year, to help you find the ones that suit you best.

Looking for a hotel, guesthouse, inn, B&B or farmhouse? Look for the **CROWN**. The classifications: 'Listed', and then **ONE to FIVE CROWN,** tell you the range of facilities and services you can expect. The more Crowns, the wider the range.

Looking for somewhere convenient to stop overnight on a motorway or major road route? Look for the 'Lodge' **MOON**. The classifications: **ONE to THREE MOON** tell you the range of facilities you can expect. The more Moons, the wider the range.

Looking for a self-catering holiday home? Look for the **KEY**. The classifications: **ONE to FIVE KEY,** tell you the range of facilities and equipment you can expect. The more Keys, the wider the range.

THE GRADES: **APPROVED, COMMENDED, HIGHLY COMMENDED and DE LUXE,** whether alongside the **CROWNS**, **KEYS** or **MOONS** show the quality standard of what is provided. If no grade is shown, you can still expect a high standard of cleanliness.

Looking for a holiday caravan, chalet or camping park? Look for the **Q** symbol. The more ✓s in the Q (from one to five), the higher the quality standard of what is provided.

English Tourist Board

We've checked them out before you check in!

More detailed information on the **CROWNS**, the **KEYS** and the **Q** is given in free *SURE SIGN* leaflets, available at any Tourist Information Centre.

South of England

With its ancient forests, heathlands and an alternately rugged and gentle coastline, the South of England is an area of spectacular beauty. But there's much more, too. Inland there is Beaulieu, the stately home and motor museum, and the ponderous might of Carisbrooke Castle where Charles I was imprisoned for a time during the Civil War. The coast pays homage to England's maritime history as it gazes sternly over the English Channel. In Portsmouth there is the chance to view the great ships Victory, Mary Rose and Warrior, or to escape to the holiday pleasures that lie on the Isle of Wight. Whatever you need, the beautiful South of England can provide it.

WHERE TO GO, WHAT TO SEE

The number against each name will help you locate it on the map (page 316).

❶ Broughton Castle
Banbury, Oxfordshire OX15 5EB
Tel: Banbury (0295) 262624
Medieval moated house built in 1300 and enlarged between 1550 and 1600. The home of Lord and Lady Saye and Sele. Civil War connections.

❷ Blenheim Palace
Woodstock, Oxfordshire
OX20 1PX
Tel: Woodstock (0993) 811091
Birthplace of Sir Winston Churchill, designed by Vanbrugh with park designed by Capability Brown. Adventure play area, maze, butterfly house, garden centre and Churchill exhibition.

❸ The Oxford Story
6 Broad Street, Oxford,
Oxfordshire OX1 3AJ
Tel: Oxford (0865) 728822
Heritage centre depicting 800 years of university history in sights, sounds, personalities and smells. Visitors are transported in moving desks with commentary of their choice.

❹ Waterperry Gardens
Waterperry, Oxfordshire OX33 1JZ
Tel: Ickford (0844) 339254
Ornamental gardens covering 6 acres of 83-acre 18th C Waterperry House estate. Saxon village church, garden shop, tea shop.

Ancient Gold Hill in Shaftesbury has a 700ft slope.

South of England

⑤ Didcot Railway Centre
Great Western Railway, Didcot, Oxfordshire OX11 7NJ
Tel: Didcot (0235) 817200
Living museum recreating the golden age of the Great Western Railway. Steam locomotives and trains, engine shed and small relics museum. Steam days and gala events.

⑥ Beale Wildlife Gardens
Church Farm, Lower Basildon, Berkshire RG8 9NH
Tel: Reading (0734) 845172
Established 36 years ago, the park features wildfowl, pheasants, Highland cattle, rare sheep, llamas. Narrow gauge railway and pets' corner.

⑦ Royalty and Empire
Windsor Station, Windsor, Berkshire SL4 1PJ
Tel: Windsor (0753) 857837
Adjacent to Windsor Castle, the exhibition celebrates 60 years of Queen Victoria and 40 years of Queen Elizabeth II. Waxworks and special effects are used to bring Royalty to life.

⑧ Stratfield Saye House
The Wellington Office, Stratfield Saye, Hampshire RG7 2BT
Tel: Basingstoke (0256) 882882
Built in 1630, the house displays many personal possessions of the Iron Duke, including funeral hearse (part of Wellington Exhibition). Gardens and pleasure grounds.

⑨ Marwell Zoological Park
Colden Common, Winchester, Hampshire SO21 1JH
Tel: Owslebury (0962) 777407
Large zoo breeding endangered species. Over 800 animals including big cats, giraffes, deer, zebras, monkeys, hippos and birds.

⑩ Broadlands
Romsey, Hampshire SO51 9ZD
Tel: Romsey (0794) 516678
Home of the late Lord Mountbatten. Magnificent 18th C house and contents. Superb views across River Test. Mountbatten exhibition and audio-visual presentation.

⑩ Paultons Park
Ower, Romsey, Hampshire SO51 6AL
Tel: Southampton (0703) 814442
A day out for all the family in beautiful surroundings. Lots of fun activities with over 40 different attractions, including bumper boats, kids' kingdom, astroglide.

Admiral Horatio Nelson and his flagship HMS Victory at Portsmouth.

⑪ Breamore House
Breamore, Hampshire SP6 2DF
Tel: Downton (0725) 22233
Elizabethan manor house built 1583, with fine art collection. Furniture, tapestries, needlework, paintings – mainly Dutch School of 17th and 18th C.

⑫ Tudor House Museum
St Michael's Square, Bugle Street, Southampton SO1 0AD
Tel: Southampton (0703) 332513
Large half-timbered Tudor house. Exhibits include Victorian kitchen, sewing tools, Tudor Hall and garden.

⑬ New Forest Butterfly Farm
Longdown, Ashurst, Hampshire SO4 4UH
Tel: Ashurst (0703) 292166
Large indoor tropical garden housing numerous exotic free-flying butterflies and moths from all over the world. Dragonfly ponds, adventure playground, insectarium.

⑭ The Dorset Heavy Horse Centre
Grains Hill, Edmondsham, Verwood, Dorset BH21 5RJ
Tel: Verwood (0202) 824040
Heavy horses (Shire, Percheron, Suffolk). Old farm wagons and implements. Parades of horses. Demonstrations of plaiting and harnessing. Miniature ponies.

⑮ Sir George Staunton Country Park
Leigh Park, Havant, Hampshire PO9 5HB
Tel: Havant (0705) 453405
Beautiful Victorian estate created by Sir George Staunton (Bart), complete with farm animals, buildings, trees and shrubs. All-year interest.

⑯ Royal Signals Museum
Blandford Camp, Blandford Forum, Dorset DT11 8RH
Tel: Blandford (0258) 482248
History of Army communication from Crimea to the Gulf. Vehicles, uniforms, medals and badges on display.

⑰ The New Forest Owl Sanctuary
Crow Lane, Crow, Ringwood, Hampshire BH24 3EA
Tel: Ringwood (0425) 476287
Sanctuary for barn owls destined to be released into the wild. Incubation room, hospital unit and 100 aviaries.

⑱ Beaulieu Palace House
Beaulieu, Hampshire SO42 7ZN
Tel: Beaulieu (0590) 612345
Home of Lord and Lady Montagu, the house has been in the family since it was acquired in 1538 following the dissolution of the monasteries by Henry VIII. National Motor Museum, monastic life exhibition, shops.

South of England

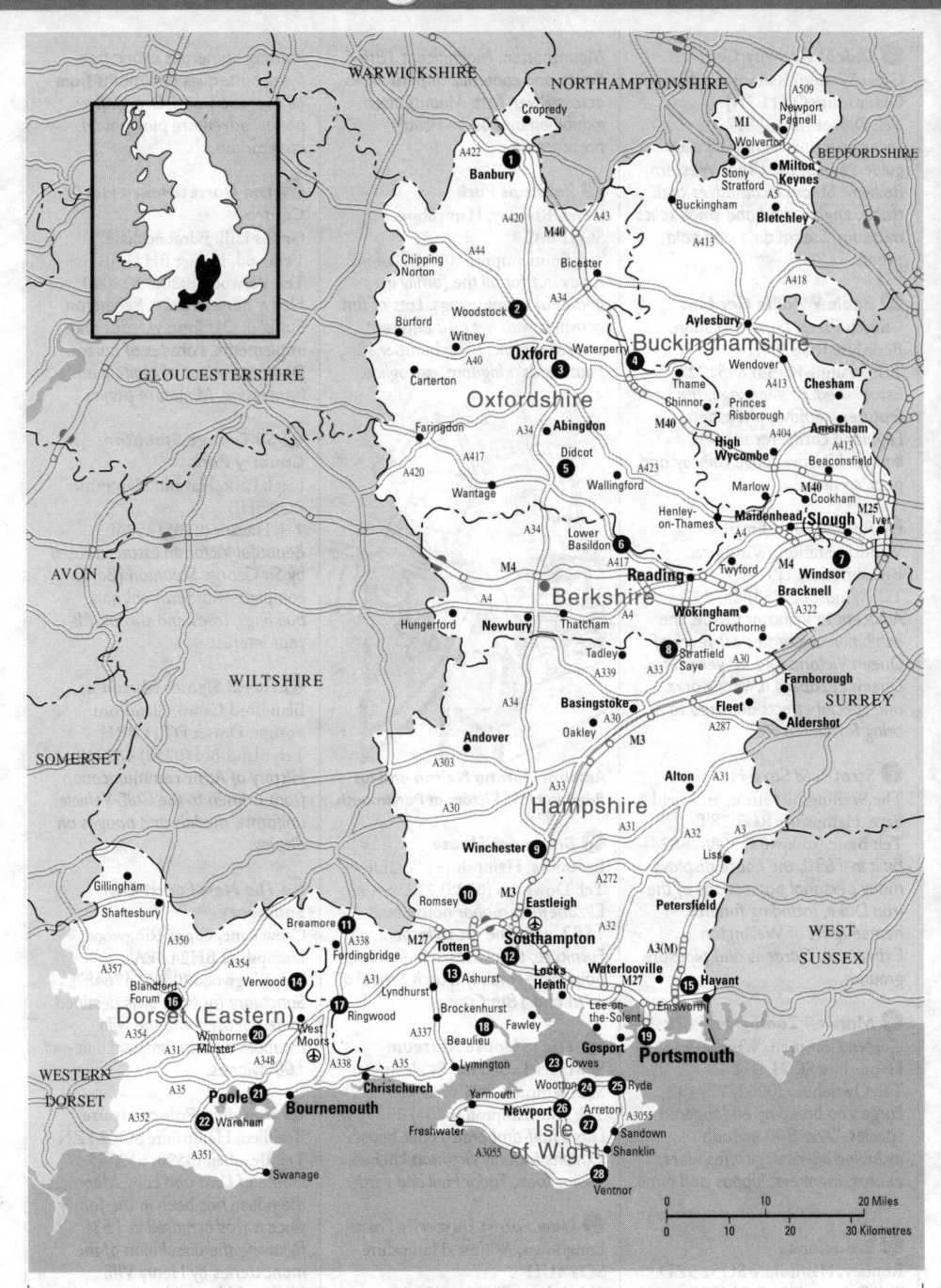

South of England

19 Mary Rose Ship Hall and Exhibition
HM Naval Base, Portsmouth, Hampshire PO1 3PZ
Tel: Portsmouth (0705) 812931
Reconstruction and conservation of Henry VIII's warship, and exhibition of the ship's treasures.

20 The D Day Museum and Overlord Embroidery
Clarence Esplanade, Portsmouth, Hampshire PO5 3PA
Tel: Portsmouth (0705) 827261
Incorporates Overlord embroidery which depicts Allied invasion of Normandy. Displays of D Day action and some of the vehicles that took part.

21 Kingston Lacy
Wimborne Minster, Dorset BH21 4EA
Tel: Wimborne (0202) 883402
17th C house designed for Sir Ralph Bankes by Sir Roger Pratt, altered by Sir Charles Barry in the 19th C. Collection of paintings, 250 acres of wooded park and herd of Devon cattle.

22 Compton Acres
Canford Cliffs, Poole, Dorset BH13 7ES
Tel: Canford Cliffs (0202) 700778
Nine separate and distinct gardens of the world. The gardens include Italian, Japanese, sub-tropical glen, rock, water and heather. Collection of statues.

22 The Tank Museum
Bovington Camp, Wareham, Dorset BH20 6JG
Tel: Bindon Abbey (0929) 403463
Largest and most comprehensive museum collection of armoured fighting vehicles in the world. Over 250 vehicles on show, with supporting displays and video theatres.

23 Osborne House
East Cowes, Isle of Wight PO32 6JY
Tel: Isle of Wight (0983) 200022
Queen Victoria and Prince Albert's seaside holiday home. Victorian carriage service to Swiss cottage where royal children learnt cooking and gardening.

24 Butterfly World and Fountain World
Staplers Road, Wootton, Ryde, Isle of Wight PO33 4RW
Tel: Isle of Wight (0983) 883430
Tropical indoor garden with butterflies from around the world. Fountain World has water features and huge fish. Italian and Japanese garden.

25 Isle of Wight Steam Railway
Railway Station, Havenstreet, Ryde, Isle of Wight PO33 4DS
Tel: Isle of Wight (0983) 882204
Five-mile steam railway using Victorian and Edwardian locomotives and carriages. Souvenir shop, refreshments, children's playground.

26 Calbourne Watermill and Rural Museum
Newport, Isle of Wight PO30 4JN
Tel: Calbourne (098 378) 227
Fine example of an early 17th C watermill still in working order. Granary, waterwheel, water and pea fowl.

27 Haseley Manor
Arreton, Isle of Wight PO30 3AN
Tel: Isle of Wight (0983) 865420
Historic manor house dating from medieval times through to the Victorian period. Large working pottery, sweet factory with demonstrations, craft village, garden, pets.

28 Ventnor Botanic Garden
The Undercliffe Drive, Ventnor, Isle of Wight PO38 1SZ
Tel: Isle of Wight (0983) 855397
22-acre garden containing some 10,000 plants including rare and exotic trees, shrubs, alpines, perennials, succulents and conifers.

FIND OUT MORE

Further information about holidays and attractions in the South of England region is available from:
Southern Tourist Board
40 Chamberlayne Road, Eastleigh, Hampshire SO5 5JH
Tel: (0703) 620006

Winchester Cathedral is the longest medieval church in Europe.

SOUTH OF ENGLAND

Places to stay

Accommodation entries in this regional section are listed in alphabetical order of place name, and then in alphabetical order of establishment.

The map references refer to the colour maps at the back of the guide. The first figure is the map number; the letter and figure which follow indicate the grid reference on the map.

The symbols at the end of each accommodation entry give information about services and facilities. A 'key' to these symbols is inside the back cover flap, which can be kept open for easy reference.

ABBOTTS ANN

Hampshire
Map ref 2C2

Abbotts Law
HIGHLY COMMENDED
Abbotts Ann, Andover SP11 7DW
☎ Andover (0264) 710350
Elegant country house in 3 acres of beautiful gardens on edge of village. Quarter of a mile from junction of A303 and A343 Salisbury road near Andover. Cordon Bleu cuisine, heated pool and tennis court. B & B price is per room. Ideal centre for exploring Wessex.
Bedrooms: 2 double, 1 twin
Bathrooms: 3 private

Bed & breakfast
per night:	£min	£max
Double	42.00	48.00

Half board
per person:	£min	£max
Daily	38.00	42.00
Weekly	250.00	275.00

Evening meal 1930 (last orders 1930)
Parking for 10
Open April-October

Virginia Lodge
COMMENDED
Salisbury Road, Abbotts Ann, Andover SP11 7NX
☎ Andover (0264) 710713
Spacious, comfortable bungalow with large gardens on edge of attractive village. On A343, one mile from A303. Central for Stonehenge, Winchester and Salisbury. "Half-way house" on east/west route.
Bedrooms: 1 double, 2 twin
Bathrooms: 1 private, 1 public

Bed & breakfast
per night:	£min	£max
Single	18.00	24.00
Double	30.00	34.00

Parking for 6

ABINGDON

Oxfordshire
Map ref 2C1

Attractive former county town on River Thames with many interesting buildings, including 17th C County Hall, now a museum, in the market-place and the remains of an abbey.
Tourist Information Centre
☎ (0235) 522711

Crooked Chimney Cottage

Little Wittenham, Abingdon OX14 4QX
☎ Clifton Hampden (0867) 307477 changing to (0865) 407477
18th C cottage in Thameside village of Little Wittenham at foot of Wittenham Clumps (nature reserve). Close to Oxford, Abingdon, Wallingford and Didcot; convenient for the Cotswolds and Blenheim Palace.
Bedrooms: 1 twin
Bathrooms: 1 private

Bed & breakfast
per night:	£min	£max
Single	20.00	24.00
Double	33.00	36.00

Parking for 3

1 Long Barn
Listed
Sutton Courtenay, Abingdon OX14 4BQ
☎ (0235) 848251

17th C village house 8 miles from Oxford, 2 miles from Abingdon. Easy access to Henley and the Cotswolds.
Bedrooms: 1 twin
Bathrooms: 1 private

Bed & breakfast
per night:	£min	£max
Single	13.00	13.00
Double	26.00	26.00

Parking for 3

ALTON

Hampshire
Map ref 2C2

Pleasant old market town standing on the Pilgrim's Way, with some attractive Georgian buildings. The parish church still bears the scars of bullet marks, evidence of a bitter struggle between the Roundheads and the Royalists.
Tourist Information Centre
☎ (0420) 88448

Glen Derry
Listed COMMENDED
52 Wellhouse Road, Beech, Alton GU34 4AG
☎ (0420) 83235
Peaceful, secluded family home set in 3.5 acres of garden. Warm welcome assured. Ideal base for Watercress Steam Railway, Winchester and Portsmouth.
Bedrooms: 1 twin, 1 family room
Bathrooms: 1 private, 1 public

Bed & breakfast
per night:	£min	£max
Single	18.00	25.00
Double	28.00	35.00

Parking for 12

SOUTH OF ENGLAND

AMERSHAM
Buckinghamshire
Map ref 2D1

Old town with many fine buildings, particularly in the High Street. There are several interesting old inns.

The Barn
Listed HIGHLY COMMENDED
Rectory Hill, Old Amersham, Amersham HP7 0BT
☎ (0494) 722701
17th C tithe barn with a wealth of beams. 6 minutes' walk from Amersham station. Easy access to M25 and M40.
Bedrooms: 2 single, 1 twin
Bathrooms: 1 public
Bed & breakfast

per night:	£min	£max
Single	27.50	30.00
Double	45.00	47.50

Parking for 5

63 Hundred Acres Lane
Listed
Amersham HP7 9BX
☎ (0494) 433095
Semi-detached house on estate. 5 minutes' drive to Amersham old town and half-an-hour to High Wycombe and Rickmansworth.
Bedrooms: 1 single, 1 double, 1 twin
Bathrooms: 1 public
Bed & breakfast

per night:	£min	£max
Single	22.00	22.00
Double	38.50	38.50

Parking for 3

AMPORT
Hampshire
Map ref 2C2

Broadwater
Amport, Andover SP11 8AY
☎ Andover (0264) 772240
Fax (0264) 772240
Grade II listed thatched cottage. From A303 (from Andover) take turn off to Hawk Conservancy/Amport. At T junction, turn right, take first road right (East Cholderton), Broadwater is first cottage on the right.
Bedrooms: 2 twin
Bathrooms: 2 private, 1 public
Bed & breakfast

per night:	£min	£max
Single	15.00	20.00
Double	36.00	40.00

Half board

per person:	£min	£max
Daily	23.00	28.00
Weekly	160.00	195.00

Evening meal 1830 (last orders 2030)
Parking for 3

ANDOVER
Hampshire
Map ref 2C2

Town that achieved importance from the wool trade and now has much modern development. A good centre for visiting places of interest.
Tourist Information Centre
☎ *(0264) 324320*

Malt Cottage
HIGHLY COMMENDED
Upper Clatford, Andover SP11 7QL
☎ (0264) 323469
Country house with idyllic 6-acre garden, lake and stream. Set in charming Hampshire village within easy reach of Salisbury, Romsey, Stonehenge and London/Exeter road.
Bedrooms: 1 double, 1 twin
Bathrooms: 2 private
Bed & breakfast

per night:	£min	£max
Single	30.00	38.00
Double	36.00	44.00

Half board

per person:	£min	£max
Daily	31.50	35.00

Evening meal from 1800
Parking for 5

The Old Barn
Listed HIGHLY COMMENDED
Amport, Andover SP11 8AE
☎ (0264) 710410
Converted old barn, in small village approximately 3 miles south west of Andover. Secluded, but only three-quarters of a mile from A303.
Bedrooms: 2 double
Bathrooms: 2 private
Bed & breakfast

per night:	£min	£max
Single	18.00	20.00
Double	29.00	31.00

Parking for 4

National Crown ratings were correct at the time of going to press but are subject to change. Please check at the time of booking.

ASCOT
Berkshire
Map ref 2C2

Small country town famous for its racecourse which was founded by Queen Anne. The race meeting each June is attended by the Royal Family.

Birchcroft House
HIGHLY COMMENDED
Birchcroft, Brockenhurst Road, South Ascot, Ascot SL5 9HA
☎ (0344) 20574
Edwardian country house, wooded gardens. Quality en-suite accommodation within easy reach of Windsor, Bracknell, M25, M3, M4, Ascot races and golf at Wentworth, Sunningdale or Berkshire courses. Heathrow 25 minutes.
Bedrooms: 1 double, 2 twin
Bathrooms: 3 private
Bed & breakfast

per night:	£min	£max
Single	28.00	44.00
Double	38.00	55.00

Parking for 6

J & W Glynn
Listed
56 King Edwards Road, North Ascot, Ascot SL5 8NY
☎ Winkfield Row (0344) 883229
Chalet bungalow in very quiet area. Convenient for Heathrow Airport, trains to London, Windsor, Ascot races, Wentworth, Sunningdale and Berkshire golf-courses. Near Ramblers' Way.
Bedrooms: 3 single, 1 twin
Bathrooms: 1 private, 2 public
Bed & breakfast

per night:	£min	£max
Single	15.00	
Double	30.00	

Parking for 6

Tanglewood
Birch Lane, off Longhill Road, Chavey Down, Ascot SL5 8RF
☎ Winkfield Row (0344) 882528
En-suite bedrooms in spacious, modern bungalow. Quiet secluded location, large wooded garden. Four miles from Windsor and 15 miles from Heathrow (pick up possible). Convenient for Wentworth, Sunningdale, Ascot, Thames Valley and London.
Bedrooms: 1 single, 2 twin
Bathrooms: 2 private, 1 public

Continued ▶

Please mention this guide when making a booking.

SOUTH OF ENGLAND

ASCOT
Continued

Bed & breakfast
per night:	£min	£max
Single	15.00	25.00
Double	30.00	50.00

Evening meal 1900 (last orders 2000)
Parking for 6

ASTHALL LEIGH
Oxfordshire
Map ref 2C1

Warwick House
Listed

Asthall Leigh, Witney OX8 5PX
☎ (099 387) 336 changing to (0993) 878336

5-acre mixed farm. Charming country home in quiet village, overlooking open farmland on edge of Windrush Valley in the Cotswolds, between Witney and Burford. All rooms en-suite.
Bedrooms: 2 double, 1 twin
Bathrooms: 3 private

Bed & breakfast
per night:	£min	£max
Single	20.00	25.00
Double	30.00	35.00

Parking for 4
Open April-September

ASTON CLINTON
Buckinghamshire
Map ref 2C1

Village far-spread on the escarpment of the Downs, with many Jacobean thatched cottages and an inn which has been receiving travellers since John Hampden's days. 14th C church with its original chancel and fine arch still stands today.

The Haven
Listed

7 Lower Icknield Way, Aston Clinton, Aylesbury HP22 5JS
☎ Aylesbury (0296) 630751
Friendly, comfortable and homely bungalow 300 yards from A41 on the B489 to Dunstable. Ideal for touring adjoining counties and Chilterns. Non-smokers only please.
Bedrooms: 1 single, 1 twin
Bathrooms: 1 public

Bed & breakfast
per night:	£min	£max
Single	15.00	17.00
Double	30.00	34.00

Parking for 2

AYLESBURY
Buckinghamshire
Map ref 2C1

Historic county town in the Vale of Aylesbury. The cobbled market square has a Victorian clock tower and the 15th C King's Head Inn (National Trust). Interesting county museum and 13th C parish church. Twice-weekly livestock market.

Apsley Manor Farm
HIGHLY COMMENDED

North Lee Lane, Marsh, Aylesbury HP22 5YA
☎ (0296) 613209

300-acre arable & dairy farm. 15th C Grade II listed manor farmhouse with oak beams, inglenook fireplaces. Lovely views of the Chiltern Hills. 3 miles from Stoke Mandeville.
Bedrooms: 1 double, 1 twin
Bathrooms: 2 private

Bed & breakfast
per night:	£min	£max
Single		25.00
Double		40.00

Parking for 12

The Old Wheatsheaf Inn
Listed

Weedon, Aylesbury HP22 4NS
☎ (0296) 641581
Old Elizabethan coaching inn, furnished with antiques. Courtyard surrounded by self-catering cottage and stable-cots. Home-from-home treatment and atmosphere. Garden with National Gardens Scheme.
Bedrooms: 3 single, 3 double, 2 twin
Bathrooms: 2 private, 3 public

Bed & breakfast
per night:	£min	£max
Single	30.00	35.00
Double	60.00	70.00

Lunch available
Evening meal 1830 (last orders 2200)
Parking for 14

Wallace Farm

Dinton, Aylesbury HP17 8UF
☎ (0296) 748660
Fax (0296) 748851
150-acre mixed farm. 16th C farmhouse offers comfortable en-suite accommodation in a quiet rural setting. Self-catering cottages also available for weekly rental.
Bedrooms: 1 double, 1 twin, 1 triple
Bathrooms: 3 private

Bed & breakfast
per night:	£min	£max
Single	28.00	
Double	36.00	38.00

Parking for 6
Cards accepted: Access, Visa

BAMPTON
Oxfordshire
Map ref 2C1

Small market town, well known for its Spring Bank Holiday Monday Fete with Morris Dance Festival.

The Elephant & Castle

Bridge Street, Bampton, Oxford OX18 2HA
☎ (0993) 850316
Grade II listed country pub with chalet-style rooms. Oak beams and open fires. Easy access to the Cotswolds.
Bedrooms: 1 double, 2 twin
Bathrooms: 3 private

Bed & breakfast
per night:	£min	£max
Single	18.00	20.00
Double	32.00	36.00

Parking for 10
Cards accepted: Access, Visa

Romany Inn
Listed

Bridge Street, Bampton, Oxford OX18 2HA
☎ (0993) 850237

Family-run 17th C listed inn, with friendly local clientele and reputation for food. Lounge bar, separate restaurant, log fires.
Bedrooms: 4 double, 2 twin, 2 triple
Bathrooms: 8 private

Bed & breakfast
per night:	£min	£max
Single	21.00	21.00
Double	30.00	30.00

Lunch available
Evening meal 1830 (last orders 2200)
Parking for 6
Cards accepted: Access, Visa

National Crown ratings were correct at the time of going to press but are subject to change. Please check at the time of booking.

SOUTH OF ENGLAND

BANBURY
Oxfordshire
Map ref 2C1

Famous for its cattle market, cakes and nursery rhyme Cross. Founded in Saxon times, it has some fine houses and interesting old inns. A good centre for touring Warwickshire and the Cotswolds.
Tourist Information Centre
☎ (0295) 259855

The Lodge
COMMENDED

Main Road, Middleton Cheney, Banbury OX17 2PP
☎ (0295) 710255
200-year-old lodge in lovely countryside, on outskirts of historic village, 3 miles east of Banbury on A422.
Bedrooms: 1 double, 1 twin
Bathrooms: 2 private
Bed & breakfast

per night:	£min	£max
Double	40.00	42.00

Parking for 5

The Mill Barn

Lower Tadmarton, Banbury OX15 5SU
☎ Swalcliffe (029 578) 349
Family home offering en-suite ground floor accommodation in a beautifully converted stone barn, set in an acre of grounds. Convenient for Oxford, Stratford-upon-Avon and the Cotswolds.
Bedrooms: 1 double, 1 triple
Bathrooms: 2 private
Bed & breakfast

per night:	£min	£max
Single	20.00	25.00
Double	35.00	40.00

Parking for 4

The Old Manor
Listed HIGHLY COMMENDED

Cropredy, Banbury OX17 1PS
☎ (0295) 750235
Fax (0295) 758479
Partially moated manor house alongside Oxford Canal and in centre of village. Rare breed farm animals and private motor museum.
Bedrooms: 1 double, 1 twin
Bathrooms: 2 private
Bed & breakfast

per night:	£min	£max
Single	22.50	25.00
Double	40.00	44.00

Parking for 20
Cards accepted: Access, Visa

"Roxtones"
Listed

Malthouse Lane, Shutford, Banbury OX15 6PB
☎ (0295) 788240
Stone-fronted semi-bungalow with garden surrounds, orchard and lawns. 6 miles from Banbury, 16 miles from Stratford-upon-Avon and 2 miles from Broughton Castle.
Bedrooms: 2 single, 1 double
Bathrooms: 1 public
Bed & breakfast

per night:	£min	£max
Single		15.00
Double		25.00

Half board

per person:	£min	£max
Daily		21.50
Weekly		150.00

Evening meal 1900 (last orders 2100)
Parking for 3
Open April-September

BASINGSTOKE
Hampshire
Map ref 2C2

Rapidly developing commercial and industrial centre. The town is surrounded by charming villages and places to visit.
Tourist Information Centre
☎ (0256) 817618

Cedar Court

Reading Road, Hook, Basingstoke RG27 9DB
☎ (0256) 762178
Comfortable ground floor accommodation with delightful gardens. On the B3349 between the M3 and M4. Six miles east of Basingstoke, 1 hour from London and the coast.
Bedrooms: 3 single, 1 double, 1 twin, 1 triple
Bathrooms: 2 private, 1 public
Bed & breakfast

per night:	£min	£max
Single	17.00	25.00
Double	28.00	35.00

Parking for 6
Cards accepted: Access, Visa, Diners

Street Farm House
COMMENDED

The Street, South Warnborough, Basingstoke RG25 1RS
☎ (0256) 862225
Charming Jacobean farmhouse, offering comfortable facilities. Well situated in a pretty, rural village within easy reach of London, Guildford and the south coast.
Bedrooms: 2 twin, 1 triple
Bathrooms: 1 private, 1 public, 1 private shower

Bed & breakfast

per night:	£min	£max
Double	32.00	42.00

Half board

per person:	£min	£max
Daily	26.00	31.00

Evening meal from 1930
Parking for 9
Cards accepted: Amex

BEAULIEU
Hampshire
Map ref 2C3

Beautifully situated among woods and hills on the Beaulieu river, the village is both charming and unspoilt. The 13th C ruined Cistercian abbey and 14th C Palace House stand close to the National Motor Museum. There is a maritime museum at Bucklers Hard.

Coolderry Cottage
Listed

Masseys Lane, East Boldre, Beaulieu SO42 7WE
☎ Lymington (0590) 612428
Charming New Forest cottage in quiet lane. Friendly family home. Cosy rooms. Cot available. Ideal for motor museum, Bucklers Hard and Exbury Gardens. Pub meals within walking distance. Half-price winter breaks. Non-smoking.
Bedrooms: 1 double, 1 twin
Bathrooms: 1 public
Bed & breakfast

per night:	£min	£max
Double	25.00	32.00

Parking for 4

Leygreen Farm House

Lyndhurst Road, Beaulieu, Brockenhurst SO42 7YP
☎ Lymington (0590) 612355
Comfortable Victorian farmhouse with large garden. Convenient for Beaulieu, Bucklers Hard museums and Exbury Gardens.
Bedrooms: 2 double, 1 twin
Bathrooms: 2 private, 1 public
Bed & breakfast

per night:	£min	£max
Single	16.00	20.00
Double	28.00	36.00

Parking for 6

Please check prices and other details at the time of booking.

321

SOUTH OF ENGLAND

BICESTER
Oxfordshire
Map ref 2C1

Market town with large army depot and well-known hunting centre with hunt established in the late 18th C. The ancient parish church displays work of many periods. Nearby is the Jacobean mansion of Rousham House with gardens landscaped by William Kent.

Manor Farm
Listed

Poundon, Bicester OX6 0BB
☎ (0869) 277212
300-acre arable and mixed farm. 400-year-old farmhouse, tranquil, spacious and comfortable, a warm welcome to all. Take A421 Bicester to Buckingham road. Poundon turn is 3 miles along on right.
Bedrooms: 1 single, 1 double, 1 triple
Bathrooms: 1 private, 2 public

Bed & breakfast
per night:	£min	£max
Single	16.00	18.00
Double	32.00	36.00

Parking for 12

BLANDFORD FORUM
Dorset
Map ref 2B3

Almost completely destroyed by fire in 1731, the town was rebuilt in a handsome Georgian style. The church is large and grand and the town is the hub of a rich farming area.
Tourist Information Centre
☎ *(0258) 454770*

Church House
COMMENDED

Church Road, Shillingstone, Blandford Forum DT11 0SL
☎ Child Okeford (0258) 860646
Fax (0258) 860646

Charming, 18th C thatched farmhouse, near Blandford. Pretty gardens, en-suite bathrooms, four-poster, log fires, home cooking. Ideal for touring, walking, exploring.
Bedrooms: 1 double, 1 triple
Bathrooms: 2 private, 2 public

Bed & breakfast
per night:	£min	£max
Single	18.00	24.00
Double	32.00	44.00

Half board
per person:	£min	£max
Daily	27.00	34.00
Weekly	160.00	230.00

Lunch available
Evening meal 1800 (last orders 1930)
Parking for 3

Fairfield House
HIGHLY COMMENDED

Church Road, Pimperne, Blandford Forum DT11 8UB
☎ (0258) 456756
Fax (0258) 480053
Distinctive, Grade II, Georgian manor house with licensed a la carte restaurant, in 1.5 acres of gardens in peaceful village. Bedrooms tastefully furnished, retaining much antiquity whilst offering modern facilities. Riding, clay shooting and golf arranged. Stables available.
Wheelchair access category 3
Bedrooms: 1 single, 2 double, 2 twin
Bathrooms: 5 private, 1 public

Bed & breakfast
per night:	£min	£max
Single		29.50
Double		52.00

Half board
per person:	£min	£max
Daily		36.50
Weekly		230.00

Lunch available
Evening meal 1900 (last orders 2100)
Parking for 20
Cards accepted: Access, Visa, Diners, Amex

Meadow House
Listed

Tarrant Hinton, Blandford Forum DT11 8JG
☎ Tarrant Hinton (025 889) 498
Brick and flint farmhouse on historic Cranborne Chase. Double glazed, quiet and comfortable accommodation. Home-produced English breakfast.
Bedrooms: 1 single, 1 double, 1 triple
Bathrooms: 3 public

Bed & breakfast
per night:	£min	£max
Single	15.00	20.00
Double	30.00	40.00

Parking for 6

We advise you to confirm your booking in writing.

BLETCHINGDON
Oxfordshire
Map ref 2C1

Thatched and stone-roofed cottages surround the village green with magnificent views of Ot Moor and the hills beyond.

Stonehouse Farm
Listed

Weston Road, Bletchingdon, Oxford OX5 3EA
☎ (0869) 350585
560-acre arable farm. 17th C Cotswold farmhouse. Ideal touring centre. 15 minutes north of Oxford, 20 minutes south of Banbury and 10 minutes from Blenheim Palace. Between the A4260 and A34, junction 9 of M40. 1 hour from Heathrow.
Bedrooms: 1 single, 1 double, 1 twin, 1 triple
Bathrooms: 2 public

Bed & breakfast
per night:	£min	£max
Single	15.00	18.00
Double	30.00	40.00

Parking for 11

BOURNEMOUTH
Dorset
Map ref 2B3

Seaside town set among the pines with a mild climate, sandy beaches and fine coastal views. The town has wide streets with excellent shops, a pier, a pavilion, museums and conference centre.
Tourist Information Centre
☎ *(0202) 789789*

The Cottage
COMMENDED

12 Southern Road, Southbourne, Bournemouth BH6 3SR
☎ (0202) 422764

Charming character family-run hotel. Restful location. Noted for home-prepared fresh cooking, cleanliness and tastefully furnished accommodation. Ample parking. Non-smoking.
Bedrooms: 1 single, 1 double, 2 twin, 1 triple, 2 family rooms
Bathrooms: 4 private, 2 public, 1 private shower

Bed & breakfast
per night:	£min	£max
Single	16.00	24.00
Double	32.00	44.00

SOUTH OF ENGLAND

Half board per person:	£min	£max
Daily	23.00	31.00
Weekly	152.00	174.00

Evening meal 1800 (last orders 1800)
Parking for 8

Downside Private Hotel
Listed

52 Westbourne Park Road,
Bournemouth BH4 8HQ
☎ (0202) 763109
Small friendly hotel in quiet position near chines, close to sea, shops, entertainments. Personal service, long or short stays welcome.
Bedrooms: 2 single, 2 double, 1 twin, 4 family rooms
Bathrooms: 2 public, 4 private showers

Bed & breakfast per night:	£min	£max
Single	11.50	15.50
Double	23.00	31.00

Half board per person:	£min	£max
Daily	17.50	21.50
Weekly	110.25	135.00

Evening meal from 1830
Parking for 5
Open April-September and Christmas

The Garthlyn Hotel
COMMENDED

6 Sandbourne Road, Alum Chine,
Westbourne, Bournemouth BH4 8JH
☎ (0202) 761016
Hotel of character with lovely gardens. Good quality beds. 4 minutes' walk to beaches (hut available). Car park in grounds.
Bedrooms: 6 double, 1 twin, 1 triple, 2 family rooms
Bathrooms: 8 private, 1 public

Bed & breakfast per night:	£min	£max
Single	21.00	26.50
Double	42.00	48.00

Half board per person:	£min	£max
Daily	28.50	35.00
Weekly	169.00	205.00

Evening meal 1800 (last orders 1900)
Parking for 9
Cards accepted: Access, Visa, Switch

The Golden Sovereigns Hotel

97 Alumhurst Road, Alum Chine,
Bournemouth BH4 8HR
☎ (0202) 762088

Attractive Victorian hotel of character, in a quiet yet convenient location 4 minutes' walk from beach. Comfortable rooms, traditional home-cooked food. Old English specialities by arrangement.
Bedrooms: 1 single, 3 double, 2 twin, 1 triple, 2 family rooms
Bathrooms: 5 private, 2 public

Bed & breakfast per night:	£min	£max
Single	15.00	27.00
Double	29.00	44.00

Half board per person:	£min	£max
Daily	22.50	35.50
Weekly	150.00	185.00

Lunch available
Evening meal 1800 (last orders 1630)
Parking for 9
Cards accepted: Access, Visa

Mayfield Private Hotel

46 Frances Road, Bournemouth
BH1 3SA
☎ (0202) 551839
Overlooking public gardens with tennis, bowling, putting greens. Central for sea, shops and main rail/coach stations. Some rooms with shower or toilet/shower. Licensed.
Bedrooms: 1 single, 4 double, 2 twin, 1 family room
Bathrooms: 4 private, 2 public, 2 private showers

Bed & breakfast per night:	£min	£max
Single	13.50	16.00
Double	27.00	32.00

Half board per person:	£min	£max
Daily	19.00	21.00
Weekly	110.00	127.00

Evening meal from 1800
Parking for 5
Open January-November

Pinecrest Guest House
COMMENDED

13 Fishermans Avenue, Southbourne,
Bournemouth BH6 3SQ
☎ (0202) 424966
Pinecrest has a bright and friendly atmosphere, comfortable rooms and good home cooking. 2 minutes' walk to the sea.
Bedrooms: 2 single, 1 double, 1 twin
Bathrooms: 1 private, 2 public

Bed & breakfast per night:	£min	£max
Single	14.00	17.00
Double	28.00	34.00

Evening meal 1800 (last orders 1800)

Pinewood
Listed COMMENDED

197 Holdenhurst Road, Bournemouth
BH8 8DG
☎ (0202) 292684
Friendly guesthouse, close to rail, coach stations and all amenities. Tea, coffee and satellite TV in all rooms.
Bedrooms: 1 single, 3 double, 1 twin, 3 triple
Bathrooms: 2 public

Bed & breakfast per night:	£min	£max
Single	14.00	15.00
Double	28.00	30.00

Parking for 8

Sun Haven

39 Southern Road, Southbourne,
Bournemouth BH6 3SS
☎ (0202) 427560
150 yards to sandy beach. Colour TV in bedrooms, central heating, snacks and tea/coffee facilities. Parking. Ideal for Bournemouth, Christchurch, New Forest and local beauty spots.
Bedrooms: 2 single, 3 double, 1 twin, 2 triple
Bathrooms: 3 public

Bed & breakfast per night:	£min	£max
Single	14.00	17.00
Double	28.00	33.00

Parking for 6
Open April-September

Willowdene Hotel
HIGHLY COMMENDED

43 Grand Avenue, Southbourne,
Bournemouth BH6 3SY
☎ (0202) 425370
Detached Edwardian house, completely refurbished, for those who require quality accommodation with a happy relaxed atmosphere. 200 yards from beautiful sandy beach.
Bedrooms: 3 double, 1 twin, 1 triple
Bathrooms: 4 private, 1 public

Bed & breakfast per night:	£min	£max
Single	15.00	16.50
Double	28.00	33.00

Parking for 8
Open April-October

SOUTH OF ENGLAND

BRACKNELL
Berkshire
Map ref 2C2

Designated a New Town in 1949, the town has ancient origins. Set in heathlands, it is an excellent centre for golf and walking. South Hill Park, an 18th C mansion, houses an art centre.
Tourist Information Centre
☎ (0344) 868196

Bear Farm
Binfield, Bracknell RG12 5QE
☎ Twyford (0734) 343286
65-acre mixed farm. 17th C oak-beamed farmhouse surrounded by 2 acres of well kept gardens, with en-suite guest bedrooms in an adjoining converted farm building.
Bedrooms: 1 double, 1 twin
Bathrooms: 2 private

Bed & breakfast
per night:	£min	£max
Single	22.50	23.50
Double		40.00

Parking for 6
Cards accepted: Access, Visa

BRAMDEAN
Hampshire
Map ref 2C3

Village astride the A272, 1 mile west of the site of a Roman villa.

Dean Farm
Listed
Kilmeston, Alresford SO24 0NL
☎ (0962) 771286
200-acre mixed farm. Comfortable, 18th C farmhouse in Kilmeston, a small and peaceful village 1.5 miles off the A272 between Petersfield and Winchester.
Bedrooms: 2 double, 1 triple
Bathrooms: 1 public

Bed & breakfast
per night:	£min	£max
Single	17.00	20.00
Double	34.00	34.00

Parking for 3

BRIGHTWELL-CUM-SOTWELL
Oxfordshire
Map ref 2C2

Small's House
Listed COMMENDED
Mackney, Brightwell-cum-Sotwell, Wallingford OX10 0SJ
☎ Wallingford (0491) 839167
Grade I listed, stone, Tudor manor house with beautiful garden, in rural situation 3 miles from Wallingford.

Bedrooms: 2 twin
Bathrooms: 1 private, 2 public, 1 private shower

Bed & breakfast
per night:	£min	£max
Single	20.00	22.00
Double	34.00	36.00

Half board
per person:	£min	£max
Daily	26.00	28.00

Parking for 6

BRIMPTON
Berkshire
Map ref 2C2

Manor Farm
Listed
Brimpton, Reading RG7 4SQ
☎ Woolhampton (0734) 713166
600-acre mixed farm. Family farm in Brimpton village. Interesting house and chapel, once of the Knights Hospitallers. Close to A4, M4 and M3.
Bedrooms: 1 double, 1 twin
Bathrooms: 1 public

Bed & breakfast
per night:	£min	£max
Single	17.50	20.00
Double	33.00	40.00

Parking for 4

BROCKENHURST
Hampshire
Map ref 2C3

Attractive village with thatched cottages and a ford in its main street. Well placed for visiting the New Forest.

The Watersplash Hotel
The Rise, Brockenhurst SO42 7ZP
☎ Lymington (0590) 22344
Fax (0590) 24047
Quiet, Victorian country house hotel set in beautiful gardens, renowned for its family-run atmosphere, good food, service and accommodation.
Bedrooms: 3 single, 9 double, 8 twin, 3 family rooms
Bathrooms: 23 private

Bed & breakfast
per night:	£min	£max
Single	39.00	49.00
Double	60.00	80.00

Half board
per person:	£min	£max
Daily	45.00	55.00
Weekly	260.00	280.00

Lunch available
Evening meal 1930 (last orders 2030)

Parking for 33
Cards accepted: Access, Visa

BUCKINGHAM
Buckinghamshire
Map ref 2C1

Interesting old market town surrounded by rich farmland. It has many Georgian buildings, including the Town Hall and Old Jail and many old almshouses and inns. Stowe School nearby has magnificent 18th C landscaped gardens.

Folly Farm
COMMENDED
Padbury, Buckingham MK18 2HS
☎ Winslow (0296) 712413
Fax (0296) 712413
500-acre arable farm. On A413 between Winslow and Padbury, 4 miles south of Buckingham. Substantial farmhouse opposite Folly Inn. Convenient for Stowe Landscape Gardens, Silverstone circuit and Addington Equestrian Centre.
Bedrooms: 2 double, 1 twin
Bathrooms: 3 private

Bed & breakfast
per night:	£min	£max
Single	17.50	17.50
Double	30.00	30.00

Parking for 10

BURFORD
Oxfordshire
Map ref 2B1

One of the most beautiful Cotswold wool towns with Georgian and Tudor houses, many antique shops and a picturesque High Street sloping to the River Windrush.
Tourist Information Centre
☎ (0993) 823558

The Dower House
Westhall Hill, Fulbrook, Oxford OX18 4BJ
☎ (0993) 822596
Elegant, newly-restored period accommodation in an imposing Cotswold dower house. Superb and tranquil setting, with commanding views over Burford and beautiful surrounding countryside. South-facing bedrooms and picturesque gardens.
Bedrooms: 2 double
Bathrooms: 1 private, 1 public

Bed & breakfast
per night:	£min	£max
Double	32.00	34.00

Parking for 3

SOUTH OF ENGLAND

Glenthorne House

174 The Hill, Burford, Oxford
OX18 4QY
☎ (0993) 822418
14th C Cotswold stone house with many medieval features but modern comforts. Private parking and garden. No smoking.
Bedrooms: 1 double, 2 twin
Bathrooms: 1 private, 1 public
Bed & breakfast

per night:	£min	£max
Single	25.00	35.00
Double	35.00	45.00

Parking for 3

The Highway Hotel

High Street, Burford, Oxford OX8 4RG
☎ (0993) 822136
Telex Hussey 838736
Beamed medieval Cotswold hotel offering en-suite rooms with TV. Ideal touring base for Cotswolds. Incorporating acclaimed needlecraft centre.
Bedrooms: 7 double, 2 twin, 2 triple
Bathrooms: 9 private, 1 public
Bed & breakfast

per night:	£min	£max
Single	25.00	35.00
Double	35.00	40.00

Cards accepted: Access, Visa, Diners, Amex

Rookery Farm
Listed COMMENDED

Burford Road, Brize Norton, Oxford
OX18 3NL
☎ Carterton (0993) 842957

2-acre smallholding. 18th C Cotswold farmhouse, pleasantly situated in small Oxfordshire village with lovely views of surrounding countryside. Generous farmhouse breakfast.
Bedrooms: 2 double, 1 twin
Bathrooms: 1 public
Bed & breakfast

per night:	£min	£max
Single	17.00	17.00
Double	34.00	34.00

Parking for 4

The Royal Oak
COMMENDED

26 Witney Street, Burford, Oxford
OX18 4SN
☎ (0993) 823278

17th C inn situated in a quiet position, approximately 100 yards from High Street. Off-street parking available.
Bedrooms: 1 double, 1 twin
Bathrooms: 2 private
Bed & breakfast

per night:	£min	£max
Single	20.00	40.00
Double	40.00	60.00

Lunch available
Evening meal 1900 (last orders 2130)
Parking for 6
Cards accepted: Access, Visa

Warwick House
APPROVED

25 Lower High Street, Burford, Oxford
OX8 4RN
☎ (0993) 823438
Grade II listed building with a Georgian facade, dating from 1590. En-suite facilities, TV in all rooms.
Bedrooms: 1 double, 2 twin
Bathrooms: 3 private
Bed & breakfast

per night:	£min	£max
Single	17.50	25.00
Double	25.00	35.00

BURLEY

Hampshire
Map ref 2B3

Attractive centre from which to explore the south-west part of the New Forest. There is an ancient earthwork on Castle Hill nearby, which also offers good views.

Forest Tea House & Restaurant

Pound Lane, Burley, Ringwood
BH24 4ED
☎ (0425) 402305
Tea rooms and restaurant offering en-suite bed and breakfast accommodation, colour TVs and beverage facilities. Evening meal by prior arrangement.
Bedrooms: 2 double, 1 twin
Bathrooms: 3 private
Bed & breakfast

per night:	£min	£max
Single	30.00	30.00
Double	40.00	40.00

Half board

per person:	£min	£max
Daily	30.00	30.00
Weekly	200.00	200.00

Lunch available
Evening meal 1900 (last orders 2000)
Parking for 20

Holmans
HIGHLY COMMENDED

Bisterne Close, Burley, Ringwood
BH24 4AZ
☎ (0425) 402307
Charming family house in 4 acres, overlooking New Forest and near golf-course. Marvellous horseriding and stabling available. Before White Buck Inn, turn right into Bisterne Close, fourth house on right.
Bedrooms: 1 single, 2 twin
Bathrooms: 2 private, 1 public
Bed & breakfast

per night:	£min	£max
Single	18.00	18.00
Double	36.00	40.00

Parking for 12

CADNAM

Hampshire
Map ref 2C3

Village with numerous attractive cottages and an inn close to the entrance of the M27.

Budd's Farm
Listed APPROVED

Winsor Road, Winsor, Southampton
SO4 2HN
☎ Southampton (0703) 812381
200-acre dairy farm. Well-modernised, thatched farmhouse in pretty country garden. Located off A336.
Bedrooms: 2 triple
Bathrooms: 1 public
Bed & breakfast

per night:	£min	£max
Single	15.50	16.00
Double	31.00	32.00

Parking for 3
Open April-October

CHANDLERS FORD

Hampshire
Map ref 2C3

Landfall
Listed

133 Bournemouth Road, Chandlers Ford, Eastleigh SO5 3HA
☎ Southampton (0703) 254801
Three bedroom, detached, family home. Situated in service road, with easy access to all routes. Pleasant garden with solar heated swimming pool.
Bedrooms: 1 single, 1 double
Bathrooms: 1 public
Bed & breakfast

per night:	£min	£max
Single	15.00	16.00
Double	26.00	28.00

Parking for 2

325

SOUTH OF ENGLAND

CHANDLERS FORD
Continued

St Lucia
Listed COMMENDED

68 Shaftesbury Avenue, Chandlers Ford, Eastleigh SO5 3BP
☎ (0703) 262995
Fax (0703) 262995

Homely accommodation well placed for touring, near Winchester, the south coast and the New Forest. Evening meals, home-grown produce in season. Non-smokers only please.
Bedrooms: 1 single, 2 twin
Bathrooms: 1 public

Bed & breakfast per night:

	£min	£max
Single	13.00	16.00
Double	28.00	30.00

Half board per person:

	£min	£max
Daily	16.50	19.50
Weekly	105.00	125.00

Evening meal 1830 (last orders 1830)
Parking for 5

CHIPPING NORTON
Oxfordshire
Map ref 2C1

Old market town set high in the Cotswolds and an ideal touring centre. The wide market-place contains many 16th C and 17th C stone houses and the Town Hall and Tudor Guildhall.

The Crown & Cushion Hotel Leisure Centre ₥
COMMENDED

23 High Street, Chipping Norton OX7 5AD
☎ (0608) 642533
Fax (0608) 642926

15th C coaching inn with indoor pool and leisure complex. Convenient for M40 motorway, Warwick, Blenheim, Stratford-upon-Avon, Cheltenham, Oxford and the Cotswolds.
Bedrooms: 29 double, 11 twin
Bathrooms: 40 private

Bed & breakfast per night:

	£min	£max
Single	19.50	59.00
Double	39.00	90.00

Half board per person:

	£min	£max
Daily	32.50	69.00
Weekly	189.00	420.00

Lunch available
Evening meal 1900 (last orders 2100)
Parking for 23
Cards accepted: Access, Visa, Diners, Amex

CHRISTCHURCH
Dorset
Map ref 2B3

Tranquil town lying between the Avon and Stour just before they converge and flow into Christchurch Harbour. A fine 11th C church and the remains of a Norman castle and house can be seen.
Tourist Information Centre
☎ *(0202) 471780*

The Beech Tree
COMMENDED

2 Stuart Road, Highcliffe, Christchurch BH23 5JS
☎ Highcliffe (0425) 272038

Warm, family-run guesthouse offering quality accommodation. Ground-floor rooms available. Perfect touring base for Dorset and Hampshire. 5 minutes from beach, shops and New Forest.
Bedrooms: 5 double, 1 twin
Bathrooms: 4 private, 1 public

Bed & breakfast per night:

	£min	£max
Single	16.00	18.00
Double	32.00	36.00

Half board per person:

	£min	£max
Daily	24.00	26.00
Weekly	168.00	182.00

Evening meal 1800 (last orders 1800)
Parking for 7

Individual proprietors have supplied details of accommodation. Although we do check for accuracy, we advise you to confirm the information at the time of booking.

COMPTON
Berkshire
Map ref 2C2

Village lies above a hollow on the eastern slope of the Berkshire Downs, a little south of the Ridgeway and the ancient British stronghold of Perborough Castle.

The Compton Swan Hotel ₥

High Street, Compton, Newbury RG16 0NH
☎ Newbury (0635) 578269
Fax (0635) 578269

Recently refurbished country hotel with games room, lounge, restaurant, extensive a la carte menu, large garden and a bar with a range of real ales. Close to the Ridgeway.
Bedrooms: 1 double, 3 twin, 1 family room
Bathrooms: 3 private, 2 public, 2 private showers

Bed & breakfast per night:

	£min	£max
Single	32.00	32.00
Double	42.00	42.00

Half board per person:

	£min	£max
Daily	37.00	45.00
Weekly	210.00	250.00

Lunch available
Evening meal 1800 (last orders 2200)
Parking for 30
Cards accepted: Access, Visa

COMPTON
Hampshire
Map ref 2C3

Mrs P Neyroud
Listed

Manor House, Place Lane, Compton, Winchester SO21 2BA
☎ Twyford (0962) 712162

Comfortable country house, 8 minutes from Shawford railway station and 2 miles west of Winchester. Non-smokers preferred.
Bedrooms: 1 double
Bathrooms: 1 public

Bed & breakfast per night:

	£min	£max
Single	10.50	10.50
Double	21.00	21.00

Parking for 1

Establishments should be open throughout the year unless otherwise stated in the entry.

SOUTH OF ENGLAND

COOMBE KEYNES
Dorset
Map ref 2B3

West Coombe Farmhouse
Listed

Coombe Keynes, Wareham BH20 5PS
☎ Bindon Abbey (0929) 462889

Former farmhouse in quiet hamlet near coast. Turn off B3071 midway between Wool and Lulworth, first house on left in village.
Bedrooms: 1 single, 1 double, 1 twin
Bathrooms: 1 public
Bed & breakfast

per night:	£min	£max
Single	18.00	20.00
Double	30.00	33.00

Evening meal from 1900
Parking for 3

CORFE CASTLE
Dorset
Map ref 2B3

One of the most spectacular ruined castles in Britain. Norman in origin, the castle was a Royalist stronghold during the Civil War and held out until 1645. The village had a considerable marble-carving industry in the Middle Ages.

Kimmeridge Farmhouse
Listed

Kimmeridge, Wareham BH20 5PE
☎ (0929) 480990
750-acre mixed farm. Farmhouse built in the 16th C, with lovely views of surrounding countryside and sea. Warm family atmosphere and spacious facilities. Evening meals by arrangement with local inn.
Bedrooms: 2 double, 1 twin
Bathrooms: 1 private, 1 public
Bed & breakfast

per night:	£min	£max
Single	20.00	25.00
Double	32.00	37.00

Parking for 3

Symbols are explained on the flap inside the back cover.

COWES
Isle of Wight
Map ref 2C3

Regular ferry and hydrofoil services cross the Solent to Cowes. The town is the headquarters of the Royal Yacht Squadron and Cowes Week is held every August.
Tourist Information Centre
☎ *(0983) 291914*

Mrs J Gibbons

14 Milton Road, Cowes PO31 7PX
☎ Isle of Wight (0983) 295723
Close to town centre and cycle track, on bus route. Continental or English breakfast. Quiet river views, parking. Free pick-up.
Bedrooms: 1 single, 1 twin
Bathrooms: 1 private, 1 public
Bed & breakfast

per night:	£min	£max
Single	14.00	22.00
Double	28.00	44.00

Half board

per person:	£min	£max
Daily	24.00	28.00
Weekly	100.00	148.00

Evening meal 1900 (last orders 2100)
Parking for 2

CRANBORNE
Dorset
Map ref 2B3

Village with an interesting Jacobean manor house. Lies south-east of Cranborne Chase, formerly a forest and hunting preserve.

The Fleur de Lys
APPROVED

5 Wimborne Street, Cranborne, Wimborne Minster BH21 5PP
☎ (072 54) 282
Charming old-world coaching inn, close to the New Forest, with a cosy atmosphere and friendly hospitality. Restaurant and bar. En-suite accommodation.
Bedrooms: 1 single, 4 double, 3 twin
Bathrooms: 7 private, 1 private shower
Bed & breakfast

per night:	£min	£max
Single	25.00	35.00
Double	38.00	50.00

Half board

per person:	£min	£max
Daily	32.00	48.00
Weekly	200.00	300.00

Lunch available
Evening meal 1900 (last orders 2145)
Parking for 35
Cards accepted: Access, Visa, Amex

CUDDESDON
Oxfordshire
Map ref 2C1

The Bat & Ball Inn
28 High Street, Cuddesdon, Oxford OX44 9HJ
☎ Oxford (0865) 874379
Old coaching inn with scenic views and interesting collection of cricket memorabilia. Cuddesdon is an attractive small village, well placed for Oxford and the M40.
Bedrooms: 5 double, 1 twin
Bathrooms: 6 private
Bed & breakfast

per night:	£min	£max
Single	35.00	35.00
Double	40.00	40.00

Lunch available
Evening meal 1830 (last orders 2100)
Parking for 15
Cards accepted: Access, Visa

DEDDINGTON
Oxfordshire
Map ref 2C1

Attractive former market town with a large market square and many fine old buildings.

Hill Barn
Listed

Milton Gated Road, Deddington, Banbury OX15 4TS
☎ (0869) 38631
Converted barn set in open countryside with views overlooking valley and hills. Banbury-Oxford road, half a mile before Deddington, turn right to Milton Gated Road. Hill Barn is 100 yards on the right.
Bedrooms: 1 double, 2 twin
Bathrooms: 1 public
Bed & breakfast

per night:	£min	£max
Single	15.00	20.00
Double	30.00	30.00

Parking for 6

Unicorn Hotel
APPROVED

Market Place, Deddington, Banbury OX15 0SE
☎ (0869) 38838
Fax (0869) 38036
17th C Cotswold border coaching inn, 10 minutes from M40 junctions 10 and 11, on A4260 Banbury to Oxford road.
Bedrooms: 4 single, 3 double, 1 twin, 1 triple

Continued ▶

SOUTH OF ENGLAND

DEDDINGTON
Continued

Bathrooms: 9 private
Bed & breakfast

per night:	£min	£max
Single	35.00	35.00
Double	45.00	45.00

Half board

per person:	£min	£max
Daily	41.00	41.00
Weekly	250.00	250.00

Lunch available
Evening meal 1900 (last orders 2100)
Parking for 33
Cards accepted: Access, Visa, Diners, Amex

DENMEAD
Hampshire
Map ref 2C3

Comparatively modern town, south-west of the original settlement.

Forest Gate
Listed

Hambledon Road, Denmead, Waterlooville PO7 6EX
☎ Waterlooville (0705) 255901
Georgian house in 2 acre garden, on main Hambledon road B2150, halfway between Denmead and Hambledon. Dinner by arrangement.
Bedrooms: 2 twin
Bathrooms: 2 private
Bed & breakfast

per night:	£min	£max
Single	18.00	20.00
Double	32.00	36.00

Half board

per person:	£min	£max
Daily	29.50	31.50
Weekly	200.00	215.00

Evening meal from 1930
Parking for 4

DIBDEN
Hampshire
Map ref 2C3

Small village on the edge of the New Forest with a full recreation centre. Picturesque 13th C church overlooks Southampton Water.

Dale Farm Guest House

Manor Road, Applemore Hill, Dibden, Southampton SO4 5TJ
☎ Southampton (0703) 849632
Friendly, family-run 18th C converted farmhouse, in wooded setting with large garden. 250 yards from A326, adjacent

to riding stables and 15 minutes from beach.
Bedrooms: 1 single, 2 double, 2 twin, 1 triple
Bathrooms: 1 public, 1 private shower
Bed & breakfast

per night:	£min	£max
Single	16.50	19.50
Double	30.00	34.00

Half board

per person:	£min	£max
Weekly	145.00	

Evening meal 1800 (last orders 1100)
Parking for 10

DIDCOT
Oxfordshire
Map ref 2C2

Important railway junction where steam engines can still be seen at the Didcot Railway Centre, together with a recreated station and a small relics museum.

North Croft Cottage
Listed COMMENDED

North Croft, East Hagbourne, Didcot OX11 9LT
☎ (0235) 813326

17th C low white cottage with oak beams inside and out, inglenook fireplace and leaded windows. Set in the heart of Oxfordshire countryside yet only 10 minutes from Didcot main line railway station.
Bedrooms: 3 single, 1 double
Bathrooms: 2 public
Bed & breakfast

per night:	£min	£max
Single		25.00
Double		38.00

Parking for 4

EAST HENDRED
Oxfordshire
Map ref 2C2

Monks Court
Listed

Newbury Road, East Hendred, Wantage OX12 8LG
☎ Abingdon (0235) 833797 & 815907 (office)
Comfortable family house on outskirts of beautiful village. Only 1.5 miles from the Ridgeway and 3 miles from A34. Convenient for Oxford and Newbury.

Bedrooms: 1 double, 1 twin
Bathrooms: 1 public
Bed & breakfast

per night:	£min	£max
Single	15.00	19.00
Double	32.00	34.00

Parking for 3

FAREHAM
Hampshire
Map ref 2C3

Lies on a quiet backwater of Portsmouth Harbour. The High Street is lined with fine Georgian buildings.
Tourist Information Centre
☎ (0329) 221342

Manor House

Church Path, Fareham PO16 7DT
☎ (0329) 287775 & Mobile (0850) 800906
Grade II listed Victorian manor house, situated in town centre with easy access to M27.
Bedrooms: 1 single, 1 double, 2 twin
Bathrooms: 1 public, 3 private showers
Bed & breakfast

per night:	£min	£max
Single	29.00	35.00
Double	58.00	70.00

Parking for 10
Cards accepted: Access, Visa

FLEET
Hampshire
Map ref 2C2

Tourist Information Centre
☎ (0252) 811151

The Webbs
Listed

12 Warren Close, Fleet, Aldershot GU13 9LT
☎ Aldershot (0252) 615063
Homely, friendly atmosphere. Families welcome (no age limit). Close to Fleet station, A30 and M3, exit 4A.
Bedrooms: 2 single, 1 twin
Bathrooms: 2 public
Bed & breakfast

per night:	£min	£max
Single	17.00	17.00
Double	34.00	34.00

Half board

per person:	£min	£max
Daily	25.00	25.00

Evening meal 1830 (last orders 1700)
Parking for 2

SOUTH OF ENGLAND

FORDINGBRIDGE
Hampshire
Map ref 2B3

On the north-west edge of the New Forest. A medieval bridge crosses the Avon at this point and gave the town its name. A good centre for walking, exploring and fishing.

Hillbury
Listed

2 Fir Tree Hill, Camel Green Road, Alderholt, Fordingbridge SP6 3AY
☎ (0425) 652582
Quiet situation with easy access to M27. Ideal touring base for New Forest and south coast. Riding, swimming, golf and fishing nearby. Non-smokers only please.
Bedrooms: 1 single, 1 twin, 1 triple
Bathrooms: 1 private, 1 public
Bed & breakfast

per night:	£min	£max
Single	15.00	17.00
Double	30.00	34.00

Parking for 5

Partridge Piece
Listed

Ogdens, Fordingbridge SP6 2PZ
☎ (0425) 655365
8-acre smallholding. Attractive house in heart of New Forest, 3 miles from Fordingbridge. Superb walking, birdwatching and riding. Catering for horses and riders a speciality.
Bedrooms: 1 twin
Bathrooms: 1 private
Bed & breakfast

per night:	£min	£max
Double	30.00	35.00

Parking for 4
Open March-November

FRITHAM
Hampshire
Map ref 2C3

Chapel Lane Cottage
Listed

Fritham, Lyndhurst SO43 7HL
☎ Southampton (0703) 812359
Friendly, comfortable accommodation in small hamlet. Easy access from M27, but very quiet and with direct access to beautiful forest. Non-smokers only please.
Bedrooms: 1 double
Bathrooms: 1 private
Bed & breakfast

per night:	£min	£max
Double	34.00	34.00

Parking for 1

Fritham Farm
COMMENDED

Fritham, Lyndhurst SO43 7HH
☎ Southampton (0703) 812333
Fax (0703) 812333

51-acre mixed farm. Lovely farmhouse in quiet situation in heart of glorious New Forest. Large comfortable lounge, TV. Warm welcome, wonderful walking, cycling and touring centre.
Bedrooms: 1 double, 2 twin
Bathrooms: 3 private
Bed & breakfast

per night:	£min	£max
Double	33.00	35.00

Half board

per person:	£min	£max
Daily	25.00	26.00

Parking for 3

GERRARDS CROSS
Buckinghamshire
Map ref 2D2

On the London Road, Gerrards Cross is distinguished by its wide gorse and beech tree common.

Dovetails
Listed

Upway, Chalfont Heights, Chalfont St Peter, Gerrards Cross SL9 0AS
☎ (0753) 882639
60-year-old detached house in its own garden, on a quiet, private estate.
Bedrooms: 2 twin
Bathrooms: 1 public
Bed & breakfast

per night:	£min	£max
Single	20.00	25.00
Double	35.00	40.00

Half board

per person:	£min	£max
Daily	27.50	32.50
Weekly	185.00	200.00

Evening meal 1800 (last orders 2000)
Parking for 2

Tree Tops
Listed

Main Drive, Bulstrode Park, Gerrards Cross SL9 7PR
☎ (0753) 887083

Large house with picturesque gardens in exclusive residential area of Gerrards Cross, close to village and station (for Marylebone, London). Convenient for Ascot, Windsor, Heathrow, M40, M25, M4. Guest lounge with TV. Parking. Evening meals by arrangement.
Bedrooms: 1 single, 1 double, 1 twin
Bathrooms: 1 public, 1 private shower
Bed & breakfast

per night:	£min	£max
Single	22.00	27.00
Double	39.00	48.00

Parking for 3

GORING
Oxfordshire
Map ref 2C2

Riverside town on the Oxfordshire/Berkshire border, linked by an attractive bridge to Streatley with views to the Goring Gap.

The John Barleycorn

Manor Road, Goring, Reading, Berkshire RG8 9DP
☎ (0491) 872509
16th C inn with exposed beams. Real ale, home-cooked food. Close to the river, lovely walks.
Bedrooms: 1 single, 1 double, 1 triple
Bathrooms: 2 public
Bed & breakfast

per night:	£min	£max
Single	21.00	
Double	35.00	

Lunch available
Evening meal 1900 (last orders 2200)
Parking for 2

GREAT HORWOOD
Buckinghamshire
Map ref 2C1

Mill Farm
Listed

Winslow Road, Great Horwood, Milton Keynes MK17 0NY
☎ Winslow (0296) 712527
52-acre livestock farm. House in a quiet location, with views across open country. On B4033 between Winslow and Great Horwood. Access to North Bucks Way. Non-smokers only please.
Bedrooms: 1 double, 1 triple
Bathrooms: 1 public

Continued ▶

SOUTH OF ENGLAND

GREAT HORWOOD
Continued

Bed & breakfast
per night:	£min	£max
Single	15.00	15.00
Double	29.00	29.00

Parking for 25

HAMBLE
Hampshire
Map ref 2C3

Set almost at the mouth of the River Hamble, this quiet fishing village has become a major yachting centre.

Braymar
Listed

35 Westfield Close, Hamble, Southampton SO3 5LG
☎ Southampton (0703) 453831
Private house, in peaceful position, 5 minutes from quiet beach and pretty, sailing village of Hamble, where "Howards Way" was filmed. 15 minutes' drive from Southampton and Portsmouth. Near M27.
Bedrooms: 1 single, 1 double, 2 twin
Bathrooms: 1 public

Bed & breakfast
per night:	£min	£max
Single	12.00	13.00
Double	24.00	26.00

Parking for 3

HAMBLEDON
Hampshire
Map ref 2C3

In a valley, surrounded by wooded downland and marked by an air of Georgian prosperity. It was here that cricket was given its first proper rules. The Bat and Ball Inn at Broadhalfpenny Down is the cradle of cricket.

Cams

Hambledon, Waterlooville PO7 4SP
☎ Portsmouth (0705) 632865
Fax (0705) 632691
Comfortable, listed family house in beautiful setting with large garden on the edge of Hambledon village. Two pubs within walking distance. Evening meal by arrangement.
Bedrooms: 1 double, 2 twin
Bathrooms: 1 private, 1 public, 1 private shower

Bed & breakfast
per night:	£min	£max
Single	15.00	17.00
Double	30.00	34.00

Half board
per person:	£min	£max
Daily	23.00	27.00
Weekly	147.00	165.00

Evening meal from 1900
Parking for 6

Mornington House
Listed

Speltham Hill, Hambledon, Waterlooville PO7 4RU
☎ Portsmouth (0705) 632704
18th C private house with 2 acres of garden and paddock, in the centre of Hambledon behind the George Inn, 2 miles from famous Bat and Ball Inn.
Bedrooms: 2 twin
Bathrooms: 1 public

Bed & breakfast
per night:	£min	£max
Single	15.00	15.00
Double	28.00	28.00

Parking for 6

Nightingale Cottage
HIGHLY COMMENDED

Hoegate, Hambledon, Waterlooville PO7 4RD
☎ Portsmouth (0705) 632447
Country house on outskirts of Hambledon, adjacent to Hoegate Common. A quarter of a mile from Rudley Mill and half a mile from B2150. In Area of Outstanding Natural Beauty.
Bedrooms: 2 double, 1 twin
Bathrooms: 3 private, 1 public

Bed & breakfast
per night:	£min	£max
Single	20.00	25.00
Double	36.00	50.00

Parking for 8
Cards accepted: Access, Visa

HAVANT
Hampshire
Map ref 2C3

Once a market town famous for making parchment. Nearby at Leigh Park extensive early 19th C landscape gardens and parklands are open to the public. Right in the centre of the town stands the interesting 13th C church of St Faith.

Tourist Information Centre
☎ (0705) 480024

Holland House Guest House

33 Bedhampton Hill, Havant PO9 3JN
☎ Portsmouth (0705) 475913
Fax (0705) 470134
Comfortable, friendly guesthouse, ideal for touring, continental ferry port, business and the sea.
Bedrooms: 2 single, 1 double, 1 twin
Bathrooms: 1 private, 1 public

Bed & breakfast
per night:	£min	£max
Single	15.00	25.00
Double	27.00	35.00

Evening meal 1700 (last orders 1845)
Parking for 6

The Old Mill Guest House

Mill Lane, Bedhampton, Havant PO9 3JH
☎ Portsmouth (0705) 454948
Georgian house in large grounds by a lake abundant in wildlife. Modernised, comfortable retreat. John Keats rested here.
Bedrooms: 1 twin, 4 triple
Bathrooms: 5 private

Bed & breakfast
per night:	£min	£max
Single	25.00	25.00
Double	39.00	39.00

Parking for 10

HAYLING ISLAND
Hampshire
Map ref 2C3

Small, flat island of historic interest, surrounded by natural harbours and with fine sandy beaches, linked to the mainland by a road.

Newtown House Hotel

Manor Road, Hayling Island PO11 0QR
☎ Portsmouth (0705) 466131
Fax (0705) 461366

Set in own grounds, a quarter of a mile from seafront. Indoor leisure complex with heated pool, gym, jacuzzi and sauna. Tennis.
Bedrooms: 10 single, 11 double, 4 twin, 3 triple
Bathrooms: 28 private, 2 public

Half board
per person:	£min	£max
Daily	45.00	45.00
Weekly	270.00	270.00

Lunch available
Evening meal 1900 (last orders 2130)
Parking for 45

SOUTH OF ENGLAND

Cards accepted: Access, Visa, Diners, Amex

HENLEY-ON-THAMES
Oxfordshire
Map ref 2C2

The famous Thames Regatta is held in this prosperous and attractive town at the beginning of July each year. The town has many Georgian buildings and old coaching inns and the parish church has some fine monuments.
Tourist Information Centre
☎ (0491) 578034

Alftrudis
HIGHLY COMMENDED

8 Norman Avenue, Henley-on-Thames RG9 1SG
☎ (0491) 573099
Friendly detached Victorian house in quiet, private road, centrally situated two minutes' walk from the station, town centre and the river. Easy parking.
Bedrooms: 1 double, 1 twin, 1 triple
Bathrooms: 1 private, 1 public
Bed & breakfast
per night:	£min	£max
Single	18.00	22.00
Double	28.00	35.00

Parking for 2

Crowsley House
Listed

Crowsley Road, Shiplake, Henley-on-Thames RG9 3JT
☎ Wargrave (0734) 403197
Attractive house in quiet riverside village, close to Henley-on-Thames. Convenient for Oxford, London, Windsor and Heathrow.
Bedrooms: 1 double, 2 twin
Bathrooms: 2 public
Bed & breakfast
per night:	£min	£max
Single	17.00	20.00
Double	34.00	40.00

Parking for 4

The Elms
COMMENDED

Gallowstree Road, Rotherfield Peppard, Henley-on-Thames RG9 5HT
☎ Reading (0734) 723164
Bed and breakfast near Henley. Heated swimming pool. All normal services, large garden, good parking. Excellent pub close by.
Bedrooms: 1 double, 1 twin
Bathrooms: 2 private
Bed & breakfast
per night:	£min	£max
Single	15.00	25.00
Double	30.00	50.00

Half board
per person:	£min	£max
Daily	24.50	34.50

Evening meal 1930 (last orders 2000)
Parking for 13

Little Parmoor Farm
Listed HIGHLY COMMENDED

Loreparmoor, Frieth, Henley-on-Thames RG9 6NL
☎ High Wycombe (0494) 881600
220-acre mixed farm. Retreat to the Hambledon Valley. 16th C farmhouse with oak beams and log fires. Peaceful walks in magnificent beechwoods. Ten minutes from Henley and Marlow.
Bedrooms: 1 double, 2 twin
Bathrooms: 1 private, 1 public
Bed & breakfast
per night:	£min	£max
Single	20.00	25.00
Double	35.00	40.00

Parking for 4
Cards accepted: Access, Visa

Mervyn House

4 St Marks Road, Henley-on-Thames RG9 1LJ
☎ (0491) 575331 & 411747
Victorian house, situated in a residential road, close to Henley town centre, station, restaurant, pubs and river. Convenient for Windsor, Oxford and London, M4 and M40.
Bedrooms: 1 double, 1 twin
Bathrooms: 1 public
Bed & breakfast
per night:	£min	£max
Single	18.00	20.00
Double	30.00	

New Lodge
COMMENDED

Henley Park, Henley-on-Thames RG9 6HU
☎ (0491) 576340
Small Victorian lodge in parkland in Area of Outstanding Natural Beauty. Lovely walks and views. Only 1 mile from Henley, 45 minutes from Heathrow.
Bedrooms: 2 double
Bathrooms: 1 private, 1 public
Bed & breakfast
per night:	£min	£max
Single	22.00	26.00
Double	29.00	39.00

Parking for 7

Pennyford House

Peppard Common, Henley-on-Thames RG9 5JE
☎ Rotherfield Greys (0491) 628272 & 628232
Family home offering evening meals and packed lunches, by prior arrangement.
Bedrooms: 1 single, 3 double, 1 twin
Bathrooms: 3 private, 1 public
Bed & breakfast
per night:	£min	£max
Single	15.00	22.00
Double	30.00	45.00

Half board
per person:	£min	£max
Daily	25.00	32.00

Parking for 7

3 Western Road
COMMENDED

Henley-on-Thames RG9 1JL
☎ (0491) 573468
A Victorian house in quiet surroundings, within walking distance of the River Thames.
Bedrooms: 1 double, 2 twin
Bathrooms: 3 private
Bed & breakfast
per night:	£min	£max
Single	20.00	25.00
Double	30.00	35.00

Parking for 2

Windy Brow
Listed

204 Victoria Road, Wargrave, Reading, Berkshire RG10 8AJ
☎ Reading (0734) 403336
Friendly accommodation in a spacious Victorian house with garden overlooking farmland. 3 miles from Henley-on-Thames, 12 miles from Windsor. Heathrow Airport half an hour away. Colour TV and tea/coffee facilities in rooms. Excellent pub food locally.
Bedrooms: 2 single, 1 double, 1 twin, 1 triple
Bathrooms: 3 private, 2 public
Bed & breakfast
per night:	£min	£max
Single	18.50	30.00
Double	38.00	45.00

Parking for 7

National Crown ratings were correct at the time of going to press but are subject to change. Please check at the time of booking.

SOUTH OF ENGLAND

HOOK NORTON
Oxfordshire
Map ref 2C1

Quiet town with a history dating back 1000 years when the Normans built and buttressed its chancel walls against attack from the invading Danes.

Pear Tree Inn
COMMENDED

Scotland End, Hook Norton, Banbury OX15 5NU
☎ (0608) 737482
Old beamed pub, near famous Hook Norton brewery. 5 miles from Chipping Norton, close to Banbury and the Cotswolds.
Bedrooms: 1 double
Bathrooms: 1 private
Bed & breakfast

per night:	£min	£max
Single	20.00	20.00
Double	35.00	35.00

Lunch available
Evening meal 1800 (last orders 2000)
Parking for 11

HORTON
Dorset
Map ref 2B3

The Horton Inn
COMMENDED

Horton, Wimborne Minster BH21 5AD
☎ Witchampton (0258) 840252
18th C coaching inn set in the beautiful Dorset downlands, with scenic views. High standard of cuisine using fresh local produce. Warm welcome.
Bedrooms: 1 double, 4 twin
Bathrooms: 2 private, 1 public
Bed & breakfast

per night:	£min	£max
Single	16.00	29.00
Double	36.00	44.00

Half board

per person:	£min	£max
Daily	28.00	32.00
Weekly	168.00	192.00

Lunch available
Evening meal 1900 (last orders 2200)
Parking for 150
Cards accepted: Access, Visa

National Crown ratings were correct at the time of going to press but are subject to change. Please check at the time of booking.

HUNGERFORD
Berkshire
Map ref 2C2

Attractive town on the Avon Canal and the River Kennet, famous for its fishing. It has a wide High Street and many antique shops. Nearby is the Tudor manor of Littlecote with its large Roman mosaic.

Marshgate Cottage Hotel ♨

Marsh Lane, Hungerford RG17 0QX
☎ (0488) 682307
Fax (0488) 685475
Family-run canalside hotel ranged around south-facing walled courtyard, linked to 350-year-old thatched cottage. Overlooks marshland and trout streams. Lovely walks, bike hire, bird watching. Important antiques centre. 1 hour from Heathrow. French, German and Scandinavian languages spoken.
Bedrooms: 1 single, 4 double, 3 twin, 1 family room
Bathrooms: 7 private, 2 public
Bed & breakfast

per night:	£min	£max
Single	25.50	35.50
Double	39.50	48.50

Evening meal 1900 (last orders 2100)
Parking for 9
Cards accepted: Access, Visa, Amex

HYTHE
Hampshire
Map ref 2C3

Changri-La
HIGHLY COMMENDED

12 Ashleigh Close, Hythe, Southampton SO4 6QP
☎ Southampton (0703) 846664
Spacious comfortable home, in unique position on edge of New Forest, a few minutes' drive from Beaulieu and other places of interest. Golf-course, pony trekking and sports complex nearby.
Bedrooms: 1 single, 1 double, 1 twin
Bathrooms: 2 public
Bed & breakfast

per night:	£min	£max
Single	14.00	14.00
Double	28.00	28.00

Parking for 3

ISLE OF WIGHT
See under Cowes, Ryde, Ryde-Wootton, Shanklin

Please mention this guide when making a booking.

KINGSCLERE
Hampshire
Map ref 2C2

Cleremede
COMMENDED

Fox's Lane, Kingsclere, Newbury, Berkshire RG15 8SL
☎ (0635) 297298
Near Watership Down and Wayfarers Walk. Breakfast in conservatory in summer overlooking large garden.
Bedrooms: 2 single, 1 twin
Bathrooms: 1 private, 2 public
Bed & breakfast

per night:	£min	£max
Single	18.00	19.00
Double	36.00	38.00

Parking for 6

KINGSTON BAGPUIZE
Oxfordshire
Map ref 2C1

Village close to the River Thames which is crossed by a very pretty 13th C bridge called Newbridge. The fine Queen Anne Kingston House and the splendid 15-acre garden at Pusey House are nearby.

Fallowfields ♨

Southmoor, Kingston Bagpuize, Abingdon OX13 5BH
☎ Longworth (0865) 820416
Fax (0865) 820629
12-acre mixed farm. A country house situated on the old A420, midway between Oxford and Swindon. Easy access to the Cotswolds and London.
Bedrooms: 3 double
Bathrooms: 3 private
Bed & breakfast

per night:	£min	£max
Single	36.50	44.00
Double	56.00	62.00

Half board

per person:	£min	£max
Daily	46.00	49.00

Evening meal 2000 (last orders 1830)
Parking for 15
Open April-September
Cards accepted: Access, Visa

KNOWL HILL
Berkshire
Map ref 2C2

Laurel Cottage
Listed

Bath Road, Knowl Hill, Reading RG10 9UP
☎ Littlewick Green (0628) 825046

SOUTH OF ENGLAND

Attractive oak-beamed cottage on the A4. Convenient for Bath, London, Henley, Ascot and Heathrow Airport. Evening meal by arrangement only.
Bedrooms: 1 single, 2 double, 1 triple
Bathrooms: 1 public
Bed & breakfast

per night:	£min	£max
Single	17.50	
Double	35.00	

Half board

per person:	£min	£max
Daily	21.50	

Parking for 3

LAMBOURN
Berkshire
Map ref 2C2

Attractive village among the Downs on the River Lambourn. Famous for its racing stables.

Lodge Down
COMMENDED
Lambourn, Newbury RG16 7BJ
☎ Marlborough (0672) 40304
Fax (0672) 40304

70-acre arable farm. Substantial house in own grounds overlooking the gallops. Take B4000 from junction 14, M4. Ignore turnings to Lambourn - drive towards Baydon. Lodge Down is situated just before driving over M4.
Bedrooms: 1 single, 1 twin, 1 triple
Bathrooms: 2 private, 1 public
Bed & breakfast

per night:	£min	£max
Single	16.00	20.00
Double	32.00	40.00

Evening meal 1830 (last orders 2030)
Parking for 5

LINWOOD
Hampshire
Map ref 2B3

An area of New Forest farms with camp sites.

High Corner Inn
COMMENDED
Linwood, Ringwood BH24 3QY
☎ Ringwood (0425) 473973
Fax (0425) 480015
Situated down a drovers' track, in 7 secluded acres in the heart of the New Forest, 4 miles north-east of Ringwood.
Bedrooms: 1 double, 1 twin

Bathrooms: 2 private
Bed & breakfast

per night:	£min	£max
Single	40.00	47.50
Double	59.00	69.00

Half board

per person:	£min	£max
Daily	39.25	44.25

Lunch available
Evening meal 1900 (last orders 2200)
Parking for 203
Cards accepted: Access, Visa, Diners, Amex

LITTLE WITTENHAM
Oxfordshire
Map ref 2C2

Rooks Orchard
HIGHLY COMMENDED
Little Wittenham, Abingdon OX14 4QY
☎ Clifton Hampden (0865) 407765
Comfortable listed 17th C house surrounded by gardens, in beautiful Thameside village next to Wittenham Clumps and nature reserve. "Superlative breakfasts". 4 miles Wallingford and Didcot, 5 miles Abingdon.
Bedrooms: 1 single, 1 double, 1 twin
Bathrooms: 3 private, 1 public
Bed & breakfast

per night:	£min	£max
Single	22.00	24.00
Double	38.00	42.00

Parking for 6

LYFORD
Oxfordshire
Map ref 2C2

Lyford Manor Farm
HIGHLY COMMENDED
Lyford, Wantage OX12 0EG
☎ Abingdon (0235) 868204
Fax (0235) 868204
400-acre dairy farm. Comfortable Elizabethan stone farmhouse set in peaceful unspoilt hamlet. Breakfast in conservatory overlooking large garden. Within easy reach of many attractions.
Bedrooms: 1 double, 2 twin
Bathrooms: 3 private
Bed & breakfast

per night:	£min	£max
Single	21.00	25.00
Double	36.00	40.00

Parking for 10
Cards accepted: Access, Visa

LYMINGTON
Hampshire
Map ref 2C3

Small, pleasant town with bright cottages and attractive Georgian houses, lying on the edge of the New Forest with a ferry service to the Isle of Wight. A sheltered harbour makes it a busy yachting centre.

Altworth
Listed APPROVED
12 North Close, Lymington SO41 9BT
☎ (0590) 674082
Near centre of town in quiet residential street, 5 minutes from bus/railway stations and Isle of Wight ferry. Within 30 minutes of Southampton and Bournemouth, with Brockenhurst and New Forest area only 10 minutes away.
Bedrooms: 1 single, 1 double, 1 triple
Bathrooms: 1 public
Bed & breakfast

per night:	£min	£max
Single	13.00	13.00
Double	23.00	23.00

Open April-October

Cedars
Listed
2 Linden Way, Highfield, Lymington SO41 9JU
☎ (0590) 676468
Bungalow accommodation in quiet, secluded area, ideal for forest and coastal walks. Ground floor annexe rooms, free access and off-street garage parking. Close to High Street, marinas and ferry.
Bedrooms: 1 double, 2 twin
Bathrooms: 2 private, 1 public
Bed & breakfast

per night:	£min	£max
Single	16.00	18.00
Double	32.00	36.00

Parking for 4

Our Bench
COMMENDED
9 Lodge Road, Pennington, Lymington SO41 8HH
☎ (0590) 673141
Fax (0590) 673141

Some en-suite ground floor bedrooms, separate TV lounge, indoor heated pool, jacuzzi and sauna. Non-smokers only please and, sorry, no children.
Bedrooms: 1 single, 2 double

Continued ▶

333

SOUTH OF ENGLAND

LYMINGTON
Continued

Bathrooms: 2 private, 1 public
Bed & breakfast
per night:	£min	£max
Single	16.00	18.00
Double	34.00	37.00

Half board
per person:	£min	£max
Daily	22.00	25.00

Evening meal 1900 (last orders 2100)
Parking for 5

LYNDHURST
Hampshire
Map ref 2C3

The "capital" of the New Forest, surrounded by attractive woodland scenery and delightful villages. The town is dominated by the Victorian Gothic-style church where the original Alice in Wonderland is buried.
Tourist Information Centre
☎ (0703) 282269

Burton House
Romsey Road, Lyndhurst SO43 7AA
☎ Southampton (0703) 282445
Lovely house in half-acre garden, near the village centre. All rooms en-suite shower, WC and washbasin. Parking.
Bedrooms: 1 single, 2 double, 1 twin, 2 triple
Bathrooms: 6 private
Bed & breakfast
per night:	£min	£max
Single	20.00	
Double	30.00	36.00

Parking for 8

Forest Cottage
Listed
High Street, Lyndhurst SO43 7BH
☎ Southampton (0703) 283461

Charming 300-year-old cottage with welcoming atmosphere in the village, yet open forest only yards away. Guest lounge with open fire.
Bedrooms: 1 single, 1 double, 1 twin
Bathrooms: 2 public
Bed & breakfast
per night:	£min	£max
Single	16.00	16.00
Double	30.00	30.00

Parking for 3

Little Hayes
HIGHLY COMMENDED
43 Romsey Road, Lyndhurst
SO43 7AR
☎ Southampton (0703) 283000

Lovely Victorian home, beautifully restored and furnished. Spacious rooms, friendly atmosphere and wonderful breakfast. Close to village centre and forest walks.
Bedrooms: 2 double, 1 twin
Bathrooms: 1 private, 1 public
Bed & breakfast
per night:	£min	£max
Single	20.00	25.00
Double	30.00	36.00

Parking for 4
Open February-October
Cards accepted: Access, Visa, Switch

The Penny Farthing Hotel
COMMENDED
Romsey Road, Lyndhurst SO43 7AA
☎ Southampton (0703) 284422
Fax (0703) 284488

This elegantly refurbished family hotel offers every comfort. Ideally situated 1 minute's walk from the village centre shops, restaurants and 2 minutes from open forest. A real treat!
Bedrooms: 3 single, 5 double, 1 twin, 1 triple, 1 family room
Bathrooms: 11 private
Bed & breakfast
per night:	£min	£max
Single	25.00	37.50
Double	45.00	70.00

Parking for 15
Cards accepted: Access, Visa

Display advertisement appears on this page

MAIDENHEAD
Berkshire
Map ref 2C2

Attractive town on the River Thames which is crossed by an elegant 18th C bridge and by Brunel's well-known railway bridge. It is a popular place for boating with delightful riverside walks. The Courage Shire Horse Centre is nearby.
Tourist Information Centre
☎ (0628) 781110

Cartlands Cottage
APPROVED
Kings Lane, Cookham Dean, Cookham, Maidenhead SL6 9AY
☎ Marlow (0628) 482196
Family room in self-contained garden studio. Meals in delightful timbered character cottage with exposed beams. Traditional cottage garden. National Trust common land. Very quiet.
Bedrooms: 1 triple
Bathrooms: 1 private, 1 public

It's service with a smile at
The Penny Farthing Hotel

Surrounded by some of the most beautiful English countryside this family run Hotel features comfortably furnished bedrooms with ensuite, colour TV and tea/coffee facilities. Lyndhurst being the centre of the New Forest provides the main Tourist Information Centre and New Forest Museum as well as a charming selection of shops, restaurants, cafes and bistros on the high street all within a couple of minutes walk. We also provide family rooms, licensed bar, residents lounge, car park and a warm welcome to all. Call for a brochure.

**Romsey Road, Lyndhurst, Hampshire,
SO43 7AA Telephone: 0703 284422.
Facsimile: 0703 284488**

SOUTH OF ENGLAND

Bed & breakfast
per night:	£min	£max
Single	16.50	18.50
Double	32.00	36.00

Parking for 4

Moor Farm
HIGHLY COMMENDED

Ascot Road, Holyport, Maidenhead SL6 2HY
☎ (0628) 33761
100-acre mixed farm. 700-year-old medieval manor in picturesque Holyport village. 4 miles from Windsor, 12 miles from Heathrow.
Bedrooms: 2 twin
Bathrooms: 2 private

Bed & breakfast
per night:	£min	£max
Double	36.00	45.00

Parking for 4

MARLOW
Buckinghamshire
Map ref 2C2

Attractive Georgian town on the River Thames, famous for its 19th C suspension bridge. The High Street contains many old houses and there are connections with writers including Shelley and the poet T S Eliot.

Acha Pani
Listed COMMENDED

Bovingdon Green, Marlow SL7 2JL
☎ (0628) 483435
Modern house with large garden, in quiet location 1 mile north of Marlow. No children or dogs please.
Bedrooms: 1 single, 1 double, 1 twin
Bathrooms: 1 private, 1 public

Bed & breakfast
per night:	£min	£max
Single	15.00	17.00
Double	30.00	35.00

Parking for 3

Holly Tree House
HIGHLY COMMENDED

Burford Close, Marlow Bottom, Marlow SL7 3NF
☎ (0628) 891110
Fax (0628) 481178
Detached house set in large gardens with fine views over the valley. Quiet yet convenient location. Large car park. All rooms fully en-suite. Outdoor heated swimming pool.
Bedrooms: 1 single, 4 double
Bathrooms: 5 private

Bed & breakfast
per night:	£min	£max
Single	60.00	
Double	70.00	75.00

Parking for 10
Cards accepted: Access, Visa, Amex

2 Hyde Green
Listed

Marlow SL7 1QL
☎ (0628) 483526
Comfortable family home a few minutes' level walk from town centre and River Thames.
Bedrooms: 1 double, 2 twin
Bathrooms: 2 private, 1 public

Bed & breakfast
per night:	£min	£max
Single	20.00	25.00
Double	30.00	35.00

Parking for 2

Little Parmoor
Listed

Frieth, Henley-on-Thames, Oxfordshire RG9 6NL
☎ High Wycombe (0494) 881447
Fax (0494) 883012
Period country house in Area of Outstanding Natural Beauty in the Chiltern Hills. Close to Marlow and Henley.
Bedrooms: 1 single, 1 twin
Bathrooms: 1 private, 1 public

Bed & breakfast
per night:	£min	£max
Single	18.00	22.50
Double	36.00	45.00

Evening meal 1930 (last orders 2100)
Parking for 5

Monkton Farmhouse
Listed COMMENDED

Monkton Farm, Little Marlow, Marlow SL7 3RF
☎ High Wycombe (0494) 521082
Fax (0494) 443905
150-acre dairy farm. 14th C cruckhouse set in beautiful countryside, easily reached by motorway, and close to shopping and sporting facilities.
Bedrooms: 1 single, 1 twin, 1 triple
Bathrooms: 1 public

Bed & breakfast
per night:	£min	£max
Single	18.00	20.00
Double	36.00	40.00

Parking for 6

5 Pound Lane
Listed

Marlow SL7 2AE
☎ (0628) 482649
Older style house, just off town centre, 2 minutes from River Thames and leisure complex. Double room has own balcony with delightful view.
Bedrooms: 1 double, 1 twin
Bathrooms: 1 public

Bed & breakfast
per night:	£min	£max
Single	20.00	25.00
Double	32.00	38.00

Parking for 2

MARNHULL
Dorset
Map ref 2B3

Has a fine church and numerous attractive houses.

Moorcourt Farm

Moorside, Marnhull, Sturminster Newton DT10 1HH
☎ Sturminster Newton (0258) 820271
117-acre dairy farm. Friendly, welcoming farmhouse in the Blackmore Vale, 4 miles from Sturminster Newton and 5 miles from Shaftesbury. Central for coast and many places of interest. Children over 10 welcome. Sorry, no pets.
Bedrooms: 2 double, 1 twin
Bathrooms: 2 public

Bed & breakfast
per night:	£min	£max
Single	13.00	13.00
Double	26.00	26.00

Parking for 6
Open March-November

Wisteria House
Listed

New Street, Marnhull, Sturminster Newton DT10 1PZ
☎ Sturminster Newton (0258) 820778
Large Georgian former rectory between Shaftesbury and Sturminster Newton.
Bedrooms: 2 double, 1 twin
Bathrooms: 1 private, 2 public

Bed & breakfast
per night:	£min	£max
Single	16.00	16.00
Double	32.00	32.00

Parking for 6

There are separate sections in this guide listing groups specialising in farm holidays and accommodation which is especially suitable for young people and organised groups.

335

SOUTH OF ENGLAND

MILTON KEYNES
Buckinghamshire
Map ref 2C1

Designated a New Town in 1967, Milton Keynes offers a wide range of housing and is abundantly planted with trees. It has excellent shopping facilities and 3 centres for leisure and sporting activities. The Open University is based here.
Tourist Information Centre
☎ *(0908) 232525*

Chantry Farm
COMMENDED
Pindon End, Hanslope, Milton Keynes MK19 7HL
☎ (0908) 510269
600-acre mixed farm. Stone farmhouse built in 1650 with inglenook fireplaces, surrounded by open countryside. 15 minutes to city centre. Swimming pool, trout lake, table tennis, clay pigeon shooting.
Bedrooms: 1 double, 2 twin
Bathrooms: 2 public, 1 private shower
Bed & breakfast

per night:	£min	£max
Single	16.00	20.00
Double	32.00	40.00

Parking for 7

Conifers Bed & Breakfast
Listed
29 William Smith Close, Woolstone, Milton Keynes MK15 0AN
☎ (0908) 674506
Every bedroom has a door leading to guests' garden patio. Only 1 mile from junction 14 of M1. Close to city centre and BR station.
Bedrooms: 1 single, 1 double, 1 twin
Bathrooms: 1 public
Bed & breakfast

per night:	£min	£max
Single	16.00	16.00
Double	35.00	35.00

The Croft
Little Crawley, Newport Pagnell MK16 9LT
☎ North Crawley (0234) 391296
Spacious bungalow in open countryside, 15 minutes' drive from city centre. Nearby inns serve evening meals. Convenient for Bedford or Northampton.
Bedrooms: 1 single, 2 double, 1 twin
Bathrooms: 2 private, 1 public
Bed & breakfast

per night:	£min	£max
Single	14.00	16.00
Double	26.00	28.00

Parking for 6

Grange Barn
Listed HIGHLY COMMENDED
Haversham, Milton Keynes MK19 7DX
☎ (0908) 313613

Attractively converted period barn with modern facilities. Comfortable accommodation in a rural setting, 10 minutes from city centre. Non-smokers only please.
Bedrooms: 1 single, 1 double, 1 twin
Bathrooms: 1 public
Bed & breakfast

per night:	£min	£max
Single	17.00	19.00
Double	30.00	32.00

Parking for 6

The Grange Stables
Winslow Road, Great Horwood, Milton Keynes MK17 0QN
☎ Winslow (0296) 712051
Fax (0296) 714991
A recently converted stable block offering comfortable and spacious accommodation. Conveniently situated opposite the Swan pub.
Bedrooms: 3 twin
Bathrooms: 1 public, 1 private shower
Bed & breakfast

per night:	£min	£max
Single	25.00	28.20
Double	35.00	41.12

Parking for 5
Cards accepted: Access, Visa

Michelville House
Newton Road, Bletchley, Milton Keynes MK3 5BN
☎ (0908) 371578
Clean compact establishment within easy reach of railway station, M1, shopping and sporting facilities. 10 minutes from Milton Keynes shopping centre.
Bedrooms: 10 single, 6 twin
Bathrooms: 4 public
Bed & breakfast

per night:	£min	£max
Single	15.00	20.00
Double	30.00	36.00

Parking for 16

Mill Farm
COMMENDED
Gayhurst, Newport Pagnell MK16 8LT
☎ Newport Pagnell (0908) 611489

505-acre mixed farm. 17th C farmhouse. Tennis, riding and fishing available on the farm. Good touring centre.
Bedrooms: 1 single, 1 twin, 1 triple
Bathrooms: 1 private, 2 public
Bed & breakfast

per night:	£min	£max
Single	15.00	20.00
Double	30.00	35.00

Half board

per person:	£min	£max
Daily	22.50	27.50

Evening meal 1900 (last orders 1600)
Parking for 12

Oldhams Field House
Listed COMMENDED
Nash Road, Beachampton, Milton Keynes MK19 6EA
☎ (0908) 568094
235-acre arable farm. Views over open countryside, yet 10 minutes' drive from Milton Keynes centre on the B4033, Stony Stratford to Winslow road. Guests welcome to walk on the farm.
Bedrooms: 1 single, 2 twin
Bathrooms: 2 public
Bed & breakfast

per night:	£min	£max
Single	20.00	
Double	30.00	

Evening meal (last orders 1930)
Parking for 6

Spinney Lodge Farm
Forest Road, Hanslope, Milton Keynes MK19 7DE
☎ (0908) 510267
350-acre arable and mixed farm. Victorian farmhouse in secluded situation. Superb walking facilities in Salcey Forest. 15 minutes Milton Keynes, 8 minutes M1 junction 15.
Bedrooms: 1 double, 1 twin
Bathrooms: 2 private
Bed & breakfast

per night:	£min	£max
Single	15.00	20.00
Double	30.00	40.00

Evening meal 1830 (last orders 1930)
Parking for 4

Vignoble
Listed COMMENDED
2 Medland, Woughton Park, Milton Keynes MK6 3BH
☎ (0908) 666804
Fax (0908) 666626
In a quiet cul-de-sac within walking distance of the Open University and 2.5 miles from the city centre. A warm welcome in three languages.
Bedrooms: 1 single, 1 double, 1 twin
Bathrooms: 1 private, 2 public

336

SOUTH OF ENGLAND

Bed & breakfast per night:	£min	£max
Single	18.00	20.00
Double	36.00	48.00

Parking for 3

MINSTEAD

Hampshire
Map ref 2C3

Cluster of thatched cottages and detached period houses. The church, listed in the Domesday Book, has private boxes - one with its own fireplace.

Acres Down Farm ⋒
Listed

Minstead, Lyndhurst SO43 7GE
☎ Southampton (0703) 813693

50-acre mixed farm. Homely New Forest working commoners' farm, in quiet surroundings opening directly on to open forest. Also self-catering cottage.
Bedrooms: 2 double, 1 twin
Bathrooms: 1 public

Bed & breakfast
per night:	£min	£max
Single	14.00	
Double	28.00	

Parking for 6

Grove House
Listed

Newtown, Minstead, Lyndhurst SO43 7GG
☎ Southampton (0703) 813211
9-acre smallholding. Attractive family home, set in quiet, rural position 3 miles from Lyndhurst, with superb walking, birdwatching and riding (stabling available).
Bedrooms: 1 family room
Bathrooms: 1 private

Bed & breakfast
per night:	£min	£max
Double	30.00	35.00

Parking for 1

The national Crown scheme is explained in full in the information pages towards the back of this guide.

MOULSFORD ON THAMES

Oxfordshire
Map ref 2C2

White House
Listed

Reading Road, Moulsford, Wallingford OX10 9JD
☎ Cholsey (0491) 651397
Fax (0491) 651397
Homely accommodation in private location with picturesque surroundings. Close to the River Thames, attractive 18-hole golf-course and the Ridgeway path.
Bedrooms: 1 double, 1 twin
Bathrooms: 2 public

Bed & breakfast
per night:	£min	£max
Single	18.00	24.00
Double	36.00	48.00

Parking for 4

NETHER WALLOP

Hampshire
Map ref 2C2

Winding lane leads to thatched cottages, cob walls of clay and straw and colourful gardens with the Wallop Brook running by St Andrew's Church. This has 11th C origins and a fine mural urging Sunday observance.

The Great Barn

Five Bells Lane, Nether Wallop, Stockbridge SO20 8EN
☎ Andover (0264) 782142
16th C barn, self-contained unit with private bathrooms. In beautiful village of Nether Wallop, setting for Agatha Christie's "Miss Marple" stories.
Bedrooms: 1 double, 1 twin
Bathrooms: 2 private

Bed & breakfast
per night:	£min	£max
Single	20.00	20.00
Double	33.00	33.00

Parking for 2

NEW FOREST

See under Beaulieu, Brockenhurst, Burley, Cadnam, Dibden, Fordingbridge, Fritham, Hythe, Linwood, Lymington, Lyndhurst, Minstead, Ringwood, Sway, Tiptoe, Totton, Woodgreen

---

Half board prices shown are per person but in some cases may be based on double/twin occupancy.

NEWBURY

Berkshire
Map ref 2C2

Ancient town surrounded by the Downs and on the Kennet and Avon Canal. It has many buildings of interest, including the 17th C Cloth Hall, which is now a museum. The famous racecourse is nearby.
Tourist Information Centre
☎ *(0635) 30267*

Little Paddocks
Listed

Woolhampton Hill, Woolhampton, Reading RG7 5SY
☎ Woolhampton (0734) 713451
Warm welcome to family home with superb views. Good food available in village. Easy access M4, Oxford, Bath, Heathrow. Excellent walks. Situated 6 miles east of Newbury.
Bedrooms: 1 double, 1 twin
Bathrooms: 2 private

Bed & breakfast
per night:	£min	£max
Single	15.00	18.00
Double	30.00	36.00

Parking for 10

The Old Farmhouse

Downend Lane, Chieveley, Newbury RG16 8TN
☎ Chieveley (0635) 248361
Small country farmhouse on edge of village. Within 1 mile of M4/A34 (junction 13) and close to Newbury. Accommodation in self-contained annexe.
Bedrooms: 1 double, 1 triple
Bathrooms: 2 private, 1 public

Bed & breakfast
per night:	£min	£max
Single	18.00	20.00
Double	34.00	36.00

Parking for 5

NEWTON LONGVILLE

Buckinghamshire
Map ref 2C1

The Old Rectory ⋒

Drayton Road, Newton Longville, Milton Keynes MK17 0BH
☎ Milton Keynes (0908) 375794

Continued ▶

337

SOUTH OF ENGLAND

NEWTON LONGVILLE
Continued

Brick built, listed Georgian house (1769), 6 miles south of Milton Keynes in village setting.
Bedrooms: 2 double, 1 twin
Bathrooms: 1 private, 2 public, 1 private shower

Bed & breakfast per night:	£min	£max
Single	15.00	15.00
Double	30.00	40.00

Half board per person:	£min	£max
Daily	20.00	25.00
Weekly	99.00	99.00

Parking for 6

NORTH LEIGH
Oxfordshire
Map ref 2C1

Small village with an ancient church whose tower was built in Anglo-Saxon times. There is a disused windmill on a hilltop and remains of a Roman villa nearby with a hypocaust and a tessellated pavement.

The Woodman Inn
Listed COMMENDED

New Yatt Road, North Leigh, Witney OX8 6TT
☎ Freeland (0993) 881790
Traditional village inn set amidst picturesque countryside, offering fine ales and good food. Convenient for Oxford, Blenheim and the Cotswolds.
Bedrooms: 2 double
Bathrooms: 1 public

Bed & breakfast per night:	£min	£max
Single	23.00	27.00
Double	30.00	35.00

Lunch available
Evening meal 1900 (last orders 2200)
Parking for 4
Cards accepted: Access, Visa

OWSLEBURY
Hampshire
Map ref 2C3

Small farming village with Marwell Conservation Zoo close by.

Miss E A Lightfoot
Listed HIGHLY COMMENDED

Tayinloan, Owslebury, Winchester SO21 1LP
☎ Winchester (0962) 777259
Private house with extensive rural views. 4 miles from M3, 11 miles from M27. Easy access to Eastleigh Airport, 9 miles away, and Portsmouth ferries. Non-smokers only please.

Bedrooms: 3 twin
Bathrooms: 3 private, 1 public

Bed & breakfast per night:	£min	£max
Single	16.50	18.00
Double	33.00	36.00

Parking for 3

Ridgeway
HIGHLY COMMENDED

Lower Baybridge Lane, Owslebury, Winchester SO21 1JN
☎ Winchester (0962) 777601
Peaceful country house offering delightful self-contained accommodation with bedroom/sitting room, kitchen and shower room/WC. Comfortably accommodates up to 3 people. Set in 8 acres surrounded by beautiful countryside, yet only 6 miles south of Winchester. Superb walking and riding area. Ideal touring location.
Bedrooms: 1 triple
Bathrooms: 1 private, 1 public

Bed & breakfast per night:	£min	£max
Double	36.00	40.00

Parking for 5
Cards accepted: Access, Visa

OXFORD
Oxfordshire
Map ref 2C1

Beautiful university town with many ancient colleges, some dating from the 13th C, and numerous buildings of historic and architectural interest. The Ashmolean Museum has outstanding collections. Lovely gardens and meadows with punting on the Cherwell.
Tourist Information Centre
☎ (0865) 726871

Acorn Guest House
Listed

260 Iffley Road, Oxford OX4 1SE
☎ (0865) 247998
Situated midway between the centre of town and the ring-road and so convenient for local amenities and more distant attractions.
Bedrooms: 2 single, 1 twin, 3 triple
Bathrooms: 2 public

Bed & breakfast per night:	£min	£max
Single	19.00	24.00
Double	34.00	42.00

Parking for 5
Cards accepted: Access, Visa

All Views
COMMENDED

67 Old Witney Road, On main A40, Eynsham, Oxford OX8 1PU
☎ (0865) 880891

7-acre livestock farm. 1991-built Cotswold-stone chalet bungalow, adjacent A40 between Oxford and Witney. Designed with guests' comfort in mind. All rooms have full facilities.
Bedrooms: 1 single, 2 double, 1 twin
Bathrooms: 4 private

Bed & breakfast per night:	£min	£max
Single	30.00	
Double	40.00	

Parking for 30

Arden Lodge
Listed

34 Sunderland Avenue, Oxford OX2 8DX
☎ (0865) 52076
Modern detached house in select part of Oxford. Within easy reach of country inns, river, city centre and meadows. Excellent position for Blenheim, Stratford-upon-Avon, Cotswolds, London.
Bedrooms: 1 single, 1 double, 1 twin
Bathrooms: 3 private

Bed & breakfast per night:	£min	£max
Single	22.00	25.00
Double	34.00	40.00

Parking for 3

Bronte Guest House

282 Iffley Road, Oxford OX4 4AA
☎ (0865) 244594
Close to Iffley village and church, 1 mile from city centre. Bus stop outside, but easy walking distance to city centre and colleges.
Bedrooms: 2 double, 2 twin, 1 triple
Bathrooms: 2 private, 1 public

Bed & breakfast per night:	£min	£max
Single	16.00	25.00
Double	28.00	42.00

Parking for 5

The Bungalow
Listed

Cherwell Farm, Mill Lane, Old Marston, Oxford OX3 0QF
☎ (0865) 57171
Modern bungalow set in 5 acres, in quiet location with views over open countryside, but within 3 miles of city centre. No smoking.
Bedrooms: 2 double, 1 twin
Bathrooms: 1 private, 1 public

Bed & breakfast per night:	£min	£max
Single	20.00	27.00
Double	34.00	45.00

Parking for 4
Open April-October

SOUTH OF ENGLAND

Cherwell Croft ⋒
COMMENDED
72 Church Street, Kidlington
OX5 2BB
☎ Kidlington (086 75) 3371
Georgian stone-built house in its own grounds. Quiet and attractive part of Kidlington by St Mary's Church. 4 miles from Oxford and 2 miles from Blenheim.
Bedrooms: 1 single, 1 double, 1 twin
Bathrooms: 1 public
Bed & breakfast
per night: £min £max
Single 13.00 16.00
Double 25.00 30.00
Parking for 3

Gables ⋒
COMMENDED
6 Cumnor Hill, Oxford OX2 9HA
☎ (0865) 862153
Very attractive detached house in a select residential area of the city. Easy access to ring road and only 5 minutes' drive into city centre.
Bedrooms: 1 single, 2 double, 2 twin, 1 triple
Bathrooms: 5 private, 2 public
Bed & breakfast
per night: £min £max
Single 18.00 24.00
Double 36.00 44.00
Parking for 8

High Hedges
COMMENDED
8 Cumnor Hill, Oxford OX2 9HA
☎ (0865) 863395
Close to city centre, offering a high standard of accommodation for a comfortable and happy stay in Oxford.
Bedrooms: 2 double, 1 twin
Bathrooms: 3 private, 1 public
Bed & breakfast
per night: £min £max
Double 34.00 38.00
Parking for 3

Isis Guest House ⋒
COMMENDED
45-53 Iffley Road, Oxford OX4 1ED
☎ (0865) 248894 & 242466
Modernised, Victorian, city centre guesthouse within walking distance of colleges and shops. Easy access to ring road.
Bedrooms: 12 single, 6 double, 17 twin, 2 triple
Bathrooms: 14 private, 10 public
Bed & breakfast
per night: £min £max
Single 19.00 25.00
Double 38.00 42.00

Parking for 18
Open June-September
Cards accepted: Access, Visa

Mount Pleasant ⋒
APPROVED
76 London Road, Headington, Oxford
OX3 9AJ
☎ (0865) 62749
Fax (0865) 62749
Small, family-run hotel offering full facilities. On the A40 and convenient for Oxford shopping, hospitals, colleges, visiting the Chilterns and the Cotswolds.
Bedrooms: 2 double, 5 twin, 1 triple
Bathrooms: 8 private
Bed & breakfast
per night: £min £max
Single 35.00 55.00
Double 48.00 75.00
Half board
per person: £min £max
Daily 35.00 52.50
Lunch available
Evening meal 1800 (last orders 2130)
Parking for 6
Cards accepted: Access, Visa, Diners, Amex

Newton House ⋒
82-84 Abingdon Road, Oxford
OX1 4PL
☎ (0865) 240561
Centrally located, Victorian townhouse with comfortable homely accommodation, warm welcome and friendly atmosphere. Special diets catered for on request.
Bedrooms: 7 double, 4 twin, 1 triple, 1 family room
Bathrooms: 5 private, 3 public
Bed & breakfast
per night: £min £max
Single 18.00 34.00
Double 30.00 45.00
Parking for 8
Cards accepted: Access, Visa

Pickwicks Hotel
COMMENDED
17 London Road, Headington, Oxford
OX3 7SP
☎ (0865) 750487 & 69413
Fax (0865) 742208
Licensed hotel, furnished to a high standard, on the main London road and easy to find. Fax available.
Bedrooms: 3 single, 5 double, 2 twin, 3 triple
Bathrooms: 9 private, 2 public
Bed & breakfast
per night: £min £max
Single 18.00 32.00
Double 35.00 52.00

Half board
per person: £min £max
Daily 24.00 40.00
Weekly 160.00 270.00
Evening meal 1800 (last orders 1930)
Parking for 18
Cards accepted: Access, Visa, Diners, Amex

7 Princes Street
Listed
Oxford OX4 1DD
☎ (0865) 726755
Restored Victorian artisan's cottage, furnished with many antiques. Short walk from Magdalen Bridge and central Oxford.
Bedrooms: 1 single, 1 double
Bathrooms: 1 public
Bed & breakfast
per night: £min £max
Single 14.00 18.00
Double 28.00 32.00
Parking for 2

PETERSFIELD
Hampshire
Map ref 2C3

Grew prosperous from the wool trade and was famous as a coaching centre. Its attractive market square is dominated by a statue of William III. Close by are Petersfield Heath with numerous ancient barrows and Butser Hill with magnificent views.
Tourist Information Centre
☎ *(0730) 268829*

Westmark House
Listed
Sheet, Petersfield GU31 5AT
☎ (0730) 263863
Pleasant Georgian country house, with hard tennis court and heated pool. Take the A3 north from Petersfield. Turn right on to A272 towards Rogate and Midhurst. Westmark House is first house on the left.
Bedrooms: 1 single, 1 double, 1 twin
Bathrooms: 1 public
Bed & breakfast
per night: £min £max
Single 20.00 26.00
Double 40.00 50.00
Half board
per person: £min £max
Daily 30.00 35.00
Weekly 210.00 245.00
Parking for 3

339

SOUTH OF ENGLAND

POOLE
Dorset
Map ref 2B3

Tremendous natural harbour makes Poole a superb boating centre. The harbour area is crowded with historic buildings including the 15th C Town Cellars housing a maritime museum.
Tourist Information Centre
☎ *(0202) 673322*

The Inn in the Park
26 Pinewood Road, Branksome Park, Poole BH13 6JS
☎ Bournemouth (0202) 761318
Small, friendly, family-owned pub with sun terrace, log fire and easy access to the beach.
Bedrooms: 3 double, 1 twin, 1 triple
Bathrooms: 5 private
Bed & breakfast

per night:	£min	£max
Single	27.50	35.00
Double	35.00	45.00

Lunch available
Evening meal 1900 (last orders 2130)
Parking for 15
Cards accepted: Access, Visa

PORTSMOUTH & SOUTHSEA
Hampshire
Map ref 2C3

The first dock was built in 1194. HMS Victory, Nelson's flagship, is here and Charles Dickens' former home is open to the public. Neighbouring Southsea has a promenade with magnificent views of Spithead.
Tourist Information Centre
☎ *(0705) 826722*

Amberly
Listed APPROVED
37 Castle Road, Southsea, Hampshire PO5 3DE
☎ (0705) 830563
Ideal location for that holiday or short break, centrally situated for all arrival and departure terminals. Traditional cooked meals at reasonable rates.
Bedrooms: 2 twin, 1 triple, 2 family rooms
Bathrooms: 2 private, 2 public
Bed & breakfast

per night:	£min	£max
Single	16.00	18.00
Double	35.00	38.00

We advise you to confirm your booking in writing.

Half board

per person:	£min	£max
Daily	22.00	24.00
Weekly	150.00	160.00

Evening meal 1800 (last orders 1500)
Cards accepted: Access, Visa, Amex

Bristol Hotel
55 Clarence Parade, Southsea, Hampshire PO5 2HX
☎ (0705) 821815
Small family-run licensed hotel overlooking gardens and Southsea Common. En-suite rooms with colour TV. Convenient for continental ferries. Central for tourist attractions.
Bedrooms: 2 single, 3 double, 7 triple, 1 family room
Bathrooms: 12 private, 1 public
Bed & breakfast

per night:	£min	£max
Single	18.00	32.00
Double	36.00	46.00

Parking for 7
Cards accepted: Access, Visa, Amex

Fortitude Cottage
Listed HIGHLY COMMENDED
51 Broad Street, Portsmouth, Hampshire PO1 2JD
☎ (0705) 823748
Charming waterside cottage near ancient fortifications, with prettily furnished bedrooms. Good breakfasts, high standard of comfort. Opposite waterbus for historic ships.
Bedrooms: 1 double, 2 twin
Bathrooms: 1 private, 1 public
Bed & breakfast

per night:	£min	£max
Single	25.00	28.00
Double	38.00	42.00

Hamilton House
COMMENDED
95 Victoria Road North, Southsea, Portsmouth, Hampshire PO5 1PS
☎ (0705) 823502
Fax (0705) 823502
Delightful family-run guesthouse, 5 minutes by car to ferry terminals and tourist attractions. Some en-suite rooms also available. Breakfast served from 6am.
Bedrooms: 1 single, 2 double, 2 twin, 1 triple, 2 family rooms
Bathrooms: 4 private, 2 public
Bed & breakfast

per night:	£min	£max
Single	15.00	17.00
Double	30.00	34.00

Evening meal from 1800

The Lady Hamilton
21 The Hard, Portsmouth, Hampshire PO1 3DU
☎ (0705) 870505
Early Victorian frontage, set in the heritage area of Portsmouth.
Bedrooms: 1 single, 7 double
Bathrooms: 7 private, 2 public
Bed & breakfast

per night:	£min	£max
Single	16.00	22.00
Double	28.00	40.00

Half board

per person:	£min	£max
Daily	20.50	26.50

Lunch available
Evening meal 1830 (last orders 2230)
Cards accepted: Access, Visa, Diners

The Saltings
HIGHLY COMMENDED
19 Bath Square, Portsmouth, Hampshire PO1 2JL
☎ (0705) 821031
Elegant town house on waterfront, overlooking Portsmouth Harbour entrance. Attractively furnished rooms with spectacular views. Within strolling distance of Maritime Heritage and museums.
Bedrooms: 1 double, 1 twin
Bathrooms: 1 public
Bed & breakfast

per night:	£min	£max
Single	28.00	30.00
Double	36.00	40.00

Open February-December

READING
Berkshire
Map ref 2C2

Busy, modern county town with large shopping centre and many leisure and recreation facilities. There are several interesting museums and the Duke of Wellington's Stratfield Saye is nearby.
Tourist Information Centre
☎ *(0734) 566226*

Mrs Sally Arnot
Listed HIGHLY COMMENDED
Belstone, 36 Upper Warren Avenue, Caversham, Reading RG4 7EB
☎ (0734) 477315
Friendly welcome in elegant Victorian family house. Quiet tree-lined avenue near river and farmland. Convenient for town centre by car. Non-smokers only please.
Bedrooms: 1 double, 1 twin
Bathrooms: 1 public

SOUTH OF ENGLAND

Bed & breakfast per night:	£min	£max
Single	25.00	27.00
Double	35.00	40.00

Parking for 2

Dittisham Guest House
Listed COMMENDED

63 Tilehurst Road, Reading RG3 2JL
☎ (0734) 569483
Renovated Edwardian property with garden, in a quiet, but central location.
Bedrooms: 4 single, 1 twin
Bathrooms: 3 private, 1 public

Bed & breakfast per night:	£min	£max
Single	17.50	27.50
Double	27.50	40.00

Half board per person:	£min	£max
Daily	23.50	33.50
Weekly	130.00	200.00

Evening meal 1830 (last orders 1945)
Parking for 7
Cards accepted: Access, Visa

10 Greystoke Road
Listed COMMENDED

Caversham, Reading RG4 0EL
☎ (0734) 475784
Private home in quiet, residential area. TV lounge, tea and coffee-making facilities. Non-smokers only please.
Bedrooms: 1 single, 1 double
Bathrooms: 2 public

Bed & breakfast per night:	£min	£max
Single	18.00	20.00
Double	28.00	30.00

Parking for 2

The Six Bells
COMMENDED

Beenham Village, Beenham, Reading RG7 5NX
☎ Woolhampton (0734) 713368
Village pub, overlooking farmland. Four miles from Theale M4 junction 12, 1 mile off A4. Newly-built bedrooms. Home cooking always available.
Bedrooms: 1 single, 2 double, 1 twin
Bathrooms: 4 private

Bed & breakfast per night:	£min	£max
Single		36.00
Double		49.00

Lunch available
Evening meal 1830 (last orders 2130)
Parking for 35
Cards accepted: Access, Visa

Please mention this guide when making a booking.

RINGWOOD
Hampshire
Map ref 2B3

Market town by the River Avon comprising old cottages, many of them thatched. Although just outside the New Forest, there is heath and woodland nearby and it is a good centre for horse-riding and walking.

Homeacres
COMMENDED

Homelands Farm, Three Legged Cross, Wimborne Minster, Dorset BH21 6QZ
☎ Verwood (0202) 822422
Fax (0202) 822422

270-acre mixed farm. Large chalet bungalow of traditional design, with inglenook fireplace in drawing room. Extensive garden, with access to large patio from drawing room.
Bedrooms: 1 single, 1 twin, 3 triple
Bathrooms: 4 private, 1 public

Bed & breakfast per night:	£min	£max
Single	15.00	19.50
Double	28.00	39.00

Parking for 8

ROMSEY
Hampshire
Map ref 2C3

Town grew up around the important abbey and lies on the banks of the River Test, famous for trout and salmon. Broadlands House, home of the late Lord Mountbatten, is open to the public.
Tourist Information Centre
☎ *(0794) 512987*

Miss R K Chambers
Listed

8 The Meads, Romsey SO51 8HB
☎ (0794) 512049
Small town house in pleasant, quiet location in town centre, with view of the abbey.
Bedrooms: 1 double, 1 twin
Bathrooms: 1 public

Bed & breakfast per night:	£min	£max
Single		18.00
Double		30.00

Parking for 1
Open April-October

Country Accommodation M
COMMENDED

The Old Post Office, New Road, Michelmersh, Romsey SO51 0NL
☎ (0794) 68739

In pretty village location, interesting conversion from old forge, bakery and post office. All ground floor rooms, some beamed. On-site parking.
Bedrooms: 1 double, 2 twin, 1 triple
Bathrooms: 4 private

Bed & breakfast per night:	£min	£max
Single	25.00	25.00
Double	35.00	35.00

Parking for 10
Cards accepted: Access, Visa

Highfield House
HIGHLY COMMENDED

Newtown Road, Awbridge, Romsey SO51 0GG
☎ (0794) 340727
Fax (0794) 341450
Recently-built house, overlooking golf-course, in unspoilt rural village. Delightful setting and charming gardens. Home cooking a speciality.
Bedrooms: 1 double, 2 twin
Bathrooms: 3 private, 1 public

Bed & breakfast per night:	£min	£max
Double	40.00	40.00

Evening meal from 1900
Parking for 10

RYDE
Isle of Wight
Map ref 2C3

The island's chief entry port, connected to Portsmouth by ferries and hovercraft. 7 miles of sandy beaches with a half-mile pier, esplanade and gardens.
Tourist Information Centre
☎ *(0983) 562905*

Sillwood Acre

Church Road, Binstead, Ryde PO33 3TB
☎ Isle of Wight (0983) 563553
Large Victorian house near Ryde, convenient for the ferry and hovercraft terminals. Two spacious en-suite rooms. Non-smoking.
Bedrooms: 1 double, 1 triple
Bathrooms: 2 private

Continued ▶

341

SOUTH OF ENGLAND

RYDE
Continued

Bed & breakfast per night:	£min	£max
Single	15.00	17.00
Double	30.00	34.00

Parking for 3

RYDE-WOOTTON

Isle of Wight
Map ref 2C3

Village runs uphill from Wootton Creek, popular with yachtsmen for its sailing school and boatyards.

Bridge House
HIGHLY COMMENDED

Kite Hill, Wootton Bridge, Ryde PO33 4LA
☎ Isle of Wight (0983) 884163
Georgian listed building with gardens down to water's edge. Traditional English breakfast with home-made preserves. A no-smoking haven!
Bedrooms: 2 double, 1 twin
Bathrooms: 1 public, 1 private shower

Bed & breakfast per night:	£min	£max
Double	30.00	38.00

Parking for 4

SELBORNE

Hampshire
Map ref 2C2

Village made famous by Gilbert White, who was a curate here and is remembered for his classic book "The Natural History of Selborne", published in 1788. His house is now a museum.

Mrs A Rouse
Listed HIGHLY COMMENDED

8 Goslings Croft, Selborne, Alton GU34 3HZ
☎ (0420) 511285
Fax (0420) 587451
Family home, set on edge of historic village, adjacent to National Trust land. Ideal base for walking and touring. Non-smokers only please.
Bedrooms: 1 twin
Bathrooms: 1 private

Bed & breakfast per night:	£min	£max
Single	19.50	19.50
Double	29.50	29.50

Parking for 1
Cards accepted: Access, Visa

SHANKLIN

Isle of Wight
Map ref 2C3

Set on a cliff with gentle slopes leading down to the beach, esplanade and marine gardens. The picturesque, old thatched village nestles at the end of the wooded chine.
Tourist Information Centre
☎ (0983) 862942

Culham Lodge Hotel

31 Landguard Manor Road, Shanklin PO37 7HZ
☎ Isle of Wight (0983) 862880
Charming hotel in beautiful tree-lined road, with heated swimming pool, solarium, conservatory, home cooking and personal service.
Bedrooms: 6 double, 4 twin
Bathrooms: 8 private, 2 public

Bed & breakfast per night:	£min	£max
Single	15.00	16.50
Double	30.00	33.00

Half board per person:	£min	£max
Daily	22.00	23.50
Weekly	135.00	150.00

Evening meal 1800 (last orders 1600)
Parking for 8
Open April-September

Hazelwood Hotel

14 Clarence Road, Shanklin PO37 7BH
☎ Isle of Wight (0983) 862824
Small, friendly comfortable hotel in a quiet tree-lined road, close to all amenities. Daily bookings taken. Parking available.
Bedrooms: 1 single, 3 double, 2 twin, 1 triple, 3 family rooms
Bathrooms: 8 private, 1 public

Bed & breakfast per night:	£min	£max
Single	16.00	19.50
Double	32.00	39.00

Half board per person:	£min	£max
Daily	21.00	24.50
Weekly	132.00	159.50

Evening meal 1800 (last orders 1600)
Parking for 5
Open March-October
Cards accepted: Access, Visa, Amex

Rosemere
COMMENDED

31 Queens Road, Shanklin PO37 6DQ
☎ Isle of Wight (0983) 862394

Close to sea, town centre and all amenities, with off-street parking. Supplement for en-suite rooms.
Bedrooms: 2 single, 3 double, 2 twin, 1 triple
Bathrooms: 5 private, 2 public

Bed & breakfast per night:	£min	£max
Single	15.00	18.00
Double	30.00	36.00

Half board per person:	£min	£max
Daily	21.00	24.00
Weekly	126.00	147.00

Evening meal from 1800
Parking for 6
Open March-October

Summercourt Hotel

6 Popham Road, Shanklin PO37 6RF
☎ Isle of Wight (0983) 863154
Spacious Tudor-style house with large pleasant garden, in a quiet position in Shanklin Old Village. Near sea and shops, adjacent to Rylstone Gardens and Shanklin Chine.
Bedrooms: 1 double, 2 twin, 2 triple, 1 family room
Bathrooms: 3 private, 1 public

Bed & breakfast per night:	£min	£max
Single	15.00	20.00
Double	28.00	38.00

Parking for 6

SHIPTON BELLINGER

Hampshire
Map ref 2B2

Parsonage Farm
COMMENDED

Shipton Bellinger, Tidworth SP9 7UF
☎ Stonehenge (0980) 42404
Former farmhouse of 16th/17th C origins. Walled garden, stables, paddocks. Situated off A338 opposite parish church and Boot Inn.
Bedrooms: 2 twin, 1 triple
Bathrooms: 1 private, 2 public

Bed & breakfast per night:	£min	£max
Single	15.00	18.00
Double	30.00	35.00

Parking for 6

All accommodation in this guide has been inspected, or is awaiting inspection, under the national Crown scheme.

SOUTH OF ENGLAND

SIXPENNY HANDLEY
Dorset
Map ref 2B3

The Barleycorn House
Deanland, Sixpenny Handley, Salisbury, Wiltshire SP5 5PD
☎ Handley (0725) 552583
Fax (0725) 552090
Converted 17th C inn retaining original period features, in peaceful surroundings with many nearby walks. Relaxed atmosphere and home cooking.
Bedrooms: 1 single, 1 double, 1 twin
Bathrooms: 2 private, 1 public

Bed & breakfast
per night:	£min	£max
Single	17.00	17.00
Double	34.00	34.00

Half board
per person:	£min	£max
Daily	25.00	25.00
Weekly	163.10	163.10

Evening meal from 1830
Parking for 5

SOUTHAMPTON
Hampshire
Map ref 2C3

One of Britain's leading seaports with a long history, now a major container port. In the 18th C it became a fashionable resort with the assembly rooms and theatre. The old Guildhall and the Wool House are now museums. Sections of the medieval wall can still be seen.
Tourist Information Centre
☎ (0703) 221106

Ashelee Lodge ⋈
Listed COMMENDED
36 Atherley Road, Shirley, Southampton SO1 5DQ
☎ (0703) 222095
Homely guesthouse, garden with pool. Half a mile from city centre, near station, M27 and Sealink ferryport. Good touring base for New Forest, Salisbury and Winchester.
Bedrooms: 2 single, 1 double, 1 twin
Bathrooms: 1 public

Bed & breakfast
per night:	£min	£max
Single	13.00	14.00
Double	27.00	28.00

Evening meal from 1800
Parking for 2
Cards accepted: Access, Visa

La Valle Guest House
Listed
111 Millbrook Road East, Freemantle, Southampton SO1 0HP
☎ (0703) 227821

Close to city centre, bus and railway stations. All rooms have central heating and colour TV.
Bedrooms: 2 single, 2 twin, 1 triple
Bathrooms: 2 public

Bed & breakfast
per night:	£min	£max
Single	11.00	
Double	22.00	

Parking for 6

SOUTHSEA
Hampshire

See under Portsmouth & Southsea

STANDLAKE
Oxfordshire
Map ref 2C1

13th C church with an octagonal tower and spire standing beside the Windrush. The interior of the church is rich in woodwork.

Blenheim Cottage
Listed
47 Abingdon Road, Standlake, Witney OX8 7QH
☎ Oxford (0865) 300718
Recently extended and modernised cottage in a rural setting on the A415. Situated at the Witney end of Standlake.
Bedrooms: 1 twin
Bathrooms: 1 private

Bed & breakfast
per night:	£min	£max
Single		18.00
Double		28.00

Parking for 1
Open May-September

STEEPLE ASTON
Oxfordshire
Map ref 2C1

Oxfordshire village whose church has one of the finest examples of church embroidery in the world. Nearby is the Jacobean Rousham House which stands in William Kent's only surviving landscaped garden.

Westfield Farm Motel
Fenway, Steeple Aston, Oxford OX5 3SS
☎ (0869) 40591 & 47594
Converted stable block with comfortable en-suite bedroom units. Combined lounge, dining room and bar. TV all rooms. Good touring centre. Fringe of Cotswolds, off A4260, 9 miles from Banbury and 5 miles from Woodstock.
Bedrooms: 2 single, 3 double, 4 twin, 1 triple
Bathrooms: 10 private

Bed & breakfast
per night:	£min	£max
Single	32.00	38.00
Double	42.00	46.00

Half board
per person:	£min	£max
Daily	39.00	48.00

Parking for 24
Cards accepted: Access, Visa

STOCKBRIDGE
Hampshire
Map ref 2C2

Set in the Test Valley which has some of the best fishing in England. The wide main street has houses of all styles, mainly Tudor and Georgian.

Carbery Guest House ⋈
COMMENDED
Salisbury Hill, Stockbridge SO20 6EZ
☎ Andover (0264) 810771
Fine old Georgian house in an acre of landscaped gardens and lawns, overlooking the River Test. Games and swimming facilities, riding and fishing can be arranged. Ideal for touring the south coast and the New Forest.
Bedrooms: 4 single, 4 double, 2 twin, 1 triple
Bathrooms: 8 private, 1 public

Bed & breakfast
per night:	£min	£max
Single	20.00	28.50
Double	40.00	47.00

Half board
per person:	£min	£max
Daily	30.50	39.00
Weekly	135.00	194.50

Evening meal 1900 (last orders 1800)
Parking for 12

STONY STRATFORD
Buckinghamshire
Map ref 2C1

Fegan's View
Listed
119 High Street, Stony Stratford, Milton Keynes MK11 1AT
☎ Milton Keynes (0908) 562128 & 564246
18th C town-house, near local amenities and convenient for central Milton Keynes, Woburn, Silverstone and Cranfield.
Bedrooms: 1 single, 3 twin
Bathrooms: 1 private, 2 public

Continued ▶

SOUTH OF ENGLAND

STONY STRATFORD
Continued

Bed & breakfast
per night:	£min	£max
Single	17.00	25.00
Double	32.00	40.00

Parking for 5

STUDLAND
Dorset
Map ref 2B3

On a beautiful stretch of coast and good for walking, with a National Nature Reserve to the north. The Norman church is the finest in the country, with superb rounded arches and vaulting. Brownsea Island, where the first scout camp was held, lies in Poole Harbour.

Bankes Arms Hotel
Manor Road, Studland, Swanage BH19 3AU
☎ (092 944) 225
Old inn in coastal village with sea views and miles of sandy beaches. Morning and evening bar meals, en-suite accommodation. Live bands, all watersports, golf, horse riding, own moorings in bay.
Bedrooms: 1 single, 3 double, 2 twin, 3 triple
Bathrooms: 5 private, 1 public

Bed & breakfast
per night:	£min	£max
Single	30.00	
Double	48.00	52.00

Lunch available
Evening meal 1900 (last orders 2130)
Parking for 12
Cards accepted: Access, Visa

SUTTON SCOTNEY
Hampshire
Map ref 2C2

Dever View
COMMENDED
17 Upper Bullington, Sutton Scotney, Winchester SO21 3RB
☎ Winchester (0962) 760566
Modernised, warm, comfortable cottage with large, pretty garden, in quiet country lane surrounded by fields, but only half-a-mile from main roads, A34, A303. A real home-from-home.
Bedrooms: 2 twin
Bathrooms: 2 public

Bed & breakfast
per night:	£min	£max
Single	18.00	20.00
Double	30.00	33.00

Parking for 7

Mrs V Keel
HIGHLY COMMENDED
Knoll House, Wonston, Sutton Scotney, Winchester SO21 3LR
☎ Winchester (0962) 760273 & 883550
Take Andover road from Winchester to Sutton Scotney. Turn right at village hall to Wonston. Situated on right hand side almost opposite Wonston Arms.
Bedrooms: 1 double, 1 twin
Bathrooms: 2 private

Bed & breakfast
per night:	£min	£max
Single	15.00	15.00
Double	30.00	30.00

Half board
per person:	£min	£max
Daily	22.00	22.00
Weekly	148.00	148.00

Evening meal 1830 (last orders 2030)
Parking for 2

SWANAGE
Dorset
Map ref 2B3

Began life as an Anglo-Saxon port, then a quarrying centre of Purbeck marble. Now the safe, sandy beach set in a sweeping bay and flanked by downs is good walking country, making it an ideal resort.
Tourist Information Centre
☎ (0929) 422885

Maycroft
Old Malthouse Lane, Langton Matravers, Swanage BH19 3HH
☎ (0929) 424305
Comfortable Victorian home in quiet village position, with magnificent views of sea and countryside. Close to coastal path and the amenities of the Isle of Purbeck, 2 miles from Swanage.
Bedrooms: 1 double, 1 twin
Bathrooms: 1 public

Bed & breakfast
per night:	£min	£max
Single	20.00	25.00
Double	28.00	32.00

Parking for 4
Open February–November

SWAY
Hampshire
Map ref 2C3

Small village on the south-western edge of the New Forest. It is noted for its 220-ft tower, Peterson's Folly, built in the 1870s by a retired Indian judge to demonstrate the value of concrete as a building material.

The Forest Heath Hotel
Listed
Station Road, Sway, Lymington SO41 6BA
☎ Lymington (0590) 682287
Victorian village inn with good food and lively bars. Lots to do, close to coast and scenic areas. Large garden. Families welcome.
Bedrooms: 2 double, 1 twin, 2 triple
Bathrooms: 3 private, 2 public

Bed & breakfast
per night:	£min	£max
Single	20.00	30.00
Double	30.00	45.00

Half board
per person:	£min	£max
Daily	27.50	37.50
Weekly	190.00	220.00

Lunch available
Evening meal 1830 (last orders 2145)
Parking for 24
Cards accepted: Access, Visa

Squirrels
COMMENDED
Broadmead, (off Silver Street), Sway, Lymington SO41 6DH
☎ Lymington (0590) 683163
Between forest, sea and yachting centre. Modern house with large woodland garden. Tranquil setting in private road adjoining Broadmead Trees Nursery. No smoking please.
Bedrooms: 1 single, 1 double, 1 family room
Bathrooms: 2 private, 1 public

Bed & breakfast
per night:	£min	£max
Single	15.00	20.00
Double	30.00	34.00

Parking for 8

We advise you to confirm your booking in writing.

Please mention this guide when making a booking.

Individual proprietors have supplied all details of accommodation. Although we do check for accuracy, we advise you to confirm the information at the time of booking.

SOUTH OF ENGLAND

THAME
Oxfordshire
Map ref 2C1

Historic market town on the River Thame. The wide, unspoilt High Street has many styles of architecture with medieval timber-framed cottages, Georgian houses and some famous inns.
Tourist Information Centre
☎ *(0844) 212834*

Crowell End
Listed COMMENDED
Crowell Hill, Chinnor, Oxford OX9 4BT
☎ Kingston Blount (0844) 352726
Family house in beautiful and peaceful surroundings, in an Area of Outstanding Natural Beauty. Ideal base for walking, riding and touring. Lovely rose gardens. 45 minutes Heathrow.
Bedrooms: 1 single, 1 double, 1 twin
Bathrooms: 1 private, 1 public

Bed & breakfast

per night:	£min	£max
Single	17.50	25.00
Double	32.50	35.00

Parking for 6

Manor Farm
Listed
Shabbington, Aylesbury, Buckinghamshire HP18 9YJ
☎ Long Crendon (0844) 201103
188-acre livestock farm. In rural setting, within 20 minutes of historic Oxford, on the fringes of the scenic Thames Valley, Chilterns and Cotswolds.
Bedrooms: 2 single, 2 double
Bathrooms: 1 private, 2 public

Bed & breakfast

per night:	£min	£max
Single	17.50	20.00
Double	35.00	40.00

Parking for 10

TIPTOE
Hampshire
Map ref 2C3

Candleford House
Listed
Middle Road, Tiptoe, Lymington SO41 0FX
☎ Lymington (0590) 682069
Modern, Georgian-style house, not overlooked, on edge of New Forest. Central for Lymington, Milford-on-Sea, Bournemouth and Southampton.
Bedrooms: 1 double, 1 twin
Bathrooms: 1 public

Bed & breakfast

per night:	£min	£max
Single		14.00
Double		28.00

Parking for 3
Open January-November

TOTTON
Hampshire
Map ref 2C3

Jubilee Cottage
303 Salisbury Road, Totton, Southampton SO4 3LZ
☎ Southampton (0703) 862397
Victorian house convenient for Romsey, M27, New Forest, continental and Isle of Wight ferries. Bed and breakfast accommodation with private facilities.
Bedrooms: 1 twin, 1 family room
Bathrooms: 2 private, 1 public

Bed & breakfast

per night:	£min	£max
Single	13.50	15.00
Double	28.00	30.00

Parking for 2

UFFINGTON
Oxfordshire
Map ref 2C2

Village famous for the great White Horse cut in the chalk, possibly dating from the Iron Age. Above it is Uffington Castle, a prehistoric hill fort.

Shotover House
Uffington, Faringdon SN7 7RH
☎ Faringdon (0367) 820351

Traditional 19th C chalkstone cottage in pretty rose-filled garden, on edge of peaceful village and with views of the White Horse.
Bedrooms: 1 single, 1 double
Bathrooms: 2 private

Bed & breakfast

per night:	£min	£max
Single		22.50
Double		45.00

Half board

per person:	£min	£max
Daily	30.00	35.00
Weekly	180.00	210.00

Evening meal from 1900

Parking for 3
Open March-October

WALLINGFORD
Oxfordshire
Map ref 2C2

Site of an ancient ford over the River Thames, now crossed by a 900-ft-long bridge. The town has many timber-framed and Georgian buildings, Gainsborough portraits in the 17th C Town Hall and a few remains of a Norman Castle.
Tourist Information Centre
☎ *(0491) 826972*

North Farm
HIGHLY COMMENDED
Shillingford Hill, Wallingford OX10 8NB
☎ Warborough (0865) 858406

500-acre mixed farm. Comfortable farmhouse close to River Thames, in a quiet position with lovely views and walks. Pygmy goats, chickens and sheep.
Bedrooms: 1 double, 1 twin
Bathrooms: 2 private

Bed & breakfast

per night:	£min	£max
Single	25.00	33.00
Double	37.00	43.00

Parking for 4

WARBOROUGH
Oxfordshire
Map ref 2C2

Blenheim House
COMMENDED
11-13 The Green North, Warborough, Wallingford OX10 7DW
☎ (086 732) 8445
Fax (086 732) 8445
Old village house set in 2.5 acres of garden. Swimming pool.
Bedrooms: 1 double, 1 twin
Bathrooms: 2 private

Bed & breakfast

per night:	£min	£max
Single	20.00	22.00
Double	40.00	44.00

Parking for 4

SOUTH OF ENGLAND

WARNFORD
Hampshire
Map ref 2C3

Paper Mill
Listed COMMENDED

Peake Lane, Warnford, Southampton SO3 1LA
☎ West Meon (0730) 829387

Self-contained mill house in unique setting on River Meon. Take A272 from Petersfield or Winchester to West Meon Hut traffic lights, turn south on A32, follow road to Warnford, past George and Falcon and turn left into Peake Lane.
Bedrooms: 1 double
Bathrooms: 1 private

Bed & breakfast per night:	£min	£max
Single	24.00	
Double	44.00	

Parking for 1
Open April-September

WARSASH
Hampshire
Map ref 2C3

On the edge of Southampton Water. Warships were built here in Napoleonic times.

The Jolly Farmer Country Inn

Fleet End Road, Warsash, Southampton SO3 6JH
☎ Locks Heath (0489) 572500 & 575118
Fax (0489) 885847
Country inn close to the banks of the River Hamble and Warsash Pier. Ample car parking, large garden and patio.
Bedrooms: 2 single, 1 double, 1 twin
Bathrooms: 1 public, 4 private showers

Bed & breakfast per night:	£min	£max
Single	32.50	35.00
Double	42.50	46.00

Lunch available
Evening meal 1900 (last orders 2300)
Parking for 41
Cards accepted: Access, Visa, Amex

WEST LULWORTH
Dorset
Map ref 2B3

Well-known for Lulworth Cove, the almost landlocked circular bay of chalk and limestone cliffs.

Cromwell House Hotel
APPROVED

Lulworth Cove, West Lulworth, Wareham BH20 5RJ
☎ (092 941) 253 & 332
Fax (092 941) 566

Family hotel on the Dorset Heritage Coast footpath. Outstanding views over Lulworth Cove. Sea views. Secluded garden. Good walking country.
Bedrooms: 1 single, 7 double, 5 twin, 2 triple
Bathrooms: 15 private

Bed & breakfast per night:	£min	£max
Single	18.50	33.50
Double	37.50	57.00

Half board per person:	£min	£max
Daily	25.50	39.50
Weekly	175.00	210.00

Evening meal 1900 (last orders 2030)
Parking for 15
Cards accepted: Access, Visa, Amex

Graybank Guest House

Main Road, West Lulworth, Wareham BH20 5RL
☎ (092 941) 256
Victorian guesthouse in beautiful countryside, 5 minutes' walk from Lulworth Cove. TV in most bedrooms. Ideal walking and touring base.
Bedrooms: 1 single, 2 double, 2 twin, 2 family rooms
Bathrooms: 3 public

Bed & breakfast per night:	£min	£max
Single	16.00	18.00
Double	32.00	36.00

Parking for 7
Open January-November

Newlands Farm
Listed COMMENDED

West Lulworth, Wareham BH20 5PU
☎ (092 941) 376
750-acre arable & livestock farm. 19th C farmhouse, with outstanding views to sea and distant Purbeck Hills. At Durdle Door, 1 mile west of Lulworth Cove.
Bedrooms: 1 double, 1 twin
Bathrooms: 1 public, 2 private showers

Bed & breakfast per night:	£min	£max
Double	36.00	40.00

Parking for 10
Open February-November

The Old Barn
Listed

West Lulworth, Wareham BH20 5RL
☎ (092 941) 305

Converted old barn in peaceful, picturesque coastal village. Choice of rooms with continental breakfast or please-yourself-rooms. Large gardens. Ideal base for touring Dorset.
Bedrooms: 2 single, 2 double, 1 twin, 1 triple, 1 family room
Bathrooms: 3 public

Bed & breakfast per night:	£min	£max
Single	15.00	18.50
Double	30.00	40.00

Parking for 9
Cards accepted: Access, Visa

WESTBURY
Buckinghamshire
Map ref 2C1

Mill Farm House
Listed

Westbury, Brackley, Northamptonshire NN13 5JS
☎ Brackley (0280) 704843
1000-acre mixed farm. Grade II listed farmhouse, overlooking a colourful garden including a covered heated swimming pool. Situated in the centre of Westbury village.
Bedrooms: 2 double, 1 triple
Bathrooms: 1 private, 1 public

Bed & breakfast per night:	£min	£max
Single	18.00	20.00
Double	36.00	40.00

Half board per person:	£min	£max
Daily	30.00	40.00
Weekly	180.00	240.00

Evening meal 1930 (last orders 2130)
Parking for 6

SOUTH OF ENGLAND

WICKHAM
Hampshire
Map ref 2C3

Lying in the Meon Valley, this market town is built around the Square and in Bridge Street can be seen some timber-framed cottages. Still the site of an annual horse fair.

Montrose ⚑
🏠🏠 HIGHLY COMMENDED

Solomons Lane, Shirrell Heath, Southampton SO3 2HU
☎ (0329) 833345
Attractive, comfortable accommodation in lovely Meon Valley, offering comfort and personal attention. Equidistant from main towns and convenient for continental ferries and motorway links.
Bedrooms: 2 double, 1 twin
Bathrooms: 1 private, 1 public

Bed & breakfast
per night:	£min	£max
Single	20.00	25.00
Double	40.00	45.00

Parking for 6

WIMBORNE MINSTER
Dorset
Map ref 2B3

Market town centred on the twin-towered Minster Church of St Cuthberga which gave the town the second part of its name. Good touring base for the surrounding countryside, depicted in the writings of Thomas Hardy.
Tourist Information Centre
☎ *(0202) 886116*

Acacia House
🏠🏠 HIGHLY COMMENDED

2 Oakley Road, Wimborne Minster BH21 1QJ
☎ Bournemouth (0202) 883958
Fax (0202) 881943

Beautifully decorated rooms are what the discerning traveller expects. What comes as a surprise is Eveline Stimpson's tea and cake welcome.
Bedrooms: 1 single, 1 double, 1 twin, 1 triple
Bathrooms: 3 private, 1 public

We advise you to confirm your booking in writing.

Bed & breakfast
per night:	£min	£max
Single	16.00	16.00
Double	32.00	38.00

Parking for 3

Ashton Lodge
🏠🏠 COMMENDED

10 Oakley Hill, Wimborne Minster BH21 1QH
☎ Bournemouth (0202) 883423
Large, detached, family house, with attractive gardens and relaxed, friendly atmosphere. Off-street parking available. Pay phone. Children welcome.
Bedrooms: 1 single, 1 double, 1 twin, 1 triple
Bathrooms: 3 private, 3 public

Bed & breakfast
per night:	£min	£max
Single	17.00	17.00
Double	37.00	37.00

Parking for 4

Northill House ⚑
🏠🏠 COMMENDED

Horton, Wimborne Minster BH21 7HL
☎ Witchampton (0258) 840407

Mid-Victorian former farmhouse, modernised to provide comfortable bedrooms, all en-suite. Log fires and cooking using fresh produce. Ideal touring centre.
Wheelchair access category 1 ♿
Bedrooms: 5 double, 3 twin, 1 triple
Bathrooms: 9 private

Bed & breakfast
per night:	£min	£max
Single	36.00	36.00
Double	63.00	63.00

Half board
per person:	£min	£max
Daily	44.50	49.00
Weekly	280.35	308.70

Evening meal 1930 (last orders 1830)
Parking for 12
Open February-December
Cards accepted: Access, Visa, Amex

Map references apply to the colour maps at the back of this guide.

WINCHESTER
Hampshire
Map ref 2C3

King Alfred the Great made Winchester the capital of Saxon England. A magnificent Norman cathedral, with one of the longest naves in Europe, dominates the city. Home of Winchester College founded in 1382.
Tourist Information Centre
☎ *(0962) 840500*

Cathedral View ⚑
🏠🏠🏠 COMMENDED

9A Magdalen Hill, Winchester SO23 8HJ
☎ (0962) 863802
Edwardian guesthouse with views across historic city and cathedral. 5 minutes' walk from city centre. En-suite facilities, TV, parking.
Bedrooms: 3 double, 1 twin, 1 triple
Bathrooms: 3 private, 1 public

Bed & breakfast
per night:	£min	£max
Single	25.00	30.00
Double	36.00	44.00

Evening meal 1900 (last orders 0900)
Parking for 4

Mrs V Edwards ⚑
Listed COMMENDED

Sycamores, 4 Bereweeke Close, Winchester SO22 6AR
☎ (0962) 867242
Detached house with open garden, in a quiet area 10 minutes' walk from the railway station. Family home.
Bedrooms: 2 double, 1 twin
Bathrooms: 1 private, 2 private showers

Bed & breakfast
per night:	£min	£max
Single	16.00	16.00
Double	32.00	32.00

Parking for 2

The Farrells ⚑
🏠

5 Ranelagh Road, St Cross, Winchester SO23 9TA
☎ (0962) 869555
Comfortable Victorian house close to city centre, St Cross Hospital and water meadows.
Bedrooms: 1 double, 1 twin, 1 triple
Bathrooms: 2 private, 2 public

Bed & breakfast
per night:	£min	£max
Single	15.00	15.00
Double	30.00	40.00

Parking for 2

SOUTH OF ENGLAND

WINCHESTER
Continued

Mrs O M Fetherston-Dilke
COMMENDED
85 Christchurch Road, Winchester
SO23 9QY
☎ (0962) 868661
Comfortable, friendly Victorian family house in St Cross, Winchester. Ideal for exploring city and Hampshire. Off-street parking. Non-smokers only please.
Bedrooms: 1 single, 1 double, 1 twin
Bathrooms: 1 private, 2 public

Bed & breakfast
per night:	£min	£max
Single	16.50	18.00
Double	33.00	36.00

Parking for 3

Leckhampton
COMMENDED
62 Kilham Lane, Winchester
SO22 5QD
☎ (0962) 852831

Peacefully sits in a large, delightful, secluded garden with pleasant surroundings, overlooking open countryside on the city boundary, only 1.5 miles from city centre. Ground floor twin and double bedrooms can be converted to family suite if required.
Bedrooms: 2 double, 1 twin
Bathrooms: 1 private, 1 public

Bed & breakfast
per night:	£min	£max
Single	21.00	25.00
Double	32.00	36.00

Parking for 3

Mrs Christine Leonard
COMMENDED
Dellbrook, Hubert Road, St Cross,
Winchester SO23 9RG
☎ (0962) 865093
Fax (0962) 865093
Comfortable, spacious, welcoming Edwardian house in quiet area of Winchester close to water meadows and 12th C St Cross Hospital.
Bedrooms: 1 twin, 2 family rooms
Bathrooms: 2 private, 1 public

Bed & breakfast
per night:	£min	£max
Double	34.00	38.00

Half board
per person:	£min	£max
Daily	29.00	31.00
Weekly	189.00	203.00

Evening meal 1800 (last orders 1400)
Parking for 4
Cards accepted: Visa

The Royal Hotel
COMMENDED
St Peter Street, Winchester SO23 8BS
☎ (0962) 840840
Fax (0962) 841582
Telex 477071 ROYAL G
Historic hotel in a quiet location 100 yards from the high street, close to famous cathedral. Good food, managed by owners.
Bedrooms: 52 double, 22 twin, 1 triple
Bathrooms: 75 private

Bed & breakfast
per night:	£min	£max
Single	75.00	95.00
Double	85.00	105.00

Half board
per person:	£min	£max
Daily	49.00	65.00
Weekly	343.00	413.00

Lunch available
Evening meal 1900 (last orders 2200)
Parking for 60
Cards accepted: Access, Visa, Diners, Amex, Switch

Shawlands
COMMENDED
46 Kilham Lane, Winchester
SO22 5QD
☎ (0962) 861166

Attractive, modern house, situated in a quiet, elevated position overlooking open countryside. Delightful garden. 1.5 miles from city centre.
Wheelchair access category 3
Bedrooms: 2 double, 1 twin
Bathrooms: 1 private, 2 public

Bed & breakfast
per night:	£min	£max
Single	18.00	
Double	32.00	36.00

Parking for 4

Stratton House
Stratton Road, St Giles Hill,
Winchester SO23 8JQ
☎ (0962) 863919 & 864529
Fax (0962) 842095

A lovely old Victorian house with an acre of grounds, in an elevated position on St Giles Hill.
Bedrooms: 2 double, 1 twin, 2 triple
Bathrooms: 1 private, 3 public,
2 private showers

Bed & breakfast
per night:	£min	£max
Single	20.00	25.00
Double	40.00	50.00

Half board
per person:	£min	£max
Daily	26.00	31.00
Weekly	165.00	200.00

Evening meal 1800 (last orders 1600)
Parking for 8

Mrs S Tisdall
32 Hyde Street, Winchester SO23 7DX
☎ (0962) 851621
Attractive 18th C town house close to city centre and recreational amenities.
Bedrooms: 1 double, 1 triple
Bathrooms: 1 public

Bed & breakfast
per night:	£min	£max
Single	16.00	17.00
Double	26.00	28.00

The Wessex Centre Sparsholt College
Sparsholt, Winchester SO21 2NF
☎ (0962) 776441
Agricultural college, offering comfortable accommodation. Picturesque surroundings, good food, sports facilities. Special weekly rates. Hostel accommodation also available.
Bedrooms: 31 single, 1 double
Bathrooms: 32 private

Bed & breakfast
per night:	£min	£max
Single	18.25	24.35
Double	36.50	48.70

Half board
per person:	£min	£max
Daily	25.50	28.00

Lunch available
Parking for 50
Cards accepted: Access, Visa

Individual proprietors have supplied all details of accommodation. Although we do check for accuracy, we advise you to confirm the information at the time of booking.

348

SOUTH OF ENGLAND

WINDSOR
Berkshire
Map ref 2D2

Town dominated by the spectacular castle and home of the Royal Family for over 900 years. Parts are open to the public. There are many attractions including the Great Park, Eton, Windsor Safari Park and trips on the river.
Tourist Information Centre
☎ (0753) 852010

Chasela
Listed
30 Convent Road, Windsor SL4 3RB
☎ (0753) 860410
Warm, modern house a mile from Windsor Castle. Easy access M4, M40, M25, M3, Heathrow. TV, tea and coffee facilities in rooms. Breakfast room overlooks lovely garden. Payphone.
Bedrooms: 1 single, 1 twin
Bathrooms: 1 public
Bed & breakfast

per night:	£min	£max
Single	16.00	18.00
Double	32.00	36.00

Parking for 5

Clarence Hotel M
APPROVED
9 Clarence Road, Windsor SL4 5AE
☎ (0753) 864436
Fax (0753) 857060
Comfortable licensed hotel near town centre, castle and Eton. All rooms en-suite, TV, hairdriers, radio and tea makers. Convenient for Heathrow Airport.
Bedrooms: 2 single, 4 double, 9 twin, 5 triple
Bathrooms: 20 private, 1 public
Bed & breakfast

per night:	£min	£max
Single	33.00	36.00
Double	49.00	54.00

Parking for 4
Cards accepted: Access, Visa, Diners, Amex

Halcyon House
COMMENDED
131 Clarence Road, Windsor SL4 5AR
☎ (0753) 863162
A warm welcome at a family-run guesthouse, 10 minutes' walk from the town centre and river. Ideal base for London. Off-street parking.
Bedrooms: 2 double, 2 twin
Bathrooms: 3 private, 1 public

Bed & breakfast

per night:	£min	£max
Single	25.00	35.00
Double	33.00	39.00

Parking for 6

49 Longmead
Windsor SL4 5PZ
☎ (0753) 866019
Fax (0753) 830964
A home-from-home with private facilities in quiet residential area. 1.25 miles from town centre and Windsor Castle.
Bedrooms: 1 double, 1 twin
Bathrooms: 2 private
Bed & breakfast

per night:	£min	£max
Single	21.00	21.00
Double	38.00	38.00

Parking for 2

Tanglewood
Listed HIGHLY COMMENDED
Oakley Green, Windsor SL4 4PZ
☎ (0753) 860034
Picturesque chalet-style guesthouse in beautiful garden. Rural area overlooking open fields on B3024. Windsor 10 minutes' drive, Heathrow 15 miles. Excellent meals at nearby pub.
Bedrooms: 2 twin
Bathrooms: 1 public
Bed & breakfast

per night:	£min	£max
Single	20.00	20.00
Double	34.00	34.00

Parking for 2
Open May-September

Trinity Guest House M
18 Trinity Place, Windsor SL4 3AT
☎ (0753) 831283
Fax (0753) 862640
Comfortable guesthouse in the heart of Windsor, close to castle, river and stations, run by traditional English family and with a worldwide reputation.
Bedrooms: 1 single, 3 double, 2 twin, 3 family rooms
Bathrooms: 4 private, 2 public
Bed & breakfast

per night:	£min	£max
Single	20.00	25.00
Double	40.00	45.00

Cards accepted: Access, Visa

The enquiry coupons at the back will help you when contacting proprietors.

WINSLOW
Buckinghamshire
Map ref 2C1

Small town with Georgian houses, a little market square and a fine church with 15th C wall-paintings. Winslow Hall, built to the design of Sir Christopher Wren in 1700, is open to the public.

Manor Farm Stables
High Street, North Marston, Buckingham MK18 3PS
☎ North Marston (0296) 67252 & 67720
Comfortable converted stables within easy reach of National Trust properties, Milton Keynes and Aylesbury. Breakfast served in farmhouse.
Bedrooms: 2 double, 2 twin
Bathrooms: 4 private
Bed & breakfast

per night:	£min	£max
Single	20.00	25.00
Double	39.00	45.00

Parking for 8

WINTERBORNE STICKLAND
Dorset
Map ref 2B3

Restharrow
HIGHLY COMMENDED
North Street, Winterborne Stickland, Blandford Forum DT11 0NH
☎ Milton Abbas (0258) 880936
Comfortable accommodation in pretty village at head of Winterborne Valley, in the "Heart of Dorset." Friendly base for exploring the county.
Bedrooms: 2 double
Bathrooms: 2 private
Bed & breakfast

per night:	£min	£max
Single	22.00	27.00
Double	32.00	37.00

Parking for 3

WINTERBORNE ZELSTON
Dorset
Map ref 2B3

Village 4 miles north-east of Bere Regis with several picturesque cottages.

Brook Farm
Listed
Winterborne Zelston, Blandford Forum DT11 9EU
☎ Morden (0929) 459217
150-acre mixed farm. Friendly, comfortable accommodation in quiet, picturesque village, midway between
Continued ▶

SOUTH OF ENGLAND

WINTERBORNE ZELSTON
Continued

Wimborne and Bere Regis. Nearby inns for excellent food. Access to rooms at all times. Weekly terms available.
Bedrooms: 2 triple
Bathrooms: 1 public

Bed & breakfast
per night:	£min	£max
Single	15.00	18.00
Double	30.00	32.00

Parking for 6

WITNEY
Oxfordshire
Map ref 2C1

Town famous for its blanket-making and mentioned in the Domesday Book. The market-place contains the Butter Cross, a medieval meeting place, and there is a green with merchants' houses.
Tourist Information Centre
☎ (0993) 775802

Ambury Close Farm
COMMENDED

Barnard Gate, Witney OX8 6XE
☎ Oxford (0865) 881236
75-acre hill farm. Off the A40, on the edge of the Cotswolds. Witney 3 miles, Burford 10 miles, Oxford 7 miles, Blenheim Palace 4 miles. Public telephone available.
Bedrooms: 2 double, 1 twin, 3 family rooms
Bathrooms: 2 private, 2 public

Bed & breakfast
per night:	£min	£max
Single	22.00	24.00
Double	34.00	40.00

Evening meal 1830 (last orders 2030)
Parking for 10

Field View
COMMENDED

Wood Green, Witney OX8 6DE
☎ (0993) 705485
Situated in two acres on edge of the bustling market town of Witney. Ideal for Oxford University and the Cotswolds.
Bedrooms: 1 double, 2 twin
Bathrooms: 2 private, 1 private shower

Bed & breakfast
per night:	£min	£max
Single	18.00	22.00
Double	36.00	40.00

Parking for 10

Greystones Lodge Hotel
HIGHLY COMMENDED

34 Tower Hill, Witney OX8 5ES
☎ (0993) 771898

Quiet, comfortable private hotel set in three-quarters of an acre of pleasant garden. Conveniently located for visiting Oxford and the Cotswolds.
Bedrooms: 3 single, 4 double, 3 twin, 1 triple, 1 family room
Bathrooms: 3 private, 1 public, 9 private showers

Bed & breakfast
per night:	£min	£max
Single	25.00	29.00
Double	37.00	45.00

Half board
per person:	£min	£max
Daily	33.00	37.00

Evening meal 1900 (last orders 1930)
Parking for 20
Cards accepted: Access, Visa, Diners, Amex

WOODGREEN
Hampshire
Map ref 2B3

Typical New Forest village, with brick and thatch cottages surrounded by thick hedges to keep out the cattle and ponies. A reminder of the village's way of life in the 1930s is depicted by murals inside the village hall.

Cottage Crest

Castle Hill, Woodgreen, Fordingbridge SP6 2AX
☎ Downton (0725) 22009 changing to 512009
Secluded country cottage offering quality bed and breakfast. Set in 4 acres of picturesque grounds with glorious views of the River Avon and surrounding forest.
Bedrooms: 2 double, 1 twin
Bathrooms: 3 private

Bed & breakfast
per night:	£min	£max
Double	36.00	38.00

Parking for 5

Please mention this guide when making a booking.

There are separate sections in this guide listing groups specialising in farm holidays and accommodation which is especially suitable for young people and organised groups.

WOODSTOCK
Oxfordshire
Map ref 2C1

Small country town clustered around the park gates of Blenheim Palace, the superb 18th C home of the Duke of Marlborough. The town has well-known inns and an interesting museum. Sir Winston Churchill was born and buried nearby.

Gorselands Farmhouse Auberge

Boddington Lane, Long Hanborough, Witney OX8 6PU
☎ Freeland (0993) 881895
Fax (0993) 882799
Stone country farmhouse with exposed beams, snooker room, conservatory. Near delightful hamlet of East End and Roman villa remains. Evening meals available. Licensed for wine and beer. Grass tennis court.
Bedrooms: 1 single, 2 double, 1 twin, 1 triple
Bathrooms: 2 private, 1 public

Bed & breakfast
per night:	£min	£max
Single	19.00	20.00
Double	25.00	35.00

Half board
per person:	£min	£max
Daily	22.45	27.45
Weekly	130.00	190.00

Evening meal 1900 (last orders 2100)
Parking for 8
Cards accepted: Access, Visa, Amex

The Laurels
HIGHLY COMMENDED

Hensington Road, Woodstock OX20 1JL
☎ (0993) 812583
Fine Victorian house, located in the historic town of Woodstock. A short walk from Blenheim Palace.
Bedrooms: 1 double, 1 twin, 1 triple
Bathrooms: 3 private

Bed & breakfast
per night:	£min	£max
Single	25.00	32.00
Double	35.00	45.00

Parking for 3
Cards accepted: Access, Visa

Punch Bowl Inn
Listed

12 Oxford Street, Woodstock, Oxford OX20 1TR
☎ (0993) 811218
Fax (0993) 811393
Family-run pub in the centre of Woodstock, close to Blenheim Palace. A

350

SOUTH OF ENGLAND

good touring centre for Oxford and the Cotswolds.
Bedrooms: 2 single, 4 double, 2 twin, 1 triple, 1 family room
Bathrooms: 3 private, 2 public

Bed & breakfast
per night:	£min	£max
Single	25.00	29.00
Double	35.00	39.00

Lunch available
Evening meal 1800 (last orders 2130)
Parking for 20
Cards accepted: Access, Visa

The Ridings

32 Banbury Road, Woodstock, Oxford OX20 1LQ
☎ (0993) 811269
Detached house in a quiet, rural setting. 10 minutes' walk to town centre and Blenheim Palace. Go past the Tourist Information Centre for 300 yards then take left fork along Banbury Road.
Bedrooms: 2 twin, 1 triple
Bathrooms: 1 private, 1 public

Bed & breakfast
per night:	£min	£max
Single	15.00	20.00
Double	30.00	40.00

Parking for 4
Open March-November

Shepherds Hall Inn

Witney Road, Freeland, Witney OX8 8HQ
☎ Freeland (0993) 881256
Well-appointed inn offering good accommodation. Ideally situated for Oxford, Woodstock and the Cotswolds, on the A4095 Woodstock to Witney road.
Bedrooms: 1 single, 1 double, 2 twin, 1 triple
Bathrooms: 5 private

Bed & breakfast
per night:	£min	£max
Single	20.00	30.00
Double	35.00	40.00

Lunch available
Evening meal 1900 (last orders 2200)
Parking for 50
Cards accepted: Access, Visa

Wynford House

Listed

79 Main Road, Long Hanborough, Oxford OX8 8JX
☎ Freeland (0993) 881402
Charming guesthouse, close to Bladon and Blenheim Palace on A4095. A warm and friendly welcome, comfortable beds and colour TV and tea/coffee facilities in all rooms.
Bedrooms: 1 double, 1 twin, 1 triple
Bathrooms: 1 private, 1 public

Bed & breakfast
per night:	£min	£max
Single	22.00	30.00
Double	34.00	38.00

Half board
per person:	£min	£max
Daily	30.00	38.00

Evening meal 1800 (last orders 2000)
Parking for 4

Key to symbols

Information about many of the services and facilities at accommodation listed in this guide is given in the form of symbols. The key to these symbols is inside the back cover flap. You may find it helpful to keep the flap open when referring to the accommodation listings.

Check the maps

The colour maps at the back of this guide show all cities, towns and villages which have accommodation listings in the guide. They will enable you to check if there is suitable accommodation in the vicinity of the place you plan to visit.

South East England

Discover the romance and mystery of South East England with its maritime heritage. Walk the beaches that were once a smugglers' meeting-place, and smell the tang of mystery that hangs in the salty air; or enjoy the friendly seaside resorts that line the coast. With more stately homes and castles than perhaps any other region in England, the rolling splendour of the Downs and the sleepy Weald of Kent, the South East offers something for all. Experience Chaucer in Canterbury, shop in the market town of Guildford, or enjoy the chintz of the Pantiles in Kent. Hang on to your hat at Thorpe Park, or enjoy a leisurely cream tea in Rye – the choice is yours.

WHERE TO GO, WHAT TO SEE

The number against each name will help you locate it on the map (page 355).

❶ Powell Cotton Museum
Quex House and Gardens, Quex Park, Birchington, Kent CT7 0BH
Tel: Thanet (0843) 42168
Regency house with period furniture. Museum with ethnograhic collections, diorama of African and Asian animals, weapons, archaeology, Chinese porcelain.

❷ Royal Engineers Museum
Gillingham, Kent
Tel: Medway (0634) 406397
The characters, lives and work of Britain's soldier-engineers, 1066–1945. Medals, uniforms, scientific and technical equipment. Collection of ethnography and decorative arts.

❸ The Historic Dockyard
Chatham, Kent ME4 4TE
Tel: Medway (0634) 812551
Historic 18th C 80-acre dockyard, now a living museum. Former HMS Gannet undergoing restoration. Sail and colour loft, ordnance mews, 'Wooden Walls' gallery.

❹ Brogdale Horticultural Trust
Faversham, Kent ME13 8XZ

Harold, King of England, killed at the Battle of Hastings.

Tel: Faversham (0795) 535286
National Fruit Collection with 4,000 varieties of fruit in 30 acres of orchard: apples, pears, cherries, plums, currants, quinces, medlars, etc.

❺ The Royal Horticultural Society's Garden
Wisley, Surrey GU23 6QB
Tel: Guildford (0483) 224234
World famous RHS establishment with 250 acres of vegetable, fruit and ornamental gardens. Trial grounds, glasshouses, rock garden, ponds, rose gardens, model and specialist gardens.

❻ Belmont
Throwley, Kent ME13 0HH
Tel: Eastling (0795) 890202
Late 18th C country mansion designed by Samuel Wyatt, seat of the Harris family since 1801.

South East England

Harris clock collection, mementoes of connections with India. Gardens and pinetum.

⑦ Howletts Zoo Park
Bekesbourne, Canterbury, Kent
CT4 5EL
Tel: Canterbury (0227) 721286
55-acre parkland with large gorilla and tiger collection and many other animals.

⑧ Guildford Cathedral
Guildford, Surrey GU2 5UP
Tel: Guildford (0483) 65287
Anglican cathedral, foundation stone laid in 1936 and consecrated in 1961. Notable glass engravings, embroidered kneelers, modern furnishings. Brass rubbing centre.

⑨ Birdworld and Underwaterworld
Farnham, Surrey GU10 4LD
Tel: Bentley (0420) 22140
20 acres of garden and parkland with ostriches, flamingoes, hornbills, parrots, emus, pelicans, etc. Penguin island, tropical fish, plant area, seashore walk.

⑩ Headcorn Flower Centre and Vineyard
Grigg Lane, Headcorn, Kent
TN27 9LX
Tel: Headcorn (0622) 890250
Walk around 6 acres of vines, pausing at the reservoir to watch wildlife. Visit flowerhouses with chrysanthemums and orchid lilies flowering all year. Wine tastings, group tours.

⑪ Whitbread Hop Farm
Beltring, Paddock Wood, Kent
TN12 6PY
Tel: Maidstone (0622) 872068
Largest collection of Victorian oasts in the world, rural museums, play area, animal village, birds of prey, pottery workshop, Whitbread shire horses. Hop story exhibition.

⑫ Iden Croft Herbs
Frittenden Road, Staplehurst, Kent
TN12 0DH

Oast-houses in Kent: used for drying hops.

Tel: Staplehurst (0580) 891432
Large herb farm with walled garden and variety of aromatic gardens, demonstrating the beauty and use of herbs. Thyme rockery of special interest.

⑬ Dover Castle and Hellfire Corner
Dover, Kent CT16 1HU
Tel: Dover (0304) 201628
One of most powerful medieval fortresses in Western Europe. St Mary in Castro Saxon church, Roman lighthouse, Hellfire Corner. All the Queen's Men exhibition and Battle of Waterloo model.

⑭ Leonardslee Gardens
Lower Beeding, West Sussex
RH13 6PP
Tel: Lower Beeding (0403) 891212
Renowned spring-flowering shrub garden in a valley: rhododendrons, camellias, azaleas, lakes, paths. Good views, autumn tints, rock garden, bonsai exhibition, alpine house.

⑮ Brickwall House and Gardens
Northiam, East Sussex TN31 6NL
Tel: Rye (0797) 223529
Formal garden with terracotta entrance gates. 18th C bowling alley, sunken topiary garden, yew hedges, chess garden. Jacobean house with 17th C plaster ceilings.

⑯ Great Dixter House and Gardens
Northiam, Rye, East Sussex
TN31 6PH
Tel: Northiam (0797) 253160
Fine example of 15th C manor house with antique furniture and needlework. Unique great hall restored by Lutyens, who also designed the garden – topiary, meadow garden, flower beds.

⑯ The Bluebell Railway – Living Museum
Sheffield Park Station, Sheffield Park, East Sussex TN22 3QL
Tel: Newick (082 572) 2370
7½-mile standard gauge track from Sheffield Park to Horsted Keynes with extension to New Coombe Bridge. Largest collection of engines in the south. Victorian stations and museum.

⑰ Rye Town Model Sound and Light Show
Strand Quay, Rye, East Sussex
TN31 7AY
Tel: Rye (0797) 226696
Fascinating combination of detailed town model of the ancient town with dramatic sound and light effects, telling the story of Rye through the ages.

⑱ Buckleys Yesterday's World and The Museum of Shops
89–90 High Street, Battle, East Sussex TN33 0AQ

South East England

Tel: Battle (042 46) 4269
Over 50,000 exhibits in a Wealden hall house recall shopping and domestic life from 1850 to 1950. Includes post-office, toy shop, grocer, chemist, railway station and garden.

⑲ Weald and Downland Open Air Museum
Singleton, West Sussex PO18 OEU
Tel: Singleton (0243) 811348
Open-air museum of rescued historic buildings from South East England reconstructed on downland country park site. 35 buildings include medieval farmstead and watermill.

⑳ The Old Needlemakers
West Street, Lewes, East Sussex BN7 2NZ
Tel: Lewes (0273) 471582
Converted 19th C candle factory housing craft workshops. Candle makers, stained glass, leather crafts and other specialist shops.

㉑ A Smuggler's Adventure at St Clement's Caves
Hastings, East Sussex TN34 3HY
Tel: Hastings (0424) 422964
One acre of caves, housing the largest smuggling exhibition in the country. Museum, audio-visual show and 50 life-size figures with dramatic sound and lighting effects.

㉒ The Wildfowl and Wetlands Centre
Mill Road, Arundel, West Sussex BN18 9PB
Tel: Arundel (0903) 883355
Wildfowl and Wetlands Trust's reserve in 60 acres of watermeadows. Tame swans, ducks, geese and many wild birds. Film theatre and visitor centre with gallery.

㉓ Denmans Garden
Fontwell, West Sussex BN18 0SU
Tel: Eastergate (0243) 542808
Walled, gravel and water gardens, natural layout of trees, climbers and wall shrubs for all-year interest. Glass areas. School of Garden Design.

㉔ Pallant House
Chichester, West Sussex PO19 1TJ
Tel: Chichester (0243) 774557
Queen Anne residence containing Bow Porcelain collection, Hussey and Kearley painting collections, Rembrandt to Picasso, sculptures by Moore, temporary exhibitions. Old kitchen.

㉕ Charleston Farmhouse
Firle, Lewes, East Sussex BN8 6LL
Tel: Ripe (0323) 811265
17th–18th C farmhouse, home of Vanessa and Clive Bell and Duncan Grant. House and contents decorated by the artists. Newly restored garden room. Traditional flint-walled garden.

㉖ Brighton Sea Life Centre
Brighton, East Sussex BN2 1TB
Tel: Brighton (0273) 604234
Ocean life on a grand scale

First and largest seaside resort in the south-east, Brighton still has a fun-filled pier.

South East England

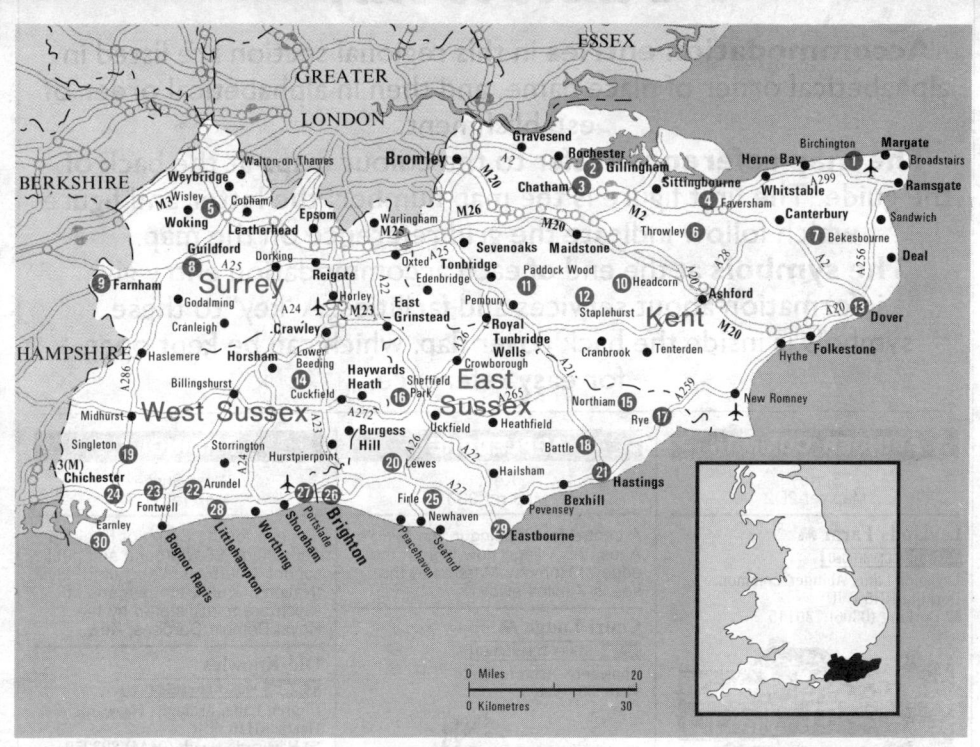

featuring over 35 displays of fascinating marine creatures, a whale and dolphin exhibition and underwater tunnel.

㉗ Foredown Tower Countryside Centre
Portslade, East Sussex BN41 2EW
Tel: Brighton (0273) 422540
Converted water tower 1909, housing exhibitions on the Downs and water. Camera obscura gives views of South Downs and coast. Touch screen computer. Local history exhibitions.

㉘ Smarts Amusement Park
Littlehampton, West Sussex
BN17 5LL
Tel: Littlehampton (0903) 721280
Large indoor and outdoor amusement park for all ages. Many rides including dodgems, Waltzer, Cyclone Roller Coaster, waterslides, sandy beaches and river.

Use the map above to locate places in the 'Where to Go, What to See' section.

㉙ Eastbourne Pier
Grand Parade, Eastbourne, East Sussex BN21 3EL
Tel: Eastbourne (0323) 410466
Well-preserved Victorian seaside pier with coastal views, family amusement arcade, disco, family entertainment room, shops, fishing and boats.

㉚ Earnley Butterflies and Gardens
Earnley, West Sussex PO20 7JR
Tel: Birdham (0243) 512637
Ornamental butterfly house, covered theme gardens, bird garden, children's play area, small animal farm.

FIND OUT MORE

Further information about holidays and attractions in the South East England region is available from:
South East England Tourist Board
The Old Brew House, Warwick Park, Tunbridge Wells, Kent
TN2 5TU
Tel: (0892) 540766

These publications are available free from the South East England Tourist Board:
South East England Accommodation Guide
Holiday Selector
Take a Break 1993/94
Diary of Events
Places to Visit in Winter
Favourite Gardens and Garden Hotels

Also available are (prices include postage and packing):
Hundreds of Places to Visit in the South East £2.35
Leisure Map for South East England £4

355

SOUTH EAST ENGLAND

Places to stay

Accommodation entries in this regional section are listed in alphabetical order of place name, and then in alphabetical order of establishment.

The map references refer to the colour maps at the back of the guide. The first figure is the map number; the letter and figure which follow indicate the grid reference on the map.

The symbols at the end of each accommodation entry give information about services and facilities. A 'key' to these symbols is inside the back cover flap, which can be kept open for easy reference.

ABINGER COMMON
Surrey
Map ref 2D2

Leylands Farm
Listed COMMENDED
Leylands Lane, Abinger Common, Dorking RH5 6JU
☎ Dorking (0306) 730115

Large family home built in 1800s set amidst Surrey hills, close to Leith Hill, 10 minutes from Dorking. Take A25 from Guildford to Dorking, turning right just after signpost Abinger Common, Friday Street. Follow road for 3 miles, take 3rd turn on left, signposted Broadmoor. Farm is half-a-mile on left. Prices are per room.
Bedrooms: 1 double
Bathrooms: 1 private
Bed & breakfast per night:

	£min	£max
Single	40.00	40.00
Double	40.00	40.00

Parking for 4

National Crown ratings were correct at the time of going to press but are subject to change. Please check at the time of booking.

APPLEDORE
Kent
Map ref 3B4

A centre for shipping in the Middle Ages, this village now lies on the edge of Romney Marsh and the sea is 7 miles away.

Court Lodge
HIGHLY COMMENDED
Appledore, Ashford TN26 2DD
☎ (0233) 83403

900-acre arable farm. Victorian farmhouse set in 4 acres of mature garden and farmland, in the picturesque village of Appledore overlooking Romney Marsh. Close to Rye, Tenterden and Channel ports.
Bedrooms: 1 double, 1 twin
Bathrooms: 2 private
Bed & breakfast per night:

	£min	£max
Single	25.00	
Double	36.00	39.00

Parking for 2

Colour maps at the back of this guide pinpoint all places which have accommodation listings in the guide.

ARDINGLY
West Sussex
Map ref 2D3

Famous for the South of England Agricultural Showground and public school. Nearby is Wakehurst Place (National Trust), the gardens of which are administered by the Royal Botanic Gardens, Kew.

Old Knowles
Listed HIGHLY COMMENDED
Church Lane, Ardingly, Haywards Heath RH16 6UR
☎ Haywards Heath (0444) 892259
Fax (0444) 892259
14th C country house situated in rural surroundings. Good access to Gatwick Airport, London and National Trust locations.
Bedrooms: 2 double, 1 twin
Bathrooms: 3 private
Bed & breakfast per night:

	£min	£max
Single	20.00	22.00
Double	38.00	40.00

Parking for 6

There are separate sections in this guide listing groups specialising in farm holidays and accommodation which is especially suitable for young people and organised groups.

SOUTH EAST ENGLAND

ARUNDEL
West Sussex
Map ref 2D3

Picturesque, historic town on the River Arun, dominated by Arundel Castle, home of the Dukes of Norfolk. There are many 18th C houses and the Toy and Military Museum, Wildfowl Trust Reserve and Heritage Centre.
Tourist Information Centre
☎ (0903) 882268

Arundel Park Inn & Travel Lodge

Station Approach, Arundel BN18 9JL
☎ (0903) 882588
Fax (0903) 883803
Refurbished to high standard, three bedrooms on ground floor. Pleasant lounge bar, informal restaurant serving home-cooked food to suit all tastes. Central for travel to many places of interest. Two minutes from main line railway station.
Bedrooms: 1 single, 8 double, 2 twin, 1 family room
Bathrooms: 11 private

Bed & breakfast

per night:	£min	£max
Single	29.00	35.00
Double	39.50	48.00

Lunch available
Evening meal 1900 (last orders 2100)
Parking for 60
Cards accepted: Access, Visa, Switch

Arundel Vineyards
Listed COMMENDED

The Vineyard, Church Lane, Lyminster, Arundel BN17 7QF
☎ (0903) 883393
3-acre fruit farm. Modern farmhouse in English vineyard in beautiful countryside. From Arundel, turn south on to A284 Littlehampton/Lyminster road (new split junction). Signposted 1 mile on right.
Bedrooms: 2 twin
Bathrooms: 1 private, 1 private shower

Bed & breakfast

per night:	£min	£max
Single	22.00	24.00
Double	32.00	36.00

Parking for 15

Mill Lane House

Slindon, Arundel BN18 0RP
☎ Slindon (0243) 65440 & 814440
18th C house in beautiful National Trust village. Magnificent views to coast. Pubs within easy walking distance. One mile from A29/A27 junction.
Bedrooms: 1 single, 3 double, 2 twin, 1 triple
Bathrooms: 7 private, 1 public

Bed & breakfast

per night:	£min	£max
Single	23.00	23.00
Double	35.00	35.00

Half board

per person:	£min	£max
Daily	26.50	32.00
Weekly	173.00	209.00

Evening meal 1900 (last orders 1000)
Parking for 7

Pindars
HIGHLY COMMENDED

Lyminster, Arundel BN17 7QF
☎ (0903) 882628
Charming country house in small village offers comfortable bedrooms, good food and warm hospitality. Beautiful garden. Non-smoking. Convenient for A27.
Bedrooms: 1 double, 1 twin, 1 triple
Bathrooms: 1 private, 1 public

Bed & breakfast

per night:	£min	£max
Double	30.00	40.00

Parking for 8

ASHFORD
Kent
Map ref 3B4

Once a market centre for the farmers of the Weald of Kent and Romney Marsh. The town centre has a number of Tudor and Georgian houses.
Tourist Information Centre
☎ (0233) 629165

Barnfield
HIGHLY COMMENDED

Pested Lane, Challock, Ashford TN25 4BQ
☎ Challock (0233) 740380
Set in beautiful Kent countryside close to Leeds Castle, Chilham and Canterbury. Easy access to M25 and M2.
Bedrooms: 2 double, 2 family rooms
Bathrooms: 4 private, 1 public

Bed & breakfast

per night:	£min	£max
Single	20.00	25.00
Double	35.00	40.00

Half board

per person:	£min	£max
Daily	27.00	30.00
Weekly	150.00	200.00

Evening meal 1900 (last orders 2100)
Parking for 10

Fishponds Farm

Pilgrims Way, Brook, Ashford TN25 5PP
☎ (0233) 812398
Rural farmhouse with lake in Wye Downs Nature Reserve, 3 miles south-east of Wye on lane to Brabourne.
Bedrooms: 1 double, 1 twin
Bathrooms: 2 private

Bed & breakfast

per night:	£min	£max
Single	15.00	15.00
Double	30.00	30.00

Parking for 10

Meadowside

Church Road, Mersham, Ashford TN25 6NT
☎ (0233) 626458
Two miles from M20, convenient for Channel ports, Canterbury, Rye and Weald. Large comfortable rooms en-suite (shower), tea-making, colour TV. Non-smokers only please.
Bedrooms: 1 double, 1 twin
Bathrooms: 2 private

Bed & breakfast

per night:	£min	£max
Single	18.00	20.00
Double	36.00	40.00

Parking for 2

One Mile Oast
Listed

Church Hill, Kingsnorth, Ashford TN23 3EX
☎ (0233) 624576

In pleasant rural surroundings 1 mile from Kingsnorth crossroads and 2.5 miles from Ashford. Converted Kent oast with circular bedrooms. Good centre for exploration.
Bedrooms: 2 double, 1 twin
Bathrooms: 2 public

Bed & breakfast

per night:	£min	£max
Single	16.00	18.00
Double	28.00	30.00

Parking for 5

Warren Cottage
APPROVED

136 The Street, Willesborough, Ashford TN25 0NB
☎ (0233) 621905 & 632929
Fax (0233) 623400

Continued ▶

357

SOUTH EAST ENGLAND

ASHFORD
Continued

300-year-old guesthouse with oak beams, open fireplaces and a cosy atmosphere. On old coaching route with easy access to M20 and a short drive from many places of interest.
Bedrooms: 2 single, 1 double, 1 twin
Bathrooms: 4 private, 1 public

Bed & breakfast
per night:	£min	£max
Single	25.00	50.00
Double	50.00	100.00

Half board
per person:	£min	£max
Daily	34.00	59.00
Weekly	170.00	295.00

Lunch available
Evening meal 1830 (last orders 2130)
Parking for 7
Cards accepted: Access, Visa

AYLESFORD
Kent
Map ref 3B3

Wickham Lodge
COMMENDED
73 High Street, Aylesford ME20 7AY
☎ Maidstone (0622) 717267

Period house fronting river by Aylesford Bridge. Lawns to river bank in front, walled garden to rear. Quiet position close to M2/M20 motorways. French spoken.
Bedrooms: 1 double, 1 triple
Bathrooms: 2 private, 1 public

Bed & breakfast
per night:	£min	£max
Single	20.00	20.00
Double	40.00	45.00

Half board
per person:	£min	£max
Daily	24.00	27.50
Weekly	168.00	192.50

Evening meal 1900 (last orders 2100)
Parking for 3

The town index towards the back of this guide gives page numbers of all places with accommodation.

BATTLE
East Sussex
Map ref 3B4

The Abbey at Battle was built on the site of the Battle of Hastings, when William defeated Harold II and so became the Conqueror in 1066. The museum has a fine collection relating to the Sussex iron industry.
Tourist Information Centre
☎ *(0424) 773721*

Kitchenham Farm
Listed
Ashburnham, Battle TN33 9NP
☎ Ninfield (0424) 892221
700-acre arable and mixed farm. Friendly family atmosphere in beautiful 18th C farmhouse. Traditional buildings offer perfect backdrop for stunning views. Large comfortable rooms.
Bedrooms: 1 double, 2 twin
Bathrooms: 2 public

Bed & breakfast
per night:	£min	£max
Double	30.00	34.00

Half board
per person:	£min	£max
Daily	28.00	28.00
Weekly	180.00	190.00

Evening meal from 1900
Parking for 7

Moons Hill Farm
The Green, Ninfield, Battle TN33 9LH
☎ Ninfield (0424) 892645
10-acre mixed farm. Modernised farmhouse in Ninfield village centre, in the heart of "1066" country. A warm welcome and Sussex home cooking. Pub opposite.
Bedrooms: 2 double, 1 twin
Bathrooms: 3 private, 1 public

Bed & breakfast
per night:	£min	£max
Single	15.00	17.50
Double	30.00	35.00

Parking for 12
Open January-November

BETCHWORTH
Surrey
Map ref 2D2

Gadbrook Old Farm
Wellhouse Old Lane, Betchworth RH3 7HH
☎ (0737) 842183
Picturesque 500-year-old farmhouse, oak beams and inglenook fireplaces. Large garden. Near village of Brockham and Betchworth off A25.
Bedrooms: 1 double, 1 twin
Bathrooms: 1 public

Bed & breakfast
per night:	£min	£max
Single	15.50	18.00
Double	30.00	36.00

Half board
per person:	£min	£max
Daily	25.00	
Weekly	140.00	

Lunch available
Evening meal 1900 (last orders 2100)
Parking for 4

BIDDENDEN
Kent
Map ref 3B4

Perfect village with black and white houses, a tithe barn and a pond. Part of the village is grouped around a green with a village sign depicting the famous Biddenden Maids. It was an important centre of the Flemish weaving industry, hence the beautiful Old Cloth Hall.

Bettmans Oast
HIGHLY COMMENDED
Hareplain Road, Biddenden, Ashford TN27 8LJ
☎ (0580) 291463
Grade II listed oast house and converted barn set in 10 acres near Sissinghurst Castle, quarter mile from Three Chimneys pub. Lovely gardens and log fires in winter.
Bedrooms: 1 family room
Bathrooms: 1 private

Bed & breakfast
per night:	£min	£max
Single	20.00	20.00
Double	40.00	40.00

Half board
per person:	£min	£max
Daily	32.00	35.00
Weekly	200.00	220.00

Evening meal 1830 (last orders 2100)
Parking for 4

BILLINGSHURST
West Sussex
Map ref 2D3

Small town lying 100 ft above sea level in undulating and unspoilt countryside.

Blue Idol Guest House
Old House Lane, Coolham, Horsham RH13 8QP
☎ Coolham (0403) 741241
Historic building founded by William Penn, set in lovely grounds up quiet lane off the A272 between Billingshurst and Coolham.
Bedrooms: 3 single, 2 double, 1 triple
Bathrooms: 2 public

358

SOUTH EAST ENGLAND

Bed & breakfast per night:	£min	£max
Single	17.00	22.00
Double	30.00	32.00

Evening meal 1800 (last orders 1800)
Parking for 20

Wooddale Cottage
Listed

Billingshurst RH14 9DU
☎ (0403) 782996
100-acre arable farm. Delightful old farmhouse set in large water gardens surrounded by over 100 acres of wooded farmland, 1 mile north east of Billingshurst.
Bedrooms: 1 single, 1 double, 1 twin
Bathrooms: 1 public

Bed & breakfast per night:	£min	£max
Single	18.00	20.00
Double	30.00	36.00

Half board per person:	£min	£max
Daily	28.00	32.50
Weekly	175.00	203.00

Parking for 3

BIRCHINGTON
Kent
Map ref 3C3

Town on the north coast of Kent with sandy beaches and rock pools. Powell Cotton Museum is in nearby Quex Park.

Woodchurch Farmhouse
Listed

Woodchurch, Birchington CT7 0HE
☎ Thanet (0843) 832468
6-acre arable farm. This Elizabethan farmhouse provides a warm welcome and ensures a comfortable stay. An excellent base for exploring south-east Kent.
Bedrooms: 1 double, 2 twin
Bathrooms: 1 public

Bed & breakfast per night:	£min	£max
Single	14.50	14.50
Double	29.00	29.00

Half board per person:	£min	£max
Daily	22.00	22.00
Weekly	145.00	145.00

Parking for 6

Check the introduction to this region for Where to Go, What to See.

BOXGROVE
West Sussex
Map ref 2C3

Meadow Corner
Listed APPROVED

The Street, Boxgrove, Chichester PO18 0DY
☎ Chichester (0243) 774134
Comfortable accommodation in pleasant home. In village 3 miles east of Chichester and well-placed for the city, theatre, Goodwood and the Downs. English or continental breakfast.
Bedrooms: 1 single, 1 twin
Bathrooms: 2 private, 2 public

Bed & breakfast per night:	£min	£max
Single	15.00	16.00
Double	32.00	36.00

Parking for 2
Open March-August, October-November

BRAMLEY
Surrey
Map ref 2D2

Jolly Farmer
Listed

High Street, Bramley, Guildford GU5 0HB
☎ Guildford (0483) 893355
Ancient attractive village freehouse. Family-run for two generations. On A281 Horsham road 3 miles from Guildford.
Bedrooms: 1 double, 2 twin
Bathrooms: 1 public, 2 private showers

Bed & breakfast per night:	£min	£max
Single	25.00	35.00
Double	40.00	55.00

Lunch available
Evening meal 1900 (last orders 2200)
Parking for 20
Cards accepted: Access, Visa

BRENCHLEY
Kent
Map ref 3B4

In the centre of this village is a small green, around which stand half-timbered, tile-hung and weatherboarded houses.

Bull Inn at Brenchley
COMMENDED

High Street, Brenchley, Tonbridge TN12 7NQ
☎ Tunbridge Wells (0892) 722701
Fax (0892) 723248
Victorian village inn set in the heart of the Weald of Kent. Comfortable accommodation with traditional English

---

ales and home-cooked food. 10 per cent discount for weekly half-board.
Bedrooms: 3 double, 1 twin
Bathrooms: 4 private, 1 public

Bed & breakfast per night:	£min	£max
Single	24.00	40.00
Double	30.00	45.00

Half board per person:	£min	£max
Daily	30.00	56.00

Lunch available
Evening meal 1830 (last orders 2130)
Parking for 10

BRIGHTON & HOVE
East Sussex
Map ref 2D3

Brighton's attractions include the Royal Pavilion, Volks Railway, Sea Life Centre and Marina, Conference Centre and "The Lanes" and several theatres. Neighbouring Hove is a resort in its own right.
Tourist Information Centre
☎ *(0273) 323755: for Hove (0273) 778087*

Albany Hotel

St. Catherine's Terrace, Kingsway, Hove BN3 2RR
☎ (0273) 773807

Situated on Kingsway (no parking restrictions), 1 mile west of West Pier. Just cross the road to the sea. All rooms en-suite with colour TV.
Bedrooms: 1 single, 5 double, 2 twin, 1 triple
Bathrooms: 9 private

Bed & breakfast per night:	£min	£max
Single	16.00	26.00
Double	30.00	37.00

Evening meal 1830 (last orders 1700)
Cards accepted: Access, Visa

'Brighton' Marina House Hotel

8 Charlotte Street, Marine Parade, Brighton BN2 1AG
☎ (0273) 605349 & 679484
Fax (0273) 605349
Cosy, well-maintained elegant hotel, offering a warm welcome, cleanliness, comfort and hospitality. English breakfast, licensed restaurant. Central

Continued ▶

359

SOUTH EAST ENGLAND

BRIGHTON & HOVE
Continued

for Palace Pier, conferences and exhibitions, adjacent to sea and a few minutes from Marina, Royal Pavilion and all amenities. Flexible breakfast, check-in and check-out times.
Bedrooms: 3 single, 4 double, 3 triple
Bathrooms: 7 private, 1 public

Bed & breakfast

per night:	£min	£max
Single	14.00	23.00
Double	33.00	43.00

Half board

per person:	£min	£max
Daily	24.00	33.00
Weekly	154.00	193.00

Lunch available
Evening meal 1830 (last orders 1700)
Cards accepted: Access, Visa, Diners, Amex

Cavalaire House
COMMENDED

34 Upper Rock Gardens, Brighton BN2 1QF
☎ (0273) 696899
Fax (0273) 600504
Victorian townhouse, close to sea and town centre. Resident proprietors offer comfortably furnished rooms with or without private facilities. Book 7 nights and get 1 night free.
Bedrooms: 1 single, 3 double, 3 twin, 2 triple
Bathrooms: 3 private, 1 public, 2 private showers

Bed & breakfast

per night:	£min	£max
Single	15.00	19.00
Double	26.00	44.00

Cards accepted: Access, Visa, Diners, Amex

Diana House
Listed

25 St. Georges Terrace, Brighton BN2 1JJ
☎ (0273) 605797
Warm and friendly, conveniently situated for town, conference centre and marina. Tea/coffee facilities, colour TV and central heating. Own key for access.
Bedrooms: 4 double, 2 twin, 2 triple, 1 family room
Bathrooms: 1 private, 6 private showers

Bed & breakfast

per night:	£min	£max
Single	15.00	19.00
Double	30.00	38.00

Cards accepted: Access, Visa

Melford Hall Hotel

41 Marine Parade, Brighton BN2 1PE
☎ (0273) 681435
Listed building well positioned on seafront and within easy walking distance of all the entertainment that Brighton has to offer. Many rooms with sea views.
Bedrooms: 4 single, 14 double, 7 twin, 3 triple, 1 family room
Bathrooms: 27 private, 2 public, 2 private showers

Bed & breakfast

per night:	£min	£max
Single	28.00	35.00
Double	44.00	54.00

Parking for 12
Cards accepted: Access, Visa, Diners, Amex

BURWASH
East Sussex
Map ref 3B4

Village of old houses, many from the Tudor and Stuart periods. One of the old ironmasters' houses is Bateman's (National Trust) which was the home of Rudyard Kipling.

Woodlands Farm
Listed

Heathfield Road, Burwash, Etchingham TN19 7LA
☎ (0435) 882794
55-acre mixed farm. Modernised 16th C farmhouse set away from road, amidst fields and woods. Friendly welcome and fresh food. Near Batemans.
Bedrooms: 2 double, 2 twin
Bathrooms: 1 private, 2 public

Bed & breakfast

per night:	£min	£max
Single	15.00	
Double	30.00	35.00

Parking for 4
Open April-December

There are separate sections in this guide listing groups specialising in farm holidays and accommodation which is especially suitable for young people and organised groups.

CANTERBURY
Kent
Map ref 3B3

Place of pilgrimage since the martyrdom of Becket in 1170 and the site of Canterbury Cathedral. Visit St Augustine's Abbey, St Martin's (the oldest church in England), Royal Museum and the Canterbury Tales. Nearby is Howletts Wild Animal Park.
Tourist Information Centre
☎ (0227) 766567

Abberley House
Listed

115 Whitstable Road, Canterbury CT2 8EF
☎ (0227) 450265
Family-run guesthouse within easy walking distance of the city and university. Tea/coffee-making facilities, wash-basins. Non-smokers please.
Bedrooms: 1 single, 1 double, 1 twin
Bathrooms: 1 public

Bed & breakfast

per night:	£min	£max
Single	17.00	20.00
Double	32.00	34.00

Parking for 2

Alicante Guest House
Listed COMMENDED

4 Roper Road, Canterbury CT2 7EH
☎ (0227) 766277
Family-run for 10 years, the Alicante offers friendly, helpful and comfortable surroundings. Competitive prices for long and short stays.
Bedrooms: 1 single, 2 double, 1 twin, 2 triple
Bathrooms: 2 public, 1 private shower

Bed & breakfast

per night:	£min	£max
Single	17.00	19.00
Double	32.00	36.00

Cards accepted: Access, Visa

Bower Farm House
Listed

Stelling Minnis, Canterbury CT4 6BB
☎ Stelling Minnis (022 787) 430
Delightful heavily beamed 17th C farmhouse between the villages of Stelling Minnis and Bossingham. Canterbury and Hythe are approximately 7 miles away.
Bedrooms: 1 single, 1 double, 1 twin
Bathrooms: 2 private, 1 public

Bed & breakfast

per night:	£min	£max
Single	17.50	19.00
Double	35.00	38.00

Parking for 8

360

SOUTH EAST ENGLAND

Bridge House
Listed

The Green, Chartham, Canterbury
CT4 7JW
☎ (0227) 738354
Well-equipped house on banks of River Stour, next to village green. Tea/coffee upon request. Colour TV. Canterbury 3 miles on A28.
Bedrooms: 2 twin
Bathrooms: 2 public

Bed & breakfast per night:	£min	£max
Single	16.00	
Double	28.00	

Parking for 5

Cathedral Gate Hotel
APPROVED

36 Burgate, Canterbury CT1 2HA
☎ (0227) 464381
Fax (0227) 462800
Central position at main entrance to the cathedral. Car parking nearby. Baby listening service. Old world charm at reasonable prices. English breakfast extra.
Bedrooms: 5 single, 7 double, 8 twin, 2 triple, 2 family rooms
Bathrooms: 12 private, 3 public, 2 private showers

Bed & breakfast per night:	£min	£max
Single	24.00	45.00
Double	44.00	68.50

Evening meal 1900 (last orders 2100)
Parking for 12
Cards accepted: Access, Visa, Diners

Clare-Ellen Guest House
HIGHLY COMMENDED

9 Victoria Road, Wincheap, Canterbury
CT1 3SG
☎ (0227) 760205
Victorian house with large, elegant en-suite rooms, 8 minutes' walk from city centre. 5 minutes to BR Canterbury East station. Car park and garage available.
Bedrooms: 1 single, 2 double, 1 twin, 1 family room
Bathrooms: 4 private, 2 public

Bed & breakfast per night:	£min	£max
Single	20.00	24.00
Double	40.00	46.00

Parking for 9
Cards accepted: Access, Visa

The Corner House
Listed

113 Whitstable Road, Canterbury
CT2 8EF
☎ (0227) 761352

Just a few minutes' walking distance from city, university, shops and restaurants. Spacious family house and friendly hospitality.
Bedrooms: 1 double, 2 twin
Bathrooms: 2 public

Bed & breakfast per night:	£min	£max
Single	18.00	25.00
Double	28.00	34.00

Parking for 4

Crossways

Field Way, Sturry, Canterbury
CT2 0BH
☎ (0227) 711059
Small family-run early Victorian home 3 miles from Canterbury on A28 Margate road. On main bus and rail routes.
Bedrooms: 1 single, 1 double, 1 twin
Bathrooms: 2 private, 1 public, 1 private shower

Bed & breakfast per night:	£min	£max
Single	15.00	17.00
Double	30.00	34.00

Parking for 6

Deerson Farmhouse
Listed

Deerson Lane, Preston, Canterbury
CT3 1EX
☎ (0227) 722241
130-acre mixed farm. Bed and breakfast in 17th C farmhouse. From Canterbury/Sandwich road at Wingham take left turn to Preston, third turn left, half-a-mile on, white farmhouse with three dormer windows.
Bedrooms: 2 double
Bathrooms: 1 public

Bed & breakfast per night:	£min	£max
Single	15.00	20.00
Double	30.00	40.00

Half board per person:	£min	£max
Daily	23.00	28.00

Evening meal 1800 (last orders 2200)
Parking for 5

The Farmhouse, Upper Mystole Park Farm
HIGHLY COMMENDED

Pennypot Lane, Mystole, Canterbury
CT4 7BT
☎ (0227) 730589

90-acre fruit farm. Modern farmhouse in the heart of Kent and with magnificent views. Set between historic Canterbury and beautiful Chilham (A28). Dover 25 minutes.
Bedrooms: 1 double, 1 twin, 1 triple
Bathrooms: 1 private, 1 public

Bed & breakfast per night:	£min	£max
Single	18.00	20.00
Double	32.00	35.00

Half board per person:	£min	£max
Daily	24.00	26.00
Weekly	165.00	175.00

Evening meal 1830 (last orders 2000)
Parking for 6

Iffin Farmhouse
Listed

Iffin Lane, Canterbury CT4 7BE
☎ (0227) 462776
Fax (0474) 569036
A warm welcome awaits you in this 18th C farmhouse, renovated to high standards in the mid-fifties. Well-appointed accommodation set in 10 acres of gardens, paddocks and orchards, in a quiet rural setting, only 6 minutes' drive to centre of the historic city of Canterbury.
Bedrooms: 2 double
Bathrooms: 1 private, 1 public

Bed & breakfast per night:	£min	£max
Single	30.00	50.00
Double	40.00	60.00

Parking for 6
Open March-November

Kenfield House

Kenfield, Petham, Canterbury
CT4 5RN
☎ Petham (0227) 700721
Fax (0227) 456345
Large Georgian former farmhouse with Tudor origins set in own grounds of 6 acres in valley, 4.5 miles from Canterbury.
Bedrooms: 1 double, 1 twin, 1 triple
Bathrooms: 1 private, 1 public

Bed & breakfast per night:	£min	£max
Single		18.00
Double	36.00	36.00

Half board per person:	£min	£max
Daily	25.00	30.00

Evening meal from 1900
Parking for 6

We advise you to confirm your booking in writing.

SOUTH EAST ENGLAND

CANTERBURY
Continued

Magnolia House
HIGHLY COMMENDED
36 St Dunstans Terrace, Canterbury CT2 8AX
☎ (0227) 765121
Fax (0227) 765121

Georgian house in attractive city street. Close to university, gardens, river and city centre. Very quiet house within a walled garden, ideal for guests to relax in. Four-poster suite available.
Bedrooms: 1 single, 3 double, 1 twin
Bathrooms: 5 private

Bed & breakfast
per night:	£min	£max
Single	34.00	38.00
Double	48.00	55.00

Half board
per person:	£min	£max
Daily	44.00	48.00

Parking for 4
Cards accepted: Access, Visa, Amex

Old Stone House
Listed
The Green, Wickhambreaux, Canterbury CT3 1RQ
☎ (0227) 728591

One of the oldest houses in Kent, parts dating from 12th C. Once the home of Joan Plantagenet, wife of the Black Prince. Ten minutes west of Canterbury, 30 minutes from Folkestone and Dover.
Bedrooms: 1 single, 2 double, 1 twin
Bathrooms: 2 private, 1 public

Bed & breakfast
per night:	£min	£max
Single	15.00	20.00
Double	32.00	40.00

Parking for 4

Oriel Lodge
COMMENDED
3 Queens Avenue, Canterbury CT2 8AY
☎ (0227) 462185

Warm and comfortable period house in residential road near city centre. Lounge area with log fire. Smoking in lounge area only.
Bedrooms: 1 single, 3 double, 1 twin, 1 triple
Bathrooms: 2 private, 2 public

Bed & breakfast
per night:	£min	£max
Single	18.00	23.00
Double	32.00	52.00

Parking for 6

Pointers Hotel
COMMENDED
1 London Road, Canterbury CT2 8LR
☎ (0227) 456846
Fax (0227) 831131

Family-run Georgian hotel close to city centre, cathedral and university.
Bedrooms: 2 single, 8 double, 2 twin, 2 triple
Bathrooms: 8 private, 2 public, 2 private showers

Bed & breakfast
per night:	£min	£max
Single	30.00	38.00
Double	42.00	58.00

Half board
per person:	£min	£max
Daily	35.00	51.00
Weekly	217.00	280.00

Evening meal 1930 (last orders 2030)
Parking for 10
Cards accepted: Access, Visa, Diners, Amex

Raemore House
Listed COMMENDED
33 New Dover Road, Canterbury CT1 3AS
☎ (0227) 769740

Family-run guesthouse close to city centre. Four-poster and en-suite rooms with TV and tea/coffee facilities. Private car park.
Bedrooms: 1 single, 5 double, 2 twin, 1 triple
Bathrooms: 3 private, 2 public

Bed & breakfast
per night:	£min	£max
Single	18.00	25.00
Double	32.00	44.00

Parking for 9
Cards accepted: Access, Visa

St Stephens Guest House
Listed COMMENDED
100 St Stephens Road, Canterbury CT2 7JL
☎ (0227) 767644

Mock-Tudor house set in attractive garden within easy walking distance of the city centre and cathedral. Colour TV in rooms. Car park.
Bedrooms: 3 single, 8 double, 1 twin
Bathrooms: 4 private, 3 public

Bed & breakfast
per night:	£min	£max
Single	18.50	
Double	37.00	

Parking for 8
Cards accepted: Access, Visa

Thanington Hotel
HIGHLY COMMENDED
140 Wincheap, Canterbury CT1 3RY
☎ (0227) 453227
Fax (0227) 453225

Beautiful bed and breakfast hotel with indoor heated swimming pool and games room. 5 minutes' walk city centre, 30 minutes' drive from Dover. Colour brochure available.
Bedrooms: 5 double, 3 twin, 2 family rooms
Bathrooms: 10 private

Bed & breakfast
per night:	£min	£max
Single	38.00	45.00
Double	55.00	60.00

Parking for 12
Cards accepted: Access, Visa, Amex

Upper Ansdore
COMMENDED
Duckpit Lane, Petham, Canterbury CT4 5QB
☎ Petham (0227) 700672

En-suite accommodation in Tudor farmhouse in secluded, elevated position on the North Downs, overlooking nature reserve. 5 miles south of Canterbury. Bedrooms also available as family or twin.
Bedrooms: 3 double
Bathrooms: 3 private

SOUTH EAST ENGLAND

Bed & breakfast per night:	£min	£max
Double	36.00	37.00

Parking for 5
Open February-November

Well House

The Green, Chartham, Canterbury
CT4 7JW
☎ (0227) 738762
In a very quiet position, on village green next to 15th C church. Just off A28, 2 miles from Canterbury.
Bedrooms: 1 double, 1 twin
Bathrooms: 2 private

Bed & breakfast per night:	£min	£max
Single	18.00	
Double	30.00	

Parking for 2

The Willows

HIGHLY COMMENDED

Howfield Lane, Chartham Hatch,
Canterbury CT4 7HG
☎ (0227) 738442
A friendly welcome awaits you at The Willows. Situated in a quiet lane, 2 miles from cathedral. Breakfast is taken in the conservatory overlooking a garden for enthusiasts.
Bedrooms: 1 single, 1 double, 1 twin
Bathrooms: 1 public

Bed & breakfast per night:	£min	£max
Single	15.00	15.00
Double	36.00	38.00

Parking for 6

York Cottage

Listed

57 Hackington Road, Tyler Hill,
Canterbury CT2 9NE
☎ (0227) 471253
Delightful cottage with friendly welcome in small village 2 miles from Canterbury. Near university. Lovely gardens. Tea and coffee making facilities. No smoking.
Bedrooms: 2 double
Bathrooms: 1 public

Bed & breakfast per night:	£min	£max
Single	18.00	25.00
Double	28.00	30.00

Parking for 4

Yorke Lodge

COMMENDED

50 London Road, Canterbury CT2 8LF
☎ (0227) 451243
Fax (0227) 462006
Spacious, elegant Victorian town house close to city centre. Relax and enjoy a special bed and breakfast.

Bedrooms: 1 single, 4 double
Bathrooms: 5 private

Bed & breakfast per night:	£min	£max
Single	22.00	24.00
Double	40.00	45.00

Parking for 4
Cards accepted: Access, Visa, Amex

Zan Stel Lodge

Listed

140 Old Dover Road, Canterbury
CT1 3NX
☎ (0227) 453654
A warm welcome awaits you at this comfortable family-run guesthouse. TV, tea/coffee-making facilities in all the spacious bedrooms. Close to city centre and Kent County Cricket Ground. Non smoking.
Bedrooms: 2 triple
Bathrooms: 2 public

Bed & breakfast per night:	£min	£max
Double	34.00	42.00

Parking for 4

CHARING

Kent
Map ref 3B4

Delightful village with many 15th C houses. The parish church has a fine timbered roof with painted beams and a medieval pulpit.

Barnfield

Listed **COMMENDED**

Charing, Ashford TN27 0BN
☎ (0233) 712421
500-acre arable farm. Kent hall farmhouse built 1420 with wealth of character. On A20, leave Charing roundabout by Maidstone exit. After 400 yards take first left signed Hook Lane, continue for 2.5 miles to house on left with white metal rail fence.
Bedrooms: 2 single, 1 double, 1 twin
Bathrooms: 1 public

Bed & breakfast per night:	£min	£max
Single	18.00	20.00
Double	36.00	40.00

Half board per person:	£min	£max
Daily	30.50	32.50
Weekly	183.00	195.00

Evening meal 1900 (last orders 1900)
Parking for 21
Cards accepted: Visa

CHICHESTER

West Sussex
Map ref 2C3

The county town of West Sussex with a beautiful Norman cathedral. Noted for its Georgian architecture but also has modern buildings like the Festival Theatre. Surrounded by places of interest, including Fishbourne Roman Palace and Weald and Downland Open-Air Museum.
Tourist Information Centre
☎ (0243) 775888

Abelands Barn

Listed **COMMENDED**

Bognor Road, Merston, Chichester
PO20 6DY
☎ (0243) 533826
Listed converted agricultural barns on A259 just 2 miles outside Chichester on coast road to Bognor Regis. Close to Festival Theatre and Goodwood.
Bedrooms: 2 double, 1 twin
Bathrooms: 3 private

Bed & breakfast per night:	£min	£max
Single	20.00	20.00
Double	40.00	40.00

Parking for 4
Cards accepted: Access, Visa

Barford

Listed

Bosham Lane, Bosham, Chichester
PO18 8HL
☎ (0243) 573393
Comfortable cottage-style bungalow in the centre of a picturesque village and within a few minutes' walk of the harbour. Cycle hire available.
Bedrooms: 2 double, 1 twin
Bathrooms: 1 public

Bed & breakfast per night:	£min	£max
Single	15.00	17.00
Double	30.00	34.00

Half board per person:	£min	£max
Daily	22.50	24.50
Weekly	157.50	171.50

Evening meal 1800 (last orders 2100)
Parking for 1

Hedgehogs

Listed

45 Whyke Lane, Chichester PO19 2JT
☎ (0243) 780022
About half-a-mile from city centre, bus/railway stations and theatre. Secluded garden. Guests' own bathroom, TV lounge. Weekly terms available. Cyclists and hikers welcome. No smoking.
Bedrooms: 2 double, 1 twin

Continued ▶

363

SOUTH EAST ENGLAND

CHICHESTER
Continued

Bathrooms: 2 public
Bed & breakfast
per night:	£min	£max
Single	13.00	17.00
Double	26.00	34.00

Parking for 4

CHIDDINGSTONE
Kent
Map ref 2D2

Pleasant village of 16th and 17th C, preserved by the National Trust, with an 18th C "castle" and attractive Tudor inn.

Hoath Holidays
Listed APPROVED

Hoath House, Chiddingstone Hoath, Edenbridge TN8 7DB
☎ Cowden (0342) 850362
Tudor family house with beamed and panelled rooms and extensive gardens.
Bedrooms: 2 twin
Bathrooms: 1 public, 1 private shower
Bed & breakfast
per night:	£min	£max
Single	13.50	19.50
Double	27.00	39.00

Parking for 8

CHILHAM
Kent
Map ref 3B3

Extremely pretty village of mostly Tudor and Jacobean houses. The village rises to the spacious square with the castle and the 15th C church. The grounds of the Jacobean House, laid out by Capability Brown, are open to the public.

Jullieberrie House

Canterbury Road, Chilham, Canterbury CT4 8DX
☎ Canterbury (0227) 730488
Modern house with lovely views over lake and woodland. On the A28 Ashford to Canterbury road, close to Chilham village.
Bedrooms: 2 double, 1 twin
Bathrooms: 2 private, 1 public, 1 private shower
Bed & breakfast
per night:	£min	£max
Single	20.00	25.00
Double	27.00	33.00

Parking for 5

The Woolpack Inn
APPROVED

High Street, Chilham, Canterbury CT4 8DL
☎ Canterbury (0227) 730208
Fax (0227) 751090
A fine bed and victuals have been offered here for 200 years. Dine on Kentish fare and enjoy the friendly bar.
Bedrooms: 8 double, 4 twin, 1 triple
Bathrooms: 13 private
Bed & breakfast
per night:	£min	£max
Single	35.00	45.00
Double	45.00	55.00

Lunch available
Evening meal 1900 (last orders 2130)
Parking for 40
Cards accepted: Access, Visa, Diners, Amex, Switch

CLIFTONVILLE
Kent

See under Margate

COPTHORNE
Surrey
Map ref 2D2

Residential village on the Surrey/West Sussex border, near Crawley and within easy reach of Gatwick Airport.

Broad Oak
Listed

West Park Road, Copthorne, Crawley, West Sussex RH10 3EX
☎ (0342) 714882
Modernised country house built in early 1920s, set in beautiful secluded grounds. Courtesy transport provided for Gatwick travellers. Dining-out facilities nearby. Non-smokers only please.
Bedrooms: 1 single, 1 twin, 1 triple
Bathrooms: 1 public
Bed & breakfast
per night:	£min	£max
Single	22.50	24.00
Double	37.50	39.00

Parking for 6

CRANBROOK
Kent
Map ref 3B4

Old town, a centre for the weaving industry in the 15th C. The 72-ft high Union Mill is a 3-storeyed windmill, still in working order.

Hallwood Farm House
Listed

Hallwood Farm, Cranbrook TN17 2SP
☎ (0580) 713204

10-acre arable farm. 15th C hall house with beams and open inglenook.
Bedrooms: 1 double, 1 twin, 1 triple
Bathrooms: 1 public
Bed & breakfast
per night:	£min	£max
Single	18.00	18.00
Double	36.00	36.00

Half board
per person:	£min	£max
Daily	30.00	30.00
Weekly	190.00	190.00

Evening meal 1930 (last orders 2030)
Parking for 3
Open April-October

Tolehurst Barn
COMMENDED

Cranbrook Road, Frittenden, Cranbrook TN17 2BP
☎ (0580) 714385

Converted 17th C beamed barn in farmland - quiet and rural, all modern conveniences. On A229, convenient for the heart of Kent and places of historic interest. Only 5 minutes from Sissinghurst. Languages spoken.
Bedrooms: 2 double, 1 triple
Bathrooms: 3 private
Bed & breakfast
per night:	£min	£max
Single	15.00	17.00
Double	30.00	34.00

Half board
per person:	£min	£max
Daily	23.00	25.00

Evening meal 1900 (last orders 2100)
Parking for 6

The White Horse Inn
Listed

High Street, Cranbrook TN17 3EX
☎ (0580) 712615
Victorian public house and restaurant in the centre of the smallest town in Kent, once the capital of the Weald.
Bedrooms: 1 single, 1 twin, 1 triple
Bathrooms: 1 public
Bed & breakfast
per night:	£min	£max
Single		20.00
Double		32.00

Half board
per person:	£min	£max
Daily	24.00	28.00

SOUTH EAST ENGLAND

Lunch available
Evening meal 1830 (last orders 2130)
Parking for 12
Cards accepted: Access, Visa

CRAWLEY
West Sussex
Map ref 2D2

One of the first New Towns built after World War II, but it also has some old buildings. Set in magnificent wooded countryside.

Caprice Guest House
Listed COMMENDED

Bonnetts Lane, Ifield, Crawley RH11 0NY
☎ (0293) 528620
Small, friendly, family-run guesthouse surrounded by farmland and close to all amenities. 10 minutes south of Gatwick Airport.
Bedrooms: 1 double, 2 twin
Bathrooms: 1 private, 1 public

Bed & breakfast per night:	£min	£max
Single	25.00	30.00
Double	35.00	45.00

Parking for 6

CUCKFIELD
West Sussex
Map ref 2D3

The High Street is lined with Elizabethan and Georgian shops, inns and houses and was once part of the London to Brighton coach road. Nearby Nymans (National Trust) is a 30-acre garden with fine topiary work.

Ousedale

Brook Street, Cuckfield, Haywards Heath RH17 5JJ
☎ Haywards Heath (0444) 450548
Comfortable quiet family chalet bungalow home with lovely gardens and views, one mile north of Cuckfield on B2036. Easy parking.
Bedrooms: 1 single, 1 double, 1 twin
Bathrooms: 2 public

Bed & breakfast per night:	£min	£max
Single	20.00	20.00
Double	33.00	33.00

Parking for 6

Please mention this guide when making a booking.

DEAL
Kent
Map ref 3C4

Coastal town and popular holiday resort. Deal Castle was built by Henry VIII as a fort and the museum is devoted to finds excavated in the area. Also the Time-Ball Tower Museum. Angling available from both beach and pier.
Tourist Information Centre
☎ (0304) 369576

Beggars Leap
Listed

Lower Mill Lane, Deal CT14 9AG
☎ (0304) 373263
Large Spanish-style house. From Dover take A258 to Deal Castle, turn left, Gilford Road, past Tides Leisure Pool, turn right then 1st left, 1st house on right.
Bedrooms: 1 double
Bathrooms: 1 public

Bed & breakfast per night:	£min	£max
Single	18.00	22.00
Double	36.00	40.00

Parking for 4

Finglesham Grange
HIGHLY COMMENDED

Finglesham, Deal CT14 0NQ
☎ Sandwich (0304) 611314

Grade 2 listed country house in secluded grounds away from the noise of town and traffic. Spacious rooms, pleasant atmosphere, personal service. Ample parking. Just 4 miles from both Deal and Sandwich.
Bedrooms: 1 double, 2 twin
Bathrooms: 3 private

Bed & breakfast per night:	£min	£max
Single	22.50	25.00
Double	40.00	45.00

Evening meal 1900 (last orders 1700)
Parking for 5

Hardicot Guest House
COMMENDED

Kingsdown Road, Walmer, Deal CT14 8AW
☎ (0304) 373867
Large, quiet, detached Victorian house with Channel views and secluded garden. Ideal for sea fishing, cliff walks and golfing.
Bedrooms: 1 double, 1 twin, 1 triple

Bathrooms: 1 public, 1 private shower

Bed & breakfast per night:	£min	£max
Single	18.00	20.00
Double	34.00	40.00

Parking for 4

DIAL POST
West Sussex
Map ref 2D3

Small village on the main road from Horsham to the coast at Worthing.

Swallows Farm

Swallows Lane, Dial Post, Horsham RH13 8NN
☎ Partridge Green (0403) 710385
210-acre mixed farm. Georgian farmhouse in the quiet Sussex countryside half a mile off A24, within easy reach of coast, downs and many places of historic interest. Gatwick Airport 35 minutes' drive.
Bedrooms: 2 double, 1 twin
Bathrooms: 2 public

Bed & breakfast per night:	£min	£max
Single	18.00	22.00
Double	30.00	36.00

Half board per person:	£min	£max
Daily	25.00	29.00

Evening meal from 1830
Parking for 4
Open March-October

DORKING
Surrey
Map ref 2D2

Ancient market town and a good centre for walking, delightfully set between Box Hill and the Downs.

Bulmer Farm

Holmbury St Mary, Dorking RH5 6LG
☎ (0306) 730210
30-acre beef farm. 17th C character farmhouse with beams and inglenook fireplace, in the Surrey hills. Choice of twin rooms in the house or double/twin en-suite rooms in tastefully converted barn adjoining the house. Village is 5 miles from Dorking.
Wheelchair access category 3
Bedrooms: 3 double, 5 twin
Bathrooms: 5 private, 2 public, 3 private showers

Continued ▶

365

SOUTH EAST ENGLAND

DORKING
Continued

Bed & breakfast
per night:	£min	£max
Single	18.00	
Double	32.00	

Parking for 12

Crossways Farm
Raikes Lane, Abinger Hammer, Dorking RH5 6PZ
☎ (0306) 730173
200-acre arable & livestock farm. 17th C listed farmhouse in a small village south-west of Dorking. Good centre for London, the South East and airports. Large comfortable rooms.
Bedrooms: 1 twin, 1 triple
Bathrooms: 2 private, 1 public

Bed & breakfast
per night:	£min	£max
Double	28.00	32.00

Half board
per person:	£min	£max
Daily	22.00	30.00
Weekly	154.00	165.00

Evening meal 1900 (last orders 1900)
Parking for 3

Mark Ash
Listed COMMENDED
Abinger Common, Dorking RH5 6JA
☎ (0306) 731326
Victorian house in lovely garden opposite village green. Area of Outstanding Natural Beauty. One mile off A25. Dorking 4 miles, Guildford 8 miles. Convenient for Gatwick Airport.
Bedrooms: 1 double, 1 twin
Bathrooms: 2 private, 1 public

Bed & breakfast
per night:	£min	£max
Single	25.00	
Double	40.00	

Parking for 4
Open March-November

Steyning Cottage
Listed
Horsham Road, South Holmwood, Dorking RH5 4NE
☎ (0306) 888481
Detached tile-hung house adjacent to A24 and within walking distance of Leith Hill. Gatwick Airport approximately 20 minutes away, Heathrow 45 minutes. French spoken.
Bedrooms: 1 single, 2 twin
Bathrooms: 1 public

Bed & breakfast
per night:	£min	£max
Single	14.00	20.00
Double	28.00	32.00

Half board
per person:	£min	£max
Daily	20.00	28.00
Weekly	91.00	180.00

Evening meal 1900 (last orders 2000)
Parking for 4

The Waltons
Listed
5 Rose Hill, Dorking RH14 2EG
☎ (0306) 883127
House retains all its period features. Central location with beautiful views. Surrounded by National Trust land. Friendly atmosphere.
Bedrooms: 1 double, 1 twin
Bathrooms: 2 public

Bed & breakfast
per night:	£min	£max
Single	15.00	20.00
Double	30.00	35.00

Half board
per person:	£min	£max
Daily	23.50	28.50
Weekly	94.00	178.50

Evening meal 1800 (last orders 2100)
Parking for 3

DOVER
Kent
Map ref 3C4

A Cinque Port and busiest passenger port in the world. Still a historic town and seaside resort beside the famous White Cliffs. The White Cliffs Experience attraction traces the town's history through the Roman, Saxon, Norman and Victorian periods.
Tourist Information Centre
☎ *(0304) 205108*

Coldred Court Farm
HIGHLY COMMENDED
Church Road, Coldred, Dover CT15 5AQ
☎ (0304) 830816
7-acre mixed farm. 1620 farmhouse full of old world charm, with modern facilities. Situated 1 mile from the A2, 10 minutes from Dover.
Bedrooms: 2 double, 1 twin
Bathrooms: 3 private

Bed & breakfast
per night:	£min	£max
Single	18.50	32.00
Double	37.00	42.00

Half board
per person:	£min	£max
Daily	28.50	42.00
Weekly	178.50	273.00

Evening meal 1800 (last orders 2030)
Parking for 13

Esther House
Listed COMMENDED
55 Barton Road, Dover CT16 2NF
☎ (0304) 241332
Non-smoking B and B with warm Christian atmosphere. Close to ferries and town centre. Ideal for short breaks and overnight stops to Continent. Early breakfasts. Evening meals by arrangement.
Bedrooms: 1 single, 1 twin, 1 triple
Bathrooms: 1 public

Bed & breakfast
per night:	£min	£max
Single	12.00	16.00
Double	24.00	32.00

Messines Guest House
Listed
Upper Road, Dover CT16 1HP
☎ (0304) 209744
Spanish-style bungalow in large garden, situated below Dover Castle between Bleriot Memorial and Langdon Cliffs.
Bedrooms: 1 double, 1 twin
Bathrooms: 2 public

Bed & breakfast
per night:	£min	£max
Single	12.00	14.00
Double	30.00	34.00

Parking for 6

Number One Guest House
1 Castle Street, Dover CT16 1QH
☎ (0304) 202007
Georgian town house, in an historic street, ideally situated for the port, Heritage Centre, restaurants, banks. Garage parking available.
Bedrooms: 2 double, 2 twin, 1 triple
Bathrooms: 5 private

Bed & breakfast
per night:	£min	£max
Double	32.00	38.00

Parking for 10

Woodpeckers
Chapel Lane, St-Margarets-at-Cliffe, Dover CT15 6BQ
☎ (0304) 852761

10 minutes from Dover docks, in the quiet village of St Margarets, behind the village pond. En-suite facilities.

SOUTH EAST ENGLAND

Bedrooms: 1 twin, 1 triple
Bathrooms: 2 private

Bed & breakfast
per night:	£min	£max
Single	19.00	19.00
Double	32.00	32.00

Parking for 4

EAST DEAN
East Sussex
Map ref 2D3

Pretty village on a green near Friston Forest and Birling Gap.

Birling Gap Hotel
APPROVED

East Dean, Eastbourne BN20 0AB
☎ Eastbourne (0323) 423197
Fax (0323) 423030

Magnificent Seven Sisters clifftop position, with views of country, sea, beach. Superb downland walks. Old world "Thatched Bar" and "Oak Room Restaurant". Coffee shop and games room, function and conference suite.

Bedrooms: 1 single, 4 double, 2 twin, 2 triple
Bathrooms: 9 private, 1 public

Bed & breakfast
per night:	£min	£max
Single	20.00	50.00
Double	30.00	55.00

Half board
per person:	£min	£max
Weekly	172.50	287.00

Lunch available
Evening meal 1830 (last orders 2130)
Parking for 100
Cards accepted: Access, Visa, Diners, Amex, Switch

EAST GRINSTEAD
West Sussex
Map ref 2D2

A number of fine old houses stand in the High Street, one of which is Sackville College, founded in 1609.

Middle House Cookhams
COMMENDED

Sharpthorne, East Grinstead
RH19 4HU
☎ (0342) 810566

Central portion of large 100-year-old country house, with open southerly aspect. In village south of East Grinstead.

Bedrooms: 1 single, 1 double, 1 twin
Bathrooms: 2 private, 1 public

Bed & breakfast
per night:	£min	£max
Single	20.00	22.00
Double	40.00	45.00

Parking for 4

EASTBOURNE
East Sussex
Map ref 3B4

One of the finest, most elegant resorts on the south-east coast situated beside Beachy Head. Long promenade, plenty of gardens, theatres, Towner Art Gallery, "How We Lived Then" museum of shops and social history. ☎ *(0323) 411400*

Bay Lodge Hotel
COMMENDED

61-62 Royal Parade, Eastbourne
BN22 7AQ
☎ (0323) 732515
Fax (0323) 735009

Small seafront hotel opposite Redoubt Gardens, close to bowling greens, sailing clubs and entertainments. Large sun-lounge. All double/twin bedrooms are en-suite.

Bedrooms: 3 single, 5 double, 4 twin
Bathrooms: 9 private, 2 public

Bed & breakfast
per night:	£min	£max
Single	16.00	23.00
Double	34.00	45.00

Half board
per person:	£min	£max
Daily	27.00	33.00
Weekly	158.00	189.00

Evening meal 1800 (last orders 1800)
Open March-October and Christmas
Cards accepted: Access, Visa

Edelweiss Private Hotel

10-12 Elms Avenue, Eastbourne
BN21 3DN
☎ (0323) 732071

Family-run hotel 50 yards from the pier. Comfortable bedrooms with TV, tea-making and hair-dryer. En-suite rooms available. Licensed bar, guests' lounge.

Bedrooms: 2 single, 6 double, 5 twin, 1 family room
Bathrooms: 3 private, 4 public

Bed & breakfast
per night:	£min	£max
Single	13.50	15.00
Double	27.00	34.00

Half board
per person:	£min	£max
Daily	17.00	20.50
Weekly	99.00	139.00

Evening meal 1800 (last orders 1500)
Cards accepted: Access, Visa

We advise you to confirm your booking in writing.

ELHAM
Kent
Map ref 3B4

In the Nailbourne Valley on the chalk downlands, this large village has an outstanding collection of old houses. Abbot's Fireside, built in 1614, has a timbered upper storey resting on brackets carved into figures.

Tye
Listed

Collards Lane, Elham, Canterbury
CT4 6UF
☎ (0303) 840271

Country house, less than a mile from the village, beautifully situated on top of a hill with lovely views and walks. Very quiet.

Bedrooms: 1 single, 2 twin
Bathrooms: 1 public

Bed & breakfast
per night:	£min	£max
Single	17.00	17.00
Double	34.00	34.00

Parking for 6

EWHURST
Surrey
Map ref 2D2

Village in the heart of the Surrey countryside, with Hurtwood Common, Winkworth Aboretum and Leith Hill nearby.

High Edser
Listed COMMENDED

Shere Road, Ewhurst, Cranleigh, Surrey GU6 7PQ
☎ Guildford (0483) 278214

14th-15th C family home set in area of outstanding natural beauty. 6 miles from Guildford and Dorking, within easy reach of airports and many tourist attractions. Non-smokers only please.

Bedrooms: 1 single, 1 double, 1 twin
Bathrooms: 1 public

Bed & breakfast
per night:	£min	£max
Single	20.00	22.00
Double	35.00	40.00

Parking for 7

National Crown ratings were correct at the time of going to press but are subject to change. Please check at the time of booking.

SOUTH EAST ENGLAND

FARNHAM
Surrey
Map ref 2C2

Town noted for its Georgian houses. Willmer House (now a museum) has a facade of cut and moulded brick with fine carving and panelling in the interior. The 12th C castle has been occupied by Bishops of both Winchester and Guildford.
Tourist Information Centre
☎ *(0252) 715109*

The Bishop's Table Hotel ♏
♛♛♛♛ COMMENDED
27 West Street, Farnham GU9 7DR
☎ (0252) 710222
Fax (0252) 733494
Telex 94016743 BISH G
An 18th C inn, once used as a training school for clergy, well situated for exploring Surrey and Hampshire.
Bedrooms: 8 single, 8 double, 2 twin
Bathrooms: 18 private

Bed & breakfast
per night:	£min	£max
Single	55.00	70.00
Double	70.00	85.00

Half board
per person:	£min	£max
Daily	66.25	80.00

Lunch available
Evening meal 1900 (last orders 2130)
Cards accepted: Access, Visa, Diners, Amex

FAVERSHAM
Kent
Map ref 3B3

Historic town, once a port, dating back to prehistoric times. Abbey Street has more than 50 listed buildings. Roman and Anglo-Saxon finds and other exhibits can be seen in a museum in the Maison Dieu at Ospringe. Fleur de Lis Heritage Centre.
Tourist Information Centre
☎ *(0795) 534542*

Leaveland Court ♏
♛
Leaveland, Faversham ME13 0NP
☎ Challock (0233) 740596
300-acre arable farm. Enchanting Grade II listed 15th C timbered farmhouse in quiet rural setting adjacent to Leaveland church. 5 minutes from M2 Faversham, 20 minutes from Canterbury.*
Bedrooms: 1 double, 2 twin
Bathrooms: 3 private, 1 public

Bed & breakfast
per night:	£min	£max
Single	18.00	20.00
Double	36.00	38.00

Half board
per person:	£min	£max
Daily	28.00	32.00
Weekly	190.00	218.00

Evening meal 1830 (last orders 1800)
Parking for 6

The Oaks
Listed
Abbotts Hill, Ospringe, Faversham ME13 0RR
☎ (0795) 532936
In quiet rural setting with attractive gardens, 1 mile south of Ospringe, via Water Lane. Excellent base for touring Kent.
Bedrooms: 1 twin
Bathrooms: 1 private

Bed & breakfast
per night:	£min	£max
Single	18.00	18.00
Double	30.00	32.00

Parking for 3

Owens Court Farm
♛ COMMENDED
Selling, Faversham ME13 9QN
☎ Canterbury (0227) 752247
265-acre fruit farm. Quiet, pretty Georgian farmhouse set amidst Kentish hop gardens. Off the A2, 3 miles from Faversham, 9 from Canterbury.
Bedrooms: 1 single, 1 twin, 1 triple
Bathrooms: 1 public

Bed & breakfast
per night:	£min	£max
Single	15.00	16.00
Double	30.00	32.00

Parking for 4
Open January-August, October-December

Preston Lea ♏
♛♛
Canterbury Road, Faversham ME13 8XA
☎ (0795) 535266
Fax (0795) 533388

An imposing large Gothic Victorian house with turrets and other interesting features, set in large secluded grounds. Only 15 minutes from Canterbury and 30 minutes from Channel ports and Eurotunnel.
Bedrooms: 1 double, 2 twin, 1 triple
Bathrooms: 4 private

Bed & breakfast
per night:	£min	£max
Single	25.00	30.00
Double	45.00	60.00

Parking for 11

White Horse Inn ♏
♛♛♛ COMMENDED
Boughton, Faversham ME13 9AX
☎ Canterbury (0227) 751700 & 751343
Fax (0227) 751090
15th C coaching inn with oak beams and inglenook fireplace. In centre of village yet only 10 minutes' drive from Canterbury.
Bedrooms: 7 double, 6 twin
Bathrooms: 13 private

Bed & breakfast
per night:	£min	£max
Single	35.00	45.00
Double	45.00	55.00

Lunch available
Evening meal 1900 (last orders 2130)
Parking for 50
Cards accepted: Access, Visa, Diners, Amex, Switch

FINDON
West Sussex
Map ref 2D3

Downland village well-known for its annual sheep fair and its racing stables. The ancient landmarks, Cissbury Ring and Chanctonbury Ring, and the South Downs Way, are nearby.

Findon Tower
♛♛ COMMENDED
Cross Lane, Findon, Worthing BN14 0UG
☎ (0903) 873870
Elegant Edwardian country house in large secluded garden. Spacious accommodation with en-suite facilities. Warm, friendly welcome, relaxed and peaceful atmosphere. Rural views, snooker room. Excellent selection of food in village restaurants and pubs.
Bedrooms: 1 double, 1 twin, 1 family room
Bathrooms: 3 private, 1 public

Bed & breakfast
per night:	£min	£max
Single	20.00	30.00
Double	35.00	40.00

Parking for 10

Establishments should be open throughout the year unless otherwise stated in the entry.

SOUTH EAST ENGLAND

FOLKESTONE
Kent
Map ref 3C4

Popular resort and important cross-channel port. The town has a fine promenade, the Leas, from where orchestral concerts and other entertainments are presented. Horse-racing at Westenhanger.
Tourist Information Centre
☎ (0303) 258594

Beachborough Park ⋒
APPROVED
Newington, Folkestone CT18 8BW
☎ (0303) 275432
Beautiful setting, ideal for sightseeing and convenient for the continent. Very comfortable for both active people and those just seeking peace and quiet.
Bedrooms: 3 double, 2 twin
Bathrooms: 5 private
Bed & breakfast

per night:	£min	£max
Single	25.00	35.00
Double	35.00	50.00

Half board

per person:	£min	£max
Daily	30.00	37.50
Weekly	175.00	227.50

Lunch available
Evening meal 1900 (last orders 2130)

FOREST ROW
East Sussex
Map ref 2D2

On a hillside overlooking the River Medway, this village is a good centre from which to explore Ashdown Forest.

Roebuck Hotel ⋒
COMMENDED
Wych Cross, Forest Row RH18 5JL
☎ (0342) 823811
Fax (0342) 824790
16th C smugglers' inn set in the Ashdown Forest.
Bedrooms: 12 double, 18 twin
Bathrooms: 30 private
Bed & breakfast

per night:	£min	£max
Single	70.00	75.00
Double	85.00	90.00

Half board

per person:	£min	£max
Daily	85.95	
Weekly	600.00	

Lunch available
Evening meal 1900 (last orders 2115)
Parking for 150
Cards accepted: Access, Visa, Diners, Amex, Switch

FULKING
West Sussex
Map ref 2D3

Small, pretty village nestling on the north side of the South Downs near the route of the South Downs Way.

Downers Vineyard ⋒
Listed
Clappers Lane, Fulking, Henfield BN5 9NH
☎ Brighton (0273) 857484
18-acre vineyard & grazing farm. Quiet rural position, 1 mile north of the South Downs and Devil's Dyke, 8 miles from Brighton.
Bedrooms: 2 triple
Bathrooms: 2 public
Bed & breakfast

per night:	£min	£max
Single	17.00	20.00
Double	30.00	32.00

Evening meal 1930 (last orders 1930)
Parking for 6

GATWICK AIRPORT
West Sussex
Map ref 2D2

See under Copthorne, Crawley, East Grinstead, Horley, Horsham, Reigate, Smallfield

GODALMING
Surrey
Map ref 2D2

Several old coaching inns are reminders that the town was once a staging point. The old Town Hall is now the local history museum. Charterhouse School moved here in 1872 and is dominated by the 150-ft Founder's Tower.

Fairfields
Listed
The Green, Elstead, Godalming GU8 6DF
☎ Farnham (0252) 702345
High quality facilities in quiet modern detached house with 1 acre of grounds in centre of village. Guildford 8 miles, Farnham and Godalming 5 miles. Excellent pub food adjacent. Non-smokers only please.
Bedrooms: 1 double, 2 twin
Bathrooms: 3 public
Bed & breakfast

per night:	£min	£max
Single	17.50	25.00
Double	35.00	40.00

Parking for 6

GUILDFORD
Surrey
Map ref 2D2

Bustling town with many historic monuments, one of which is the Guildhall clock jutting out over the old High Street. The modern cathedral occupies a commanding position on Stag Hill.
Tourist Information Centre
☎ (0483) 444007

Beevers Farm
Listed
Chinthurst Lane, Bramley, Guildford GU5 0DR
☎ (0483) 898764
In peaceful surroundings 2 miles from Guildford, in village with pubs and restaurants. Convenient for Heathrow and Gatwick. Friendly atmosphere. Non-smokers only please.
Bedrooms: 3 twin
Bathrooms: 1 public
Bed & breakfast

per night:	£min	£max
Double	26.00	37.00

Parking for 10
Open March-November

The Old Malt House ⋒
Bagshot Road, Worplesdon, Guildford GU3 3PT
☎ Worplesdon (0483) 232152
Old country house in extensive grounds with swimming pool and ancient trees. Easy access to Heathrow, Gatwick and central London.
Bedrooms: 1 double, 1 twin, 1 family room
Bathrooms: 2 public
Bed & breakfast

per night:	£min	£max
Single	18.00	20.00
Double	28.00	30.00

Parking for 4

HAILSHAM
East Sussex
Map ref 2D3

An important market town since Norman times and still one of the largest markets in Sussex. Two miles west, at Upper Dicker, is Michelham Priory, an Augustinian house founded in 1229.
Tourist Information Centre
☎ (0323) 840604

Sandy Bank ⋒
COMMENDED
Old Road, Magham Down, Hailsham BN27 1PW
☎ (0323) 842488

Continued ▶

369

SOUTH EAST ENGLAND

HAILSHAM
Continued

Well-appointed en-suite rooms in recent development adjacent to cottage, plus one en-suite in cottage in attractive Sussex countryside with easy access to Downs and sea. Ideal base for touring Sussex. Friendly atmosphere. Evening meals by prior arrangement.
Bedrooms: 3 twin
Bathrooms: 3 private

Bed & breakfast
per night:	£min	£max
Single	22.00	
Double	38.00	

Evening meal 1900 (last orders 2030)
Parking for 2

HARRIETSHAM
Kent
Map ref 3B4

Village beneath the North Downs, close to the North Downs Way. Of interest are many old houses and the church with its fine Norman font.

Mannamead

Pilgrims Way, Harrietsham, Maidstone ME17 1BT
☎ Maidstone (0622) 859336
Quiet, comfortable home with pretty garden. Situated on peaceful and historic Pilgrims' Way, 4 miles from Leeds Castle. Excellent base for touring.
Bedrooms: 1 single, 1 double, 1 twin
Bathrooms: 1 private, 1 public

Bed & breakfast
per night:	£min	£max
Single	15.00	20.00
Double	28.00	34.00

Parking for 4

HARTFIELD
East Sussex
Map ref 2D2

Pleasant village in Ashdown Forest, the setting for A A Milne's "Winnie the Pooh" stories.

Bolebroke Watermill
HIGHLY COMMENDED

Edenbridge Road, Hartfield TN7 4JP
☎ (0892) 770425
Watermill (1086) and miller's barn with Honeymooners' Hayloft in romantic, secluded woodland. Accommodation of great rustic charm set around mill machinery. Regret, some very steep stairs!
Bedrooms: 4 double
Bathrooms: 4 private

Bed & breakfast
per night:	£min	£max
Double	49.00	63.00

Half board
per person:	£min	£max
Daily	40.50	

Evening meal 1900 (last orders 1000)
Parking for 8
Open March-November
Cards accepted: Access, Visa, Amex

Stairs Farmhouse
Listed COMMENDED

High Street, Hartfield TN7 4AB
☎ (0892) 770793
17th C modernised farmhouse with various period features, in picturesque village. Close to Pooh Bridge and Hever Castle. Views over open countryside. Home produced additive free breakfast provided. Tea room and farm shop.
Bedrooms: 1 double, 1 twin, 1 triple
Bathrooms: 2 public

Bed & breakfast
per night:	£min	£max
Single	25.00	32.00
Double	38.00	42.00

Half board
per person:	£min	£max
Daily	24.00	40.00

Lunch available
Parking for 10

HASLEMERE
Surrey
Map ref 2C2

Town set in hilly, wooded countryside, much of it in the keeping of the National Trust. Its attractions include the educational museum and the annual music festival.

Town House
Listed COMMENDED

High Street, Haslemere GU27 2JY
☎ (0428) 643310
Period house in centre of quiet town. Panelled reception rooms, period furniture throughout. Easy walking to restaurants and pubs.
Bedrooms: 2 single, 1 double, 1 twin
Bathrooms: 2 private, 1 public

Bed & breakfast
per night:	£min	£max
Single	18.00	20.00
Double	35.00	38.00

Parking for 3
Open February-December

HASTINGS
East Sussex
Map ref 3B4

Ancient town which became famous as the base from which William the Conqueror set out to fight the Battle of Hastings. Later became one of the Cinque Ports, now a leading resort. Castle, Hastings Embroidery inspired by the Bayeux Tapestry and Sealife Centre.
Tourist Information Centre
☎ *(0424) 718888*

Argyle Guest House

32 Cambridge Gardens, Hastings TN34 1EN
☎ (0424) 421294
Over 16 years of hospitality ensures a warm welcome. Homely and pleasantly furnished guesthouse offering bed and breakfast only. Ideally situated near seafront, stations and all amenities.
Bedrooms: 2 single, 3 double, 2 twin, 1 triple
Bathrooms: 4 private, 1 public

Bed & breakfast
per night:	£min	£max
Single	16.00	
Double	28.00	

Grand Hotel

Grand Parade, St Leonards-on-Sea, Hastings TN38 0DD
☎ (0424) 428510
Fax (0424) 722387
Family-run seafront hotel, close to all amenities. Licensed, international cooking. Parking for disabled guests. Radio room call/baby listening in all rooms. Ici on parle francais.
Bedrooms: 4 single, 7 double, 7 twin, 2 triple
Bathrooms: 7 private, 3 public

Bed & breakfast
per night:	£min	£max
Single	14.00	50.00
Double	28.00	95.00

Half board
per person:	£min	£max
Daily	22.00	65.00
Weekly	154.00	450.00

Lunch available
Evening meal 1800 (last orders 1900)

Parkside House
DE LUXE

59 Lower Park Road, Hastings TN34 2LD
☎ (0424) 433096
Elegant Victorian house opposite Alexandra Park. 10 minutes' walk to town centre and beaches. Quiet location.

370

SOUTH EAST ENGLAND

No parking restrictions. Drinks licence.
No smoking throughout.
Bedrooms: 2 single, 1 double, 2 twin
Bathrooms: 4 private, 1 public,
1 private shower

Bed & breakfast
per night:	£min	£max
Single	20.00	40.00
Double	40.00	50.00

Half board
per person:	£min	£max
Daily	30.00	35.00
Weekly	190.00	225.00

Evening meal 1800 (last orders 1200)
Cards accepted: Access, Visa

HAWKHURST
Kent
Map ref 3B3

Village in 3 parts: Gill's Green, Highgate and the Moor. There is a colonnaded shopping centre, large village green, church and inn which is associated with the Hawkhurst smuggling gang.

Conghurst Farm
HIGHLY COMMENDED

Conghurst Lane, Hawkhurst,
Cranbrook TN18 4RW
☎ (0580) 753331

500-acre arable & livestock farm. Georgian farmhouse on Kent/Sussex border 2 miles from Hawkhurst, in peaceful countryside.
Bedrooms: 1 double, 2 twin
Bathrooms: 3 private

Bed & breakfast
per night:	£min	£max
Double	35.00	40.00

Half board
per person:	£min	£max
Daily	29.50	32.00
Weekly	178.50	193.50

Evening meal 1900 (last orders 1100)
Parking for 8
Open March-November

Half board prices shown are per person but in some cases may be based on double/twin occupancy.

HAYWARDS HEATH
West Sussex
Map ref 2D3

Busy market town and administrative centre of mid-Sussex, with interesting old buildings and a modern shopping centre.

The Anchorhold
Listed

35 Paddock Hall Road, Haywards Heath RH16 1HN
☎ (0444) 452468
Religious community providing bed and breakfast in a separate cottage within the grounds. Main line station is a quarter of a mile away.
Bedrooms: 2 single, 2 twin
Bathrooms: 1 public

Bed & breakfast
per night:	£min	£max
Single		14.00
Double		28.00

Parking for 3

HEADCORN
Kent
Map ref 3B4

Small town with timbered houses used in the 17th C as cloth halls by Flemish weavers. Headcorn Vineyards and Flower Nursery are open to visitors.

Bletchenden Manor Farm
Listed

Headcorn TN27 9JB
☎ Maidstone (0622) 890228
50-acre livestock farm. Listed farmhouse in peaceful position on outskirts of Headcorn village, surrounded by farmland, a mile from mainline station. Gardens, ponds and woodland. Ideal for touring. Close to Sissinghurst and many National Trust properties.
Bedrooms: 3 twin
Bathrooms: 1 private, 1 public

Bed & breakfast
per night:	£min	£max
Double	37.00	44.00

Parking for 2
Open January-November

Vine Farm

Waterman Quarter, Headcorn, Ashford TN27 9JJ
☎ (0622) 890203
50-acre livestock farm. Stay in the old world charm of our quietly situated, comfortable 16th C farmhouse. Close to Leeds and Sissinghurst castles. Ample parking.
Bedrooms: 2 double, 1 twin
Bathrooms: 3 private

Bed & breakfast
per night:	£min	£max
Double	40.00	44.00

Evening meal from 1900

HERSTMONCEUX
East Sussex
Map ref 3B4

Pleasant village noted for its woodcrafts and the beautiful 15th C moated Herstmonceux Castle.

The Stud Farm
COMMENDED

Bodle Street Green, Herstmonceux, Hailsham BN27 4RJ
☎ (0323) 833201
70-acre mixed farm. Upstairs, 2 bedrooms and bathroom let as one unit to party of 2, 3 or 4. Downstairs, twin-bedded room with shower, WC and handbasin en-suite, sunroom.
Bedrooms: 1 double, 2 twin
Bathrooms: 1 private, 1 public

Bed & breakfast
per night:	£min	£max
Single	22.00	25.00
Double	34.00	38.00

Half board
per person:	£min	£max
Daily	27.50	33.50
Weekly	178.50	213.50

Evening meal from 1830
Parking for 3

HOLLINGBOURNE
Kent
Map ref 3B3

Pleasant village near romantic Leeds Castle in the heart of the orchard country at the foot of the North Downs. Some fine half-timbered houses and a flint and ragstone church.

Woodhouses
Listed

49 Eyhorne Street, Hollingbourne, Maidstone ME17 1TR
☎ Maidstone (0622) 880594
Interconnected listed cottages dating from 17th C, with inglenook fireplace and exposed wooden beams. Well stocked cottage garden.
Bedrooms: 2 double, 1 twin
Bathrooms: 2 private, 1 public

Bed & breakfast
per night:	£min	£max
Single	16.00	16.00
Double	33.00	33.00

Evening meal 1800 (last orders 2000)
Parking for 1

371

SOUTH EAST ENGLAND

HORLEY
Surrey
Map ref 2D2

Town on the London to Brighton road, just north of Gatwick Airport, with an ancient parish church and 15th C. inn.

Chalet Guest House M
COMMENDED

77 Massetts Road, Horley RH6 7EB
☎ (0293) 821666
Fax (0293) 821619
Comfortable modern guesthouse. Convenient for Gatwick Airport, motorways, railway station, local bus, shops, pubs and restaurants.
Bedrooms: 3 single, 1 double, 1 twin, 1 triple
Bathrooms: 5 private, 1 public
Bed & breakfast
per night:	£min	£max
Single	22.00	30.00
Double		42.00

Parking for 14
Cards accepted: Access, Visa

Crutchfield Farm M
COMMENDED

Hookwood, Horley RH6 OHT
☎ Norwood Hill (0293) 863110
Fax (0293) 863233
Listed 15th C farmhouse set in 10 acres, 3 miles from Gatwick. Well-appointed accommodation, tennis court and swimming pool. Parking, transport to airport.
Bedrooms: 1 double, 2 twin
Bathrooms: 1 private, 1 public
Bed & breakfast
per night:	£min	£max
Single	30.00	35.00
Double	40.00	50.00

Evening meal 1930 (last orders 2100)
Parking for 10

The Gables Guest House M
Listed

50 Bonehurst Road, Horley RH6 8QG
☎ (0293) 774553
Approximately 2 miles from Gatwick and the railway station. Long term parking. Transport to the airport available.
Bedrooms: 3 single, 7 double, 9 twin, 3 triple
Bathrooms: 7 private, 4 public
Bed & breakfast
per night:	£min	£max
Single	25.00	25.00
Double	33.00	40.00

Parking for 25

Gainsborough Lodge M
COMMENDED

39 Massetts Road, Horley RH6 7DT
☎ (0293) 783982
Fax (0293) 785365
Extended Edwardian house set in attractive garden. Five minutes' walk from Horley station and town centre. Five minutes' drive from Gatwick Airport.
Bedrooms: 3 single, 2 double, 5 twin, 2 triple
Bathrooms: 12 private
Bed & breakfast
per night:	£min	£max
Single	25.00	35.00
Double	37.00	44.00

Parking for 16
Cards accepted: Access, Visa, Amex

Gorse Cottage M
66 Balcombe Road, Horley RH6 9AY
☎ (0293) 784402
Fax (0293) 784402
Small, friendly, private accommodation in pleasant residential area 5 minutes from Horley station, 40 minutes from London and 2 miles from Gatwick. English breakfast after 7am. Private parking.
Bedrooms: 2 single, 1 twin, 1 triple
Bathrooms: 1 public
Bed & breakfast
per night:	£min	£max
Single	20.00	21.00
Double	30.00	32.00

Parking for 4

Latchetts Cottage M
Listed

Ricketts Wood Road, Norwood Hill, Horley RH6 OET
☎ Norwood Hill (0293) 862831
Cosy country cottage situated midway between Leigh and Charlwood. Very rural, yet only 10 minutes from Gatwick Airport.
Bedrooms: 1 single, 1 double
Bathrooms: 1 public
Bed & breakfast
per night:	£min	£max
Single		18.50
Double		37.00

Parking for 5

The Lawn Guest House M
HIGHLY COMMENDED

30 Massetts Road, Horley RH6 7DE
☎ (0293) 775751

Ideal for travellers using Gatwick. Pleasantly situated, few minutes' walk to town centre, pubs and restaurants. Good base for London and the south coast. Non-smokers only please.
Bedrooms: 1 double, 4 twin, 1 triple, 1 family room
Bathrooms: 3 private, 2 public
Bed & breakfast
per night:	£min	£max
Single	24.00	31.00
Double	35.00	42.00

Parking for 10
Cards accepted: Access, Visa, Diners, Amex

Prinsted Guest House
Listed

Oldfield Road, Horley RH6 7EP
☎ (0293) 785233
Detached, Edwardian guesthouse in a quiet position with spacious accommodation, including large family rooms. Close to Gatwick, London 30 minutes by train.
Bedrooms: 1 double, 2 twin, 2 triple, 1 family room
Bathrooms: 3 public, 1 private shower
Bed & breakfast
per night:	£min	£max
Single	27.00	37.00
Double	37.00	40.00

Parking for 10
Cards accepted: Amex

Springwood Guest House

58 Massetts Road, Horley RH6 7DS
☎ (0293) 775998
Elegant detached Victorian house in pleasant residential road close to Gatwick Airport. Long-term car parking, with transport.
Bedrooms: 2 single, 1 double, 3 twin, 1 family room
Bathrooms: 1 private, 2 public
Bed & breakfast
per night:	£min	£max
Single	21.00	26.00
Double	32.00	38.00

Parking for 10
Cards accepted: Access, Visa

Stone Court

64 Smallfield Road, Horley RH6 9AT
☎ (0293) 774482
Quiet country location. Comfortable pretty bedrooms, antiques, fruit and flower gardens, fish pools, terrace and fountains, guest TV lounge. National Trust gardens nearby. Gatwick 5 minutes, London and coast 35 minutes. Ample car parking, long term arranged.
Bedrooms: 2 twin, 1 triple
Bathrooms: 2 public

SOUTH EAST ENGLAND

Bed & breakfast per night:

	£min	£max
Single	20.00	35.00
Double	35.00	45.00

Parking for 9
Open March-October

Victoria Lodge Guest House
Listed APPROVED
161 Victoria Road, Horley RH6 7AS
☎ (0293) 785459
Edwardian detached house, in town centre close to shops, restaurants and pubs. One mile from Gatwick Airport and close to Horley station with direct service to Victoria. Colour TV and tea/coffee in rooms. Full English breakfast.
Bedrooms: 1 single, 1 twin, 1 triple
Bathrooms: 1 public, 1 private shower
Bed & breakfast per night:

	£min	£max
Single	23.00	23.00
Double	35.00	35.00

Parking for 3

HORSHAM
West Sussex
Map ref 2D2

Busy town with much modern development but still retaining its old character. The museum in Causeway House is devoted chiefly to local history and the agricultural life of the county.
Tourist Information Centre
☎ (0403) 211661

Saxtons Farm
HIGHLY COMMENDED
Nuthurst, Horsham RH13 6LG
☎ Lower Beeding (0403) 891231
100-acre mixed farm. Family-run farm with home cooking, close to Gatwick Airport and within easy reach of south coast resorts and London. Non-smokers preferred.
Bedrooms: 1 single, 1 double, 1 twin
Bathrooms: 2 public
Bed & breakfast per night:

	£min	£max
Single	21.00	23.00
Double	36.00	40.00

Parking for 8

Westlands Guest House
HIGHLY COMMENDED
Brighton Road, Monks Gate, Horsham RH13 6JD
☎ (0403) 891383

Elegant large Victorian house, situated in Sussex countryside on A281 Horsham/Cowfold/Brighton road. Close to village pubs, Gatwick, coast and places of interest.
Bedrooms: 1 single, 1 double, 2 twin
Bathrooms: 4 private
Bed & breakfast per night:

	£min	£max
Single	30.00	30.00
Double	37.50	42.50

Parking for 8

HOVE
East Sussex

See under Brighton & Hove

LENHAM
Kent
Map ref 3B4

Shops, inns and houses, many displaying timber-work of the late Middle Ages, surround a square which is the centre of the village. The 14th C parish church has one of the best examples of a Kentish tower.

Dog and Bear Hotel
COMMENDED
The Square, Lenham, Maidstone ME17 2PG
☎ Maidstone (0622) 858219
Fax (0622) 859415
15th C coaching inn retaining its old world character and serving good Kent ale, lagers and fine wines with home cooking. En-suite rooms. Large car park and function room.
Wheelchair access category 3
Bedrooms: 5 single, 12 double, 5 twin, 3 triple
Bathrooms: 25 private
Bed & breakfast per night:

	£min	£max
Single	35.00	45.00
Double	45.00	55.00

Lunch available
Evening meal 1900 (last orders 2130)
Parking for 26
Cards accepted: Access, Visa, Diners

Please mention this guide when making a booking.

LEWES
East Sussex
Map ref 2D3

Historic county town with Norman castle. The steep High Street has mainly Georgian buildings. There is a folk museum at Anne of Cleves House and the archaeological museum is in Barbican House.
Tourist Information Centre
☎ (0273) 483448

Felix Gallery
Listed
2 Sun Street, (Corner Lancaster Street), Lewes BN7 2QB
☎ (0273) 472668
Fully-modernised period house in quiet location 3 minutes' walk from town centre, Records Office and castle. Colour TV.
Bedrooms: 1 single, 1 twin
Bathrooms: 1 public
Bed & breakfast per night:

	£min	£max
Single	21.00	23.00
Double	34.00	36.00

Cards accepted: Access, Visa

Wootton Cottage
Listed
Hamsey Road, Barcombe, Lewes BN8 5TG
☎ Brighton (0273) 400486
Old family home set in heart of the Sussex countryside with extensive orchard and gardens. 3.5 miles from county town of Lewes and 11 miles from Brighton and Haywards Heath.
Bedrooms: 1 single, 1 double, 1 twin
Bathrooms: 1 private, 1 public
Bed & breakfast per night:

	£min	£max
Single	13.00	15.00
Double	26.00	32.00

Parking for 12

LYMINSTER
West Sussex
Map ref 2D3

Sandfield House
COMMENDED
Lyminster, Littlehampton BN17 7PG
☎ Littlehampton (0903) 724129
Spacious country-style family house in 2 acres. Between Arundel and sea, in area of great natural beauty.
Bedrooms: 1 double
Bathrooms: 1 public

Continued ▶

SOUTH EAST ENGLAND

LYMINSTER
Continued

Bed & breakfast

per night:	£min	£max
Double	32.00	40.00

Parking for 4

MAIDSTONE
Kent
Map ref 3B3

Busy county town of Kent on the River Medway has many interesting features and is an excellent centre for excursions. Museum of Carriages, Museum and Art Gallery, Archbishop's Palace, Mote Park.
Tourist Information Centre
☎ (0622) 673581

Wealden Hall House

East Street, Hunton, Maidstone
ME15 0RA
☎ (0622) 820246
16th C Grade II Wealden hall house offering comfortable accommodation. Four-poster bed. Set in 1 acre of gardens, 8 miles from Leeds Castle. Two-night winter breaks available November-February.
Bedrooms: 1 single, 3 double
Bathrooms: 4 private, 1 public

Bed & breakfast

per night:	£min	£max
Single	18.00	
Double		36.00

Parking for 6

Willington Court ♙
COMMENDED

Willington Street, Maidstone
ME15 8JW
☎ (0622) 738885

17th C Tudor-style house, traditionally furnished. Antiques, four-poster bed. Adjacent to Mote Park and near Leeds Castle.
Bedrooms: 1 single, 2 double, 1 twin
Bathrooms: 2 private, 1 public

Bed & breakfast

per night:	£min	£max
Single	17.00	27.00
Double	34.00	42.00

Parking for 6

Cards accepted: Access, Visa, Diners, Amex

MARDEN
Kent
Map ref 3B4

The village is believed to date back to Saxon times, though today more modern homes surround the 13th C church.

Great Cheveney Farm ♙
Listed HIGHLY COMMENDED

Goudhurst Road, Marden, Tonbridge
TN12 9LX
☎ Maidstone (0622) 831207
Fax (0622) 831786

300-acre arable & fruit farm. 16th C farmhouse in Kent Weald, between Marden and Goudhurst villages on B2079. Comfortable, friendly accommodation in peaceful surroundings. Close to Sissinghurst, Scotney and Leeds Castle.
Bedrooms: 1 single, 1 double
Bathrooms: 2 private showers

Bed & breakfast

per night:	£min	£max
Single	18.00	21.00
Double	33.00	36.00

Parking for 3
Open April-October

Tanner House ♙

Tanner Farm, Goudhurst Road,
Marden, Tonbridge TN12 9ND
☎ Maidstone (0622) 831214
Fax (0622) 832472
105-acre mixed farm. Tudor farmhouse in centre of attractive family farm. Inglenook dining room. Off B2079. Car essential. Shire horses bred on farm.
Bedrooms: 1 double, 2 twin
Bathrooms: 3 private

Bed & breakfast

per night:	£min	£max
Double	33.00	40.00

Half board

per person:	£min	£max
Daily	28.50	32.00
Weekly	190.00	210.00

Evening meal 1900 (last orders 1800)
Parking for 3
Cards accepted: Access, Visa, Amex

MARGATE
Kent
Map ref 3C3

Oldest and most famous resort in Kent. Many Regency and Victorian buildings survive from the town's early days. There are 9 miles of sandy beach. "Dreamland" is a 20-acre amusement park and the Winter Gardens offers concert hall entertainment.
Tourist Information Centre
☎ (0843) 220241

The Malvern Hotel ♙

29 Eastern Espl, Cliftonville, Margate
CT9 2HL
☎ Thanet (0843) 290192
Overlooking the sea, promenade and lawns. Close indoor/outdoor bowls complex, Margate Winter Gardens, amenities and Channel ports. Parking (unrestricted) outside and opposite hotel. TV and tea-making facilities - most rooms en-suite with shower and toilet (no baths).
Bedrooms: 1 single, 5 double, 3 twin, 1 family room
Bathrooms: 8 private, 1 public

Bed & breakfast

per night:	£min	£max
Single	18.00	20.00
Double	32.00	40.00

Evening meal 1800 (last orders 1000)
Cards accepted: Access, Visa, Diners, Amex

Raymonde Hotel ♙
APPROVED

1-7 Ethelbert Road, Cliftonville,
Margate CT9 1SH
☎ Thanet (0843) 223991
Privately-owned family hotel with homely atmosphere and entertainment most evenings. Two minutes from beach and central for amenities. Lift to all floors. Group bookings most welcome.
Bedrooms: 7 single, 9 double, 9 twin, 3 triple
Bathrooms: 16 private, 5 public, 2 private showers

Bed & breakfast

per night:	£min	£max
Single	17.00	21.00
Double	33.50	41.00

Half board

per person:	£min	£max
Daily	22.00	28.00
Weekly	120.00	160.00

Lunch available
Evening meal from 1800

SOUTH EAST ENGLAND

OSPRINGE
Kent
Map ref 3B3

Village close to Faversham with the Maison Dieu, a medieval hostel open to visitors.

The Granary
Listed HIGHLY COMMENDED
Plumford Lane, Ospringe, Faversham ME13 ODS
☎ Faversham (0795) 538416
Delightfully converted granary in peaceful setting with large garden. Own lounge with colour TV. Close M2 and Canterbury. Friendly welcome.
Bedrooms: 2 double, 1 twin
Bathrooms: 1 public

Bed & breakfast
per night:	£min	£max
Single	15.00	23.00
Double	30.00	36.00

Parking for 8

OXTED
Surrey
Map ref 2D2

Pleasant town on the edge of National Trust woodland and at the foot of the North Downs. Chartwell, the former home of Sir Winston Churchill, is close by.

The New Bungalow
Listed
Old Hall Farm, Tandridge Lane, Oxted RH8 9NS
☎ South Godstone (0342) 892508
44-acre mixed farm. Spacious, modern bungalow set in green fields and reached by a private drive. 5 minutes' drive from M25.
Bedrooms: 1 double, 1 twin, 1 family room
Bathrooms: 1 public

Bed & breakfast
per night:	£min	£max
Single	22.00	25.00
Double	32.00	35.00

Parking for 5
Open January-November

PARTRIDGE GREEN
West Sussex
Map ref 2D3

Small village between Henfield and Billingshurst.

The Bushes
COMMENDED
Littleworth Lane, Littleworth, Partridge Green, Horsham RH13 8JF
☎ Horsham (0403) 710495
Detached small country house in the hamlet of Littleworth, near Partridge

Green. Landscaped garden. Gatwick Airport 20 minutes by car. Near Horsham.
Bedrooms: 1 single, 2 double, 1 twin
Bathrooms: 1 private, 2 public

Bed & breakfast
per night:	£min	£max
Single	16.00	21.00
Double	30.00	36.00

Parking for 7

Pound Cottage Bed and Breakfast
Mill lane, Littleworth, Partridge Green, Horsham RH13 8JU
☎ (0403) 710218 & 711285
Pleasant country house in quiet surroundings. 8 miles from Horsham, 20 minutes from Gatwick. Just off the West Grinstead to Steyning road.
Bedrooms: 1 single, 1 double, 1 twin
Bathrooms: 1 public

Bed & breakfast
per night:	£min	£max
Single	15.00	15.00
Double	30.00	30.00

Half board
per person:	£min	£max
Daily	20.00	20.00
Weekly	140.00	140.00

Evening meal from 1830
Parking for 8

PETWORTH
West Sussex
Map ref 2D3

Town dominated by Petworth House, the great 17th C mansion, set in 2000 acres of parkland laid out by Capability Brown. The house contains wood-carvings by Grinling Gibbons.

White Horse Inn
HIGHLY COMMENDED
The Street, Sutton, Pulborough RH20 1PS
☎ Sutton (079 87) 221
Fax (079 87) 291

Pretty Georgian village inn close to South Downs Way. Roman villa 1 mile. Garden, log fires. 4 miles Petworth, 2 miles Pulborough. Prices below are from 1 April 1994.
Bedrooms: 4 double, 2 twin
Bathrooms: 6 private

Bed & breakfast
per night:	£min	£max
Single	48.00	48.00
Double	58.00	58.00

Half board
per person:	£min	£max
Daily	41.00	60.00
Weekly	206.00	290.00

Lunch available
Evening meal 1900 (last orders 2140)
Parking for 10
Cards accepted: Access, Visa

POYNINGS
West Sussex
Map ref 2D3

Set in the South Downs behind Brighton, with Dyke Hill above, on which there was an Iron Age camp, and the Devil's Dyke along the southern side.

Poynings Manor Farm
Poynings, Brighton BN45 7AG
☎ Brighton (0273) 857371
260-acre mixed farm. Charming old farmhouse in quiet scenic surroundings. Ideal for walkers, riders and country lovers. Coast 15 minutes, Gatwick 30 minutes.
Bedrooms: 1 double, 2 twin
Bathrooms: 2 public

Bed & breakfast
per night:	£min	£max
Single	20.00	25.00
Double	36.00	

Evening meal from 1900
Parking for 6

RAMSGATE
Kent
Map ref 3C3

Popular holiday resort with good sandy beaches. At Pegwell Bay is the replica of a Viking longship. Terminal for car-ferry service to Dunkirk.
Tourist Information Centre
☎ *(0843) 591086*

Eastwood Guest House
Listed COMMENDED
28 Augusta Road, Ramsgate CT11 8JS
☎ Thanet (0843) 591505
Comfortable, homely guesthouse with sea views, on east side of Ramsgate harbour. Satellite TV in all rooms. Some en-suite rooms available.
Bedrooms: 1 single, 5 twin, 2 triple, 5 family rooms
Bathrooms: 8 private, 3 public

Continued ▶

375

SOUTH EAST ENGLAND

RAMSGATE
Continued

Bed & breakfast per night:	£min	£max
Single	15.00	25.00
Double	25.00	35.00

Half board per person:	£min	£max
Daily	20.00	30.00
Weekly	105.00	145.00

Evening meal 1830 (last orders 1930)
Parking for 20

REIGATE
Surrey
Map ref 2D2

Old town with modern developments, on the edge of the North Downs. Just outside the town on Reigate Heath stands an old windmill, which has been converted into a church.

Beechwood House

39 Hatchlands Road, Redhill RH1 6AP
☎ Redhill (0737) 761444 & 764277
Small, friendly, licensed hotel. Five minutes' walk to town centre and railway station. 30 minutes by train to Victoria station, 20 minutes to Gatwick Airport.
Bedrooms: 2 single, 2 double, 2 twin, 2 triple, 1 family room
Bathrooms: 7 private, 1 public, 2 private showers

Bed & breakfast per night:	£min	£max
Single	25.00	38.00
Double	35.00	55.00

Half board per person:	£min	£max
Daily	40.00	45.00
Weekly	280.00	290.00

Lunch available
Evening meal 1900 (last orders 2100)
Parking for 9
Cards accepted: Access, Visa, Diners, Amex

There are separate sections in this guide listing groups specialising in farm holidays and accommodation which is especially suitable for young people and organised groups.

ROBERTSBRIDGE
East Sussex
Map ref 3B4

Small town in well-wooded country near the River Rother, with a number of old timber and boarded houses. An important local industry is the making of Gray-Nicolls cricket bats.

Parsonage Farm
Listed
Salehurst, Robertsbridge TN32 5PJ
☎ (0580) 880446
300-acre arable & livestock farm. 15th C farmhouse with beams and panelling. Relaxed atmosphere. Within easy reach of south coast resorts and many places of historic interest and natural beauty.
Bedrooms: 1 twin, 1 triple
Bathrooms: 1 public

Bed & breakfast per night:	£min	£max
Single	16.00	18.00
Double	32.00	32.00

Half board per person:	£min	£max
Daily	23.50	
Weekly	148.00	

Evening meal from 1830
Parking for 20
Open January-August, October-December

ROGATE
West Sussex
Map ref 2C3

Trotton Farm
COMMENDED
Trotton, Petersfield, Hampshire GU31 5EN
☎ Midhurst (0730) 813618
Fax (0730) 816093
Farmhouse just off the A272, access through yard. Accommodation and lounge/games room in a converted cart shed adjoining farmhouse. All rooms with en-suite shower.
Bedrooms: 2 twin
Bathrooms: 2 private

Bed & breakfast per night:	£min	£max
Single	25.00	25.00
Double	35.00	40.00

The national Crown scheme is explained in full in the information pages towards the back of this guide.

ROTTINGDEAN
East Sussex
Map ref 2D3

The quiet High Street contains a number of fine old buildings and the village pond and green are close by.

Braemar Guest House

Steyning Road, Rottingdean, Brighton BN2 7GA
☎ Brighton (0273) 304263
Family-run guesthouse, proud of its cheerful atmosphere, in an old world village where Rudyard Kipling once lived.
Bedrooms: 5 single, 6 double, 3 twin, 2 triple
Bathrooms: 3 public, 2 private showers

Bed & breakfast per night:	£min	£max
Single	14.00	15.00
Double	28.00	30.00

RYE
East Sussex
Map ref 3B4

Cobbled, hilly streets and fine old buildings make Rye, once a Cinque Port, a most picturesque town. Noted for its church with ancient clock, potteries and antique shops, and the Ypres Tower Museum. Town Model sound and light show gives a good introduction to the town.
Tourist Information Centre
☎ *(0797) 226696*

Aviemore Guest House
APPROVED
28/30 Fishmarket Road, Rye TN31 7LP
☎ (0797) 223052

Owner-run, friendly guesthouse offering a warm welcome and hearty breakfast. Overlooking "Town Salts" and the River Rother. 2 minutes from town centre.
Bedrooms: 1 single, 4 double, 3 twin
Bathrooms: 4 private, 2 public

Bed & breakfast per night:	£min	£max
Single	15.00	28.00
Double	28.00	38.00

SOUTH EAST ENGLAND

Half board per person:	£min	£max
Daily	21.00	26.00
Weekly	144.00	182.00

Evening meal 1800 (last orders 2200)
Cards accepted: Access, Visa, Amex

Green Hedges
HIGHLY COMMENDED
Hillyfields, Rye Hill, Rye TN31 7NH
☎ (0797) 222185
Country house in a private road. 1.5 acres of landscaped gardens with heated swimming pool. Short stroll to town centre. Ample parking. Home grown organic produce.
Bedrooms: 2 double, 1 twin
Bathrooms: 3 private, 1 public

Bed & breakfast per night:	£min	£max
Single	35.00	45.00
Double	45.00	55.00

Evening meal 1900 (last orders 2300)
Parking for 7

Holloway House
HIGHLY COMMENDED
High Street, Rye TN31 7JF
☎ (0797) 224748
Creeper-covered Tudor building in heart of conservation area. Heavily beamed, Caen stone fireplaces, oak panelling, antique beds and furnishings. Hearty breakfasts.
Bedrooms: 5 double
Bathrooms: 5 private, 1 public

Bed & breakfast per night:	£min	£max
Single	39.00	60.00
Double	50.00	90.00

Lunch available
Evening meal 1800 (last orders 2100)
Cards accepted: Access, Visa

Jeake's House
HIGHLY COMMENDED
Mermaid Street, Rye TN31 7ET
☎ (0797) 222828
Fax (0797) 222623

Recapture the past in this historic building, in a cobblestoned street at the heart of the old town. Honeymoon suite available.
Bedrooms: 1 single, 7 double, 1 twin, 2 triple, 1 family room
Bathrooms: 11 private, 2 public

Bed & breakfast per night:	£min	£max
Single	21.50	21.50
Double	39.00	55.00

Cards accepted: Access, Visa, Amex

Kimblee
COMMENDED
Main Street, Peasmarsh, Rye
TN31 6UL
☎ Peasmarsh (0797) 230514
Country house with views from all aspects, 250 metres from pub/restaurant and 5 minutes' drive on the A268 from Rye. Warm welcome.
Bedrooms: 3 double
Bathrooms: 3 private

Bed & breakfast per night:	£min	£max
Single	15.00	17.50
Double	30.00	35.00

Parking for 4
Cards accepted: Access, Visa

The Old Vicarage
Listed COMMENDED
Rye Harbour, Rye TN31 7TT
☎ (0797) 222088
Imposing Victorian former vicarage, quietly situated close to sea and nature reserve. Antique furniture and open fires. Good English breakfast.
Bedrooms: 1 double, 1 twin
Bathrooms: 1 public

Bed & breakfast per night:	£min	£max
Single	16.00	20.00
Double	32.00	36.00

Parking for 4

Saint Margarets
Listed
Dumbwomans Lane, Udimore, Rye
TN31 6AD
☎ (0797) 222586
Comfortable, friendly chalet bungalow with sea views. Car parking. En-suite facilities. B2089, 2 miles west of Rye.
Bedrooms: 2 double, 1 twin
Bathrooms: 3 private

Bed & breakfast per night:	£min	£max
Double	26.00	28.00

Parking for 3

Strand House
COMMENDED
Winchelsea TN36 4JT
☎ (0797) 226276
Fine old 15th C house with oak beams and inglenook fireplaces. Located just off A259. 10% discount for weekly terms except in high season.
Bedrooms: 8 double, 1 twin, 1 triple
Bathrooms: 8 private, 1 public

Bed & breakfast per night:	£min	£max
Single	25.00	30.00
Double	40.00	55.00

Evening meal 1830 (last orders 1900)
Parking for 15

Top o'The Hill at Rye
COMMENDED
Rye Hill, Rye TN31 7NH
☎ (0797) 223284
Fax (0797) 227030

Small friendly inn offering fine traditional food and accommodation. Central for touring Kent and Sussex, Channel ports nearby. Large car park, garden.
Bedrooms: 3 double, 2 twin, 1 triple
Bathrooms: 6 private

Bed & breakfast per night:	£min	£max
Single	22.00	24.00
Double	36.00	40.00

Lunch available
Evening meal 1900 (last orders 2100)
Parking for 32
Cards accepted: Access, Visa

ST NICHOLAS AT WADE
Kent
Map ref 3C3

Village in the Isle of Thanet with ancient church built of knapped flint.

Streete Farm House
Listed
Court Road, St Nicholas at Wade, Birchington CT7 0NH
☎ Thanet (0843) 47245
90-acre arable and mixed farm. 16th C farmhouse on the outskirts of the village, with original oak-panelled dining room.
Bedrooms: 1 single, 2 double
Bathrooms: 1 public

Bed & breakfast per night:	£min	£max
Single	15.00	16.00
Double	30.00	32.00

Parking for 4

SOUTH EAST ENGLAND

SARRE
Kent
Map ref 3C3

Crown Inn (The Famous Cherry Brandy House)
COMMENDED

Ramsgate Road, Sarre, Birchington CT7 0LF
☎ Birchington (0843) 47808
Fax (0843) 47914

An ideal centre for exploring Canterbury, Thanet and east Kent. Our unique liqueur has been available here since 1650.
Wheelchair access category 3
Bedrooms: 9 double, 2 twin, 1 triple
Bathrooms: 12 private

Bed & breakfast
per night:	£min	£max
Single	35.00	45.00
Double	45.00	55.00

Lunch available
Evening meal 1900 (last orders 2200)
Parking for 40
Cards accepted: Access, Visa

SEVENOAKS
Kent
Map ref 2D2

Set in pleasant wooded country, with a distinctive character and charm. Nearby is Knole (National Trust), home of the Sackville family and one of the largest houses in England, set in a vast deer park.
Tourist Information Centre
☎ *(0732) 450305*

The Bull Hotel
APPROVED

Wrotham, Sevenoaks TN15 7RF
☎ (0732) 885522 & 883092
Fax (0732) 886288

Privately-run 14th C coaching inn, in secluded historic village 15 minutes from Sevenoaks. Just off M20 and M25/26, 30 minutes from Gatwick and London. Oak beams and inglenook fireplaces. Ideal for local places of interest.
Bedrooms: 1 single, 3 double, 6 twin
Bathrooms: 5 private, 1 public

Bed & breakfast
per night:	£min	£max
Single	35.00	40.00
Double	45.00	50.00

Lunch available
Evening meal 1900 (last orders 2200)
Parking for 50
Cards accepted: Access, Visa, Diners, Amex

Moorings Hotel

97 Hitchen Hatch Lane, Sevenoaks TN13 3BE
☎ (0732) 452589
Fax (0732) 456462

Friendly family hotel offering high standard accommodation for tourists and business travellers. 30 minutes from London. Close to BR station.
Bedrooms: 5 single, 3 double, 12 twin, 2 triple
Bathrooms: 20 private, 2 public, 1 private shower

Bed & breakfast
per night:	£min	£max
Single	24.00	42.00
Double	36.00	59.00

Half board
per person:	£min	£max
Daily	29.00	55.00
Weekly	170.00	325.00

Evening meal 1900 (last orders 2100)
Parking for 22
Cards accepted: Access, Visa

Stone Ridge

168 Maidstone Road, Borough Green, Sevenoaks TN15 8JD
☎ Borough Green (0732) 882053
Fax (0732) 885903

Edwardian country house with friendly atmosphere in beautiful surroundings of 7 acres. Convenient for famous Kentish attractions, motorways and London. Non-smokers preferred.
Bedrooms: 1 double, 1 family room
Bathrooms: 2 private

Bed & breakfast
per night:	£min	£max
Single	22.00	26.00
Double	32.00	38.00

Half board
per person:	£min	£max
Daily	23.00	33.00
Weekly	135.00	195.00

Parking for 4
Cards accepted: Access, Visa

National Crown ratings were correct at the time of going to press but are subject to change. Please check at the time of booking.

SHEERNESS
Kent
Map ref 3B3

Commercial port, formerly a naval base and now a holiday resort with a long promenade and a sand and shingle beach. Terminal for car-ferry service to Vlissingen in Holland.
Tourist Information Centre
☎ *(0795) 665324*

Alexandra Guest House

122 Alexandra Road, Sheerness ME12 2AU
☎ (0795) 666888

Attractive family house providing accommodation of a high standard. Close to Olau Line ferry, town centre, rail and bus station.
Bedrooms: 1 single, 1 double, 1 twin, 1 triple
Bathrooms: 1 public

Bed & breakfast
per night:	£min	£max
Single	12.00	14.00
Double	24.00	28.00

Evening meal 1800 (last orders 2000)
Parking for 3

SIDLESHAM
West Sussex
Map ref 2C3

Muttons Farmhouse
Listed

Keynor Lane, Sidlesham, Chichester PO20 7NG
☎ (0243) 641703

18th C listed house off B2145, 4 miles south of Chichester. Rural surroundings near Pagham Harbour reserve. Ideal for Goodwood, beach and countryside.
Bedrooms: 2 single, 2 twin
Bathrooms: 2 public

Bed & breakfast
per night:	£min	£max
Single	13.50	14.50
Double	28.00	32.00

Parking for 7

There are separate sections in this guide listing groups specialising in farm holidays and accommodation which is especially suitable for young people and organised groups.

SOUTH EAST ENGLAND

SITTINGBOURNE
Kent
Map ref 3B3

The town's position and its ample supply of water make it an ideal site for the paper-making industry. Delightful villages and orchards lie round about.

The Beaumont
COMMENDED

74 London Road, Sittingbourne
ME10 1NS
☎ (0795) 472536
Fax (0795) 425921

Friendly, family-run establishment in a convenient location close to Canterbury and Maidstone. Sheerness ferry terminal only 20 minutes away. Easy access to M2 and M20.
Bedrooms: 3 single, 2 double, 2 twin, 1 triple, 1 family room
Bathrooms: 3 private, 1 public, 5 private showers
Bed & breakfast
per night:	£min	£max
Single	22.00	36.00
Double	40.00	48.00

Parking for 9
Cards accepted: Access, Visa

SMALLFIELD
Surrey
Map ref 2D2

Small village between Horley and Lingfield, named after local estate.

Chithurst Farm
Listed

Chithurst Lane, Horne, Smallfield, Horley RH6 9JU
☎ (0342) 842487

92-acre dairy farm. Recently renovated 16th C listed farmhouse, with genuine beamed rooms, inglenook fireplaces and attractive garden. Set in a quiet country lane, yet convenient for Gatwick and motorways.
Bedrooms: 1 single, 1 double, 1 triple
Bathrooms: 1 public
Bed & breakfast
per night:	£min	£max
Single	14.00	19.50
Double	28.00	33.00

Parking for 3
Open February-November

SMARDEN
Kent
Map ref 3B4

Pretty village with a number of old, well-presented buildings. The 14th C St Michael's Church is sometimes known as the "Barn of Kent" because of its 36-ft roof span.

Chequers Inn

Smarden, Ashford TN27 8QA
☎ Ashford (0233) 770217 & 770623
15th C inn with oak beams, centrally situated for visiting many stately homes. 5 golf-courses nearby. Food always available - speciality is fresh fish.
Bedrooms: 1 single, 1 twin, 1 family room
Bathrooms: 2 public
Bed & breakfast
per night:	£min	£max
Single	20.00	25.00
Double	35.00	45.00

Lunch available
Evening meal 1800 (last orders 2200)
Parking for 18
Cards accepted: Access, Visa, Switch

STELLING MINNIS
Kent
Map ref 3B4

Off the Roman Stone Street, this quiet, picturesque village lies deep in the Lyminge Forest, south of Canterbury.

Great Field Farm
Listed

Misling Lane, Stelling Minnis, Canterbury CT4 6DE
☎ (022 787) 223
42-acre mixed farm. Lovely spacious farmhouse with wealth of old pine, fine furnishings, pleasant gardens, paddocks with friendly ponies. Self-contained flat available for B&B or self catering. Quiet location midway Canterbury/Folkestone, adjacent B2068.
Bedrooms: 2 double, 1 twin
Bathrooms: 2 private, 1 public
Bed & breakfast
per night:	£min	£max
Single	15.00	18.00
Double	30.00	36.00

Parking for 6

The enquiry coupons at the back will help you when contacting proprietors.

STORRINGTON
West Sussex
Map ref 2D3

Small town within easy reach of walks over the South Downs and the popular Sussex coast.

Greenacres Farm
COMMENDED

Washington Road, Storrington, Pulborough RH20 4AF
☎ Worthing (0903) 742538

Family-run bed and breakfast set in 6 acres at the foot of the downs, 20 minutes from Worthing and the sea. Central for touring the south. Swimming pool.
Bedrooms: 1 single, 2 twin, 3 triple, 1 family room
Bathrooms: 6 private, 1 public
Bed & breakfast
per night:	£min	£max
Single	20.00	27.00
Double	40.00	50.00

Half board
per person:	£min	£max
Daily	29.00	35.00
Weekly	168.00	198.00

Evening meal 1830 (last orders 2000)
Parking for 30
Cards accepted: Access, Visa, Amex

SUTTON VALENCE
Kent
Map ref 3B4

Built on a ridge with tiered streets and some interesting 16th C houses. The village commands superb views across the Weald.

Richmond House
Listed

Rectory Lane, Sutton Valence, Maidstone ME17 3BS
☎ Maidstone (0622) 842217

Quietly situated with panoramic views of the Weald. Half mile from Kings Head on A274.

Continued ▶

379

SOUTH EAST ENGLAND

SUTTON VALENCE
Continued

Bedrooms: 1 twin
Bathrooms: 1 public
Bed & breakfast
per night: £min £max
Single 18.00 20.00
Double 34.00 36.00
Parking for 6

SWANLEY
Kent
Map ref 2D2

The Dees
Listed COMMENDED
56 Old Chapel Road, Crockenhill, Swanley BR8 8LJ
☎ (0322) 667645
Crockenhill is adjacent to M25, M20. Easy access to Brands Hatch, London, Kent and Sussex coast and country. Nice double room with full private facilities.
Bedrooms: 1 double
Bathrooms: 1 private, 1 public
Bed & breakfast
per night: £min £max
Single 12.50 15.00
Double 25.00 30.00
Parking for 2

TENTERDEN
Kent
Map ref 3B4

Most attractive market town with a broad main street full of 16th C houses and shops. The tower of the 15th C parish church is the finest in Kent.

Finchden Manor
HIGHLY COMMENDED
Appledore Road, Tenterden TN30 7DD
☎ (0580) 764719
Early 15th C manor house, Grade II listed, with inglenook fireplaces, panelled rooms and beams. Set in 4 acres of gardens and grounds.*
Bedrooms: 1 single, 2 double
Bathrooms: 3 private, 3 public
Bed & breakfast
per night: £min £max
Single 22.00 24.00
Double 44.00 48.00
Parking for 3

West Cross House Hotel
COMMENDED
2 West Cross, Tenterden TN30 6JL
☎ (0580) 762124

Private hotel in fine, spacious Georgian house on wide tree-lined main street of attractive Kent town, convenient for touring.
Bedrooms: 1 single, 2 double, 2 twin, 2 triple
Bathrooms: 2 public
Bed & breakfast
per night: £min £max
Single 16.00 16.00
Double 32.00 34.00
Parking for 7
Open March-October

TONBRIDGE
Kent
Map ref 2D2

Ancient town, built on the River Medway, has a long history of commercial importance and is still a thriving town. Attractive gardens surround the remains of the Norman castle.
Tourist Information Centre
☎ *(0732) 770929*

Poplar Farm Oast
Listed COMMENDED
Three Elm Lane, Golden Green, Tonbridge TN11 0LE
☎ (0732) 850723
Kentish oast in a quiet position overlooking surrounding farmland. Situated off A26 and central for touring this historic area.
Bedrooms: 2 double, 1 twin
Bathrooms: 1 public
Bed & breakfast
per night: £min £max
Double 32.00 38.00
Parking for 4
Open January-November

TUNBRIDGE WELLS
Kent
Map ref 2D2

This "Royal" town became famous as a spa in the 17th C and much of its charm is retained, as in the Pantiles, a shaded walk lined with elegant shops. Heritage attraction "A Day at the Wells". Rich in parks and gardens and a good centre for walks.
Tourist Information Centre
☎ *(0892) 515675*

Chequers
HIGHLY COMMENDED
Camden Park, Tunbridge Wells TN2 5AD
☎ (0892) 532299
Friendly family house, origins 1840. Part-walled garden. Unique private location, 10 minutes from Pantiles, high street, railway station. Peaceful,

comfortable, central base. Non-smokers only please.
Bedrooms: 1 single, 1 twin
Bathrooms: 2 private
Bed & breakfast
per night: £min £max
Single 18.00 20.00
Double 30.00 35.00
Parking for 5

Cheviots
COMMENDED
Cousley Wood, Wadhurst, East Sussex TN5 6HD
☎ Wadhurst (0892) 782952

On B2100 between Lamberhurst and Wadhurst. Comfortable bed and breakfast in modern country house with extensive garden. Home cooking. Convenient base for walking and motoring. Close to Bewl Water.
Bedrooms: 1 single, 1 double, 2 twin
Bathrooms: 3 private, 1 public
Bed & breakfast
per night: £min £max
Single 17.00 22.00
Double 34.00 44.00
Half board
per person: £min £max
Daily 30.00 35.00
Weekly 210.00 245.00
Evening meal from 1800
Parking for 4
Open May-October

Jordan House
COMMENDED
68 London Road, Tunbridge Wells TN1 1DT
☎ (0892) 523983
17th C town house with old world ambience, overlooking Tunbridge Wells Common and near town centre and station. Non-smokers preferred.
Bedrooms: 1 double, 1 twin
Bathrooms: 2 private
Bed & breakfast
per night: £min £max
Single 18.00 20.00
Double 36.00 40.00
Evening meal 1830 (last orders 2030)

Manor Court Farm
Ashurst, Tunbridge Wells TN3 9TB
☎ Fordcombe (0892) 740 279
350-acre mixed farm. Georgian farmhouse. Guests welcome to explore the farm. Many footpaths and lovely views. Tennis and fishing by

380

arrangement with owner. On the A264, half a mile east of Ashurst village (Tunbridge Wells to East Grinstead road).
Bedrooms: 1 double, 2 twin
Bathrooms: 2 public
Bed & breakfast

per night:	£min	£max
Single	18.00	20.00
Double	36.00	40.00

Parking for 15

Nellington Mead

Nellington Road, Tunbridge Wells TN4 8SQ
☎ (0892) 545037
A comfortable modern house with extensive garden. Easy access to Kent/Sussex countryside, historic houses and gardens. London and coast easily accessible.
Bedrooms: 1 twin
Bathrooms: 1 private
Bed & breakfast

per night:	£min	£max
Single	17.50	17.50
Double	35.00	35.00

Evening meal from 1900
Parking for 5
Open January-November

St. Martins

31 Broadwater Down, Tunbridge Wells TN2 5NL
☎ (0892) 536857
Victorian detached mansion house quietly situated along a tree-lined road yet close to the Pantiles, mainline station and town centre. Friendly family atmosphere. Reduced rates for children.
Bedrooms: 1 single, 1 twin, 1 triple
Bathrooms: 3 private
Bed & breakfast

per night:	£min	£max
Single	27.50	36.50
Double	42.50	52.50

Parking for 7
Cards accepted: Visa

UCKFIELD
East Sussex
Map ref 2D3

Once a medieval market town and centre of the iron industry, Uckfield is now a busy country town on the edge of the Ashdown Forest.

Old Mill Farm

High Hurstwood, Uckfield TN22 4AD
☎ Buxted (0825) 732279
50-acre beef farm. Situated in picturesque valley, off A26. Gatwick,

Crowborough, Uckfield and Ashdown Forest nearby.
Bedrooms: 1 single, 1 double, 2 twin
Bathrooms: 3 private, 2 public
Bed & breakfast

per night:	£min	£max
Single	17.00	17.00
Double	34.00	34.00

Half board

per person:	£min	£max
Daily	24.00	24.00
Weekly	168.00	168.00

Evening meal 1800 (last orders 2030)
Parking for 6

South Paddock
HIGHLY COMMENDED

Maresfield Park, Uckfield TN22 2HA
☎ (0825) 762335
Comfortable quiet country house accommodation set in 3.5 acres of landscaped gardens. Home-made preserves and log fires. Within easy reach of Gatwick, Brighton, Glyndebourne, Ashdown Forest.
Bedrooms: 2 twin
Bathrooms: 1 public
Bed & breakfast

per night:	£min	£max
Single	30.00	34.00
Double	45.00	50.00

Parking for 6

WALTON-ON-THAMES
Surrey
Map ref 2D2

Busy town beside the Thames, retaining a distinctive atmosphere despite being only 12 miles from central London. Close to Hampton Court Palace, Sandown Park racecourse and Claremont Landscape Garden, Esher.

Beech Tree Lodge

7 Rydens Avenue, Walton-on-Thames KT12 3JB
☎ (0932) 242738
Edwardian house in tree-lined avenue near buses, trains, shops, pubs. Handy for London, Hampton Court, Kingston and country.
Bedrooms: 2 twin, 1 triple
Bathrooms: 2 public
Bed & breakfast

per night:	£min	£max
Single		15.00
Double		30.00

Parking for 8

We advise you to confirm your booking in writing.

SOUTH EAST ENGLAND

WARNINGLID
West Sussex
Map ref 2D3

Gillhurst

The Street, Warninglid, Haywards Heath RH17 5SZ
☎ Haywards Heath (0444) 461388
Quiet setting outside beautiful village. Extensive grounds, hard tennis court, lovely decor, large rooms. Walks and lovely gardens in vicinity.
Bedrooms: 1 double, 2 twin
Bathrooms: 3 private
Bed & breakfast

per night:	£min	£max
Single	30.00	40.00
Double	40.00	60.00

Parking for 10

WEST CHILTINGTON
West Sussex
Map ref 2D3

Well-kept village caught in the maze of lanes leading to and from the South Downs.

New House Farm
COMMENDED

Broadford Bridge Road, West Chiltington, Pulborough RH20 2LA
☎ (0798) 812215
50-acre mixed farm. 15th C farmhouse with oak beams and inglenook for log fires. 40 minutes' drive from Gatwick. Within easy reach of local inns and golf-course.
Bedrooms: 1 double, 2 twin
Bathrooms: 3 private
Bed & breakfast

per night:	£min	£max
Single	25.00	35.00
Double	36.00	44.00

Parking for 6
Open January-November

WEST CLANDON
Surrey
Map ref 2D2

Ways Cottage
Listed

Lime Grove, West Clandon, Guildford GU4 7UT
☎ Guildford (0483) 222454
Rural detached house in quiet location, five miles from Guildford. Easy reach of A3 and M25. Close to station on Waterloo/Guildford line.
Bedrooms: 1 single, 1 double
Bathrooms: 1 private, 1 public

Continued ▶

381

SOUTH EAST ENGLAND

WEST CLANDON
Continued

Bed & breakfast
per night:	£min	£max
Single	15.00	18.50
Double	30.00	30.00

Half board
per person:	£min	£max
Daily	22.50	26.00

Evening meal 1800 (last orders 2100)
Parking for 2

WEST MALLING
Kent
Map ref 3B3

Became prominent in Norman times when an abbey was established here.

Westfields Farm
Listed
St. Vincents Lane, Addington, West Malling ME19 5BW
☎ (0732) 843209
A farmhouse of character, approximately 500 years old, in rural setting. Within easy reach of London, Canterbury, Tunbridge Wells and the coast. Reductions for children. Golf nearby.
Bedrooms: 1 single, 1 double, 1 twin
Bathrooms: 2 public

Bed & breakfast
per night:	£min	£max
Single	16.00	16.00
Double	32.00	32.00

WHITSTABLE
Kent
Map ref 3B3

Seaside resort and yachting centre on Kent's north shore. The beach is shingle and there are the usual seaside amenities and entertainments and a museum.
Tourist Information Centre
☎ (0227) 275482

15 Newton Road
Listed
Whitstable CT5 2JD
☎ (0227) 274283

In quiet residential area, 5 minutes' walk to seafront. Bus route on seafront to Herne Bay/Canterbury.
Bedrooms: 1 single, 1 double
Bathrooms: 1 public

Bed & breakfast
per night:	£min	£max
Single	14.00	15.50
Double	28.00	30.00

Parking for 1

WOKING
Surrey
Map ref 2D2

One of the largest towns in Surrey, which developed with the coming of the railway in the 1830s. Old Woking was a market town in the 17th C and still retains several interesting buildings.

Elm Lodge
Listed
Elm Road, Horsell, Woking GU21 4DY
☎ (0483) 763323
Fax (0344) 845656
Comfortable Victorian home in a quiet location overlooking woodland, yet 5 minutes from town centre and main line station.
Bedrooms: 3 twin
Bathrooms: 1 public

Bed & breakfast
per night:	£min	£max
Single	25.00	28.00
Double	35.00	40.00

Evening meal 1800 (last orders 2000)
Parking for 6

Oakhill ♠
Listed HIGHLY COMMENDED
Trotters Lane, Sandpit Hall Road, Chobham, Woking GU24 8HA
☎ (0276) 858021
Fax (0276) 858021
Comfortable, secluded country home in extensive gardens, with tennis court. Rooms with private bathrooms available. Evening meals by prior arrangement. Good access to M25, M3 and Woking rail line.
Bedrooms: 1 double, 1 twin
Bathrooms: 2 private

Bed & breakfast
per night:	£min	£max
Single	25.00	30.00
Double	44.00	50.00

Evening meal 1900 (last orders 2100)
Parking for 17

WORTHING
West Sussex
Map ref 2D3

Largest town in West Sussex, a popular seaside resort with extensive sand and shingle beaches. Seafishing is excellent here. The museum contains finds from Cissbury Ring.
Tourist Information Centre
☎ (0903) 210022

Tudor Guest House ♠
Listed
5 Windsor Road, Worthing BN11 2LU
☎ (0903) 210265

Comfortable bedrooms, satellite TV, English or continental breakfast. 1 minute from seafront, restaurants. Close to town centre, entertainment, bowling greens, Beach House Park. Parking on premises.
Bedrooms: 7 single, 1 twin, 1 family room
Bathrooms: 1 public

Bed & breakfast
per night:	£min	£max
Single	11.00	14.50
Double	22.00	29.00

Parking for 5
Cards accepted: Access, Visa

Individual proprietors have supplied all details of accommodation. Although we do check for accuracy, we advise you to confirm the information at the time of booking.

SURE SIGNS
OF WHERE TO STAY

Throughout Britain, the tourist boards now inspect over 30,000 places to stay, every year, to help you find the ones that suit you best.

Looking for a hotel, guesthouse, inn, B&B or farmhouse? Look for the **CROWN**. The classifications: 'Listed', and then **ONE to FIVE CROWN,** tell you the range of facilities and services you can expect. The more Crowns, the wider the range.

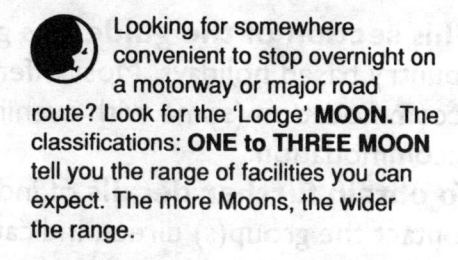

Looking for somewhere convenient to stop overnight on a motorway or major road route? Look for the 'Lodge' **MOON**. The classifications: **ONE to THREE MOON** tell you the range of facilities you can expect. The more Moons, the wider the range.

Looking for a self-catering holiday home? Look for the **KEY**. The classifications: **ONE to FIVE KEY,** tell you the range of facilities and equipment you can expect. The more Keys, the wider the range.

THE GRADES: **APPROVED, COMMENDED, HIGHLY COMMENDED and DE LUXE,** whether alongside the **CROWNS**, **KEYS** or **MOONS** show the quality standard of what is provided. If no grade is shown, you can still expect a high standard of cleanliness.

Looking for a holiday caravan, chalet or camping park? Look for the **Q** symbol. The more ✓s in the Q (from one to five), the higher the quality standard of what is provided.

English Tourist Board

We've checked them out before you check in!

More detailed information on the **CROWNS**, the **KEYS** and the **Q** is given in free *SURE SIGN* leaflets, available at any Tourist Information Centre.

383

farm holiday groups

This section of the guide lists groups specialising in farm and country based holidays. Most offer bed and breakfast accommodation (some with evening meal) and self-catering accommodation.

To obtain further details of individual properties please contact the group(s) direct, indicating the time of the year when the accommodation is required and the number of people to be accommodated. You may find the booking enquiry coupons helpful when making contact.

The cost of sending out brochures is high, and the groups would appreciate written enquiries being accompanied by a stamped and addressed envelope (at least 9" x 4½").

The 'b&b' prices shown are per person per night; the self-catering prices are weekly terms per unit.

The symbol 🐄 before the name of a group indicates that it is a member of the Farm Holiday Bureau, set up by the Royal Agricultural Society of England in conjunction with the English Tourist Board.

🐄 Cream of Cornwall
Mrs J. Nancarrow, Poltarrow Farm, St Mowan, St Austell, Cornwall PL26 7DR
Tel: (0726) 67111
Range of traditional farmhouses, from those nestling under the hills of out-of-the-way villages to the granite lintels of those perched high on the cliffs of the Atlantic coastline.
35 properties offering bed and breakfast: £11–£26 b&b.
25 self-catering units: low season £90–£150; high season £250–£600.
Short breaks also available.

🐄 Heart of Devon Farm Holiday Group
Mrs R. Hill, Quoit-at-Cross Farm, Stoodleigh, Tiverton, Devon EX16 9PJ
Tel: (039 85) 280
Variety of working farms in and around the lovely Exe Valley, offering self-catering accommodation or bed and breakfast with optional evening meal. Friendly, welcoming atmosphere assured.
12 properties offering bed and breakfast: £12–£18 b&b.
8 self-catering units: £80–£500 depending on season.
Short breaks also available.

🐄 Isle of Wight Farm and Country Holidays
Mrs D. Harvey, Newbarn Farm, Gatcombe, Newport, Isle of Wight PO30 3EQ
Tel: (0983) 721202
Picturesque farms and manor houses in the 'Garden Isle'. Seaside, countryside and many island attractions. Ideal walking country at any season.
9 properties offering bed and breakfast: £14–£18 b&b.
22 self-catering units: low season (November–March) £80–£200; high season (April–October) £150–£500.
Short breaks also available.

🐄 Kent Farm Holidays
Mrs D. Day, Great Cheveney Farm, Goudhurst Road, Marden, Tonbridge, Kent TN12 9LX
Tel: (0622) 831207
Fax: (0622) 831786
Mrs R. Bannock, Court Lodge Farm, Teston, Maidstone, Kent ME18 5AQ
Tel: (0622) 812570
Fax: (0622) 814200
Wide selection, from traditional farm cottages to modern farm-building conversions. Many with interesting architectural features and leisure facilities, many welcome non-smokers. Peaceful touring caravan and camping park.
19 properties offering bed and breakfast: £16–£30 b&b.
27 self-catering units: low season (October–April) from £90; high season (May–September) £125–£450.
Discounted short breaks available in low season.

farm holiday groups

Lincolnshire Farming Families Group
Mrs G. Grant, East Farm, Buslingthorpe, Market Rasen, Lincolnshire LN3 5AQ
Tel: (0673) 842283
High quality farmhouse and farm cottage accommodation in Lincolnshire, all in quiet rural settings. En-suite facilities available. Brochure on request.
12 properties offering bed and breakfast: £12.50–£20 b&b.
6 self-catering units: £140–£250.
Short breaks also available.

South Cotswold Holidays Agency
Mrs Victoria Jennings, Apple Orchard House, Springhill, Nailsworth, Stroud, Gloucestershire GL6 0LX
Tel: Stroud (0453) 832503
Fax: (0453) 836213
Variety of superior quality bed and breakfast establishments including inns and hotels, ranging from 17th C to modern, in the centre of an area with many visitor attractions, half an hour from Bath and Cirencester and convenient for Cheltenham, Gloucester, Stratford-upon-Avon, Oxford, Wells and Worcester. All have private bathrooms, tea/coffee facilities, friendly, helpful hosts. Colour brochure. Immediate bookings by fax.
39 properties offering bed and breakfast: £15–£21 b&b. Some rooms for disabled guests.
6 self-catering units: low season (November–April) £100–£180; high season (May–October) £150–£280.
Short breaks also available.

South Pennine Farm Holiday Group
Mrs A. Heathcote, Higher Quick Farm, Lydgate, Oldham OL4 4JJ
Tel: (0457) 872424
Mrs Jean Mayall, Globe Farm, Huddersfield Road, Delph, Oldham OL3 5LU
Tel: (0457) 873040
Pennine hill farms in Hawkshaw (Bury), Rochdale, Saddleworth, Werneth Low and Marple. Remote moorland and dramatic scenery, yet only 30 minutes from Manchester city and airport. Caravan and tent pitches also available.
7 properties offering bed and breakfast: £18–£22 b&b.
7 self-catering units: £100–£300.
Short breaks also available.

Teesdale Farm and Country Holiday Group
Mrs G. Wall, Kleine Cottage, Romaldkirk, Barnard Castle, Co Durham DL12 9ED
Tel: (0833) 50794
Range of holiday accommodation in one of the most picturesque and historic dales of County Durham. Many properties date back to the 14th C and have been modernised without losing their charm. Tent pitches also available.
8 properties offering bed and breakfast: £12–£16 b&b.
7 self-catering units: low season (October–April) £80–£120; high season (April–September) £120–£350.
Short breaks also available.

Warwickshire Farm Holidays
The Secretary, Crandon House, Avon Dassett, Leamington Spa, Warwickshire CV33 0AA
Tel: (0295) 770652
A warm welcome at farmhouses offering serviced and self-catering accommodation in comfortable and homely surroundings, situated in historic and picturesque 'Shakespeare country'. Caravan and tent pitches also available.
27 properties offering bed and breakfast: £12–£27 b&b.
25 self-catering units: low season (October–April) £70–£350; high season (May–September) £80–£450.

group & youth section

Most of the accommodation establishments listed in this guide are particularly suitable for people looking for relatively low-cost places to stay in England.

Some establishments make a special point of providing safe, budget-priced accommodation for young people, for families or for large groups. These places, ranging from Youth Hostels, YMCA and YWCA residences and budget and student hotels to the seasonally available campuses of universities and colleges, are listed individually in the pages which follow.

Information on organisations which specialise in this type of accommodation is given below – please contact them direct for further details.

YOUTH HOSTELS

The Youth Hostels Association (England and Wales) provides basic accommodation, usually in single-sex bunk-bedded rooms or dormitories, with self-catering facilities. Most hostels also provide low-cost meals or snacks. At the time of going to press, a night's stay at a Youth Hostel will cost between £3.50 and £16.50.

In spite of the word "youth" in the name, there is in fact no upper age limit. Indeed, many Youth Hostels also offer family accommodation, either in self-contained annexes (with kitchen, living room and bathroom) or by letting the smaller, four-to-six bed dormitories as private units.

Groups are very welcome at Youth Hostels, whether for educational or leisure pursuits: some hostels offer field study facilities and many more have classrooms. The YHA also offers a wide range of adventure holidays and special interest breaks.

Youth Hostels – from medieval castles to shepherds' huts – can be found all over the country, both in countryside and coastal locations and in towns and cities.

You need to be a member of the YHA in order to take advantage of the facilities. Membership entitles you to use not only the 240 hostels in England and Wales but also the thousands of Youth Hostels in other parts of the British Isles and around the world. Membership costs £3 (under 18) or £9 (over 18). Family membership is available at £9 (single-parent family) or £18 (two-parent family).

Further information from:
Youth Hostels Association
Trevelyan House, 8 St Stephen's Hill, St Albans, Hertfordshire
AL1 2DY
Tel: (0727) 855215
Fax: (0727) 844126

YWCA & YMCA

The Young Women's Christian Association, founded in 1855, has grown into the world's largest women's organisation. Among its many activities is the running of over 60 houses in Britain which offer safe, reasonably priced self-catering accommodation, mostly in single rooms, either on a permanent or temporary basis.

Most houses take short-stay visitors only during the summer months. However, some of the houses do accept short-stay visitors all the year round.

Although the word "women" appears in the name of the organisation, many of the residences now take men and boys as well as women and girls.

The Young Men's Christian Association (YMCA), founded in 1844, operates on much the same basis as the YWCA, taking people of both sexes at its 50-plus residences around the country either on a permanent or short-stay basis.

Special budget accommodation is also available in July and August at some YMCAs as part of the Inter-Point Programme, set up to provide accommodation and advice for Inter-Railers.

Further information from:
YWCA HQ
Clarendon House, 52 Cornmarket Street, Oxford OX1 3EJ
Tel: (0865) 726110
YMCA
National Council, 640 Forest Road, Walthamstow, London E17 3DZ
Tel: 081-520 5599

For details of the Inter-Point Programme, please contact Brian Welters at YMCA.

group & youth section

UNIVERSITIES & COLLEGES

Accommodation in universities and colleges offers excellent value for money at dozens of city centre, seaside and countryside campus locations around England.

This type of accommodation is particularly suitable for groups, whether on a leisure trip or participating in a conference or seminar. Beds available on campus vary from 30 to 3,000. There is a wide selection of meeting room facilities to choose from, with a maximum capacity of 2,000 people, and banqueting facilities for up to 1,500.

Most accommodation is in single "study bedrooms", with a limited number of twin and family rooms.

Availability is mainly during the academic vacation periods (usually July to September and for four-week periods at Christmas and Easter), with some venues offering short-stay accommodation throughout the year.

For relaxation, there is a wide choice of recreational facilities, with most venues providing TV rooms, bars and restaurants and a variety of sporting activities, ranging from tennis, squash and swimming to team sports.

Activity and special interest holidays are also on offer as are many self-catering flats and houses.

Further information from:
British Universities Accommodation Consortium (BUAC)
Box No 1006, University Park, Nottingham NG7 2RD
Tel: (0602) 504571
Fax: (0602) 422505

Connect Venues
36 Collegiate Crescent, Sheffield
S10 2BP
Tel: (0742) 683759
Fax: (0742) 661203

OTHER ACCOMMODATION

In addition to the above main providers on a countrywide basis of budget accommodation for young people and groups, there are, of course, the many individual student and budget hotels around England and also such places as outdoor and field study centres.

Some of these feature in the following pages but for more information on what is available in a particular area, please contact a local Tourist Information Centre.

GROUP & YOUTH SECTION

Places to stay

Accommodation entries in this section are listed in alphabetical order of place name, and then in alphabetical order of establishment.

The map references refer to the colour maps at the back of the guide. The first figure is the map number; the letter and figure which follow indicate the grid reference on the map.

The symbols at the end of each accommodation entry give information about services and facilities. A 'key' to these symbols is inside the back cover flap, which can be kept open for easy reference.

AMBLESIDE
Cumbria
Map ref 5A3

Market town situated at the head of Lake Windermere and surrounded by fells. The historic town centre is now a conservation area and the country around Ambleside is rich in historic and literary association. Good centre for touring, walking and climbing.
Tourist Information Centre
☎ (053 94) 32582

Iveing Cottage Holiday Centre
YWCA, Old Lake Road, Ambleside LA22 0DJ
☎ (053 94) 32340
Contact: The Director
Centrally located on old coaching road between Ambleside and lake. Ideal for fell-walking, rambling or climbing. Parties or individuals.
Bedrooms: 1 single, 3 double/twin, 6 dormitories. Total number of beds: 50
Bathrooms: 7 public
Bed & breakfast
per person:	£min	£max
Daily	11.25	12.75

Lunch available
Evening meal 1800 (last orders 1800)
Parking for 9
Open February-November

Colour maps at the back of this guide pinpoint all places which have accommodation listings in the guide.

BASSENTHWAITE
Cumbria
Map ref 5A2

Standing in an idyllic setting, nestled at the foot of Skiddaw and Ullock Pike, this village is just a mile from Bassenthwaite Lake, the one true "lake" in the Lake District. The area is visited by many varieties of migrating birds.

Kiln Hill Barn
Bassenthwaite, Keswick CA12 4RG
☎ (076 87) 76454
Contact: Mr. J K Armstrong
Farmhouse and converted barn in the country. Owned and run by the Armstrongs. Meals served in the barn dining room.
Bedrooms: 1 single, 2 double/twin, 2 dormitories. Total number of beds: 39
Bathrooms: 2 public
Bed & breakfast
per person:	£min	£max
Daily	17.50	17.50

Full board
per person:	£min	£max
Weekly	150.00	150.00

Evening meal 1830 (last orders 1830)
Parking for 15
Open February-October

Individual proprietors have supplied all details of accommodation. Although we do check for accuracy, we advise you to confirm the information at the time of booking.

BATH
Avon
Map ref 2B2

Georgian spa city beside the River Avon. Important Roman site with impressive reconstructed baths, uncovered in 19th C. Bath Abbey built on site of monastery where first king of England was crowned (AD 973). Fine architecture in mellow local stone. Pump Room and museums.
Tourist Information Centre
☎ (0225) 462831

The City of Bath YMCA
International House, Broad Street Place, Bath BA1 5LN
☎ (0225) 460471
Contact: Mr T Durbidge
Open to those of both sexes and all ages. Centrally located and only minutes away from Bath's major attractions. A convenient base for city and west country tours.
Minimum age 17
Bedrooms: 69 single, 13 double/twin, 4 triple, 2 dormitories. Total number of beds: 135
Bathrooms: 26 public
Bed & breakfast
per person:	£min	£max
Daily	9.50	12.00

Full board
per person:	£min	£max
Weekly	116.00	144.20

Lunch available
Evening meal 1700 (last orders 1800)

Please mention this guide when making a booking.

GROUP & YOUTH SECTION

BIRMINGHAM
West Midlands
Map ref 4B3

Britain's second city, with many attractions including the City Art Gallery, Barber Institute of Fine Arts, 17th C Aston Hall, science and railway museums, Jewellery Quarter, Cadbury World, 2 cathedrals and Botanical Gardens. Good base for exploring Shakespeare country.
Tourist Information Centre
☎ 021-643 2514

The University of Birmingham
Edgbaston, Birmingham B15 2TT
☎ 021-454 6022
Fax 021-456 2415
Telex 338938
Contact: Mr E Farrar, Residences & Conferences
Accommodation is provided in single and twin study bedrooms with washbasins, in parkland area in the attractive suburb of Edgbaston.
Bedrooms: 1050 single, 300 double/twin. Total number of beds: 1650
Bathrooms: 160 private, 100 public

Bed & breakfast
per person:	£min	£max
Daily	28.85	

Lunch available
Evening meal 1800 (last orders 2000)
Parking for 1000
Open January, March-April, July-September, December

BISHOP AUCKLAND
Durham
Map ref 5C2

Busy market town on the bank of the River Wear. The Palace, a castellated Norman manor house altered in the 18th C, stands in beautiful gardens. Open to the public and entered from the market square by a handsome 18th C gatehouse, the park is a peaceful retreat of trees and streams.

Weardale House
Ireshopeburn, Bishop Auckland, County Durham DL13 1HB
Contact: Mr Chris Jones, Y.M.C.A. Residential Office, Herrington Burn, Houghton-le-Spring, Tyne and Wear DH4 4JW
☎ 091-385 2822 & 385 3085
Fax 091-385 2267
Multi-activity outdoor centre.
Minimum age 7
Bedrooms: 3 single, 8 dormitories
Total number of beds: 70
Bathrooms: 8 public

Full board
per person:	£min	£max
Weekly	99.00	99.00

Lunch available
Parking for 10

BRADFORD
West Yorkshire
Map ref 4B1

City founded on wool, with fine Victorian and modern buildings. Attractions include the cathedral, city hall, Cartwright Hall, Lister Park, Moorside Mills Industrial Museum and National Museum of Photography, Film and Television.
Tourist Information Centre
☎ (0274) 753678

University of Bradford
Richmond Road, Bradford BD7 1DP
☎ (0274) 733466
Telex 51309
Contact: Ms. C Robinson, Conference Officer
Attractive, compact campus in a convenient location for touring the peaks, dales and Bronte country. Sports facilities including swimming pool, sauna and solarium.
Minimum age 10
Bedrooms: 1100 single. Total number of beds: 1100
Bathrooms: 5 private, 190 public

Bed only
per person:	£min	£max
Daily	13.00	23.00

Bed & breakfast
per person:	£min	£max
Daily	17.00	27.00

Lunch available
Evening meal from 1800
Open January, March-April, July-September, December

CAMBRIDGE
Cambridgeshire
Map ref 2D1

A most important and beautiful city on the River Cam with 31 colleges forming one of the oldest universities in the world. Numerous museums, good shopping centre, restaurants, theatres, cinema and fine bookshops.
Tourist Information Centre
☎ (0223) 322640

Cambridge Y.M.C.A.
Queen Anne House, Gonville Place, Cambridge CB1 1ND
☎ (0223) 356998
Fax (0223) 312749
Contact: Mrs P Bishop
A young people's residency, in the centre of Cambridge overlooking Parkers Piece. Near railway and bus stations. Very busy - not suitable for guests expecting peace and quiet.
Minimum age 16
Bedrooms: 95 single, 31 double/twin.
Total number of beds: 157
Bathrooms: 24 public

Bed & breakfast
per person:	£min	£max
Daily	15.90	19.60

Full board
per person:	£min	£max
Weekly	143.26	158.62

Lunch available
Evening meal 1715 (last orders 1845)

COVENTRY
West Midlands
Map ref 4B3

Modern city with a long history. It has many places of interest including the post-war and ruined medieval cathedrals, art gallery and museums, some 16th C almshouses, St Mary's Guildhall, Lunt Roman fort and the Belgrade Theatre.
Tourist Information Centre
☎ (0203) 832303

Coventry University
Priory Halls of Residence, Priory Street, Coventry CV1 5FB
☎ (0203) 838445
Fax (0203) 838445
Contact: Miss J Payne
University student halls of residence, offering out-of-term accommodation. Situated in the city centre beside Coventry Cathedral and sports centre.
Bedrooms: 546 single, 2 double/twin.
Total number of beds: 550
Bathrooms: 2 private, 200 public

Bed & breakfast
per person:	£min	£max
Daily	16.50	

Lunch available
Open January, March-April, July-September, December
Cards accepted: Access, Visa

The town index towards the back of this guide gives page numbers of all places with accommodation.

Symbols are explained on the flap inside the back cover.

389

GROUP & YOUTH SECTION

DURHAM
Durham
Map ref 5C2

Ancient city with its Norman castle and cathedral set on a bluff high over the Wear. A market and university town and regional centre, spreading beyond the market-place on both banks of the river. July Miners' Gala is a celebrated Durham tradition.
Tourist Information Centre
☎ 091-384 3720

College of St. Hild & St. Bede ⋒
University of Durham, Leazes Road, Durham DH1 1SZ
☎ 091-374 3069
Contact: Mr P A Warburton
College set in spacious grounds in the medieval City of Durham, providing a splendid base for exploring Northumbria.
Minimum age 10
Bedrooms: 364 single, 45 double/twin, 1 triple. Total number of beds: 457
Bathrooms: 53 public

Bed & breakfast
per person:	£min	£max
Daily	12.00	15.00

Full board
per person:	£min	£max
Weekly	165.20	186.20

Lunch available
Evening meal 1800 (last orders 1900)
Parking for 200
Open March-April, July-September

Collingwood College ⋒
South Road, Durham, County Durham DH1 3LT
☎ 091-374 4565
Fax 091-374 4595
Contact: Mrs Sylvia Hall
Durham's newest residential college set in woodland one mile south of the city.
Bedrooms: 295 single, 3 double/twin.
Total number of beds: 301
Bathrooms: 56 public

Bed & breakfast
per person:	£min	£max
Daily		14.19

Full board
per person:	£min	£max
Weekly		178.57

Lunch available
Evening meal 1800 (last orders 1900)
Parking for 70
Open January, March-April, July-September, December

We advise you to confirm your booking in writing.

Durham University Business School ⋒
Mill Hill Lane, Durham, County Durham DH1 3LB
☎ 091-374 2202
Contact: Ms Alison Fairlamb
Modern university complex offering 60 en-suite bedrooms and full conference facilities. Close to the centre of historic Durham with pleasant woodland surroundings.
Minimum age 15
Bedrooms: 58 single, 2 double/twin.
Total number of beds: 62
Bathrooms: 60 private

Bed only
per person:	£min	£max
Daily	14.10	28.79

Bed & breakfast
per person:	£min	£max
Daily	17.62	33.66

Lunch available
Parking for 60
Cards accepted: Access, Visa

Grey College ⋒
University of Durham, South Road, Durham, County Durham DH1 3LG
☎ 091-374 2900
Contact: Mrs V Hamilton
An attractive location in the University of Durham. Equipped with lounges, TV room, bar, lecture hall (150) and seminar rooms.
Bedrooms: 275 single, 12 double/twin, 1 dormitory. Total number of beds: 300
Bathrooms: 28 public

Bed & breakfast
per person:	£min	£max
Daily		15.75

Lunch available
Evening meal from 1900
Parking for 60
Open March-April, June-October

St. Aidans College ⋒
University of Durham, Windmill Hill, Durham, County Durham DH1 3LJ
☎ 091-374 3269
Contact: Lt. Cdr. J C Bull
A modern college in beautifully landscaped gardens overlooking the cathedral. Comfortable standard and en-suite single and twin-bedded rooms, bar, TV lounge, free tennis and croquet.
Bedrooms: 293 single, 66 double/twin.
Total number of beds: 425
Bathrooms: 94 private, 48 public

Bed only
per person:	£min	£max
Daily	12.00	17.00

Bed & breakfast
per person:	£min	£max
Daily	15.00	25.00

Full board
per person:	£min	£max
Weekly	176.00	205.00

Lunch available
Evening meal 1830 (last orders 1900)

Parking for 80
Open January, March-April, July-September, December

Saint Chad's College University of Durham ⋒
18 North Bailey, Durham, County Durham DH1 3RH
☎ 091-374 3370 & 374 3364
Contact: Mr I Blacklock
Historic college welcomes conferences, groups or individuals at its quiet central location beside the cathedral, overlooking gardens and river.
Bedrooms: 79 single, 54 double/twin, 5 triple. Total number of beds: 202
Bathrooms: 10 private, 38 public

Bed only
per person:	£min	£max
Daily	8.00	15.00

Bed & breakfast
per person:	£min	£max
Daily	11.00	18.50

Full board
per person:	£min	£max
Weekly	120.00	180.00

Lunch available
Evening meal 1800 (last orders 1930)
Parking for 15
Open January, March-April, June-September, December

St. Cuthberts Society
12 South Bailey, Durham, County Durham DH1 3EE
☎ 091-374 3464
Contact: Mrs H Bowler
3 old stone houses with riverside gardens, 5 minutes' walk from the city centre and close to the cathedral.
Bedrooms: 50 single, 23 double/twin, 3 triple. Total number of beds: 114
Bathrooms: 21 public

Bed & breakfast
per person:	£min	£max
Daily	15.00	15.00

Full board
per person:	£min	£max
Weekly	140.00	140.00

Open July-September

St. John's College ⋒
University of Durham, 3 South Bailey, Durham DH1 3RJ
☎ 091-374 3566
Contact: Mr Martin Clemmett
College buildings are skilfully adapted 18th C houses adjacent to Durham Cathedral and Castle.
Bedrooms: 96 single, 12 double/twin, 1 triple. Total number of beds: 120
Bathrooms: 25 public

Bed only
per person:	£min	£max
Daily	13.00	13.00

GROUP & YOUTH SECTION

Bed & breakfast per person:	£min	£max
Daily	15.50	15.50

Full board per person:	£min	£max
Weekly	185.50	185.50

Evening meal 1800 (last orders 1930)
Open March-April, July-September, December

Van Mildert College
University of Durham, Durham, County Durham DH1 3LH
☎ 091-374 3963
Fax 091-384 7764
Contact: Mr Sawyer
College buildings grouped around a small lake, in pleasant surroundings, 1 mile from the historic cathedral and city centre.
Minimum age 17
Bedrooms: 390 single, 48 double/twin.
Total number of beds: 438
Bathrooms: 48 private, 68 public

Bed & breakfast per person:	£min	£max
Daily	16.50	26.50

Lunch available
Evening meal from 1800
Parking for 100

GUILDFORD
Surrey
Map ref 2D2

Bustling town with many historic monuments, one of which is the Guildhall clock jutting out over the old High Street. The modern cathedral occupies a commanding position on Stag Hill.
Tourist Information Centre
☎ (0483) 444007

University of Surrey
Guildford GU2 5XH
☎ (0483) 509158
Fax (0483) 579266
Contact: Mr. R Paxton
The university and cathedral occupy commanding positions on a hill overlooking this historic town. London 30 miles, coast 40 miles. Self-catering accommodation also available.
Minimum age 14
Bedrooms: 1989 single, 86 double/twin. Total number of beds: 2161
Bathrooms: 260 private, 491 public

Bed & breakfast per person:	£min	£max
Daily	15.24	18.46

Lunch available
Evening meal 1800 (last orders 1930)
Parking for 1400
Open January, March-April, July-September, December
Cards accepted: Access, Visa

HEBDEN BRIDGE
West Yorkshire
Map ref 4B1

Originally a small town on packhorse route, Hebden Bridge grew into a booming mill town in 18th C with rows of "up-and-down" houses of several storeys built against hillsides. Ancient "pace-egg play" custom held on Good Friday.
Tourist Information Centre
☎ (0422) 843831

Hebden Hey Activity and Training Centre
Hardcastle Crags, Hebden Bridge HX7 7AW
Contact: Mr & Mrs A P Garside, 26 Carlton House Terrace, Haugh Shaw Road, Halifax, West Yorkshire HX7 3LD
☎ (0422) 347408
Two purpose-built hostels providing accommodation for up to 28 and 46 persons, in bunk rooms. Price is per person as part of group.
Bedrooms: 8 dormitories. Total number of beds: 74
Bathrooms: 7 public

Bed only per person:	£min	£max
Daily	9.00	

Parking for 15

LITTLEDEAN
Gloucestershire
Map ref 2B1

Village in the Forest of Dean close to the River Severn with magnificent views of the Severn Valley. Traces of a Roman paved road leading to the mines can be seen near the village.

Littledean House Hotel
Littledean, Cinderford GL14 3JT
☎ Dean (0594) 822106
Contact: Mrs J R Felton
Large, rambling old hotel in Forest of Dean. Informal atmosphere. Catering for individuals, families and educational and recreational groups.
Bedrooms: 15 single, 21 double/twin, 18 quadruple, 8 dormitories. Total number of beds: 100
Bathrooms: 11 public

Bed & breakfast per person:	£min	£max
Daily	14.80	24.00

Full board per person:	£min	£max
Weekly	165.00	210.00

Evening meal 1830 (last orders 2000)
Parking for 20
Open March-November

LIVERPOOL
Merseyside
Map ref 4A2

Exciting city, famous for the Beatles, football, the Grand National, theatres and nightlife. Liverpool has a magnificent waterfront, 2 cathedrals, 3 historic houses, museum, galleries and a host of attractions.
Tourist Information Centre
☎ 051-709 3631

Embassie Youth Hostel
1 Faulkner Square, Toxteth, Liverpool L8 7NU
☎ 051-707 1089
Contact: Mr Kevin Murphy
Large Georgian hostel 10 minutes' walk from Liverpool's Anglican Cathedral. Cheap, clean and friendly.
Bedrooms: 1 double/twin, 3 dormitories. Total number of beds: 32
Bathrooms: 4 public

Bed & breakfast per person:	£min	£max
Daily	7.50	

Full board per person:	£min	£max
Weekly	50.00	

Parking for 10

LONDON
Greater London
Colour maps 6 & 7 at the back of the guide show place names and London Postal Area codes and will help you to locate accommodation in your chosen area of London.

Anne Elizabeth House Hostel
30 Collingham Place, London SW5
☎ 071-370 4821
Contact: Mrs. M Lopes
Convenient for Earl's Court and within easy reach of the West End.
Bedrooms: 4 single, 5 double/twin, 8 triple, 4 quadruple, 2 dormitories. Total number of beds: 64
Bathrooms: 7 public

Bed & breakfast per person:	£min	£max
Daily	7.50	21.00

Baden Powell House Hostel
Queen's Gate, South Kensington, London SW7 5JS
☎ 071-584 7031
Fax 071-581 9953
Contact: Miss A Watson
International scout hostel with accommodation ranging from single to dormitory rooms. Limited to scouts, schools, students and organisations affiliated to NCVYO.

Continued ▶

391

GROUP & YOUTH SECTION

LONDON
Continued

Bedrooms: 9 single, 15 double/twin, 4 triple, 4 quadruple, 6 dormitories.
Total number of beds: 112
Bathrooms: 3 private, 23 public

Bed & breakfast
per person:	£min	£max
Daily	8.40	29.00

Full board
per person:	£min	£max
Weekly	58.80	203.00

Lunch available
Evening meal 1800 (last orders 1915)
Parking for 14
Cards accepted: Access, Visa, Switch

Brunel University Conference Centre ⚑
Conference Office, Brunel University, Uxbridge, Middlesex UB8 3PH
☎ Uxbridge (0895) 274000
Fax (0895) 203142
Telex 261173 G
Contact: Mr Carl Woodall
En-suite or standard bedrooms, cafeteria or silver service meals, purpose-built theatres and classrooms, audio and visual aids and sports facilities all available.
Minimum age 12
Bedrooms: 790 single. Total number of beds: 790
Bathrooms: 400 private, 85 public

Bed only
per person:	£min	£max
Daily	15.35	20.95

Bed & breakfast
per person:	£min	£max
Daily	18.87	24.48

Full board
per person:	£min	£max
Weekly	207.20	286.30

Lunch available
Evening meal 1800 (last orders 2000)
Parking for 2000
Open April-September

Campbell House
Taviton Street, London WC1H 0BX
☎ 071-380 7079
Contact: Mr. R L Sparvell
Specially reconstructed Georgian housing providing self-catering accommodation in a peaceful, central London location.
Minimum age 10
Bedrooms: 60 single, 40 double/twin.
Total number of beds: 140
Bathrooms: 25 public

Bed only
per person:	£min	£max
Daily	13.00	15.25

Open June-September

Central University of Iowa Hostel
7 Bedford Place, London WC1B 5JA
☎ 071-580 1121
Contact: Ms. W Bristow
Old Georgian house near the British Museum. Closest underground stations are Russell Square and Holborn.
Bedrooms: 1 single, 6 double/twin, 5 dormitories. Total number of beds: 30
Bathrooms: 7 public

Bed & breakfast
per person:	£min	£max
Daily	17.00	18.00

Open May-August

Driscoll House Hotel
172 New Kent Road, London SE1 4YT
☎ 071-703 4175
Fax 071-703 8013
Contact: Mr. T Driscoll

Long or short term accommodation offered to teachers, students and tourists. Weekly full-board price excludes weekday lunch.
Minimum age 18
Bedrooms: 200 single. Total number of beds: 200
Bathrooms: 14 public

Full board
per person:	£min	£max
Weekly-	140.00	

Lunch available
Evening meal 1730 (last orders 1900)
Parking for 1

Ealing YMCA
25 St Marys Road, Ealing, London W5 5RE
☎ 081-579 6946
Fax 081-579 1129
Contact: Mr J Burch
A new residential centre. Each room with colour TV. Le Jardin restaurant on premises.
Minimum age 16
Bedrooms: 129 single, 13 double/twin, 13 triple. Total number of beds: 157
Bathrooms: 13 private, 28 public

Bed & breakfast
per person:	£min	£max
Daily	22.88	23.80

Lunch available
Evening meal 1745 (last orders 1855)
Cards accepted: Access, Visa

Holy Trinity Urban Centre (Peter Ward Hostel)
Carlisle Lane, London SE1 7LG
☎ 071-928 5447
Contact: Mr Demitri Maldonado

Residential centre behind St Thomas's Hospital, adjacent to Archbishops Park. Groups and individuals of all ages welcome.
Minimum age 6
Bedrooms: 6 dormitories. Total number of beds: 40
Bathrooms: 2 private, 4 public

Bed only
per person:	£min	£max
Daily	15.00	

Bed & breakfast
per person:	£min	£max
Daily	17.00	

Full board
per person:	£min	£max
Weekly	122.50	189.00

Lunch available
Evening meal from 1800
Parking for 40

Ingram Court ⚑
King's College London, Chelsea Campus, 552 Kings Road, London SW10 0AU
Contact: Ms Lindsay Elliot Smith, King's Campus Vacation Bureau, King's College London, 552 Kings Road, London SW10 0UA
☎ 071-351 6011
Fax 071-352 7376
Student bedrooms in small residences grouped around a quiet courtyard, on a spacious green campus. Other halls of residence available in Westminster, Wandsworth, Champion Hill and the Sloane Square end of the King's Road.
Bedrooms: 107 single, 7 double/twin. Total number of beds: 121
Bathrooms: 30 public

Bed & breakfast
per person:	£min	£max
Daily	16.50	22.50

Parking for 20
Open March-April, July-September, December

International House Woolwich ⚑
109 Brookhill Road, London SE18 6RZ
☎ 081-854 1418
Fax 081-855 9257
Contact: Mr B Siderman
Purpose-built student hostel. Self-contained flats for married couples and children. Full en-suite facilities also available. Short-term visitor accommodation available July-September.
Bedrooms: 85 single, 21 double/twin. Total number of beds: 127
Bathrooms: 21 private, 18 public

Bed & breakfast
per person:	£min	£max
Daily	8.68	12.67

Parking for 21
Open April, July-September, December

GROUP & YOUTH SECTION

International Students Hostel
99 Frognal, London NW3 6XR
☎ 071-794 6893 & 794 8095
Contact: Sr. P S Taylor

Historic, listed building in attractive grounds. Family atmosphere. Five minutes Hampstead Heath and underground, 15 minutes central London. Budget rates for long-term students.
For females only
Minimum age 16
Bedrooms: 17 single, 2 double/twin, 4 dormitories. Total number of beds: 40
Bathrooms: 14 public

Bed only
per person:	£min	£max
Daily	8.50	16.00

Bed & breakfast
per person:	£min	£max
Daily	9.50	16.50

Evening meal from 1845

International Students House
229 Great Portland Street, London W1N 5HD
☎ 071-631 3223
Fax 071-636 5565
Contact: Ms Ursula Lydon

10 minutes' walk from the West End and next to Regents Park. Numerous facilities available in a modern building.
Minimum age 17
Bedrooms: 157 single, 110 double/twin, 4 triple, 5 quadruple. Total number of beds: 409
Bathrooms: 10 private, 40 public

Bed & breakfast
per person:	£min	£max
Daily	12.00	22.70

Lunch available
Evening meal 1800 (last orders 1930)
Parking for 10
Cards accepted: Access, Visa, Switch

John Adams Hall (Institute of Education)
15-23 Endsleigh Street, London WC1H ODH
☎ 071-387 4086
Fax 071-383 0164
Telex 94016519 DICE G
Contact: Ms Sue Waller

An assembly of Georgian houses, the hall has retained its old glory. Close to Euston, King's Cross and St Pancras stations.
Bedrooms: 127 single, 22 double/twin, 13 triple. Total number of beds: 171
Bathrooms: 1 private, 26 public

Bed & breakfast
per person:	£min	£max
Daily	18.00	22.50

Evening meal 1730 (last orders 1830)
Open January, March-April, July-September, December
Cards accepted: Access, Visa

Kent House
325 Green Lanes, London N4 2ES
☎ 081-802 0800 & 802 9009
Fax 081-802 9070
Contact: Mr M L Metin

Special off-season and weekly rates for young tourists. Facilities for self-catering. Adjacent to Manor House underground station and 10 minutes from central London.
Minimum age 16
Bedrooms: 3 single, 13 double/twin, 3 dormitories. Total number of beds: 34
Bathrooms: 6 public

Bed only
per person:	£min	£max
Daily	10.00	25.00

Bed & breakfast
per person:	£min	£max
Daily	11.50	27.00

Parking for 4

London Student Hotel
14 Penywern Road, London SW5 9ST
☎ 071-244 6615
Contact: Ms Annika McWilliams

Small budget hotel close to Earl's Court underground station. Non-students and travellers welcome.
Bedrooms: 1 single, 5 double/twin, 6 quadruple, 2 dormitories. Total number of beds: 47
Bathrooms: 1 private, 5 public

Bed & breakfast
per person:	£min	£max
Daily	10.00	15.00

London Student Housing Friendship House
1 Nicholas Glebe, Rectory Lane, London SW17 9QH
☎ 081-672 2262
Contact: Mrs S White

Friendship House offers accommodation to visitors, from Britain and overseas, in a modern purpose-built hostel. Students are particularly welcome.
For individuals only
Minimum age 18
Bedrooms: 76 single. Total number of beds: 76
Bathrooms: 21 public

Bed & breakfast
per person:	£min	£max
Daily	15.00	20.00

Lunch available
Evening meal 1745 (last orders 1830)
Parking for 10

Lords Hotel
20-22 Leinster Square, London W2 4PR
☎ 071-229 8877
Fax 071-229 8317
Telex 298716 LORDS G
Contact: Mr. N G Ladas

Bed and breakfast accommodation in central London. Residents' bar, direct-dial telephone, radio. Most rooms with private facilities.
Bedrooms: 11 single, 28 double/twin, 12 triple, 14 quadruple. Total number of beds: 161
Bathrooms: 36 private, 12 public

Bed & breakfast
per person:	£min	£max
Daily	14.00	40.00

Cards accepted: Access, Visa, Diners, Amex, Switch

O'Callaghan's
205 Earls Court Road, London SW5 9AN
☎ 071-370 3000 & 081-540 5958
Contact: Mr. B J Browning

Central London low-budget guesthouse for tourists and students. Open all year round.
Minimum age 16
Bedrooms: 4 double/twin, 3 triple, 3 quadruple. Total number of beds: 26
Bathrooms: 3 public

Bed & breakfast
per person:	£min	£max
Daily	8.00	10.00

Passfield Hall
1 Endsleigh Place, London WC1H 0PW
☎ 071-387 7743 & 387 3584
Contact: Ms. J Martin

University hall of residence with washbasin in all rooms, suitable for families. Central for Oxford Street and the West End.
Bedrooms: 100 single, 34 double/twin, 10 triple. Total number of beds: 198
Bathrooms: 36 public

Bed & breakfast
per person:	£min	£max
Daily	17.50	22.50

Open March-April, July-September

Queen Alexandra's House
Bremner Road, Kensington Gore, London SW7 2QT
☎ 071-589 3635
Fax 071-589 3177
Contact: Mrs. V E Makey

A hostel for women students of all ages.
For females only
Minimum age 17
Bedrooms: 75 single, 2 double/twin. Total number of beds: 81
Bathrooms: 20 public

Continued ▶

GROUP & YOUTH SECTION

LONDON
Continued

Bed & breakfast
per person:	£min	£max
Daily	20.00	

Open July-August

Ramsay Hall
20 Maple Street, London W1P 5GB
☎ 071-387 4537
Contact: Mr Hugh Ewing
Central London location, good value, comfortable accommodation in pleasant surroundings.
Minimum age 11
Bedrooms: 364 single, 20 double/twin, 2 triple. Total number of beds: 410
Bathrooms: 70 public

Bed & breakfast
per person:	£min	£max
Daily	18.00	19.50

Evening meal 1800 (last orders 1900)
Open January, March-April, June-September, December

Rotherhithe Youth Hostel and Conference Centre
Island Yard, Salter Road, London SE16 1PP
☎ 071-232 2114
Fax 071-237 2919
Contact: Mr Frank Velander
Ultra-modern building with every facility for families and individuals. All rooms have en-suite facilities, there is a restaurant and ample street parking. Special prices for family rooms.
Minimum age 5
Bedrooms: 22 double/twin, 16 quadruple, 32 dormitories. Total number of beds: 320
Bathrooms: 70 private

Bed only
per person:	£min	£max
Daily	14.50	17.95

Bed & breakfast
per person:	£min	£max
Daily	18.00	20.50

Full board
per person:	£min	£max
Weekly	153.70	180.00

Lunch available
Evening meal 1730 (last orders 2030)
Cards accepted: Access, Visa, Switch

Rywin House
36 Christchurch Avenue, Brondesbury, London NW6 7BE
☎ 081-459 5134
Contact: Mr. P Horsley
In a quiet residential area with British Rail and London Transport stations nearby. Short walk to local tennis courts.
Bedrooms: 2 single, 1 double/twin, 6 dormitories. Total number of beds: 23
Bathrooms: 3 public

Bed & breakfast
per person:	£min	£max
Daily	14.50	14.50

Tent City
Old Oak Common Lane, East Acton, London W3 7DP
Contact: Ms Maxine Lambert, Tent City Limited, P O Box 1197, Shepherd's Bush, London W3 7ZA
☎ 081-749 9074 & 885 5402
A tented hostel in a large park providing cheap, simple accommodation for summer visitors to London. East Acton underground station.
Bedrooms: 14 dormitories. Total number of beds: 448
Bathrooms: 24 public

Bed only
per person:	£min	£max
Daily	4.00	5.00

Parking for 30
Open June-September

TUC National Education Centre
77 Crouch End Hill, London N8 8DG
☎ 081-341 6161
Fax 081-348 3961
Contact: Ms Penny Bromfield
65 single bedded rooms each with en-suite facilities plus a small number of twin bedded rooms. Restaurant, bar, games room and gardens.
Bedrooms: 65 single, 2 double/twin, 1 triple. Total number of beds: 71
Bathrooms: 67 private

Bed only
per person:	£min	£max
Daily	31.00	31.00

Bed & breakfast
per person:	£min	£max
Daily	36.00	36.00

Full board
per person:	£min	£max
Weekly	252.50	252.50

Lunch available
Evening meal 1800 (last orders 1845)
Parking for 15
Open May-September
Cards accepted: Access, Visa

University of Westminster
Hall of Residence, 35 Marylebone Road, London NW1 5LS
Contact: Ms N Chanson, University of Westminster, Luxborough Suite, 35 Marylebone Road, London NW1 5LS
☎ 071-911 5000
Fax 071-911 5141
Telex 25964
Three halls of residence in central London and one in the Highgate/Hampstead area, offering well-appointed single and twin study bedrooms on self-catering or meals basis.
For groups only

Minimum age 7
Bedrooms: 220 single. Total number of beds: 220
Bathrooms: 131 public

Bed only
per person:	£min	£max
Daily	13.50	17.50

Bed & breakfast
per person:	£min	£max
Daily	15.75	19.75

Full board
per person:	£min	£max
Weekly	175.00	221.95

Lunch available
Evening meal 1700 (last orders 1900)
Parking for 7
Open March-September
Cards accepted: Access, Visa, Switch

Wimbledon YMCA
200 The Broadway, Wimbledon, London SW19 1RY
☎ 081-542 9055
Fax 081-542 1086
Contact: Mr. A C Rothery
Modern, purpose-built residence with sports hall, fitness studio, saunas and sunbeds, coffee bar, restaurant, laundry.
Minimum age 12
Bedrooms: 106 single, 30 double/twin, 4 quadruple. Total number of beds: 170
Bathrooms: 1 private, 20 public

Bed & breakfast
per person:	£min	£max
Daily	11.25	19.50

Lunch available
Evening meal 1700 (last orders 1850)
Parking for 30
Cards accepted: Access, Visa

Y.M.C.A.
Rush Green Road, Romford RM7 0PH
☎ Romford (0708) 766211
Fax (0708) 754211
Contact: Ms Audrey Hylton
8 minutes' walk from Romford British Rail station, 25 minutes from Liverpool Street station. Easy access to M25 and south coast. Easy travel into London by underground (Elm Park). International hostel with many sports facilities.
Minimum age 18
Bedrooms: 148 single, 2 double/twin. Total number of beds: 150
Bathrooms: 4 private, 24 public

Bed & breakfast
per person:	£min	£max
Daily	16.80	

Full board
per person:	£min	£max
Weekly	68.75	106.80

Lunch available
Evening meal 1730 (last orders 1845)
Parking for 120
Cards accepted: Access, Visa

GROUP & YOUTH SECTION

YWCA Elizabeth House
118 Warwick Way, London SW1
☎ 071-630 0741
Contact: Ms. F McGinlay
Clean and secure basic bed and breakfast accommodation in central London for men, women and families. Garden available for guests.
Minimum age 5
Bedrooms: 10 single, 13 double/twin, 1 triple, 3 quadruple. Total number of beds: 51
Bathrooms: 9 private, 8 public

Bed & breakfast
per person:	£min	£max
Daily	15.00	22.50

MANCHESTER
Greater Manchester
Map ref 4B1

Manchester, City of Drama 1994, is full of variety and vitality. It offers the liveliest nightlife in Britain; exclusive restaurants jostle with pavement cafes; shops range from boutiques to antiques. The city is rich in historic interest.
Tourist Information Centre
☎ 061-234 3157/8

University of Manchester
Dept C684, Oxford Road, Manchester M13 9PL
☎ 061-275 2156
Fax 061-275 3000
Contact: Miss. C S Bolton
Accommodation for groups and facilities for conferences and exhibitions in university halls of residence. Small or large groups - long or short stay, flexible arrangements, friendly staff.
Minimum age 12
Bedrooms: 3530 single, 169 double/twin. Total number of beds: 3868
Bathrooms: 360 private, 1031 public

Bed only
per person:	£min	£max
Daily	13.00	15.28

Bed & breakfast
per person:	£min	£max
Daily	18.90	34.55

Full board
per person:	£min	£max
Weekly	260.38	372.00

Lunch available
Parking for 1500
Open January, March-April, June-September, December

Colour maps at the back of this guide pinpoint all places which have accommodation listings in the guide.

MATFIELD
Kent
Map ref 3B4

Village with Georgian houses, green and pond.

Old Cryals
Cryals Road, Matfield, Tonbridge TN12 7HN
☎ Brenchley (089 272) 2372
Fax (089 272) 3311
Contact: Mr C Charrington
Hostel-type accommodation for 12, in two rooms for 4 and 8. Comfortable sitting/dining room with microwave oven, TV, freezer, dishwasher. Self-catering only.
Bedrooms: 2 dormitories. Total number of beds: 12
Bathrooms: 2 public

Bed only
per person:	£min	£max
Daily		5.50

Parking for 12
Open March-November

NEWCASTLE UPON TYNE
Tyne and Wear
Map ref 5C2

Commercial and cultural centre of the North East, with a large indoor shopping centre, Quayside market, museums and theatres which offer an annual 6 week season by the Royal Shakespeare Company. Norman castle keep, medieval alleys, old Guildhall.
Tourist Information Centre
☎ 091-261 0691 or 230 0030

North Eastern YWCA Hostel
Jesmond House, Clayton Road, Newcastle upon Tyne, Tyne & Wear NE2 1UJ
☎ 091-281 1233
Contact: Mr B Garnon
New, custom-built accommodation in a good residential area with easy access by Metro and bus to the city centre. All bedrooms have wash basins.
Minimum age 18
Bedrooms: 80 single. Total number of beds: 80
Bathrooms: 12 public

Bed & breakfast
per person:	£min	£max
Daily		15.00

Full board
per person:	£min	£max
Weekly		75.00

Parking for 20

University of Northumbria At Newcastle
Coach Lane Campus Halls of Residence, Coach Lane, Newcastle upon Tyne NE7 7XA

Contact: Mrs S Cowell, University of Northumbria, At Newcastle, Ellison Place, Newcastle upon Tyne, Tyne & Wear NE1 8ST
☎ 091-227 4024
Fax 091-227 8017
Accommodation in modern halls of residence, set in pleasant grounds, 3 miles from the city centre. Bed and breakfast with or without evening meal for groups or parties.
Bedrooms: 186 single, 50 double/twin. Total number of beds: 286
Bathrooms: 44 public

Bed only
per person:	£min	£max
Daily	9.65	12.80

Bed & breakfast
per person:	£min	£max
Daily	14.30	18.00

Full board
per person:	£min	£max
Weekly	135.70	246.45

Lunch available
Evening meal 1730 (last orders 1930)
Parking for 200
Open April, July-September

NEWPORT
Shropshire
Map ref 4A3

Small market town on the Shropshire Union Canal has a wide High Street and a church with some interesting monuments. Newport is close to Aqualate Mere which is the largest lake in Staffordshire.

Harper Adams College
Newport TF10 8NB
☎ (0952) 820280 & 24 hours (0860) 810698
Fax (0952) 814783
Contact: Mr Ian Barnard

A country estate of 600 acres. Renaissance architecture with 200 en-suite rooms (300 others). Conference, tutorial and all sports. Groups only (4 plus).
Minimum age 10
Bedrooms: 443 single, 60 double/twin. Total number of beds: 503
Bathrooms: 180 private, 60 public

Bed only
per person:	£min	£max
Daily		12.00

Continued ▶

GROUP & YOUTH SECTION

NEWPORT
Continued

Bed & breakfast
per person:	£min	£max
Daily	15.00	

Full board
per person:	£min	£max
Weekly	90.00	

Lunch available
Evening meal 1700 (last orders 2200)
Parking for 4000
Open January, April, July-September, December

NORWICH
Norfolk
Map ref 3C1

Beautiful cathedral city and county town on the River Wensum with many fine museums and medieval churches. Norman castle, Guildhall and interesting medieval streets. Good shopping centre and market.
Tourist Information Centre
☎ (0603) 666071 or (accommodation) 761082

YWCA
Marjorie Hinde House, 61 Bethel Street, Norwich NR2 1NR
☎ (0603) 625982
Contact: Mrs Sylvia Phillips
Comfortable hostel for long or short stays. Central position near shops, theatres, gardens, library and public transport.
For females only
Bedrooms: 20 single, 7 double/twin.
Total number of beds: 34
Bathrooms: 7 public

Bed only
per person:	£min	£max
Daily	7.70	9.30

OTTERBURN
Northumberland
Map ref 5B1

Small village set at the meeting of the River Rede with Otter Burn, the site of the Battle of Otterburn in 1388. A peaceful tradition continues in the sale of Otterburn tweeds in this beautiful region, which is ideal for exploring the Border country and the Cheviots.

Otterburn Hall
Otterburn NE19 1HE
☎ Freephone 0800 591527
Fax 091-385 2267
Contact: Mrs K Hutchinson
Family holiday hotel, conference venue and training establishment in 100 acres. Offering special interest holidays. Prices quoted include dinner.

Minimum age 8
Bedrooms: 3 single, 33 double/twin, 16 triple, 7 quadruple, 1 dormitory.
Total number of beds: 136
Bathrooms: 33 private, 8 public

Bed & breakfast
per person:	£min	£max
Daily	33.00	36.00

Lunch available
Evening meal 1900 (last orders 1900)
Parking for 60
Cards accepted: Visa

POOLE
Dorset
Map ref 2B3

Tremendous natural harbour makes Poole a superb boating centre. The harbour area is crowded with historic buildings including the 15th C Town Cellars housing a maritime museum.
Tourist Information Centre
☎ (0202) 673322

Rockley Point Sailing School
Rockley Park, Hamworthy, Poole
BH15 4LZ
☎ Bournemouth (0202) 677272
Fax (0202) 668268
Contact: Ms Barbara Gordon

RYA sailing school catering for all abilities and ages. Accommodation of various types available and residential children's courses. Also windsurfing and yacht courses. Adult all-in courses in bed and breakfast accommodation.
Minimum age 8
Bedrooms: 30 single, 16 dormitories.
Total number of beds: 80
Bathrooms: 5 public

Bed & breakfast
per person:	£min	£max
Daily	10.00	12.00

Full board
per person:	£min	£max
Weekly	110.00	125.00

Lunch available
Parking for 10
Open March-October
Cards accepted: Access, Visa

Please mention this guide when making a booking.

PORTSMOUTH & SOUTHSEA
Hampshire
Map ref 2C3

The first dock was built in 1194. HMS Victory, Nelson's flagship, is here and Charles Dickens' former home is open to the public. Neighbouring Southsea has a promenade with magnificent views of Spithead.
Tourist Information Centre
☎ (0705) 826722

Portsmouth Y M C A
Penny Street, Portsmouth, Hampshire
PO1 2NN
☎ (0705) 864341
Contact: Mr D S Butler
Comfortable, reasonably priced accommodation adjacent to beaches and road/rail interchange. Family and youth groups most welcome. Brochure available.
Bedrooms: 80 single, 20 double/twin, 5 dormitories. Total number of beds: 130
Bathrooms: 15 public

Bed only
per person:	£min	£max
Daily	6.00	

Bed & breakfast
per person:	£min	£max
Daily	12.50	

Full board
per person:	£min	£max
Weekly	82.50	

Evening meal 1715 (last orders 1800)

SHEFFIELD
South Yorkshire
Map ref 4B2

Local iron ore and coal gave Sheffield its prosperous steel and cutlery industries. The modern city centre has many interesting buildings - cathedral, Cutlers' Hall, Crucible Theatre, Graves and Mappin Art Galleries - and Meadowhall shopping centre nearby.
Tourist Information Centre
☎ (0742) 734671 or 795901

University of Sheffield
Conference Office, Octagon Centre, Sheffield S10 2TQ
☎ (0742) 768555
Fax (0742) 729097
Telex 547216
Contact: Ms C Davies
Six halls of residence in a quiet suburb near the city centre and adjacent to the Peak District National Park.
Bedrooms: 2100 single, 100 double/twin. Total number of beds: 2300
Bathrooms: 300 public

GROUP & YOUTH SECTION

Bed & breakfast		
per person:	£min	£max
Daily	14.00	19.75

Full board		
per person:	£min	£max
Weekly	120.00	240.00

Lunch available
Parking for 600
Open January, March-April, July-September, December

SOUTHAMPTON
Hampshire
Map ref 2C3

One of Britain's leading seaports with a long history, now a major container port. In the 18th C it became a fashionable resort with the assembly rooms and theatre. The old Guildhall and the Wool House are now museums. Sections of the medieval wall can still be seen.
Tourist Information Centre
☎ *(0703) 221106*

Southampton YMCA
George Williams House, Cranbury Place, Southampton SO2 0LG
☎ (0703) 221202
Contact: The Executive Director
Educational groups welcome from home and overseas. Bookings also welcome from individuals and couples.
Minimum age 10
Bedrooms: 74 single, 4 double/twin.
Total number of beds: 82
Bathrooms: 15 public

Bed & breakfast		
per person:	£min	£max
Daily	12.00	14.00

Parking for 10

SOWERBY BRIDGE
West Yorkshire
Map ref 4B1

Busy little town in the Calder Valley near the Calder Hebble Canal.

Mill Bank Centre
AMIT (Personal and Training Services), Mill Bank, Sowerby Bridge HX6 3DY
☎ Halifax (0422) 824388 & 824189
Contact: Mr J Haymer
Well-equipped residential centre with conference facilities, in a converted chapel overlooking a Pennine conservation village. Centrally heated, with carpets and Continental quilts. Prices vary according to number in group - please ask for details.
For groups only
Minimum age 10

Bedrooms: 1 single, 3 double/twin, 3 dormitories. Total number of beds: 32
Bathrooms: 6 public

Bed only		
per person:	£min	£max
Daily	18.00	

Lunch available
Parking for 10

STANLEY
Durham
Map ref 5C2

Small town on the site of a Roman cattle camp. At the Beamish North of England Open Air Museum numerous set-pieces and displays recreate industrial and social conditions prevalent during the area's past.

Beamish Hall
Stanley, County Durham DH9 0RG
☎ (0207) 233147
Fax (0207) 281723
Contact: Mr T M McKeon
Weekend and holiday courses for adults. Residential facilities for groups of all ages, close to Beamish Museum.
For groups only
Bedrooms: 18 single, 10 double/twin, 6 dormitories. Total number of beds: 80
Bathrooms: 6 public

Bed & breakfast		
per person:	£min	£max
Daily	17.50	

Full board		
per person:	£min	£max
Weekly	196.00	

Lunch available
Evening meal 1830 (last orders 1830)
Parking for 40

STOKE ROCHFORD
Lincolnshire
Map ref 3A1

Stoke Rochford Hall
Stoke Rochford, Grantham NG33 5EJ
☎ Great Ponton (047 683) 337
Fax (0476) 83534
Contact: Peter Robinson
Elegant Victorian mansion house in 28 acres of beautiful parkland and formal gardens, an idyllic setting for that sought-after country holiday retreat. Creche and activity weeks for children in summer, extensive leisure club with indoor heated swimming pool, 18-hole golf-course adjacent.
Bedrooms: 86 single, 100 double/twin.
Total number of beds: 233
Bathrooms: 68 private, 10 public

Bed & breakfast		
per person:	£min	£max
Daily	27.00	41.00

Lunch available
Evening meal 1900 (last orders 2015)
Parking for 500
Cards accepted: Access, Visa, Diners, Amex, Switch

WICK
Avon
Map ref 2A2

Wick Court Centre
Wick, Bristol BS15 5RB
☎ Bristol (0272) 373562
Contact: Mr N Chiswell Jones
Low cost accommodation especially suitable for young people. Minimum group size 25. Beautiful surroundings. Adventure playground, hard tennis court, river.
For groups only
Bedrooms: 2 double/twin, 13 dormitories. Total number of beds: 58
Bathrooms: 1 private, 9 public

Bed only		
per person:	£min	£max
Daily	7.25	7.25

Bed & breakfast		
per person:	£min	£max
Daily	9.25	12.25

Full board		
per person:	£min	£max
Weekly	109.00	120.00

Parking for 15

YORK
North Yorkshire
Map ref 4C1

Ancient walled city nearly 2000 years old containing many well-preserved medieval buildings. Its Minster has over 100 stained glass windows. Attractions include Castle Museum, National Railway Museum, Jorvik Viking Centre and York Dungeon.
Tourist Information Centre
☎ *(0904) 620557 or 621756 or 643770*

Fairfax House
99 Heslington Road, York YO1 5BJ
☎ (0904) 432095
Contact: Mrs. A E Glover
Student residence in quiet spacious grounds, within walking distance of town centre. Reduced rates for children under 12 and senior citizens.
Bedrooms: 93 single. Total number of beds: 93
Bathrooms: 14 public

Bed & breakfast		
per person:	£min	£max
Daily	16.00	18.00

Open March-April, July-September

397

GROUP & YOUTH SECTION

YORK
Continued

York Youth Hotel
11-13 Bishophill Senior, York
YO1 1EF
☎ (0904) 625904 & 630613
Fax (0904) 612494
Contact: Ms Maureen Sellers

Dormitory-style accommodation in the city centre. Private rooms, TV lounge, snack shop, evening meals, packed lunches, games room, residential licence, disco and 24-hour service.

Minimum age 2
Bedrooms: 7 single, 14 double/twin, 1 triple, 4 quadruple, 5 dormitories.
Total number of beds: 120
Bathrooms: 8 public

Bed only
per person:	£min	£max
Daily	8.00	12.00

Bed & breakfast
per person:	£min	£max
Daily	9.30	14.30

Full board
per person:	£min	£max
Weekly	115.00	126.00

Evening meal 1700 (last orders 1900)
Cards accepted: Access, Visa

Use your *i*'s

There are more than 550 Tourist Information Centres throughout England offering friendly help with accommodation and holiday ideas as well as suggestions of places to visit and things to do.

In your home town there may be a centre which can help you before you set out. You'll find the address of your nearest Tourist Information Centre in your local Phone Book.

information pages

National Rating Scheme — **page 400**
All you need to know about the national Crown and Lodge ratings.

National Accessible Scheme for Wheelchair Users — **page 402**
Information on the national scheme which categorises places to stay accessible to wheelchair users and others who may have difficulty in walking.

General advice and information — **page 403**
Things to note when making a booking and helpful advice on cancellations, late arrival, complaints, etc.

About the guide entries — **page 406**
How to get the best out of the detailed accommodation entries in this guide, covering locations, prices, symbols, pets, credit cards, etc.

What's on in England 1994 — **page 409**
A guide to some of the major cultural, sporting and other events that will be taking place in England during 1994.

Enquiry coupons — **page 415**
To help you when making contact with individual establishments or advertisers.

Town index — **page 425**
Page numbers for all the cities, towns and villages with accommodation listings.

Index to advertisers — **page 431**
A quick-reference index to all display advertisements.

Mileage chart — **page 432**
Distances by road between key cities and towns in Britain.

Colour maps of England — **page 433**
Apart from being useful route planners, these colour maps pinpoint all the cities, towns and villages with accommodation listings in this guide.

InterCity rail map — **page 447**
A guide to BR InterCity rail services.

National Rating Scheme

The Tourist Boards in Britain operate a national rating scheme for all types of accommodation. The purpose of the scheme is to identify and promote those establishments that the public can use with confidence. The system of facility classification and quality grading also acknowledges those that provide a wider range of facilities and services and higher quality standards.

Over 30,000 places to stay are inspected under the scheme and offer the reassurance of a national rating.

For 'serviced' accommodation (which includes hotels, motels, guesthouses, inns, B&Bs and farmhouses) there are six classification bands, starting with LISTED and then from ONE to FIVE CROWN. For the new generation of 'lodges', offering budget accommodation along major roads and motorways, there are three classification bands, from ONE to THREE MOON.

Quite simply, the more Crowns or Moons, the wider the range of facilities and services offered.

To help you find accommodation that offers even higher standards than those required for a Crown or Moon rating, there are four levels of quality grading, using the terms APPROVED, COMMENDED, HIGHLY COMMENDED and DE LUXE.

Wherever you see a national rating sign, you can be sure that a Tourist Board inspector has been there before you, checking the place on your behalf – and will be there again, because every place with a national rating is inspected annually.

Establishments that apply for quality grading – which is optional – are subject to a more detailed inspection that assesses the quality standard of the facilities and services provided. The initial inspection invariably involves the Tourist Board inspector staying overnight, as a normal guest, until the bill is paid the following morning.

The quality assessment includes such aspects as warmth of welcome and efficiency of service, as well as the standard of the furnishings, fittings and decor. The standard of meals and their presentation is also taken into account. Everything that impinges on the experience of a guest is included in the assessment.

Tourist Board inspectors receive careful training to enable them to apply the quality standards consistently and fairly. Only those facilities and services that are provided are assessed, and due consideration is given to the style and nature of the establishment.

B&Bs, farmhouses and guesthouses are not expected to operate in the style of large city centre hotels, and vice versa. This means that all types of establishment, whatever their classification, can achieve a high quality grade if the facilities and services they provide, however limited in range, are to a high quality standard.

The quality grade that is awarded to an establishment is a reflection of the overall standard, taking everything into account. It is a balanced view of what is provided and, as such, cannot acknowledge individual areas of excellence.

Quality grades are not intended to indicate value for money. A high quality product can be over-priced; a product of modest quality, if offered at a low price, can represent good value. The information provided by the combination of the classification and quality grade will enable you to determine for yourself what represents good value for money.

All establishments listed in this 'Where to Stay' guide have been inspected or are awaiting inspection under the national rating scheme. The ratings that appear in the accommodation entries were correct at the time of going to press but are subject to change. If no rating appears in an entry it means that the inspection had not been carried out by the time of going to press.

An information leaflet giving full details of the national rating scheme – which also covers self-catering holiday homes and caravan, chalet and camping parks – is available from any Tourist Information Centre.

Lodge ratings

In a One Moon 'Lodge', your bedroom will have at least a washbasin and radio or colour TV. Tea/coffee may be from a vending machine in a public area.

Your bedroom in a Two Moon 'Lodge' will have colour TV, tea/coffee-making facilities and en-suite bath or shower with WC.

In a Three Moon 'Lodge', you will find colour TV and radio, tea/coffee-making facilities and comfortable seating in your bedroom and there will be a bath, shower and WC en-suite. The reception area will be manned throughout the night.

INFORMATION PAGES

Your at-a-glance guide to the minimum facilities and services available at each Listed and Crown rating.

THE GRADES: APPROVED, COMMENDED, HIGHLY COMMENDED and **DE LUXE** indicate the quality standard of what is provided. If no grade is shown you can still expect a high standard of cleanliness.

	Listed	One Crown	Two Crown	Three Crown	Four Crown	Five Crown
Clean and comfortable accommodation	✓	✓	✓	✓	✓	✓
Adequate heating at no extra charge	✓	✓	✓	✓	✓	✓
No extra charge for baths or showers	✓	✓	✓	✓	✓	✓
Clean towels, fresh soap	✓	✓	✓	✓	✓	✓
Breakfast	✓	✓	✓	✓	✓	✓
Fire Certificate (where required)	✓	✓	✓	✓	✓	✓
Comfortable lounge or sitting area		✓	✓	✓	✓	✓
A washbasin in your room or private bathroom		✓	✓	✓	✓	✓
Beds no smaller than 6' 3" x 3' (single) or 6' 3" x 4' 6" (double)		✓	✓	✓	✓	✓
No nylon sheets		✓	✓	✓	✓	✓
Cooked breakfast		✓	✓	✓	✓	✓
Use of telephone		✓	✓	✓	✓	✓
Tourist information		✓	✓	✓	✓	✓
Private bathrooms for at least 20% of the bedrooms			✓	✓	✓	✓
Help with your luggage			✓	✓	✓	✓
Colour TV in the lounge or your bedroom			✓	✓	✓	✓
Double beds with access and table at both sides			✓	✓	✓	✓
Bedside lights			✓	✓	✓	✓
Early morning tea/coffee in your room, hot beverage in the evening			✓	✓	✓	✓
En-suite bathrooms for at least 50% of the bedrooms				✓	✓	✓
Easy chair, full length mirror, luggage rack, tea/coffee in your bedroom				✓	✓	✓
Hairdryer, shoe cleaning equipment and ironing facilities available				✓	✓	✓
A public telephone or one in your room				✓	✓	✓
A hot evening meal				✓	✓	✓
En-suite bathrooms for at least 90% of the bedrooms, many with bath and shower					✓	✓
Colour TV, radio and telephone in your bedroom					✓	✓
Room service – drinks and light snacks between 7am and 11pm					✓	✓
Lounge service of drinks and snacks to midnight					✓	✓
Evening meals, with wine, last orders 8.30pm or later					✓	✓
A quiet sitting area					✓	✓
Laundry services					✓	✓
Toiletries, message taking, newspapers on request					✓	✓
All bedrooms with bath, shower and WC en-suite						✓
Direct dial telephone, writing table						✓
Shoe cleaning and daily clothes pressing service						✓
24-hour lounge service and room service with meals up to midnight						✓
Restaurant open for breakfast, lunch and dinner, with last orders 9pm or later						✓
Full liquor licence						✓
Night porter and porterage						✓

Please bear in mind that all Crown classified establishments will provide at least some of the facilities of a higher classification.

National Accessible Scheme for Wheelchair Users

Throughout England, the Tourist Boards are inspecting all types of places to stay, on holiday or business, that provide accessible accommodation for wheelchair users and others who may have difficulty walking. Those that meet the criteria can display their wheelchair access category and symbol at their premises and in their advertising – so look for the symbol when choosing where to stay.

The criteria the Tourist Boards have adopted do not, necessarily, conform to British Standards or to Building Regulations. They reflect what the boards understand to be acceptable to meet the practical needs of wheelchair users.

The Tourist Boards recognise three categories of accessibility:

Category 1
Accessible to all wheelchair users including those travelling independently

Category 2
Accessible to a wheelchair user with assistance

Category 3
Accessible to a wheelchair user able to walk short distances and up at least three steps

If you have additional needs or special requirements of any kind, we strongly recommend that you make sure these can be met by your chosen establishment before you confirm your booking.

❑ The National Accessible Scheme forms part of the Tourism for All Campaign that is being promoted by all three national Tourist Boards. Additional help and guidance on finding suitable holiday accommodation for those with special needs can be obtained from:
Holiday Care Service
2 Old Bank Chambers, Station Road, Horley, Surrey RH6 9HW.
Tel: (0293) 774535.
Fax: (0293) 784647.
Minicom: (0293) 776943 (24-hour answering).

The following establishments listed in this 'Where to Stay' guide had been inspected and given an access category at the time of going to press. Use the Town Index at the back of the guide to find page numbers for their full entries.

Category 1
Wimborne Minster, *Dorset*
  Northill House

Category 3
Ambleside, *Cumbria*
  Borrans Park Hotel
Beverley, *Humberside*
  Rudstone Walk Farm, Country House and Conference Centre
Blandford Forum, *Dorset*
  Fairfield House

Boscastle, *Cornwall*
  The Old Coach House
Dorking, *Surrey*
  Bulmer Farm
Earlstoke, *Wiltshire*
  Longwater
Lenham, *Kent*
  Dog and Bear Hotel
Lincoln, *Lincolnshire*
  Garden House
Nailsworth, *Gloucestershire*
  Apple Orchard House
Parkend, *Gloucestershire*
  The Fountain Inn
Richmond, *N. Yorkshire*
  Mount Pleasant Farm
Sarre, *Kent*
  Crown Inn (The Famous Cherry Brandy House)
Thirsk, *N. Yorkshire*
  Doxford House
Thoralby, *N. Yorkshire*
  High Green House
Ullswater, *Cumbria*
  Waterside House
Warwick, *Warwickshire*
  Fulbrook Edge
Winchester, *Hampshire*
  Shawlands
Windermere, *Cumbria*
  The Burn How Garden House Hotel & Motel

General advice and information

MAKING A BOOKING

When enquiring about accommodation, as well as checking prices and other details you will need to state your requirements clearly and precisely – for example:
1. Arrival and departure dates with acceptable alternatives if appropriate.
2. The accommodation you need. For example: double room with twin beds, private bath and WC.
3. The terms you want. For example: room only; bed & breakfast; bed, breakfast and evening meal (half board); bed, breakfast, lunch and evening meal (full board).
4. If you will have children with you give their ages, state whether you would like them to share your room or have an adjacent room and mention any special requirements such as a cot.
5. Tell the management about any particular requirements such as a ground floor room or special diet.

Misunderstandings can occur very easily over the telephone so we recommend that all bookings should be confirmed in writing if time permits.

When first enquiring in writing about a reservation you may find it helpful to use the booking enquiry coupons (pages 415–419) which can be cut out and mailed to the establishment(s) of your choice.

Remember to include your name and address and please enclose a stamped and addressed envelope – or an international reply coupon if writing from outside Britain.

Please note that the English Tourist Board does not make reservations. You should address your enquiry direct to the establishment.

DEPOSITS AND ADVANCE PAYMENTS

For reservations made weeks or months ahead a deposit is usually payable and the amount will vary according to the length of booking, time of year, number in party and so on. The deposit will be deducted from the total bill at the end of your stay.

Some establishments, particularly larger hotels in big towns, now require payment for the room on arrival if a prior reservation has not been made – especially from guests arriving late and/or with little luggage. Regrettably this practice has become necessary because of the number of guests who have left without paying their bills.

If you are asked to pay on arrival it may be advisable to see your room first to ensure that it meets your requirements.

If you book by telephone and are asked for your credit card number, you should note that the proprietor may charge your credit card account if you subsequently cancel the booking.

CANCELLATIONS

When you accept offered accommodation, on the telephone or in writing, you are entering into a legally binding contract with the proprietor. This means that if you cancel a reservation, fail to take up the accommodation or leave prematurely the proprietor may be entitled to compensation if the accommodation cannot be re-let for all or a good part of the booked period. If a deposit has been paid it is likely to be forfeited and an additional payment may be demanded.

However, no such claim can be made by the proprietor until after the booked period, during which time every effort should be made to re-let the accommodation. Any circumstances which might lead to repudiation of a contract may also need to be taken into account and, in the case of a dispute, legal advice should be sought by both parties.

It is therefore in your own interests to advise the management immediately if you have to change your travel plans, cancel a booking or leave prematurely.

Travel and holiday insurance protection policies are available quite cheaply and will safeguard you in the event of your having to cancel or curtail your holiday. Your insurance company or travel agent can advise you further on this. Some hotels also offer insurance schemes.

ARRIVING LATE

If you will be arriving late in the evening it is advisable to say so at the time of booking; if you are

INFORMATION PAGES

delayed on your way, a telephone call to inform the management that you will be late might help to avoid problems on arrival.

SERVICE CHARGES AND TIPPING

Many establishments now levy a service charge automatically and if so this fact must be stated clearly in the offer of accommodation at the time of booking. If the offer is then accepted by you the service charge becomes part of the contract.

At establishments where a service charge of this kind is made there is no need for you to give tips to the staff unless some particular or exceptional service has been rendered. In the case of meals the usual amount is 10% of the total bill.

TELEPHONE CALL CHARGES

There is no restriction on the charges that can be made by hotels for telephone calls made through their switchboard or via direct-dial telephones in bedrooms. Unit charges are frequently considerably higher than telephone companies' standard charges. Hoteliers claim that they need to charge higher rates to defray the cost of providing the service.

Although it is a condition of a national Crown rating that a hotel's unit charges are displayed alongside telephones, it is not always easy to see how these compare with the standard charges. Before using a hotel telephone for long-distance calls within Britain or overseas, you may wish to ask how the charges compare.

SECURITY OF VALUABLES

Property of value may be deposited for safe-keeping with the proprietor or manager of the establishment who should give you a receipt and who will then generally be liable for the value of the property in the case of loss. For your peace of mind we advise you to adopt this procedure. In establishments which do not accept articles for safe custody, you are advised to keep valuables under your personal supervision.

You may find that proprietors of some establishments disclaim, by notice, liability for property brought on to their premises by a guest; however, if a guest engages overnight accommodation in a hotel the proprietor is only permitted to restrict his liability to the minimum imposed upon him under the Hotel Proprietors Act, 1956. Under this Act, a proprietor of a hotel is liable for the value of the loss or damage to any property (other than a motor car or its contents) of a guest who has engaged overnight accommodation, but if the proprietor has a notice in the form prescribed by that Act, liability is limited to the sum of £50 in respect of one article and a total of £100 in the case of any one guest.

These limits do not apply, however, if you have deposited the property with the proprietor for safe-keeping or if the property is lost through the default, neglect or wilful act of the proprietor or his staff.

To be effective, any notice intended to disclaim or restrict liability must be prominently displayed in the reception area of, or in the main entrance to, the premises.

CODE OF CONDUCT

All establishments appearing in this guide have agreed to observe the following Code of Conduct:
1. To ensure high standards of courtesy and cleanliness; catering and service appropriate to the type of establishment.
2. To describe fairly to all visitors and prospective visitors the amenities, facilities and services provided by the establishment, whether by advertisement, brochure, word of mouth or any other means. To allow visitors to see accommodation, if requested, before booking.
3. To make clear to visitors exactly what is included in all prices quoted for accommodation, meals and refreshments, including service charges, taxes and other surcharges. Details of charges, if any, for heating or for additional services or facilities available should also be made clear.
4. To adhere to, and not to exceed, prices current at time of occupation for accommodation or other services.
5. To advise visitors at the time of booking, and subsequently of any change, if the accommodation offered is in an unconnected annexe, or similar, or by boarding out, and to indicate the location of such accommodation and any difference in comfort and amenities from accommodation in the main establishment.
6. To give each visitor, on request, details of payments due and a receipt if required.
7. To deal promptly and courteously with all enquiries, requests, reservations, correspondence and complaints from visitors.
8. To allow an English Tourist Board representative reasonable access to the establishment, on request, to confirm that the Code of Conduct is being observed.

INFORMATION PAGES

COMMENTS AND COMPLAINTS

Accommodation establishments have a number of legal and statutory responsibilities to their customers in areas such as the provision of information on prices, the provision of adequate fire precautions and the safeguarding of valuables. Like other businesses, they must also meet the requirements of the Trade Descriptions Acts 1968 and 1972 when describing and offering accommodation and facilities. All establishments appearing in this guide have declared that they fulfil all applicable statutory obligations.

The establishment descriptions and other details appearing in this guide have been provided by proprietors and they have paid for their entries to appear.

The English Tourist Board cannot guarantee the accuracy of the information in this guide and accepts no responsibility for any error or misrepresentation. All liability for loss, disappointment, negligence or other damage caused by reliance on the information contained in this guide, or in the event of bankruptcy or liquidation or cessation of trade of any company, individual or firm mentioned, is hereby excluded. Prices and other details should always be carefully checked at the time of booking.

We naturally hope that you will not have any cause for complaint but problems do inevitably occur from time to time. If you are dissatisfied, make your complaint to the management at the time of the incident. This gives the management an opportunity to take action at once to investigate and to put things right without delay. The longer a complaint is left the more difficult it is to deal with effectively.

In certain circumstances the English Tourist Board may look into complaints. However, the Board has no statutory control over establishments or their methods of operation and cannot become involved in legal or contractual matters.

We find it very helpful to receive comments about establishments in 'Where to Stay' and suggestions on how to improve the guide. We would like to hear from you. Our address is on page 17.

Key to symbols

Information about many of the services and facilities at accommodation listed in this guide is given in the form of symbols. The key to these symbols is inside the back cover flap. You may find it helpful to keep the flap open when referring to the accommodation listings.

405

About the guide entries

LOCATIONS

Establishments are listed in this guide under the name of the place where they are situated or, in the case of isolated spots in the countryside, under the nearest village or town. Place names are listed alphabetically within each regional section together with the county name.

Map references are given against each place name. These refer to the colour maps at the back of the guide. The first figure is the map number; the letter and figure which follow indicate the grid reference on the map. Some entries were included just before the guide went to press and therefore may not appear on the maps.

ADDRESSES

County names are not normally repeated in the entries for each establishment but you should ensure that you use the full postal address and postcode when writing.

TELEPHONE NUMBERS

The telephone number, exchange name (where this differs from the name of the town under which the establishment is listed) and STD code (in brackets) are given immediately below the establishment address in the listings pages of this guide. The STD code applies to calls made anywhere in the UK except for local calls.

PRICES

The prices appearing in this publication will serve as a general guide, but we strongly advise you to check them at the time of booking. This information was supplied to us by proprietors in the summer of 1993 and changes may have occurred since the guide went to press.

Prices are shown in pounds sterling and include Value Added Tax if applicable.

Some, but not all, establishments include a service charge in their standard tariff so this should also be checked at the time of booking. There are many different ways of quoting prices for accommodation and in order to make this as clear as possible and provide a basis for comparison we have adopted a standardised approach.

For example, we show:

1. Bed and breakfast. Price for overnight accommodation with breakfast – single room and double room.

The double room price is for two people. If a double room is occupied by one person there is normally a reduction in the quoted tariff, but some establishments may charge the full rate.

2. Half board. Price for room, breakfast and evening meal, per person per day and per person per week.

Some establishments provide a continental breakfast only in the quoted tariff and may make an extra charge for full English breakfast.

There is a statutory requirement for establishments which have at least four bedrooms, or eight beds, to display overnight accommodation charges in the reception area or at the entrance. This is to ensure that prospective guests can obtain adequate information about prices before taking up accommodation. When you arrive it is in your own interests to check prices and what they include.

A reduced price is often quoted for children, especially when sharing a room with their parents. Some establishments, however, charge the full price when a child occupies a room which might otherwise have been let at the full rate to an adult.

The upper age limit for reductions for children may vary according to the establishment and should therefore be checked at the time of booking.

Prices often vary according to the time of year and may be substantially lower outside the peak holiday weeks. Many hotels and other establishments offer special 'package' rates (for example, fully inclusive weekend rates) particularly in the autumn, winter and spring.

Further details of bargain packages can be obtained from the establishments themselves or from the English Tourist Board and England's Regional Tourist Boards. Your local travel agent may also have information about these packages and can help you make bookings.

BATHROOMS

Each accommodation entry shows the number of private bathrooms available, the number of public bathrooms and the number of

INFORMATION PAGES

private showers. The term 'private bathroom' means a bath and/or shower plus a WC en suite with the bedroom or a bathroom with bath and/or shower plus a WC solely for the occupant(s) of one bedroom; 'private shower' means a shower en suite with the bedroom but no WC.

Public bathrooms are normally equipped with a bath and sometimes also a shower attachment. Some establishments, however, have showers only. If the availability of a bath is an important factor, this should be checked before booking.

MEALS

Where an establishment serves evening meals, the starting time and last orders time are shown in each entry. At some smaller establishments you may be asked at breakfast time or midday whether you will require a meal that evening. So, the last orders time for an evening meal could be, say, 0900 or 1330.

Although the accommodation prices shown in each entry are for bed and breakfast and/or half board, many establishments also offer luncheon facilities and this is indicated by the words 'Lunch available'.

OPENING PERIODS

Except where an opening period is shown (e.g. Open March–October), the establishment should be open throughout the year.

SYMBOLS

Information about many of the services and facilities available at establishments is given at the end of each entry in the form of symbols.

The key to these symbols can be found inside the back cover flap. You may find it helpful to fold out the flap when referring to the entries.

ALCOHOLIC DRINKS

Alcoholic drinks are available at all types of accommodation listed in this guide unless the symbol [UL] appears. However, the licence to serve drinks may be restricted, for example to diners only, so you may wish to check this when enquiring about accommodation.

SMOKING

Many establishments offer facilities for non-smokers, ranging from no-smoking bedrooms and lounges to a no-smoking area of the restaurant/dining room. Some establishments prefer not to accommodate smokers and in such cases the establishment description makes this clear.

PETS

Many establishments will accept guests with pets but we advise you to confirm this at the time of booking when you should also enquire about any extra charges and any restrictions on movement within the establishment. Some establishments will not accept dogs in any circumstances and these are marked with the symbol 🐾.

Visitors from overseas should not bring pets of any kind into Britain unless they are prepared for the animals to go into lengthy quarantine. Owing to the continuing threat of rabies, penalties for ignoring the regulations are extremely severe.

CREDIT/CHARGE CARDS

Indicated immediately above the line of symbols at the end of each accommodation entry are credit/charge cards that are accepted by the establishment. However, you are advised to confirm this at the time you make a booking if you intend to pay by this method. The abbreviations are:

Access – Access/Eurocard/Mastercard
Visa – Visa/Barclaycard
Diners – Diners
Amex – American Express
Switch – Direct debit card

Where payment for the accommodation is made by credit card, proprietors may charge a higher rate than for payment by cash or cheque. The difference is to cover the percentage paid by the proprietor to the credit card company.

Not all proprietors make this additional charge but if you intend to pay by credit card, it is worth asking whether it would be cheaper to pay by cash or cheque.

When making a booking by telephone you may be asked to give your credit card number as 'confirmation'. You should note that the proprietor may charge your credit card account if you cancel the booking. If this is the policy, it must be made clear to you at the time you make the booking.

CONFERENCES AND GROUPS

Establishments which can cater for conferences and meetings have been marked with the symbol ⚑ (numbers following show capacity). Rates are often negotiable and the price may be affected by a number of factors such as the time of year, number of people and any special requirements stipulated by the organiser.

THE ENGLAND FOR EXCELLENCE AWARDS 1992 WINNERS

The England for Excellence Awards were created by the English Tourist Board to recognise and reward the highest standards of excellence and quality in all major sectors of tourism in England. The coveted Leo statuette, presented each year to winners, has become firmly established as the ultimate accolade in the English tourism industry.

Over the past five years, the Leo has been won by all types and sizes of business with one common attribute – excellence in the facilities and services they offer.

Thames Tower
Black's Road
London W6 9EL

English Tourist Board

Resort of the Year sponsored by Marks & Spencer
BOURNEMOUTH

Bed and Breakfast Award sponsored by Le Shuttle
THE OLD RECTORY, Ripon

Attraction of the Year sponsored by Blackpool Pleasure Beach Limited
NATIONAL FISHING HERITAGE CENTRE

Hotel of the Year sponsored by Horwath Consulting
THE LANESBOROUGH

TIC of the Year sponsored by Holiday Property Bond Limited
FONTWELL TIC

Self-Catering Holiday of the Year sponsored by Hoseasons Holidays Limited
ANGLERS' PARADISE HOLIDAYS

Tourism and the Environment Award sponsored by Center Parcs Limited
LOSEHILL HALL, PEAK NATIONAL PARK CENTRE

Travel Journalist of the Year sponsored by Forte Plc
PAUL GOGARTY

Hotel Company of the Year sponsored by RCI Europe Limited
HILTON UNITED KINGDOM

Tourism for all Award sponsored by RAC Enterprises Limited
MUSEUM OF SCIENCE AND INDUSTRY IN MANCHESTER

Tourism and the Arts Award sponsored by First Leisure Corporation Plc
GREATER MANCHESTER VISITOR AND CONVENTION BUREAU/MANCHESTER INTERNATIONAL FESTIVAL OF EXPRESSIONISM

Caravan Holiday Park Award sponsored by the National Caravan Council
FOXHUNTER PARK

Tourism Training Award sponsored by The Tussauds Group Limited
LUCKETTS TRAVEL

English Travel Company of the Year sponsored by BTTF
BUTLIN'S LIMITED

Outstanding Contribution to English Tourism Award sponsored by Hilton UK
SIR ANDREW LLOYD WEBBER

INFORMATION PAGES

What's on in England 1994

This is a selection of the many cultural, sporting and other events that will be taking place in England during 1994. Dates marked with an asterisk (✻) were provisional at the time of going to press. For details of local events please enquire at the local Tourist Information Centre.

JANUARY 1994

1 January–31 December
TOWER CENTENARY YEAR 1994
Tower World, Promenade, Blackpool, Lancashire

5–30 January
HOLIDAY ON ICE '94
Brighton Centre, Kings Road, Brighton, East Sussex

6–16 January
LONDON INTERNATIONAL BOAT SHOW
Earl's Court Exhibition Centre, Warwick Road, London SW5

FEBRUARY 1994

4–19 February
JORVIK FESTIVAL
Various venues, York, North Yorkshire

13 February
CHINESE NEW YEAR CELEBRATIONS
'Chinatown', Gerrard Street and Leicester Square, London W1

19–27 February
BOAT, CARAVAN AND LEISURE SHOW
National Exhibition Centre, Birmingham, West Midlands

MARCH 1994

5–6 March
DOLLS, DOLLS' HOUSES AND MINIATURES FAIR
Dunham Massey Hall, Altrincham, Greater Manchester

10–13 March
CRUFTS DOG SHOW
National Exhibition Centre, Birmingham, West Midlands

15–17 March
HORSE RACING: CHELTENHAM GOLD CUP MEETING
Cheltenham Racecourse, Prestbury, Cheltenham, Gloucestershire

17 March–10 April
DAILY MAIL IDEAL HOME EXHIBITION
Earl's Court Exhibition Centre, Warwick Road, London SW5

18–20 March
INTERNATIONAL CLOWNS CONVENTION
Various venues, Bognor Regis, West Sussex

19 March
NATIONAL SHIRE HORSE SHOW
East of England Showground, Alwalton, Peterborough, Cambridgeshire

21–24 March
BOWLING: BRITISH ISLES CHAMPIONSHIPS AND INTERNATIONAL SERIES
Blackpool Borough Indoor Bowls Club, Lark Hill Street, Blackpool, Lancashire

26 March
ROWING: OXFORD v CAMBRIDGE UNIVERSITY BOAT RACE
Putney to Mortlake, River Thames, London

409

INFORMATION PAGES

30 March–6 April
HARROGATE INTERNATIONAL YOUTH MUSIC FESTIVAL
Various venues, Harrogate, North Yorkshire

APRIL 1994

2–4 April
EASTER EGG HUNT
Leeds Castle, Maidstone, Kent

3–4 April
MEDIEVAL JOUSTING TOURNAMENTS
Knebworth Park, Stevenage, Hertfordshire

4 April
WORLD COAL CARRYING CHAMPIONSHIP
Gawthorpe, Ossett, West Yorkshire

7–9 April ✽
HORSE RACING: GRAND NATIONAL MEETING
Aintree Racecourse, Liverpool, Merseyside

7–13 April
BRITISH INTERNATIONAL ANTIQUES FAIR
National Exhibition Centre, Birmingham, West Midlands

21–24 April
HARROGATE SPRING FLOWER SHOW
Valley Gardens, Harrogate, North Yorkshire

22–24 April
CHESHIRE SPRING SHOW
Marbury Country Park, Comberbach, Northwich, Cheshire

24 April
TEESDALE COUNTRY FAIR
Lartington Park, Barnard Castle, Durham

27 April
INTERNATIONAL ANTIQUES AND COLLECTORS FAIR
The Showground, South of England Centre, Ardingly, West Sussex

30 April–1 May
GOLF: LYTHAM TROPHY
Royal Lytham and St Anne's Golf Course, Links Gate, Lytham St Anne's, Lancashire

MAY 1994

May–September
CHICHESTER FESTIVAL THEATRE SEASON
Chichester, West Sussex

5–8 May
BADMINTON HORSE TRIALS
Badminton, Avon

5–8 May ✽
GOLF: BENSON AND HEDGES INTERNATIONAL OPEN
St Mellion Golf and Country Club, St Mellion, Saltash, Cornwall

5–8 May
LIVING CRAFTS AT HATFIELD HOUSE
Hatfield House, Hatfield, Hertfordshire

6–7 May
NOTTINGHAMSHIRE COUNTY SHOW
Newark Showground, Winthorpe, Nottinghamshire

6–8 May
MALVERN SPRING GARDEN SHOW
Three Counties Centre, The Showground, Malvern, Hereford and Worcester

7 May
HELSTON FURRY DANCE
Helston, Cornwall

7–9 May
SPALDING FLOWER PARADE AND FESTIVAL
Various venues, Spalding, Lincolnshire

11–15 May
ROYAL WINDSOR HORSE SHOW
Home Park, Windsor, Berkshire

12–15 May
BEVERLEY EARLY MUSIC FESTIVAL
Various venues, Beverley, Humberside

19–21 May
DEVON COUNTY SHOW
Westpoint Showground, Clyst St Mary, Exeter, Devon

20–21 May
SHROPSHIRE AND WEST MIDLANDS AGRICULTURAL SHOW
The Showground, Berwick Road, Shrewsbury, Shropshire

INFORMATION PAGES

20–22 May
KESWICK JAZZ FESTIVAL
Keswick, Cumbria

24–27 May
CHELSEA FLOWER SHOW
Royal Hospital, Royal Hospital Road, Chelsea, London SW3
(Members only 24–25 May)

27 May–3 June
BRITISH OPEN BALLROOM AND LATIN AMERICAN DANCE CHAMPIONSHIPS
Winter Gardens, Church Street, Blackpool, Lancashire

27 May–12 June
BATH INTERNATIONAL FESTIVAL
Various venues, Bath, Avon

28–29 May
AIR FETE '94
RAF Mildenhall, Bury St Edmunds, Suffolk

28–30 May
KNEBWORTH COUNTRY SHOW
Knebworth Park, Stevenage, Hertfordshire

28–30 May ✻
NORTH SHIELDS FISHQUAY FESTIVAL
Various venues, North Shields, Tyne and Wear

28–31 May
BRACKENFIELD WELL DRESSINGS
Brackenfield Church Hall, Church Lane, Brackenfield, Derby, Derbyshire

30 May
NORTHUMBERLAND COUNTY SHOW
Tynedale Park Rugby Ground, Corbridge, Northumberland

JUNE 1994

1–2 June
SUFFOLK SHOW
Suffolk Showground, Bucklesham Road, Ipswich, Suffolk

1–4 June
HORSE RACING:
THE DERBY (1st);
CORONATION CUP (2nd);
INTERNATIONAL DAY (3rd);
OAKS STAKES (4th)
Epsom Racecourse, Epsom, Surrey

1–4 June
ROYAL BATH AND WEST SHOW
Royal Bath and West Showground, Shepton Mallet, Somerset

2–6 June
CRICKET:
FIRST TEST MATCH – ENGLAND v NEW ZEALAND
Nottinghamshire County Cricket Club, Trent Bridge, Nottingham, Nottinghamshire

2–8 June
APPLEBY HORSE FAIR
Appleby, Cumbria

5–6 June
D-DAY ANNIVERSARY AIR DISPLAY
Aeroplane and Armament Experimental Establishment, Boscombe Down Airfield, Amesbury, Salisbury, Wiltshire

9–12 June
BRAMHAM INTERNATIONAL HORSE TRIALS AND YORKSHIRE COUNTRY FAIR
Bramham Park, Bramham, West Yorkshire

10–26 June
ALDEBURGH FESTIVAL OF MUSIC AND THE ARTS
Various venues, Aldeburgh, Suffolk

11–12 June ✻
DURHAM REGATTA
River Wear, Durham, Durham

12 June
VINTAGE VEHICLE GALA
King George Playing Field, Uppermill, Greater Manchester

13–18 June
TENNIS:
VOLKSWAGEN CUP
Devonshire Park, College Road, Eastbourne, East Sussex

14–16 June
THREE COUNTIES AGRICULTURAL SHOW
Three Counties Agricultural Showground, Malvern, Hereford and Worcester

14–17 June
HORSE RACING:
ROYAL ASCOT
Ascot Racecourse, Ascot, Berkshire

17 June–9 July
BRADFORD FESTIVAL
Various venues, Bradford, West Yorkshire

20 June–3 July ✻
LAWN TENNIS CHAMPIONSHIPS
All England Lawn Tennis and Croquet Club, Wimbledon, London SW19

411

INFORMATION PAGES

22–23 June
LINCOLNSHIRE SHOW
Lincolnshire Showground, Grange-de-Lings, Lincoln, Lincolnshire

24–26 June
UPTON JAZZ FESTIVAL
Various venues, Upton-upon-Severn, Hereford and Worcester

25 June–10 July
LUDLOW FESTIVAL
Various venues, Ludlow, Shropshire

26 June–2 July
ALNWICK FAIR
Various venues, Alnwick, Northumberland

29–30 June
ROYAL NORFOLK SHOW
The Showground, Dereham Road, Norwich, Norfolk

29 June–3 July
HENLEY ROYAL REGATTA
Henley-on-Thames, Oxfordshire

30 June
CENTENARY OF TOWER BRIDGE
Tower Bridge, London SE1

JULY 1994

1–10 July
BIRMINGHAM INTERNATIONAL JAZZ FESTIVAL
Various venues, Birmingham, West Midlands

2–3 July
BATTLE OF MARSTON MOOR
Long Marston and Tockwith, North Yorkshire

4–7 July
ROYAL INTERNATIONAL AGRICULTURAL SHOW
National Agricultural Centre, Stoneleigh, Kenilworth, Warwickshire

6–7 July
CYCLING: TOUR DE FRANCE (BRITISH STAGES)
Various venues, Kent to East Sussex (6th) and Hampshire (7th)

10 July
AMERICAN AUTO CLUB RALLY
Knebworth House, Knebworth Park, Stevenage, Hertfordshire

10 July ✶
MOTOR RACING: BRITISH GRAND PRIX
Silverstone Circuit, Towcester, Northamptonshire

12–14 July
GREAT YORKSHIRE SHOW
Great Yorkshire Showground, Hookstone Oval, Wetherby Road, Harrogate, North Yorkshire

13–17 July
CLAREMONT LANDSCAPE GARDEN FETE CHAMPETRE
Claremont Landscape Garden, Old Portsmouth Road, Esher, Surrey

15 July–10 September
HENRY WOOD PROMENADE CONCERTS
Royal Albert Hall, Kensington Gore, London SW7

16–17 July ✶
DURHAM COUNTY AGRICULTURAL SHOW
Lambton Park, Chester-le-Street, Durham

16–17 July
MASHAM STEAM ENGINE AND FAIR ORGAN RALLY
Lowburton Hall, Masham, North Yorkshire

17 July
TOLPUDDLE MARTYRS RALLY
Tolpuddle, Dorset

19–21 July
EAST OF ENGLAND SHOW
East of England Showground, Peterborough, Cambridgeshire

20–23 July
FETE CHAMPETRE – STOURHEAD'S ENCHANTED GARDEN
Stourhead House and Gardens, Stourton, Wiltshire

23 July
CLEVELAND COUNTY SHOW
Stewart Park, Middlesbrough, Cleveland

26–28 July
NEW FOREST AND HAMPSHIRE COUNTY SHOW
New Park, Brockenhurst, Hampshire

29 July–5 August
INTERNATIONAL FESTIVAL OF FOLK ARTS
Various venues, Sidmouth, Devon

30 July–6 August
SAILING: COWES WEEK
Cowes, Isle of Wight

30 July–13 August
LAKE DISTRICT SUMMER MUSIC FESTIVAL
Charlotte Mason College, Rydal Road, Ambleside, Cumbria

412

INFORMATION PAGES

AUGUST 1994

3–4 August
BAKEWELL SHOW
The Showground, Coombe Road, Bakewell, Derbyshire

4 August
LAKE DISTRICT SHEEPDOG TRIALS
Hill Farm, Ings, Windermere, Cumbria

5–7 August
CLASSIC MOTOR BOAT RALLY
Windermere Steamboat Museum, Rayrigg Road, Windermere, Cumbria

5–7 August
LOWTHER HORSE DRIVING TRIALS AND COUNTRY FAIR
Lowther Castle, Penrith, Cumbria

5–7 August
PORTSMOUTH AND SOUTHSEA SHOW
Southsea Common, Southsea, Hampshire

13–20 August
BILLINGHAM INTERNATIONAL FOLKLORE FESTIVAL
Various venues, Billingham, Cleveland

18 August
GRASMERE SPORTS
Sports Field, Stock Lane, Grasmere, Cumbria

20 August
ASHBOURNE SHOW
The Polo Ground, Osmaston, Ashbourne, Derbyshire

20–21 August
GARLIC FESTIVAL
Fighting Cocks, Cross Roads, Bathingbourne, Isle of Wight

20–29 August
INTERNATIONAL BRASS FESTIVAL
Various venues, Wensleydale, North Yorkshire

21–26 August
THREE CHOIRS FESTIVAL
Hereford Cathedral, Hereford, Hereford and Worcester

23–29 August *
BEATLES FESTIVAL
Various venues, Liverpool, Merseyside

25–27 August
PORT OF DARTMOUTH ROYAL REGATTA
Dartmouth, Devon

28–29 August
CLASSIC CAR SHOW
Knebworth House, Knebworth Park, Stevenage, Hertfordshire

28–29 August
NOTTING HILL CARNIVAL
Ladbroke Grove, London W11

29 August
KESWICK SHOW
Keswick Showground, Crossings Field, Keswick, Cumbria

SEPTEMBER 1994

1–4 September
BURGHLEY HORSE TRIALS
Burghley House, Stamford, Lincolnshire

2–18 September *
SALISBURY FESTIVAL
Various venues, Salisbury, Wiltshire

2 September–6 November *
BLACKPOOL ILLUMINATIONS
The Promenade, Blackpool, Lancashire

3–4 September
ENGLISH WINE FESTIVAL AND REGIONAL FOOD FAIR
English Wine Centre, Alfriston Roundabout, Alfriston, East Sussex

9 September–5 November *
SUNDERLAND ILLUMINATIONS
Roker and Seaburn, Sunderland, Tyne and Wear

10–11 September
BEAULIEU INTERNATIONAL AUTOJUMBLE
National Motor Museum, Beaulieu, Hampshire

10–11 September
FARNBOROUGH INTERNATIONAL – AEROSPACE EXHIBITION AND FLYING DISPLAY
Defence Research Agency, Farnborough, Hampshire

10–12 September
STANHOPE AGRICULTURAL SHOW
Unthank Park, Stanhope, Durham

15–18 September
BLENHEIM INTERNATIONAL HORSE TRIALS
Blenheim Palace, Woodstock, Oxfordshire

16–24 September
SOUTHAMPTON INTERNATIONAL BOAT SHOW
Mayflower Park, Southampton, Hampshire

17 September
EGREMONT CRAB FAIR
Baybarrow, Egremont, Cumbria

OCTOBER 1994

3–16 October *
NORFOLK AND NORWICH FESTIVAL
Various venues, Norwich, Norfolk

4–9 October *
HORSE OF THE YEAR SHOW
Wembley Arena, Empire Way, Wembley, Middlesex

6–8 October
NOTTINGHAM GOOSE FAIR
Forest Recreation Ground, Nottingham, Nottinghamshire

413

INFORMATION PAGES

8 October
ALWINTON BORDER SHEPHERDS' SHOW
The Haugh, Alwinton, Morpeth, Northumberland

8–22 October
CANTERBURY FESTIVAL
Various venues, Canterbury, Kent

9 October
WORLD CONKER CHAMPIONSHIP
Village Green, Ashton, Oundle, Northamptonshire

13–28 October
LEEDS INTERNATIONAL FILM FESTIVAL
Various venues, Leeds, West Yorkshire

17–20 October
BLACKPOOL SEQUENCE DANCE FESTIVAL
Winter Gardens, Church Street, Blackpool, Lancashire

17–21 October
POWERBOAT RACING: WINDERMERE RECORD ATTEMPTS
Low Wood Watersports Centre, Low Wood, Windermere, Cumbria

21–23 October
SOUTHERN COUNTIES CRAFT AND DESIGN SHOW
The Maltings, Bridge Square, Farnham, Surrey

NOVEMBER 1994

3 November
BRIDGWATER GUY FAWKES CARNIVAL
Bridgwater, Somerset

5 November
ALNWICK NORTHUMBRIAN GATHERING
Duchess's School, Alnwick Castle, Alnwick, Northumberland

10–12 November
BLACKPOOL CLOSED DANCE FESTIVAL
Winter Gardens, Church Street, Blackpool, Lancashire

11–13 November
HOLKER HALL ANTIQUES FAIR
Holker Hall, Cark-in-Cartmel, Grange-over-Sands, Cumbria

12 November ✻
LORD MAYOR'S PROCESSION AND SHOW
The City, London

DECEMBER 1994

3–4 December
DICKENSIAN CHRISTMAS
Various venues, Rochester, Kent

15–18 December ✻
LINCOLN CHRISTMAS MARKET
Lincoln, Lincolnshire

16–20 December ✻
OLYMPIA INTERNATIONAL SHOWJUMPING CHAMPIONSHIPS
Olympia, Hammersmith Road, London W14

Use your *i*'s

There are more than 550 Tourist Information Centres throughout England offering friendly help with accommodation and holiday ideas as well as suggestions of places to visit and things to do. In your home town there may be a centre which can help you before you set out. You'll find the address of your nearest Tourist Information Centre in your local Phone Book.

booking coupons

▶ **Complete this coupon and mail it direct to the establishment in which you are interested. Do not send it to the English Tourist Board. Remember to enclose a stamped addressed envelope (or international reply coupon).**

▶ **Tick as appropriate and complete the reverse side if you are interested in making a booking.**

❑ Please send me a brochure or further information, and details of prices charged.

❑ Please advise me, as soon as possible, if accommodation is available as detailed overleaf.

Name: _____ (BLOCK CAPITALS)

Address: _____

_____

_____ Postcode: _____

Telephone number: _____ Date: _____

Where to Stay 1994
BED & BREAKFAST, FARMHOUSES, INNS & HOSTELS   English Tourist Board

---

▶ **Complete this coupon and mail it direct to the establishment in which you are interested. Do not send it to the English Tourist Board. Remember to enclose a stamped addressed envelope (or international reply coupon).**

▶ **Tick as appropriate and complete the reverse side if you are interested in making a booking.**

❑ Please send me a brochure or further information, and details of prices charged.

❑ Please advise me, as soon as possible, if accommodation is available as detailed overleaf.

Name: _____ (BLOCK CAPITALS)

Address: _____

_____

_____ Postcode: _____

Telephone number: _____ Date: _____

Where to Stay 1994
BED & BREAKFAST, FARMHOUSES, INNS & HOSTELS   English Tourist Board

booking coupons

▶ **Complete this side if you are interested in making a booking.**
Please advise me if accommodation is available as detailed below.

From (date of arrival): _____ To (date of departure): _____

or alternatively from: _____ To: _____

Adults _____ Children _____ (ages _____)
Please give the number of people and ages of children

Accommodation required: _____

_____

_____

Meals required: _____

Other/special requirements: _____

▶ Please enclose a stamped addressed envelope (or international reply coupon).
▶ Please read the information on pages 403–407 before confirming any booking.

▶ **Complete this side if you are interested in making a booking.**
Please advise me if accommodation is available as detailed below.

From (date of arrival): _____ To (date of departure): _____

or alternatively from: _____ To: _____

Adults _____ Children _____ (ages _____)
Please give the number of people and ages of children

Accommodation required: _____

_____

_____

Meals required: _____

Other/special requirements: _____

▶ Please enclose a stamped addressed envelope (or international reply coupon).
▶ Please read the information on pages 403–407 before confirming any booking.

booking coupons

▶ **Complete this coupon and mail it direct to the establishment in which you are interested. Do not send it to the English Tourist Board. Remember to enclose a stamped addressed envelope (or international reply coupon).**

▶ **Tick as appropriate and complete the reverse side if you are interested in making a booking.**

❏ Please send me a brochure or further information, and details of prices charged.

❏ Please advise me, as soon as possible, if accommodation is available as detailed overleaf.

Name: _____ (BLOCK CAPITALS)

Address: _____

_____

_____ Postcode: _____

Telephone number: _____ Date: _____

Where to Stay 1994
BED & BREAKFAST, FARMHOUSES, INNS & HOSTELS   English Tourist Board

---

▶ **Complete this coupon and mail it direct to the establishment in which you are interested. Do not send it to the English Tourist Board. Remember to enclose a stamped addressed envelope (or international reply coupon).**

▶ **Tick as appropriate and complete the reverse side if you are interested in making a booking.**

❏ Please send me a brochure or further information, and details of prices charged.

❏ Please advise me, as soon as possible, if accommodation is available as detailed overleaf.

Name: _____ (BLOCK CAPITALS)

Address: _____

_____

_____ Postcode: _____

Telephone number: _____ Date: _____

Where to Stay 1994
BED & BREAKFAST, FARMHOUSES, INNS & HOSTELS   English Tourist Board

booking coupons

▶ **Complete this side if you are interested in making a booking.**
Please advise me if accommodation is available as detailed below.

From (date of arrival): To (date of departure):

or alternatively from: To:

Adults   Children   (ages   )
Please give the number of people and ages of children
Accommodation required:

Meals required:

Other/special requirements:

▶ **Please enclose a stamped addressed envelope (or international reply coupon).**
▶ **Please read the information on pages 403–407 before confirming any booking.**

▶ **Complete this side if you are interested in making a booking.**
Please advise me if accommodation is available as detailed below.

From (date of arrival): To (date of departure):

or alternatively from: To:

Adults   Children   (ages   )
Please give the number of people and ages of children
Accommodation required:

Meals required:

Other/special requirements:

▶ **Please enclose a stamped addressed envelope (or international reply coupon).**
▶ **Please read the information on pages 403–407 before confirming any booking.**

booking coupons

▶ **Complete this coupon and mail it direct to the establishment in which you are interested. Do not send it to the English Tourist Board. Remember to enclose a stamped addressed envelope (or international reply coupon).**

▶ **Tick as appropriate and complete the reverse side if you are interested in making a booking.**

❏ Please send me a brochure or further information, and details of prices charged.

❏ Please advise me, as soon as possible, if accommodation is available as detailed overleaf.

Name: _____ (BLOCK CAPITALS)

Address: _____

_____

_____ Postcode: _____

Telephone number: _____ Date: _____

Where to Stay 1994
BED & BREAKFAST, FARMHOUSES, INNS & HOSTELS   English Tourist Board

---

▶ **Complete this coupon and mail it direct to the establishment in which you are interested. Do not send it to the English Tourist Board. Remember to enclose a stamped addressed envelope (or international reply coupon).**

▶ **Tick as appropriate and complete the reverse side if you are interested in making a booking.**

❏ Please send me a brochure or further information, and details of prices charged.

❏ Please advise me, as soon as possible, if accommodation is available as detailed overleaf.

Name: _____ (BLOCK CAPITALS)

Address: _____

_____

_____ Postcode: _____

Telephone number: _____ Date: _____

Where to Stay 1994
BED & BREAKFAST, FARMHOUSES, INNS & HOSTELS   English Tourist Board

booking coupons

▶ **Complete this side if you are interested in making a booking.**

Please advise me if accommodation is available as detailed below.

From (date of arrival): _____ To (date of departure): _____

or alternatively from: _____ To: _____

Adults _____ Children _____ (ages _____)
Please give the number of people and ages of children

Accommodation required: _____

_____

Meals required: _____

Other/special requirements: _____

▶ **Please enclose a stamped addressed envelope (or international reply coupon).**
▶ **Please read the information on pages 403–407 before confirming any booking.**

▶ **Complete this side if you are interested in making a booking.**

Please advise me if accommodation is available as detailed below.

From (date of arrival): _____ To (date of departure): _____

or alternatively from: _____ To: _____

Adults _____ Children _____ (ages _____)
Please give the number of people and ages of children

Accommodation required: _____

_____

Meals required: _____

Other/special requirements: _____

▶ **Please enclose a stamped addressed envelope (or international reply coupon).**
▶ **Please read the information on pages 403–407 before confirming any booking.**

advertisement coupons

▶ **Complete this coupon and mail it direct to the advertiser from whom you would like to receive further information. Do not send it to the English Tourist Board.**

To (advertiser's name): _____

Please send me a brochure or further information on the following, as advertised by you in the English Tourist Board's *Where to Stay 1994* Guide:

_____

_____

My name and address are on the reverse.

▶ **Complete this coupon and mail it direct to the advertiser from whom you would like to receive further information. Do not send it to the English Tourist Board.**

To (advertiser's name): _____

Please send me a brochure or further information on the following, as advertised by you in the English Tourist Board's *Where to Stay 1994* Guide:

_____

_____

My name and address are on the reverse.

▶ **Complete this coupon and mail it direct to the advertiser from whom you would like to receive further information. Do not send it to the English Tourist Board.**

To (advertiser's name): _____

Please send me a brochure or further information on the following, as advertised by you in the English Tourist Board's *Where to Stay 1994* Guide:

_____

_____

My name and address are on the reverse.

advertisement **coupons**

Name: _____ (BLOCK CAPITALS)

Address: _____

_____

_____ Postcode: _____

Telephone number: _____ Date: _____

Where to Stay 1994
BED & BREAKFAST, FARMHOUSES, INNS & HOSTELS — English Tourist Board

---

Name: _____ (BLOCK CAPITALS)

Address: _____

_____

_____ Postcode: _____

Telephone number: _____ Date: _____

Where to Stay 1994
BED & BREAKFAST, FARMHOUSES, INNS & HOSTELS — English Tourist Board

---

Name: _____ (BLOCK CAPITALS)

Address: _____

_____

_____ Postcode: _____

Telephone number: _____ Date: _____

Where to Stay 1994
BED & BREAKFAST, FARMHOUSES, INNS & HOSTELS — English Tourist Board

advertisement coupons

▶ **Complete this coupon and mail it direct to the advertiser from whom you would like to receive further information. Do not send it to the English Tourist Board.**

To (advertiser's name):

Please send me a brochure or further information on the following, as advertised by you in the English Tourist Board's *Where to Stay 1994* Guide:

_____

_____

My name and address are on the reverse.

▶ **Complete this coupon and mail it direct to the advertiser from whom you would like to receive further information. Do not send it to the English Tourist Board.**

To (advertiser's name):

Please send me a brochure or further information on the following, as advertised by you in the English Tourist Board's *Where to Stay 1994* Guide:

_____

_____

My name and address are on the reverse.

▶ **Complete this coupon and mail it direct to the advertiser from whom you would like to receive further information. Do not send it to the English Tourist Board.**

To (advertiser's name):

Please send me a brochure or further information on the following, as advertised by you in the English Tourist Board's *Where to Stay 1994* Guide:

_____

_____

My name and address are on the reverse.

advertisement **coupons**

Name: _____ (BLOCK CAPITALS)

Address: _____

_____

_____ Postcode: _____

Telephone number: _____ Date: _____

Where to Stay 1994
BED & BREAKFAST, FARMHOUSES, INNS & HOSTELS

[English Tourist Board]

Name: _____ (BLOCK CAPITALS)

Address: _____

_____

_____ Postcode: _____

Telephone number: _____ Date: _____

Where to Stay 1994
BED & BREAKFAST, FARMHOUSES, INNS & HOSTELS

[English Tourist Board]

Name: _____ (BLOCK CAPITALS)

Address: _____

_____

_____ Postcode: _____

Telephone number: _____ Date: _____

Where to Stay 1994
BED & BREAKFAST, FARMHOUSES, INNS & HOSTELS

[English Tourist Board]

Town index

The following cities, towns and villages all have accommodation listed in this guide. If the place where you wish to stay is not shown, the colour maps (starting on page 433) will help you to find somewhere suitable in the same area.

A	page no
Abberton *Essex*	216
Abbotsbury *Dorset*	253
Abbotts Ann *Hampshire*	318
Abingdon *Oxfordshire*	318
Abinger Common *Surrey*	356
Abthorpe *Northamptonshire*	196
Acaster Malbis *North Yorkshire*	104
Acle *Norfolk*	216
Adstone *Northamptonshire*	196
Alcester *Warwickshire*	138
Alderley Edge *Cheshire*	88
Aldham *Essex*	216
Aldwark *Derbyshire*	196
Alford *Lincolnshire*	196
Alkmonton *Derbyshire*	196
Allerford *Somerset*	253
Alnmouth *Northumberland*	66
Alnwick *Northumberland*	66
Alston *Cumbria*	42
Alton *Hampshire*	318
Alton *Staffordshire*	138
Altrincham *Greater Manchester*	88
Alvechurch *Hereford and Worcester*	139
Amble-by-the-Sea *Northumberland*	67
Ambleside *Cumbria*	42
Amersham *Buckinghamshire*	319
Amesbury *Wiltshire*	253
Ampney Crucis *Gloucestershire*	140
Amport *Hampshire*	319
Ampthill *Bedfordshire*	216
Ancaster *Lincolnshire*	197
Andover *Hampshire*	319
Appleby-in-Westmorland *Cumbria*	44
Appledore *Kent*	356
Ardingly *West Sussex*	356
Arundel *West Sussex*	357
Ascot *Berkshire*	319
Ashbourne *Derbyshire*	197
Ashbrittle *Somerset*	254
Ashburton *Devon*	254
Ashford *Kent*	357
Ashford in the Water *Derbyshire*	197
Ashover *Derbyshire*	197
Ashton Keynes *Wiltshire*	254
Askrigg *North Yorkshire*	104
Asthall Leigh *Oxfordshire*	320
Aston Clinton *Buckinghamshire*	320

Avon Dassett *Warwickshire*	140
Aylesbury *Buckinghamshire*	320
Aylesford *Kent*	358
Aylsham *Norfolk*	217
Aysgarth *North Yorkshire*	105

B	page no
Bacup *Lancashire*	88
Bainbridge *North Yorkshire*	105
Bakewell *Derbyshire*	198
Baldersdale *Durham*	67
Balk *North Yorkshire*	105
Balsall Common *West Midlands*	140
Bamburgh *Northumberland*	67
Bampton *Oxfordshire*	320
Banbury *Oxfordshire*	321
Bantham *Devon*	254
Bardfield Saling *Essex*	217
Barlaston *Staffordshire*	140
Barnard Castle *Durham*	67
Barnetby *Humberside*	105
Barnstaple *Devon*	255
Barrow *Suffolk*	217
Basingstoke *Hampshire*	321
Bassenthwaite *Cumbria*	388
Bath *Avon*	255
Battle *East Sussex*	358
Beadnell *Northumberland*	68
Beaminster *Dorset*	260
Beamish *Durham*	68
Beaulieu *Hampshire*	321
Beccles *Suffolk*	217
Beckington *Somerset*	260
Bedale *North Yorkshire*	105
Bedford *Bedfordshire*	217
Beetley *Norfolk*	218
Belford *Northumberland*	68
Bellingham *Northumberland*	69
Belper *Derbyshire*	198
Berkeley *Gloucestershire*	140
Berrynarbor *Devon*	260
Berwick-upon-Tweed *Northumberland*	69
Betchworth *Surrey*	358
Betley *Staffordshire*	140
Beverley *Humberside*	106
Bibury *Gloucestershire*	141
Bicester *Oxfordshire*	322
Bickington *Devon*	260
Biddenden *Kent*	358
Bideford *Devon*	261
Billericay *Essex*	218
Billingshurst *West Sussex*	358
Bingley *West Yorkshire*	106
Birchington *Kent*	359

Birmingham *West Midlands*	141
Birmingham Airport (See under Balsall Common, Coleshill, Coventry, Hampton in Arden, Meriden, Solihull)	
Bishop Auckland *Durham*	70
Bishop Sutton *Avon*	261
Bishop Thornton *North Yorkshire*	106
Bishop's Lydeard *Somerset*	261
Blackburn *Lancashire*	89
Blackpool *Lancashire*	89
Blakeney *Norfolk*	218
Blandford Forum *Dorset*	322
Bledington *Gloucestershire*	141
Bletchingdon *Oxfordshire*	322
Blockley *Gloucestershire*	141
Blunsdon *Wiltshire*	261
Blyth *Nottinghamshire*	198
Blythburgh *Suffolk*	218
Bodenham *Hereford and Worcester*	142
Bodmin *Cornwall*	261
Bolton *Greater Manchester*	89
Bolton-le-Sands *Lancashire*	89
Borley *Essex*	218
Boroughbridge *North Yorkshire*	107
Borrowdale *Cumbria*	45
Boscastle *Cornwall*	261
Boston *Lincolnshire*	198
Bournemouth *Dorset*	322
Bourton-on-the-Water *Gloucestershire*	142
Bovey Tracey *Devon*	262
Bowes *Durham*	70
Boxford *Suffolk*	218
Boxgrove *West Sussex*	359
Brackley *Northamptonshire*	198
Bracknell *Berkshire*	324
Bradford *West Yorkshire*	107
Bradford-on-Avon *Wiltshire*	262
Braintree *Essex*	219
Braithwaite *Cumbria*	45
Bramdean *Hampshire*	324
Bramley *Surrey*	359
Brampton *Cumbria*	45
Branston *Lincolnshire*	199
Bredenbury *Hereford and Worcester*	143
Bredon's Norton *Hereford and Worcester*	144
Brenchley *Kent*	359

Brendon *Devon*	262
Bretforton *Hereford and Worcester*	144
Bridestowe *Devon*	262
Bridgerule *Devon*	263
Bridgnorth *Shropshire*	144
Bridgwater *Somerset*	263
Bridlington *Humberside*	107
Bridport *Dorset*	263
Brigg *Humberside*	107
Brighton & Hove *East Sussex*	359
Brightwell-cum-Sotwell *Oxfordshire*	324
Brimpton *Berkshire*	324
Bristol *Avon*	264
Brixham *Devon*	264
Broad Chalke *Wiltshire*	265
Broad Hinton *Wiltshire*	265
Broadhembury *Devon*	265
Broadway *Hereford and Worcester*	145
Brockenhurst *Hampshire*	324
Bromsgrove *Hereford and Worcester*	146
Bromyard *Hereford and Worcester*	147
Broseley *Shropshire*	147
Broughton Astley *Leicestershire*	199
Broughton-in-Furness *Cumbria*	46
Broxton *Cheshire*	90
Bruisyard *Suffolk*	219
Buckfastleigh *Devon*	265
Buckingham *Buckinghamshire*	324
Bucknell *Shropshire*	147
Bude *Cornwall*	265
Budleigh Salterton *Devon*	266
Bulphan *Essex*	219
Bungay *Suffolk*	219
Burbage *Wiltshire*	266
Bures *Suffolk*	219
Burford *Oxfordshire*	324
Burgh St Peter *Norfolk*	219
Burley *Hampshire*	325
Burnley *Lancashire*	90
Burton Bradstock *Dorset*	266
Burton Latimer *Northamptonshire*	199
Burton upon Trent *Staffordshire*	147
Burwash *East Sussex*	360
Bury *Greater Manchester*	90
Bury St Edmunds *Suffolk*	220
Buttermere *Cumbria*	46
Buxton *Derbyshire*	199

425

TOWN INDEX

C — page no

Cadnam *Hampshire*	325
Caldbeck *Cumbria*	46
Callington *Cornwall*	266
Calne *Wiltshire*	266
Cambridge	
Cambridgeshire	220
Cannington *Somerset*	267
Canterbury *Kent*	360
Cardington *Shropshire*	148
Carlisle *Cumbria*	47
Cartmel *Cumbria*	48
Cartmel Fell *Cumbria*	48
Castle Bytham	
Lincolnshire	200
Castle Carrock *Cumbria*	48
Castle Cary *Somerset*	267
Castle Donington	
Leicestershire	200
Castle Hedingham *Essex*	222
Castleside *Durham*	70
Castleton *Derbyshire*	200
Castleton	
North Yorkshire	108
Cawston *Norfolk*	222
Chacewater *Cornwall*	267
Chagford *Devon*	267
Chandlers Ford	
Hampshire	325
Chard *Somerset*	267
Charing *Kent*	363
Chatteris *Cambridgeshire*	222
Cheadle	
Greater Manchester	90
Cheddar *Somerset*	268
Chediston *Suffolk*	222
Chelmsford *Essex*	222
Cheltenham	
Gloucestershire	148
Chester *Cheshire*	90
Chester-Le-Street	
Durham	71
Chew Magna *Avon*	268
Chewton Mendip	
Somerset	268
Chichester *West Sussex*	363
Chickerell *Dorset*	268
Chiddingstone *Kent*	364
Chilham *Kent*	364
Chippenham *Wiltshire*	268
Chipping Campden	
Gloucestershire	149
Chipping Norton	
Oxfordshire	326
Chiselborough *Somerset*	268
Chittoe Heath *Wiltshire*	269
Chorley *Lancashire*	91
Choseley *Norfolk*	223
Christchurch *Dorset*	326
Chudleigh *Devon*	269
Church Stretton	
Shropshire	150
Cirencester	
Gloucestershire	150
Clare *Suffolk*	223
Clevedon *Avon*	269
Cliftonville *Kent*	
(See under Margate)	
Clitheroe *Lancashire*	91
Clophill *Bedfordshire*	223
Cloughton	
North Yorkshire	108
Clovelly *Devon*	269
Clun *Shropshire*	151
Clungunford *Shropshire*	152
Coddenham *Suffolk*	223
Codicote *Hertfordshire*	223
Codsall *Staffordshire*	152
Colchester *Essex*	223
Coleshill *Warwickshire*	152
Colne *Lancashire*	91
Coltishall *Norfolk*	224
Colwall	
Hereford and Worcester	152
Colyton *Devon*	269
Combe Martin *Devon*	270
Compton *Berkshire*	326
Compton *Hampshire*	326
Congleton *Cheshire*	92
Coniston *Cumbria*	48
Consett *Durham*	71
Constantine *Cornwall*	270
Coombe Bissett *Wiltshire*	270
Coombe Keynes *Dorset*	327
Copthorne *Surrey*	364
Corbridge	
Northumberland	71
Corfe Castle *Dorset*	327
Corse *Gloucestershire*	152
Corsham *Wiltshire*	270
Cotgrave	
Nottinghamshire	200
Cotherstone *Durham*	71
Cotswolds	
(See under Ampney Crucis, Bibury, Bledington, Blockley, Bourton-on-the-Water, Bretforton, Broadway, Cheltenham, Chipping Campden, Cirencester, Cowley, Donnington, Fairford, Gloucester, Great Rissington, Guiting Power, Lechlade, Long Compton, Mickleton, Minchinhampton, Moreton-in-Marsh, Nailsworth, Naunton, Northleach, Nympsfield, Painswick, Rendcomb, Slimbridge, Stonehouse, Stow-on-the-Wold, Stroud, Teddington, Tetbury, Tewkesbury, Winchcombe)	
Coventry *West Midlands*	153
Coverack *Cornwall*	270
Cowes *Isle of Wight*	327
Cowley *Gloucestershire*	153
Coxwold *North Yorkshire*	108
Crackington Haven	
Cornwall	271
Crakehall	
North Yorkshire	108
Cranborne *Dorset*	327
Cranbrook *Kent*	364
Cranford St Andrew	
Northamptonshire	201
Crawley *West Sussex*	365
Crayke *North Yorkshire*	109

Use your i's

There are more than 550 Tourist Information Centres throughout England offering friendly help with accommodation and holiday ideas as well as suggestions of places to visit and things to do.

In your home town there may be a centre which can help you before you set out. You'll find the address of your nearest Tourist Information Centre in your local Phone Book.

TOWN INDEX

D — page no *(continued at top)*

Crediton *Devon*		271
Crewkerne *Somerset*		271
Cromer *Norfolk*		224
Crook *Durham*		72
Cropton *North Yorkshire*		109
Croyde *Devon*		272
Croydon *Greater London*		36
Cuckfield *West Sussex*		365
Cuddesdon *Oxfordshire*		227

D — page no

Dalston *Cumbria*		49
Danbury *Essex*		224
Darsham *Suffolk*		225
Dartmoor		
(See under Ashburton, Bickington, Bovey Tracey, Bridestowe, Buckfastleigh, Chagford, Dunsford, Holne, Lustleigh, Lydford, Moretonhampstead, Okehampton, Peter Tavy, Poundsgate, Tavistock, Two Bridges, Widecombe-in-the-Moor, Yelverton)		
Dartmouth *Devon*		272
Dawlish *Devon*		272
Deal *Kent*		365
Debden Green *Essex*		225
Deddington *Oxfordshire*		327
Dedham *Essex*		225
Deerhurst *Gloucestershire*		154
Denmead *Hampshire*		328
Derby *Derbyshire*		201
Dereham *Norfolk*		225
Desborough *Northamptonshire*		201
Devizes *Wiltshire*		273
Dial Post *West Sussex*		365
Dibden *Hampshire*		328
Dickleburgh *Norfolk*		225
Didcot *Oxfordshire*		328
Diddlebury *Shropshire*		154
Diss *Norfolk*		225
Doddiscombsleigh *Devon*		273
Doncaster *South Yorkshire*		109
Donnington *Gloucestershire*		154
Dorchester *Dorset*		273
Dorking *Surrey*		365
Dover *Kent*		366
Doveridge *Derbyshire*		201

E — page no

Droitwich *Hereford and Worcester*		154
Dulverton *Somerset*		274
Dunsford *Devon*		275
Dunster *Somerset*		275
Durham *Durham*		72
Dutton *Lancashire*		92

Easingwold *North Yorkshire*		109
East Barkwith *Lincolnshire*		202
East Budleigh *Devon*		275
East Dean *East Sussex*		367
East Grinstead *West Sussex*		367
East Hendred *Oxfordshire*		328
Eastbourne *East Sussex*		367
Ebberston *North Yorkshire*		109
Ebchester *Durham*		73
Eccleshall *Staffordshire*		155
Eckington *Hereford and Worcester*		155
Edmundbyers *Durham*		73
Edwinstone *Nottinghamshire*		202
Eggesford *Devon*		275
Eggleston *Durham*		73
Egremont *Cumbria*		49
Elham *Kent*		367
Ellerby *North Yorkshire*		110
Ellesmere *Shropshire*		155
Elmdon *Essex*		225
Elmesthorpe *Leicestershire*		202
Elmley Castle *Hereford and Worcester*		156
Elmswell *Suffolk*		226
Elsing *Norfolk*		226
Elstree *Hertfordshire*		226
Ely *Cambridgeshire*		226
Embleton *Northumberland*		73
English Bicknor *Gloucestershire*		156
Epping *Essex*		226
Erlestoke *Wiltshire*		275
Evesham *Hereford and Worcester*		156
Ewen *Gloucestershire*		156
Ewhurst *Surrey*		367
Exeter *Devon*		276
Exford *Somerset*		277

F — page no

Exmoor		
(See under Allerford, Brendon, Combe Martin, Dulverton, Dunster, Exford, Kentisbury, Lynmouth, Lynton, Simonsbath, West Anstey, Winsford)		
Exmouth *Devon*		277
Eyam *Derbyshire*		202
Eye *Suffolk*		227
Eyke *Suffolk*		227

Fairford *Gloucestershire*		157
Falstone *Northumberland*		73
Fareham *Hampshire*		328
Farnham *Surrey*		368
Faversham *Kent*		368
Feckenham *Hereford and Worcester*		157
Felixstowe *Suffolk*		227
Fenny Bridges *Devon*		277
Figheldean *Wiltshire*		277
Findon *West Sussex*		368
Flamborough *Humberside*		110
Flaxton *North Yorkshire*		110
Fleet *Hampshire*		328
Folkestone *Kent*		369
Fonthill Gifford *Wiltshire*		278
Fordingbridge *Hampshire*		329
Forest-in-Teesdale *Durham*		74
Forest of Dean		
(See under Corse, English Bicknor, Newent, Newland, Parkend)		
Forest Row *East Sussex*		369
Foxton *Leicestershire*		202
Framlingham *Suffolk*		227
Fressingfield *Suffolk*		228
Frinton-on-Sea *Essex*		228
Fritham *Hampshire*		329
Froggatt *Derbyshire*		202
Frome *Somerset*		278
Fulking *West Sussex*		369

G — page no

Garboldisham *Norfolk*		228
Garforth *West Yorkshire*		110
Garstang *Lancashire*		92
Gatwick Airport		
(See under Copthorne, Crawley, East Grinstead, Horley, Horsham, Reigate, Smallfield)		
Gerrards Cross *Buckinghamshire*		329
Giggleswick *North Yorkshire*		110
Gillamoor *North Yorkshire*		110
Gissing *Norfolk*		228
Glastonbury *Somerset*		278
Glooston *Leicestershire*		202
Gloucester *Gloucestershire*		157
Goathland *North Yorkshire*		111
Godalming *Surrey*		369
Goring *Oxfordshire*		329
Gorleston-on-Sea *Norfolk*		229
Gosfield *Essex*		229
Grafton *North Yorkshire*		111
Grampound *Cornwall*		278
Grantham *Lincolnshire*		203
Grasmere *Cumbria*		49
Grassington *North Yorkshire*		111
Grayrigg *Cumbria*		50
Grays *Essex*		229
Great Bircham *Norfolk*		229
Great Dunmow *Essex*		229
Great Eccleston *Lancashire*		92
Great Horwood *Buckinghamshire*		329
Great Rissington *Gloucestershire*		157
Great Yarmouth *Norfolk*		229
Green Hammerton *North Yorkshire*		111
Greenhead *Northumberland*		74
Greinton *Somerset*		279
Guildford *Surrey*		369
Guildford *Surrey*		391
Guiting Power *Gloucestershire*		158
Gunnerside *North Yorkshire*		111

H — page no

Hacheston *Suffolk*		230
Hadleigh *Suffolk*		230
Hadstock *Essex*		230
Hailsham *East Sussex*		369

BARCHESTER?

Check the maps

The colour maps at the back of this guide show all cities, towns and villages which have accommodation listings in the guide. They will enable you to check if there is suitable accommodation in the vicinity of the place you plan to visit.

427

TOWN INDEX

Hainton *Lincolnshire*	203	
Halifax *West Yorkshire*	112	
Halsetown *Cornwall*	279	
Haltwhistle		
Northumberland	74	
Hamble *Hampshire*	330	
Hambledon *Hampshire*	330	
Hampsthwaite		
North Yorkshire	112	
Hampton in Arden		
West Midlands	158	
Hamsterley Forest		
(See under Barnard		
Castle, Bishop Auckland,		
Crook, Tow Law)		
Hardwick		
Cambridgeshire	231	
Harmby *North Yorkshire*	112	
Harmer Hill *Shropshire*	158	
Harrietsham *Kent*	370	
Harrogate		
North Yorkshire	112	
Harrow *Greater London*	36	
Hartfield *East Sussex*	370	
Hartland *Devon*	279	
Hartoft End		
North Yorkshire	113	
Haslemere *Surrey*	370	
Hastings *East Sussex*	370	
Hathersage *Derbyshire*	203	
Havant *Hampshire*	330	
Haverthwaite *Cumbria*	50	
Hawes *North Yorkshire*	113	
Hawkhurst *Kent*	371	
Hawkshead *Cumbria*	50	
Haworth *West Yorkshire*	113	
Haydon Bridge		
Northumberland	75	
Hayling Island		
Hampshire	330	
Haywards Heath		
West Sussex	371	
Headcorn *Kent*	371	
Heathrow Airport		
(See under West		
Drayton)		
Hebden Bridge		
West Yorkshire	391	
Heighington *Durham*	75	
Hellifield		
North Yorkshire	114	
Helmsley		
North Yorkshire	114	
Helston *Cornwall*	279	
Hemingford Grey		
Cambridgeshire	231	

Henley-in-Arden		
Warwickshire	158	
Henley-on-Thames		
Oxfordshire	331	
Henstridge *Somerset*	280	
Hereford		
Hereford and Worcester	158	
Hermitage *Dorset*	280	
Herstmonceux		
East Sussex	371	
Hertford *Hertfordshire*	231	
Hesleden *Durham*	75	
Hethersett *Norfolk*	231	
Hevingham *Norfolk*	231	
Hexham *Northumberland*	75	
Higham *Suffolk*	231	
Highworth *Wiltshire*	280	
Hinckley *Leicestershire*	203	
Hindolveston *Norfolk*	231	
Hintlesham *Suffolk*	232	
Hitcham *Suffolk*	232	
Hollingbourne *Kent*	371	
Holmes Chapel *Cheshire*	92	
Holmfirth *West Yorkshire*	114	
Holne *Devon*	280	
Holnest *Dorset*	280	
Holsworthy *Devon*	280	
Holt *Norfolk*	232	
Holy Island		
Northumberland	76	
Hook Norton *Oxfordshire*	332	
Horley *Surrey*	372	
Horsham *West Sussex*	373	
Horton *Dorset*	332	
Horton-in-Ribblesdale		
North Yorkshire	114	
Hove *East Sussex*		
(See under Brighton &		
Hove)		
Hoylake *Merseyside*	93	
Hubberholme		
North Yorkshire	115	
Huddersfield		
West Yorkshire	115	
Hungerford *Berkshire*	332	
Hunstanton *Norfolk*	232	
Huntingdon		
Cambridgeshire	233	
Hunton *North Yorkshire*	115	
Husbands Bosworth		
Leicestershire	203	
Husthwaite		
North Yorkshire	115	
Hyde *Greater Manchester*	93	
Hythe *Hampshire*	332	

I	**page no**
Ickleton *Cambridgeshire*	233
Ilfracombe *Devon*	280
Ilkley *West Yorkshire*	115
Ilmington *Warwickshire*	159
Ingatestone *Essex*	233
Ingleby Greenhow	
North Yorkshire	116
Ingleton *North Yorkshire*	116
Inglewhite *Lancashire*	93
Ipswich *Suffolk*	233
Ironbridge *Shropshire*	159
Isle of Wight	
(See under Cowes, Ryde,	
Ryde-Wootton, Shanklin)	
Isles of Scilly	281
Ivybridge *Devon*	281

K	**page no**
Kendal *Cumbria*	50
Kenilworth *Warwickshire*	159
Kentisbeare *Devon*	281
Kentisbury *Devon*	281
Kersey *Suffolk*	233
Kessingland *Suffolk*	234
Keswick *Cumbria*	51
Kettlewell	
North Yorkshire	116
Kidderminster	
Hereford and Worcester	160
Kielder Forest	
(See under Bellingham,	
Falstone, Wark)	
Kineton *Warwickshire*	160
King's Lynn *Norfolk*	234
King's Nympton *Devon*	282
Kingsand *Cornwall*	282
Kingsbridge *Devon*	282
Kingsclere *Hampshire*	332
Kingston Bagpuize	
Oxfordshire	332
Kingstone	
Hereford and Worcester	160
Kirby Muxloe	
Leicestershire	203
Kirkby *North Yorkshire*	116
Kirkby Stephen *Cumbria*	53
Kirkbymoorside	
North Yorkshire	116
Knaresborough	
North Yorkshire	116
Kneesworth	
Cambridgeshire	234
Knowl Hill *Berkshire*	332
Knutsford *Cheshire*	93

L	**page no**
Lambourn *Berkshire*	333
Lamplugh *Cumbria*	53
Lancaster *Lancashire*	93
Langdale *Cumbria*	54
Langport *Somerset*	283
Launceston *Cornwall*	283
Lavenham *Suffolk*	234
Lawshall *Suffolk*	235
Leamington Spa	
Warwickshire	160
Lechlade *Gloucestershire*	161
Ledbury	
Hereford and Worcester	161
Leeds *West Yorkshire*	117
Leeds/Bradford Airport	
(See under Bingley,	
Bradford, Leeds, Otley)	
Leek *Staffordshire*	161
Leigh *Wiltshire*	283
Leintwardine	
Hereford and Worcester	162
Lenham *Kent*	373
Leominster	
Hereford and Worcester	162
Lewes *East Sussex*	373
Lichfield *Staffordshire*	163
Lincoln *Lincolnshire*	204
Linwood *Hampshire*	333
Liskeard *Cornwall*	283
Little Bedwyn *Wiltshire*	284
Little Tey *Essex*	235
Little Walsingham	
Norfolk	235
Little Wittenham	
Oxfordshire	333
Littledean	
Gloucestershire	391
Littleport *Cambridgeshire*	235
Liverpool *Merseyside*	94
Loddon *Norfolk*	235
London	25
Long Buckby	
Northamptonshire	204
Long Compton	
Warwickshire	163
Long Marston	
North Yorkshire	117
Longhorsley	
Northumberland	76
Longnor *Staffordshire*	163
Longtown *Cumbria*	54
Looe *Cornwall*	284
Lorton *Cumbria*	54
Louth *Lincolnshire*	204

Country Code

♣ Enjoy the countryside and respect its life and work
♣ Guard against all risk of fire ♣ Fasten all gates
♣ Keep your dogs under close control ♣ Keep to public paths across farmland ♣ Use gates and stiles to cross fences, hedges and walls ♣ Leave livestock, crops and machinery alone ♣ Take your litter home ♣ Help to keep all water clean ♣ Protect wildlife, plants and trees ♣ Take special care on country roads ♣ Make no unnecessary noise

TOWN INDEX

Low Row *North Yorkshire*	118
Lowestoft *Suffolk*	235
Loweswater *Cumbria*	54
Lowick *Northumberland*	76
Ludford *Lincolnshire*	204
Ludlow *Shropshire*	163
Lund *Humberside*	118
Lustleigh *Devon*	284
Lydford *Devon*	285
Lyford *Oxfordshire*	333
Lyme Regis *Dorset*	285
Lymington *Hampshire*	333
Lyminster *West Sussex*	373
Lyndhurst *Hampshire*	334
Lynmouth *Devon*	286
Lynton *Devon*	286

M — page no

Macclesfield *Cheshire*	94
Maidenhead *Berkshire*	334
Maidstone *Kent*	374
Malham *North Yorkshire*	118
Malmesbury *Wiltshire*	286
Malpas *Cheshire*	94
Malton *North Yorkshire*	118
Malvern *Hereford and Worcester*	165
Manchester *Greater Manchester*	95
Manchester Airport (See under Alderley Edge, Altrincham, Hyde, Knutsford, Manchester, Salford, Stockport, Wilmslow)	
Marden *Kent*	374
Margaret Roding *Essex*	236
Margate *Kent*	374
Market Deeping *Lincolnshire*	204
Market Drayton *Shropshire*	165
Market Harborough *Leicestershire*	205
Market Lavington *Wiltshire*	286
Market Rasen *Lincolnshire*	205
Market Weighton *Humberside*	118
Marlborough *Wiltshire*	287
Marlow *Buckinghamshire*	335
Marnhull *Dorset*	335
Martinstown *Dorset*	287
Martock *Somerset*	287

Marton *Warwickshire*	166
Maryport *Cumbria*	54
Masham *North Yorkshire*	119
Matfield *Kent*	395
Matlock *Derbyshire*	205
Maulds Meaburn *Cumbria*	55
Maxstoke *Warwickshire*	166
Medbourne *Leicestershire*	205
Melksham *Wiltshire*	287
Melton Mowbray *Leicestershire*	205
Mere *Wiltshire*	287
Meriden *West Midlands*	166
Mevagissey *Cornwall*	287
Mickleton *Gloucestershire*	166
Middleham *North Yorkshire*	119
Middlesbrough *Cleveland*	76
Middleton *Northamptonshire*	205
Middleton-in-Teesdale *Durham*	77
Milton Keynes *Buckinghamshire*	336
Minchinhampton *Gloucestershire*	166
Minehead *Somerset*	288
Minstead *Hampshire*	337
Minsterley *Shropshire*	166
Modbury *Devon*	288
Moreton-in-Marsh *Gloucestershire*	167
Moretonhampstead *Devon*	288
Morpeth *Northumberland*	77
Morwenstow *Cornwall*	289
Moulsford on Thames *Oxfordshire*	337
Much Hadham *Hertfordshire*	236
Much Wenlock *Shropshire*	168
Mullion *Cornwall*	289
Mungrisdale *Cumbria*	55
Mylor Bridge *Cornwall*	289
Mytholmroyd *West Yorkshire*	119
Myton-on-Swale *North Yorkshire*	119

N — page no

Nailsworth *Gloucestershire*	168
Nantwich *Cheshire*	95
Naunton *Gloucestershire*	169
Neatishead *Norfolk*	236
Nether Wallop *Hampshire*	337
New Forest (See under Beaulieu, Brockenhurst, Burley, Cadnam, Dibden, Fordingbridge, Fritham, Hythe, Linwood, Lymington, Lyndhurst, Minstead, Ringwood, Sway, Tiptoe, Totton, Woodgreen)	
Newark *Nottinghamshire*	206
Newbury *Berkshire*	337
Newcastle-under-Lyme *Staffordshire*	169
Newcastle upon Tyne *Tyne and Wear*	77
Newent *Gloucestershire*	169
Newland *Gloucestershire*	170
Newmarket *Suffolk*	236
Newport *Shropshire*	170
Newquay *Cornwall*	290
Newton Abbot *Devon*	290
Newton Ferrers *Devon*	290
Newton Longville *Buckinghamshire*	337
Norfolk Broads (See under Acle, Aylsham, Beccles, Bungay, Burgh St Peter, Cawston, Coltishall, Gorleston-on-Sea, Great Yarmouth, Hevingham, Loddon, Lowestoft, Neatishead, North Walsham, Norwich, Oulton Broad, Rackheath, Rollesby, Salhouse, Wroxham)	
Norham *Northumberland*	77
North Leigh *Oxfordshire*	338
North Tawton *Devon*	291
North Walsham *Norfolk*	236
Northallerton *North Yorkshire*	120
Northleach *Gloucestershire*	170
Northwich *Cheshire*	96
Norwich *Norfolk*	237

Nottingham *Nottinghamshire*	206
Nuneaton *Warwickshire*	170
Nunnington *North Yorkshire*	120
Nympsfield *Gloucestershire*	171

O — page no

Oakamoor *Staffordshire*	171
Oakham *Leicestershire*	206
Oakington *Cambridgeshire*	238
Oakworth *West Yorkshire*	120
Okehampton *Devon*	291
Oldham *Greater Manchester*	96
Ombersley *Hereford and Worcester*	171
Onneley *Staffordshire*	172
Orford *Suffolk*	238
Orton *Cumbria*	55
Osmotherley *North Yorkshire*	120
Ospringe *Kent*	375
Oswestry *Shropshire*	172
Otley *West Yorkshire*	120
Otterburn *Northumberland*	396
Otterton *Devon*	291
Ottery St Mary *Devon*	291
Oulton Broad *Suffolk*	238
Oundle *Northamptonshire*	207
Owslebury *Hampshire*	338
Oxford *Oxfordshire*	338
Oxted *Surrey*	375

P — page no

Padstow *Cornwall*	292
Paignton *Devon*	292
Painswick *Gloucestershire*	172
Parkend *Gloucestershire*	172
Parracombe *Devon*	292
Partridge Green *West Sussex*	375
Pateley Bridge *North Yorkshire*	120
Patterdale *Cumbria*	55

Key to symbols

Information about many of the services and facilities at accommodation listed in this guide is given in the form of symbols. The key to these symbols is inside the back cover flap. You may find it helpful to keep the flap open when referring to the accommodation listings.

429

TOWN INDEX

Peak District
(See under Aldwark, Ashbourne, Ashford in the Water, Bakewell, Buxton, Castleton, Eyam, Froggatt, Hathersage, Tideswell, Winster)
Peasenhall *Suffolk* 238
Pelynt *Cornwall* 292
Pendeen *Cornwall* 292
Penrith *Cumbria* 55
Penruddock *Cumbria* 56
Pensford *Avon* 293
Pentewan *Cornwall* 293
Penzance *Cornwall* 293
Perranuthnoe *Cornwall* 294
Peter Tavy *Devon* 294
Peterborough
Cambridgeshire 238
Petersfield *Hampshire* 339
Petworth *West Sussex* 375
Pickering
North Yorkshire 121
Piddletrenthide *Dorset* 294
Plymouth *Devon* 294
Polzeath *Cornwall* 295
Poole *Dorset* 340
Porthleven *Cornwall* 295
Portishead *Avon* 295
Portland *Dorset* 295
Portreath *Cornwall* 295
Portsmouth & Southsea
Hampshire 340
Potton *Bedfordshire* 238
Poundsgate *Devon* 296
Powerstock *Dorset* 296
Poynings *West Sussex* 375
Preston *Lancashire* 96
Priddy *Somerset* 296
Pulham Market *Norfolk* 238
Purley *Greater London* 36
Putley
Hereford and Worcester 172

Q — page no
Quidenham *Norfolk* 239

R — page no
Rackheath *Norfolk* 239
Radwinter *Essex* 239
Ramsey *Cambridgeshire* 239
Ramsgate *Kent* 375
Ravenscar
North Yorkshire 121
Reading *Berkshire* 340
Redcar *Cleveland* 78
Redlynch *Wiltshire* 296
Redmire *North Yorkshire* 121
Reepham *Norfolk* 239
Reeth *North Yorkshire* 122
Reigate *Surrey* 376
Rendcomb
Gloucestershire 172
Ribble Valley
(See under Clitheroe, Dutton)
Richmond
North Yorkshire 122
Ringwood *Hampshire* 341
Ripon *North Yorkshire* 122
Roadwater *Somerset* 296
Robertsbridge
East Sussex 376
Rochdale
Greater Manchester 97

Rock
Hereford and Worcester 173
Rode *Somerset* 297
Rogate *West Sussex* 376
Rollesby *Norfolk* 239
Romsey *Hampshire* 341
Ross-on-Wye
Hereford and Worcester 173
Rothbury
Northumberland 78
Rottingdean *East Sussex* 376
Rowland *Derbyshire* 207
Rowlands Gill
Tyne and Wear 78
Rufforth *North Yorkshire* 123
Rugby *Warwickshire* 174
Rushall *Norfolk* 239
Ruyton-XI-Towns
Shropshire 175
Ryde *Isle of Wight* 341
Ryde-Wootton
Isle of Wight 342
Rye *East Sussex* 376
Ryton *Tyne and Wear* 79

S — page no
Saffron Walden *Essex* 240
St Agnes *Cornwall* 297
St Albans *Hertfordshire* 240
St Austell *Cornwall* 297
St Dominick *Cornwall* 297
St Ives *Cornwall* 297
St Kew *Cornwall* 297
St Mawgan *Cornwall* 298
St Michael's on Wyre
Lancashire 97
St Nicholas at Wade
Kent 377
Salcombe *Devon* 298
Salford
Greater Manchester 97
Salhouse *Norfolk* 241
Salisbury *Wiltshire* 298
Salisbury Plain
(See under Amesbury, Figheldean, Market Lavington, Salisbury, Shrewton, Winterbourne Stoke)
Saltburn-by-the-Sea
Cleveland 79
Sandbach *Cheshire* 97
Sandy *Bedfordshire* 241
Sarre *Kent* 378
Scarborough
North Yorkshire 123
Seahouses
Northumberland 79
Seaton *Devon* 299
Sedbergh *Cumbria* 56
Selborne *Hampshire* 342
Selby *North Yorkshire* 123
Settle *North Yorkshire* 124
Sevenoaks *Kent* 378
Severn Stoke
Hereford and Worcester 175
Shaldon *Devon* 299
Shanklin *Isle of Wight* 342
Sheerness *Kent* 378
Sheffield *South Yorkshire* 124
Shelsley Beauchamp
Hereford and Worcester 175
Shepton Mallet *Somerset* 300
Sherborne *Dorset* 300
Sheringham *Norfolk* 241

Sherwood Forest
(See under Edwinstowe, Newark, Southwell, Upton)
Shifnal *Shropshire* 175
Shipton Bellinger
Hampshire 342
Shiptonthorpe
Humberside 124
Shirwell *Devon* 300
Shrewsbury *Shropshire* 175
Shrewton *Wiltshire* 300
Sidlesham *West Sussex* 378
Sidmouth *Devon* 300
Silloth *Cumbria* 56
Simonsbath *Somerset* 301
Singleton *Lancashire* 98
Sinnington
North Yorkshire 124
Sittingbourne *Kent* 379
Sixpenny Handley
Dorset 343
Skegness *Lincolnshire* 207
Slaley *Northumberland* 79
Slapton *Devon* 301
Slimbridge
Gloucestershire 177
Smallfield *Surrey* 379
Smarden *Kent* 379
Solihull *West Midlands* 177
South Mimms
Hertfordshire 241
South Molton *Devon* 301
Southampton *Hampshire* 343
Southend-on-Sea *Essex* 241
Southport *Merseyside* 98
Southsea *Hampshire*
(See under Portsmouth & Southsea)
Southwell
Nottinghamshire 207
Southwold *Suffolk* 242
Sowerby Bridge
West Yorkshire 397
Spennithorne
North Yorkshire 124
Spennymoor *Durham* 79
Stafford *Staffordshire* 177
Staindrop *Durham* 80
Staintondale
North Yorkshire 125
Stamford *Lincolnshire* 207
Standlake *Oxfordshire* 343
Stanley *Durham* 80
Stanway *Essex* 242
Stathe *Somerset* 301
Staveley *Cumbria* 57
Stawell *Somerset* 302
Steel *Northumberland* 80
Steeple Aston
Oxfordshire 343
Steeple Bumpstead
Essex 242
Stelling Minnis *Kent* 379
Stiperstones *Shropshire* 177
Stockbridge *Hampshire* 343
Stockport
Greater Manchester 98
Stocksfield
Northumberland 80
Stoke Holy Cross
Norfolk 242
Stoke Lacy
Hereford and Worcester 177
Stoke-on-Trent
Staffordshire 178

Stoke Rochford
Lincolnshire 397
Stoke St Gregory
Somerset 302
Stokesley
North Yorkshire 125
Stone *Staffordshire* 178
Stonehouse
Gloucestershire 178
Stony Stratford
Buckinghamshire 343
Storrington *West Sussex* 379
Stourbridge
West Midlands 179
Stourport-on-Severn
Hereford and Worcester 179
Stow-on-the-Wold
Gloucestershire 179
Stratford St Mary
Suffolk 242
Stratford-upon-Avon
Warwickshire 180
Stroud *Gloucestershire* 183
Studland *Dorset* 344
Sunderland
Tyne and Wear 80
Sutton-on-Trent
Nottinghamshire 208
Sutton Scotney
Hampshire 344
Sutton Valence *Kent* 379
Swanage *Dorset* 344
Swanley *Kent* 380
Sway *Hampshire* 344
Swindon *Wiltshire* 302
Sydling St Nicholas
Dorset 302
Symonds Yat West
Hereford and Worcester 183

T — page no
Tadcaster
North Yorkshire 125
Taunton *Somerset* 303
Tavistock *Devon* 303
Teddington
Gloucestershire 184
Telford *Shropshire* 184
Tenterden *Kent* 380
Terrington
North Yorkshire 125
Tetbury *Gloucestershire* 184
Tewkesbury
Gloucestershire 184
Thame *Oxfordshire* 345
Thaxted *Essex* 243
Thetford *Norfolk* 243
Thirsk *North Yorkshire* 125
Thompson *Norfolk* 243
Thoralby *North Yorkshire* 126
Thornham *Norfolk* 243
Thornton Dale
North Yorkshire 126
Thornton Watlass
North Yorkshire 126
Threlkeld *Cumbria* 57
Throcking *Hertfordshire* 243
Thurlstone
South Yorkshire 127
Tideswell *Derbyshire* 208
Tintagel *Cornwall* 303
Tiptoe *Hampshire* 345
Tiptree *Essex* 244
Tiverton *Devon* 304
Tonbridge *Kent* 380
Torquay *Devon* 304

430

TOWN INDEX

Torrington *Devon*	305
Totnes *Devon*	306
Totton *Hampshire*	345
Tow Law *Durham*	80
Tring *Hertfordshire*	244
Troutbeck *Cumbria*	57
Trowbridge *Wiltshire*	306
Truro *Cornwall*	306
Tunbridge Wells *Kent*	380
Two Bridges *Devon*	307
Tynemouth	
Tyne and Wear	81

U — page no

Uckfield *East Sussex*	381
Uffington *Oxfordshire*	345
Ugley *Essex*	244
Ullswater *Cumbria*	57
Underbarrow *Cumbria*	58
Upper Hulme	
Staffordshire	185
Uppingham	
Leicestershire	208
Upton *Nottinghamshire*	209
Upton-upon-Severn	
Hereford and Worcester	185
Uttoxeter *Staffordshire*	186

V — page no

Vowchurch	
Hereford and Worcester	186

W — page no

Wallingford *Oxfordshire*	345
Walton-on-Thames	
Surrey	381
Warborough *Oxfordshire*	345
Ware *Hertfordshire*	244
Wark *Northumberland*	81
Warkworth	
Northumberland	81

Warnford *Hampshire*	346
Warninglid *West Sussex*	381
Warsash *Hampshire*	346
Warter *Humberside*	127
Warwick *Warwickshire*	186
Wasdale *Cumbria*	58
Watchet *Somerset*	307
Waterhouses	
Staffordshire	187
Watford *Hertfordshire*	244
Watton *Norfolk*	244
Weedon	
Northamptonshire	209
Weeton *Lancashire*	98
Wellington *Somerset*	307
Wellow *Avon*	307
Wells *Somerset*	308
Wells-next-the-Sea	
Norfolk	244
Wem *Shropshire*	188
Wembley *Greater London*	37
Weobley	
Hereford and Worcester	188
Wessington *Derbyshire*	209
West Anstey *Devon*	308
West Bagborough	
Somerset	309
West Bergholt *Essex*	245
West Chiltington	
West Sussex	381
West Clandon *Surrey*	381
West Drayton	
Greater London	37
West Grafton *Wiltshire*	309
West Haddon	
Northamptonshire	209
West Lulworth *Dorset*	346
West Malling *Kent*	382
West Stow *Suffolk*	245
West Witton	
North Yorkshire	127
Westbury	
Buckinghamshire	346

Westgate-in-Weardale	
Durham	81
Weston-super-Mare *Avon*	309
Weston Underwood	
Derbyshire	209
Wetherby *West Yorkshire*	127
Wetherden *Suffolk*	245
Weybread *Suffolk*	245
Weymouth *Dorset*	309
Whitby *North Yorkshire*	127
Whitley Bay	
Tyne and Wear	82
Whitstable *Kent*	382
Whittington *Shropshire*	188
Wick *Avon*	397
Wick St Lawrence *Avon*	309
Wickham *Hampshire*	347
Widecombe-in-the-Moor	
Devon	310
Wilmslow *Cheshire*	98
Wimborne Minster	
Dorset	347
Wincanton *Somerset*	310
Winchcombe	
Gloucestershire	188
Winchester *Hampshire*	347
Windermere *Cumbria*	58
Windsor *Berkshire*	349
Winsford *Somerset*	310
Winslow	
Buckinghamshire	349
Winster *Derbyshire*	209
Winterborne Stickland	
Dorset	349
Winterborne Zelston	
Dorset	349
Winterbourne	
Steepleton *Dorset*	310
Winterbourne Stoke	
Wiltshire	310
Wirksworth *Derbyshire*	209
Wirral *Merseyside*	
(See under Hoylake)	

Wisbech *Cambridgeshire*	245
Witney *Oxfordshire*	350
Wix *Essex*	245
Woking *Surrey*	382
Wolverhampton	
West Midlands	189
Woodbridge *Suffolk*	246
Woodbury *Devon*	311
Woodgreen *Hampshire*	350
Woodham Ferrers *Essex*	246
Woodstock *Oxfordshire*	350
Wookey *Somerset*	311
Woolacombe *Devon*	311
Woolley *Cambridgeshire*	246
Woolpit *Suffolk*	246
Wootton Wawen	
Warwickshire	189
Worcester	
Hereford and Worcester	189
Workington *Cumbria*	61
Worthing *West Sussex*	382
Wroxham *Norfolk*	247
Wye Valley	
(See under Hereford,	
Ross-on-Wye, Symonds	
Yat West)	
Wylam *Northumberland*	82
Wymondham *Norfolk*	247

Y — page no

Yardley Gobion	
Northamptonshire	210
Yelverton *Devon*	311
Yeovil *Somerset*	311
Yeovilton *Somerset*	312
York *North Yorkshire*	128
Yoxall *Staffordshire*	190

Z — page no

Zeals *Wiltshire*	312

Index to Advertisers

You can obtain further information from any display advertiser in this guide by completing an advertisement enquiry coupon. You will find these coupons on pages 421–423.

Abbey Court Hotel, *London W2*	33, IBC	King's Head Hotel, *Keswick*	15
The Abbotts Hotel, *London NW2*	29	New Inn, *Winterbourne Monkton*	276
Alcott Farm, *Alvechurch*	139	Old Mill Hotel & Restaurant, *Bath*	13, 256, IBC
Apple Orchard House, *Nailsworth*	169	Oxstalls Farm Stud, *Stratford-upon-Avon*	180
The Beeches, *Doveridge*	201	The Penny Farthing Hotel, *Lyndhurst*	334
Hotel Cornelius, *Manchester*	14, 95	The Round House, *Ecclesall*	155
Corona Hotel, *London SW1*	27	Sass House Hotel, *London W2*	33, IBC
Craig Manor Hotel, *Windermere*	15	Sidney Hotel, *London SW1*	28
Croydon Hotel, *Croydon*	36	Westpoint Hotel, *London W2*	33, IBC
Elizabeth Hotel, *London SW1*	27	Windsor House Hotel, *London SW5*	29
Granada Lodges	IFC		

431

mileage chart

The distances between towns on the mileage chart are given to the nearest mile, and are measured along routes based on the quickest travelling time, making maximum use of motorways or dual-carriageway roads.
The chart is based upon information supplied by the Automobile Association.

432

WHERE TO STAY 1994

colour maps

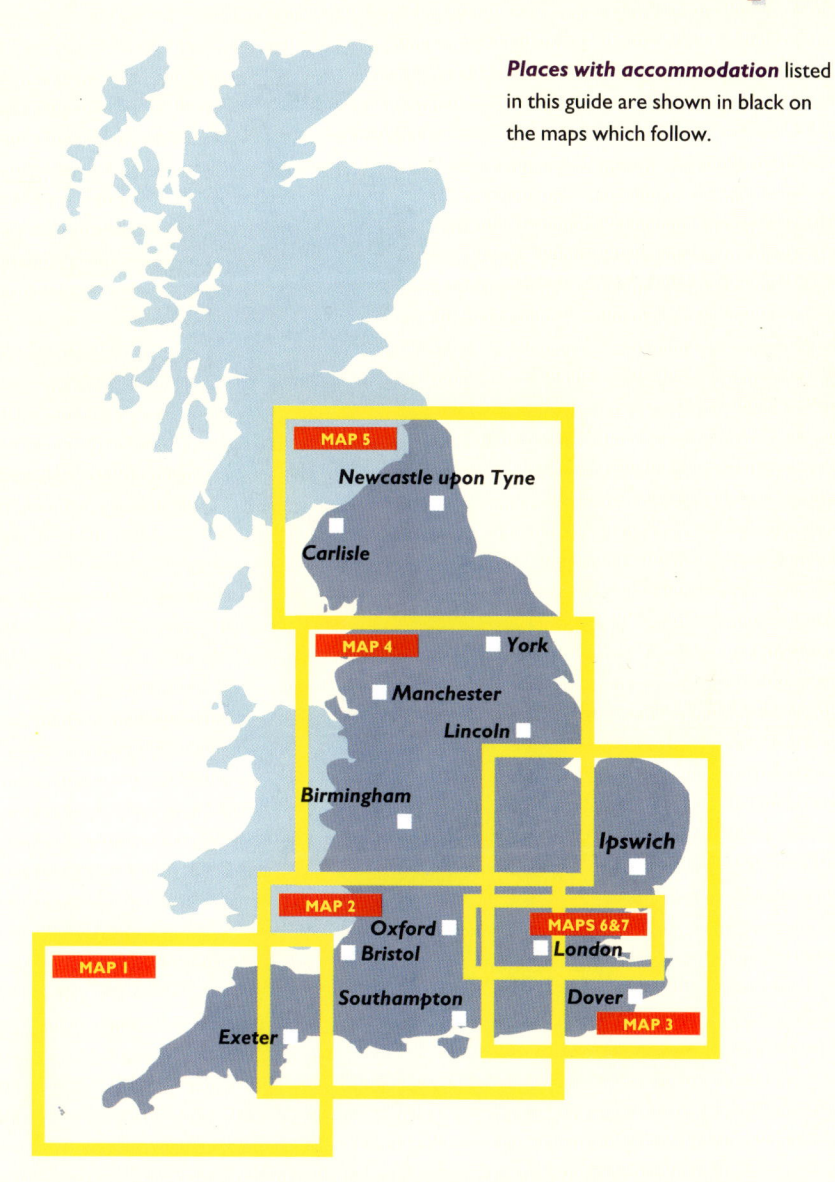

Places with accommodation listed in this guide are shown in black on the maps which follow.

MAP 5
Newcastle upon Tyne
Carlisle

MAP 4
York
Manchester
Lincoln
Birmingham
Ipswich

MAP 2
Oxford
Bristol
MAPS 6 & 7
London
Southampton
Dover
MAP 3

MAP 1
Exeter

map 1

map 1

map 2

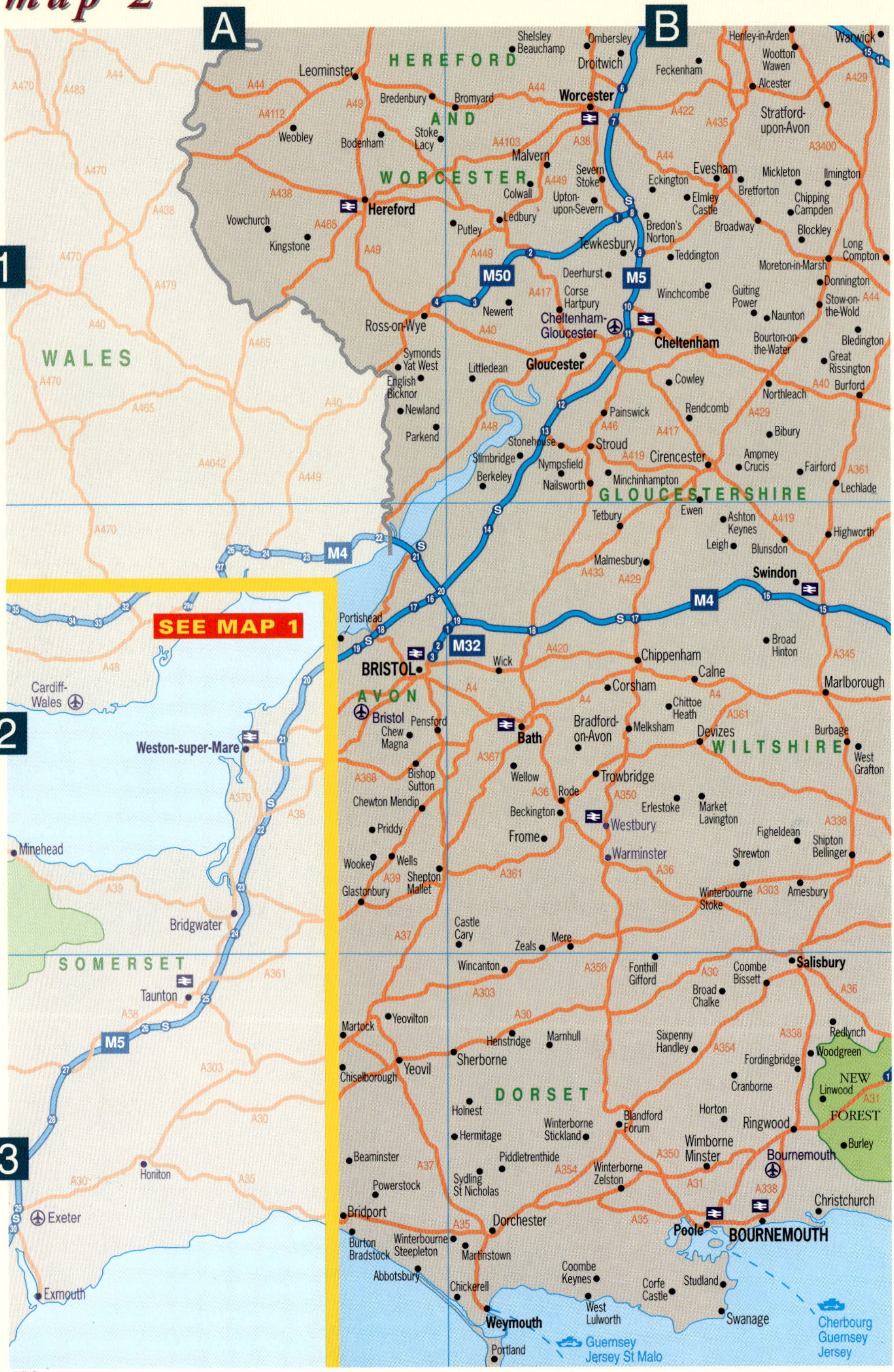
A
B
1
2
3
SEE MAP 1
WALES
HEREFORD AND WORCESTER
GLOUCESTERSHIRE
AVON
WILTSHIRE
SOMERSET
DORSET
NEW FOREST
Leominster
Weobley
Bodenham
Bredenbury
Bromyard
Stoke Lacy
Shelsley Beauchamp
Ombersley
Droitwich
Worcester
Feckenham
Henley-in-Arden
Wootton Wawen
Alcester
Warwick
Stratford-upon-Avon
Malvern
Colwall
Severn Stoke
Upton-upon-Severn
Eckington
Evesham
Elmley Castle
Mickleton
Bretforton
Ilmington
Chipping Campden
Broadway
Blockley
Vowchurch
Kingstone
Hereford
Putley
Ledbury
Tewkesbury
Bredon's Norton
Teddington
Moreton-in-Marsh
Long Compton
Donnington
Stow-on-the-Wold
Deerhurst
Corse Hartpury
Newent
Cheltenham-Gloucester
Cheltenham
Winchcombe
Guiting Power
Naunton
Bourton-on-the-Water
Bledington
Great Rissington
Burford
Ross-on-Wye
Symonds Yat West
English Bicknor
Newland
Parkend
Littledean
Gloucester
Cowley
Rendcomb
Northleach
Bibury
Painswick
Stroud
Stonehouse
Slimbridge
Berkeley
Nympsfield
Nailsworth
Minchinhampton
Cirencester
Ampney Crucis
Fairford
Lechlade
Tetbury
Ewen
Ashton Keynes
Leigh
Blunsdon
Highworth
Malmesbury
Swindon
Portishead
BRISTOL
Wick
Chippenham
Calne
Broad Hinton
Marlborough
Corsham
Chittoe Heath
Bristol
Pensford
Chew Magna
Bath
Bradford-on-Avon
Melksham
Devizes
Burbage
West Grafton
Bishop Sutton
Wellow
Trowbridge
Chewton Mendip
Rode
Beckington
Erlestoke
Market Lavington
Westbury
Priddy
Frome
Fighelden
Shipton Bellinger
Warminster
Shrewton
Wookey
Wells
Shepton Mallet
Glastonbury
Winterbourne Stoke
Amesbury
Castle Cary
Zeals
Mere
Wincanton
Fonthill Gifford
Coombe Bissett
Salisbury
Broad Chalke
Yeovilton
Martock
Henstridge
Marnhull
Sixpenny Handley
Redlynch
Woodgreen
Fordingbridge
Chiselborough
Yeovil
Sherborne
Cranborne
Linwood
Holnest
Blandford Forum
Horton
Ringwood
Hermitage
Winterborne Stickland
Wimborne Minster
Burley
Beaminster
Piddletrenthide
Bournemouth
Sydling St Nicholas
Winterborne Zelston
Powerstock
Bridport
Dorchester
Christchurch
Poole
BOURNEMOUTH
Burton Bradstock
Winterbourne Steepleton
Martinstown
Abbotsbury
Coombe Keynes
Chickerell
Corfe Castle
Studland
Weymouth
West Lulworth
Swanage
Portland
Guernsey Jersey St Malo
Cherbourg Guernsey Jersey
Cardiff-Wales
Weston-super-Mare
Minehead
Bridgwater
Taunton
Honiton
Exeter
Exmouth
M4
M5
M50
M32

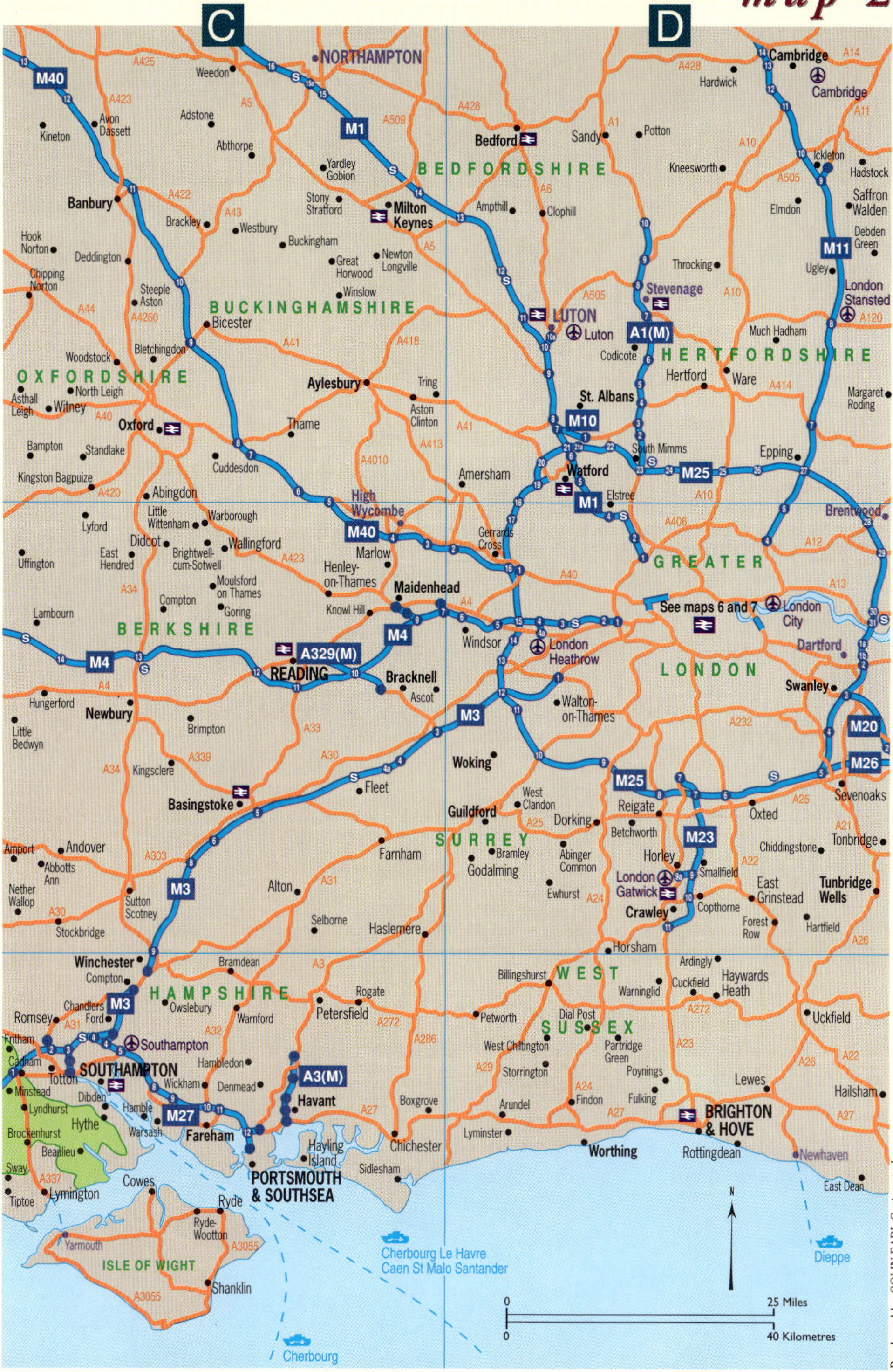

Produced by COLIN EARL Cartography

map 3

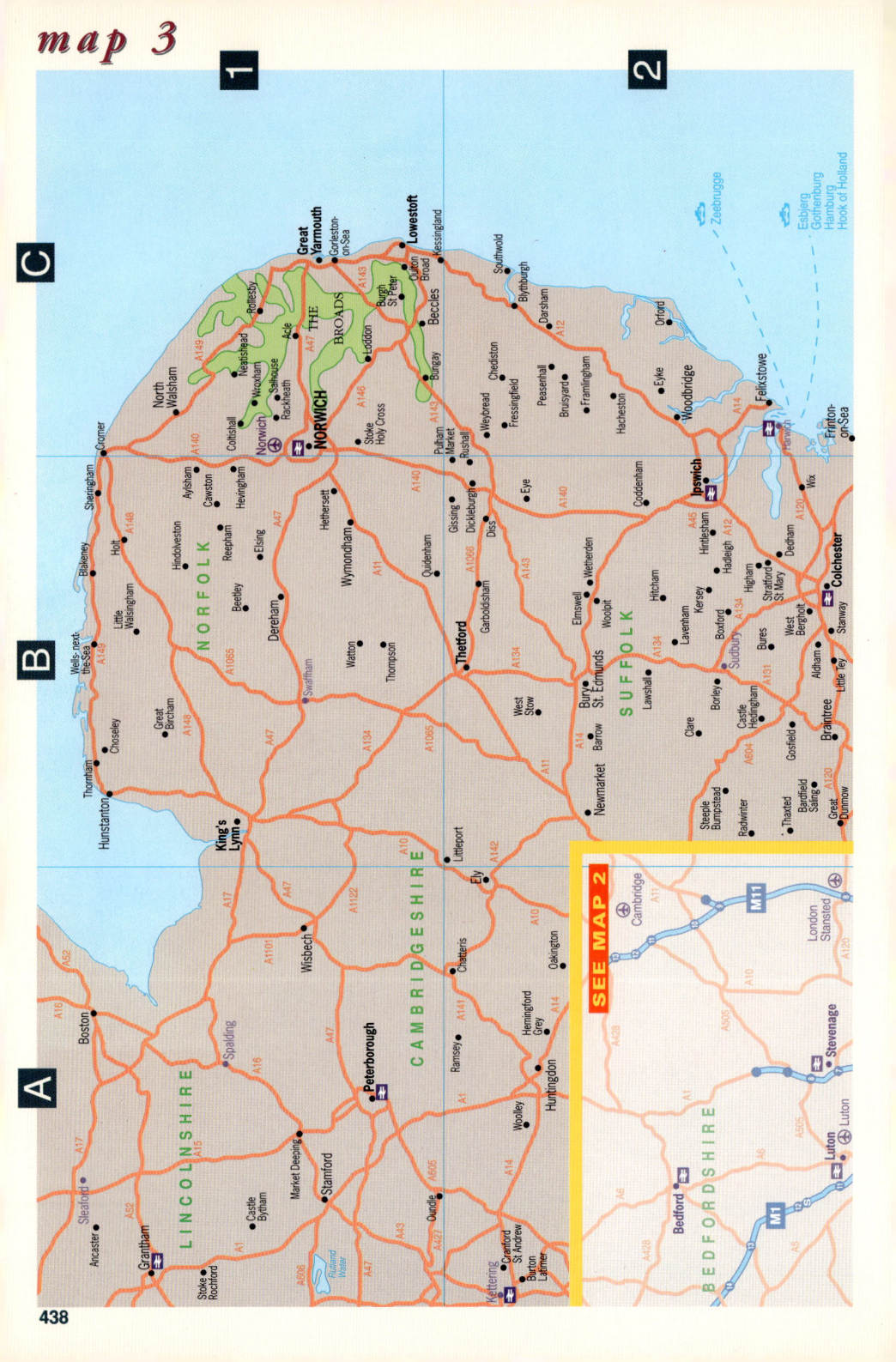

map 3

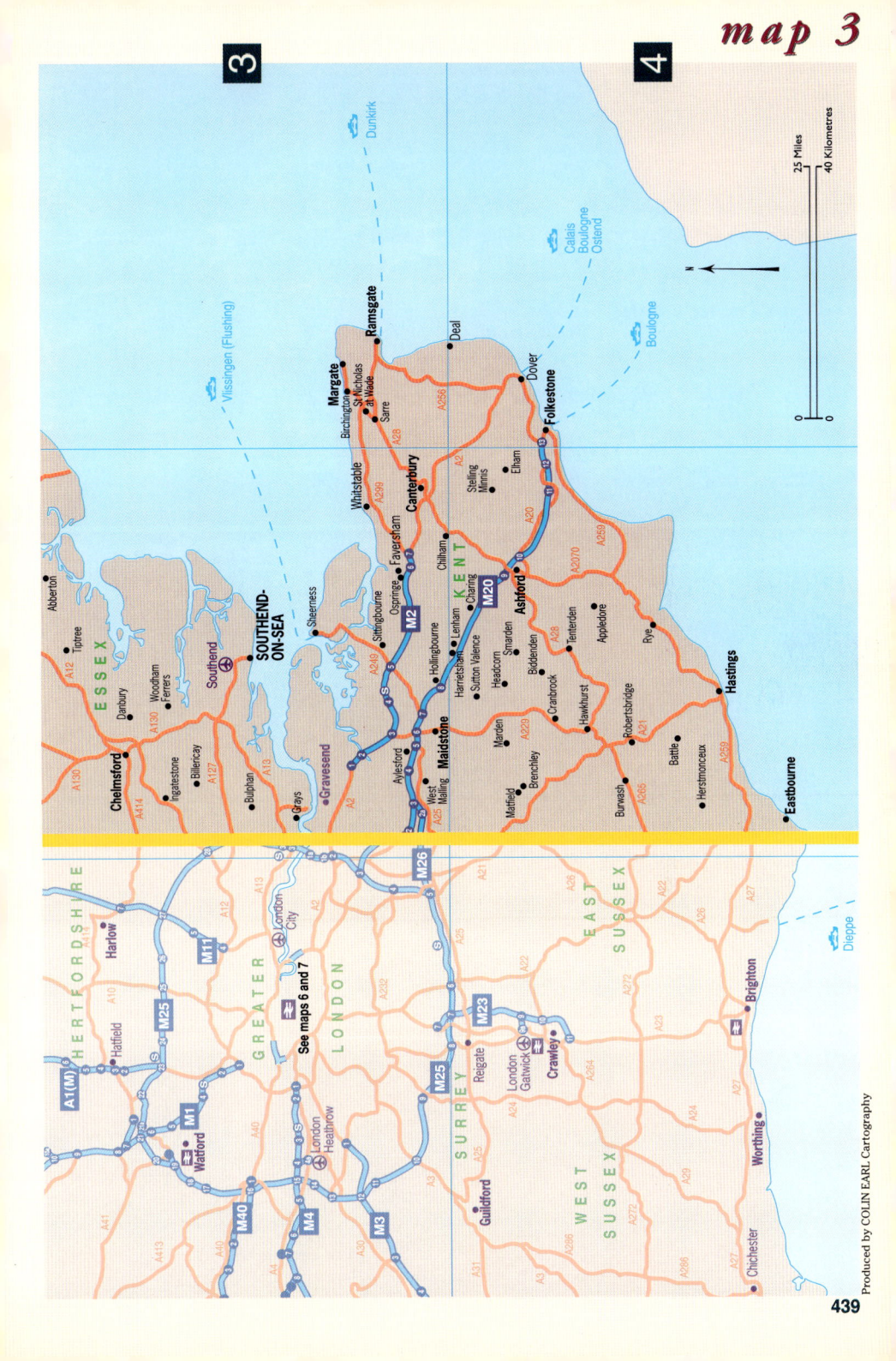

map 4

A
B
1
2
3
Lancaster
Douglas
LANCASHIRE
Garstang
St Michael's on Wyre
Singleton
Great Eccleston
Inglewhite
Weeton
BLACKPOOL
Lytham St. Anne's
M55
M6
PRESTON
Clitheroe
Dutton
Blackburn
M65
Colne
Burnley
YORKSHIRE DALES NATIONAL PARK
Hellifield
Hampsthwaite
Knaresborough
Harrogate
NORTH YORKSHIRE
Wetherby
Ilkley
Otley
Keighley
Leeds-Bradford
Oakworth
Haworth
Bingley
BRADFORD
LEEDS
Garforth
Hebden Bridge
Halifax
Mytholmroyd
Sowerby Bridge
Bacup
HUDDERSFIELD
WEST YORKSHIRE
Wakefield
M62
M1
Southport
Chorley
M61
M66
Rochdale
Bury
Bolton
Wigan
Oldham
Holmfirth
Thurlstone
Douglas
M58
GREATER MANCHESTER
MANCHESTER
Salford
MERSEYSIDE
M57
LIVERPOOL
Hoylake
Birkenhead
M62
Warrington
Runcorn
Liverpool
M56
M53
M63
Hyde
Stockport
Altrincham
Cheadle
Manchester
Knutsford
Wilmslow
Alderley Edge
SOUTH YORKSHIRE
PEAK DISTRICT NATIONAL PARK
SHEFFIELD
Castleton
Hathersage
Eyam
Froggatt
Tideswell
Rowland
Buxton
Ashford in the Water
Bakewell
Chesterfield
Macclesfield
Northwich
M6
Holmes Chapel
CHESHIRE
Chester
Sandbach
Congleton
Upper Hulme
Longnor
Winster
Matlock
Ashover
Aldwark
Wirksworth
Wessington
Leek
Crewe
Broxton
Nantwich
WALES
Malpas
Betley
Newcastle-under-Lyme
STOKE-ON-TRENT
Onneley
Waterhouses
DERBYSHIRE
Ashbourne
Belper
Weston Underwood
Oakamoor
Alton
Barlaston
Alkmonton
STAFFORDSHIRE
DERBY
Ellesmere
Whittington
Market Drayton
Stone
Uttoxeter
Doveridge
Oswestry
Wem
Ruyton-XI-Towns
Harmer Hill
Eccleshall
Stafford
Burton upon Trent
Yoxall
Newport
Telford
Shrewsbury
M54
Lichfield
Minsterley
Shifnal
Ironbridge
Codsall
Stiperstones
Broseley
Much Wenlock
WALSALL
Church Stretton
Cardington
WOLVERHAMPTON
M6
Hinckley
Nuneaton
Coleshill
Maxstoke
Bridgnorth
SHROPSHIRE
WEST MIDLANDS
BIRMINGHAM
Birmingham
Diddlebury
Stourbridge
M42
Meriden
Clun
Clungunford
M5
Solihull
Hampton in Arden
Balsall Common
COVENTRY
Bucknell
Ludlow
Leintwardine
Kidderminster
WARWICKSHIRE
Alvechurch
Rock
Stourport-on-Severn
Bromsgrove
M40
Kenilworth
Marton
Leamington Spa

map 4

map 5

map 5

C   **D**

0 — 25 Miles
0 — 40 Kilometres

N

Bergen
Esbjerg
Gothenburg
Hamburg
Stavanger

- Bamburgh
- Seahouses
- Beadnell
- Embleton
- Alnwick
- Alnmouth
- Warkworth
- Amble-by-the-Sea
- Longhorsley
- Morpeth
- Whitley Bay
- Newcastle
- **NEWCASTLE UPON TYNE**
- Tynemouth
- Ryton
- Gateshead
- Rowlands Gill
- **TYNE AND WEAR**
- Beamish
- Stanley
- Washington
- **SUNDERLAND**
- Chester-le-Street
- Durham
- Hesleden
- Crook
- Spennymoor
- Bishop Auckland
- A1(M)
- Hartlepool
- Heighington
- Stockton-on-Tees
- Darlington
- Tees-side
- Redcar
- Saltburn-by-the-Sea
- **CLEVELAND**
- **MIDDLESBROUGH**
- Ellerby
- Stokesley
- Ingleby Greenhow
- Kirkby
- Castleton
- Whitby
- Richmond
- Goathland
- Ravenscar
- Harmby
- Hunton
- Spennithorne
- Crakehall
- Osmotherley
- **NORTH YORK MOORS NATIONAL PARK**
- Staintondale
- Cloughton
- Middleham
- Bedale
- Thornton Watlass
- Northallerton
- Gillamoor
- Hartoft End
- Masham
- Thirsk
- **NORTH YORKSHIRE**
- Kirkbymoorside
- Cropton
- Sinnington
- Ebberston
- Scarborough
- Helmsley
- Pickering
- Thornton Dale
- Balk
- Coxwold
- Husthwaite
- Nunnington
- Terrington
- Malton
- Ripon
- Crayke
- Flamborough
- Pateley Bridge
- Boroughbridge
- Easingwold
- Myton-on-Swale
- Bishop Thornton
- Grafton
- Flaxton
- Bridlington

Produced by COLIN EARL Cartography

443

map 6

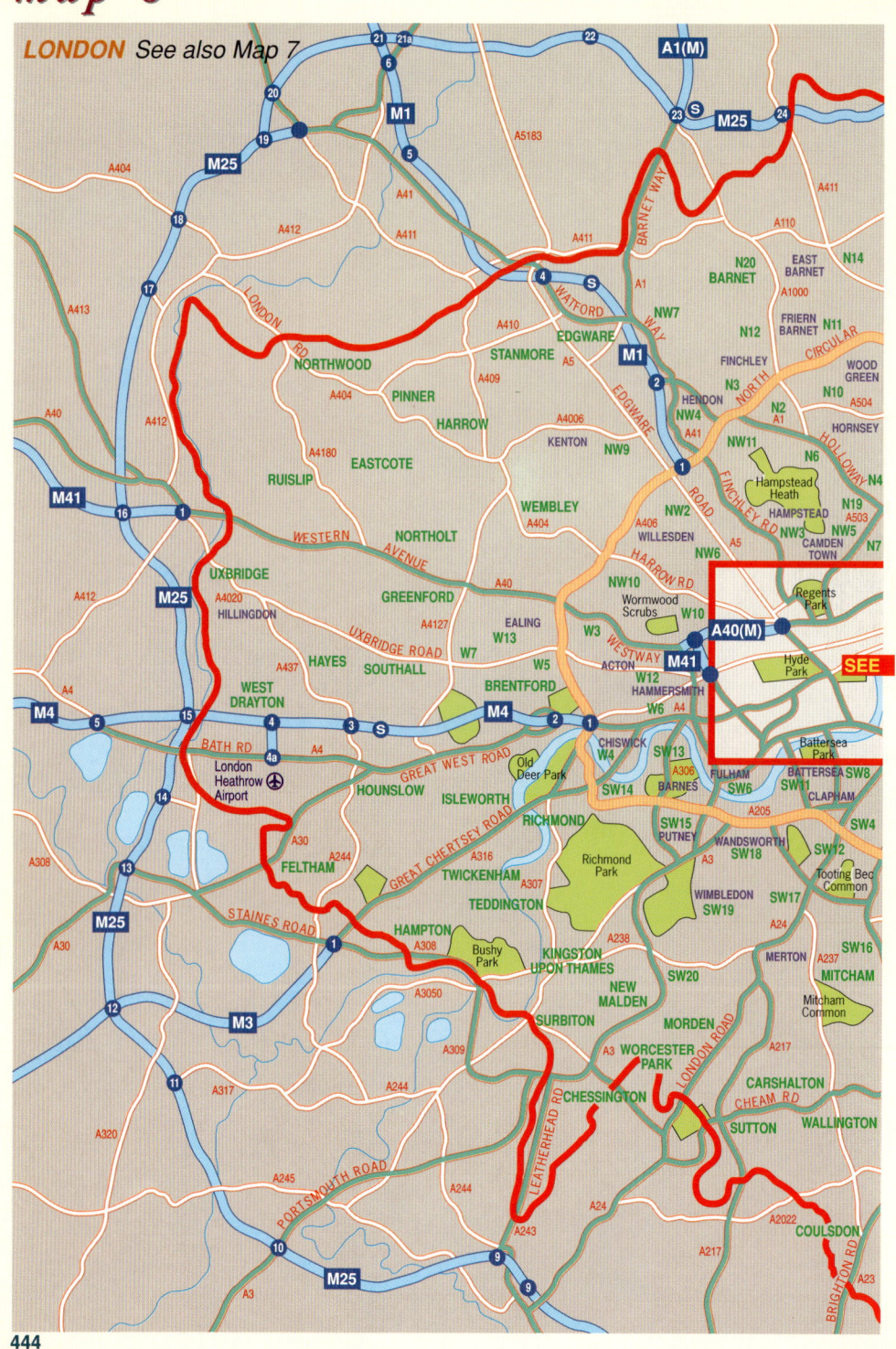

LONDON See also Map 7

444

map 6

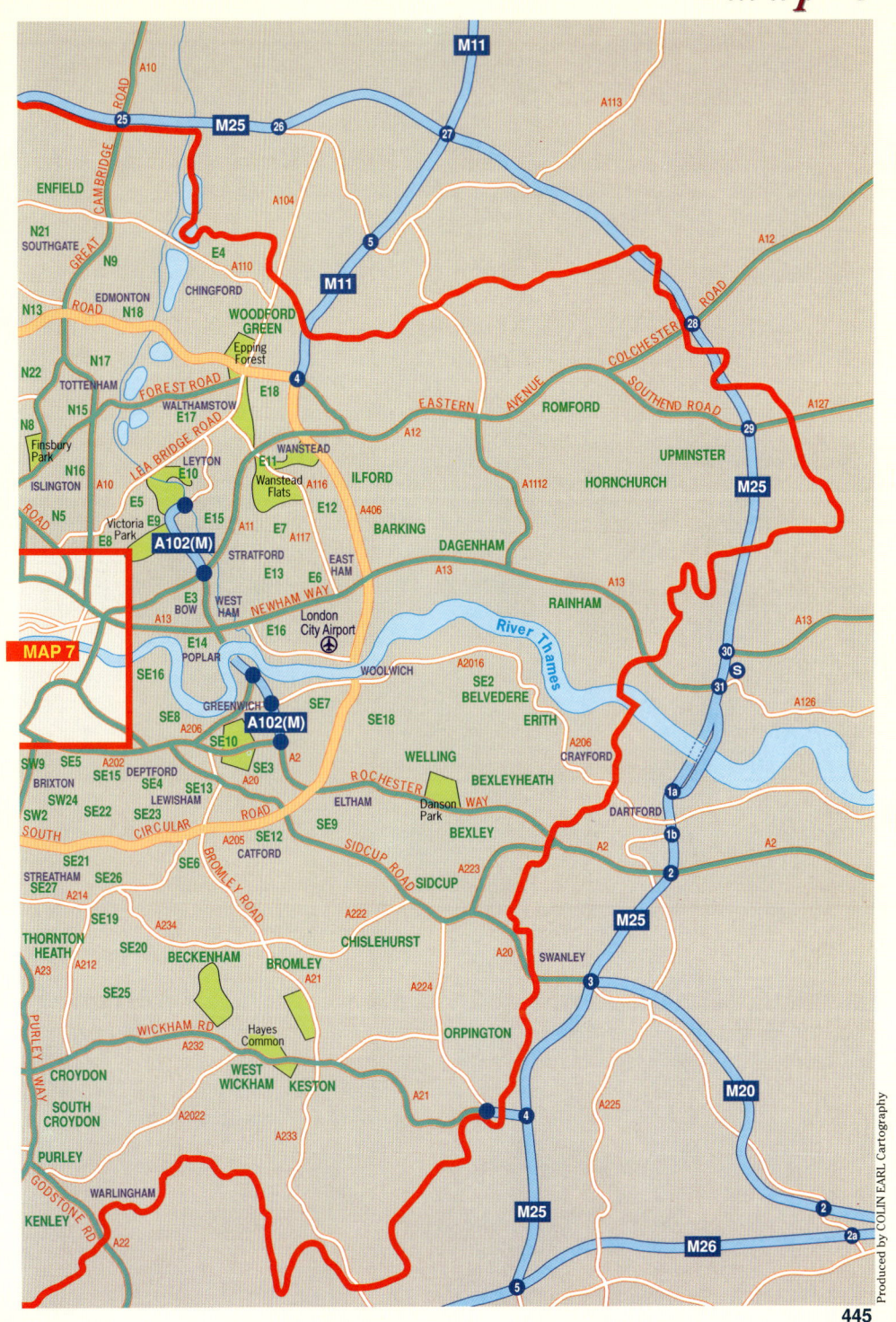

445

map 7

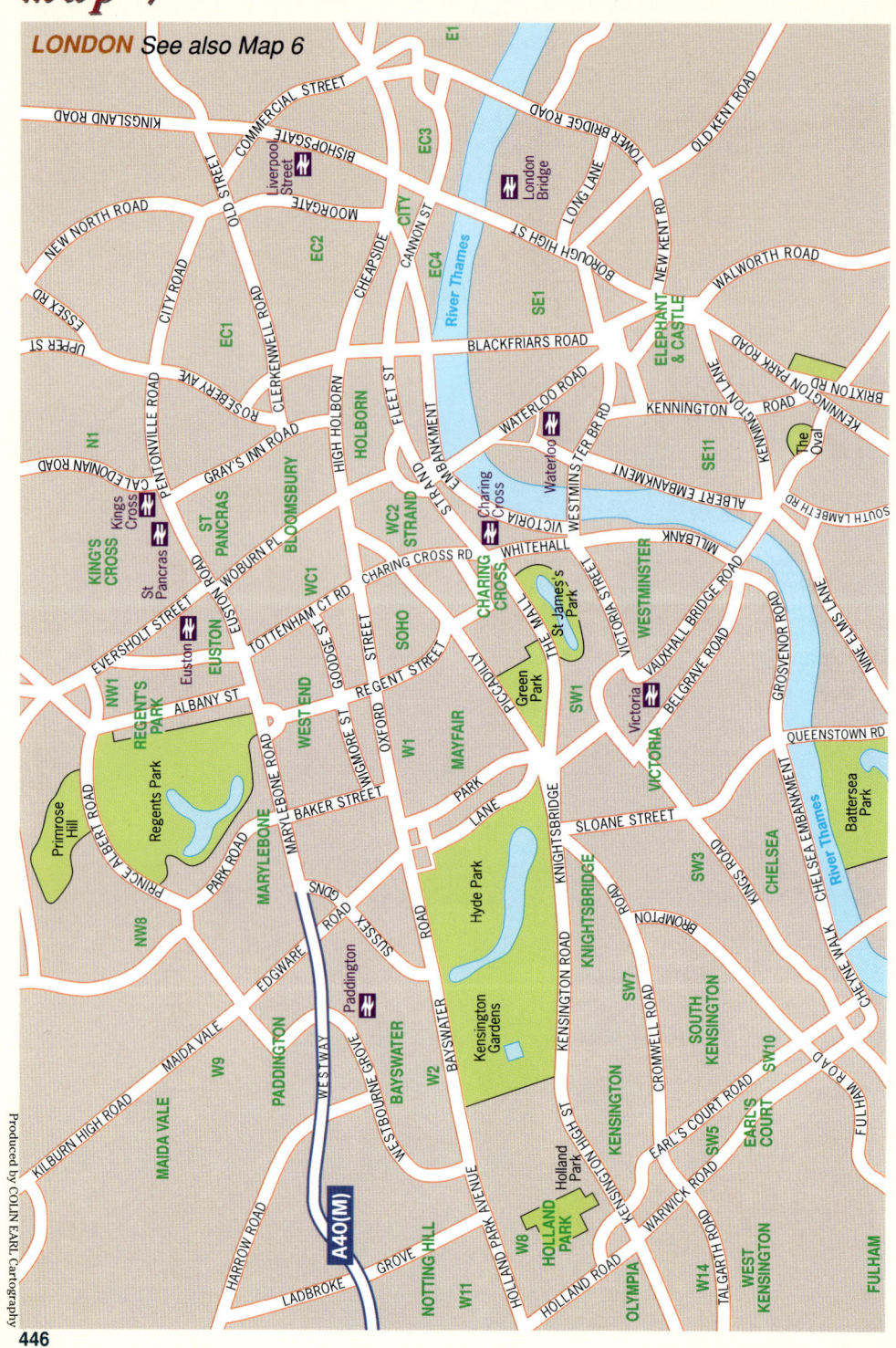

LONDON See also Map 6

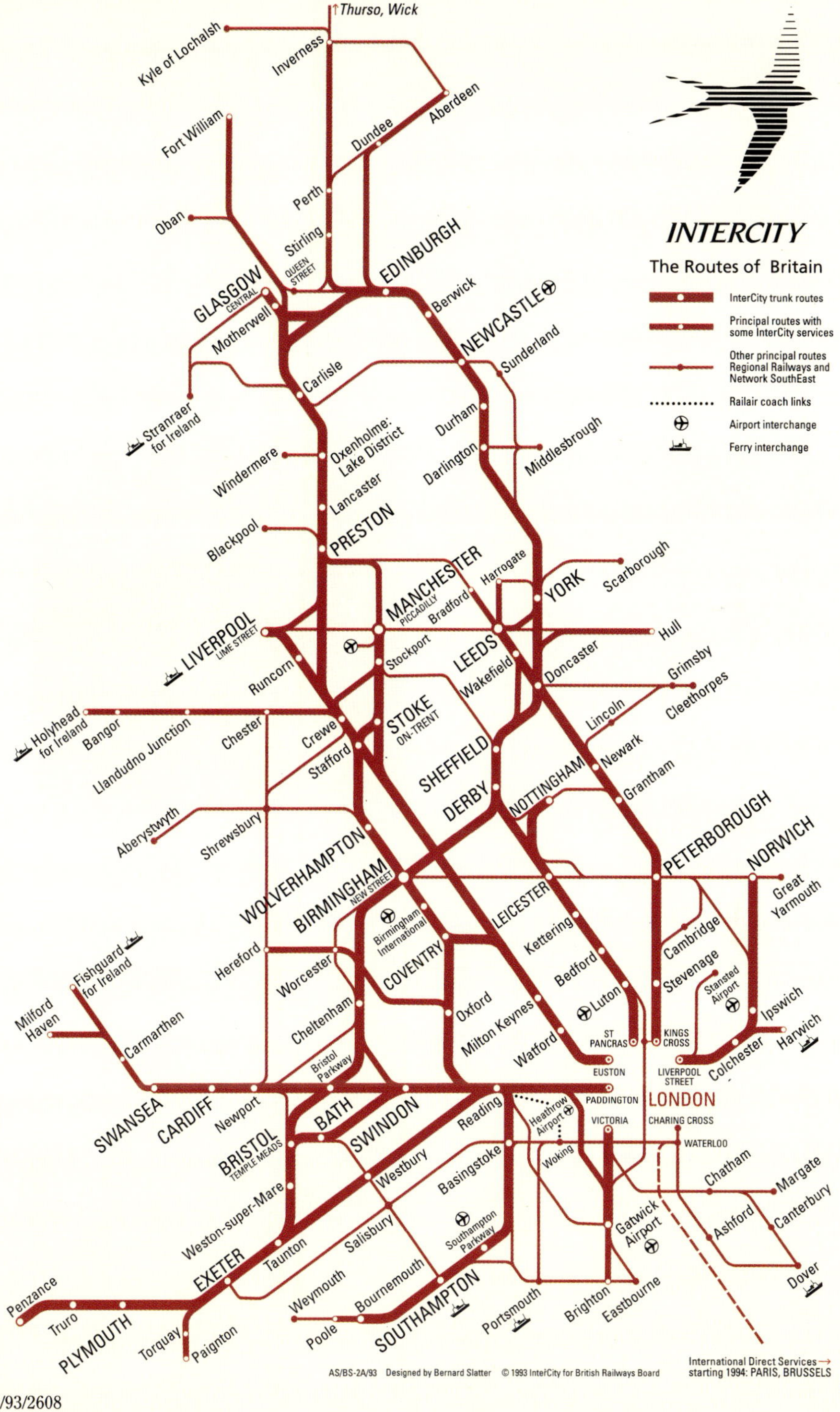

AS/BS-2A/93 Designed by Bernard Slatter

TLB/93/2608

WHERE TO STAY 1994

This 'Where to Stay' guide makes it quick and easy to find somewhere suitable to stay.

quick guide
to finding a place to stay

The town index (starting on page 425) and the colour maps (starting on page 433) show all cities, towns and villages with accommodation listings in this guide.

① *If the place you plan to visit* is included in the town index, turn to the page number given to find accommodation available there. Also check that location on the colour maps to find other places nearby which also have accommodation listings.

nthwaite *Cumbria*		388
Avon		255
Battle *East Sussex*		358
Beadnell *Northumberland*		68
Beaminster *Dorset*		260
Beamish *Durham*		68
Beaulieu *Hampshire*		321
Beccles *Suffolk*		217
Beckington *Somerset*		260
Bedale *North Yorkshire*		105
Bedford *Bedfordshire*		217
Beetley *Norfolk*		218
Belford *Northumberland*		68
Bellingham *Northumberland*		69
Belper *Derbyshire*		198
Berkeley *Gloucestershire*		140
Berrynarbor *Devon*		260

② *If the place you want* is not in the town index – or you only have a general idea of the area in which you wish to stay – use the colour maps to find places in the area which have accommodation listings.

When you have found suitable accommodation, check its availability with the establishment and also confirm any other information in the published entry which may be important to you (price, whether bath and/or shower available, children/dogs/credit cards welcome, months open, etc).

If you are happy with everything, make your booking and, if time permits, confirm it in writing.